Sorry!

CASES AND MATERIALS ON THE REGULATION OF INTERNATIONAL BUSINESS AND ECONOMIC RELATIONS

Alan C. Swan

Professor of Law
University of Miami

John F. Murphy

Professor of Law
Villanova University

CASES AND MATERIALS SERIES

1991

 **Matthew Bender**

 **Printed On Recycled Paper**

 Times Mirror Books

MATTHEW BENDER & CO.
EDITORIAL OFFICES
11 PENN PLAZA, NEW YORK, NY 10001 (212) 967-7707
2101 WEBSTER ST., OAKLAND, CA 94612 (510) 446-7100

LEGAL EDUCATION PUBLICATIONS

_____

ADVISORY BOARD

_____

Preface

The law of transnational business and economic relations is a vast subject, even when narrowed to matters of principal concern to American lawyers. Necessarily a text on such a subject will reflect some difficult choices; choices in organization, topic selection and on the relative emphasis to be given the multitude of questions that each topic is certain to raise.

Organizationally we have followed what would seem a very straight-forward approach. When a business first enters international markets it will typically do so by trading goods, services or technology with enterprises abroad. Hence the book starts with trade: trade in goods, trade in technology. It turns first to the law that most directly determines the rights and obligations of the immediate parties to the transaction and then moves on to the regulatory framework that sets the larger context within which trade in goods and technology takes place. This latter encompasses both national regulatory legislation and the public and private international law that constrains and directs exercises in national law making, especially the GATT and the several treaties pertaining to intellectual property rights.

Beyond trade, the next step for a business "going international" will most likely be the establishment of one or more productive operations abroad through direct foreign investment. Hence, the second major area covered by the book. Again, we start with the more purely private transactional elements involved in making foreign investments and then turn to consider the more general framework of international economic law. Under the latter heading we focus on two subjects: the international law of state responsibility governing host government interventions in either the ownership or management of foreign investments, including techniques for the settlement of disputes occasioned by such interventions, and the international monetary system. Understanding that system is important not only because of its influence on currency values, national exchange controls and the availability of vital foreign exchange but also because it can be a major force in shaping the overall macro-economic climate in which investment takes place.

Between these two major subject areas — trade and direct foreign investment — are two transitional chapters. The first takes a historical and broad theoretical look at the international law that delineates the permissible transnational reach of national economic regulation; i.e., the law of prescriptive jurisdiction. This body of law can influence, often decisively, what elements of private transnational business conduct — whether relating to trade or to investments — individual nations will attempt to regulate. In this context we examine a number of U.S. regulatory initiatives, including seamen's welfare legislation, labor relations, and export controls.

The second transitional chapter takes an extended look at the transnational applications of American antitrust law. No serious discussion of policies regarding international trade and investment can proceed without an understanding of how

v

growth in trade and in international capital flows depends upon the existence of open and competitive markets and of how readily private firms — often with governmental connivance — can impair the maintenance of such markets.

Against the background of this transactional learning and its broader international law context, the book then turns to examine problems relating to the settlement of international business disputes; canvassing both informal methods of settlement such as mediation and conciliation and the problems likely to arise when formal adjudication or arbitration is used.

Finally, the last two chapters address yet another aspect of the broader legal context in which U.S. foreign economic relations are conducted. This time U.S. Constitutional law is the focal point of interest, and the study examines both the allocation of governmental power to make foreign economic policy and the constraints that the Constitution imposes upon state and federal regulation of transnational business undertakings.

In assembling these materials the authors have been guided — we hope with some success — by a number of basic precepts. Recognizing the difficulties of offering anything approximating a genuinely comprehensive yet rigorous semester-long course covering both the international economic law and the transactional law aspects of international business, we have chosen to develop materials that will permit an in depth exploration of the central issues under each topic heading. As a consequence the materials lend themselves to development of at least three or even four separate semester-long courses, assuming for this purpose careful coverage of about 500-600 pages of material. These courses include: a straight forward international transactions course,[1] a general international economic law course,[2] an international trade course,[3] and perhaps a course with a somewhat distinctive emphasis on the law of U.S. foreign economic relations.[4]

In addition, preparation of these materials has been guided by the authors' firm conviction that careful attention must be paid to certain fundamental economic principles, especially when examining the international economic law context in which trade and investment take place. The subject, after all, is international economic law and it is sheer folly to think that legal issues can be understood without a sound grasp of the basic economic forces giving rise to the problems which the law seeks to address. Experience also suggests that law professors can often teach the basic, essentially rudimentary, economics required for such an understanding as effectively as trained economists.

More important, the law in these matters is changing because the world is changing at headlong speed: Europe and 1992; the Uruguay Round of the GATT which promises to bring vast new areas of international economic life under greater multilateral control; the first cautious moves toward a new regime in

---

[1] Chapters 1, 2, 6, 7, 8, 9 and 11 with variations including Sections 2-4 of Chapter 5 and Chapter 13 in lieu of Chapter 7.

[2] Chapters 3, 4, 5, 6, 7, 9 and 10 with the possible addition of Sections 3 and 7 of Chapter 11 and Section 1 of Chapter 13 or even of Chapter 12.

[3] Chapters 1, 2, 3, 4, 5, 6 and 7 with variations such as Chapter 10 in lieu of Chapter 7.

[4] Chapters 12, 13, 3, 5, 6, 7, 9 and 11. Variations include Chapter 4 in lieu of 5, Sections 3, 5 and 6 only of Chapter 11 with Chapter 10 added.

agricultural trade; changes in ideological orientation that are certain to bring Eastern Europe into a new economic, and hence legal, relationship with Western Europe and the United States; the expansion of U.S.-Canadian free trade and the attendant experiments in new techniques for exercising bilateral control over national trade policies; continued changes in Japan's role in the world economy that even now are forcing changes in the political and legal structures that heretofore governed world economic affairs; and the continued challenge of third world development made more difficult by the overwhelming burdens of third world debt. This is the setting for our study. And while any attempt at a full account of these developments would be seriously misplaced, our purpose, nevertheless, requires that we take cognizance of them.

To state the point more fully, our purpose is to examine the basic institutional, normative, and procedural structures underlying the existing international economic order, to become sensitive to how our thinking about those structures has been influenced by certain concepts and rhetorical forms and then to understand how the failures and the successes of those structures have contributed to the forces of change now challenging and reshaping those very same structures. Manifestly, such a study can not proceed without a sound grasp of at least the rudimentary economic principles that help explain the changes. Certainly without a handle on the economics one cannot adequately understand the politics of the international economic order. And for the student of the law, failure to understand the political and economic forces bearing down on the social arrangements which the law seeks to regulate, usually means a failure to understand the law in anything other than the most aridly formalistic terms.

Lastly, some care has been taken to assure that materials from foreign legal systems are used sparingly and very discriminatingly. Too often the study of foreign legal materials unguided by someone schooled in the systems from which they emanate can give rise to serious, even dangerous, misapprehensions about that law. Moreover, this is not a study in comparative law; it is a study of American law, including international law as part of the law of the United States, and a study of international law in its more distinctively international sense. Comparative materials, therefore, appear not for the purpose of teaching the substance of foreign law or even teaching the methods and techniques used in the interpretation and application of foreign law. Comparative materials are used only to illustrate the kinds of complications American lawyers are likely to encounter when they handle transactions with foreign legal implications, to show how their decisions on questions of American law can either minimize or exacerbate those complications and then to impress upon students the need in such cases to seek advice from others expert in foreign law.

Needless to say that as work on an enterprise of this magnitude spread out over the years, it drew into its orbit increasing numbers of people for whose help and support the authors are deeply grateful. There are, first of all, our colleagues who critiqued parts of the manuscript offering many a helpful suggestion or who, in discussions too many to count, offered ideas that opened up new and fruitful lines of analysis. At Miami, special mention should be made of Professors Kenneth Casebeer, Garcia-Amador, Pat Gudridge, Marc Fager, Steven Halpert, Richard Hyland, George Mundstock and Bernard Oxman. At Villanova special thanks are due to adjunct faculty members Manuel Angulo and James Dinnage. Others include Professor Swan's former colleague Professor Jeremy Paul, now at the University of Connecticut, Professor Cynthia Lichtenstein of Boston College, Professor Ken Abbott of Northwestern and Professor David Gerber of the Chicago Kent School of Law. We are also indebted to Ms. Charlene Barchefsky of the District of Columbia bar, for her helpful comments on the subsidies materials, to Daniel Price of the Pennsylvania Bar for his help on the materials on international arbitration, and to Messrs. Keith Highet, of the New York Bar, and Robert Starr, an American lawyer practicing in London, for supplying us with ideas from unpublished sources. A special note of appreciation is due to Mr. Evan R. Berlack of the District of Columbia Bar, and to his law partners, for making office space and legal materials available to Professor Murphy in the summer of 1983.

Nor can we repay the debt owed our students who diligently searched out materials, checked citations and who, in our classes, suffered through various iterations of the text suggesting many a needed clarification. Of special note, at Miami, are Loraine Brennan, Paula Day, Douglas Dimmock, Elizabeth Egan, Gerry Edens, Jorge Guerra, Kathleen Karelis, Till Mueller-Ibold and Suzanna Laos. At Kansas and Villanova we would be remiss if we failed to acknowledge the assistance of Marguerite Trossevin, now of the District of Columbia Bar, Laura Sunstein Murphy, now of the Pennsylvania Bar, and Fred Sand.

Behind any such endeavor there are always members of the administration performing the often thankless tasks of mobilizing needed institutional support and arranging teaching schedules to accommodate the time demands of the enterprise. Here Dean Mary Doyle, Associate Dean Bernard Oxman, Mrs. Eileen Walsh, Mrs. Enis Del Riego, Mr. Oscar Carbajal all of Miami and former Dean Michael Davis of Kansas and former Dean John E. Murray, Jr., now President of Duquesne University, and Dean Steven P. Frankino of Villanova merit our special appreciation.

No endeavor in legal scholarship is possible without librarians, and no expression of gratitude can ever fully measure the debt we owe our librarians. They responded cheerfully to all our requests and met our more impossible demands with a diligence and imagination that was, at times, heroic. To the Director of the Law Library at Miami, Professor Westwell Daniels, for his work in bringing together a superb staff imbued with a spirit of service, to Miami's International Law Librarian, Ms. Amber Smith, for the skill with which she applied on our behalf her extraordinary knowledge of international sources and to Ms. Nora De La Garza for the diligence with which she searched out sometimes stubbornly elusive materials we express our deepest appreciation. At Kansas and Villanova we owe thanks to Professor Anita K. Head, former Director of the Law Library at the University of Kansas and now Director of the Law Library at George Washington University, to Professor Alan S. Holoch, formerly Director of the Law Library at Villanova University and now Director of the Law Library at Ohio State University, to Professor William James, Director of the Law Library at Villanova University, and to Ms. Nancy Armstrong and Ms. Mary Cornelius, reference librarians at the Villanova Law Library.

In the end, of course, the people closest to the enterprise were our long-suffering secretaries. Without their patience in the face of countless revisions of the text, their skill in handling the vagaries of the modern computer, their cheerfulness, their persistent reminders and even their mild reproaches the enterprise could never have been accomplished. To Ms. Julie Skokan, Mrs. Joan Maiocco and Ms. Stephanie Olsen at Miami and Mrs. Joan DeLong, Mrs. Terri LaVerghetta, and Ms. Lori Hallman at Villanova the authors extend their most heartfelt thanks.

Coral Gables, Fl.

Villanova, Pa.

January, 1990

TABLE OF CONTENTS

CHAPTER 4

THE INTERNATIONAL CONTROL OF NATIONAL TRADE POLICIES — AN OVERVIEW OF THE GENERAL AGREEMENT ON TARIFFS AND TRADE

CHAPTER 5

THE INTERNATIONAL CONTROL OF NATIONAL TRADE POLICIES — OF "SAFEGUARDS" AND "UNFAIR" TRADE PRACTICES

CHAPTER 7

THE UNITED STATES ANTITRUST LAWS AND TRANSNATIONAL BUSINESS

CHAPTER 8

UNITED STATES BUSINESS IN FOREIGN COUNTRIES THROUGH FOREIGN DIRECT INVESTMENT

CHAPTER 9

INTERNATIONAL CLAIMS FOR ECONOMIC INJURIES TO ALIENS

CHAPTER 12

THE CONSTITUTIONAL AUTHORITY OF THE PRESIDENT AND CONGRESS IN THE MAKING OF FOREIGN POLICY

CHAPTER 13

CONSTITUTIONAL AND OTHER LIMITATIONS ON THE REGULATION OF TRANSNATIONAL BUSINESS

CHAPTER 1

THE INTERNATIONAL SALE OF GOODS

Introduction

International economic transactions generally consist of the transfer of goods, money, ideas or people across national boundaries or, if no boundary is crossed, between residents of different states. Our study is of the legal arrangements that facilitate or regulate these movements. We start that study with the movement of goods. We do so because, from the days of the ancient Phoenicians up until the vast expansion of foreign capital investment in the last decade or so, the international trading of goods constituted the single most important international economic activity. Trade — the reasons for trade, lessons learned from governmental interference with or efforts to expand trade, the impact of trade on domestic economic arrangements and on the management of domestic economies — is the stuff from which much of our learning about the international economy has been and will continue to be derived.

In this Chapter we begin our study of trade with the commercial law that most directly impacts the trader in goods. While we cannot canvas all the questions that the almost infinite variety of transactions might raise, there are a number of arrangements, central to the conduct of international trade, the fundamentals of which can be mastered through the examination of certain basic issues.

First, we will examine the new United Nations' Convention on Contracts for the International Sale of Goods (hereinafter called "the United Nations' Sales Convention"). The Convention has been signed by twenty one nations including the United States. It came into force for the United States and ten other signatories on January 1, 1988.[1]

In this Chapter we will examine two problems to compare the likely resolution of each under the Convention with their resolution under the Uniform Commercial Code. Next, we turn to the commercial terms of trade under which virtually all international sales transactions are conducted, and examine the effect of those terms on the allocation of rights and responsibilities between buyer and seller. Later we shall examine the effect of those terms on the computation of damages. We then turn to the rules that pertain to the primary documents of title used in the international movement of goods: bills of lading, delivery orders and the like. This sets the ground work for examining the Carriage of Goods by Sea Act, and

---

[1] Twenty-one nations were signatories to the Convention. Ratification by ten of those signatories brought the Convention into effect for those ten nations on January 1, 1988. Since then one additional signatory has ratified and, as of October 31, 1989, six additional nations have acceded to the Convention, bringing the total number of parties to seventeen. They are: Argentina, Australia, Austria, China, Egypt, Finland, France, Hungary, Italy, Lesotho, Mexico, Norway, Sweden, Syria, United States, Yugoslavia, and Zambia.

1

other related legislation, which define the carrier's responsibility for the safe transport of goods. Our next subject is generated by the hazards of international trade; the use of force majeure and the doctrines of impossibility and frustration of purpose. Lastly, we turn to the letter of credit — that ingenious device used, in the case of commercial letters of credit, for paying the seller of goods and, in the case of stand-by letters of credit, for providing the buyer with a guarantee of performance by the seller.

§ 1.01 An Introduction to the International Sales Convention

[A] The Formation of Contracts; Also the Choice of Law

UNITED NATIONS CONVENTION ON CONTRACTS FOR THE INTERNATIONAL SALE OF GOODS (1980)[2]

Chapter I

Sphere of Application

Article 1

(1) This Convention applies to contracts for sale of goods between parties whose places of business are in different States:

   (a) when the States are Contracting States; or

   (b) when the rules of private international law lead to the application of the law of a Contracting State.

(2) The fact that the parties have their places of business in different States is to be disregarded whenever this fact does not appear either from the contract or from any dealings between, or from information disclosed by, the parties at any time before or at the conclusion of the contract.

(3) Neither the nationality of the parties nor the civil or commercial character of the parties or of the contract is to be taken into consideration in determining the application of this Convention.

Articles 2 and 3

[These two Articles identify certain types of contracts that are exempt from the Convention. They are: sales involving goods bought for personal or household use, goods bought by auction or pursuant to execution under law, sales of securities, negotiable instruments, money, ships, aircraft and electricity (Article 2), contracts for goods to be manufactured where the buyer

---

[2] To date the text of the Convention has not been made available in either the United States Treaty Series, the TIAS ("Treaties and Other International Agreement Series," issued by the U.S. Department of State) or the U.N. Treaty Series. The text given here is taken from Honnold, Uniform Law for International Sales; Under the 1980 United Nations Convention, Kluwer (1982), Appendix A at page 469 (Hereinafter cited as Honnold). See also: 52 Fed Reg. 6262 (March 2, 1987).

supplies a substantial part of the materials necessary to that manufacture and contracts under which the seller's obligation pertains in preponderant part to the supply of labor and other services (Article 3).]

Article 4

This Convention governs only the formation of the contract of sale and the rights and obligations of the seller and the buyer arising from such a contract. In particular, except as otherwise expressly provided in this Convention, it is not concerned with:

(a)   the validity of the contract or any of its provisions or of any usage;

(b)   the effect which the contract may have on the property in the goods sold.

Article 5

This Convention does not apply to the liability of the seller for death or personal injury caused by the goods to any person.

Article 6

The parties may exclude the application of this Convention or, subject to article 12,[3] derogate from or vary the effect of any of its provisions.

NOTES AND QUESTIONS

(1) Under Article 95 of the Convention, a signatory State may, at the time of depositing its ratification, declare that it will not be bound by subparagraph (1)(b) of Article 1. The United States has issued such a declaration. While, as we shall see, this simplifies matters considerably for the American courts, it still leaves open possibilities for some intricate choice of law questions.

---

[3] Article 12 provides: "Any provision of article 11, article 29 or Part II of this Convention that allows a contract of sale or its modification or termination by agreement or any offer, acceptance or other indication of intention to be made in any form other than in writing does not apply where any party has his place of business in a Contracting State which has made a declaration under article 96 of this Convention. The parties may not derogate from or vary the effect of this article."

This provision was precipitated by the unwillingness of certain Contracting Parties to allow certain formal requirements imposed by their domestic law to be superceded by the rules of the Convention. For example, article 11 provides that a "contract of sale need not be included in or evidenced by writing and is not subject to any other requirement as to form." Article 11 applies only as between the parties. It would not apply, for example, to vitiate a government regulation that required a written contract as a condition of obtaining a license to export the goods under the contract. Nevertheless, article 11 was still objectionable to some parties. The solution was to allow those Contracting Parties, wishing to retain a domestic legislative requirement for a writing, to issue a declaration under article 96 stating that any provision of article 11, article 29 and Part II of the Convention that obviated the need for a writing would not apply in cases where, under normal choice of law principles, the law of the declaring state was otherwise applicable.

(2) Paragraph 2 of Article 1 is addressed to the case where one party contracts with an agent of an undisclosed principal and it later turns out that the latter has his place of business abroad.

(3) If one party to a contract has a place of business in both Country A and Country B and the other party has its place of business in Country A alone, Article 10(a) provides:

For purposes of this Convention:

(a) **if a party has more than one place of business, the place of business is that which has the closest relationship to the contract and its performance, having regard to the circumstances known to or contemplated by the parties at any time before or at the conclusion of the contract;**

---

(4) Under Article 4(a) the Convention would not supersede a rule of domestic law that, for example, prohibits the sale of specified products, such as cocaine, or invalidates contracts relating to such illegal sales. Nor would the Convention displace domestic rules on capacity to contract (*i.e.*, insanity, infancy or other disability) or rules with regard to the effect of mistake[4] or the absence of consideration on the validity of the contract. On the other hand, the Convention does modify the traditional common law rule requiring new consideraton to support modification of a contract[5] or to render an offer irrevocable.[6] Likewise, the Convention does not interfere with the special rights and remedies that domestic law gives to persons who have been induced to enter into a contract by fraud. The Convention governs only obligations "arising from [the] contract," and the rule against fraud is not a contractual obligation. Note, however, that innocent misstatements of quality are governed by the Convention.[7]

---

[4] This point needs some clarification. The traditional common law rules concerning the recision of contracts for mutual mistake undoubtedly survive as a result of Article 4(a). On the other hand, rules on unilateral mistake concerning the quality of the goods which, in some civil law jurisdictions, tend to cover much the same ground as warranty law should, in the interests of the uniformity which the Convention seeks to achieve, be considered superceded by the conformity provisions of the Convention (Part III, Chapter II, Section II, Articles 35-44).

[5] Article 29 which follows Section 2-209(1) of the Uniform Commerical Code.

[6] Article 16(2) which embodies the so-called "firm offer" rule of Section 2-205 of the Uniform Commercial Code.

[7] See Honnold, page 96.

A HYPOTHETICAL CASE[8]

HEINZ-KOPPER, G. m.b. H v. ATLANTIC SULPHUR COMPANY

(1974)

Before CHILDERS, PEAL, and ROBBINS, CIRCUIT JUDGES.

PEAL, CIRCUIT JUDGE. . . . Heinz-Kopper, GmbH (Heinz-Kopper) in its complaint sought damages for breach of an alleged contract. The defendant New York Atlantic Sulphur Company (Atlantic) counterclaimed for the price of . . . fertilizer sold . . . to Heinz-Kopper but not the transaction involved in plaintiff's complaint. . . .

I. FACTS

Heinz-Kopper is engaged in the business of selling grain and fertilizer throughout the European Economic Community. Its main office and plant are located at Frankfurt-am-Main, West Germany, but it maintains offices and warehouses elsewhere in Europe. Atlantic supplied phosphates and potash to Heinz-Kopper for resale several years prior to 1969. During this period, the parties conducted business on an order basis without written contracts. Pursuant to orders placed by Heinz-Kopper, Atlantic shipped fertilizer from mines under its control either to Heinz-Kopper at Frankfurt or occasionally directly to other recipients designated by Heinz-Kopper. Sometime in mid-October 1969 Friedrich Kopper, General Manager of Heinz-Kopper, . . . [and] Charles Odum, Atlantic's European sales manager in Brussels, [discussed] . . . the availability [and price] of potash for sale by Atlantic. Odum indicated that he would send Kopper a written sales contract.

Approximately November 20, 1969, Kopper received two copies of the proposed contract by mail. A brief cover letter instructed Kopper as follows: "Please sign the enclosed contracts and return to the Brussels office. We will return a copy to you for your files." The two documents already bore the signatures of B. W. Guess . . . Atlantic's general sales manager for potash and phosphates, with an office in [New York, N.Y.]. . . . Kopper signed both copies, made a photostatic copy of one of them, and returned both originals to Odum in Brussels about November 25. The documents apparently were received in Brussels but were misplaced shortly thereafter [and were only found] . . . two weeks prior to trial . . . in Odum's office in Brussels. There was no evidence that the documents ever were sent from Brussels to New York.

The document signed by Guess and Kopper was an Atlantic printed form contract. By its terms, Atlantic agreed to sell and ship and Heinz-Kopper agreed to buy and receive at its plant, for the period November 1, 1969 through June 30, 1970 . . . 10,000 tons of coarse and 2,000 tons of granular [potash]. The sale

---

[8] What is set-out here is an edited version of the actual opinion in *Neal-Cooper Grain Co. v. Texas Gulf Sulphur*, 508 F. 2d 283 (7th Cir, 1974) with only the names of the parties and the location of their businesses changed in order to render it an international sale of goods. In the actual case the panel was composed of Judges Pell, Fairchild and Stevens, with Judge Pell writing the opinion.

was to be "in accordance with the terms and conditions stipulated herein and with the seller's attached Price List dated which is hereby made a part of this contract." . . . No date was shown for the price list, and no price list as such was attached to the agreement. Rather, the following terms were typed near the bottom of the agreement's front side:

> "2% 30, Net 180 Days
> Coarse at 21c per unit through January 31, 1970
> Granular at 23c per unit through January 31, 1970"

stipulations in the k

Immediately thereunder appeared . . . the signatures of Kopper and Guess each on a separate signature line. Guess's signature appeared . . . over the printed title, "Manager of Sales." It was stipulated [at trial] that both Guess and Kopper "had the authority to execute contracts for their respective companies."

The contract form stated it was "made in the City and State of New York, this Fifth day of November 1969," between [Atlantic and Heinz-Kopper]. . . . Shipment was to be "F.O.B. cars seller's plant Potash, Utah." The printed front portion of the document further provided that the "contract shall not be binding upon the seller until duly accepted at its New York Office."

price increase

Among the printed terms and conditions appearing on the reverse side of the form was a provision which enabled Atlantic to institute a general price increase effective fifteen days after receipt by the buyer of a revised Atlantic price list. The agreement also contained a general exculpatory clause excusing the parties from any failures to perform caused by, *inter alia*, "the operation of statutes or of law."

* * * *

Between November 12 and December 4, 1969, Atlantic shipped and billed to Heinz-Kopper three shipments of . . . 278.63 tons of coarse and 300.14 tons of granular [potash]. Two of the three shipments occurred prior to the time Kopper executed the purported sales contract. According to the invoices, the granular potash, priced at 23c per unit, was shipped directly to Heinz-Kopper at Frankfurt, while the coarse, at a price of 21c per unit was sent to [Heinz-Kopper's customers] . . . in Dusseldorf, West Germany and Reims, France . . . respectively. All shipments were shipped freight prepaid; however, Heinz-Kopper was billed for the amount of the freight charges.

On December 2, 1969, Kopper sent . . . [a] teletype order for potash to Atlantic in Brussels . . . "as per contract agreement." The Order was for 10,000 tons of coarse potash to be delivered in the "first 25 working days of January" to several specified destinations in Germany. At the end of the Order it was stipulated:

> If There Are Any Changes Or Amendments To Our Contract We Would Reserve The Right To Change These Shipping Instructions.

Kopper admitted at trial that a ten thousand ton order was "larger than normal," and that he had never previously ordered potash in such quantity for shipment within thirty days.

Atlantic made no response to the December 2 order. On January 17, 1970, Heinz-Kopper received a price list from Atlantic which listed new prices for coarse (35c) and granular potash (37c) effective January 1, 1970. The price list stated, *inter alia*, that shipments were to be "at Seller's option from either Allan, Saskatchewan; Moab, Utah or Seller's warehouses."

On January 20, 1970, Kopper sent a second teletype message to the Atlantic Brussels office . . . [indicating that Heinz-Kopper was] "waiting for your [sic] to start shipping". . . . In late January or early February 1970, Kopper saw Guess and Odum . . . in Brussels. Guess told Kopper that Atlantic would not ship potash to Heinz-Kopper at the old prices listed in the sales contract.

On February 7, 1970, Kopper sent a photostatic copy of the contract to Dr. Guy McBride, Vice President of Atlantic in New York where Atlantic had its World-Wide headquarters. On February 20 Guess responded with a letter to Kopper, in which he stated that Atlantic had "never received the original signed copy of the contract." The letter, however, did not deny the existence of a contractual relationship but merely referred to the fact that the orders of December 2 "were not accepted or confirmed to you." The letter further stated that Atlantic "did not have the product to ship or the capability to ship this tonnage to just one customer if we had the product available." The letter concluded by referring to certain Canadian government regulations [and by stating] . . . that "we cannot promise any fixed tonnage for shipment in the future." The letter did not deny that such promises had been made in the past.

In his deposition Guess admitted that there was no time during 1969 and 1970 when Atlantic did not have a source of potash. During 1969, Atlantic purchased an interest in a Canadian mine located at Allan, Saskatchewan. . . . As of . . . January 1, 1970 the Allan mine apparently became Atlantic's principal source of potash. During January and February 1970 the Moab mine continued to produce but at a reduced rate most of which was derived from "cleaning up" operations.

By Order of Council 1733/69, dated November 17, 1969, the Province of Saskatchewan promulgated certain "Potash Conservation Regulations," . . . pursuant to [which] the Saskatchewan Minister of Natural Resources established a floor price of 33.75c (Canadian) per unit for potash produced in Saskatchewan. Adherence to the floor price apparently was a prerequisite to obtaining a license to produce or dispose of potash.

Kopper testified that during January and February 1970 he attempted to obtain potash from several sources other than Atlantic . . . [but was only partially successful]. He . . . also testified [with regard to the prevailing price of granular potash in January] . . . that . . . some [was] being shipped at twenty-one cents and some at thirty-five cents [and] that on February 20, 1970, the date on which Guess wrote the letter indicating the order would not be filled, the prevailing prices were 35c and 37c.

The only other evidence pertaining to market price was supplied by Bryan Guess, who testified that the price during January, in and around Frankfurt, was 21c to 26c for coarse and 2c higher for granular. Guess indicated that "some" potash was available at these prices from suppliers other than Atlantic during January and February 1970. . . . We do not know whether the[se] prices . . . were market prices for sales made in January or whether these were merely prices on delivery in January pursuant to contracts made earlier and still in effect.

The action was tried before the district court without a jury. Seventeen months after trial, on March 30, 1973, the court filed its memorandum opinion finding for defendant Atlantic on the plaintiff's complaint and ordering that judgment be . . . entered for the defendant on its counterclaim in the stipulated amount of $105,907.85.

II. FORMATION OF THE CONTRACT

Atlantic argued . . . [*inter alia*] that the document signed by Guess and Kopper in November 1969 never ripened into a contract because it was never accepted at Atlantic's New York office. . . .

The district court found that the parties' minds never met and no contract, therefore, came into being. The court [concluded that] there . . . [had been no acceptance] in New York; [that] even if there was a custom for Guess . . . to have final authority to approve contracts, Heinz-Kopper was unaware of the custom and had no cause to rely upon it; [that] plaintiff returned both copies at defendant's request, indicating that it did not believe it had a contract; and [that this] . . . lack of belief was further evidenced by the words on the December order referring to "any changes or amendments to our contract.". . . .

We need look no further than the deposition of Guess to determine that . . . [there was a contract]. . . . Whether Heinz-Kopper knew or not of the internal corporate protocol for contract approval by Atlantic is immaterial. The plain fact is that Atlantic as a corporation did approve the contract and chose to disregard the printed words in its contract concerning New York geographical approval. Guess's authority to execute the contract on behalf of Atlantic was stipulated. At the time in question he was sales manager for all international sales. It was his title of "manager of sales" that was printed on the Atlantic form of sales contract. He had the ultimate authority in the corporation to determine prices and, of course, the bone of contention in the present case is whether Atlantic was obligated to the prices in the written contract. In his own words, "[no] one had the authority to set prices but me" and the salesmen would have to sell at a price that he had set.

The normal procedure had been to have the contract go first to the customer "for his signing, returned to the area office (*i.e.* Brussels) and the area office sends it to . . . New York for final execution and then the executed copy is returned to the customer." In the present case, the order of signing was reversed but the Atlantic approval was just as complete and final as it would have been if the reverse and normal order of signing had been observed. . . . [I]f the area office in the present case instead of losing the contract had forwarded it to New York . . . it is not unreasonable to believe that . . . Guess would have been wondering why it was coming back to him when he had already executed it.

We do not give any significance to the fact that someone in the field, apparently following normal practice and overlooking the fact that Atlantic had already approved, requested both copies be returned. . . . We find it more significant that there was no place on the form contract for approval by New York. The only place for signature on behalf of Atlantic was the one line which was in fact signed by Guess who had the final authority in setting prices.

As to the reference to changes or amendments contained in the December teletyped order, this was nothing more than a recognition that if Atlantic exercised its contractual right to impose a general price increase upon 15 days notice, Atlantic reserved the right to change the shipping instructions.

Since we find that neither of the last two mentioned matters upon proper analysis have any bearing on whether a contract had been entered because they do not reflect a lack of belief on Heinz-Kopper's part that it had a contract, we need not decide whether a subjective belief that a contract has not been entered can have the effect of negativing the existence of a contract legally executed.

* * * *

NOTES AND QUESTIONS

(1) Note the approach taken by the District Court on the question of contract formation. Of critical importance to that court was the question of whether Friedrich Kopper, when he signed the form sent him by Atlantic, thought he had a contract. The approach is highly subjective. What is the key circumstance relied *Atlantic's* upon by the District Court in reaching its conclusion? What additional circum- *approval.* stances might have confirmed Mr. Kopper in the belief attributed to him by that Court? Note the stipulation found at the end of Heinz-Kopper's teletype order of *"As per k* December 2, 1969. Are you satisfied that the Appeals Court adequately refuted *agreement"* the District Court's interpretation of that stipulation?

(2) Does the Appeals Court quarrel with the District Court's assessment of Mr. Kopper's state of mind? Or, does it take a different approach altogether? Can the Appeals Court's approach be squared with Section 2-204(1) of the UCC, which stipulates as follows:

(1) A contract for sale of goods may be made in any manner sufficient to show agreement, including conduct by both parties which recognizes the existence of such a contract.

(3) Note that the floor on prices for potash from Saskatchewan established by the Minister of Natural Resources was some 47%-60% higher than the price contained in Atlantic's proposed contract with Heinz-Kopper. The latter, we can assume, was a competitive price. If so, how could Saskatchewan expect to sell its potash after such a large increase? Might these circumstances have affected the Appeals Court's perception of the case? Might your answer implicate UCC Section 1-203, which stipulates that: "Every contract or duty within this Act imposes an obligation of good faith in its performance or enforcement." Is Heinz-Kopper's conduct completely free of similar suspicions?

(4) If the question of contract formation was determined according to the United Nations' Sales Convention, would the result be the same as that reached by the Appeals Court? For this purpose consider the following provisions of the Convention:

General Provisions

Article 7

(1) In the interpretation of this Convention, regard is to be had to its international character and to the need to promote uniformity in its application and the observance of good faith in international trade.[9]

(2) Questions concerning matters governed by this Convention which are not expressly settled in it are to be settled in conformity with the general principles on which it is based or, in the absence of such principles, in conformity with the law applicable by virtue of the rules of private international law.

Article 8

(1) For the purposes of this Convention statements made by and other conduct of a party are to be interpreted according to his intent where the other party knew or could not have been unaware what that intent was.

(2) If the preceding paragraph is not applicable, statements made by and other conduct of a party are to be interpreted according to the understanding that a reasonable person of the same kind as the other party would have had in the same circumstances.

(3) In determining the intent of a party or the understanding a reasonable person would have had, due consideration is to be given to all relevant circumstances of the case including the negotiations, any practices which the parties have established between themselves, usages and any subsequent conduct of the parties.

Article 14

(1) A proposal for concluding a contract addressed to one or more specific persons constitutes an offer if it is sufficiently definite and indicates the intention of the offeror to be bound in case of acceptance. A proposal is

---

[9] In his treatise on the Convention, Honnold offers the following commentary on Article 7:

"To read the words of the Convention with regard to their "International Character" requires that they be projected against an international background. With time, a body of international experience will develop through international case law and scholarly writing. . . . In the meantime, the only international setting for the Convention's words is its legislative history — its genetic background. . . .

Paragraph (1) of Article 7 concludes with the statement that in interpreting the Convention there shall be regard for promoting "the observance of good faith in international trade". . . . This was a compromise worked out in the late stages of drafting the Convention between those who thought that, in the formation of a contract, the parties should be held to a standard of "good faith" and "fair dealing" and those who thought that these terms had no fixed meaning and would lead to uncertainty. [This means that the Convention is not as broad as some national legislation, for example, Sec. 1-203 of the UCC.]. . . . [T]he Sales Convention . . . rejects "good faith" as a general requirement and uses "good faith" solely as] a principle for interpreting the provisions of the Convention. Honnold, pages 114-115 and 123-124.

sufficiently definite if it indicates the goods and expressly or implicitly fixes or makes provision for determining the quantity and the price.

(2) A proposal other than one addressed to one or more specific persons is to be considered merely as an invitation to make offers, unless the contrary is clearly indicated by the person making the proposal.

A CHOICE OF LAW PROBLEM

As already noted the United States has, pursuant to Article 95 of the Convention, declared that it will not be bound by subparagraph 1(b) of Article 1. This means that in an action on a contract between a party with its place of business in the United States and a party with its place of business abroad, the Convention will only be applied by the American courts if the State in which the non-U.S. party to the contract has its place of business is also a State party to the Convention. But change the facts of the *Heinz-Kopper* Case along the following lines:

Assume Atlantic has two places of business, one in New York, the other in Brussels. Assume also that the New York office was not involved by way of negotiations, approvals or otherwise, with the alleged contract between Atlantic and Heinz-Kopper (*i.e.*, everthing on Atlantic's side was done in Brussels), that the potash was to be shipped directly from Canada to Germany and payment was to be made through banking channels directly to the Brussels office. Under these circumstances, the rule in Article 10(a) would certainly seem to indicate that, for purposes of the Convention, Atlantic's place of business was in Belgium. Furthermore Belgium is not a party to the Convention. Assume that Germany is a party, but has not issued a declaration under Article 95 similar to the U.S. declaration. If Heinz-Kopper then sued Atlantic in a U.S. court, the latter may have to decide, at the very threshold of the case, which law was to govern the question of whether a contract existed between Atlantic and Heinz-Kopper; German law (*i.e.*, the Convention), Belgian law (*i.e.*, non-Convention law) or U.S. law (doubtful).

In making this decision assume the U.S. court turned to the principles contained in the Restatement, Conflicts of Laws (Second) as follows:

RESTATEMENT, CONFLICTS OF LAWS (SECOND) (1971)

Section. 6. Choice of Law Principles

(1) A court, subject to constitutional restrictions, will follow a statutory directive of its own state on choice of law.

(2) When there is no such directive, the factors relevant to the choice of the applicable rule of law include

    (a) the needs of the interstate and international systems,

(b)   the relevant policies of the forum,

(c)   the relevant policies of other interested states and the relative interest of those states in the determination of the particular issue,

(d)   the protection of justified expectations,

(e)   the basic policies underlying the particular field of law,

(f)   certainty, predictability and uniformity of result, and

(g)   ease in the determination and application of the law to be applied.

Section 188. Law Governing [Contracts] in Absence of Effective Choice by the Parties

(1)   The rights and duties of the parties with respect to an issue in contract are determined by the local law of the state which, with respect to that issue, has the most significant relationship to the transaction and the parties under the principles stated in Section 6.

(2)   In the absence of an effective choice of law by the parties (See Section 187), the contacts to be taken into account in applying the principles of Section 6 to determine the law applicable to an issue include:

(a)   the place of contracting,

(b)   the place of negotiation of the contract,

(c)   the place of performance,

(d)   the location of the subject matter of the contract, and

(e)   the domicile, residence, nationality, place of incorporation and place of business of the parties.

These contacts are to be evaluated according to their relative importance with respect to the particular issue.

* * * *

With regard to the "place of contracting," the "Comment" on Subsection (2) states, in part, as follows:

> *The Place of Contracting.* As used in the Restatement of this Subject, the place of contracting is the place where occurred the last act necessary, under the forum's rules of offer and acceptance, to give the contract binding effect, assuming, hypothetically, that the local law of the state where the act occurred rendered the contract binding.

> Standing alone, the place of contracting is a relatively insignificant contact. To be sure, in the absence of an effective choice of law by the parties, issues involving the validity of a contract will, in perhaps the majority of situations, be determined in accordance with the local law of the state of contracting. In such situations, however, this state will be the state of the applicable law for reasons additional to the fact that it happens to be the place where

occurred the last act necessary to give the contract binding effect. The place of contracting, in other words, rarely stands alone and, almost invariably, is but one of several contacts in the state. Usually, this state will be the state where the parties conducted the negotiations [or have] a . . . common domicile. . . . By way of contrast, the place of contracting will have little significance, if any, when it is purely fortuitous and bears no relation to the parties and the contract, such as when a letter of acceptance is mailed in a railroad station in the course of an interstate trip.

NOTES AND QUESTIONS

(1) Observe that under the Restatement of Conflicts, Section 188, the law of the state of the place of contracting would appear, potentially at least, to have a "significant relationship" to the issue of whether or not there was a contract between Heinz-Kopper and Atlantic. Yet, the place of contracting can only be established if one first concludes that there is a contract. How does the Restatement resolve this apparent circularity?

(2) Turn now to the facts of the *Heinz-Kopper* Case as we varied those facts above. Plainly, under the variation, the place of contracting will be either in Germany or in Belgium. To ascertain that place, however, the American court must, as the comments to the Restatement of Conflicts quoted above indicate, look to the substantive United States law of offer and acceptance (see answer to question (1)). Does that mean the law as laid down in the Convention or the law that would apply absent the Convention (*i.e.* traditional American contract law)? Note, in this connection, that if you looked to the substantive law of the Convention, Article 18(2) provides that:

> An acceptance of an offer becomes effective at the moment the indication of assent reaches the offeror.[10]

Under this rule where is the place of contracting?

On the other hand, if you look to the substantive law of the United States that would apply in the absence of the Convention, Section 63 of the Restatement (Second) Contracts provides:

> Unless the offer provides otherwise,
>
> (a)   an acceptance made in a manner and by a medium invited by an offer is operative and completes the manifestation of mutual assent as soon as put out of the offeree's possession, without regard to whether it ever reaches the offeror.

---

[10] Article 24 of the Convention further elaborates as follows: "For the purposes of this Part of the Convention, an offer, declaration of acceptance or any other indication of intention 'reaches' the addressee when it is made orally to him or delivered by any other means to him personally, to his place of business or mailing address or, if he does not have a place of business or mailing address, to his habitual residence."

Under this rule where is the place of contracting?

Is the Restatement's injunction to choose the substantive law with the most significant relationship to the transaction helpful in deciding which U.S. law to use in determining the place of contracting; the law of the Convention or the more traditional U.S. contract law? Or, is that putting the cart before the horse?

(3) In order to avoid all of this, what initial line of inquiry might the U.S. court be well advised to undertake?

(4) Among the principal reasons for having the United Nations' Convention was the desire to avoid this kind of "choice of law" inquiry. Would that objective necessarily be achieved if Belgium acceded to the Convention? In answering, return to the earlier discussion of the merits of the contract formation issue under the Convention. What should a U.S. court do if it were clear that under the variation of the actual facts in the case, the German courts would conclude that under the Convention a valid contract did exist between Heinz-Kopper and Atlantic and the Belgian courts also interpreting the Convention would reach the opposite conclusion?

[B] The Battle of the Forms: The U.N. Sales Convention Contrasted with the Uniform Commercial Code

A great of deal of international trade moves under standard form contracts which, while initially drafted by lawyers, are not reviewed by lawyers each time they are used. To do so would only increase the time and costs of contracting that is the very purpose of the forms to avoid. This, however, can give rise to the familiar "battle of the forms," which Professors James White and Robert Summers, in their treatise on the Uniform Commercial Code,[11] describe in the following terms:

> It is a sad fact that many sales contracts are not fully bargained, not carefully drafted, and not understandingly signed or otherwise acknowledged by both parties. Often here is what happens: underlings of seller and buyer each sit in their respective offices with a telephone and a stack of form contracts. Seller's lawyer has drafted seller's forms to give him advantage. Buyer's lawyer has drafted buyer's forms to give him advantage. The two sets of forms naturally diverge. They may diverge not only in substantive terms but also in permissible methods of contract formation. The process of "contracting" begins with underling telephoning underling or with the dispatch of a form. When the process ends, there will usually be two forms involved, seller's and buyer's, and each form may even be signed by both underlings. The deal may coincide with respect to the few bargained terms such as price, quality and quantity terms, and delivery terms. But on other terms, the respective forms will diverge in important respects. Frequently this will pose no problem, for the deal will go forward without breakdown. But sometimes the parties will fall into dispute even before the occasion for performance. More often, one or both will perform or start to perform and a dispute will break out. In all such cases the parties will then haul out their forms and read them — perhaps

---

[11] J. White and R. Summers, Uniform Commercial Code 24 (3rd ed., 1980).

for the first time — and they will find that their forms diverge. Is there a contract? If so, what are its terms?

[At this point UCC Sec. 2-207 comes into play]. . . . The original draftsman of 2-207 designed it mainly to keep the welsher in the contract. . . . But unfortunately . . . [p]arties to sales much more often call on courts to use 2-207 to decide the terms of their contract after they exchange documents, perform, or start to perform and then fall into dispute. This is not only a different but also a more difficult problem for the law than that of keeping the welsher in.

Section 2-207 of the Uniform Commercial Code provides as follows (See Documentary Supplement for Official Comments):[12]

Section 2-207. Additional Terms in Acceptance or Confirmation

(1) A definite and seasonable expression of acceptance or a written confirmation which is sent within a reasonable time operates as an acceptance even though it states terms additional to or different from those offered or agreed upon, unless acceptance is expressly made conditional on assent to the additional or different terms.

(2) The additional terms are to be construed as proposals for addition to the contract. Between merchants such terms become part of the contract unless:

   (a) the offer expressly limits acceptance to the terms of the offer;

   (b) they materially alter it; or

   (c) notification of objection to them has already been given or is given within a reasonable time after notice of them is received.

(3) Conduct by both parties which recognizes the existence of a contract is sufficient to establish a contract for sale although the writings of the parties do not otherwise establish a contract. In such case the terms of the particular contract consist of those terms on which the writings of the parties agree, together with any supplementary terms incorporated under any other provisions of this Act.

Articles 18 and 19 of the United Nations' Sales Convention provide, in pertinent part, as follows:

Article 18

(1) A statement made by or other conduct of the offeree indicating assent to an offer is an acceptance. Silence or inactivity does not in itself amount to acceptance.

---

[12] Documentary Supplement.

* * * *

(3) . . . if, by virtue of the offer or as a result of practices which the parties have established between themselves or of usage, the offeree may indicate assent by performing an act, such as one relating to the dispatch of the goods or payment of the price, without notice to the offeror, the acceptance is effective at the moment the act is performed, provided that the act is performed within the period of time laid down in the preceding paragraph. [*i.e.* within the time fixed in the offer or within a reasonable time.]

Article 19

(1) A reply to an offer which purports to be an acceptance but contains additions, limitations or other modifications is a rejection of the offer and constitutes a counter-offer.

(2) However, a reply to an offer which purports to be an acceptance but contains additional or different terms which do not materially alter the terms of the offer constitutes an acceptance, unless the offeror, without undue delay, objects orally to the discrepancy or dispatches a notice to that effect. If he does not so object, the terms of the contract are the terms of the offer with the modifications contained in the acceptance.

(3) Additional or different terms relating, among other things, to the price, payment, quality and quantity of the goods, place and time of delivery, extent of one party's liability to the other or the settlement of disputes are considered to alter the terms of the offer materially.

Consider the results that might be reached in the following problems under the Uniform Commercial Code and under the United Nations Sales Convention.

PROBLEM 1

A buyer in Great Britain sent to a seller in the United States a printed document entitled "Purchase Order No. 258900" containing, in typewritten entries under printed headings, the following: under the heading "Seller," the latter's name and address; under "Quantity," a specified number of yards of cotton piece goods; under "Description," specifications relating to the type and quality of goods; under "Price" a stated dollar amount per yard; under "Terms" the words "payment at sight against confirmed letter of credit to be opened on or before" a stated date; and under the heading "Delivery," the words "c.i.f. Manchester on or before" a named date. Immediately under these entries were the printed words: "This order is subject to all the terms and conditions contained on the reverse side hereof." On the reverse side were some ten numbered paragraphs in small print. Paragraph 9 stated:

> All disputes relating to this Order shall be settled by arbitration in London under the rules of the London Cotton Exchange as then in effect.

The Purchase Order was signed by one Robert Smith purporting to be buyer's "General Manager."

Some ten days' later buyer received from the seller a printed form entitled "Acknowledgment of Order" stating in print: "We hereby acknowledge receipt and our acceptance of your Purchase Order No." Then typewritten was the buyer's Purchase Order number, date and entries repeating precisely all of the terms regarding quantity, quality, price, delivery and payment contained in the buyer's purchase order. The "Acknowledgement" was signed by one William Jones purporting to be seller's "General Sales Manager." On the reverse side of the form were eight unnumbered paragraphs in small print, one of which stated:

> All disputes arising out of or otherwise relating to the order described above shall be settled exclusively by submission to the courts of the State of New York, and for that purpose all parties hereto shall be deemed to have consented to the jurisdiction of said courts.

Shortly before the date set for delivery of the goods, seller cabled buyer stating that it would be unable to deliver the material described in the latter's purchase order. The buyer immediately replied that it considered seller in breach of contract, that it was purchasing the piece goods from an alternative source at a considerably higher price and demanding that seller remit to it the difference between the contract price and its cost of cover. After several inconclusive exchanges of correspondence in which seller maintained that no contract existed between it and the buyer, the latter, following the rules of the London Cotton Exchange, sent seller a "Notice of the Commencement of Arbitration" stating the nature of its claim, appointing one arbitrator and demanding that seller appoint a second arbitrator. Seller then filed a motion in the Supreme Court of New York asking that court to issue an order staying the London arbitration. In response, the buyer appeared and moved the court to order arbitration. In the alternative, the buyer asked the court to judge the seller in breach of contract and to award it damages.

(1) Is there a valid contract between buyer and seller, under the UCC? under the United Nations' Sales Convention? With respect to the UCC how might Section 2-207(2)(b) influence your answer?

(2) Suppose that in its purchase order buyer had stated a price of $2.00 per yard and in its acknowledgement seller had stated $2.20 per yard. Would there be a contract? Can you reconcile your answers to questions (1) and (2)?

(3) If there is a valid contract under either the United Nation's Sales Convention or the UCC, should the court order arbitration or not? With regard to the UCC, assume that the clause in seller's form calling for judicial settlement of disputes "materially alters" the terms of buyer's purchase order within the meaning of Section 2-207(2)(b). How might Comments 2 and 6 to Section 2-207 bear on your answer?[13]

---

[13] Documentary Supplement.

PROBLEM 2

Assume all the facts in Problem 1 except that neither buyer's purchase order nor seller's acknowledgment contain any provision regarding the settlement of disputes and that buyer's purchase order contains, in small print on the reverse side, an express warranty pertaining to the "strength and tightness of weave" of all goods subject to its order. The seller's acknowledgment contains the following words, again in small print on the back but in bolder type than the other provisions of the form:

> [Seller] hereby disclaims all warranties, express or implied, with respect to the goods described in this acknowledgment, including, without limitation, all warranties of merchantability or of fitness for a particular purpose.

Shortly after dispatch of its acknowledgment, seller, in accordance with the delivery terms contained in the purchase order, shipped the goods to buyer. Upon inspection after arrival the buyer claimed that the goods not only failed to meet the terms of the express warranty contained in its purchase order but in other respects did not conform to the contract description. After several inconclusive discussions of settlement, buyer sued seller in a U.S. court for breach of warranty.

(1) What result under the UCC? In addition to Section 2-207, examine UCC Sections 2-313 through 2-316.[14] Again consider Comments 2 and 6 to Section 2-207.

(2) What result under the United Nations' Sales Convention? Note that the Convention contains no provision similar to UCC Section 2-316 regarding the disclaimer of warranties. Review Article 4 of the Convention. Honnold, in his treatise on the Convention, takes the position that this omission would not, by reason of Article 4, render UCC 2-316(2) applicable in a case otherwise governed by the Convention. In Honnold's view, the disclaimer issue does not go to the validity of the contract within the meaning of Article 4.[15]

PROBLEM 3

Assume all the facts in Problem 2, except that the buyer's purchase order is completely silent with regard to warranties, express or implied. Again what result under the UCC? under the United Nations' Sales Convention? With regard to the UCC, upon what question does the applicability of Section 2-207(2) turn?

---

[14] Documentary Supplement.

[15] Honnold, page 233. For a contrary view see: Note, Disclaimers Of Implied Warranties: The 1980 United Nations Convention On Contracts For The International Sale Of Goods, 53 Fordham L. Rev. 863-87 (1985). For a view agreeing with the result reached by Honnold but arguing that even if UCC 2-316(2) concerns the validity of disclaimer clauses, it concerns formal rather than substantive validity and that, while the Convention leaves questions of substantive validity to domestic law, questions of formal validity are preempted by Article 11, see Hyland, Conformity Of Goods To The Contract Under the United Nations Sales Convention And The Uniform Commercial Code, in "Einheitliches Kaufrecht und Nationales Obligationenrecht" (Schlechtriem, Editor) Nomos Verlagsgesellschaft, Baden-Baden, 1987, note at page 315.

PROBLEM 4

Again assume all the facts in Problem 2, except that seller attaches to its acknowledgment a letter, on the company letterhead and signed by Jones, stating in part:

> We note some minor differences between the terms contained in your purchase order and in the attached acknowledgment. It should be understood that our willingness to fill your order is subject to your acceptance of our terms.

Buyer never responded to this note, the goods were dispatched and a dispute ensued. Again what result under the UCC? under the United Nations' Sales Convention? With regard to the UCC, see Comment 7.[16]

§ 1.02   The Commercial Terms of Trade; C.I.F., F.O.B. and Related Terms

In some respects the risks assumed by buyer and seller in an international sales transaction differ completely from those entailed in a purely domestic transaction (*e.g.*, risk of exchange rate fluctuations and of governmental embargoes). In other respects the difference is merely a matter of degree. Yet that difference can be important. In an international sale the buyer and the seller may not only be at a greater distance from each other but are very likely to be working out of different commercial cultures and with far less information about each other. Sellers, as a consequence, are more likely to insist upon payment as soon as they ship or even before that (*e.g.*, when they commence to manufacture or assemble the goods). Buyers, on the other hand, are likely to want to defer payment until the goods have arrived and been inspected.

To meet this problem the international trading community has developed a number of devices, most of which can be and are used in domestic sales, but all of which were primarily a response to the needs of international trade and are used with much greater frequency in the latter context. The central innovation is the so-called "documentary transaction."

Broadly speaking in a "documentary transaction," the seller ships the goods but is paid upon tender, not of the goods, but of documents to the buyer or, if a letter of credit is being used, to a bank. The documents required for this purpose will be specified in the contract of sale or letter of credit. Thus, for the seller the time between the shipment of goods and the receipt of payment is foreshortened to the time it takes to forward the documents to the buyer or bank. The buyer, in turn, can protect itself by specifying the documents that the seller must present before being entitled to payment (*e.g.*, a bill of lading which guarantees that the goods have been shipped, an inspection certificate showing that the goods are of the quality contracted for, a policy of insurance against loss or damage to the goods in transit). Also, once in possession of the documents and having paid for the goods the buyer can, if the documents are in proper form, turn around and deal in the goods as though they were actually in his possession even though they may still be at sea.

---

[16] Documentary Supplement.

At this point the reader should turn to the Documentary Supplement and examine samples of the documents frequently used in international "documentary transactions," especially the draft or bill of exchange and the bill of lading.[1] These documents, along with the seller's invoice are almost invariably present in any such transaction. Other documents that may be employed, although not as frequently, include inspection certificates, packing lists, insurance policies, consular certificates, certificates of origin, and various commercial "visas" (*e.g.*, a "quota" visa) or governmentally required licences (*e.g.* export license).

While the invoice is self explanatory and other of these documents, particularly the bill of lading, will be dealt with at greater length in this and later Sections of this Chapter, a word concerning the "draft" or "bill of exchange" is in order.

In its most straightforward form where there is no bank involved in the transaction, a draft is an order by the seller (the "drawer" or "maker") on the buyer (the "drawee") to pay a stated sum of money to the "payee" who may be the "drawer" itself or the drawer's agent. Where a bank is involved as issuing or confirming bank under a letter of credit the drawee will often be the bank and the drafts and other documents will be handled as described in Section 1.07 *infra*. In either event, the order to pay may call for payment at "sight" (*i.e.*, upon presentation to the "drawee"), upon the expiration of a specified period thereafter (i.e., "thirty-days after sight") or on a stated date. Under UCC Sec. 3-104 a draft to be negotiable must be payable on demand (*e.g.*, at "sight") or at a definite time, including a specified period after "sight."

In addition to the hazards of distance and lack of familiarity, the increased hazards of an ocean voyage, the greater chance that a war or civil disturbance will render shipment impossible, the imposition of new duties or other governmentally imposed barriers to trade are all possibilities likely to make international sales transactions riskier than purely domestic sales. As a consequence the assignment of the risks of these hazards is a matter of vital importance in framing any contract for the international sale of goods. Critical to fixing these responsibilities and hence in determining the documents which the seller will have to present under a documentary transaction in order to get paid are the commercial terms specified in the contract of sale. The principal terms used are C & F, CIF, FAS, and FOB although others may also be employed such as "Ex Factory" or "Ex Works" or "Delivered Duty Paid." While, as a result of usage, these terms have taken on well acknowledged general meanings, the reader should consult UCC Sections 2-319 through 2-324,[2] the INCOTERMS promulgated by the International Chamber of Commerce and the Revised American Foreign Trade Definitions,[3] and note that there are some important differences between these authorities.

What follows is the leading English case on the meaning and incidences of a CIF contract and of the once contending theories concerning those incidences. While the theory ultimately adopted by the House of Lords is no longer subject to doubt, the argument is instructive and a useful point of departure in identifying the differences between CIF (C & F) contracts and FOB (FAS) contracts.

---

[1] Documentary Supplement.
[2] Documentary Supplement.
[3] Documentary Supplement

BIDDELL BROTHERS v. E. CLEMENS HORST COMPANY

Court of Appeals
[1911] 1 K.B. 934

APPEAL from the judgment of Hamilton J. in an action tried by him without a jury.

The action was brought to recover damages for alleged breaches of two contracts, dated respectively October 13, 1904, and December 21, 1904.

The first contract, which was made at Sunderland between the defendants, of San Francisco and London, parties of the first part, and [plaintiff's assignor] Vaux & Sons, Limited, of the city of Sunderland, parties of the second part, provided that:

> . . . the parties of the first part [defendants] agree to sell to the parties of the second part [plaintiff's assignor] one hundred (100) bales, equal to or better than choice brewing Pacific Coast hops of each of the crops of the years 1905 to 1912 inclusive.
>
> The said hops to be shipped to Sunderland.
>
> The parties of the second part shall pay for the said hops at the rate of ninety (90) shillings sterling per 112 lbs., c.i.f. to London, Liverpool, or Hull (tare 5 lbs. per bale).
>
> Terms net cash.
>
> It is agreed that this contract is severable as to each bale.
>
> The sellers may consider entire unfulfilled portion of this contract violated by the buyers in case of refusal by them to pay for any hops delivered and accepted hereunder or if this contract or any part of it is otherwise violated by the buyers.
>
> Time of shipment to place of delivery, or delivery at place of delivery, during the months (inclusive) of October to March following the harvest of each year's crop.
>
> If for any reason the parties of the second part shall be dissatisfied with or object to all or any part of any lot of hops delivered hereunder, the parties of the first part may, within thirty days after receipt of written notice thereof, ship or deliver other choice hops in place of those objected to.

The second contract was between the same parties, and in the same terms, except that it provided for the sale by the defendants to [the plaintiff's assignor], of fifty bales [of a slightly different hops], c.i.f. London. . . .

Correspondence passed between the parties as to the shipment of the 150 bales of the 1909 crop, and on January 29, 1910, the defendants wrote to the plaintiffs stating that they were ready to make shipment of the 150 bales of the 1909 crop of the contracted quality, and that:

> . . . for the invoice price less freight we will value on your good selves at sight with negotiable bills of lading and insurance certificates attached to draft, and if you wish we will also attach certificates of quality of the Merchants'

Exchange, San Francisco, or other competent authority to cover the shipment.

On February 1 the plaintiffs replied that they were prepared to take delivery on the terms of the contract, and that it was:

> . . . in accordance with the universal practice of the trade and the custom adopted by you in your dealings with other purchasers of your hops, and it has also been your custom with our assignors to submit samples, and the samples having been accepted to give delivery in bulk in accordance with the samples; but if you decline to adopt the usual and undoubtedly most convenient course, we can only pay for the hops against delivery and examination of each bale. We cannot fall in with your suggestion of accepting the certificate of quality of the Merchants' Exchange, San Francisco.

On February 5 the defendants' solicitors wrote to the plaintiffs' solicitors that the refusal of the plaintiffs to pay for the hops except upon terms which were not in accordance with the contracts was a clear breach of the contract by the plaintiffs, and, that being so, the defendants would not now ship to the plaintiffs the 150 bales of the 1909 crop, and they reserved all their rights in respect of the breach of contract by the plaintiffs.

> [Plaintiffs then commenced this action claiming damages for breach of contract in refusing to ship or deliver the 150 bales of hops. The defendants, in turn, alleged that plaintiffs had violated the entire unfulfilled portion of the agreement by refusing to pay in accordance with the contract and counterclaimed for damages by reason of plaintiffs refusal to take and pay for the 150 bales]

The following judgments were read —

VAUGHAN WILLIAMS L.J. . . . It was argued before Hamilton J., on behalf of the defendants that the terms "net cash" in a c.i.f. contract necessarily mean "cash against documents," and that a c.i.f. contract is performed by the vendor shipping goods of the description specified in the contract, effecting a proper insurance thereon, and then tendering to the buyer the documents representing the goods, namely, the indorsed bill of lading, invoice, and policy, and that thereupon the buyer has to pay for the goods whether they have arrived or not. Hamilton J. affirmed [this] . . . proposition . . . but in no way based his conclusion on the assumption that "terms net cash" means "cash against documents," and expressed his opinion that the words "terms net cash" in themselves mean only . . . no credit and no deduction by way of discount or rebate or otherwise. . . .

There is no evidence as to the practice or course of business between the parties . . . [so I] seek only to determine what is the obligation of payment under a c.i.f. contract which does not state when or under what conditions the payment of the price is to be made, and which does not contain a provision that payment of the price is to be made against shipping documents. . . .

It is suggested, as one of the reasons why [c.i.f. implies an obligation of payment against shipping documents] . . . that the goods under a c.i.f. contract are carried at the risk of the buyer, and must be paid for whether the goods are lost at sea or not, because the policy is taken out on behalf and in the interest of the buyer. I do not think that any such implication ought to be made, seeing that "cash against documents" is a term which is frequently included in a c.i.f. contract by express words, and, moreover, because I do not think that the admitted fact that an object of the c.i.f. policy is to enable the goods at sea to be commercially dealt with before the ship arrives compels the buyer to take advantage of this opportunity, if for any reason he is not disposed to do so.

There is no evidence in the present case of any law merchant or custom which reads such words as "payment to be made against shipping documents" . . . into the contract. . . . [But even if that were understood in some circles] I do not think we ought to allow [it] to be the basis of a decision between litigants in an action in a case where there is no evidence whatsoever either as to local usage in England or as to such general usage in England or foreign countries as is a condition of the admission and adoption as part of the law merchant of England. . . . When it is said that mercantile law is acted upon by the Courts without proof of usage, this means after it has in earlier cases been proved and adopted. . . .

As to the construction of the contract, I certainly think that the [last three paragraphs of the contract as quoted above] . . . taken together make it very difficult to construe this c.i.f. contract as containing an implied condition for payment of "cash against documents."

The appeal, therefore, must be allowed, and judgment entered for the plaintiffs. . . .

FARWELL L.J. The first question in this case is whether a contract for hops "c.i.f. to London, terms net cash," but without the words "against documents," means that the price is to be paid against documents, or after the buyer has had the opportunity of inspecting the goods. Hamilton J. has held, and I agree with him, that "terms net cash" adds nothing to the contract to pay. . . .

Now, . . . there are three ways only in which a provision not expressed in a written document can be added to it. The first is where the words used are elliptical; the second is usage: . . . and the third is necessary implication. . . . The words of the contract here . . . are obviously elliptical so far as "c.i.f." is concerned, and on construction mean that the 90s is to include cost insurance and freight . . . but they express no time or term of payment: payment is dealt with in the next sentence — "terms net cash" — and here is the natural and usual place to add "against documents" . . . if the parties so intend. . . . It is in my opinion equally impossible to add any term by usage . . . [since] no evidence was tendered, nor was it suggested, that there was any usage or law merchant.

There remains, therefore, only the third ground. At common law the delivery of goods by the seller and acceptance and payment by the buyer are regarded as concurrent acts, the buyer being entitled to a reasonable opportunity for inspection before he accepts and pays. . . . The general rule, therefore, is payment against inspected goods; and this is simple enough where both parties and the goods are together in the same place. But when goods are shipped from across seas, the contract becomes complicated by the fact that the delivery, although not complete until acceptance, commences on a c.i.f. contract on shipment, and the property passes, subject to certain qualifications not necessary now to consider, when the goods are shipped; if the seller fails to ship, or ships goods not according to contract, the breach by him is committed there and then. . . . But the buyer's acceptance and duty to pay is not on shipment. The c.i.f. contract usually provides for payment against documents, a practice convenient for both parties as the bill of lading enables financial dealings on the credit of the goods to be carried out before the arrival of the goods; but no one has ever suggested that on a c.i.f. contract, silent as to time of payment, the buyer is bound to pay on shipment of the goods. The result must therefore be that the ordinary rule of law is not displaced, namely, payment against examined goods. It is said that this cannot be so, because under the contract in common form "c.i.f. payment against documents" the buyer has to unload and warehouse the goods at his own expense; whereas the seller would have to bear such expense if he has to afford the buyer an opportunity of inspection before payment can be required. But this is only to state the different consequences flowing from two contracts expressed in different terms: there is no such necessity for any implication as to justify the Court in altering the usual incidence of burdens under a contract silent as to this particular burden. . . .

. . . I will assume that as a matter of usage the seller is bound to tender the bill of lading to the buyer when it arrives, and, if the buyer accepts it, he must, of course, pay for the goods on such acceptance, because the delivery of the bill of lading is a symbolical delivery of the goods, and, if the goods are accepted, the right of antecedent (though not of subsequent) inspection before payment is thereby waived, just as it would be in the case of acceptance of the goods themselves without inspection. But I fail to follow the consequence said by the learned judge to ensue. The duty on A to tender to B a document before he can require payment does not impose on B a duty to accept such document as equivalent to goods, if he has a right to inspect such goods before accepting and paying for them. B has the option of choosing between two alternative rights: he may accept symbolical delivery or actual delivery, but in the absence of express contract it is at his option, not at the seller's. . . . If the goods were lost at sea, the option would at once cease because inspection would have been rendered impossible, and the buyer would be bound to pay against documents. . . .

The basis of my judgment is that the buyer has a common law right (now embodied in the Sale of Goods Act) to have inspected goods against payment, and this cannot be taken away from him without some contract expressed or implied, and here I can find neither.

In my opinion the appeal should be allowed and judgment entered for the plaintiffs.

KENNEDY L.J. So far as regards the claim of the plaintiffs, which Hamilton J. has dismissed, his judgment was in my opinion right, and but for the contrary opinion of the other members of this Court, from whom I have the misfortune to differ, I should have ventured to think the case a reasonably simple one. . . .

Let us . . . leave out of sight altogether for the present all question of usage or judicial recognition of usage. The application of the principles and rules of the common law, now embodied in the Sale of Goods Act, 1893, to the business transaction embodied in the c.i.f. contract appears to me decisive of the issue between these parties. . . .

At the port of shipment — in this case San Francisco — the vendor ships the goods intended for the purchaser under the contract. Under the Sale of Goods Act,

1893, s. 18, by such shipment the goods are appropriated by the vendor to the fulfillment of the contract, and by virtue of s. 32[5] the delivery of the goods to the carrier . . . for the purpose of transmission to the purchaser is prima facie to be deemed to be a delivery of the goods to the purchaser. Two further legal results arise out of the shipment. The goods are at the risk of the purchaser, against which he has protected himself by the stipulation . . . that the vendor shall, at his own cost, provide him with a proper policy of marine insurance . . . if the goods should be lost in transit; and the property in the goods has passed to the purchaser. . . . But the vendor, in the absence of special agreement, is not yet in a position to demand payment from the purchaser; his delivery of the goods to the carrier is . . . only "prima facie deemed to be a delivery of the goods to the buyer;" and under s. 28 . . . a tender of delivery entitling the vendor to payment of the price must, in the absence of contractual stipulation to the contrary, be a tender of possession. How is such a tender to be made of goods afloat under a c.i.f. contract? By tender of the bill of lading, accompanied in case the goods have been lost in transit by the policy of insurance. The bill of lading in law and in fact represents the goods. Possession of the bill of lading places the goods at the disposal of the purchaser. . . . The meaning of "delivery" under Sale of Goods Act is defined by s. 62 to be "voluntary transfer of possession from one person to another." Such delivery . . . may be either actual or constructive and . . . in the case of seaborne goods, the delivery of the bill of lading operates as a symbolical delivery of the goods. But then I understand it to be objected on behalf of the plaintiffs: "Granted that the purchaser might, if he pleased, take this constructive delivery and pay against it the price of the goods; what is there in the 'cost freight and insurance' contract which compels him to do so? Why may he not insist on an option of waiting for a tender of delivery of the goods themselves after having had an opportunity of examining them after their arrival?"

There are, I think, several sufficient answers to such a proposition. In the first place, an option of a time of payment is not a term which can be inferred, where the contract itself is silent. . . . Secondly, if there is a duty on the vendor to tender the bill of lading, there must, it seems to me, be a corresponding duty on the part of the purchaser to pay when such tender is made. . . . [As] expounded by Bowen L.J. in the *Moorcock* . . .: "The stipulations which are inferred in mercantile contracts are always that the party will do what is mercantilely reasonable"; and, if it be the duty implied in the c.i.f. contract . . . that the vendor shall make every reasonable exertion to send forward and tender the bill of lading as soon as possible after he has destined the cargo to the particular vendee, it is, I venture to think, "mercantilely reasonable" that the purchaser should be held bound to make the agreed payment when delivery of the goods is constructively tendered to him by the tender of the bill of lading. . . .

[Moreover] . . . the plaintiffs' assertion of the right . . . to withhold payment until delivery of the goods themselves, and until after an opportunity of examining them, cannot possibly be effectuated except in one of two ways. Landing and delivery can rightfully be given by the shipowner only to the holder of the bill of lading. Therefore, if the plaintiffs' contention is right, one of two things must

---

[5] Documentary Supplement.

happen. Either the seller must surrender to the purchaser the bill of lading . . . without receiving payment, which, as the bill of lading carries with it an absolute power of disposition, is, in the absence of a special agreement . . . so unreasonable as to be absurd; or, alternatively, the vendor must himself retain the bill of lading, himself land and take delivery of the goods, and himself store the goods on quay . . . or, warehouse the goods, for such time as may elapse before the purchaser has an opportunity of examining them. But this involves a manifest violation of the express terms of the contract "90s per 112 lbs cost freight and insurance." The parties have in terms agreed that for the buyer's benefit the price shall include freight and insurance, and for his benefit nothing beyond freight and insurance. . . .

Finally, . . . suppose the goods . . . during the ocean transit . . . [had] been lost by the perils of the sea. The vendor tenders the bill of landing, with the insurance policy and the other shipping documents (if any) to the purchaser, to whom from the moment of shipment the property has passed, and at whose risk, covered by the insurance, the goods were at the time of loss. Is it, I ask myself, arguable that the purchaser could be heard to say, "I will not pay because I cannot have delivery of and an examination of the goods?" But it is just this which is necessarily involved in the contention of these plaintiffs. The seller's answer, and I think conclusive answer, is, "You have the bill of lading and the policy of insurance."

I have only to add as to this . . . a few words in regard to ss. 28 and 34 of the Sale of Goods Act. As I have already said, my own view as to s. 28 is that the section is satisfied by the readiness and willingness of the seller to give possession of the bill of lading. I am, however, far from saying that the view . . . suggested . . . [by] Hamilton J., namely, that when the parties have entered into a c.i.f. contract they have "otherwise agreed," is not one which could be supported, as I hold that a similar view is the true view also in regard to s. 34, sub-s. 2. As to s. 34, sub-s. 1, there is no difficulty. No one suggests that the plaintiffs, if they pay against documents, become thereby precluded from rejecting the goods if, on examination after their arrival, they are found to be not goods in accordance with the contract, or from recovering damages for breach of contract if they prefer that course.

[Furthermore] . . . the judgment of the Court of Appeal . . . in the case of *Parker v. Schuller* cannot, in my judgment, be reconciled with [the] contention of the present appellants. In *Parker v. Schuller* . . . the contract was in every essential point identical with the contract in the present case. It was a simple c.i.f. contract, without mention of payment against documents, the goods sold being goods to be shipped from Germany to Liverpool. The goods had not been shipped. The breach alleged by the plaintiffs . . . was the non-delivery of the goods themselves to the buyers in Liverpool. [On this count they obtained judgment below, but] . . . the Court of Appeal reversed . . . holding that th[e] non-delivery of the goods themselves . . . did not constitute a breach of the c.i.f. contract. . . . [Indeed on appeal] counsel for the plaintiff expressly . . . declined even to argue the point upon which his clients had [won in the court below]. . . . [As noted in] the judgment of the Master of the Rolls:

> Upon the appeal the alleged contract to deliver the goods at Liverpool was dropped, the contract being c.i.f. Liverpool. . . . That was abandoned. . . .

It was not contended that a c.i.f. contract was a contract to deliver goods in this country.

The case of the plaintiffs on the present appeal that the defendants can demand payment only upon delivery of the goods logically depends upon the alleged obligation of the defendants to delivery the goods themselves in this country, and we cannot, it appears to me, reverse the judgment of Hamilton J. in this case without holding, as a necessary conclusion, that this Court decided wrongly in *Parker v. Schuller.* . . .

In my judgment, the judgment of Hamilton J. was right, and this appeal, so far as relates to the plaintiff's claim, should be

Dismissed.

From the judgment of the Court of Appeals, the defendants E. Clemens Horst Company took an appeal to the House of Lords, with the following results.

E. CLEMENS HORST COMPANY v. BIDDLE BROTHERS

House of Lords
[1912] Appeals Cases 18

EARL LOREBURN L.C. My Lords, in this case there has been a remarkable divergence of judicial opinion. . . . For my part I think it is reasonably clear that this appeal ought to be allowed; and the remarkable judgment of Kennedy L.J., illuminating, as it does, the whole field of controversy, relieves me from the necessity of saying much upon the subject. . . .

Now, s. 28 of the Sale of Goods Act says in effect that payment is to be against delivery. . . . But when is there delivery of goods which are on board ship? . . . The answer is that delivery of the bill of lading when the goods are at sea can be treated as delivery of the goods themselves, this law being so old that I think it is quite unnecessary to refer to authority for it.

Now in this contract there is no time fixed at which the seller is entitled to tender the bill of lading. He therefore may do so at any reasonable time; and it is wrong to say that he must defer the tender of the bill of lading until the ship has arrived; and it is still more wrong to say that he must defer the tender of the bill of lading until after the goods have been landed, inspected and accepted. . . .

Accordingly, Hamilton J.'s order ought to be restored so far as the [plaintiffs'] claim is concerned. As regards the counter-claim, I think there ought to be judgment for the defendants with one shilling damages, and no costs on either side.

LORD ATKINSON. My Lords, I concur.

LORD GORELL. My Lords, I also concur.

LORD SHAW OF DUNFERMLINE. My Lords, I desire to express my adherence to the opinion delivered by Kennedy L.J. the value of which has not been overstated by the noble Earl on the woolsack.

NOTES AND QUESTIONS

(1) When seller, rather quaintly, writes to the buyer "we will value on your good selves at sight," what document was it referring to? The amount of this document was to be "invoice price less freight." What arrangement with the carrier did this indicate the seller intended to make? If, instead of being at "sight," the contract of sale required the document to be "sixty days after sight," would you, as buyer's lawyer, object to seller's anticipated arrangement with the carrier? What more would you need to know? On this point consult, UCC Section 2-320, Comment 5[6] and Revised American Foreign Trade Definitions, C.I.F. Comment 6.[7]

(2) Note that the contract of October 13, 1904, was for seven years at a fixed price of 90 shillings (*i.e.*, then £4 1/2) per 112 pounds. If at the time of contracting the exchange rate between the dollar and pound sterling was £1 = $5 who would lose if later the pound devalues against the dollar to where £1 = $4? Who gains if the dollar devalues against the pound to where £1 = $6? Now restate the general principle as to who takes the exchange risk under an international sales contract.

(3) In deciding whether the words "c.i.f. at London" standing alone entitled the seller to payment against documents, all of the judges in the Court of Appeals disclaimed any reliance upon usage of the trade, general commercial usage or any course of dealing between these particular parties. If so, what are they relying upon? In the court below, Hamilton, J. thought that the meaning of those terms was "well settled and well understood." By whom? Kennedy J. does cite *Parker v. Shuller* but more particularly notes that the majority position would either require the seller to (i) surrender the bill of lading before getting paid or (ii) land and store the goods at its own expense until the buyer had inspected them. The first option he calls "absurd." To Whom? The second option he finds contrary to the contract. Circular? How might Farwell J. respond to this last point? How does Kennedy J. square his result with Section 28 of the English Sale of Goods Act?[8] Again, what are the Judges relying upon in reaching their differing interpretations? Their disagreement certainly suggests that the question was not "well settled" in law, although one may question why so at so late a date. In all events Kennedy's position as adopted by the House of Lords is now well settled. See UCC Sec. 2-320(4) particularly Comment 1. As redrafted, new INCOTERMS do not make the point as they did under the old version.

---

[6] Documentary Supplement.
[7] Documentary Supplement.
[8] Documentary Supplement.

(4) If the contract in *Biddle Brothers* had been FOB Vessel, would the precise issue in that case have been decided differently? Compare UCC Sec. 2-320(4) with Sec. 2-319(4). Under FOB vessel the responsibilities of the parties to arrange for ocean transport, insurance, etc. would be different, but how would the allocation of commercial risks differ? Who would bear the risk of loss of the goods at sea? Who will ultimately pay the costs of ocean freight and the costs of marine insurance? Who can divert the cargo while at sea under CIF? under FOB Vessel? Note this is a fairly long-term contract. What other element in the total delivered cost of the goods could, indeed is likely to, change over that term and who bears the risk of that change under CIF? under FOB Vessel?

§ 1.03   Documents of Title; Bills of Lading, Delivery Orders and Other Documents

In connection with your study of the next cases examine the sample standard form Bill of Lading found in the Documentary Supplement.[1]

BARCLAYS BANK, LTD. v. COMMISSIONERS OF CUSTOMS AND EXCISE

Queen's Bench Division (Commercial Court),
[1963] 1 Lloyd's List Law Rep. 82

[In this case, the bank claimed to be entitled to possession as pledgee of two consignments of washing machines shipped from Rotterdam to Cardiff in early 1961, and seized, while in a bonded warehouse at Cardiff, in execution of a judgment for back taxes by the Goverment.

The washing machines had been purchased by Bruitrix Electric Company, Ltd. (Bruitrix) from a Dutch supplier, c.i.f. Cardiff, delivery against acceptance of bills of exchange. The bill of lading issued by the shipowners was an "order" bill which stipulated:

This Bill of Lading duly endorsed to be given in exchange for delivery order if required. . . .

The draft was accepted by Bruitrix in March 1961 who was then given the bill of lading and invoices. The goods were discharged from the vessel, put into a transit warehouse and there held to the order of the shipowners. Bruitrix, however, took no steps to obtain possession or clear the goods through customs. In May, with the goods still in the warehouse, the shipowners wrote Bruitrix asking for "clearance documents (*i.e.* the invoices), as soon as possible, to avoid trouble with Customs." Bruitrix did nothing.

On June 2, 1961, Bruitrix pledged the bills of lading with the bank as security on an overdraft, and executed a memorandum of pledge. The bills of lading and invoices were deposited with the bank. Ultimately the invoices were obtained by the shipowners from the bank, the goods were cleared through customs and were moved to a bonded warehouse still in the name of the

---

[1] Documentary Supplement.

shipowners who would not issue a delivery order without presentation of the bill of lading. In August, the Government recovered judgment against Bruitrix for back taxes. On September 28, the shipowners issued delivery orders to the bank upon presentation of the bills of lading. The next day, at 3:00 p.m. the Sheriff took possession of the goods on behalf of the Government. The Bank then took the delivery orders to the bonded warehouse which issued dock warrants at 5:00 p.m. By that time the Sheriff had the goods. Accordingly, the bank commenced this action.]

Before LORD JUSTICE DIPLOCK (sitting as an additional judge of the Queens' Bench Division)

LORD JUSTICE DIPLOCK. . . .[T]he question which I have to decide is whether on June 2, 1961, the bills of lading were still documents of title for the goods to which they related, so that effective pledge of the goods could be made by deposit of the bills of lading indorsed in blank with the Bank. . . .

* * * *

The contention of the [Government] is that as soon as (1) . . . the contract of carriage by sea . . . evidenced by the bill of lading is complete, and (2), the bill of lading is in the hands of the person entitled to . . . possession of the goods, and is in a form which would entitle him upon mere presentation to obtain delivery of the goods from the shipowner . . . it ceases to be a document of title by . . . which the rights and property in the goods can be transferred. This is indeed a startling proposition of law which, if correct, would go far to destroy the value of a bill of lading as an instrument of overseas credit. It would mean that no bank could safely advance money on the security of a bill of lading without first making inquiries at the port of delivery, which may be at the other side of the world, as to whether the goods had been landed with the shipowner's lien, if any, discharged or released. It would also mean that no purchaser of goods could rely upon delivery and indorsement to him of the bill of lading as conferring upon him any title to the goods without making similar inquiries, for it would follow that once the goods had been landed and any lien of the shipowner released or discharged, the owner of the goods could divest himself of the property in them without reference to the bill of lading. It would also follow that the shipowner, once the goods had been landed in the absence of any lien, could not safely deliver the goods to the holder of the bill of lading upon presentation because the property in and right to possession of the goods, might have been transferred by the owner to some other person. . . .

The contract for the carriage of goods by sea, which is evidenced by a bill of lading, is a combined contract of bailment and transportation under which the shipowner undertakes to accept possession of the goods from the shipper, to carry them to their contractual destination and there to surrender possession of them to the person who, under the terms of the contract, is entitled to obtain possession of them from the shipowners. Such a contract is not discharged by performance until the shipowner has actually surrendered possession (that is, has divested himself of all powers to control any physical dealing in the goods) to the person entitled under the terms of the contract to obtain possession of them.

So long as the contract is not discharged, the bill of lading, in my view, remains a document of title by indorsement and delivery of which the rights of property in the goods can be transferred. . . .

In the present case, the contract of carriage . . . had not been discharged on June 2, 1961, when Bruitrix purported to pledge the goods to the Bank. . . . The goods were in the constructive possession of the [carrier]. . . . The [carrier was] under no obligation to surrender [its] constructive possession and control to deal with the goods, except on production of the bill of lading and had no intention of doing so. In those circumstances it seems to me beyond argument that the bills of lading were at all material times effective documents of title for the goods by deposit of which to the Bank a valid pledge of the goods for security on advances could be made.

The argument to the contrary is really based upon some isolated passages . . . [in] the case of *Barber v. Meyerstein*. . . . The relevant question in that case was whether a valid pledge of goods could be made by deposit of a bill of lading after the goods had been delivered by the shipowner at a sufferance-wharf in London, and there held by the wharfinger in the name of the consignee subject to a lien on the freight made effective by notice given by the shipowner to the wharfinger. . . . The principle decided in that case is generally accepted as that laid down succinctly by Mr. Justice Willes in the Court of Common Pleas [as follows]:

> . . . the bill of lading remains in force [—as I elicit it was a document of title for delivery by indorsement of which property can be transferred—] at least so long as complete delivery of possession of the goods has not been made to some person having a right to claim them under it. . . .

It is not necessary in this case to consider what is a much more difficult question of law . . . as to what the position would be if the shipowners had given a complete delivery to Bruitrix of the goods without production of the bill of lading, at the date when they were entitled under its terms to delivery, and Bruitrix had subsequently purported to pledge the goods by deposit of the bill of lading. . . . In my opinion the pledge made on June 2, by deposit of the bill of lading was a valid pledge and as a consequence I think that I can give judgment for the plaintiffs in this case.

COMPTOIR D'ACHAT ET DE VENTE DU BOERENBOND BLEGE S/A/ v. LUIS DE RIDDER LTDA.

(THE JULIA)

House of Lords
[1949] A.C. 293

[In April 24, 1940 Luis de Ridder, Ltda. an Argentine grain exporting firm sold 500 tons of rye to Comptoir d'Achat et de Vente du Boerenbond Belge, S.A. under a contract calling for "shipment per steamer . . . *Julia* afloat as per . . . bills of lading dated . . . accordingly at a price of [$20,250] . . . c.i.f. Antwerp" and providing further:

> Payment to be made by net cash on first presentation of and in exchange for first arriving copy/ies of bill/s of lading and/or delivery order/s and policy/ies and/or certificate/s and/or letter/s of insurance at Antwerp by first rate cable transfer at New York, unless the vessel carrying the goods arrives before the said time, in which case payment is to be made on arrival of vessel at port of discharge.

On April 18, before contracting with the buyers, the sellers chartered the *Julia*, loaded her with 1,120 tons of rye and received from the ship's master a bill of lading for the full 1,120 tons. The bill of lading provided for delivery at Antwerp to the order of the sellers agent in that city, the Belgian Grain & Produce Company ("Belgian Grain"), upon payment of the freight.

On April 29, 1940, while the *Julia* was at sea, Belgian Grain sent the buyers a "provisional invoice" for approximately $5,000 representing the cost of the goods and insurance (*i.e.* total contract price less $15,250 of freight cost). The next day Belgian Grain also sent the buyer a delivery order instructing F. Van Bree S.A. ("Van Bree"), a firm of Antwerp cargo superintendents employed by the sellers, to release 500 tons of rye from the *Julia* upon presentation of the delivery order. The delivery order also stated, "We give a share to the bearer of the present order . . . in a certificate of insurance" on the rye aboard the Julia. The "share" specified was 2% over the invoice value of the rye that the buyers had contracted to purchase.

On April 30, the buyers accepted the "provisional invoice" and delivery order and paid the $5,000. The same day the seller delivered to Van Bree the certificate of insurance referred to in the delivery order. The certificate provided that it represented the original policy and conveyed all the rights of the original policy-holder for the purpose of collecting claims and that it could be exchanged for a stamped policy if and when required.

On May 10, 1940, while the *Julia* was still at sea, Germany invaded Belgium and shortly afterward occupied Antwerp. Whereupon, the owners, with the concurrence of the seller, diverted the ship to Lisbon and there the cargo was sold for substantially less than the contract price agreed to by the buyer. The seller offered to pay the buyer the amount realized on this sale, but the buyer refused claiming a right to the full $5,000 paid. After the war, the case went to arbitration before an Umpire on a claim by the buyer for 1,243 Pounds representing the Sterling equivalent of $5,000. The buyer contended that the non-delivery of the rye at Antwerp constituted a total failure of consideration for the payment made by it. In his award the Umpire concluded that the contract was a genuine c.i.f. contract and, subject to a decision of the court on the point, that the sellers had delivered as per the contract, that the property and all risk attendant thereto had passed to the buyer and that the buyer was not, as a consequence, entitled to the recovery sought. The Umpire's award was upheld by the court of first instance and by the Court of Appeals from which decision the present appeal was taken.

The Umpire also found that, for more than ten years, the buyer and the seller had been doing business this way in what they called their "c.i.f. business."

That "business typically involved the following steps, all of which would have occurred had the Julia not been diverted to Lisbon. (i) Typically the seller would load a ship with cargoes of grain in bulk and then, usually while the ship was at sea, sell parts of the cargo to different buyers. Payment equal to the invoice value of the goods plus insurance would be made by each buyer, usually before the ship arrived, on the basis of a provisional invoice and a delivery order. (ii) After the ship arrived the buyer in this case would give the delivery order with its check for the freight to Carga, S.A., another Antwerp cargo superintendent firm, employed by the buyer as its agent. (iii) Carga would present Belgian Grain with the check and the delivery order and Belgian Grain would acknowledge receipt of the check by signing at the bottom of the order. (iii) Carga would then present the counter-signed delivery order to Van Bree, seller's agent, who would file the order and issue a release instructing its own employees at the dock to deliver to Carga the quantity of grain described in the release. (iv) Before Carga could take actual possession of the goods, however, Van Bree had to have received from agents of the shipowner a so-called "captain's release" indicating that the ship's agents had actually received or were satisfied that they would receive payment of the freight. This "captain's release" was directed to the crew of the ship and instructed them to deliver the grain described therein. Thereupon representatives of Carga and Van Bree would go aboard the vessel and take samples of the cargo. If Carga was satisfied, the appropriate amount of grain was transferred from the ship to a lighter and transported to the buyer's warehouse or to designated customers. Also, according to the Umpire, the "captain's release" was the "effective document upon which Van Bree obtained physical possession of the goods." This "release" was issued to Van Bree and was never physically in the buyers' hands. The same was also true of the certificate of insurance. In the past, two instances had occurred where ships had been lost at sea. In both cases each buyer received from Belgian Grain a remittance for the insured value of their portion of the lost cargo.]

LORD PORTER. . . .

My Lords, the obligations imposed upon a seller under a c.i.f. contract are well known, and in the ordinary case include the tender of a bill of lading . . . coupled with an insurance policy in the normal form and accompanied by an invoice which shows the price and, as in this case, usually contains a deduction of the freight which the buyer pays before delivery at the port of discharge. Against tender of these documents the purchaser must pay the price. In such a case the property may pass either on shipment or on tender, the risk generally passes on shipment . . . but possession does not pass until the documents which represent the goods are handed over in exchange for the price. . . . The strict form of c.i.f. contract may, however, be modified: a provision that a delivery order may be substituted for a bill of lading or a certificate of insurance for a policy would not, I think, make the contract concluded upon something other than c.i.f. terms, but . . . [n]ot every contract which is expressed to be a c.i.f. contract is such. . . . The true effect of all [the contract] . . . terms must be taken into account, though, of course, the description c.i.f. must not be neglected. [In the end, I do not construe the contract in this case as a c.i.f. contract] . . . even when illuminated by the practice adopted by the parties. That practice seems to me rather to show that the payment was not made for the documents but as an advance payment for a contract afterwards to be performed. . . . I can see no sufficient reason for supposing either that the delivery order had some commercial value or that Van Bree undertook a personal liability by their indorsement of the document. . . . In my view, if [Belgian Grain] . . . were sued upon the document they would rightly reply that they were acting only as agents and Van Bree could make the same defense. The document appears to me to be no more than an indication that a promise already made by the sellers would be carried out in due course, but in no way increases their obligations or adds to the security of the buyers.

. . . No doubt the contract could have been so performed as to make it subject to the ordinary principles which apply to a c.i.f. contract. The tender of a bill of lading or even of a delivery order upon the ship, at any rate if attorned to by the master, and a policy or a certificate of insurance delivered to or even held for them might well put it in that category. But the type of delivery order tendered in the present case was a preliminary step only. . . . [B]efore physical delivery of the goods could take place Van Bree must have received a "Captain's laissez suivre" authorizing delivery to them. "It was thus," as the umpire says, "the effective document upon which Van Bree obtained physical possession of the goods; it was issued to Van Bree and was never physically in the buyers' hands."

My Lords, the object and the result of a c.i.f. contract is to enable sellers and buyers to deal with cargoes or parcels afloat and to transfer them freely from hand to hand by giving constructive possession of the goods which are being dealt with. Undoubtedly the practice of shipping and insuring produce in bulk is to make the process more difficult. . . .

[W]here, as, in my opinion, is the case here, no further security beyond that contained in the original contract passed to the buyers as a result of payment, where the property and possession both remained in the sellers' possession until delivery in Antwerp, where the sellers were to pay for deficiency in bill of lading weight, guaranteed condition on arrival and made themselves responsible for all averages, the true view, I think, is that it is not a c.i.f. contract even in a modified form but a contract to deliver at Antwerp. . . . What the buyers wanted was delivery of the goods in Antwerp. What the sellers wanted was payment of the price before that date, and the delivery of the documents furnished the date for payment, but had no effect on the property or possession of the goods or the buyers' rights against the sellers. If this be the view there was plainly a frustration of the adventure. . . . The buyers are accordingly entitled to recover the money which they have paid. I would allow the appeal and pronounce for the alternative award with costs in your Lordships' House and in the courts below.

LORD SIMONDS . . . [I]t was urged, that the sellers had done all, and I emphasize the word "all," they were bound to do if and when they handed over a delivery order and certificates of insurance. I do not pause to examine the factual basis of this contention, for it seems to me to be wholly unsound in law. The fact that a seller at a certain stage in the carrying out of his contract is entitled by its terms to demand payment does not mean that at that stage he has fully performed his contract. Confusion, as I think, has arisen from the fact that had the sellers been in a position and elected to tender shipping documents by virtue of which the property in the goods passed to the buyers, then the latter could not have contended that there had been failure of consideration. But this result would have ensued not because a clause in the contract provided for payment against documents, but because in law there cannot be failure of consideration if the property has passed. . . .

But then, it was said, . . . that there could not be total failure of consideration if the sellers had done something towards carrying out this contract and that they had done something, viz., handed over a delivery order . . . [It was also] . . . said that something was itself of value, therefore there was not a total failure of consideration. In its first aspect this contention appears to suffer from the same fallacy as that which I have already tried to expose. . . . But in its second aspect it demands closer attention, for here it has the support of the learned judges in the courts below.

My Lords, there is, in my opinion, no finding of fact by the umpire which would justify your Lordships in holding that the delivery order which was handed to the buyers had any commercial value in the ordinary sense. That it was not a document of title by itself entitling the buyers to delivery of the goods was expressly found. It is a matter of conjecture whether in these circumstances it had any commercial value, and your Lordships cannot found on conjecture . . . I come, then, to the conclusion that the sellers performed neither all nor, in any material sense, a part of what they were required to do under the contract and that the buyers obtained no part of that which they had contracted to buy. There was therefore total failure of consideration.

LORD NORMAND. What then is the basis of the contention that the buyers received consideration for the part of the price paid by them? The main proposition advanced by the sellers was that the delivery order must be treated as equivalent to the goods, though neither the property nor the risk passed, because the contract so provides. But there were independent and subsidiary contentions that the risk of marine loss had passed to the buyers, and, failing all else, that the delivery order was valuable consideration on one of two grounds, either that it was a document of commercial value or that it contained a promise by Van Bree that they personally would honour the delivery order in accordance with the terms of the bill of lading which they held for the inspection of the bearer.

I propose to consider first whether these subordinate contentions have any validity and relevance. . . . The agreement of parties that the buyers should bear the risk of a loss against which the insurance was provided for by the contract is not evidence of an intention that the buyers were also to take the risk of a frustration which was not within the contemplation of the contract. I have also difficulty in attaching any intelligible meaning in this case to the proposition that the marine risk passed though the property did not pass.

It may be conceded that the parties can agree to some purely artificial allocation of the risk and if they express that agreement in suitable language in the contract it must somehow be given effect. But the parties to commercial contracts are practical people and in those cases in which it has been held that the risk without the property has passed to the buyer it has been because the buyer rather than the seller was seen to have an immediate and practical interest in the goods. . . . But in the present case the buyers had no more than a promise to deliver a part of the bulk cargo. . . . The sellers' practical and real interest in the goods at risk is also evidenced by clauses in the contract by which they assumed liability for deficiency at discharge on bill of lading weight and guaranteed condition on arrival, and by a clause providing that all average should be for sellers' account. Nor is it immaterial to observe that if the contract had been completely performed the buyers would never have had in their hands any document entitling them to sue underwriters. The fact that on two occasions when there was a total loss the sellers collected the insured value and remitted it to the buyers . . . is of no importance, because that was done without the buyers' instructions and, since the sum remitted was not less than the price paid, the buyers had no interest to question the sellers' conduct. The clause obliging the sellers to give to the buyers all policies and certificates of insurance . . . is not in harmony with a contract intended to be performed as this contract was. It seems, indeed, that this clause and perhaps some others, though appropriate where it was intended that the sale should be implemented by tender of shipping documents . . . do not fit the course of dealing by the parties which by imposing a special meaning on "delivery order" required the sellers to accept a document which was not in law a symbol of the goods. It is not necessary to deny all effect to the clause dealing with policies of insurance and certificates. The buyers had a double interest in the insurance. First, the cost of the policies was a component of the price and they therefore had an interest to know that proper insurance had been effected and at what cost. Second, the marine risk policies would cover the risk from the time the rye was delivered to them by the ship till it reached their warehouse. Beyond these two interests I think that the buyers had no concern with the insurance. . . .

The other subsidiary arguments for the sellers all depend on the attribution of some value to the delivery order. I again question the relevance of the line of argument. It is agreed that the delivery order was not the equivalent of the goods in the sense that its possession conferred on the holder the right of property in the goods valid against all the world. But the consideration for the price is nothing less than that right, unless there are special terms in the contract. If the delivery order had some value otherwise than as the equivalent of the goods the fact has not been proved, and if proved it would be without relevance. . . .

These subsidiary arguments by themselves therefore avail nothing, and the sellers must rely on their contention that the contract by its special terms provides that between the sellers and the buyers the delivery order shall be treated as equivalent to the goods. The sellers laid weight on the description of the price as a c.i.f. price and on the description of the business as c.i.f. business. . . . I think, however, that the explanation of the description c.i.f. in relation to the price and the business carried on by these two parties is that the contract stipulates for a price the components of which were cost, insurance and freight. . . . The stipulation that the price or part of it was to be paid in exchange for a bill of lading and policy or in exchange for a delivery order and certificate does not carry with it the implication that in relation to the rights of the parties inter se the delivery order is to have the effect of a bill of lading. . . . But I think that if the words "delivery order" had to be construed without the aid of the previous course of dealing, it would have been held to mean a document addressed to and accepted by one in physical possession of the goods. The sellers would then have been bound to tender a document which was in fact the legal equivalent of the goods.

The effect of the course of dealing was to release the sellers from that obligation and to entitle them to payment on tender of a document which contains no more than a personal obligation. I do not find evidence in the contract that the parties have undertaken to treat this document as a document of title as between themselves. I would therefore allow the appeal, with costs, both here and in the courts below.

Appeal allowed.

NOTES AND QUESTIONS

(1) Why did the parties use this complex system of delivery orders and releases?

(2) All three Law Lords concluded that under the contract "illuminated" by the practice of the parties, "property in the goods had not passed" from the seller to the buyer at the time of the diversion of the *Julia* to Lisbon. Presumably this means that the seller had not done all that was legally necessary to confer on the buyer a right to obtain possession of the goods. This, as we have seen, is the function of a bill of lading — whether negotiable or not. Also, because the bill of lading is a symbolic tender of possession, the buyer is obligated, unless the parties otherwise agree, to pay for the goods upon tender of the bill. Furthermore, to say that "property in goods" has passed to the buyer is also to conclude that the buyer bears the risk of loss of the goods during transit, a risk against which insurance is required under a c.i.f. arrangement. Against this background consider a few preliminary points:

(a) Lord Simonds makes much of the absence in the record of any evidence showing that the delivery orders employed in the *Julia* case had commercial value. The seller's contention that they had value was based, he said, on pure conjecture, and the House of Lords could not "found" its decision on conjecture. What is the Lord Justice suggesting? Does he mean to say that the document which purports to confer on the buyer the right to obtain possession of the goods from the seller (*i.e.*, to pass "the property" in the goods) must also confer on the buyer a commercially valuable right to deal in the goods with third parties? If this is what he means, do you agree? In answering, remember that the issue being discussed is only to locate "the property" in the goods as between buyer and seller. Remember also, that a negotiable bill of lading is often commercially more valuable than a non-negotiable bill precisely because it facilitates further dealings in the goods by the buyer. Non-negotiable bills of lading can be transferred only by an assignment to which the other party to the instrument — the carrier — must consent. Yet, the non-negotiable form is equally effective to convey the right of possession in the goods ("the property") as between buyer and seller.

(b) Alternatively, is Lord Simond merely saying that the absence of commercial value in the delivery order is some evidence that the parties, in using that device, did not intend for "the property" to pass; *i.e.*, that the parties intended a contract for delivery at destination with pre-payment by the buyer. What more might you want to know before ascribing such an intention to the parties merely because the delivery order lacked commercial value?

(3) To further test the Law Lord's conclusion that the delivery order did not convey to the buyer a right of possession to the goods, go through each step that would have been followed, according to prior practice, had the *Julia* actually arrived in Antwerp and identify the precise purpose of each step. Specifically, (i) why would Carga take the delivery order to Belgian Grain for the latter's counter-signature; (ii) why would Van Bree then take up the counter-signed delivery order and issue its own delivery order; (iii) why was it necessary to obtain the "captain's release" — the "Captain laissez-suivre?"

Now, suppose that the seller in the *Julia* Case had obtained from the carrier a non-negotiable bill of lading "freight collect" naming Belgian Grain as consignee and that thereafter, while the *Julia* was still at sea, the buyer purchased the entire cargo of rye. Assume further that Belgian Grain, at the time of payment by the buyer, assigned the non-negotiable bill to the buyer, with the carrier's consent.

(a) Under these circumstances, what steps would the buyer, through Carga its agent, have had to take in order to obtain possession of the rye after the ship arrived in Antwerp? With the possible exception of issuance of its check to Belgian Grain (this would depend on the terms of the assignment), is there any step that the buyer would not have had to take if it held a non-negotiable bill of lading, that it was required to take under the delivery order system traditionally used by the parties? If, in the case where a bill of lading was used, the buyer's check would not be issued to Belgian Grain, to whom would it be issued? Would this make any difference in terms of the efficacy of the document in question — the delivery order v. the bill of lading — to confer a right of possession on the buyer?

(b) Lord Porter makes much of the umpires finding that the "Captain's release was the effective document upon which Van Bree obtained possession of the goods" and that document was never in the buyer's possession. Mechanically, would this not be equally true if the buyer held a non-negotiable bill of lading?

(4) Turn now to the question of the allocation of risk and consider the following:

(a) Lord Normand admits that the parties "can agree to some purely artificial allocation of the risk." Presumably he means by this an agreement by the buyer to assume the risk of loss of the goods before receiving "the property" in the goods. But if that is "artificial," isn't Lord Normand's analysis badly flawed? Doesn't the buyer's assumption of the risk of loss suggest something about the parties' intentions with respect to "the property" in the goods?

(b) Lord Normand also states that: "if the contract had been completely performed the buyers would never have had in their hands any document entitling them to sue underwriters." It is, of course, true that under a c.i.f contract the buyer normally receives, at the time of payment, a policy of insurance. Note, however, that Lord Porter thought that a certificate of insurance, in lieu of the policy, would not be inconsistent with the c.i.f. form. If so, does the arrangement actually employed in the case (*i.e.*, statement in the delivery order promising the buyer either the certificate or the policy, if needed) combined with past practice represent a significant deviation from the normal course of conduct under a c.i.f. contract? How would the buyer have proceeded had it needed to sue the underwriter?

(c) Observe, Lord Normands' discomfiture at this point. He states: "It seems, indeed, that this clause (*i.e.*, the promise to make the policy available) . . . do[es] not fit the course of dealing by the parties which by imposing a special meaning on "delivery order" required the buyers to accept a document which was not in law a symbol of the goods." Again, isn't the mode of analysis flawed? What does the clause concerning the insurance policy tell you about the delivery order?

(5) Lord Porter notes, as evidence that the property in the goods was retained by the seller, that under the contract the "sellers were to pay for deficiency in bill of lading weight [and] guaranteed condition on arrival." What would sellers' responsibilities be if, under our non-negotiable bill of lading hypothetical, Carga and Van Bree discovered after the ship arrived that the cargo did not actually weigh out to the tonnage stated in the bill of lading or that its condition did not conform to the contract? What do you make of the fact that sellers retained responsibility for "all averages?"

(6) What is the significance of the fact that when it issued the delivery order Belgian Grain presumably gave none of the warranties that normally accompany negotiation of a negotiable bill of lading? Note, that the assignment of a non-negotiable bill of lading does not normally carry with it the warranties that accompany endorsement of a negotiable bill. Explain. Again, have the Law Lord's confused the issue of the commercial utility of the document with its function as between buyer and seller?

(7) Was the House of Lords decision a triumph of formalism over function and commercial utility? Note the arbitrator, the court of first instance and the Court of Appeals all thought that this was a true c.i.f. contract.

NOTE ON THE FEDERAL BILL OF LADING ACT

49 U.S.C. Secs. 81-124

While this Note focuses on the Federal Bill of Lading Act, it is well to recognize the close relationship of that Act to the Federal Carriage of Goods by Sea Act (COGSA), which we examine in the next Section. The basic purposes of the Federal Bill of Lading Act are to perfect the negotiability of order bills of lading, to prescribe more precisely the responsibilities of carriers in delivering goods covered by a bill of lading and to prohibit certain practices in the issuance of bills of lading.[2] COGSA, on the other hand, regulates the responsibilities of carriers with respect to the handling and transport of cargoes. As such, it necessarily regulates certain aspects of the bill of lading. Finally, there is Article 7 of the Uniform Commercial Code which covers much of the same ground as the Federal Bill of Lading Act and, as State law, governs in cases not within the scope of the Federal law.

As to scope, the Federal Bill of Lading Act applies, by its terms, to all bills of lading issued by a common carrier for transportation between States of the United States or from a place in such a State to a place in a foreign country. It does not apply to bills of lading (i) for carriage *originating* in a foreign country, (ii) to *intrastate* carriage or (iii) to *interstate* carriage that originates and ends in the same State.[3]

The latter two cases are governed by the UCC. Cases where the carriage to the United States originates abroad, however, might very well require choosing between the law of the country of origin and the appropriate State UCC. Also, a choice of law issue could theoretically arise even in cases where the Federal Act by its terms applies, if the Act differed in substance from the law of some other country with a close relationship to the transaction. Following the tradition established under COGSA,[4] however, one would generally expect the American courts to treat the statutory definition of the scope of the Bill of Lading Act as a Congressionally mandated choice of law foreclosing any independent judicial choice under normal conflicts principles.

COGSA, on the other hand, has a somewhat different and, for purposes of international trade, broader scope than the Bill of Lading Act. It applies to:

> Every bill of lading or similar document of title which is evidence of a contract for the carriage of goods by sea to or from the ports of the United States, in foreign trade. . . .[5]

Again, as already noted, the courts have tended to treat this provision as foreclosing any independent judicial choice of foreign law in cases within its scope, although we will note some possible erosion of that tendency.

Turning next to the substance of the Federal Bill of Lading Act, it starts with some definitions and a number of rules concerning the form of negotiable bills. Thus, a bill of lading stating that the goods are consigned to a specified person is called a "straight bill" (Section 82). A bill stating that the goods are consigned "to the order of any person named," is an "order bill." Any provision in an order

---

[2] For example, Section 84 prohibits issuance in a State of order bills of lading in parts or sets if the goods are to be transported to any place in the United States but not to foreign countries. See Comment to UCC Section 7-304. Documentary Supplement.

[3] See: J. White and R. Summers, Uniform Commercial Code, (2d ed., 1980) at page 830.

[4] See page 49 *infra.*

[5] 46 U.S.C. Sec. 1312, provides in pertinent part as follows:
The term "foreign trade" means the transportation of goods between the ports of the United States and ports of foreign countries. Nothing in this chapter shall be held to apply to contracts for carriage of goods by sea between any port of the United States or its possessions, and any other port of the United States or its possession; provided, however, that [if] any bill of lading . . . for carriage . . . between such ports . . . [expressly provides that this chapter is to apply] . . . . it shall be subjected hereto. . . .

bill or any notice, contract, or tariff stating that such a bill is "non-negotiable" is null and void, unless the fact of non-negotiability appears on the face of the bill and is agreed to by the shipper (Section 83). A "straight" bill must have the words "non-negotiable" placed plainly on its face.

The term "negotiability" can mean a number of things. Its most familiar context is in connection with short term instruments for the payment of money. In that context it is most commonly understood to mean that a holder of a negotiable instrument may occupy a privileged status. If he paid value for it and took without knowledge of any defect in the transaction that led to the issuance of the instrument (fraud, ultra vires, lack of consideration, etc.), he is a "holder in due course" and, as a consequence, defects in the underlying transaction may not be interposed as a defense in any action he may bring against the issuer to collect the promised payment. Secondly, and equally important, negotiability of an instrument for the payment of money means that the instrument (the piece of paper) represents the debt itself; the debt is "merged" in the instrument. Commercially this has a number of consequences. In most circumstances, if the instrument is discharged, so is the debt. Moreover, the only payment that will discharge the debt is payment to the holder — one who is in physical possession of the instrument. Also, the instrument — and hence the debt — is discharged by that payment even if made to someone with no right to the instrument, such as a thief. In other words, while the holder is protected by possession of the instrument, the issuer is protected by the rule allowing him to pay any holder. Third, creditors of the holder who seek to reach the instrument as part of their debtor's assets can do so only by attaching the instrument itself, not by serving process on the issuer. Plainly, the combination of these circumstances has helped to covert a simple promise to pay money to a particular creditor into a readily salable asset capable of circulating with great facility. Negotiability, in short, is a legal construct that has contributed importantly to the expansion of credit. Accordingly, when the Federal Bill of Lading Act sought to enhance the negotiability of bills of lading its purpose was to lend to instruments representing goods the same characteristics that had made instruments to pay money so important a facility of commerce. In furtherance of this purpose, the principal provisions of the Bill of Lading Act are as follows:

Section 88. Duty to Deliver Goods on Demand; Refusal

A carrier, in the absence of some lawful excuse, is bound to deliver goods upon a demand made either by the consignee named in the bill for the goods or, if the bill is an order bill, by the holder thereof, if such a demand is accompanied by —

(a) An offer in good faith to satisfy the carrier's lawful lien upon the goods;

(b) Possession of the bill of lading and an offer in good faith to surrender, properly indorsed, the bill which was issued for the goods, if the bill is an order bill; and

(c) A readiness and willingness to sign, when the goods are delivered, an acknowledgment that they have been delivered, if such signature is requested by the carrier.

In case the carrier refuses or fails to deliver the goods, in compliance with a demand by the consignee or holder so accompanied, the burden shall be upon the carrier to establish the existence of a lawful excuse for such refusal or failure.

Sec. 89. Delivery; When Justified

A carrier is justified, subject to the provisions of sections 90-92 of this title, in delivering goods to one who is —

(a) A person lawfully entitled to the possession of the goods, or

(b) The consignee named in a straight bill for the goods, or

(c) A person in possession of an order bill for the goods, by the terms of which the goods are deliverable to his order; or which has been indorsed to him, or in blank by the consignee, or by the mediate or immediate indorsee of the consignee.

Sec. 90. Liability for Delivery to Person Not Entitled Thereto

Where a carrier delivers goods to one who is not lawfully entitled to the possession of them, the carrier shall be liable to anyone having a right of property or possession in the goods if he delivered the goods otherwise than as authorized by subdivisions (b) and (c) of section 89 of this title; and, though he delivered the goods as authorized by either of said subdivisions, he shall be so liable if prior to such delivery he —

(a) Had been requested, by or on behalf of a person having a right of property or possession in the goods, not to make such delivery, or

(b) Had information at the time of the delivery that it was to a person not lawfully entitled to the possession of the goods.

Such request or information, to be effective within the meaning of this section, must be given to an officer or agent of the carrier, the actual or apparent scope of whose duties includes action upon such a request or information, and must be given in time to enable the officer or agent to whom it is given, acting with reasonable diligence, to stop delivery of the goods.

Sec. 91. Liability for Delivery Without Cancellation of Bill

Except as provided in section 106 of this title, and except when compelled by legal process, if a carrier delivers goods for which an order bill had been issued, the negotiation of which would transfer the right to the possession of the goods, and fails to take up and cancel the bill, such carrier shall be liable for failure to deliver the goods to anyone who for value and in good faith purchases such bill, whether such purchaser acquired title to the bill before or after the delivery of the goods by the carrier and notwithstanding delivery was made to the persons entitled thereto.

Next, the Act stipulates when and how "order" bills may be negotiated through delivery or by endorsement (Sections 107 and 108). It then states that order bills may be negotiated by any person in possession thereof regardless of how that possession was acquired if the bill was made out to the order of that person or if it was negotiable by delivery. The Act then provides:

Sec. 111. Title and Right Acquired by Transferee of Order Bill

A person to whom an order bill has been duly negotiated acquires thereby —

    (a)   Such title to the goods as the person negotiating the bill to him had or had ability to convey to a purchaser in good faith for value and also such title to the goods as the consignee and consignor had or had power to convey to a purchaser in good faith for value; and

    (b)   The direct obligation of the carrier to hold possession of the goods for him according to the terms of the bill as fully as if the carrier had contracted directly with him.

Sec. 114. Warranties Arising Out of Transfer of Bill

A person who negotiates or transfers for value a bill by indorsement or delivery, unless a contrary intention appears, warrants —

    (a)   That the bill is genuine;

    (b)   That he has a legal right to transfer it;

    (c)   That he has knowledge of no fact which would impair the validity or worth of the bill;

    (d)   That he has a right to transfer the title to the goods, and that the goods are merchantable or fit for a particular purpose whenever such warranties would have been implied if the contract of the parties had been to transfer without a bill the goods represented thereby.

Sec. 117. Negotiation of Bill; Impairment of Validity

The validity of the negotiation of a bill is not impaired by the fact that such negotiation was a breach of duty on the part of the person making the negotiation, or by the fact that the owner of the bill was deprived of the possession of the same by fraud, accident, mistake, duress, loss, theft, or conversion, if the person to whom the bill was negotiated, or a person to whom the bill was subsequently negotiated, gave value therefore in good faith, without notice of the breach of duty, or fraud, accident, mistake, duress, loss, theft, or conversion.

[NOTE: Compare UCC Sec. 7-501 - 7-504.[6]]

---

[6] Documentary Supplement.

A good summary of the significance and extent of the negotiability of bills of lading is contained in the following excerpt from Gilmore and Black, The Law of Admiralty, Chapter III the "Carriage of Goods Under Bills of Lading."

The Negotiability of Bills of Lading

In the adaptation of the law of money instruments to documents of title, the proposition of greatest commercial importance has been the documentary analogue to the rule that the only payment which will discharge an instrument is payment to the holder.

. . . A carrier which has issued a non-negotiable bill of lading normally discharges its duty by delivering the goods to the named consignee; the consignee need not produce the bill or even be in possession of it; the piece of paper on which the contract of carriage is written is of no importance in itself. A carrier which has issued a negotiable or order bill thereby places itself in a radically different situation. Just as the maker of a note effects his discharge only by payment to the holder, so the carrier will be discharged only by delivery to the holder of the bill. The piece of paper on which the bill is written now becomes indispensable; the goods are locked up in the bill, in the same way that the debt is merged in the instrument. A seller who ships on an order bill can, by insisting on payment before the bill is delivered to his buyer, protect himself against an insolvent's obtaining possession of the goods much more effectually than by his common-law remedy of stoppage in transit. A bank which advances money against goods covered by a negotiable bill of lading has the goods as security so long as it or a correspondent retains possession of the bill. The carrier which delivers goods without taking up and canceling its order bill remains liable to anyone who has purchased the bill for value and in good faith, before or after the improper delivery, and even though the delivery was made to a person legally entitled to possession of the goods.

To the rule just discussed there is one exception whose theoretical interest is greater than its commercial importance. A bill may be issued to a shipper who has no title to the goods. The thief, who has procured the bill to be issued, will seek to obtain advances against it, so there are good chances that the bill will end up in the hands of a good faith purchaser. On this state of facts the law protects the true owner of the goods and, incidentally, the carrier which has innocently issued its bill to the thief. The true owner may replevy the goods from the carrier or from anyone into whose hands they have passed after delivery. The carrier is doubly protected: if, without knowledge of the true owner's claim, it delivers the goods to the holder of the bill, the carrier is discharged. If, on the other hand, it delivers the goods to the true owner without taking up the outstanding bill, it is equally protected against any good faith purchaser of the bill. [Sections 89 and 90 of the Bill of Lading Act] which make the carrier liable to the holder of an order bill for delivery of the goods without cancellation of the bill provides that the carrier is to be so liable only with respect to bills "the negotiation of which would transfer the right to the possession of the goods," and a bill issued to one without title is not such a bill. The issuance of a bill to one who has voidable title, — that is, one who has acquired the goods by fraud rather than by theft — does carry the title to the goods with it, and in disputes between defrauded owner of the goods and good faith purchaser of the bill, the title derived from the bill will prevail. The determination of who owns the goods is not, and ought not to be, any business of the carrier; in all such cases it will be well advised to require the claimants to interplead, and in most cases it does just that.

Other aspects of negotiability do not require extended discussion here. A person to whom a bill has been "duly negotiated" acquires title to the goods, as well as title to the document itself, except in the single case of the bill issued by one without title to the goods; the taker by due negotiation also, and subject to the same exception, acquires "the direct obligation of the carrier" under its bill. An order bill properly endorsed may be negotiated "by any person in possession of the same, however such possession may have been acquired" and the validity of the negotiation is not impaired by its being a breach of duty on the part of the transferor or "by the fact that the owner of the bill was deprived of the possession of the same by fraud, accident, mistake, duress, loss, theft, or conversion." The purchaser who is protected is, of course, the purchaser for value, in good faith and without notice of claims. By analogy to the Negotiable Instrument Law rule that a holder in due course must take the instrument before maturity, the documentary case law, in the absence of specific statutory language, has developed an analogous concept of "staleness" with reference to bills of lading: one who purchases a bill outstanding more than a reasonable time after its issue does not take by "due negotiation" and receives only the title of his transferor. The cases have been few and it is far from clear how old a bill must be to be stale. Under the N.I.L. every instrument was presumed to have been issued for a valuable consideration and every holder was presumed to be a holder in due course; thus the burden of proof normally borne by plaintiff in a contract action was cast on the defendant. No doubt the same presumptions run in favor of purchasers of order bills; the statutes, however, are blank and the issue has not been litigated. Negotiation of order bills is made by indorsement of the order party plus delivery: the indorsement may be blank or special, and, as under the Negotiable Instrument Law, a blank indorsement converts the bill to "bearer paper" so that subsequent negotiation may be by delivery alone. Unlike the general indorser of a negotiable instrument, who engages that if the bill is not paid on due presentment he will pay it, the indorser of a bill does not engage to take back the bill if the carrier fails to make delivery. The indorser warrants only the genuiness of the bill and, in substance, his own good faith and authority to transfer both bill and goods; if the indorser is a seller of goods, but not if he is a bank to which the bill has been pledged, he also makes the standard sales warranties with respect to the quality and condition of the goods. The warranty as to the goods obviously does not cover damage to the goods in transit unless, by the terms of the contract of sale, the risk of loss remains on the seller during the transit period. Where a purchaser of a bill fails to secure his transferor's indorsement and such an indorsement is necessary for negotiation, the statutes provide that the missing indorsement may be compelled; as under the Negotiable Instrument Law the indorsement (for purposes of the "dueness" of the negotiation) takes effect when made and not at the time when the bill was transferred. Finally, when an order bill has been issued, the goods may no longer be attached or levied upon; a creditor seeking to reach the goods must by appropriate process first obtain possession of the document. To the rule just stated there is the recurrent exception in favor of the true owner whose goods have been stolen; he may disregard the outstanding bill and replevy the goods directly from the carrier.

PROBLEM

A is the owner of goods. B obtains possession of the goods either by (i) stealing them, (ii) committing a fraud on A or (iii) as A's bailee, converting them. B then ships the goods with Carrier who issues to B a negotiable bill of lading without knowledge of B's wrongdoing. B then promptly negotiates the bill to C who pays value and has no knowledge of the circumstances under which B acquired possession of the goods.

(1) Suppose before C presents the bill of lading, A goes to the Carrier and after offering proof of B's wrongdoing sufficient to satisfy the Carrier induces the latter to turn the goods over to him. C later presents the bill of lading. Is Carrier liable to C if (i) B stole the goods, or (ii) obtained the goods through fraud or conversion. What can Carrier do to protect itself? If Carrier is not liable to C, can C now replevy the goods in A's hands?

(2) Suppose that C presents the bill of lading before A makes any request of the Carrier. If Carrier turns the goods over to C and takes up the bill of lading, may Carrier be liable to A, if (i) B stole the goods, or (ii) obtained the goods through fraud or conversion? If Carrier is not liable to A, can A replevy the goods in C's hands?

[NOTE: The same result would obtain under UCC Section 2-403.[7] Also compare UCC Section 7-502[8] with Section 117 of the Bill of Lading Act, relating to the holder of the bill of lading who takes from a thief of the bill rather than the goods.]

WABCO TRADE COMPANY, v. S.S. INGER SKOU et al

United States District Court (S.D.N.Y.)
482 F. Supp. 444 (1979)

SWEET, DISTRICT JUDGE.

Wabco . . . a Delaware Corporation has sued GCC Shipping Co., Ltd. (GCC), a Greek corporation, and Constellation Navigation, Inc. (Constellation), a New York corporation, for damages in the amount of $212,984.96, plus interest . . . resulting from the loss of four motor graders. . . .

. . . [P]laintiff shipped four motor graders from Charleston, South Carolina aboard the S.S. INGERSKOU, bound for Beirut, Lebanon. Defendant GCC was the . . . carrier [and] . . . Constellation was the agent of GCC, and issued a negotiable bill of lading for the shipment of [the] . . . graders.

Due to political disturbances in Beirut, the INGERSKOU discharged plaintiff's motor graders at Piraeus, Greece on or about October 20, 1975. Shortly thereafter, Constellation sent the following undated letter to Wabco:

---

[7] Documentary Supplement.
[8] Documentary Supplement.

Dear Sirs:

We very much regret to advise that because of the current state of affairs in Beirut we have been compelled to discharge the captioned cargo at Piraeus, Greece. While we have taken this step pursuant to our rights under clause 5 and 6 of the bill of lading, and reserve all of our rights under said bill of lading and those clauses, it is our intention for the time being to bear the expense of storage at the Piraeus Free Zone in the hope that the situation in Beirut will stabilize in the reasonably near future and the cargo can be reloaded onto one of our vessels and transhipped to Beirut. Although we shall pay the cost of storage, all risk during the storage is and will continue to be for the account of cargo.

If there is any change in this arrangement, or if final delivery will in fact have to be made at Piraeus, we shall notify you.

On December 3, 1975, Wabco instructed Constellation to hold the motor graders in Piraeus until Wabco advised Constellation of a further destination. . . . Constellation's manager and part owner, testified that he forwarded a photocopy of plaintiff's letter to GCC in Greece and that he agreed orally that GCC would hold the goods in Piraeus. . . . GCC made no written reply, but did hold the graders in Piraeus for three months following Wabco's request. . . .

In early March, 1976, GCC, without notifying Wabco or the consignee designated in the bill of lading, transshipped the goods from Piraeus to Beirut on board [another vessel] . . . [Upon arrival] . . . in Beirut . . . GCC's agent took custody of the goods and delivered them to the Beirut Port Authority in exchange for a warehouse receipt.

. . . Wabco did not learn of any change in status of its goods until . . . over two weeks after [their] arrival . . . in Beirut [and] . . . did not verify that its goods had been sent on . . . [until] three weeks after the date of shipment from Piraeus.

The government warehouse in which the graders were bailed was apparently ransacked, the graders seized, and despite efforts by the parties, were never recovered. There is some suggestion that they were used as armored vehicles during the civil disorder.

GCC . . . has asserted that the bill of lading remained in force following the discharge of the graders in Piraeus, and that GCC acted in accordance with the bill in transhipping the goods to Beirut. Wabco . . . has urged that the contract of carriage contained in the bill of lading was terminated when the graders were discharged in Piraeus and notices were exchanged by GCC and Wabco and that the subsequent on shipment to Beirut constituted an unjustified conversion. . . .

GCC relies upon clauses 6(a)[9] and 7[10] of the original bill of lading. . . . In fact,

---

[9] Clause 6(a) of the bill provides:

"6(a) In any situation . . . during the voyage, which in the carrier's judgment may give rise to risk of damage, delay or disadvantage to the ship . . . or make it imprudent to . . . continue the voyage, or to enter or discharge at any port . . . the carrier . . . may discharge the goods into depot . . . or may proceed or return . . . to such other port or place as the carrier may select and discharge the goods or any part thereof there; . . . or may forward or transship the goods by any means, but always at the risk and expense of the goods; or

the parties agreed otherwise, and the contract of carriage was terminated in Piraeus. . . . In view [of what transpired between the parties they effectively] . . . agreed to terminate the original bill of lading as of December, 1975. There was a mutual assent to the new arrangement proposed by Wabco whereby GCC would hold the goods in Piraeus until Wabco advised it of further plans. GCC's on shipment of the graders represented not an attempt to comply with its original contract of carriage, but rather an inadvertent error in violation of its new agreement.

GCC has further contended that under the Federal Bills of Lading Act, 49 U.S.C Secs. 81-124, it had no choice but to deliver the goods in accordance with the terms of the bill and that as long as the negotiable bill of lading remained outstanding, it acted at its peril in complying with the instructions of the shipper, Wabco. While GCC had a right to demand the surrender of the bill of lading from Wabco in order to protect itself from liability to a good faith purchaser of the bill of lading, GCC chose not to do so and never questioned Wabco's ownership of the goods or possession of the bill of lading.

Furthermore, Section 90 of the Bills of Lading Act provides:

Where a carrier delivers goods to one who is not lawfully entitled to the possession of them, the carrier shall be liable to anyone having a right of property or possession in the goods if he delivered the goods [other than to a person in possession of an order bill for the goods indorsed to him]; and, though he delivered the goods [to such a person], he shall be so liable if prior to such delivery he —

(a) Had been requested by or on behalf of a person having a right of property or possession in the goods, not to make such delivery.

Such request or information, to be effective . . . [must] be given to an officer or agent of the carrier in time to enable the officer or agent to whom it is given, acting with reasonable diligence, to stop delivery of the goods. 49 U.S.C. Sec. 90.

The Act permits a person having a right of possession in goods to exercise a right of stoppage in transit. If the carrier delivers goods — even to the holder of a negotiable bill of lading — in violation of the owner's request, it is liable for loss of the goods. Accordingly, even if GCC's contention that the bill of lading was not terminated prior to transhipment were accepted; GCC would still not have been justified in delivering the goods to Beirut, in contravention of Wabco's instructions.

---

may require the shipper or consignee to take delivery at port of shipment or elsewhere, and if he has to do so, carrier may warehouse, store or hold the goods."

10 Clause 7 of the bill provided:

"7. Whenever the carrier . . . may deem it advisable or in any case where the goods are consigned to a point where the ship does not expect to discharge, the carrier or master may, without notice, forward the whole or any part of the goods, before or after loading at the original or at any intermediate port of shipment or at any other place . . . even beyond the port of discharge or the destination of the goods, by any vessel. . . . The carrier, in making any arrangements for transshipments under the bill of lading by any means of transportation not operated by it, shall be deemed the forwarding agent of the shipper and consignee without any other responsibility whatsoever. . . . Pending or during transshipment the goods may be stored ashore or afloat at their risk and expense."

A conversion is a "disposition of the property of another, without right, as if it were [one's] own." . . . The tort of conversion does not require defendant's knowledge that he is acting wrongfully, but "merely an intent to exercise dominion or control over property in a manner inconsistent with the rights of another" . . . The absence of benefit to GCC does not preclude liability. An action for conversion may be based on transferring possession of the owner's property to one not authorized to receive it. . . . In particular, a bailee who transfers goods in a manner inconsistent with an owner's instruction is liable for conversion to his bailor. . . .

Here, GCC acting as bailee of the motor graders . . . transhipped the[m] . . . in contravention of its agreement with Wabco to hold them in Piraeus. Under these circumstance, GCC is liable for conversion of Wabco's motor graders.

Plaintiff shall submit a judgment, on notice, within ten days, consistent with this opinion.

NOTES AND QUESTIONS

(1) Note the court asserts that even if the bill of lading were not terminated, the carrier under Section 90 of the Bill of Lading Act would be liable to Wabco for the loss of the graders. Do you agree? If the bill of lading was not terminated, would the transhipment to the Government warehouse in Beirut for the account of Wabco constitute a conversion?

(2) In *Atei v. M/V Barber Tonsberg*,[11] it was held that had carrier refused to off load and store goods at an intermediate port and delivered them instead to plaintiff consignee under the bill of lading, the carrier would have been liable under Section 90 to the shipper named in the bill. The named shipper had notified carrier that the goods were stolen from it and shipment to the plaintiff consignee arranged by the thief in shipper's name. Also authorities investigating the theft requested that the goods be off-loaded and stored. Is *Wabco* distinguishable?

§ 1.04   Carrier's Liability for Safe Carriage of Goods; Carriage of Goods by Sea Act (COGSA) and the Harter Act

The Statute.

Title 46 of the United States Code, Sections 1300-1315, constitute what is known as the Carriage of Goods by Sea Act (COGSA). The basic purpose of the Act is to regulate the responsibilities of carriers with respect to the handling and transport of cargoes. Its history, its relationship to similar enactments by other countries and to certain international conventions, is adequately explained in the cases set out below. As already noted, COGSA applies to all bills of lading or similar documents evidencing a contract for the carriage of goods by sea to or from ports of the United States as part of the foreign commerce of the United States.

---

[11] 639 F. Supp. 993 (S.D.N.Y., 1986).

The heart of COGSA is found in two sections, 1303 and 1304, which provide in pertinent part as follows:

Sec. 1303. Responsibilities and Liabilities of Carrier and Ship.

(1) **The carrier shall be bound, before and at the beginning of the voyage, to exercise due diligence to —**

    (a) **Make the ship seaworthy;**

    (b) **Properly man, equip, and supply the ship;**

    (c) **Make the holds, refrigeration and cooling chambers, and all other parts of the ship in which goods are carried, fit and safe for their reception, carriage, and preservation.**

(2) **The carrier shall properly and carefully load, handle, stow, carry, keep, care for and discharge the goods carried.**

(3) **After receiving the goods into his charge the carrier, or the master or agent of the carrier, shall, on demand of the shipper, issue to the shipper a bill of lading showing among other things —**

[(a) marks necessary for identification of the goods, (b) the number of packages or pieces, or the quantity or weight, (c) the apparent order and condition of the goods.]

(4) [The bill of lading is expressly made prima facie evidence of receipt by the carrier of the goods as described in accord with Paragraphs 3 (a)-(c) above.]

(5) [The shipper is held to have guaranteed to the carrier the accuracy of any "marks, number, quantity and weight" supplied by the shipper and must indemnify the carrier for any loss due to inaccuracies in that information.]

(6) [Unless written notice of loss or damage to the goods is given the carrier before transfer of the goods to the custody of the person entitled to delivery, their removal constitutes prima facie evidence of the delivery of the goods as described in the bill of lading. If the loss or damage is not apparent, the notice must be given within three days of delivery. No notice is required if the goods have been the subject of joint survey or inspection.]

In any event the carrier and the ship shall be discharged from all liability in respect of loss or damage unless suit is brought within one year after delivery of the goods or the date when the goods should have been delivered: Provided, [that failure to give the notice referred to above shall not prejudice the shipper's right to sue within the one-year statutory period.]

(7) [After loading, the shipper has a right to demand a "shipped" bill of lading upon surrender of any other document of title pertaining to the goods. A carrier may convert an ordinary bill into a "shipped" bill by appropriate notations thereon.]

(8) Any clause, covenant, or agreement in a contract of carriage relieving the carrier or the ship from liability for loss or damage to or in connection with the goods, arising from negligence, fault, or failure in the duties and obligations provided in this section, or lessening such liability otherwise than as provided in this chapter, shall be null and void and of no effect. A benefit of insurance in favor of the carrier, or similar, clause, shall be deemed to be a clause relieving the carrier from liability.

Sec. 1304. Rights and Immunities of Carrier and Ship

(1) Neither the carrier nor the ship shall be liable for loss or damage arising or resulting from unseaworthiness unless caused by want of due diligence on the part of the carrier to . . . [fulfill the responsibilities imposed by] . . . the provisions of paragraph (1) of section 1303 of this title. Whenever loss or damage has resulted from unseaworthiness, the burden of proving the exercise of due diligence shall be on the carrier or other persons claiming exemption under this section.

(2) Neither the carrier nor the ship shall be responsible for loss or damage arising or resulting from —

[Here are listed in paragraphs (a) through (p) some sixteen potential causes of loss or damage to which the exemption applies, including:][1]

(a) Act, neglect or default of the master, mariner, pilot, or the servants of the carrier in the navigation or in the management of the ship;

(b) Fire, unless caused by the actual fault or privity of the carrier;

(c) Perils, dangers, and accidents of the sea or other navigable waters;

* * * *

(p) Any other cause arising without the actual fault and privity of the carrier and without the fault or neglect of the agents or servants of the carrier, but the burden of proof shall be on the person claiming the benefit of this exception to show that neither the actual fault or privity of the carrier nor the fault or neglect of the agents or servants of the carrier contributed to the loss or damage.

(3) The shipper shall not be responsible for loss or damage sustained by the carrier or the ship arising or resulting from any cause without the act, fault, or neglect of the shipper, his agents, or his servants.

(4) Any deviation in saving or attempting to save life or property at sea, or any reasonable deviation shall not be deemed to be an infringement or breach of this chapter or of the contract of carriage, and the carrier shall not be liable for any loss or damage resulting therefrom: Provided,

---

[1] The other listed causes are: perils, dangers, and accidents of the sea; acts of God, war and public enemies; arrest of princes; quarantine; act or omission of the shipper or owner of the goods; strikes; riots and civil commotions; saving or attempting to save life or property at sea; wastage arising from inherent defects in the goods; insufficient packing; insufficient or inadequate marks; latent defects not discoverable by due diligence.

however, That if the deviation is for the purpose of loading or unloading cargo or passengers it shall, prima facie, be regarded as unreasonable.

(5) Neither the carrier nor the ship shall in any event be or become liable for any loss or damage to or in connection with the transportation of goods in an amount exceeding $500 per package lawful money of the United States, or in case of goods not shipped in packages, per customary freight unit, or the equivalent of the sum in other currency, unless the nature and value of such goods have been declared by the shipper before shipment and inserted in the bill of lading. This declaration, if embodied in the bill of lading, shall be prima facie evidence, but shall not be conclusive on the carrier.

By agreement between the carrier, master, or agent of the carrier, and the shipper another maximum amount than that mentioned in this paragraph may be fixed; Provided, That such maximum shall not be less than the figure above named. In no event shall the carrier be liable for more than the count of damage actually sustained.

[The next clause exonerates the carrier for all loss if the nature or value of the goods has been "knowingly and fraudulently" misstated by the shipper.]

(6) [The carrier, without having to compensate the shipper, is authorized to off-load at any place and destroy or render innocuous any inflammable, explosive or dangerous cargo shipped without the carrier's consent knowing the "nature and character" of the cargo. If shipped with the carrier's consent and knowledge such a cargo may nevertheless be landed and destroyed if it should "become a danger to the ship or cargo."]

———————

Other provisions of COGSA: (i) permit a carrier, by stipulation in the bill of lading, to limit its immunities or increase its liabilities (Section 1305); (ii) authorize a carrier and shipper to negotiate their own terms under special circumstances not involving a commercial shipment made in the ordinary course of trade and not involving the issuance of a bill of lading (Section 1306); and (iii) stipulate that nothing in the act prohibits a carrier and shipper from making an agreement fixing their mutual rights and responsibilities in connection with the care and handling of goods prior to loading and after discharge from the ship (Section 1307).

———————

The Structure of COGSA

For the historical reasons explained in the cases, COGSA seeks to strike a balance between the competing interests of carriers and shippers. To accomplish this it first changed the common law which held carriers to an absolute standard of liability for loss of or damage to goods. Under the act a carrier is liable only if it, or its servants, are at fault through negligence or, what amounts to the same thing, the lack of due diligence.

Beyond this change, the act imposes two principal duties on the carrier. It must, first of all, exercise due diligence in putting the vessel into good shape for the voyage (*i.e.*, it must be "seaworthy" in the three respects set out in Section 1303(1)). If it supplies a seaworthy vessel — a responsibility fulfilled when the ship "breaks ground" (*i.e.*, leaves its moorings)[2] — the carrier is not responsible for any default by those whom it puts in charge of running the ship (Section 1304(2)(a)). The rationale for drawing the line at this point is that the safety of the carrier's own vessel was thought to be a sufficient incentive to ensure that those entrusted with its operation would use due care in the vessel's navigation and management.

The second important duty imposed on the carrier is to care for the cargo from the time it is loaded to the time it is discharged from the ship (Section 1303(2)). The search for a balance between carrier and shipper interests, however, resulted in the creation of a number of exceptions to this duty, exceptions that have vastly complicated the task of drawing the line between losses for which the carrier is responsible and those that must be borne by the shipper or its insurer. For example, the duty to properly load, handle and discharge the cargo has had to be reconciled with the exemption from liability for the defaults of the master or crew in the navigation and management of the ship. Likewise, a line must be drawn between the exemption from liability for crew negligence and the carrier's obligation to provide a seaworthy vessel, including a properly trained crew. While the carrier is not responsible for any damage or loss to the cargo resulting from fire or the perils of the sea (Section 1304(2)(b) and (c)), both exceptions must be read in conjunction with the overriding responsibility for seaworthiness. Also the carrier is not responsible for damage or loss from any cause not attributable to the fault of the carrier or its servants (Section 1304(2)(q). However, while crew negligence will defeat the carrier's effort to invoke this exception, that does not necessarily imply carrier liability; there is still the exemption from liability for defaults of the master and crew in navigating and managing the ship (Section 1304(2)(a).

Finally, in a number of places the act shifts the burden of proof from the shipper, normally a plaintiff, to the defendant carrier in ways that are contrary to the normal allocation of burdens under the tort law and, as the cases illustrate, with possibly decisive effect.

---

[2] In *Mississippi Shipping Co. v. Zander & Co., Inc.*, 270 F. 2d 345 (5th Cir. 1959), vacated 361 U.S. 115, conformed to and revised in part 273 F. 2d 618 (2d Cir., 1960), it was held that the voyage had begun when undocking maneuvers commenced, so that a failure to stop and repair damage caused during that maneuver did not constitute a failure to provide a seaworthy vessel.

SUNKIST GROWERS, INC. v. ADELAIDE SHIPPING LINES

United States Court of Appeals, Ninth Circuit
603 F. 2d 1327 (1979)

BEFORE DUNIWAY and KILKENNY, CIRCUIT JUDGES and McGOVERN, DISTRICT JUDGE.

KILKENNY, CIRCUIT JUDGE.

Facts

The facts are not seriously in dispute. [Sunkist] is a California corporation engaged in packing and shipping citrus fruit. [Adelaide] is a [British] corporation and is the owner of the vessel GLADIOLA. . . . Salen is a [Swedish] corporation . . . and . . . the charterer of the GLADIOLA.

[In late] . . . August and [early] . . . September, 1974, [the GALDIOLA took on a cargo of fresh lemons owned by Sunkist at Long Beach, California] . . . for refrigerated transportation to Gdansk, Poland . . . [By agreement] . . . Salen provided vessels once or twice a week to transport Sunkist's citrus cargoes. Occasionally, Sunkist would not fill the entire vessel with its cargo and in those instances . . . Salen could arrange for additional cargo to be shipped and would make stops en route to load this extra cargo. . . . When additional cargo was to be transported, Sunkist was informed by telex of the type of cargo . . . and the additional stops that would be made. . . . As long as the additional loading stops did not unduly delay the ship's arrival in Northern Europe . . . Sunkist did not object to deviations from a direct course to Northern Europe. In this instance, Sunkist was informed by telex that the vessel would be stopping in Ecuador to load bananas. It did not object [and, as a result,] the GLADIOLA . . . [arrived] . . . in Guayaquil Harbor, [Ecuador] on September 10th.

[Later] that day . . . a fire broke out in the engine room . . . [caused by] . . . a separation of a . . . compression pipe fitting and a . . . ferrule in the low pressure diesel fuel line. . . . The diesel fuel sprayed on to hot surfaces of the numbers 1 and 2 generators.

Cummings, an extra third engineer . . . upon hearing the fire alarm . . . proceeded to the generator flat [where] [h]e observed . . . oil splashing onto the hot exhaust turbo chargers of . . . the generators, [but saw] . . . no flames. Then occurred what might well be described as a Shakespearean comedy of errors, with a result akin to one of his tragedies. Because he had [not been trained] . . . on what to do in such an emergency, Cummings failed to use the diesel oil turn off screw . . . nor did he turn off another valve [a few feet away]. . . . The second engineer arrived at the scene about this time but, inasmuch as his . . . training was no better . . . he also failed to close either valve. . . . [He then] . . . attempted to use . . . [a] fire extinguisher but turned the control valve . . . in the wrong direction and broke it. . . . Cummings [then] went back to the control room and reported the generator on fire [and finally] . . . shut off the fuel to the pumps . . . by means of a simple switch.

The fire spread rapidly . . . filling the engine room with dense smoke. Within minutes the vessel blacked out and the engine room had to be evacuated.

[Cummings then attempted] to locate the chief engineer [and, in so doing,] stumbled over his body. He appeared to be dead. After attempts to save the engineer failed, the captain finally ordered the remotely controlled . . . fire extinguisher system in action, but the fire was out of control and . . . [was] not extinguished . . . until three days later, [after extensive] . . . damage. The chief engineer died in the fire and the captain suffered a fatal heart attack a couple of days later.

Although the lemons had not been damaged in the fire, the destruction of the refrigeration equipment made it necessary to . . . give the lemons to the military authorities for distribution to the people. The value of the lost lemon crop was stipulated at $350,784.00.

[[Sunkist then sued Adelaide for this loss, and Adelaide pleaded the exemption from liability for fire losses contained in Sec. 1304(2)(b) of COGSA. Sunkist claimed that Adelaide could not benefit from the fire exemption because it had failed to exercise due diligence in making the vessel seaworthy and because of the deviation of the vessel to Ecuador.]

District Court's Findings and Conclusion

In its findings of fact, the district court found, among other things, that the GLADIOLA, prior to the commencement of the voyage, could have been made safe in the following respects:

(1) The lining on the electrical cables could have been sheathed in metal to reduce smoke. . . .

(2) A flange joint, rather than a compression joint, could have been used on the fuel pipe leading into the generator, making a stronger connection;

(3) Fewer joints could have been used in the pipe. . . .

(4) Protective shields could have been placed around the generators to reduce the spray of hot fuel. . . . ;

(5) A serto ferrule could have been maintained in the fuel pipe joint that caused the leak, rather than the emerto ferrule replacement that had been inserted;

(6) Barriers and fire dampers could have been placed along the electric cabling. . . .

(7) Suits of protective fire clothing could have been maintained on board.

After making these findings, the court went on to say that a prudent vessel owner and/or charterer would not necessarily have made most of these modifications, including a statement that although a serto ferrule should be maintained in the particular joint, "A failure to maintain the proper ferrule would be the fault of the crew in failing to report ferrule replacement, rather than the fault of the owner in failing to notice that a replacement had been made."

The court also found that the crew should have been given specific instructions on the proper way to deal with engine room fires and the exact method of handling fire extinguishers. Nonetheless, the court went on to say that a reasonable vessel owner and or charterer, in preparing to deal with fire, would have relied on the certification of its crew members, along with their prior fire fighting experience and training, ship drills and equipment labelled with instructions for use.

Based on its findings of fact, the district court concluded, among other things:

* * * *

4. In a fire loss case under [COGSA] . . . the owner or charterer has the burden of proving that the loss resulted from the fire. The burden then switches to the shipper to show that the fire was the result of the design, neglect, fault, or privity of the owner or charterer. In a fire case, the charterer and/or vessel owner do not have the burden of initially proving that they exercised due diligence in making the vessel seaworthy.

5. While this allocation of the burden of proof runs contra to the general scheme of proofs in shipping cases . . . American authority is clear that the fire exemption provisions shift the burden of proof to the shipper. The plaintiff's reliance on the Canadian authority of *Maxine Footwear Company v. Canadian Government Merchant Marine* . . . is misplaced. Although the Court in that case did place the burden of proving initial seaworthiness on the carrier, that case was dealing with a Canadian statute fashioned on the Hague Rules."

Historical Background

In order to fully understand . . . the legal problems presented, we must view them in their historical context, including the Common Law of Maritime Carriage of Goods at Sea, the Limitation of Liability Act of 1851,[3] the Harter Act of 1893,[4] . . . The Hague Rules as formulated by the Brussels Convention of 1924 and the Carriage of Goods by Sea Act of 1936 (COGSA)[5] . . . .

The Act of 1851[6] was passed by the Congress to promote the expansion of the American Merchant Marine and to protect the capital investment of those engaged in maritime shipping. It is clear that the legislation was enacted for the purpose of placing American ship owning interests on a competitive basis with British interests insofar as limitation of liability was concerned. . . .

The subsequent history of maritime common carriage makes it obvious that the COGSA Fire Exemption of 1936, as distinguished form the 1851 Fire Statute, was part of an overall plan to settle the adverse interests of carriers and cargo shippers.

From that history, we gather that the British courts generally upheld the validity of what was then commonly known as the "negligence" exceptions in bills of lading, while the federal courts in the United States held it against public policy for the carrier to contract itself out of liability for its own negligence. Consequently, when goods were carried under a bill of lading containing such a clause,

---

[3] (46 U.S.C. Secs. 181-189).

[4] (46 U.S.C. Secs. 190-196).

[5] (46 U.S.C. Sec. 1300, et. seq.).

[6] Sec. 182 of the 1851 "Fire Statute" provided that; "No owner of any vessel shall be liable to answer for or make good to any person any loss or damage, which may happen to any merchandise whatsoever, which shall be shipped, taken in, or put on board any such vessel, by reason or by means of any fire happening to or on board the vessel, unless such fire is caused by the design or neglect of such owner."

the accessibility of courts or amenability to service of process made a crucial difference in the outcome of the litigation. In part as a result of this difference, the British Merchant Marine became dominant in the Atlantic. The United States, of course, was vitally interested in seagoing cargo, both export and import. Therefore, to partially solve this problem, the Congress in 1893 enacted the Harter Act, 46 U.S.C. Secs. 190-96, which Act attempted to strike a balance between the interests of the carrier in being free from all claims based upon its negligence, and the shippers who wished to hold the carriers responsible for the consequences of any sort of negligence. In effect, the Harter Act declared "negligence" exceptions in the bills of lading to be null and void, but carriers would not be liable for goods damaged due to the shippers acts or omissions or for errors of the crew, if the carrier did exercise due diligence to make the vessel seaworthy and to properly maintain, equip and supply the vessel.[7]

While this compromise served to protect a cargo shippers' interest with respect to litigation in American courts, shippers in most of the other countries of the world were still at the mercy of the exoneration clauses in the bills of lading, or at least of the different judicial interpretations of the clauses which carriers continued to carefully insert in the bills. As an outgrowth of the conflicts between these two warring factions, the interested antagonists, which included banking and underwriting interests, met at the World's Shipping Conference of 1920 to put the Harter Act principle into effect generally. As an outgrowth of these meetings, the Brussels Convention of August 25, 1924, promulgated what are commonly known as The Hague Rules which, with important additions, amounted to an international adaptation of the Harter Act. However, the United Sates did not ratify the Convention or enact COGSA, a statutory codification of The Hague Rules, until 1936.

It is well recognized that The Hague Rules or COGSA have superseded the Harter Act with respect to foreign trade and are incorporated by reference in every bill of lading[8] for foreign transport to and from the United States. It has been said

---

[7] While the Harter Act is less comprehensive than COGSA (*e.g.* Section 1 and 2 of Harter lays down no positive rules of law, but simply forbids certain stipulations in the bill of lading), the basic responsibilities of the carrier are much the same and Section 3 grants the carrier certain immunities from liability. Indeed, at many points the two acts are so much alike that their differences have come to be treated as more stylistic than substantive (*e.g.* the definition of seaworthiness). The scope of their applicability, however, does differ, although where they overlap COGSA supercedes Harter. Thus, COGSA applies only to foreign commerce while Harter applies to both foreign and domestic water carriage under bills of lading. This means that Harter still applies to all "coastwise" trade unless the parties expressly stipulate for the application of COGSA as they are entitled to do. Also, as already noted, COGSA applies from the time when the goods are loaded to when they are discharged from the vessel. Harter, however, applies from receipt of the goods by the carrier to delivery to the shipper or other party entitled thereto. During the period from loading to discharge Harter has been superceded by COGSA, but COGSA expressly saves Harter from repeal during the period, even in foreign commerce, when the goods are in the carrier's hands prior to loading and after discharge. Ed.

[8] It is specifically incorporated into the two bills of lading covering this particular shipment . . . which reads:

" Paramount Clause, The Hague Rules contained in the international Convention for unification of certain rules relating to bills of lading, dated Brussels the 25th August, 1924, as enacted in the country of shipment shall apply to this contract. . . ."

that the primary purpose of COGSA is to protect carriers engaged in foreign trade to and from the United States against all-encompassing liability, while protecting the shipper's interest by assuring that due care is exercised in making the ship seaworthy. The intent of the Congress in passing COGSA is made absolutely clear by the language of [what is now Sec. 1303(8) of the act.]

Discussion

As we read the record . . . there is overwhelming evidence that [Adelaide was] . . . in violation of . . . Secs. 1303 and 1304 of COGSA before and at the inception of the voyage in two respects:

It is undisputed that the carrier failed to provide a proper . . . ferrule fitting in the low compression fuel joint that separated . . .; that the fitting had not been touched after the commencement of the voyage [and that the] separation permitted the diesel oil to spray upon the hot generator parts, thus causing the fire. Moreover, the failure to use a . . . [proper] . . . compression joint in the fuel line is a clear violation of Lloyd's Rule, Chapter E, Sec. 312 . . . [and] there is no evidence that Lloyd's ever granted a variance of this rule. The fact that the district court said that compression joints [used on the GLADIOLA] . . . were used on "many British ships" is of no importance. Mere compliance with a custom which falls below the United States' and Lloyd's standards is not sufficient.

Furthermore, we hold that there is overwhelming evidence that there was lack of due diligence on the part of the appellees in their failure to man the vessel with a crew properly trained in engine room fire fighting. The engineers' reactions to the fire . . . indicated a lack of fundamental preparation and knowledge of the various means available to efficiently control this type of fire.

A case closely in point and misread by the district court is *Asbestos Corp. Ltd. v. Compagnie de Navigation*[9] . . . There the vessel . . . suffered an engine room fire. Unlike the case at bar, there was no fault on the part of the owner with respect to the cause of the fire. The claimed unseaworthiness involved the location of the fire fighting equipment and its controls in the engine room. At trial, the owners contended that they could be liable only if their personal negligence caused the fire. . . . In speaking of the 1851 Fire Statute and the COGSA fire exemption, the . . . court said:

Appellants urge . . . a narrow reading of the exception to the exemption. Under their construction, a fire ignited because of lack of due diligence by the shipowner would result in liability, but failure to maintain equipment adequate to extinguish a non-negligently ignited fire before it causes the damage would not. . . . [We reject] . . . this construction. . . . [A]n inexcusable condition of unseaworthiness of a vessel, which in fact causes the damage — either by starting a fire or by preventing its extinguishment — will exclude the shipowners from the exemption of the Fire Statue and COGSA.

The "inexcusable condition of unseaworthiness" mentioned in *Asbestos Corp.* no doubt refers to a condition of unseaworthiness where the carrier did not use due diligence. That is to say, if the carrier used due diligence, the unseaworthiness would be excusable. . . .

---

[9] 480 F.2d 669 (2d Cir. 1973).

Our own court in *New York Mdse. Co. v. Liberty Shipping Corp.*[10] . . . has placed *Asbestos Corp.* in proper perspective. In Liberty Shipping, we held there was substantial evidence supporting the trial court's findings that the damage to the cargo resulted from the unseaworthiness of the vessel consisting of the incompetence of the master and the crew who were not properly trained in the use of the vessel's fire fighting equipment.

[Also] in *Liberty Shipping* the [carrier's further contention was answered in the following terms] . . . :

[Carrier] . . . next contends that the district court has, contrary to the statutory exemptions, placed upon the owner strict liability for the loss suffered by cargo. [Carrier] . . . reasons that the court, by attributing responsibility for cargo damage jointly to the fire and to unseaworthiness, has placed upon the owner the traditional nondelegable duty to make the ship seaworthy and thus has imposed strict liability. The statutory exemptions, it is contended, do not permit the imposition of liability by nondelegable duty.

[However] . . . in the case before us liability was not based on the traditional elements by which an owner is held liable for unseaworthiness of his vessel — those related to warranty and nondelegable duty. Here there was owner neglect and actual fault constituting failure to exercise the due diligence required by COGSA through permitting the vessel to put to sea without having properly trained the master and crew in the use of fire-fighting equipment and without having remedied deficiencies in the vent closing devices. Where the unseaworthy conditions that were the cause of the fire damage existed by reason of owner neglect or actual fault, the exemptions created by the Fire Statute and COGSA do not apply.

Of more than ordinary significance is the fact that the *Liberty Shipping* court did not place upon the shipper the burden of proof on the issue of due diligence. To the contrary, *Liberty Shipping*, by the use of the language: "Here there was owner neglect and actual fault constituting failure to exercise the due diligence required by COGSA . . . .," clearly was referring to the due diligence required by . . . Sec. 1303(1) and 1304(1). In Sec. 1304(1) the burden of proof is placed directly on the carrier by the following language: ". . . Whenever loss or damage has resulted from unseaworthiness, the burden of proving the exercise of due diligence shall be on the carrier or other persons claiming exemptions under this section." . . .

Appellees argue that the language "this section" ending the last sentence of Sec. 1304(1) limits the vitality of the "due diligence" provision to that paragraph and does not apply to paragraph (2), the Fire Exemption Clause of COGSA. This contention is groundless. . . . That the Congress was aware of the distinction between "paragraph" and "section" is made crystal clear by the use of the language "in accordance with the provision of paragraph (1) of Section [1303] of this title." This language is used in the same paragraph as the word "section" in . . . [Section 1304]. Obviously, both paragraphs must be read and construed together.

---

[10] 509 F.2d 1249 (CA 9, 1975).

* * * *

Conclusion

We adopt, as the law of our circuit, the [conclusion] that the provisions of Sec. [1303] . . . paragraph 1, COGSA, create an overriding obligation and if that obligation is not fulfilled and the nonfulfillment causes the damage, the fire immunity of Sec. [1304], Paragraph 2(b) cannot be relied upon by [Adelaide]. This overriding obligation to exercise due diligence to: (a) make the ship seaworthy, and (b) properly man, equip, and supply the ship applies to the master and those in the management of the ship, as well as to the owners or charterers personally, or those who act for the owners in a managerial capacity.

Our analysis of the record convinces us that the appellees also failed to carry their burden of proof on the issue of exercising due diligence to make the ship seaworthy as required by Sec. [1304], Paragraph 1. . . . Consequently, the district court's findings of fact rested upon an erroneous view of the law as expressed in its conclusions. It is practically conceded that the improper ferrule in place at the commencement of the voyage, permitted the volatile diesel oil to spray on the generators. . . . Moreover, as in *Asbestos Corp.*, it was not "crew negligence" that either started the fire or prevented its extinguishment, but a failure to properly train the crew in what to do in case of engine room fires and in the use of fire fighting equipment. This unperformed obligation required by Sec. [1303](1)(b) also was a cause of the damage. Therefore, the overall cause of the breakdown of the vessel's refrigeration equipment, which . . . [caused the loss of the fruit] . . . was the failure of [Adelaide] . . . to fulfill [its] obligations as required by COGSA. It was not the fire. . . .

NOTES AND QUESTIONS

(1) Section 1304(2)(b) is based on the so-called "Fire Statute" of 1851 [11] under which the shipowner lost the exemption if the fire was "caused by the design or neglect of the owner." The words used in COGSA, "the actual fault or privity" of the owner, have been construed to have the same meaning as "design or neglect." Both formulations have been held to require that the fault through which the owner loses the exemption must be personal to him. Negligence by the master, crew or other agents will not be attributed to the shipowner under the doctrine of *respondeat superior*. In the case of a corporate owner the fault must have been that of managers with responsibility for inspecting vessels, deciding on the precautions to take and similar duties. [12]

(2) Plainly the crew's inept response to the fire on the Gladiola amounted to negligence, if not gross negligence. In everyday terms that negligence could, in turn, be taken as probative of the shipowner's failure to assure, through training or otherwise, that the crew was competent to fight the fire. But under COGSA this poses a problem, does it not? Specifically:

---

[11] Rev. Stat. Section 4282 (1875) 46 U.S.C.A. Sec. 182.
[12] See, Gilmore and Black, The Law of Admiralty (Second Edition) at page 161.

(a) Under COGSA can this "proof," standing alone, be sufficient to sustain a claim of unseaworthiness? If so, what has happened to the great compromise that underlies COGSA as explained by the *Adelaide* court in its discussion of the history of that statute?

(b) Is *Asbestos Corp.*, relied on by the Appeals Court, of much help?

(c) Note the argument made by counsel in *Liberty Shipping*. Under the "nondelegable duty" doctrine a shipowner who contracts out the work necessary to prepare a ship for sea remains liable for lack of seaworthiness if the contractor is negligent even though the owner was itself not guilty of any negligence in selecting the contractor. In *Adelaide*, even more than in *Liberty Shipping*, the Appeals Court decision comes close, does it not, to extending this doctrine to crew negligence.

(3) Juxtapose the crew's behavior with the evidence relied upon by the trial court in concluding that the shipowner had not failed to properly man the ship, one of the requirements of seaworthiness. Does this suggest that the burden of proof, especially the burden of persuasion, may have been the crucial issue in the case? Is this the only way to square the outcome in *Adelaide* with the basic assumption that underlay Congress' (and The Hague conferees') decision to confine owner responsibility to supplying a seaworthy vessel?

(4) A similar problem exists in drawing the line between the shipowner's duty to supply a seaworthy vessel and its exemption from liability for damages or loss caused by the "perils of the sea." In *Gerber & Co. Inc. v. the Sabine Howaldt et al.* [13] plaintiff sued for water damage to the cargo which could only have come through the hatches. Plaintiff alleged that the vessel was unseaworthy because the carrier failed to supplement the MacGregor hatch covers with tarpaulin. Expert testimony established that both upon departure and arrival the MacGregor hatch covers were completely watertight. The District Court held that the storm encountered by the ship in transit was not sufficiently severe to constitute a "peril of the sea" so that the very existence of water damage demonstrated that the carrier's failure to supplement the hatch covers with tarpaulin constituted negligence. In reversing this decision, the Second Circuit noted that it was not the customary practice, even on trips across the North Atlantic in winter, to supplement MacGregor hatch covers with tarpaulin. The District Court had also misread the ship's log and the captain's testimony with regard to the severity of the storm. It was a genuine hurricane requiring the ship to "hove to" and not merely a storm with occasional gusts of hurricane force. The appeals court went on to observe:

> The standard of seaworthiness must remain uncertain because of the imponderables of the forces exerted upon a ship by the winds and seas. Ship design and construction . . . have evolved to meet the dangers inherent in violent winds and tempestuous seas. But for the purpose of deciding whether or not they constitute perils of the sea [under] . . . the statutory exception there is the question of how violent and how tempestuous. These are matters of degree and not amenable to precise definition. Moreover, there are variations in kind; . . . whether the winds are steady for a number of hours from one direction or are in frequent gusts . . . or are cyclonic and shifting. . . . As

[13] 437 F.2d 580 (2d Cir, 1971).

there is a direct relationship between the wind velocity and the build up and size and shape of waves, a very important measure considered on perils of the sea issue is the wind velocity in terms of the Beaufort Scale. . . . No exact Beaufort Scale wind force can be referred to as the dividing line which will determine those cases in which a peril of the sea is present and those . . . in which it is not. There are, however, few cases in which the winds are force 9 or below (*i.e.* 54 land miles per hour) in which there has been found to have been a peril of the sea, whereas there are many where the force has been 11 or above. This is still, however, a rough measure at best and not sufficient standing by itself. Other indicia are, assuming a seaworthy ship, the nature and extent of the damages to the ship itself, whether or not the ship was buffeted by cross-seas which wrenched and wracked the hull and set up unusual stresses in it and like factors. While the seaworthiness of a ship presupposes that she is designed, built and equipped to stand up under reasonably expectable conditions this means no more than the usual bad weather which is normal for a particular sea area at a particular time. It does not, however, include an unusual combination of the destructive forces of wind and sea which a skilled and experienced ship's master would not expect and which the ship encountered as a stroke of bad luck. . . . We are satisfied that the Sabine Howaldt was a seaworthy vessel when she left Antwerp on Dec. 19, 1965. Through-out the voyage she was operated in a good and seamanlike manner. There was no negligence on the part of the carrier. The damage to the cargo was caused by violence of the wind and sea and particularly by the resulting cross-seas which, through wrenching and twisting the vessel, set up torsions within the hull which forced up the hatch covers and admitted sea water to the holds.

PRUDENTIAL LINES, INC. v. GENERAL TIRE INTERNATIONAL CO., et. al

United States District Court, Southern District of New York
448 F. Supp. 202 (1978)

[In this action, plaintiff Prudential Lines, Inc. ("Prudential"), an ocean carrier, sought indemnity from a number of defendants for monies paid to the consignee of goods shipped to Rumania in settlement of the latter's claim for cargo damage. Defendant General Tire International Inc. ("General") had contracted with I.S.C.E. Romchim, State Enterprise for Foreign Trade of Rumania, to sell equipment for use in a Rumanian tire factory. General engaged two of the defendants to prepare and package the equipment for ocean shipment. The packaged cargoes were delivered to Prudential at its pier and were loaded aboard six Prudential "Lash"[14] barges by a third defendant. Carpenters employed by a fourth defendant were responsible for bracing and chocking the cargo in the barges and the employees of a fifth defendant for

---

[14] "Lash" is an acronym for "Lighter Aboard Ship."

lashing the cargo to the barges. Finally the loaded barges were lifted aboard plaintiff's mother vessel the "Lash Italia."

The bill of lading issued by Prudential to General, as the shipper, incorporated COGSA and also contained a "Himalaya" clause which extended to the agents of the carrier "all exemptions and immunities from and limitations of liability which the carrier has" under COGSA. En route to Rumania, the Lash Italia encountered rough weather and the cargo was damaged. Romchim initially claimed damages of $16 million. Prudential finally settled this claim for $2 million, and it is this sum for which Prudential seeks indemnification alleging negligence and breach of warranty by the defendants in their failure to package and secure the cargo properly.

The defendants all countered by claiming that Plaintiff should have limited its liability to Romchim to the $500 per package limitation contained in COGSA. Those covered by the Himalaya Clause argued that, in all events, under the clause they were entitled to that limitation even upon a claim of indemnification. The defendants not covered by the clause argued that Prudential, by settling with Romchim for an amount in excess of the $500 per package, made a gratuitous or voluntary payment for which it was not entitled to indemnification.

At an initial hearing on the case (440 F. Supp. 556 (1977)), the court accepted defendants' contention that their liability would be limited to $500 per package, if plaintiff could have limited its liability to Romchim by that amount, adding

"Whether the plaintiff could have done so turns on the law of Rumania; specifically, whether the Rumanian courts would have enforced COGSA, either under its own choice of law rules or as a matter of contract law." (at page 560).

In a subsequent hearing, after the parties had submitted expert testimony on Rumanian law, the court reached the following conclusions.]

MacMahon, District Judge.

". . . [The] witnesses concluded unanimously that the courts of Rumania would enforce a contractual choice of law clause, even where such a clause mandates the application of the law of another nation. . . . Thus, since the bill of lading represents the parties' contract of carriage, and since that contract specifies the application of COGSA, we can only conclude that the Rumanian courts would have applied COGSA in Romchim's action against plaintiff.

This does not mean, however, that COGSA would have been applied *as a statute* in the Rumanian action. On the contrary, by virtue of their incorporation into the bill of lading, the provisions of COGSA would have been applied by the Rumanian court merely *as terms of a contract*. Under Rumanian choice of law rules, the terms of the contract would have been interpreted under the law of the place of performance. Since the cargo was to be delivered in Rumania, a court of Rumania would have deemed Rumania to have been the place of performance. Accordingly, the substantive law of Rumania would have been applied in interpreting the terms of the contract of carriage, including the $500 per package damage limitation incorporated from COGSA.

Substantive Rumanian law provides that gross negligence on the part of a carrier vitiates any contractual damage limitation. In the instant case, the record contains substantial evidence indicating a complete failure on the part of the carrier and his agents to chock, lash or brace the cargo in the barges. This evidence, the experts agree, would have led to a finding in the Rumanian action that plaintiff had been grossly negligent. Therefore, we must conclude that plaintiff's liability would not have been limited to $500 per package in Rumania. . . .

[The court then went on to deny all of the defendants benefit of the $500 per package limit.]

NOTES AND QUESTIONS

(1) Is there a certain confusion in the case? A law, such as COGSA, represents an exercise of authority by a sovereign state to prescribe rules of conduct for those within its "prescriptive" jurisdiction. A contract term, on the other hand, is merely the act of the parties. It has the force of law, if at all, only if a sovereign state is prepared under its domestic contract law to enforce the terms of the contract as between those parties. Therefore, if as the court asserts, Rumania, under its choice of law rules, was prepared to enforce COGSA, it would be contradictory to say that it would do so only as a contract term. The former is a matter controlled by Rumanian *conflict of laws rules*, the latter by its *domestic contract law*. Indeed, to say that COGSA was enforceable only as a contract term, actually implies that Rumania would not, under its conflict of laws rules, apply COGSA as a law of the United States.

Most nations, under their conflict of laws rules, refuse to apply a foreign law deemed repugnant to their fundamental public policy (ordre public). But this has generally come to mean that the foreign law must be repugnant to some very basic moral or ethical precept of the forum state. Not every difference of policy violates the forum's public policy in this sense. On the other hand, if a certain contractual undertaking is declared, by the contract law of the forum, to be invalid, the forum court, acting under its own contract law, is under a duty not to enforce that undertaking even if would not, under its conflicts law, violate the forum's public policy. Query, did the court's inclination in Prudential to equate application by the Roumanian courts of COGSA as a statute with their application of COGSA as a contract term show an adequate appreciation of how the difference might have affected the outcome?

(2) Can the result in *Prudential Lines, Inc.* be reconciled with *Indussa Corporation v. S.S. Ranborg?*[15] There the Second Circuit declined to honor a clause in a bill of lading requiring all disputes to be settled in, and according to the law of, the country where the carrier had its headquarters. The court concluded that by making COGSA applicable to "every bill of lading . . . for the carriage of goods

---

[15] 377 F.2d 200 (2d Cir., 1967).

by sea . . . in the foreign trade," of the United States, Congress effectively "forbid an American court from a holding that a bill of lading covering an ocean shipment to or from the United States . . . [was subject to] . . . foreign rather than American law." Also, if the foreign law chosen by the parties was more generous to the carrier than COGSA, the choice of law clause would, in the court's view, run afoul of COGSA Section 1303(8) invalidating any clause in the bill of lading lessening the carrier's liabilities. The court then expressed the view that a choice of forum clause was "almost as objectionable" as a choice of law clause. "There would seem to be no way, [the court thought,] save perhaps stipulation by the parties, that would bind the foreign court in its choice of applicable law." And even if the foreign court were to apply COGSA, forcing the American shipper to assert its claim in a foreign court could "lessen the liability of the carrier quite substantially."

(3) In *The Bremen v. Zapata Off-Shore Co.*,[16] the Supreme Court expressed a broadly receptive attitude toward choice of forum clauses — even where those clauses implicitly carried with them a choice of foreign law — which contrasts sharply with the Second Circuit's more hostile perspective in *Indussa*. While technically COGSA was not applicable in *The Bremen*, the contrast has not gone unmarked by the lower courts. Thus, in an action by a German carrier against a German shipper alleging the latter's failure to properly prepare the cargo for shipment and seeking indemnification for injuries incurred by a longshoreman while unloading that cargo in the United States, the court upheld a clause in the bill of lading designating Hamburg as the forum for the settlement of the dispute. *Roach v. Hapag-Lloyd et. al.*[17] The *per se* rule of *Indussa* would not, the court thought, be particularly "efficacious" under these circumstances. To ignore the choice of forum clause would require the shipper to defend itself in the United States, a burden that would effectively lessen the carrier's responsibilities. And while technically Section 1303(8) was not applicable to the case, that added burden would be contrary to the broad policy of that Section. Accordingly, even though by the terms of COGSA, the bill of lading was subject to that Act — a point the court ignored — it felt free to apply *The Breman* analysis, pointing to the German nationality of the parties, issuance of the bill of lading in Germany and the presence of evidence in Germany. At this point the reader will want to consider the possibilities of bringing to bear on this issue the approach and methodology employed by the Supreme Court in *Lauritzen v. Larsen*[18] *infra* page 541.

(4) In *Komatsu Ltd. v. States Steamship Co.*,[19] the court refused to apply the $500 per package limitation in a claim by a shipper for damages to a tractor sustained while being unloaded. According to the court, the carrier could take advantage of the $500 limit only if it first gave "a fair opportunity to choose between a higher or lower liability by paying a correspondingly greater or lesser charge," an option conferred on the shipper by Section 1304(5). The burden of proving "fair opportunity" was upon the carrier. The court then rejected the argument that a carrier could meet this burden merely by incorporating COGSA

---

[16] 407 U.S. 1, 92 S. Ct. 1907 (1972), text at page 935 *infra*.
[17] 358 F. Supp. 481 (N.D. Calif., 1973).
[18] 345 U.S. 751, 73. S. Ct. 921 (1953)
[19] 674 F. 2d 806 (9th Cir., 1982).

by reference in the Paramount Clause of the bill of lading. Even in the case of "an experienced shipper" mere incorporation of COGSA by reference, as distinguished from incorporating the language of Section 1304(5) verbatim, would not, the court held, sustain the carrier's burden of proof. The court also rejected the carrier's claim that its burden of proving "fair opportunity" had been met with another clause that stated:

> Reference is hereby made specifically to value limitations (46 U.S. Code 1304(5)) . . . which shall apply and are incorporated herein by reference.

This clause failed, the court thought, to meet the requirement that the opportunity to declare a higher value " 'present itself on the face of the bill of lading' ".

§ 1.05   Terms of Sale and Fixing Damages for Breach

SEAVER v. LINDSAY LIGHT CO.

Court of Appeals (New York)
233 N.Y. 273, 135 N.E. 329 (1922)

McLAUGHLIN, J.

The defendant, in October, 1915, was located and doing business at Chicago, Ill., and plaintiff's assignor was located and doing business in London, England. About the time named they entered into a written contract . . . by which defendant agreed to sell and deliver to plaintiff's assignor 5,544 pounds of thorium in six monthly shipments at the price of $4 per pound, c.i.f. London dock. Each shipment was to be paid for in Chicago in advance. Three shipments were made and paid for according to the contract, but defendant refused to ship the balance, 2,772 pounds. This action was thereupon brought to recover the damages alleged to have been sustained. At the trial the sole issue was the proper measure of damages; the plaintiff contending it was the difference between the contract and market price at London dock at the time of the breach, and defendant contending it was the difference between the contract and market price at Chicago at that time.

If the former contention were correct, then plaintiff was entitled to recover $8,316, besides interest: if the latter contention were correct, then he was entitled to recover only $868.50, besides interest, the different amounts being the difference between the market price at London dock and Chicago at the time of the breach.

The trial court held that defendant's contention was correct, and thereupon gave judgment for the plaintiff in accordance therewith. Plaintiff appealed to the Appellate Division which reversed the judgment and ordered a new trial, holding that the measure of damage was as contended by plaintiff. Defendant now appeals to this court.

The meaning of the letters "c.i.f." in an executory contract is, and at the time the contract in question was made were, well understood in the commercial world. They mean the cost of the merchandise, insurance thereon, and freight charges to point of destination. . . . Unless there is something in a c.i.f. contract to indicate to the contrary, the seller completes his contract when he delivers the merchandise called for to the shipper, pays the freight thereon to point of destination, and forwards to the buyer bill of lading, invoice, insurance policy, and receipt showing payment of freight. . . .

Where was the delivery of the thorium in the present case to be made? Was it at Chicago or at London dock? If delivery were to be made at the former place, then the measure of damage was as found by the trial court. If at London dock, then it was as found by the Appellate Division.

I am of the opinion that the trial court was right. [The contract] . . . clearly indicate[d] an intention on the part of both parties that the delivery was to be made at Chicago, and when defendant delivered to a carrier at that point, paid the freight to point of destination, and forwarded the other necessary documents, he had fully completed his part of the contract. Failure to make delivery at that place obligated it to respond in damages in an amount corresponding to the difference there between the contract and market price of thorium at the time of the breach plus the cost of insurance and freight. There certainly is nothing in this contract to indicate that a delivery was to be made only at point of destination. Concededly, if the merchandise had been lost intermediate the delivery to the carrier and point of destination, the loss would have fallen upon the buyer and not upon the seller. That Chicago was to be the place of delivery seems to me not only to follow from the contract itself, but especially from that provision of it which required each shipment to be paid for in advance at Chicago. The trial court found as a fact that was the meaning and intention of the agreement. This finding is sustained by the evidence, and a finding to the contrary would be against the evidence.

* * * *

The judgment appealed from should be reversed, and the judgment of the trial court reinstated, with costs in this court and in the Appellate Division.

HISCOCK, C.J., AND HOGAN, CARDOZO, POUND, CRANE, AND ANDREWS, JJ., CONCUR.

C. SHARPE & CO. LIMITED v. NOSAWA & CO.

King's Bench Division
[1917] 2 K.B. 814

[In early 1914, C. Sharpe & Co. Limited ("Sharpe") agreed to buy and Nosawa & Co., ("Nosawa") agreed to sell 93 tons of Japanese peas at 10 Pounds 15 shillings a ton, c.i.f. London June shipment. Sale was based upon a sample ("the contract sample") sent by the seller to the buyer. Sometime prior to June 16, Sharpe received from Nosawa a bulk "shipment sample" together with the documents. Then between June 16 and July 29 the following communications occurred between the parties: *June 16*, Sharpe cabled that it would refuse to accept the goods because the shipment sample was inferior to the contract sample; Nosawa cabled that the two samples were of the same quality and that he would cancel the balance; Sharpe cabled that the quality was not equal and that he would claim damages; *June 17* Sharpe wrote asking Nosawa to send goods of the quality required by the contract; *June 18* Nosawa confirmed its June 16 cable with a letter; *July 29*, Sharpe replied by letter asking if it were to understand that Nosawa had not shipped the balance of the goods and requesting immediate cable response, otherwise it would have to buy against them. Nosawa never answered this last letter.

Sharpe claimed damages for non-delivery of the 93 tons of peas. An arbitrator determined that the shipping sample was indeed inferior to the contract sample. Accordingly, the only question for the court was the measure of damages. Had the goods been shipped on the last possible date for a June shipment and the shipping documents forwarded in the normal course, the documents would have arrived in London on or about July 21 and the goods on or about August 30. Nosawa paid into court 12 Pounds per ton for 93 tons, alleging that to be the value of similar goods obtainable on the London market on July 21. Sharpe claimed damages on the basis of 17 Pounds 10 shillings per ton, that being the London price of similar goods on August 30, World War I having started August 1-4, 1914.]

ATKIN J.

The question is whether the damages are to be measured by the price of peas in July, when the documents would have arrived in the ordinary course, or the price in August, when the goods would have arrived on a June shipment, assuming that the voyage took two months. The answer depends upon the true meaning of a c.i.f. contract of this kind. It is reasonably plain that such a contract is performed by the vendor taking reasonable steps to deliver as soon as possible after shipment the shipping documents, including the bill of lading and policy of insurance, and the buyer paying the price against the documents unless there is some other stipulation as to payment in the contract. But performance by the seller is by delivery of the documents which represent the goods. . . . The delivery intended by the contract is a constructive delivery. The bill of lading is, in the words of Bowen L.J., . . . "a key which in the hands of a rightful owner is intended to unlock the door of the warehouse, floating or fixed, in which the goods may chance to be," and is therefore a constructive delivery of the goods to the buyer, who from the time he receives the documents has control of the goods and can deal with them relying on their receipt, or, by virtue of the insurance their value, so that there can be no doubt in his mind that he has the control of existing goods or their value. . . . [In the] judgment of Kennedy L.J. in *Biddel Brothers v. E. Clemens Horst Co.*, it was assumed . . . that if there is a mail the vendor will transmit the documents so that they will arrive before the ship. That is clearly the right view. The contract is performed in fact, and the date of its performance is the date when the documents would come forward, the vendor making every reasonable effort to forward them. In this case, on the evidence, such a period would be twenty to twenty-one days after the ship sailed. Not only from the course of business in this case, but from ordinary commercial usage, it would be reasonable for the vendor to send the documents by mail by the Trans-Siberian Railway as soon as the goods have been shipped. They would have arrived on July 21 — that is, twenty or twenty-one days after the latest possible June shipment. They did not arrive on July 21, and there was consequently a breach of the contract on that date. What, then, is the remedy of the buyer? His remedies are specified in s. 51 of the Sale of Goods Act, 1893.[1] His right is to place himself as near as possible in that position in which he would have been if the contract had been fulfilled.

. . . The damages are to be assessed on the basis of reasonable conduct on the part of the purchaser. In the circumstances of this case the reasonable thing for a merchant to do who could not buy goods coming forward would be to go into the market and buy goods on the spot. In that way he would put himself as nearly as may be in the same position as if the contract had been fulfilled, and would have got control of an equivalent amount of goods. It is true he may incur further expense by reason of having to take up goods at once, the cost of warehousing, insuring &c., but that would be a part of his damages. It has been suggested that he might and ought to wait until the goods would have arrived. That, in my view, puts him into a different position. If the contract had been performed he would have had control of the goods at the time when the documents would have arrived. If he awaits the arrival of the goods, inasmuch as that may not happen for weeks or months, he is in the meantime subjecting the vendor to the risk of fluctuations in the market not contemplated by the parties and not reasonable. The reasonable course was for the plaintiffs to go into the market and buy goods. There is no doubt that they could have bought Japanese peas on the spot in July. They would have bought ex wharf and would have had to pay more in respect of landing charges, but they would have got a month's credit. In the normal course the goods would have arrived toward the end of August. The plaintiffs could have warehoused the substituted goods for fourteen days free of charge. The cost of warehousing till the end of August, so as to put themselves in the same position as if the goods had arrived in the ordinary course, would be a small matter.

* * * *

The only other question is as to "the time or times when they" — *i.e.* the goods — "ought to have been delivered" within the meaning of s. 51 of the Sale of Goods Act, 1893. Those words mean the time or times when they ought to be delivered according to the mode of delivery contemplated by the contract. If the contract provides for delivery of goods by means of documents, or by handing over the key of a warehouse, the date for that event is the "time . . . when they ought to have been delivered." In this case the date on which the documents ought to have arrived, that is to say July 21, is the important date in considering when the plaintiffs ought to have bought in the market. No doubt the plaintiffs ought to have a reasonable time in which to consider their position. The time cannot be indefinitely extended on the assumption that the plaintiffs could waive the term that the shipment should be in June. The matter has to be considered as between vendor and vendee on a contract to be performed strictly as to time. In these circumstances I fix the time for ascertaining the market or current price as somewhere about the last week in July. It is not necessary to fix the price very definitely, because the defendants have paid into court the equivalent of 12 Pounds a ton, and that is a sufficient allowance for all extra considerations. If August is the proper time to fix the market price, the price then was 17 Pounds, 10 shillings. But in my view the end of July is the proper time, and the defendants

---

[1] Documentary Supplement.

are entitled to judgment, but the plaintiffs get the costs of the action up to the date of payment into court by the defendants.

NOTES AND QUESTIONS

(1) Ignore for the moment the fact that in *Seaver v. Lindsay Light Co.* payment was to be made in Chicago. The court mentions but essentially ignores this fact, relying instead on the c.i.f. terms of the contract. In *Seaver* it was held that the market whose price is to be used in fixing damages is the market in which delivery was to occur. Under a c.i.f. contract that was Chicago, the point of shipment: straight-forward enough. But *C. Sharpe & Co. Ltd. v. Nosawa & Co.* also involved a c.i.f. contract, and the court, without discussion, assumes that damages should be based upon the price in London (the point of destination) not the price at the point of shipment (Japan). This is because London, not Japan, was the place of "delivery" of the goods. We have two possible explanations for this divergence. Either: (i) one of the courts doesn't understand a c.i.f. contract, or (ii) each has a very different concept of what constitutes "delivery" under such a contract. Which is it? If the latter, identify the difference.

(2) Which of these concepts is more appropriate to the issue being addressed? In deciding, note the following: If the issue were whether the risk of loss had passed to the buyer, which would be the controlling concept of delivery? If the issue were which party had the right of stoppage in transit, which version would control? Does this necessarily mean that the same concept of delivery should control when the issue is the measure of damages? In answering, consider the *purposes* of a damage award. The *Seaver* case makes the point rather dramatically, does it not? Consider the inverse situation; suppose the market price in Chicago had risen to approximately $7, the price in London to $4.31 and the contract price was $4.

(3) Now, *Seaver* contained an additional wrinkle. Payment was to be made against delivery of documents in Chicago. In light of this fact, would the court in *C. Sharpe and Co. Ltd.*, have necessarily reached the same result as the court in *Seaver*? In answering consider generally whether the purposes served by the delivery of documents to the buyer's agent in the seller's city are the same as the purposes served by delivery to the buyer at its principal place of business? If there are differences, which is the more appropriate "point" of delivery in assessing damages?

(4) Examine UCC Section 2-713, especially Comment 1.[2] For the rules on "tender" see: UCC Sections 2-301, 2-503, 2-504 and 2-507.

(5) In *Standard Casing Company, Inc. v. California Casing Company, Inc.*,[3] the buyer contracted for the purchase of the goods f.o.b. San Francisco, "sight draft, bill of lading attached with the privilege of examining the goods on arrival" in New York. The seller made no shipments, its breach of the contract was conceded and the only issue was the extent of the buyer's recovery; whether the damages were

---

[2] Documentary Supplement.
[3] 233 N.Y. 413 (1922).

to be measured by the market price of the goods in San Francisco, as the seller contended, or in New York, as the buyer claimed. The Court of Appeals, per Cardozo J., adopted the seller's view on the ground that it found nothing in this contract revealing an intention inconsistent with the general rule that:

> . . . upon a sale f.o.b. the point of shipment, title passes from the seller at the moment of delivery to the carrier and the subject of the sale is thereafter at the buyer's risk. . . . The reservation by a consignee of the privilege of inspection does not place the goods while in transit at the risk of the consignor. . . . The incidence of the risk is unaffected also by the right, retained by the defendant, to determine whether the bill of lading should run to consignor or to consignee. . . . If [all this] . . . is so, the seller's performance would be complete upon the beginning of the transit. The place where that [occurred] . . . must be the place also of default when performance was refused. Market values in California, and not market values in New York, must, therefore, be the measure of the value of the bargain (*Seaver v. Lindsay Light Co., supra*).

Are you persuaded? Recall the discussion of the differences between a c.i.f. and a f.o.b. contract *supra* page 29.

§ 1.06   Excuse for Non-Performance: Force Majeure, Commercial Impracticability and Frustration of Purpose

TSAKIROGLOU & CO. LTD. v. NOBLEE THORL G.m.b.H.

House of Lords
[1962] A. C. 93

VISCOUNT SIMONDS: My Lords . . . [this is an appeal from a judgment by DIPLOCK J, affirmed by the Court of Appeals upholding an] . . . award of an umpire in an arbitration between . . . [Tsakiroglou & Co. Inc., as sellers, and Noblee Thorl G.m.b.H, as buyers] . . . awarding the latter the sum of 5,625 Pounds against the former as damages for breach of contract. . . .

[Under] the contract made on Oct. 4, 1956. . . the appellants agreed to sell to the respondents 300 tons of Sudanese groundnuts at 50 [Pounds] per 1,000 kilos (*i.e.* per ton) including bags c.i.f. Hamburg, shipment during November/ December, 1956. No goods were shipped by the appellants. . . .

All groundnuts exported from the Sudan to Europe are shipped from Port Sudan . . . [T]he usual and normal route for the shipment [is] . . . via the Suez Canal. [At the time of contracting] . . . both parties contemplated [use of] . . . that route. It would have been unusual and rare for any substantial parcel of Sudanese groundnuts from Port Sudan to Europe to be shipped via the Cape of Good Hope. Before the closure of the Suez Canal, the [sellers] acquired [and held in warehouses in Port Sudan] 300 tons of Sudanese groundnuts . . . [for which they] booked space in one or other of four vessels scheduled to call at Port Sudan between Nov. 10 and Dec. 26, 1956. British and French armed forces began military operations against Egypt on Oct. 29, 1956. The Suez Canal was blocked on Nov. 2, and remained closed for effective purposes until at least Apr. 9, 1957. The shipping company canceled [seller's] . . . bookings on Nov. 4, 1956. But the [sellers] . . . could have transported the goods from Port Sudan to Hamburg via the Cape of Good Hope during November and December, 1956.

The distance from Port Sudan to Hamburg via the Suez Canal is about 4,386, and via the Cape about 11,137, miles. The freight ruling at the time of the contract for the shipment of groundnuts from Port Sudan to Hamburg via the Canal was about 7 [Pounds] 10 [shillings] per ton. After the closure of the canal . . . goods supplied on vessels proceeding via the Cape . . . [were subject to a surcharge from] . . . Nov. 10, 1956, [of] twenty-five per cent., and as from Dec. 13, 1956, one hundred per cent. The market price of Sudanese nuts in shell shipped from Port Sudan c.i.f. Hamburg was 68 [Pounds] 15 [shillings] per ton between Jan. 1 and 15, 1957. As has been already said, the [sellers] did not ship any nuts. They claimed that they were entitled to consider the contract as canceled, and to this view they adhered.

The contract provided, by clause 6, that:

> In case of prohibition of import or export, blockade or war, epidemic or strike, and in all cases of force majeure preventing the shipment within the time fixed for the delivery, the period allowed for shipment or delivery shall be extended by not exceeding two months. After that, if the case of force majeure be still operating, the contract shall be canceled.

The [arbitration] award [concluded that: 1] . . . "neither war nor force majeure prevented shipment of the contract goods during the contract period if the word 'shipment' means placing the goods on board a vessel destined for the port of Hamburg . . .; if the word shipment' includes . . . transportation to the contract destination . . . via the Suez Canal [then shipment] was prevented . . . by reason of force majeure . . .;" [(2)] " . . . it was not an implied term of the contract that shipment . . . should be made via the Suez Canal . . ." [and hence] " . . . the contract was not frustrated by the closure of the Suez Canal;" and [(3)] " . . . the performance of the contract by shipping the goods on a vessel routed via the Cape of Good Hope was not commercially or fundamentally different from its being performed by shipping the goods on a vessel routed via the Suez Canal."

The first . . . of these findings relate to the claim of the [sellers] . . . that . . . clause 6 . . . of the contract absolved them from performance of the contract. I will deal with this at once and shortly.

Similar words . . . fell to be construed in *Re Comptoir Commercial Anversois v. Power, Son & Co.*[1] BAILHACHE, J., said:

> Now, if I give to the word "shipment" the widest meaning of which it is capable, it cannot mean more than bringing the goods to the shipping port and then loading them on board a ship prepared to carry them to their contractual destination.

His judgment on this point was affirmed in the Court of Appeal. It has never been questioned, and I see no reason for questioning it. . . .

I come, then, to the main issue and . . . I find two questions interlocked: (i) What does the contract mean? In other words, is there an implied term that the goods shall be carried by a particular route? (ii) Is the contract frustrated?

---

[1] [1920] 1 K.B. 868.

It is convenient to examine the first question first, though the answer may be inconclusive. . . . It is put in the forefront of the [sellers'] case that the contract was a contract for the shipment of goods via Suez. . . . To say that . . . is . . . its meaning is to say in other words that the term must be implied. For this I see no ground. It has been rejected . . . in two other cases, *Carapanayoti & Co., Ltd. v. E. T. Green, Ltd.*[2] and *Albert D. Ganon & Co. v. Societe Interprofessionelle des Oleagineux Fluides Alimentaires*[3] . . . . A variant of this contention was that there should be read into the contract by implication the words "by the usual and customary route" and that, as the only usual and customary route at the date of the contract was via Suez, the contractual obligation was to carry the goods via Suez. Though this contention has been viewed somewhat differently, I see as little ground for the implication . . . for it seems to me that there are precisely the same grounds for rejecting the one as the other. Both of them assume that sellers and buyers alike intended and would have agreed that, if the route via Suez became impossible, the goods should not be shipped at all. In as much as the buyers presumably wanted the goods and might well have resold them, the assumption appears wholly unjustified. Freight charges may go up or down. If the parties do not specifically protect themselves against change, the loss must lie where it falls.

* * * *

I turn now to what was the main argument for the appellants, that the contract was frustrated by the closure of the canal from Nov. 2, 1956, till April, 1957. Were it not for the decision of MCNAIR, J., in *Green's* case,[4] I should not have thought this contention arguable, and I must say with the greatest respect to that learned judge that I cannot think he has given full weight to the decisions old and new of this House on the doctrine of frustration. He correctly held . . . that "where a contract expressly, or by necessary implication, provides that performance, or a particular part of the performance, is to be carried out in a customary manner, the performance must be carried out in a manner which is customary at the time when the performance is called for." But he concluded that the continued availability of the Suez route was a fundamental assumption at the time when the contract was made, and that to impose on the sellers the obligation to ship by an emergency route via the Cape would be to impose on them a fundamentally different obligation, which neither party could, at the time when the contract was made, have dreamed that the sellers would be required to perform. Your Lordships will observe how similar this line of argument is to that which supports the implication of a term that the route should be via Suez and no other. I can see no justification for it. We are concerned with a c.i.f. contract for the sale of goods, not a contract of affreightment, though part of the sellers' obligation will be to procure a contract of affreightment. There is no evidence that the buyer attached any importance to the route. He was content that the nuts should be shipped at any date in November or December. There was no evidence and, I suppose, could not be that the nuts would deteriorate as the result of a longer voyage and a double crossing of the Equator, nor any evidence that the market was seasonable. In a word, there was no evidence that the buyer cared by what route or, within

---

[2] [1959] 1 Q.B. 131; [1958] 3 W.L.R. 390; [1958] 3 All E.R. 115.
[3] [1960] 2 Q.B. 318, 341; [1959] 3 W.L.R. 622; [1959] 2 All E.R. 693.
[4] [1959] 1 Q.B. 131.

reasonable limits, when, the nuts arrived. What, then, of the seller? I recall the well-known passage in the speech of LORD ATKINSON in *Johnson v. Taylor Bros. & Co., Ltd.*,[5] where he states the obligations of the vendor of goods under a c.i.f. contract, and asks which of these obligations is . . . "fundamentally" altered by a change of route. Clearly the contract of affreightment will be different and so may be the terms of insurance. In both these respects, the seller may be put to greater cost; his profit may be reduced or even disappear. But it hardly needs reasserting that an increase of expense is not a ground of frustration. . . .

Nothing else remains to justify the view that the nature of the contract was "fundamentally" altered or . . . "radically different" . . . Whatever expression is used . . . the doctrine of frustration must be applied within very narrow limits. In my opinion, this case falls far short of satisfying the necessary conditions. . . .

On this part of the case, I have not thought it necessary to deal with the decision in *Societe Franco Tunisienne d'Armement v. Sidermar S.P.A.*[6] There the question was whether a charter party was frustrated by the blocking of the Suez Canal. The learned judge held that it was, but was at pains to point out that the position was very different in a contract for the sale of goods. On that point, I agree with him and need not discuss the matter further.

I come finally to a question which has given me some trouble. . . . It will be remembered that the vital words [in the arbitral award] were "not commercially or fundamentally different." Diplock, J., regarding this as a finding of fact, thought that the case was thereby concluded. I cannot regard this as a correct decision. It is a question of law whether a contract has been frustrated, and it is commonly said that frustration occurs when conditions arise which are fundamentally different from those contemplated by the parties. But it does not follow from the use by the arbitrator of the word "fundamentally" in describing the difference between the actual and the contemplated conditions that the court is precluded from forming its own judgment whether or not a contract has been frustrated. It is of great value to the court to know that lay arbitrators with special knowledge do or do not regard the new circumstances as so different from those contemplated that they think "fundamental" an appropriate word to use. But the value is evidential only. It has not the sanctity of a finding of fact. . . .

In my opinion, the appeal should be dismissed with costs.

LORD REID:

The [sellers'] first argument was that it was an implied term of the contract that shipment should be via Suez. . . . [B]ut I find nothing in the contract or in the case to indicate that they intended to make this a term of the contract, or that any such term should be implied; they left the matter to the ordinary rules of law.

> [Admitting that the "ordinary rule" is that a shipper must ship by the usual and customary route, or, if there is no such route, then by a practicable and reasonable route, Lord Reid concurred with Viscount Simonds that this means the usual and customary route at the time of performance not the date of the contract, giving the following reason for this conclusion.]:

[5] [1920] A.C. 144, 155; 36 T.L.R. 62, H.L.
[6] [1961] 2 Q.B. 278; [1060] 3 W.L.R. 701; [1960] 2 All E.R. 529.

If [the date of contracting is the reference point and if] . . . the new route made necessary by the closing of the old is substantially different, the contract would be at an end, however slight the effect of the change might be on the parties. That appears to me to be quite unreasonable; in effect, it means writing the old route into the contract, although the parties have chosen not to say anything about the matter. On the other hand, if the rule is to ascertain the route at the time of performance, then the question whether the seller is still bound to ship the goods by the new route does depend on the circumstances as they affect him and the buyer; whether or not they are such as to infer frustration of the contract. That appears to me much more just and reasonable and, in my opinion, that should be held to be the proper interpretation of the rule.

I turn then to consider the position after the canal was closed, and to compare the rights and obligations of the parties . . . if the canal had remained open. As regards the sellers, the only difference to which I find reference in the Case . . . was that they would have had to pay . . . [an increased freight.] They had no concern with the nature of the voyage. In other circumstances, that might have affected the buyers, [for example] if the market price of groundnuts had fallen instead of rising, it might have been the buyers who alleged frustration, [or] . . . where damage to the goods was a likely result of the longer voyage which twice crossed the Equator, or, perhaps, the buyer could be prejudiced by the fact that the normal duration of the voyage via Suez was about three weeks, whereas the normal duration via the Cape was about seven weeks. But there is no suggestion in the case that the longer voyage could damage the groundnuts or that the delay could have caused loss to these buyers of which they could complain. Counsel for the appellants rightly did not argue that this increase in the freight . . . was sufficient to frustrate the contract, and I need not, therefore, consider what the result might be if the increase had reached an astronomical figure. The route by the Cape was certainly practicable. There could be, on the findings in the case, no objection to it by the buyers and the only objection to it from the point of view of the sellers was that it cost them more and it was not excluded by the contract. Where, then, is there any basis for frustration?

. . . I, therefore, agree that this appeal should be dismissed.

LORD RADCLIFFE:

[Lord Radcliffe first agrees with the seller that, broadly speaking, under a c.i.f. contract the seller must obtain a bill of lading for transport of the goods by the "customary or usual route." He then declines to concur in the seller's further proposition that if that route, as it existed at the time of contracting, subsequently became unavailable, the contract would be unenforceable either because it was impossible of performance or because its purpose had been frustrated. His Lordship continued:]

. . . .

. . . This contract was a sale of goods which involved despatching the goods from Port Sudan to Hamburg. . . . There was nothing to prevent the vendors from despatching the goods as contracted, unless they were impliedly bound as a term of the contract to use no other route than that of the Suez Canal. I do not see why that term should be implied; and, if it is not implied, the true question seems to me to be . . . whether it was a reasonable action for a mercantile man to perform his contract by putting the goods on board a ship going round the Cape of Good Hope and obtaining a bill of lading on this basis. A man may habitually leave his house by the front door to keep his appointments; but, if the front door is stuck, he would hardly be excused for not leaving by the back. The question, therefore, is what is the reasonable mercantile method of performing the contract at a time when the Suez Canal is closed, not at a time when it is open. To such a question the test of "the usual and customary route" is ex hypothesi inapplicable.

On the facts found [in the arbitration] . . . I think that the answer is inevitable. The voyage would be a much longer one in terms of miles; but length reflects itself in such matters as time of arrival, condition of goods, increase of freight rates. A change of route may, moreover, augment the sheer hazard of the transport. There is nothing in the circumstances of the commercial adventure represented by the [sellers'] . . . contract which suggests that these changes would have been material. Time was plainly elastic. . . . With all these facts before them, as well as the measure of freight surcharge that would fall to the vendors' account, the [umpire in the arbitration found] . . . that performance by shipping on the Cape route was not "commercially or fundamentally different" from shipping via the Suez Canal. We have no material which would make it possible for us to differ from that conclusion.

It has been a matter of debate whether this finding ought to be treated as a finding of fact, by which a court would be bound, or as a holding of law . . . open to review. . . .

Since Lord Mansfield's day, commercial law has been ascertained by a cooperative exchange between judge and jury and, now that arbitrators have taken the place of juries I do not think that we can start all over again with an absolute distinction between the respective spheres of judge and arbitrator. Generally speaking, I do not think that a finding in the form which we have here can ever be conclusive on the legal issue. . . . [But] it would be contrary to common sense that a court, which cannot uninstructed assess the commercial significance of, say, a surcharge of 7 [Pounds] 10 [shillings] per ton for freight in a c.i.f. contract of this kind, should not pay careful attention to such a view from [persons familiar with the trade] . . . just as it would be, I think, contrary to principle that a court should regard a view so expressed as finally conclusive of the legal issue.

I would dismiss the appeal.

LORD HODSON:

[After concluding that the issue was whether, after closure of the Suez canal, performance of the contract was "fundamentally different in kind" from the performance promised, Lord Hodson states:]

* * * *

. . . The freight was higher than that involved in the Suez route but . . . [f]reight rates go up and down and it is exceedingly difficult in a commercial contract to escape from its terms on the ground of frustration by the increased expense involved when the time of performance is reached as compared with that contemplated when the contract is made. Indeed, the [sellers'] . . . did not rest their frustration argument on the increase of freight, . . . but maintained that "the long haul round the Cape" was so fundamentally different from what had earlier been the usual route that the c.i.f. contract which included the obligation to procure a contract of affreightment had been frustrated by the closure of the canal.

I see no ground as a matter of law on the true construction of this contract and the facts found in the [arbitration] . . . on which frustration can stand. . . .

I would dismiss the appeal.

LORD GUEST:

* * * *

[The thrust of Lord Guest's speech is contained in his commentary on the decision of McNair J in *Carapanayoti & Co., Ltd. v. E. T. Green, Ltd.*[7] He states:]

The circumstance [of that case] were almost precisely similar to the present. The learned judge held that the nature and extent of the sellers' obligation in relation to the route was to be ascertained at the time of performance. He then proceeded, however, to find that the contract was frustrated because to impose on the sellers an obligation to ship via the Cape was to impose on them a fundamentally different obligation from that which they undertook when the contract was made. The learned judge, I think, fell into the error which he had previously corrected in the sellers' argument by treating the date of the contract as the date when the sellers' obligation had to be ascertained. If the critical date is the time when performance is called for, there cannot be frustration.

* * * *

I would dismiss the appeal.

Appeal dismissed.

NOTES AND QUESTIONS

(1) As several Law Lords noted, both parties assumed that the peanuts would be shipped from Port Sudan to Hamburg via the Suez Canal, yet, none of them were willing to make that route an "implied term" of the contract. Viscount Simonds sets out the test for such a term to be implied. Why, in spite of the parties' assumption, was that test not met? Be specific. These considerations suggest, do they not, that the House of Lords was actually engaged in allocating the risk between the parties and that the decision on whether the term should be implied as well as on whether the performance of the contract was impossible was a function of that allocation.

(2) Note that several of the Law Lords pointed to the fact that time was not of the essence under the contract of sale. They note that the seller had a two month

---

[7] [1959] 1 Q.B. 131.

long period within which to ship the goods, that the groundnuts would not be damaged by the longer voyage around the Cape and that there was no evidence to suggest that the delay occasioned by a longer voyage would give the buyer a problem. These discussions plainly seem to imply that had this not been the case — had time been of the essence because, for example, cargo deterioration was a serious possibility or the buyer had commitments to resell — then a claim that closure of the Canal made performance impossible, might well have succeeded. Do you agree? In answering, assume time was of the essence and consider the following:

> (a) Seller refuses to ship and buyer is forced to purchase on the open market at a much higher price in order to cover its obligations to its customers. Buyer then sues seller for the difference between the contract price and the cost of cover. Seller defends on the ground that closure of the Canal made its performance impossible and that hence the contract was unenforceable. ·

> (b) Seller ships via the Cape, goods are delayed and, as a consequence, buyer is forced to purchase on the open market to cover its obligations to its customers. However, it succeeds in doing so at or below the contract price. Seller, forced to sell at the lower market price, then sues buyer for the difference between the market and the contract price. Buyer defends on the ground that closure of the Canal made performance of the contract impossible and hence unenforceable.

Now consult your answer to Question (1) and decide whether the defense of impossibility should succeed in both of these cases, or in only one. If so, which one? Explain. Does your answer suggest that, taken literally, the impossibility or frustration of purpose doctrine as articulated by the House of Lords is seriously lacking in substantive content?

(3) In *Florida Power and Light Company v. Westinghouse Electric Corporation*,[8] FP&L sued for breach of a 1966 contract under which Westinghouse had undertaken to build a nuclear power plant and furnish ten years of uranium at a fixed price and had also granted FP&L the option of either disposing of spent fuel itself or having Westinghouse do so. The latter option was exercised by FP&L in 1972, just before the plant "went critical," in the following terms:

> Westinghouse will remove the irradiated fuel from the Plant site and dispose of it as Westinghouse sees fit.

Anticipating FP&L's choice, Westinghouse entered into a "letter of intent" with Allied General Nuclear Services (AGNS) for the construction by the latter of a plant in Barnwell, South Carolina to process FP&L's waste. By 1974, however, AGNS was pleading that it could not meet the agreed price because of cost increases occasioned by new government regulations. Then, anticipating that there would be no federal support for the expansion of AGNS's Barnwell plant (see discussion below), the Westinghouse-AGNS negotiations were broken off in late 1975. As a result Westinghouse declined to remove the spent fuel and FP&L sued. As its defense Westinghouse pleaded impossibility or impracticability of performance, relying on the following events.

---

[8] 826 F. 2d 239 (4th Cir., 1987).

When the government began promoting the private uses of atomic power it was generally thought that reprocessing would be the way to dispose of irradiated fuel. Yet, not until the late 1960's — after the Westinghouse-FP&L contract had been signed — did private firms show any interest in entering the commercial reprocessing business. As a consequence, no private nuclear power plants were constructed until the government, in 1957, assured the industry that if private commercial facilities were not available, it would take responsibility for reprocessing spent fuel from private power plants. This also meant that throughout the 1950's and 1960's it was not only assumed that safe reprocessing was feasible but that permanent storage — the only other recognized option — was impracticable (some components of spent fuel have a half-life of 25,000 years). Both Westinghouse and FP&L shared these assumptions when they entered into the 1966 contract. In fact, Westinghouse estimated a recovery of between $14-$19 million from the sale of reprocessed fuel.

The situation soon changed however. Although several commercial reprocessing plants were licensed in the late 1960's, by 1972, when a number of private concerns applied for licenses to construct new reprocessing facilities, they were strenuously opposed by environmentalist groups. Then, in 1976 the courts struck down the Nuclear Regulatory Commission's attempt to issue these applicants interim licenses pending formulation of a generic environmental impact statement. Whereupon President Carter ordered the indefinite deferral of all licenses for the commercial reprocessing of spent fuel from private nuclear power plants and committed his administration to exploring ways of providing permanent storage for the waste.

In 1981, the incoming Reagan administration adverted back to reprocessing as the solution. By this time, however, the commercial reprocessing industry had collapsed and there was no permanent or even interim storage facilities in sight. The power companies' only option was to expand their temporary on-site storage capabilities. Finally, in 1982, Congress passed the Nuclear Waste Policy Act (NWPA) providing for permanent deep repositories to hold nuclear waste and authorizing several interim measures including expansion of on-site "re-racking" storage. Also under the Act all nuclear power companies were required to negotiate contracts with the government fixing the amount each would pay for future storage once permanent facilities were in place, an event not expected to occur until, according to the District Court, 1994 or, according to the Appeals Court writing three years later, 2009. Later FP&L did enter into a contract with the government agreeing to pay $80 million for future storage of its waste.

Over a period of four years the District Court per Judge Merhige issued three opinions in the case.[9] Turning to the Restatement of Contracts (Second), Section 265, the District Court noted that the defense of impracticability would require that performance was frustrated by the occurrence of an event "the non-occurrence of which was a basic assumption upon which the contract was made."[10] Applying this criteria the Judge reached three separate conclusions.

---

[9] The first opinion is reported at 517 F. Supp 440 (E.D. Va., 1981), the second opinion is unreported, the third opinion is reported at 597 F. Supp 1456 (E.D. Va., 1984).

[10] The bulk of this summary is taken from the third opinion, 597 F. Supp 1456 (E.D. Va., 1984).

First, that with respect to spent fuel accumulated up to 1976 there was no impracticability of performance. The contract committed Westinghouse to "remove" the spent fuel. Admitting that the parties both assumed that the fuel would be disposed of by reprocessing, the Judge emphasized that Westinghouse's ability to dispose of it in that manner was not a condition of the contract. With respect to the fuel accumulated up to 1976, therefore, Westinghouse could have complied with the contract terms because:

> . . . had [it] acted with diligence, it could have removed [that] portion of the spent fuel to the existing storage space at AGNS facility or to similar space at a number of other sites summarized in the expert's report.

Second, that as respects the period after 1976 the Judge rejected Westinghouse's claim of impracticability on the basis that:

> Westinghouse [could] now ultimately meet its obligation in reference to removal and disposal of the spent fuel as a consequence of [FP&L's] having contracted with the [Department of Energy] for its removal to the permanent federal repository.

The costs of removal under the contract with the Department of Energy would not, the Judge concluded, support a finding of excessive expense considering the profit that Westinghouse stood to make on other parts of its contract with FP&L. More broadly, on Westinghouse's' plea of impracticability, the District Court held that notwithstanding the parties assumption regarding disposal through reprocessing, the unavailability of reprocessing was something foreseeable and therefore not an "unforeseen occurrence" within the impracticability doctrine. Citing a long line of AEC reports, the court observed that commercial reprocessing was an unproven technology and one likely to be subjected, for safety reasons, to more stringent and expensive regulations which could destroy the viability of a commercial reprocessing industry. Either Westinghouse did foresee this possibility, or should have done so because under the contract it alone had voluntarily assumed the risk of the nonavailability of commercial reprocessing.

The court also rejected Westinghouse's contention that the Government's 1957 promise to reprocess spent fuel if commercial facilities were not available constituted an assurance that disposal of its nuclear waste would not involve substantial costs to the nuclear power industry. The Government only undertook, according to the Judge, to provide reprocessing services "at their estimated cost" not "at a subsidized level."

Third, turning to Westinghouse's "implicit timeliness obligation" to FP&L, Judge Merhige noted that as the prospects for viable commercial reprocessing collapsed, the Government in October 1977 announced that it would take title to spent fuel for interim and long-term storage for a one-time fee, a policy that impliedly at least would take effect within five years. By the time the NWPA was enacted it was clear that no federal repository would be available at least until 1998. The Judge went on:

> Perhaps Westinghouse should reasonably have been aware in the mid-1960's that the Government might not be in a position to take the spent fuel off the industry's hands immediately . . . but Westinghouse could reasonably have assumed that the service would have been available in a commercially

reasonable time so as to minimize expenditures on temporary, stop-gap solutions. . . . Hence, Westinghouse is correct in asserting that the Government unforeseeably did not fulfill this timeliness aspect of its implied commitment to the industry.

No one could have anticipated the poor planning, delays, and policy reversals that have added up to more than twenty years of delay, after the outlook for commercial reprocessing became clouded, before the Government will be providing any alternative. Both [FP&L] and Westinghouse were aware that reprocessing might not be available, but neither of them anticipated that no alternative means of removal would be available until 1998 or after.

Accordingly, the court determined that "an equitable allocation" of the interim on-site storage costs was in order, with Westinghouse to absorb the costs of the first re-racking at the South Florida plant and FP&L the costs of the second re-racking.

Neither party appealed that part of the District Court judgment apportioning the interim costs of "re-racking" the South Florida plant. With regard to the remainder of the judgment, however, the Fourth Circuit Court of Appeals reversed both the District Court's decision that for the period up to 1976 Westinghouse had not been diligent in seeking alternative methods of disposal and the decision requiring Westinghouse to pay for future storage with the Government.

In reversing on the question of Westinghouse's diligence, the Appeals Court noted that storage at AGNS facilities would have required the conversion of those facilities and an AEC license; that in light of the AEC's failed experiments with "away from reactor storage" in the early 1970's, it was "unreasonable to assume that Westinghouse could" have constructed its own storage facilities; that had Westinghouse in 1970 desired to build a reprocessing facility it, like AGNS, would have had to have an AEC license and would doubtless have suffered the same delays and ultimate failure that AGNS experienced; and that the failure of Westinghouse to secure a reprocessing contract with AGNS was not the fault of Westinghouse but was due to AGNS's understandable unwillingness to name a firm price in the changing regulatory climate.

Then, calling the case a "textbook illustration of the circumstances warranting the application of the doctrine of impracticability/impossibility of performance," the Appeals Court summarized in the following terms:

> We are unable to distill from this record the slightest credible evidence that at the time this contract was executed both parties had not assumed (1) that reprocessing was a practical and available method for disposing of spent fuel, (2) that it was the method of disposal by which it was intended that . . . the party obligated would dispose of the spent fuel, and (3) that, if commercial reprocessing was not available on reasonable terms, the Government would reprocess the plants' spent fuel.

The Appeals Court distinguished *Transatlantic Financing Corp. v. United States*,[11] a Suez Canal closing case, upon which the District Court had relied, by arguing that in *Transatlantic*:

---

[11] 363 F. 2d 312 (D.C. Cir., 1966).

. . . there was always a foreseeable and reasonable alternative means of carriage of the cargo existing both at the time the contract of carriage was executed and at the time performance was called for. In this case, however, there was neither a reprocessing plant nor . . . a storage facility available to Westinghouse. . . .

The Appeals Court then continued by concluding that:

. . . the promise of storage, as made by the Government under the [NWPA] . . . [did not] represent a reasonable alternative to the reprocessing, the availability of which was . . . [under] the Government's 1957 assurance, "an implied commitment."

With regard to the $80 million Government charge for future storage of spent fuel, the Appeals Court again held that the District Court had erred. The latter had compared the $80 million Government storage contract with the total project costs, including $222 million of plant construction costs and had concluded that the storage cost was not sufficiently excessive to render performance of the contract impracticable. In the Appeals Court's view the "only thing to be considered" [was] the cost or profit to be realized by Westinghouse if reprocessing had been available compared with the cost of storage." On this basis a performance which would have netted Westinghouse just under $20 million compared with a burden of $80 million was, the court concluded, "obvious[ly] . . . unreasonable and excessive."

Finally, since the doctrine of impracticability is an "equitable defense," the Appeals Court, after noting that the rate-payers of Florida had greatly benefited from the lower cost of nuclear generated electricity, concluded that it was as fair to impose on those ratepayers the costs of spent fuel storage during the period for which Westinghouse had disposal responsibility, as it was to impose those costs on the rate-payers thereafter, when FP&L would be responsible for disposal.

At this point consider the following questions:

(a) The Appeals Court thought that Judge Merhige contradicted himself when he acknowledged that, at the time of contracting, both parties assumed that spent fuel would be reprocessed and then concluded that Westinghouse should have foreseen the possible nonavailability of reprocessing facilities. Do you agree? Does your answer turn on whether you take a formalistic approach to the impracticability doctrine or consider it, initially at least, an invitation to a risk allocation analysis? In this connection the Appeals Court, at one point, noted that the American courts had rejected the theory that the impracticability doctrine rested on an "implied condition" of the contract. This meant, the court said, that, "the language of the contract is irrelevant." Is it?

(b) Can you square the Appeals Court decision with *Tsakiroglou*? At the time of contracting which was the more improbable, the nonavailability of reprocessing for FP&L's spent fuel or the carriage of Tsakiroglou's peanuts around the Cape of Good Hope?

(c) Unlike *Tsakiroglou* the contract in the *Westinghouse* case contemplated a long-term relationship in a venture (nuclear power) the future of which was admittedly clouded with uncertainties. Under these circumstances consider what purpose the impracticability doctrine might properly serve. Which decision best served that purpose? In this connection how do you evaluate the Appeals Court's assessment of the equities of the case?

(4) In *American Trading and Production Corp. v. Shell International Marine Ltd.*,[12] the parties entered into a voyage charter under which the tanker "Washington Trader" was to carry lube oil from Beaumont, Texas to Bombay, India. The freight rate was to be in accordance with the prevailing American Tanker Rate Schedule (ATRS) of $14.25 per ton, plus seventy five percent and a charge of $.85 per ton for passage through the Suez Canal. After the ship sailed the owner advised the captain to take on extra "bunker" in Spanish Morocco because of possible diversion due to the Canal crisis. This the ship did on May 31, thereafter sailing to a point about 84 miles North of the Canal. On the day the Canal was closed, the owners first warned the ship and then sought the charterer's permission to divert the vessel. The latter left it for the owner to decide. The next day the owner ordered the ship to sail around the Cape of Good Hope "reserving all rights for extra compensation." It then billed the charterer $131,978 over the $417,327 already paid at the time of original hire. The charterer refused to pay and the owner sued, claiming commercial impracticability. The owner argued that the rate was expressly based on a voyage through the Suez Canal in as much as the parties had stipulated that for a trip around the Cape the negotiations would have started at an ATRS rate of $17.35 per ton instead of $14.25 and the contract rate expressly included Canal tollage. The court rejected the argument stating: " . . . all the ATRS rate establishes is that the parties obviously expected a Suez passage but there is no indication at all in the instrument or dehors that it was a condition of performance." The court also thought an increase of less than one-third in the contract price was not so excessive as to render performance impracticable. Can you square the decision of the Court of Appeals in *Westinghouse* with this reasoning?

(5) In *Societe Franco Tunisienne D'Armement v. Sidermar S.P.A. (The Messalia)*[13] a voyage charter rate of 134s per ton for 5,000 tons of iron ore had been calculated for a voyage from India to Italy via the Canal. The Canal was closed before the ship sailed and the owners elected to make the longer voyage around the Cape of Good Hope. Pearson J. held that the charter had been frustrated and that the owners were entitled to be compensated for the reasonable costs of the longer voyage, awarding them 195s per ton.

(6) *Ocean Tramp Tankers Corp v. V/O Sovfracht (The Eugenia)*[14] involved a time, not a voyage charter, under which the charterer pays (usually monthly) for as long as it is entitled to use the ship. During that time the ship is, unlike a vessel under a voyage charter, subject to the charterer's orders. The Eugenia sailed from Odessa on the Black Sea bound for India via the Suez. On October 30 when it was widely known that the Canal was about to be attacked, the charterer (a Russian trading company) ordered the ship into the Canal over the owners objection, where it became trapped until the following January when a channel

---

[12] 453 F. 2d 939 (2d Cir., 1972).
[13] [1961] 2 Q.B. 278 (1960).
[14] [1964] 2 Q.B. 226 (CA, 1963).

was cleared back to the Mediterranean end of the Canal. The charterer, claiming that the charter had been frustrated, refused to pay the charter hire for the three months that the ship was trapped in the Canal. The owners denied the claim of frustration and then terminated the charter on the ground that the ships entry into the Canal violated the "war clause" in the charter party. Whereupon the parties negotiated a new charter at a higher rate, the ship proceeded to India via the Cape of Good Hope and the owners sued for the three months charter hire that had not been paid. The Court of Appeals held for the owner. Lord Denning, who delivered the principal opinion, concluded that the charterers could not claim frustration since they had been responsible for sending the ship into the Canal. "Self-induced frustration" was, his Lordship said, unknown to the law. Moreover, the order to enter the Canal also violated the war clause and the owner properly terminated the charter party. He then went on to consider what the legal situation would have been if the Eugenia had not entered the Canal and the charterers sought an exemption from payment of the charter hire for the extra time taken for the voyage around the Cape on the ground that the loss of that time constituted frustration of the charter party. Relying on *Tsakiroglou*, he decided that the charter would not have been frustrated and overruled the decision in *The Sidermar*. He could not, Denning said, find any difference between a c.i.f. contract of sale and a charter party or, for that matter, between a voyage and a time charter. Consider the following:

(a) If you employ a risk allocation analysis, how do you evaluate Lord Denning's statement that in judging the impossibility of performance there is no difference between a c.i.f. contract and a voyage charter; between a voyage and a time charter? In spite of his statement he correctly over-ruled *The Sidermar*, did he not? Explain. Note that under a voyage charter the charterer pays, usually in one lump sum, for however long it takes to complete the voyage. Under a time charter the charterer pays, often monthly, for the time stipulated in the contract.

(b) Can the Suez Canal closing cases be reconciled with the Fourth Circuit's decision in *Westinghouse*?

CZARNIKOW LTD. v. ROLIMPEX

House of Lords
[1979] A.C. 351

[Czarnikow Ltd. appealed from a judgment of the Court of Appeals affirming the judgment of Kerr J. which upheld an award by a panel of arbitrators of the Council of the Refined Sugar Association. The arbitrators dismissed the appellants' claims for damages for non-delivery of about 14,300 tons of Polish white sugar f.o.b. Polish ports in November/December 1974.]

The facts are stated in their Lordships' opinions.

LORD WILBERFORCE. My Lords, this appeal arises out of two contracts for the purchase of sugar by the appellant from the respondent. Each contract was made subject to the rules of the Refined Sugar Association and expressly provided that the performance of the contract was subject to *force majeure* as defined in the association's rules. There are two relevant rules. Rule 18(a)[15] applies if the delivery in whole or in part within the delivery time should be prevented or delayed directly or indirectly by *inter alia* government intervention and provides, as is usual, for an extension and ultimately for cancellation of the contract. Rule 21 deals with licences and is in the following terms:

> The buyer shall be responsible for obtaining any necessary import licence and the seller shall be responsible for obtaining any necessary export licence. The failure to obtain such licence/s shall not be sufficient grounds for a claim of force majeure if the regulations in force at the time when the contract was made, called for such licence/s to be obtained.

The contracts were made in May and July 1974 (subject to addenda of later dates) and were forward sales for delivery in November/December 1974. The seller thus assumed the risk of a rise in the price of sugar between the contract date and the date of delivery.

Since the seller failed to deliver any of the 11,000 m.t. provided for by the first contract and part of the tonnage provided for by the second contract, it would be liable to the buyer for substantial damages unless it could rely on force majeure.

The respondent seller Rolimpex is a state trading organization of the Polish state: it obtains sugar required for export from the Sugar Industry Enterprises represented by the Union of Sugar Industries in Poland. The relation between the latter body and Rolimpex is that Rolimpex sells as "commission merchant," *i.e.*, it sells in its own name but only for a commission and on account of the Sugar Industry Enterprises concerned. The contracts now in question were no doubt intended to be satisfied from the 1974 sugar crop in Poland. It is found that the Polish National Economic Plan required a total sugar production of 1,835,000 m.t. for the season 1974/75. Of this, 1,500,000 m.t. was required for the domestic market and the balance was authorized for export. In May 1974 Rolimpex was authorized to contract for the export of 200,000 m.t.

In August 1974 there was heavy rain and flooding in the sugar beet producing areas: the result was that only 1,432,000 m.t. were produced — a shortfall even on the amount required for domestic consumption. On November 5, 1974, a resolution of the Council of Ministers was passed banning the export of sugar with effect from November 5, 1974, and canceling export licences. This resolution was found not to [have] the force of law. However, later on November 5, 1974, the Minister of Foreign Trade and Shipping signed a decree providing:

> 1. From November 5, 1974, it is prohibited to release export deliveries of sugar specified by present contracts.

> 2. Customs authorities shall immediately stop the deliveries of sugar prepared for export and notify disposers about the prohibition of sugar export.

> 3. The rule is in force from the date of its signature.

This made the export of sugar illegal by Polish law.

---

[15] Full text of this rule is found on page 88 in the speech by Viscount Dilhourne. Ed.

It is found by the arbitrators that on November 5, 1974, there was a considerable quantity of sugar at the port of Gdynia and a further quantity on the way to Gdynia by rail. But for the ban, sugar would have been available for the performance by Rolimpex of both contracts. It was also found that both before and after November 15, 1974 (the date when the buyer was able to ship) there was Polish sugar of the contract quality available on the market. If there were insufficient quantities available, there was a market for the purchase and sale of other sugar of equivalent quality. In the condition of the market any purchaser would have accepted any sugar of equivalent quality in substitution for Polish sugar. The market value of the relevant quality of sugar on November 15 was however FF. 7,500 per m.t. as compared with FF. 3,064 the price fixed for one contract and about FF. 4,000 for the other.

The export ban remained in operation until July 1, 1975. Rolimpex declared *force majeure* on November 6, 1974, and, if it was entitled to do so, both contracts became void.

. . . In their award the arbitrators found [*inter alia*] that sugar was available on the world market to meet the shortage in the Polish market but the Council of Ministers resolved not to purchase sugar on the world market because of the high price and the loss of foreign exchange that such a purchase would have entailed; that the ban was imposed to relieve the anticipated shortage in the domestic market; that its effect was to throw the losses caused by the partial failure of the Polish sugar crop on overseas traders and consumers, thus saving the Polish state having to bear any financial loss in replacing the sugar sold well in advance of the 1974/75 campaign. They added this unusual observation:

(a)(v) We very much regret that the Council of Ministers authorized the ban rather than permitting the purchase of sugar on the world market, so enabling Rolimpex to honour its contractual obligations.

A further group of findings contained the following:

(b) The persons employed in Rolimpex did not induce the Council of Ministers to authorize the ban and did not influence its continuance or effect. (c) Rolimpex is an organization of the Polish state. (d) Rolimpex is not so closely connected with the Government of Poland that it is precluded from relying on this ban . . . as "government intervention" within rule 18(a) of the rules of the Refined Sugar Association. (e) Rolimpex is accordingly entitled to rely on rule 18(a) as a defense to Czarnikow's claims."

. . . The matter came before the court with two main questions for decision. 1. Was this a case of government intervention within rule 18(a)? 2. Was the case taken out of rule 18(a) by the provisions of rule 21? There was also a question (of very considerable difficulty) as to the measure of damages.

Consideration of Question 1 can conveniently start from the arbitrators' finding (b) above. It was the case of the buyer before the arbitrators that there was some kind of collusion or conspiracy between Rolimpex and the government of Poland by which the government was persuaded, in the interest of Rolimpex, to impose the ban. In order to deal with this, Rolimpex produced a quantity of evidence to show that there was no such collusion or conspiracy; on the contrary, when the possibility of a ban on exports was mentioned to the director and general manager of Rolimpex before November 6, 1974, he protested about it and the persons employed in Rolimpex were not consulted about the imposition of the ban and were not informed of the ban until after its imposition. The arbitrators found that Czarnikow had failed to prove its allegation that the ban was imposed after consultation between the persons employed in Rolimpex and the Ministry of Foreign Trade and Shipping. The ban was in fact requested by the Minister of Food and Agricultural Industries on the grounds that it was unacceptable to put the people of Poland on short rations and other alternative views were unacceptable. There being disagreement among the ministers (including the Minister for Foreign Trade and Shipping who supervises Rolimpex) the matter was referred to the Council of Ministers which passed the resolution of November 5, 1974 (see above). There was thus ample evidence to support the arbitrators' finding against collusion or conspiracy.

Before the courts and this House the buyer took a different line. It appealed to a group of English cases dealing with actions taken by or on behalf of the Crown in which a distinction has been made, broadly, between the acts which are performed by a government for the public good or for a general executive purpose and acts which a government does so as to avoid liability under a contract or contracts . . . [In the Court of Appeals] Lord Denning M.R. was disposed to hold that this distinction might be applied to the present case if, but only if, Rolimpex was to be regarded as a department of government: he then proceeded to hold that it was not. I have very great doubt whether the doctrine developed by these cases, which is very much one of English constitutional law, can viably be transplanted into the constitutional structure of foreign States — particularly such states as Poland which we are entitled to know have an entirely different constitutional structure from ours. Such a transplantation, if possible at all, would involve English courts in difficult and delicate questions as to the motivation of a foreign State, and as to the concept of public good, which would be unlikely to correspond with ours. I am not saying that there may not be cases when it is so clear that a foreign government is taking action purely in order to extricate a state enterprise from contractual liability, that it may be possible to deny to such action the character of government intervention, within the meaning of a particular contract, but that result cannot, in my opinion, be achieved by means of the doctrine mentioned above: it would require clear evidence and definite findings. It is certain that no such evidence or findings exist in the present case. On the contrary, the evidence is that the action was taken to avoid serious domestic, social and political effects and to avoid loss of foreign exchange if high price sugar were to be brought on the world market. The arbitrators indeed so found.

I agree, however, wholly with Lord Denning M.R. that Rolimpex cannot on the evidence be regarded as an organ of the Polish state. . . . The independence of Rolimpex from the government is in my opinion amply demonstrated by the facts set out at length in the award. Together with all four learned judges who have considered this point, I find the conclusion clear, and I therefore hold that the seller makes good the contention that there was government intervention within rule 18.

The second question is whether rule 21 operates as a savings clause which, in the circumstances, takes the case out of rule 18. I am afraid that I can find no substance in this argument. Rule 21 appears in a section of the rules headed "Licences." In my opinion it does no more than to place on the seller the obligation to obtain an export licence (and on the buyer to obtain an import licence) and to state that failure to fulfill this obligation shall not be a sufficient ground for a claim of force majeure. The word "obtain" in this context means "obtain" or "get" and I cannot read in to it any obligation or warranty to maintain it in force. The seller complied with this obligation and the clause is satisfied. I agree entirely with the disposition of this point by Kerr J.

I would dismiss the appeal.

VISCOUNT DILHORNE. . . .

The rules of the Refined Sugar Association contain a chapter headed "Force Majeure." The chapter contains rules 17-20. Rule 18 (a) is relevant to this case and so far as material reads as follows:

> Should the delivery in whole or in part within the delivery time specified by prevented or delayed directly or indirectly by government intervention . . . beyond the seller's control, the seller shall immediately advise the buyer . . . of such fact and of the quantity so affected, and the period of delivery shall be extended by 30 days for such quantity. . . . If delivery is still prevented by the end of the extended period, the buyer shall have the option of canceling the contract for the affected quantity or of taking delivery at the contract price without claiming damages as soon as the sugar can be delivered. . . . Should the buyer elect not to cancel the contract but delivery of the sugar in whole or in part still remains impossible 60 days after the last delivery date provided for by the contract, the contract shall be void for such quantity without penalty payable or receivable.

It is in my opinion clear beyond all doubt that delivery of the sugar in pursuance of the contracts within the delivery time was prevented by the intervention of the government of Poland. It is, I think, equally clear that the action taken by the government was beyond the respondents' control. The facts found by the arbitrators show, as I have said, that the respondents had insisted on the export of the 200,000 tons they had contracted to sell, and also that on November 5 when informed of the possibility of the ban, the respondents' director and general manager had protested. Nevertheless the ban was imposed.

The appellants contended that "government intervention" in rule 18(a) should be interpreted to mean only intervention for what was called a general executive purpose; that the decree was imposed to achieve a particular result in relation to the contracts for the export of sugar, and that intervention for such a purpose was not to be regarded as government intervention within the meaning to be given to those words in rule 18(a).

The particular result which it was the respondents' purpose to achieve was, it was alleged, to throw the losses caused by the failure of the sugar crop on to overseas traders and consumers and to avoid it being borne by the Polish state.

Rule 18(a) clearly requires it to be established, if the force majeure relied on is government intervention, that the cause of the delivery being prevented or delayed was government intervention. It does not stipulate that, if there is such intervention, one has to go on to consider for what purpose the intervention was made. I do not find it necessary in this case to consider whether a government intervention, which in fact occurred, can be treated as not having occurred if it be established that it was to secure a particular result such as that alleged by the appellants, for the facts found by the arbitrators in their award, in my view clearly negative the contention that it was for that particular purpose. They found that Poland was faced with a shortage of sugar if all contracts for the export of sugar were performed, that the Council of Ministers feared that the shortage of sugar in the home market would have serious domestic social and political effects, that sugar was available on the world market to meet the shortage but that the Council of Ministers resolved not to purchase on the world market because of the high price of sugar and the loss of foreign exchange that such a purchase would have entailed and that the ban "was accordingly imposed to relieve the anticipated shortage in the domestic market." Presumably this purpose was achieved. The arbitrators say that the effect of the ban was:

> to throw the losses caused by the partial failure of the Polish sugar crop on overseas traders and consumers thus saving the polish state having to bear any financial loss in replacing the sugar sold well in advance of the 1974/75 campaign.

While this was a consequence of the ban, its purpose as stated by the arbitrators was not that but to relieve the anticipated shortage on the home market.

The foundation for this contention by the appellants is not there and so it is unnecessary to consider what effect, if any, it would have had it been.

* * * *

The appellants also asserted that the respondents bought and sold for the state. This while no doubt true, does not in my view help the appellants. The facts found by the arbitrators stated above show that they were not a department of the government but have a separate identity. They were, it was found as a fact, employed as "a commission merchant" to sell sugar intended for export on behalf of Sugar Industry Enterprises which were also state enterprises.

The fact that they did so cannot in my opinion invalidate the decree made on November 5.

So if rule 18(a) stood alone, the respondents are in my opinion entitled to rely on it as excusing them from liability for non-delivery of the sugar within the period stipulated in the contract.

The appellants, however, say that they are prevented from doing so by rule 21. . . .

If this is the right construction of the rule, it would mean that where a licensing system was in force at the time of the contract, the words "government intervention" in rule 18(a) would have little, if any, significance. Never could the seller in any country rely on that rule if the government of that country placed an embargo on export and a licence for export was required both at the time of the contract and at the time for delivery. . . .

In this case the cause of the non-delivery was government intervention not failure to obtain an export licence.

For these reasons in my opinion this appeal fails and should be dismissed. . . .

LORD SALMON. . . .

I do not express any concluded opinion as to what the position might have been, in law, had the facts as found by the arbitrators established that the sellers were an organ or department of the government or of the state. I am inclined to the view that, in such circumstances, the facts as found in paragraph 50(a)(v) of the award may nevertheless have been expressed without sufficient clarity to establish with the necessary certainty that the ban was not imposed "for the public good" or for "a general executive purpose" but only for the purpose of extricating the government from its obligation under the contracts of sale. If the findings had been so expressed, I would agree with Lord Denning M.R. that the sellers, in the circumstances postulated, would have been precluded from relying on rule 18(a). . . .

Paragraph 50(a) (iv) of the award makes it plain that the ban had been imposed to relieve the anticipated shortage in the domestic market: but this step was taken only because it had been decided not to buy the sugar which was readily available on the world market and would equally have relieved any home shortage. For my part I am not at all surprised by the comment in paragraph 50(a) of the award: "We very much regret that the Council of Ministers authorized the ban rather than permitting the purchase of sugar on the world market, so enabling [the sellers] to honour [their] contractual obligations."

Since, however, the sellers were not found to be an organ or department of the government or the state, it is unnecessary to express any concluded view on what should have been the result had such a finding been made.

I now turn to consider the effect of rule 21 of the Refined Sugar Association's rules which was also incorporated in the contracts of sale. . . . The regulations in force in Poland at the time the contracts were made called for [export] . . . licences to be obtained.

Someone had to take the risk that the necessary export licences might become unobtainable or be canceled. In my opinion, it was the sellers who accepted the responsibility for obtaining such licences and the risk that they might fail to do so. If they failed from any cause, obviously, they could not deliver the sugar they had sold: but they would then be liable to compensate the buyers for any damage the buyers had suffered as a result of the non-delivery.

At the time when these forward contracts were entered into, it must have been foreseen that before the stipulated delivery date, the Polish government might well intervene by preventing export licences from being issued and canceling any such licences as had been issued. This, in my opinion, was a risk which fell upon the sellers under rule 21. To construe this rule otherwise emasculates it and deprives the buyers of the protection which it purports to afford them.

Rule 18(a) cites, first, government intervention and then ten other specific examples of force majeure. Any of these, unless excluded by some provision in the contract, would afford a valid defense to the sellers if it prevented or delayed delivery under the contract. So far as the sellers' contractual obligations are concerned, Rule 21 preserves only their obligation to obtain the necessary export licences, otherwise, the sellers' escape routes under Rule 18(a) for failure to deliver, or a delay in delivery, are left intact. I consider, however, that Rule 21 makes it plain that the sellers cannot escape from their failure to obtain the necessary export licence on the ground of government intervention or any other ground of force majeure; certainly not without implying or writing into Rule 21 after the words "force majeure," the words "unless caused by government intervention." I cannot find any justification for doing so. Far from it being necessary to emasculate Rule 21 in order to give business efficacy to the contract, I consider that it makes far better commercial sense as it stands.

I would accordingly allow the appeal.

LORD FRASER OF TULLYBELTON. My Lords, I have had the advantage of reading in draft the speech of my noble and learned friend, LORD WILBERFORCE, and I agree with it.

On the arbitrators' findings in this case there is no doubt that there was government intervention in the sense of Rule 18. At one time I was inclined to attribute more importance than some of your Lordships do to Rule 21, and to think that it was intended to place on the seller an obligation to obtain an export licence which would be effective at the time of exporting. But further reflection has satisfied me that for the reasons stated by my noble and learned friend, Viscount Dilhorne, to construe Rule 21 in that way would involve reading into the word "obtain" more than it can fairly bear. Nor does it seem to me that the word "necessary" helps the appellants. In the context of Rule 21, the word must imply that there is in force a licensing system of such a character that, if the necessary licence is obtained, it would be effective to allow the seller to export the goods which he had contracted to sell. But if the licensing system is abolished or (as in the present case) superseded, with the result that no licence can be effective during the period of suspension, Rule 21 does not have the effect of imposing on the seller an absolute obligation to obtain government permission to export the goods; if it did, it would remove almost the whole of the protection against government intervention given to him by rule 18. I agree with Cumming-Bruce L.J. in the Court of Appeal [1978] Q.B. 176, 204 that:

> His [the seller's] obligation though absolute is more restricted, and is only to obtain from the licensing department or authority evidence of such permission to export as is within the ordinary scope of the licensing system that department is concerned with.

I would dismiss the appeal.

LORD KEITH OF KINKEL. My Lords, I have had the opportunity of reading in draft the speech of my noble and learned friend, Lord Wilberforce. I agree with it, and for the reasons he gives I too would dismiss the appeal.

NOTES AND QUESTIONS

(1) Note that counsel for Czarnikow argued that even if there was no conspiracy between the government of Poland and Rolimpex, the government ban on sugar

exports was not for the "public good" but just to escape liability on a contract and hence did not constitute "government intervention" within the meaning of the force majeure clause. Lord Denning in the Court of Appeals and Lord Salmon, in the House of Lords, turns this around and indicates that the issue of the government's purpose would only arise if Rolimpex were found to be a "department of government." Suppose there had been such a finding or a finding that Rolimpex induced the Council of Ministers to issue and continue in effect the ban on sugar exports. What result would the House of Lords have likely reached? By way of dicta each Law Lord intimates the answer, does he not? What reason would there be for such a doctrine? It is a dangerous doctrine, is it not, in an age where governments, through agencies and wholly owned corporations, often engage in commercial ventures? Do we see here a British version of the American "Act of State" doctrine?[16]

(2) Suppose the Council of Ministers had issued a 90 day ban on sugar exports under the following circumstances: the international sugar market was in short supply, the international price of sugar had risen well above Rolimpex's contract price and was projected to rise even further. At the same time all Polish production targets had been met. What result?

(3) What result if all the facts of the *Rolimpex* case were the same except that Rule 21 of the Refined Sugar Association provided as follows:

> The buyer shall be responsible for obtaining and maintaining in full force and effect throughout the period required for performance of this contract any necessary import license and the seller shall be responsible for obtaining and maintaining during the same period any necessary export license. The failure to obtain and/or maintain such license/s shall not be sufficient grounds for a claim of force majeure if the regulations in force at the time when the contract was made, called for such license/s to be obtained.

§ 1.07   The Letter of Credit

Introduction

In this section we turn to examine the letter of credit, one of the most pervasive and useful devices found in international trade where it is employed more frequently than in domestic sales. As noted earlier (§ 1.02 *supra*), in a documentary transaction documents serve for a time in lieu of goods. The seller ships the goods and gets paid upon presentation, not of the goods, but of documents. The buyer, in turn, can protect itself by specifying the documents that the seller must present in order to be paid. All of this, of course, helps facilitate international trade. That facility, however, can be greatly enhanced when banks enter the picture through the issuance of commercial letters of credit. While persons other than banks can issue letters of credit, banks are so preponderantly the source of those credits that we will simply confine our discussion to bank issued credits.

A letter of credit is an undertaking by the issuing bank to pay the seller upon the presentation of the documents specified in the credit. It is wholly separate from

---

[16] This doctrine is discussed in Chapter 13 at page 1083.

the underlying contract between buyer and seller. (At this point examine the sample letter of credit found in the Documentary Supplement).[1] From the seller's viewpoint, not only does it get paid against documents but, with a letter of credit, it ships against the credit of both the buyer and the issuing bank. Particularly when the buyer is in another country this can afford the seller an important measure of additional security. For this reason letters of credit are generally made "irrevocable" for a stated period. While a credit can be "revocable," it simply cannot perform the same commercial function as the "irrevocable" credit.

From the buyer's viewpoint a letter of credit has a number of advantages. The buyer arranges for the issuance of the credit, normally with a bank in its country. The very fact that the buyer is able to secure bank credit of this type enhances its negotiating position with the seller. In addition, since the buyer initiates issuance of the credit it normally has substantial control over the types and content of the documents which the seller must present. Finally, the buyer may, in the context of arranging for the letter of credit, be able to obtain bank financing for its purchase.

At this point it is important to note, however, that the arrangement between the buyer and the issuing bank is no part of the letter of credit itself and will reflect the broader bank - customer relationship between the two. The bank will, of course, charge the buyer a fee for its service. In addition, since the bank is obligated to pay the seller or a prior paying bank upon the presentation of conforming documents and thereafter has recourse only against the buyer, the bank may require the buyer to post some type of security or maintain sufficient deposits to cover payments under the credit or obtain a guaranty of payment from a third party. If, however, the buyer is a particularly valued customer the bank may be willing to extend what is in effect an unsecured line of credit against which the buyer can draw by applying for the issuance of one or more letters of credit.

Obviously, the facility of a letter of credit can be further enhanced by bringing in yet another bank; this time a bank in the seller's country. The latter may be just an "advising" bank, or it may be a "paying" or "confirming" bank. We will examine each type more fully below. Suffice it to note here that there will normally be a correspondent relationship (*i.e.*, each maintains one or more accounts with the other) between the issuing bank and the bank in the seller's country and if the latter is a "paying" or "confirming" bank, the lapsed time between the seller's shipment of the goods and receipt of payment is foreshortened by the time it would otherwise take to transmit the documents to the issuing bank abroad.

Against this general background consider the following diagram.

---

[1] Documentary Supplement.

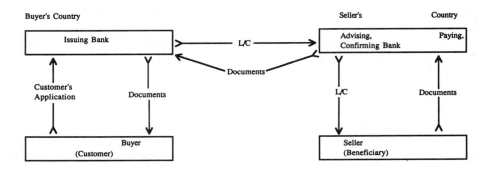

As the diagram indicates, the buyer, as "customer," applies to a bank, usually in its country, for the issuance of a letter of credit to the seller, the "beneficiary." Since the letter will recite that it is issued for the account of the named buyer, the buyer is also sometimes referred to as the "account party." While the letter can be issued directly to the seller, more frequently it is sent to a bank in the seller's country and the latter bank advises the seller that the credit has been issued in its favor. The "advising" bank may also undertake to pay the seller (*i.e.*, become a "paying" bank) or it may go further and confirm the credit (*i.e.*, become a "confirming" bank). This latter is usually stipulated for in the contract between the buyer and seller. After receiving the letter of credit the seller ships the goods, presents its draft accompanied by the required documents either to the issuing bank directly or to a paying or confirming bank and receives payment all as described more fully below. If the documents are presented to a paying or confirming bank, the latter will take responsibility for forwarding them to the issuing bank who, in turn, will send them on to the buyer.

Issuing Bank. As already noted the issuing bank, pursuant to a separate contract with the buyer, agrees to issue to the seller or beneficiary the bank's undertaking (the letter of credit) to honor drafts drawn on it or on the customer if accompanied by specified documents. (Examine the standard form letter of credit application contained in the Documentary Supplement.[2]) If it is a "straight" letter of credit, the undertaking runs only to the beneficiary and not to any endorser or other purchaser of the draft. If it is a "negotiation" credit,[3] the undertaking also runs to any other drawer of a draft under the credit as well as to endorsers and purchasers of the draft. The issuing bank is liable to the beneficiary, other drawer, endorser or purchaser if it dishonors a demand for payment that otherwise complies with all the conditions stated in the credit. On the other hand, since the customer is not a party to the undertakings contained in the letter of credit, the issuing bank is not liable in damages to the customer if it pays against documents which do not conform to the terms of the letter or if it pays with knowledge that the documents were false or fraudulent. Rather, under its separate contract with

---

[2] Documentary Supplement.

[3] It will contain language along the following lines: "We hereby engage with the drawer, endorsers, and bona fide holders of drafts drawn under and in compliance with the terms of this credit that the same will be duly honored on due presentation."

the customer, improper payment either forecloses the issuing bank's right of reimbursement from the customer or, if it has charged the customer's account, entitles the latter to have the funds restored.

Confirming Bank. Since the issuing bank is likely to be some distance from, and may have had no prior relationship with, the seller, the latter in its contract with the buyer may stipulate that the letter of credit is to be "confirmed" by the seller's own bank or at least a bank in its locality. A confirming bank independently assumes all of the obligations undertaken by the issuer of the credit. A confirmed letter of credit, in other words, is backed by the credit of two separate banks. Once it has made payment to the beneficiary, the confirming bank will look to the issuing bank for reimbursement. Like the issuer, if a confirming bank wrongfully dishonors a demand for payment it will be liable to the beneficiary and, since all confirmed credits must be "negotiation" credits, it will also be liable to other drawers, endorsers and purchasers of drafts drawn under the credit. Likewise, it will be foreclosed from obtaining reimbursement from the issuing bank if it pays against non-conforming documents or documents known to be fraudulent.

Advising Bank. Again because of distance and lack of familiarity, an issuing bank may, if confirmation is not called for, request a bank in the seller's locality to act simply as an advising bank. An advising bank merely advises the seller that a letter of credit has been opened naming it the beneficiary and informs the latter of the terms and conditions of the credit. Such a bank incurs no liability to the seller and does not put out any money. If, however, the advice calls for the seller to draw its draft on the advising bank, the latter automatically becomes a paying bank as well.

Paying Bank. Not infrequently the advice to the seller will indicate that the advising bank will also pay the seller upon presentation of the required documents; will act as a paying, but not a confirming, bank. Like an advising bank, a paying bank takes its instructions from the issuing bank and undertakes no liability to the seller.

Payment and Reimbursement. If the letter of credit calls for a sight draft, an issuing, confirming or paying bank will, upon presentation of the documents by the beneficiary, examine those documents and if it finds them in order make immediate payment. If a time draft is called for, both an issuing and a confirming bank will examine the documents and, finding them to be in order, will mark the draft "accepted." A paying bank, on the other hand, will simply forward the documents to the issuing bank for acceptance and await the latter's instructions. In either event, payment will follow automatically on the due date of the draft.

If the credit calls for the seller's draft to be drawn on a bank in the seller's country (*i.e.* a paying or confirming bank), the latter will, after paying the beneficiary, draw its draft on the issuing bank and receive reimbursement by a credit to its account in that bank. If the draft is drawn on the issuing bank or the customer, a paying or confirming bank will simply endorse the seller's draft and forward it on to the issuing bank.

Transfer and Assignment of Credits. Letters of credit can be "transferred" only if they expressly so provide. To transfer a credit means to convey to the transferee the right to perform all or some of the conditions stated in the credit, to receive directly all or a stated portion of the payments due thereunder and to enforce that right of payment. An "assignment," on the other hand, confers on the assignee only a right to some or all of the proceeds of a letter of credit after all of the conditions precedent to payment have been performed by the assignor or by a subsequent purchaser or endorser of the assignor's draft. An assignee does not have the right to enforce the terms of the letter credit against a party obligated thereunder, such as an issuing or confirming bank. The assignee must look strictly to its assignor. Unlike the transfer, an assignment does not have to be expressly authorized by the terms of the letter of credit itself. Sometimes the words "transfer" and "assignment" are used interchangeably, and one must be careful to understand the precise nature of the conveyance being authorized.

Transferable credits are especially useful where the seller is a distributor or other middleman who intends to fill his buyer's order by purchase from a third-party supplier. For example, suppose a buyer abroad and a seller in the United States enter into a contract to purchase specified goods in the amount of $500,000, c.i.f. port city in the buyer's country. The buyer obtains from a bank in its country a transferable letter of credit in that amount naming the seller as beneficiary. The letter is confirmed by the seller's bank. The seller, in turn, contracts with a third party supplier in the United States to supply the goods for $450,000 on the same terms, *i.e.* c.i.f. port city in the buyer's country. The seller then simply transfers the letter of credit up to the amount of $450,000 to the supplier. The supplier ships the goods under an order bill of lading naming one of the banks or the buyer as consignee. It then draws its draft for $450,000 on the confirming bank and presents that draft accompanied by its invoice, the bill of lading and such other documents as the letter of credit may require. In the meantime, the seller will have drawn its draft on the confirming bank in the amount of $500,000. If the confirming bank finds the documents in order, it will pay the seller's draft ($500,000) by credit to the latter's account, charge that account with $450,000 in order to pay the third party supplier, replace the latter's invoice with the seller's invoice, draw its draft on the issuing bank and forward the documents, properly endorsed, to the issuer.

Even if a letter of credit is transferable, a seller may prefer to use "back-to-back" credits in order to keep its relationship with the buyer confidential or to keep greater control or more readily divide the sums due it from the buyer among a number of third party suppliers. Thus, under our example, in lieu of a transfer, the bank in the seller's country would, after having confirmed the buyer's $500,000 letter of credit (Credit 1), issue its $450,000 letter of credit (Credit 2) for the account of the seller, naming the third party supplier as beneficiary. The documentation and other requirements under Credit 2 would have to be tailored to satisfy the requirements of Credit 1. Thereafter the transaction would proceed essentially as described above. The confirming/issuing bank will pay $450,000 on the third party supplier's draft under Credit 2, charge that amount to the seller's account after having credited the seller with $500,000 represented by the latter's draft under Credit 1, replace the invoices and forward the documents under Credit 1 to the issuer.

[A]   The Letter of Credit and the Underlying Contract

URQUHART LINDSAY AND COMPANY, LTD. v. EASTERN BANK, LTD.

King's Bench Division
[1922] 1 K.B. 318

Action in the Commercial Court before ROWLETT J.

The plaintiffs were manufacturers of machinery, and the defendants were bankers with various branches in the East, including Calcutta. In December, 1919, the plaintiffs agreed to manufacture for the Benjamin Jute Mills Co., Ltd., who were customers of the defendants, a quantity of machinery for delivery f.o.b. Glasgow to the amount of 64,942 [Pounds].

This contract contained (inter alia) the following terms: (1) that in the event of any increase taking place in wages or cost of materials or transit rates or any further reduction taking place in working hours, the plaintiffs' prices would be correspondingly increased; and (2) that the Benjamin Jute Co., Ld., should open in this country a confirmed irrevocable banker's credit to the extent of 70,000 [Pounds].

On February 14, 1920, the defendants wrote to the plaintiffs the following letter:—

4 Crosby Square,
London.

To MESSRS. URQUHART LINDSAY & CO.

Dundee.

Dear Sirs,

We beg to advise you that under instructions received from our Calcutta branch we are prepared to pay you the amounts of your bills on B. N. Elias, managing agent, the Benjamin Jute Mills Co., Ld., Calcutta, to the extent of, but not exceeding 70,000 [Pounds] in all (say seventy thousand pounds). The bills are to be accompanied by the following complete documents covering shipments of machinery to Calcutta, are to be drawn payable 30 days after sight, and are to be received by us for payment on or before April 14, 1921:—

Signed Invoices in duplicate.

Complete set of bills of lading made out "to order" indorsed in blank and marked by the shipping company "freight paid."

Policies of insurance against marine or war risks

This is to be considered a confirmed and irrevocable credit, and the bills should bear a clause to the effect that they are drawn under credit No. 102 dated Calcutta, January 15, 1920. Kindly acknowledge receipt.

M. HARKNESS,
Manager.

The plaintiffs thereupon bought raw material and in 1920 began to manufacture the goods. They made two shipments under the contract in February and March, 1921, and tendered to the defendants bills of exchange together with shipping documents, which the defendants duly paid. On February 18, 1921, the defendants wrote to the plaintiffs, in reference to their former letter of February 14, 1920, a further letter advising them that they had heard from Calcutta that should it be necessary for the plaintiffs to include in their invoice for extra cost of labour, this extra amount must be referred to the buyers, before they (the defendants) would be at liberty to pay the same. The defendants then refused to meet the bills of exchange presented by the plaintiffs on the third shipment, and only did so, under protest on May 9, 1921, when the confirmed credit had expired.

The plaintiffs meantime on April 12, 1921, issued a writ in the action, and in their points of claim, dated June 29, 1921, alleged that the defendants' letter of February 18, 1921, was a breach of the contract contained in their letter of February 14, 1920, and that they (plaintiffs) had suffered damage, and lost the profit which they would otherwise have made, and that there was no available market for the goods.

The defendants in their points of defense (July 30, 1921) alleged that it was a term or condition in the contract between the plaintiffs and the Benjamin Jute Mills Co., Ld., that the plaintiffs should not draw bills of exchange for more than shippers' current prices in December, 1919, and in particular that they should not include in such bills any increased cost over the price in 1919 on which the agreed credit of 70,000 [Pounds] was calculated. They contended that the plaintiffs had acted in breach of this term or condition; and further that the damage (if any) was too remote and was not recoverable.

ROWLETT J. read the following judgment: . . . [The defendant's letter of] credit was by its terms to be irrevocable and the invoices were to be for machinery. There can be no doubt that upon the plaintiffs acting upon the undertaking contained in this letter of credit consideration moved from the plaintiffs, which bound the defendants to the irrevocable character of the arrangement; . . . nor was it contended before me that this had not become the position when the circumstances giving rise to this action took place.

. . . .

In my view the defendants committed a breach of their contract with the plaintiffs when they refused to pay the amount of the invoices as presented. Mr. Stuart Bevan contended that the letter of credit must be taken to incorporate the contract between the plaintiffs and their buyers; and that according to the true meaning of that contract the amount of any increase claimed in respect of an alleged advance in manufacturing costs was not to be included in any invoice to be presented under the letter of credit, but was to be the subject of subsequent independent adjustment. The answer to this is that the defendants undertook to pay the amount of invoices for machinery without qualification, the basis of this form of banking facility being that the buyer is taken for the purposes of all questions between himself and his banker or between his banker and the seller to be content to accept the invoices of the seller as correct. It seems to me that so far from the letter of credit being qualified by the contract of sale, the latter must accommodate itself to the letter of credit. The buyer having authorized his banker to undertake to pay the amount of the invoice as presented, it follows that any adjustment must be made by way of refund by the seller, and not by way of retention by the buyer.

There being thus in my view a breach of contract, the question arises what damages the plaintiffs can recover. The point is a new one, and not free from difficulty. It is, of course, elementary that as a general rule the amount of damages for non-payment of money is only the amount of the money itself. If, for instance, the defendants had merely undertaken to pay the price of goods as and when shipped, nothing being said about the undertaking being irrevocable within limits of time and amount, such undertaking would become binding only in respect of each shipment upon its being made, the successive shipments being the separable considerations for the separable undertakings referring to them respectively; and the engagement could be revoked at any time as to future shipments. In such a case the damages in case of a refusal to pay for any shipment made before revocation would be merely the amount owing in respect of the shipment. In the present case, however, the credit was irrevocable; and the effect of that was that the bank really agreed to buy the contemplated series of bills and documents representing the contemplated shipments just as the buyer agreed to take and pay for by this means the goods themselves. Now, if a buyer under a contract of this sort declines to pay for an installment of the goods, the seller can cancel and claim damages upon the footing of an anticipatory breach of the contract of sale as a whole. These damages are not for nonpayment of money. It is true that non-payment of money was what the buyer was guilty of; but such non-payment is evidence of a repudiation of the contract to accept and pay for the remainder of the goods; and the damages are in respect of such repudiation. I confess I cannot see why the refusal of the bank to take and pay for the bills with the documents representing the goods is not in the same way a repudiation of their contract to take the bills to be presented in future under the letter of credit; nor, if that is so, why the damages are not the same. Mr. Stuart Bevan argued that the sellers should go on shipping and sue the bank *toties quoties*.[4] Why should they be put in this position as against the bank any more than as against the seller? What is the difference for this purpose between the obligation to take the goods and pay the invoice, and the obligation to take bills and documents representing the goods and pay the invoice? The whole purpose of the arrangement is that the seller shall have a responsible paymaster in this country to protect him against the very contingency which has occurred and the very damages which he claims.

Mr. Stuart Bevan, however, further argued that the plaintiffs ought to have minimized their damages by tendering bills only for so much of the invoices as in view of the attitude of the buyer the bank would pay, letting their goods and relative documents go against this reduced payment, and drawing other bills for the balance. These bills they would have to discount without documents, and of course without excluding recourse against themselves; but if the buyers refused them acceptance and the plaintiffs had to pay them they could then, if right in their position, says Mr. Stuart Bevan, still sue the defendants. This is merely to contend that the plaintiffs should have let their documents go against such part of their invoices as the bank would pay, and sue them for the rest. This is not minimizing damages but abandoning their right to be paid against documents.

---

[4] As often as it occurs. Ed.

The damages to which the plaintiffs are entitled are the difference between on the one hand the value of the materials left on their hands and the cost of such as they would have further provided, and, on the other hand, what they would have been entitled to receive for the manufactured machinery from the buyers, the whole being limited to the amount they could in fact have tendered before the expiry of the letter of credit.

A subsidiary question arose whether the plaintiffs are entitled to interest on the money paid after action for the goods that had actually been shipped. I do not see upon what ground I can award this interest.

Judgment for plaintiffs.

NOTES AND QUESTIONS

(1) Obviously the seller bargained for some flexibility in the price. That flexibility, in turn, created a problem of control. How might the buyer have handled that problem more effectively when it came to formulating the letter of credit?

(2) Having failed to protect itself in formulating the letter of credit, the buyer obviously turned to the bank for help. At this point the bank faced a dilemma. It ultimately decided to oblige the buyer because, we may presume, the latter was a valued customer. Accordingly, counsel for the bank attempted to cure the buyer's carelessness by advancing a theory concerning the relationship between the letter of credit and the underlying contract of sale. Had the court adopted counsel's theory what effect would that have had on the utility of commercial letters of credit generally?

(3) Is the court's award of damages based upon the plaintiff's loss due to the bank's failure to pay, or upon some other measure? Work out the damages that the court would award in the following example; Contract calls for five shipments at a total contract price of £70,000; breach occurs with the third shipment; including that shipment £50,000 remained to be paid under the contract; attributable to the unpaid portion of the contract are: £10,000 overhead and labor; £10,000 for material yet to be acquired; and £25,000 representing material on hand having a salvage value of £10,000. On the issue of damages see UCC Sec. 5-115 in the Documentary Supplement.[5]

(4) Suppose Urquhart Lindsay had, prior to suit, found another company in India willing to buy the machinery ordered by Benjamin Jutes Mills at a total price of £60,000. Assume further that, as a result, Urquhart Lindsay completed fabrication of the machinery and shipped it to the new buyer receiving £40,000 in payment. Meanwhile Benjamin Jute Mills transferred the machinery shipped under the first two installments to the new buyer for which it received £20,000.

---

[5] Documentary Supplement.

How much should Urquhart Lindsay recover in damages against the bank? See UCC Sec. 2-708(2).[6]

MAURICE O'MEARA CO. v. NATIONAL PARK BANK OF NEW YORK

Court of Appeals of New York
239 N.Y. 386, 146 N.E. 636 (1925)

McLAUGHLIN, J. This, action was brought to recover damages alleged to have been sustained by the plaintiff's assignor, Ronconi & Millar, by defendant's refusal to pay three sight drafts against a confirmed irrevocable letter of credit. The letter of credit was in the following form:

The National Park Bank of New York.
Our Credit No. 14956, October 28, 1920.

Messrs. Ronconi & Millar,
49 Chambers Street,
New York City, N.Y.

Dear Sirs: In accordance with instructions received from the Sun-Herald Corporation of this city, we open a confirmed or irrevocable credit in your favor for account of themselves, in amount of $224,853.30, covering the shipment of 1,322 2/3 tons of newsprint paper in 72 1/2" and 36 1/2" rolls to test 11-12 [points], 32 lbs. at 8 1/2c per pound net weight — delivery to be made in December 1920, and January 1921.

Drafts under this credit are to be drawn at sight on this bank, and are to be accompanied by the following documents of a character which must meet with our approval:

Commercial invoice in triplicate.

Weight returns.

Negotiable dock delivery order actually carrying with it control of the goods.

This is a confirmed or irrevocable credit, and will remain in force to and including February 15, 1921, subject to the conditions mentioned herein.

When drawing drafts under this credit, or referring to it, please quote our number as above.

Very truly yours,

R. Stuart,
Assistant Cashier.

The complaint alleged the issuance of the letter of credit; the tender of three drafts, the first on the 17th of December, 1920, for $46,301.71, the second on January 7, 1921, for $41,416.34, and the third on January 13, 1921, for $32,968.35. Accompanying the first draft were the following documents:

----

[6] Documentary Supplement.

1. Commercial invoice of the said firm of Ronconi & Millar in triplicate, covering . . . 300, 36 1/2 inch rolls of newsprint and . . . 300, 72 1/2 inch rolls of newsprint paper, aggregating a net weight of . . . 544,726 pounds, to test . . . 11, 12, 32 pounds.

2. Affidavit of Elwin Walker, verified December 16, 1920, to which were annexed samples of newsprint paper, which the said affidavit stated to be representative of the shipment covered by the accompanying invoices and to test . . . 12 points . . . 32 pounds.

3. Full weight returns in triplicate.

4. Negotiable dock delivery order on the Swedish American Line, directing delivery to the order of the National Park Bank of . . . 300 rolls of newsprint paper, 72 1/2 inches long and . . . 300 half rolls of newsprint paper.

The documents accompanying the second draft were similar to those accompanying the first, except as to the number of rolls, weight of paper, omission of the affidavit of Walker, but with a statement: "Paper equal to original sample in test 11/12-32 pounds;" and a negotiable dock delivery order on the Seager Steamship Company, Inc.

The complaint also alleged defendant's refusal to pay; a statement of the amount of loss upon the resale of the paper due to a fall in the market price; expenses for lighterage, cartage, storage, and insurance amounting to $3,045.02; an assignment of the cause of action by Ronconi & Millar to the plaintiff; and a demand for judgment.

The answer denied, upon information and belief, many of the allegations of the complaint, and set up (a) as an affirmative defense, that plaintiff's assignor was required by the letter of credit to furnish to the defendant "evidence reasonably satisfactory" to it that the paper shipped to the Sun-Herald Corporation was of a bursting or tensile strength of eleven to twelve points at a weight of paper of thirty-two pounds; that neither the plaintiff nor its assignor, at the time the drafts were presented, or at any time thereafter, furnished such evidence; (b) as a partial defense, that, when the draft for $46,301.71 was presented, the defendant notified the plaintiff there had not been presented "evidence reasonably satisfactory" to it, showing that the newsprint paper referred to in the documents accompanying said drafts was of the tensile or bursting strength specified in the letter of credit; that thereupon an agreement was entered into between plaintiff and defendant that the latter should cause a test to be made of the paper . . . and, if such test showed that the paper was up to the specifications of the letter of credit, defendant would make payment of the draft; (c) for a third separate and distinct defense that the paper tendered was not, in fact, of the tensile or bursting strength specified in the letter of credit; (d) for a fourth separate and distinct defense that on or about January 15, 1921, and after the respective drafts referred to in the complaint had been presented . . . and payment refused, and at a time when the paper was owned and possessed by plaintiff or Ronconi & Millar, the Sun-Herald Corporation . . . offered to the plaintiff that it would accept the newsprint paper . . . at a price of eight and one-half cents per pound, provided the plaintiff . . . would promptly and reasonably satisfy the Sun-Herald Corporation that the newsprint paper tested as much as eleven points to thirty-two pounds as specified in the letter of credit, and was of the sizes specified therein; that the plaintiff refused to accept said offer; and (e) as a fifth separate and partial defense, all of the allegations of the fourth defense were repeated.

After issue had been joined the plaintiff moved, upon the pleadings and affidavits . . . to strike out the answer and for summary judgment.

The claim for damages for the nonpayment of the third draft was, apparently, abandoned at or prior to the time the motion was made. . . .

The motion for summary judgment was denied and the defendant appealed to the Appellate Division, where the order denying the same was unanimously affirmed, leave to appeal to this court granted, and the following question certified: "Should the motion of the plaintiff for summary judgment herein have been granted?"

. . . .

I am of the opinion that the order of the Appellate Division and the Special Term should be reversed and the motion granted. The facts set out in defendant's answer and in the affidavits used by it in opposition to the motion are not a defense to the action.

The bank issued to plaintiff's assignor an irrevocable letter of credit, a contract solely between the bank and plaintiff's assignor, in and by which the bank agreed to pay sight drafts to a certain amount on presentation to it of the documents specified in the letter of credit. This contract was in no way involved in or connected with, other than the presentation of the documents, the contract for the purchase and sale of the paper mentioned. That was a contract between buyer and seller, which in no way concerned the bank. The bank's obligation was to pay sight drafts when presented if accompanied by genuine documents specified in the letter of credit. If the paper when delivered did not correspond to what had been purchased, either in weight, kind or quality, then the purchaser had his remedy against the seller for damages. Whether the paper was what the purchaser contracted to purchase did not concern the bank and in no way affected its liability. It was under no obligation to ascertain, either by a personal examination or otherwise, whether the paper conformed to the contract between the buyer and seller. The bank was concerned only in the drafts and the documents accompanying them. This was the extent of its interest. If the drafts, when presented, were accompanied by the proper documents, then it was absolutely bound to make the payment under the letter of credit, irrespective of whether it knew, or had reason to believe, that the paper was not of the tensile strength contracted for. This view, I think, is the one generally entertained with reference to a bank's liability under an irrevocable letter of credit of the character of the one here under consideration. . . .

The defendant had no right to insist that a test of the tensile strength of the paper be made before paying the drafts; nor did it even have a right to inspect the paper before payment, to determine whether it in fact corresponded to the description contained in the documents. The letter of credit did not so provide. All that the letter of credit provided was that documents be presented which described the paper shipped as of a certain size, weight and tensile strength. To hold otherwise is to read into the letter of credit something which is not there, and this the court ought not to do, since it would impose upon a bank a duty which in many cases would defeat the primary purpose of such letters of credit. This primary purpose is an assurance to the seller of merchandise of prompt payment against documents.

It has never been held, so far as I am able to discover, that a bank has the right or is under an obligation to see that the description of the merchandise contained in the documents presented is correct. A provision giving it such right, or imposing such obligation, might, of course, be provided for in the letter of credit. The letter under consideration contains no such provision. If the bank had the right to determine whether the paper was of the tensile strength stated, then it might be pertinent to inquire how much of the paper must it subject to the test. If it had to make a test as to tensile strength, then it was equally obligated to measure and weigh the paper. No such thing was intended by the parties and there was no such obligation upon the bank. The documents presented were sufficient. The only reason stated by defendant in its letter of December 18, 1920, for refusing to pay the draft, was that: "There has arisen a reasonable doubt regarding the quality of the newsprint paper. . . . Until such time as we can have a test made by an impartial and unprejudiced expert we shall be obliged to defer payment." This being the sole objection, the only inference to be drawn therefrom is that otherwise the documents presented conformed to the requirements of the letter of credit. All other objections were thereby waived. . . .

. . . .

Some criticism is made as to the statement contained in the documents when the second draft was presented. The criticism, really, is directed towards the expression "in Test 11/12, 32 Lbs" and "Paper equal to original sample in test 11/12, 32 pounds." It is claimed that these expressions are not equivalent to "rolls to test 11-12, 32 Lbs." I think they are. I do not see how any one could have been misled by them or misunderstood them. The general rule is that an obligation to present documents is complied with if any of the documents attached to the draft contain the required description. The purpose, obviously, was to enable defendant to know that dock delivery orders had been issued for the paper. . . .

The alleged oral agreement for a test was unenforceable against plaintiff. It is not alleged that Ronconi & Millar, the beneficiaries of the letter of credit, were parties to this alleged modification of it. They did not assign it to the plaintiff until May 25, 1921, five months after the agreement is alleged to have been made. The letter of credit could not have been modified in this way by parol. . . . Since the defendant was already bound by its letter of credit to pay the drafts on presentation of the documents, without any inspection of the goods, there was no consideration for the alleged new promise and the same, even if made, was invalid. . . .

. . . .

Finally, it is claimed that the plaintiff was not entitled to a summary judgment since there was an issue raised as to the amount of damages. It appears from the affidavits in support of the motion that after the defendant had refused to pay the drafts, due notice was given to it by the plaintiff of its intention to sell the paper for the best price possible, although no notice of such resale was necessary. . . . No attention was paid to the notice and the paper was sold as soon as practicable thereafter and for the best price obtainable, which represented the fair market value at the time of the sale. The plaintiff's damages were, primarily, the face amount of the drafts. Plaintiff, of course, was bound to minimize such damage so far as it reasonably could. This it undertook to do. . . . There was absolutely no statement in defendant's affidavits to the effect that the plaintiff did not act in the utmost good faith or with reasonable care and diligence in making the resale. The only reference thereto is that defendant did not get the best price possible. The defendant gave no evidence, however, of a market value at the time and the plaintiff submitted the affidavits of three dealers in paper that the paper was sold at the fair market value at the time of the sale. Plaintiff's damages were therefore liquidated by a resale on notice. . . . This is the rule which has long prevailed between seller and buyer. The only requirement is that the resale must be a fair one. . . .

. . . .

There was a loss on the resale of the paper called for under the first draft of $5,447.26, and under the second draft of $14,617.53, making a total loss of $20,064.79, for which amount judgment should be directed in favor of the plaintiff.

The orders appealed from should therefore be reversed and the motion granted, with costs in all courts. The question certified is answered in the affirmative.

CARDOZO, J. (dissenting). I am unable to concur in the opinion of the court.

I assume that no duty is owing from the bank to its depositor which requires it to investigate the quality of the merchandise . . . I dissent from the view that, if it chooses to investigate and discovers thereby that the merchandise tendered is not in truth the merchandise which the documents describe, it may be forced by the delinquent seller to make payment of the price irrespective of its knowledge. We are to bear in mind that this controversy is not one between the bank on the one side and on the other a holder of the drafts who has taken them without notice and for value. The controversy arises between the bank and a seller who has misrepresented the security upon which advances are demanded. Between parties so situated payment may be resisted if the documents are false.

I think we lose sight of the true nature of the transaction when we view the bank as acting upon the credit of its customer to the exclusion of all else. It acts not merely upon the credit of its customer, but upon the credit also of the merchandise which is to be tendered as security. The letter of credit is explicit in its provision that documents sufficient to give control of the goods shall be lodged with the bank when drafts are presented. I cannot accept the statement of the majority opinion that the bank was not concerned with any question as to the character of the paper. If that is so, the bales tendered might have been rags instead of paper, and still the bank would have been helpless, though it had knowledge of the truth, if the documents tendered by the seller were sufficient on their face. A different question would be here if the defects had no relation to the description in the documents. In such circumstances it would be proper to say that a departure from the terms of the contract between the vendor and the vendee was of no moment to the bank. That is not the case before us. If the paper was of the quality stated in the defendant's answer the documents were false.

I think the conclusion is inevitable that a bank which pays a draft upon a bill of lading misrepresenting the character of the merchandise may recover the payment when the misrepresentation is discovered, or at the very least, the difference between the value of the thing described and the value of the thing received. If payment might have been recovered the moment after it was made, the seller cannot coerce payment if the truth is earlier revealed.

We may find persuasive analogies in connection with the law of sales. One who promises to make payment in advance of delivery and inspection may be technically in default if he refuses the promised payment before inspection has been made. None the less, if the result of the inspection is to prove that the merchandise is defective, the seller must fail in an action for the recovery of the price. The reason is that "the buyer would have been entitled to recover back the price if he had paid it without inspection of the goods" . . .

I think the defendant's answer and the affidavits submitted in support of it are sufficient to permit a finding that the plaintiff's assignors misrepresented the nature of the shipment. The misrepresentation does not cease to be a defense, partial if not complete, though it was innocently made.

The order should be affirmed and the question answered "No."

HISCOCK, C. J., and POUND and ANDREWS, JJ., concur with MCLAUGHLIN.

CARDOZO, J., reads dissenting opinion, in which CRANE, J., concurs; LEHMAN J, not sitting.

NOTES AND QUESTIONS

(1) Note that with respect to the alleged agreement to have the paper tested (second defense) Judge McLaughlin states "since the defendant was already bound by the letter of credit to pay the drafts . . . there was no consideration for the alleged promise and the same, if made, was invalid." This is the so-called "pre-existing duty doctrine" found in Section 73, Restatement of the Law (Second), Contracts. This, however, raises a larger question concerning the theoretical basis for concluding that upon issuance an irrevocable letter of credit gives rise to an enforceable contract between the seller-beneficiary and the issuing bank. Certainly issuance of the credit does not create a bilateral contract; the seller makes no promise and incurs no obligation to the bank. Perhaps it is a third party beneficiary contract. But that would scarcely do because the contract between the buyer (customer) and the bank is wholly separate from the contract (letter of credit) between the bank and seller (beneficiary) and the buyer is not a party to this latter contract. Alternatively, perhaps the letter of credit gives rise to a unilateral contract, or what the Restatement calls an "Option Contract" (See Section 45, Restatement of the Law (Second) Contracts[7]) However, an "option contract"

---

[7] Section 45. "(1) Where an offer invites an offeree to accept by rendering a performance and does not invite a promissory acceptance, an option contract is created when the offeree tenders or begins the invited performance or tenders a beginning of it.

would require acceptance by the optionee (the seller) through a tender of performance (*i.e.* submission of documents). Until then the option is presumably revocable unless supported by a separate consideration. In the case of the letter of credit, however, there certainly is no consideration flowing from the optionee (the seller) to the optioner (the bank) to support the issuance of the credit, yet it is irrevocable. Note that UCC Sec. 5-105 simply states: "No consideration is necessary to establish a credit or to enlarge or otherwise modify its terms." Perhaps this recognizes that letters of credit are sui generis.

Consider, however, the following possibility. Some cases, drawing upon Corbin, ascribe to an option a dual character. From the optioner's point of view it is a unilateral contract subject to the performance of a condition by the optionee. From the optionee's viewpoint, however, it is only an "offer" subject to acceptance by performance (*Palo Alto Town & Country Village v. BBTC Company*[8] Perhaps the best analysis, therefore, is to take the optionee's viewpoint and consider the letter of credit an offer subject to acceptance by performance which, until performance is tendered, is subject to the "firm offer rule." That rule holds that an express promise to hold an offer open for a stated period is enforceable without separate consideration (*e.g.* UCC Sec. 2-205,[9] applicable to offers by merchants to buy or sell goods).

With this analysis in mind return to *O'Meara*. Would the alleged agreement to have the paper tested, if proven, constitute a good defense? If so, would that undermine the purpose of the letter of credit?

(2) Note that Judge Cardozo draws a distinction between a case, like *O'Meara*, in which the seller seeks payment under a letter of credit on the strength of fraudulent documents, and a case in which payment is sought by "a holder of the drafts who has taken them without notice and for value." Presumably in the latter case Cardozo would conclude that, in spite of knowing that the documents were fraudulent, a bank that refused payment would be liable to the holder in due course. Does this create a difficult situation for an issuing bank? Remember Cardozo only says that a bank may, not "must," refuse payment on fraudulent documents sought by a party who is not a holder in due course. Consider the position of an issuing bank confronted with a demand for payment by a confirming bank that has already paid the seller on the strength of documents conforming on their face but known by the issuing bank to be fraudulent.

(3) Where does Cardozo draw the line? Suppose buyer and seller genuinely and in good faith disagree about the quality of the goods. Would a bank that heeds the buyer, its customer, and withholds payment from the seller be liable even if it later turns out that the goods were defective? How can the bank assure itself of the bona fides of each party?

---

(2) The offeror's duty of performance under any option contract so created is conditional on completion or tender of the invited performance in accordance with the terms of the offer."

[8] 11 Cal. 3d. 494, 521 P.2d 1097, 113 Cal. Rpt 705 (1974).

[9] Documentary Supplement.

[B]   Enjoining Payment Under Letters of Credit

In **SZTEJN v. J. HENRY SCHRODER BANKING CORPORATION et. al.,**[10] Plaintiff buyer sought to enjoin the defendant J. Henry Schroder Banking Corporation ("Schroder") issuer of a letter of credit, from making payments on drafts presented under the credit and to enjoin the Chartered Bank of India, Australia and China ("Chartered Bank"), from presenting the draft for payment. Plaintiff had purchased a quantity of bristles from Transea Traders Ltd. (Transea), a company in India, and pursuant to the contract had obtained issuance of the credit by Schroder in favor of Transea. Transea then purported to ship fifty crates of bristles. It obtained a bill of lading, drew its draft on Schroder to the "order" of Chartered Bank and delivered these documents to the latter "for collection" for the account of Transea. Before the documents could be forwarded for payment to Schroder, Plaintiff discovered that the crates contained cowhide and other "worthless rubbish" and brought this action to enjoin payment and presentation for payment of Transea's draft. Defendant Chartered Bank moved to dismiss for failure to state a cause of action and the court, in denying the motion, stated in part as follows:

> It is well established that a letter of credit is independent of the primary contract of sale between the buyer and the seller. The issuing bank agrees to pay upon presentation of documents, not goods. This rule is necessary to preserve the efficiency of the letter of credit as an instrument for the financing of trade[;] . . . to furnish the seller with a ready means of obtaining prompt payment for his merchandise. . . . However, I believe that a different situation is presented in the instant action. This is not a controversy between the buyer and the seller concerning a mere breach of warranty . . . ; on the present motion, it must be assumed that the seller has intentionally failed to ship any goods ordered by the buyer. In such a situation, where the seller's fraud has been called to the bank's attention before . . . [presentation of the documents,] the principle of the independence of the bank's obligation . . . should not be extended to protect the unscrupulous seller. . . . The distinction between a breach of warranty and active fraud on the part of the seller is supported by authority and reason. . . . [And] no hardship will be caused by permitting the bank to refuse payment where fraud is claimed . . . where the draft and the accompanying documents are in the hands of one who stands in the same position as the fraudulent seller, . . . where the bank has been given notice of the fraud before being presented with the . . . documents . . . and . . . itself does not wish to pay pending an adjudication of the rights and obligations of the other parties. . . . On this motion only the complaint is before me and I am bound by its allegation that the Chartered Bank is not a holder in due course but is a mere agent for collection for the account of the seller charged with fraud. Therefore, the Chartered Bank's motion to dismiss the complaint must be denied. . . .

---

[10] 177 Misc. 719, 31 N.Y.S. 2d. 631 (Sup. Ct., 1941)

UNITED BANK LIMITED et al. v.
CAMBRIDGE SPORTING GOODS CORP.

Court of Appeals of New York
41 N.Y. 2d 254, 392 N.Y.S. 2d 265, 360 N.E. 2d 943 (1976)

GABRIELLI, JUSTICE.

On this appeal, we must decide whether fraud on the part of a seller-beneficiary of an irrevocable letter of credit may be successfully asserted as a defense against holders of drafts drawn by the seller pursuant to the credit. If we conclude that this defense may be interposed . . . we must also determine whether the courts below improperly imposed upon . . . buyer the burden of proving that . . . [those holders] were not holders in due course. . . .

In April, 1971 appellant Cambridge Sporting Goods Corporation (Cambridge) entered into a contract for the manufacture and sale of boxing gloves with Duke Sports (Duke), a Pakistani corporation. Duke committed itself to the manufacture of 27,936 pairs of boxing gloves at a sale price of $42,576.80; and arranged with its Pakistani bankers, United Bank Limited (United) and The Muslim Commercial Bank (Muslim), for the financing of the sale. Cambridge was requested by these banks to cover payment of the purchase price by opening an irrevocable letter of credit with its bank in New York, Manufacturers Hanover Trust Company (Manufacturers). Manufacturers issued an irrevocable letter of credit obligating it, upon the receipt of certain documents . . . to accept and pay, 90 days after acceptance, drafts drawn upon Manufacturers for the purchase price of the gloves.

Following confirmation of the opening of the letter of credit, Duke informed Cambridge that it would be impossible to manufacture and deliver the merchandise within the time period required by the contract, and sought an extension of time for performance until September 15, 1971 and a continuation of the letter of credit, which was due to expire on August 11. Cambridge replied on June 18 that it would not agree to a postponement of the manufacture and delivery of the gloves because of its resale commitments and, hence, it promptly advised Duke that the contract was canceled and the letter of credit should be returned. Cambridge simultaneously notified United of the contract cancellation.

Despite the cancellation of the contract, Cambridge was informed on July 17, 1971 that documents had been received at Manufacturers from United purporting to evidence a shipment of the boxing gloves under the terms of the canceled contract. The documents were accompanied by a draft, dated July 16, 1971, drawn by Duke upon Manufacturers and made payable to United, for the amount of $21,288.40, one half of the contract price of the boxing gloves. A second set of documents was received by Manufacturers from Muslim, also accompanied by a draft, dated August 20, and drawn upon Manufacturers by Duke for the remaining amount of the contract price.

An inspection of the shipments upon their arrival revealed that Duke had shipped old, unpadded, ripped and mildewed gloves rather than the new gloves to be manufactured as agreed upon. Cambridge then commenced an action against Duke in the Supreme Court, New York County, joining Manufacturers as a party, and obtained a preliminary injunction prohibiting the latter from paying drafts drawn under the letter of credit; subsequently, in November, 1971 Cambridge levied on the funds subject to the letter of credit and the drafts, which were delivered by Manufacturers to the Sheriff in compliance therewith. Duke ultimately defaulted in the action and judgment against it was entered in the amount of the drafts, in March, 1972.

The present proceeding was instituted by the Pakistani banks to vacate the levy made by Cambridge and to obtain payment of the drafts on the letter of credit. The banks asserted that they were holders in due course of the drafts which had been made payable to them by Duke and, thus, were entitled to the proceeds thereof irrespective of any defenses which Cambridge had established against their transferor, Duke, in the prior action which had terminated in a default judgment. The banks' motion for summary judgment on this claim was denied and the request by Cambridge for a jury trial was granted. Cambridge sought to depose the petitioning banks, but its request was denied and, as an alternative, written interrogatories were served on the Pakistani banks to learn the circumstances surrounding the transfer of the drafts to them. At trial, the banks introduced no evidence other than answers to several of the written interrogatories which were received over objection by Cambridge to the effect that the answers were conclusory, self-serving and otherwise inadmissible. Cambridge presented evidence of its dealings with Duke including the cancellation of the contract and uncontested proof of the subsequent shipment of essentially worthless merchandise.

The trial court concluded that the burden of proving that the banks were not holders in due course lay with Cambridge, and directed a verdict in favor of the banks on the ground that Cambridge had not met that burden; the court stated that Cambridge failed to demonstrate that the banks themselves had participated in the seller's acts of fraud, proof of which was concededly present in the record. The Appellate Division affirmed, agreeing that while there was proof tending to establish the defenses against the seller, Cambridge had not shown that the seller's acts were "connected to the petitioners [banks] in any manner." The Appellate Division also held that CPLR 3117 "seemingly" authorized the introduction of the challenged interrogatories into evidence.

We reverse and hold that it was improper to direct a verdict in favor of the petitioning Pakistani banks. We conclude that the defense of fraud in the transaction was established and in that circumstance the burden shifted to petitioners to prove that they were holders in due course and took the drafts for value, in good faith and without notice of any fraud on the part of Duke (Uniform Commercial Code, Sec. 3-302). Additionally, we think it was improper for the trial court to permit petitioners to introduce into evidence answers to Cambridge's interrogatories to demonstrate their holder in due course status.

This case does not come before us in the typical posture of a lawsuit between the bank issuing the letter of credit and presenters of drafts drawn under the credit seeking payment. . . . Because Cambridge obtained an injunction against payment of the drafts and has levied against the proceeds of the drafts, it stands in the same position as the issuer, and, thus, the law of letters of credit governs the liability of Cambridge to the Pakistani banks.[11] Article 5 of the Uniform

---

[11] Cambridge has no direct liability on the drafts because it is not a party to the drafts which were drawn on Manufacturers by Duke as drawer; its liability derives from the letter

Commercial Code, dealing with letters of credit, and the Uniform Customs and Practice for Documentary Credits promulgated by the International Chamber of Commerce set forth the duties and obligations of the issuer of a letter of credit.[12] A letter of credit is a commitment on the part of the issuing bank that it will pay a draft presented to it under the terms of the credit, and if it is a documentary draft, upon presentation of the required documents of title (see Uniform Commercial Code, Sec. 5-103). Banks issuing letters of credit deal in documents and not in goods and are not responsible for any breach of warranty or nonconformity of the goods involved in the underlying sales contract (see Uniform Commercial Code, Sec. 5-114, subd. (1); Uniform Customs and Practice, General Provisions and Definitions (c)) . . . Subdivision (2) of section 5-114,[13] however indicates certain limited circumstances in which an issuer may properly refuse to honor a draft drawn under a letter of credit or a customer may enjoin an issuer from honoring such a draft.[14] Thus, where "fraud in the transaction" has been shown and the holder has not taken the draft in circumstances that would make it a holder in due course, the customer may apply to enjoin the issuer from paying drafts drawn under the letter of credit. . . . This rule represents a codification of precode case law most eminently articulated in the landmark case of *Sztejn v. Schroder Banking Corp.* . . . Even prior to the *Sztejn* case, forged or fraudulently procured documents were proper grounds for avoidance of payment of drafts drawn under a letter of credit . . .; and cases decided after the enactment of the code have cited *Sztejn* with approval. . . .

---

of credit which authorizes the drafts to be drawn on the issuing bank. Since Manufacturers has paid the proceeds of the drafts to the Sheriff pursuant to the levy obtained in the prior proceeding, it has discharged its obligation under the credit and is not involved in this proceeding.

[12] It should be noted that the Uniform Customs and Practice controls, in lieu of Article 5 of the code, where, unless otherwise agreed by the parties, a letter of credit is made subject to the provisions of the Uniform Customs and Practice by its terms or by agreement, course of dealing or usage of trade (Uniform Commercial Code, Sec. 5-102, subd. [4]). No proof was offered that there was an agreement that the Uniform Customs and Practice should apply, nor does the credit so state. . . . Neither do the parties otherwise contend that their rights should be resolved under the Uniform Customs and Practice. However, even if the Uniform Customs and Practice were deemed applicable to this case, it would not, in the absence of a conflict, abrogate the precode case law (now codified in Uniform Commercial Code, Section 5—114) and that authority continues to govern even where Article 5 is not controlling. . . . Moreover, the Uniform Customs and Practice provisions are not in conflict nor do they treat with the subject matter of Section 5—114 which is dispositive of the issues presented on this appeal. . . . Thus, we are of the opinion that the Uniform Customs and Practice, where applicable, does not bar the relief provided for in Section 5—114 of the Code.

[13] Documentary Supplement.

[14] Subdivision (2) of Section 5—114 of the Uniform Commercial Code provides that, "[u]nless otherwise agreed when documents appear on their face to comply with the terms of a credit but . . . there is fraud in the transaction (a) the issuer must honor the draft or demand for payment if honor is demanded by a . . . holder of the draft . . . which has taken the draft . . . under the credit and under circumstances which would make it a holder in due course (Section 3—302) . . .; and (b) in all other cases as against its customer, an issuer acting in good faith may honor the draft . . . despite notification from the customer of fraud, forgery or other defect not apparent on the face of the documents but a court of appropriate jurisdiction may enjoin such honor."

. . . Although precisely speaking there was no specific finding of fraud in the transaction by either of the courts below, . . . we hold upon the facts as established, that the shipment of old, . . . rather than the new boxing gloves as ordered by Cambridge, constituted fraud in the transaction within the meaning of subdivision (2) of section 5-114. It should be noted that the drafters of section 5-114, in their attempt to codify the *Sztejn* case and in utilizing the term "fraud in the transaction," have eschewed a dogmatic approach and adopted a flexible standard to be applied as the circumstances of a particular situation mandate.[15] It can be difficult to draw a precise line between cases involving breach of warranty (or a difference of opinion as to the quality of goods) and outright fraudulent practice on the part of the seller. To the extent, however, that Cambridge established that Duke was guilty of fraud in shipping, not merely nonconforming merchandise, but worthless fragments of boxing gloves, this case is similar to *Sztejn*.

If the petitioning banks are holders in due course they are entitled to recover the proceeds of the drafts but if such status cannot be demonstrated their petition must fail.[16] The parties are in agreement that section 3-307[17] of the code governs the ple ing and proof of holder in due course status and that section provides:

(1) Unless specifically denied in the pleadings each signature on an instrument is admitted. When the effectiveness of a signature is put in issue

    (a) the burden of establishing it is on the party claiming under the signature; but

    (b) the signature is presumed to be genuine or authorized except where the action is to enforce the obligation of a purported signer who has died or become incompetent before proof is required.

(2) When signatures are admitted or established, production of the instrument entitles a holder to recover on it unless the defendant establishes a defense.

(3) After it is shown that a defense exists a person claiming the rights of a holder in due course has the burden of establishing that he or some person under whom he claims is in all respects a holder in due course.

Even though section 3-307 is contained in Article 3 of the code dealing with negotiable instruments rather than letters of credit, we agree that its provisions should control in the instant case. Section 5-114 (subd. (2), par. (a)) utilizes the holder in due course criteria of section 3-302 of the code to determine whether a presenter may recover on drafts despite fraud in the sale of goods transaction. It is logical, therefore, to apply the pleading and practice rules of section 3-307 in the situation where a presenter of drafts under a letter of credit claims to be

---

[15] In its original version Section 5—114 contained the language "fraud in a required document" (see 1955 Report of N.Y. Law Rev. Comm., pp. 1655— 1658).

[16] Although several commentators have expressed a contrary view, the weight of authority supports the proposition that fraud on the part of the seller-beneficiary may not be interposed as a defense to payment against a holder in due course to whom a draft has been negotiated. . . . This approach represents the better view that as against two innocent parties (the buyer and the holder in due course) the former, having chosen to deal with the fraudulent seller, should bear the risk of loss. . . .

[17] Documentary Supplement.

a holder in due course. In the context of section 5-114 and the law of letters of credit, however, the "defense" referred to in section 3-307 should be deemed to include only those defenses available under subdivision (2) of section 5-114. . . . In the context of a letter of credit transaction and, specifically subdivision (2) of section 5-114, it is these defenses which operate to shift the burden of proof of holder in due course status upon one asserting such status. . . . Thus, a presenter of drafts drawn under a letter of credit must prove that it took the drafts for value, in good faith and without notice of the underlying fraud in the transaction [18]. . . .

Turning to the rules of section 3-307 as they apply to this case, Cambridge failed to deny the effectiveness of the signatures on the draft in its answer and, thus, these are deemed admitted and their effectiveness is not an issue in the case. However, this does not entitle the banks as holders to payment of the drafts since Cambridge has established "fraud in the transaction." The courts below erroneously concluded that Cambridge was required to show that the banks had participated in or were themselves guilty of the seller's fraud in order to establish a defense to payment. But, it was not necessary that Cambridge prove that United and Muslim actually participated in the fraud, since merely notice of the fraud would have deprived the Pakistani banks of holder in due course status.

In order to qualify as a holder in due course, a holder must have taken the instrument "without notice . . . of any defense against . . . it on the part of any person" [19] . . . Pursuant to subdivision (2) of section 5-114 fraud in the transaction is a valid defense to payment of drafts drawn under a letter of credit. Since the defense of fraud in the transaction was shown, the burden shifted to the banks by operation of subdivision (3) of section 3-307 to prove that they were holders in due course and took the drafts without notice of Duke's alleged fraud. As indicated in the Official Comment to that subdivision, when it is shown that a defense exists, one seeking to cut off the defense by claiming the rights of a holder in due course "has the full burden of proof by a preponderance of the total evidence" on this issue. This burden must be sustained by "affirmative proof" of the requisites of holder in due course status. . . . It was error for the trial court to direct a verdict in favor of the Pakistani banks because this determination rested upon a misallocation of the burden of proof; and we conclude that the banks have not satisfied the burden of proving that they qualified in all respects as holders in due course, by any affirmative proof. The only evidence introduced by the banks consisted of conclusory answers to the interrogatories which were improperly admitted by the Trial Judge. . . . The failure of the banks to meet their burden is fatal to their claim for recovery of the proceeds of the drafts and their petition must therefore be dismissed.

[The court goes on to conclude that the trial court erred in admitting the Pakistani banks' answers to Cambridge's interrogatories as proof of the banks' holder in due course status.]

. . . [A]s we have noted, in the absence of this evidence, there is absolutely no proof in the record on the part of the banks to sustain their burden of demonstrating holder in due course status; therefore, their petition to obtain the proceeds of the drafts and to set aside Cambridge's levy thereupon should be dismissed.

[18] Uniform Commercial Code, Section 3-302.
[19] Uniform Commercial Code, Section 3-302, subd. (1), par. (c).

BREITEL, C. J. and JASEN, JONES, WACHTER, FUCHSBERG and COOKE, JJ., concur.

NOTES AND QUESTIONS

(1) How does the *Cambridge* court's reading of the UCC solve the problem that Judge Cardozo's position in *O'Meara* would have created for issuing banks? Note this problem did not exist in *Sztejn*. Why so?

(2) If there is "fraud in the transaction" and the party demanding payment under the letter of credit is not a holder in due course, UCC Section 5-114(2)(b) empowers the courts to enjoin payment by the issuer. "Fraud in the transaction" is ambiguous. What transaction: the *letter of credit transaction* or the *underlying transaction* between buyer and seller? Since the letter of credit is wholly separate from the underlying contract, the bank is not a party to the latter and Section 5-114(2)(b) is addressed to the customer-bank relationship, that section could arguably be referring only to fraud in the letter of credit transaction. Yet, in *Cambridge* the fraud, in the first instance, was in the underlying transaction. Is this necessarily inconsistent with a finding of fraud in the letter of credit transaction? In light of your answer, could a court enjoin payment to a seller who makes a demand knowing that there was a genuine dispute between himself and the buyer over the quality of the goods? Suppose the description of the goods in the seller's invoice would be false if the defects claimed by the buyer actually exist.

(3) The Uniform Customs and Practice for Documentary Credits (UCP) was developed by the International Chamber of Commerce, a private organization headquartered in Paris, in an effort to codify bank practices in the handling of letters of credit. First issued in 1920, the UCP has gone through three subsequent revisions, the latest being the 1983 version, with each version purporting to reflect changes in customs and usage. The UCP has no official status or sanction. It does not apply to any transaction as a direct consequence of being made applicable through the operation of a statute, treaty, government regulation or judicial decision. It only applies as a rule of law if banks expressly provide for its applicability in letters of credit which they issue. The practice of doing so, however, is widespread, especially with credits issued or confirmed by New York banks. In addition, the UCP may be looked to by a court as a definitive statement of banking custom and usage whenever the court is called upon to decide questions by reference to such usage. When the UCC was being proposed to State legislatures through out the country, there was widespread bank objection to the inclusion in the Code of an article on letters of credit. Some bankers simply argued that the availability of the UCP made such an article unnecessary. Others wanted the right to opt out of the UCC altogether. Only the New York bankers, however, succeeded in obtaining this latter privilege, with the result that Section 5-102 of the New York Version of the UCC provides as follows:

> Unless otherwise agreed, this Article 5 does not apply to a letter of credit or a credit if by its terms or by agreement, course of dealing or usage of trade such letter of credit or credit is subject in whole or in part to the Uniform

Customs and Practice for Commercial Documentary Credits fixed by the Thirteenth or by any subsequent Congress of the International Chamber of Commerce.

The court in *Cambridge* first noted that nothing in the letter of credit, course of dealing or trade usage rendered the letter subject to the UCP. It concluded, however, that even were the UCP applicable, UCC Article 5 would still control unless it conflicted with the UCP. There was, the court stated, no such conflict in so far as UCC Section 5-114 was concerned. After consulting Articles 8 and 9 of the UCP, do you agree?

In all other states, the UCC will, in the case of credits expressly made subject to the UCP, prevail over an inconsistent provision in the latter, unless, under the UCC, the parties agreement sets the prevailing norm. This, however, is not a point of great concern since the areas of divergence between the UCC and the UCP are not great.

(4) Does UCC Section 5-114(2)(b) fully answer the dilemma which an issuing bank faces when a valued customer, alleging fraud, asks the bank to dishonor a demand for payment under a letter of credit? Why might the customer resist the bank's request that it seek an injunction against payment? If the bank yields to the customer, what damages might it have to pay if the party demanding payment successfully sues the bank? Recall the discussion of damages following *Urquhart Lindsay & Co. Ltd. v. Eastern Bank, Ltd. supra.* Does UCC Section 5-114(3) protect the bank? If not, how can the bank protect itself? Consult the Application for Letter of Credit Form in the Documentary Supplement.[21]

In the following case and attendant notes we encounter another form of letter of credit; the "stand-by" letter of credit. Under a stand-by credit it is the seller of goods or services, not the buyer, that arranges for issuance of the credit (*i.e.* is the account party) and it is the buyer who is the beneficiary. The purpose of the credit is to provide the buyer with what is in effect a guaranty of performance by the seller. Also, if the underlying contract between the buyer and seller contains a liquidated damage clause, the purpose of the credit may be to give the buyer ready access to payment of those damages. While stand-by credits can certainly be used in connection with a simple purchase and sale of goods, more typically they accompany a sales contract only if the seller is also required to provide services, such as installation, testing, and training of the buyer's personnel. While perhaps their widest use is to be found in connection with long-term construction contracts, stand-by credits are also employed under pure service contracts and in connection with a variety of financing agreements.

Necessarily, of course, the documents that must accompany a beneficiary's demand for payment under a stand-by credit are very different from those the seller must present under a commercial letter of credit. Sometimes all that is required, in addition to the beneficiary's draft, is the latter's certification that the seller has defaulted on the underlying contract in a manner which, under the terms

---

[21] Documentary Supplement.

of the stand-by credit, entitles the beneficiary to payment. At other times the beneficiary's certification must be accompanied by statements, verified or otherwise, from independent experts (architects, engineers, laboratories, auditors, etc.) attesting to the default. Apart, however, from the reversal of the position of the parties and differences in documentation, the basic procedures and principles that govern commercial letters of credit are applicable to stand-by credits.

HARRIS CORPORATION v. NATIONAL IRANIAN RADIO AND TELEVISION and BANK MELLI, IRAN

United States Court of Appeals, (Eleventh Circuit)
691 F. 2d 1344 (1982)

Before HILL and KRAVITCH, CIRCUIT JUDGES and MORGAN, SENIOR CIRCUIT JUDGE.

JAMES C. HILL CIRCUIT JUDGE:

I. The Facts

On February 22, 1978, the Broadcast Products Division of Harris Corporation entered into a contract with NIRT ("the contract") to manufacture and deliver 144 FM broadcast transmitters to Teheran, Iran, and to provide related training and technical services for a total price of $6,740,352. Harris received an advance payment of $1,331,470.40, which was to be amortized over the life of the contract by deducting a percentage of the payment due upon shipment of the equipment or receipt of the services and training from the balance of the advance.

Pursuant to the contract, Harris obtained a performance guarantee in favor of NIRT from Bank Melli, an agency of the State of Iran.[22] The guarantee provides that Melli is to pay NIRT any amount up to $674,035.20 upon Melli's receipt of NIRT's written declaration that Harris has failed to comply with the terms and conditions of the contract. The contract between Harris and NIRT makes the guarantee an integral part of the contract and provides that NIRT must release the guarantee upon termination of the contract due to force majeure.[23] Before

---

[22] The agreement is a standby letter of credit; it will be referred to herein as a performance guarantee or a guarantee letter of credit in order more easily to distinguish it from the standby letter of credit issued by Continental Bank in favor of Bank Melli. For an explanation of the operation of standby letters of credit and a comparison of standbys with traditional, commercial letters of credit, see Comment, Enjoining the International Standby Letter of Credit: The Iranian Letter of Credit Cases, 21 Harv. Int'l L. J. 189, 190-200 (1980).

[23] The following paragraphs in the contract deal with force majeure and termination of the contract:

"11-5 The contractor shall not be liable for any excess cost or for liquidated damage for delay if any failure to perform the contract arises out of force majeure acts of nature, or of government, fires, floods, epidemics, quarantines [sic] restrictions, to [sic] any such causes unless NIRT shall determine that the materials or equipment or services to be

Melli issued the guarantee it required that Harris obtain a letter of credit in Melli's favor. Continental Bank issued this standby, which provides that Continental is to reimburse Melli to the extent that Melli pays on the guarantee it issued. Harris, in turn, must indemnify Continental Bank to the extent that Continental pays Melli.

From August 1978 through February 1979, Harris shipped to Iran 138 of the 144 transmitters (together with related equipment for 144 transmitters) and also conducted a 24-week training program in the United States for NIRT personnel. In February 1979, the Islamic Republic of Iran overthrew the Imperial Government of Iran. After the overthrow, one shipment of goods which Harris sent could not be delivered safely in Iran. Harris notified NIRT, by telex dated February 27, that those goods were taken to Antwerp, Belgium, and Sharjah, United Arab Emirates.

Frank R. Blaha, the Director of Customer Products and Systems Operations of the Broadcast Products Division of Harris Corporation, met with NIRT officials in Teheran in early May, 1979, to help them obtain the goods in Antwerp, to discuss amendments to the contract, and to discuss a revised delivery schedule made necessary by Iranian events. Harris, offering Blaha's affidavit, contends that all parties at those meetings acknowledged the existence of force majeure as defined in the contract provisions set forth in [the note *supra*].

Blaha worked in May to obtain the Antwerp goods for NIRT, then returned to Teheran to continue discussions with NIRT officials. At these discussions, NIRT agreed to delay shipment of the final six transmitters until the fall of 1979 due to the conditions in Iran.

Negotiations on contract modifications continued during the summer and fall of 1979. On August 18, 1979, Harris formally advised NIRT of the additional costs it had incurred with respect to the goods that had been reshipped from

---

furnished by the contractor were obtainable from other source [sic] in sufficient time to permit the contractor to meet the required time schedule, provided that the contractor shall within (10) ten days from the beginning of such delay, notify NIRT in writing of the causes of the delay. NIRT shall ascertain the facts and the extent of the delay and extend the time for completing the work as its judgment and finding justify. In any event the contractor shall make every effort to overcome the causes of delay or to arrange substitute procedure and shall continue to perform his obligations to the extent he can."

"11-6. If, arriving at any cause as set forth in paragraph 11-5 above, the contractor finds it impractical to continue operations, or if owing to force majeure or to any cause beyond NIRT's control, NIRT finds it impossible to continue operations, then prompt notification, in writing, shall be given by the party affected to the other. If the difficulties or delay caused by force majeure cannot be expected to ease or become available, or if operations cannot be resumed within (6) six months, then either party shall have the right to terminate the contract upon (10) ten days written notice to the other. In the event of termination of the contract under this paragraph, payment will be made to the contractor as follows:" [Here detailed provisions are made primarily to assure payment to Harris for work completed. Sub-paragraph (c) in this Paragraph 11-6, then states as follows:] "(c) NIRT will also release all bonds and guarantee unless the total amount of payment previously paid to the contractor exceeds the final amount due him, in which case, the contractor shall refund the excess within (60) days after termination, against the release of bonds and guarantee furnished to NIRT."

Antwerp, and Harris requested payment for the additional amount in accordance with the contract's force majeure clause and with a letter from NIRT authorizing Harris to reship the goods.

On November 4, 1979, Iranian militants took 52 hostages at the United States Embassy in Teheran. Harris received no further communications from NIRT after the seizure of the hostages.

Harris completed the remaining six transmitters in November 1979 and inventoried them for future delivery. Harris, supported by Blaha's affidavits, has argued that disruptive conditions created by the Iranian revolution initially prevented shipment of the final six transmitters. Subsequently, Harris contends, it was unable to ship the materials as a result of the Iranian Assets Control Regulations [issued] effective November 14, 1979 [by the United States' Treasury Department]. In particular, Harris points out, the Treasury voided all general licenses to ship to Iran and required sellers to obtain special license on a case-by-case basis before exporting goods. . . . An affidavit submitted by Blaha states that Harris's counsel was advised by the Office of Foreign Assets Control that special licenses would be issued only in emergency situations or for humanitarian reasons and would not be issued for the transmitters. This request is not documented, and Harris did not inform NIRT of its inability to ship. On April 7, 1980, Treasury Regulation 535.207 became effective and prohibited the shipment of nonessential items to Iran. . . .

On June 3, 1980, Continental Bank received a telex from Melli reporting that NIRT had presented Melli with a written declaration that Harris had failed to comply with the terms of the contract and stating that NIRT had demanded that Melli extend or pay the guarantee. Melli demanded that it be authorized to extend the guarantee and that Continental Bank extend its corresponding letter of credit to Melli, or else Melli would pay the guarantee and demand immediate payment from Continental.

In response to the demand by Melli, Harris . . . [o]n July 11, 1980 . . . filed a verified complaint against NIRT and Melli in the United States District Court for the Middle District of Florida, seeking to enjoin payment and receipt of payment on the guarantee and receipt of payment on the letter of credit. The complaint also sought a declaratory judgment that the contract underlying the guarantee and the letter of credit had been terminated by force majeure. The court granted a temporary restraining order on June 13, 1980, pending a hearing on Harris' motion for a preliminary injunction.

On June 16, 1980, a copy of the TRO was mailed to Melli's counsel and on the following day was hand-delivered to Melli's branch office in Manhattan. On June 20, 1980, three days after receipt of the June 13th TRO at its Manhattan branch office, and despite the restraint against payment contained in the TRO, Melli telexed Continental Bank that it had paid the full amount of the guarantee "after receipt of a demand for payment from the National Iranian Radio and Television stating that there has been a default by Harris Corporation . . . to comply with the terms and conditions of contract F-601-1 . . . ." The telex also demanded that Continental pay Melli by crediting Melli's London office with the amount of the letter of credit. After a hearing on August 15, 1980, the district court issued the preliminary injunction at issue here.

. . . .

IV. The Preliminary Injunction

A. The Framework for Review

The appellants contend that the district court erred in entering the preliminary injunction against payment or receipt of payment on the NIRT-Melli guarantee letter of credit and against receipt of payment on the Melli-Continental letter of credit. The four prerequisites for the injunction are: (1) a substantial likelihood that the plaintiff will prevail on the merits; (2) a substantial threat that the plaintiff will suffer irreparable injury if the injunction is not granted; (3) threatened injury to the plaintiff must outweigh the threatened harm that the injunction may cause to the defendant; and (4) granting the preliminary injunction must not disserve the public interest. . . .

B. Substantial Likelihood of Success on the Merits

The merits of this case involve letter of credit law. Harris asserts that the existence of force majeure terminated its obligations under the contract with NIRT, making illegitimate NIRT's subsequent attempt to draw upon the performance guarantee issued by Melli. The appellants respond by relying upon a fundamental principle of letter of credit law: the letter of credit is independent of the underlying contract . . . Harris advanced two ways to overcome this barrier to enjoining a letter of credit transaction.

First, Harris asserts that the independence principle was modified by the parties here. It points to those paragraphs of its contract with NIRT which made "the bank guarantees" an "integral part" of the contract and which state that NIRT shall release all guarantees upon termination of the contract due to force majeure . . . Harris contends that it has demonstrated a substantial likelihood that force majeure occurred and terminated both the contract and the guarantee. Harris cites *Touche Ross & Co. v. Manufacturers Hanover Trust Co.*[24] . . . where, under similar facts, the court enjoined payment on a guarantee letter of credit because it found that the underlying contract had been terminated by force majeure and held that the guarantee had thus been released.

We choose not to rely upon Harris's first line of argument, for we hesitate to hold that the letters of credit were automatically terminated by the operation of the contractual provisions. Accepting Harris's first argument would create problems; a bank could honor a letter of credit only to find that it had terminated earlier. While parties may modify the independence principle by drafting letters of credit specifically to achieve that result . . . there is no assertion by Harris that the performance guarantee or the letter of credit contain provisions (conditions) which would modify the independence of the banks' obligations. Since the banks were not parties to the underlying contract, it would appear that the contractual provisions relied upon by Harris would have the same effect as a warranty by NIRT that it would not draw upon the letter of credit issued by Melli if the contract were to terminate due to force majeure.

---

[24] 107 Misc. 2d 438, 434 N.Y.S. 2d 575 (Sup. Ct. 1980), modified 18 N.Y.L.J. 11 (May 5, 1981).

The second avenue pursued by Harris is the doctrine of "fraud in the transaction." Under this doctrine, a court may enjoin payment on a letter of credit, despite the independence principle, where there is shown to be fraud by the beneficiary of the letter of credit. . . . Unfortunately, one unsettled point in the law is what constitutes fraud in the transaction, *i.e.*, what degree of defective performance by the beneficiary justifies enjoining a letter of credit transaction in violation of the independence principle?

Contending that a narrow definition of fraud is appropriate, the appellants assert that an injunction should issue only upon a showing of facts indicating egregious misconduct. They argue that fraud in the transaction should be restricted to the type of chicanery present in the landmark case of *Sztejn v. Henry Schroder Banking Corp.*[25] . . . .

The appellants further contend that Harris does not and cannot allege conduct on the part of NIRT or Melli that would justify a finding of fraud under *Sztejn*. The egregious conduct, they assert, was by Harris. They state that it was Harris which failed to ship the remaining goods, unreasonably refused to extend the letter of credit obtained from Continental, and deliberately abandoned and destroyed the underlying contract. In contrast, they point out that they informed Continental that they would have been satisfied if the letter of credit had been extended long enough for Harris to complete performance. According to the view of NIRT and Melli, all that Harris has — taking its assertions as true — is an impossibility defense to an action on the underlying contract.

Appellants' arguments are not persuasive in the context of this case. *Sztejn* does not offer much direct guidance because it involved fraud by the beneficiary seller in the letter of credit transaction in the form of false documentation covering up egregiously fraudulent performance of the underlying transaction. That does not mean that the fraud exception should be restricted to allegations involving fraud in the underlying transaction, nor does it mean that the exception should be restricted to protecting the buyer in the framework of the traditional letter of credit. The fraud exception is flexible, *e.g.*, *United Bank v. Cambridge Sporting Goods Corp.*[26] . . . and it may be invoked on behalf of a customer seeking to prevent a beneficiary from fraudulently utilizing a standby (guarantee) letter of credit. [cases cited]. . . .

Thus, the independent contracts rule does not make a fraudulent demand completely irrelevant to a bank's obligation to honor a standby. The differences between the allegations in this case and those in *Sztejn* merely require us to focus on the conduct of the buyer rather than the seller as we evaluate the beneficiary's conduct in light of the terms of the particular documents involved in the demand.

In order to collect upon the guarantee letter of credit, NIRT was required to declare that Harris had failed to comply with the terms and conditions of the contract. Harris contends that NIRT intentionally misrepresented the quality of Harris's performance; Harris thus asserts fraud as it has been defined traditionally.

We find that the evidence adduced by Harris is sufficient to support a conclusion that it has a substantial likelihood of prevailing on the merits. The facts suggest

---

[25] 177 Misc. 719, 31 N.Y.S. 2d. 631 (Sup. Ct., 1941).
[26] 41 N.Y. 2d 254, 392 N.Y.S. 2d 265, 360 N.E. 2d 943 (1976).

that the contract in this case broke down through no fault of Harris's but rather as a result of problems stemming from the Iranian revolution. NIRT apparently admitted as much during its negotiations with Harris over how to carry out the remainder of the contract. Nonetheless, NIRT sought to call the performance guarantee. Its attempt to do so necessarily involved its representation that Harris had defaulted under the contract. Yet the contract explicitly provides that it can be determined due to force majeure. Moreover, NIRT's demand was made in a situation that was subtly suggestive of fraud. Since NIRT and Bank Melli had both become government enterprises, the demand was in some sense by Iran upon itself and may have been an effort by Iran to harvest undeserved bounty from Continental Bank. Under these circumstances, it was within the district court's discretion to find that, at a full hearing Harris might well be able to prove that NIRT's demand was a fraudulent attempt to obtain the benefit of payment on the letter of credit in addition to the benefit of Harris's substantial performance.[27]

C. Irreparable Injury

The district court did not abuse its discretion in finding a substantial likelihood of irreparable injury to Harris absent an injunction. Harris has sufficiently demonstrated that its ability to pursue a legal remedy against NIRT and Melli (*i.e.* to recover the proceeds of the standby) has been precluded. It is clear that the Islamic regime now governing Iran has shown a deep hostility toward the United States and its citizens, thus making effective access to the Iranian courts unlikely. . . . Similarly, the cooperative response of agencies of Iran to orders of a United States court would be unlikely where the court's order would impose a financial obligation on the agencies . . . Harris's possible resort to the Iran-United States Claims Tribunal does not, in our eyes, ameliorate the likelihood of irreparable injury for purposes of this requirement for preliminary relief.

D. The Balance of Harms

Neither appellant argues that the preliminary injunction has caused or will cause it any harm. Since there would otherwise be a likelihood that Harris would suffer irreparable injury, the balance of harms weighs heavily in Harris's favor.

---

[27] The appellants have, of course, cited other cases involving Iranian letters of credit where courts have found that the "fraud in the transaction" exception did not apply. The cases presented, however, do not involve the same, or even a very similar, combination of the beneficiary's conduct, the terms of the contract, and the terms of the demand document as we have before us. See, *e.g.*, *KMW Int'l v. Chase Manhattan Bank*, 606 F. 2d 10 (2d Cir. 1979) (no demand on the letter of credit); *American Bell Int'l Inc. v. Islamic Republic of Iran*, 474 F. Supp. 420, 424-25 (S.D.N.Y. 1979) (insufficient showing of fraud where letter of credit provided for immediate payment on demand, without regard to cause); *United Technologies Corp. v. Citibank*, 469 F. Supp. 473 (S.D.N.Y. 1979) (no recognition by beneficiary of any condition excusing contract performance); *Balfour Machine Int'l, Ltd. v. Manufacturers Hanover Trust Co.*, No. S/B 20801/78 (N.Y.Sup. Ct., N.Y. County July 13, 1979) (lacked requisite allegations of fraud). . . . We reject any implication, purportedly drawn from the opinions in such cases, that an injunction should not be available under the facts of this case.

E. The Public Interest

In a Statement of Interest filed with the district court on July 16, 1982, the United States indicated, that new amendments to the Iranian Assets Control Regulations governing letter of credit claims still permit American litigants to proceed in United States Courts and to obtain preliminary injunctive relief. The supplementary information explaining the changes provides a good indication that preliminary injunctions such as the one entered here are in the public interest:

> Iran filed more than 200 claims with the Iran-U.S. Claims Tribunal (the "Tribunal") based on standby letters of credit issued for the account of United States parties. United States nationals have filed with the Tribunal a large number of claims related to, or based on, many of the same standby letters of credit at issue in Iran's claims. Other United States nationals have litigation pending in United States courts concerning some of these same letters of credit.
>
> The purpose of the amendment is to preserve the status quo by continuing to allow U.S. account parties to obtain preliminary injunctions or other temporary relief to prevent payment on standby letters of credit, while prohibiting, for the time being, final judicial action permanently enjoining, nullifying or otherwise permanently disposing of such letters of credit.
>
> Preservation of the status quo will provide an opportunity for negotiations with Iran regarding the status and disposition of these various letter of credit claims. Preservation of the status quo for a period of time also permits possible resolution in the context of the Tribunal of the matters pending before it. The amendment will expire by its terms on December 31, 1982[28]
>
> . . . .

Melli has charged, however, that the entry of a preliminary injunction here would threaten the function of letters of credit in commercial transactions. Admittedly, that has given us pause, for it would be improper to impose relief contrary to the intentions of parties that have contracted to carry out their business in a certain manner. Some might contend that the use of the fraud exception in a case such as this damages commercial law and that Harris could have chosen to shift the risks represented in this case. Under the circumstances, however, we disagree. First, the risk of a fraudulent demand of the type which Harris has demonstrated a likelihood of showing is not one which it should be expected to bear in light of the manner in which the documents in this transaction were structured. Second, to argue that Harris could have protected itself further by inserting special conditions in the letters of credit and should be confined to that protection is to ignore the realities of the drafting of commercial documents. Third, unlike the first line of argument presented by Harris, the issuance of a preliminary injunction based on a showing of fraud does not create unfortunate consequences for a bank that honors letters of credit in good faith; it is up to the customer to seek and obtain an injunction before a bank would be prohibited from paying on a letter of credit. Finally, foreign situations like the one before us are

---

[28] Supplementary Information, Iranian Assets Control Regulations, "Judicial Action involving standby letters of credit," to be codified at 31 C.F.R. 535.222(g) and 535.504 (July 1, 1982).

exceptional. For these reasons, the district court's holding is not contrary to the public interest in maintaining the market integrity and commercial utility of guarantee letters of credit.Accordingly, the decision of the district court is

Affirmed.

NOTES AND QUESTIONS

(1) Recall that in *Cambridge* the latter on June 18, 1971 had cancelled its contract with Duke. The letter of credit, however, did not expire until August 11, 1971, and presumably could not be terminated because to do so would require the consent of all the parties to the credit (see UCP Article 3(c)) and Duke would not or had not been asked to consent. In other words, in spite of cancellation of the contract Cambridge still faced the exposure represented by the outstanding letter of credit. Recall also that Cambridge had to go elsewhere to fill its customers' orders. It undoubtedly, therefore, wanted to avoid any payment to Duke even if the latter had shipped goods fully in compliance with the contract. Does the *Harris* Case suggest a way that Cambridge might have achieved this objective? Note that the draft presented to Manufacturers Hanover was dated July 16, 1971. We can presume that the bill of lading and seller's invoice were likewise issued after the June notice of cancellation. What additional steps does your answer suggest Cambridge should have taken at the time it cancelled the contract with Duke? Would this application of the *Harris* reasoning to commercial letters of credit be sound?

(2) In *Harris* the court argued that Harris was likely to prevail on the merits of the fraud issue because the contract with NIRT had "broke[n] down" due to no fault of Harris and yet NIRT, after acknowledging that fact, called the performance guaranty thereby representing that Harris was in default. In addition, the court said, NIRT's conduct was subtly suggestive of fraud because Bank Melli and NIRT "had both become government enterprises." Are you convinced? Consider the following:

   (a) Harris and NIRT both acknowledged the existence of force majeure in May of 1979. Presumably that agreement was based on Paragraph 11-5 of the contract (see footnote 23). Consider also the parties conduct in the months that followed but before the hostages were seized. Was that conduct consistent with Paragraph 11-5? If so, does it support the court's conclusion that the contract had "broken down" in the sense that Harris would be excused if it failed to ship the transmitters?

   (b) After that what prevented shipment? Assume that because of those events Harris would be excused for non-shipment on the grounds of impracticability. Would NIRT's demand for payment, in the face of that excuse, constitute fraud in the absence of a declaration of force majeure? Note that at no time after May, 1979 did Harris invoke force majeure (Paragraph 11-6 of the contract) until, in resisting Bank Melli's demand for payment, it asked the court to declare force majeure. Close question?

(c) How should the question be resolved in light of the purpose of the stand-by letter of credit? Is the "Statement of Interest" filed by the government sufficient to resolve the matter? Was the court convinced? Are you convinced by the court?

(3) Compare *Harris* with *American Bell International, Inc. v. Islamic Republic of Iran and Manufacturers Hanover Trust Co.*[29] In that case Iran had made a $38 million down payment on a $280 million contract with Bell for the installation of a national telecommunications system. The down payment was to be returned to Iran upon the latter's demand, although the amount to be returned was reduced as payments were made to Bell under the contract. Securing the obligation to return the down payment was the guaranty of an Iranian bank. The bank, in turn, was secured by Manufacturers Hanover's irrevocable stand-by letter of credit. In August of 1979 the Iranian bank, claiming to have honored its guaranty to Iran, demanded payment from Manufacturers Hanover for the full amount of the then returnable portion of the down payment ($30.2 million). Bell, claiming Iran had repudiated the contract on which it was still owed substantial sums, sought to enjoin Manufacturers from paying under the credit. The court denied the injunction. It concluded that even if the demands for payment, under either the guaranty or letter of credit, were wrongful, Bell had an adequate remedy in law. It could sue the Iranian parties in a U.S. court under the Foreign Sovereign Immunities Act. Moreover, on the fraud question, Bell had failed to show probable success on the merits. If, as Manufacturers argued, that required a showing of fraud in the letter of credit transaction, Bell failed because it could not show fraud in the issuance of the credit, the terms of the credit or in the demand for payment. If, as Bell contended, it meant fraud in the underlying transaction, Bell still failed. Bell had argued that it was per se fraud for Iran to demand payment under a contract which Iran itself had repudiated. In response, the court first noted that Bell's evidence of repudiation — an intragovernmental decree ordering termination of the Bell contract — was off-set by official Iranian statements showing an intent to honor all legitimate contracts. The evidence failed, in the court's judgment, to show an irrevocable decision to repudiate. However, even if Iran had repudiated the contract, Bell failed to prove fraud since, according to the court, not every person who repudiates or breaches a contract is guilty of fraud. The court found the evidence ambivalent as to "whether the purported repudiation result[ed] from a non-fraudulent economic calculation [*i.e.* get back the down payment to which it was entitled on demand] or from a fraudulent intent to mulct Bell."[30]

[29] 474 F. Supp 420 (S.D.N.Y., 1979).

[30] Unlike the court in *Harris*, the court in *American Bell International Inc.*, was required to weigh the balance of hardships prior to the Hostage seizure and the breach of diplomatic relations between Iran and the United States. Under these circumstances it concluded that any hardship that Bell might suffer (*i.e.* loss of $30.2 million with no assurance of recouping that amount from Iran) was outweighed by the potential hardships facing Manufacturers if the latter were barred from making payment on the letter of credit. The Iranian Bank could initiate suit and attach $30.2 million of Manufacturers assets in Iran. It could seek consequential damages beyond that sum. Iran might retaliate by nationalizing other of Manufacturers Iranian assets which far exceeded Bell's $30.2 million. And Manufacturers failure to make good on a letter of credit could result in its "loss of credibility in the international banking community."

Was NIRT's demand for payment predicated on a claim of default by Harris any more probative of fraud than Iran's demand for payment after repudiating the contract with Bell?

(4) Consider, on the other hand, the function of the stand-by credit in allocating risks between the parties to the underlying contract. Note that, at the time of suit, there were still remedial possibilities available to Bell at least in the American courts and perhaps in Iran as well. For Harris, on the other hand, Iran was completely closed and any recovery on a judgment by a United States court against Bank Melli or NIRT would have had to run the gauntlet of the Government's blocking orders. While still unsettled when the case came before the district court, by the time of the appeal it was clear that all Iranian assets in the United States would either be returned to Iran, placed in a special fund for the payment of awards issued by the Iran-United States Tribunal or subject to Treasury blocking orders.[31] Harris would, therefore, have had to start all over again in that Tribunal. Consult, *Touche Ross & Co. v. Manufacturers Hanover Trust Co.*,[32] holding that where payments under a letter of credit would be subject to government blocking orders plaintiff lacked an adequate remedy at law. Perhaps, in other words, the disruption of the relationship between the United States and Iran had destroyed all possibility of achieving the intended effect of the stand-by letter of credit in allocating risks between the parties. Query, however, is this conclusion, even if correct, relevant to the "fraud in the transaction" requirement of UCC Sec. 5-114(2)? On this point, one commentator has suggested that:

> . . . a sovereign, when demanding payment on a standby letter of credit, implicitly represents that it has taken no action counter to its international duty of state responsibility. When it is established that the sovereign beneficiary has denied the private party a previously existing legal means of challenging the retention of the proceeds, the representation implicit in the demand for payment is false.[33]

(5) At an earlier point in the unfolding Iranian crisis, the courts were called upon to deal with requests for pre-demand injunctive relief. While almost invariably they denied requests to fully enjoin payment under these circumstances, they did grant "notice" injunctions. *Pan American World Airways Inc and Pan American Technical Services Inc. v. Bank Melli Iran and Citicorp N.A.*,[34] is instructive. There the court granted plaintiff Pan Am a preliminary injunction against Bank Melli prohibiting payment for a period of twenty days after notice on two guarantees issued by Bank Melli securing plaintiff's performance under a technical services contract with the Government of Iran. While, at the time of suit, no demand for payment under the guarantees had been made, Pan Am argued that the political chaos in Iran created a fear that unauthorized persons might call for payment under the guarantees and that it had fully performed under the technical

[31] See *Dames & Moore v. Regan*, 453 U.S. 654, 101 S. Ct. 2972, 69 L. Ed. 2d 918 (1981) (Chapter 12 *infra*), upholding the constitutionality of the Declarations of Algeria disposing of blocked Iranian assets here and abroad.

[32] 107 Misc. 2d 438 (Sup. Ct., N.Y. Co., 1980) 434 N.Y.S. 2d 575.

[33] Getz, Enjoining The International Standby Letter Of Credit: The Iranian Letter Of Credit Cases, 21 Harv. Int'l L. J. 189 at page 239 (1980).

[34] Slip op., 79 Civ. 1190 (WCC), (S.D.N.Y., April 3, 1979).

services contract until February 22, 1979 when it had invoked force majeure. The twenty-day period would enable Pan Am to investigate whether any requests for payment under the guarantees were fraudulent. The court concluded that Bank Melli would suffer no prejudice from such limited relief; that plaintiffs had no adequate remedy at law because if Bank Melli paid on the guarantees, in good faith, they would have to locate the individuals who made the fraudulent demand; and that plaintiffs had demonstrated the existence of "questions going to the merits" that were "sufficiently serious" to constitute "a favorable ground for litigation." The court then observed that while the relief requested would require reading a non-existent notice provision into Bank Melli's guarantees, " 'the fluid and precarious circumstances now prevailing in Iran justif[ied] deviation from what would otherwise be a strong reluctance to do so.' " Quoting *Stromberg-Carlson Corporation v. Bank Melli Iran*[35] and *Harris International Telecommunications, Inc. v. Bank Melli Iran.*[36]

At the same time, however, the court denied Pan Am's request for a similar twenty-day "notice" injunction against payment by Citicorp on a stand-by letter of credit issued to Bank Melli as security for payments made under the guarantees. According to the court, the "notice" injunction against Bank Melli gave plaintiff substantial protection even if Bank Melli were deemed a holder in due course, a point which the court refused to decide (*i.e.*, could the beneficiary of a letter of credit be a holder in due course). Citicorp, on the other hand, could suffer substantial injury because even a twenty day delay in payment would constitute a dishonor of the standby credit and, as a result, Citicorp could be denied the opportunity to do a banking business in Iran. Also, Pan Am had an adequate remedy at law since Bank Melli had substantial assets in the United States.

(a) Assuming that UCC Section 5-114(2) was technically inapplicable to the Bank Melli guarantees, what traditional source of judicial power could be invoked as a basis for the "notice" injunction? Who benefits from that injunction? Since the guarantees and the stand-by letter of credit are so closely linked, does this detract from or add to the commercial utility of the stand-by credit? Is there a ripeness issue here?

(b) Suppose Pan Am had not joined Bank Melli in its action and had only requested a "notice" injunction against payment on Citicorp's stand-by letter of credit? What result? Consider the benefit analysis under (a) above. Assume a beneficiary can be a holder in due course, what problems would that pose under UCC Sec. 5-114(2)?, under an alternative theory of judicial power? Consult, *KWM International v. Chase Manhattan Bank, N.A.*,[37] *reversing* the district court's[38] grant of a preliminary injunction against any payment on the stand-by credit but ordering Chase to give plaintiff three days notice before payment. Note that UCC Section 5-112(1)(a) authorizes a bank to defer honoring a demand for payment "until the close of the third banking day following receipt of the documents."

[35] 467 F. Supp. 530. (S.D.N.Y., March 23 1979).
[36] No. 79-802 (S.D.N.Y., Feb. 22, 1979).
[37] 606 F. 2d 10 (Cir. 2d, 1979).
[38] Slip Op., No. 79-1067, Mar. 9, 1979 aff'd on rehearing Mar. 16, 1979.

[C]   The Meaning of Strict Compliance

J.H. RAYNER AND COMPANY, LTD. v. HAMBRO'S BANK LTD.

Court of Appeal
[1943] 1 K.B. 37

Appeal from ATKINSON J.

On March 29, 1940, the defendants, Hambro's Bank, Ltd., received a cable from correspondents in Denmark, which was not then in enemy occupation, requesting them to open an irrevocable sight credit expiring June 1, 1940, in favour of J.H. Rayner & Co., the plaintiffs. The material words of the . . . cable were:

. . . account Aarhus Oliefabrik for about 16,957L against invoice full set straight clean bills of lading to Aarhus Oliefabrik dated Madras during April, 1940, covering about 1400 tons Coromandel groundnuts in bags at 12L 2s 6d per ton f.o.b. Madras shipment motorship Stensby to Aarhus.

On April 1, the defendants issued a letter of credit to the plaintiffs in these terms:

Confirmed credit No. 14597.

We beg to inform you that a confirmed credit has been opened with us in favour of yourselves for an amount of up to about 16,975L account of Aarhus Oliefabrik available by drafts on this bank at sight to be accompanied by the following documents:

— invoice,

— clean on board bills of lading in complete set issued to order Aarhus Oliefabrik, dated Madras during April, 1940, covering a shipment of about 1400 tons Coromandel groundnuts in bags at 12L. 2s. 6d. per ton f.o.b. Madras per m.s. Stensby to Aarhus.

This credit is valid until June 1, 1940. All drafts drawn here against must contain the clause "Drawn under confirmed credit No. 14597." We undertake to honour drafts on presentation, if drawn in conformity with the terms of this credit.

On April 15, the plaintiffs presented to the defendant bank a draft, accompanied by an invoice of the same date for "17,724 bags Coromandel groundnuts. Bill of lading dated 2.4.40," and three bills of lading, differing only as to the number of bags, which totalled 17,724, each of which the goods were described in these terms: in the margin were the marks:

OTC CRS Aarhus,

and in the body of the bill [the words]:

. . . bags machine-shelled groundnut kernels, each bag said to weigh 177 lb. nett. Country of origin, British India. Country of final destination, Denmark. Goods are Danish property.

Those documents, having been presented to the defendants, they refused to accept the draft, on the ground that the terms of the letter of credit called for an invoice and bill of lading both covering a shipment of "Coromandel groundnuts" whereas the bills of lading presented described the goods as "machine-shelled groundnut kernels. Country of origin British India." The plaintiffs thereupon brought this action, alleging that the defendants' refusal to honour their draft was wrongful, and a breach of the undertaking in the letter of credit. At the trial before Atkinson J. evidence was given and accepted by him that "machine-shelled groundnut kernels" were the same commodity as "Coromandel groundnuts" and would be universally understood to be so in the trade in London, and, further, that the marginal mark "C.R.S." was short for "Coros" or "Coromandels" and would be so understood in the trade. Atkinson J. gave judgment for the plaintiffs, and the defendants appealed.

MACKINNON L.J. The legal result of a banker issuing a letter of credit has been considered in various cases . . . but two passages . . . seem to me to sum up the position in general terms with the greatest accuracy. In *English, Scottish and Australian Bank, Ltd. v. Bank of South Africa*[39] . . . it was said:

> It is elementary to say that a person who ships in reliance on a letter of credit must do so in exact compliance with its terms. It is also elementary to say that a bank is not bound or indeed entitled to honour drafts presented to it under a letter of credit unless those drafts with the accompanying documents are in strict accord with the credit as opened.

. . . Lord Sumner in *Equitable Trust Co. of New York v. Dawson Partners, Ltd.*[40] . . . said:

> It is both common ground and common sense that in such a transaction the accepting bank can only claim indemnity if the conditions on which it is authorized to accept are in the matter of the accompanying documents strictly observed. There is no room for documents which are almost the same, or which will do just as well. Business could not proceed securely on any other lines. The bank's branch abroad, which knows nothing officially of the details of the transaction thus financed, cannot take upon itself to decide what will do well enough and what will not. If it does as it is told, it is safe; if it declines to do anything else, it is safe; if it departs from the conditions laid down, it acts at its own risk.

The defendant bank were told by their Danish principals to issue a letter of credit under which they were to accept documents . . . covering "Coromandel groundnuts in bags." They were offered bills of lading covering "machine-shelled groundnut kernels." The country of origin was stated to be British India. The words in that bill of lading clearly are not the same as those required by the letter of credit. The whole case of the plaintiffs is, in the words of Lord Sumner, that "they are almost the same, or they will do just as well." The bank, if they had accepted that proposition, would have done so at their own risk. I think on pure principle that the bank were entitled to refuse to accept this sight draft on the ground that the documents tendered, the bill of lading in particular, did not comply precisely with the terms of the letter of credit which they had issued.

---

[39] [1921] 13 Ll. L. Rep. 21 at 24 Bailache J.
[40] [1927] Ll. L. Rep. 49 at 52.

Atkinson J., however, in his judgment says:

A sale of Coromandel groundnuts is universally understood to be a sale of machine-shelled kernels, that is, dry decorticated, and there is a standard form of contract, No. 37, used in the trade. The marking C.R.S is short for "Coros," which is itself an abbreviation for "Coromandels." If a bag of kernels is marked "C.R.S." it means that it is a bag of Coromandel groundnuts.

That is stating the effect of evidence given by persons who deal in groundnuts in Mincing Lane, and when Atkinson J. says that it is "universally understood," he means that these gentlemen from Mincing Lane have told him: "We dealers in Mincing Lane all understand these things. We understand that 'Coromandel groundnuts' are machine-shelled groundnut kernels, and we understand when we see 'C.R.S.' that means 'Coromandels' ." It is suggested that as a consequence the bank, . . . when this bill of lading was brought to them, ought to be affected with this special knowledge of those witnesses who deal in these things on contracts in Mincing Lane. I think that is a perfectly impossible suggestion. To begin with, this case does not concern any transaction in Mincing Lane. It is a transaction with Denmark, and for aught I know, and for aught the evidence proved, the people in Denmark know nothing about this business usage of Mincing Lane. Moreover, . . . it is quite impossible to suggest that a banker is to be affected with knowledge of the customs and customary terms of every one of the thousands of trades for whose dealings he may issue letters of credit. A homely illustration is suggested by the books in front of me. If a banker were ordered to issue a letter of credit with respect to the shipment of so many copies of the "1942 Annual Practice" and were handed a bill of lading for so many copies of the "1942 White Book," it would be entirely beside the mark to call a lawyer to say that all lawyers know that the "1942 White Book" means the "1942 Annual Practice." It would be quite impossible for business to be carried on, and for bankers to be in any way protected in such matters, if it were said that they must be affected by a knowledge of all the details of the way in which particular traders carry on their business. . . . For these reasons, I think that this appeal succeeds, that the judgment in favour of the plaintiffs must be set aside, and judgment entered for the defendants with costs, here and below.

GODDARD L.J., I agree. It seems to me that Atkinson J. has based his judgment on the consideration that the bank was affected in some way by this custom of the trade, and, secondly, that he has considered whether what the bank required was reasonable or unreasonable. I protest against the [first point] . . . but, quite apart from that, even if the bank did know of this trade practice by which "Coromandel groundnuts" can be described as "machine-shelled groundnuts kernels" I do not think that would be conclusive of the case.

There are three parties concerned in a banker's credit — the person who requests the bank to establish the credit, the bank which establishes it, and the beneficiary who can draw on it. The person who requests the bank to establish the credit can impose what terms he likes. If he says to the bank: "I want a bill of lading in a particular form," he is entitled to it. If the bank accepts the mandate which its customer gives it, it must do so on the terms which he imposes. The bank, as between itself and the beneficiary can impose extra terms if it likes. . . . [But] . . . if it has only been authorized by its customer to pay on certain terms it must see that those terms are included in the notification which it gives to the beneficiary, and it must not pay on any other terms. If it does pay on any other terms, it runs the risk of its customer refusing to reimburse it. . . . If the customer says: "I require a bill of lading for Coromandel groundnuts," the bank is not justified, in my judgment, in paying against a bill of lading for anything except Coromandel groundnuts, and it is no answer to say: "You know perfectly well that machine-shelled groundnut kernels are the same as Coromandel groundnuts.' " For all the bank knows, its customer may have a particular reason for wanting "Coromandel groundnuts" in the bill of lading. . . .

In my opinion, in this case, whether the bank knew or did not know that there was this trade practice to treat "Coromandel Groundnuts" and "machine-shelled groundnut kernels" as interchangeable terms, is nothing to the point. . . . The question is . . . [what promise did the bank make to the beneficiary and whether the beneficiary availed himself of that promise.] In my opinion, . . . he did not, and, therefore, I think that the bank was justified in refusing to pay. . . .

Appeal allowed

DIXON, IRMAOS & CIA., LTDA. v. CHASE NATIONAL BANK OF THE CITY OF NEW YORK

United States Court of Appeals, Second Circuit
144 F. 2d 759 (1944), cert. denied 324 U.S. 850 (1945)

Before L. HAND, SWAN, and FRANK, CIRCUIT JUDGES.

SWAN, CIRCUIT JUDGE.

This appeal raises interesting and important questions as to letters of credit covering C.I.F. shipments abroad. The plaintiffs, an exporter of cotton in Sao Paulo, Brazil, contracted to sell cotton to a purchaser in Belgium. A Belgian bank requested the Chase Bank to issue in favor of the plaintiff two irrevocable letters of credit for $7,000 and $3,500 respectively to finance such sales. Chase Bank did so and mailed them to Sao Paulo, where they were received by the plaintiff on May 2, 1940. They bound Chase Bank to honor 90 day drafts drawn under the credits, if presented at its office on or before May 15, 1940 and accompanied by specified documents, including a "full set of bills of lading" evidencing shipment of a stated quantity and quality of cotton "C.I.F. Ghent/Antwerp." One of the letters of credit (both being the same in form) is set out in the margin.[41] The

---

[41] The Chase National Bank of The City of New York

April 8, 1940.

Confirmed Irrevocable Straight Credit
Dixon Irmaos and Cia. Ltda.,
Sao Paulo, Brazil
Gentlemen:
    We are instructed by Banque de Bruxelles, S.A., Brussels, Belgium to advise you that

plaintiff duly shipped the cotton to its Belgian customer in two lots, receiving for each shipment two originals of the bills of lading. Instead of prepaying freight the plaintiff shipped the goods freight collect and deducted the freight charges from the invoice price. Through the Guaranty Trust Company of New York, the plaintiff's representative, drafts and documents were presented to Chase Bank on May 15, 1940, but only one of the set of two bills of lading was delivered. In lieu of the other, which was in the mail and not yet arrived in New York, an indemnity agreement or guaranty against loss resulting from its absence was tendered by the Guaranty Trust Company.[42]

Chase Bank had no objection to the form of the guaranty or to the responsibility of the guarantor, but it refused the drafts on two grounds: (1) Absence of a full set of the bills of lading and (2) failure to prepay the freight. The plaintiff then brought the present action to recover the amount of its drafts, $5,587.15 under the larger letter of credit and $2,757.49 under the smaller. The case was tried without a jury. At the conclusion of the evidence each side moved for judgment. Decision being reserved, the district judge thereafter rendered an opinion and filed findings of fact and law. He gave judgment for the defendant on the ground that

---

they have opened their irrevocable credit in your favor for account of George Alost under their credit Number 40466 for a sum or sums not exceeding a total of about $7000.00 (Seven Thousand Dollars) U.S. Currency available by your drafts on us at 90 days sight, in duplicate to be accompanied by

Commercial invoice in triplicate, or invoice copy

Insurance certificate which must cover land and sea risks into the mills, and showing merchandise covered on board the steamer named and/or other steamer or steamer

Full set bills of lading. Port or custody bills of lading acceptable evidencing shipment of 22 tons Brazilian Sao Paulo Cotton type MINI shipped during April 1940, CIF Ghent/Antwerp

All documents in name of La Georgie.

All drafts so drawn must be marked "Drawn under Chase National Bank Credit No. E71582"

The above mentioned correspondent engages with you that all drafts drawn under and in compliance with the terms of this credit will be duly honored on delivery of documents as specified if presented at this office on or before May 15, 1940; we confirm the credit and thereby undertake that all drafts drawn and presented as above specified will be duly honored by us.

Unless otherwise expressly stated, this credit is subject to the uniform customs and practice for commercial documentary credits fixed by the Seventh Congress of the International Chamber of Commerce and certain guiding provisions.

Your very truly,
C. F. Wellman
Assistant Manager

[42] The Guaranty Trust Company's indemnity agreement stated: "In consideration of your accepting the above described draft, we hereby agree to hold you harmless from any and all consequences which might arise due to the following discrepancy: Only 1 copy presented out of a set of 2 bills of lading issued. It is understood that this guarantee will remain in force until such time as you may obtain a release from your clients. We shall thank you to take the necessary steps to obtain this release as soon as possible and inform us promptly when it has been obtained."

the tender of less than a full set of bills of lading did not comply with the terms of the letters of credit.

Assuming for the moment that a C.I.F. shipment does not require the shipper to prepay freight if the freight charges are credited against the invoice price, the Guaranty Trust Company's tender to Chase Bank of drafts and documents fully met the requirements of the letters of credit, except for the fact that one original bill of lading out of each set of two was missing. The plaintiff contends that this fact did not defeat the adequacy of its tender because the evidence established the existence of a custom among New York banks issuing letters of credit to finance a shipment from outside the United States and calling for a "full set of bills of lading," to accept in lieu of a missing part of the set a guaranty by a responsible New York bank against any loss resulting from the absence of the missing part. On this subject the trial judge made the following findings of fact:

12. The letters of guaranty of the Guaranty Trust Company tendered to the defendant are in the usual form of guaranties tendered by and accepted by leading New York banks issuing commercial credits, when less than all bills of lading are presented under credits calling for a full set of bills of lading.

12A. The Guaranty Trust Company was and is a prime and leading New York bank with sound financial standing.

12B. The defendant raised no objection to the form of the guaranties tendered by the Guaranty Trust Company nor with the financial responsibility of the Guaranty Trust Company.

13. On May 15, 1940, and for some time prior thereto, there existed a general and uniform custom among New York banks, exporters and importers to the effect that in lieu of a missing bill or missing bills of lading presented under credits calling for a full set of bills of lading, that the bank issuing the credits would accept in lieu of the missing bill or bills of lading, a guaranty of a leading New York bank, if it determined the guaranty to be satisfactory in form and if it was satisfied as to the responsibility of the bank issuing the guaranty. The bank issuing the credit was, however, free to exercise its own discretion and make its own determinations as to whether it would accept a guaranty in lieu of a missing bill of lading.

We are not entirely clear as to the meaning of the final sentence of finding 13. If it means that the issuer of credit is free to reject the tendered guaranty if doubts are entertained regarding the guarantor's financial responsibility or the sufficiency of the form of the document, it is not inconsistent with the custom stated in the first sentence and may be disregarded; in these respects Chase Bank was satisfied with the guaranty tendered by Guaranty Trust Company. But if it means that even when so satisfied the bank issuing the credit may reject the tendered guaranty and refuse to accept the draft, it is inconsistent with the stated custom and is unsupported by the evidence. . . . Indeed, it is clear that the Chase Bank would in this very case have honored the drafts, had they been presented before the German invasion of Belgium. One of its witnesses naively said that before May 15, 1940 it was the custom to accept such a guaranty as was tendered, but not on that date or thereafter. . . . In short, the existence of the custom was established beyond dispute.

It is true, as the defendant argues, that . . . numerous cases . . . declare that evidence of a custom is not admissible to contradict the unambiguous terms of a written contract. . . . But it is also well settled "that parties who contract on a subject-matter concerning which known usages prevail, incorporate such usages by implication into their agreements, if nothing is said to the contrary" . . . In our opinion the custom under consideration explains the meaning of the technical phrase "full set of bills of lading" and is incorporated by implication into the terms of the defendant's letters of credit. No authority on the precise point has come to our attention. The statement of Bankes, L. J. in *Scott & Co., Ltd. v. Barclay's Bank, Ltd.*[43] . . . upon which the defendant relies, is inapposite because no custom such as the court found here was there proved or attempted to be proved. Finally, the defendant urges that the reference in the concluding paragraph of the letters of credit to the [UCP] . . . excludes incorporation into the contracts of any other custom. We do not think so. Those customs do not deal with the meaning of a "full set of bills of lading." Hence the problem whether the New York custom gives meaning to those words is unaffected by the reference to those other customs. The reasonableness and utility of the local New York custom is obvious. It is absolutely essential to the expeditious doing of business in overseas transactions in these days when one part of the bill of lading goes by air and another by water. Unless an indemnity can be substituted for the delayed part, not only does quick clearance of such transactions become impossible but also the universal practice of issuing bills of ladings in sets and sending the different parts by separate mails loses much of its purpose. We conclude therefore that the defendant's first ground for dishonor of the drafts was not a valid reason.

The second ground for dishonor was that while the credits specified a C.I.F. shipment, the plaintiff deducted freight charges from the invoices and shipped the goods freight collect. On this subject the court made the following findings:

15. . . . The term [c.i.f.] does not imply the time when or the place where the freight is to be paid and there was no uniform practice in New York on May 15, 1940 or prior thereto of prepaying freight to the point of destination under a c.i.f. shipment. The practice was that it was sometimes prepaid and sometimes deducted from the invoice.

16. The "American Foreign Trade Definitions" are incorporated by reference in the letter of credit. . . . Under the definition of a c.i.f. contract as [therein] defined . . . there is no requirement that a shipper must prepay freight.[44]

18. The tender of documents showing a deduction of freight from the invoices was not a deviation from the requirement of defendant's credits calling for C.I.F. shipment.

We agree with this conclusion. In the case of a sight draft, it is wholly immaterial to the buyer whether freight is prepaid or credit given on the invoice price. In the case of a time draft, it is true that the buyer may be deprived of the credit period as to part of the purchase price, that is, so much of it as the freight amounts to. In the case at bar the freight was $1,359.14. The measure of any possible loss to the buyer is the interest upon this sum for the period between arrival of the goods

---

[43] [1923] 2 K.B. 1, 11.

[44] Documentary Supplement, especially Comment 6. Ed.

and the date the drafts would fall due and the possible inconvenience of being called upon for early payment in cash of this portion of the price. The bills of lading were endorsed "on board" on May 5th and, if we assume the voyage would take 30 days, the buyer would not be called upon for the freight until June 5th. The draft if accepted on May 15th would have been due 90 days later, that is, the buyer would have had to pay freight about 70 days earlier than he would otherwise have paid such sum. Interest at 6% would amount to about $17. On a transaction involving about $9,700 such a sum is insignificant. The law has not cut so fine. The point of possible inconvenience is taken care of by ancient usage. The seller has so long had the option of shipping either freight collect or freight prepaid that the cases recognize the option as part of the standard meaning of the term C.I.F., making no distinction between prepayment or shipping freight collect and crediting it on the invoice irrespective of whether the draft be time or sight. . . . Furthermore, if the buyer sells the documents before arrival of the goods, as frequently happens in C.I.F. transactions, whether freight was prepaid will be wholly immaterial to him.

The judgment for the defendant is reversed and judgment directed in favor of the plaintiff.

NOTES AND QUESTIONS

(1) Why might the custom of bankers on Wall Street change after May 15, 1940, at least for Belgian customers? Was something similar at work in *Rayner*?

(2) If, in *Dixon, Irmaos* custom was admissible to explain the meaning of the phrase "full set of bills of lading," why was it not admissible to explain the meaning of "C.R.S.?" Can *Rayner* be reconciled with *Dixon, Irmaos*? Consult UCC Section 5-109.[45]

(3) Note that in *Rayner* the letter of credit required that the full description of the goods be included in the bill of lading: "full set straight clean bills of lading to Aarhus Oliefabrik . . . covering a shipment of about 1400 tons Coromandel groundnuts in bags. . . ." This was dangerous from the seller's viewpoint, was it not? Who prepares the bill of lading? If the seller had any control over the matter to what document should the full description be confined? More generally, the beneficiary of a letter of credit may encounter problems in assuring that all the documents conform to the terms of the credit. Consider the following typical documents and consider who is likely to prepare each of them: (i) invoice, (ii) bill of lading, (iii) policy or certificate of insurance, (iii) inspection certificate, (iv) export license or declaration, (v) packing list, (v) consular invoice required by the country of import, (vi) certificate of origin?

(4) UCP Article 41(c) may be thought of as a partial response to the problem discussed in the previous Note. Would that Article require a different result in *Rayner*? See *Soproma S.p.A. v. Marine & Animal By-Products Corporation*,[47] for

---

[45] Documentary Supplement.
[47] [1966] 1 Lloyd's Rep. 367 at page 389.

the conclusion that it would change the result. Can that decision be squared with the argument made by Lord Goddard in *Rayner*? In this connection reexamine the cable sent by Oliefabrik to Hambro's Bank on March 29, 1940.

(5) In *Laudisi v. American Exchange National Bank*,[48] the account party, in its application to the bank for a letter of credit, covering a shipment of "Alicante Bouchez" grapes, stipulated for: "Invoice and a bill of lading showing destination to Eighth street yard Long Island railroad." The letter of credit contained essentially the same terms. The court held that the bank had properly paid upon the presentation of an invoice that fully described the "Alicante Bouchez grapes" and a bill of lading which merely described the goods as "grapes." In so doing, the court noted however, that if a customer "requires that the bill of lading shall . . . on its face show that certain described goods have been shipped, a bank will not be protected which pays on the faith of a bill which does not comply with this requirement." Where, however, all that was required was an "invoice and negotiable bill of lading showing destination," the Bank was justified, according to the court, in acting on a bill of lading which "so far as its description goes, shows the shipment of required goods, and is then supplemented by a proper invoice which completes the description and shows that the goods are the ones mentioned in the letter of credit." Can you reconcile this decision with the conclusion that UCP Article 41(c) reverses the decision in *Rayner*? If not, considering the commercial function of a letter of credit, how should Article 41(c) be interpreted?

(6) What is the purpose of issuing a bill of lading in a set of parts? Note that UCC Sec. 7-304[49] prohibits such issue "except where customary in overseas transportation."

---

[48] 239 N.Y. 234, 146 N.E. 347 (1924).
[49] Documentary Supplement.

CHAPTER 2

UNITED STATES BUSINESS IN FOREIGN COUNTRIES OTHER THAN THROUGH FOREIGN DIRECT INVESTMENT

If one wishes to sell goods manufactured in the United States to purchasers in foreign countries, there are two basic ways one can do so: either sell the goods directly to purchasers in foreign countries — often through a U.S. intermediary such as an export trading company — or arrange for their distribution in the foreign country through an outlet there. We turn now to a consideration of the first of these two alternatives. The second we take up in § 2.02, *infra*.

§ 2.01 Export Departments, Exporters, and Export Trading Companies

Because the United States itself serves as a vast continental market, U.S. businesses have been slow — in comparison with countries in Western Europe and Japan — to develop foreign markets for their goods and services. Only about eight percent of the more than 250,000 businesses in the United States export regularly, and of these about 100 companies are responsible for more than half of the exports of manufactured goods.

Many of these 100 companies are large enough in size to have their own export departments to analyze foreign markets and distribution channels to handle the financing, transportation and insurance that exports require, to prepare the necessary documents and to take any steps necesssary to comply with export controls.

Few of the 10,000 or so small or medium-sized firms that export their products have such resources available. These companies therefore employ the services of various intermediaries principally "export companies" and Webb-Pomerene Associations (associations formed solely for the export of goods and exempt in certain ways from U.S. antitrust laws). These intermediaries, however, have not proven adequate to service the small or medium-sized firms in the United States desiring to export. Ninety-two percent of the 4,000 export firms in this country employ fewer than five people; most are limited to a single product line or geographical area and have not been able to secure lines of credit adequate for financing exports on a large scale. Of $217 billion total U.S. exports in 1980, these export firms accounted for an estimated $17-22 billion of exports of manufactured products and $25 billion of agricultural commodities. As of 1979, Webb-Pomerene Associations accounted for only two percent of U.S. exports, mostly agricultural commodities, chemicals and motion pictures.

In an effort to improve the export performance of small and medium-sized American businesses, on October 8, 1982, President Reagan signed the Export

Trading Act of 1982.[1] The Act attempts to do this through changes in federal banking and antitrust law.

Req. to benefit by the Act

To receive the benefits of the Act, an export trading company must be "exclusively engaged in activities related to international trade" and must be "organized and operated principally" either to export goods or services produced in this country or to facilitate the export of goods or services that have been produced in the United States by unaffiliated persons. When only facilitating exports, an export trading company must do so by providing one or more "export trade services." These include, *inter alia*, consulting, international market research, advertising, marketing, insurance (limited to risks outside the United States and to risks associated with transportation of goods whose final destination is outside the United States), product research and design, legal assistance, transportation (including documentation and freight forwarding), the communication and processing of orders originating abroad, warehousing, foreign exchange, financing, and, when done to facilitate the export of U.S. produced goods or services, taking title to goods.

Traditionally, U.S. law has limited banking institutions to activities such as taking deposits, making loans, and acting as trustees and has excluded them from "commercial" activities not strictly "banking" in character. Accordingly, federal law generally forbids banks and bank holding companies (a firm that owns 25 percent or more of the voting shares of, or otherwise controls, one or more banks) from having equity positions in "commerce." Title II of the Export Trading Act, however, permits bank holding companies and their affiliates to have ownership interests in export trading companies, subject to prior approval by the Federal Reserve Board.

The ability of bank holding companies to invest in export trading companies would, it was hoped, greatly strengthen the latter as a vehicle for expanding U.S. exports. Banks provide a range of services that are indispensable to the success of an export trading company: international correspondent relationships, knowledge of foreign markets, extensive operations and communications systems, financing and related services, especially letters of credit, knowledge about foreign currency transactions, and the kind of managerial expertise necessary for large-scale inventory control operations. The law, however, placed limits on the involvement of bank holding companies in export trading companies. A bank

Req. to bank holding Companies

holding company may not invest more than five percent of its consolidated capital and surplus in export trading companies. Any extension of credit by a bank holding company to an export trading company in which it has an interest must be on the same terms as those given to other borrowers, and the total extension of credit by the bank holding company must not exceed ten percent of its consolidated capital and surplus at any one time.

Also, an export trading company in which bank holding companies have ownership interests generally cannot engage in manufacturing or in agricultural production, although they may modify products to the extent necessary to ensure conformity with foreign country requirements or to facilitate foreign sales. More

---

[1] P.L. 97-290, 96 Stat. 1233 (1982) (codified at 12 U.S.C. Sections 372, 635-4, 1843(c)(14), 15 U.S.C. Sections 6a, 45(a), 4001-4003, 4011-4021 (1982); for regulations and guidelines, see 12 C.F.R. Sections 211.31-34 (1985), 50 Fed. Reg. 1786 (1985).

than one bank holding company may invest in an export trading company as long as each one and the company comply with the requirements of the Act.

By way of improving the financing of exports, Title II of the Act establishes an export trading company loan guarantee program at the Export-Import Bank that provides guarantees for loans made by financial institutions or other public or private creditors to export trading companies or to other exporters when such loans are secured by export accounts receivable or inventories of exportable goods. Provision of these guarantees is contingent upon the Board of Directors of the Export-Import Bank finding both that the private credit market is not providing adequate financing to export trading companies and that such guarantees will facilitate an expansion of exports that would not otherwise take place.

The Act also permits an export trading company or other U.S. entity to secure a limited exemption from the antitrust laws for its activities by obtaining an Export Trade Certificate of Review from the Department of Commerce.[2]

QUESTION

On the basis of the admittedly sketchy information set forth above, would you conclude that the Export Trading Company Act is an unmitigated blessing for small and medium companies in this country desiring to export? What cost, if any, might be involved in taking advantage of the Act?

§ 2.02 The Distributorship Arrangement

As an alternative to direct exports or exports through an intermediary such as an export trading company, the distributorship arrangement may be attractive for high volume and long-term exporting. With their knowledge of local conditions, distributors may be able to develop a foreign market. Indeed, over half the world's foreign trade is handled by distributors or agents.

Developing a productive relationship with a foreign distributor takes time and effort and requires an understanding and appreciation of the nuances of local culture. The rights and obligations arising out of this relationship are governed by the distributorship agreement between the parties, and this must be negotiated with a knowledge of United States law, the law of the distributor's country, and

---

[2] For commentary on the Export Trading Company Act of 1982, see *e.g.*, Garvey, *Exports, Banking And Antitrust: The Export Trading Company Act — A Modest Tool For Export Promotion*, 5 Nw. J. Int'l L. & Bus. 818 (1983); Zarin, *The Export Trading Company Act: Reducing Antitrust Uncertainty In Export Trade*, 17 Geo. Wash. J. Int'l L. & Econ. 297 (1983); Golden & Kolb, *The Export Trading Company Act Of 1982: An American Response To Foreign Competition*, 58 Notre Dame Law. 743 (1983); Victor, *The Export Trading Company Act Of 1982: New Antitrust Protection For Exporters (and New Opportunities For Lawyers)*, 52 Antitrust L.J. 917 (1984); Unkovic, *Joint Ventures And The Export Trading Company Act*, 5 J.L. & Com. 373 (1985); Lacy, *The Effect Of The Export Trading Company Act Of 1982 On U.S. Export Trade*, 23 Stan. J. Int'l L. 177 (1987).

any applicable international law. Because a distributorship arrangement contemplates a long term relationship it is important that both parties be happy with the agreement and that the agreement provide for periodic updating of its terms.

It is important to distinguish between agents and distributors. Generally, the distributor buys goods for his own account and resells them. The distributor normally operates at his own risk and in his own name. By contrast, an agent is an intermediary who procures business for another enterprise and who acts for the account of that enterprise. His compensation is usually based on a percentage commission, and usually the agent's principal provides the invoice covering the sale and sends it to the customer. In practice, however, the distinction between an agent and a distributor may be difficult to draw. Moreover, laws in many countries regulating agency agreements have been extended by analogy to distributorships, or conversely, laws regulating distributorships have been extended by analogy to agency agreements.

It is also important (especially for tax reasons) to distinguish between a commercial agent and a sales representative. Unlike a commercial agent, a sales representative normally does not have the authority to bind the foreign principal to a contract with a third party; rather, a sales representative merely solicits orders, and the principal decides whether to accept them.

The terms of the agreement will vary depending upon whether the foreign representative is acting solely as a sales person, or is purchasing the goods on his own account for resale, or stocking goods on consignment and selling them on commission. When the goods are delivered on consignment, the commission agent is not buying the goods, nor taking responsibility for goods or credit. Where goods are delivered on consignment, the contract has to make clear, for example, that they remain the property of the principal if the agent goes bankrupt. If the foreign representative is a distributor buying the products himself, then the contract is more a contract of sale subject to certain conditions regarding the operation of the distributor's business.

The following have been suggested[1] as possible key questions to be resolved in an agreement between a principal and a true agent (not a distributor):

1. Is the agreement with the individual or his firm?

2. Can the agent assign the agreement to his successor or sell it as part of the goodwill of his business, leaving the principal represented by someone else?

3. Where the document is in two languages, which is authoritative in case of a difference of interpretation?

4. If the principal brings out a new, related product, is he at liberty to appoint another agent to handle it?

5. Is the agent appointed for the whole of the principal's program, representing the firm rather than the products?

---

[1] McMillan and Paulden, Signing Up Your Agent, V International Trade Forum 12, 13 (Oct. 1969).

6. What is the definition of the origin of an order? If it is placed by, say, a buying house in Paris, for delivery to Chad, does the African or French agent qualify for commission?

7. Is the principal at liberty to negotiate with buyers from the agent's territory who refuse to purchase through a local agent? Does the agent earn commissions on such sales?

8. Is commission invoiced on the gross sum or only on the net value of goods (less freight charges, insurance, etc.)?

9. What is the size, quality and location of the establishment that the agent must maintain? What type of service capability? What, if any, inventory must it keep on hand?

10. Who, the principal or agent, will be responsible for advertising in the agent's territory?

11. What is the agreed method of quoting?

12. Who is responsible for payment of inland carriage?

13. Who is responsible for insurance on stocks held on consignment? (No use arguing after the fire!)

14. If urgent cables are required for a contract, which party defrays the cost?

15. If the principal is unable to fulfill a sales contract or cannot accept an order due to production or delivery problems, can the agent buy from an alternative source to satisfy a customer?

16. What notice is required to terminate an agreement, and what are the compensation terms for premature termination?

17. Is the agreement for a fixed period, and what is the procedure for renewal?

The freedom of the principal and agent to contract may be sharply circumscribed by the law of the agent's country. It is important, for example, to confirm that the agent is competent to enter into an agreement. Many countries in the developing world require agents to be local citizens, registered for trading with some commercial authority, solvent, etc. In Eastern Europe only state trading companies or state agency companies have been permitted to act as agents. (At this writing the situation is in an extreme state of flux).

Many countries have also enacted laws protective of agents' interests that limit the principal's options in contract negotiations. Such laws may require the principal to compensate the agent according to scheduled rates for damages or losses caused by termination of the agency agreement without just cause. They may then list and describe the reasons and situations under which an agency agreement may be validly terminated, i.e., incompetence of the agent and serious decrease in sales due to circumstances attributable to the agent. Some laws, for example, declare non-waivable the compensation and other rights granted to the agent; establish the law of the forum as the sole applicable law, thus precluding the parties from validly electing some other country's laws to govern the contract; place agents on the same footing as employees, thus entitling them to the benefits of the local labor laws governing dismissal and compensation for a discharge without just cause (in some jurisdictions incorporation of the agent will avoid a requirement that the agent be given notice of the termination prior to its effective date); condition the refusal to extend an expired agency agreement upon a showing of just cause.

Foreign principals seeking to do business in member countries of the European Economic Community (EEC) must be aware that on December 18, 1986, the EEC Council adopted a directive[2] that contains provisions on self-employed commercial agents (but not distributors) to which legislation of member states will have to be adapted. Article 189 of the EEC Treaty provides that a directive shall be binding, as to the result to be achieved, on each member state to which it is addressed. However, national authorities may decide on the form and method to be used to implement a directive. For member states other than Italy, Ireland and the United Kingdom, the directive is to be implemented before January 1, 1990. Because Ireland and the United Kingdom will have to effect fundamental changes in order to adapt their legal systems to the directive, they have been granted an additional four years; they must implement the directive, as to both future and existing contracts, by 1994. Italy has been granted an extension to 1993. The directive covers such matters, among others, as the commission to be paid the agent, termination of the agency agreement, and the agent's right to an indemnity or compensation for damages upon termination of the agreement.

Additionally, within the framework of EEC antitrust laws and regulations, the EEC Commission has prohibited certain practices of suppliers, such as parallel import restrictions and other forms of export-import restrictions established in distributorship agreements.

Next, consider, with a critical eye, the draft distributorship agreement below. As an aid to your analysis, refer to the Notes and Questions following the draft agreement.

DISTRIBUTORSHIP AGREEMENT

THIS AGREEMENT, made in Philadelphia, Pennsylvania, U.S.A. this _____ day of _____, 1990, by and between BOILO, INC. (hereinafter "MANUFAC-TURER"), a company organized and existing under the laws of the State of Pennsylvania U.S.A., and ARGEN, A.G. (hereinafter "DISTRIBUTOR"), a corporation organized and existing under the laws of the Federal Republic of Germany,

WITNESSETH:

WHEREAS, DISTRIBUTOR desires to sell and distribute certain models of the Products hereinafter described in accordance with the terms and conditions hereof;

NOW, THEREFORE, in consideration of the mutual promises contained herein and other good and valuable consideration, the receipt and sufficiency of which is hereby acknowledged, the parties hereto agree as follows:

---

[2] Directive 86/653, O.J.L. 382/17, December 31, 1986. For discussion of the directive, see Guy-Martial Weijer, Ed., Commercial Agency and Distribution Agreements: Law and Practice in the Member States of the European Community (1989).

ARTICLE I - DEFINITIONS

For the purpose of this Agreement:

A. The term "Products" shall mean the products manufactured by MANUFAC-TURER and catalogued in MANUFACTURER's literature, together with certain service equipment.

B. The term "Person" shall mean any natural person, corporation, company, partnership or other association.

C. The expression "Term of This Agreement" shall mean a period of three and one-half (3-1/2) years beginning on the date first above written and ending three and one-half (3-1/2) years after such date or upon termination of this Agreement in accordance with Article VIII hereof, whichever first occurs.

ARTICLE II — GRANT OF RIGHTS

(2.1) MANUFACTURER hereby grants to DISTRIBUTOR the exclusive right to sell and distribute the Products throughout the Federal Republic of Germany for the Term of this Agreement.

(2.2) DISTRIBUTOR agrees that it shall not, during the Term of this Agreement, manufacture, use or sell any products within the field of this Agreement other than sale or use of the Products to the extent specifically authorized herein.

ARTICLE III — PERFORMANCE BY DISTRIBUTOR

(3.1) DISTRIBUTOR hereby agrees to purchase from MANUFACTURER 100 percent of DISTRIBUTOR's requirements for the Products during the Term of this Agreement, provided that DISTRIBUTOR agrees to purchase not less than the following quantities:

First 18 months following
the date of execution of
this Agreement: _____

Next 12 months: _____

Next 12 months: _____

(3.2) DISTRIBUTOR agrees to place an initial order for not less than 2,000 units of the Products within thirty (30) days from the date of execution of this Agreement.

(3.3) DISTRIBUTOR agrees to use its best efforts to promote the sale and use of the Products throughout the Federal Republic of Germany.

ARTICLE IV - PURCHASE OF PRODUCTS

(4.1) Each order for the Products shall be submitted to MANUFACTURER at its office in Philadelphia, Pennsylvania, U.S.A., or at such other place as MANU-FACTURER may direct by notice to DISTRIBUTOR.

(4.2) Each order placed by DISTRIBUTOR shall be for no less than one full container shipment, and shall be placed three months in advance.

(4.3) The prices for the Products shall be MANUFACTURER's price in U.S. dollars as set forth in the attached price list, said prices subject to change by MANUFACTURER on July 1 of each year within the term of this Agreement, beginning July 1, 1990.

(4.4) Payment by DISTRIBUTOR shall be made by bill of exchange, 45 days from date of shipment.

ARTICLE V - SERVICE AND MARKETING ASSISTANCE

(5.1) MANUFACTURER shall provide to DISTRIBUTOR, at no cost, operating and installation instruction manuals to accompany each unit of the Products sold to DISTRIBUTOR hereunder, which DISTRIBUTOR shall provide to its customers.

(5.2) MANUFACTURER agrees to sell to DISTRIBUTOR, at DISTRIBUTOR's request, spare parts for the Products at MANUFACTURER's published list prices in the Federal Republic of Germany. The provisions of Article IV hereof shall govern shipment of and payment for spare parts.

(5.3) MANUFACTURER shall provide to DISTRIBUTOR, at no cost, sufficient manuals per Contract Year, containing instructions for the maintenance and repair of the Products.

ARTICLE VI — WARRANTIES AND LIABILITY

(6.1) MANUFACTURER hereby warrants that the Products which MANUFACTURER sells to DISTRIBUTOR will be free from defects in material and workmanship for a period of twelve (12) months from the date of shipment by DISTRIBUTOR to its customer; provided that this warranty shall not apply to any defects resulting from normal wear and tear, improper or unreasonable use, or improper installation.

(6.2) The sole obligation of MANUFACTURER under this warranty is expressly limited to replacement or repair of defective Products or parts or components thereof.

(6.3) THIS WARRANTY IS EXPRESSLY IN LIEU OF ANY OTHER EXPRESS OR IMPLIED WARRANTIES, INCLUDING ANY IMPLIED WARRANTY OF MERCHANTABILITY OR FITNESS FOR ANY PARTICULAR PURPOSE, WITH RESPECT TO ANY PRODUCT SOLD BY MANUFACTURER UNDER THIS AGREEMENT.

(6.4) Neither MANUFACTURER nor DISTRIBUTOR shall make any agreements, representations or warranties in the name of or on behalf of the other, and neither MANUFACTURER nor DISTRIBUTOR shall be obligated by or have any liability under any agreements, representations or warranties made by the other, nor shall MANUFACTURER be obligated for any damages to any person or property directly or indirectly arising out of the use or sale of the Products by DISTRIBUTOR or any other person.

ARTICLE VII — ASSIGNMENT, SUBLEASE AND TRANSFER

(7.1) No assignment or sublicensing of this Agreement, either in whole or in part, or of any of the rights or obligations hereunder, may be made by

DISTRIBUTOR without the prior written consent of MANUFACTURER, which consent may be withheld by MANUFACTURER in its absolute discretion.

ARTICLE VIII - TERMINATION

(8.1) This Agreement shall continue in force from the date hereof for a period of three and one-half (3-1/2) years, unless sooner terminated pursuant to the provisions of this Article, and shall be automatically renewable provided that DISTRIBUTOR has fully performed all of its obligations hereunder.

(8.2) During the initial three and one-half (3-1/2) years, this Agreement may be terminated at any time during such period by either party without cause upon the expiration of ninety (90) days after written notice to the other party.

(8.3) If DISTRIBUTOR shall default in the performance or observance of any of its obligations under this Agreement, including purchase of the Products under Article III or timely payment therefor under Article IV hereof, and such default shall continue for sixty (60) days after notice specifying such default has been sent to DISTRIBUTOR by MANUFACTURER, MANUFACTURER may terminate this Agreement, at its option, by notice in writing to DISTRIBUTOR, such termination to take effect upon expiration of the sixty (60) day period.

(8.4) If MANUFACTURER shall default in performance or observance of any of its obligations under this Agreement, and such default shall continue for sixty (60) days after notice specifying such default has been sent to MANUFAC-TURER, DISTRIBUTOR may terminate this Agreement by notice in writing to MANUFACTURER, such termination to take effect on expiry of the sixty (60) day period.

(8.5) MANUFACTURER may terminate this Agreement at any time by written notice to DISTRIBUTOR, if DISTRIBUTOR shall discontinue business or become bankrupt or insolvent, or apply for or consent to the appointment of a trustee, receiver, or liquidator of its assets, or seek relief similar to the foregoing under the laws of the Federal Republic of Germany; or if shares representing a majority of the voting power of DISTRIBUTOR or substantially all of the assets of DISTRIBUTOR are transferred to or acquired by any person or persons other than the present shareholders of DISTRIBUTOR.

(8.6) Termination of this Agreement for any cause shall not release DISTRIBU-TOR from its obligations to pay MANUFACTURER for any Products sold to DISTRIBUTOR prior to such termination nor from any other obligations incurred as a result of operations conducted under this Agreement.

ARTICLE IX - ARBITRATION

(9.1) All disputes arising in connection with this Agreement shall be finally settled by arbitration in New York under the Rules of the American Arbitration Association.

ARTICLE X - NOTICE

(10.1) Any written notice or statement required or desired to be given by either party to the other shall be by airmail postage prepaid or by telex, telegram or cable.

(10.2) Notice given by airmail shall be effective upon receipt. Notice given by telex, telegram or cable shall be effective upon the dispatch or transmission of same.

ARTICLE XI - MISCELLANEOUS

(11.1) No delay or omission of MANUFACTURER to enforce any of the covenants, terms or stipulations contained in this Agreement shall be construed as a waiver thereof. No waiver by MANUFACTURER of any breach of this Agreement shall be effective unless it be in writing and signed by an authorized officer of MANUFACTURER. No waiver of any breach shall be construed or deemed to be a waiver of any other or subsequent breach.

(11.2) If any provision of this Agreement shall be determined to be void by any court of competent jurisdiction, such determination shall not affect any other provision of this Agreement, all of which provisions shall remain in full force and effect: Provided, however, that in the event of any such court determination which materially affects MANUFACTURER's rights hereunder, MANUFACTURER shall have the right to terminate this Agreement by written notice to DISTRIBUTOR.

(11.3) Neither party hereto is to be considered the agent of the other party, for any purpose whatsoever, and neither party has any authority to enter into any contracts or assume any obligations for the other party or make any warranties or representations on behalf of the other party.

(11.4) This Agreement shall be governed by and construed in accordance with the laws of the State of Pennsylvania, U.S.A. The English language text of this Agreement shall be the authorized text for all purposes.

In witness whereof, the parties hereto have caused this Agreement to be duly executed as of the date first above written.

BOILO, INC.

By: _____   Date:_____

ARGEN, A.G.

By: _____   Date:_____

GERMAN STATUTES RELEVANT TO DISTRIBUTORSHIP AGREEMENTS

Commercial Code Section 84 [Definition]

(1) **A commercial agent is one who as an independent conductor of a business is consistently entrusted with acting as intermediary for another entrepreneur in transactions or in concluding them in the latter's name.**

One is "independent" who basically can freely regulate his own activity and determine his own hours of work.

* * * *

Commercial Code Section 89 [Cancellation]

(1) If the contractual relation is entered into for an unspecified time it can be cancelled in the first three years of the duration of the contract on six weeks' notice at the end of a calendar quarter. If a different period of notice is agreed on it must amount to a month at least; it can only be cancelled at the end of a calendar month.

(2) After a three-year duration of the contract the contractual relation can only be terminated upon at least three months' notice at the end of a calendar quarter.

(3) An agreed upon period of notice must be the same for both parties. If unequal notice is agreed upon the longer period is effective for both parties.

Commercial Code Section 89a [Cancellation for Important Cause]

(1) The contract relations can be cancelled by either party for important cause without observing any notice period. This right cannot be excluded or limited.

(2) If the cancellation is caused by conduct, for which the other side is responsible, the latter is obligated to make good the damage caused by the termination of the contract relation.

Commercial Code Section 89b [Claim for Settlement]

(1) The commercial agent can demand of the entrepreneur, after the termination of the contractual relationship, a suitable settlement, if and insofar as:

1. The entrepreneur has derived significant advantages from the business relationship with new customers, whom the commercial agent has obtained, even after the termination of the contractual relationship,

2. The commercial agent as a result of the termination of the contractual relationship loses claims to compensation which he would have had, if it had continued, from transactions already concluded with the customers obtained by him or from transactions to have arisen with them in the future, and

3. The payment of a settlement is fair considering all the circumstances. It is equivalent to obtaining a new client if the commercial agent has extended the business relation with a customer so substantially that this economically corresponds to the obtaining of a new customer.

(2) The settlement amounts at the most to an annual compensation or other annual payment calculated on the basis of the average of the last five

years of activity of the commercial agent; in case of a shorter duration of the contract the average during the term of the activity is controlling.

(3) The claim does not exist if the commercial agent has cancelled the contractual relationship without the entrepreneur's conduct having given an adequate basis therefor. The same is true if the entrepreneur cancelled the contractual relationship and there existed for the cancellation an important reason because of the delinquency of the commercial agent.

* * * *

(4) The claim cannot be excluded by advance agreement. . . .

Commercial Code Section 90a [Agreement not to Compete]

(1) An agreement which limits the commercial agent in his business activity after the end of the contractual relationship (agreement not to compete) must be in writing and requires the delivery to the commercial agent of a copy signed by the entrepreneur containing the agreed upon conditions. The Agreement can only be made for, at the longest, two years from the end of the contractual relationship. The entrepreneur is obligated to pay the commercial agent an appropriate compensation for the term of the restraint on competition. . . .

(4) Agreements deviating from the above to the disadvantage of the commercial representative cannot be made.

Commercial Code Section 92c [Commercial Agent Abroad]

(1) If the commercial agent has no branch within the country an agreement can be made contravening all of the prescriptions of this section. . . .

Introduction to the Civil Code Section 30

The application of a foreign law is not permitted if the application would be contra bonos mores, or contrary to the object of a German law.

Civil Code Section 134

A Jural act which is contrary to a statutory prohibition is void, unless a contrary intention appears from the statute.

NOTES AND QUESTIONS

(1) Assume that products are lost at sea during a violent storm. Which party to the distributorship agreement bears the risk of such loss? What result if the products are damaged in storage in the United States while awaiting shipment? Or suppose that the Common Market imposes a high tariff or a quota on the importation of Manufacturer's products. Which party bears the burden of the

increased cost or the reduced number of items imported? Would it make any difference if the source of the loss was United States export controls or limits on manufacture due to scarcity of materials? Can one find the answer to these questions in the terms of the distributorship agreement?

Suppose the draft distributorship agreement had provisions along the lines set forth below,[3] would these help in answering the questions in the preceding paragraph? Would they be satisfactory from the perspective of the manufacturer? From the perspective of the distributor? How would you redraft them?

> Manufacturer shall in good faith supply requirements of distributor for products and make shipments promptly in accordance with Distributor's orders. Whenever Manufacturer shall deliver to a common carrier any products ordered by Distributor, Manufacturer shall not be responsible for any delays or damages in shipment. Distributor may specify the routing as well as consignees for shipments ordered, but in all cases billings shall be directed to Distributor by Manufacturer.

> Distributor shall purchase products from Manufacturer F.O.B. its plant at Philadelphia, Pennsylvania, at such United States dollar prices as are scheduled in Manufacturer's export price list, payable in United States currency and upon terms of payment net 30 days from date of invoice with a ____% distributorship discount from list price.

(2) Compare Article I(c) of the draft distributorship agreement with Article VIII(8.1). Any problems?

(3) Note that under Article II(2.1), Boilo grants to Argen the exclusive right to distribute the products throughout the Federal Republic of Germany. Suppose Boilo enters into a distributorship arrangement with a distributor in France knowing that the French distributor intends to export some of the products to Germany? Has Boilo violated its agreement with Argen?

(4) With respect to Article VI's provisions on warranties and disclaimers it should be noted that Germany has ratified the United Nations Convention on Contracts for the International Sale of Goods, discussed in Chapter 1. Accordingly, Articles 35 and 36 of the Convention would apply.[4] While on the face of

---

[3] These provisions are taken, in slightly revised form, from Moore, *Agreements For The Transmission Of Technology Abroad: The Distributor Relationship*, 45 Denver L.J. 43, 60 (1968).

[4] These Articles provide as follows:

Article 35. (1) The seller must deliver goods which are of the quantity, quality and description required by the contract and which are contained or packaged in the manner required by the contract.

(2) Except where the parties have agreed otherwise, the goods do not conform with the contract unless they:

(a) are fit for the purposes for which goods of the same description would ordinarily be used;

(b) are fit for any particular purpose expressly or impliedly made known to the seller at the time of the conclusion of the contract, except where the circumstances show that the buyer did not rely, or that it was unreasonable for him to rely, on the seller's skill and judgment.

(c) possess the qualities of goods which the seller has held out to the buyer as a

it Article 35 covers much the same ground as UCC Sections 2-313 through 2-315, it does not explicitly draw a distinction between express and implied warranties. Because of this and because the Convention will undoubtedly be read by courts in different countries against the background of very different legal traditions concerning warranties, great care will have to be taken by those courts if the Convention's goal of uniformity is to be achieved in this important area. What is critical, of course, is that the American lawyer cannot, in spite of the facial similarities between Article 35 and the UCC, rely on the Convention being interpreted in accordance with American traditions under the UCC if the issue ends up in a foreign court. As already suggested in Chapter 1, the question arises whether a court in the United States or elsewhere will honor a choice of law clause selecting the law of the other applicable state party to the Convention if its attention is brought to the possibility of a disparate interpretation by the courts of that state.

(5) Note further the disclaimer of warranties in Article 6.3 of the draft distributorship agreement. This was obviously drafted to meet the requirements laid down by Section 2-316 of the UCC. Should the Convention become applicable to that agreement, its *substantive* validity will, by reason of Article 4(a) of the Convention, continue to be controlled by the applicable domestic law.[5] Hence a choice of law clause remains an important provision of the agreement. As already noted, however, there is some dispute over whether the requirements as to the form of the disclaimer set out in Section 2-316 of the UCC will continue to apply.[6]

(6) Evaluate the termination provisions in Article VIII of the draft distributorship agreement. Are they consistent with the German Statutes reproduced above? Do these statutes apply to the draft distributorship agreement? Does Article XI (Section 11.4) of the draft distributorship agreement resolve any problems? See in this connection Note 8 below.

(7) In considering the German statutes reproduced above, it should be noted that, while these statutes protect "commercial agents," they do not specifically

---

sample or model;
    (d) are contained or packaged in the manner usual for such goods, or, where there is no such manner, in a manner adequate to preserve and protect the goods.
(3) The seller is not liable under subparagraphs (a) to (d) of the preceding paragraph for any lack of conformity of the goods if at the time of the conclusion of the contract the buyer knew or could not have been unaware of such lack of conformity.
Article 36. (1) The seller is liable in accordance with the contract and this Convention for any lack of conformity which exists at the time when the risk passes to the buyer, even though the lack of conformity becomes apparent only after that time.
(2) The seller is also liable for any lack of conformity which occurs after the time indicated in the preceding paragraph and which is due to a breach of any of his obligations, including a breach of any guarantee that for a period of time the goods will remain fit for their ordinary purpose for some particular purpose or will retain specified qualities or characteristics.
[5] Hyland, *Conformity Of Goods To The Contract Under the United Nations Sales Convention And The Uniform Commercial Code*, in Einheitliches Kaufrecht und nationales Obligationenrecht (Schlechtriem, Hrsg.), Nomos Verlagsgesellschaft, Baden-Baden, (1987) at page 313.
[6] See § 1.01 , note 16 and accompanying text.

refer to, and there are, at this writing, no German legislative provisions governing, distributorship agreements. However, the German Supreme Court has ruled that these provisions apply by way of analogy to exclusive distributorships. *Judgment of April 5, 1962.*[7] Query whether the ruling would be the same in the case of a non-exclusive distributorship agreement.

In Belgium, statutory provisions regarding distributors are applicable only if the arrangement is exclusive, quasi-exclusive, or has an indefinite duration. Belgian courts, moreover, will "stretch" their construction of a distributorship agreement to find it exclusive or quasi-exclusive or of indefinite duration. These provisions are often applied by analogy to agents as well as to distributors.

(8) The German Courts have handed down decisions relevant to termination of distributorship agreements. In particular, in the *Decision of 30 January 1961,*[8] a German plaintiff had acted as general representative in the Federal Republic and West Berlin for defendant, a Netherlands Corporation, which produced bathing suits and knitted garments. The German Supreme Court held plaintiff was not entitled to a settlement from defendant under Commercial Code Section 89b when the contract between them provided that all litigation involving the contract was to be brought in a Netherlands court and that Netherlands law should govern all legal relations between the parties arising from the contract. The Court rejected plaintiff's contention that application of Netherlands law in this instance would be *contra bonos mores* or contrary to the object of a German law within the meaning of Section 30 of the Introduction to the German Civil Code or a juristic act contrary to a statutory prohibition under Section 134 of the German Civil Code. The court also rejected plaintiff's argument *ex contrario* based on Commercial Code Section 92c that with respect to a commercial agent with a domestic branch an agreement for foreign law and a foreign forum is ineffective because of the mandatory nature of Commercial Code Section 89b.

In early decisions German courts were willing to grant a distributor a cancellation settlement under Commercial Code Sec. 89b only if he could show that he was completely dependent upon the principal like a typical commercial agent. If the distributor expended substantial amounts of his own capital during the term of the distributorship, he was not regarded as being "in need of protection." However, the Bundesgerichtshof (The German Supreme Court) recently ruled that the distributor's need for protection is irrelevant to his right to goodwill compensation. This right exists from the moment the relationship between manufacturer and distributor becomes more than a seller-buyer relationship and the distributor is contractually obligated to perform tasks and live up to the standards normally applicable to agents. *Judgment of Feb. 11, 1977.*[9]

(9) A number of countries have laws that limit or circumscribe the termination of distributorship arrangements, and some are more stringent than those of the Federal Republic of Germany. Costa Rica, for example, has a non-waivable statute that mandates an indemnity be paid equal to four months' average gross profit for each year or fraction thereof that the distributor agreement has been in

---

[7] [1962] Der Betriebs Berater 543.
[8] [1961] 2 Neue Juristische Wochenschrift, 1061.
[9] [1977] Neue Juristiche Wochenschrift 896.

force, if a foreign supplier unilaterally terminates or refuses to renew a distributorship agreement for a definite period at the end of the original term.[10] The indemnity can be as high as nine years' average gross profit of the distributor, and the supplier has to repurchase the inventory of the terminated distributor at prices set by the Costa Rican Government. For its part a Costa Rican distributor can terminate a distributorship agreement and claim compensation for a wide variety of reasons. A foreign supplier can terminate without paying compensation only for "just cause," a concept defined narrowly by the statute.

Although this is not the case in Costa Rica, some contractual provisions may avoid or at least mitigate the application of local law protecting the distributor. Some suggested examples include:

(a) The inclusion of a notice period for unilateral termination. Such periods are often required by statute or judicial doctrine.

(b) The insistence by a U.S. manufacturer of the use of the corporate form by foreign distributors.

(c) A contractual provision for the automatic termination of the distributorship agreement one day before the effective date of a new protective statute in the country of the distributor.

(d) A specific contractual list of obligations of a distributor which, if not met, may be used to define "just cause." Such a list may include sales quotas or objectives.

(e) The express waiver by the distributor of the benefits of local protective legislation.

(f) The choice of the law of the country of the foreign manufacturer, or of a third country which does not have protective legislation or judicial doctrine.[11]

(g) The use of an indefinite term, or a specific term. The laws of some countries are by their terms inapplicable to contracts of indefinite term or contracts for a specific term.

(h) The use of a provision that requires that enhancements to the value of a distributor's goodwill inure to the benefit of the foreign supplier.

---

[10] Law for the Protection of Representatives of Foreign Firms, Costa Rican Law No. 6209 of April 3, 1978.

[11] But see: *Southern International Sales v. Potter & Brumfield Division*, 410 F. Supp. 1339 (S.D.N.Y., 1976) refusing to honor the parties' choice of Indiana law to govern a distributorship agreement between an Indiana manufacturing company and its Puerto Rican distributor. Indiana law permitted a principal to terminate a distributorship for any reason whatsoever. The court, relying on Section 187(2)(b) of the Restatement (Second) of Conflicts of Law and the "most significant contacts test", concluded that termination was controlled by the "just cause" requirement of the Puerto Rican Dealer's Contracts Act. Although the equipment sold by the distributor was manufactured in Indiana and shipped from there to Puerto Rico, the court thought that the parties' choice of law "would pale" when seen against the fact that most of the equipment sold by the distributor was sold in Puerto Rico, for Puerto Rican accounts and for use in Puerto Rico after solicitation there and because the distributor signed the contract in Puerto Rico and the application of Indiana law would "frustrate the fundamental policy" of Puerto Rico.

(i)   The use of a provision expressly stipulating that the foreign distributor is neither the employee nor the agent of the U.S. manufacturer.

(j)   The appointment of a non-exclusive distributor. Some foreign termination laws only apply to exclusive distributorships. Furthermore, the right to appoint a second distributor can obviate the necessity of terminating a distributorship agreement in the first place.

(k)   The express provision for the existence and amount of a termination indemnity.[12]

(10) In the United States, the Automobile Dealers Act of 1956,[13] is roughly comparable to the German statutes reproduced above, although it applies only to truck and car dealers resident in the United States, and it is arguable whether they are "in need of protection" in the sense indicated by the German courts.

(11) Read the materials on choice of forum and arbitration, *infra*, Chapter 11. What advantages, if any, are there in submitting disputes arising under the agreement to arbitration? Would Argen be likely to resist Article IX's choice of New York as a place of arbitration? What arguments might Boilo advance to justify such a selection? In light of the adoption by both the United States and the Federal Republic of Germany of the U.N. Convention on Arbitral Awards, Chapter 11, *infra*, should Article IX be redrafted to improve its enforceability?

(12) An important consideration in the drafting of a distributorship agreement is the tax implications. In particular, the question arises whether Boilo might be subject to German taxes on the sale of its products by Argen. Here the Convention Between the United States and the Federal Republic of Germany for the Avoidance of Double Taxation with Respect to Taxes on Income[14] comes into play. Article III of that Convention, in pertinent part, provides that "industrial or commercial profits of an enterprise of one of the Contracting States shall be exempt from tax by the other State unless the enterprise is engaged in trade or business in such other State through a permanent establishment therein." Under Article II(1)(c)(ee) of the Convention, "[a]n enterprise of one of the Contracting States shall not be deemed to have a permanent establishment in the other State merely because it is engaged in trade or business in that other State through a broker, general commission agent or any other agent of an independent status, where such person is acting in the ordinary course of business."

It might also be possible for Boilo to minimize United States taxes on these earnings by the use of a Foreign Sales Corporation (FSC). (See discussion Chapter 5 pages 424-428 *infra*.)

(13) Consider, from the perspective of a counsel for Boilo, the provisions of Article III, Section 3.3 and Article IV, Sections 4.3 and 4.4. Are they satisfactory? If not, how would you redraft them?

(14) Local law may limit the ability of a supplier to appoint a distributor the exclusive seller of its goods. For example, French law requires that exclusive distributorships be for a period of no more than ten years.

---

[12] Lake, *Foreign Business Organization*, 1 The Law Of Transnational Business Transactions 2-30 (V.P. Nanda, ed. 1987).
[13] 15 U.S.C.A. Sections 1221-1225.
[14] Signed at Washington, July 22, 1954, U.S.T. & O.I. 2768, T.I.A.S. No. 3133.

(15) Deliberately omitted from the draft distributorship agreement, for purposes of illustration of its need, but an important provision in distributorship arrangements is a force majeure clause. Such a clause might read, for example, along the following lines:

> Neither party hereto shall be liable to the other on account of any loss, damage or delay occasioned or caused by strikes, riots, fire, insurrection, war, peril of the seas, embargoes, failure of carriers, compliance with any law, regulation or other governmental order, import or export prohibitions or other causes beyond the reasonable control of the affected party, despite its best efforts to insure performance of all its obligations hereunder.

(16) An equally important provision omitted from the draft distributorship agreement is a clause along the following lines:

> Distributor represents and agrees that it has not offered, given, promised to give or authorized giving, and will not offer, give, promise to give or authorize giving, directly or indirectly, any money or anything else of value to any government official, political party, political official or candidate for political office in connection with its activities hereunder.

Such a provision is advisable because of the U.S. Foreign Corrupt Practices Act, which requires U.S. suppliers to ensure that those who act on their behalf do not engage in bribes or other forms of corrupt activity. Another advisable step to assure compliance with the FCPA is to exercise care in checking distributor references and reputations.

(17) Missing from the draft distributorship agreement above but, depending upon the particular circumstances, worthy of consideration for possible inclusion are provisions regarding liability for local taxes, the right of the manufacturer to repurchase a distributor's inventory upon termination, trademarks and patents, freight, insurance, handling and other similar costs, product liability, and import and export procedures.[15] Also in drafting a distributorship agreement one must be especially cognizant of the importance of the local law of the distributors country.[16]

---

[15] For examples of distributorship agreements see 3 W.P. Streng & J.W. Salacuse, *International Business Planning: Law and Taxation Appendix 11B (1988)*; 1 The Law of Transnational Business Transactions 2-31 V.P. Nanda, ed. (1987).

[16] For a look at the laws of several countries, see Puelinck & Tielemans, *The Termination Of Agency And Distributorship Agreements: A Comparative Survey*, 3 Nw. J. Int'l L. & Bus. 452 (1981). For further reading on distributorship arrangements, see *e.g.*, Graupner, Sole Distributorship Agreements — A Comparative View, 18 Int. & Comp. L.Q. 879 (1969); Burkard, Termination Compensation To Distributors Under German Law, 7 Int'l Law. 185 (1973); Juncadella, Agency, Distribution And Representative Contracts In Central America And Panama, 6 Law. Am. 35 (1974); Carbonneau, Exclusive Distributorship Agreements in French Law, 28 Int. & Comp. L.Q. 91 (1979); King, Legal Aspects Of Appointment And Termination Of Foreign Distributors And Representatives, 17 Case W. Res. J. Int'l L. 91 (1984); Vorbrugg & Mahler, Agency And Distribution Agreements Under German Law, 19 Int'l Law 607 (1985); Herold & Knoll, Negotiating And Drafting International Distribution, Agency, And Representative Agreements: The United States Exporter's Perspective, 21 Int'l Law. 939 (1987); Nelson, Selling from the United States to Japan: Representation, Sales and Distribution Agreements with Japanese Businesses, 2 Int'l Q. 31 (1990).

§ 2.03   The Transfer of Technology

Streng and Salacuse have aptly defined "technology" and the role it may play in an international business transaction as follows:

> [Technology] includes not only scientific and industrial knowledge which is protected by a patent, but also unpatented know-how necessary for the organization, operation and management of industrial, agricultural, or other economic activities. Closely related to technology are trademarks, which are necessary or at least useful in marketing a particular good or service produced by virtue of the exported technology. Thus, the export of the technology for manufacturing widgets may include the patented rights to produce the widget itself, the unpatented know-how for organizing and managing a widget factory, and the trademark under which the widget will be marketed.[1]

The transfer of technology — which includes, among other things, transactions between parties that have as one of their purposes the licensing or assignment of industrial property rights, the sale or any other type of transfer of technical knowledge, and the supply of technical services — has become an issue in a great number of international forums and in the context of diverse subject matters. For example, transfer of technology issues have arisen in the ten year deliberations on the law of the sea, in debates over the law of outer space, and in general discussions on trade and investment in United Nations bodies and are a major area of negotiation in the current Uruguay Round of the GATT.

In this Section our focus is more narrowly confined to arrangements by which technology is transferred pursuant to licensing agreements. Of particular concern to the parties to a licensing agreement are national and international arrangements for the protection of trademarks and patents. We explore these arrangements in the first two subsections below. In the last two subsections we turn to special problems in drafting a license agreement and in structuring franchising arrangements.

[A]   International Licensing of Technology

Licensing is an increasingly popular method of exploiting technology in a foreign country. There are, of course, other means available for such exploitation. An American business may simply export its products. However, the cost of transportation, import and export regulatory barriers, or the nature of the product may make exporting difficult. Or, as we consider in Chapter 8, an American business might decide to set up a manufacturing operation abroad for the sale of goods. Here, too, the problems may be formidable. A firm may not want to expose its capital to the risks of such an investment abroad, and the difficulties in maintaining an adequate staff may be considerable. Also, some countries require a foreign firm operating locally to meet "working requirements" for technology sharing in order to gain governmental assent to do business in the national market. Under these conditions, licensing may be the only way for a firm to operate internationally.

---

[1] 3 W. P. Streng & J.W. Salacuse, International Business Planning: Law And Taxation Sec. 12.01, 12-2 (1988).

Yet, licensing is not a sure method of avoiding restraints. Foreign governments increasingly intervene in licensing arrangements, and the entire agreement may be subject to governmental approval (for example, in Latin America and Japan). Moreover, developing country governments often place severe limitations on the repatriation of royalties.

Recently, developing countries have been pressing hard in international forums for a variety of restraints on technology transfers. Many of these demands have called for radical changes in the terms of international protection for trademarks and patents, and we shall explore these below. Some of the more sweeping attacks on current arrangements have taken place in the United Nations Conference on Trade and Development (UNCTAD), which is attempting to draft an International Code of Conduct on Transfer of Technology.[2] At this time the code is still in the drafting stage.

By definition licenses have restrictive effects on international trade and business. As we shall see *infra*, in Chapter 7, some of the restraints associated with the use of patents may attract the attention of United States or foreign antitrust authorities. Other restraints arising out of licensing agreements may be rejected by the authorities of the licensee's country. These problems we consider in Subsection C.

[B] International Protection of Trademarks and Patents

Trademarks and patents constitute the primary form of intellectual property involved in international business transactions. After a brief discussion of trademarks, we will consider the elaborate legal framework that has developed with respect to the international protection of patents.

Trademarks

The twin purposes of a trademark are to identify the source of the products to which it is affixed and to assure consumers that products bearing the same trademark issue from a common source. When a trademark and a manufacturer have a common name, *e.g.*, Coca Cola, the mark serves both purposes. Well established trademarks may also connote quality, efficiency and reliability ("good-will").

In protecting trademarks, the law grants a limited monopoly to the owner over a word or symbol. The owner alone is authorized to employ it to designate a particular product. Trademark protection has its roots in the common law tort of unfair competition or "passing off." At common law the tort might consist of imitating an organization's mark or copying the shape or manner of packaging a product. However, towards the beginning of the twentieth century, the common law in the United States was largely supplanted by federal legislation, primarily the Trademark Act of 1905. The current legislation is the Lanham Act of 1946.[3]

Under the Lanham Act, the Patent Office maintains a register of trademarks. The proper registration of a trademark allows its owner to exercise rights against

---

[2] For drafts of this effort, see 17 Int'l Legal Mat. 453 (1978); U.N. Doc. TD/Code, TOT/33 (April 10, 1981).

[3] 60 Stat. 427, as amended, 15 U.S.C.A. sections. 1051-1127.

infringement upon the mark. Enforcement of these rights may be through litigation in the federal courts, which can grant various kinds of remedies, including changes in the register, issuance of injunctions, or monetary relief, either in the amount of the damages suffered by the trademark holder or of the profits made from the infringing activity.

In addition, Section 526 of the Tariff Act of 1930[4] provides that it is unlawful to import merchandise bearing a registered trademark:

> . . . owned by a citizen of, or by a corporation or association . . . organized within the United States . . . unless written consent of the owner of such trademark is produced.

Section 526 also authorizes the Customs Service to seize goods imported in violation of that Section. If, after seizure, the U.S. trademark owner does not consent to importation of the goods, they are forfeit. For some time a controversy has existed with regard to the scope of this provision as applied to the so-called "gray-market" problem. "Gray-market" goods are genuine goods manufactured and trademarked abroad by the owner or licensee of a trademark registered in a foreign country so that their sale abroad is perfectly legal. They are not counterfeit goods. Then, bearing that mark, which is identical to the U.S. trademark, they are imported into the United States by someone — frequently a discount house — who is not the owner or licensee of the U.S. trademark owner and are sold in competition with goods marketed by the latter. While the imported product is the genuine article, and in this respect the consumer is not deceived, concern has been expressed that the importer is free riding on the good will built-up by the holder of the U.S. trademark. Also, the importer may not stand ready to provide the same warranty or other service that consumers may have come to associate with the trademarked product. To preserve that reputation the holder of the U.S. mark will sometimes meet its usual warranty or other service obligations even though it was not compensated through the sale of the product. If this seems unfair, it is also possible that by excluding imports of these otherwise genuine articles the holder of the U.S. trademark can preserve such monopoly power as it might have in the American market.

The Supreme Court in *K Mart Corporation v. Cartier, Inc.*[5] upheld Customs Service Regulations under which "gray market" goods would be exempt from seizure under Section 526 if the holder of the U.S. trademark was the subsidiary, the parent or the same company as the foreign manufacturer. The Court also upheld the Regulations calling for seizure if the U.S. trademark holder had purchased the U.S. mark from an independent foreign manufacturer. Finally, the Court invalidated the Customs Regulations in so far as they exempted "gray-market" goods from seizure where the holder of the U.S. trademark had authorized the foreign manufacturer to use the mark in one or more foreign countries.

Like patents, trademarks are basically territorial. The international attorney must therefore examine the laws of each country where a client might use the trademark to ascertain who can obtain a trademark within a territory and what protections are afforded such a mark. The requirements of individual countries

---

[4] 19 U.S.C. Section 1526.
[5] 486 U.S. 281, 108 S. Ct. 1811 (1988).

vary widely, especially with respect to registration or use within the territory. However, all countries allow a mark to be renewed indefinitely if there is use of the mark, and since trademarks may have unlimited terms, they often outlive any patent. Accordingly, an agreement for the licensing of trademarks should contain clauses clearly specifying how the trademark license will terminate. Such clauses should also provide that all advertising material, literature and signs will be returned to the licensor when the agreement terminates.

An increasingly frequent problem is the counterfeiting of trademarks. Potential licensors, therefore, should be aware of the source of counterfeit merchandise. Counterfeiting is especially prevalent in the Far East; investigative services in Hong Kong can run a check on the reputation of a prospective licensee.

Some mitigation of the problems created by diversity among national laws on trademarks is afforded by treaties. For example, the United States is a party to numerous bilateral Treaties of Friendship, Commerce and Navigation which set down general principles with respect to obtaining and protecting patents, trademarks, tradenames and other industrial property. The most important of these principles is that of "national treatment" which assures nationals and companies of one contracting party national treatment with respect to trademarks in the other party's territory.[6] The United States has also entered into bilateral treaties devoted specifically to trademarks.[7]

The International Convention for the Protection of Industrial Property, originally signed in Paris in 1883, and last revised in Stockholm in 1967[8] (the Paris Convention), is the primary multilateral convention relevant to the international dimension of trademarks as well as patents. As of January 1, 1988, the United States and 97 other countries were parties to the Paris Convention, which we consider in greater detail in the next subsection on patents. With respect to trademarks, the Paris Convention guarantees national treatment for owners from treaty countries and protects foreign registrations of trademarks by allowing a domestic application — if filed within six months — to be dated back to the date of the foreign filing. Article 6 *bis* of the Paris convention allows the cancellation at any time of a fraudulently obtained mark.

The Nice Agreement, as revised, Concerning the International Classification of Goods and Services for the Purposes of the Registration of Marks,[9] which entered into force for the United States on February 29, 1984, provides a single classification system for the registration of marks, thus bringing a measure of uniformity to national administrative procedures previously noted for their diversity. On a regional basis the United States is a party, with several Latin American countries, to the General Inter-American Convention of 1920.[10] This Convention is closely modeled after the Paris Convention.

---

[6] See, *e.g.*, Article X of Treaty of Friendship, Commerce and Navigation, April 2, 1953, United States-Japan, 4 U.S.T. 2063, T.I.A.S. No. 2863.

[7] See, *e.g.*, Declaration Affording Reciprocal Protection to Trademarks, Oct. 24, 1877, United States-United Kingdom, 20 Stat. 703, T.S. No. 138.

[8] 13 U.S.T. 1, T.I.A.S. No. 4031, as Revised, July 14, 1967; 21 U.S.T. 1583, T.I.A.S. No. 6923.

[9] — U.S.T. — , T.I.A.S. No. —.

[10] 46 Stat. 2907, T.S. No. 833.

The United States does not participate in the so-called Madrid Arrangement of 1891. However, the Arrangement may be utilized by an American attorney if filing a trademark in the name of a European company located in a signatory country. Related to the Paris Convention, the Arrangement provides that a trademark registered in any signatory country may, through the International Office for the Protection of Industrial Property Rights at Berne, Switzerland, also be registered in the trademark offices of all other signatory countries.[11] Also, on December 21, 1988, the European Community adopted the First Directive to approximate the laws of the Member States relating to trademarks.

United States economic regulations applicable to trademarks raise issues of prescriptive jurisdiction along the lines of those discussed *infra* in Chapter 6. For cases where United States courts have had to decide whether U.S. trademark law applies when all or some of the activity takes place abroad, see, *e.g.*, *Steele v. Bulova Watch Co.*[12] and *Vanity Fair Mills, Inc. v. T. Eaton Co.*[13]

Patents

Today's patent laws may be traced at least back to 15th century Venice. In order to encourage innovation and invention among its own citizens, as well as the importation of special skills from abroad, the city granted a monopoly to the maker of any device who could show that (1) the device was constructive and useful, (2) was new, and (3) was inventive. These grants to inventors are today called patents. They constitute an exclusive privilege granted to an inventor to manufacture, use or sell a patented product or to use a patented process. The privilege, however, can only be exercised in accord with conditions prescribed by law that constitute an effort to protect the freedom of commerce and industry and to avoid the creation of an economic, as distinct from a technological, monopoly harmful to the public. Patent laws specify the conditions with which the inventor must comply, fix the duration of the privilege, and impose certain obligations on the patentee.

During the Industrial Revolution of the 19th century, countries underwent industrial transformation at varying paces — with a resultant gap in technology between industrialized and non-industrialized countries. Even in the industrialized countries legal developments took different paths. Although these countries had similar goals — to encourage progress while avoiding excessive restrictions on the freedom of commerce and industry — their legislatures reacted to particular interests in each country and often produced laws in conflict with those of neighboring countries. With the expansion of trade, however, these conflicting laws often meant that foreigners' industrial property rights were not protected.

---

[11] Off. J. of the European Communities, 1989, L40/1. Article 189, of the Rome Treaty provides, "A directive shall be binding, as to the result to be achieved, upon each member state to which it is addressed, but shall leave to the national authorities the choice of form and methods." Under this provision, the implementing legislation — not the directive itself — is the enforceable law within member countries. However, the member country itself is under an obligation to enact such implementing legislation, and in several instances where a member country has failed to do so, the Commission has brought a suit against the country before the European Court of Justice, the judicial organ of the Community.

[12] 344 U.S. 280, 73 S.Ct. 252, 97 L. Ed. 319 (1952).

[13] 234 F.2d 633 (2d Cir. 1956).

Yet, industrial progress, economic growth and improved communication require that they be protected. Foreigners were often discriminated against in favor of nationals in the acquisition and enforcement of those rights. In short, it was at the international level that protection had to be granted if there was going to be a system that would encourage the investment in new ideas and in the creative efforts that social and economic progress required.

Accordingly, we first consider United States patent law as a reference point for the national approach. Then we turn to an examination of the primary international instruments relevant to patents. In so doing, we explore conventions recently concluded in Europe that represent a step beyond those adopted on a worldwide basis.

United States Patent Law

Under Article I, Sec. 8, of the United States Constitution, Congress is authorized "to promote the Progress of Science and the Useful Arts by securing for limited Times to Authors and Inventors the exclusive right to their respective Writings and Discoveries." Pursuant to this authority Congress has adopted patent laws [14] that are illustrative of a highly developed national patent system.

Procedurally, the life of a United States patent may be divided into two periods. During the first period an inventor files a patent application with the patent office on an invention that claims to be new, useful and non-obvious.[15] A patent application is considered complete and is assigned a priority date when it contains a specification, a drawing (when applicable), the required oath, and the requisite filing fee.[16] To be accepted, a specification, at a minimum, must describe at least one specific embodiment of the invention and must conclude with "one or more claims particularly pointing out and distinctly claiming the subject matter which the applicant claims as his invention." These claims, which are brief one-sentence statements describing the inventive concept, establish the parameters of the property right protected by the patent.

An applicant needs to obtain an early priority date, since a patent may issue only to the first inventor. If two inventors describe and claim the same subject matter in their patent application, the Patent Office will call an interference proceeding to determine who is the prior inventor.

Only in the United States may an applicant obtain a filing date earlier than the actual filing date in the patent office, i.e., the date he "conceived" the invention. To obtain thisearly priority date, an applicant must proceed with diligence to reduce his conception to practice, and then to file the patent application.

At the Patent Office, the application is "examined" against the complete body of available technical literature, including United States and foreign patents and technical journals throughout the world. Only after the Patent Office is satisfied that the invention is novel, will a patent be allowed to issue. From that moment, the inventor may prevent others from making, using, or selling the subject matter of his patent for 17 years.

[14] Codified in Title 35 of the United States Code.
[15] 35 U.S.C. Section 101.
[16] 35 U.S.C. Section 111.

After the patent is granted, the second procedural period begins, and the right to exclude others from the property covered by the patent vests. As in the case of trademarks, foreign goods covered by a United States product patent or produced abroad by a process subject to a United States process patent can be barred from importation.[17] The right to exclude encompasses the right to include as well, and when a patentee elects to allow others to exploit his property, he grants a license, usually in exchange for some kind of consideration. The patent may also be sold by formal assignment which is recorded in the Patent Office.

In litigation to prevent infringement of the patent, the patentee has the advantage that his patent is presumed valid. This presumption may be rebutted by the party challenging the patent's validity through a showing that the idea was obvious, that the patentee was not the inventor, that the patent was issued on a non-novel invention, that the patentee was not diligent in filing his application, etc.

Worldwide Conventions on Patents

As already noted, the primary worldwide convention on patents is the Paris Convention for the Protection of Industrial Property (Paris Convention) of March 20, 1883. The Paris Convention covers patents, industrial designs, trademarks, and tradenames and as of January 1, 1988 had 98 parties who form the Paris Union. It does not establish a worldwide patent or trademark registration system. Rather, it requires member countries to follow certain principles in applying their own laws on industrial property, and it simplifies procedures for obtaining protection.

Thus, Article 2(1) of the Convention adopts the principle of "national treatment." This obliges member countries to treat the nationals of other member countries applying for patent or trademark protection no less favorably than their own nationals. It prohibits discrimination against foreigners.

The Convention's second, and most important, principle is the "right of priority." Under Article 4(C)(I) of the Convention, a person who receives a patent or registers a trademark in a member country will have priority over any other applicant filing for the same invention or seeking to register the same trademark in any other state party to the Convention, provided he files his patent claim or registers his mark in the latter country within six months for trademarks and twelve months for patents (*i.e.*, the "period of priority").

Under the patent law of many countries, the prior publication of an invention anywhere in the world prevents an applicant from obtaining a patent, on the ground that the invention is no longer original. The right of priority, however, precludes a state party to the Convention from invoking this objection to the grant of a patent in its own jurisdiction. Within the period of priority an applicant may file for a patent in a state party to the Convention, even if the invention has already received a patent and is in production in another country. In effect, an applicant may use the filing date of his first application in a state party to the Convention as the effective date of all subsequent applications filed in other state parties during the one-year period of priority.

---

[17] Section 337 of the Tariff Act of 1930, 46 Stat. 703, as amended, and 54 Stat. 724 (1940), 19 U.S.C.A. Sections 1337, 1337a.

The World Intellectual Property Organization (WIPO), a specialized agency of the United Nations located in Geneva, Switzerland is charged with carrying out the objectives of the Paris Convention and, as such, functions as the central organ for the development of international industrial property rights. It attempts, through research, educational programs and conferences, to develop a more effective international system for the protection and transfer of intellectual property. Among its activities, WIPO maintains an international registry for trademarks and a depository of industrial designs, provides legal services for countries drafting and revising legislation and treaties on industrial property, and administers a computerized International Patent Documentation Center in Vienna.

It was through efforts by WIPO that the Patent Cooperation Treaty of June 19, 1970[18] was promulgated. As of January 1, 1988, the United States and thirty-nine other states were parties to the treaty, the primary purpose of which is to facilitate international patent filing procedures. Toward this end, the treaty provides, in separate chapters, for two sets of procedures.

Under Chapter I of the treaty, an applicant may file an "international application" that has the effect of a national application in all state parties in which the applicant seeks protection. An applicant does this by filing with one of the national patent offices of Japan, Sweden, the Soviet Union, or the United States, which have been designated International Searching Authorities, as has the European Patent Office at Munich/The Hague. The countries in which the applicant seeks patent protection are referred to as "designated states." The application then undergoes a novelty search conducted by an International Searching Authority. The results of this examination are sent with a copy of the application to the national patent offices of the designated states. The applicant may amend his application, or evaluate whether he wishes to proceed in foreign countries, after reviewing the prior art disclosed by the search. He is given a 20-month period of priority.

The second procedural phase afforded by Chapter II of the treaty is optional in two respects. First, states may become parties to the treaty without accepting this set of procedures. Second, even if a state accepts Chapter II, an applicant from that state may decide for himself whether he wants to take advantage of it. Under Chapter II, an applicant may submit his international application accompanied by the international search report, and any changes made as a result of the report, to an International Preliminary Examining Authority. The Authority will issue a non-binding report on whether the invention meets the criteria for patentability established by the treaty. The findings of the report provide a strong indication of patentability and may be accepted, or at least save time, in the examination process by other states. Thus, the Patent Cooperation Treaty does not create a truly international patent system. The final decision whether to grant a patent is still made by national patent offices rather than by an international body.

Moreover, the patent laws of countries vary considerably. Some regard certain products — such as medicines or food stuffs — as unpatentable. Others provide for a shorter duration of the patent than the 17 years granted by the U.S. Many

---

[18] 28 U.S.T. 7645, T.I.A.S. No. 8733 (PCT).

states insist that the patentee exploit the patent, and provide penalties, such as compulsory licensing or forfeiture, after nonuse for a stated period.

As a result of these varying approaches, a product patented in one country might turn out to be unpatentable elsewhere. Also, courts in one country (including the United States) normally will regard themselves as incompetent to enjoin alleged infringements of foreign patents and will decline to rule on the validity of foreign patents.

Regional Initiatives: The European Patent Convention And The Community Patent Convention

The impetus for the Convention on the Grant of European Patents, commonly called the European Patent Convention (EPC) of October 5, 1973,[19] came from the Commission of the European Communities. The Commission considered the divergencies in national patent laws to be incompatible with the Community goal of creating a single trading unit. To remedy the situation, the Commission established a working group of experts to draft a convention that would centralize application procedures and substantive law throughout Europe. These efforts ultimately produced the European Patent Convention.

The purpose of the European Patent Convention is to rationalize and simplify the procedures for granting patents by enabling a person to file a single patent application in a single language, have it subjected to a single examination procedure, and obtain a patent having the effect of a national patent in some or all (depending on the countries designated by the applicant) of the state parties to the Convention.

Under the Convention, a European patent has a term of twenty years from the date of filing and the effect of a national patent. The Convention, however, does not replace European national patent systems whose substantive law may conflict with the European Patent Convention, although many countries have changed their laws to conform to the Convention. Indeed, Article 64(1) of the Convention provides that the European patent confers upon its holder the same rights as a national patent. This means national courts are competent to hear actions for infringement and decide the case under the national law of the state for which the European patent has been granted.

On the other hand, a European patent is governed by the law of the Convention in certain key areas. For example, as noted above, the European patent has a duration of twenty years from the date of filing. This is true even if the national patent for the designated country has a shorter duration. Also, the scope of protection of a European patent is defined by the Convention under its rules of patentability. (Unless a state party has made a reservation on this point.) Further, a European patent may only be revoked for reasons contained in the Convention. One of the grounds for revoking a European patent is that the invention is not patentable under Articles 52 to 57 of the Convention. A national court deciding the validity of a European patent will look to these provisions and disregard national law.

---

[19] Reprinted in Common Mkt. Rpt. (CCH) Par. 5503-5790L (May 7, 1974).

The entire procedure for the grant of a European patent is carried out by a single entity, the European Patent Office (EPO). The EPO is located in Munich, Germany, with a branch office in The Hague, The Netherlands. No national patent offices participate in the grant proceedings — the EPO grants a single patent and publishes only a single specification.

Americans filing in Europe can take advantage of this procedure under the Patent Cooperation Treaty by designating the EPO instead of individual countries in the application. Under the Patent Cooperation Treaty this converts the application into a European Patent Application.

There is, in addition, the European Community Patent Convention (Community Patent Convention).[20] When that convention goes into effect, it will go beyond the European Patent Convention by creating a unitary patent for all EEC countries.[21] A Community Patent will have the same effect in member states regardless of national law, and will be subject only to the provisions of the Convention. In this regard a Community Patent resembles a United States patent that takes effect in 50 States. Products protected by the Community Patent may circulate freely in all member states once they have been put on the market in one of them. Patents may be granted, transferred, revoked, or allowed to lapse only with respect to all of the Community countries. For a transitional period, however, an applicant for a patent will have a choice between a Community Patent and a European Patent that may designate only one or two member states. Moreover, the Community Patent Convention does not replace the national patent laws of the contracting states. States may maintain national law concurrently with the Community Patent Convention. But an inventor who has both a Community Patent and a national patent cannot have simultaneous protection. Under Article 80 of the Convention, where both a national patent and a Community Patent have been granted to the same inventor for the same invention, with the same priority date, the Community Patent prevails on the date it is granted.

Under Article 69 of the Convention, national courts are competent to deal with patent infringement actions. However, if infringement is based on rights conferred by a published Community Patent application, and patentability of the invention is contested, the national court must suspend the action until the European Patent Office decides whether to grant a Community Patent. Under Article 73(2), a national court may suspend an infringement action at the request of one of the parties if an application for a revocation of the patent has been filed in the European Patent Office. Pursuant to procedures at the Community level, an EPO decision to revoke a Community Patent may be appealed to the European Court of Justice.

Under current conditions the American firm seeking patent protection in Europe must decide whether to pursue a group of national patents or a European patent, or both. Although maximum protection would be achieved by obtaining both the national patent and a European patent, the expense would be prohibitive. Accordingly, the prudent firm must carefully analyze its business, the product and

---

[20] Off. J. of the European Communities, 1976, L17/1, reprinted in Common Mkt. Rpt. (CCH) pars. 5795-5815L.

[21] Because of constitutional problems in some member states, it may be sometime before the Convention becomes effective.

the market in order to determine the appropriate procedure for its invention. Factors such as the cost of translation and the retention of agents in each country are reduced when filing under the European Patent Convention. Moreover, since the European patent is examined for patentability, validity contests in registration countries may be simplified.

In order to qualify for a European patent, an applicant must satisfy four criteria: invention, novelty, non-obviousness, and industrial applicability. This list is exhaustive, and no other requirement may be added.

Article 52(2) of the European Patent Convention carefully avoids any attempt to define the term "invention." Rather, it sets forth a non-exhaustive list of subject matter that may not be considered inventions. Excluded are scientific theories, discoveries, mathematical models, aesthetic creations, presentations of information, and non-technical mental processes, including computer programs. Also, Article 53 of the Convention excepts inventions whose publication would be contrary to *ordre public* or public morality and inventions in the area of plant cultivation and animal breeding. On the other hand, included within the scope of possible inventions under the Convention's approach are microbiological inventions and the processes and implementation thereof. The Convention also does not exclude or restrict patent protection for chemical and pharmaceutical inventions.

Under Article 54(1) of the EPC, "an invention shall be considered to be new if it does not form part of the state of the art." Paragraph (2) of Article 54 provides that the state of the art consists of all the information disclosed by any means on the date of the European patent application, and thereby the EPC adopts the system of absolute novelty. That is, disclosure by any means, at any time or in any place destroys novelty, subject to a few exceptions spelled out in the Convention. As defined by Article 56 of the EPC, novelty involves an inventive step that does not proceed from the state of the art in a manner evident to a person skilled in the art. This test requires a qualitative analysis that involves a subjective determination whether one skilled in the art would be able to conceive of the invention through standard professional capacities.

Finally, under Article 57 of the EPC, an invention is viewed as susceptible of industrial application if it may be manufactured or used in any kind of industry or agriculture. "Industry" includes "any human enterprise aimed at the transformation or the use of nature."

NOTES AND QUESTIONS

(1) The Paris Convention has been sharply criticized by the developing countries and, to a lesser extent, by the socialist and communist countries. As a result, conferences have been held under WIPO auspices with a view to possible revision of the convention.[22] To date these efforts have not been successful.[23]

---

[22] See *WIPO: Revision Of The Paris Convention*, 16 J. World Trade L. 180 (1982).

[23] For a provocative article concluding that the institution of a patent system in a developing country may confer significant costs, see Oddi, *The International Patent System and Third World Development: Reality or Myth?*, 1987 Duke L.J. 831.

(2) Assume that, as an American attorney, you have a client, a citizen of the United States, who has filed an application with the U.S. Patent Office for a new type of widget and for a process adapted to its manufacture. The client wishes to have the patent officially approved and registered in Italy, Belgium, France, and the United Kingdom, since she plans to arrange for the manufacture of the invention in those countries. What steps must you and your client take to achieve this end?[24]

[C] Select Problems in Drafting a Licensing Agreement

As already noted, international licensing of technology may allow the holder of industrial property — patents, trademarks and unpatented trade secrets and "know-how" — an alternative path toward entering a foreign market. However, the steps that must be taken toward this goal are not free from difficulty. The very first step — finding a suitable licensee in a foreign country — can be a time-consuming and frustrating enterprise. Although in the case of a large company there may be a natural match of licensor and licensee (*e.g.*, Dupont/Imperial Chemical Industries, Ltd.), the antitrust barriers to such an arrangement may be formidable. Smaller firms, in particular, may have to explore a variety of sources to identify potential licensees. Such sources might include, among others, friendly firms or local commercial banks and trade associations in the licensee's country. Especially if the licensor is considering several countries as possible locations for licensees, it may wish to turn to international sources of information, such as the International Chamber of Commerce, or the United Nations Industrial Development Organization (UNIDO). Also helpful are international licensing consultants or brokers. International licensing or trade forums, several of which have been held in recent years, are an excellent meeting place for licensors and licensees.

Once a suitable licensee is discovered, there remains what may be difficult negotiations regarding the licensing agreement itself. As noted above these negotiations may in effect be trilateral, since the government of the licensee's country may demand that certain clauses be included or excluded from the agreement. Indeed, in the case of a license agreement with an East European

---

[24] Guidelines for use of the European Patent system may be found in A. Turner, The Law of the New European Patent (1979). The leading treatise in the field of international trademark and patent protection is the three volume work by Stephen P. Ladas, Patents, Trademarks, and Related Rights: National and International Protection (1975). Some other leading publications include: W. W. White, Patents Throughout the World (1978); Cawthra, Patent Licensing in Europe (1978); W.R. Brookhard, S.M. Leach & B.D. Trober (eds), Current International Legal Aspects of Licensing and Intellectual Property (1980). Some helpful articles are: WIPO: Revision of the Paris Convention, 16 J. World Trade L. 180 (1982); Haar, *Revision of the Paris Convention: A Realignment of Private and Public Interests in the International Patent System*, 8 Brooklyn J. Int'l 77 (1982); Schmidt, *A New Instrument of Technology Transfer: The European Patent*, 3 Houston J. Int'l L. 185 (1981); Editorial, *Revision of the Paris Convention*, 15 J. World Trade L. 93 (1981); *Note, The United States Position on Revision of the Paris Convention: Quid Pro Quo or Denunciation*, 5 Fordham Int'l L. J. 411 (1982); Braendli, Haertel & Singer, The European Patent Convention 10 Years On - Review Of The Past And Prospects For The Future, 26 Indus. Prop. (WIPO) 369 (1987); Bumbak, *Industrial Property Rights And The Free Movement Of Goods In The European Community*, 16 Case W. Res. J. Int'l L. 381 (1984).

licensee, one negotiates directly with an official state trade agency (this may change because of the revolutionary developments in Eastern Europe). Other government agencies also may become involved from time to time during the negotiations.

License agreements may take many forms and be concluded in a variety of contexts. These include, for example, sales, distributorship, and related agreements; agreements to develop and market new technology; straight patent licenses; know-how licenses; trademark licenses and trade name agreements; technical assistance agreements; franchise agreements; university licensing; joint venture agreements; special industry agreements; consulting and management contracts; and computer software licenses.[25] In this Section we consider select problems in negotiating a straight patent license; in § 2.04 *infra*, we turn to some special problems associated with a franchise agreement.

One major consideration the drafter of an international licensing agreement must keep in mind is taxation, and the agreement should include provisions covering the handling of taxes. In particular, many countries impose heavy taxes on royalties. As discussed more extensively *infra*, in Chapter 8, tax treaties may provide some relief from the tax burden, and the lawyer should ascertain whether a double taxation treaty exists between the United States and the licensee's country. These treaties either eliminate or greatly reduce foreign taxes, such as the withholding tax on royalties and other types of income received by a United States taxpayer from the treaty country. The absence of a tax treaty may result in the licensor losing up to half his royalties in taxes. In such situations, the licensor must be forewarned that he will receive only a net royalty after taxes and not the full royalty set forth in the agreement.

From the United States tax perspective, it may be possible to structure the licensing agreement to ensure that the gain from the transaction to the U.S. licensor is characterized as a long-term capital gain. The question which arises on this point is whether the transfer of a patent or other form of industrial property constitutes a "sale or exchange" of a capital asset under Sections 1001 and 1221-23 of the Internal Revenue Code of 1986. The issue also arises as to what qualifies as a "transfer of all substantial rights" under Section 1235 of the Code. The case law on these issues is indecisive. But it does appear that non-exclusive licensing always fails to qualify for capital gains treatment and hence revenues received for the transfer of a patent are treated as ordinary income. On the other hand, a sale or exchange of a patent as a capital asset always results in capital gains treatment. Transactions that fall between these two extremes may or may not qualify as a sale or exchange or transfer of all substantial rights depending on the nature and number of restrictions the licensor imposes on the licensee.[26] It should also be noted that under current law, long-term capital gains are taxed at the same marginal rate as ordinary income, but still have advantage in that they can be offset by long-term capital losses. Currently, however, Congress is considering a number of possible ways of extending other advantages to capital gains.

---

[25] See 1 and 2 Eckstrom's, Licensing In Foreign And Domestic Operations (Szczepanski, ed. 1986).

[26] For a discussion of these and other taxation problems, see J. Bischel, Taxation of Patents, Trademarks, Copyrights and Know-how (1974).

Another important consideration the drafter of an international transfer of technology agreement should keep in mind is that the scope of protection available under local law for the technology varies greatly from country to country. For example, many countries will grant a patent for a much shorter duration than the 17 years available in the United States. Similarly, some countries will not grant a patent for food, medicine, medical devices, or certain items relating to nuclear energy. In other countries proprietary information (*e.g.*, trade secrets and industrial know-how) may be given no protection or only protection of short duration. Finally, some countries are much more likely than others to enforce patent and proprietary information rights.

Read the following draft licensing agreement critically. Several of the provisions would create difficulties under United States or foreign antitrust law or both, and several other provisions would create additional practical and legal difficulties. Consider also whether there may be some critical provisions *omitted* from the draft agreement. We explore these problems in the notes and questions that follow.

AGREEMENT[27]

AN AGREEMENT made this ____ day of _____, 19____, between Sonar Corporation, a corporation organized and existing under the laws of Ohio, having a place of business at Columbus, Ohio, U.S.A. (hereinafter called Licensor), and Compania Garciado, S.A., a company duly incorporated under the Laws of Panaduras, having a place of business at Estacia, Panaduras (hereinafter called Licensee).

PREAMBLE

WHEREAS: Licensor is the owner of patents on certain ultrasonic sensing systems in the United States, and in Panaduras and elsewhere as set forth in Annex A.

WHEREAS: Licensee is interested in the manufacture and sale of ultrasonic sensing systems in Panaduras and in other countries as set forth in Annex B (hereinafter called the Territory), and in that connection seeks to avail itself of the patents and patent applications owned by Licensor in Panaduras and these other countries.

NOW, THEREFORE, in consideration of a down payment of one thousand United States dollars (U.S. $1,000) having been made by Licensee to Licensor and of the covenants and agreements herein contained, it is agreed as follows:

Article I. Definitions

(1) A "Licensed System" will mean and include any ultrasonic sensing system which is manufactured, used, or sold in one of the countries set forth in Annexes A & B, and which embodies or is made by or with the use of, in whole or in part, inventions covered by the patent existing in the particular country at the time of its manufacture, use, or sale therein, and including the particular systems set forth in Annexes A & B.

---

[27] The license agreement is adapted from Eckstrom's Licensing In Foreign And Domestic Operations (Szczepanski, ed. 1 through 3, 1986) and Goldschmid, International License Contracts, A Practical Guide (1986).

(2) "Unit System" will mean a Licensed System, or that part thereof, comprising the ultrasonic transmitting and receiving transducers, their housings and mountings, cables, and conductors, and the associated indicator and control unit, including the components of an amplifier, detector relay driver, relay, and basic enclosures therefore; or comprising any subassembly of the foregoing parts particularly adapted for use in a Licensed System.

(3) "License Year" will mean each twelve (12) month calendar period commencing with January 1 and beginning with the year 19____ and continuing during the existence in force of the exclusive licenses.

Article II. Grants

(1) Licensor hereby agrees to grant to Licensee exclusive licenses to manufacture, use, and sell in the Territory, ultrasonic sensing systems and the existing patents and patents to issue on applications in other countries as set forth in Annexes A & B. These exclusive licenses are subject to any and all provisions and conditions of this Agreement.

(2) Licensor hereby agrees to grant to Licensee the right to grant sublicenses within the Territory. The Licensee's choice of sublicensees shall, however, be subject to the review and approval of the Licensor.

Article III. Royalties

(1) Licensee, in consideration of the grant of the licenses hereunder, will pay to Licensor the sum of twenty thousand United States dollars (U.S. $20,000) (in the manner provided in paragraph (4) below) within one month of the date hereof, less any taxes assessed against Licensor on the payment which Licensee may be required by law to deduct. In the absence of any clearly defined legal restrictions, Licensor will have the right to determine how any taxes will be paid.

(2) During the continuance of these licenses, Licensee will pay to Licensor on all sales by it of a Licensed System a royalty of ten percent (10%) of the selling price for each Unit System or part thereof manufactured by or on behalf of Licensee and sold by Licensee, its affiliates, and subsidiaries, provided that:

(a) If to meet competition within any country forming part of the Territory in which no patent or application for patent for the time being exists (hereinafter referred to as an Open Country) Licensee is required to reduce the selling price therein of all or any of the Licensed Systems then the rate of royalty payable hereunder by Licensee to Licensor in respect of sales of the Licensed System in an Open Country during that quarter will be reduced by one twentieth (1/20) (up to a maximum of ten twentieths (10/20) for each reduction by one one hundredth (1/100) in the selling price of the Unit System at that time over the average selling price of the Unit System during the two preceding quarters.

(3) During the continuance of these licenses, Licensee will pay an annual minimum royalty for each License Year:

(a) During the first year, counted from the date of this agreement — twenty thousand United States dollars (U.S. $20,000); during the second year — thirty thousand United States dollars (U.S. $30,000); during the third year and thereafter — one hundred thousand United States dollars (U.S. $100,000) or seven percent (7%) of the aggregate invoiced value of sales of the Licensed System effected in the United States of America by Licensor during the year ended on the December 31 preceding the License Year in respect of which royalty is payable by Licensee, whichever is the lower.

(b) It is presently contemplated that Licensee will initially purchase a number of Licensed Systems from Licensor to fill its need until Licensee's manufacturing operation reaches its full capacity. These sales and all further supplementary sales will be credited toward the minimum royalties at the rate of the number of Unit Systems purchased during the given License Year times ten percent (10%) of the selling price of a Unit System from Licensee to the purchasers.

(c) Royalties paid under the separate Know-How Agreement between the parties hereto will be credited toward the annual minimum royalties set forth in paragraph (3)(a) under "Royalties."

(4) Royalties are to be paid in quarterly installments (less taxes as aforesaid) within sixty (60) days after the close of each quarter of the License Year. Any payment required to be made by Licensee to ensure that the aggregate royalties paid in respect of any License Year are equal to the minimum royalty for that License Year will become due and payable by Licensee with the quarterly installment of royalties due and payable for the quarter ending on December 31 of that License Year.

Each of these installment payments will be converted to U.S. dollars by reference to the official rates between Panaduran pesos and U.S. dollars prevailing on the date of remittance and will be paid at Licensor's office in Columbus, Ohio, U.S.A., or at such other places as Licensor may specify from time to time.

Each installment payment shall be accompanied by a statement specifying the number of Licensed Systems manufactured and sold during that quarter, the sales price, the amount of royalty due thereon and the income tax paid. Each statement shall be duly verified by a responsible accounting officer in Licensee's firm.

Should remittance of royalties be delayed by Licensee beyond the sixty (60) days grace period, any loss caused thereby to Licensor due to decline of Panaduran currency shall be made good by Licensee.

(5) For as long as royalties are due under this Agreement, Licensee will keep true and accurate records adequate to permit royalties due to Licensor to be computed and verified, which records shall once during each financial year be audited and certified by Licensee's own auditor and submitted to Licensor. Any expenses incurred due to such certification shall be borne by Licensor.

Article IV. Maintenance

(1) Licensor will pay all fees in connection with the obtaining, issuance, and maintenance of patents and patent applications to be licensed by Licensor to Licensee in the Territory.

(2) Licensor will pay all fees in connection with the registration and maintenance of all trademarks to be licensed by Licensor to Licensee in the Territory and the expense of appointing Licensee a Registered User thereof.

Article V. Diligence

Licensee agrees to be diligent and to use its best endeavors to promote and develop the sale of and the market for the Licensed Systems within the Territory.

Article VI. Manufacture and Marking

(1) Licensee agrees to manufacture the Licensed Systems in accordance with the designs, specifications, drawings, and other information supplied or approved by Licensor, in accordance with standards set by Licensor. Licensor will not unreasonably withhold approval of improvements suggested by Licensee.

(2) Licensor will have the right to inspect the production facilities and processes used by Licensee in manufacturing the Licensed Systems and to test the finished products sold under any trademark of Licensor.

(3) Licensee agrees to mark the Licensed Systems and the packages or containers in which the Licensed systems are sold and shipped in a manner which conforms with the patent and trademark law and practice of the various countries in the Territory with respect to notice or other matters relating to patent and trademark ownership license and infringement.

Article VII. Term

(1) The licenses granted pursuant to the provisions of paragraphs (1) and (2) of Article II of this Agreement will take effect from the date hereof and will continue in force up to the date of expiry of Licensor's latest patent in the Territory relating to the Licensed System, unless sooner terminated as provided herein.

(2) If Licensee defaults in making royalty payments in accord with the provisions of paragraph (2) of Article III or commits any other material breach of the terms of this Agreement, Licensor, at its option (to be exercised within thirty (30) days of knowledge of the occurrence of the breach), can give written notice of its intention to terminate to Licensee, specifying the default or breach and a termination date not earlier than thirty (30) days from the date of the mailing of that notice, in the case of default in making royalty payments, and not earlier than ninety (90) days from the date of mailing of that notice for any other breach.

If Licensee fails to repair the default or breach prior to the specified date of termination, the licenses hereunder will then terminate. No failure by Licensor to exercise the option hereunder upon any occurrence therefore will be a waiver of Licensor's right to exercise the option respecting a subsequent default or breach.

(3) In the event either party commits any act of bankruptcy, becomes insolvent, enters into any arrangements with creditors, or goes into liquidation (other than for purposes of amalgamation or reconstruction), the other party will be entitled to terminate this Agreement forthwith by notice in writing without prejudice to the rights and remedies of either party against the other which accrued prior thereto.

(4) The licenses under this Agreement cannot be terminated because either Licensor or Licensee undergoes a reorganization, provided that the obligations under this Agreement are fulfilled.

(5) Subject to the royalty provisions of this Agreement, Licensee, for a period of one hundred and twenty (120) days following upon termination of the licenses

hereunder for cause by Licensor, can sell all Licensed Systems in inventory and finish and sell all thereof in process of manufacture. Upon termination for other than cause by Licensor, the period will be one (1) year.

Article VIII. Infringement and Warranty

(1) If any infringement or threatened infringement of any patents licensed hereunder comes to the notice of Licensee, it shall forthwith notify Licensor giving particulars thereof and Licensor will have the first right to sue all infringers. Licensor may, at its discretion, take legal steps to enforce its patent rights, but is under no obligation to do so.

(2) Licensor warrants that all Licensed Systems sold pursuant to this Agreement do not infringe any patent or other rights in the Territory of any person, firm, or company, and agrees to indemnify Licensee against all actions, costs, claims and demands made against Licensee in respect to any infringement or alleged infringement, provided that Licensee notifies Licensor immediately of any suits, charges, or prospective problems coming to Licensee's attention. Licensor will forthwith undertake the defense thereof with the cooperation of Licensee or, at Licensor's option, will permit Licensee to defend, at Licensor's expense, provided, however, that without prejudice to the foregoing, if Licensor reasonably anticipates that the expenses of Licensor in indemnifying Licensee and defending any actions, claims, or demands may exceed the total royalty payable by Licensee to Licensor on sales of the Licensed System in respect of the License Year preceding the License Year in which the infringement arose for the country in which it arose, Licensor shall have the option to terminate its liability forthwith by not less than thirty (30) days prior notification in writing to Licensee insofar as it relates to the country in which the infringement arose, Licensor being liable to Licensee for indemnification up to the date of termination. If Licensee chooses to continue the claimed infringement after this notification becomes effective, Licensee will assume the full liability of both Licensor and Licensee for any further claims and costs on account of the infringement and will continue to pay royalties. If the defense proves successful, Licensee can deduct from said royalties the costs of defense up to the amount of the royalties paid on sales in the particular country between the effective date of notification and the completion of the defense. If sales are finally terminated in that country, then, with effect from the date of final termination in respect of that country, the minimum annual royalty payable hereunder by Licensee relating to the grant of patent licenses will be reduced by an amount proportional to the sales volume in that country up to the date of termination as compared with the total sales volume of the Licensed System in the Territory up to the date of termination.

Article IX. Improvements

(1) Licensor agrees to notify Licensee promptly of any improvements or inventions relating to the Licensed Systems developed or in the process of development by Licensor. Licensee will have the right to use those improvements. In the event that Licensor secures patents on any of these improvements within the Territory, Licensee will have the right, at its option, to include those patents within the terms of the present Agreement. Only one (1) royalty per Licensed

System will be due regardless of the number of patents involved in a Licensed System.

(2) Licensee shall promptly disclose to Licensor any improvement or invention pertaining to the Licensed Systems. At Licensor's request, Licensee shall assign to Licensor the entire right, title and interest in any such improvement or invention, as well as the right to file any patent applications therefor, including the right to sublicense, free of any royalty.

Article X. Trademarks

(1) Licensor agrees to register and maintain, at its expense, in the Territory any Licensor trademarks relating to the Licensed Systems in use during the continuance of this Agreement if so requested by Licensee from time to time.

(2) The term of use of any trademark licensed in connection with this Agreement will be coincident with the life of this Agreement.

Article XI. Construction

(1) Any delay or omission on the part of any party in the strict exercise of its rights hereunder will not impair those rights, nor will it constitute a waiver or renunciation of those rights. Any waiver by any party in respect of one breach of this Agreement will not constitute an acquiescence in any subsequent breach nor in any other default under this Agreement.

(2) The terms and provisions of this Agreement will be construed in accordance with the laws of Ohio.

(3) In the event of a dispute arising out of any of the clauses hereunder, or in the case of a breach of any of those clauses, the parties shall try, in the first instance, to arrive at an amicable settlement. Should this fail, the dispute shall be submitted to arbitration, which shall take place at the residence of the opponent to the party seeking arbitration. Both parties shall nominate an arbitrator within a fortnight; should one party fail to do so, the other party shall name the other arbitrator also. Both arbitrators shall name a third arbitrator who shall be a member of the legal profession. The decision of the arbitrators shall be final and both parties agree to abide by the same. The arbitrators shall also decide on each party's share of the expenses of arbitration. The arbitration shall follow the Rules of the International Chamber of Commerce in Paris.

(4) If any provision of this Agreement is declared invalid by a court of last resort or by any court from the decision of which an appeal is not taken within the time provided by law, then and in such an event, this Agreement will be deemed to have been terminated only as to the portion thereof which relates to the provision invalidated by that judicial decision, but this Agreement, in all other respects, will remain in force.

(5) Licensee will not contest, nor assist others in contesting, (a) the validity of the patents and patent applications which are the subject of the Agreement, (b) the title of Licensor thereto, nor (c) the novelty, utility, or patentability of any subject matter of any of the patents. The patents, throughout their respective terms and for all purposes, will be deemed in force and valid unless declared invalid by a court of last resort or by any court from the decision of which an appeal is not taken within the time provided by law.

Article XII. Notice

Any notice required to be given hereunder to any party will be served by letter sent to the above indicated place of business or last known address of that party by registered airmail, prepaid, return receipt requested and will be deemed to have been served on the fourth day following the date of posting.

NOTES AND QUESTIONS

(1) It is important that a licensing agreement be drafted with the particular economic, social and political climate of the licensee's country in mind. Thus, the practical problems one faces in drafting a licensing agreement may differ considerably, depending upon whether the licensee is located in a developed country in Western Europe, a country in Eastern Europe, or a country in the developing world. We have already noted that in an Eastern European country the U.S. licensor may, in effect, be negotiating directly with the government (although, as also already noted, this situation in Eastern Europe is at present greatly in flux). This makes the negotiations almost invariably long and difficult, but the involvement of the government also provides some advantages to the arrangement. The backing of the state of each arrangement ensures, with the exception of Yugoslavia, which has a mixed economy, that the licensee will not go bankrupt. Moreover, licensees tend to adhere strictly to the letter of the license agreement since the licensee's undertaking has the official sanction of the state.

Some of the difficulties a U.S. licensor may encounter in its negotiations with East European licensees include the following. Eastern European countries greatly favor lump-sum payments, barter, or a combination of the two as a method of payment. The reason for this is the nature of the budgetary process in a centrally planned economy and the scarcity of hard currency reserves. In the relatively rare situation where the Eastern European licensee will agree to a so-called running royalty based on sales of the product, it may be difficult to agree on the appropriate royalty base. Royalty bases such as the net sales prices, net profit, gross profit, etc., common in the non-Socialist world, are concepts contrary to the idea of a centrally planned economy. Also, Eastern European government officials have resisted independent audit of the books of their licensees.

One possible way to avoid conceptual problems regarding a royalty base is to specify the United States sales price of the licensed product as the appropriate base. Reportedly, too, a running royalty with an East European licensee may be negotiable if the licensor agrees to a ceiling on the amount of the royalty for any given year. At all events, the license agreement should specify that payment of agreed amounts be made in hard currency at a United States bank.

Territorial limitations are generally accepted by Eastern European licensees. However, they require that territorial restraints in a license permit the licensee to market the licensed product at least throughout member countries of the Council for Mutual Economic Assistance (COMECON) and occasionally in a few additional countries. The reason for this insistence is that the technology transferred under East-West license agreements sometimes results in production levels far exceeding the consuming capacity of the individual country's market.

With respect to dispute settlement procedures, East European licensees prefer to designate Swiss law (especially that of the Cantons of Bern or Zurich) as the applicable law governing the agreement. They refuse to accept a designation of United States law as the applicable law because of their unfamiliarity with it. Most commonly, East-West license agreements refer disputes to an arbitral tribunal under the auspices of the International Chamber of Commerce in Paris, Basel, Stockholm, or some other commercial center designated as appropriate.

Another unusual environment the potential United States licensor should be aware of is that of the developing countries. Here, the concern on the part of the licensee's government is that the licensing agreement, at a minimum, not undermine the economic development of the country, and, ideally, contribute to furthering the development process through the smooth transfer of technology. Many of the developing countries believe strongly that the terms of standard licensing agreements greatly frustrate the transfer of technology and maintain the developing countries in an economic condition subservient to the developed countries.

One commentator has summarized the developing countries' complaints as follows:

> (i) The technology transferred is inappropriate, that is, not harmonized with the socioeconomic goals of the recipient country.

> (ii) Developed country transferors seek to perpetuate the developing country's technological dependence by making no effort to establish or promote the development of indigenous research and development or to train developing country personnel.

> (iii) The monopolistic power of developed country transferors and the resultant inequalities in bargaining strength lead to the negotiation of onesided, unconscionable transfer agreements. . . .[28]

At the international level the developing countries have been working through the so-called Group of 77 (now numbering well over 100 developing countries) in the United Nations and its specialized agencies. In particular, the United Nations Conference on Trade and Development (UNCTAD) has been working on An International Code for the Transfer of Technology (see Chapter 8). In its present form, the code incorporates many of the developing countries' views. The proposals of the developing countries, however, have been strongly resisted by the developed countries, and the final form and fate of the Code is not clear.

The developing countries, especially in Latin America, have also been active in expressing their viewpoint in regional and national forums. For example, in 1969 six South American countries (Bolivia, Chile, Columbia, Ecuador, Peru and Venezuela) formed the Andean Subregional Market (ANCOM). In 1971, the Andean countries drafted common rules for the treatment of foreign patents,

---

[28] Finnegan, Practical and Legal Considerations in the International Licensing of Technology, III W. Surrey & D. Wallace, A Lawyer's Guide to International Business Transactions 44 (Folio 8, 1981).

licenses and royalties, and agreed upon the application of these rules by each member government in its review of international license agreements. The fundamental purpose of this approach was to avoid foreign investors attempting to divide and conquer the individual Andean member nations. In particular, Articles 20 and 21 of the directive adapted by the Andean Commission provide:

DECISION 24 —

December 31, 1970

10 Int'l Leg. Mat. 159 (1971)

* * * *

Article 20

The member countries shall not authorize the execution of those contracts on transfer of external techniques or patents which contain:

a. Clauses whereby the supply of techniques involves an obligation for the member country or for the recipient enterprise to acquire capital assets, intermediate assets and raw materials from a specific source or make permanent use of the personnel appointed by the enterprise supplying the techniques. In exceptional cases, the recipient country may accept this type of clauses for acquisition of capital assets, intermediate products or raw materials providing that their prices correspond to the normal levels in the international market.

b. Clauses whereby the technique selling enterprise keeps its right to set prices for sale or resale of the products manufactured on the basis of the respective technique.

c. Clauses whereby restrictions are established on volume and structure for production.

d. Clauses prohibiting the use of competitive techniques.

e. Clauses establishing an option for total or partial purchase in favor of the supplier of the technology.

f. Clauses which commit the purchaser of technology to disclose to the supplier the inventions or improvements accomplished through utilization of said technology.

g. Clauses whereby the [licensees] of patents are obligated to pay royalties on un-used patents. And

h. Other clauses with similar effects.

Except in specific cases, duly qualified as such by the corresponding organism in the recipient country, those clauses which in whatever manner prohibit or limit exportation of the products manufactured on the basis of the respective technique, shall not be accepted.

In no case shall this type of clause be accepted with reference to subregional exchange or for exportation of similar products to third countries.

Article 21

The intangible technical contributions shall be entitled to payment of royalties upon previous authorization of the corresponding national organization but may not be computed as a contribution of capital.

When any of such contributions are to be supplied to a foreign enterprise by its home office or by any of the subsidiaries of said home office, the payment of royalties shall not be approved nor any deductions accepted on such account for taxation purposes.

Decision 24 had a rocky history. Because of dissatisfaction with its constraints, Chile withdrew from ANCOM in 1977; special treatment was accorded Ecuador and Bolivia, because of their greater dependency on foreign investments; and Venezuela passed a foreign investment law that clearly violated Decision 24's provisions. Finally, in 1987, ANCOM repealed Decision 24, replacing it with a directive that allows each of the five remaining member states of ANCOM to adopt its own foreign investment and transfer of technology rules.

Nonetheless, as to transfer of technology rules, the approach adopted by Decision 24 continues to be followed, in the main, by the five ANCOM countries and is a good vehicle for illustrating some of the particular practices that developing countries tend to find objectionable. It has, moreover, served as a model for other Latin American states. Mexico is a prominent example.

MEXICO

Law For

THE CONTROL OF REGISTRATION OF THE TRANSFER OF TECHNOLOGY

and the

USE AND EXPLOITATION OF PATENTS AND TRADEMARKS

Official Gazette, January 11, 1982.

* * * *

Article 2

For the purposes of this Law, all agreements, contracts and all other acts that are contained in documents to be effective in Mexico in connection with the following, shall be registered in the National Technology Transfer Registry:

    (a)   Trademark licenses;

    (b)   Licenses on patents of invention or of improvements and on certificates of invention;

    (c)   License on industrial models or drawings;

(d) Trademark assignments;

(e) Patent assignments;

(f) Tradename licenses;

(g) Transfer of know-how through plans, diagrams, models, instruction manuals, formulas, specifications, educating and training of personnel and otherwise;

(h) Technical assistance, however provided;

(i) Supply of basic or detail engineering;

(j) Company operation or administration services;

(k) Advisory, consultory and supervisory services, when rendered by foreign individuals or corporations or their subsidiaries regardless of their domicile;

(l) Copyright licenses that imply industrial exploitation; and

(m) Computer programs.

[NOTE: Failure to register a transfer of technology agreement in accordance with Article 2 renders the agreement unenforceable in Mexico and may result in the imposition of criminal penalties. Such an agreement must be filed with the Ministry of Patrimony and Industrial Development within sixty days from the date of its conclusion. To be registrable, however, agreements must be compatible with the following provisions:]

* * * *

Article 15

The Ministry of Patrimony and Industrial Development shall not register the acts, agreements or contracts referred to in Article Second hereof in the following cases:

I. If clauses are included which allow the supplier to regulate or intervene, directly or indirectly, in the management of the acquirer of the technology;

II. If the obligation is set forth to assign or grant a licence, onerously or free of charge to the supplier of the technology, in connection with the patents, trademarks, innovation or improvements that are obtained by the acquirer, except when there is reciprocity or a benefit for the acquirer in the exchange of the information;

III. If limitations are imposed on the acquirer's technological research or development;

IV. If the obligation is set forth to acquire equipment, tools, parts or raw materials, from a specific origin exclusively, when other sources exist in the national or international market;

V. If the export of the acquirer's goods or services is forbidden in a manner contrary to the interests of Mexico;

VI. If the use of complementary technologies is forbidden;

VII. If the obligation is set forth to sell the goods produced by the acquirer to an exclusive customer;

VIII. If the acquirer is under an obligation to use, permanently, personnel appointed by the supplier of the technology.

IX. If production volumes are limited or if selling or reselling prices are imposed for the national production or for the exports of the acquirer;

X. If the acquirer is under the obligation to execute sale or exclusive representation contracts with the supplier of the technology, unless exports are involved, and the acquirer accepts and it is proven to the satisfaction of the Ministry of Patrimony and Industrial Development that the supplier has proper distribution outlets or the good commercial standing necessary to sell the products in better conditions than the acquirer;

XI. If the acquirer is under the obligation to keep secret the technical information given by the supplier, beyond the duration of the acts, agreements or contracts or beyond the time established by the applicable laws;

XII. If it is not expressly established that the supplier shall be liable for the infringement of Industrial Property rights of third parties;

XIII. If the supplier does not warrant the quality and results of the contracted technology.

Article 16

The acts, agreements or contracts referred to in Article Second will not be registered either in the following cases:

I. When their purpose is the transfer of technology from abroad which is already available in Mexico;

II. When the price or counterservice is out of proportion to the acquired technology or constitutes an unwarranted or excessive burden for the national economy or for the acquiring company;

III. When excessive durations are established. In no case may such durations exceed ten years, obligatory for the acquirer; and

IV. When litigation that may arise in connection with the interpretation or fulfillment of the acts, agreements or contracts is submitted to foreign courts, except in cases of exportation of Mexican technology or of express submission to private international arbitration, provided that the arbitrator applies Mexican substantive law to the controversy, and in accordance with the international agreements on the subject signed in Mexico.

Article 17

In the cases provided for in the two preceding Articles, the Ministry of Patrimony and Industrial Development through the National Technology Transfer

Registry, shall determine in accordance with its judgment those cases which shall be granted exceptions, taking into account the benefits for the country.

———————————

Mexican law requires that patents granted in Mexico be worked within three years. If they are not, compulsory licenses may be rewarded to others, with a government board setting the royalty.

In January, 1990, the Government of Mexico enacted a regulation concerning the transfer of technology. The new regulation, among other things, streamlines the red tape necessary to export technology to Mexico and allows the parties to a transfer of technology transaction greater flexibility in structuring the arrangement. Under the previous approach the government decided whether the technology would be valuable to Mexico, if the terms of the deal were acceptable, and how much in royalties would be paid. The new regulation permits these matters to be determined by the parties themselves free of governmental interference. Also, at this writing the Government of Mexico has announced its intention to introduce new legislation to improve the legal framework for the protection of intellectual property in Mexico and to bring it into line with the level of protection afforded in the industrialized countries.

As illustrated by the Andean Code and Mexican transfer of technology provisions quoted above, a primary thrust of the developing countries' constraints on licensing agreements is toward the prevention of so-called restrictive business practices, such as tie-ins, tie-outs, exclusive grant backs, territorial restrictions, etc. Another area where the developing countries place substantial limitations on licensing arrangements is the amount of royalties that can be paid to the licensor. The Andean Code, for example, placed a limit on the amount of royalties that could be expatriated to a licensor of 14% of invested capital. Moreover, under the local legislation of developing countries, it may be difficult or impossible to arrange alternative forms of consideration, since these may be subject to approval or simply prohibited. An example would be the prohibition of capital participation as consideration by the Andean Group.

(1) Other examples of constraints developing countries may place on licensing arrangements include prohibiting the acquisition of technology that is indigenously available, limiting the duration of license agreements, and providing generally that all technology transfer agreements shall be in keeping with the social and economic goals of the recipient country. Also, many countries, both developing and developed, require that patents be worked and in the event of inadequate utilization within a prescribed period of time, forfeiture and compulsory licensing. Lastly, many developing countries fail to accord legal recognition to the protection of know-how and trade secrets, thereby greatly complicating arrangements for their protection.

(2) Under the draft license agreement, set forth above, what constraints are placed on the ability of the licensee to export from Panaduras? See the two "whereas" clauses in the preamble and paragraphs (1) and (2) under the "Grants" section. May the licensee sell the Licensed Systems outside of the Territory

covered by the agreement? May the licensee export Licensed Systems to the United States? Conversely, may the Licensor export Licensed Systems from the United States to Panaduras? What would be the position of Panaduran officials (assuming Panaduras has a local law and practice similar in its thrust to that of the Andean Code and of Mexico)?

(3) A most important part of any license agreement, from the perspective of all interested parties, is the provision regarding royalties. Evaluate the provision on royalties of the draft license agreement. Note that Paragraph 2 of Article III of the agreement provides that the royalty is to be based on 10% of the selling price of each system. Is this a satisfactory arrangement from the perspective of the licensor, the licensee, the government of Panaduras?

One way to avoid potential problems with royalties is to pay the royalty in one lump sum at the beginning of a license agreement. What advantages and disadvantages do you see in this arrangement?

The most common manner of paying for licensed technology under a license agreement is on a so-called running royalty basis. Running royalties may be computed on a percentage or a straight money basis, *e.g.*, 1 cent per pound, 5 cents per square yard, or 25 cents per barrel. What advantages, if any, do you see in using a percentage royalty arrangement as compared with a straight money basis?

One of the most common methods of calculating a running royalty is as a percentage of the net sales price of licensed products. Why? If this method is used, it is important to define exactly what is included in the "net sales price." Taxes, credits for returned products, quantity discounts, freight allowances, cash discounts, and agents' commissions are normally omitted from the net sales price. A definition of "net selling price" might read: "gross amount invoiced by licensee on sales of licensed product, less returns, rebates, trade discounts, cash discounts, sales taxes, and transportation charges allowed to purchaser."

If the law of the distributor's country will permit it, an alternative to royalty payments is a grant of a license by the licensor in exchange for voting shares in the licensee's company. An advantage of this approach is that it may permit the licensor to exercise more control over the licensee's operations.

Consider the provisions in paragraph (5) of Article III of the agreement. Is it satisfactory from the perspective of the Licensor? If not, what changes would you advise?

(4) Another major difficulty with royalty payments is the rapid rate of fluctuation in currency values. For example, if the Licensee receives 1,000,000 Panaduran pesos from a purchaser of a Licensed System when 10 pesos equals $1, and then remits a royalty payment pursuant to the license agreement when the rate is 15 to 1, the Licensor has suffered a 33-1/3% decline in the value of its royalty payment. A common way of protecting the Licensor or Licensee against currency fluctuations is to provide for an adjustment of the royalty to correspond to the devaluation or revaluation.

It is often advisable to insert a clause in the licensing agreement that provides for periodic renegotiation of the provisions on royalties, especially if a long term arrangement is contemplated. Such a clause may also be looked upon with favor by the government of the licensee's country.

(5) Consider paragraph (1) of Article VII and paragraphs (1) and (2) of Article IX of the license agreement. Under these provisions how long is the licensing agreement likely to last? Will these provisions be acceptable to the government of Panaduras? To the United States Government? If these provisions raise problems, how might they be revised?

(6) Would paragraph (5) of Article XI of the agreement raise any objections from the government of Panaduras? From United States authorities? As counsel for the Licensor, how would you respond to such objections?

(7) Consider the provisions on choice of law and arbitration in paragraphs (2) and (3) of Article XI. Are they satisfactory from the perspective of the Licensor? Suppose the government of Panaduras does not recognize the validity of such provisions. Should the Licensor refuse to go ahead with the licensing arrangement?

(8) United States export controls must be taken into account in most licensing arrangements. Especially if the product licensed qualifies as high technology, one must be concerned about the possible imposition of so-called national security controls. Under such controls it would be the responsibility of the licensor to ensure that the licensee did not export the licensed product to a prohibited designation (various communist countries or other countries deemed unfriendly to the United States).

(9) There are a number of provisions not included in the draft license agreement but worthy of serious consideration for inclusion. Some of these we have seen in Section A, *supra* at pages 148-154, in the draft distributorship agreement. For example, a license agreement should probably contain a *force majeure* clause.

Often a potential licensor and licensee enter into an option agreement *before* entering into the license agreement itself. Under this arrangement, the license agreement goes into effect only if the licensee decides to exercise the option. This arrangement allows the licensee a period of time (say 90 days to 6 months) in which to evaluate the licensed technology.

Most major international license agreements provide that the licensor will render technical assistance to the licensee. Assistance in the design, construction, and operation of a complex facility may be indispensable to the success of licensee's operations. The agreement should also state clearly whether the licensee or licensor is responsible for the salaries and expenses of technical personnel furnished by the licensor to the licensee. A common arrangement is for the licensor to bear such expenses for an initial period of time; thereafter, the licensor provides technical personnel only if the licensee agrees to pay their salaries and expenses. Conversely, a license agreement may provide that the licensee may send technical personnel and members of its own staff to the licensor's plant for on–the–site training.

In a country like Panaduras, the license agreement would almost surely have to be approved by a government agency or at least registered with a government agency. The license agreement would normally require the licensee to obtain the necessary approvals, since it will be more knowledgeable than the licensor about local procedures and government personnel.[29]

---

[29] For information on international licensing, see *inter alia*, Technology Exports, 3 W.P. Streng, J.W. Salacuse, International Business Planning: Law and Taxation 12-1 (1988);

§ 2.04   Select Problems in Franchising

International franchising is similar to, but distinguishable from, both distribution and licensing arrangements. An international distributorship arrangement involves a foreign distributor marketing a United States manufacturer's product in the distributor's country. By contrast, under an international franchising arrangement, a foreign franchisee operates the franchisor's business in the franchisee's country. That business may involve the manufacture, processing or distribution of goods or the rendering of services. Prominent U.S. companies engaged in extensive foreign franchising include, among others, McDonald's, Holiday Inn, and Coca-Cola. One commentator has suggested the following reasons for franchising internationally:

1. To utilize local management personnel and thus overcome problems of language and culture;

2. To overcome problems of detailed supervision often otherwise insuperable because of distance;

3. To leave compliance with local laws to those familiar with such laws and thus be able to market a product in a target country without incurring liability under the laws of such country;

4. To avoid laws which may inhibit or control foreign direct investment in particular countries. Franchising enables a product to be marketed in a country with restrictive direct investment laws without a direct investment being made by the franchisor in that country;

5. To overcome political difficulties such as the possibility of expropriation of overseas investment. The franchisee will normally be a resident of the target country and probably less vulnerable to such threats. In any event, if the property is expropriated, it is the franchisee's and not the franchisor's loss;

6. To take advantage of revenue, tax planning and similar financial considerations.

The terms "franchising" and "licensing" are sometimes, mistakenly, used interchangeably. By definition, a license is a right granted by a licensor to a licensee which enables the licensee to make use of the licensor's property, which in the international context usually involves intellectual property, including patents, designs, trademarks, and know-how. The term "license" is improperly used in the context of contractual relationships "which do not involve the grant of a right in property, such as distribution agreements, sales agency or representation agreements, or concessions granted by governments for the installation of an industry."[1] Franchising may be a viable option for the international business firm that

---

Bard & Peters, International Technology Transfer Agreements, 1 The Law of Transnational Business Transactions 6-1 (V.P. Nanda, ed. 1987); Eckstrom, Licensing In Foreign And Domestic Operations (Szczepanski ed., 1 through 3 1986); International Licensing Agreements (2d ed. G. Pollzien & E. Langen, eds. 1973); L M. Finnegan & R. Goldscheider, The Law and Business of Licensing Part II (1975); Finnegan, Practical and Legal Considerations in the International Licensing of Technology, III A Lawyer's Guide to International Business Transactions (2d ed. W. Surrey & D. Wallace, eds. 1981).

[1] Ladas, Problems Of Licensing Abroad, 1965 U. Ill. L. F. 411.

possesses technology and marketing expertise, finds itself barred by tariffs and other barriers from exporting, yet hesitates to risk capital investment and direct manufacture or providing services in a foreign country. Before deciding to enter into an international franchising agreement, however, the following factors, among others, should be considered: (1) the business climate affecting franchising; (2) the presence or absence of foreign legislation affecting foreign franchising; (3) antitrust implications; (4) foreign trademark laws; (5) the tax aspects of foreign franchising; (6) the available forms of doing business; (7) the presence or absence of investment incentives; (8) customs and import-export controls; (9) the availability of liability insurance; (10) the absence or presence of laws, regulations, or other limitations respecting employment; and (11) any restrictions on ownership or leasing of real property by foreigners or companies controlled by foreigners.

Many of these factors, it should be noted, need to be considered as well with respect to licensing agreements. Franchising arrangements give rise to some particular problems of their own, however. Because of the close control exercised by a franchisor, it may be subject to potential liability under local law by either the franchisee or customers of the franchisee. Provisions in the franchise agreement that the franchisor and franchisee are independent contractors, that neither the franchisor nor the franchisee shall have any liability under any agreements, representations, or warranties made by the other, or that the franchisor shall not be obligated for any damages to any person or property directly or indirectly arising out of the operation of the franchisee's business may help to limit liability, but they are hardly airtight. As an added protection, the franchise agreement should provide that the franchisee will reimburse the franchisor for any damages, obligations, or taxes for which it is held liable, as well as any costs incurred by the franchisor in defending itself against such claims. In the event these protections fail, the availability of liability insurance would be a crucial factor for the franchisor in deciding whether to enter into the franchise agreement.

Restrictive customs and import-export controls may render it impossible for the franchisee to conduct the franchisor's business. That is, there may be extraordinary tariff rates, import quotas, import licensing requirements, or other restrictions that affect imports of machinery, equipment, food products, packing supplies, etc. Similarly, extraordinary customs restrictions, visa requirements, or other limitations (e.g., on the length of stay), may frustrate the ability of the franchisor to send its employees to the franchisee's country to supervise business arrangements, training, etc. More generally, franchising is much closer than either a distributorship or licensing arrangement to direct investment in a foreign country. In particular, the amount of control a franchisor exercises over the franchisee's business operations may raise the suspicion of the host country's government. The host country's government may regard franchising as a method of frustrating real transfers of technology to the host country. In keeping with local economic development plans, it may favor or disfavor certain industries or products, e.g., the fast food industry, tourist industry, high technology items, food products, soft drinks, etc.

Because of perceived inequality between the parties, the host country legislation or practice may place severe limitations on the termination, cancellation, or non-renewal of a franchise agreement. The franchisor may be required to compensate the franchisee, for example, or repurchase items from the franchisee upon termination, cancellation, or non-renewal of the franchise agreement. Similarly, the franchisor may need the approval of a government agency to sell the franchise.

In the same vein, the host government may scrutinize carefully or disapprove control exerted by the foreign franchisor over the franchisee by means such as inspection; the length of the contract term; requirements that the franchisor be given proprietary information, technology, or know-how at the expiration of the franchise agreement; and requirements that restrict the franchisee to operating exclusively the franchised business. The host country may also restrict ownership or leasing of real property by foreigners or companies controlled by foreigners.

Effective protection of tradenames in the franchisee's country is indispensable to the success of a franchise arrangement. Hence, with respect to trademarks, local law and practice should be examined to ascertain, *inter alia*, whether a foreign franchisor is entitled to register; whether use is required prior to issuance of registration; whether use must be shown to renew the mark; whether foreign marks must be used in association with marks originally registered in the franchisee's country; whether the registration will be extinguished or lapse if the mark is not used for a specified period of time; whether a franchisee of a registered mark can sublicense use of the mark. Local law should also be surveyed to determine if a franchisor can bring suit against a third party for infringement of a trademark without joining the franchisee as a party to the suit.

Local law should also be examined to ascertain the extent of copyright protection available for the franchisor's operations manual. Moreover, the franchise agreement should contain a provision stating that no copies, photographs, or reproductions may be made of the manual, that the manual remains the property of the franchisor, and that the manual will be returned to the franchisor at the termination of the agreement.

Research into local law should further determine whether the franchisee's country is a party to the Universal Copyright Convention, September 16, 1955.[2] Under the Universal Copyright Convention copyright holders receive, among other benefits, national treatment, translation rights, and a minimum term of 25 years of copyright protection. On October 31, 1988, the United States became a party to the Berne Convention of 1886, as revised, which provides for additional benefits. The United States is a party to Latin American conventions which afford protections along the lines of those granted by the Universal Copyright Convention.

The franchise agreement should also contain a provision enjoining the franchisee to keep secret the contents of the agreement, the manual, advertising instructions, and any other information divulged to him in confidence. The only exceptions should be when the information is necessary to carrying out the agreement, to obtaining a lease, bank credit or responding to the demands of a government agency or court of law.

---

[2] 6 U.S.T. 2731, T.I.A.S. No. 3324, 216 U.N.T.S. 132.

NOTES AND QUESTIONS

(1) Assume that a draft license agreement prepared by counsel for the franchisor contains a provision along the following lines:

> Franchisor can terminate this agreement if gross sales are less than $150,000 per year after the first year.[3]

As counsel for the franchisee, what would be your reaction? If you would wish to make some revisions to this provision, what would these be?

(2) Assume further that you are counsel for a Canadian franchisee who is engaged in negotiating a franchise agreement with a New York franchisor. You learn that the New York franchisor, a fast food establishment, has opened twenty outlets in the state of New York during the last five years. Does receipt of this information suggest to you the need for a particular provision to be included in the agreement to protect your client?

(3) A standard provision in a franchise agreement permits the franchisor to terminate the agreement in the event of the franchisee's bankruptcy. From the franchisee's perspective it is important that the agreement contain a correlative provision permitting the franchisee to terminate the agreement in the event of the franchisor's bankruptcy.

(4) Tax aspects of foreign franchising are a matter of crucial importance to the success of the enterprise. In some countries a foreign franchisor may not be able to directly license franchisees, but must instead establish a branch or subsidiary. This may have tax consequences under both U.S. law and the law of the franchisee's country.[4]

---

[3] See G. Berlinski, *Franchising In The United States and Canada*, 13 Rev. Juridique Themis 543, 581 (1978).

[4] For writings on international franchising, see generally, American Bar Association, Franchising Committee. Section of Antitrust Law, Survey of Foreign Law and Regulations Affecting International Franchising (1982), 15 Glickman, Business Organization: Franchising, Sec. 11.08 (1983); Rosenfield, The Law of Franchising (1970); Pengilley, *International Franchising Arrangements and Problems in Their Negotiation*, 7 Nw. J. Int'l L. & Bus. 185 (1985). Berlinski, *Franchising in the United States and Canada*, 13 Rev. Juridique Themis 543 (1978); Ladas, Problems of Licensing Abroad, 1965 U. Ill. L.F. 411; P. Hearn, International Business Agreements (1987); R. Baldi, Distributorship, Franchising, Agency: Community And National Law And Practice In The EEC (1987); Schmitz & Van Hemme, Franchising In Europe — The First Practical EEC Guidelines, 22 Int'l Law 717 (1988).

CHAPTER **3**

THE INTERNATIONAL CONTROL OF NATIONAL TRADE POLICIES
— THE ECONOMICS OF INTERNATIONAL TRADE

Introduction to Chapters 3, 4 and 5

In Chapters 3, 4 and 5 we focus upon the institutions and other less formal arrangements through which the international community seeks to control or otherwise influence national policies that impact international trade. While the General Agreement on Tariffs and Trade (the "GATT")[1] occupies much of our attention, these chapters also introduce the reader to the United Nations Conference on Trade and Development ("UNCTAD"), the Organization for Economic Development ("OECD"), various regional groups, such as the European Economic Community ("EEC") and the ACP[2] States under the Lome Accords and to a host of purely bilateral arrangements. In the context of particular issues our purpose is to examine the role these organizations play in the overall institutional (*i.e.*, legal) framework within which national trade policies are formulated and carried out.

We start in this Chapter with an introduction to certain basic economic principles. In Chapter 4 we turn to a study of the GATT itself, paying particular attention to those provisions that establish GATT as the principal vehicle for the exercise of multilateral control over national trade policies. Chapter 4 then continues with what might roughly be considered two case studies. The first concerns the GATT review of the Treaty of Rome which established the EEC and with the aftermath of that encounter: the Dillon and Kennedy Rounds of tariff negotiations. This sequence is historically important in the evolution of GATT as a source of law and as a constraint upon nations who, for political, ideological or economic reasons, seek to form special, discriminatory trading relationships. Here also we take a closer look at the "reciprocity" principle which, although developed in the context of traditional tariff negotiations, may have a wider, contemporary application as our next study illustrates.

Next, in Chapter 4 we examine the evolution of the Generalized System of Preferences (GSP) and briefly the American legislation on the subject. While the GSP may not be particularly significant in terms of the proportion of world trade that it covers, the development of the idea, and its implementation, is a useful vehicle for studying the special trade problems confronting the less developed countries of the world. Against the background of those problems we also introduce the UNCTAD and take a quick look at the problem of agricultural trade.

---

[1] 61 Stat. Parts (5) and (6); TIAS 1700; 55-61 UNTS; 4 Bevans 639.
[2] ACP stands for African, Caribbean and Pacific.

Then, in Chapter 5, we turn to three very fundamental problems which, perhaps better than any others, illustrate the threat now confronting the liberal multilateral trading order embodied in GATT. The first is the so-called "safeguards" problem; a problem which today is among the most important pieces of unfinished business on the international trade agenda. To understand the problem we must examine the causes and effects of the rising tide of protectionism that has engulfed the major trading nations of the world during the last decade and which threatens to tear apart the GATT system of multilateral control over national trade policies. Ultimately the "safeguards" problem brings us to the question of whether the international trading community can deal with the casualties of increased trade liberalization without destroying the process of liberalization itself, and, if so, how.

Secondly, in Chapter 5, we turn to efforts by the international community to cabin the growing propensity of nations to effectively change their relative comparative advantage (*i.e*, to expand exports and curtail imports) by subsidizing their own producers. Related to this problem are the issues that arise when, under its countervailing duty laws, the United States' seeks to offset the competitive impact of subsidized imports.

Finally, in Chapter 5, we turn to the so-called "dumping" problem. "Dumping" occurs whenever a foreign producer sells abroad at a price lower than that charged in its own domestic market. Often thought of as "international price discrimination," the critical inquiry is whether there is any justification whatsoever for an "anti-dumping" law.

The subsidization of exports and "dumping" have been lumped together under the label of "unfair" trade practices. Whether justified or not — a question that remains to be explored — the label itself speaks eloquently to why "dumping" and subsidy cases have given rise to some of the most acrimonious trade disputes of recent years.

Much of the work of the institutions studied in this three chapter sequence involves law making in the formal sense of promulgating and interpreting rules of conduct to which nations are expected to adhere. Much of what they do involves the application of those rules through established procedures. But there is more. At times these institutions seek to influence national policies through processes in which legal rules play little or no role at all — except as they prescribe the process itself — and in which economic and political considerations are the accepted currency of discourse. Yet, even when this is the case, the discourse is often cast in the forms of legal thought and argument. At other times the institutions employ processes where rules, although important, perform functions that cannot be subsumed within the more traditional view of law as rules for judging the legality of particular conduct. Here the challenge is jurisprudential; to understand the function that law performs and to become aware of the limitations on the efficacy of law implicit in the functional analysis.

Introduction to Chapter 3

Any study that engages the law of international trade at such varied levels, and in such varied forms as in these three chapters, must begin by examining the basic theoretical economic rationale for international trade; the welfare gains from trade liberalization, the economic consequences of protectionism, the impact of exchange rates on the direction and flow of trade and the reasons, political as well as economic, behind efforts by the international community to control national trade policies. This preliminary excursus provides a basis for exploring, at various places throughout Chapters 4 and 5, the economic consequences of particular trade policies and of the political forces upon which those consequences are likely to play in the ultimate resolution of policy issues. Out of this stuff the study will hopefully elicit a fuller understanding of how the institutions, the rules, the processes and the forms of legal argument can and do influence the resolution of those issues; the role of law in the governance of international trade.

§ 3.01   The Growth of and Reasons for Trade

The Growth of Trade

International trade has played an increasingly important role in the world economy, doubling in nominal dollar amount about every ten years between 1938 and 1958 and more rapidly thereafter. In 1938 total world exports amounted to $24.1 billion; by 1948 the figure had grown to $53.7 billion and it reached $96 billion in 1958. In 1970 exports were valued at $282 billion internationally but by 1975 had almost tripled to $789.2 billion and by 1985 had more than doubled again to $1 trillion, 785.1 billion.[1] Of this total in world exports, twenty industrialized countries[2] accounted for $1 trillion, 285.6 billion, or 70%, while sixty-two developing countries accounted for $526.5 billion, or 30%. Of the latter, $111 billion represented exports by countries over two-thirds of whose export trade consisted of petroleum.

Much of the growth in the value of trade in the 1970's was due to worldwide inflation, and especially to the price increases obtained by oil-producing countries. In 1970 those countries accounted for less than 7% of the value of world exports, but by 1975 they produced 20%. Regardless of the reason, however, it is clear that world trade is a factor of mounting importance. In 1946 the value of imports and exports was equivalent to about 10% of the Gross National Product (GNP) of the United States. By 1985 that value exceeded 20%. In the case of some countries, such as the Federal Republic of Germany and South Korea, imports and exports

---

[1] Source: International Financial Statistics, May 1987. International Financial Statistics is a publication of the International Monetary Fund. The trade figures given do not include exports or imports for the USSR, the Communist countries of Eastern Europe (except Hungary, Rumania and Yugoslavia), Cuba, Vietnam or Cambodia. Included are figures for the Peoples Republic of China but not Taiwan. In addition the values given are not in constant dollars.

[2] These countries are: United States, Canada, Australia, Japan, New Zealand, Austria, Belgium, Luxembourg, Denmark, Finland, France, Germany, Ireland, Italy, Netherlands, Norway, Spain, Sweden, Switzerland and United Kingdom.

exceed 50% of GNP. Needless to add that the growing importance of international trade in the overall economic life of most nations of the world means that the rising tide of protectionism, which we will examine in Chapter 5, is a matter of increasingly grave concern.

The Reasons for Trade

While the magnitude and direction of growth in world trade is the product of a complex set of economic and political factors and of the legal order which is the subject of our study, its mainspring (as is true in economics generally) is prices. A country engages in trade because its producers can fetch a higher price abroad, while domestic consumers may be able to purchase some of their wants more cheaply outside the country. As these advantages to both producers and consumers increase so will that country's volume of international trade. What is important here is to observe precisely that structure of international prices which leads a nation to trade and to observe the gains to national welfare that are to be derived from such trade.

The underlying importance of prices in international trade can be demonstrated with the use of a simple supply and demand graph. Figure 1 presents a typical supply curve for watch producers in what we shall call Country A. It shows the various quantities (horizontal axis "Q") of watches they will be willing to produce at various prices (vertical axis "P").

Figure 1

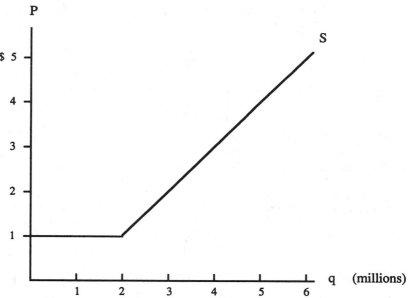

The supply curve (S) for watches shows the different amounts of watches that producers will supply at different prices. At some point, producers' marginal costs increase, meaning that increased supply is forthcoming only at higher prices. Thus the supply curve is upward sloping.

For example, Figure 1 shows that producers will deliver up to 2 million watches if the price received is $1. To produce more, however, they will require a higher price. This is so because beyond some point (2 million in our example) producers' costs begin to increase. Economists refer to this as the "law of increasing marginal costs" and it means nothing more than that producers trying to increase output will eventually find their costs increasing.[3] In effect, the watchmakers' higher costs mean that they cannot produce unless offered a higher price. This is the derivation of the supply curve (S) in Figure 1.

Consumers are different, however; lower prices lead them to buy more. This is shown in Figure 2.

Figure 2

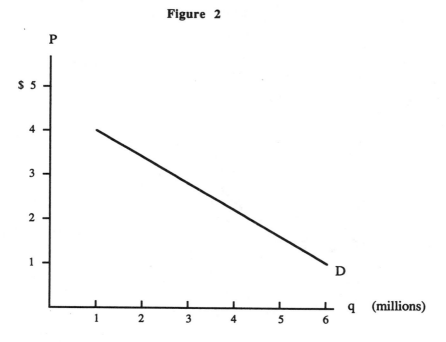

The demand curve (D) is based upon the proposition that consumers will want to buy more of a good the lower its price.

In Figure 2, consumer demand is such that only 1 million watches will be purchased if the price is $4, even though producers will be willing to make 5 million watches for that price. At $4 there would be a surplus of watches. If the price fell to $1, people would want to buy 6 million watches. The problem would

---

[3] More labor will be needed, for example, but to compete resources away from their current employment, higher prices to labor (wages) must be offered. Obtaining additional parts, more machinery and other required resources will also be more costly for similar reasons.

then be that producers would supply only 2 million watches and there would be a shortage.

How are producers and consumers to agree on the price and quantity? In fact, they do not have to. If producers provide 4 million watches and charge $3, only 2.5 million will be bought. There will be a *surplus* which will lead producers to cut back production and lower prices. On the other hand, if only 2 million watches are produced, consumers will want 6 million at the price of $1. There will be a *shortage* that will induce consumers to bid more for the short supply and ultimately lead manufacturers to step up production. Whether the price is too high or too low, whether too much or too little is produced, the system has a built-in mechanism pushing it towards the equilibrium solution shown in Figure 3: 3.5 million watches selling for $2.50 each. The efficient, low-cost solution to the two questions of how much to produce and what price to charge are obtained through the use of the market.

Figure 3

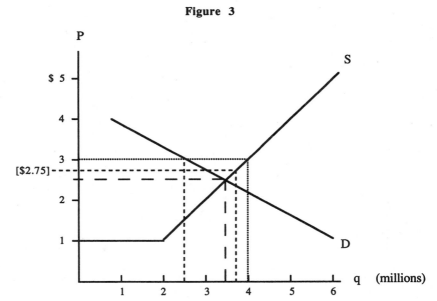

The supply (S) and demand (D) curves intersect at $2.50. At that price the market is in equilibrium; producers will supply just as many watches as consumers are willing to purchase at that price.

Thus far we have presupposed a closed economy, one in which all watches consumers want are manufactured at home and in which the price of watches without trade is $2.50. Suppose, however, that the possibility of international trade is introduced and that the price abroad for watches of equivalent quality is $3. The watches made in Country A are perfect substitutes for those selling abroad, so the home product can sell abroad just as easily as at home. Ignoring transportation costs (which today are quite low per item sold) the price of watches in Country A will have to adjust to the $3 world price.[4] Producers will not sell in one market for $2.50 what they can sell in another for $3.

To illustrate this last point, observe that at a price of $3, producers in country A will, as Figure 3 indicates, produce 4 million watches. At $3 per watch, however, consumers in Country A will purchase only 2.5 million watches. But this won't deter producers in Country A from charging $3 so long as they can sell the rest of their production (*i.e.*, 1.5 million watches) abroad. In that event, the price of watches in Country A will rise to the prevailing world price of $3. Suppose, however, that at $3 producers in Country A can only sell 500,000, rather than 1.5 million, watches abroad. Under these circumstances a price of $3 will mean a surplus of watches; producers will make 4 million watches but consumers at home and abroad will buy only 3 million (2.5 million at home and 500,000 abroad). Producers will accordingly have to lower their price. Note, again from Figure 3, that at a price of $2.75 consumers in Country A will purchase 3 million watches and producers will make 3.75 million watches. If by dropping their price to $2.75, producers in Country A can increase their sales abroad from 500,000 to 750,000, the market — this time the world market — will be in equilibrium, and consumers the world over will have to pay the prevailing world price of $2.75.

In all of this we have not expressly mentioned, but we have not ignored, foreign producers. Our assumptions about how many watches producers in Country A can sell abroad, reflect not only what quantities foreign consumers will buy at particular prices but also what quantities foreign producers will offer at those prices. For example, to say that producers in Country A can sell 1.5 million watches abroad at a price of $3, means that the quantity of watches foreign producers will offer at $3 falls 1.5 million short of the quantity foreign consumers will purchase at that price.

Now, we can summarize by observing that if the world price is $3 and if at that price Country A is exporting watches and other countries are importing watches from Country A, we may conclude that, at $3, there is a surplus of watches in Country A, a fact confirmed by Figure 3, and a shortage of watches abroad. If international trade were then terminated, producers in Country A, facing a surplus, would have to lower their price to $2.50 and curtail their production to 3.5 million watches, which means that consumers in A would get more watches at less cost. On the other hand if trade were terminated, the price abroad would have to rise above $3 in order to induce producers to increase production and eliminate the shortage. This can be shown by Figure 4.

---

[4] It is assumed in these examples that we are dealing both at home and abroad with competitive markets in which all producers are "price-takers" in that no one producer's contribution to total supply is significant enough to affect the prevailing price. If any one producer attempts to raise his price above that prevailing in the market, there are plenty of producers around who will take the business away from him. Likewise we assume each country is a "price-taker" meaning that no one country's contribution to total world supply is so significant as to have an effect on the prevailing world price. Each country thus takes world prices as given.

Figure 4

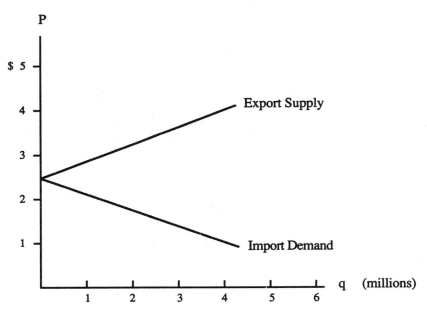

A world price above the closed market equilibrium price in Country A of
$2.50 will lead to exports; a price below $2.50 to imports.

As Figure 4 indicates, at a world price above $2.50 (the closed market equilib-
rium price in Country A), producers in A will want to produce more than the home
market will absorb and so will export their surplus. The surplus in fact becomes
the export supply; at a world price of $3, the home country will export 1.5 million
watches. Should the world price instead be $2, producers in Country A will not
produce enough to fill the demand and Country A will import a total of 1.5 million
watches. Prices will determine the direction and quantity of trade.

§ 3.02 Comparative Advantage and the Gains from Trade

It will be observed from what we have said so far that when one introduces the
possibilities of international trade into once closed national markets, certain
groups of people benefit and others appear, at first blush, to be less well off.
Consumers abroad and producers in Country A appear to benefit. Consumers in
Country A and producers abroad seem to lose. What is the net of welfare gains
and loses; do the benefits from trade outweigh the losses? Is there any theoretical
formulation that will tells us, or is it a question to be answered on the facts of each
case?

First, one rough observation from our example is worth noting. When we
hypothesized that producers in Country A could, at a price of $3, produce watches
that could be sold abroad, we were also in effect saying that producers abroad were
not able, because of their costs, to make the additional watches that their own
consumers would buy at $3. This, in effect, means a number of things: (i) at $3
there is an unsatisfied consumer demand outside country A, (ii) that demand can

only be met by devoting additional resources to the manufacture of watches, (iii) if produced outside country A it will require *more than $3* of additional resources per watch to meet the demand, and (iv) at a cost in excess of $3 some of the demand will remain unsatisfied. On the other hand, if because trade is possible, the added production takes place in Country A it will require *only $3* of additional resources per watch to fill the unsatisfied demand. Trade is the mechanism for allocating resources to the lowest cost producer; the producer who will use those resources most efficiently. This, in turn, is a clue that there may indeed be a broader theoretical formulation to tell us whether the welfare gains from international trade are likely to exceed the welfare losses, or not.

That theory was first articulated by several of the great 19th Century, Classical British economists, most notably David Ricardo. They called it the "doctrine of comparative advantage" — not, as we shall see, "absolute" advantage. Few, if any theoretical economic formulations have been as thoroughly vindicated by actual events as has this doctrine. The extraordinary extent to which world trade in industrial products has been liberalized since World War II, matched with the extraordinary growth in that trade itself and in the domestic economies of the major trading nations, compared with the disasters bred by the protectionism of the interwar period, offer as much "proof" of the efficacy of the doctrine as any practical statesman or lawyer needs. Certainly, to ignore the teachings of the doctrine is to court disaster. What follows, therefore, is a series of simple numerical examples that illustrate the operation of the doctrine of comparative advantage.

First we must simplify things. Assume that there were only two nations in the world — United States and Japan — each producing only two products; the same two products — watches and cloth — and that no trade was possible between the two countries. Assume further, that the United States could produce, using all its resources, 3 million watches in one year if it produced only watches, or 2 million bolts of cloth if it devoted all its resources to the textile sector. A smaller country, Japan, could produce only 2 million watches or 1 million bolts of cloth by directing all its resources to one or the other. The United States is thus able to produce more of both commodities than Japan. The production possibilities of both countries are summarized in Table I.

Table I

Inputs	Production Possibilities		Domestic Exchange (Price) Ratio
	Watches	Cloth	
U.S.A.			
3 mill. man/hrs + 3 mill. capital	3 million	2 million	1w = .67c (1c = 1 1/2w)

Japan

| 2.5 mill, man/hrs
+ 2.5 mill. capital | 2 million | 1 million | 1w = .50c
(1c = 2w) |

Note first that the United States is the larger of the two economies. It has 3 million man hours and 3 million units of capital available to produce watches or cloth or some mix of the two, while Japan has only 2.5 million man hours and units of capital available. Secondly, note that measured by quantity of output per unit of input the United States is a more efficient producer of both watches and cloth than Japan. In other words, the United States has the absolute advantage in the production of both products. This is shown more precisely in Table II.

Table II

Inputs	Output of Watches		Output of Cloth
U.S.A.			
1 man/hr +1 capital	1 watch	or	.67 cloth
Japan			
1 man/hr +1 capital	.8 watch	or	.4 cloth

The most important point to note, however, is that while the United States is a larger economy and has the *absolute advantage* in both products, it has the *comparative advantage* only in the production of cloth, while Japan has the *comparative advantage* in the manufacture of watches. This can be seen by comparing the Domestic Exchange or Price Ratios in Table I for each country. To get 3 million watches, the United States must forego production of 2 million bolts of cloth. Or, stated more fully, for each watch the United States' may want to produce it must take resources that would otherwise produce .67 (2/3) of a bolt of cloth. The *opportunity cost* (*i.e.*, the amount of one product that must be given-up in order to produce another) of one watch made in the United States is 2/3's (.67) of a bolt of cloth. On the other hand, the *opportunity cost* of one watch in Japan is only half (.50) a bolt cloth. To produce watches, Japan will have to forego production of cloth to a lesser extent than will the United States. Conversely, for each additional bolt of cloth produced, the United States will have to forego the production of 1 1/2 watches while Japan will have to forego the production of 2 watches. To produce cloth the United States will have to forego the production of fewer watches than Japan. Thus, Japan is *comparatively* (*i.e.*, in terms of its own internal opportunity cost structure) more efficient (*i.e.*, has the "*comparative advantage*") in the production of watches and the United States has the comparative advantage in the production of cloth.

Keeping these conditions in mind, first suppose that there is no possibility of trade between the two countries. Each country will want to consume some of both goods and will have to produce its own requirements. Suppose each decides upon the following mix:

	Watches	Cloth
United States	1 million	1.33 million
Japan	1 million	.50 million
Totals	2 million	1.83 million
	(3.83 million)	

Between the two countries, 2 million watches and 1.83 million bolts of cloth will be produced. Note that the opportunity cost of producing watches is reflected in the amounts of cloth that each country can produce.

Now, assume that we introduce the possibility of international trade. The result is that because the United States has the *comparative advantage* in making cloth and Japan in producing watches, both countries will gain by each specializing where their advantage lies and then engaging in trade. Production of both products will be increased (valuable resources will be put to their best use) by letting the principle of *comparative advantage* work. For example, specialization might yield the following pattern of production:

	Watches	Cloth
United States	100,000	1,943,000
Japan	2,000,000	0
Totals	2,100,000	1,943,000
	(4,043,000)	

Note that with trade between the two countries exactly the same resources yield more cloth and more watches than was possible in the absence of trade. From the same resource base specialization according to comparative advantage has made it possible for the world to achieve a net increase in the total goods and services available to satisfy human need. For another example see note below.[1] At this point there are two important points to make.

No Trade	Watches	Cloth
United States	2 million	.67 million
Japan	1 million	.50 million
Totals	3 million	1.17 million
	(4.17 million)	

With Trade	Watches	Cloth
United States	1 million	1.33 million
Japan	2 million	0
Totals	3 million	1.33 million
	(4.33 million)	

First, by allocating resources to the most efficient producer, both countries will gain. The gain may not be divided exactly evenly, but both will share in the increase in global welfare. This is then the answer to our earlier question. While some groups within trading countries may lose, the over-all gain to each trading nation will be greater than the loss.

Secondly it is important to note that the doctrine of *comparative advantage* applies between and among countries of all sizes. It underscores the point that *all* countries benefit from trade, regardless of their size or degree of *absolute* efficiency, since it permits specialization in the areas of greater comparative efficiency, or (so to speak) lesser inefficiency. Absolute economic size is irrelevant. In more political terms — terms highly relevant to the lawyer interested in the institutions that govern world trade — this means that the process of trade liberalization is not a *zero-sum game*, where one party's gain must be matched by another's loss. It is a *positive-sum game*, where all stand to gain. To this must be added yet another point. In spite of the affluence of many in the developed countries of the world, the vast majority of the world's people live in poverty. Many face an ever present threat of starvation. There is a vast unmet need for the essentials of a better life; for food, housing, health and education. In this setting a demand that the world as a whole order its affairs in such a way as to maximize the efficient use of all of the world's resources begins to take on the aspect of a moral imperative.

At the same time, one cannot ignore the fact that with trade, under our example, some American watchmakers will go out of business, their plants idled and their employees forced to look for other work. The same is true of Japanese clothmakers. There are clearly adjustments to be made when countries liberalize trade, and it is this fact that introduces a powerful element into the politics of trade. American watchmakers and Japanese clothmakers are not likely to stand idly by and watch the market, operating according to the dictates of an abstract economic principle, determine their fate. They are likely to go to their governments and seek protection. The point to keep in mind, however, is that if they are protected, society as a whole is very likely to be worse off. We say "likely to be" because we will want later to consider further whether there are any situations in which the curtailment of trade can enhance national welfare. For the present, however, it is important to observe that in the broadest terms the issue is not so much should trade be liberalized than how can society use the welfare gains that trade makes possible to ameliorate the costs of adjustment that particular groups within the society must bear. While theoretically it is sometimes argued that these adjustment costs could be so great as to swallow-up all the welfare gains from trade, that is problematic at best. Empirical studies increasingly make clear that the costs to society of protection, especially consumer costs, are very likely to out strip any benefit the protected industry might reap from not having to adjust to a more liberal trading climate.

Since Japan is using all its resources to make watches and, under our assumed production possibilities, can make no more, the remaining 1 million of world-wide demand for watches must be produced in the United States. The welfare gain, therefore, comes from the U.S. shifting resources from making 1 million watches to making cloth, and Japan shifting resources from making .50 million bolts of cloth to making watches.

§ 3.03 The Role of Money and the Flow of Trade

Exchange Rates

Now, of course a very small part of world trade takes the form of barter (*e.g.*, watches for cloth). The relative value of goods and the opportunity costs of their production are not generally measured in exchange ratios between alternate production mixes, but in terms of money prices. In our discussion of prices we used only one currency, the United States' dollar, and yet trade actually occurs between countries with different currencies. This then introduces the very basic fact that in international trade, as distinguished from purely domestic trade, there are two prices, not just one price to be considered. There is first the price of the goods denominated in the currency of the contract. Secondly, there is the price that one of the parties to the contract must pay to acquire the currency of the contract: the "exchange rate." Suppose, a Japanese seller agrees to sell and an American buyer agrees to buy 1,000 watches at 1,000 yen per watch. Since typically the American will be earning dollars by selling the watches in the United States, he has two prices to cope with. He has to pay the seller 1,000 yen, but he must also take his dollars and buy those yen. If $1 will buy 200 yen (an "exchange rate" of $1 = 200 yen), the price to the buyer of a 1,000 yen watch is $5. On the other hand, if $1 will buy 250 yen, then that very same watch will cost the American buyer only $4. The same is true of the seller if the contract is denominated in dollars. Most of his costs are likely to be payable in yen and so the price he gets on a $5 watch will be very different if $1 will buy only 200 yen rather than 250 yen (if $1 = Y200 a $5 watch will yield Y1000; if $1 = Y250 a $5 watch will yield Y1,250).

This then raises a basic question. As we noted, under the principle of comparative advantage, trade yields gains to efficiency through the specialization of production when two nations have different opportunity costs (*i.e.*, domestic exchange ratio's). Since those costs are likely to be expressed in money price terms, the question is what effect can exchange rates have on the operation of the principle of comparative advantage.

Suppose the prices for watches and cloth in the United States and Japan were as follows:

	Watches	Cloth	Exchange Ratio
United States	$2	$3	1w = .67c
Japan	300 yen	600 yen	1w = .5c

Again we can see that the United States has comparative advantage in cloth and Japan in watches.[1] Assume now that the exchange rate is $1 = 250 yen. At that

---

[1] In the U.S. the price of one watch is 2/3's the price of a bolt of cloth, but in Japan a watch costs only one half the price of a bolt of cloth. In the U.S. a bolt of cloth costs one half again as much as a watch, but in Japan it costs twice as much as a watch.

rate of exchange the Japanese cloth buyer would need 750 yen in order to obtain the $3 he needs to buy American cloth and the Japanese watch buyer will need 500 yen to obtain the $2 he needs for an American watch. Since both can buy the Japanese products cheaper (*i.e.,* cloth at 600 yen and watches at 300 yen), neither will import the American product. On the other hand, at that rate, the American watch buyer must pay only $1.20 to buy the 300 yen needed for the Japanese watch and the American cloth buyer will need only $2.40 to buy the 600 yen he needs for the Japanese cloth. They will be happy to purchase both watches and cloth from Japan and pocket the change. In spite of comparative advantage, we will have only one-way trade; Japanese watches and cloth to the United States.

Now suppose the dollar devalues against the yen to where $1 = 125 yen. At this point the Japanese cloth buyer needs only 375 yen to buy the $3 needed for American cloth and the Japanese watch buyer needs only 250 yen to obtain the $2 he needs for an American watch. Both will be happy to buy from the United States. The American watch buyer now needs $2.40 to purchase the 300 yen needed for the Japanese watch and the American cloth buyer needs $4.80 to purchase the 600 yen required for Japanese cloth. The Americans will obviously not buy. Again we will have one way trade: U.S. cloth and watches to Japan.

In sum at an exchange rate of $1 = 250 yen the dollar is too expensive for Japanese buyers and the yen is cheap to American buyers (*i.e.,* the dollar is over-valued relative to the yen), while at $1 = 125 yen, the dollar is under-valued (the dollar is cheap to the Japanese and the yen is too expensive for Americans). Quite obviously, if one nation wants to expand its exports to another country and curtail imports from the latter, it will want its currency to be under-valued relative to its trading partner's currency.

This, however, cannot go on forever. Built into the mechanism is at least a partial corrective. Assume, the dollar is under-valued at $1 = 125 yen and Japanese buyers are buying American cloth and watches at record levels but Americans are not buying Japanese products. So long as we have a free-market in foreign exchange where governments are not intervening to maintain a particular rate, this means that Japanese buyers are offering yen to the market (increasing the supply of yen) and buying dollars (increasing the demand for dollars) at a rate much faster than American buyers are increasing the supply of dollars and the demand for yen. With the demand for dollars out-stripping the supply and with the supply of yen out-stripping the demand, it will soon take more yen to buy a dollar; the yen value of the dollar will start to rise from $1 = 125 yen, to say, $1 = 175 yen. At that exchange rate, the Japanese cloth buyer will now need 525 yen to purchase the $3 American cloth where his own cloth will cost him 600 yen. The American watch buyer will need only $1.72 to purchase the Japanese watch at 300 yen while an American watch would cost him $2. By the same token the Japanese watch buyer will not spend 350 yen to buy the $2 American watch nor will the American cloth buyer spend the $3.43 necessary to buy the 600 yen Japanese cloth. In short, at an exchange rate of $1 = 175 yen the U.S. will sell cloth to Japan and Japan will sell watches to the United States and we will have the two-way trade that comparative advantage dictates.

Unhappily, the self adjusting system doesn't always work, or doesn't work as quickly or as decisively as it might. The reasons are complex but at least two of them should be noted. First, governments do intervene and more often than otherwise they intervene to keep their currencies either over or under-valued. Some of the reasons for this we shall turn to presently in our discussion of the balance of payments. Second, we have simplified by treating the only persons buying and selling foreign exchange as buyers and seller of goods. There are, of course, other people buying and selling each others currencies and it is quite possible that their actions might counteract those of traders in goods. Suppose, for example, the dollar is overvalued so that American cloth is too expensive for Japanese cloth buyers but Japanese watches are very cheap to American watch buyers and the latter are selling dollars and buying yen, thereby helping to drive the value of the dollar down. At the same time, however, suppose interest rates in the United States are higher than in Japan or there is political unrest in Japan. Both of these circumstances may cause Japanese investors to sell yen and buy dollars, thereby countering the effects of the American watch buyers.

The International Monetary System

At this point it is well to state some of what we have just described concerning exchange rates a bit more rigorously and then relate the discussion to the broader context of the international monetary system, including the problem of the balance of payments. As we have seen trade is dependent on the existence of the "right" exchange rate. And since an exchange rate is simply the price of one currency denominated in terms of another, one would expect the exchange rate to be determined by the laws of supply and demand. And so it is, as shown in Figure 5.[2]

---

[2] For simplicity, it is again assumed that we are operating in a world of only two countries. Multi-country exchange markets operate on the same principles of supply and demand for each currency traded, although additional theoretical discussion is required to explain why the same rates emerge on each market. An excellent introductory text is Leland Yeager, International Monetary Mechanism.

Figure 5

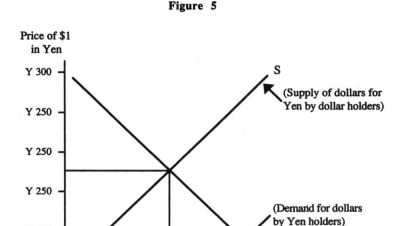

The exchange rate of dollars for yen is the result of a process equilibrating the quantity supplied with that demanded. This figure shows the supply of and demand for dollars and the "price," expressed in terms of yen, at which equilibrium occurs.

Figure 5 portrays the situation facing yen-holders (presumably, Japanese buyers and investors)[3] interested in converting their yen into dollars. If the price of one dollar is 250 yen, relatively few dollars will be demanded because the high price of dollars makes American goods, services and investments relatively unattractive to Japanese buyers.[4] On the other hand, a low exchange rate of 125 yen for one dollar means that American goods will be cheaper to Japanese buyers than at the higher rate, and those buyers will increase the number of dollars demanded. In other words, the demand for U.S. currency is a function of foreigners' desire to use dollars. The lower the price the more they will demand.

On the supply side, Figure 5 also shows that as more yen are offered per dollar, the supply of dollars trading on the market for yen will increase. This reflects the fact that as American dollar holders are offered more yen per dollar (*i.e.*, the dollar will revalue against the yen) Japanese goods, investments and so forth will be correspondingly cheaper to Americans. Dollar holders will, as a result, put more

---

[3] Obviously, demanders of dollars for yen might include Americans holding yen, but these will be a smaller portion of all yen-holders than the Japanese.

[4] The Japanese yen-holders demand for dollars is not necessarily linked to a desire to purchase goods and services from Americans. The Japanese yen-holders may want to buy dollars for investment in the United States, especially if interest rates in the United States are higher than in Japan or elsewhere in the world. They may want to hold their wealth in the United States because political conditions in Japan make them fearful of losing their savings. Whatever the reasons, they are all part of the demand for dollars by yen-holders.

dollars into the supply offered for yen. The supply curve thus has its usual upward slope.

Eventually, the market will settle down at a rate of $1 = 175 yen, as shown. If more dollars are offered than the Japanese want to purchase (which occurs when the dollar trades for more than 175 yen), the oversupply means that the price will fall — just as an oversupply in any market produces a falling price. On the other hand, if the dollar exchanges for a time at less than 175 yen, more dollars will be demanded than American dollar holders are willing to part with. The shortage will lead dollar demanders to bid up the price — the exchange rate — until the equilibrium rate of $1 = 175 yen is attained. Once again, the provision of a market guiding transaction means an efficient, low-cost solution to the problem of the "right" rate for the exchange of dollars and yen.

Now, Figure 5 portrays the supply and demand for dollars at various yen prices prevailing so long as the basic economic conditions influencing yen-holders' decisions remained relatively stable. Suppose, however, that those conditions begin to change; interest rates in the United States begin to fall, prices in the U.S. begin to rise more rapidly than in Japan, the Japanese economy grows more rapidly than the American, the investment climate in Japan improves relative to that of the United States. If these circumstances occur then, as shown in Figure 6, the previous demand curve (D) will shift to (D¹), indicating a decreased demand by the Japanese for dollars. This means in turn that the exchange rate should change, with the new rate being $1 = 150 yen (the dollar will devalue). This is only what one would expect to emerge on any market, since whenever demand decreases — for watches or dollars — a lower price for that item is the normal result.

Figure 6

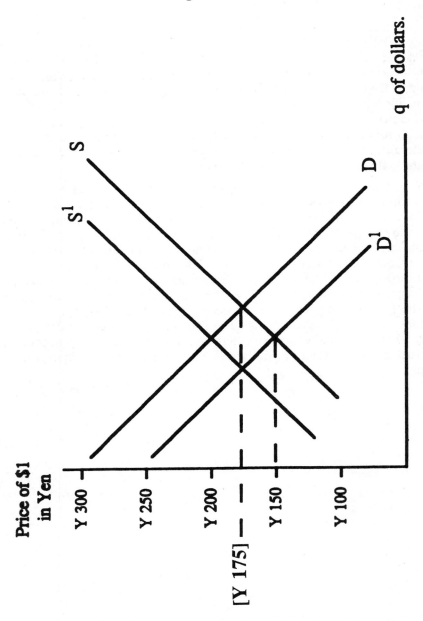

In response to a fall in demand for dollars, from (D) to (D¹), the exchange rate should fall to $1 = 150 yen. The government can avoid this drop in the exchange rate by buying up dollars in the market, shifting supply back from (S) to (S¹) until the old exchange rate is reestablished.

Note that in response to a decline in the demand for dollars we say the exchange rate "should fall." The problem is that we have included the supply and demand of dollars only on the part of private parties active on the foreign exchange market. There is a third actor: the government. Because it holds large stocks of gold and foreign currency, the government can intervene on foreign exchange markets and influence the exchange rate of the dollar. Suppose that for "prestige" or some other reason, the American government does not want the exchange rate to be anything less than $1–175 yen. It can enter the market itself,[5] *selling yen and buying dollars.* The purchase of dollars by the government effectively reduces the supply of dollars on the market, shifting the supply schedule to (S^1), as shown in Figure 6. The purchase of dollars will continue until a new equilibrium is reached by the intersection of D^1 and S^1, where the governmentally desired exchange rate of $1 = 175 yen is reestablished. By continually intervening in foreign exchange markets the government can support its currency at a predetermined rate — but only for as long as it has liquid assets (gold and foreign currencies) to buy up dollars.

The Balance of Payments

Our discussion of government intervention will proceed more smoothly once we have a basic idea of that much misunderstood concept, the balance of payments. The most important point to make at the outset is that there is no magic attached to the word "balance." Because balance–of–payments accounting is a double–entry system, debits and credits must automatically match. A country's international trade and monetary affairs might be in utter chaos, yet the account of international payments would be balanced, since every entry on the plus side is matched on the minus side. Simplifying a bit, a typical balance-of-payments statement resembles that shown in Table III. The international transactions are divided into account groups: merchandise (goods), services, investment income (earnings from investments already made), unilateral transfers (foreign aid, private gifts and so forth), and capital, both long and short-term. There is also a settlement account to which we return in a moment.

---

[5] In the United States, intervention in foreign exchange markets is handled by the New York Federal Reserve Bank. Intervention refers only to those transactions undertaken by government in support of its exchange rate; the U.S. government also purchases and sells abroad, but such transactions are treated the same as purchases and sales by private consumers and producers.

Table III

Hypothetical Balance of Payments Statement
(Billions of Dollars)

	Minus (Debit)	Plus (Credit)
1. Merchandise	100	50
2. Services	70	70
3. Investment Income	60	80
4. Unilateral Transfer	10	0
5. Long-term Capital	50	40
6. Short-term Capital	50	70
7. Sub-Total, "above the line"	340	310
8. Settlement Transactions	-0-	30
	340	340

Note that for each type of transaction, there is a minus (debit) and plus (credit) side of the ledger. *Minus or debit transactions are those which ordinarily entail payment by residents to foreigners*; an import of watches is thus a minus item. Plus (credit) items are the reverse, *involving ordinarily the payment by foreigners to residents*; thus the export of cloth is a credit item. To see the necessary "balancing" of the balance of payments, just think what happens when an international transaction occurs. If a Japanese consumer purchases cloth from the United States, an American producer exports the cloth, which is a plus transaction. But before the foreign buyer could pay for the cloth, he had to buy dollars, which he does on the foreign exchange market. Since this entailed a payment of dollars by Americans to foreigners, *it constitutes a minus item of the same magnitude recorded on the capital account.* Or suppose a private citizen sends money abroad as a gift to foreign relatives. That is a minus item, since payment moves from a resident to a foreigner. But what will the foreigner do with the dollar–denominated gift? Most probably he will cash it in for his home currency. The foreign bank where he does this will then exchange the dollars for home currency at the country's central bank (a government agency that stands ready to exchange foreign for home currencies), which then ships the dollars back to the United States to be reimbursed in the home currency by our central bank (the Federal Reserve). This last stage is a plus item, involving payment from foreigners to residents. Or perhaps the dollars sent abroad will be used to purchase American exports, or repay a dollar repayable loan, both plus items. In any case, there is a necessary balancing of plus and minus items. Implicit in our examples and obvious from Table III is the fact that each separate account need not balance. What is important is the aggregate of accounts 1 through 6; the so-called "above the line" accounts referring to an imaginary line separating ordinary transactions from the official settlement account in line 7. Also because it takes time for a transaction recorded as a debit to work through to a corresponding credit transaction, and vice versa, the overall payments account between the U.S. and another country need not be, and is not likely to be, "in balance" at any one time. Indeed, such "above the line" imbalances can persist for protracted periods of time.

This brings us to the last account in the statement, settlement transactions. These are the official operations of the government necessary to settle any *imbalance of plus and minus totals that occur within a stated accounting period* on ordinary transactions in accounts 1 through 6. Government settlement transactions involve the receipt or the payment of "official reserves" (principally gold and foreign reserve currencies held by the government) from or to foreigners. In the case of the gift of money sent abroad, we saw that the foreign recipient could cash it in for his own currency with his central bank and the latter will then transfer the dollars to the Federal Reserve and receive its currency. The net result is the loss of foreign currency from our official holdings of currency reserves. It is important to note that the loss of the foreign currency (or gold) is a *plus* transaction. Surrender of our assets like foreign currency or gold ordinarily entails payment of dollars by foreigners (in the example, the foreign gift recipient) to residents, which is the definition of a plus or credit transaction. The easiest way to remember this is to think of the loss of reserves or gold as an *export* just like an export of goods. Both are plus transactions.

It is the information contained in the settlement account that gives meaning to the concepts of balance–of–payment surplus and deficit. When the aggregate of accounts reflecting the ordinary economic transactions of society (accounts 1 through 6 in Table III) balance out, there is neither a surplus nor deficit. This is known as a balance "above the line." When it is necessary for government settlement operations to resolve any imbalance in the ordinary transactions above the line, we have either a surplus or deficit. Surplus is defined as a debit (minus) on the settlement account, whereby the government has a net *intake* of gold or foreign reserves. Deficit is correspondingly defined as the net *outflow* of gold and reserves (as in our example), which is a credit (plus) in balance-of-payments accounting.

Why is there such a pejorative connotation attached to the term deficit? There are at least two reasons, one of which is totally without foundation. It holds that it is the wealth of the state itself which is the important indicator of national well being. This was the Mercantilist view, which was dominant in Europe from the early sixteenth to the end of the eighteenth centuries. Deficits were *per se* undesirable, since they involved a diminution of the government's holdings of gold and reserves. But what is the state if not the totality of its citizens, who in no way benefit from the stacks of gold bars and paper money in the national coffers? As a matter of fact, deficits are in themselves *desirable*, as long as they can be sustained, since they indicate that the citizenry is receiving in goods, services, gifts and investment capital ("above the line" transactions) more than they are having to give up.

But this can be sustained for only so long, and it is this fact that underlies the real reason to regard deficits in the long run with some dismay. Deficits can only be sustained as long as there are sufficient gold and foreign currency in the national treasury to continue the outpayment to foreigners.

Correction of Disequilibria

We saw earlier that by buying dollars for yen, the American government could keep the exchange rate where it wanted it, $1=175 yen. We now know that it cannot do so forever. For the *amount of yen of which it must use to buy dollars every year and thereby keep the dollar artificially expensive is the size of the deficit that will show up at year's end on the balance of payments statement.* Now consider Figure 7, which is based on Figure 6.

Figure 7

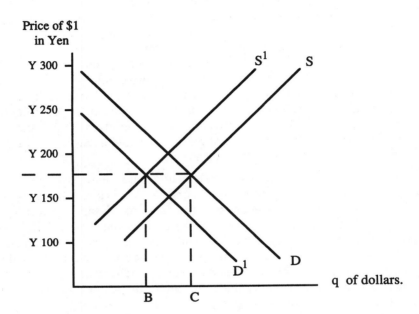

Absent government intervention on the foreign exchange market, the exchange rate for $1 will fall from 175 yen to 150 yen when the demand for dollars falls. By selling its liquid assets government can reduce the supply of dollars to bouy their price. Only when BC dollars have been purchased will the exchange rate be reestablished at the old level of $1 = 175 yen.

As Figure 7 shows, once yen holders' demand for dollars has fallen to D¹, the government must sell BC dollars worth of yen annually to keep the exchange rate of the dollar at 175 yen. As long as it has gold or foreign currencies, it can sell these to keep supporting the dollar. But its resources are not unlimited. At some point, should the supply of and demand for dollars remain as pictured, the government will have to cease its support and let the dollar find its value in the exchange markets at 150 yen. At this point, there will be no deficit or surplus (since there will be no settlement transactions) and so no balance-of-payment worries. This should explain why countries chronically running a balance-of-payments deficit are referred to as having an "overvalued currency." The price of the currency is pegged artificially high by government intervention, producing deficits in the balance of payments. For currencies kept artificially low, such as Germany's during much of the post-war period, the result of the "undervalued currency" is a chronic surplus.

If this is not clear, recall that an overvalued currency makes imports cheaper for the home country, but exports of home country products to foreigners more expensive. A deficit should result. Undervaluation produces the reverse price incentives and should lead to a surplus.

Fixed Versus Floating Exchange Rates

The system whereby exchange rates are left free to find their own level is known as a "floating rate" regime; the system of government supported rates is known as a "fixed rate" system. Until 1971 post-World War II international monetary affairs took place against a backdrop of fixed exchange rates. The reasons for this are many, but one in particular deserves attention.

During the 1930's depression national governments adopted draconian measures to try to increase exports and so create jobs at home without a concomitant increase in imports. One means was very high tariffs, such as those contained in the Tariff Act of 1930 (the Smoot-Hawley Act). Another was "competitive devaluation." This was not devaluation to attain the equilibrium value of one's currency, but rather to create the undervaluation that leads to surpluses. Of course, as one nation imposed new tariffs or devalued, another would retaliate by doing the same thing. The result was the dismemberment of the system of relatively free trade that had previously prevailed, and the sort of loss of individual wealth that the theory of comparative advantage posits will accompany the destruction of trade. It was largely the experience of the depression years that led to the formation of the International Monetary Fund (IMF), the ill-fated International Trade Organization (ITO) and the General Agreement on Tariffs and Trade (GATT). In the field of international monetary affairs, it is the IMF that played the predominant role. By the rules of the IMF as originally formulated, member countries were required to state the schedule of rates (known as "parities") at which they would convert their own currencies for foreign currencies. These parities had to be maintained by intervention, except when there developed a "fundamental disequilibrium," an imprecise term to be sure. Essentially, the large-scale gain or loss of foreign reserves over a long period would suffice to prove that one's currency was in "fundamental disequilibrium" and revaluation or devaluation was called for. But for the most part, fixity was the rule of the day.

Economic events are no respecter of institutions, however, and the Bretton Woods system (so-called for the New Hampshire town where the plan for the IMF was established) which was designed to prevent unnecessary competitive devaluations ultimately proved to be powerless to ensure that the necessary devaluations were made. A full-fledged monetary history of the past eighteen years is not possible here, but suffice it to say that member nations' unwillingness to officially alter their parities (primarily the refusal of surplus countries to revalue their currencies) made the system so brittle that between 1971 and 1973 the Bretton Woods rules collapsed. By 1976 these were replaced by the so-called Jamaican Agreements, which we will have a chance to examine more closely in Chapter 10. Suffice it here to say we now have what some have called a "managed float." Exchange rates are generally allowed to fluctuate according to the dictates of supply and demand, but governments intervene periodically usually in furtherance of their macro-economic goals and increasingly only after a good deal of consultation with each other.

§ 3.04   Tariffs, Quotas

If the underlying basis for trade is simply the price advantage to trading abroad, then manipulation of prices is one way to manipulate trade. That is the effect of and reason for tariffs. Here consult Figure 8.

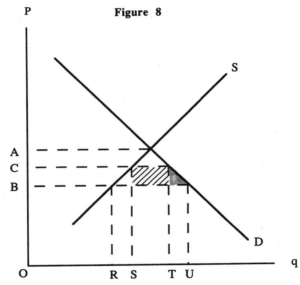

Assume that, as shown in Figure 8, the domestic price of watches in the absence of trade would be A. But suppose that with trade, the world price is B. At that price the home country would be an importer of watches; consumers will demand U watches, but only R will be produced by home manufacturers. The rest (U minus R) will be supplied by foreign manufacturers in the world market.

A tariff does nothing more than increase domestic production and decrease importation by imposing a tax on every good imported. The tax becomes part of the price paid. In our example, assume that Congress imposes a tax of BC on watches. Since watches now cost more, consumers demand fewer of them, only T, but the higher price means that consumers will be willing to pay up to C dollars (the price of foreign watches with the tariff) for domestically produced watches. So home production expands to S, leaving T minus S as the new level of imports.

All other things being equal, the net effect of increasing the price of imports is the same as increasing the price of any good — less is purchased. Producers are better off, consumers worse off, the national treasury richer by the proceeds of the tariff paid by consumers, which is represented by the shaded area in Figure 8 [1] and overall national welfare reduced (since we are paying more for what we could have gotten cheaper abroad). This is shown by the dotted area in Figure 8. Before the tariff consumers obtained U watches at a price per watch of B. After the tariff consumers obtained only T watches at a price of C per watch. Producers gained and the government gained, but the dotted area represents the amount by which the loss to consumers exceeds the combined gains to producers and the government.

Quotas will achieve much the same result as tariffs, although they involve different administrative problems for the government and are even more beneficial to producers. Quotas are mandatory ceilings on the absolute amount of a certain product that can be legally imported into the country. We see that without governmental interference, consumers would find it advantageous to import U watches at the going price. Suppose that a ceiling is now set on watch imports, allowing no more than T (See Figure 8) to be imported. Since, with fewer imports, the quantity demanded would exceed the quantity supplied at the prevailing world price of B, prices of watches would begin to climb. As prices begin to rise, increased production at home would accompany the reduction in quantities demanded by consumers, until once again the quantity supplied (home manufactures plus imports) equals the quantity demanded. This will only happen at the price C. From the consumers' standpoint the end result is the same as if a tariff had been imposed. The price has increased by BC and the quantity consumed and imported are both correspondingly lower.

There is, however, one big difference between a tariff and a quota; the revenue effect. Under a tariff, the shaded area in Figure 8 would be collected as government revenue by the importing country. If a quota were imposed allowing only ST watches to be imported, the price of the imported product would rise, but who will capture that increase cannot be determined in advance. If the exporters have a strong position in the market and importers are unorganized, the exporters are likely to capture the bulk of that increase and vice versa. Indeed, as we shall see in some of the more notable cases of protectionist quotas imposed by the United States, exporter's abroad reaped large "rents." Where this occurs, it also has an adverse effects on the importing country's "terms of trade." [2]

Alternatively the government may establish a system of import licenses, sometimes with quite unintended consequences. [3] The government might even

---

[1] Since an additional BC is paid on T minus S items imported, the total tariff revenue is ST × BC, or the area of the rectangle.

[2] A country's terms of trade refers to the prices it pays for imported goods relative to the prices it earns on exports. Thus, if the "terms of trade" are running against a country, it means that, measured over some period, prices paid for imports are increasing more rapidly, or decreasing more slowly, than prices earned on its exports.

[3] For example, the Eisenhower administration changed the U.S. system of oil import licenses from one where licenses were issued to previous importers to one where only oil refineries received licenses. The change made little difference for companies which both imported and refined, but the difference for others approached or surpassed a hundred million dollars a year. Inland refineries which had never used imported oil gained and coastal refineries built to use imported crude oil lost, as the latter had to acquire the license to buy oil at the world price, which was about a dollar a barrel below the domestic price.

auction off import licenses, so that it would capture for itself the bulk of the increase in price. This would make the quota the exact equivalent of the tariff, down to and including the revenue effect. Bureaucrats, however, do not favor auctions and they are not widely used. Thus, the increased price resulting from the quota will most often accrue to either exporter or importer, depending upon the proximate conditions in the market. In any event, if the government does not auction off licenses to importers, it must decide who imports on some basis: first come, first served; traditional importers; or some even more arbitrary system.

§ 3.05   The Costs of Protectionism and the Arguments Against Free Trade

The discussion thus far has identified in theory some of the costs that the protection of domestic producers against foreign competition is likely to visit upon the domestic economy. To lend theory a certain creditability, however, some recent empirical studies of the use by the United States of quotas have produced conclusions that, on their face, are quite startling, although there are also reasons to think that the studies may understate those costs.

As we have seen quotas will result in: (i) increased costs to consumers, (ii) increased returns to domestic producers, (iii) increased returns to foreign producers (unless the quotas are auctioned off), (iv) a loss of revenue to the government to the extent the excluded goods would have entered under a tariff, and (v) a deadweight welfare loss to the nation as a whole through the less then most efficient use of its resources. Thus, Hufbauer, Berliner and Elliott[1] have calculated that the third phase of protection granted the U.S. Carbon Steel industry beginning in 1980 imposed a total recurring annual cost on American consumers of $6.8 billion dollars. That worked out to be a cost of $750,000 annually for every steelworker's job that the protection was thought to have saved. The same program yielded a gain to U.S. steel producers of $3.8 billion annually, a gain to foreign steel producers of $2 billion annually, an anuual revenue loss to the government of $560 million and loss to efficiency of $330 million each year.

The same study shows that the Voluntary Restraint Agreements (VRAs) limiting imports of automobiles beginning in 1981 visted an annual cost of $5.8 billion on consumers. This meant it cost consumers $105,000 annually for every auto worker's job saved. American automobile producers gained $2.6 billion, foreign automobile manufacturers gained $4.3 billion, $790 million of government revenue was lost each year and the annual welfare loss to the nation was $200 million.

In spite of all we have said there have always been those, including professional economists, who have argued for various forms of protection, some for more or less permanent forms, others for more temporary measures that will enable domestic industries to adjust to changing patterns of import competition. These latter we will take a closer look at in Chapter 5 when we consider the "safeguards"

These licenses turned out to be worth just about the difference between the world and the domestic prices.

[1] Hufbauer, Berliner & Elliott, Trade Protection In The United States: 31 Case Studies, Institute For International Economics, Washington, D.C., (1986) at page 14.

problem. But at this point a more general survey of the arguments for protection of domestic industry and a brief critique of those arguments is instructive. For this purpose consider the following excerpt:

Robert Z. Lawrence & Robert E. Litan,[2]
SAVING FREE TRADE: A PRAGMATIC APPROACH

* * * *

With rare exceptions, freer trade provides gains for each trading nation that outweigh any losses because it enables countries to specialize in the production of goods and services in which they enjoy a comparative advantage. Under the principle of comparative advantage, nations can maximize the economic welfare of their citizens by concentrating in the production of goods and services where limited resources are best employed. They can then export the excess not consumed domestically and import other goods.

Some economists, however, have advocated interfering with free trade on grounds of efficiency — namely, that under certain conditions, intervention will actually improve economic performance. In particular, three types of arguments based on efficiency merit consideration: that intervention is needed to preserve essential production, that it serves to protect so-called infant industries, and that it is necessary to compensate for private costs of dislocation that may not fully reflect total social costs.

Essential Industries

The first set of arguments favoring trade intervention suggests that the international marketplace can damage the nation's industrial structure. Specifically, by harming certain key domestic industries, trade can allegedly impair national defense. U.S. policy makers accepted this reasoning in imposing quotas on crude oil imports between 1959 and 1973 to protect domestic oil production. Recently, advocates of protection for the American steel industry have resurrected the national defense rationale to justify restrictions on steel imports.

This argument is flawed. After the current defense buildup has been completed, the American steel industry will retain far more capacity than is necessary for protecting national security. Perhaps more important, trade protection is an inefficient means of preserving the production capacity of an industry deemed essential to national defense. A far less costly mechanism is to pay for the capacity and necessary stockpiles of defense materials directly out of the federal expenditure budget.

Others have justified special government treatment by asserting a need to protect and support certain basic industries (again, such as steel) considered essential to the performance of other industries. The government, they argue, must subsidize or shelter these industries from import competition in order to prevent the American industries that rely on them from becoming vulnerable to price hikes or supply disruptions.

---

[2] Lawrence & Litan, Saving Free Trade; A Pragmatic Approach, Brookings Institution, Washington D. C. (1986) pages 16-23. Copyright © 1986. Reprinted by permission.

The first problem with the argument for protecting basic industries is that it applies only, if at all, to those products for which international competition is weak, such as crude oil in the 1970s, when the OPEC cartel had effective control over world oil prices. Strong competition in the international marketplace assures a steady supply of imported products at competitive prices. With such competition, American purchasers should not be concerned that domestic suppliers may be driven out of business or forced to shrink capacity. Indeed, American business will suffer if government misguidedly imposes import restrictions on relevant inputs. Restrictions only raise the price on such products and thereby reduce or destroy any competitive advantage American manufacturers of finished goods may enjoy in world markets.

Nevertheless, it is sometimes argued that domestic capacity should be subsidized to prevent foreigners from gouging during periods of shortage. But this argument, too, rests on questionable grounds. Participants in private markets can foresee such possibilities as well as the government and are able to protect themselves in various ways — by agreeing to long-term contracts, stockpiling inventories, and using futures markets, among other devices.

The rationale of protecting basic industries contains another flaw: no clear basis exists for distinguishing "basic" from "nonbasic" industries. Many industries produce goods for other industries — lumber for wood products, copper for finished metal products, cotton for textiles. There is no principled basis for singling out one or two of these sectors of the economy for subsidies or protection from imports.

Infant and Recuperating Industries

Another classic rationale for protection is that new domestic industries need to be shielded from import competition until they can become viable international competitors. Given the developed nature of the U.S. economy, the argument for protecting infant industries is rarely invoked. Proponents of protection do, however, frequently claim that a major objective of trade policy should be to allow import-damaged industries some breathing room in order to recuperate and modernize.

Although it is rarely stated as such, the rationale for special trade assistance to rejuvenate faltering industries implies a major failure in the capital market. If an industry can be profitable once it has attained sufficient capacity or experience (an infant industry) or when it has modernized and retooled itself (a recuperating industry), what prevents it from entering the capital market to obtain funds to tide itself over until it can compete? The answer must be that private participants in the capital market are, for some reason, systematically unable to recognize these opportunities. But this proposition is difficult to accept. The United States has the most well-developed capital market in the world, with nearly 15,000 commercial banks, more than 2,100 insurance companies and pension funds, and highly talented and well capitalized investment banking houses, let alone the largest network of stock and bond exchanges in the world. With so many potential suppliers of capital and such a highly sophisticated system of financial intermediation to channel funds efficiently to capital users, the market should not systematically fail to recognize and finance industries that could become competitors in the international marketplace. And even if such systematic errors occur, we are not aware that government officials or lawmakers have superior forecasting ability or, by releasing such information, that they cannot convince private participants of its value.

Others justify government support of efforts to rejuvenate industry by arguing that the recovery of individual firms may generate positive external benefits for an entire industry. In the case of underdeveloped countries in which capital markets remain relatively primitive, this argument may be valid. But even in these cases the best approach would be to provide direct production subsidies rather than to use costly tariffs or quotas.

Market Failures and Dislocation Costs

Politicians who seek to intervene to protect domestic industries often maintain that by doing so they will save jobs, implying that the sole alternative to current employment is permanent unemployment. This assumption is valid only from an extremely short-term perspective. Given sufficient time, most workers will find alternative employment, albeit often at lower wages. Some politicians also claim that protection can improve the trade balance. In a world of flexible exchange rates, however, restricting imports will not create employment. Import barriers may protect specific job slots, but since they will cause the dollar to appreciate, they will also induce job losses and cause erosion in international competitiveness elsewhere in the economy.

More sophisticated arguments for trade intervention therefore focus on the costs of dislocation. Ordinarily, market forces determine decisions to lay off workers, to scrap equipment, and to close plants or companies. The market will allocate resources to their most efficient uses, however, only if the firms and workers immediately involved bear all the costs of plant shutdown or worker layoffs and if the relevant actors respond to prices that accurately reflect social as well as private costs. Nevertheless, under certain circumstances other parties may bear some of the costs of scrapping capacity in depressed sectors, and government policies, market rigidities, and monopolies may distort prices. These market failures are frequently cited as grounds for providing special assistance to victims of intense foreign competition. Accordingly, each bears further scrutiny.

Externalities and Public Goods

The costs of major plant shutdowns or large worker layoffs are often not confined to the parties immediately affected. When a local firm adds to the unemployment rolls with significant layoffs, dislocation costs of other workers and job seekers in the region may dramatically increase. Because private firms do not pay these costs when laying off workers and shedding capacity, purely private decisions may lead to the premature shrinkage or elimination of industries. Targeted government assistance may be able to prevent unnecessary shutdowns, or at least slow the rate of decline.

Other Policies

Other government policies may also inhibit the optimal adjustment to slumps caused by strong import competition. In a dynamic context a proportional tax on capital income will distort the adjustment process because it reduces incentives for private sector decision makers to redeploy capital that is no longer socially productive.

Imperfections in the unemployment insurance program also distort layoff decisions. Because tax levels for unemployment compensation do not fully take into account differences in layoff experiences among firms, many firms lack incentives to lower their layoff rates.

Inappropriate Prices

Price signals facing individual actors will also be inappropriate if they are set by monopolies in product or factor markets or when markets fail to clear in the short run. If, for example, wages have been set too high in a unionized industry that competes with imports under the initial protection of a tariff, removing the tariff could impose enough damage on the industry to lower national income. If markets fail to clear, that is, if wage rates do not fully adjust to eliminate any labor surplus, layoffs in an industry experiencing a decline in demand can be excessive because wages elsewhere are too high to induce other firms to hire displaced workers. In the short run, free trade will result in a decline in national income from an incomplete use of resources.

That each of the foregoing market failures may exist, however, does not necessarily justify the adoption of policies intended specifically for easing or preventing trade-related injury. If markets fail to allocate or to adjust resources because of inherent failures such as imperfect capital markets and externalities, the appropriate response would be to correct these failures generally rather than to single out trade induced dislocations for special treatment. And these corrective policies may themselves be subject to imperfections, introducing distortions in their attempts to achieve conflicting goals.

The problems can be compounded by attempts to isolate trade-induced economic injury for special treatment. . . . Programs that ensure against trade induced injury have discouraged the movement of resources into more productive activities. Temporary protection from import competition can discourage firms from shrinking their capacity, particularly if that protection takes the form of quotas, which guarantee domestic producers a certain market share regardless of their ability to compete. Similarly, by making . . . assistance available only as long as unemployment continues, previous [Trade Adjustment Assistance[3]] programs have failed to encourage workers to search actively for new employment. Furthermore, trade assistance can actually attract labor to trade-sensitive industries and thus increase the pool of workers eligible to receive supplemental aid in the future.

Finally, programs of assisting the victims of foreign competition often suffer from contradictory objectives. Arguments supporting industrial modernization could produce policies designed to accelerate the pace of change; at the same time,

---

[3] This refers to programs initially established under the Trade Expansion Act of 1962 and continued, with some interruptions, ever since. The programs involved grants by the Government to laid off workers in an industry to finance retraining or to supplement unemployment compensation, or both and grants to industry for modernization and retooling. Ed.

however, arguments stressing the external costs of plant closures and worker layoffs could lead to policies designed to slow the rate of adjustment. In principle, an omniscient planner could simultaneously apply some instruments such as investment subsidies to encourage modernization, while using others such as employment subsidies to prevent the dislocation that modernization might cause. But the mix of policies would have to be extremely complex and the goals understood with great precision.

CHAPTER 4

THE INTERNATIONAL CONTROL OF NATIONAL TRADE POLICIES — AN OVERVIEW OF THE GENERAL AGREEMENT ON TARIFFS AND TRADE

Introduction

Even before the tide had turned for the allies in World War II, allied officials led by the British and Americans were laying plans for the post-war international economic order; one that would avoid the disasters of the interwar period. Three basic institutions were projected; the International Monetary Fund (IMF), the International Bank for Reconstruction and Development (the World Bank) and the International Trade Organization (ITO). The IMF and World Bank were, in due course, established and remain vital parts of the contemporary system. The ITO, however, effectively died in 1948 when President Truman declined to submit the proposed ITO Charter — known as the Havana Charter — to the Senate for its advise and consent. Senate opposition had grown steadily as compromises were increasingly grafted onto what the American planners had initially envisioned as a bold and comprehensive effort at multilateral governance of the world economy.[1]

In spite of the demise of the ITO, twenty-three of the world's major trading nations had met in Geneva the year before to conduct the first of what came to be known as negotiating "rounds" concerned with reducing tariffs and other barriers to trade. Both to record the agreements reached and to insure that participants did not, in their trade policies, subvert those agreements, the parties to the Geneva conference drew-up the General Agreement on Tariffs and Trade (GATT), incorporating many of the substantive trade policy provisions of the Havana Charter. Updated in 1957, the GATT is today the principal body of substantive international law governing the trade policies of its members. As of this writing, one hundred and five nations are full members of GATT and more than twenty other nations apply the General Agreement on Tariffs and Trade to their trade relations of a *de facto* basis.

Because GATT was only intended to record the agreements reached at one trade conference and was not thought of as a permanent framework for the multilateral governance of international trade, it was given over almost entirely to setting forth

---

[1] In addition to the commercial policy provisions that were picked up in the General Agreement on Tariffs and Trade (GATT), the Havana Charter contained extensive chapters on "Employment and Economic Activity," "Economic Development and Reconstruction," "Restrictive Business Practices," and "Intergovernmental Commodity Agreements." Also provision was made for an elaborate organization with rules for its governance, a Secretariat, and a variety of dispute resolution devices, including consultation, arbitration and submissions to the International Court of Justice for advisory opinions.

substantive rules of law. No provision was made for any kind of organization or for its governance. Initially no procedures were specified for the conduct of future trade negotiating "rounds" and such procedures as were set forth for policing the agreement and resolving disputes were rudimentary. Moreover, the coverage of GATT, especially in the early years, was limited by the Protocol of Provisional Application and by the Protocols under which individual nations acceded to the GATT in the years following the initial 1947 conference. Broadly stated, the Protocol of Provisional Application exempts from the trade policy rules of Part II of the General Agreement any inconsistent legislation of a Contracting Party in effect on January 1, 1948. As time has passed and new legislation has come on the books of member countries the Protocol has, of course, become an increasingly less important limitation on the coverage of GATT rules.

Amendment of the General Agreement is difficult. It has only been amended twice, once in 1957 and then in 1966 with the addition of Part IV dealing with the trade of developing nations. Growth in the substantive law of GATT, therefore, has taken a number of forms. Interpretive traditions and a "practice of GATT" has grown-up around many of the subjects with which particular Articles treat. A so-called "pragmatic" approach has at times prevailed. The Contracting Parties, responding to changing political and economic realities, have not infrequently backed away from a strict enforcement of the rules and sought more to facilitate a practical adjustment between the conflicting policies of its members. Needless to add, this approach has been both lauded as the great strength of GATT and attacked as a singular weakness that has forestalled the fuller development of "hard" law. In addition, waivers have been granted with some frequency.

Most significant of all, however, in the evolution of GATT law, has been the development of a series of special agreements usually negotiated within the framework of a formal GATT "round." These agreements either elaborate upon the rules already embodied in the General Agreement or address some important trade problem for the first time. No Contracting Party is required to adhere to these agreements once promulgated. Many wait to see how the agreement works in practice before signing. Non-signatories retain all of their rights under the General Agreement, a situation that leaves open the issue of which controls in the event of a conflict between the GATT proper and one of these special agreements. The issue has been largely solved — or perhaps ignored — by resort to the "pragmatic approach." In all events, these special agreements have become an important device for growth in GATT law. One such agreement — a so-called "Anti-dumping Code" — emerged from the Kennedy Round (1963-67). Nine so called MTN (Multinational Trade Negotiations) agreements emerged from the Tokyo Round (1974-1979),[2] several of which we shall examine quite closely. Also, starting in 1962, the several agreements concerning trade in textiles and

---

[2] These included an Agreement on Technical Barriers to Trade, an Agreement on Government Procurement, Agreement on Interpretation and Application of Article VI, XVI, and XXIII (the so-called "Subsidies Code"), the Arrangement Regarding Bovine Meat, an International Dairy Agreement, an Agreement on Implementation of Article VII (customs valuation), an Agreement on Import Licensing Procedures, an Agreement on Trade in Civil Aircraft, and an Agreement on Implementation of Article VI (a revised "Anti-Dumping" Code). For text see GATT, BISD, 26th Supp., pages 8-188 (1980).

apparel and now known as the "Multi-Fiber Arrangement" have been promulgated outside the framework of any formal "round."

Since the General Agreement establishes no organization to administer its provisions and contains very few rules of procedure, the membership of GATT — the "Contracting Parties" as they are called — has had to innovate, often without any sanction whatsoever in the text of the Agreement itself. A permanent Secretariat, headed by a Director-General has been established. Since the Contracting Parties formally meet only once a year, a Council of Representatives has been established to handle problems that arise between sessions. Composed of representatives of the Contracting Parties that choose to join, staffed by permanent representatives of those parties stationed in Geneva, where GATT has its headquarters, the Council has increasingly become the principal body guiding GATT activities. There is also the Consultative Group of Eighteen, ten of whom represent developing countries. Staffed by senior civil servants from its member governments, the Group is charged with following global trade developments with an eye toward identifying emerging problems, moving to forestall sudden disturbances that might pose a threat to the trading system and coordinating GATT action with the IMF. Much of the work of the GATT, however, is carried out through three different types of groups: committees, working parties and panels.

Committees are established by the Contracting Parties to study important trade questions usually on a continuing basis[3] or as part of a "Work Programme."[4] There are also committees established under the special agreements mentioned above. Normally composed of all members who choose to join, committees, in their discussions and debates with countries whose policies are a source of special concern, can play an important part in the broader GATT function of subjecting national trade practices to multilateral surveillance and discipline.

Working Parties are groups established by the Council at the request of a Contracting Party to study and report to the Contracting Parties on a particular matter that raise issues under the General Agreement, including, on occasion, to make recommendations regarding a dispute under Article XXIII. For this latter purpose, however, Panel's are preferred (see: "Understanding Regarding Notification, Consultation, Dispute Settlement and Surveillance" (hereinafter the "Understanding on Dispute Settlement")).[5] Any Contracting Party interested in the matter may participate in the deliberations of a working party. Hence working parties vary greatly in size. When working parties are used to hear disputes

---

[3] Examples include the Committee on Balance of Payments Restrictions, the Committee on Tariff Concessions, Committee on Trade and Development and the Budget Committee.

[4] The "Work" or "Action Programme" is an interesting device used by GATT and many other international organizations. As a consensus develops among the members of the organization that a particular problem needs systematic attention a "Work Programme" will be formulated which usually begins by an intensified study of the issues and then progresses through to the negotiated formulation of a set of principles that are to guide members in conducting their own national policies. While often the final product is only hortatory — raising interesting jurisprudential questions concerning its legal status — a "Work Programme" will at times lead to the development of a text that is then submitted to the members for adoption as legally binding.

[5] L/4907, adopted 28 November 1979, GATT, BISD 26th Supp. page 210, *et. seq.* (1980).

between GATT members, the disputants always participate in the decision. This is not the case when panels are used. Moreover, unlike panels, all participants in a working party act as representatives of their governments and, because of the emphasis on reaching a consensus, working party decisions are frequently the product of negotiation and compromise.

Panels are used to hear and judge particular trade disputes between GATT members and to make recommendations to the Contracting Parties. According to the Understanding on Dispute Settlement, panels are to be composed of three or five members. They may be private individuals but government officials are preferred. In no event, however, may they be citizens of countries involved in the dispute and if they are government officials they do not act as representatives of their governments, but as independent experts.

GATT, in sum, is a body of substantive international trade law. But it is much more. It is an institution for multilateral trade negotiations, for the study of trade problems and for the formulation of principles to guide members in the resolution of those problems, for the "adjudication" of disputes and an institution through which the international community can examine and confront the trade practices of particular nations. In all of this GATT has had some remarkable successes and equally notable failures. Today it faces challenges perhaps greater than ever before in its history. The adequacy of GATT law and GATT processes to meet these challenges is a matter of considerable concern.

GATT's success in fostering a multilateral, "neo-liberal"trading order has largely been achieved through the vehicle of periodic negotiating "rounds". The so-called "Geneva Round" in 1947 produced the General Agreement. The "Annecy Round" of 1949 in Annecy, France and the "Torquay Round" in Torquay, England in 1951 were concerned primarily with the accession to the GATT of countries that did not participate in the Geneva Round. After this, there followed a minor round in 1956 and then three very significant rounds; the Dillon Round (1960-62), the Kennedy Round (1964-67) and the Tokyo Round (1974-79), all of which we will consider in varying detail later in these materials. Then, in September 1986, the Contracting Parties announced their decision to conduct yet another major round of trade negotiations, the "Uruguay Round," so-called because the announcement was issued at a Ministerial level meeting of GATT in Punta Del Este, Uruguay.

Currently underway and scheduled to be completed by December 31, 1990, the Uruguay Round is an ambitious undertaking. In addition to negotiating further reductions in both tariff and non-tariff barriers to trade in goods, the Contracting Parties have committed themselves to developing, in the Uruguay Round, a regime of rules governing international trade in services (*e.g.*, financial services, including banking, shipping, insurance, telecommunications, to name a few). This would vastly broaden the economic reach and significance of GATT. Also in the Round the Contracting Parties have mounted a new attack on the safeguards problem, on strengthening GATT's dispute resolution machinery, and on ways to bring textile trade back within the basic multilateral framework of GATT, to mention only some of the more important areas under active negotiation.

At this writing, one encounters a wide variety of opinion regarding the chances that this ambitious agenda will actually be completed by the December 1990 target date, although characteristically in GATT Rounds agreements tend to come with a rush as deadlines approach. Neverthless there appear to be some serious problems. The United States and Europe appear virtually deadlocked on the question of how fast to eliminate agricultural subsidies. Without some agreement on agriculture, the fate of the entire Round could be in jeopardy. Also, a growing number of American industries now appear to want exemption from a so-called GATS (General Agreement on Trade in Services). This presents a serious embarrassment to the United States, the principal champion of a service agreement in the first place. The safeguards question is still stymied on the problem of selectivity and on how to bring so-called "grey-area" measures under multilateral discipline. This is a critical item in the larger effort to maintain a system of multilateral control over national trade policies.[6]

With regard to overall progress in the Uruguay Round, Mr. Arthur Dunkel, Director General of the GATT, recently observed that "we are collectively behind schedule." Much of this was attributable, he thought, to the "absence of new instructions from a number of capitals," and to:

> . . . the phenomenon of linkages within and among subjects which arise from the Uruguay Round being one single undertaking. Linkages can, and should be used positively to push the whole process forward. Unfortunately, up until now, they have been used negatively with negotiators largely playing hide-and-seek with each other and not revealing their hand.[7]

Perhaps this latter phenomenon is not too hard to understand; the stakes are high. On the other hand, failure of the Uruguay Round to make genuine and well noted progress on the more vexing problems that bedevil world trade could lead to a major restructuring of the way the free-world governs its international trade relations. Increasingly, the basic GATT system of multilateral control under neo-liberal free-trade principals has been under attack. Should the Uruguay Round fail, or be perceived to have failed, some believe that there is a real danger that the world will move increasingly into a multi-polar trading system dominated by at least three great inward looking, protectionist centers — the European Community, Japan with links around the Pacific rim and North America — conducting, as between themselves and with the rest of the world, what has come to be called "managed trade;" bilaterally negotiated sectoral agreements fixing the direction and quantity of trade without any multilateral surveillance and largely without regard for either the dictates of the free-market, the theory of comparative advantage or the effects of those agreements on global efficiency. Examples of what such a system would look like already exist in the Multi-Fibre Arrangement (MFA)[8] and the various Voluntary Restraint Agreements that the United States has used to control imports of automobiles and steel.[9] The reader can judge for himself what such a sytem might portend for global welfare.

Against this general background, we turn first to examine certain concepts that are at the core of the "neo-liberal" orientation of the General Agreement: the

---

[6] We shall look at these and other specific problems that are the subject of the Uruguay Round negotiations at various points in the ensuing materials.

[7] GATT, "News of the Uruguay Round," NUR 039, 30 July 1990 at page 2.

[8] Discussed at page 236 *infra*.

[9] Discussed in Chapter 5

principle of non-discrimination embodied in the most-favored nation (MFN) clause and some exceptions to that principle; the basic scheme outlawing most non-tariff barriers to trade and subjecting tariff barriers to negotiated reductions; the concepts of reciprocity and national treatment and the foundations of GATT adjudications under the "nullification or impairment" of benefits concept of Article XXIII. Then, in our study of the Generalized System of Preferences, we will encounter the modification of certain core principles in the case of developing country trade.

§ 4.01   Some Basic Elements: Non-Discrimination (Most-Favored Nation (MFN)); GATT Tariff Negotiations

A cornerstone of the General Agreement is the requirement that in the administration of their tariffs and other national regulations of trade GATT members not discriminate between their trading partners; that they accord each unconditional most-favored nation ("MFN") status. Later in our consideration of the GATT deliberations on the European Economic Community we will take a closer look at the economics and the politics of discrimination. Here we focus on a bit of history, some of the practical considerations that underlie the MFN idea and how the unconditional form of MFN affects the GATT tariff negotiating process. In this latter context we shall also encounter other key concepts such as "reciprocity" and "trade coverage." Later we shall also take-up certain of those provisions of the General Agreement that prohibit discrimination in favor of domestic products as against imports; the so-called "national treatment" requirement.

Article I:1 of the General Agreement states the MFN principle in its broadest terms as follows:

Article I

1. **With respect to customs duties and charges of any kind imposed on or in connection with importation or exportation or imposed on the international transfer of payments for imports or exports, and with respect to the method of levying such duties and charges, and with respect to all rules and formalities in connection with importation and exportation . . . any advantage, favour, privilege or immunity granted by any Contracting Party to any product originating in or destined for any other country shall be accorded immediately and unconditionally to the like product originating in or destined for the territories of all other Contracting Parties.[1]**

---

[1] Article I:2 contains what was, at the formation of GATT, thought to be a major exception to the MFN principle of Article I:1. The American negotiators' determination to rid the world of all preferential trading arrangements immediately encountered the British insistence upon preserving the system of Commonwealth preferences established in 1932. As a consequence, Article I:2 grants an exception to all then existing preferential arrangements most of which were between Britain, France, Belgium, Italy and their former colonial possessions, including the Commonwealth nations. At the same time it was agreed that the margin of preference could not be increased beyond that existing, in most cases, on April 10, 1947. Reflecting these arrangements Article II establishes two schedules: Paragraph (1) a schedule showing the bound MFN rate and Paragraph (2) showing the

To better understand both the background and operational importance of the MFN principle, a brief excursion into pre-GATT practice is instructive.

WHITNEY et. al. v. ROBERTSON

United States Supreme Court
124 U.S. 190, 8 S.Ct. 456 (1888)

[Plaintiffs imported sugar from the Dominican Republic that was similar to Hawaiian sugar. The latter was regularly being admitted duty free under a treaty with the "king" of Hawaii and Plaintiffs claimed that their sugar was also entitled to enter duty free because of the following provision in a treaty with the Dominican Republic:

> Art. 9th: No higher or other duty shall be imposed on the importation into the United States of any article the growth, produce or manufacture of the Dominican Republic . . . than are or shall be payable on the like articles the growth, produce or manufacture of any other foreign country[2] . . . .

Article 9th also contained a reciprocal undertaking by the Dominican Republic with respect to American products.

Under the treaty with Hawaii the United States extended duty free treatment to a long list of Hawaiian products, including sugar, in exchange for a like exemption upon the importation of specified American products into Hawaii. The first two articles of that treaty declared that these reciprocal undertakings were made in consideration "of the rights and privileges" which the parties conceded to each other and "as an equivalent therefore".

The customs collector denied Plaintiffs' claim and assessed a duty of $21,936 against the Dominican sugar. After taking their administrative appeals, Plaintiffs paid the duty under protest and then sued in the Federal Circuit Court for the Southern District of New York to recover the sum paid. That court upheld the collector's decision and Plaintiffs appealed.]

---

bound preferential rate. Article I(4) then imposes a limit on the margin of preference. For a number of practical reasons this accommodation has not seriously affected the broader GATT goal of minimizing, and eventually eliminating, discrimination in international trade. With regard to *ad velorum* tariffs, the general reduction of the MFN rates through successive GATT "rounds" has undermined the value of the preference. Moreover, under the rules, while unbound preferential rates and unbound MFN rates could be increased, the margin of preference could not be increased. Finally inflation has seriously eroded the value of preferences for products subject to specific duties. These latter were widely used in the Commonwealth system.

[2] 15 Stat. 473, 478.

FIELD, J. . . . In *Bartram v. Robertson*[3] . . . decided last term, we held that . . . sugars . . . [from] St. Croix, which is part of the dominions of the king of Denmark, were not exempt from duty by force of the treaty with that country, because similar goods from the Hawaiian islands were thus exempt. The . . . treaty with Denmark provided that the Contracting Parties should not grant " . . . any particular favor" to other nations in respect to commerce and navigation, which should not immediately become common to the other party, who should:

> . . . enjoy the same freely if the concession were freely made, and upon allowing the same compensation if the concession were conditional.[4] . . . .

The fourth article . . . [of the Danish treaty] provided that no "higher or other duties" should be imposed by either party on the importation of any article which is its produce or manufacture into the country of the other party than is payable on like articles, being the produce or manufacture of any other foreign country. And we held . . . [in *Bartram v. Robertson*] that . . . :

> those stipulations . . . do not cover concessions like those made to the Hawaiian islands for a valuable consideration. They were pledges of the two Contracting Parties, the United States and the king of Denmark, to each other, that, in the imposition of duties on goods imported into one of the countries which were the produce or manufacture of the other, there should be no discrimination against them in favor of goods of like character imported from any other country. They imposed an obligation upon both countries to avoid hostile legislation in that respect, but they were not intended to interfere with special arrangements with other countries founded upon a concession of special privileges.

The counsel for the plaintiffs meet this position by pointing to the omission in the treaty with the [Dominican Republic] . . . of the provision as to free concessions, and concessions upon compensation [quoted above], contending that the omission precludes any concession in respect of commerce and navigation by our government to another country, without that concession being at once extended to [the Dominican Republic]. We do not think that the absence of this provision changes the obligations of the United States. The ninth article of the treaty with [the Dominican Republic] . . . is substantially like the fourth article in the treaty with the king of Denmark; and as we said of the latter, we may say of the former, that it is a pledge of the contracting parties that there shall be no discriminating legislation against the importation of articles which are the growth, produce or manufacture of their respective countries, in favor of articles of like character, imported from any other country. It has no greater extent. It was never designed to prevent special concessions, upon sufficient consideration, touching the importation of specific articles into the country of the other. It would require the clearest language to justify a conclusion that our government intended to preclude itself from such engagements with other countries, which might in the future be of the highest importance to its interests.

---

[3] (122 U.S. 116).
[4] (11 Stat. 719).

But, independently of considerations of this nature, there is another and complete answer to the pretensions of the plaintiffs. The act of congress under which the duties were collected, authorized their exaction. It is of general application, making no exception in favor of goods of any country. It was passed after the treaty with the Dominican Republic, and, if there be any conflict between the stipulations of the treaty and the requirements of the law, the latter must control. . . . By the constitution, a treaty is placed on the same footing, and made of like obligation, with an act of legislation. Both are declared by that instrument to be the supreme law of the land, and no superior efficacy is given to either over the other. When the two relate to the same subject, the courts will always endeavor to construe them so as to give effect to both, if that can be done without violating the language of either; but, if the two are inconsistent, the one last in date will control the other. . . .

Judgment Affirmed.

NOTES AND QUESTIONS

(1) The overtones of the "mercantilist's" zero-sum-game are plain enough in the language used by the *Whitney* Court to characterize tariff reductions and to insist that any MFN clause must be construed as "conditional" unless an intent to grant the kind of "unconditional" MFN treatment, which plaintiff claimed for the Dominican Treaty, is clearly expressed. A tariff reduction is a "concession". Tariff negotiations are not, explicitly at least, a search for the welfare gains of freer trade but a search for "equivalency" in what each must give-up. And the plain fact is that the Court's rhetoric mirrors the political perspective that today, as in 1888, still dominates much practical discussion of trade policy. How much it continues to play a role in GATT negotiations is a matter we shall explore further when we look closer at the concept of "reciprocity." For the time being, however, consider the following problem:

> You are counsel to the negotiator for Country A who has negotiated an agreement with Country B giving B a 50% reduction in tariffs on imports of Product X, in exchange for a like reduction in B's tariff on Product Y. Why would you, from the "quasi-mercantilist" perspective of the *Whitney* decision, advise your client to include a clause in the agreement extending MFN status to Country B?

(2) The clause, of course, would have to be reciprocal. Assuming also that any tariff negotiations that your client might conduct with third countries would be on a purely bilateral basis, what problems might an unconditional MFN clause in the agreement with Country B present? What considerations would determine your preference for the conditional or unconditional form? Would you be comfortable with the following argument by Viner in favor of an unconditional undertaking.

> Country A has no ground for complaint if concessions to it from Country B, for which it has given compensation, are extended gratuitously to Countries

C and D, for during the life of A's treaty with B Country A will in like manner receive gratuitous concessions which were granted by B to C and D for compensation.[5]

Would you find the following statement by the British Foreign Minister Lord Granville, in 1885, objecting to the traditional American position reflected in *Whitney* more on point:

> From this [the American] interpretation, Her Majesty's government entirely and emphatically dissent. The most-favored-nation clause has now become the most valuable part of the system of commercial treaties, and exists between almost all the nations of the earth. . . . It is . . . obvious that the interpretation now put forward [by the United States] . . . would nullify the most-favored-nation clause; for any country . . . though bound by the most-favored-nation clause . . . [in one treaty] might make treaties with any other country involving reductions of duties on both sides, and by merely inserting the statement that these were granted reciprocally and for consideration, might yet refuse to grant them [to the first country] unless the latter granted what [it] might consider an equivalent. Such a system would press most hardly on those nations which have already reformed their tariffs and have not an equivalent concession to offer, and therefore Great Britain, which has reformed her tariff is most deeply interested in resisting it.

(3) From mid-19th Century until 1925, the United States, virtually alone of all major trading countries in the world, held to a policy of giving only conditional MFN undertakings in its commercial treaties. As Lord Granville's statement illustrates, this policy was a recurring source of diplomatic friction between this country and its principal trading partners.[6] We finally abandoned the policy in a treaty with Germany dated October 14, 1925. Secretary of State Hughes explained the change by noting that the conditional form of MFN upset the "equilibrium of conditions which it was the interest of this country to maintain" and rendered "reciprocal commercial arrangements . . . but temporary makeshifts, because constant negotiations then created uncertainty." Quoted in, *John T. Bill Co. v. United States.*[7] The Secretary's reference to the "equilibrium of conditions" is a reference to the potential for a highly discriminatory tariff structure implicit in the conditional form of MFN, the consequences and growing American abhorrence of which we will examine at a later point.

GATT TARIFF NEGOTIATIONS

Background. Many of the problems posed by a system of purely bilateral tariff negotiations could only be addressed through a new institutional framework that would transform those negotiations into a more nearly multilateral process. To

---

[5] Viner, *The Most-Favored-Nation Clause In American Commercial Treaties*, 32 J. of Pol. Econ. 101 (1924).

[6] See generally Viner *id.*

[7] 104 F. 2d 67., 27 C.C.P.A. 26 (1939).

the post-war economic planners this was precisely what the ITO was intended to accomplish and the Havana Charter reflected that expectation. GATT, however, was only intended to be a temporary measure and not a permanent framework for future negotiations. As a result, it was not until Article XXVIII *bis* was added in 1957 that the General Agreement made express provision for periodic comprehensive efforts at tariff reduction.[8] The omission, however, did not, deter the process of tariff liberalization. Even before 1957, the Contracting Parties engaged in four multilateral tariff negotiating "rounds".[9]

While both the Kennedy and Tokyo Rounds reformed traditional GATT tariff negotiating procedures in significant ways, on both occasions the core of the system remained intact. An understanding of that core is important. It illustrates one significant linkage between the principle of non-discrimination embodied in the MFN clause of Article I:1 and GATT as an institution for the exercise of multilateral surveillance and discipline over national trade policies. Moreover, it is in the area of tariff reductions on industrial products that GATT has registered its greatest success. By 1985, with the final Tokyo Round reductions fully in effect, the original United States Smoot-Hawley average tariff of 60% on industrial products had been reduced to approximately 5%, with corresponding reductions by the other industrialized trading nations of the world. While the effort to liberalize trade in agricultural products has been far less successful, past success in reducing tariffs on industrial goods, had, by 1974, caused attention to shift away from tariffs to so-called "non-tariff barriers" (NTB's) as the chief obstacles to free trade.

Bindings. Under Article II:1(a) of the General Agreement each Contracting Party undertakes to extend to all other parties, tariff treatment "no less favourable" than that provided for in the annexed Schedules described in Subparagraphs (b) and (c). The undertakings recorded in the Schedules are known as "bindings". A "binding" either commits a Contracting Party not to raise an existing rate, which may be zero, or to reduce an existing tariff to a specified rate and then (i) not raise it above that rate, or (ii) not raise it above a specified higher rate that is nevertheless below the existing rate.

---

[8] Article XXVIII *bis* provides, in part, as follows: 1. The Contracting Parties recognize that customs duties often constitute serious obstacles to trade; thus negotiations on a reciprocal and mutually advantageous basis, directed to the substantial reduction of the general level of tariffs and other charges on imports and exports and in particular to the reduction of such high tariffs as discourage the importation even of minimum quantities, and conducted with due regard to the objectives of this Agreement and the varying needs of individual Contracting Parties, are of great importance to the expansion of international trade. The Contracting Parties may therefore sponsor such negotiations from time to time. 2. (a) Negotiations under this Article may be carried out on a selective product-by-product basis or by the application of such multilateral procedures as may be accepted by the Contracting Parties concerned. . . .
   (b) The Contracting Parties recognize that in general the success of multilateral negotiations would depend on the participation of all Contracting Parties which conduct a substantial proportion of the external trade with one another.
   3. [This paragraph lists certain considerations that are to be taken into account in the conduct of negotiations under Article XXVIII *bis*, such as the needs of developing countries and the fiscal, strategic and developmental needs of particular parties.]
[9] See Chapters 4-5 *supra*.

Remedies. The basic GATT approach to violations of the General Agreement is reflected in Article XXIII. Under that Article violations of GATT obligations are to be met first by attempts at a negotiated adjustment between the injured party and the alleged violator. If that proves unsuccessful, the Contracting Parties, after an investigation, may authorize the injured party to suspend or withdraw such of its own concessions or obligations as the Contracting Parties deem appropriate. (For a more detailed examination of Article XXIII see page — *infra.*)

Against the background of this basic remedial structure, Article XXVIII establishes a special regime by which the Contracting Parties are allowed to adjust the legal commitments made in their Article II tariff "bindings". The concepts used in this regime have, in turn, supplied the conceptual core of the more comprehensive tariff reduction efforts in the several "Rounds" mentioned above, albeit with important modifications in the Kennedy and Tokyo Rounds. Article XXVIII provides in pertinent part as follows:

Article XXVIII

Modification of Schedules

1. **On the first day of each three-year period . . . beginning 1 January 1958 . . . a Contracting Party . . . (the "applicant contracting party") may, by negotiation and agreement with any Contracting Party with which such concession was initially negotiated and with any other Contracting Party . . . hav[ing] a principal supplying interest[10] ([the foregoing collectively called] . . . the "Contracting Parties primarily concerned"), and subject to consultation with any other Contracting Party . . . [with] a substantial interest in such concession, modify or withdraw a concession included in the appropriate Schedule annexed to this Agreement.**

[Note: The Contracting Parties must designate the Party with a principal supplying interest or with a substantial interest.]

2. **In such negotiations and agreement, which may include provision for compensatory adjustment with respect to other products, the Contracting Parties concerned shall endeavour to maintain a general level of reciprocal and mutually advantageous concessions not less favourable to trade than that provided for in this Agreement prior to such negotiations.**

---

[10] To avoid making the negotiations unduly difficult and complicated Ad Article XXVIII:4 & 5 state:

    4. . . . the Contracting Parties should only determine that a Contracting Party has a principal supplying interest if that . . . party has had, over a reasonable period of time prior to the negotiations, a larger share in the market of the applicant . . . than a Contracting Party with which the concession was initially negotiated or would . . . have had such a share in the absence of discriminatory quantitative restrictions maintained by the applicant. . . . It would, therefore, not be appropriate [to designate] more than one contracting party, or in those exceptional cases where there is near equality more than two [such] parties.

    5. Notwithstanding the [foregoing] . . . the Contracting Parties may exceptionally determine that a Contracting Party has a principal supplying interest if the concession in question affects trade which constitutes a major part of the total exports of such . . . party.

3.   (a) If agreement between the Contracting Parties primarily concerned
cannot be reached before . . . expiration of a period envisaged in paragraph 1 . . . the [applicant] Contracting Party . . . shall, nevertheless,
be free . . . [to modify or withdraw the concession] and if such action is
taken any [of the three other Contracting Parties described in paragraph
1] . . . shall then be free not later than six months after such action is
taken, to withdraw, . . . [upon 30 days' notice], substantially equivalent
concessions initially negotiated with the applicant contracting party.

[Paragraph 3(b) gives a party with a substantial interest the right to withdraw
or modify substantially equivalent concessions if it is not satisfied with any
agreement reached between the applicant and the parties primarily
concerned.]

4.   The Contracting Parties may, at any time, in special circumstances,
authorize a Contracting Party to enter into negotiations for modification
or withdrawal of a [scheduled] concession . . . subject to the following
procedures and conditions:

[(a) The negotiations are to be conducted in accord with Paragraphs 1 and
2 above.]

[(b) If the parties primarily concerned reach agreement Paragraph 3(b)
applies.]

[(c) If no agreement is reached within 60 days, the applicant may refer the
matter to the Contracting Parties.]

[(d) Upon such reference the Contracting Parties are to examine the matter
and make recommendations to the parties primarily concerned. If that results
in settlement, Paragraph 3(b) applies. If not, the applicant may go ahead and
withdraw or modify the concession unless the Contracting Parties determine
that the applicant has "unreasonably failed to offer adequate compensation."
In the event of such a determination any of the three other Contracting Parties
may respond as provided in Paragraph 3(a).]

5.   Before . . . the end of any period envisaged in paragraph 1 a Contracting
Party may elect . . . to reserve the right, for the duration of the next
period, to modify the appropriate Schedule in accordance with the
procedures of paragraphs 1 and 3. If a Contracting Party so elects, other
Contracting Parties shall have the right, during the same period, to
modify or withdraw, in accordance with the same procedures, concessions
initially negotiated with that Contracting Party.

NOTES AND QUESTIONS

(1) The regime established by Article XXVIII illustrates a certain pragmatic
approach which characterizes much of what GATT does. Contrary to the normal
rule of international law under which a party to a treaty is expected to continue
to abide by its treaty obligations even when to do so becomes contrary to its

interests, Article XXVIII has written a good measure of flexibility into the obligation represented by a "binding". In appraising this scheme, assume that it is intended to facilitate two broad objectives (i) to get as many tariff reducing agreements as possible and (ii) to assure as much continuity as possible to commitments once made. Consider how a regime more attuned to the traditional postulates of international law might affect these objectives. In light of this, identify that concept which is the key to the compromise implicit in Article XXVIII. Is it a regime that legitimates retaliation? How else might you characterize it?

(2) Note that the Contracting Parties affected by an applicant's withdrawal or modification of a concession, may respond by withdrawing "substantially equivalent concessions." The practice has developed of measuring equivalency by the volume of trade that entered under the bound rate being withdrawn during some representative period prior to withdrawal (*i.e.*, trade coverage). What are the problems with this approach? Consider the following:

> Suppose Country A, the applicant, proposes to withdraw a concession by which it had earlier reduced the tariff on product X from 15% ad velorum to 5% and that A's imports of X from Country B had, under the 5% rate, averaged $50 million per year over the past three years. Suppose that during the same period Country B had imported from A, $50 million per year of product Y and proposes to respond to A's action by withdrawing a concession which had earlier reduced the tariff on Y from 25% to 15% ad velorum. In spite of the equivalency of trade coverage, is Country B necessarily withdrawing a "substantially equivalent concession? What more must you know?

(3) Prior to the enactment of Article XXVIII *bis*, Article XXVIII set the basic ground rules not only for periodic adjustment of tariff concessions but also for the more comprehensive tariff negotiating rounds. Consider first the "principal supplier" rule. In the more comprehensive rounds this was taken to mean that only the principal supplier of a product to a particular country could request the latter for a concession on that product. This tended to render those rounds essentially a series of bilateral negotiations. As such they could well have encountered the same problems that plagued pre-GATT bilateral negotiations under an unconditional MFN policy; namely, the improbability of a country that is giving a concession gaining compensation from two different countries on two different occasions, since the second country will have already received the concession *gratis*. Reflect upon how the institutional structure of a GATT negotiating round — with Article I:1 in the background — might be used to forestall this problem. For this purpose the following case is instructive.

EUROPEAN ECONOMIC COMMUNITY
IMPORTS OF BEEF FROM CANADA

Report of the Panel
adopted on 10 March 1981
(L/5099)

GATT, BISD, 28th Supp., page 92

[In the Tokyo Round of tariff negotiations the EEC, as a result of negotiations with the United States, bound a global tariff quota for 21,000 tons of "high quality" bovine meat, of which 10,000 tons was to be "grained-fed, fresh, chilled or frozen beef." When it came to implementing this concession the EEC promulgated regulations which set standards for determining the quality of beef entitled to enter under the tariff quota and then stipulated, "Beef Graded USDA 'choice' or 'prime' automatically meets the definition above." The Regulation also required importers to produce a "certificate of authentication" endorsed by the appropriate issuing authority and then went on to name the "Food Safety and Quality Service (FSQS) of the U.S. Department of Agriculture" as the only appropriate authority listed. Canada appealed to the GATT claiming that the EEC had violated Articles I:1 and II:1(a) because the Regulation effectively foreclosed Canadian exporters from participating in the 10,000 ton tariff quota. Canada pointed out that in another agreement between Canada and the United States, the latter had recognized Canadian Grades A2, A3 and A4, as equal to USDA "choice" and "prime." A Panel was appointed and in the arguments to the Panel the EEC representative made the following point:]

* * * *

. . . [A]t no time in the Multilateral Trade Negotiations — including the final phase when there were close contacts between the Community and Canada during which lists of priorities were exchanged and negotiated — did Canada make any request concerning high-quality [beef].

He further said that Canada was not unaware that the EEC was engaged in negotiations with the United States on a concession concerning high-quality meat. Other GATT Contracting Parties, interested in exporting high-quality meat to the Community, were careful, in the framework of the [Tokyo Round] . . . to enter into negotiations with the [Community] in time, so as to secure the benefits of a very specific concession in this sector when the mutual concessions were finalized. During the negotiations, the Community could not but note that by its passive attitude Canada showed a certain disinterest in the subject.

He observed that a small number of developed countries "participants" in the negotiations were expecting indirect benefits for themselves deriving from concessions paid for by others, without necessarily always making sure to contribute their share to the maintenance of an even balance between their rights and obligations. Such an attitude was in contradiction with the Tokyo Declaration . . . [which called upon the participants in the negotiations to] "jointly endeavour . . . to achieve, by appropriate methods, an overall balance of advantage at the highest possible level. . . ."

NOTES AND QUESTIONS

(1) Note the EEC representative's description of how the MTN was conducted. Is there an aspect of conditional MFN in that process? Even if so, has the EEC representative overstated the case in an attempt to draw a normative principle out of an institutional process? The Panel seemed to think so. It upheld Canada's claim, concluding that the EEC's contention could not override "the relevant provisions of the General Agreement."

(2) One commentator has suggested that this process probably has had a ratchet effect resulting in greater tariff reductions than would have otherwise occurred under the pre-GATT system.[11] If so, it would be one example of how multilateral processes can be important to trade liberalization. In this context, compare the incentives of the principal supplier with the incentives of other participants that might be interested in receiving a particular concession? With this mind, how might the principal supplier rule have further enhanced the tariff reducing potential of the process?

(3) With the Dillon round it became obvious that the GATT tariff negotiating process was seriously impaired by the complexity of the product-by-product mode of negotiation dictated by the principal supplier rule. Accordingly, Congress in 1962 authorized the President to negotiate linear reductions in U.S. tariffs subject to certain exceptions covering approximately 12% of U.S. imports. A linear reduction, as the name implies, involves a uniform percentage cut across the entire spectrum of a nation's tariff schedule, so that a 50% linear reduction would cut all 20% tariffs to 10% and all 60% tariffs to 30% and so forth.[12] In 1964 the GATT Ministers agreed to hold the so-called Kennedy Round on the basis of "a plan of substantial linear tariff reductions,"[13] with 50% as a "working hypothesis" for the size of the reduction. The Ministers recognized, however, that if the participants were denied the right to exempt some sensitive products from that "hypothesis," it would prejudice the prospects for achieving the full reduction on a broader spectrum of items. It was agreed, therefore, that the participants could "table" lists of exceptions but were to keep the list to a "bare minimum" and each exception was to "be subject to confrontation and justification."[14] In practical effect these rules tended to have two opposing effects. The linear cut eliminated the distortions endemic to a rule of product-by-product reciprocity measured principally by trade coverage. It also tended to make the negotiations more manageable. On the other

---

[11] Dam, The GATT, Law and Economic Organization, University of Chicago Press (1970), at page 63.

[12] For an excellent overview of the course of the Kennedy Round, see Rehm, *Development in the Law and Institutions of International Economic Relations*, 62 A.J.I.L. 403 (1968).

[13] GATT, BISD, 12th Suppl. (1964), at page 47.

[14] GATT, BISD, 13th Suppl. (1965), at page 110.

hand, the extensiveness of some of the exceptions lists and the confrontation and justification requirement all tended to reintroduce the traditional haggling over specific items guided by the traditional measures of reciprocity. Further inroads on the linear approach occurred when it was decided to exclude agriculture from the linear process.[15] This, in turn, threatened to disadvantage a number of developed countries whose principal exports consisted of agricultural products. They were expected to reduce duties on their industrial imports in accordance with the "linear 50% formula," yet were to be denied benefit of that formula for their agricultural exports. The problem was only solved by designating those countries — Australia, Canada, New Zealand and South Africa — "non-linear countries" and authorizing them to negotiate on the traditional product-by-product basis.

(4) Nowhere does GATT deny to a Contracting Party the right to refuse to give tariff concessions. Each party is free to pursue its own self-interest. This, in turn, has led to the concept of "reciprocity" which, although nowhere defined, has become a central tenet of the General Agreement. Indeed, when Article XXVIII *bis* was added it acknowledged that negotiations were to be conducted on a "reciprocal and mutually advantageous" basis. In addition, "trade coverage", as described in Note (2) above, has come to be used as the controlling measure of what constitutes a "reciprocal" undertaking. Recall the discussion under Note (2) and the inadequacies of "trade coverage" when used to equate concession withdrawals pursuant to the adjustment process of Article XXVIII. Reflect upon whether the same critique can be applied when "trade coverage" is used as a measure of "reciprocity" in more comprehensive tariff-cutting negotiations. Are there practical considerations that distinguish the two situations? More importantly, does "reciprocity" have a somewhat different function in this latter context; a function for which an inexact measure — what some have called a "diffuse reciprocity" — is quite adequate?

(5) In light of the propensity, even under a system of linear reductions, to fall back into a good deal of product-by-product negotiating, may Lord Granville's complaint continue to represent a problem for certain countries? Explain. While the so-called "disparities" problem evoked a good deal of inconclusive debate in the Kennedy Round, nothing was done until the Tokyo Round. There the so-called Swiss formula was adopted.

---

[15] The decision was based in part upon the fact that the principal obstacles to expanded agricultural trade were non-tariff barriers, rather than tariffs. It also was symptomatic of the intractable conflict between the EEC which, under its Common Agriculture Policy, had determined to move from being a major food importer to self-sufficiency, and the United States for whom Europe was a major agricultural market. In fact, the growing American concern with the emerging European policy led Congress, in the Trade Expansion Act of 1962, to empower the President to reduce American tariffs to zero for specified agricultural products provided that the EEC agreed to accord the United States "acceptable conditions of access" to the EEC market in those products. The strategy failed. The Europeans were less forthcoming on the agricultural question than the strategists had hoped and the authority was never used.

§ 4.02 Prohibition on Quantitative Restrictions and Its Exceptions: More On Non-Discrimination

In the negotiations leading-up to the Havana Charter the United States proposed that all quantitative restrictions on trade be outlawed and that the only permissible form of protection be tariffs, the reduction of which would be the subject of periodic negotiations. The United States argued that tariffs were far more transparent, left greater room for the operation of market forces and were less subject to being administered in a covertly discriminatory manner. The opposition to this position was broadly based and vocal, especially on the part of those participants who viewed quantitative restrictions as a useful mechanism for improving their balance of payments position. The result was a compromise embodied in Articles XI, XII, XIII and XIV.

The Basic Prohibition (Article XI)

Article XI

1. **No prohibitions or restrictions other than duties, taxes or other charges, whether made effective through quotas, import or export licenses or other measures, shall be instituted or maintained by any Contracting Party on the importation of any product of the territory of any other Contracting Party or on the exportation or sale for export of any product destined for the territory of any other Contracting Party.**

Paragraph 2 introduces a number of exceptions covering export controls to relieve food shortages, prohibitions to assure adherence to standards for classifying, grading or marketing goods and, in subparagraph (c), quotas necessary to protect domestic agricultural programs. The latter was instituted largely at the insistence of the United States, but soon became outdated.[1] Also, as we shall see later, Article XIX — the so-called "escape clause" provision of GATT — sanctions the use of quantitative restrictions.

The Multi-Fiber Arrangement (MFA): A Major Exception to the Prohibition on Quantitative Restrictions

Responding to competitive pressures on their own apparel and textile industries by cheap imports, first from Japan and later from a growing number of developing countries, the industrialized countries in GATT led the way in obtaining the Contracting Parties' approval of what is now called the Multifiber Arrangement (MFA). The bilateral agreements negotiated within the framework of the MFA

---

[1] Article XI:2(c) exempts from the broad prohibition of Article XI:1 import restrictions on agricultural products that are necessary to the enforcement of domestic programs which have any of the following effects: (i) limit production of a like domestic product, or (ii) remove a temporary surplus in the domestic product through grants or concessional sales to "certain groups of domestic consumers," or (iii) limit the production of domestic animal products, the production of which is dependent upon the imported commodity. If, at the time, this provision was adequate to exempt quotas imposed by the United States in order to insulate its domestic agricultural programs from foreign imports, that soon changed as the United States increasingly turned away from production control measures to subsidizing domestic production. (See discussion *infra* page 317.)

represent what is perhaps the most sweeping departure from the prohibition contained in Article XI and from the original GATT philosophy of minimizing the use of quantitative restrictions in favor of tariffs that would be subject to negotiated reductions. The history of the MFA and some reflections on its costs and its purposes are contained in the following excerpt.

The Future in World Trade In Textiles and Apparel[2]

William C. Cline

* * * *

Evolution and Impact of Protection

In the postwar period Japan first placed pressure on [the apparel and textile markets of the industrialized countries] . . . Europe responded with exemptions to liberalization for Japan. . . . Following the resulting spillover of supply to new sourcing from Hong Kong, by 1961 the United States led the international negotiation of the Short Term Arrangement for trade in cotton textiles and apparel, followed in 1962 by the corresponding Long Term Arrangement. . . . As trade in man-made fibers mushroomed, by the early 1970's there was intense pressure to extend coverage to non-cotton textiles. . . . [This led, in 1974, to the Multi-Fiber Arrangement (MFA) which] combined dual objectives: implementing new restraints while at the same time imposing some uniform limits on how severe the restraints could be. . . . Designed mainly to legitimize emerging bilateral restraints, the MFA incorporated compensatory liberalizing moves: the identification of a 6 percent annual growth as a target for imports under quota . . . and flexibility provisions ("swing" across categories, "carry-forward" over time). The MFA also provided for a phase down of bilateral European restrictions against Eastern Europe and developing countries.

From the beginning of the MFA, it has been the specific limitations in bilateral agreements negotiated under its auspices with individual supplier countries that have constituted the operational core of the Arrangement. Because the European nations were slow to reach bilateral agreements, by 1977 they contended they had borne a disproportionate burden of imports under MFA-I and they led the demand for tightening in the 1977 renewal (MFA-II), [principally] . . . by provid[ing] for "reasonable departures" from the 6 percent quota growth target, thereby fundamentally backing down on the liberalization compromise originally embedded in the mechanism. . . . In the renewal of 1981 (MFA-III) the EC again complained of an undue burden of imports, and sought actual cutbacks of imports from the key East Asian suppliers. GATT analysts subsequently judged that the renewal brought another round of tightening.

By the early 1980's, the United States had bilateral restraint agreements with 34 countries, covering 80 percent of textile and apparel imports from the developing countries. Worldwide, the MFA covered some 14 percent of textile trade and 40 percent of trade in apparel. Other quantitative restraints . . . raised the total

---

[2] The title is that of a book by William C. Cline published by the Institute for International Economics © (1987). Reprinted by permission. What follows is an excerpt from the "Introduction and Summary" of that book.

trade subject to restraints to approximately 60 percent in textiles and 65 percent in apparel. The remainder, . . . dominated by trade among the industrial countries, was restraint free but subject to relatively high tariffs. . . . On the basis of various studies but most importantly evidence on the price of quota rights traded in Hong Kong, [it is possible to estimate] the tariff equivalent of MFA quotas at approximately . . . 25 percent in apparel and 15 percent in textiles.

The structure of the MFA has been such (especially as administered by the United States) that there have been loopholes that do permit more rapid import growth when the economic forces increase. . . . The case of Korea illustrates how imports could rise briskly even from a country with relatively tight controls. Apparel imports rose by 38 percent in value from 1982 to 1984. Categories controlled by quotas in 1982 (representing approximately two-thirds of import value) advanced only 2 percent in quantity but rose 28 percent in value, showing rapid upgrading. Categories subject only to surveillance in 1982 showed, in contrast, a quantity increase of 42 percent and a value increase of 61 percent. In the Korean case, it was neither quota growth nor "adjusted utilization rates" . . . that made the difference, but upgrading where quotas applied and increased volume where looser surveillance existed.

Key changes in the administration of US bilateral agreements in 1986 sharply curtailed the scope for such increases. . . . [T]he categories subject only to surveillance [were] seriously cutback and shifted to quota control. [I]n addition . . . [adoption of] a system of layered category and subcategory quotas further removed flexibility. New bilateral agreements with Hong Kong, Korea and Taiwan cut the annual growth of import quotas to 1 percent or less and extended coverage to . . . [additional] products. It would be a serious mistake to conclude, on the basis of experience in the early 1980s, that textile and apparel protection has minimal restrictive effect; all indications are that the flexibility that permitted rapid growth in imports in this period has by now been largely eliminated.

[Finally] . . . in July 1986 the United States and 53 other nations renewed the Multi-Fiber Arrangement for another five years. At US insistence, the renewal provided for new tightening. It extended product coverage, . . . facilitated measures to guard against import surges, . . . opened the door further to outright reduction in quotas from large supplier countries and [authorized] . . . departures from the original target of 6 percent quota growth. At the same time . . . the United States concluded new bilateral agreements with Hong Kong, Taiwan, and Korea. As always, the bilaterals were the scene of the real protective content, and the MFA only an umbrella. These new bilaterals broadened product coverage, . . . imposed extremely low quota growth rates of one-half of a percent to 1 percent annually [and] in the case of Taiwan actually rolled back imports by 7 percent . . . from the May 1986 [level].

Costs of Protection

Protection imposes costs on consumers and the economy at large. Restriction of the supply of imports tends to raise their price. In addition, as import prices rise, the prices of competing domestic goods tend to rise in response; consumers shift demand away from imports and toward domestic goods, and US producers can raise prices when relieved from import competition. The increase in consumer prices causes a transfer of income away from consumers to domestic producers. . . . In addition, part of the consumer cost accrues not to US citizens but to foreign suppliers, in the form of "quota rents" — the scarcity value of import quotas (as illustrated by the Hong Kong quota premiums). There is a further economic loss from the inefficient allocation of additional resources to produce goods that could be more cheaply purchased abroad.

The net national cost of protection, after deducting transfers to producers (and, in the case of tariff protection, to government revenue), must be compared to the net benefits arising from avoidance of temporary unemployment of workers who would be displaced from the textile and apparel sectors in the absence of protection. This loss from temporary unemployment occurs on a one-time basis, whereas the consumer and efficiency costs recur year after year.

[Using a model which] treats imports as partial substitutes for domestic goods[3] [and applying that model] . . . to 1986 data . . . [t]ariff and quota protection raised import prices by an estimated 53 percent for apparel and 28 percent for textiles. Total consumer costs of protection amount[ed] to $17.6 billion annually in apparel and $2.8 billion in textiles. Total protection preserved 214,200 direct jobs in apparel and 20,700 jobs in textiles. The average American household thus paid $238 every year to retain some 235,000 jobs in the textile and apparel sectors rather than elsewhere in the economy. The consumer cost per job saved [was] approximately $82,000 in apparel and $135,000 in textiles.[4]

The net welfare cost to all Americans was smaller; after deducting transfers to producers and government, the net national cost annually amounted to $7.3 billion in apparel and $811 million in textiles. However, the employment benefits of protection are far smaller than this cost. Evaluated on the basis of average duration of unemployment and average wage, the annualized cost of transitional unemployment resulting from elimination of protection would amount to only about 3 percent to 4 percent of the net welfare costs of protection. Of the total net national cost of approximately $8 billion, almost half arises from the transfer of income to foreign suppliers in the form of quota rents.

These estimates of protection costs are broadly comparable to those of other major recent studies. The calculations here should be interpreted as conservative, because they assume that retailing firms pass along to consumers only the absolute cost increase imposed by protection, but do not apply their normal percentage marketing margins to these costs. (Otherwise, the consumer costs could be as much as twice the level estimated here.)

. . . Despite the frequent justification of this protection for apparel and textiles on grounds that it shelters low-income workers, the [fact appears to be that] . . . that protection has a regressive income distribution impact. It reduces the income of the lowest 20 percent of households by 3.6 percent, cuts income by about 1

---

[3] Under the model, prices of domestic goods rise partially but by less than the full percentage by which imported prices increase as the result of protection.

[4] If the more conservative measure incorporating indirect employment in intermediate inputs is used, the consumer cost is approximately $46,000 per job in apparel and $52,000 in textiles. However, as there would be alternative indirect employment associated with other sectors, if some resources were shifted out of textiles and apparel, the cost per direct job is the more meaningful figure for policy purposes.

percent for the next three quintiles, and increases income by one-third of 1 percent for the richest 20 percent (who own the shares of textile and apparel firms). Textile and apparel workers generally fall in the second and third quintiles, and these income classes might be expected to gain; but because of the inefficiency of protection, even these income groups suffer on balance because the gains for textile and apparel workers are smaller than the losses of others in the same income classes.

Quantitative Restriction for Balance of Payments Purposes (Article XII): A Further Exception

Another significant exception to the prohibitions of Article XI is found in Article XII which authorizes quantitative restrictions imposed for balance of payments purposes. Whenever a government is unwilling to let the market completely dictate exchange rates for its currency and also experiences chronic balance of payments deficits, it means that the demand for foreign currencies by holders of the deficit currency chronically exceeds the supply of those foreign currencies at a price acceptable to the government. A government in this position is constantly required to use its own reserves of foreign exchange to buy up the surplus in its own currency thereby depleting its reserves. Moreover, efforts to cure such a situation through internal fiscal and monetary restraints (budget cuts and tight money) or devaluation of the currency (*i.e.*, making imports of goods not produced locally more expensive), can have political consequences that governments find hard to accept. Understandably they may prefer to raise tariffs selectively, impose quantitative restrictions on imports or resort to exchange controls.

Exchange controls usually require residents who earn scarce foreign currencies to surrender the latter to the government in exchange for the deficit currency. The government then rations the scarce foreign currencies on the basis of some predetermined criteria to importers and others who need them. This renders the deficit currency "inconvertible." An "inconvertible" currency in this sense is often spoken of as a "soft" currency, while a currency that is freely convertible is a "hard" currency.[5]

At the end of World War II, the vast majority of industrialized nations, except the United States, had in place elaborate exchange control mechanisms that

---

[5] While it is somewhat easier to explain "inconvertibility" in the context of a "par value system", the demise of that system has not meant that balance of payments problems, and the consequent use of exchange controls, quantitative restrictions and the like have also disappeared from the world scene. A number of countries, especially less developed countries, have turned to these restrictions and to the controls that render their currencies "inconvertible" because the more or less automatic devaluations that occur under a "floating exchange rate system" have not always provided as rapid a cure for their deficits as they might have liked, especially where the terms-of-trade have turned against them. In addition, some have turned to exchange controls in order to avoid domestic fiscal and monetary reforms or to gain "breathing room" for those often painful and politically unpopular measures.

rendered their currencies "inconvertible." Most of these controls reflected the "dollar shortage" brought about by the war's devastation. At the same time, most of the countries suffering from this "shortage" were determined to pursue full employment policies, rebuild their war torn economies, erect costly social service systems and adopt a par-value system that would make competitive currency devaluations difficult. As a result, most post-war international monetary planners accepted the fact that exchange controls would, for a time at least, be a fixture of the international monetary order. They also recognized, however, that exchange controls, along with high tariffs, quantitative restrictions and the like would, if allowed to become a permanent fixture of the international economic order, constitute a serious barrier to the long run economic growth of the major industrialized countries of the world — a reversion to precisely those strictures that added to the misery of the pre-war depression.

Accordingly, the economic planners stipulated in the IMF Articles of Agreement that the members of that organization would dismantle their exchange controls and render their currencies fully convertible as rapidly as conditions would permit.[6] But this, the planners knew, would not happen overnight. They also anticipated that for less developed countries the transition might take much longer and that even after the major trading nations had attained a general condition of currency convertibility, individual nations might periodically experience payments difficulties warranting the imposition of some controls.[7]

Once all of this was recognized in the context of negotiating the post-war monetary system, it was possible for those who otherwise favored the retention of quantitative restrictions, to obtain from the United States one very basic concession: a balance of payments corollary for trade. Nations suffering chronic payments difficulties might, for a time, maintain quantitative limitations on imports.[8] Hence Article XII.

Under Paragraphs 1 and 2(a) of that Article a Contracting Party may impose quantitative limits on imports to the extent necessary to "forestall the imminent threat of or to stop a serious decline" in its monetary reserves or, where reserves are "very low," to increase those reserves. Paragraph 2(b) requires that these restrictions be "progressively" relaxed as conditions improve and eliminated altogether when no longer justified.

Paragraph 3 contains a series of stipulations regarding domestic policies that may have adverse balance of payments affects and enjoins upon parties employing quantitative restrictions to do so in a manner that will avoid unnecessary damage to the interests of other States. Most notably, however, Paragraph 3(d) excuses

---

[6] Consult Article VIII, Section 2 and Article XIV of the Articles of Agreement of the International Monetary Fund (Original Version, as entered into effect, December 27, 1945, 60 Stat. 1401, TIAS, 2 U.N.T.S. 39.

[7] Consult Article VIII, Section 2, of the Articles of Agreement of the International Monetary Fund, as amended effective April 1, 1978, 29 U.S.T. 2203, TIAS 8937. These provisions authorize the maintenance of exchange restriction with "the approval of the Fund." Also consult Article XIV, regarding transitional measures.

[8] Obviously nations might also find it expedient to respond to balance of payments difficulties with tariff increases. Such increases, however, could be handled through the periodic adjustments anticipated under Article XXVIII of the GATT.

any Contracting Party pursuing domestic full employment or economic development policies from having to withdraw or modify its quantitative restrictions merely because those restrictions would be unnecessary if it changed its domestic policies.

Procedural Provisions Paragraph 4 sets forth a series of procedural provisions which nations invoking Article XII must follow, including initial notification to, and, where feasible, prior consultation with GATT and mandatory annual consultations thereafter. *Remedial measures may be taken* Remedial measures may also be taken if GATT finds that any quantitative restriction is being applied inconsistent with the requirements of Article XII and is causing damage to the trade of any Contracting Party.

These procedural provisions set the framework for one of the more notable chapters in early GATT history, one that illustrates how the GATT process of multilateral surveillance and discipline can work and the impact it can have. Many of the immediate post-war quantitative restrictions imposed for balance of payments purposes were maintained on a highly discriminatory basis, a reality which largely explains the inclusion of Article XIV to which we shall turn shortly. Yet, the commitment made by these nations to restore their currencies to full convertibility (IMF Article VIII), the undertakings contained in GATT Article XII:2 and 3 and the restrictions imposed by Article XIV on their right to discriminate, all combined to provide the essential underpinnings for a process that Gardner Patterson has described in the following terms:[9]

> [The commitments] . . . meant that in the consultations the fact and extent of the discrimination were made evident and the burden of proof for the practice was on those who wished to discriminate. They were in the open and on the defensive. . . . Contracting parties which discriminated did so with certain knowledge that in the GATT . . . those whose exports suffered . . . would ask "is this still necessary?" and would have a "right" to expect specific and detailed answers which said more than that the policy was an easy answer to the discriminating country's immediate problems. The commitment to consult required that the interests of third countries be weighed. As it happened, the practice developed early of asking blunt and searching questions, and national spokesmen who year after year could not provide answers convincing to third countries often found themselves in acutely embarrassing positions. The replies given in successive years as to recent policy changes show that governments were responsive to findings that their actions conflicted with their international obligations and were hurtful to others.

By the mid-to-late 1960's most of the post-war balance of payments based quantitative restrictions imposed by the developed countries on imports of industrial products had been abolished, and the focus of attention under Article XII and Article XIV shifted to the developing countries. This is not to say, however, that quantitative restrictions disappeared from the lexicon of developed country protectionism. Quite the contrary was true,[10] but with respect to

---

[9] Gardner Patterson, Discrimination In International Trade; The Policy Issues, 1945-1965, Princeton University Press, Princeton, N.J. (1965) at page 64.

[10] If anything, quantitative restrictions on agricultural goods and other primary products flourished either by virtue of a waiver of the GATT prohibitions or in open violation of the General Agreement. Also, GATT itself by sponsoring the Cotton Textile Arrange-

restrictions imposed for balance of payments purposes under Article XII and also Article XVIII, Section B, several steps were taken in 1970 and 1972 to improve the consultative process outlined in Article XII:4 and Article XVIII. Then, in the Tokyo Round, the Contracting Parties adopted a "Declaration on Trade Measures Taken for Balance of Payments Purposes."[11] In addition, to a number of strongly worded principles[12] and some procedural innovations, the Declaration's principal substantive contribution lay in bringing within the consultative process of Articles XII and XVIII "all restrictive import measures taken for balance of payments purposes." For historical reasons, GATT, while permitting balance of payments based quantitative restrictions, had prohibited other measures, most notable tariff surcharges. In certain circumstances, however, such surcharges, because they give greater latitude to market forces, are to be preferred and had come into fairly wide use inspite of the GATT prohibition. Given the pragmatic way in which GATT often acts, it may be doubted whether the Declaration can be read as lending implied sanction to such measures, but it does bring them within the GATT system of multilateral surveillance.

Non-Discrimination in the Administration of Quantitative Restrictions (Article XIII)

Article XIII of the General Agreement provides in pertinent part as follows:

Article XIII

Non-discriminatory Administration of Quantitative Restrictions

1. **No prohibition or restriction shall be applied by any Contracting Party on the importation of any product of the territory of any other Contracting Party or on the exportation of any product destined for the territory of any other Contracting Party, unless the importation of the like product of all third countries or the exportation of the like product to all third countries is similarly prohibited or restricted.**

2. **In applying import restrictions to any product, Contracting Parties shall aim at a distribution of trade in such product approaching as closely as possible the shares which the various Contracting Parties might be**

---

ment of 1962 and its successor the Multifiber Arrangement (MFA), endorsed a system under which discriminatory quantitative restrictions became the rule of the day for international trade in textiles and apparel (See page 236, *infra*). Moreover, today the widespread use of bilateral Voluntary Restraint Agreements (VRAs) and Orderly Marketing Agreements (OMAs), negotiated outside the GATT framework, pose a major threat to a non-discriminatory trading system (See page 349 *infra*).

[11] GATT, BISD, 26th Supp. (1980), at page 205.

[12] Among the stated principles, all relating to balance of payments based quantitative restrictions were the following: (i) such restrictions are in general an "inefficient" means of restoring balance of payments equilibrium, (ii) they should not be used to protect particular industries, (iii) Contracting Parties should avoid restrictions that stimulate new investments which cannot otherwise survive, and (iv) a recognition that less-developed countries must take into account their "individual development, financial and trade situation" in determining whether to employ such restrictions. *Id.* at pages 205-206.

expected to obtain in the absence of such restrictions, and to this end shall observe the following provisions:

(a) [provides that whenever possible quotas covering the total amount of permitted imports should be fixed, whether allocated among supplying countries or not.]

(b) [allows the use of import licenses if quotas are not practicable.]

(c) [import licenses may not be required for the importing of a product from a particular country or source, unless used in connection with quotas allocated as provided in subparagraph (d).]

(d) **In cases in which a quota is allocated among supplying countries, the Contracting Party applying the restrictions may seek agreement with respect to the allocation of shares in the quota with all other Contracting Parties having a substantial interest in supplying the product concerned. In cases in which this method is not reasonably practicable, the Contracting Party concerned shall allot to Contracting Parties having a substantial interest in supplying the product, shares based upon the proportions, supplied by such Contracting Parties during a previous representative period, of the total quantity or value of imports of the product, due account being taken of any special factors which may have affected or may be affecting the trade in the product. . . .**

NORWAY — RESTRICTIONS ON IMPORTS OF CERTAIN TEXTILE PRODUCTS

Report of the Panel
adopted on 18 June 1980
(L/4959)

GATT, BISD 27th Supp., at page 119

[Until the end of 1977, Hong Kong's shipments to Norway of the textiles involved in this dispute were subject to the limitations contained in a bilateral restraint agreement concluded within the framework of the MFA. In October 1977 Norway requested Hong Kong to negotiate a further bilateral agreement for 1978, but after consultations no agreement was reached. Therefore, in January 1978, Norway imposed temporary unilateral control measures on imports from a number of countries including Hong Kong. By the end of April 1978 Norway had concluded long-term bilateral restraint agreements with six textile-supplying developing countries, but was still unable to reach agreement with Hong Kong.

In July of 1978 Norway informed the Contracting Parties that it had decided to invoke Article XIX [13] and that it was preparing to introduce global import

-----

[13] Article XIX is the so-called "escape clause" which we shall examine more closely *infra*. It provides that if, as a result of "unforeseen developments," any obligation incurred

quotas on nine textile items for 1979. Shortly thereafter Norway, in conducting consultations under Article XIX:2, informed Hong Kong that imports from the EEC and EFTA, together with imports from the six developing countries with whom Norway had concluded long-term bilateral arrangements, would not be covered by the global quotas. Hong Kong objected. Relying on Article XIII it requested that, as a substantial supplier of the products involved, (i) it be allocated for the year 1979 a share of the global quota "similar" to the shares which had been allotted to the six countries with which Norway had signed bilateral agreements, and (ii) it be compensated for export trade lost in the year 1978. Norway declined to honor the request.

In late 1978, Norway notified GATT that the size of the global quotas for 1979 had been calculated on the basis of average imports in 1974–76 from the countries included in those quotas, *i.e.*, all countries except the six developing countries and the EEC and EFTA.

The matter was then referred to the Contracting Parties pursuant to Article XXIII by the United Kingdom, acting on behalf of Hong Kong. The Contracting Parties agreed to the appointment of a Panel and subsequently adopted the Panel Report set out below.]

* * * *

III. Main Arguments

Hong Kong

6. . . . Concerning [Norway's] invocation of Article XIX, Hong Kong argued that while it was prepared to assume that Norway had the necessary justification for taking this action, the latter was nevertheless inconsistent with the General Agreement and in particular Article XIII. Norway had excluded from the global quotas . . . [(i)] the EEC and EFTA countries . . . [and (ii)] the six countries with which it had concluded bilateral agreements. . . . [As to (i)] while stating that it did not agree with Norway's explanation . . . Hong Kong believed that the basis of its complaint did not necessitate a finding by the Panel. . . .

[As to (ii)] Hong Kong contended that . . . the maintenance of [the six bilateral] . . . agreements outside Norway's global quotas had adversely affected Hong Kong's interests because the size of the global quotas had as a result been reduced. To make the quotas established under the six agreements consistent with GATT, they must be regarded as part of Norway's Article XIX action and country shares allotted under Article XIII:2(d). In view of its substantial interest in supplying the products concerned, Hong Kong requested that Norway should either immediately terminate its Article XIX action or make it consistent with Article XIII:2(d) by allotting an appropriate quota to Hong Kong. Hong Kong stressed, however, that in making this request, [it] . . . had no intention of questioning Norway's

---

under GATT, including a tariff concession, causes a product to be imported by a Contracting Party in increased quantities sufficient to cause serious injury to domestic producers, that Contracting Party may suspend the obligation for so long as is necessary to prevent or remedy the injury.

motive in maintaining the six bilateral agreements . . . nor was Hong Kong asking Norway to suspend those agreements.

7. Hong Kong further stated that it had more than met its obligations . . . [to] Norway under the MFA. The restraints covered by bilateral agreements entered into by the two parties under the MFA had expanded rapidly in scope so that by 1977 . . . Hong Kong's last bilateral agreement with Norway covered fifteen broad groups of products representing 73 percent of Hong Kong's total exports of textiles and clothing to Norway. Furthermore, Hong Kong had accepted, between 1975 and 1977, annual growth rates of only token amounts (one percent) in respect of certain products in which Hong Kong had a significant export interest, and this was done in a situation where Norway's imports *of other than "low-price" products* . . . which had been excluded from any action so far taken by Norway, had increased at the rate of 120 percent from 1973 to 1977, which was not much lower than the rate of increase of *"low-price" imports* in the same period. Hong Kong contended that its textile exports in 1974–1977 had therefore not been inequitable and unforeseen. At any rate, cut-backs as requested by Norway of a magnitude of 25.5 percent to 76.9 percent on existing restraint limits could not be considered "reasonable departures" from the MFA which provided for an annual growth rate of not less than 6 percent. Under these circumstances it had not been possible to reach an agreement with Norway.

8. Hong Kong finally stated that the latest twelve-month period should be used as a representative base period both for establishing the size of the global quotas and for allocating country shares. In Hong Kong's view, the latest period in which imports of the products in question from Hong Kong into Norway had taken place within a legitimate framework was the year 1977.

9. On this basis, Hong Kong . . . [claimed that] as a result of Norway's failure to carry out its obligations under Article XIII, . . . [its] benefits under the General Agreement have been, and continue to be, nullified or impaired . . . [and that] the Contracting Parties should recommend that the Government of Norway should either immediately terminate its Article XIX action, or immediately make it consistent with the provisions of Article XIII:2(d) by allotting an appropriate quota to Hong Kong."

Norway

10. As to the general background of its import restrictions, Norway stated that total *low-priced imports* of clothing had gone up from NKr 225 million in 1973 to NKr 581 million in 1977, representing an increase of 159 percent and threatening its "minimum viable production of textiles" (MFA Article 1, paragraph 2). For Hong Kong the corresponding figures were NKr 93 million and NKr 307 million, an increase of 230 percent and an annual growth of 35 percent; Hong Kong's share of clothing imports had risen from 41.5 percent in 1973 to 52.9 percent in 1977. Under these circumstances temporary unilateral import restrictions effective from 1 January 1978 had proved to be necessary in order to limit the injury to Norway's textile industry while pursuing further bilateral consultations.

11. . . . As a member of the MFA . . . Norway was entitled to take the unilateral measures put into force . . . [in] 1978. . . . [T]his was done on the basis

of the provisions of the . . . Protocol extending the MFA [because it was] . . . still involved in bilateral consultations with a number of textile supplying countries, aimed at concluding the necessary agreements allowing . . . accession [to the extended MFA]. . . . Norway did, therefore, not specify the provisions on which its import restrictions were based until it became evident that the possibility of reaching a bilateral solution on the basis of the extended MFA . . . with Hong Kong had vanished. . . . Only after a final attempt to reach a bilateral solution with Hong Kong in June 1978 had failed, did Norway invoke Article XIX.

12. Norway maintained that its Article XIX action was in full conformity with the GATT. Imports from EEC and EFTA countries had been excluded because Norway had entered into agreements with these countries under Article XXIV of the GATT. The six bilateral agreements with the developing countries had been concluded before a decision to invoke Article XIX had been taken; and Norway stated that, on inquiry, all six countries had expressed their firm wish to maintain the agreements. Furthermore a suspension of these agreements would not facilitate Norway's accession to the extended MFA and in addition would not be in conformity with the spirit and objective of Part IV of the GATT. Against this background Norway stated that the bilateral quotas under these agreements were not to be considered as country shares within the meaning of Article XIII:2(d). If, however, the Contracting Parties found that imports from the six countries should be included in the global quota system, Norway would act accordingly and suspend these agreements.

* * * *

IV. Conclusions

14. The Panel based its consideration of the case on Articles XIX and XIII of the GATT:

(a) The Panel noted . . . and consequently based its decision on the statements by Hong Kong that the latter was prepared to assume that Norway had the necessary justification for taking [its Article XIX] . . . action and that a finding concerning the exclusion from the quotas of the EEC and EFTA countries was not necessary.

(b) The Panel was of the view that the type of action chosen by Norway . . . under Article XIX was subject to the provisions of Article XIII which provides for non-discriminatory administration of quantitative restrictions. In this connection, the Panel noted [that] . . . paragraph 2 . . . stipulates that in applying an import restriction on a product, a Contracting Party "shall aim at a distribution of trade in such product approaching as closely as possible the shares which the various Contracting Parties might be expected to obtain in the absence of such restrictions. . . ." To this end, paragraph 2(a) of Article XIII further prescribes that wherever practicable, quotas representing the total amount of permitted imports (whether allocated among supplying countries or not) shall be fixed.

15. . . . The Panel noted that Norway had concluded these [six] agreements with the intention of acceding to the MFA. . . . [H]owever, in the event Norway had not acceded to the MFA . . . no derogation from the provisions of Parts I–III

of GATT had ever been invoked by Norway [with respect to these six agreements]. While . . . [some] provision . . . for assured increase in access [by developing countries] to Norway's textile and clothing markets might be consistent . . . with the spirit and objective of Part IV of the GATT, this cannot be cited as justification for actions which would be inconsistent with a country's obligations under Part II of the GATT. The Panel held that Norway's reservation of market shares for these six countries therefore represented a partial allocation of quotas under an existing regime of import restrictions of the products in question and that Norway must therefore be considered to have acted under [the first sentence] of Article XIII:2(d).

16. Since Hong Kong has a substantial interest in supplying eight of the nine product categories in question to the Norwegian market, it had the right to expect the allocation of a share of the quotas in accordance with Article XIII:2(d) . . . [and] to the extent that Norway had allocate[d] import quotas . . . to six countries but had failed to allocate a share to Hong Kong, its Article XIX action was not consistent with Article XIII.

17. In accordance with established GATT practice, the Panel held that where a measure had been taken which was judged to be inconsistent with the provisions of the General Agreement, this measure would *prima facie* constitute a case of nullification or impairment of benefits which other Contracting Parties were entitled to expect under the General Agreement.

18. On the basis of the conclusions reached above, the Panel finds that Norway should immediately either terminate its action taken under Article XIX or make it consistent with the provisions of Article XIII.

19. The Panel expresses the hope that in the light of this report the parties will be able to arrive at a mutually acceptable agreement.

NOTES AND QUESTIONS

(1) Suppose the United States extended "escape clause" relief (Article XIX of the GATT and Section 201 et. seq. of the Omnibus Trade and Competitiveness Act of 1988) to its automobile industry, and then attempted to implement that relief through bilaterally negotiated Voluntary Restraint Agreements. Does the decision in the *Norwegian Textile* Case mean that in the negotiation of those VRAs the U.S. would be subject to Article XIII and hence to GATT discipline? Who might bring the issue to GATT? See GATT Article XXIII on "nullification and impairment," page 270 *infra*.

(2) The Panel noted the introductory language to Article XIII:2 calling for a distribution of trade under a quota "approaching as closely as possible" the distribution that would obtain in the absence of the quota. Paragraph 2(d), however, calls for quota allocations "based upon the proportions supplied [by each exporting country] during a previous representative period." Norway apparently was suggesting that the years 1974-1976 constituted just such a period. Hong Kong counters with the suggestion that 1977 alone should be the reference point. From

the data contained in the Panel's Report explain why Hong Kong took this position. Why should Norway object?

(3) As counsel for Hong Kong, formulate your legal argument and then support it with a policy argument. Note the reference in Paragraph 2(d) to "special factors." According to Ad Article XIII:4 such factors include "changes in relative efficiency . . . between different foreign producers."

(4) Assume that the scheme originally proposed by Norway would have passed muster under the MFA, how would you formulate Norway's response to Hong Kong? Note, that both Norway and the Panel referred to Part IV of the General Agreement. Examine that Part in the Documentary Supplement.[14] How would you use it to bolster Norway's argument?

(5) Observe that the Panel left the issue posed in Note (2) essentially unresolved, leaving it for the parties to work the problem out. Reflect on what was accomplished by this all too typical exercise in GATT dispute resolution. What contribution to an ultimate resolution did the Panel make? Should they have gone further?

(6) In the case of *EEC Restrictions on Imports of Apples from Chile*,[15] the GATT Panel, after determining, "in accordance with GATT practice," that a three year representative period was appropriate, calculated that the 42,100 ton EEC quota for 1979, which Chile was contesting, gave the latter almost exactly the 13.6% average share of imports that Chile had enjoyed during that period. It then noted, however, that during the period Chile's share had been rising rapidly from 5% in the first year to 17% in the last and concluded that "Chile's increased export capacity should have been taken into account" in fixing its allocation, especially since Chilean suppliers already had contracts for 60,500 tons.

Discriminatory Quantitative Restrictions for Balance of Payments Purposes (Article XIV)

Having accepted the principle that, for countries in balance of payment difficulties, an exception from the rule against quantitative restrictions was a necessary trade corollary to the right to maintain exchange controls, the GATT framers necessarily confronted the fact that, as in the case of exchange controls, those quantitative trade restrictions might also justifiably be maintained on a discriminatory basis.

As already noted, most of the industrialized nations of the West emerged from World War II faced with a chronic "dollar shortage". They were utterly dependent upon goods from the United States to rebuild their wartorn economies. The United States, through its fiscal, monetary and foreign aid policies controlled the supply of dollars available to meet this demand. All of these countries had pegged their currency values to the dollar and much of the earnings from trade with their traditional European partners was in the form of currencies as inconvertible as their own. With these circumstances in mind examine Article XIV.

---

[14] Documentary Supplement.
[15] GATT, BISD 27th Supp., at page 98 (1980).

Article XIV

1. A Contracting Party which applies restrictions under Article XII or under Section B of Article XVIII may, in the application of such restrictions, deviate from the provisions of Article XIII in a manner having equivalent effect to restrictions on payments and transfers for current international transactions [*i.e.,* exchange controls — *ed.*] which that Contracting Party may at that time apply under Article VIII or XIV of the Articles of Agreement of the International Monetary Fund. . . .[16]

NOTES AND QUESTIONS

(1) Assume that country A is a "hard currency" country and that B and C are "soft currency" countries but are also traditional trading partners. Suppose that, relative to its own demand for the two currencies, C has a shortage of currency A and a relatively abundant supply of currency B and fully expends its holdings of currency A to purchase imports from A. Under a system of fixed exchange rates, what would be the effect if, under a rule of non-discrimination, C's restrictions on imports from B (whether in the form of exchange controls or quantitative restrictions) had to be the same — as harsh as — the controls it imposes on imports from A? Would any reduction in purchases from B, because of those controls, be offset by increased purchases from A? What effect would such a rule of nondiscrimination have on the overall level of trade and of economic activity in the three countries? Assuming that C were given the right, under these circumstances, to maintain discriminatory exchange and trade controls, what longer term dangers inhere in that right?

(2) Admittedly the conditions giving rise to the discrimination permitted by Article XIV were very particular to the situation confronting the major industrialized nations of the West in the immediate post-war years. Nevertheless, can you formulate a more contemporary setting in which that discrimination might also be justified? Does the advent of floating exchange rates obviate that justification altogether or only render it less compelling? Explain. Are the dangers inherent in permitting discrimination greater or less in the historical setting that gave rise to Art. XIV or under your more contemporary application of that provision?[17]

---

[16] Paragraph 2 of Article XIV deals with small deviations from the rule of Article XIII; Paragraph 3 deals with countries having a common quota in the IMF; Paragraph 4 allows a country to direct its exports in a manner designed to aid its balance of payments; and Paragraph 5 permits deviations from Article XIII which have the equivalent effect of exchange restrictions maintained under yet other provisions of the IMF Articles of Agreement.

[17] For the discriminatory imposition of countervailing duties and antidumping duties see Chapter 5. For the problems regarding discrimination in the application of "safeguard" measures, including Article XIX, see discussion at page 368 *infra.*

§ 4.03   The Concept of National Treatment

Scattered throughout Part II of the General Agreement are a number of provisions designed to prevent the circumvention, through other means, of obligations incurred in furtherance of the liberalizing objectives of the General Agreement. Many, but not all, of these reflect the so-called "national treatment" concept. They are directed at preventing governments, in their internal taxing and regulatory policies, from extending more favorable treatment to domestic products than to imports thereby impairing the anticipated benefits of a tariff binding or other GATT obligation. A quick perusal of these provisions can be instructive, for they serve to illustrate the extraordinary variety of ways that nations can inhibit or otherwise distort trade, unless legally prohibited from doing so.[1] Some of them, such as the provisions authorizing so-called "buy-America" legislation (Article III:8(a)), we examine in other Chapters of the book. Here, in the context of a recent and very notable case, we examine Article III:4 and, in the notes that follow, we consider the limitations placed on internal taxation by Article III:1 and 2.

UNITED STATES — SECTION 337 OF THE TARIFF ACT OF 1930

GATT Document, L/6439

16 January 1989

Background

[In this case, the EEC filed a complaint with the GATT contending that a U.S. statute, Section 337 of the Tariff Act of 1930 (19 U.S.C. Section 1337) — the provisions of which are fully described in the ensuing Panel Report — violated Article III:4 of the General Agreement.

The EEC's complaint was occasioned by a case in which E.I. DuPont de Nemours and Company (Dupont) filed a complaint with the United States International Trade Commission (ITC) under Section 337 alleging the importation, sale and marketing in the United States of aramid fibres produced by Akzo N.V. (Akzo) in the Netherlands using a process for which DuPont held the U.S. patent. Following failure by the EEC and U.S. to settle the case, the GATT Council, on October 7, 1987, agreed to establish a Panel to hear the dispute and to make recommendations to the Contracting Parties. While DuPont and Akzo settled their dispute before the Panel had concluded its deliberations, the Panel nevertheless proceeded to examine Section 337, along with the related Section 337a, in the abstract. Also, while the Panel was deliberating, Section 337 was amended by the Omnibus Trade and

---

[1] In addition to the provisions discussed in the text, the remainder of Article III, Article VIII ("Formalities Connected with Importation and Exportation"), Art. IX ("Marks of Origin"); Article X ("Publication and Administration of Trade Regulations"), Article XVII ("State Trading Enterprises") are worth examining .

Competitiveness Act of 1988. The Panel, however, based its findings on Section 337 as it stood in October 1987, although it took note of the amendments.

While Section 337 is not limited to patent disputes — it does not even mention patents but merely speaks of "unfair methods of competition and unfair acts in the importation of articles into the United States" — the EEC complaint and the submissions made to the Panel by the parties to the dispute concentrated on the application of Section 337 to patent-based cases. Accordingly, the Panel's findings and conclusions were limited to such cases.

Applicable Provisions of the GATT

Article III:4 provides in pertinent part as follows:

> The products of the territory of any contracting party imported into the territory of any other contracting party shall be accorded treatment no less favourable than that accorded to like products of national origin in respect of all laws, regulations and requirements affecting their internal sale, offering for sale, purchase transportation, distribution or use. . . .

Also, Ad Article III states, in part, as follows:

> . . . any law, regulation or requirement . . . which applies to an imported product and to the like domestic product and is . . . enforced in the case of the imported product at the time or point of importation, is . . . subject to the provisions of Article III.

Article XX provides in relevant part as follows:

> Subject to the requirement that such measures are not applied in a manner which would constitute a means of arbitrary or unjustifiable discrimination between countries where the same conditions prevail, or a disguised restriction on international trade, nothing in this Agreement shall be construed to prevent the adoption or enforcement by any contracting party of measures:
>
> * * * *
>
> (d) necessary to secure compliance with laws, or regulations which are not inconsistent with the provisions of this Agreement, including those relating to . . . the protection of patents, trademarks and copyrights. . . .

In its "Findings" the Panel stated the broad issue in the case in the following terms:

> The central and undisputed facts before the Panel are that, in patent infringement cases, proceedings before the ITC under Section 337 are only applicable to imported products alleged to infringe a United States patent; and that these proceedings are different, in a number of respects, from those applying before a federal district court when a product of United States origin is challenged on the grounds of patent infringement. The [EEC] . . . maintained that the differences between the two proceedings are such that the treatment accorded to imported products is less favourable than that accorded to like products of United States origin, inconsistently with Article III:4 of the General Agreement, and that this less favourable treatment cannot be justified under

Article XX(d) of the General Agreement. The United States maintained that Section 337 is justifiable under Article XX(d) and, in any event, is not inconsistent with Article III:4 since it does not accord imported products less favourable treatment than that accorded to like products of United States origin.]

Report by the Panel

* * * *

II. Factual Aspects

(i) Section 337

2.2 Under Section 337 . . . unfair methods of competition and unfair acts in the importation of articles into the United States, or in their sale, are unlawful if these unfair acts or methods of competition have the effect or tendency to (i) . . . substantially injure an industry efficiently and economically operated in the United States. . . . The unfair acts and methods of competition in question include the importation or sale of goods that infringe valid United States patents. Section 337a specifically applies Section 337 to the importation or sale of products produced abroad by a process covered by a United States patent. . . .[2]

2.3 Remedies available under Section 337 . . . consist of orders excluding the articles concerned from importation into the United States (exclusion orders) and/or cease and desist orders directing parties violating Section 337 to stop the act or method of competition found to be unfair. The exclusion order may be a general order covering all imports that . . . infringe the United States patent in question, or may be limited to goods produced by a respondent in the case.

* * * *

(iv) Differences Between Section 337 and Federal District Court Proceedings

2.8. Much of the argumentation developed before the Panel concerned the relationship and differences between patent-based Section 337 actions and litigation in federal district courts under United States patent law. The following are the main features of this relationship and of these differences as understood by the Panel.

---

[2] Section 1342(c) of the Omnibus Trade and Competitiveness Act of 1988 (Pub. L. 100-418) repealed Section 337a while, at the same time, amending Section 337 to make clear that the latter was applicable to imports made by a process covered by a U.S. patent. See 19 U.S.C. Section 1337(a)(1)(B)(ii). ED.

* * * *

(d) *Jurisdiction*:

(i) The USITC has jurisdiction only over unfair practices in import trade, such as patent infringement, that have stated effects on an industry (or trade and commerce) in the United States. Thus in order to have standing to bring a complaint the complainant, whether a United States or foreign national, must be using the patented invention in question for an industrial activity in the United States.[3] Complaints of infringement of United States patents may be filed before federal district courts by any owner or exclusive licensee of a United States patent, whether or not the plaintiff is using the patent in manufacturing in the United States (or anywhere else), and whether or not injury, as defined in Section 337, is claimed.

(ii) A Section 337 action may be brought only in respect of imports of articles alleged to infringe a United States product or process patent — that is the actual importation or the subsequent sale of those articles. A federal district court patent action may be brought in respect of imported goods and/or domestically produced goods, with one exception: as the law stood in October 1987, the owner of a United States process patent could not bring a cause of action in a federal district court against imports of products that are produced outside the United States by a process patented in the United States, based solely on alleged infringement of the process patent.

(iii) In cases over which the two fora have jurisdiction, the complainant has the right to file a complaint in either forum or in both. This may be done either simultaneously or consecutively, with one exception — a final negative finding on the patent (invalidity/non-infringement) by a federal district court precludes a subsequent Section 337 investigation on the same cause of action. A negative Section 337 determination, even when based on the patent issues, does not, at least formally, preclude relitigation of the same issues under United States patent law, because USITC determinations are not formally considered to have *res judicata* or collateral estoppel effect. For the same reasons, a disappointed respondent in a Section 337 case is not, at least formally, prevented from relitigating defences on patent issues before a federal district court, by seeking a declaratory judgment of invalidity of the complainant's patent.

(iv) Under Section 337, it is not necessary to establish *in personam* jurisdiction over all parties, as is required for federal district court litigation, except with respect to cease and desist orders directed against a party. The jurisdiction of federal district courts under existing law extends only to parties that can be served with valid process in accordance with Rule 4 of the Federal Rules of Civil Procedure. Under Section 337, the proceeding is initiated by publication of the notice of the institution of the investigation in the Federal

---

[3] This observation by the Panel still generally holds true in spite of repeal of the injury requirement in patent-based cases. The 1988 Act provides that a Section 337 exclusion order may only be issued if "an industry in the United States, relating to the articles protected by the patent . . . exists or is in the process of being established." See 19 U.S.C. Section 1337(a)(2).

Register. In addition, copies of the complaint and of the notice in the Federal Register are mailed to all respondents named in the notice and to the government of each country of foreign respondents.

(e) *Default:* Under a Section 337 proceeding, if a respondent fails to respond to a complaint the complainant is required to establish a *prima facie* case of violation of Section 337 for relief to be ordered. Federal district courts have the authority to enter a judgment by default to establish patent infringement.

(f) *Time-limits:* The USITC is required by statute to complete Section 337 investigations and make its final determination within twelve months or, in . . . "more complicated" [cases], within eighteen months, of the . . . publication of the notice of investigation. The maximum time allowed from filing to disposition of a Section 337 case, including the period . . . for Presidential review, is thus fifteen months (twenty one months in more complicated cases). Patent litigation in federal district courts does not proceed according to a statutorily determined time-schedule, and the period taken varies considerably from case to case. In the year 1 July 1986 — 30 June 1987, the average time for disposition of the patent cases in federal district courts that completed trial was thirty-one months . . .

* * * *

(h) *Counterclaims:* The USITC does not have jurisdiction in Section 337 proceedings to entertain counterclaims. In federal district court proceedings, counterclaims, whether or not related to the principal claim, may be raised in the same legal action. Assertions which constitute defences to patent infringement, for example inequitable conduct or antitrust violations, may, however, be raised as defences in Section 337 proceedings.

(i) *Economic requirements:* The complainant in a Section 337 action has to show that the effect or tendency of the patent infringement is to destroy or to substantially injure an industry efficiently and economically operated in the United States, or to prevent the establishment of such an industry. No comparable requirement exists in patent litigation in federal district courts.[4]

(j) *Public interest considerations:* Before issuing an order under Section 337, the USITC is required to consider the effect of its order on: public health and welfare; competitive conditions in the United States; the production of like or directly competitive articles in the United States; and United States consumers. No comparable requirement exists in litigation in federal district courts.

(k) *Presidential review:* . . . No Presidential review exists for federal district court decisions.

(1) *Remedies:* The principal remedy available under Section 337 is an *in rem* exclusion order. . . . The Commission may also issue cease and desist orders, typically to parties in the United States such as importers or vendors. In patent actions in federal district courts remedies operate *in personam*. . . . The main remedies are injunctions, accounting for profits, and damages,

---

[4] See footnote 3, *supra.* Ed.

either compensatory or, in case of willful infringement, multiple. In exceptional cases, attorney's fees may be awarded in federal district court litigation e.g., in cases of willful infringement by the defendant or inequitable conduct by the patentee.

(m) *Enforcement of remedies:* Section 337 exclusion orders are enforced, without any further action by the complainant, by the United States Customs Service at ports of entry into the United States. A cease and desist order by the USITC may be addressed directly to a party over which it has *in personam* jurisdiction . . . Sanctions for violation of such an order, including civil penalties and mandatory injunctions (enforceable by contempt proceedings), may be enforced in a civil action brought by the USITC in a federal district court. In federal district court patent actions, injunctions may be enforced through a contempt proceeding in that court usually initiated by the plaintiff.

(n) *Preliminary relief:* Preliminary relief under Section 337 consists of a temporary exclusion order (or a temporary cease and desist order). Such relief lasts only as long as the investigation. . . . In federal district court litigation, preliminary injunctions may be issued against an alleged infringer and normally cannot be suspended by the posting of a bond by the defendant; however, the plaintiff is required to post a bond which can be used to compensate the defendant in the event that the defendant ultimately prevails. Under Section 337, the complainant is not required to post a bond and no damages for any losses to legitimate interests resulting from a temporary exclusion order can be recovered where the respondent prevails in the final determination.

(o) *Judicial review:* Both USITC Section 337 determinations and federal district court decisions are subject to judicial review, on appeal, by the Court of Appeals for the Federal Circuit. The Court of Appeals applies the same standard of review for issues of law to decisions of either forum. On questions of fact, USITC determinations are reviewed on the basis of the "substantial evidence" standard. . . . The same standard is used to review the factual findings of juries in federal district court litigation; factual findings by federal district judges are subject to a "clearly erroneous" standard.

* * * *

V. Findings

* * * *

(iii) Relation of Article III to Article XX(d)

5.8 The parties to the dispute agreed that Article III:4 applies to substantive patent law . . . that the consistency of the substantive provisions of United States patent law with the General Agreement is not at issue . . . [and] that Section 337, when applied in cases of alleged patent infringement, is a means to secure compliance with United States patent law in respect of imported products. They disagreed, however, on the question of whether [such] a measure . . . — in contrast to the substantive patent law itself — is covered by Article III:4. In the view of the United States, measures to secure compliance with patent legislation are covered only by Article XX(d). The [EEC] took the position that Article III:4 requires national treatment also for procedures designed to enforce internal legislation, and that Article XX(d) provides for an exception to be considered only after conduct inconsistent with another provision of the General Agreement has been established.

5.9 The Panel noted that Article XX is entitled "General Exceptions" and that the central phrase in the introductory clause reads: "nothing in this Agreement shall be construed to prevent the adoption or enforcement . . . of measures . . . " Article XX(d) thus provides for a limited and conditional exception from obligations under other provisions. The Panel therefore concluded that Article XX(d) applies only to measures inconsistent with another provision of the General Agreement, and that, consequently, the application of Section 337 has to be examined first in the light of Article III:4. If any inconsistencies with Article III:4 were found, the Panel would then examine whether they could be justified under Article XX(d).

(iv) Article III:4

(a) Meaning of "laws, regulations and requirements" in Article III:4

5.10 . . . The Panel first addressed the issue of whether only substantive laws, regulations and requirements or also procedural laws, regulations and requirements can be regarded as "affecting" the internal sale of imported products. The positions of the United States and the [EEC] on this were different. . . . The Panel noted that the text of Article III:4 makes no distinction between substantive and procedural laws . . . and it was not aware of anything in the drafting history that suggests that such a distinction should be made. . . . In the Panel's view, enforcement procedures cannot be separated from the substantive provisions they serve to enforce. If the procedural provisions of internal law were not covered by Article III:4, contracting parties could escape the national treatment standard by enforcing substantive law, itself meeting the national treatment standard, through procedures less favourable to imported products than to like products of national origin. The interpretation suggested by the United States would therefore defeat the purpose of Article III, which is to ensure that internal measures "not be applied to imported or domestic products so as to afford protection to domestic production" (Article III:1). The fact that Section 337 is used as a means for the enforcement of United States patent law at the border does not provide an escape from the applicability of Article III:4 [as Ad Article III quoted above makes clear]. . . . Nor could the applicability of Article III:4 be denied on the ground that most of the procedures in the case before the Panel are applied to persons rather than products, since the factor determining whether persons might be susceptible to Section 337 proceedings or federal district court procedures is the source of the challenged products, that is whether they are of United States origin or imported. For these reasons, the Panel found that the procedures under Section 337 come within the concept of "laws, regulations and requirements" affecting the internal sale of imported products, as set out in Article III of the General Agreement.

(b) The "no less favourable" treatment standard of Article III:4

5.11 The Panel noted that . . .the "no less favourable" treatment requirement set out in Article III:4, is unqualified. . . . [Accordingly,] contracting parties may apply to imported products different formal legal requirements if doing so would accord imported products more favourable treatment. On the other hand . . . there may be cases where application of formally identical legal provisions would in practice accord less favourable treatment to imported products and a contracting party might thus have to apply different legal provisions to imported products to ensure that the treatment accorded them is in fact no less favourable. For these reasons, the mere fact that imported products are subject under Section 337 to legal provisions that are different from those applying to products of national origin is in itself not conclusive in establishing inconsistency with Article III:4. . . . [I]t is incumbent on the contracting party applying differential treatment to show that, in spite of such differences, the no less favourable treatment standard of Article III is met.

5.12 The Panel noted the differing views of the parties on how [this] assessment should be made. . . . In brief, the United States believed that [it] . . . could only be made on the basis of an examination of the *actual results* of past Section 337 cases [so that] . . . any unfavorable elements of treatment of imported products could be offset by more favourable elements of treatment, provided that the results, as shown in past cases, have not been less favourable. The [EEC's] interpretation of Article III:4 would require that Section 337 not be *capable* of according imported products less favourable treatment; elements of less and more favorable treatment could thus only be offset against each other to the extent that they always would arise in the same cases and necessarily would have an offsetting influence on each other.

5.13 The Panel examined these arguments carefully. It noted that a previous Panel had found that the purpose of the first sentence of Article III:2, dealing with internal taxes and other internal charges, is to protect "expectations on the competitive relationship between imported and domestic products".[5] Article III:4, which is the parallel provision of Article III dealing with the "non-charge" elements of internal legislation, has to be construed as serving the same purpose. Article III:4 would not serve this purpose if the United States interpretation were adopted, since a law, regulation or requirement could then only be challenged in GATT after the event as a means of rectifying less favourable treatment of imported products rather than as a means of forestalling it. In any event, the Panel doubted the feasibility of an approach that would require it to be demonstrated that differences between procedures under Section 337 and those in federal district courts had actually caused, in a given case or cases, less favourable treatment. The Panel therefore considered that, in order to establish whether the "no less favorable" treatment standard of Article III:4 is met, it had to assess whether or not Section 337 in itself may lead to the application to imported products of treatment less favorable than that accorded to products of United States origin.

---

[5] Report of Panel on United States-Taxes on Petroleum and Certain Imported Substances (L/6175, paragraph 5.1.9), adopted by the Council on 17 June 1987.

It noted that this approach is in accordance with previous practice of the Contracting Parties in applying Article III. . . .[6]

5.14 The Panel further found that the "no less favorable" treatment requirement of Article III:4 has to be understood as applicable to each individual case of imported products. The Panel rejected any notion of balancing more favorable treatment of some imported products against less favorable treatment of other imported products. If this notion were accepted, it would entitle a contracting party to derogate from the no less favourable treatment obligation in one case, or indeed in respect of one contracting party, on the ground that it accords more favorable treatment in some other case, or to another contracting party. . . .

(c) Appraisal of Section 337 in Terms of Article III:4 — Contentions by the United States that More Favorable Treatment is Accorded to Imported Products

5.15 The United States contended . . . that Section 337 accords imported products more favorable treatment than that accorded to domestic products in district court proceedings because of:

— the substantive economic elements relating to injury [of an] industry that a Section 337 complainant has to prove and that do not have to be proved in patent litigation in federal district courts;

— the possibility that relief under Section 337 might be modified or not applied on public interest or policy grounds, which possibility does not exist in federal district courts; and

— certain procedural differences from federal district court procedures that accord Section 337 respondents more favorable treatment.

The Panel examined whether these elements of claimed more favorable treatment could within the meaning of Article III:4 offset any elements of less favorable treatment of imported products alleged by the Community.

5.16 As has already been stated above, an element of more favorable treatment would only be relevant if it would always accompany and offset an element of differential treatment causing less favorable treatment. The Panel had no difficulty in recognizing that the economic requirements and the possibility of denial or limitation of relief on public interest or policy grounds could decisively influence the outcome of certain Section 337 cases in favor of imported products, as might the requirement on a complainant to make a *prima facie* case in a default situation, and that no equivalent advantages are enjoyed by defendants in federal district court litigation in respect of products of United States origin.[7] However, the Panel

---

[6] For example: Working Party on Brazilian Internal Taxes (BISD II/184-5, paragraph 13-16): Panel on Italian Discrimination against Imported Agricultural Machinery (BISD 7S/63-64, paragraph 11-12); Panel on EEC-Measures on Animal Feed Proteins (BISD 25S/65, paragraph 4.10); Panel on Canada-Administration of the Foreign Investment Review Act (BISD 30S/167, paragraph 6.6); Panel on United States-Taxes on Petroleum and Certain Imported Substances (L/6175, paragraphs 5.1.1-5.1.9).

[7] The Panel noted that several of the elements said to give advantages to respondents-notably the requirement that a complainant must show injury to an industry and the requirement that a complainant must show that the industry was being "efficiently and economically operated" — were repealed, at least as far as certain intellectual property based cases are concerned, by the Omnibus Trade and Competitiveness Act adopted by the United States in the Summer of 1988 (see Annex II).

found, on the one hand, that these requirements may involve the respondent in litigation, defence and discovery of business secrets unrelated to the underlying patent issue; and, on the other hand, there is no reason to believe that such dispositive influences would always operate in each individual case where a negative effect on the respondent might result from the operation of an element of less favorable treatment claimed by the [EEC]. Further, the Panel noted that, in each case over which both the USITC and federal district courts have jurisdiction, the complainant has the choice whether to proceed before the USITC or before the regular courts (see paragraph 5.18 below).

5.17 The Panel noted that some of the procedural advantages that, according to the United States . . . are given to respondents could operate in all cases. The Panel also recognized that the substantive economic requirements put procedural burdens not only on the respondent but also on the complainant, which has the burden of proof on these matters, and that these procedural burdens could operate in all cases. The Panel took these factors into account to the extent that they might be capable of exerting an offsetting influence in each individual case of less favourable treatment resulting from an element cited by the [EEC].

Contentions By the Community That Less Favourable Treatment is Accorded to Imported Products

5.18 In cases concerning imported products over which both federal district courts and the USITC have jurisdiction, the complainant has the choice of which forum to use, or possibly to initiate a complaint in both fora; no equivalent choice of forum is available to a plaintiff in a case concerning products of United States origin. . . . The Panel found that, given the differences between the proceedings of the USITC and of federal courts, to provide the complainant with the choice of forum where imported products are concerned and to provide no corresponding choice where domestically-produced products are concerned is in itself less favourable treatment of imported products and is therefore inconsistent with Article III:4. It is also a reason why in practice . . . [t]he complainant will tend to avoid recourse to Section 337 in cases where elements of more favourable treatment of the respondent than that accorded in federal district court litigation might play a role, for example where public interest or policy considerations might be expected to intervene.

5.19 The Panel considered the specific differences between Section 337 proceedings and those in federal district courts referred to by the [EEC]. . . .:

> Time-limits . . . The Panel found that the relatively short and fixed time-limits for the completion of proceedings under Section 337 could put the respondent in a significantly less favourable position than it would have been in before a federal district court where no fixed time-limits apply, both because the complainant has a greater opportunity . . . to prepare his case before bringing the complaint and because defence in general benefits from delay. It is true that the short time-limits might benefit the respondent in cases where a negative finding is made, since any damage to his business resulting from the uncertainty generated by the litigation would be ended more quickly, but this does not justify the less favourable treatment in other cases. The Panel did not accept the argument of the United States that the appropriate

comparison with Section 337 time-limits is the time taken for issuing preliminary injunctions in federal district courts. A Section 337 final order is not comparable to a preliminary injunction since it is not subject to review by the same forum nor is it accompanied by the safeguards usually attached to preliminary orders to protect the legitimate interests of defendants. The Panel noted the arguments of the United States that a complainant was required to provide more detailed information in a Section 337 complaint — a point contested by the [EEC] — and that an additional ten days was given to foreign respondents for service by mail, but concluded that these factors could not significantly offset the disadvantage that the respondent could suffer from the tighter Section 337 time-limits.

Inadmissibility of counterclaims . . . The Panel found that the inability of the respondent to make counterclaims in a Section 337 action . . . deprives the respondent of an option that is available *where products of United States origin rather than imported products are concerned.* Moreover, the existence of this option, which applies to unrelated as well as related counterclaims, could act as a dissuasive factor on a potential complainant in filing a complaint in the first place. The Panel noted the observation of the United States that many of the points that might be the subject of a related counterclaim in court proceedings could be made in USITC proceedings by way of defence. However, the complainant runs no risk of an affirmative adverse finding on these points, or of adverse findings or need to litigate in respect of unrelated issues, and in the Panel's view this gives complainants before the USITC advantages that might well be significant. The Panel therefore found that the non-availability of the opportunity to raise counterclaims constitutes less favourable treatment of imported products within the meaning of Article III:4.

In rem exclusion orders . . . The [EEC] . . . raised two issues concerning . . . exclusion orders . . . [First,] [w]hile exclusion orders are automatically enforced by the United States Customs Service, enforcement of an injunction ordered by a federal district court, the equivalent relief in respect of products of United States origin, requires individual proceedings brought by the successful plaintiff. The Panel found that this difference results in less favourable treatment of imported products within the meaning of Article III:4 of the GATT. [Second] [i]n respect of . . . general exclusion orders [orders applicable to products found to be infringing produced by any person] the Panel noted that relief against persons other than the parties to a proceeding is not generally available to successful plaintiffs in actions against domestic infringers. This difference therefore results in less favourable treatment of imported products within the meaning of Article III:4 of the General Agreement.

Double proceedings . . . The [EEC] raised the question of the possibility of simultaneous proceedings. . . . [I]mported products might be faced with double proceedings . . . whereas like products of United States origin can only be challenged in proceedings in federal district courts.[8] The Panel found

---

[8] As a result of the Omnibus Trade and Competitiveness Act of 1988, this possibility now also applies where process patents are concerned. See Annex II for details.

that, while the likelihood of having to defend imported products in two fora is small, the existence of the possibility is inherently less favourable than being faced with having to conduct a defence in only one of those fora. . . .

[The Panel concluded that the techniques used under Section 337 to protect confidential information were not effectively different from those generally employed in the federal district courts; . . . and that any nominal difference in the standard used by the Federal Circuit to review findings of fact by the USITC and by federal judges was not likely to result in less favourable treatment of imported products.]

* * * *

[After summarizing the particular respects in which imports were, as a result of Section 337, treated less favorably than products of domestic origin, the Panel asked whether these differences could be traced back to the fact that the USITC was fundamentally not a court of law but an administrative agency, and whether this structural difference could itself constitute treatment incompatible with the requirements of Article III. It then declined to answer the question since it had not been raised in such general terms by the EEC.]

(v) Article XX(d)

(a) The Conditions Attached to the Use of Article XX(d)

5.22 . . . The Panel . . . then examined whether, in respect of the elements of Section 337 found to be inconsistent with Article III:4 of the General Agreement, the conditions specified in Article XX(d) to justify measures otherwise inconsistent with the GATT are met. These are:

— that the "laws or regulations" with which compliance is being secured are themselves "not inconsistent" with the General Agreement;

— that the measures are "necessary to secure compliance" with those laws or regulations;

— that the measures are "not applied in a manner which would constitute a means of arbitrary or unjustifiable discrimination between countries where the same conditions prevail, or a disguised restriction on international trade."

5.23-5.24 [After noting that each of the foregoing conditions had to be met before the U.S. could properly invoke the Article XX(d) exception,] . . . the Panel then considered whether the inconsistencies with Article III:4 are "necessary" to secure compliance with those laws, this being the issue on which the discussion had mainly concentrated.

(b) The "Necessary to Secure Compliance" Condition

5.25 The Panel noted that the United States and the Community interpret the term "necessary" differently. They differ as to whether it requires the use of the least trade-restrictive measure available. They also differ as to whether "necessity" to use measures that accord less favourable treatment to imported products can be created by a contracting party's choice, in its national legislation, of enforcement measures against domestic products that would not be effective against imports.

5.26 It was clear to the Panel that a contracting party cannot justify a measure inconsistent with another GATT provision as "necessary" in terms of Article XX(d) if an alternative measure which it could reasonably be expected to employ and which is not inconsistent with other GATT provisions is available to it. By the same token, in cases where a measure consistent with other GATT provisions is not reasonably available, a contracting party is bound to use, among the measures reasonably available to it, that which entails the least degree of inconsistency with other GATT provisions. The Panel wished to make it clear that this does not mean that a contracting party could be asked to change its substantive patent law or its desired level of enforcement of that law, provided that such law and such level of enforcement are the same for imported and domestically-produced products. However, it does mean that, if a contracting party could reasonably secure that level of enforcement in a manner that is not inconsistent with other GATT provisions, it would be required to do so.

5.27 Bearing in mind the foregoing and that it is up to the contracting party seeking to justify measures under Article XX(d) to demonstrate that those measures are "necessary," . . .[9] the Panel considered whether the inconsistencies that it had found with Article III:4 can be justified as "necessary" in terms of Article XX(d). The Panel first examined the argument of the United States that the Panel should consider not whether the individual elements of Section 337 are "necessary" but rather whether Section 337 as a system is "necessary" for the enforcement of United States patent laws. . . . The Panel did not accept this contention since it would permit contracting parties to introduce GATT inconsistencies that are not necessary simply by making them part of a scheme which contained elements that are necessary. In the view of the Panel, what has to be justified as "necessary" under Article XX(d) is each of the inconsistencies with another GATT Article found to exist . . . are necessary.

(c) The Necessity of the Specific Inconsistencies With Article III:4

5.28 . . . The Panel did not consider that a different scheme for imports alleged to infringe process patents is "necessary" [within the terms of Article XX(d),] since many countries grant to their civil courts jurisdiction over imports of products manufactured abroad under processes protected by patents of the importing country. The Panel noted that, in the 1988 Omnibus Trade and Competitiveness Act, the United States has in fact amended its law to this effect.[10]

5.29 The United States also suggested that certain features of Section 337 are necessary in order to permit Presidential review, which is in the interests of respondents (paragraph 3.66). The Panel did not believe that this provided an argument for necessity in terms of Article XX(d), since Presidential review is not

---

[9] See Report of the Panel on Canada-Administration of the Foreign Investment Review Act, paragraph 5.20 (BISD 30S/164), adopted on 7 February 1984.

[10] See Section 9003 of the Omnibus Trade and Competitiveness Act of 1988, Pub. L. 100-418 adding new subsection (g) to 35 U.S.C. Section 271. Ed.

necessary in order to secure compliance with United States patent legislation; it is not, of course, available in United States patent litigation involving challenged products of domestic origin.

5.30–5.31 The United States suggested that Section 337 is needed because of difficulties with service of process on and enforcement of judgments against foreign manufacturers. . . . As regards service of process, the difference in procedures between Section 337 and federal district courts was not itself alleged to be inconsistent with any GATT provision. . . . However, . . . [in view of the Panel's conclusion that the availabilty under Section 337 of *in rem* general exclusion orders against imported products when no equivalent remedy was available against products of United States origin, was inconsistent with Article III:4 and in view of the importance placed by the United States on its sytem of *in rem* orders, the Panel considered this difference "at some length."]. . . . The Panel agreed with the United States that taking action against infringing products at the source, that is at the point of their production, would generally be more difficult in respect of imported products than in respect of products of national origin: imported products are produced outside the jurisdiction of national enforcement bodies and it is seldom feasible to secure enforcement of the rulings of a court of the country of importation by local courts in the country of production. *In personam* action against importers would not in all cases be an adequate substitute for action against the manufacturer, not only because importers might be very numerous and not easily brought into a single judicial proceeding, but also, and more importantly, because as soon as activities of known importers were stopped it would often be possible for a foreign manufacturer to find another importer. For these reasons the Panel believed that there could be an objective need in terms of Article XX(d) to apply limited *in rem* exclusion orders to imported products, although no equivalent remedy is applied against domestically-produced products.

5.32 A limited *in rem* order applying to imported products can thus be justified, for the reasons presented in the previous paragraph, as the functional equivalent of an injunction enjoining named domestic manufacturers. However, these reasons do not justify as "necessary" in terms of Article XX(d) the inconsistency with Article III:4 found in respect of general exclusion orders. . . . The United States informed the Panel that the situations which under Section 337 could justify a general exclusion order against imported products are a widespread pattern of unauthorized use of the patented invention or process and a reason to infer that manufacturers other than respondents to the investigation might enter the United States market with infringing products. However, the Panel saw no reason why these situations could not also occur in respect of products produced in the United States. Nevertheless, the Panel did not rule out entirely that there could sometimes be objective reasons why general *in rem* exclusion orders might be "necessary" . . . against imported products even though no equivalent measure was needed against products of United States origin. For example, in the case of imported products it might be considerably more difficult to identify the source of infringing products or to prevent circumvention of orders limited to the products of named persons, than in the case of products of United States origin. Of course, the United States could bring the provision of general exclusion orders into consistency with

Article III:4 by providing for the application in like situations of equivalent measures against products of United States origin.

5.33 As noted above, the Panel found an inconsistency with Article III:4 in the fact that Section 337 exclusion orders are automatically enforced by the Customs Service, whereas the enforcement of injunctions against products of United States origin requires the successful plaintiff to bring individual proceedings. However, in this case the Panel accepted the argument of necessity in terms of Article XX(d). A United States manufacturer which has been enjoined by a federal district court order can normally be expected to comply with that injunction, because it would know that failure to do so would incur the risk of serious penalties resulting from a contempt proceeding brought by the successful plaintiff. An injunction should therefore normally suffice to stop enjoined activity without the need for subsequent action to enforce it. As far as imported products are concerned, enforcement at the border by the customs administration of exclusion orders can be considered as a means necessary to render such orders effective.

5.34 The Panel considered the argument of the United States that many of the procedural aspects of Section 337 reflect the need to provide expeditious prospective relief against infringing imports. . . . The Panel understood this argument to be based on the notion that, in respect of infringing imports, there would be greater difficulty than in respect of infringing products of domestic origin in collecting awards of damages for past infringement, because foreign manufacturers are outside the jurisdiction of national courts and importers might have little by way of assets. In the Panel's view, given the issues at stake in typical patent suits, this argument could only provide a justification for rapid *preliminary* or conservatory action against imported products, combined with the necessary safeguards to protect the legitimate interests of importers in the event that the products prove not to be infringing. The tight time-limits for the *conclusion* of Section 337 proceedings, when no comparable time-limits apply in federal district court, and the other features of Section 337 inconsistent with Article III:4 that serve to facilitate the expeditious completion of Section 337 proceedings, such as the inadmissibility of counterclaims, cannot be justified as "necessary" on this basis.

5.35 . . . On the basis of the preceding review and analysis, the Panel *found* that the system of determining allegations of violation of United States patent rights under Section 337 of the United States Tariff Act cannot be justified as necessary within the meaning of Article XX(d). . . .

VI. *Conclusions*

[6.1-6.3. After noting that while it had found that certain elements of Section 337 were inconsistent with the U.S.'s GATT obligations, the Panel emphasized that it found no evidence that these elements had been deliberately introduced so as to discriminate against foreign products. It then concluded that:]

. . . Section 337 of the United States Tariff Act of 1930 is inconsistent with Article III:4, in that it accords to imported products challenged as infringing United States patents treatment less favourable than the treatment accorded to products of United States origin similarly challenged, and that these inconsistencies cannot be justified in all respects under Article XX(d).

6.4 The Panel *recommends* that the Contracting Parties request the United States to bring its procedures applied in patent infringement cases bearing on imported products into conformity with its obligations under the General Agreement.

NOTES AND QUESTIONS

(1) The United States contended that the Panel could only determine whether, under Section 337, imports alleged to infringe a United States patent were accorded "less favorable treatment" than domestic products by looking at the results in actual cases. The EEC countered by arguing that Section 337 could pass muster under Article III:4 only if it were incapable of according imports less favorable treatment than domestic products. The Panel rejected the U.S. approach. Are you persuaded by the Panel's reasoning? (See Paragraphs 5.13 and 5.14.) To what extent is the decision predicated on other GATT principles not expressly alluded to in the Panel's Report?

(2) The Panel was also careful to observe a number of respects in which an imported product subject to a Section 337 proceeding was likely to be treated more favorably than a domestic product subject to an infringement suit in a U.S District Court. The Panel also noted ways in which the import was likely to receive less favorable treatment, but then went on and expressly refused to balance the more favorable treatment against less favorable treatment. At this point the United States had lost the case, had it not? Or, was it lost when the Panel declined to adopt the U.S. result oriented approach? In light of the Panel's concerns discussed under note (1) above, was it really necessary for the Panel effectively to foreclose the United States from demonstrating — assuming it had the evidence — that in a large majority of cases the differences between Section 337 and an infringement proceeding in the courts worked to the distinct advantage of the imported product? What does the Panel's decision imply for any two-track enforcement procedure such as the U.S. employed in these patent infringement cases? In spite of what the Panel said (see Paragraph 5.11), can there, under the Panel's decision, really be any difference between the two procedures unless all of those differences favor the imported product over the domestic?

(3) How would you recommend that the United States amend its law to bring it into compliance with GATT while keeping as many of the present features of Section 337 as possible? Note, that if Section 337 were repealed and the federal district courts given exclusive jurisdiction over infringing imports, it is highly doubtful that Congress could Constitutionally confer on the President power to deny effect to judicially issued exclusion orders. In like vein, could one grant District Courts' power to issue general injunctions similar to general exclusion orders? Would it be practicable to give the ITC jurisdiction to hear unrelated counterclaims in the context of a Section 337 proceeding?

(4) In subsequent discussions in the GATT Council on whether to adopt the Panel's recomendations — which as of this writing has not occurred — the United States took the position that "the Panel requires that contracting parties ensure

de facto equality of treatment for imports in all instances." The U.S. cited Paragraph 5.11 of the Report in support of this conclusion.[11] The U.S statement came in response to a statement by the EEC in which, relying on the same Paragraph in the Panel's Report, the Community characterized the Panel's approach to the case in the following terms:

> The Panel thus examined whether the legal provisions under Section 337 establishing *de jure a difference in the treatment* of imported and domestic products in fact amount to a less favourable treatment of imported goods.[12]

Which characterization more nearly conforms to the Panel's refusal to adopt a result oriented approach? Does this dispute over how to characterize the Panel's interpretive approach to Article III:4 adequately capture the analytic method employed by the Panel? How would you characterize that method?

(3) Among the more important applications of Article III has been in the area of internal taxation. Article III Paragraphs 1 and 2 provide as follows:

Article III

1. **The Contracting Parties recognize that internal taxes and other internal charges . . . should not be applied to imported or domestic products so as to afford protection to domestic production.**

2. **The products of the territory of any Contracting Party imported into the territory of any other Contracting Party shall not be subject, directly or indirectly, to internal taxes or other internal charges of any kind in excess of those applied, directly or indirectly, to like domestic products. Moreover, no Contracting Party shall otherwise apply internal taxes or other internal charges to imported or domestic products in a manner contrary to the principles set forth in paragraph 1.**

Note that, at the threshold, these provisions raise a basic problem of characterization. A tariff is, of course, a tax. It is a tax the whole purpose of which is to discriminate against imports in favor of domestic production. Yet, tariffs are permitted by GATT subject to being "bound" if the taxing party negotiates a concession. When, therefore, is a tax a "tariff" which, be definition, discriminates between imports and domestic products, and when is it an "internal tax" which cannot discriminate? An interpretive note (Ad Article III) makes clear that a charge may still be an internal tax, subject to Article III:1 and 2, even if collected at the border. No satisfactory definition has been developed, so that generally the matter is left to the nomenclature that the taxing government chooses to place upon it. This may, however, constitute a very sensible solution to the problem. If a Contracting Party chooses to characterize a tax collected at the border as a "tariff" it can discriminate by imposing the tax only on imports, but then it must be willing to submit the tax for possible reduction through the GATT negotiating process. If, on the other hand, it chooses to insulate the tax from that process it can call it an "internal tax" but must then levy the tax on both domestic and

---

[11] See Communication from the United States, GATT Document L/6500, 12 May 1989.

[12] See Communication from the European Communities, GATT Document L/6487, 11 April 1989.

imported products. In addition, it should be noted that the words "directly or indirectly" do not refer to what is commonly called "direct taxes" (i.e., income taxes) and "indirect taxes" (i.e., sales and other excise taxes).[13] Article III simply does not apply to income taxes, but only to so-called "indirect taxes."

PROBLEM 1

THE AMERICAN WINE-GALLON METHOD OF TAXATION

Under the Internal Revenue Code distilled spirits, both domestic and imported, were taxed at $10.50 per gallon whether "proof" or "wine" gallon. A gallon contained 231 cubic inches. A "proof" gallon was one containing spirits with an alcoholic content of at least 50% (i.e., the spirits had to be rated "100 Proof" or more). If the alcohol content was less than 50% (i.e., the spirits were less than "100 Proof") it was classified as a "wine" gallon. In *Bercut-Vandervoort & Co., Inc. v. United States*,[14] the importer of 90 Proof Dutch gin contended that the $10.50 per gallon tax violated Articles II:2 and III:2 of the GATT. His imported 90 Proof gin bottled and ready for shipment to customers had been taxed as a "wine" gallon. Competing domestic gin, however, was taxed when withdrawn from bond but still in "proof" gallon form. After paying the tax, domestic producers diluted their gin to 90 Proof and sold in competition with the imported product. Thus, for every 10 gallons of 100 Proof gin taxed, domestic producers obtained one additional gallon of 90 Proof gin free of tax. Effectively, the importer was taxed $10.50 for every gallon of 90 Proof gin sold to customers in this country while domestic producers were taxed $9.55 for every such gallon sold. The court concluded that this differential did not run afoul of Article III:2 of GATT.

In denying the importer's appeal, the court reasoned that at the time the tax accrued the imported and domestic gin were two different products; one 90 Proof gin the other 100 Proof gin, adding: "The domestic producer controls the composition of his products in the same fashion that the importer can control the composition of his product when he imports it. He can import . . . [100 Proof] spirits and have the product taxed accordingly."

In light of what the doctrine of comparative advantage teaches regarding the location of productive enterprises and the GATT as a mechanism for furthering the establishment of a liberal trading order, how would you assess the court's decision?[15]

---

[13] For an explanation of the distinction between "direct" and "indirect" taxes see discussion page 423 *infra*.

[14] 46 C.C.P.A. 28 (1958).

[15] At the Tokyo Round negotiations the United States agreed with the EEC to eliminate use of the so-called "wine gallon" method of taxation upheld in *Bercut-Vandervoort*. Agreements Reached in the Tokyo Round of the Multilateral Trade Negotiations, H. Doc. 95-153, Part I, 96th Cong. 1st Sess., June 19, 1979 at page 665. To implement this

PROBLEM 2

MARGARINE AND BUTTER

Suppose Country A, after binding itself to a 5% *ad velorum* tariff for imports of oleomargarine, imposed on all margarine sales — domestic as well as imported — a 10% internal sales tax while exempting butter from all such taxes. Assume that prior to the imposition of the internal sales tax on margarine no sales tax was imposed on either margarine or butter and that within a short period following the imposition of that tax domestic consumption of butter increased by at least 10% and that of margarine declined by a comparable amount. Note that an interpretive note (Ad Article III:2) states as follows: "A tax conforming to the requirements of the first sentence of paragraph 2 would be considered to be inconsistent with the provisions of the second sentence only in cases where competition was involved between, on one hand, the taxed product and, on the other hand, a directly competitive or substitutable product which was not similarly taxed." Under these circumstances would the internal sales tax run afoul of Article II of the GATT? In answering consider the following possibilities:

(a) The combined consumption of butter and margarine in Country A before the internal tax was imposed consisted of 40% domestically produced butter, 45% domestically produced margarine and 15% imported margarine. No butter was imported.

(b) The combined pre-tax consumption of butter and margarine in Country A was 5% domestically produced butter, 5% imported butter, 75% domestically produced margarine and 15% imported margarine.

§ 4.04　The GATT System of Adjudication: Article XXIII and "Nullification or Impairment"

Article XXIII of the General Agreement is the foundation upon which the GATT system of adjudication has been built. Paragraph 1 grants a Party, claiming that a benefit accruing to it under the General Agreement is being "nullified or impaired," a right to demand that any Party whose actions are the basis of the claim engage in an effort to reach a "satisfactory adjustment" of the matter. Paragraph 1 also defines the several grounds upon which a claim of "nullification or impairment" may be based. Paragraph 2 provides for an appeal to the Contracting Parties if the efforts at settlement do not succeed. It also prescribes the measures that the Contracting Parties may authorize as a "remedy" for any well-founded claim. To assist in discharging their responsibilities under Paragraph 2 the Contracting Parties have established the general practice of forming Panels — or, on occasion, working parties — to hear and make recommendations on unsettled disputes. Since, however, only the Contracting Parties have the authority to make a decision under Article XXIII, Panel interpretations of the General

---

undertaking, Section 801 of the Trade Agreements Act of 1979, (P.L. 96-39, 93 Stat. 144 at 273) amended Section 5001(a)(1) of the Internal Revenue Code of 1954. By virtue of the amendment under proof spirits, imported as well as domestic, are taxed at a rate proportional to the tax on the proof gallon.

Agreement are not, in any formal sense, authoritative until adopted by the Contracting Parties or by the Council acting on behalf of the Contracting Parties. Those interpretations, in other words, do not represent "GATT law" until adopted. Moreover, since the Council operates under a consensus rule, any Party, determined to do so, can block adoption of a Panel's recommendations. And while this has not happened with great frequency, it is nevertheless considered by many a major weakness in the GATT adjudication process.[1]

Article XXIII
Nullification or Impairment

1. If any Contracting Party should consider that any benefit accruing to it directly or indirectly under this Agreement is being nullified or impaired or that the attainment of any objective of the Agreement is being impeded as the result of:

(a) the failure of another Contracting Party to carry out its obligations under this Agreement, or

(b) the application by another Contracting Party of any measure, whether or not it conflicts with the provisions of this Agreement, or

(c) the existence of any other situation,

the Contracting Party may, with a view to the satisfactory adjustment of the matter, make written representations or proposals to the other Contracting Party or parties which it considers to be concerned. Any Contracting Party thus approached shall give sympathetic consideration to the representations or proposals made.

2. If no satisfactory adjustment is effected . . . within a reasonable time, or if the difficulty is of the type described in paragraph 1(c) of this Article, the matter may be referred to the Contracting Parties. The Contracting Parties shall promptly investigate any matter so referred to them and shall make appropriate recommendations to the Contracting Parties which they consider to be concerned, or give a ruling on the matter, as appropriate. . . . If the Contracting Parties consider that the circumstances are serious enough to justify such action, they may authorize a Contracting Party or parties to suspend the application to any other Contracting Party or parties of such concessions or obligations under this Agreement as they determine to be appropriate in the circumstances. If the application to any Contracting Party of any concession or other obligation is in fact suspended, that Contracting Party shall then be free, not later than sixty days after such action is taken, to give written notice to the Executive Secretary to the Contracting

---

[1] For the rules and understandings governing GATT use of Panels, their formation and modes of deliberation, see "Understanding, Regarding Notification, Consultation, Dispute Settlement and Surveillance." L/4907, adopted 28 November 1979, GATT, BISD 27th Supp., at page 210 (1980). For a thorough and informative discussion of how GATT Panel's are formed and tend to conduct their work also consult Plank, *An Unofficial Description Of How A GATT Panel Works And Does Not*, Swiss R. Int'l Comp., Feb. 1987 at page 81, reprinted in 4 J. of Int'l Arb. 53 (1987).

Parties[2] **of its intention to withdraw from this Agreement and such withdrawal shall take effect upon the sixtieth day following the day on which such notice is received by him.**

THE AUSTRALIAN SUBSIDY ON AMMONIUM SULPHATE

Report adopted by the Contracting Parties
3 April 1950

(GATT/CP.4/39)

GATT, BISD Volume II (1952)

Background

[Prior to the outbreak of war in 1939, *ammonium sulphate* was distributed in Australia by a commercial pooling arrangement operated by Nitrogenous Fertilizers Proprietary, Ltd. (NFPL), a private enterprise. NFPL bought *ammonium sulphate* from both local and foreign producers and sold the product from whatever source at a uniform price. The distribution of *sodium nitrate*, on the other hand, was through independent commercial channels. When a wartime shortage of *ammonium sulfate* arose, the Australian government purchased *sodium nitrate* from abroad and resold it to NFPL for distribution to retailers. Thereafter NFPL sold both products at a uniform price. When NFPL experienced losses on these sales, the Australian government undertook to make up the deficit on both products.

On July 1, 1949, Australia ceased subsidizing and NFPL ceased selling *sodium nitrate* and the trade in that product reverted to its pre-war commercial channels. However, the government continued to purchase *ammonium sulfate* for distribution through NFPL and while the government did not fix NFPL's price it continued to meet the company's losses. The result was that by 1949/50 the retail price of *sodium nitrate*, all from foreign sources, was approximately £A 31 33s. The subsidized retail price of *ammonium sulfate*, primarily from domestic sources, was £A 22 10s. It was estimated that unsubsidized the latter would have risen to £A 28. Among the reasons for the different treatment of the two products was the fact that some growers who used *ammonium sulfate* would have been prevented by price control regulations and long term supply contracts from raising prices charged for their crops in response to increases in their fertilizer costs. These users, according to the Australian representative, preferred ammonium sulfate for technical reasons "irrespective of price". Users of *sodium nitrate* apparently were not subject to price controls. In response to these developments, Chile invoked the provisions of Article XXIII claiming that Australia had nullified

---

[2] By decision of 23 March 1965, the title of the head of the GATT Secretariat was changed from "Executive Secretary" to "Director General." The General Agreement, however, has not been formally amended to reflect this change. Ed.

or impaired the tariff concession on *sodium nitrate* granted by Australia to Chile in 1947. A working party was appointed and reported, in pertinent part, as follows:]

* * * *

III. Consistency of the Australian Measures with the Provisions of the General Agreement

7. The removal of [the subsidy for] nitrate of soda . . . did not involve any prohibition or restriction on the import of sodium nitrate and did not institute any tax or internal charge on that product. The working party concluded, therefore, that the provisions of Article XI, paragraph 1, and of Article III, paragraph 2, were not relevant.

8. As regards the applicability of Article I . . . the working party noted that the General Agreement made a distinction between "like products" and "directly competitive or substitutable products." . . . [Article I] is limited to "like products." Without trying to give a definition of "like products," and leaving aside the question of whether the two fertilizers are directly competitive, the working party reached the conclusion that they were not to be considered as "like products" within the terms of Article I. In the Australian tariff the two products are listed as separate items and enjoy different treatment. . . . Whereas nitrate of soda is admitted free [under] . . . the most-favored-nation tariff, sulphate of ammonia is admitted free only for the preferential area [*i.e.*, from British Commonwealth sources *ed.*]; . . . moreover, in the case of nitrate of soda the rate is bound whereas no binding has been agreed upon for sulphate of ammonia. In the tariffs of other countries the two products are listed separately.

9. In view of the fact that Article III, paragraph 4, applies to "like products," the provisions of that paragraph are [likewise] not applicable to the present case. . . . As regards the provisions of paragraph 9[3] of the same article the working party was informed that a maximum selling price for ammonium sulphate was no longer fixed by governmental action and, in any event, noted that Australia had considered the Chilean complaint and had made an offer within the terms of that paragraph. Since it was not found that any of the substantive provisions of Article III were applicable, the exception contained in paragraph 8(b)[4] is not relevant.

10. The working party then examined the question of whether the Australian Government had complied with the terms of Article XVI on subsidies. . . . Even

---

[3] Article III:9 provides as follows: "9. The Contracting Parties recognize that internal maximum price control measures, even though conforming to the other provisions of this Article, can have effects prejudicial to the interests of Contracting Parties supplying imported products. Accordingly, Contracting Parties applying such measures shall take account of the interests of exporting Contracting Parties with a view to avoiding to the fullest practicable extent such prejudicial effects."

[4] Article III:8(b) provides: "8(b). The provisions of this Article shall not prevent the payment of subsidies exclusively to domestic producers, including payments to domestic producers derived from the proceeds of internal taxes or charges applied consistently with the provisions of this Article and subsidies effected through governmental purchases of domestic products."

if it assumed that the maintenance of the . . . subsidy on ammonium sulfate is covered by the terms of Article XVI, it does not seem that the Australian Government's action can be considered as justifying any claim of injury under this article. . . .

11. . . . [T]he examination of the relevant provisions of the General Agreement thus led [the working party] . . . to the conclusion that no evidence had been presented to show that the Australian Government had failed to carry out its obligations under the Agreement.

IV. Nullification or Impairment of the Concession Granted to Chile on Sodium Nitrate

12. The working party next considered whether the injury which the Government of Chile said it had suffered represented a nullification or impairment of a benefit accruing to Chile directly or indirectly under the General Agreement and was therefore subject to the provisions of Article XXIII. It was agreed that such impairment would exist if the action of the Australian Government which resulted in upsetting the competitive relationship between sodium nitrate and ammonium sulphate could not reasonably have been anticipated by the Chilean Government, taking into consideration all pertinent circumstances and the provisions of the General Agreement, at the time it negotiated for the duty-free binding on sodium nitrate. The working party concluded that the Government of Chile had reason to assume, during these negotiations, that the wartime fertilizer subsidy would not be removed from sodium nitrate before it was removed on ammonium sulfate. In reaching this conclusion, the working party was influenced in particular by the combination of the circumstances that:

(a) The two types of fertilizer were closely related;

(b) Both had been subsidized and distributed through the same agency and sold at the same price;

(c) Neither had been subsidized before the war, and the wartime system of subsidization and distribution had been introduced in respect of both at the same time and under the same war powers of the Australian Government.

(d) This system was still maintained in respect of both fertilizers at the time of the 1947 tariff negotiations.

For these reasons, the working party also concluded that the Australian action should be considered as relating to a benefit accruing to Chile under the Agreement, and that it was therefore subject to the provisions of Article XXIII. . . .

The situation in this case is different from that which would have arisen from the granting of a new subsidy on one of the two competing products. In such a case, given the freedom under the General Agreement of the Australian Government to impose subsidies and to select the products on which a subsidy would be granted, it would be more difficult to say that the Chilean Government had reasonably relied on the continuation of the same treatment for the two products. In the present case, however, the Australian Government, in granting a subsidy on account of the wartime fertilizer shortage and continuing it in the post-war period, had grouped the two fertilizers together and treated them uniformly. . . .

13. Having thus concluded that there was a *prima facie* case that the value of a concession granted to Chile had been impaired as a result of a measure which did not conflict with the provisions of the General Agreement, the working party came to the conclusion that there was no infringement of the Agreement by Australia. Since Chile had not applied for a release from any of its obligations, under the provisions of the last two sentences of Article XXIII, paragraph 2 . . . it was not necessary for the working party to consider whether the above-mentioned provisions were applicable to the case.

* * * *

16. In the light of the considerations set out above, the working party wishes to submit to the Contracting Parties the following draft recommendation:

> The Contracting Parties recommend that the Australian Government consider, with due regard to its policy of stabilizing the cost of production of certain crops, means to remove any competitive inequality between nitrate of soda and sulphate of ammonia for use as fertilizers which may in practice exist as a result of the removal of nitrate of soda from the operations of . . . [its subsidy system] and communicate the results of their consideration to the Chilean Government, and that the two parties report to the Contracting Parties at the next session.

Statement by the Australian Representative

* * * *

2. The working party . . . went to considerable trouble to show why Chile *could not reasonably expect* that Australia, in abolishing its wartime emergency subsidies, would do so as the needs of its economy dictated rather than in accordance with the anticipation of Chile that these two fertilizers, possessing substantially different characteristics and uses and not being like products, would be treated in an identical manner. The question of what obligations with respect to ammonium sulphate Australia could reasonably have expected when she consented to a binding of the free-duty rate on sodium nitrate would seem to be no less relevant. Equally relevant is the question of whether Australia could reasonably have anticipated the needs which would give rise to her present subsidy policy.

3. In view of the above and the fact that the working party has also found that the Australian subsidy on ammonium sulphate is completely in accordance with the provisions of the Agreement — including the provisions specifically relating to subsidies — Australia cannot consider it a sound argument that what a country might now say was its *reasonable expectation* three years ago in respect of a particular tariff concession should be the determining factor in establishing the existence of impairment in terms of Article XXIII. If it were accepted by the Contracting Parties, then this interpretation of Article XXIII would require a complete reexamination of the principles on which Australia (and, we had supposed, all other countries) had hitherto granted tariff concessions. The history and practice of tariff negotiations show clearly that if a country seeking a tariff

concession on a product desires to assure itself of a certain treatment for that product in a field apart from rates of duty *and to an extent going further than is provided for in the various articles of the General Agreement*, the objective sought must be a matter for negotiation in addition to the actual negotiation respecting the rates of duty to be applied.

[NOTE: The dispute was settled by an agreement under which Australia adjusted its subsidy on ammonium sulfate.]

NOTES AND QUESTIONS

(1) Removal of the subsidy on sodium nitrate clearly put imports of Chilean nitrate at a disadvantage in the Australian market. As the working party observed, removal upset the "competitive relationship" that had existed between ammonium sulfate and sodium nitrate when Chile and Australia negotiated a tariff reduction on the latter. Australia's action plainly "nullified or impaired" the expected benefits that Chile had paid for in that negotiation. On the other hand, the working party also states that had neither product been subsidized at the time of the tariff negotiations and had Australia subsequently subsidized ammonium sulfate but not sodium nitrate, no nullification or impairment of benefits within the meaning of Article XXIII would have occurred. Is there any rational basis for this distinction? Economically, the granting of a new subsidy would have upset the "competitive relationship" between the two products as surely as removal of a pre-existing subsidy. In answering this question, consider Australia's separate statement. It effectively accuses the working party of ignoring the fact that when it bound the tariff on sodium nitrate, Australia did not expect that it was thereby foreclosed from responding to the changing needs of its economy merely because that response might change the competitive relationship between the two products adverse to Chile. This argument raises a fundamental problem that lies at the heart of the working party's interpretation of Article XXIII, does it not? Consider the following possibilities:

(a) That when two countries exchange reciprocal tariff concessions, they thereby implicitly "freeze" in place all economic policies that might affect the competitive relationships that were used in calculating the anticipated benefits of those concessions, unless they are willing either to compensate their trading partners or accept a reciprocal suspension of concessions by the latter. The working party seemed to think that this would go too far. It drew a distinction. If a nation has linked two products together under the same market distorting policy and then negotiates concessions with respect to those products, subsequent abandonment of that policy with respect to one of the products but not the other will, if it adversely effects imports, open that nation to a charge of "nullification or impairment." If, however, it has not linked the products before negotiating the concession and subsequently adopts new market distorting measures for one of the products but not the other, no such charge can be made, even if the new policy disadvantages imports of one of the products. Does this distinction make any sense in light of the trade liberalizing purposes of GATT? as a political matter?

(b) The far-reaching implications of the working party's conclusion may be the inescapable corollary of subparagraph 1(b) of Article XXIII. Under that subparagraph Article XXIII remedies may be invoked even if the actions which cause the "nullification or impairment" do not violate the General Agreement. Since Australia's removal of the subsidy on sodium nitrate plainly disadvantaged Chilean nitrates in the Australian market, once the working party found that Australia had not violated any express prohibition of the GATT, it faced a difficult task. It had to find a way of limiting the far reaching implications of Article XXIII:1(b) or, if it could not do so, either accepting those implications or rendering subparagraph 1(b) utterly meaningless. In short, perhaps the whole problem lies with subparagraph 1(b)?

(c) On the other hand, subparagraph 1(b) may be essential to maintaining the integrity of any trade liberalizing measure negotiated in GATT. Consider Article III:4 (*see* Documentary Supplement). It prohibits virtually any form of national regulatory discrimination against imports in favor of domestic products. But it applies only if the discrimination is against "like" products. It does not forestall discriminatory regulations against imports that are not "like" the domestic product but are nevertheless directly and immediately competitive with that product. If "like" products are only those that exhibit the same physical characteristics and generally fall within the same customs nomenclature, Article III:4 leaves a gaping hole through which a flood of discriminatory regulations could flow with potentially devastating effects on tariff and other concessions. Strict health regulations on beef, for example, if accompanied by the virtual non-regulation of chicken, could readily destroy the value of any concession given to beef but would not run afoul of Article III:4 — or any other provision of GATT — so long as both sets of regulations were applied even-handedly to domestic and imported products. Note also that Article III:2, relating to internal taxes, unlike Article III:4, implicitly recognizes this point. Surely, the drafters of the General Agreement had to close this loophole. Hence Article XXIII:1(b). But if so, the working party's effort to limit Pargraph 1(b) is badly flawed, is it not? Note, had there been no subsidies when Chile and Australia exchanged concessions and had Australia thereafter subsidized ammonium sulfate but not sodium nitrate, that "domestic" subsidy would not have violated any provision of GATT (See Article XVI:1). Nevertheless under Article XVI:1, if the subsidy caused "serious prejudice" to Chile's interests, Australia would, at Chile's request, have been required to "discuss with [Chile] . . . or with the Contracting Parties, the possibility of limiting the subsidization." See also the impact of the GATT Subsidies Code, discussed in § 4.06 *infra*.

(2) While the hypothetical domestic subsidy in Note (1)(c) above is not illegal under GATT, it is subject to the constraints of Article XVI:1. Contrast, for example, Article III:8(a) which expressly permits discrimination against imports in the case of laws "governing the procurement by governmental agencies of products purchased for governmental purposes . . . " Consider the follow problem:

Suppose that Country A grants Country B a tariff concession on a product a substantial portion of the domestic demand for which is accounted for by government agencies in Country A; that because of this concession Country B realistically expects to supply 70% or more of that demand; that the reciprocal concessions given by Country B to Country A reflect this expectation; and that subsequently Country A, in conformity with Article III:8(a), enacts a statute requiring that 50% of its government agency purchases of the product be from domestic sources. Can Country B, relying on subparagraph 1(b), now make a claim against Country A of "nullification or impairment" under Article XXIII:2, in spite of the fact that Country A's law is expressly authorized by the General Agreement? Should it be able to advance such a claim?

(3) Contrast the working party's decision with that of the Panel in *Uruguayan Recourse to Article XXIII.* [5] In 1961 Uruguay charged fifteen developed countries [6] with maintaining a variety of restrictive measures that adversely affected its exports. With respect to any measure which was not in violation of the GATT, the Panel appointed to hear the case nevertheless went on to ascertain whether "there [were] a priori grounds for assuming that [the measure in question] could have an adverse effect on Uruguay's exports." Each time it found that adverse effects could occur, however, the Panel contented itself with suggesting that the nation maintaining the restriction engage in consultations with Uruguay under Article XXII, expressly declining, in each instance, "to make any specific recommendations based on nullification or impairment" under Article XXIII:2. Only with respect to those measures whose consistency with GATT was "not established," did the Panel decide that Uruguay's benefits were presumptively being "nullified or impaired." As to these measures, the Panel recommended that the governments responsible be given until March 1, 1963 to either remove the restrictions or make some other "adjustment, such as the provision of suitable concessions acceptable to Uruguay." Failure to meet the deadline would, according to the Panel's recommendation, give rise to "circumstances . . . deemed to be serious enough' to justify action under the penultimate sentence" of Article XXIII:2." The Contracting Parties accepted this recommendation. Are you satisfied that this was an appropriate way of avoiding some of the problems alluded to in the prior Notes?

§ 4.05   The Economics-Politics of Discrimination, Article XXIV of the GATT and GATT Review of the Treaty of Rome Establishing the European Economic Community (EEC)

In this section we first set out certain very basic economic postulates underlying the GATT prohibition on discrimination in trade relations between member nations (*i.e.,* the unconditional MFN requirement) and identify some of the political implications of those postulates. It is the politics of discrimination that will be our principal concern here and throughout the remainder of this Chapter.

---

[5] Report Adopted on 16 November 1962, L/1923, GATT, BISD, 11th Supp., (1963) at pages 56 and 95.

[6] Austria, Belgium, Canada, Czechoslovakia, Denmark, Finland, France, Federal Republic of Germany, Italy, Japan, Netherlands, Norway, Sweden, Switzerland and the United States.

We then look briefly at Article XXIV of the General Agreement which creates an exception to the rule against discrimination for free trade areas and customs unions. This, in turn, sets the stage for our examination of the GATT debate on the question of whether the Treaty of Rome, establishing the European Economic Community (EEC), conformed to the requirements of Article XXIV. In the Notes that follow we review briefly the aftermath of that encounter; the Dillon and Kennedy Rounds of tariff negotiations. Historically important in the development of GATT, this episode introduces some of the key issues raised when nations, for political, ideological and economic reasons, seek to form new, larger trading blocs that necessarily discriminate against nations that are not members of the bloc. It also affords a good opportunity to examine some broader issues concerning the role of law, especially GATT law, in the governance of the international economic order.

[A] The Economic-Political Case Against Discrimination

The economic argument against discrimination — against allowing a country to give one or more of its trading partners a preference over others — is at bottom an argument from the "second best". Assuming that nations will, for the indefinite future, maintain some barriers to trade that yield less than an optimal allocation of global resources, the nondiscrimination principle is designed to assure that there are no further losses to efficiency; that the world attains the most efficient allocation of resources as is possible within such levels of protection as exist at any one time.

In order to develop the argument in an orderly way it is necessary to distinguish between partial and unregulated preferential trading systems, where each nation has an unlimited choice of the products and trading partners in whose favor it will discriminate, and broader based arrangements, such as customs unions and free trade areas. First, we address the dangers attendant to a partial and unregulated system. Thereafter we will examine whether customs unions and free trade areas conforming to the requirements of Article XXIV of the General Agreement are likely to exhibit characteristics that make out an exception to the fundamental case against discrimination.

Consider, at this point, Table IV which shows (i) for each of three countries (A, B and C) the cost at which producers in each of those countries can, within a certain output range, deliver product X for sale in Country C and (ii) the total delivered price of each group of producers after Country C imposes a $10 tariff on all imports from Countries A and B.

Table IV

Country A		Country B	
Producers' Cost	$49	Producers' Cost	$55
Tariff	10	Tariff	10
Delivered Price	59	Delivered Price	65

Country C

Producers'Cost	$60
Tariff	0
Delivered Price	60

Plainly Country A is the most efficient producer of product X within the assumed output range upon which these figures are based. Assume that under these conditions producers in Country A fill 70% of the total demand for product X in Country C and that the remainder of that demand is filled by producers in Country C (*i.e.*, domestic producers).[1] Since imports from Country B are also subject to the $10 tariff they will cost $65 and are, therefore, out of the market altogether.

Suppose next, that Country C decides to eliminate the $10 tariff on imports from Country B but not on imports from Country A. It decides to discriminate in favor of imports from Country B. Under these circumstances producers in Country B will be able to offer product X to consumers in Country C at a price which, depending upon their cost structure, will range from $55 to $60, at which point they will encounter competition from producers in Country C. This, in turn, will have the following effects:

— So long as the price offered remains below $59, the quantity of product X purchased by consumers in Country C will increase.

— So long as producers in Country B can offer product X at a price of less than $59, imports from B will (i) displace imports from Country A and (ii) displace sales by domestic producers. It is, of course, possible that producers in B will take over the entire market in Country C.

How should these changes be evaluated? We must assume, of course, that Country C has not acted irrationally; that from its perceived national interest a discriminatory lowering of the tariff is preferable to a nondiscriminatory reduction. Perhaps the discriminatory reduction is the most economical way to reciprocate for a trade benefit received from Country B. Perhaps for foreign policy, or domestic political reasons, Country C wants to fashion closer relations with B or distance itself from A.[2]

It is, of course, possible that confronted with a rule of international law barring discriminatory tariffs, Country C would opt to eliminate the $10 per ton tariff altogether. For now, however, we shall assume the worst case; that if not allowed to discriminate Country C will simply leave the tariff in place on all imports, those from B as well as A. The question then is whether a discriminatory elimination of the tariff is better or worse than leaving the nondiscriminatory tariff intact.

---

[1] Recall the "law of increasing marginal costs". At an output in excess of that required to capture 70% of the market in Country C, the costs of producers in Country A are likely to start rising and, since their product is subject to a tariff, they can no longer meet the domestic producer's price of $60.

[2] Note that while consumers in C gain and producers lose under both a discriminatory and a nondiscriminatory reduction, the relative gains and losses are likely to be greater under the non-discriminatory cutback. Perhaps then, the discriminatory reduction was the only "deal" between consumer and producer interests that could be worked out through the political process in Country C.

One way of answering this question is to observe the consequent changes in output — both quantity and source — that will occur in response to the discriminatory tariff cut and then determine whether each change contributes to or detracts from a more efficient allocation of world resources. For ease of reference, a change that yields a more efficient allocation of resources is called "trade creating" and a change that yields a less efficient allocation, "trade diverting." In our example the discriminatory lowering of the $10 tariff, will result in three basic changes in output, some "trade creating" some "trade diverting."

> *First,* the discriminatory tariff reduction will increase the total output of product X in order to meet the increased demand by consumers in Country C. This increase will enhance the efficient allocation of world resources. It is "trade creating," because when elimination of the tariff opened the market in C to producers in B, the latter were able to bid productive resources away from other less valued uses.

> *Second,* the discriminatory tariff reduction will shift production from producers in C to producers in B, a shift that could be as large as that 30% of C's market which was previously supplied by domestic producers. The shift will be "trade creating" because it will substitute production costing $55 dollars per unit for production which previously cost $60 per unit.[3]

> *Third,* the discriminatory tariff reduction will cause production to shift from Country A to Country B. This will represent a loss to efficiency — a "trade diverting" effect — because output that now costs $55 per unit will replace output that previously cost only $49 per unit. Stated another way, the shift, which is likely to equal at least 70% of the market in C (*i.e.*, A's prior share), will cause resources previously devoted to the production of X to be transferred to less productive alternative uses.

In sum, unless the gains to efficiency represented by (i) increased consumption in C and (ii) the substitution of production from Country B for domestic production exceed the losses to efficiency represented by the shift of production from Country A to Country B, a highly unlikely prospect,[4] the discriminatory reduction of the $10 tariff by C will result in a net loss to global efficiency.

Put more dramatically, more than likely the maintenance of a nondiscriminatory $10 tariff on all imports of product X into Country C will result in a more efficient allocation of resources and a higher net social welfare than the discriminatory elimination of that tariff on imports from B. In the world of the second best

---

[3] This can be stated another way: because the producers in C could bid the resources needed to make product X away from alternative uses only so long as they were protected by the tariff, the release of those resources to their alternative uses will represent a move toward a more efficient allocation of resources.

[4] In speaking of a shift of production representing 70% of the market in C from the most efficient (Country A) to a less efficient source (Country B) and a shift of 30% of the market from the least efficient (Country C) to a more efficient source (Country B) we do not purport to quantify the actual net loss to efficiency. However, in order for the discriminatory tariff reduction to have a net "trade creating" effect, the efficiency gained by the increased consumption and by the 30% of output that shifted from C to B, must be more than double the efficiency lost on 70% of the market that moved from A to B. This is improbable to say the least.

(a world with tariffs) it is better to apply the tariff across the board to all imports than to eliminate the tariff on imports from some but not all sources.

Now, of course, our example presents only one possible set of supply and demand conditions. One could readily envision another product (say, Product Y) the supply and demand for which are such that a discriminatory tariff reduction would have a net "trade creating" effect (*e.g.*, before the tariff reduction imports from Country A commanded only 20% of the market in Country C and domestic producers supplied 80%). In short, the economic analysis suggests a policy standoff. Under certain conditions a discriminatory lowering of a preexisting tariff can improve global efficiency. Under other conditions it can result in a loss to efficiency. And there is no general principle of economic theory that will predict which effect is likely to predominate in any particular case.[5] This being so, the argument against discrimination necessarily changes from a matter of economic theory to a political one. Yet, for purposes of developing the political argument note the following points that emerge from the economic analysis.

(1) Note that if a country, anticipating reciprocal trade benefits, or for political or other reasons, is prepared to reduce tariffs on imports from the most efficient foreign producer, it is unlikely to find any advantage in discriminating against other less efficient foreign producers.[6] In other words, a country will find discrimination advantageous only if it can discriminate against the most efficient and in favor of a less efficient foreign producer.

(2) While the "trade diverting" affect of a discriminatory tariff structure is derived from the shifting of production *from one group of foreign producers to another* — from the more to the less efficient — the "trade creating" effect is dependent upon a shift from *domestic producers to foreign producers* and from the consequent reductions in price and increases in domestic demand that will accompany that shift.

(3) Third, the chances of a discriminatory tariff reduction having a net "trade creating" affect will increase the smaller the difference between domestic and foreign producers costs (*i.e., the lower the relative inefficiency of domestic producers*) and the more elastic the demand for the product in question (*i.e., the greater the increase in quantity demanded as a result of the discriminatory tariff reduction*).

---

[5] The matter is an empirical question to be decided case by case. See material page 285 *infra* and footnote 8 for a discussion of some of the difficulties that are likely to be encountered in conducting an empirical study and for references to some of the studies of the European Economic Community.

[6] If Country C, for example, had been prepared to eliminate the tariff on imports from Country A, there would have been no reason not to do so on imports from B as well, unless, of course, it feared that B might, as a result of scale economies, become the more efficient producer. If this latter were true, then the refusal to lower tariff for B (the decision to discrimination against B) would be tantamount to a shift away from the most to the less efficient producer.

NOTES AND QUESTIONS

(1) Observe that under a rule of international law prohibiting discrimination, all tariff reductions are "trade creating." In our example, producers in A — the most efficient producers — would simply displace producers in C — the least efficient producers.[7] This means that the only situation in which a rule permitting discrimination may be of value is where, confronted with a rule prohibiting discrimination, a country would refuse to reduce a tariff altogether. Assume that in such a situation we do not know — as is very likely the case — whether the "trade diverting" effect of a discriminatory reduction for product X would be greater or less than the "trade creating" effect of such a reduction on product Y. If this is so, the issue is whether we should allow discrimination and take the chance that, in the context of a bilateral trade negotiation, offers to reduce tariffs on products where a discriminatory reduction is "trade creating" would outnumber the offers on products where a discriminatory reduction is "trade diverting." In assessing whether the chance is worth taking consider the following:

(a) In terms of the adverse effect on producers in C, which product — the "trade diverting" product X or the "trade creating" product Y — will Country C prefer to offer for a possible tariff reduction, if it knows it can discriminate between foreign countries?

(b) In terms of gains to consumers in C, which product (X or Y) will Country C prefer to offer for a possible tariff reduction?

(c) If there are going to be winners and losers in Country C, which is likely to be larger: the amount *each* winner stands to gain or the amount *each* loser stands to lose? What are the political implications of this disparity viewed in terms of the resources that the winners and losers are likely to commit to advancing their own interests in the political arena? Hence, which product (X or Y) is Country C likely to offer for a tariff reduction, if permitted to discriminate among foreign sources of supply?

(d) If Country C is willing to offer for a nondiscriminatory tariff reduction products for which a discriminatory reduction would be "trade creating," what position is it likely to take with regard to tariff reductions on products which, under discrimination, are likely to yield a "trade diverting" effect?

(2) Possibly the more inelastic demand for a product with a "trade diverting" effect means that it is a "necessity" for which national self-sufficiency is considered important. Perhaps also a product yielding a "trade creating" effect, with its more elastic demand, is not viewed in this way. If this is so, how do you assess the possibility that, if allowed to discriminate, Country C will prefer to reduce tariffs on products which have a "trade creating" effect (i.e., non-necessities) rather than on products which have a "trade diverting" effect (*i.e.*, necessities). How is a rule against discrimination likely to affect this behavior?

---

[7] The only difference between a non-discriminatory cutting of the tariff on a product which, in the event of a discriminatory reduction, would yield a "trade creating" effect and cutting the tariff on a product that, under discrimination, would yield a "trade diverting" effect, lies in the magnitude of the gains to efficiency that the nondiscriminatory reduction would produce.

(3) How does the principle of reciprocity affect the likelihood that a country will refuse to make any tariff reduction whatsoever unless permitted to discriminate?

(4) Suppose Country C maintains identical quotas on imports of product X from both Country A and Country B. Assume that C then removes the quota on imports from B but not A. Observe that two consequences, or a combination of both, are possible: (i) imports from Country B could displace domestic production in C, a clear "trade creating" effect, or (ii) imports from B, now free from any quantitative restraint, could displace imports from A. But this latter could only occur if producers in B offered a lower price than producers in A (*i.e.*, if they were the more efficient producers). If they could not offer a lower price, producers in A will continue to hold their pre-existing share of the market in C. In all events, discriminatory removal of the quota will contribute to global efficiency. Does this mean Article XIII:1 is a complete anomaly? Note that we started out with the assumption that Country C had allocated identical quotas to A and B. Is this a likely event if C is free to discriminate?

[B] Customs Unions and Free-Trade Areas: An Exception to the Rule Against Discrimination

When the post-war economic planners came to consider the possibility of groups of nations forming customs areas — generally regional in scope — that would systematically discriminate in favor of intermember trade and against trade from nonmembers, economic theory on the subject was still in its formative stage. Much alert to the trade diverting possibilities of partial and unregulated discrimination, they were far less cognizant of the comparable dangers inherent in broader regional arrangements. They tended, instead, to share a general sense that the latter were a good thing; trade barriers would be reduced, trade would expand and the cooperation implicit in the arrangement would yield desirable political by-products. This latter was of singular importance. The promotion of European unity had become a major tenet of American foreign policy, manifest most directly in the administration of the Marshall Plan, and a goal increasingly espoused by European leaders themselves. The result was Article XXIV which provides in pertinent part as follows:

Article XXIV

Customs Unions and Free-Trade Areas

* * * *

4. **The contracting parties recognize the desirability of increasing freedom of trade by the development, through voluntary agreements, of closer integration between the economies of the countries parties to such agreements. They also recognize that the purpose of a customs union or of a free-trade area should be to facilitate trade between the constituent territories and not to raise barriers to the trade of other contracting parties with such territories.**

5. **Accordingly, the provisions of this Agreement shall not prevent, as between the territories of contracting parties, the formation of a customs union or of a free-trade area. . . . Provided that:**

(a) with respect to a customs union . . . the duties and other regulations of commerce imposed at the institution of any such union . . . in respect of trade with contracting parties not parties to such union . . . shall not on the whole be higher or more restrictive than the general incidence of the duties and regulations of commerce applicable in the constituent territories prior to the formation of such union. . . .

[(b) in the case of a free-trade area, the duties and other regulations of commerce established upon formation of the area "shall not be higher or more restrictive" than the duties and regulations existing in the constituent territories prior to formation of the free-trade area.]

6. If, in fulfilling the requirements of subparagraph 5(a), a Contracting Party proposes to increase any rate of duty inconsistent with the provisions of Article II, the procedure set forth in Article XXVIII shall apply. Inproviding for compensatory adjustment, due account shall be taken of the compensation already afforded by the reductions brought about in the corresponding duty of the other constituents of the union.

[7. This paragraph requires that GATT be notified if a Contracting Party plans to enter into a customs union or free-trade area, authorizes GATT to insist on changes to assure that the parties' plans are carried out within a reasonable period and provides for notice to GATT of any changes in those plans.]

8. For purposes of this Agreement:

(a) A customs union shall be understood to mean the substitution of a single customs territory for two or more customs territories, so that

(i) duties and other restrictive regulations of commerce (except, where necessary, those permitted under Articles XI, XII, XIII, XIV, XV and XX) are eliminated with respect to substantially all the trade between the constituent territories of the union or at least with respect to substantially all the trade in products originating in such territories, and,

subject to the provisions of paragraph 9, substantially the same duties and other regulations of commerce are applied by each of the members of the union to the trade of territories not included in the union;

(b) A free-trade area shall be understood to mean a group of two or more customs territories in which the duties and other restrictive regulations of commerce (. . . [with the exceptions noted in (a) above]) are eliminated on substantially all the trade between the constituent territories in products originating in such territories.

[9. This Paragraph provides that the preferences referred to in Article I:2 (See footnote 1, page 224) are not to be affected by formation of a customs union or free-trade area but may be adjusted.]

[10. This Paragraph authorizes the Contracting Parties to permit deviations from the foregoing rules upon a two-thirds vote.]

NOTES AND QUESTIONS

(1) Describe the technical difference between a customs union and a free trade area.

(2) Note the "substantially all the trade" requirement in Paragraph 8. It is a rule of thumb that "substantially" means 80%. How do you interpret the requirement? Does it mean that a customs union or free trade area must reduce to zero all duties on 80% of the products traded between the member states, or that 80% of the tariff must be eliminated on all of those products? Generally, the higher levels of a tariff provide the most protection (*e.g.*, on a 55% tariff, the duty levied as a result of percentage points 20-55 has a more protective effect than the duty levied as a result of percentage points 5-10). With this in mind, and drawing on your knowledge of the economics of discrimination *supra*, how should the "substantially all" requirement be formulated in order to most effectively counter the "trade diverting" bias that a rule allowing discrimination could foster?

(3) In formulating the economic argument against discrimination *supra* we held to a rather static model. Much of the argument favoring customs unions and free trade areas relies upon a more dynamic analysis. While the question of whether these dynamic effects will prevail over the losses to efficiency that the static model demonstrates is ultimately an empirical question,[8] it is well to note some of the major elements upon which the dynamic analysis relies. Consider the following:

    (a)   Assume that there are scale economies that manufacturers in Country B have not been able to exploit. To the extent those manufacturers each produce a somewhat specialized and differentiated product and hence face a downward sloping demand curve (*i.e.*, unlike a "price taker" under pure competition, who faces a horizontal demand curve), how are they likely to respond if Country B forms a customs union with Country C that conforms to the GATT standards? Will this response tend to be "trade creating" or "trade diverting?"

    (b)   Assume that the market structure of product X in Country C has all the hallmarks of an oligopoly. What is likely to occur to that structure if Country C and Country B establish a customs union? Will the effect of the change be "trade diverting" or "trade creating?"

---

[8] Empirical studies on this subject are fraught with difficulty. Comparison of preunion and postunion trade flows — internal and external — can be affected by a number of factors other than the impact of a newly created preference for member trade, such as overall growth in national income both within and without the union, changes in technology, and changes in consumer preferences. Likewise, studies comparing preunion and postunion sources of supply can be gravely complicated by differential movements in price levels and incomes both within and without the union. Nevertheless, most of the studies of the European Economic Community — even those done after the expansion from the six to nine — have concluded that over-all the trade created by the EEC has exceeded the trade diverted, although in agriculture the diversion has been pronounced. For a survey of the studies consult: Mayes, *The Effects Of Economic Integration On Trade*, 17 J. Of Common Mkt. Stud. 1 (1978); For an update, see MacBean & Snowden, International Institutions In Trade And Finance, Ch. 8., Allen & Unwin, London, 1981.

(c) Given that new business investment is always attended with uncertainty, what is likely to happen to the level of new business investment by citizens of C, if all other things remain constant, but Country C joins a customs union with Country B? Again, is this change likely to create or divert trade?

[C] GATT Debates On the Treaty of Rome Establishing the European Economic Community (EEC)

INTRODUCTORY NOTE ON THE SCOPE AND STRUCTURE OF THE EUROPEAN COMMUNITIES

The vision of a united Europe is an old one. But only after having suffered, in less than one fifty year span, the devastation of two great European civil wars and only after having the United States' challenge their historic dominance of the world economy, did the Europeans embark upon the first measured steps toward making that vision a reality peacefully without benefit of military conquest. The years immediately following World War II saw the formation of the Organization for European Economic Cooperation (OEEC),[9] initially established for the cooperative management of Marshall Plan aid, which through the European Payments Union soon developed into a major instrument for returning European currencies to full convertibility. This was followed by the Benelux Customs Union. Next, the Council of Europe was established.[10] Then came the Schumann Plan and, in 1951, formation of the European Coal and Steel Community (ECSC) — the first of the "European Communities" — by Belgium, France, Italy, Luxembourg, Netherlands and West Germany (the "Six"). In 1952 the Six signed a treaty creating the European Defense Community (EDC) and instructed the ECSC Assembly to commence planning a European Political Community (EPC). The defeat of the EDC Treaty in the French National Assembly in 1954, however, spelled the end of these bold steps toward greater political union. But the integration movement was not dead. In 1957 the Six signed the Treaty of Rome[11] establishing the European Economic Community (EEC) and a separate treaty

---

[9] In 1960, with European recovery accomplished, the OEEC was reconstituted and renamed the Organization for Economic Cooperation and Development (OECD) and its membership expanded to include the other major industrialized countries of the world. The membership as of January 1, 1989 consisted of Australia, Austria, Belgium, Canada, Denmark, Finland, France, West Germany, Greece, Iceland, Ireland, Italy, Japan, Luxembourg, Netherlands, New Zealand, Norway, Portugal, Spain, Sweden, Switzerland, Turkey, United Kingdom and United States. The OECD is concerned with issues pertaining to the maintenance of economic growth and development worldwide. It sponsors important studies of these questions, develops policy proposals and is often used as a forum through which its members, all developed countries, formulate common positions on issues being considered in other arenas, such as the United Nations and UNCTAD.

[10] Under the auspices of the Council of Europe there eventually emerged the European Convention for the Protection of Human Rights, the Human Rights Commission and the European Court of Human Rights.

[11] The Treaty of Rome was signed March 5, 1957 and came into force January 1, 1958 (298 U.N.T.S. 11 (1958)).

establishing the European Atomic Energy Community (EURATOM).[12] Together the ECSC, EEC and EURATOM are known as the European Communities (EC) or, as used herein, the "Community." As the centerpiece in the continuing process of European unification the Community has grown from the original Six[13] to twelve members. The United Kingdom, Denmark and Ireland[14] joined in 1973, Greece in 1981 and Portugal and Spain in January of 1986.

The heart of the EEC, of course, is the formation of a customs union among its members; the progressive abolition of all barriers to trade between Member States, the establishment of a common external tariff and other common regulations governing trade with nonmembers. But the EEC is much more than a customs union. From the start it was seen as leading, over time, to the full economic and monetary union of its members. This promise is far from having been fulfilled and progress towards its fulfillment has until recently proceeded fitfully. In 1986, however, the Single European Act was adopted and with it the integration movement received a strong new impetus. Article 13 of that Act added a new Article 8a to the EEC Treaty pledging the Community to adopt measures that would "progressively establish the internal market . . . by 31 December 1992," and stating that:

> The internal market shall comprise an area without internal frontiers in which the free movement of goods, persons, services and capital is ensured in accordance with the provisions of this Treaty.[15]

With this action the Community set itself a formidable task. Although a good deal of integration had already been achieved, before passage of the Single European Act such measures as differential indirect tax rates and border tax adjustments, origin requirements necessary to police national restrictive trade agreements with non-Member countries, national product registration requirements, state trading monopolies and vast amounts of differential and sometimes discriminatory national regulation of banking, insurance, capital markets, communications and transport, to mention only a few, had been viewed as necessary or had been, at least, tolerated. Formidable as the task of dismantling these barriers may be, by March 1990, 60% of the necessary Community legislation had been adopted. It is fully expected that Community institutions will complete their legislative work by the end of 1990. That would give the member states two years to pass and implement the estimated 279 pieces of national legislation necessary to complete the internal market.

---

[12] 298 U.N.T.S. 167.

[13] Although initially invited to join the EEC, the United Kingdom declined and, instead, took the lead in forming the "European Free Trade Association (EFTA), a much less ambitious free trade area established under the Stockholm Convention of January 4, 1960 between Austria, Denmark, Norway, Portugal, Sweden, Switzerland and the United Kingdom. (370 U.N.T.S. 5 (1960).)

[14] The United Kingdom, joined by Denmark, Ireland and Norway first applied for membership in the EEC in 1961. In 1963 France announced that it would effectively veto that application. Likewise France vetoed a second application submitted in 1967. After DeGaulle left the Presidency of France, the second application was reexamined by the EEC in 1969 and negotiations were commenced that resulted in a decision to admit all four nations. By referendum, however, the Norwegians declined to join.

[15] Article 13, Single European Act, EC Bulletin, Supp. February, 1986.

In addition, the heads of government of the twelve, meeting in Dublin in June 1990, agreed that two intergovernmental conferences were to commence in the Winter 1990-91 drafting two new treaties; one on monetary union, which would look to the eventual establishment of a single European currency and a single "central-bank," and another treaty reforming existing community institutions to achieve a higher degree of political union.

What all of this tends to dramatize is the fact that the EC exercises broad influence over the economic affairs of its members. On certain subjects, the treaties establishing the EC either themselves lay down substantive rules of law or set the framework within which the institutions of the Community (principally the Council and the Commission) are empowered to make law through "regulations," and "decisions" binding not only on Member States but also, in appropriate circumstances, on individuals and private enterprises and enforceable both by the European Court of Justice and by national courts. On other topics the EC, acting through "directives," serves to harmonize and coordinate the laws and policies of the members.[16] Finally, on matters within its competence, the Community possess a preclusive power over its members to conduct "foreign relations".

The breadth of its law making powers, combined with its "foreign relations" power, lend to the Community many of the aspects of a supra-national, "federal-type" governmental structure. Among its most influential and earliest proponents

---

[16] Besides calling for the elimination of all tariff and other trade barriers between the Member States and establishment of a common external tariff, Article 3 of the Treaty of Rome stipulates that the "activities of the Community" shall include:

(i) Establishment of a common commercial policy towards third countries (one of the principal underpinnings to the EEC's "foreign relations" power);

(ii) The abolition of obstacles to the free movement of persons, services and capital between Member States (an activity which includes assuring to nationals of one Member State a right, subject to exceptions, "of establishment" in any other Member State (Articles 52-58);

(iii) The inauguration of a common agricultural policy and a common transport policy;

(iv) Enforcement of the "antitrust" law of the EEC (Articles 85-94 set out the basic elements of that law);

(v) Establishing procedures for coordinating the economic policies and remedying the balance of payments problems of Member States (under this heading the EEC has fostered close member collaboration on monetary matters and established a mechanism for maintaining close alignment of their individual exchange rates);

(vi) Approximating (i.e., harmonizing) the national laws of the Member States "to the extent necessary for the functioning of the Common Market" (under this charter, inter alia, Articles 117-122 expressly call upon the Commission to promote close Member collaboration in the labor and social welfare field);

(vii) Creation of a European Social Fund to improve employment opportunities and the standard of living of workers in the Community;

(viii) Establishment of a European Investment Bank to promote economic growth. Articles 123-128 set out the basic mandate of the European Social Fund to be administered by the Commission, while the Statute of the European Investment Bank is set forth as a Protocol to the Treaty of Rome;

(ix) The promotion of an association between the EEC and "overseas territories and countries" (an activity to which we shall make more detailed reference later).

were those who saw it as a giant step toward a true union of European states. While in the past the dream has, at times, seemed to fade, it never died. Indeed, the European Parliament in particular has worked to keep the dream alive.[17] The measure of the will to make that dream a reality and the shape that union will take, however, are matters that must await the negotiations scheduled to begin in the Winter of 1990-91. For the time being, a better measure of the Community as a supra-national entity is to be found in the operation of its principal organs; their structure, powers, interrelationships and modes of operation. These organs are the European Parliament,[18] the Council, the Commission and the European Court of Justice.

Parliament has, since 1979, been popularly elected.[19] Its members sit and act not by national designation but by party (they may not be instructed by Member States). While in structure, Parliament is a truly supra-national body — not merely representative of member governments — it plays only a limited role in the law making process of the Community. That power still resides primarily in the Council and the Commission.

Under the treaties as originally drafted the lawmaking powers of Parliament were virtually non-existent. It only had to be consulted — not followed — by the Council and only on certain subjects. The first formal step towards genuine Parliamentary participation in Community decision-making was the establishment of new budget procedures starting in 1970. As finally evolved, Parliament now has the right to either "make" or "propose" amendments to the draft budget. With respect to expenditures "which result necessarily from [the treaties] or from acts in accordance therewith" (*i.e.*, "obligatory expenditures"), Parliament can now propose amendments but the Council has the final word.[20] With regard to "non-obligatory expenditures," Parliament can amend the budget in what is effectively a power to override the Council, subject only to certain limitations on the appropriation of additional funds.[21] Finally, Parliament has the power to

---

[17] See *Draft Treaty Establishing The European Union, Resolution of the European Parliament of 14 February 1984* (Spinelli Initiative), Off. J. (49 March 1984, C. 77, page 32, *et. seq.*). See also the so called Genscher/Colombo Initiative for a European Union, 20 CML Rev. 685 (1983). More generally see, J.P. Jaque, *The Draft Treaty Establishing The European Union*, 22 CML Rev. 49 (1985).

[18] The European Parliament is referred to in the original treaties as the "Assembly." It was the "Assembly" that initiated the practice of referring to itself as the European Parliament. The other institutions then followed suit. Recently this practice was given "de jure" recognition in Article 6 et. seq. of the "Single European Act" (EC Bulletin, Supp. February, 1986).

[19] The Plan for popular election was adopted in 1976 and the first election held in June of 1979. (See Council Decision 76/787 and the attached "Act Concerning the Election of the Representatives of the Assembly by Direct Universal Suffrage" (Off. J., No. L278, October 8, 1976, page 1; 3 CCH Common Market Rep. P-4308)). Prior to that time members of the Parliament were elected by the national legislatures of the Member States. Parliament currently consists of 518 members elected for five-year terms including the 60 Spanish members and 24 Portuguese members. (See Article 28 of an "Act Concerning the Conditions of Accession of the Kingdom of Spain and the Portuguese Republic and the Adjustments to the Treaties." 3 CCH Common Market Rep. P-7709T.)

[20] Article 203 (4) of the Treaty of Rome.

[21] Article 203 (10) of the Treaty of Rome.

reject the draft budget in toto, a decision which cannot be over-riden by the Council.[22]

Another important change came with adoption of the Single European Act. In certain specified areas[23] that Act requires the Council, acting on a proposal of the Commission, to follow a "cooperation procedure" which has increased Parliament's participation in the lawmaking process.[24] Finally, the Council must obtain the formal assent of Parliament to all treaties of accession to or association with the Community.[25]

The Council consists of the Member States usually represented either by their foreign ministers when "general questions" are under discussion or, when specialized topics are at issue, by that cabinet officer charged, in the member government, with the subject being considered. Of particular importance, however, is the fact that since 1974 the heads of government have met at least once a year to consider both Community and other matters in what is called the European Council. When, in such meetings, the heads of government exercise the powers conferred by the treaties on the Council of the EC, the European Council becomes effectively the Council of the Community.

The Commission, on the other hand, consists of 17 members who, although appointed by the Member States,[26] are to be chosen for their "general

---

[22] Article 23 (8) of the Treaty of Rome. This right has only been exercised once (1980 budget). For details and the difficulties which arose from that deadlock see, Jorn Pipkorn, Legal Implications Of The Absence Of The Community Budget At The Beginning Of A Financial Year, 18 CML Rev. 141 (1981).

[23] The areas are: nondiscrimination (Article 7 of the EEC Treaty); free movement of people (Article 49 of the EEC Treaty); freedom of establishment (Article 54, 55, 57 of the EEC Treaty); certain procedures for harmonization of laws (Article 8a & 100a of the EEC Treaty); social policy (Article 118a of the EEC Treaty); regional development (Article 130e of the EEC Treaty); and research and technical development (Article 130q of the EEC Treaty).

[24] First, in acting on a proposal from the Commission in any designated area, the Council must first obtain Parliament's "opinion." Then the Council, instead of making a decision, must adopt what is called a "common position" which must be communicated to Parliament. Parliament within a specified period may either approve, reject or amend the proposal. If Parliament rejects or amends the proposal, the Commission must reexamine the proposal in light of Parliament's action. If the Commission accepts Parliament's amendments, the Council may adopt the amended proposal by a qualified majority but cannot change what is in effect a joint Commission-Parliament position except by an unanimous vote. If the Commission does not accept Parliament's amendments, the Council can either, by a qualified majority, adopt the proposal as originally submitted by the Commission or, by an unanimous vote, adopt the proposal as amended by Parliament. In all events, the Council cannot amend a proposal itself, except upon an unanimous vote. Articles 6, 7 of the Single European Act. More importantly, the Commission can no longer ignore Parliament's position. In addition, Parliament may propound "parliamentary questions" to both the Council and Commission and may, by two-thirds vote, dismiss the Commission en bloc (a power never exercised).

[25] Articles 8 & 9 of the Single European Act and Article 237 & 238 of the EEC Treaty.

[26] All members of the Commission must be nationals of a Member State, and no more than two may be nationals of the same State (Article 157(1)). In practice, France, Germany, Italy, Spain and the United Kingdom each nominate two members of the Commission and the other States one each. The nominees must all be accepted by the Member States.

competence," must " . . . [be] of indisputable independence," must act "in the general interest of the Community" and may not seek or receive instruction from Member States (EEC Treaty Article 157). Commissioners serve for four-year renewable terms and may not be removed from office except *en bloc* by Parliament or individually for cause by the Court of Justice.

As to the powers and modes of operation of Council and Commission virtually all important questions of policy are reserved to the Council — except, of course, as the treaties themselves set out the applicable substantive rule. The Council, in short, is the principal legislative organ of the Community, subject, however, to several critical reservations.

First, in most part the Council cannot exercise its law making power except upon a proposal from the Commission, which proposal it cannot amend except by a unanimous vote. In an important sense the legislative power of the EC is shared by Council and Commission. At the same time, it would be over stating the case to say that the Commission proposes and the Council disposes. In practice, the exercise of Council powers by the heads of government — the European Council — has so added to the stature of the Council that it effectively sets the Community agenda and establishes the basic framework for all policies. This has undermined the power and independence of the Commission — the Community's principal supra-national organ — and strengthened the "international" rather than "supra-national" attributes of the Community.

The power and independence of the Commission has been further eroded by establishment of the "Committee of Permanent Representatives;" a body of civil servants with Ambassadorial rank who represent the Member States. The Committee carries out preparatory work for the Council and can, if it chooses, decisively affect the timing and content of any Commission proposal.

Second, while the Commission acts by a simple majority, voting by the Council is carefully structured to reflect the relative powers of the Member governments, underscoring how immediately and directly the Community is viewed as answerable to those governments. Even more than this, however, while formally under the Treaty, unanimity is rarely required and most important decisions are to be taken by a "qualified majority"[27] or a special majority, actual practice has up until recently been quite different.

---

[27] Where a "qualified majority" is required, the Member States' votes are weighted as follows: France, Germany, Italy and the United Kingdom each receive a weight of 10 votes; Spain 8 votes; Belgium, Greece, Netherlands and Portugal each receive a weight of 5 votes; Denmark and Ireland 3 votes each; and Luxembourg 2 votes. The total of all weights is 76 votes. In all cases for an act of the Council to be adopted by a "qualified majority", it must be approved by 54 votes. If the act is upon a Commission proposal, 54 affirmative votes is sufficient. In all other cases the 54 approving votes must be cast by no less than eight members. Note that weighting the votes prevents the eight smaller countries, including Spain, from adopting a measure over the combined opposition of the big four. But weighting without the 54 vote minimum would require that the big four hold a united front against the eight. One defection and the measure would pass. Weighting, plus the minimum, means that at least two of the big four must join the eight. Conversely, once weighting was established to protect the big four, weighting alone would have allowed the big four to pass a measure over the opposition of a united eight. The 54 vote minimum compels the four to enlist some mix of at least three other countries, excluding Luxembourg

In 1965 General DeGaulle, unhappy with some far reaching Commission proposals with distinct supra-national implications, absented France from all Council deliberations. This threw the EC into a constitutional crisis that remains even today the most ominous that it has ever confronted. The crisis was resolved only after the then Six agreed, in January 1966, to issue the "Luxembourg Accords."[28] While not legally binding and far from unambiguous, the Accords have had a major influence on Community governance. In the Accords the Six agreed on the essentiality of greater Council-Commission cooperation, including prior consultations on important proposals through the Committee of Permanent Representatives. Then, with regard to majority voting, the Six agreed that where "the very important interests" of a "partner" were at stake "Members of the Council will endeavour:"

. . . to reach solutions which can be adopted by all the Members of the Council while respecting their mutual interests and those of the Community.

This agreement was followed by two clauses. The first recorded France's interpretation. On issues to which the agreement was applicable, "discussion [was to] continue," in France's view, "until unanimous agreement [was] reached." In the second clause the Six noted that there was a "divergence of views" on what should occur if unanimity could not be attained.

Although not a legal commitment in the sense of a formal binding derogation from the Treaty or Rome, the endeavour to reach unanimity pledged by the Luxembourg Accords has been a major factor in Community decision making for many years. In practice it has been tempered by an understanding that no one should, or could afford to be, unduly obstructive.[29] Nevertheless, it represented an important retreat from the power of the Community, implicit in its majoritarian voting structure, to override the sovereignty of its individual members and has meant that certain critical issues were never addressed.[30] For this reason, more recent developments represent important steps in putting the EC back on a path toward the more nearly "supra-national" structure of governance originally envisioned by the treaties.

In 1982, Britain, in a dispute over the Community agricultural budget, sought to invoke the Accords on the question of setting agricultural prices. The other Members demurred and, after long negotiations, the issue went to a vote. Since then a goodly number of votes have been taken, and while the Luxembourg Accords are not yet dead,[31] the practice of majority voting when called for by the Treaty has been affirmed in the amended rules of Procedure of the Council.[32] This

---

(i.e., obtain a simple majority of States). This three becomes four if Luxembourg is counted with the big four or the matter did not originate with the Commission. (Article 14 of the Spanish and Portuguese Accession Act, id. note 5, P-7708U.)

[28] Bulletin of the European Communities, March, 1966, No. 3, at pages 5-9.

[29] See Hartly, The Foundations of Community Law (Clarendon Press, Oxford, 1981) at page 13.

[30] As a good example see, European Court of Justice, Judgment of 4 October 1979, France v. United Kingdom, Case 141/78, [1979] ECR at 2923, concerning fishing rights.

[31] During debates on the ratification of the Single European Act (SEA), the French and British governments both represented to their respective parliaments that the SEA did not affect the validity of the Luxembourg Accords.

[32] Off. J. 15 October 1987, L 291, p. 27.

latter step was necessary in order to implement the "cooperation procedure" mandated by the Single European Act. Indeed, under the amended Procedures, a vote must be taken if requested by either a Member State or the Commission and that request is approved by a simple majority of the Council.

Finally, further limiting the supra-national attributes of the Community are some of the limitations placed on the exercise by the Commission of what otherwise could have been two separate and important sources of an independent power to shape Community law.

First, the Commission has a general mandate under the Treaty to supervise execution of the Treaty and all "legal acts" issued thereunder — to act as the Community Executive. Necessarily, in a complex modern state, the power to execute the law is often the power to give definitive content to the law. In the EC, however, the Commission exercises this power directly in only select areas.[33] On most matters administration of Community Law is in the hands of the Member States. Here the Commission has only supervisory authority although, in so doing, it can often issue decisions in specific cases, withhold payments to either individuals or Member States and challenge alleged breaches of Community Law by either Member States or individuals before the European Court of Justice.

Second, the Treaty envisions the delegating of considerable power to the Commission to make law within the framework of broad policies set by the Council.[34] The Council, however, in delegating "lawmaking" power to the Commission has very often tied the delegation, in one way or another, to a series of Committees composed of civil servants appointed by and responsible to the Member States. In some cases (Advisory Committees) the Commission is only required to consult with the Committee. Management and Regulatory Committees, on the other hand, have a veto power over the exercise by the Commission of its delegated authority. In the case of a veto by a Management Committee, the Council may take up the matter directly. In the case of a Regulatory Committee veto, the Commission's only recourse is to make a proposal to the Council in accordance with the normal procedure. Necessarily, this system has greatly affected the Commission's ability to set aside the parochial interests of one or more Member States and to take a more independent perspective based on the interests of the Community as a whole — the perspective of a truly "supra-national" executive.

Promptly after the Treaty of Rome was signed in 1957 it was submitted by the Member States to the GATT. The Contracting Parties resolved into a Committee of the Whole and appointed four Sub-Groups each to study and report on a particular aspect of the Treaty. Portions of two of these Reports, one concerned with the proposed common external tariff (CXT) and the other with the establishment of the Associated Overseas Territories (AOT), are set-out below.

---

[33] The principal areas are: management of the coal and steel price and production quota policy, antitrust, administration of antidumping and antisubsidy measures.
[34] Consult Article 155 of the EEC Treaty, Article 145 last paragraph as amended by Article 10 of the Single European Act.

On November 29, 1957 the Contracting Parties adopted those reports, referred the matter to the Intersessional Committee[35] and appointed a Panel of Experts as more fully described below.[36] At no time did the Contracting Parties ever reach a final and definitive decision on whether the Treaty of Rome conformed to the requirements of the GATT. The issues were handled in quite a different way as we shall see.

In reading these Sub-Group Reports it must be remembered that the participants were dealing with a very sparse record and the EEC was then far from the complex, ongoing and wide ranging enterprise that it has since become.

THE EUROPEAN ECONOMIC COMMUNITY

Reports adopted on 29 November 1957
(L/778)

GATT, BISD, 6th Supp., at page 70 (1958)

A. Tariff Plan and Schedule

I. Introduction

1. Sub-Group A examined the provisions of the Rome Treaty relating to the establishment of a common tariff and the elimination of import and export duties among the members. . . .

2. There was extensive discussion in the Sub-Group as to the significance to be placed upon paragraph 4 [of Article XXIV of the GATT]. . . . The representatives of the Governments of the Member States of the European Economic Community stated:

> The terms of paragraph 4 on the one hand, and paragraphs 5 to 9 on the other hand must be interpreted interdependently. Paragraph 5 of Article XXIV starts with the word "accordingly" . . . [demonstrating that] . . . the conditions laid down in paragraphs 5 to 9 have the purpose of ensuring that customs unions or the free trade areas are in conformity with the general principle laid down in the second sentence of paragraph 4. In other words, a customs union or a free-trade area which fulfills the requirements of the provisions of paragraphs 5 to 9 of Article XXIV would automatically and necessarily satisfy the requirements of paragraph 4 since paragraphs 5 to 9 merely spell out the implications of paragraph 4. This interpretation is confirmed by the records of the preparatory work related to the adoption of the text of the present Article XXIV.

> The view expressed by certain contracting parties that the terms of paragraph 4 of Article XXIV require the Six to take into consideration the situation of each contracting party is furthermore in contradiction with the provisions of

---

[35] GATT, BISD Sixth Supp., at page 68 (1958).
[36] *Id.*, p. 18.

paragraph 5 *et seq.*, particularly with those of paragraphs 5(a) and (b) which deal with the general incidence of tariff rates and commercial regulations.

The objective of paragraph 6 is furthermore the maintenance of the rights of the contracting parties acquired by concessions granted to them, a fact which should take care to a large extent of the problem of the countries the trade of which depends on one or on a few products.

* * * *

II. *Common tariff*

[NOTE: Under the Treaty of Rome the common external tariff (CXT) for any product was to equal the *lower* of the "arithmetical average" of the pre-EEC tariffs of the Member States or a stated percentage ranging from 3% to 55% ad velorum depending upon the "List" to which the product was assigned. There was also a "List" (List F) fixing a separate CXT for each listed product and a List G consisting of products representing roughly 20% of total Member State imports (a higher proportion for some members), for which the CXT was yet to be negotiated (Article 49). The CXT was to be implemented in stages (Article 23). Where the difference, in either direction, between a Member's pre-EEC tariff and the CXT was 15% or less, that member had four years to implement the CXT; if the difference exceeded 15%, that difference was to be reduced by stages over a "transitional period" consisting of three, four year stages. The Commission could give limited extensions of this schedule to Members experiencing "special difficulties," but the extensions could not exceed 5% of a Member's total imports from nonmembers (Article 26). Members were free to raise or lower their tariffs in advance of this schedule (Article 24) and, by the end of the first stage, were to have harmonized their customs laws and administrative provisions (Article 27).]

* * * *

5. . . . Since the rates of duty are not yet known for a large part of the common tariff, the Sub-Group came to the conclusion that it was not possible at this time to determine whether the common tariff would be consistent with the provisions of paragraph 5(a) of Article XXIV. [Nevertheless the Sub-Group did proceed to consider "the basis on which the Contracting Parties could best make a judgment with regard to the common tariff in the light of . . ." that paragraph.]

7. The representatives of the Member States [noted that] . . . Article XXIV do[es] not exclude any method of calculation for the preparation of a common tariff, provided . . . the rates . . . are not on the whole higher than the general incidence of the duties which they replace.

The Member States base their calculation on the arithmetical average method . . . For arriving at a still lower tariff level [they] . . . provided ceiling rates for a great number of products which have to be applied even in instances where the arithmetical average would lead to higher rates.

The Member States therefore consider that they have gone further than . . . [required by] paragraph 5 of Article XXIV. Further, the Member States do not see the advantage of a product-by-product study which could lead to nothing but the confirmation that the duties of the common tariff are, as shown by the study submitted to the Contracting Parties, on the whole, of a general incidence which is not higher than the incidence of the rates which they replace. Finally, the Member States are not in a position to accept a country-by-country study for the reasons stated above (See paragraph 2). . . .

8. Most members of the Sub-Group believed that the Contracting Parties should have an opportunity to make a thorough and detailed analysis of the proposed common tariff . . . [on a commodity-by-commodity basis] . . . at the earliest practicable date. It was envisaged that, in the first instance, this examination would be carried out by each contracting party . . . [followed by] an opportunity to examine jointly the common tariff. Such joint consideration should take account of the trading interests of contracting parties, including those whose exports to the Community are made up of a small number of products.

* * * *

11. The representatives of the Members of the Community stated that they would do everything in their power to communicate as soon as practicable the rates of the common tariff. . . . One member suggested that, if possible, sections of the common tariff should be transmitted as they are completed. The representatives of the Six pointed out that this suggestion could not be accepted since the common tariff has to be judged as an entirety but they undertook to transmit this suggestion to the Commission of the European Economic Community.

12. The Sub-Group confirmed unanimously that paragraph 6 provides that if the common tariff would involve in its implementation the raising of any duty rate above that specified in the schedules, negotiations should take place under the procedure provided for in Article XXVIII. The Sub-Group agreed that the provisions of paragraphs 1, 2 and 3 of Article XXVIII apply; any modification of the procedures that might be required will be made by the Contracting Parties when they make arrangements for the negotiations. However, the representative of the Six declared that they could not commit themselves to such negotiations without prior consultations as to the methods of the application of paragraph 6 of Article XXIV.

14. . . . [In response to a question] . . . representatives of the Member States . . . [confirmed] that the Commission [of the EEC], duly authorized by the Council, would be responsible for conducting tariff negotiations with third countries concerning the common tariff.

* * * *

17. Most members of the Sub-Group felt that the Rome Treaty contained a fairly detailed plan and schedule for the elimination of tariff barriers among the Member States. . . . [H]owever, some delegations felt that no such detailed plan was yet forthcoming for the last stage of the operation. The representatives of the Member States agreed that the plan and schedule were not as detailed for the latter part of the operation as for the first two stages but pointed out that the Member States were committed to complete the customs union within a period which would in no case exceed fifteen years.

Attention was also called to the provisions in the Treaty of Rome which allowed for a delay in the transition from the first to the second stage, and it was suggested that the Contracting Parties should recommend under paragraph 7(b) of Article XXIV that the Community should inform them in the event of recourse to those provisions. The representatives of the Six, however, indicated that they were not in a position to accept this recommendation. The possible prolongation of the first stage cannot be considered to be a modification of the plan and schedule since the plan itself provides for this prolongation; paragraph 7 of Article XXIV cannot therefore be invoked.

18. The Sub-Group noted that, under paragraph 7(c) of Article XXIV, any substantial change in the plan or schedule should be communicated to the Contracting Parties which would be free to ask the Six to consult with them if the change appeared likely to jeopardize or delay unduly the formation of the customs union.

* * * *

D. Association of Overseas Territories[37]

[19][1]. Sub-group D examined, in the light of the provisions of the General Agreement on Tariffs and Trade . . . the provisions of the Treaty relating to the association with the common market of the overseas territories.

[NOTE: Part IV of the Rome Treaty established a special relationship between the original Six and what the Treaty called the "Associated Overseas Territories" (AOTs).[38] The latter were all non-European countries and

---

[37] Each of the Sub-Group Reports starts the numbering of paragraphs with (1). In order to avoid confusion in discussing these two reports, the editors have numbered all paragraphs sequentially. This is the number shown in brackets. The small number superscripted above the bracketed number is the actual number used in the Sub-Group Report.

[38] The idea of the Associated Overseas Territories may be traced back to the European Economic Conference (the "Westminister Conference") of 1948 and to the subsequent Strasbourg Plan (1951) formulated under the auspices of the Council of Europe. Both envisioned a vast, globe encircling preferential trading area encompassing the whole of Western Europe and all the overseas countries and territories politically linked to Europe, including the British Commonwealth. The Strasbourg Plan, however, failed to command the support of the Council's Committee of Ministers representing the member governments. To many of the latter, overseas possessions were indispensable to the maintenance of their influence in world affairs and they were not prepared to have their colonial prerogatives diluted by a so-called "collective colonialism." Later, as the planning for European integration continued, the bold concept of the Westminister Conference and the Strasbourg Plan receded even further into the background. The rising tide of anti-colonial sentiment and cracks in the French empire — the loss of Indo-China and the Algerian revolt — cast a pall over any enterprise that "smacked" of colonialism, even the "collective" form. Indeed, not until the negotiation of the Treaty of Rome was well along did the French finally make clear that some preferential linkage between the EEC and France d'outre mer was essential to securing French adherence to the Treaty of Rome. While, in the end, France was joined by Belgium, the latter was quite prepared to forego the linkage. The Belgian Congo and the Trust Territories of Ruanda-Burundi already operated under a "free-trade" policy that would be unaffected by formation of the EEC, and for itself Belgium was a large importer with low tariffs. Italy was more concerned for its trade relations with Latin

territories that had been or were, at the time, colonies of Belgium, France, Italy and the Netherlands.[39]

The stated purpose of the association was to " . . . promote the economic and social development of the [AOTs] . . . and to establish close economic relations between them and the Community as a whole." (Art. 131) Specifically, duties on imports from the AOTs into the EEC, and duties on imports by the AOTs from the EEC and from other AOTs were, subject to the exception noted below, to be completely abolished in accordance with the Treaty provisions governing the abolition of duties among the Six (Art. 133:1 & 2). It was, of course, expected that each AOT would maintain duties and other restrictions on trade with third countries. In addition, the Six committed themselves (i) "to contribute to the investments required by the progressive development of" the AOTs (Art. 132:3) and (ii) to apply to all commerce with the AOTs the same rules that they were, under the Rome Treaty, to apply to commerce between themselves (Art. 132:1). In return, each AOT was to apply the same rules to each of the Six and to the other AOTs as were applicable to the Member State with which it had a special relationship (Art. 132:2). The one important exception to the AOT's obligation to abolish duties on imports from the EEC, related to duties which:

> . . . correspond to the needs of their development and to the requirements of their industrialization or which, being of a fiscal nature, have the object of contributing to their budgets.

If the fiscal or development duties on imports from EEC members generally, were higher than the duties imposed on imports from the particular EEC member with which the AOT in question had a special relationship, they were to be "progressively reduced" to the latter level (Art. 133:3). If the level of duties imposed by any AOT on imports from third countries combined with the duty-free treatment given exports from that AOT to the EEC, caused trade to be diverted to the detriment of a Member State, the latter could ask the EEC Commission to propose remedial measures (Art. 134). Lastly, there was appended to the Rome Treaty a special "Implementing Convention," dealing

---

America than with the trust territory of Italian Somaliland. Sentiment in the Netherlands and West Germany, however, strongly favored resisting the French demands. Neither relished the idea of having to finance the development of France's overseas empire. It was only Chancellor Adenauer's personal stature, the concessions he obtained from France and a broader concern for the fate of the entire Treaty that finally reconciled the Germans and Dutch to a grudging acceptance of the AOT arrangement.

[39] These countries and territories were, according to the names then in use: French West Africa (Senegal, Guinea, the Ivory Coast, Dahomey, Mauretania, the Niger and the Upper Volta); French Equatorial Africa (Middle Congo, Ubangi-Shari, Chad and Gabon); other French territories (St. Pierre and Miquelon, the Comoro Archipelago, Madagascar and Dependencies, French Somali Coast, New Caledonia and Dependencies, French Settlements in Oceania, the Southern and Antarctic Territories, the Cameroons Trusteeship); the Republic of Togoland; Belgian Congo; Ruanda-Burundi (Belg.); Somaliland Trusteeship (Ital.); Netherlands New Guinea.

inter alia with quotas and other quantitative restrictions between the EEC and the AOTs.[40]]

* * * *

[21][3]. One member of the Sub-Group stated that under paragraph 5 of Article XXIV, in the case of a customs union the customs duties in the external tariff might differ . . . from the duties previously applied in the constituent territories; . . . but when a free-trade area was formed under paragraph 5(b), it was necessary to maintain . . . duties not greater than those which were previously in force. As the customs union of the Six involved certain increases in those duties, the free-trade area could not be constituted without infringing the provisions of paragraph 5(b). . . . The fact that the obstacle thus created can be easily circumvented does not prove anything against this legal situation. On the other hand, the existence of this inconsistency and the very fact that it can be circumvented show that the authors of Article XXIV did not contemplate the creation at the same time of a customs union and of a free-trade area. . . .

[23][5]. The representative of the Six and some other members could not accept this view . . . [pointing out] that . . . [i]f the authors of the Havana Charter had intended to oppose the simultaneous establishment and the co-existence of the two systems, they would have included appropriate provisions in the text which they had drafted. . . . [In addition] if the text of Article XXIV only prevented the simultaneous formation of the customs union and the free-trade area, that obstacle could be very easily and automatically overcome by staggering the establishment of the two systems over a period of time. However short the intervening period (whether a month or a day), the establishment of the two systems would no longer be simultaneous. . . . [T]he authors of the General Agreement . . . would [not] have included provisions which could so easily be circumvented.

[24][6]. [Moreover] . . . the representative of the Six pointed out that the tariff increases which might result from the Rome Treaty for certain countries in the free-trade area were not the legal consequence of the provisions establishing that area, but of those which established the customs union. Therefore, since the formation of the free-trade area was not in itself the legal cause of any increase in a national tariff, but that increase resulted only from the customs union, the free-trade area was consistent with the provisions of the relevant paragraph of Article XXIV.

---

[40] Implementing Convention Relating to the Association with the Community of the Overseas Countries and Territories, [1958] U.N.T.S. at page 157. The Implementing Convention related, in large measure, to the operation of the Development Fund that the Six were to establish for the benefit of the AOTs and to other facets of the relationship (*e.g.*, the right of establishment). However, it also contained a significant number of provisions relating to quotas that AOT's then had in place. In addition, and most importantly, it committed the Six to extend to the AOTs those provisions of the Rome Treaty providing for the progressive elimination of quantitative restrictions on commercial exchanges between the Six (Art. 10). For their part, each AOT was to convert any quota granted to imports from the Member State with which it had a special relationship to a "global quota" available without discrimination to all imports from the EEC.

* * * *

[27][9]. Most members of the Sub-Group considered that for the reasons set forth below . . . Part Four [of the Rome Treaty] and [the] Implementing Convention are incompatible with Article XXIV of the General Agreement. . . .

> [NOTE: What follows at this point is only some, and not necessarily the most important, arguments advanced by the non-EEC members against the AOT provisions of the Rome Treaty. Drawing upon what you have already learned about discriminatory trade arrangements of this type you should be able to start filling-in the arguments.]

[28][10]. Some members considered that the concept of a free-trade area did not allow for the conciliation of the divergent interest of industrialized countries with the interest of territories which exported only raw materials, and which had scarcely yet embarked on the subsequent stages of economic development. . . . [In addition] one member pointed out that the Havana Conference had not envisaged an exception to Article I of the General Agreement which would cover nearly a quarter of world trade;. . . . [It] had only envisaged a possible customs union between France and Italy, and one between Argentina and Chile . . . There was, [that member thought], a fundamental incompatibility between the principles of Article XXIV . . . and the [provisions of] . . . the Rome Treaty which, in any case, nowhere indicated that such an association would constitute a free-trade area, and whose language structure, references and technique are those of an extension of preferences.

* * * *

[33][15]. Under paragraph 8(b) of Article XXIV, it was necessary for the formation of a free-trade area to be accompanied by the elimination of the duties and restrictive regulations of commerce on "substantially all the trade" of the constituent territories . . . [subject only to] . . . the maintenance of the restrictions permitted under Articles XI, XII, XIII, XIV, XV and XX of the General Agreement. The Rome Treaty deviated from that rule, as it did not provide that the associated territories should eliminate their export duties, which were considerable, on exports to the territory of the Six. Further, the [AOTs] . . . would be empowered . . . to levy import duties on [imports from . . . the Six] when such duties correspond to their fiscal requirements or to the needs of their economic development. . . . Moreover, there is no provision in the Treaty for the complete and permanent elimination of quantitative restrictions against imports from the Six into the [AOTs]. . . .

* * * *

[36][18]. [Further along the lines of the foregoing argument it was pointed out] . . . that the association of the overseas territories, which opened up vast prospects for them both in the field of investment and as regards outlets for their exports, would give a strong impetus to the industrialization of those territories. It was natural that such development should require increasing customs protection, particularly in view of the difference between the productivity of the Six and that of the territories in question. . . .

* * * *

[39][21]. To sum up, most of the representatives thought that substantial barriers to the free movement of goods between the various constituent units would remain after the full implementation of the overseas territories provisions of the Rome Treaty (*e.g.*, on export duties) and that barriers to trade would increase progressively in view of the need to protect the industrial development of the overseas territories. For this and the other reasons . . . they remained of the view that the proposals did not conform to Article XXIV, but constituted an extension of existing preferential systems contrary to Article I:2 of the General Agreement.

[40][22]. On the other hand, the representatives of the Six considered that the rules of the Rome Treaty concerning the association of the overseas territories (Part Four) were in conformity with the provisions of the General Agreement concerning free-trade areas. The arguments put forward in support of this viewpoint can be summarized as follows:

[41][23]. At the time when the Havana Charter was drawn up, the concept of an integrated Europe was already familiar. The Charter could not have placed any limitation on the realization of such aspirations. . . .

[42][24]. The fact that the Treaty did not call the association a "free-trade area" in no way altered the nature or legal structure of the association. [Because] . . . the provisions of the Treaty related to . . . other matters (such as investments) which did not fall within the normal framework of a free-trade area . . . [that] term had . . . not been used. . . .

[43][55]. The Rome Treaty fulfilled the conditions laid down in Article XXIV of the General Agreement for free-trade areas, in that:

— substantially all trade was liberalized;

— the duties and restrictive regulations maintained by each constituent territory — in the case of a free–trade area including also a customs union — would not, on the whole, be higher or more restrictive than were the general incidence of the duties and regulations in force before the formation of the area; and

— there was a plan and schedule for the formation of the area within a reasonable length of time.

[44][26]. There was no reference to Article XVIII[41] in . . . the Rome Treaty . . . [Nevertheless] it had been stated, during the general discussion, that . . . Article 133 [of the Rome Treaty] corresponded to the same concern for the underdeveloped countries that had led to the inclusion in the General Agreement of Article

---

[41] In Article XVIII, entitled Governmental Assistance to Economic Development, the contracting parties recognized that the economic development of countries that could only support low standards of living was important to the attainment of the objectives of GATT. Accordingly, fairly elaborate provisions were set-out under which such countries might raise tariffs to promote the establishment of particular industries, employ quantitative restrictions to meet development related balance of payments problems and otherwise deviate from provisions of the General Agreement in the interests of their economic development, all, however, under strict reporting requirements and close GATT surveillance.

XVIII. But the Rome Treaty did not make any legal use of Article XVIII. Furthermore, the argument which had been drawn *a contrario* from the fact that Article XVIII was not one of those referred to in Article XXIV:8(b) did not take into account the fact that Article XXI was not mentioned either. It would be difficult, however, to dispute the right of Contracting Parties to avail themselves of that provision . . . and it must therefore be concluded that the list was not exhaustive. . . .

[45][27]. Among the import duties authorized by Article 133 were fiscal duties. They were nondiscriminatory, however, and were compensated by internal levies when there was local production. They should therefore not be taken into consideration.

[46][28]. The principle of the progressive elimination of customs duties was clearly stated in Article 133, paragraph 2. It was therefore appropriate to examine only . . . protective duties. With regard to them, the representative of the Six pointed out that . . . the General Agreement merely provided that the duties in force at a given moment should not affect more than a fraction of the trade, so as not to jeopardize the requirement that substantially all the trade should be liberalized.

[47][29]. The General Agreement did not specify what that fraction must be and it now had to be determined. Some delegations had requested proof of the existence of a free-trade area, but the representative of the Six was justified in asking first for a precise definition of the . . . fraction which constituted "substantially all" the trade. The representative of the Six stated that, for his part, he could provide [such definition]. . . .

[48][30]. [According to] the representative of the Six . . . the annual volume of trade between the territories constituting the free-trade area (including the trade between the individual Members of the customs union) was approximately $7,868 million, and the fraction which might be subjected to the protective duties provided for in Article 133, paragraph 3 of the Treaty amounted to barely $108 million, namely 1.4 per cent of the trade between the European and overseas territories constituting the free-trade area . . . [L]iberalization of 98.6 per cent certainly fulfilled the requirement of the Article [XXIV] . . . He was surprised to hear it contended that the liberalization did not apply to "substantially all" the trade while at the same time no definition of the term "substantially all" was forthcoming. For their part, the Six had proposed the following definition: a free-trade area should be considered as having been achieved for substantially all the trade when the volume of liberalized trade reached 80 per cent of total trade. . . .

* * * *

[50][32] . . . [T]he representative of the Six [also] pointed out that the industrialization of the overseas territories should normally only result in the levy of protective duties to the extent that the newly-established industries produced for the domestic market and not for export. Furthermore, any increase in the volume of trade subject to protective duties (constituting the numerator of the fraction) would only result in an increase in the percentage if it was not canceled out by a corresponding increase in total trade (constituting the denominator). There were therefore reasons for thinking that the amount of trade affected would continue

to be only a small proportion of the total trade. . . . Last, if that was not the case at a given moment in the evolution of the free-trade area, and more precisely if the percentage subject to protective duties reached 20 per cent, the . . . European Economic Community would then, but only then . . . apply for such waivers as they deemed necessary.

[51][33]. The Sub-Group considered whether or not the Contracting Parties should specify the proportion of trade on which duties could be maintained within a free-trade area. [In response] . . . [m]any members of the Sub-Group said that each case . . . had to be considered on its merits and that it was, therefore, inappropriate to fix a general figure. . . . Some members . . . thought that it would be unrealistic to apply the same criterion to a free-trade area such as that existing between Nicaragua and El Salvador and to a free-trade area the members of which were highly industrialized countries accounting for a large percentage of world trade.

* * * *

[57][39]. A member of the Sub-Group referred to the statement made to the Committee by a representative of the Six, to the effect that the Six were prepared to consider as and when it occurred any prejudice which the association of the overseas territories might cause to the trade of third countries.

[58][40]. The representative of the Six pointed out that it was necessary to determine whether any prejudice which might be caused was to be attributed to any inconsistency as between the Treaty and the rules of the General Agreement; or whether it was merely inherent in a situation resulting from a group arrangement that was consistent with the provisions of the General Agreement.

* * * *

[60][42]. The Sub-Group was of the opinion that the Contracting Parties should give consideration, inter alia, to the effects of the association of the overseas territories on the trade of third countries, and that . . . such examination should commence in January and deal first with such products as the following: cocoa, coffee, bananas, oilseeds and vegetable oils, wood and timber, tobacco, hard fibres, cotton, sugar and tea. . . .

[61][43] . . . [S]everal members of the Sub-Group asked the Six to agree to refrain until the end of 1958, by which time they felt that final decisions would have been taken by the Contracting Parties on the question [of the association of overseas territories], from applying . . . any tariff reductions in respect of products originating in the overseas territories. The representative of the Six said that . . . he could not give an answer to the above request without first consulting the Interim Committee for the Common Market.

NOTES AND QUESTIONS

(1) Consider the EEC's interpretation of Paragraph 4 of Article XXIV as set-forth in Paragraph 2 of the Debate. It is narrowly technical and formalistic.

Drawing upon your knowledge of the economics of discrimination, fashion the argument in response to the EEC's interpretation. Identify the specific language in Paragraph 4 of Article XXIV upon which you would rely.

(2) Again drawing upon your knowledge of the economics of discrimination, might the EEC have taken a broader position; one more in tune with the basic economic goals that underlie the GATT and the non-EEC parties' argument formulated above?

(3) Consider next some of the tactical problems that may have caused the EEC to adopt a narrow interpretive approach. More specifically, how might the AOT provisions of the Rome Treaty have influenced their tactical decision? Within three months of these debates a special working party appointed to study the problem produced a voluminous report studying twelve commodities representing 80% of the trade of the AOTs. The report (i) showed that the exports of many of these products by the AOTs were on the point of exceeding the total requirements of their respective pre-Rome Treaty preferential markets among the Six but were substantially below the requirements for the whole of the EEC; (ii) projected the following preferential margins under the Treaty: cocoa — 9%; coffee — 16%; bananas — 20%; tea — 35%; tobacco — 35%; sugar — 80% and (iii) found that none of the AOTs exported tea. Much of this information, if not in the same detail, was available to the non–EEC members of the GATT at the time of this debate. Frame the argument, or arguments, against the AOT provisions of the Rome Treaty that these data suggest could have been, and were in fact, made in the debates. How does the argument differ from those made against the EEC proper?

(4) Note also the EEC's insistence on a formula (the "arithmetical average") in applying Paragraph 5(a) of Article XXIV, its resistance to a product-by-product or country-by-country approach, its recognition that under Paragraph 6 of Article XXIV it would have to engage in Article XXVIII negotiations (Paragraph 12 of the Debate), to which negotiations Paragraph 2 of Article XXVIII would be applicable. Step away from the global viewpoint and consider, from a national viewpoint, what nations gain from the trade creating effects of a customs union and what nations lose from its trade diverting effects? What implications would this have for the Article XXVIII negotiations? How might the EEC's narrow, formalistic interpretation of Article XXIV have helped it avoid those implications?

(5) Examine Paragraph 28 of the Debate. The argument reflects a concern with the broader implications of the Rome Treaty — the AOT provisions in particular — for the structure of the free world economy. Identify that concern more precisely. Does it have political implications, especially for the United States and its then strategic position in the World? If so, explain. Are you persuaded by the EEC response found in Paragraph 41 of the Sub-Groups' Reports?

(6) On behalf of the United States or any other non-EEC member of GATT, how would you respond to the argument and the data given by the EEC representative in Paragraphs 45, 46 and 48 of the Debates to support the claim of EEC compliance with the "substantially all" requirement of Paragraphs 8(a)(i) and 8(b) of Art. XXIV?

(7) Even before the Contracting Parties approved the Sub-Group Reports, members of the EEC made their position clear: "There can be no question," they

said, "either of a readjustment of the Treaty [of Rome] or of any of its provisions, or of waivers or of subjecting the Six to special controls."[42] Not unexpectedly, therefore, the Contracting Parties never attempted to judge definitively whether the Treaty of Rome conformed to Article XXIV. The Intersessional Committee, to whom review of the Treaty had been referred, summed-up the prevailing opinion when it concluded that:

> . . . it would be more fruitful if attention could be directed to specific and practical problems, leaving aside for the time being questions of law and debates about the compatibility of the Rome Treaty with Article XXIV of the General Agreement.[43]

What is to be made of all of this? From the perspective of the United States and other non-Continental Western powers, European unity had important strategic implications. The Treaty of Rome was a major step forward and there was every indication that any concerted effort to revise the Treaty could well have unraveled the whole fragile political fabric out of which it had been fashioned. At the same time, as Gardner Patterson has observed, ". . . this was the first time in history that a large number of third countries, those most likely to suffer, had been given the opportunity to examine in detail the regional plans of others." As a consequence the Europeans learned how seriously they had " . . . underestimated the concern of the rest of the world over the discriminatory aspects of their scheme."[44]

One broader development, which we can only note in passing, was the institution of annual reviews of interim plans for regional groupings. As the AOT provisions of the Treaty of Rome were superseded first by the Yaounde Conventions and then the Lome Accords (see page 311, *infra*), as plans for other regional groupings proliferated, these reviews proved to be useful in constraining the activities of some groups. Yet, it may be doubted that the reviews ever really succeeded, as a normative matter, in establishing a substantive connection between the general principle of Paragraph 4 of Article XXIV — read as a broad sanction of trade creating but not trade diverting regimes — to the technical criteria of Paragraphs 5 and 8.

Also the Contracting Parties followed up their 1957 debate by appointing a panel of experts to study past and current trends in international trade.[45] Within the ensuing year the Panel produced a highly influential report, commonly known

---

[42] GATT, Press Release 357, October 6, 1957.
[43] GATT, BISD Seventh Supp., at page 70.
[44] Patterson, *op cit.*, page 155.
[45] Decision of 29 November 1957, GATT, BISD Sixth Supp., at page 18. In addition, the Intersessional Committee commissioned a sub-committee report that proved influential. GATT, BISD Seventh Supp., at page 70. The Committee also suggested resort to "normal procedures" under the General Agreement especially Art. XXII. On November 10, 1958 the Contracting Parties approved the Committee's proposed procedures for Article XXII consultations between the EEC and any nonmember wishing to engage therein. *Id.* at page 24. This was followed by a substantial number of bilateral discussions which apparently, however, had very little direct affect on the EEC's position. Patterson, *op. cit.* page 169. See also the complaints registered by India and Yugoslavia in SR.16/9, 20 June 1961.

as the Haberler Report after the Panel's chairman.[46] With regard to the EEC,[47] the Report concluded that, because the economies of the European countries were very competitive and because increases in output and real incomes in Europe should lead to a greater demand for products from outside Europe, the trade creating effects of the EEC should outweigh the trade diverting effects. To assure this result, however, the Panel also recommended that the Common Market be established over as large an area of Europe as possible and that the common external tariff be reduced below the standard set in Paragraph 5(a) of Article XXIV.[48]

(8) At about the time the Haberler Report was being issued, the United States' Congress extended the President's trade agreement making authority.[49] Thereupon Undersecretary of State Douglas Dillon proposed a new GATT tariff negotiating round which the EEC promptly endorsed.[50] At the end of May, 1959 the Contracting Parties decided to hold a two stage round of negotiations; the first was to be a renegotiation with the EEC under Article XXIV:6 of the EEC member tariffs the second was to be a general multilateral negotiation of "reciprocal and mutually advantageous concessions" under Art. XXVIII *bis* (soon known as the "reciprocal" or "Dillon Round").[51] Combined the two stages were soon to be dubbed the "1960-61 negotiations" although they were not actually completed until July of 1962.

For a number of reasons the Art. XXIV:6 negotiations proved to be more difficult than originally anticipated.[52] Most importantly, the non-EEC participants, focusing primarily upon cases where pre-EEC national tariffs were to be raised in determining the CXT, tended each to demand that its own *losses* be

---

[46] Trends in International Trade. A Report by a Panel of Experts, General Agreement on Tariffs and Trade, Geneva, October 1958.

[47] *Id.* at pages 117-117.

[48] At this point the panel added a footnote questioning whether the proposed CXT met the GATT requirement, noting that " . . . in a number of cases duties for the common tariff have been fixed by mutual agreement rather than by computing an average. . . . Some of these are actually higher than an arithmetic average would be. Furthermore, the use of an unweighted arithmetic average . . . may tend to produce an upward bias, if, as appears to be the case in most instances, the largest importers among the Six have the lowest tariffs."

[49] The Trade Agreements Extension Act of 1958, Pub. L. 85-686, 72 Stat. 673 (1958), amending Section 350 of the Tariff Act of 1930, 49 U.S.C. Sec. 1351.

[50] Also at about this time the EEC announced that it would extend to all nations enjoying most-favored-nation status the first 10% cut in internal tariffs effective January 1, 1959, and, for three quarters of all commodities, the second 10% internal tariff cut effective six months later, provided that the cut did not reduce the national tariff rate below the projected CXT. This, of course, was simply a speed up of realignment for those national tariffs scheduled to be reduced in arriving at the CXT. The speed up, however, did not apply to most agricultural products or to goods on List G for which no CXT had as yet been established. GATT, Doc. L/1099, 13 November 1959.

[51] First Report of Committee I, adopted 29 May 1959, GATT, BISD Eighth Supp., at page 101.

[52] See GATT, Doc L/1372, Rev. 1, 23 November 1960 and General Agreement on Tariffs and Trade; Analysis of United States Negotiations, State Department Publication No.7349, Commercial Policy Series 186 (1962).

matched by compensatory gains before entertaining EEC claims for reciprocal concessions. Initially, at least, the EEC would have none of this. Their duty to compensate was discharged, the EEC contended, if the trade covered by any upward adjustment of a national tariff was matched by a corresponding downward adjustment in a national tariff with comparable coverage, irrespective of the possibility that one non-EEC participant might suffer most of the loss from the increased tariff and another benefit from the decrease. Based largely upon the earlier, simple arithmetic average but taking some account of trade coverage, this formula approach conceded nothing by way of compensation for potential trade diversion. In the end, however, both sides gave way, but as one close observer of these events has put it:

> While [these differences] . . . made the negotiation of the first part of the 1960-61 tariff agreements exceedingly onerous, . . . it established GATT as a strong and reliable instrument where even such a powerful economic block as the Six could be made to conform. This became particularly obvious, when, in the course of the negotiations, the representatives of the EEC Commission did not succeed with their prearranged formula and had to make repeated requests in Brussels to be given more negotiating power for concession-making. In the end the negotiations became quite a formidable demonstration of the extent to which countries had abdicated to GATT some of the national sovereignty in the field of tariffs and commercial policy.[53]

While the trade covered by new bindings was considerable,[54] the non-EEC participants did not get all the compensation they might have wanted. Thus, from an initial CXT on machinery that yielded tariff revenues equal to 13.5% of total machinery imports, the 1960-61 negotiations resulted in a tariff that yielded revenues equal to 11.9% of machinery imports; for automotive vehicles the comparable numbers were 13.8% and 12.6%; for chemical products revenues under the original CXT equalled 14.3% of imports while the final negotiated rates

---

[53] Curzon, op cit. page 99.

[54] In addition to the overall reductions illustrated by the following examples, the trade coverage of the U.S.-EEC negotiations was substantial. In 1958 a total of $1.488 billion of U.S. exports to the EEC moved under classifications where the tariff had been bound by one or more of the Six to either the United States directly ($900 million) or to a third country ($588 million) and available to the U.S. under the MFN clause. Under the Art. XXIV:6 negotiations this coverage was replaced with the following:

    (i) the United States obtained concessions on trade of $1.677 billion of which $1.583 billion was in the form of direct bindings to the United States. This latter represented a 75 percent increase in the trade covered by direct bindings to the United States.

    (ii) On the $1.583 of trade covered by new direct bindings the United States obtained new concessions covering trade of $530 million at rates of duty below those previously applicable, while giving up $300 million of trade under pre-EEC bindings at rates below the CXT. Thus on trade of $230 million there was a net improvement in the rate structure of direct bindings to the United States.

    (iii) On the $1.583 of trade covered by new direct bindings, $584 million represented items bound under the CXT at rates equal to the pre-union national rates.

In sum, nearly three-fourths of the direct concessions obtained by the United States were at rates equivalent to or below those which the individual members of the EEC had previously applied.

yielded revenues equal to 13.6% of imports; on agricultural products the comparable numbers were 16.4% and 16%.[55] Moreover, the 1960-61 negotiations closed with a general recognition that, because of its complexity, the product-by-product approach had materially hampered the achievement of more significant tariff reductions. Accordingly, even before signature of the final Protocol, President Kennedy had called for a new round of trade negotiations based upon a "linear" or across-the-board approach and Congress was already at work on legislation authorizing the President to engage in just such negotiations.

Following the President's lead, Congress in October, 1962 enacted the Trade Expansion Act of 1962,[56] two main provisions of which reveal the extent of the American policy-makers' pre-occupation with the political dimensions of the U.S-EEC relationship.[57] When these provisions failed to produce the results they were designed to achieve the entire focus of the Kennedy Round changed. Economic objectives moved to center stage and what eventually proved to be the most significant grant in the legislation was the authority to negotiate a linear reduction of up to 50% of all existing U.S. tariffs with certain exceptions.

In the final event, and after a long wrangle over the "disparities" problem, the Kennedy Round negotiations did achieve a marked reduction in the tariffs applied by the world's major trading nations to a significant portion of their international trade in industrial products but not in agriculture. Thus, prior to the Kennedy Round $2.689 billion of U.S. imports from the EEC were either dutiable or duty free but unbound. In the Kennedy Round the United States extended concessions covering $2.216 billion of these items. On $24 million of this trade the tariff concession given by the United States exceeded 50% of the existing rate. On $1.180 billion of trade the tariff was reduced by 50%. On $119 million of imports the cut was between 25% and 49%. On $247 million the tariff reduction ranged from 1% to 24%. The United States also "bound" existing duties or the right to duty free entry on $45.8 million of imports from the EEC.

---

[55] Source: Economic Bulletin for Europe, Vol. 14, No.1, Geneva, Sept. 1962.

[56] Pub. L. 87-794, 76 Stat. 872, 49 U.S.C. Sec. 1801 *et. seq.* (1962).

[57] The two provisions of the 1962 Act were the following. First, the Act empowered the President to grant duty free entry to specified tropical agricultural and forestry products (largely products of less developed countries), provided that the EEC granted similar treatment to substantially the same products on a nondiscriminatory basis. This effort to woo the AOT's away from their special ties to the EEC and to join those territories with other developing countries in bringing pressure on the EEC to abandon its discrimination against the latter, ultimately failed, at least in the short run. France was adamant. Keeping her ex-colonies within a special EEC orbit was a cornerstone of French policy (See Curzon, *op. cit.* page 279) and the associated territories themselves were less than confident of competing on equal terms with other less developed country producers of tropical products. Secondly, the 1962 Act authorized the President to reduce U.S. tariffs to zero on any product for which the combined U.S.-EEC share of world trade was 80% or more. With the British share of world trade included, this authority encompassed almost $2 billion of trade. Without the British share there were only a few products that could qualify under the 80% rule. The measure was, in short, designed to enhance the prospects of British entry into the EEC, the application for which was then pending before the EEC Council. A political move, the strategy floundered on DeGaulle's late 1963 veto of Britain's application.

On its part, the EEC, prior to the Kennedy Round, was importing from the United States $3.465 billion of products that were dutiable or duty free but unbound. In the Kennedy Round the EEC gave concessions covering $3.029 billion of this trade. Ninety two percent of the concessions related to non-agricultural products. On $45.6 million of this trade the tariff reduction exceeded 50% of the rate then in effect. On $1.3 billion the reduction was 50% of the existing tariff. On $373 million of trade the reduction was between 2% and 49% and on $88 million the tariff was reduced by 1% to 24%. Other "bindings" covered $305 million of trade. While these figures suffer all the defects noted earlier concerning the use of "trade coverage" to measure the value of a tariff concession, the Kennedy Round was, nevertheless, a notable achievement.

(9) The non-EEC members of GATT certainly could, and doubtless would, have out-voted the EEC members on the question of whether a CXT based upon the arithmetic average of the preexisting national tariffs met the requirements of Art. XXIV. This was even more clearly the case with the projected common agricultural policy and the AOT provisions. At the very least they might have demanded that the Rome Treaty submit to the waiver procedure with the grant of the waiver circumscribed by conditions. In the final event, however, they did neither and the implementation of the Treaty of Rome proceeded in accordance with its original terms. What then does this say for the General Agreement as a body of international law?

By one account, law, or a legitimate legal regime, exhibits at least two characteristics. First, law consists of rules or, more indeterminately, of principles — rules or principles by which to judge the right and wrong of particular behavior. While this account may admit that rules are often indeterminate in application, it nevertheless insists that they constitute law, properly so called, only to the extent that there is some process for the resolution of those indeterminacies and that the pronouncements emanating from that process are taken as authoritative by, and control the actual behavior of, those to whom the rule is addressed.

Secondly, if law consists of rules or principles by which to judge the right and wrong of particular behavior, it also implies a process of fact finding by which the persons or institutions making that judgment can determine whether the behavior being judged does or does not conform to the rule.

Turning then to the GATT review of the Treaty of Rome it is apparent that the Contracting Parties: (i) never sought to resolve the interpretive questions posed by the rules found in Article XXIV; (ii) declined to judge the Treaty of Rome definitively in accordance with their final interpretation of that Article; (iii) did not demand any modification of the Treaty (assuming they had found a divergence between the Treaty terms and their interpretation of Article XXIV) or attempt to subject the EEC to the constraints of a formal waiver; or (iv) attempt to communicate to the EEC what sanctions it might encounter if it refused that demand. Having in mind the account of law as rules, this would certainly seem to constitute a failure of the GATT as a regime of law.

(10) Reflect upon some of the causes of this failure. Rules embody social choices. Like all such choices, when made by institutions of collective governance, they depend for their authoritativeness upon either, or a combination of, the following: (i) effective power in those institutions to impose their choices on those

to whom the rules are addressed and the will to exercise that power; or (ii) a sufficient consensus among the governed regarding the values to be fostered through obedience to the choices embodied in the rules. While consensus need not mean unanimity, it does imply a willingness in the dissenters to prefer obedience to existing rules over no rules at all.

With this in mind, was GATT under the circumstances of the case bound to fail as a regime of law, judged according to the account of law as rules? Specify the points in the Debate and in the circumstances surrounding the formation of the EEC upon which you base your answer. Recall the difference between the global and the national perspective; who may win from the trade creating effects of a customs union and who may lose from its trade diverting effects? How does this fit into the problem of power and consensus?

(11) The EEC argued, perhaps for tactical reasons, but not without justification, that any serious country-by-country, product-by-product attempt to ascertain whether the EEC would be on balance trade creating or trade diverting would have embarked the Contracting Parties upon a time consuming fact finding task of forbidding complexity. Even had time been available, the acknowledged limitations of a static production effects analysis and the uncertainties attendant to a more dynamic analysis would have further complicated any such detailed study.[58] Again, perhaps the nature of the problem confronting GATT in reviewing the Treaty of Rome put the case beyond its reach as a legal institution, again judged according to the account of law as rules.

(12) In light of the foregoing, but before concluding that the EEC case represented a failure of the rule of law, consider the possibility of an alternative account of law upon which to base a more charitable, and possibly more realistic and useful judgment. Perhaps rules of law are not necessarily standards by which to judge the right and wrong of particular behavior. Perhaps they may, in a more rudimentary stage of legal development, serve instead only to characterize situations where one party, perceiving that its interests may be adversely affected by actions of another, can legitimately advance a claim to engage in a process of settlement. Rules, by this account, serve not as touchstones for the resolution of disputes, but normative benchmarks that legitimate a grievance and confer a right to invoke a process of good faith settlement. The process of settlement, in turn, seeks not so much to vindicate one or another set of values but rather to explore whether a value consensus is possible, and, if not, to allocate costs and benefits in a way that will minimize losses to human welfare. While the demand for fairness and predictability may, over time, yield a consistency of settlements out of which an ever widening consensus regarding the rules may emerge, it is nevertheless settlements, not the vindication of rules, that may be the essence of the rule of

---

[58] Recall that the EEC argued that under Paragraph 5(a) the "restrictiveness" of the CXT was solely a function of its "height". The non-EEC members, on the other hand, insisted that trade effects were the key. At the heart of the nonmembers' concern was the fear of loosing their position in the burgeoning European market. Even as the debate was heating up, however, experts were beginning to doubt that there was any satisfactory statistical method for translating the "height" of a tariff into an estimate of its trade effects, *e.g.*, Viner, The Measurement of the "Height" of Tariff Levels, reprinted in his International Economics, Glencoe, Ill., 1951, pages 161-175.

law, at least in the context of an international problem of this importance. But, if this is so, then one may find that, at this rudimentary stage, it is precisely through contradiction and lack of clarity — through indeterminacy — that rules perform their essential service to the rule of law. And by this account the test for the adequacy of any legal regime is whether the rules, through their indeterminacy, sweep broadly enough to deposit before the dispute settling mechanism as great a number of potential conflicts as will avoid a serious disruption of world trade. With this account of law in mind, consider the following:

— Identify the normative standard or standards that countries concerned with the possible adverse effects of a customs union or free trade area could employ to legitimate their claim of right to a good faith negotiation of measures to minimize those effects.

— If you were advising a customs union or free-trade area, how much confidence would you place upon the basic approach taken by the EEC in the GATT debates as a tactic for resisting those claims or of circumscribing the scope of the negotiations? What might you advise your clients to expect if they were contemplating (i) a CXT based upon an arithmetic average of the pre-Union national tariffs, (ii) a free-trade area embracing both highly developed industrialized nations and less developed primary product countries?

(13) If the account of law outlined in Note (10) above (*i.e.*, law as rules) is thought to represent law at a more mature stage, how would you evaluate the argument that to dignify the second account as "law," properly so called, undermines efforts by the international community to work toward and insist upon the more mature form; it legitimates the second best and should, therefore, be rejected.

NOTE
EXPANSION OF THE EEC'S SYSTEM OF PREFERENCES FOR SELECTED DEVELOPING COUNTRIES

Since the Contracting Parties took no action against the AOT provisions of the Rome Treaty, they were implemented as originally envisioned. In 1964, after the overseas territories gained their independence, those provisions were superseded by a treaty, commonly known as Yaounde I, between the EEC Six and each of the eighteen former dependent territories. In 1968, under the aegis of the Agreement of Arusha, the free trade, but not the financial and technical assistance, provisions of Yaounde I were extended to Kenya, Uganda and Tanzania. Yaounde I was succeeded, in 1970, by Yaounde II which raised the level of EEC aid to the eighteen, largely to quiet the fears of the eighteen as the EEC moved toward adoption of a Generalized System of Preferences (GSP) the following year.

When Great Britain joined the EEC in 1972, the less developed Commonwealth countries in Africa and the Caribbean — but not Asia — were offered association status with the EEC on a variety of terms. Upon expiration of Yaounde II in 1975, the EEC Nine entered into what became known as the Lome I Agreement with the original eighteen Yaounde States, twenty-one Commonwealth countries in Africa, the Caribbean and the Pacific and seven other less developed African countries. These forty-six nations became collectively known as the ACP States. Lome I was followed, in 1979, by Lome II with fifty-nine ACP countries and in 1984 by Lome III with the EEC Ten[59] and sixty-six ACP States as signatories. Upon securing the necessary ratifications, Lome IV (signed December 15, 1989) between the EEC Twelve and sixty-nine ACP States will go into effect for 10 years from March 1, 1990.

Responding to strong pressure from the United States, Lome I largely did away with reverse preferences (*i.e.*, EEC exports were no longer to enjoy a preferential position in the ACP States, but were to enter on an MFN basis only). Also under that agreement, and the subsequent Lome accords, virtually all industrial and many agricultural products of the ACP States, with exceptions designed to protect the EEC's common agricultural policy, came to enjoy duty and quota free access to the EEC. Each agreement provided for expanded financial and technical assistance by the EEC. A fund to stabilize ACP commodity export earnings was established. Provisions progressively strengthening the right of establishment and the free movement of services and capital have been added. Lastly, by requiring the EEC to consult with the ACP States more frequently and on a broader range of issues, the Lome agreements have substantially changed the ACP States' relationship with Europe from one of associational dependency as foreshadowed by Part IV of the Rome Treaty to something more akin to an economic alliance.

Even as it was expanding, and in the process modifying, the association concept, the EEC was forging a wider network of preferential trading relationships. In 1976, the EEC Nine negotiated special trade preference and development assistance agreements with the non-ACP States of Algeria, Morocco and Tunisia. In 1977 similar agreements were made with Egypt, Syria, Jordan and Lebanon. In that year, Israel agreed that, by 1989, it would establish a free trade zone with the EEC. The agreement is now in effect. Arrangements between EFTA[60] and the EEC, also made in 1977, have resulted in duty free status for the vast bulk of Western European trade in industrial products. Turkey is, by agreement, moving to full participation in the EEC Customs Union. Cyprus and Malta have signed association agreements under Article 238 of the Rome Treaty and in 1980 Yugoslavia was extended special preferential treatment.

This expanding network has had profound effects. Forged as much for political as economic reasons, it colored everything the EEC said and did in the international forums where the broader issues of less developed country participation in world trade were being debated. It affected the positions taken by the ACP states and, with that, the ability of the less developed world to maintain a united front. It decisively influenced American and Japanese attitudes and was ultimately a major factor in shaping the EEC's own generalized system of preferences.

In the end, the decisive question is one of dynamics. What has been, or is likely to be, the ultimate outcome from a global viewpoint when one juxtaposes these

---

[59] Excluding Spain and Portugal.

[60] Austria, Finland, Iceland, Norway, Sweden and Switzerland.

arrangements along side the emerging pattern of generalized preferences? What conclusions about the process of change in the international economic order can be deduced from the way in which these arrangements unfolded, from their causes, the responses they evoked and the debates they engendered along the way?

§ 4.06   The Generalized System of Preferences

Here we turn to consider the evolution of a system under which virtually all developed country members of the GATT eventually came to grant preferential treatment to a comprehensive, although far from complete, list of imports from most less developed countries; what has come to be called the Generalized System of Preferences (GSP). In the context of this study we begin to examine some of the trade problems created by the disparities in resources, in economic and political institutions and in outlook that separate the developed from the developing countries. The topic necessarily invites inquiry into how changes in legal concepts and institutions might assist in better organizing international trade to facilitate economic development in the so-called third world.

[A]   Aftermath of the EEC Debate in GATT

If the global welfare effects of the EEC itself were ambiguous, the AOT arrangements fairly trumpeted their trade diverting propensity. Yet, the AOT debates also served to bring the plight of the less developed countries into a sharper focus than ever before in GATT history. They led to the appointment of the Panel of Experts under Gottfried Haberler's chairmanship, and to the work that followed upon the Panel's report, including the addition of Part IV to the General Agreement.

TRENDS IN INTERNATIONAL TRADE

Report by a Panel of Experts
(The "Haberler Report")
GATT, Geneva, October, 1958

[NOTE: The Haberler Panel was instructed by the Contracting Parties to study " . . . past and current international trade trends and their implications," with special reference to " . . . the failure of the trade of less developed countries to develop as rapidly as that of the industrialized countries, excessive short-term fluctuations in prices of primary products, and widespread resort to agricultural protection."[1] The picture to emerge from the report was a sobering one.]

Export-Import Trends

First, the Panel noted that exports by the non-industrialized countries, having suffered a greater decline during the depression than exports by the industrialized

-----

[1] Decision of 29 November 1957, GATT, BISD, 6th Supp., at page 18 (1958).

countries,[2] had, by 1957, returned to capture their traditional pre-depression, one-third share of total world exports.[3] The composition of the non-industrialized nations share, however, had changed radically. Petroleum exports from a handful of non-industrialized nations accounted for over 50% of the total increase. Thus, even though the *volume* of total non-industrialized country exports had risen by 51% between 1928 and 1957, the *volume* of non-petroleum exports had risen only 17-18%, compared with a 62% rise in the volume of exports by the industrialized countries.

Turning to imports, the Panel noted that compared with a threefold growth in exports between 1928 and 1957, the value of imports by the non-industrialized countries had increased nearly fourfold, from $8.71 billion to $34.31 billion. This represented a change in the over-all trade balance for these countries from a positive $1.68 billion in 1928 to a negative $3.43 billion in 1957. Once again, however, the petroleum factor tended to mask the seriousness of the problem. Hidden in the overall negative trade balance of $3.43 billion, was a positive balance of $2.22 billion for the petroleum exporting nations. This meant that the remaining non-industrialized countries had moved from a positive trade balance of $1.54 billion in 1928 to a negative balance of $5.65 billion, in 1957. In the latter year imports exceeded exports by about 23%, a deficit which, in the five years since 1953, had grown from $.26 billion to $5.65 billion.

Adding to the complexity as well as the problems suggested by these raw numbers, the Panel noted that while the prices of all primary products had risen during the Suez crisis they had, following the first quarter of 1957, started to decline. Overall for the period 1953 through the first quarter of 1958, the prices of primary products had declined 4% while prices of manufactured goods had risen 7%. The Panel also observed that the growth in exports by those non-industrialized countries that had a "privileged" (*i.e.*, preferential) position in their chief export market significantly exceeded the growth for those nations that were not so "sheltered."[4]

---

[2] The Panel classified as "industrialized" all of the member States of the Organization for European Economic Cooperation (OEEC) (*i.e.*, Western Europe), Canada, Japan and the United States and classified as "non-industrialized" the rest of the world excluding the USSR, Eastern Europe and mainland China. Data on these latter were not included in the study. Thus, included in the "non-industrialized" countries were such developed nations as Australia, New Zealand and Finland, all of whose exports were composed primarily of agricultural and other primary products. The inclusion of these countries in the "non-industrialized" category, however, meant that the Report tended at points to understate the difficulties facing the less developed "non-industrialized" nations of the world.

[3] Between 1928 — the pre-depression baseline used by the Panel — and 1957, annual exports by the non-industrialized nations had risen from $10.4 billion to $30.9 billion and those of the industrialized countries from $21.3 billion to $66.7 billion.

[4] Between 1928 and 1955 the total value of exports by the countries belonging to the overseas sterling area, by those associated with continental Europe and by Cuba — which enjoyed a preferential position in the American market — grew by 227% compared with a 113% growth rate for the "unsheltered" group.

Financing the Trade Deficit —
Implications for Development

Addressing next the matter of financing this growing trade imbalance, the Panel noted first that while the "flow of private long term capital ha[d] failed to develop in line with the value of world trade, official grants and loans" (foreign aid) from the industrialized countries had, overall, surpassed previous levels of private lending. This changing pattern, however, together with the petroleum factor, had created a further problem. The oil exporting countries were rapidly accumulating gold and foreign exchange reserves and were attracting the largest share of private capital. Of the remaining non-industrialized countries, the semi-industrialized nations confronted the "greatest difficulties." Faced with declining reserves, hard hit by the overall drop in private long term lending, and recipients of only a small fraction of the official grants and loans, many of these nations stood precisely at that point in their development where the demand for imports of industrial products was bound to increase. The rest of the non-petroleum exporting nations were only slightly better off because of foreign aid. Distribution of that aid, however, was controlled as much by political considerations as by any objective assessment of their development needs.

At this juncture it should be recognized that the problem posed by the Panel's analysis was not merely, or even primarily, a matter of rectifying trade imbalances. It was one of development. If development was the object, then the issue was, as the Panel put it, "whether in the future the non-industrialized countries will be able to finance a . . . volume of imports," adequate to sustain their economic development. Here the Panel employed an illustration to convey a general awareness of the dimensions of the problem. According to the Panel's calculations, if net annual investment in some hypothetical country was 6%, it could expect to sustain only a 1% annual increase in per capita income. If it sought to step this rate up to a modest 3%, it would not only have to double its net annual investment but would likely confront the need to increase imports by as much as 10% each year.[5]

How would such an increase be financed? The two most important sources of financing would be exports of goods and services and imports of capital. Since the amount of new capital flowing to the non-industrialized countries was only one-tenth of the value of their exports, the largest part of the financing would, barring a massive increase in private investments or official aid, have to come from expanded exports.

---

[5] The Panel's calculations were as follows: If net investment in some country was 6% of national income, if gross investment (net investment plus depreciation) was 11%, and if the capital-output ratio was 2, then the annual increase in national product obtained by a net investment of 6% would be 3%. If population increased by 2% annually, the resulting increase in per capita income would be 1%. If the country wanted to speed up its development by another modest 2%, it would have to raise net investment from 6% to 10% of its gross national income (an increase of 67%) and raise gross investment from 11% to 15% (an increase of 40%). To do this, imports of capital goods would probably also have to rise proportionally. Since imports of capital goods constituted about 28% of all imports by the semi-industrialized countries, a 2% step-up in development from 1% to 3% annually would require an increase in total imports each year of more than 10% (.28 x 40%).

Challenged to forecast the prospects for future export expansion by the non-industrialized countries, the Panel reviewed a number of factors. Concerning the possible growth of demand in the developed countries for non-industrialized country exports, the Panel had before it two studies. One study projected a five year 3.5% annual growth rate for Western Europe; another a twenty year projection of 5% annually for the United States and the rest of the world. Even if these projections were to bear out, they would, the Panel thought, translate into a much lower growth rate in purchases of primary products since the income elasticity of demand for the latter was considerably less than one.[6] With regard to technological change, those changes had thus far worked against primary product producers through the development of synthetic substitutes. The only favorable prospect was the possible exhaustion of certain competing mineral deposits in the industrialized countries.

This doleful picture brought the Panel squarely to the critical issue; the problem of protectionism in the industrialized countries. It is on this point that the Panel made its mark. Mincing no words, it placed much of the blame for the deteriorating trade position of the non-industrialized countries of the world, and the bleak prospects for their future, on the barriers to that trade erected by the industrialized nations. The Report observed that as a consequence of these protectionist measures:

> . . . the combined Western European and North American net imports of [basic] foodstuffs from the rest of the world (*i.e.*, broadly speaking, from the unindustrialized countries) was more or less halved (falling from 2.96 [billion dollars] in 1938 to 1.43 [billion dollars] in 1956) in spite of a rise of no less than 35 per cent in the total consumption of the two industrialized areas (consumption increasing from 26.28 [billion dollars] in 1938 to 35.36 [billion dollars] in 1956).[7]

The initial GATT response to the stern injunctions of the Haberler Report was promising. Three committees were established to formulate an Action Programme embracing further tariff reductions (Committee I), an attack on non-tariff barriers to trade (Committee II) and on current obstacles to the expansion of export earnings by less developed countries (Committee III).[8] Committee III, in study after study with the Haberler findings as a base, detailed, product by product, the disabling effects that the extraordinary variety of barriers raised by the industrialized nations were having on exports from the less-developed world. Out of this work came, in turn, a Ministerial Declaration (1961), an Action

---

[6] But see, page 351, footnote 13 and accompanying text for the figures on actual rates of growth and the relationship between growth in developed country GNP and growth in developing country exports to the developed nations of the world.

[7] *Id.*, at page 88. The values given by the Report are all based upon constant 1952-53 prices.

[8] Programme of Action Directed Towards An Expansion Of International Trade, Decision of 17 November 1958, GATT, BISD, 7th Supp. at page 27, (1959).

Programme (1963) and finally, in November 1964, the addition of Part IV ("Trade and Development") to the General Agreement.[9]

At one level these measures seemed to signal a new awareness by the developed nations that reform of their own commercial policies was essential to any significant export expansion by the less developed countries of the world. Awareness of the problem, important as it might be, did not, however, translate into immediate action. While the pressures for reform continued to mount and the 1963 Action Programme had some positive effects, overall the developed nations failed to deliver the needed reforms.

As a result, the less developed countries, especially those not associated with the EEC, commenced, in the early 1960s, to press their case before the United Nations, securing resolutions calling for the establishment of the United Nations' Conference on Trade and Development (UNCTAD). UNCTAD then became the principal forum for debate over the foremost item in the less developed countries' agenda, the Generalized System of Preferences. From the beginning, however, it became apparent that the developed countries would not accept a GSP that might threaten their protectionist agricultural subsidy schemes. As discussions regarding the GSP progressed it became clear that its primary impact was to be confined to manufactured and semi-manufactured products.

NOTE
THE PROBLEM OF AGRICULTURE —
A CONTEMPORARY PERSPECTIVE

In the years since the Haberler Panel and Committee III issued their dismal projections, agricultural protectionism has, if anything, become more pervasive. This has not only adversely affected less developed country exports, it has been a major cause of friction in the broader trade relations between those developed countries that are major producers of agricultural products such as Australia, Canada, New Zealand and the United States, on one hand, and Western Europe and Japan, on the other. And in those years GATT has been largely powerless to

---

[9] In 1961 the GATT Ministers adopted an eight point Declaration enjoining upon the Contracting Parties certain principles to govern their respective trade policies. Promotion of the Trade of Less-Developed Countries, Declaration of 7 December 1961, GATT, BISD 10th Suppl., at page 28 (1962). On the topic of trade preferences, the Ministers concluded: "While it is important that [the] . . . various advantages [of existing preferential arrangements] should not operate to the detriment of other less-developed countries, it is also necessary that action to deal with this problem should be on a basis that meets the marketing needs of supplying countries now enjoying preferred access to markets." (p. 31) In 1963, spurred on by the preparations for the first United Nations Conference on Trade and Development (UNCTAD), the Ministers of all the developed country members of GATT except the EEC Ministers agreed to an Action Programme formulated principally by twenty-one less developed countries thoroughly exasperated by the lack of action but still unable to garner the support of all their number. This was then followed in 1964 by the adoption of Part IV of the General Agreement.

resolve the problem. The current frightful state of affairs, and some of its causes is nicely captured in the following excerpt:

The Economist
November 15, 1986

DAIRY, PRAIRIE[10]

In the rich and mainly industrial countries farmers are paid too much, so they produce too much. In the poor and mainly agricultural countries farmers are paid too little, so they produce too little. Europeans trample Cognac grapes into industrial alcohol; Americans fill Rocky Mountain caverns with butter; Japanese pay eight to ten times the world price for their bowl of rice. Meanwhile, many million Asians and Africans live in rural poverty and go hungry to bed. Do not despair. The mistakes are so large that these contrary policies will soon collapse. Properly staged and handled, that collapse will leave the whole world better off.

The mistakes of the rich

If all the subsidies and protectionism were removed, calculates the World Bank, consumers and taxpayers in the rich OECD countries would be $100 billion a year better off, while their farmers would be only $50 billion worse off. Conclusion: win your next election by paying farmers a net $50 billion a year in a wiser way. As the worst present way, the Japanese government gives its farmers three times the world price for rice, then feeds it to pigs at half the world price, while charging human Japanese 16-20 times what it charges the pigs. . . .

The second worst system is the EEC's. It pays its farmers twice the world price for their dairy produce. As a result, the butter mountain is reaching 1.5m tonnes. . . . Storage costs of all EEC surpluses will soon go above the value of the stored products; the costs are increasing daily, while the value is declining as butter deteriorates into nasty butter oil, and grain degenerates into something indefinable. Yet European farmers are bringing even their most marginal land under the plough. . . .

Change for the better will come more quickly if critics resist the temptation to repair bad incentives. Half-free-marketmen used to argue that any quotas should be auctioned: should they, now that in western Canada the right to sell one cow's milk costs eight times as much as one cow? The best approach is to widen the cracks, hasten the collapse and then build a better system. The cracks are coming first in the United States, where farming support has mushroomed from $2.7 billion in 1980 to a record $25.8 billion in 1986. The EEC's taxpayers should

---

[10] This title is taken from the first line of the following ditty used on the cover of the November 15, 1986 issue. Copyright © 1986 by the Economist. Reprinted by permission.

Dairy, Prairie,
quite contrary
How does your surplus grow?
With lobbies strong
so prices wrong,
And subsidies
all in a row.

revolt next: they are spending around $21.5 billion on farm support this year, up from $6.2 billion ten years ago.

* * * *

. . . The United States needs to take the lead, and for once give agriculture the prominence it deserves at the top. Australasia and Argentina would support this; so should Canada, even though it has just imposed a heavy tariff on American [corn]. Everything would then depend on whether the EEC plucked up its courage to support America. If it did, Japan could not keep out of this Euro-American anti-corn-laws league. There would then be real reform, not just another tedious trans-Atlantic and trans-pacific trade row.

The political costs of bravery are diminishing every day. Britain is the big EEC country most ready to weaken the common agricultural policy, because only 2-1/2% of Britons now farm or work directly for farmers. France is the policy's shrillest supporter, but only 8% of French workers are now on the land, down from 22% in 1960. The country that matters most for European reform will probably be West Germany, where 5-1/2% work on the land — but most of them are part-timers with another job. . . .

Saving the poor

The difference in the third world is that the subsidized minority lives in town; the soaked majority in the countryside. While many farmers in rich countries receive double the world price for their produce, many peasants in poor ones are palmed off with half the world price for their produce, often by awful state marketing boards.

This is now changing for the better, as the world's two largest countries are allowing markets rather than mandarins to set agricultural prices. India was the world's basket case in the 1960s, until it ceased to rely on "food for peace". . . . Food prices then rose in India, so peasants started growing food for market. Last year, India was a net exporter of grain.

China's turnaround is even more remarkable. The average real incomes of its 800m peasants have almost trebled in the eight years since the Chinese govern-ment scrapped the communes, letting rural families earn more if they produced more. In Africa, Zimbabwe has shown what happens when farmers are given their head. It has helped feed Ethiopia, charitably, and South Africa, profitably, during their recent droughts. It need not fear any competition from Tanzania. Though 80% of Tanzanians live off the land, the government pays farmers just a quarter off the world price for their [corn].

In those third world countries where farm folk far outnumber town folk, the answer to most agricultural problems is simple: let market prices prevail. The consequent rise in farm output would slay two vultures with one stone — staunching both the flow of people off the land into urban shanties and the flow of scarce foreign exchange abroad to pay for imported food.

In industrial countries, the political aim should be to give farmers their $50 billion a year of support in ways that do not pinch $100 billion a year from everybody else. The social case for continuing some support is that the 2% who stay on the farm provide a service for the other 98% of people, both aesthetically (Hampshire looks nicer than Wolverhampton) and maybe in terms of community values (many want to believe that country people are more kindly, more neighbourly, more moral and more wise). Neither aim will be served by the present policy of using money to rig markets to get farmers to overproduce food in the most factory-farm sort of way. The surpluses mean that the EEC food cartel is now as likely to crash in 1986-96 as OPEC was to crash in 1976-86, and Europe's farmers may go down to depression in the most surly and self-defeating way. . . .

Some part of rich countries' rural support should switch to the rural tourist industry: pony–trekking, dude ranches, adventure holidays for rockclimbing and in tents. Because villages are nice, more relatively well–to–do people want to live in them. . . . "Boutique farming" has helped each farm acre in Massachusetts to bring in 3-1/2 times as much cash as the average acre under corn in Iowa; the subsidy–fed rural European should not mock at designer beetroot and the servicing of speciality restaurants for the diet conscious.

Such ideas are not as macabre as America's subsidy for tobacco, nor as the EEC's system of making some farmers pay more for feed for their cows than they would get on world markets for those cows' milk. They are less mad than the central principle in politicians' pricing policies for agriculture in the past three decades. Politicians have done most to encourage the production of food in all the countries where the main medical problem is obesity, and most to discourage it in all countries where starvation remains a threat.

> [NOTE: Since the foregoing excerpt first appeared, agriculture has moved to center stage in the Uruguay Round negotiations. While some progress has been made, the United States and the EEC, as already noted, appear at this late date in the negotiations to be at an impasse on the rate of subisdy reduction. More specifically, the United States initially proposed a definite deadline for the elimination of all domestic agricultural subsidies by the industrialized countries. This move was strongly backed by Canada, Australia and New Zealand who at one point proposed to hold the entire Uruguay Round negotiations hostage to progress on liberalizing agricultural trade. The EEC balked, with the result that until a last minute compromise was reached at the late December, 1988 Mid-Term Review in Montreal, the fate of the entire Round was at issue. Under the terms agreed upon, the negotiations turned to defining "in operational terms . . . a framework for liberalizing trade in agriculture and bringing all measures affecting import access and export competition under . . . more effective GATT discipline." It was also agreed that the "long-term objective of the agricultural negotiations was to establish a fair and market-oriented agricultural trading system" resulting in "substantial progressive reductions in agricultural support and protection over an agreed period of time . . ."[11] Hence the present impasse; how musch reduction and how fast.]

---

[11] GATT, *Mid-Term Review Agreements*, in News of the Uruguay Round, NUR 027, 24 April 1989 at page 9.

[B]   Enter UNCTAD and the OECD

In December 1961 the United Nations General Assembly designated the 1960s as the "United Nations Development Decade,"[12] declaring that trade should be the primary instrument for the achievement of that development and instructing the Secretary General to consult with member states on the advisability of holding a conference on international trade.[13] As a result of these consultations and encouraged by a conference of developing nations held in Cairo in July of 1962,[14] the General Assembly, that same year, called for the first United Nations Conference on Trade and Development (UNCTAD) to be held in 1964.

The central, and probably most influential working document of UNCTAD I was a Report prepared by the Secretary General of the Conference, Raul Prebisch, a well known Argentinian economist.

SUMMARY OF POINTS
REPORT BY THE SECRETARY GENERAL OF UNCTAD I
ENTITLED

"TOWARD A NEW TRADE POLICY FOR DEVELOPMENT"[15]

1. After noting the need for a massive expansion of less developed country exports, Prebisch observed that the GATT presumes that the only measures required for the expansion of trade are the removal of obstacles to the free play of economic forces. It espouses "an abstract notion of economic homogeneity which conceals the great structural differences between industrial centres and peripheral countries." This had, Prebisch argued, rendered GATT incapable of fashioning "the new order" required to "meet the needs of development." Foremost among the structural problems was the difference between the growth rates

---

[12] General Assembly Resolution 1710 (XVI) of 19 December 1961.

[13] General Assembly Resolution 1707 (XVI) of 19 December 1961.

[14] See Cairo Declaration of Developing Countries, quoted in Jankowitsch and Sauvant, eds. The Third World Without Superpowers: The Collected Documents Of The Non-aligned Countries (Dobbs Ferry, N.Y. Oceana, 1978), Vol. I at page 72. The Cairo Conference was the first meeting at which the less developed countries formally attempted to coordinate their policy positions on development issues before the United Nations. This attempt at the maintenance of a unified front, largely unsuccessful in the GATT, carried over into the submission of a Joint Statement to the UNCTAD Preparatory Committee in 1963, later submitted to the General Assembly as a "Joint Resolution" of 75 developing countries. The effort to affirm the unity of the developing countries continued following UNCTAD I with the issuance, in June of 1964, of the "Joint Declaration of the Seventy-Seven" marking the beginning of the so-called "Group of 77." The points of tension within the "Group of 77" were many and, at times, so palpable as to render their avowed unity no more than a rhetorical front. Nevertheless, the determination to maintain at least the appearance of unity eventually led to some important procedural innovations and had a decisive influence on the normative context surrounding the first as well as later UNCTAD deliberations.

[15] U.N., Doc. E. Conf. 4613 Vol. II, 1964.

in developing country exports of primary products and their imports of industrial goods — a difference exacerbated by the persistent deterioration in the developing countries' terms of trade. While the "elimination of protectionism in the industrial centres" and an increase in the income transferred from the industrialized to the peripheral countries would both be helpful, they would be mere "palliatives." The "absolute necessity" was, according to Prebisch, to "[build] up . . . trade in industrial exports" by the less developed countries.

2. To meet this need, the Report proposed a number of measures but is best remembered for proposing a system of trade preferences to be granted by developed countries to developing countries and by the latter to each other; what came to be known as the Generalized System of Preferences (GSP). After acknowledging both the trade-diverting as well as trade creating possibilities of the GSP, the Report argued that the system should not be judged from so narrow a frame of reference. A successful Kennedy Round could more than offset the export decline that some industrialized countries might suffer due to competition from the developing countries.

3. The preferential treatment of exports from developing countries, the Report argued, would help industries in those countries overcome the difficulties that they encounter in export markets because of their high initial costs. It would be a temporary measure and as such a logical extension of the infant industry argument under which national protection is often justified for new industries which in the long-run are likely to achieve high levels of efficiency. If infant industries need protection in the domestic market because of high costs, Prebisch argued, they obviously need even more protection in the form of preferential treatment in foreign markets.

4. The Report expressed the hope and the expectation that all developed countries would agree to grant preferences to all developing countries.

5. In deciding which countries ought to benefit from preferences, the Report listed a number of factors, such as per capita income, the size of the country, the share of agriculture and industry in total employment and output, and the impact of the primary export sector on the growth of the economy. Using these factors Prebisch thought that it would be relatively easy to decide which are and which have ceased to be developing countries, at the same time he acknowledged that there was a small group of borderline cases for which it would not be easy to establish a cut-off point. In all events the question, Prebisch argued, was not very important to the industrial countries, because imports of manufactures from the developing countries were not likely to be a matter of overwhelming consequence to them.

6. In most previous discussions it had been assumed, according to the Report, that the need to exclude products that would create domestic problems in the industrialized countries and the need to assure that developing countries put their emphasis on industries with a strong growth potential, would require granting preferences selectively to particular products. This approach, Prebisch argued, had two great disadvantages.

First, every industry in an industrialized country facing strong foreign competition would seek to be exempt from the system. If then the commodities covered by all national preference systems were to be the same, the ultimate list would likely be the lowest common denominator of all national lists.

Second, it was difficult to imagine how suitable industries in the developing countries would be selected. It was better to leave the initiative to the managers of particular enterprises.

In principle, therefore, the Report argued, preferential treatment should be granted to all imports from the developing countries subject only to certain specified exclusions and safeguards.

7. The Report conceded that, since the purpose of the proposed preferential system was to encourage infant industries, preferences would have to be eliminated once an industry was firmly established. Hence, Prebisch proposed that, in general, the preference for any given industry continue for no less than ten years. This would compel entrepreneurs to concentrate on making their industry fully competitive as rapidly as possible. It would also mean that preferences for industries established shortly after the inception of the scheme in the more advanced developing countries would give way to preferences for industries in countries that were still at an early stage of development.

8. The Report conceded that the industrialized countries would want to have a limit placed on the total volume of preferential imports and the volume of imports in any one category. Since, however, even a large expansion in exports by the developing countries would represent only a small fraction of the total manufactured goods consumed in the industrialized countries, a limit, high in relation to existing developing country exports, would still be small in relation to the markets in the preference granting countries.

9. The Report further conceded that if developing country exports exerted undue pressure on prices prevailing in an industrial country, that would demonstrate either that the developing country industry did not need the preference or that the preference was excessive. Thus, under the new preferential system each preference granting country should be able to reserve a right to withhold preferential treatment from products accounting in toto for a reasonable percentage of its aggregate imports or provide that imports cease to qualify for a preference when they exceed a certain percentage of domestic consumption.

10. Among the most difficult problems connected with the introduction of a new system was whether to give different degrees or kinds of preference to countries according to their stage of development. This would be desirable, the Report suggests, because the productivity differential between the least and most advanced developing countries is far greater than the difference between the latter and the industrially developed countries. However, the scope for the gradation of preferences would not be very great if the Kennedy Round achieved significant success.

At the close of UNCTAD I the participants adopted a Final Act,[16] "general principle eight" of which affirmed that, while international trade should normally

[16] Preamble to the Final Act, Section IV, Paragraph 45, United Nations Conference on Trade and Development, Final Act and Report, Vol. I, 1964/IIB/11, at page 8.

be conducted under the MFN principle, (i) "new preferential concessions" should be made to developing countries as a whole; (ii) preferences among developing countries *inter se* need not be extended to developed countries; and (iii) special preferences already granted by certain developed countries to a limited number of developing countries should be progressively phased out. Seventy eight countries approved this principle. Eleven developed countries, including the United States, voted against it and twenty-three, mostly developed states, abstained.[17]

Initially, at least, perhaps no country was as determined in its opposition to Prebisch's proposal as the United States. We shall return to examine the reasons for that opposition. Here the point to note is that in the years immediately following UNCTAD I the United States found itself increasingly isolated from virtually all of its developed country allies on the broad principle of a GSP. The basic strategy of the U.S. was to try and minimize the benefits of such a scheme. But that strategy did not work partly because it failed to take account of the structure of many developed country tariffs (see Notes and Questions below) and partly because it failed to recognize the symbolic importance of the idea. Moreover, with the Kennedy Round negotiations completed it became more difficult to argue that the GSP, as a discriminatory and trade diverting mode of liberalization, was no substitute for the broadly inclusive and trade creating prospects of trade liberalization under MFN auspices. Inspite of its accomplishments, the Kennedy Round had failed to even dent agricultural protectionism or address the problem of non-tariff barriers to trade.

In addition, the rapid proliferation of special preferential arrangements by the EEC brought home to American officials how rapidly the international trading community was being broken up into discriminatory spheres of influence and how, as a result of their opposition to the principle of GSP, they had lost the influence necessary to forestall this development.[18] This, in turn, played directly into the hands of those Latin American countries which, having been excluded from the EEC network, began to pressure the United States to change its position, using the Alliance for Progress framework for this purpose.[19]

---

[17] *Id.*, page 20.

[18] Consult Statement by Anthony M. Solomon, Assistant Secretary of State for Economic Affairs, before the Subcommittee on Foreign Economic Policy of the Joint Economic Committee, United States Congress, July 12, 1967. 56 Dep't of State Bull. 709 (1967)

[19] There was also the encounter in GATT over the Canadian-U.S. Automotive Products Agreement. Anxious to diffuse domestic pressures to countervail subsidized exports of Canadian automotive products (see: Order in Council Establishing Rebate Plan, 22 October 1963, P.C. 1963-1/1544; reprinted in Hearings on H.R. 6960, before the House Committee on Ways and Means, 89th Cong., 1st Sess. at page 43), the United States and Canada agreed, in 1965, to grant each other reciprocal duty free access to a broad range of automotive vehicles and original equipment parts (Agreement Concerning Automotive Products Between the Government of the United States of America and the Government of Canada, 16 January 1965; 17 U.S.T. 1372, T.I.A.S. No. 6093). When the United States applied to GATT for an Article XXV:5 waiver — a waiver that was ultimately granted — members of the GATT Working Party could hardly resist inquiring, apparently without receiving an answer, whether the automotive agreement "indicated a change in the positions of . . . [the Canadian and American] Governments with regard to the granting of new preferences, especially preferences [to] . . . less-developed countries" (Decision of the Contracting Parties, 20 December 1965, GATT, BISD, 14th Supp. at pages 37-44 and pages 181-190 (1966).

By 1967 the United States was ready to withdraw its opposition to the basic principle of a GSP.[20] Once this watershed was.crossed, work toward framing an international consensus on the subject moved forward at a goodly pace. In December of 1967 the Special Group on Trade with Developing Countries of the OECD (the OECD Special Group) submitted its final report. The Group was composed of representatives of France, Germany, Great Britain and the United States and was formed to develop a common position that the OECD States might take in UNCTAD II. In spite of strong objections on certain points by the less developed countries, the OECD Special Group's Report established most of the core elements in the framework that eventually emerged in 1971 in the form of "Agreed Conclusions" by the UNCTAD Special Committee on Preferences. Two questions considered by the Special Group are of special interest because of the agreements reached — and the disagreements revealed. First, was the question of what to do about existing preferences for developing countries (*e.g.*, the expanding European system) and second, what to do about reverse preferences. Part One of the Special Group's Report summarizes the conclusions reached on these points; Part Two elaborates.

REPORT BY THE SPECIAL GROUP ON TRADE WITH DEVELOPING COUNTRIES OF THE OECD

(Reproduced as TD/56)

Proceedings of the United Nations Conference on Trade and Development, Second Session, Vol. III, (E.68.II.D.16) at page 78 (1968)

Part One

* * * *

H. — Preferences received by some developing countries in the markets of some developed countries

It is recognized that many countries would see as an important objective of the new arrangements a movement in the direction of equality of treatment for the exports of all developing countries in developed country markets. At the same time, developing countries at present receiving.preferences in some such markets would expect the arrangements to provide them with increased export opportunities to compensate for their sharing of their present advantages.

J. — Action by developing countries

* * * *

The United States member stated that, in his view, a key element in any arrangements for the grant of special tariff treatment is the phasing out, as rapidly

---

[20] 56 State Dept Bull. 709 (1967).

as possible, of existing preferences extended by some developing countries to some developed countries.

Part Two

* * * *

Tariff arrangements now in force

38. The Group agreed it would be unrealistic to expect those developing countries which now enjoyed a preferential position in certain developed markets to accept curtailment of their existing access privileges in the context of arrangements for special tariff treatment for all developing countries. The Group recognized that the maintenance in full of existing "access" arrangements for preferred developing suppliers might mean that in certain developed markets the exports of all developing countries would not be treated in precisely the same way. . . . Although equality of treatment as between developing countries might not be fully achieved in certain markets, the movement would be in the direction of rather than away from equality.

39. One member of the Group underlined . . . his country's view [that] a key objective [was] . . . the gradual elimination of [special preferential] arrangements, in order [to] end pressure from developing countries outside existing . . . arrangements for action which might further fragment the world trading system.

40. In respect of tariff advantages enjoyed by some developed countries in the markets of some developing countries, there was a difference of view in the Group. It was maintained, on the one hand, that it would not be politically feasible for some developed countries to get legislative authority for special tariff treatment in favour of countries that were discriminating against their exports in favour of other developed countries. The opposing view was that . . . the basic idea was to confer a new benefit on the exports of developing countries without expecting any direct reciprocal benefit in return. To demand that developing countries granting [reverse preferences] . . . abandon them was in essence a demand for payment in return for conceding special tariff treatment.

Following the Report of the OECD Special Committee, UNCTAD II, meeting in New Delhi, in March, 1968, officially noted that there was "unanimous agreement" among the participants "in favor of the early establishment of a . . . system of generalized non-reciprocal and non–discriminatory preferences" for the benefit of developing countries and proceeded to establish a Special Committee on Preferences (the UNCTAD Special Committee) to carry out the consultations necessary to develop that system.[21]

While the broad outline formulated by the OECD Special Group emerged from the deliberations in UNCTAD II largely unchanged in spite of less developed

---

[21] Resolution 21 (II), Annex I to the Final Report, Proceedings of The United Nations Conference on Trade and Development, Second Session, Vol I. (E.68.II) at page 38 (1968).

country objections, differences over the future of special and reverse preferences still remained and surfaced again in the UNCTAD Special Committee.[22] With regard to existing special preferences, the African States agreed in that Committee to subscribe to the compensation formula enunciated by the OECD Special Group. The United States confined itself to expressing an assumption that GSP would "go a long way toward eliminating" these preferences but warned that should such schemes increase it would declare "the beneficiaries of such special preferences ineligible" under the American system. With this in hand the UNCTAD Special Committee was able to reach agreement in terms which:

(i) reiterated that beneficiaries of existing schemes expected compensation through access to new markets and

(ii) that in periodic UNCTAD reviews "careful consideration" would be given to whether those countries were in fact benefiting from the overall system.

The EEC was not entirely satisfied. The statement did not, in its view, fully reflect the wishes of the developing countries and that, therefore, the EEC reserved the right to adjust its GSP as necessary to redress any "adverse effects" that the overall scheme might have on its "associates."

NOTES AND QUESTIONS

(1) Suppose that the delivered price in the United States for a raw material not produced in this country was $100 dollars; that in semi-processed form the U.S. market price was $120; that in raw form the product entered the United States duty free but that in semi-processed form it was subject to a nominal duty of 5% *ad velorum*. What is the effective tariff rate on semi-processed imports (*i.e.*, how much below the American processors' costs would a foreign processor have to produce in order to compete in the American market? Express that difference (roughly) as a percentage of the American processors' costs. From a development point of view which would a less-developed country prefer to export; the raw or the semi-processed product?

(2) This problem is not fanciful. Because many developed countries do not produce certain important primary products used as industrial raw materials, there was, by the mid-1960s, a substantial trade in those materials that entered the developed countries duty free or at very low nominal rates.[23] At the same time

---

[22] In the UNCTAD Special Committee on Preferences, the United States initially took the position that developing countries granting reverse preferences should be "excluded" from GSP. It later softened this by announcing that any country giving the United States "adequate assurances" that its reverse preferences would be phased out within a reasonable time would be included in the American scheme from the outset. It then promised to be "reasonable" with regard to the "kind of assurances" required.

[23] In a study of the Kennedy Round, the GATT Secretariat noted that six developed participants in those negotiations (the EEC, Japan, Sweden, Switzerland, United Kingdom and the United States) accounted for 90% of all imports by developed countries from less

studies showed that, in the case of most products from less developed countries, developed country tariff structures were systematically higher the higher the level of processing.[24]

Why was this basic structural problem not likely to be seriously addressed in the ongoing course of the several GATT tariff negotiating rounds? In answering, consider the basic pattern of trade between the developed and less developed nations of the world as outlined in the Haberler Report, then recall the basic principles under which those negotiations occur.

(3) As the Haberler Report pointed out, another barrier against imports from less developed countries was to be found in the high levels of indirect taxes (the value added and other excise taxes) used, especially in Western Europe, as a source of revenue. Many of these products were not produced in those countries. Committee III of the GATT reported that in 1961 internal Western European taxes on coffee — then the second largest commodity in international trade accounting for 40%–70% of the foreign exchange earnings of fourteen countries — amounted to more than 100% of the ad velorum equivalent. The ad velorum equivalent for tea was even higher and for cocoa it was high in all countries reaching upwards of 50%. Together tea and cocoa accounted for the bulk of the foreign exchange earnings of four different countries. Tobacco posed an especially delicate problem. Important to a large number of less developed states, revenue was only one reason for the high internal taxes that prevailed throughout most of the developed world. In addition apart from the high level of these internal taxes and their adverse impact on demand, their administration was often attended with some not so subtle forms of discrimination (*e.g.*, the Case of the United States Wine-Gallon Method of taxing imports of liquor (*supra* page 268).

(4) Another major barrier to the expansion of less developed country exports was and continues to be the protectionist effects of developed country subsidies to their own producers of agricultural raw materials and foodstuffs.[25] All of these,

---

developed nations, and that in 1964 those six imported approximately $12.2 billion of such goods (excluding petroleum products, certain temperate foodstuffs and imports from preferential sources). Of this amount about $7.1 billion, or 58%, entered duty-free. Annex I to the Report of the Committee on Trade and Development adopted 21 November 1967 (L/2912), GATT, BISD 15th Supp. at page 149 (1968).

[24] For example, in both Great Britain and the EEC the nominal tariff rate for copper wire was 10% higher than the rate for raw cooper. This meant that the effective tariff rate on copper wire was 77%. In Sweden a nominal 3% differential yielded a 23% effective rate for copper wire while in the EEC a difference in the nominal rates for shelled groundnuts and for crude oil and cakes made from groundnuts resulted in an effective tariff on the latter of 140%.

[25] While, obviously, tropical products are not produced in the more temperate developed countries, the warmer regions of the United States and Europe do produce subsidized agricultural and forestry products important to the export earnings of many non-industrialized countries (*e.g.*, cotton, sugar, rice, tobacco, peanuts, citrus, lumber, vegetable oils and oilseeds). There are also temperate substitutes for competitive tropical products (*e.g.*, beet sugar for cane sugar, synthetic for natural fibers and rubber). Not a few developing countries are significant producers of the same temperate products as are the object of developed country subsidy schemes (*e.g.*, cereals, meats, wool, wood, leather-goods and wine). By 1968 less developed country share of total world exports was as follows: Tropical

in one way or another, provide domestic producers "a price which is to some degree divorced from the world price." Most such schemes contain a "stabilization" element and a "protective" element, which are not always easy to separate.[26] In addition, these schemes all exhibit some combination of the following features.

First, most employ measures that directly limit imports, including import duties, quantitative restrictions (mostly quotas), state-trading organizations, multiple exchange rate systems, mixing ratios and agreements with foreign exporters to limit their sales to the protected market.[27]

Second, most schemes support domestic producers in one or more of several basic ways. (i) They may make so-called "deficiency" payments equal either to the difference between the market price received by the producer for his product and some support price fixed by the government or equal to a defined shortfall in the producer's income from sales at market price. (ii) The subsidizing government may intervene directly in the market to maintain the desired or "supported" price, usually piling up substantial surpluses. Under these schemes:

(a) Identify the price that will govern the output decision of the domestic producer and the price that will govern the output decision of a foreign producer selling without benefit of a subsidy.

(b) If the latter price is on the average lower than the price governing the domestic producer, how would the output decisions of these two producers under a subsidy scheme differ from their output decisions if both operated under competition without subsidy?

(c) Identify the margin of protection that inheres in the subsidy scheme.

(5) Not infrequently domestic subsidy schemes result in pressures to subsidize exports. Assume Country A subsidizes its exports and Country B does not do so.

Products: Coffee (97%), Cocoa (98%), Tea (84%), Bananas (90%). Renewable Industrial Raw Materials: Raw Wood (43%), Leather & Skins (23%), Natural Rubber (98%); Cotton (57%), Wool (13%), Jute (95%), Heavy Fibres (97%). Agricultural Food Products and Tobacco: Fresh Meat (20%), Oilseeds (43%), Citrus (25%), Sugar (73%), Wheat (5%), Rice (40%), Other grains (12%), Tobacco (21%). Harris, The World Commodity Scene And The Common Agricultural Policy, Occasional Paper No. 1, The Centre For European Agricultural Studies, Wye College (University of London), Ashford, Kent, 1975 at page 37.

[26] The Haberler Panel Report explained: "Insofar as the price which thus accrues to the domestic producer is on the average equal to the world price but is merely more stable than the world price (being higher than the world price when the [latter] . . . is low, and lower . . . when the world price is high), the scheme may be said to be only a stabilization scheme. But insofar as [it works] . . . to keep the price paid to the domestic producer on the average above the world price, there is a "protective" element in the scheme." Report by a Panel of Experts, Trends in International Trade, General Agreement on Tariffs and Trade, Geneva, 1958 at page 67.

[27] Note that all of the devices described above are, in one way or another, subject to some constraint under the General Agreement (*e.g.*, Articles I, II, III, XI, XV, XVI). Some may be expressly outlawed and survive either through the Protocol of Provisional Application, or by waiver — usually with limiting conditions — or in sheer defiance of the GATT.

Again, identify the prices that will govern the output decisions of producers in Country A and producers in Country B. Which price is likely to be the higher and if so, how do those prices translate into a protective measure? Identify the protected market and the margin of protection? Lastly, what happens to the consumer in all of this?

(6) Turn next to Raul Prebisch's Report to UNCTAD I. His analogy between tariffs to protect infant industries and preferences for developing countries has a number of important implications. Classically the infant industry argument envisages a social investment — an investment in a country's economic development — by consumers of the country imposing the tariff. The investment — or subsidy, if you like — is financed through higher prices paid by consumers and received by those producers protected by the tariff. How does a preference differ from this? Who is making the social investment? Who is the beneficiary of that investment? In answering, assume imports from developing countries enter the preference granting country either (i) at the pre-preferential domestic price (*i.e.*, a price higher than the world price, the latter being the price that would prevail in the absence of tariffs) or (ii) at a price somewhat below the pre-preferential domestic price but above the world price. What are the political implications of this?

(7) Note that Prebisch admits that "some provision must be made for the elimination of preferences once the industries [of a less developed country] are firmly established." Obviously, they are not "infant industries" any longer. Isn't Prebisch's admission that, in such cases, the MFN tariff should be re-imposed anomalous? The political obstacles to GSP in the preference granting country have already been overcome (Recall Note (6) above). Perhaps more importantly, recall that the subsidy implicit in the preference is equal to the difference between the domestic price in the preference giving country and the world price. Thus, if an industry in a developing country succeeds in attaining some power over the domestic price in the preference granting industrialized country and, as a result, drives that price downward toward the world price, the subsidy is automatically reduced. Should that price actually reach the world price, the subsidy is automatically eliminated and, thereafter, any displacement of sales from producers outside the preference granting country constitutes trade creation.

Did Prebisch give away a potentially powerful lever for the liberalization of trade not only from the developing countries but trade more generally, especially if one considers the more highly industrialized of the developing countries (*e.g.*, what are now called the NICs such as Hong Kong, Singapore, South Korea and Taiwan) of which Prebisch was very much aware? Politically, did he have a choice?

(8) Prebisch, with good reason, was certainly concerned with how broadly or equitably the benefits of a GSP would be distributed among preference receiving countries. At this point Prebisch is skating on very thin ice and is aware of it. His concern tended to play directly into the hands of the French and the Belgians. In May of 1963 the so-called Brasseur Plan, named after the Belgian Minister of External Trade, had been submitted to GATT and later to the OECD in preparation for UNCTAD I. The Plan proposed the negotiation of "selective, temporary and digressive" preferences, product by product, between interested developed

and developing countries.[28] This was backed by a French Memorandum to UNCTAD I[29] in which it was argued that each developing country must be treated differently based upon their particular need for a preference in order to export and the extent to which they had engaged in "social" dumping (*i.e.*, keeping wages "abnormally" low) or had subsidized exports. Also, France contended, each product must be judged separately, and the grant of a preference by one developed country to a product from a particular developing country should in no way influence whether that product received a similar preference elsewhere. Preferences must be "selective as regards the countries which grant them or benefit from them" and "temporary and digressive as regards the products they effect." Transparent? Identify the opposition to this approach. Plainly it posed several problems for Prebisch. How does he attempt to address them?

(9) The United States' opposition to Prebisch's proposal stemmed, in part, from a strong belief in the MFN principle. But it was more complex than that. Consider the following:

   (a) In seeking to allay the fears his proposal might have generated, Prebisch necessarily painted the picture of a potentially new structure of trade relations cut through with possibilities for conflict. Identify those potential conflicts. Why might the United States, in particular, have viewed such a structure with special concern?

   (b) Recall that the AOT provisions of the Treaty of Rome were particularly abhorrent to the United States. Yet the United States was unprepared to force the issue of those provisions in GATT. Might not that experience have predisposed the United States' attitudes toward the GSP? If so, was the reaction sound? Might not Prebisch's ideas have been better seen as a riposte to the Rome Treaty arrangements? At one point Prebisch's makes a direct plea for the immediate elimination of all reverse preferences. There is a judgment call here. How might the French and Belgian position have influenced that judgment?

   (c) United States' implementation of a GSP would obviously require legislation. Why might the American Executive, with its deep concern for multilateralism, have viewed taking this matter to Congress with some trepidation? See discussion of U.S. legislation, *infra*.

(10) As noted, the United States, in opposing the GSP, initially tried to down play the benefits it would bring to less developed countries. Recall that in order for a less developed country industry to take advantage of a preference it must

---

[28] The essential points of the original plan are contained in a Statement by Maurice Brasseur, Minister for External Trade and Technical Assistance of Belgium, Proceedings, United Nations Conference on Trade and Development I, E/Conf.46/141, Vol II, at page 111, New York, N.Y., 1964.

[29] Memorandum Concerning Certain Items On The Agenda Of The United Nations Conference On Trade And Development, Submitted by France, Proceedings, United Nations Conference On Trade and Development, E/Conf.46/141, Vol. VI, at page 18, New York, N.Y., 1964.

at least be able to meet the domestic price in the preference granting market. With this as a base, the U.S. argument, as put by Patterson, was as follows:

> . . . it seems doubtful that the heights of the tariffs that might be reduced preferentially are now great enough to permit a large amount of help. The present average tariff level in the major developed countries amounts to only about 15 percent *ad velorum*. . . . [A]ssuming that the Kennedy round . . . is moderately successful, and that the level of tariffs on most manufactured goods is reduced by something in the neighbourhood of 35 per cent, the resulting . . . average level of *ad valorem* tariffs on all manufactured goods may turn out to be no more than 10 per cent. Account must also be taken of the fact that there will be great reluctance to give preferences that result in no tariffs at all or "zero tariffs". . . . Applying . . . [the 50% preferential rate that was most frequently talked about at the UNCTAD meetings] . . . to the assumed post-Kennedy round tariff, yields an average preference in the neighborhood of 5 per cent. . . . These calculations are, at best, only rough orders of magnitude. Still . . . [h]ow many cases are there where a 5–7 percent price advantage would be a decisive factor in making it possible for less developed countries to take markets in developed nations away from both domestic producers . . . *and* from producers of comparable manufactured goods in other industrial countries?[30]

Patterson also punctuates his argument by calling attention to the diluting effect that creation of both the EEC and EFTA would have on any preferences that the countries of Western Europe might give.

As it turned out, when the United States eventually came to establishing its GSP, the preferential rate for most products was a zero tariff. On that basis consider the following Problem concerning the sale of product X in the United States.

PROBLEM

World price of X (semi-manufacture) — $100
Cost of raw material — 70% of world price of X
U.S. tariff on X — 10% ad velorum
U.S. tariff on raw material — 8% ad velorum
U.S. has no domestic sources of raw material

Situation Confronting Producers of X

Costs (Excl. Production costs)	U.S. Producers	Preferred Foreign Prod.	Other Foreign Prod.

---

[30] Gardner Patterson, Would Tariff Preferences Help Economic Development?, Lloyds Bank Review, No. 76 (April, 1965), pp. 26-27.

Raw Material Tariff on	$70.00	$70.00	$70.00
Raw Material Tariff on	$5.60	0	0
Prod. X	0	0	10.00
Total Margin avail. for Production Costs at world price	$75.60	$70.00	$80.00
	$24.40	$30.00	$20.00

Recall the distinction drawn earlier between nominal tariff rates and effective tariff rates. With that distinction in mind and using the example above calculate:

(a) the "margin of protection" that American Producers would forfeit to Preferred Foreign Producers if the latter were given duty free entry for their products into the United States. Note that continuation of the 8% tariff on raw materials constitutes what is called a "negative tariff". Explain.

(b) The "margin of preference" that Preferred Foreign Producers would receive over Non-Preferred Foreign Producers if their products were to enter the United States duty free.

Is this of no help?[31]

(11) Turn next to the OECD Special Group's Report. Recall the Group concluded that developing nations then enjoying special preferences should be compensated for their loss of advantage by increased export opportunities in new markets under the GSP. At a practical level there is something dubious about this proposition, is there not? Explain. In spite of these doubts, reflect upon the utility of the Report's formulation and begin to reflect upon the function performed by such formulations in international relations and in the wider development of international law.

(12) Recall that the European members of the Special Group used the "no-reciprocity" argument to avoid abandoning their reverse preferences. As legal adviser to the American representative on the Special Group, what response would you make to that argument?

(13) Examine the resolution of the special preferences problem that was worked out in the UNCTAD II Special Committee on Preferences. It is a wonderful juxtaposition, is it not! Do we now have some law on the subject of special preferences? Suppose, for example, that the Lome States started losing their

---

[31] A better appreciation of the actual situation confronting UNCTAD I can be obtained by examining Table I in the Documentary Supplement at page 129 which shows for selected product groups the aggregate subsidy available to domestic value added under the corresponding pre-Kennedy (*i.e.*, 1962) nominal tariff rate. This constitutes the "margin of preference" potentially available to preference receiving producers as against non-preferred foreign sources of supply. The Table also shows the implicit tax on domestic producers; the so-called "negative tariff."

traditional share of the EEC market to the Latin Americans and that because those losses were not offset by gains in the American market the EEC adjusted its preferential rates in ways that seriously disadvantaged the Latin Americans. Can the United States, citing the EEC's action, declare the Lome States ineligible under its scheme? If so, why? Because the EEC acted illegally? Or, alternatively, because it had reserved the right to retaliate in that fashion without necessarily implying that the EEC acted illegally? If illegality is implied, what significance do you attach to the EEC's reservation of a right to adjust its system? to the United States' statement and consequent action? If there is law here, reflect on its nature and function.

(14) In contrast to their position on special preferences, the Europeans and their overseas "associates" rapidly receded on the question of reverse preferences. How might you explain this difference? Is there something of an emergent value consensus here?

Throughout the UNCTAD, GATT and OECD discussions, the question of the legal "framework" for the GSP kept recurring. The problem was how to get around the apparently unqualified nature of the MFN undertaking in Article I of the GATT. When a waiver under Article XXV:5 was suggested, the developing countries strongly objected. They argued that application of MFN to their trade relations was a discredited aberration of the past. Differential treatment was to be the rule and hence GSP, as an expression of differential treatment, could not be the subject of a waiver; it was not an "exception" but part of an emerging GATT regime. Moreover, Article XXV:5 authorized waivers of "obligations," so that a waiver for GSP would reaffirm MFN (Article I) as the obligatory element and imply that GSP was the exception, empty of any obligatory connotation whatsoever. The developing nations also argued more affirmatively that Part IV of the General Agreement already contained a limitation upon the broad mandate of Article I sufficient to sustain GSP, especially the statement in Article XXXVI:8 that the developed countries did "not expect reciprocity for commitments" in trade negotiations with the developing countries.[32] To the developed countries this line of argument came too close to being a claim of a legal right to preferential treatment by the developing countries. Accordingly, the OECD Special Group announced that the OECD states would not consider the grant of "temporary tariff advantages to developing countries . . . as constitut[ing] a binding commitment"

---

[32] In addition to the non-reciprocity undertaking, the representatives of the less developed countries contended that in Article XXXVI:1(a) the contracting parties had recognized that one objective of the GATT was the economic development of the less developed countries and that international trade, "as a means" to that end, "should be governed by such rules and procedures as are consistent with the objectives set-forth in" that Article. These broader principles had then been carried forward in the more specific undertakings for joint action in Article XXXVIII and for action by individual developed country members of GATT in Article XXXVII, including the undertaking in Paragraph 1(a) of the latter to "accord high priority to the reduction and elimination" of barriers to trade in products of special interest to less developed countries.

and should not in any way "impede the reduction of tariffs on an [MFN] basis." In all events, after the UNCTAD Committee's final report was issued (October, 1970),[33] the decision was made to invoke Article XXV:5 and, in June 1971, GATT issued a waiver of Art. I:1, authorizing individual developed countries to establish their own GSP programs extending preferential tariff treatment to developing countries for a period of ten years, provided the arrangement did not raise "barriers to the trade of other contracting parties." The Decision embodying the waiver expressly noted the point made by the OECD Special Group.[34]

On July 1, 1971 the EEC announced implementation of the first full-fledged GSP scheme and within the year ten more developed countries established their programs. The United States followed suit with the enactment of Title V of the Trade Act of 1974,[35] the provisions of which were not actually implemented, however, until January 1, 1976. As of this writing some nineteen developed country members of the OECD have established some form of GSP.

Notwithstanding the OECD members earlier opposition, by the end of the Tokyo Round attitudes had sufficiently changed to where the contracting parties were willing to promulgate a so-called "enabling clause" providing a "permanent legal basis" for preferences in favor of developing countries. The phrase "enabling clause" was employed, however, to make clear that it did not establish a legal obligation to grant preferences.[36]

[C] The United States' Generalized System Of Preferences

Here we briefly examine Title V of the Trade Act of 1974 as amended[37] (the "1974 Act"). Its stated purpose, of course, was to promote the economic development of the non-industrialized countries. Recall, however, that no industry in a preference receiving country can benefit from a tariff preference until it is sufficiently competitive to sell at the market price in the preference giving nation and that beyond that threshold point export expansion can occur only with improvements in the recipient industry's efficiency and productive capacity. If those improvements are pronounced enough the result may be substantial downward pressure on prices in the preference giving market which the domestic industry will have to match or lose market share. All too cognizant of this, the developed countries made very plain that they would not allow the GSP to

---

[33] Official Records Of The Trade And Development Board, Tenth Session, Supplement No. 6 (TD/B/300/Rev.1) and No. 6A (TD/B/329/Rev.1.) (1970).

[34] Decision of the Contracting Parties of 25 June 1971, L/3545, GATT, BISD, 18th Supp., at page 24 (1972).

[35] Pub. L. 93-618, Title V, Section 501 *et. seq.*, January 3, 1975, 88 Stat. 2066, 19 U.S.C. Section 2461 *et. seq.*

[36] Olivier Long, Law And Its Limitations In The GATT Multilateral System, Martinus Nijhoff Publishers, 1985 at page 100. In addition, while some delegations thought the clause should appear as a new Article of the General Agreement, others thought that it should stand only as a decision or declaration of the contracting parties. As a result the clause was promulgated without prejudice to the determination of its eventual legal status.

[37] Pub. L. 93-618, Title V, Section 501 *et. seq.*, Jan. 3, 1975, 88 Stat. 2066, 19 U.S.C. Section 2461 *et. seq.* as amended by Pub. L. 94-455, Oct. 4. 1976, 90 Stat 1763, Pub. L.96-39, Title XI, July 26, 1979, 93 Stat. 312, Pub L. 98-573, Title V, Oct. 30, 1984, 98 Stat. 3019 and Pub. L. 99-47, June 11, 1985, 99 Stat. 85.

seriously prejudice their own economies. Consequently as the several national GSP schemes evolved — the American, the European and the Japanese — they were cut through with manifestations of a tension between the development goals of the GSP and the autarchic propensities of the "donor" states. While it is almost impossible to measure precisely what contribution the GSP may have made to export growth by the developing countries, it is necessary to ask how rationally the American scheme has come to grips with this tension and with what results.

The American experience with the GSP should also be viewed in the broader context of the multilateral trading system. Multilateral MFN tariff reductions, negotiated under the "reciprocity" principle, are frequently "bound" and cannot be raised, except under certain safeguard procedures, without a substantial risk of retaliation. This is not so with the grant of a preference. Paradoxically, therefore, when a tariff reduction spurs improved efficiency and increased productive capacity in a developing country, that effect is more likely to have the continuity needed to further the country's overall economic development if the tariff reduction was negotiated on an MFN basis rather than being promulgated unilaterally under a GSP scheme. The legal foundation for this difference is, of course, implicit in the understandings that led to the promulgation of the "enabling clause," but there is more to it. The question is whether the difference is undergird by a more fundamental normative consensus regarding the importance of multilateralism in the conduct of trade policy. If this is so, does the GSP signal a weakening of that consensus? On the other hand, does the GSP experience tend to underscore the value of MFN? Furthermore, do the differences between the two systems — MFN and GSP — shed new light on the function of the "reciprocity" principle; has the GSP weakened the functional dynamics of that principle or, again paradoxically, has GSP given "reciprocity" both a stronger conceptual foundation and a broader practical application?

Designation of "Beneficiary Developing Countries" — (Sections 501 and 502 of the 1974 Act)

Section 501 authorizes the President, after having taken a number of broad considerations into account,[38] to provide "duty-free treatment" for "eligible article[s]" from "beneficiary developing countr[ies]," the latter constituting any country that expresses "its desire" to be designated and is then declared to be such by the President (Section 502(a)).

Next, Section 502(b) prohibits the designation of the members of the EEC, sixteen additional developed countries, communist countries, and OPEC countries.[39] That same provision also sets forth an extensive list of other disqualifying

---

[38] These are: whether such action will further the economic development of developing countries, whether other developed nations are mounting similar programs, likely impact on U.S. producers and the designated country's competitiveness with respect to eligible articles.

[39] Initially the exclusion of OPEC members resulted in the denial of beneficiary status to three countries, Ecuador, Venezuela and Indonesia, that had not participated in the 1973-74 oil boycott but did raise their prices in line with other OPEC members. This denial occasioned much criticism, especially in Latin America, with the result that Section 1111(a)(2) of the Trade Agreements Act of 1979 (Pub. L. 96-39, 93 Stat. 315) added what is now Section 502(d)(2) authorizing the President to exempt from Section 502(b)(2) any

considerations.⁴⁰ While the statute avoids fixing any hard quantitative measure of what constitutes a developing country (but see; Section 504(f) added by the 1984 Amendment), it does lay out a number of factors that the President must take into account, including, the country's level of economic development, whether other developed countries are extending GSP treatment to that country and the extent to which it has assured the United States of equitable and reasonable access to its own markets.⁴¹ As of January 1988, 112 independent nations and 29 non-independent countries and territories were designated "beneficiary developing countries" under the U.S. GSP scheme.⁴²

Designation of Eligible Articles

After receiving a list of articles from the President, the International Trade Commission (ITC) is required to determine the probable economic effect of duty free entry into the United States of each article on the list.⁴³ The Commission's

---

country that entered into a product specific agreement under Section 102 of the 1974 Act ensuring the United States "fair and equitable access to [petroleum] supplies." By dint of this provision the three countries listed above were designated beneficiary countries.

⁴⁰ These pertain to: (1) Countries that grant reverse preferences to other developed nations. This provision, of course, was directed principally at the ACP States and with regard to those States was largely resolved by the terms of the Lome I Agreement. In addition, the provision raised problems in the case of Cyprus, Greece, Israel, Portugal, Spain and Turkey. Greece, Portugal and Spain are now members of the EEC and hence ineligible. All of the others are presently designated beneficiary countries. (2) Countries that have expropriated American owned property. Shortly after enactment some 18 countries were found to have nationalized U.S. property but were determined by the President to have been taking steps to carry out their obligations under international law (Exec. Order No. 11,888, 40 Fed. Reg. 55275 (1975). More serious problems existed in the case of Somalia, Uganda and Yemen (Sana) all of which appear to have been resolved since all three are currently listed as designated beneficiary countries. In 1980 Ethiopia was removed from the list under this provision. (3) Countries that fail to cooperate with the United States in stemming the narcotics trade, (4) Countries that do not recognize arbitral awards in favor of American citizens, (5) Countries that aid or abet terrorism, and (6) Countries that fail to accord their workers "internationally recognized worker rights" (See Section 502(a)(4) for a description of these rights). Items (2) through (6) will not operate to disqualify a country if the President certifies that its designation "will be in the national economic interest of the United States".

⁴¹ Under Paragraph (5) of Section 502(c), the President must also consider whether the country is providing adequate protection to intellectual property rights. This provision was added by the 1984 Amendment in response to growing American business concern with the counterfeit goods problem. In like manner, new Paragraph (c)(6) reflects an ongoing American interest in liberalizing trade in services as well as our growing concern with new non-tariff barriers to trade in goods such as foreign laws that constrain U.S. investors from purchasing their inputs from the United States or impose export and other performance requirements that can lead to below cost pricing and other trade distorting practices.

⁴² Headnote 3(c)(ii)(A), Harmonized, Tariff Schedules of the United States, USITC Publication No 2030.

⁴³ More specifically, Section 503(a) requires the ITC to exercise the mandate contained in Section 131 of the 1974 Act under which the Commission must judge the probable economic effect that duty free entry of the article under GSP will have on domestic industries producing like or directly competitive articles and on consumers, including an assessment of its likely effect on domestic employment, profit levels and on the use of domestic productive facilities (Section 131(d)(2) of the 1974 Act).

report is then sent to the President who decides which items to designate as GSP "eligible articles" (Section 503(a)). The statute, however, explicitly forecloses the designation of a number of so-called "import-sensitive" products by name[44] and then adds to the list "any other articles which the President determines to be import sensitive in the context of . . . " the GSP (Section 503(c)(1)). Finally, the President is authorized to withdraw, suspend or limit the application of duty-free treatment with respect to the importation of any previously designated article from a specified country (Section 504(a)(1)).

Following the initial designation under Section 503(a) of some 2,724 separate articles by President Ford in 1975, the two provisions — the new designations and the withdrawals or limitations — were administratively brought together in a single annual product review.[45] By 1984 over 3,000 separate items in the Tariff Schedule of the United States had been designated eligible for GSP treatment, although a significant number of those articles were not eligible when imported from beneficiary countries that were subject either to a competitive need limit or had been graduated, all as discussed below.

Some Basic Data

Data for the years 1981 through 1985[46] show the following: (i) total imports from countries designated GSP beneficiaries rose from $79.8 billion in 1981 to $107.6 billion in 1985, averaging nearly 33% of total U.S. imports annually; (ii) of total imports from beneficiary countries in 1981, only $16.8 billion, or 21%, consisted of products eligible for GSP (duty free) treatment, (iii) by 1985 eligible

---

[44] These are: (i) textiles subject to textile agreements, watches, import sensitive electronic articles, import sensitive steel, footwear and other leather goods, import sensitive glassware.

[45] Under current regulations a request or petition by an interested party, including a foreign government, to designate a new article (Section 503(a)) or to withdraw, suspend or limit an existing designation (Section 504(a)) must be submitted by June 1 in any year. By July 15 the Trade Policy Staff Committee (TPSC) — an interagency group chaired by a representative of the Office of Trade Representative and composed of senior trade officials from nine other Executive Departments or agencies, including the ITC — determines which petitions contain the requisite information and also merit "further consideration" and hence are "accepted for review". Where required (*e.g.*, new designation) or otherwise appropriate the petition may be submitted to the ITC. In addition, hearings on the petition are held before a Sub-committee of the TPSC and an opportunity given for public comment on the ITC's report. Ultimately, recommendations go forward, first from the GSP Sub-Committee through several levels of interagency review under the chairmanship of the Office of Trade Representative and then from the Trade Representative to the President. Decisions are announced April 1 of the following year to become effective July 1 of that year. (15 C.F.R. Ch. XX, Part 2007). Judicial review of the President's decision lies within the exclusive jurisdiction of the Court of International Trade. *Barclay Industries Inc. v. Carter*, 494 F. Supp. 912 (D.D.C., 1980).

[46] Source for all the data given below is: International Trade Commission: Operation Of The Trade Agreements Program, 33d Report (1981) ITC Pub. No. 1308 at 222; 34th Report (1982) ITC Pub. No 1414 at 275; 35th Report (1983) ITC Pub. No. 1535 at 382; 36th Report (1984) ITC Pub. No. 1725 at 219; 37th Report (1985) ITC Pub. No. 1871 at 252. For a fuller statement of these data see GSP Tables, Table II in the Documentary Supplement.

imports had reached $32.7 billion, or 30% of total U.S. imports from beneficiary countries;[47] (iv) overall, GSP eligible imports as a percent of total U.S. imports from all sources, was 6.5% in 1981 and rose steadily to about 9.9% in 1985.[48]

Note that these data do not represent imports that actually entered duty free under GSP. They represent only the value of articles from beneficiary countries which were of a type that would qualify for GSP treatment if all other requirements were met and, as such, represent only a modest percentage of all imports from those countries. They represent an even more modest percentage of total U.S. imports.

In addition, for 1985, imports of products eligible for GSP (duty free) treatment from all sources (not just designated beneficiary countries) totalled $113.1 billion or 39% of total U.S. non-petroleum imports. Of these total GSP eligible imports, $80.5 billion, however, came from countries that were *not designated as GSP beneficiaries*. Only $32.7 billion came from beneficiary countries. In other words, in 1985, 71.2% of all imports of products eligible for GSP treatment came from countries not eligible for such treatment, while only 28.8% came from GSP beneficiary countries.

One way of characterizing these data is to say that the U.S. GSP Program was intended to give beneficiary developing countries an advantage in the competition to supply the $113.1 billion of GSP eligible articles imported by the U.S. in 1985. In that competition beneficiary countries have succeeded in capturing only between 29% and 32% of the potential business, percentages which roughly approximate their share of total U.S. imports.[49]

---

[47] Total beneficiary country imports includes both imports that are subject to an m.f.n. duty and those that are non-dutiable on an m.f.n. basis. Obviously, GSP, as a program designed to assist in expanding developing country exports, is important only if the goods would otherwise be dutiable. Hence, GSP eligible imports as a percent of total "dutiable" imports by beneficiary countries is a better measure of the program's coverage than the percentages stated above which are based upon total beneficiary country imports both dutiable and non-dutiable. Unfortunately, the Source Reports do not give us the breakdown and UNCTAD data which does distinguish between MFN dutiable and MFN non-dutiable imports are not available for the years following 1982. For the years 1978-1982, however, the UNCTAD data show that "MFN non-dutiable" imports from beneficiary countries ranged between 16% and 24% of total imports from those countries. If we then took 22% as a rough approximation of "non-dutiable" imports for each of the years 1981-85, reduced total beneficiary country imports by that margin and recalculated, the percentages given at this point improve as follows: 1981 increases to 27% and rises steadily thereafter until it reaches 38% for 1985. A similar adjustment to the percent of beneficiary country imports that were not eligible for GSP treatment would be misleading because the percentage of non-eligible imports that are "non-dutiable" is likely to be smaller than the percentage of total beneficiary country imports in that category. We can only say, therefore, that the 79% to 70% range given is somewhat overstated as one indicia of the Program's limitations.

[48] The figure for total U.S. imports includes imports of petroleum products. When those imports are excluded the percentages improve slightly, 1981 — 9.4%; 1985 — 11.3%.

[49] These percentages cannot be strictly compared because the sources used (see Note 46) do not break out total petroleum imports from total beneficiary country imports. Hence the value of total U.S. imports and total beneficiary country imports shown in the first set of data given above necessarily includes those products. For the second set of data, however, since petroleum products are not GSP eligible, it is possible to show the values and compute the percentages exclusive of petroleum.

Doubtless there a number of factors contributing to this situation. One factor is the erosion of the beneficiary countries' margin of preference that inevitably occurred as the Tokyo Round MFN tariff reductions took effect. In spite of this, however, and while the point has been disputed, the better analysis seems to be that the gains to developing country trade resulting from the Tokyo Round MFN reductions exceeded any losses suffered by reason of the diminished margin of preference.[50]

Another major feature of the U.S. GSP Program lies in the disparate proportion of eligible imports originating in the economically most advanced of the beneficiary countries. Thus, of the $32.7 billion of products eligible for GSP treatment imported from all beneficiary countries in 1985, $27.5 billion, or 84.1%, came from "advanced beneficiary" countries, $4.9 billion, or 15%, came from "middle income beneficiary" countries and $300 million, or .9%, came from "low income beneficiary" countries.

"Competitive Need Limits" and "Graduation"

Apart from the original designation of eligible articles, the provisions that have had the greatest affect on the scope of the U.S. Program are the "competitive-need" limits and the practice of "graduation." The 1974 Act contains two standard "competitive need" limits (Section 504(c)(1)). The first is an annual quantitative limit of $25 million increased by an amount equal to the ratio between the U.S. GNP in 1974 and the year under consideration. If the current GNP is three times the 1974 GNP, the limit for the current year would be $75 million. Any beneficiary country that exports a particular eligible article in excess of the annual limit looses its beneficiary designation with respect to that article for the ensuing year.

Under the second "competitive need" limit, any designated beneficiary that exports to the United States more than 50% of the total U.S. imports of a designated article loses its beneficiary status with respect to that article in the ensuing year. There are, however, a number of exemptions to this limit.[51]

The impact of these limitations, as well as of other exclusions, is illustrated by the fact that of the $32.7 billion of products eligible for GSP treatment imported into the United States in 1985 from beneficiary countries, only $13.3 billion actually entered duty-free under GSP. $19.4 billion did not receive that treatment. Of the $19.4 billion, $15.4 billion, or 79%, were denied duty free treatment because of the competitive need limitations and $4 billion, or 11%, were excluded for other reasons. Of the $15.4 billion of imports denied GSP treatment under the competitive need limitations, $14.5 billion, or 95%, came from the "advanced beneficiary" countries and $900 million, or 5%, came from all other beneficiary countries. In sum, in 1985 the total of beneficiary country imports that entered under the MFN rates because of the competitive need limitations exceeded the total beneficiary country imports that entered duty-free under GSP. Plainly, the

---

[50] Ballassa, *The Tokyo Round And The Developing Countries*, 14 J. World Trade L. 93 (1980).

[51] The exemptions are: one exemption applicable only to the Philippines, an exemption for the least-developed countries, an exemption where no competitive article is produced in the United States and de-minimis imports. (Section 504(c)(4) and (6) and 504(d)(1) and (2)).

advanced beneficiary developing countries have borne by far the largest portion of these exclusions.

In its Report on the 1974 Act, the Senate Finance Committee explained these competitive need limits as measures designed for "those cases where [preferential treatment] . . . can no longer be justified on grounds of promoting the development of an industry in a particular developing country" and also "to provide more opportunities to the least developed countries".[52]

In addition to the competitive need limitations contained in the original 1974 Act, the 1984 amendment added an additional exclusion. Any beneficiary country that is determined by the President to have a "sufficient degree of competitiveness" with respect to a particular eligible article will lose the right of duty free entry for that article in any year following the year in which its exports to the United States exceed either (i) 25%, rather than 50%, of total U.S. imports of the article or (ii) $25 million adjusted upwards for any increase in the U.S. GNP over the base year of 1984, rather than 1974.

With regard to these more stringent limits the statute itself makes clear that a "sufficient degree of competitiveness" with respect to any eligible product means competitiveness relative to other beneficiary countries. Note, however, that the competitiveness determination is linked to a broader Presidential review under all of the criteria in Section 501 and 502(c). The Senate Finance Committee Report accompanying the 1984 Renewal makes the linkage clear. The more stringent limits will, the Committee observed:

 . . . most affect products from the advanced developing counties [sic] that are the major program beneficiaries. These [countries] offer the greatest opportunities for U.S. export growth, but in many cases have been slow to adopt . . . the obligations and responsibilities of the international trading system. The committee thus intends that the general review emphasize opportunities for market access in its competitiveness determinations.[53]

On January 2, 1987 the President announced that nine named countries had "demonstrated a sufficient degree of competitiveness" with regard to certain designated articles (totaling for all countries 293 articles) to merit application of the reduced limits.[54] At the same time the President invoked his authority (Section 504(c)(3)) to waive the application of all competitive need limitations with respect to imports of certain other eligible articles (68 in all) from five of the

---

[52] S. Rep. No. 1298; Report on H.R. 10710, Trade Reform Act of 1974; Committee on Finance, United States Senate, 93d Cong. 2d Sess., November 26, 1974 at 227. See also: H. Rep. 1090; Report on the Generalized System of Preferences Renewal Act of 1984; Committee on Ways and Means, House of Representatives, 98th Cong. 2d Sess., September 27, 1984 at page 16.

[53] S. Rep 485; Renewal of the Generalized System of Preferences; Report of the Committee on Finance, United States Senate, 98th Cong. 2d Sess., May 24, 1984 at page 14.

[54] The countries and the number of eligible articles from each that were subjected to the reduced limit are as follows: Taiwan 139 articles; Korea 41 articles; Hong Kong 37 articles; Mexico, 36 articles; Brazil, 29 articles; Argentina, 6 articles; Singapore, 3 articles; Colombia and Yugoslavia, 1 article each. Actions Concerning The Generalized System Of Preferences; Memorandum of January 2, 1987, 52 Fed. Reg. 389 (January 6, 1987).

nine beneficiary countries to whom the reduced limitations were to apply.[55] Apparently the linkage that the Senate Committee sought to forge is not to be too rigorously applied.

Closely related to these competitive need limitations is the President's use of his authority under Section 504(a)(1) to "graduate" a beneficiary by declaring it no longer eligible to receive GSP treatment for a particular eligible article. In practical terms graduation covers: (i) a refusal to restore GSP benefits to a country that otherwise qualifies for that restoration by staying within the competitive need limits during the year of denial; (ii) excluding a particular country from receiving GSP treatment for a newly designated eligible article of which it is the leading supplier even if its exports are below the competitive need limits; and (iii) removing a country that has not exceeded the competitive need limits from eligibility for a particular product if it has otherwise demonstrated its competitiveness in the U.S. market.

The trade represented by these graduations has steadily increased since the inception of the practice in 1981. In that year graduation covered what, in 1980, had been $510 million of trade under GSP. In 1983 the figure reached $900 million, in 1984, $1.2 billion and in 1985 $1.8 billion, all based upon the immediately preceding year's GSP imports of the excluded items.

A Broader Appraisal

Because growth in the real volume of trade is a highly complex function of numerous factors, it is not possible to isolate with any degree of rigor the extent to which the United States GSP Program may have contributed to the expansion of exports by beneficiary developing countries or to the latter's economic development. Nevertheless, there are some "straws in the wind" suggesting that the contribution, at least with respect to a number of beneficiary countries, has not been negligible.

For the five years ending with 1985, the average annual nominal rate of growth in total U.S. imports, including petroleum, was 7.8%. During the same period, the average annual rate of growth of all U.S. imports from beneficiary developing countries was 8.3% while imports from those same countries of GSP eligible items grew at the average annual rate of 18.4%. Only some of this latter growth can be attributed to the addition of new articles to the GSP eligible list. Furthermore, attesting to both the overall positive effect of the program and the propensity of the competitive need and graduation limitations to constrain that effect, the average annual rate of growth in imports entering duty free under GSP was 13.4%, a figure 5.1% higher than the growth rate in total beneficiary imports but 5% below the growth rate for imports of all eligible articles.

In addition, the International Trade Commission in a survey conducted as part of its Report on the First Five Years' of the Program, noted, not surprisingly, that most of the major beneficiaries (Taiwan, Korea, Malaysia, Singapore, Israel and India) acknowledged a direct relationship between GSP and domestic economic development[56] as did a number of countries accounting for a more modest share

---

[55] Taiwan and Hong Kong each received a waiver with regard to 17 articles; Singapore, 15 articles; South Korea, 12 articles and Columbia 7 articles.

[56] Korea noted that GSP had stimulated small and medium sized industries and had led to a diminished role for textiles and footwear. Malaysia cited a diversification from raw

of total GSP imports (Haiti, Honduras, Sri Lanka and Kenya). A number of beneficiaries (Argentina, Brazil, Colombia, Costa Rica, Haiti and Uruguay) cited specific examples of "major export expansion as a result of GSP". On the other hand most Near Eastern, Asian and African countries, with only marginal trade ties to the United States, thought that the U.S. program had had no impact on their economies. Nevertheless, several (Botswana, Kenya, Lesotho and Mozambique) cited certain general benefits, and a number of ACP States which had made little use of the American program signaled a desire to do so "as a means of diversifying export markets and lessening dependence on Europe."[57]

Lastly, one UNCTAD sponsored study examined the increase in GSP imports to the United States between 1970 and 1980[58] and estimated that 65% of the increase was attributable to increases in apparent U.S. consumption, 31.2% was attributable to improvements in GSP product coverage and beneficiary country diversification, the latter partially in response to GSP, 2.3% was attributable to improvements in the beneficiary countries' competitive position and only 1.5% attributable to the displacement by GSP imports of U.S. domestic production or of imports from non-beneficiary countries because of the preferential grant of duty free treatment. Over two-thirds of this 1.5% represented displacement of non-beneficiary imports and less than one-third represented displacement of U.S. domestic production.[59]

One general conclusion suggested by these data is that, because of inadequate product coverage, the competitive need limits and "graduation," the U.S. Program has far from realized its full potential as a means of aiding the economic development of its intended beneficiaries. Moreover, an International Trade Commission study of products in which GSP imports constituted a significant factor in rising "import penetration" of the U.S. market showed that overall that penetration was modest, but that a number of specific products, within the broader categories studied, did experience large absolute gains and did capture a significantly larger portion of the American market than the aggregate figures show.[60]

---

materials to related light industry exports, Singapore a high growth of domestic value-added and upgraded technology and Taiwan indicated that 6% of its GNP was directed toward GSP exports. India noted a 41% annual increase in GSP exports to the United States between 1976 and 1978, twice the overall export growth rate to the United States, while GSP exports from Israel were 67% higher than overall exports to the United States. Hong Kong and Chile thought that their own free-trade policies were more influential in fostering economic development than was GSP, a point with which one could hardly take issue. *Id.* note 79 at page 34-35.

[57] *Id.* Note 79 at page 83.

[58] The study uses, for the year 1970, imports of articles which would have been eligible for GSP treatment had the U.S. had a program in that year comparable to the program commenced in 1976.

[59] MacPhee, Craig, Evaluation Of The Trade Effects Of The Generalized System Of Preferences, Document TD/B/C.5/87, 19 January 1984, reprinted in United Nations Conference on Trade and Development, Operation And Effects Of The Generalized System Of Preferences, selected studies submitted to the Special Committee on Preferences at its eleventh and twelfth sessions, TD/B/C.5/100, New York, 1985 at page 72.

[60] GSP imports of sugar increased from $83.3 million in 1978 to $713.7 million in 1981 representing 17% of the domestic market in the latter year. GSP imports of canned fish accounted for 21% of the domestic market in 1981, GSP imports of glass mirrors increased

The very existence of these exceptions, however, serves to raise the larger question concerning the rationality of the competitive need limits and the "graduation" policy. As the ITC study makes clear, while other factors enter in,[61] these limitations together with the statutory product exclusions and the limited product coverage have combined to provide American producers with ample protection.

In its Eighth General Report on the Implementation of the Generalized System of Preferences[62] the UNCTAD Secretariat undertook to place GSP into the larger framework of "international trade relations as a whole" and, in so doing, made the following observations:

> The likelihood of the emergence of developing countries as the most dynamic partners in international trade during the late 1970s and early 1980s was not foreseen when the GSP was established. . . . [Nevertheless] [d]eveloping country beneficiaries have become . . . the main markets for the expansion of exports of the three main preference-giving countries. For every dollar increase in the imports from beneficiaries, throughout the period 1976-1982, their increase in exports to those beneficiaries exceeded $1, being $1.12 for the United States, $1.81 for EEC and $1.69 for Japan. . . . It might be argued that the effect of the GSP has, in terms of trade balances, been to increase the mutual benefits of trade and not simply to benefit one group of countries. . . . [Thus];

> The increasing importance of beneficiary country markets for the United States is reflected by the fact that while, before 1976, EEC was the main source of United States' trade creation surplus, it has since been replaced by the developing country beneficiaries of the United States scheme;

> The EFTA countries, which actually receive greater preferential treatment in EEC than the GSP beneficiaries, . . . have ironically been replaced since 1976 [as a principal EEC export market] by those developing countries which have been subject to differentiation or graduation measures under the EEC scheme;

> In Japan, the developing countries' fast growing exporters of manufactures have become, since 1976, the second source, after the United States, of Japan's trade surpluses;

> [Moreover] among developing country beneficiaries, it is those most subject to the restriction on preferential access that have shown the greatest tendency

---

from 2.9% to 5.8% in the period studied, by 1981 GSP imports of mechanical equipment had captured 6.1% of domestic consumption, with individual items attaining even larger portions of the market, and GSP imports of electrical equipment 5.8% of the market while GSP imports of costume jewelry rose from 6.6% to 12.7% of domestic consumption in the period 1978-1981. *Id.* at pages vi-ix and page 59.

[61] The other factors cited by the ITC Study are the temporary nature of the program, manufacturing limitations in many beneficiary countries such as lack of technology, manufacturing capacity, basic infrastructure, skilled labor and adequate capital and the generally low preferential margins available to most GSP imports because of the low MFN rate. *Id.* at page vi.

[62] UNCTAD Document TD/B/C.5/90, 26 March 1984 contained in UNCTAD, Operation and Effects of the Generalized System of Preferences, Selected Studies submitted to the Eleventh and Twelfth Sessions of the Special Committee on Preferences, TD/B/C.5/100, 1985 at page 14.

to become the most dynamic markets for preference-giving countries' exports. . . . In their trade relations with the United States [for example] it is the beneficiaries affected by competitive need limitations which have shown most dynamism in creating United States surpluses. The same phenomenon is apparent in EEC.[63]

While the UNCTAD Secretariat was elsewhere careful to disclaim any suggestion that the GSP was solely or even principally responsible for the export growth described above, its argument was nevertheless clear:

Both the development needs of developing countries and the mutuality of interests are cogent arguments for doing away with all forms of graduation measures or at least for raising the competitive need limitations.[64]

NOTES AND QUESTIONS

(1) Critics, including the UNCTAD Secretariat, have claimed that certain of the conditions that a less developed country must meet in order to be designated a "beneficiary country," especially those calling for improved U.S. access to markets in that country and protection of U.S. "intellectual" and other property rights, were "at complete variance with the agreements reached in international organizations," especially the principles of "non-reciprocity" and "differential treatment".[65]

In its critique the UNCTAD Secretariat also contended that the "GSP . . . [was] designed to assist developing countries in achieving development objectives, and its use for other purposes would clearly be incompatible with the system's basic principles. . . ."

    (a)   Are you persuaded that the conditions contained in the U.S. legislation have no development implications?

    (b)   More fundamentally, evaluate the efficacy of the Secretariat's appeal to principles of "non-reciprocity" and "differential treatment" in light of the political dynamics implicit in the data about the U.S. program given above. Could it be that the less developed countries have squandered away their bargaining leverage? Have they become so preoccupied with "reciprocity" as experienced in the narrow context of tariff negotiations and so mesmerized by the rhetoric of "differential and unequal treatment," that they have failed to recognize the broader possibilities available to them under contemporary conditions?

---

[63] *Id.* at pages 24, 26-27.
[64] *Id.* at page 43.
[65] Submission by UNCTAD to the Subcommittee on International Trade of the Senate Finance Committee regarding the proposed Generalized System of Preferences Renewal Act of 1983, contained in Hearings On The Renewal Of The Generalized Systems Of Preferences — 1984 (98-697, 98th Cong. 2d Sess. January 27, 1984 at page 303).

(c) Doesn't the UNCTAD Secretariat's Report, quoted above, admit as much?

(2) The thrust of the Secretariat's argument, of course, is to suggest that notwithstanding the subsidy effects of the GSP, it is not a zero, but a positive, sum game. Yet, notwithstanding this argument and notwithstanding the interests of American consumers who would benefit from lower prices, of export industries searching for new markets and of U.S. financial interests for whom expanded developing country exports is critical to the latter's debt servicing capacity, GSP renewal in 1984 was a bitterly contested issue. Indeed, it is fair to suggest that the very grudging decision to renew owed more to broader considerations of American foreign economic policy than to any conviction concerning the merits of the GSP as such. With regard to the EEC, while the politics of preferences may have been somewhat more complex the results were not too different. In this connection, recall the primary strategic consideration that led the United States to reverse its opposition to the GSP and then consider whether the expectations underlying that strategy have been realized.

(3) With the foregoing in mind, reflect on the possibility that the GSP, in its departure from certain traditional tenets of GATT and the international trading order, suffers from a fundamental structural defect. If so, consider the underlying political function that those tenets may serve. Consider also the normative and pragmatic appeals of the GSP — the moral imperative of economic development and the pragmatic argument advanced by the UNCTAD Secretariat — and reflect on the apparent inadequacy of those appeals to rectify the GSP's basic structural defect. Identify the counteracting normative concerns that may have contributed to this weakness. Are we dealing here with only an unrepentant protectionism or something far more complex? If the latter, does the GSP experience rightly suggest we may treat these fundamental GATT tenets as rules of law and how should one characterize their role in the ordering of international trade relations?

(4) While doubtless import sensitivity may be the ground for excluding some products from the GSP "eligible" list, there are other factors that bear on the decision as well. Examine the criteria found in Section 501(a) and the type of information that the Office of Trade Representative requires in support of any petition for a new listing or for a withdrawal.[66] In short, the decision to designate

---

[66] A petition for the designation of a new article must identify the principal beneficiary country suppliers likely to benefit from the designation and, for each, (i) figures on actual production, actual capacity, capacity utilization and estimated increase in the latter if designation is forthcoming, (ii) employment figures, including number, type, wage rate, location and estimated changes in these figures if designation is granted, (iii) total sales figures — quantity, value and prices, (iv) information on total exports, including, for each principal export market, quantity, value and export trends, distribution methods and, preferences received, (v) information on exports to the United States — quantity, value and price — together with information concerning the effect that GSP status for the product under consideration would have on exports of like or directly competitive products to the United States by other beneficiary countries, (vi) information concerning overall development of the industry in beneficiary developing countries, (vii) profitability of firms and (viii) unit prices and other information bearing on the competitiveness of the product. 15 C.F.R. Ch. XX, Section 2007.1(c). Petitions to withdraw or limit GSP status for any product must provide, for all "firms producing a like or directly competitive product", information

a product can turn on variety of considerations, not merely on whether it is "import sensitive" or not. Accordingly, drawing upon material already studied — the Haberler Report, the state of the current international regime for agricultural trade, the economics of preferences and discussions in the OECD Special Group — begin to pull together some of the factors that may have contributed to the situation portrayed in the data given above.

(5) From the perspective of counsel for Hong Kong or Taiwan or any of the other major beneficiaries of the U.S. GSP Program charged with developing a case against, or a case for modification of, the competitive need limits, consider first the primary purposes that it is claimed those limitations serve. Are the limits a rationally defensible means for carrying out those purposes? If the quantitative limitation is thought to measure competitiveness — competitiveness against whom? Consider the same question in connection with the percentage of import limitation. In light of the availability of other devices to protect domestic U.S. industry and the broader developmental purposes of the GSP, how would you evaluate this narrow country-product focus for determining "competitiveness?"

---

comparable to that described above (*i.e.*, data on production, employment, sales, exports and profitability), plus a comparative analysis of costs — materials, labor and overhead — a discussion of the general competitive situation in the domestic industry, identification of major competitors and the effect that duty free entry for the product under consideration has had on the petitioner. 15 C.F.R. Ch. XX, Section 2007.1(b).

CHAPTER **5**

THE INTERNATIONAL CONTROL OF NATIONAL TRADE POLICIES —
OF "SAFEGUARDS" AND "UNFAIR" TRADE PRACTICES

§ 5.01 Safeguards and Adjustment Assistance

In this section we consider two closely related subjects. First there is the so-called "safeguards" problem. Under that heading we start by examining GATT Article XIX — the so-called "escape clause" — along with the "escape clause" provisions in the Omnibus Trade and Competitiveness Act of 1988 (the "1988 Act").[1] Then briefly we will compare the latter with other forms of protectionist U.S. legislation. Second, there is the question of whether and in what form the government should provide financial aid to American workers and firms injured by import competition — the problem of "adjustment assistance."

[A] The Dimensions of the Safeguards Problem and Its Contemporary Setting

Introduction

As concerns us here, "safeguards" consist of a great variety of protective measures extended to domestic industries threatened with foreign competition. Among these are the protections afforded by the U.S. "escape clause" legislation which is based, in turn, on Article XIX of the GATT. What marks protection under the "escape clause" off from other forms of protectionist legislation, however, is that "escape clause" aid is expressly for the purpose of giving the domestic industry time to adjust to increased import competition. The protection is, therefore, time limited, digressive and may be conditioned upon submission by the industry of a concrete plan of adjustment.

This is in sharp contrast to the other more categorical forms of protection to which the trading nations of the world are turning with increasing frequency, and in the process largely ignoring the constraints of Article XIX. Indeed, some of these measures are in open defiance of GATT. Others, if not illegal, are far more subtle than the relatively transparent measures prohibited or regulated by Part II of the General Agreement. Still others, such as Orderly Marketing Agreements (OMA's) and Voluntary Restraint Agreements (VRA's) or, as they are sometimes called, Voluntary Export Restraints (VER's),[2] are not sanctioned by GATT nor

---

[1] Pub. L. 100-418, 102 Stat. 1107, Codified in various titles of the U.S.C. (August 23, 1988).

[2] Orderly Marketing Agreements (OMA's) and Voluntary Restraint Agreements (VRA's) consist of bilaterally negotiated limitations on exports from one country to another. Under an OMA, the limitation is not infrequently enforced by the importing

subject to GATT surveillance. As such they have become a favorite instrument in the rising tide of protectionism that now grips all the major trading nations of the world and have emerged as the principal instruments of a growing propensity for nations to "manage trade" in lieu of relying upon the free-trade precepts underlying GATT.

As far as the United States is concerned, these other protectionist measures can be usefully catalogued along the following lines.[3]

First, Congress has periodically responded to protectionist pleas by fashioning general framework legislation vesting in the Executive a certain discretion to protect broad areas of the national economy. There is Section 204 of the Agriculture Act of 1956[4] used principally to protect the textile and apparel industries. There is the notable, if not notorious, Section 22 of the Agriculture Adjustment Act of 1933,[5] the fountainhead of agricultural protection in the United States. If any event marks the start of the continuing tragedy that now confronts the entire world in the matter of agricultural trade, it is the waiver of the GATT "busting" provisions of Section 22 that the United States obtained from the Contracting Parties in 1955.[6] Another example is Section 232 of the Trade Expansion Act of 1962[7] which empowers the President to protect industries deemed essential to national security, an authority used for a time to restrict petroleum imports.

Second, Congress has from time to time enacted product specific protectionist legislation; the Meat Act,[8] the Jones Act[9] and the Magnuson Fisheries Act[10] are notable examples. More notable, however, is that while attempts at such legislation have abounded, especially in recent years, the American statute books still remain, for reasons we shall touch upon briefly, remarkably free of such restrictions. How long this will continue is anybody's guess. The list grows longer if one adds those specific products that have been largely exempt from GATT tariff

---

country as a quota — essentially a bilaterally negotiated quota. VRA's or VER's typically consist of undertakings, either by the exporting country or by producer groups in that country, to limit the quantity or value of goods shipped to the importing country. To say the limitation is "voluntary" is a misnomer since ordinarily the undertaking is only given to avoid more drastic unilateral action.

[3] The classification used here is taken from G. Hufbauer, D. Berliner & K. Elliott, Trade Protection In The United States: 31 Cases (1986). It should be noted that under any one of the listed methods of establishing protective measures for American industry, including the "escape clause," the precise form of protection may be a tariff, a tariff-quota, some manner of unilaterally imposed quantitative restriction or some form of an "agreed" limit on goods or services sold in the American market.

[4] Act of May 28, 1956, 70 Stat. 200, 7 U.S.C. 1854.

[5] Act of May 12, 1933, 48 Stat. 31 as added by Section 31, Act of August 24, 1935, 49 Stat. 773, 7 U.S.C. Section 624.

[6] GATT, BISD, 3rd Supp. (1955) at page 32.

[7] Pub. L. 87-794, 19 U.S.C. Section 1862 as amended by Section 1501 of the Omnibus Trade and Competitiveness Act of 1988, Pub. L. 100-418, 102 Stat. 1107 at 1257.

[8] Meat Import Act of 1979, Pub. L. 96-177, 93 Stat. 1291.

[9] Merchant Marine Act, 1920, Act of June 5, 1920, 41 Stat. 988 (codified throughout Title 46 U.S.C.). See for example 46 U.S.C. 883.

[10] Magnuson Fishery and Conservation Act, Act of April 13, 1976, Pub. L. 94-265, 90 Stat. 331 (Codified in Title 16 U.S.C.). See for example 16 U.S.C. 1825.

reductions and remain ensconced behind the protective shields of Smoot-Hawley and its precursors.

The *third* category of protectionist measures are those taken by the Executive under a claim of independent Presidential power over foreign relations. The early VRA's rested upon this claim.

This then is the broader legislative context that lends renewed significance to the "escape clause." The question is what role "escape clause" actions should play in solving the broader "safeguards" problem — the problem of bringing all protectionist actions under multilateral surveillance and control. It is as urgent a problem as any currently facing the international trading community. And it is also a problem closely linked, as we shall see in the ensuing sections of this Chapter, to the problem of so-called "unfair trade" practices, especially subsidies and dumping.

The Causes of Protectionism: A Contemporary Perspective

The urgency of the "safeguards" problem is in major part due to the rising tide of protectionist sentiment here and abroad. That sentiment, and the measures it has spawned, pose a threat to several of the most important institutional arrangements undergirding the multilateral trading system. Yet, to some extent the protectionist tide is a tribute to the trade liberalization already achieved by that system and to the growing interdependence that has followed apace. But it is far more than just a product of past success.

Several developments in the general macro-economic climate of the 1970's and 1980's, contrasted with the more favorable climate of the 1950's and 1960's, have contributed significantly to the rising demand that domestic firms be protected against import competition. The period from the early 1950's through 1973 was characterized by steady and sustained real growth in the Gross Domestic Product (GDP) of all the OECD states.[11] This was, in turn, accompanied by an increase in imports at average annual rates nearly double the rate of GDP growth. In contrast, the period since the first OPEC[12] oil embargo has been one of severe fluctuations: the first oil shock and the consequent recession of 1974-1975; the short recovery thereafter in which the rates of GDP and import growth never matched the pre-1973 average; the second oil embargo; the stagflation of 1977-1979; the recession of 1980-1981 which saw a net decline in OECD imports; and finally the slow recovery in the years since then.[13]

---

[11] Organization For Economic Cooperation and Development. See Footnote 9 and accompanying text at page 286, *supra* for discussion of the origins, purposes and membership of the OECD.

[12] Organization of Petroleum Exporting Countries.

[13] From 1952 to 1966 the real rate of growth in the GDP of the OECD states averaged nearly 5.5% accompanied, in turn, by an average real rate of growth in imports in excess of 12%. From 1967 to 1973 the average annual rate of real growth in GDP was nearly 5% and imports grew at almost 11% annually. Then, during the recession of 1974-1975 GDP growth declined to less than 1% and the value of imports declined at an average annual rate of nearly 5%. From 1976 through 1979 the average annual rate of real growth in the GDP of these same countries was slightly over 3.9% and the annual rate of increase in

While it might be thought that periods of maximum import growth would augur for a period of maximum protectionist pressure, those pressures tend to be blunted when import growth is accompanied by internal economic expansion, as was generally the case in the 1950's and 1960's. In such a setting, even firms experiencing a loss of market share, find the protectionist argument difficult to sustain in the face of their own rising levels of output, profits and employment.

In contrast, when starting with 1974, the industrialized nations entered upon a period of sluggish growth interspersed by sharp and sometimes severe cyclical downturns, import penetration was joined with shrinking markets to accelerate plant closings, worker lay-offs and declining profits, precisely the conditions upon which the protectionist impulse feeds. Moreover, during virtually the entire period 1974-1986 the United States dollar remained seriously over-valued. This not only exacerbated the import penetration problem, it cut severely into American exports and with it the political support for trade liberalization that could otherwise be expected from export oriented industries. Finally, under these conditions firms in trouble could more readily advance a claim of fairness; that, unless given protection, they alone would bear the costs of generating for others the welfare gains from free trade.[14]

Beyond these macro-economic factors, protectionist sentiment has been fed by certain fundamental cultural and political differences that have come to occupy an increasingly decisive place in trade relations between the major industrialized nations of the world. The reduction of the more transparent border barriers to trade — tariffs and quantitative restrictions — has had the effect of uncovering a whole sub-stratum of more subtle almost, at times, invisible trade barriers rooted in the economic culture of a nation. The complex interactions — the "diffuse reciprocity" as one author labels it — among Japanese firms is only one example of the subtle and deep-set patterns of national cultural autarchy with which the forces of international trade liberalization have now become engaged.[15]

For the United States these barriers pose a special problem. The greater reliance that we tend to place on competitive markets to direct corporate action and our emphasis on transparency in governmental action, make it harder for American firms to sustain the subtle and less visible modes of protectionism that other nations find so congenial. Not unnaturally, when the U.S. encounters those modes, they evoke a sense of having been dealt with in bad faith. In this atmosphere the

---

imports averaged nearly 8.7%. Bergsten and Cline, Trade Policy In The 1980's: An Overview, In Trade Policy For The 1980s (Cline ed.), Institute for International Economics, Washington D. C. (1983) at pages 76-78.

[14] If the broader international economic setting has been conducive to the breeding of protectionist sentiment in the United States and elsewhere, the political economy virtually assured its growth to full maturity. While the benefits of free trade are broadly disbursed throughout the economy (*i.e.*, to import dependent and to export industries and ultimately to the consumer), the costs of adjusting to free trade tend, as we have seen (*supra* page 278) fall upon a much narrower range of firms. Collectively the gains from free trade may outweigh the losses, but individually the benefits to each winner tend to be dwarfed by the costs that each looser must bear. With more at stake individually, the losers can more readily mobilize the resources needed to support their cause in the political arena.

[15] See generally, Krasner, *Trade Conflicts And The Common Defense: The United States And Japan*, 101 Pol. Sci. Q. 787 (1986).

most blatantly protectionist proposals can too easily be cloaked in self righteous rhetoric; the issue becomes not "free-trade" but "fair trade" and the "reciprocity" principle gets turned on its head.

Impact of Protectionism on the Principles
and Institutions of the Liberal Trading Order

As one of the historical underpinnings of the multilateral trading order, "reciprocity" promises to become one of the first casualties of the new protectionism. As we have already seen, "reciprocity" has traditionally reflected the element of bargain in the trade negotiating process. It is part of the cement which holds trade liberalizing commitments in place. In the hands of the "fair traders," however, "reciprocity" is now used to justify erecting new barriers to trade. Under the new usage, one nation — usually the United States — claiming that it already maintains a trade regime more liberal than that of others, threatens retaliation against the latter if they fail to lower barriers against our exports. The threat of retaliation, the "fair traders" argue, is designed merely to advance the cause of "reciprocity" in world trade. Understandably this line of argument may appeal to American politicians and trade bureaucrats increasingly frustrated with the more subtle barriers that successive trade liberalizing rounds have now brought to center stage. But precisely because of the intractable nature of those barriers, its claim to be a liberalizing move is highly suspect.[16] Indeed, under the normative cloak of a distorted reciprocity, the "fair trade" argument is precisely the stuff of which trade wars are made.

Equally dangerous as the assault on the historical understanding of reciprocity, is the threat which the new protectionism poses to the multilateral structure of international trade relations. We have already examined the keystone to that structure; the non-discrimination principle of Article I of the GATT. Consistent with that principle, Article XIX has traditionally been interpreted to require the non-discriminatory application of "escape clause" relief. Nevertheless, GATT members have, virtually from the beginning, found ways to discriminate when engaged in safeguarding their domestic industries, a propensity that has accelerated dramatically in the last decade. The devices used are many,[17] with perhaps the biggest threat to multilateralism coming from the increased use of VRA's. Exact statistics are hard to come-by. Nevertheless, it has been estimated that the use of these extra-GATT arrangements exceeds the number of "escape clause" actions under Article XIX by a factor of four or more with no signs of abating.[18]

---

[16] It is highly doubtful that "risk adverse" foreign statesmen will, when threatened with retaliation, unilaterally dismantle trade barriers so deeply rooted in their business or political culture without receiving any concessions in return.

[17] Japanese accession to the GATT spawned a host of reservations. Even when purporting to apply Article XIX on a non-discriminatory basis, GATT members discriminated against particular countries through such devices as discretionary licensing systems, tariff-quotas and linking the level of duties to the price of the imported product, to name a few. For an interesting discussion of the "de facto" discrimination practiced under the purportedly non-discriminatory strictures of Article XIX, see Bronckers, Selective Safeguard Measures In Multilateral Trade Relations, Kluwer, The Hague (1985) at page 20.

[18] Wolff, Need For New GATT Rules To Govern Safeguard Actions, In Trade Policy in the 1980's (Cline ed.), Institute for International Economics, Washington, D. C. (1983) at page 390.

There are many reasons for the increasing resort to these bilateral devices.[19] Whatever the reasons, however, they enable politicians and bureaucrats to cater to protectionist pleas without having to bear the costs that multilateral surveillance and the rule of non-discrimination would otherwise exact from them. They make protectionist policies cheap and, as such, stimulate demands for a global system of "managed trade."

The third institutional structure indispensable to the liberalization of international trade since World War II and now under pressure from the new protectionism, is that complex of legal arrangements and more informal political understandings that have up to now provided a framework for the making of American trade policy. Over time Congress has crafted an intricate set of institutional arrangements the principal upshot of which has been to insulate it from product specific trade decisions and to redirect local constituency pressures for protection toward the Executive and a growing professional trade bureaucracy that are better situated to diffuse those pressures.

First, in 1934 Congress took itself out of the business of making tariffs and delegated that function to the President, confining its role to giving of general policy guidance and to prescribing procedures for making, and fixing the outer limits of, any reduction in the statutory rates.[20]

Second, principal responsibility for negotiating international trade agreements was, in 1962, taken away from the State Department and placed in the "Special Trade Representative" — now the "United States Trade Representative" — located in the Executive Office of the President. This was an important step toward building domestic political credibility for the trade negotiating function within the Executive Branch.

Third, Congress, in the years following World War II, expanded and formalized the authority of the then Tariff Commission — now the ITC. This better enabled Congress and those Executive officers charged with negotiating international trade agreements, to diffuse politically embarrassing demands by domestic industry for protection against "unfair" foreign trade practices and import penetration by

---

[19] Some of the reasons are to be found in the purported shortcomings of Art. XIX, especially the practice developed under Art XIX:(2) and (3) of giving compensation or undergoing retaliation. There are also political considerations: the desire not to undermine traditional trading patterns as might otherwise occur with restraints imposed on an MFN basis; the desire not to aggravate relations with countries whose producers are not the principal threat to a domestic industry; the propensity, especially on the part of the Europeans, to foster special economic relationships with exporting countries in certain regions of the world. Also, the very absence of accountability to any multilateral body and the lack of transparency are qualities that appeal to the bureaucratic mind.

[20] The Constitutional rationale for this delegation was found in linking the tariff making authority of Congress to the President's authority to negotiate international agreements. This linkage, in turn, converted tariff making from a unilateral matter focused almost exclusively on imports into a subject for international bargaining focused increasingly on gaining access to new export markets through "reciprocal" reductions in trade barriers.

diverting those demands to a technical bureaucracy where they would be judged in formal proceedings according to prescribed economic criteria.[21]

Lastly, the process of diffusing pressures upon Congress for product specific protection was significantly aided by the power of the principal trade policy making Committee's of Congress, especially the House Ways and Means Committee in the days when its Chairmanship was in the skillful hands of Wilbur Mills (). Ark). Individual legislators might introduce product specific protectionist legislation to appease their constituents, but such bills rarely went any further.[22]

The highpoint in the exercise of relatively independent trade negotiating authority by the Executive came under the Trade Expansion Act of 1962. By 1974, when it came time to devise authorizing legislation for the Tokyo Round, circumstances had changed. The focus of the Round was not to be tariffs but "non-tariff barriers to trade" and Congress, already feeling protectionist pressure, was loath to vest in the Executive the authority traditionally yielded on the tariff question. Thus, under the Trade Act of 1974, implementation of all Executive agreements relating to non-tariff barriers — unlike tariff cutting agreements — was made contingent upon further legislation.

Still Congress protected itself. It devised a so-called "fast track" procedure which was renewed by the 1988 Act for purposes of the Uruguay Round. Ninety-days before signature Congress is to receive a copy of any proposed "non-tariff barrier" agreement. After signature, it is to receive the signed agreement and a draft implementing bill. It then has sixty-days within which to either accept or reject the bill as written without amendment.[23] "Fast-track" plainly protected the Tokyo Round MTN Agreements from inroads by product-specific protectionist Committee and floor amendments. Indeed, in the case of those Agreements, the "fast track" provisions of the Act combined with the skill with which the Trade Representative, Robert Strauss, used the network of committees established under the 1974 Act, resulted in an institutional process by which, as one commentator has described it:

> Congress effectively forced the bureaucracy, which has the capacity to understand trade, to deal with the constituents; and forced the constituents to deal with the bureaucracy, which incidentally gave them a broader understanding of American trade problems. Congress left itself the task of

[21] One should not here minimize the protectionist pressures brought to bear, from time to time, on the ITC through the process of Congressional oversight; a process that often reflects more the political idiosyncracies and interests of powerful Committee Chairmen than any broader Congressional concensus.

[22] For an instructive discussion of the role of the Ways and Means Committee and its Chairman see, Destler op. cit. at page 25.

[23] Section 1102 of the Omnibus Trade and Competitiveness Act of 1988 extended, through June 1, 1993, the President's authority to negotiate tariff reductions (Section 1102(a)) and his authority to negotiate reductions in non-tariff barriers to trade (Section 1102(b)). Section 1103(b) of that Act also extended the "fast-track" provisions of the 1974 Act to agreements reducing non-tariff barriers. A new provision was added, however, stipulating that "fast-track" would not apply to an implementing bill if both Houses of Congress passed a "procedural disapproval resolution" stating that, with respect to the negotiation of any agreement covered by that bill, the President had failed to consult with Congress as required by the Act (Section 1103(c)(1)(E)).

assessing the results of the process. The Congressional role was a judicial
more than it was legislative.[24]

Without much doubt this was a salutary development. Yet, it should
missed that the system was, at bottom, a response to the increasing expo
domestic interests to the vicissitudes of international trade and of the er
interdependent economic order that successive rounds of trade liberalizatic
wrought. Nor can it be missed that this exposure is, in the context of ur
macro-economic conditions, the very stuff of protectionism that could pr
to its own purposes the system set-up by the 1974 Act. If the extraordinary
that the Trade Representative had to put forth to keep the proposed Omn.
Trade and Competitiveness Act of 1988 ("1988 Act") acceptably free of proc
specific protectionist measures is any portent of things to come, the prospects
a continued cabining of the new protectionism are, at best, uncertain.[25]

A Caution

Lest the picture remain unbalanced, however, it is wise to recognize that
forces of free-trade have not by any means left the field. There is still the memo
not only in the trade bureaucracy but in Congress, of the disaster that marked
trade wars of the 1930's. Protectionism is far from having won the ideologi
battle. So much so, that the chief protectionist argument — the "fair trac
argument — still wraps itself in the flag of free trade and purports only to be
argument about tactics. And finally, the United States is now strongly committe
to the success of the Uruguay Round which, if progress is made on trade in services
and in agriculture, could prove highly beneficial to this country.

[B] Article XIX of the GATT

Article XIX, also known as the "escape" clause provision of the GATT, is the
principal authority for "safeguard" action under the General Agreement although
the term "safeguard" has also been applied to a number of other actions such as
quantitative restrictions imposed under Article XII for balance of payments
reasons and anti-dumping and countervailing duties imposed under Article VI.

---

[24] Winham, *Robert Strauss, The MTN, and the Control of Faction*, 14 J. of World Trade
Law 377, 386 (1980).

[25] In 1985, more than 634 trade bills were introduced, 99 of which were openly and
seriously protectionist and 77 others potentially so. When, in 1987, an omnibus trade bill
passed the House of Representatives, the latter *inter alia* curbed Presidential discretion in
trade remedy cases, including the "escape clause", mandated retaliation against countries
who failed to open their markets and imposed quotas upon countries running large trade
surpluses with the United States. While these features did not survive in the bill that
eventually emerged from Conference as the 1988 Act, they illustrate all too clearly how,
given the causes of the new protectionism, trade policy issues have moved to the forefront
of public and hence Congressional interest and how, as a consequence, Congress seems less
and less disposed to leave product specific issues to the Executive.

ARTICLE XIX

Emergency Action on Imports of Particular Products

(a) If, as a result of unforeseen developments and of the effect of the obligations incurred by a contracting party under this Agreement, including tariff concessions, any product is being imported into the territory of that contracting party in such increased quantities and under such conditions as to cause or threaten serious injury to domestic producers in that territory of like or directly competitive products, the contracting party shall be free, in respect of such product, and to the extent and for such time as may be necessary to prevent or remedy such injury, to suspend the obligations in whole or in part or to withdraw or modify the concession.

* * * *

2. Before any contracting party shall take action pursuant to the provisions of paragraph (1) of this Article, it shall give notice in writing to the contracting parties as far in advance as may be practicable and shall afford the contracting parties and those contracting parties having a substantial interest as exporters of the product concerned an opportunity to consult with it in respect of the proposed action. . . . In critical circumstances, where delay would cause damage which it would be difficult to repair, action under paragraph 1 of this Article may be taken provisionally without prior consultation, on the condition that consultation shall be effected immediately after taking such action.

3. (a) If agreement among the interested contracting parties with respect to the action is not reached, the Contracting Party which proposes to take or continue the action shall, nevertheless, be free to do so, and if such action is taken or continued, the affected contracting parties shall then be free, not later than ninety days after such action is taken, to suspend . . . the application to the trade of the contracting party taking such action . . . of such substantially equivalent concessions or other obligations under this Agreement the suspension of which the contracting parties do not disapprove.

(b) Notwithstanding the provisions of sub-paragraph (a) of this paragraph, where action taken under paragraph 2 of this Article without prior consultation causes or threatens serious injury in the territory of a Contracting Party to the domestic producers of products affected by the action, that Contracting Party shall, where delay would cause damage difficult to repair, be free to suspend, upon the taking of the action and throughout the period of consultation, such concessions or other obligations as may be necessary to prevent or remedy the injury.

NOTES AND QUESTIONS

(1) Article XIX(1) specifies two causal relationships that must be est before that Article may be invoked to protect a domestic industry. Des two relationships.

(2) Observe that an alternative means available to a Contracting Pa "safeguarding" a domestic industry suffering injury from import competi to invoke its rights under Article XXVIII and negotiate an upward adjus in the appropriate tariff. Compare Article XXVIII with Article XIX(2) and Article XIX, unlike Article XXVIII(2), makes no mention of compensa adjustments nor does Article XIX enjoin upon the parties involved responsibi to maintain "mutually advantageous concessions not less favorable to trade" t the concessions which preceded the adjustment. Does this omission necess indicate that action under Article XIX is likely to lead to an increase in the ov level of protection? If not, may that not signal a certain weakness in Article X if it is to be an effective device for defusing some of the political forces behi the new protectionism? Note in this connection that while an upward adjustm in a tariff under Article XXVIII is permanent, a tariff increase imposed ur Article XIX is to be temporary.

REPORT ON THE WITHDRAWAL BY THE UNITED STATES OF A TARIFF CONCESSION UNDER ARTICLE XIX OF THE GENERAL AGREEMENT ON TARIFFS AND TRADE

October, 1951[26]

[At the 1947 Geneva Round of GATT negotiations, the United States had bound a 32% reduction of the tariff on women's hats, caps, bonnets and hoods of a certain description and within a certain price range. In September 1950, the U.S. Tariff Commission, after an investigation, concluded that, as a consequence of this concession, women's hats were being imported in such increased quantities and under such conditions as to cause serious injury to the domestic industry. Then, in October 1950, the United States announced its decision to invoke Article XIX of the GATT and withdraw the Geneva concessions on those items.

As required by that Article, the United States consulted with all of the contracting parties with an interest in the concession. Agreement was reached with all of them except Czechoslovakia, which, on November 7, 1950, lodged a protest against the United States alleging that the conditions of Article XIX had not been fulfilled. The contracting parties referred the matter to a Working Party which issued its report in March of 1951. The report was adopted by the contracting parties in October of the same year. Select portions of the report follow.]

---

[26] Sales No.: GATT/1951-3, (Nov. 1951).

* * * *

III. Existence of the Conditions Required for Action Under Article XIX

6. *Increase in imports.* The Working Party noted that, according to the available data, the volume of imports of women's fur felt hats and hat bodies into the United States increased substantially in 1948, 1949 and the first six months of 1950 as compared with 1946 and 1947; as from 1949 the imports also exceed those of 1937. The relevant figures are reproduced below:

(Quantity in dozens)

1937	1939	1946	1947	1948	1949	1950 (Jan–June)
52,493	6,372	36,910	15,984	44,646	120,511	61,827[27]

The increase is even more apparent if the comparison is limited to the value brackets affected by the withdrawal.

(Quantity in dozens)

1946	1947	1948	1949	1950 (Jan–June)
14,140	8,251	36,045	106,426	53,097

7. *Existence of unforeseen developments: relation of these and of the tariff concession to imports.* The concession granted at Geneva was substantial. Taking a simple average for the 4 value brackets from $9 to $24 per dozen, the duties as from January 1, 1948, were 32.3 per cent less than the rates of the 1930 Tariff Act.

8. The United States representative stated that about the time the duties were reduce there was a style change greatly favouring hats with nap or pile finishes, a development which was not and could not have been foreseen at the time the concession was granted. As a result of that style change hat bodies with special finishes were imported in increased quantities and represented more than 95 percent of the imports of women's fur felt hats and hat bodies in 1949 and in the first six months of 1950. The increased popularity of special finishes, which, as compared with the plain felt hats, require much larger amounts of hand labour . . . created a special problem for the United States producers who were not in a position to adapt themselves to the change in demand in view of a severe competition from imports. He stated that the United States negotiators at Geneva, while realizing the shifting fashions in the hat trade and expecting some increase in imports, had not been aware of the extent that this particular change in taste had then reached in Europe and had not foreseen the degree of the future shift to special finishes or the effect which it, together with the concession, would have on imports. He considered this statement was sufficient to show unforeseen developments.

---

[27] Statistics available to the Working Party indicate that total imports in the period January–November 1950 were 259,032 dozen (Source: Official Statistics of the United States Department of Commerce).

9. The Czechoslovak representative stated that the term "unforeseen developments" should be interpreted to mean developments occurring after the negotiation of the relevant tariff concession which it would not be reasonable to expect that the negotiators of the country making the concession could and should have foreseen at the time when the concession was negotiated. The other members of the Working Party (other than the United States' representative) agreed with this view.

10. On the basis of the interpretation accepted by the majority, the Czechoslovak representative maintained that:

  (a) it is universally known that fashions are subject to constant changes — "change is the law of fashion;"

  (b) . . . the change [that took place] was not due simply to a change in the taste of American women; it resulted mainly from the enterprise of the exporters . . . and of the American milliners, who deliberately produced the new designs and created the demand for them by advertisement and good salesmanship. . . .

  (c) . . . at [the time of the Geneva negotiations] it was well-known, and was commented upon in the trade journals, that velours had already become fashionable in Paris, and it could be expected that the Paris fashion would spread to other countries.

  (d) [the U.S. negotiators at Geneva knew] . . . that Czechoslovakia had for long had an important . . . interest in the export of . . . velours and other special finishes, had obtained a concession for this type of hat body in a pre-war agreement with the United States . . . and [were] desirous of [again] obtaining . . . [such a concession]. The United states representative agreed that this [was] the case.

* * * *

  (g) the other factors . . . *viz.* the level of productivity of the United States . . . [in these types of hat bodies] . . . and the high proportion of wage costs in the total cost of production, have always existed and were known to the United States negotiators.

11. The other members of the Working Party, except the representative of the United States, agreed with the Czechoslovak representative that the fact that hat styles had changed did not constitute an "unforeseen development" within the meaning of Article XIX. These members and the representative of the United States considered, however, that the United States negotiators in 1947 would not reasonably be expected to foresee that this style change in favour of velours would in fact subsequently take place, and would do so on as large a scale and last for as long a period as it in fact did. Moreover, the evidence before the Working Party appeared to indicate that the increase in United States imports of women's fur felt hat bodies in and after 1948 was due primarily to the following causes:

  (i) [The production necessary to meet the change in demand which took place] . . . requires much more labour than does the production of plain-finished hat bodies.

(ii)   As a result [of this and the relatively higher level of wages in the United States] . . . the generality of United States manufacturers were unable to produce special finishes which could compete . . . with imported hat bodies. . . .

(iii) In consequence . . . overseas suppliers were able to secure by far the greater part of the increasing United States market for special finishes; . . . Furthermore the concession . . . [had reduced] the price differential between imported special finishes and . . . plain felt hat bodies produced in the United States . . . encouraging milliners and consumers to prefer [the special finishes].

12. The members of the Working Party, with the exception of the Czechoslovak representative, accordingly considered that [under the above circumstances] . . . the degree to which the change in fashion affected the competitive situation, could not reasonably be expected to have been foreseen by the United States authorities in 1947.

13. *Existence or threat of a serious injury.* The United States representative produced the following facts. The apparent consumption of women's fur felt hat bodies was lower after the war than before, ranging from 500 to 700 thousand dozen, as compared with 900 to 1100 thousand dozen in the years 1935-1939, but a larger percentage of that reduced demand has been met by imported supplies; the ratio of imports to consumption, which averaged 4.5 percent before the war and was as low as 3.2 percent in 1947, increased to more than 17 percent in 1949 and more than 23 percent in the first half of 1950. Domestic production in the United States remained at a lower level after the war than was the case before the war. Post-war figures were of the magnitude of 5-600,000 dozen as compared with 900,000 to 1,000,000 dozen before the war.

14. Imports and production, and therefore also apparent consumption, of women's fur felt hat bodies in 1947 were all exceptionally low, and all increased from 1947 to 1948. In 1949 and the first half of 1950, however, both imports and apparent consumption continued to increase, while production declined. The following table shows this decline.

Production of Women's Fur Felt Hat Bodies

	1948	1949	1950 (Jan-June)
Quantities in dozens	629,235	565,768	203,235[28]
Percentage of decrease as compared with 1948 figures	—	10%	18%[29]

Consequently, at the time of the investigation, when imports were increasing rapidly, as indicated above, there had been a substantial decrease in production.

---

[28] These were the latest figures available at the time of the investigation. It has been subsequently determined that total production for January — November 1950 was 607,265.

[29] Based on production of 247,865 dozen for January to June 1948.

15. A substantial percentage (estimated at over 20 per cent in 1949 and at over 30 per cent in the first six months of 1950) of the apparent demand for hat bodies shifted to special finishes. 80 per cent of imports in 1949 were of these special finishes. As the total consumption did not increase substantially it would appear likely that in 1949 and the first six months of 1950 the imported hat bodies with special finishes replaced to some extent plain felt hat bodies which would have normally been supplied by domestic producers.

16. No data were available to assess the financial losses which firms producing felt hat bodies may have suffered from the increase in imports. In the industry as a whole the production of women's hat bodies represents about 25-30 per cent of the total production of hat bodies and hats, and it has not been possible to separate the financial results of the production of women's hat bodies from that of men's hat bodies and hats.

17. Inquiries by the United States Tariff Commission, however, showed that ten out of fourteen manufacturers questioned by it stated that they could not make hat bodies in special finishes at prices competitive with imports.

18. As regards the effects of increased imports on employment, the figures show a decrease in the number of productive workers on felt hat bodies (men's and women's) during the period 1947 to 1949. This reduction was substantial between 1948 and 1949 as indicated below:

Productive Workers Engaged in Making Fur Felt Hat Bodies

	1947	1948	1949
Average number of workers	4,383	4,349	3,717
Percentage decline as compared with 1947	—	1%	15%

19. It is not practicable to segregate employment in the production of women's hat bodies from that in the production of men's hat bodies and hats. Moreover, it was difficult to estimate to what extent the reduction in employment is due to increased imports of women's hat bodies and to what extent due to other factors including those affecting the production of men's hats. According to the findings of the United States Tariff Commission a considerable part of this reduction was attributable to increased imports, and this would seem to be supported by the substantial decrease in production of women's hat bodies in 1949 and in the first half of 1950.

* * * *

21. The Czechoslovak representative maintained that neither the data submitted by the United States representative nor the actual developments in the United States hat industry during the decisive period 1947-1950 proved that there was any injury or threat of it to the workers:

    (a)   The figures for changes in the average number of productive workers employed in the fur felt hat bodies industry were not conclusive. . . .

    (b)   The downward trend of employment which was slight in 1948 and more marked in 1949 was attributed by the United States authorities investigating the situation largely to factors other than the influence of increased imports. Nothing definite was adduced to support the view that the increased imports had some effect on employment. . . .

(c)   The conclusion as to whether there was any injury to the workers caused by the increased imports should necessarily take into account not only the decrease in average numbers employed but also the actual figures of unemployed hat workers. These figures were not available. . . .

(d)   . . . The statistics of employment showed an upward trend in employment during the first half of 1950. It was highly probable that this resulted from the increasing domestic production of hat bodies with special finishes.

(e)   All this, together with the fact that the wage rates of the workers in the United States industry for women's fur felt hat bodies were not affected, proved that the increased imports caused or threatened no injury to the workers.

22. The Czechoslovak representative maintained further that the increased imports of hat bodies with special finishes did not threaten the United States domestic production of those types. On the contrary, the change in fashion . . . and the resulting increase in demand for those types created an opportunity for the domestic producers to start and expand rapidly a production of these types:

(a)   Admittedly there was no production of hat bodies with special finishes in the United States in 1947. The domestic producers started to produce them in 1948 under the influence of the expanding market. The increase in the United States domestic production of hat bodies with special finishes is quite clear from the following table based on the data supplied by the United States representative:

	Production (in thousand) (dozen)	Increase compared with previous yr.	Index in comparison to 1948
1947	0	—	—
1948	15	—	100
1949	25	66%	166
1950	100	400%	666 [30]

The comparison between the rate of increase in imports and the rate of increase in the domestic production of hat bodies with special finishes shows that domestic production had increased in higher proportion than imports.

	Index of Imports	Index of Domestic Production
1948	100	100
1949	269	166
1950	580	666

. . . According to data furnished by the United States representative, . . . [only 4 of the 14 . . . U.S. producers of women's fur felt hat bodies that had

---

[30] All figures in this and the subsequent table for 1950 were based on figures obtained by the Czechoslovak representative from his own sources of information in the United States of America.

made velours, succeeded in putting their] . . . production on anything like a satisfactory basis . . . [and they] produced nearly the whole of the total production of 25,000 dozen in the first half of 1950, . . . [The other 10] . . . produc[ed] nothing but samples [indicating that their] . . . production was in an experimental stage and that this was the real cause of their high cost of production. . . .

(b)   . . . It might have been expected that the domestic production of plain hat bodies would decrease as producers switched over to special finishes and therefore part of their productive capacity would be absorbed by the production of velours. But in fact total domestic production of hat bodies in the United States did not decrease at all:

	Domestic Production (thousand doz.)	Increase as compared with previous yr.	Index in comparison with 1947
1947	487	—	100
1948	629	+29%	129
1949	566	-10%	116
1950	650 [31]	+15%	133

The domestic production of women's hat bodies was thus 33 per cent above the level of 1947 when the concession was granted.

The actual development of the domestic United States production of women's fur felt hat bodies from 1947 to the end of 1950 was such that there was no serious injury caused to it by the increasing imports of velours. The Czechoslovak representative referred to a graph drawn by him from the United States data showing the actual development of the United States production. What in fact happened was that the change in fashion created a new market and the demand was such that in 1949 and in the first half of 1950 the exporters and also the domestic producers were unable to fulfill all the orders they received for the special finishes. The market for plain felt hat bodies remained stationary; the domestic production of these types was estimated in thousand dozens by the Czechoslovak representative at 487 in 1947, 614 in 1948, 541 in 1949 and 550 in 1950. The action taken by the United States Government operated not to protect the domestic industry from a threat of injury but to protect an attempt by the domestic producers to capture and monopolize the new market by killing the import trade and to accumulate profits which previously never came their way. The application of Article XIX in this respect was improper.

24. The views of the other members of the Working Party on the question of serious injury were as follows. . . .

25 . . . [T]he statistics bearing on the relation between imports and domestic production up to mid-1950 show a large and rapidly increasing volume of imports, while at the same time domestic production decreased or remained stationary. On the whole, therefore, they constitute evidence of some weight in

---

[31] Arrived at by adding an estimate of 43,000 for December to the United States figure of 607,000 for the first eleven months in 1950.

favour of the view that there was a threat of serious injury to the United States industry.

26. On the other hand it is noteworthy that the Tariff Commission report contains the following statement:

> Imports of hat bodies of these special finishes have to some extent affected domestic production of hat bodies of plain felt, particularly those in the higher priced ranges. More especially, however, these imports have severely limited the establishment and expansion of domestic production of these special finishes.

27. In this respect, it must be commented that any proposal to withdraw a tariff concession in order to promote the establishment or development of domestic production of a new or novel type of product in which overseas suppliers have opened up a new market is not permissible under Article XIX but should be dealt with under other provisions of the Agreement, such as Article XVIII. On the other hand, it may be permissible to have recourse to Article XIX if a new or novel type of imported product is replacing the customary domestic product. . . . [T]he statistics up to mid-1950 appear on the whole to indicate a material degree of displacement of domestically produced plain felt hat bodies by imported velours and other special finishes. . . .

28. Employment and unemployment statistics are inconclusive. . . .

29. To sum up, the available data support the view that increased imports had caused or threatened some adverse effect to United States producers. Whether such a degree of adverse effect should be considered to amount to "serious injury" is another question, on which the data cannot be said to point convincingly in either direction. . . . Moreover, the United States is not called upon to prove conclusively that the degree of injury caused or threatened in this case must be regarded as serious; since the question under consideration is whether or not they are in breach of Article XIX, they are entitled to the benefit of any reasonable doubt. No facts have been advanced which provide any convincing evidence that it would be unreasonable to regard the adverse effects on the domestic industry concerned as a result of increased imports as amounting to serious injury or a threat thereof; and the facts as a whole certainly tend to show that some degree of adverse effect has been caused or threatened. It must be concluded, therefore, that the Czechoslovak Delegation has failed to establish that no serious injury has been sustained or threatened.

* * * *

[36-39. *Duration of the Action.* The United States Government had decided to place no specific time limit on the duration of the withdrawal, arguing *inter alia* that this was necessary in light of the compensatory adjustments negotiated with two other Contracting Parties, both of whom (France and Italy) said that this was "not insuperable."]

VI. CONCLUSIONS

47. The following paragraphs contain the conclusions arrived at by the members of the Working Party other than the Czechoslovak and the United States representatives.

48. These members were satisfied that the United States authorities had investigated the matter thoroughly . . . and had reached in good faith the conclusion that the proposed action fell within the terms of Article XIX. . . . Moreover, those differences of view on interpretation which emerged in the Working Party are not such as to affect the view of these members on the particular case under review. If they, in their appraisal of the facts, naturally gave what they consider to be appropriate weight to international factors and the effect of the action . . . on the interests of exporting countries while the United States authorities would normally tend to give more weight to domestic factors, it must be recognized that any view on such a matter must be to a certain extent a matter of economic judgment and that it is natural that governments should on occasion be greatly influenced by social factors, such as local employment problems. It would not be proper to regard the consequent withdrawal of a tariff concession as *ipso facto* contrary to Article XIX unless the weight attached by the government concerned to such factors was clearly unreasonably great.

* * * *

50. They wish however to point out that in their opinion, action under Article XIX is essentially of an emergency character and should be of limited duration. . . . In the case under review . . . it would be desirable for the United States Government to follow the trends of consumption, production and imports . . . with a view to restoring the concession . . . as soon as it becomes clear that its continued complete withdrawal cannot reasonably be maintained . . . under Article XIX.

NOTES AND QUESTIONS

(1) The Working Party agreed with the Czech representative that the change in women's hat fashions could have been foreseen by the U.S. negotiators at Geneva, but concluded, nevertheless, that the consequent increase in imports was the result of an "unforeseen development" within the meaning of Article XIX. In other words, although the change could be foreseen its impact on trade could not, and it is the latter to which Article XIX has reference. Consider the circumstances to which the Czech representative alludes in making his argument. In light of those circumstances how convincing is the Working Party's conclusion? What additional circumstances might have persuaded the Working Party that the trade impact was foreseeable? Plainly, in deciding not to apply the "unforeseen developments" requirement as stringently as it might otherwise have done, the Working Party made a basic policy choice. How do you evaluate that choice in light of conditions today? Would a more stringent interpretation render Article XIX a more or less effective instrument for bringing the new protectionism under multilateral control?

(2) The evidence in the *Hatter's Fur* Case, certainly indicates that, starting with 1948, imports increased dramatically after the tariff was reduced by 32% in 1947, but does this establish that the tariff reduction "caused" the increased imports.

The "cause" of the increased imports — whether unforeseen or not — would seem to have been the consequence of (i) a shift in consumption patterns to which the foreign producers were better able to respond than were domestic producers,[32] because (ii) the lower tariff allowed them to exploit (iii) their superior productive efficiency.

Again the interpretation of Article XIX would appear to involve a basic policy choice. Should the requisite causal connection between increased imports and the tariff concession turn on some standard of relative importance in the causal nexus (*i.e.* that the tariff concession was "more important than" or "equally important as" the foreign producers' superior efficiency or, if not equally important, was nevertheless a "substantial" or "material" factor)? Alternatively should it suffice that there was a coincidence in time between the tariff concession and the increased imports. Which of these alternatives did the Working Party appear to accept, at least *sub silentio*? Clearly the latter would mean a substantial lowering of the standard that a Contracting Party must meet in order to invoke Article XIX. On the other hand, it is far easier to administer and from the domestic industry's perspective the only important fact is that imports have increased. Which of these considerations should prevail if Article XIX is to be an effective instrument for cabining the new protectionism? Indeed, is there any need to link increased imports back to a one or more trade concessions?

[NOTE in 1974 the U.S. "escape clause" legislation was amended to remove any required causal relationship between increased imports and a trade concession.[33]].

(3) Assume the U.S. hat industry suffered injury. Again it would seem to be clear that any causal relationship between that injury and increased imports was produced by a change in the pattern of domestic demand for hat bodies and the fact that foreign producers were better able to respond to that change than were domestic producers. With this in mind, consider the following:

(a)   Recall that the Working Party said that it was not permissible under Article XIX to withdraw a concession "in order to promote the . . . development of domestic production of a new or novel type of product" which foreign suppliers had introduced. Does this contradict the Working Parties' broader conclusion that the United States did not violate Article XIX in the *Hatter's Fur* Case? Without tariff protection domestic hat manufacturers were apparently unable to develop the productive capacity necessary to meet the demand for a new type of product.

(b)   Consider the following alternative. Suppose through-out the period 1947-50 domestic producers' sales of the new hat bodies:

(i)   did not off-set the loss of sales in traditional bodies, thus resulting in injury; but

(ii)   were increasing and thus enabling domestic producers to capture a constant share of the growing market for those bodies.

---

[32] Note, that while imports in 1948 exceeded the 1947 figure by over 180%, those imports exceeded the 1946 figure, the first full postwar year, by only 20%, an occurrence for which the Working Party offers no explanation.

[33] Section 201(b)(1) of the Trade Act of 1974, Pub. L. 93-618, 19 U.S.C. Section 2251.

Under these circumstances would you characterize a decision to raise the level of protection as forestalling continued injury (permissible under Article XIX) or promoting the development of additional domestic production (not permissible under Article XIX)?

(c) This again is a policy choice, is it not? If you conclude that protection under Article XIX is not permissible you are simply concluding, are you not, that increased imports *are not to be* considered a legally sufficient cause of injury if domestic producers' sales of the new product are rising and their market share is holding steady? On the other hand, if you conclude that protection under Article XIX is appropriate, you are concluding that increased imports *are to be* considered a legally sufficient cause of injury until the domestic producers' share of the new market is sufficient to fully compensate them for their loss of the old market. In either case the question of "causation" is a policy question, not a question susceptible of a logically necessary or scientific resolution. As such, it a question that turns on the purposes you believe Article XIX should serve.

(4) Note the burden of proof that the Working Party placed upon Czechoslovakia. With that in mind compare the figures in paragraphs 14 and 22(b). It appears that total domestic production of women's felt hat bodies did decline between 1948 and 1949, but that, contrary to the United States' assertion, domestic production rose again in 1950 beyond the 1948 level when the full year's output is taken into account. Next, examine the second table in Paragraph 22(a) and note that apparently the U.S. producer's market share of the new special finishes was rising. Under these circumstances what possible basis was there for suggesting that increased imports were injuring the domestic industry? (See first table in Paragraph 22(a)). Stated otherwise, which of the alternative interpretations discussed in Note 3 did the Working Party implicitly adopt when it concluded that Czechoslovakia had failed to sustain its burden of proof.

(5) If as suggested, the interpretation of the causation standard in Article XIX, turns on the purposes which that Article ought to serve, how do you evaluate the Working Party's interpretation? This is a question that recurs through-out the materials in this section, but here consider two points: (i) Which interpretation would render Article XIX a more effective vehicle for subjecting the new protectionism to multilateral surveillance? (ii) Which interpretation is to be preferred if Article XIX is to remain only as authority for temporary relief; a means of facilitating an adjustment by the domestic industry to a new competitive climate?

(6) Does the MFN principle of Article I apply to actions under Article XIX? Note Paragraph (1) of Article XIX provides for an "original" suspension of obligations by a Contracting Party whose domestic industry is being injured. Paragraph 3(a) allows Parties affected by that action to retaliate. Under Paragraph 3(a), however, the retaliatory action must be directed at ". . . the trade of the contracting party taking . . . [the original] action." Similar language is not found in either Paragraph (1) or Paragraph (3)(b). What is the implication of this omission? That implication is supported by the legislative history of Article XIX.[34]

---

[34] Dam, The GATT: Law And International Economic Organization, University of Chicago Press (1970) at page 105.

The question raised is one that has been much debated in the context of the larger "safeguards" issue. What should the rule be? Among the principal reasons for the development of OMA's and VRA's is that they can be applied selectively and not on an MFN basis. Recall why countries imposing such restraints might prefer the discriminatory alternative. On the other hand, consider the likely consequences for a less developed country if a developed country could make its original suspension of an obligation owed the LDC on a discriminatory, non-MFN basis. Consider, however, the potential multiplier effect if safeguard action were required to be on an MFN basis, especially if retaliatory suspensions were also on that basis. What broader systemic considerations might warrant allowing "escape clause" actions to be taken on a discriminatory basis?

[C] Select Problems in the Application of the United States' "Escape Clause" Legislation

Historical Note

The "escape clause" concept as found in Article XIX had its origins in three Executive Orders issued by President Truman under the reciprocal trade agreements program.[35]

The first and second of the Executive Orders are to be found in Paragraph 5 of Executive Order 9832 of February 25, 1947, 3 C.F.R. (1943-1948 Compilation) 624 at 625 and Paragraph 10 of Executive Order 10004 of October 5, 1948, 3 C.F.R. (1943-48 Compilation) 819 at 821, respectively.

Congress first enters the picture with enactment of the Trade Agreements Extension Act of 1951,[36] with language that tracked much of Executive Order 10082, but with some variations.[37] Thereafter the law went through several iterations, the most stringent version of which was found in the Trade Expansion Act of 1962.[38] Only absolute increases in imports, not relative increases, could

---

[35] Paragraph 10, Executive Order 10082 of October 5, 1949, 3 C.F.R. (1949-1953 Compilation) 281 at 283 contains the final formulation. It is notable that the only substantive difference between this Executive Order and Paragraph 1(a) of Article XIX is that the latter does not expressly provide for the possibility of a "relative," as distinguished from an "absolute," increase in imports triggering escape clause relief. Parallel provisions in the Havana Charter, however, contained the word "relatively" and at the second session of GATT a Working Party recorded its understanding that the concept of a "relative" increase was intended to carry-over into the interpretation of Article XIX. GATT, BISD 2d Supp. (1952) at pages 44-45. In practical terms this means that if domestic consumption is declining as a result, for example, of a general recession, and if, as a consequence, imports are also declining in absolute terms, escape clause relief might still be available if imports are capturing an increasing share of the domestic market (i.e., are increasing relative to domestic production).

[36] Pub. L. 82-50, approved June 16, 1951, 65 Stat. 72.

[37] The cause of the increased imports had to be a "duty or other customs treatment reflecting . . . [a] concession" given under a trade agreement. The increase could not, as under the Executive Order, stem from some other obligation of the United States. Under the Act it was not necessary to show that the increase was attributable to "unforeseen developments." The Act contained a non-exclusive list of factors the Tariff Commission was to take into account in making its determination.

[38] Pub. L. 87-794 approved October 11, 1962, 76 Stat. 872.

trigger a right to escape clause relief and the increase in imports had to be caused "in major part" by a tariff concession. Query, whether the *Hatter's Fur* Case could have met this requirement? Increased imports had to be "the major factor in causing, or threatening to cause . . . injury" and in determining whether an industry was injured the Tariff Commission was required to examine all economic factors relevant to the health of the industry, not just those pertaining to the import impacted segment of the industry.

Not unexpectedly these changes were accompanied by a sharp decline in the number of successful escape clause petitions.[39] Congress' response to this experience was to substantially liberalize[40] the "escape clause" in the Trade Act of 1974. While most of the basic substantive concepts underlying the 1974 Act have been carried over into the Omnibus Trade and Competitiveness Act of 1988 (the "1988 Act"), and the decisions hereinafter examined were all rendered under the 1974 Act, the 1988 Act would modify certain of those basic concepts and would add a number of significant new provisions. The 1988 Act is more fully set-out in the Documentary Supplement. What follows is a summary of the law as it now stands.

United States "Escape Clause" Legislation

The 1988 Act recast the "escape clause" provisions of the 1974 Act in the following terms.

Under Section 202(a) a petition requesting "escape clause" relief may be filed with the Commission by a trade association, firm, certified or recognized union, or group of workers representative of an industry. The petition must include a statement of the specific purposes for which relief is being sought and may include a plan to facilitate "positive adjustment to import competition."[41] In addition, the Commission while investigating a petition must seek information regarding actions being taken, or planned, by firms or workers in the industry to adjust to import competition and any interested party, including an affected community, may make commitments to the Commission regarding actions it intends to take to facilitate that adjustment. "Positive adjustment to import competition" is defined to mean (1) that the domestic industry is either able to compete successfully with imports after receiving escape clause relief or experiences an orderly transfer of resources to other productive pursuits, including a possible reduction in the size of the industry and (2) dislocated workers experience an orderly transition to productive pursuits (Sec. 201(b)). The 1988 Act then provides:

---

[39] Between 1951 and 1962, 35% of the 116 petitions to the Tariff Commission resulted in affirmative injury determinations. In 37% of those cases the President actually granted relief, for an overall success rate of 13%. On the other hand, between 1963 and 1974 the Commission issued affirmative injury determinations in only 20% of the 40 petitions filed and the President granted relief in only 2 cases, for an overall success rate of 5%.

[40] Between 1975 and 1985, after the law was liberalized, the Commission issued affirmative determinations in 58% of the 57 petitions filed and the President granted relief in 42% of those cases for an overall success rate of 24%. Of course, these latter increases in particular reflect much more than just the changes in the law. They also reflect the troubled state of the Nation's and the World economy during the 1975-85 decade.

[41] Under Section 202(a)(5)(A) a petitioner, before submitting an adjustment plan under paragraph (4), may consult with the Trade Representative who may then, by published notice, bring in other participants to the consultations.

Section 202(b) Investigations and Determinations by Commission

(1) —

(A) Upon the filing of a petition under subsection (a)(1)[42] . . . the Commission shall promptly make an investigation to determine whether an article is being imported into the United States in such increased quantities as to be a substantial cause of serious injury or the threat thereof, to the domestic industry producing an article like or directly competitive with the imported article.

(B) For purposes of this section, the term "substantial cause" means a cause which is important and not less than any other cause.[43]

Section 202(c) Factors Applied in Making Determinations

(1) In making determinations under subsection (b), the Commission shall take into account all economic factors which it considers relevant, including (but not limited to):

(A) with respect to serious injury —

   (i) the significant idling of productive facilities in the domestic industry,

   (ii) the inability of a significant number of firms to carry out domestic production operations at a reasonable level of profit, and

   (iii) significant unemployment or underemployment within the domestic industry;

(B) with respect to threat of serious injury —

   (i) a decline in sales or market share, a higher and growing inventory (whether maintained by domestic producers, importers, wholesalers, or retailers), and a downward trend in production, profits, wages, or employment (or increasing underemployment) in the domestic industry,

   (ii) the extent to which firms in the domestic industry are unable to generate adequate capital to finance the modernization of their domestic plants and equipment, or are unable to maintain existing levels of expenditures for research and development,

------

[42] The Commission must also conduct an investigation if requested to do so by the President, the Trade Representative, or by a resolution of either the Committee on Ways and Means of the House of Representatives or the Committee on Finance of the Senate. The Commission may also act on its own motion.

[43] Section 202(b)(2) requires the Commission to make its injury determination within 120 days or, in complicated cases, within 150 days of the filing of a petition. Section 202(b)(3) specififes the time within which the Commission must make a determination regarding "critical circumstances" if alleged and Subsection (4) requires the Commission to hold open hearings. "Critical circumstances" exist if a substantial increase in imports over a short period has led to circumstances in which a delay in taking action under this chapter would "significantly impair the effectiveness of such action." Section 202(b)(3)(B).

    (iii) the extent to which the United States market is the focal point for the diversion of exports of the article concerned by reason of restraints on exports of such article into third country markets; and

  (C) with respect to substantial cause, an increase in imports (either actual or relative to domestic production) and a decline in the proportion of the domestic market supplied by domestic producers.

(2) In making determinations under subsection (b), the Commission shall —

  (A) Consider the condition of the domestic industry over the course of the relevant business cycle, but may not aggregate the causes of declining demand associated with a recession or economic downturn in the United States economy into a single cause of serious injury or threat of injury; and

  (B) examine factors other than imports which may be a cause of serious injury or threat of serious injury;

* * * *

(4) For purposes of subsection (b), in determining the domestic industry producing an article like or directly competitive with an imported article, the Commission —

  (A) to the extent information is available, shall, in the case of a domestic producer which also imports, treat as part of such domestic industry only its domestic production:

  (B) may, in the case of a domestic producer which produces more than one article, treat as part of such domestic industry only that portion or subdivision of the producer which produces the like or directly competitive article. [44]

If the Commission makes an affirmative determination under subsection (b)(1), it is then required to recommend to the President the actions that it believes would most effectively address that injury and facilitate the industry's efforts to adjust.

Actions the Commission is authorized to recommend are: the imposition or increase of a duty, imposition of a tariff quota, modification or imposition of a quantitative restriction, one or more appropriate adjustment measures, including

---

[44] Section 202(c)(4)(C) authorizes the Commission to define the relevant industry by reference to a limited geographic area of the United States when certain conditions are met. Also Section 202(c)(5) requires that if in its investigation the Commission has reason to believe that increased imports are attributable to foreign subsidies or dumping or whose importation constitutes "unfair competition" under section 337 of the Tariff Act of 1930, it must promptly notify the appropriate agency or that fact. Also, under the 1988 Act amendments, the President is authorized to take provisional measures pending the outcome of a Commission investigation, if the Commission reports a finding that "critical circumstances" require such action.

trade adjustment assistance under chapter 2. (Section 202(e)). The Commission may also recommend that the President initiate negotiations to address the underlying causes of the increased imports or take any other action authorized by law which, in the Commission's view, would facilitate a positive adjustment to import competition.[45]

In its report to the President the Commission is required to assess the short and long-term effects which the action it recommends (as well as the failure to act as it recommends) are likely to have on the petitioning industry, other domestic industries, consumers, and on the communities where production facilities are located.[46]

Within 60 days of receiving an affirmative determination from the Commission the President must decide whether to act. He is authorized to take all feasible action within his power to facilitate efforts by the domestic industry to make a positive adjustment to import competition (Sec. 201(a)).

In making his decision the President must consider whether workers and firms are benefitting from adjustment assistance, are engaged in worker retraining and are making efforts to implement adjustment plans or commitments submitted to the Commission. Also, the President must consider the short and long-term economic and social costs and benefits of any action he might take, with special reference to the costs that taxpayers, communities, workers and consumers might have to bear. He is then authorized to consider any other factor related to the national economic interest of the United States, including: (i) the effect of any action on competition in domestic markets, (ii) the impact on domestic industries of any international obligation of the United States to give compensation; and (iii) the national security interests of the United States.

In addition to the actions that the Commission is authorized to recommend, the President may decide to negotiate orderly marketing agreements with foreign countries, and/or proclaim procedures for auctioning off import licenses.

Once he has made a decision the President must submit to Congress a report explaining his decision. He must also give reasons for any differences between his decision and the actions recommended by the Commission. If he decides to take no action or the action he takes differs from the Commission's recommendation, the action recommended by the latter will take effect upon the enactment of a Joint Resolution within 90 days following receipt of the President's report.

The maximum duration for any escape clause relief is eight years. If the period of the initial action is less, the President may extend that period but the aggregate

---

[45] Under Section 202(e)(6) only those Commission members who made an affirmative determination under subsection (b) are eligible to vote on the remedies to be recommended, although the members who voted against an affirmative determination may submit their separate views regarding what action the President should take, if any.

[46] Under Section 202(g) if the Commission recommends trade adjustment assistance, the Secretaries of Labor and Commerce are required to expedite their review of any petitions for such assistance received from workers or the domestic industry. Also under Section 202(h) no investigation is to be made with respect to the subject matter of a previous investigation unless 1 year has elapsed since the Commission reported the results of the latter investigation to the President.

of the initial action and the extension may not exceed eight years.[47] If the effective period of certain actions exceeds three years, that action must, if feasible, be phased down, with the first reduction taking effect within three years.

The Commission is required to monitor all actions taken under this chapter for the purpose of reporting to the President and Congress every two years what progress workers and firms in the domestic industry are making toward a positive adjustment to import competition.

The President may at any time reduce, modify or terminate any escape clause relief (i) if he determines that the domestic industry has not made adequate efforts to adjust to import competition, (ii) the effectiveness of the relief given has been impaired by changed economic circumstances, or (iii) if a majority of representatives of the domestic industry request such action and the President finds that the industry has adjusted to import competition.

REPORT TO THE PRESIDENT ON CERTAIN MOTOR VEHICLES AND CERTAIN CHASSIS AND BODIES THEREFOR

United States International Trade Commission

Investigation No. TA-203-44
December 3, 1980

USITC Publication 1110

Determination

On the basis of the information developed in the course of the investigation, the Commission has determined (Commissioners Moore and Bedell dissenting in part) that automobile trucks, on-the-highway passenger automobiles, and bodies (including cabs) and chassis for automobile trucks . . . are not being imported into the United States in such increased quantities as to be a substantial cause of serious injury, or the threat thereof, to the domestic industries producing articles like or directly competitive with the imported articles.

Background

The Commission instituted the present investigation, . . . on June 30, 1980, following the receipt . . . of a petition for import relief filed by the International Union, United Automobile, Aerospace, and Agricultural Implement Workers (UAW).

[47] Section 203(e)(3) provides that: "No action may be taken under this section which would increase a rate of duty to (or impose) a rate which is more than 50 percent *ad valorem* above the rate (if any) existing at the time the action is taken." Section 203(e)(4) provides that: "Any action taken under this section proclaiming a quantitative restriction shall permit the importation of a quantity or value of the article which is not less than the quantity or value of such article imported into the United States during the most recent period that is representative of imports of such article."

Views of Chairman Bill Alberger

* * * *

While I find . . . for both passenger automobiles and light trucks . . . [that imports have increased and that the domestic industry has been injured], I do not find . . . [that the increased imports were a substantial cause of the injury] and therefore my determination with respect to these items is in the negative. [With regard to] medium and heavy trucks [the fact that there was no increase in imports] . . . also mandate[s] a negative determination. . . .

The Domestic Industry

This case raises a number of issues with respect to the scope of the industry or industries to be analyzed . . . The language of section 201 . . . requires an examination of serious injury to "the domestic industry producing an article like or directly competitive with the imported article."[48] . . . [T]he important thing to emphasize is that the definition of an industry under section 201 . . . may not necessarily coincide with the generic description everyone uses when they refer to "the auto industry."

* * * *

Since the phrase "like or directly competitive" is clearly expressed in the disjunctive, and since the adjectives "like" and "directly competitive" were not intended to be synonymous or explanatory of each other,[49] . . . our initial task is to draw distinctions where possible between the "like product" to the imported article (*i.e.*, that which is "the same or nearly the same in inherent or intrinsic characteristics")[50] and those which are "directly competitive" with it (*i.e.*, "substantially equivalent for commercial purposes, that is, . . . adapted to the same uses and . . . essentially interchangeable therefor").[51] If these groups of producers can clearly be treated as separate and distinct industries in terms of production, sales, employment, etc., and if such action is consistent with the realities of the marketplace, then a showing of serious injury to either group . . . will satisfy the criteria for relief and mandate an affirmative result.

Applying these principles . . . I believe we are faced with three separate and distinct industries — [namely] . . . (1) all passenger automobiles . . . (2) light trucks of under 10,000 lbs. (of the type classified as automobile trucks) . . . and (3) medium and heavy trucks . . . but not truck tractors and trailers imported together, which we specifically excluded from the scope of our investigation. . . . I reach this industry segmentation on the basis of the following rationale:

1. There is no persuasive basis on which to segment passenger automobiles into more than one industry, as requested by several importers. . . . [T]here is no clear dividing line between "large autos" and "small autos" for example.[52] [Importers also . . . argu[e] that consumer surveys show a marked lack

---

[48] Trade Act of 1974, Section 201(b)(I), 19 U.S.C. 2251(b)(I).
[49] S. Rep. 93-129, 93d Cong., 2d Sess., 121-22 (1974).
[50] *Id.*
[51] *Id.*
[52] An example would be the Ford Granada, which is classified as a small car, but which is closer to the Dodge Diplomat — a large car — than it is to the subcompact Chevette in terms of size and gas mileage.

of direct competitiveness between these classes. There appears to be an inherent contradiction here, because the same parties cite the shift in demand from large to small cars (brought on by rising fuel costs) as an important cause of injury. This shift merely demonstrates why these goods are "directly competitive" . . . [that there is] . . . a high degree of cross-elasticity. . . . Furthermore, all passenger automobiles have substantially similar uses, and there is certainly ample evidence that all are — to a greater or lesser extent — directly competitive . . . .

2. Light trucks are inherently distinct from passenger vehicles in terms of their characteristics and principal uses. All types are, to some extent, able to carry substantial [loads] . . . While many are also adapted to passenger transport, they are purchased [mostly] . . . for utilitarian purposes. I believe this is enough of an qualitative difference to make them unlike passenger vehicles. . . .

3. Medium and heavy trucks . . . are essentially distinct from either passenger vehicles or light trucks. The vast majority are commercial vehicles designed for specific commercial purposes, . . . are produced by a different group of firms and marketed separately. . . .

* * * *

The Question of Canadian Imports

[Here the Commissioner rejects an argument by Ford and the UAW that, because U.S. and Canadian manufacturing operations are part of a single industry, and because the Automotive Products Trade Act of 1965 (APTA),[53] implementing the U.S.-Canadian Automotive Agreement,[54] recognizes this fact, imports from Canada, produced almost entirely by subsidiaries of U.S. firms, should be excluded from the scope of the investigation. The Commissioner then took note of the fact that it had always been the Commission's practice to consider all imports in determining whether there are "increased imports," and not to count imports by domestic producers as domestic production in considering injury.]

* * * *

Substantial Cause

While I find the domestic industries producing passenger automobiles and light trucks to be suffering serious injury within the meaning of Section 201(b)(1), I do not find that increased imports are a substantial cause of such injury. . . . I have found the decline in demand for new automobiles and light trucks owing to the general recessionary conditions in the United States economy to be a far greater cause of the domestic industries' plight than the increase in imports. While I also believe that the rapid change in product mix necessitated by the shift of consumer preference away from large, less fuel efficient vehicles, is an important cause of

---

[53] 19 U.S.C. 2001.

[54] Agreement Concerning Automotive Products Between The Government Of The United States And The Government Of Canada, 17 U.S.T. 1372, T.I.A.S. No. 6093 (1965).

the present injury, I do not view this factor to be a more important cause than increased imports.

The Decline in Overall Demand

One noticeable factor in this case is the apparent lack of correlation between the growth in import volume and the state of health of domestic producers. Our investigation reveals that the period 1976-78 was characterized by strong domestic sales and record profits.[55] Yet it was during this period that the largest increase in total imports occurred[56] . . . Imports actually declined in 1979, when the recession began in earnest. Even Japanese imports grew most dramatically in the prior period, and remained about steady in 1979. While Japanese imports have increased by a more alarming rate in the first 6 months of 1980 (about 200,000 units over the comparable period of 1979), imports from other sources have declined. This juxtaposition of events becomes even more curious when we consider the testimony of petitioners that the injury began in early 1979 and has deepened over the past 18 months. Given the relatively slight import growth in that period, and considering how healthy the monthly sales figures were before 1979, one obviously begins to look for other explanations of the current injury.

One figure that stands out in stark contrast to the rather marginal import increases for 1979-1980 is the very large decline in overall consumption of both passenger autos and light trucks. Consumption of passenger autos fell by almost 1 million units in 1979, a decline of 7.8 percent. Moreover, consumption in January-June 1980 was 1.1 million units or 18.5 percent below the figure for January-June 1979. It is therefore clear that domestic producers faced seriously declining demand in the period January 1979 - June 1980. While imports did improve their market share substantially during this period by maintaining constant or slightly increasing volume in the face of falling demand, the downturn in demand itself is obviously a variable factor which must be independently assessed for its impact on U.S. producers.

At the most fundamental level, then, it is useful to allocate the decline in domestic producers' shipments in 1979 and 1980 into two basic components: that portion accounted for by the reduced overall consumption of autos and light trucks because of general economic conditions, and that portion attributable to the increasing market share of import vehicles. The relative magnitude of these two causes can be assessed by comparing the actual decline in domestic shipments to the decline that might have occurred if imports had not increased their market share in 1979-80. The difference between these two figures represents the maximum potential loss in sales due to increased imports. This amount can then be compared to the volume of loss attributable *solely* to reduced demand. The following tables reveal the results of this exercise for 1979 and for January-June 1980:

---

[55] This fact was essentially acknowledged by domestic industry representatives during the hearing.

[56] The Commissioner points out that: "Passenger automobile imports increased from 2 million units in 1975 to 2.9 million in 1978, while light truck imports grew from 375,000 in 1975 to 859,000 in 1978. - Ed.

Table 1

Passenger Automobiles: U.S. Apparent Consumption, U.S. Producers' Domestic Shipments, Imports for Consumption, Imports' Share, 1978 and 1979, and Relative Increases or Declines in Imports and Producers Shipments in 1979.

Item	1978	1979
Actual 1978 and 1979 data: (In 1,000 units)		
Apparent consumption	11,185.0	10,315.3
U.S. producers' domestic shipments	8,356.9	7,518.2
Imports for consumption	2,928.1	2,797.1
Ratio of imports to consumption(%)	26.2%	27.1%
Estimate for 1979, holding import share of consumption constant at 1978 level and using actual 1979 consumption data (in 1,000 units)		
Imports, if held at 1978 share of consumption	NA	2,702.6
U.S. producers' domestic shipments if held at 1978 share of consumption	NA	7,612.7
Net change from 1978 to 1979 (in 1,000 units)		
Decline in U.S. producers' shipments	NA	738.7
Net decline due to increase import share	NA	94.5
Net decline due to declining demand	NA	644.2
Share of declining U.S. shipments due to [57]declining demand (%)	NA	87.2%

I believe that these tables demonstrate graphically why imports are not a "substantial cause" of either industry's present malaise. They suggest that declining demand accounted for over 80 percent of the net decline in U.S. producers' domestic shipments of both automobiles and trucks from 1978 to 1979, as compared with less than 20 percent of the decline in U.S. producers' domestic shipments being attributable to imports' increasing share of U.S. consumption. Between January-June 1979 and January-June 1980, about two-thirds of the decline in U.S. producers' domestic shipments was attributable to declining demand . . . Thus, even if the import share had been held constant during these critical 18 months, and even if all of those sales which went into the increased import share had instead gone to U.S. producers' domestic firms' sales still would

---

[57] The Chairman's opinion contains three additional tables similar to Table 1 showing that between January-June 1979 and January-June 1980 63.5% of the decline in domestic producers' shipments of automobiles was due to declining demand (Table 2) and that with respect to light trucks, 83.9% of the decline in domestic producers shipments between 1978 and 1979 and 66.9% of the decline between January-June 1979 and January-June 1980 was due to declining demand (Tables 3 and 4).

have fallen by over 80 percent of their actual decline in 1979 and by 60 percent of their actual decline in January-June 1980. . . .

Petitioners would perhaps dispute the conclusions I draw from the above tables because the tables fail to allow for the theory that an import increase in the earlier period of 1976-78 could be accountable for injury which did not become manifest until 1979. However, even if average imports, consumption and domestic shipments for 1976-78 are compared to the 1979 figures, the decline in demand is still greater than the import factor. . . .

It has been argued . . . that the downturn in demand is itself a result of several factors, and that . . . to consider demand in the aggregate . . . is to cumulate artificially what are clearly separate causal elements in a manner inconsistent with the purposes or legislative history of Section 201. Among the separate and identifiable causes mentioned . . . are inflation, unemployment, rising interest rates, and higher energy costs. Undoubtedly, all of these factors played a part in bringing about the present recession in new vehicle sales. Supporters of the petition contend that none of these factors *alone* played as great a role in bringing about the injury as increasing imports.

All of these contentions seek to isolate and weigh separately the various components of a general economic downturn. In reality, most of the factors mentioned above have worked in unison to bring about what is commonly termed a "recession." Inflation in new vehicle prices coupled with higher credit rates have acted together to drive up the total costs of new motor vehicles. Interest rates have played a particularly important part in the volume of auto sales, because these are long-term consumer durable purchases where credit financing is the norm. Not only have transaction prices for new vehicles and monthly payments for loans increased, but credit has become "tighter," and the refusal rate on auto credit applications has grown. Unemployment and general inflation have acted to reduce the real disposable income of the average consumer, and a normal reaction has been to delay many long-term capital outlays.

All of these phenomena are part and parcel of a generalized recession. . . . But to say [that recessions] are comprised of a multitude of causes is not to say that reduced demand in a recession cannot be cited as a single cause for purposes of section 201. . . . The reason for such a policy is readily apparent; if decline in demand for the product is a consequence of an general economic downturn, then the inevitable recovery from the recession will restore health to the industry. . . . Cyclical downturns in the/economy are to be expected, and must not force a reliance on unnecessary import remedies. The problem which auto producers confront is one which confronts many sectors of the economy . . . and it cannot be solved by import relief. . . . [I]t is possible for imports to be a "substantial cause" of serious injury [during a recession] . . . only where the absolute or relative increase is of sufficient magnitude to outweigh or equal the effects of the recession itself. . . .

The Shift In Demand

[Here the Commissioner notes that there has been a major shift in demand from large to small cars due to the high cost of new cars, high interest rates, rising fuel costs and the consequent demand for more fuel-efficient models and the loss of trade-in value for the large cars currently in use. He then continues:]

This . . . consumer behavior . . . raises the inevitable question of whether shift in demand to smaller cars is itself a more important cause of serious injury than increased imports. . . . One of the difficulties in assessing such a factor quantitatively is that . . . two-thirds of the recent increase in small car sales has accrued to the benefit of importers. Ultimately, one becomes involved in a tautological debate about whether increased imports of small cars are an effect of the shift in demand or the explanation for it. Thus, it is only possible to make certain qualitative judgments about the shifting product mix within the domestic industry itself.

Ordinarily, the shift to another product within the same industry should not necessarily be injurious to that industry. However, the lead times associated with introducing new models and the magnitude of capital investments required make the auto industry unique. In order to be able to accommodate a shift, they must anticipate it by 3 to 5 years. . . . Due largely to unforeseen events such as the Iranian revolution and subsequent oil shortage, and because of the lead-time problem associated with auto production, U.S. producers' plans for expanding small car output lagged far behind the market and its needs. . . . Only General Motors [in contrast to Ford and Chrysler], with superior capital resources, was in a position to face the trend toward smaller cars. . . .

Clearly then, the rapid transition to smaller autos and trucks disturbed U.S. producers' plans for a slow, orderly transition. They had hoped to finance their plans for new, fuel-efficient models through the profits on large autos. . . . Our investigation reveals that the profit margin on small cars has traditionally been much less, so the industry found itself shifting into a product line which resulted in a lower ratio of net profits to sales. Yet, they were not producing such models on sufficient economies of scale to yield the type of profits that sales of large cars — loaded with expensive "extras" — could produce.

All of these factors unquestionably affected the profit picture of U.S. firms. . . . Thus, the shift in demand must be viewed as an "important cause" of injury separate and apart from the shift to imports. Many of the industries' costs would have been incurred even if import competition had not existed, because simple economics dictated the change in consumer preference. However, I do not believe that the problems associated with this shift in demand should be considered more important than the relative increase in imported products. First, there is the previously mentioned fact that two-thirds of the growth in small cars has accrued to the benefit of imports. Some have suggested that this merely means imports, particularly Japanese vehicles, were better situated to capitalize on the shift in demand. While this is certainly true, it does not alter the fact that the transition of domestic producers to smaller vehicles was much less profitable in the short run because a disproportionate number of small car sales were going to importers. . . . Also, U.S. firms have found themselves unable to charge sufficient markups on their small models because of import competition. Thus, I believe imports were an equal or greater problem for the industry to confront than the mere transition to small cars.

* * * *

Finally, there may be some implication . . . that we should give greater weight to the shift in demand as a cause because the industry brought injury upon itself by refusing to recognize in a timely manner the long term change in consumer preference away from "gas guzzlers." This "self inflicted injury" theory . . . ignores the fact that large car sales were exceedingly healthy in the period 1976-78. Events such as the revolution in Iran and the sudden changes in our nation's energy policy after decades of price regulation are what disturbed the pattern. . . . After the initial scare of gasoline lines and shortages in 1974, the American consumer flirted with a shift to small cars. [But soon] . . . went back to demanding large, fuel-inefficient vehicles . . . Thus, the auto industry has had considerable difficulty in judging fickle consumer wishes [and] . . . the fact remains that the American consumer was not ready for the change until 1979. . . .

* * * *

In addition to concluding that increased imports are not a substantial cause of the serious injury which presently exists, I also believe they could not be a substantial cause of any threat thereof. U.S. small car production is steadily increasing. The three major manufacturers have begun introducing their new generation of front wheel drive, fuel efficient vehicles. . . . As such products come on stream the import share of the small car market should decline, particularly if demand picks up. Of course, if we remain in a deep recession . . . it is probable that the present critical state of the industry will continue for some time. However, the adjustment already made by domestic firms . . . should act to reduce the import share . . . [The fact] . . . that monthly import sales have actually declined since August, 1980, . . . seems to suggest that import volume has peaked, and that there would only be a noticeably higher import market share if demand for automobiles continued to decline. Such a decline in demand would only dramatize the causal link to recessionary factors which I have already cited as the major problem.

Views of Commissioner Paula Stern

* * * *

Many Causes of Injury:
Imports Not a Substantial Cause

Although there is serious injury present in the passenger car industry, I have determined that increased imports do not constitute a substantial cause of the existing serious injury.

Standards and Framework

* * * *

[Under this heading Commissioner Stern makes a number of points worth noting. *First,* in the Commissioner's view the ability of imports to perform relatively better than the domestic product in a recession always demands explanation; it cannot *ipso facto* establish that imports are an important cause of serious injury as great as any other cause,[58] especially since the legislative history indicates that a shift in demand may be deemed a cause of injury alternative to imports. *Second,* she rejects both Honda's argument that the Commission has explicitly considered intra-industry shifts in negative determinations and Ford's contention that a change in consumer tastes must be a shift to a product outside the scope of the domestic industry before it can be considered as an cause of injury alternative to imports. Ford's position would make too many decisions turn on the technicality of how the industry was defined. *Third,* cyclical industries raise a special conceptual problem which the Commission had never squarely considered; namely should a "normal" business cyclical decline in overall demand be factored out of the total injury picture or alternatively should only injury beyond that expected be assessed in determining the seriousness of the injury and causation? The first approach makes it more difficult for a cyclical industry to demonstrate serious injury but easier to show substantial causation. The opposite effects occur if you factor in normal declines. Quoting from what is now Section 201(c)(1)(A), she concludes that arguably the statute envisions no elimination of injury of any sort from a "serious" injury determination.]

* * * *

Causes of Injury

. . . The injury sustained by the automobile industry can best be explained by analyzing four fundamental phenomena:

(1) A general decline in demand due to rapidly increasing costs of car ownership and operation (added to normal — if not precisely predictable — recessionary effects on consumer income and confidence);

(2) A seemingly permanent shift in consumer tastes to relatively smaller, more fuel-efficient autos;

(3) A substantially negative accounting impact on profits resulting from huge investments to transform the industry; and

(4) Success of imports in head-to-head competition.

The decline in demand and shift in demand are more important causes of injury to the auto industry than increasing imports, per se. I have not been able to evaluate fully the relative significance of the massive capital costs of transforming the industry; however, I believe that their impact on domestic industry performance is at least of the same magnitude as that of imports. It is doubtful that in the absence of the first three causes the remaining injury attributable to imports would be serious.

---

[58] Findings on such other questions as the scope of the industry can also have an impact on the causal analysis. In Mushrooms, Inv. No. TA-201-42, USITC Pub. No. 1089 (1980), the imported product was canned while a substantial portion of the domestic industry was devoted to marketing fresh mushrooms. Had the two been deemed separate industries, the determination might well have been different.

General Decline in Demand

. . . The general decline in automobile consumption by 25 percent from the first half of 1979 to the first half of 1980 is in greatest part due to factors peculiar in their severity to the present recession and quite unrelated to the presence of imports in the American market place.

Consumer demand for automobiles is determined by the need for private transportation, disposable income . . . the value of trade-in cars, and the true price of auto ownership and operation. The total costs of auto ownership consist of depreciation, finance charges, gasoline, maintenance, insurance, parking, tolls, and taxes. None of [these] have . . . advanced more slowly than general price trends. Studies [of] . . . the last five years for each class of cars . . . [show that] costs [of automobile ownership] between 1975 and 1980 rose rapidly in nominal terms . . . [and] were less marked when converted to constant dollars — a slow decline from 1975 to 1979 and then a more rapid rise from 1979 through 1980.

The underlying reasons for the growth of ownership/operation costs of autos have nothing whatever to do with imports; the three main culprits have been the explosion of gasoline prices, the rapid rise in new car prices, and the credit crunch. . . .

The rise in retail costs during the last two years has been accomplished by an erosion of per capita real disposable income, which declined from $4,536 (1972 dollars) in first-quarter 1979, to $4,425 in the second quarter of 1980. While the numbers themselves are not huge, one must remember that Americans are accustomed to an increasing living standard; any decline has a shocking effect. It is not purely psychological; people are poorer than they were two years ago.

Underneath the market phenomena lie changes in the perceived need for private transport. The domestic market in the last decade became principally a replacement market; expanded ownership became primarily a response to slow population growth rather than to growth of two and three-car families. The development of mass transit systems . . . [growth] in rental car fleets . . . [the fact that] . . . between 1972 and 1979, the average age of passenger cars on the road grew from 5.7 years to 6.4 years . . . [all mean that] . . . the penchant for additional per capita auto consumption seems to have been quenched as the domestic market reached maturity.

* * * *

Beyond any general decline in auto sales lies the phenomenal collapse of the market for the traditional large cars which have been the historic mainstay of profits for the industry. . . .

Shift in Demand

. . . [T]here are also "substitution" effects. As demand declined in 1979 and 1980, it also shifted: sales of large cars — the mainstay of the U.S. auto industry — fell faster than overall consumption from 1975 to 1979. Large cars declined to 29.2 percent of apparent consumption by 1980. The shift in demand to smaller, more fuel-efficient autos has followed the relative increase in the total cost of operation of large versus small cars. . . . All observers and industry members regard the shift to smaller, more fuel-efficient vehicles as irreversible.

* * * *

A more general phenomenon, of which the shift in mix is but one part, can be observed in the long-term trend of net profits to net sales in the auto industry. The data for the last twenty years show cyclical behavior for the aggregate profit margins, but there is also an alarming secular trend: from 1960 to 1980 each successive peak (or trough) is lower than the previous peak (or trough). Each year the industry has had to sell more cars to make the same absolute level of profits. Clearly this trend could not go on forever. The years of reckoning were 1979-1980. A readjustment was inevitable, and imports have had little to do with this ominous trend.

* * * *

Imports

Imports, particularly those from Japan, have dramatically increased their market share. The extent to which an imported product has been able to capture sales in direct competition with domestic product to the detriment of the domestic industry is the extent to which they can be considered a cause of injury.

All the pricing information suggests that the success of imported automobiles has not been based on any competitive price advantage. For example, the export price index for Japanese autos grew 38 percent from the beginning of 1976 to the end of 1979 while the producer price index for domestic sales grew only 29 percent during the same period. The price data are quite complex, but there are no indications that Japanese cars or any other imports enjoy any direct price advantage.

[With regard to] quality . . . imports, particularly Japanese autos, have enjoyed a definite advantage in the perception of quality they have been able to generate among U.S. customers. Surveys . . . clearly show that domestic cars are viewed as having lower quality than foreign ones.

[Here Commissioner Stern notes that this perception may in part be justified by the fact that none of the four largest selling Japanese car makers had a recall rate higher than one-third the lowest rate shown by a U.S. producer.]

I have treated quality considerations as an explanation of how imports may have contributed to the injury of the domestic industry. . . . I have not treated fuel-economy, a definite factor in the choice of imports, in the same fashion because imports have only been incidental beneficiaries of a more fundamental shift in demand to smaller cars. This shift has also definitely benefited domestic small cars such as the Chevrolet Chevette, whose production lines have been operating at full capacity during the last two years.

The independent contribution of imports to injury must be assessed in relation to other factors such as the decline and shift in demand. The shift/share analysis prepared by ITC staff aided such an evaluation. [See page — *supra*].

[Here the Commissioner mentions demographic considerations. Because larger domestic cars have had their best markets among blue collar workers — the consumers hardest hit by a recession — large cars tend to suffer a greater downturn in market share during a recession and the market share of small car imports is counter-cyclical.]

Serious Injury Will Continue,
Imports Not a Substantial Cause

[At this point Commissioner Stern turns to examine whether imports might be a threatened cause of future injury, offering the following summary of her conclusions.]

The unusual problems suffered by this industry in terms of sales, profits and employment will likely continue. However, imports are not threatening to become a substantial cause of any future injury. [While] the plans underway for restructuring the industry [will] address many of the industry's problems . . . continuing difficulties in the cost and availability of consumer credit and unavoidable time lags in the introduction of new fuel-efficient models may retard the industry's recovery. The continued incidence of high capital expenditures will restrain improvements in profits while rapid productivity improvements will prevent employment from ever recovering to former levels. However, in . . . the long-term prospects for the domestic industry as a whole are good as it increasingly focuses on a world rather than national market. . . .

* * * *

. . . No tangible link between [the auto-makers ambitious transformation] . . . plans and any requested import relief has been established. The transformation of the industry will take place in the absence of any import relief and would not be speeded by relief. . . . Extending a strict relief program over the next five years, using a quota of 1.7 million units could generate $4.0 billion (1979 dollars) — or less than eight percent of the projected new investment of $40 billion.[59]

Ignoring the huge cost of any remedy to the public . . . [t]he UAW and Ford have professed an interest in encouraging foreign auto producers to locate facilities in the United States. Volkswagen and Honda . . . are well down this path . . . [Both] have shown in confidential submissions that the UAW proposal . . . would set up difficult-to-administer local content rules which would make establishing a domestic plant an enormous gamble. . . .

Furthermore, there are good reasons to believe that relief would be inimical to the interests of most other U.S. producers, because they have already become so highly integrated on an international scale. General Motors . . . has begun a serious program of worldwide expansion . . . American Motors . . . is dependent on completion of major financing plans with Renault. [Both of these projects] . . . could be seriously jeopardized by import relief. Chrysler has been rather silent with respect to relief. . . . Its financial state seems to have been helped by its captive imports from Japan. . . .

---

[59] Our staff study assumes no domestic price increases; any price increases would trade off potential jobs and production for increased profits.

* * * *

*Views of Commissioners George M. Moore
and Catherine Bedell*

* * * *

[Commissioners Moore and Bedell concluded, contrary to the majority, that increased imports of *passenger automobiles* had caused serious injury to the domestic industry, but were in agreement with the majority that this was not so of *automobile trucks, bodies and chassis.*]

We agree with the Commission majority that the domestic automobile industry is seriously injured. . . . [At the same time] imports have increased significantly, in both actual and relative terms. More important, however, imports have captured an ever larger share of the domestic passenger automobile market; . . . 25 percent in 1976 and 1977, 26 percent in 1978, 27 percent in 1979 and 25 percent in the first 6 months of 1979 [compared with] . . . 34 percent in the first 6 months of 1980. . . . [While] we believe that there are a number of other individual causes of injury[60] . . . we find that none of these other causes . . . are a more important cause of serious injury to the domestic industry than increased imports. . . .

It is clear that our determination differs from the majority in the interpretation given to the provisions in section 201 of the Trade Act. . . . We believe that the law clearly and unequivocally provides that the Commission shall . . . isolate each of the economic factors relevant to the matter of serious injury for the purpose of comparing each of them with the factor of increased imports. If we were to do otherwise — that is, to aggregate the negative economic factors — . . . there would be few, if any, Commission decisions favorable to a domestic industry in section 201 cases in times of recession or economic downturn.

. . . Further, we believe that economic downturns represent the concurrence of a number of adverse factors. We do not believe that Congress envisioned that the Commission would consider an economic downturn per se to be a single economic factor. Instead, we believe that Congress intended the Commission to examine imports and their impact on the domestic industry over the course of the business cycle — during both good and bad years — in order to ascertain whether import penetration is increasing and, if so, whether the increasing penetration is seriously injuring the domestic industry. . . .

. . . We believe that the domestic industry today would be in much better condition — losses would not be so massive and plant closings and layoffs not so severe — had imports not increased their share of the market to the extent that they have. Furthermore, the surge in imports and share of the market held by imports make it likely that the industry will remain in its present state of serious injury for years to come and increase the likelihood that one or more of the major domestic producers and several of the domestic suppliers will not survive. . . .

---

[60] The other causes listed by the Commissioners were a shift in consumer preferences, high interest rates, a shortage of consumer credit, increased gasoline prices, the failure of domestic corporate management to anticipate current conditions and costly Government regulations. - Ed.

This is a classic case for an affirmative determination under section 201 of the Trade Act. . . . There are increasing imports resulting in dramatic increases in the penetration of the domestic market . . . [and] the domestic industry is suffering almost catastrophic injury. . . . Had it not been for increasing imports of passenger automobiles during the past 3 years, the domestic industry would now be well into the process of adjusting to the other, less important adverse economic conditions.

[While] . . . is not feasible to assign a number on a scale of 1 to 10 to each of the causes of serious injury and thereby discover which is the most important cause . . . it is consistent with the legislative intent to examine each individual cause to determine which one, if absent, would have had the greatest effect of alleviating the serious injury experienced by the domestic industry. On that basis the most important cause of serious injury to the domestic automobile industry is increasing imports of on-the-highway passenger automobiles. . . .

We believe reasonable quotas on imports . . . would have provided the domestic . . . industry with a much-needed opportunity to adjust to the anew competitive conditions . . . which are the result of economic factors beyond its control."

NOTES AND QUESTIONS

(1) Commissioners Moore and Bedell argue that Chairman Alberger, by aggregating into a single cause all factors contributing to the recession generally and to the decline in demand for automobiles more specifically, made it extremely difficult for any industry to receive "escape clause" relief during an economic downturn. Their criticism can be rather pointedly illustrated by the following example:

Assume a general 10% decline in aggregate sales of all automobiles (imported as well as domestic) and that, prior to the decline, imports commanded 25% of the U.S. market and domestic producers 75%. Note that, under the shift-share analysis employed by Commissioner Alberger, for imports to constitute a "cause" of injury "not less" important than the general decline in demand, import penetration (i.e., substitution of imports for domestic production) must result in a further 10% decline in sales by domestic producers. Since imports account for only 25% of the market, this level of market penetration can only be achieved if there is an absolute increase in imports. Stated another way, 10% of 75% is greater than 10% of 25%. Therefore, the *increase* in imports necessary to cause an additional 10% decline in the domestic producers market share (i.e., 10% of 75%) must necessarily exceed the *decline* in imports occasioned by the recession (i.e., 10% of 25%). More generally, any time imports in the base year command less than 50% of the U.S. market the Chairman's shift-share analysis will require an absolute, rather than relative, increase in imports before the latter could qualify as a "substantial cause" of injury.

Can this be squared with the 1974 Act?

(2) On the other hand, have Commissioners Moore and Bedell solved the problem? The task of quantifying each of the multiple forces giving rise to a recession and assaying the contribution that each may have made to a decline in product demand is enough to intimidate even the most intrepid econometrician. Note Commissioner's Moore and Bedell make no effort to do so.

There is also the problem of determining the level at which disaggregation is to occur. Consider the 1980-81 recession. That downturn could be attributed, in significant part, to the tight money policies adopted by the Federal Reserve Board in response to the inflation of the late 1970's and to the second oil embargo. Tight money yielded high interest rates; interest rates contributed to a strong dollar; a strong dollar and high interest rates then combined with inflation to produce an industrial slow-down; the slow-down increased unemployment and hence decreased the spendable income available for the purchase of automobiles. At the same time the general inflation together with the oil-embargo, large industry wage settlements, high interest rates and new governmental regulations drove up the price of purchasing and maintaining an automobile.

At what level should the ITC disaggregate? Should it separately assess the impact on demand of general inflation, wage settlements, government regulation, oil prices, rising interest rates and the strong dollar and then compare each with the adverse impact that imports may have had on the industry? Would that not virtually assure "escape clause" relief for any domestic industry whose import competition experienced even a modest increase in market share during a recession? Is this approach consistent with the purpose of the "escape clause"? Return to this question after considering Note (5) below.

Alternatively, should the ITC aggregate separately first the factors that contributed to rising automobile purchase and maintenance costs and second the factors that led to declining spendable income, and then compare each of these partial aggregates with the impact of imports on the industry? If so, why not aggregate all the factors that caused the recession?

(3) Does Commissioner's Stern's approach solve some of these problems. In the *Stainless Steel and Alloy Tool Case,* [61] she offered the following summary of the approach she took in that case:

> Cyclical industries are moving targets and hence it is more difficult to focus on them. Amidst the peaks and troughs of their cycles, we can draw an imaginary trend line which smooths out the cycles. This puts cyclical industries on the same basis as those not so exposed to the effects of recessions and booms. The criteria of section 201 may then be applied to any departure from this imaginary trend line to answer how large the departure is (the question of serious injury) and what factors are responsible (the question of substantial cause).

Suppose, in accord with this approach, we calculated the percentage *decline in aggregate U.S. demand* for automobiles — both domestic and imported — during

---

[61] International Trade Commission, Report To The President On Stainless Steel And Alloy Tool Steel Investigation No. TA-201-48, USITC Publication 1377, (May, 1983), "Additional Views of Commissioner Stern."

1974-75 and earlier recessions and extrapolated from that data a percentage representing the "normal" cyclical downturn for the industry, a downturn for which no "escape clause" relief would be available. Assume the decline in demand in the 1979-80 recession exceeded this percentage. Suppose that we then reduced the *total loss of sales by domestic producers* in 1979-80 by that percentage, treating only the excess loss as "abnormal," which if caused by imports, would merit "escape clause" relief. How would such a calculation help? Would it demonstrate that the added severity — the "abnormal" loss by domestic producers — was attributable to imports, or would the Commission still have to analyze the causes of the "abnormal" decline in precisely the way it did in the *Automobile Case*? Conversely, suppose the percentage used for the industry's "normal" cyclical decline was greater than the percentage decline in demand during the 1979-80 recession. Would that demonstrate that imports were not a significant cause of the latter? In the Automobile Case did Commissioner Stern actually address these issues, and if so how?

(4) The problem won't go away because Congress has now entered the act. Section 201(b)(10) as added by the 1988 Act provides:

> **In making a determination under paragraph (1), the Commission shall take into account the condition of the domestic industry over the course of the relevant business cycle and shall not aggregate the causes of declining demand associated with a recession or economic downturn in the United States economy into a single cause of serious injury or threat of injury.**

(5) Congress' intent was to repudiate the heavy reliance placed by Chairman Alberger on the "shift-share" analysis in the *Automobile Case*. [62] But that doesn't solve the problem.

Consider the matter from another perspective. The escape clause is designed to allow a domestic industry to adjust to a deterioration in its relative *comparative advantage* or to a loss of protection against its pre-existing *comparative disadvantage*. As such it is addressed to those industry specific market factors that determine trade flows. If, however, the injury is attributable principally to macro-economic conditions — which can, of course, also affect trade flows — the extension of escape clause relief becomes more problematic. In the latter case, any adjustment designed to meet an assumed loss of competitive efficiency by the domestic industry may well run counter to what in the longer run, when the macro-economic distortions abate, would be the most efficient solution for the industry. Thus, we cannot — as Congress recognized — ignore recessions. From this perspective, however, what would the following evidence suggest:

    (a) No factor exogenous to the general recession, such as cost-busting labor settlements, government regulations or defaults of management, was plainly at fault; and

---

[62] See Report of the Committee on Ways and Means, U.S. House of Representatives on H.R. 3, The Trade and Economic Policy Reform Act of 1987, Rep. No 100-40, Part 1, 100th Cong., 1st Sess. April 6, 1987 at page 101. The Committee Report summarizes the purposes of Section 201(b)(10) in the following terms: "The amendment would not preclude the Commission from considering the effects of a recession, but instead would direct the Commission . . . not [to] aggregate the different causes of declining demand — such as high interest rates, unemployment, reduced business investment and higher energy costs — if related to a recession, into a single cause of injury."

(b) Imports, facing the same recessionary conditions as domestic production, had significantly displaced domestic sales (*i.e.*, the domestic industry had suffered a non-trivial loss of market share), without the benefit of a plainly over-valued dollar.

How did the approach taken by Commissioners Moore and Bedell differ from this?

(6) At this point it is necessary to broaden the perspective even further and place the "escape clause" into the context of the overall "safeguards" problem as exacerbated by the new protectionism. Consider the following information. Does it suggest a political argument for the "escape clause" that might influence the solution to the problems discussed in the foregoing Notes? If so, how?

(a) After the ITC's negative decision in the *Automobile Case*, the Reagan administration, in 1981, entered into a Voluntary Export Restraint (VER) with Japan limiting Japanese automobile exports to the United States to 1.68 million cars per year. The VER was renewed for the 1984-85 period, and again for 1986-87 with only a slightly higher limits of 1.8 million and million cars, respectively, per year. In a 1984 study of the effects of these agreements, Robert Crandall points out a number of facts.[63]

— By 1983 the industry had returned to an appearance of financial health. The price of Japanese cars surged and U.S manufacturers paid substantial bonuses to their executives.

— By 1981 manufacturers had reduced the average weight of a domestic car 30 percent. Even before the VER the industry was selling 40 percent of its cars with international competition. Fuel economy was up by more than 25 percent over 1972-73 and actual fuel economy increased much more than that, as buyers shifted to smaller cars.

— Between 1975-76 and 1979-80, the companies' real investment expenditures increased by more than 88 percent. Between 1981 and the date of the study, real investment expenditures by the automobile industry had fallen by 30 percent.

— By creating an artificial scarcity of Japanese imports, the voluntary restraints have increased the prices charged for those cars. A 1983 Wharton Econometrics study estimated that as a result of the quotas, the prices of Japanese imports jumped an average of $920 to $960 per car in 1981-82 alone. With the surge in demand that took place in 1983, this price effect surely increased substantially.

— The VER's benefited Japanese producers and their dealers by at least $2 billion per year in price enhancement.

---

[63] Crandall, Import Quotas And The Automobile Industry: The Costs of Protection, The Brookings Review, Summer, 1984 at page 8.

(b) Recall the various types of "safeguard" measures traditionally employed by the United States: those promulgated by the Executive under "general framework legislation;" product specific restraints, including those that have escaped GATT negotiated tariff reductions; and those issued under the President's independent authority (See page — *supra*). In a study by Hufbauer and Rosen[64] the authors investigated all 31 cases of protection since World War II in which trade exceeded $100 million and found the following:

— In eight cases, protection was based on Executive action under general framework legislation. In all but one case — petroleum — that protection has been continuously in effect for periods ranging from 23 to 54 years.

— Three cases involved product specific legislation. In all three, protection is continuing; in two cases that protection dates back to the 19th century; in the third case, the protection has been in effect for 11 years.

— Seven cases involved high tariffs dating back 58-66 years. All but one are still in place.

— In four cases, all involving steel or automobiles, the President acted on his independent authority. Carbon Steel has been protected for 21 years, with a short four year hiatus 1974-78, and automobiles for the eight years since 1981, with no end in sight.

— In nine cases protection was extended under the "escape clause." The average length of protection was about 5 years.

(c) Finally, consider other differences between "escape clause" relief and other types of safeguards, such as the typical form of the barriers raised against imports (tariffs v. quotas) and the incidents of international surveillance.

(6) Recall that in the *Automobile* Case it was suggested to the Commission that much of the loss of market share by domestic manufacturers was due to inferior product quality. This raises the whole question of how to treat evidence of management failures in an "escape clause" causality analysis. If it appears that an industry's troubles are primarily the result of management mistakes, the mere fact that there was a coincident increase in imports would not seem to justify "escape clause" relief. Given the broader political context in which the clause might be placed and its purpose to aid domestic industries adjust to new competitive conditions, however, would you fashion an exception to this? Be specific.

(7) Manifestly, the shift from domestic automobiles to imports was a major factor in the *Automobile* Case. The domestic industry argued that the shift in consumer preference toward fuel efficient cars was a straight forward shift from the purchase of domestic to the purchase of imported cars and could not be treated

---

[64] Hufbauer & Rosen, Trade Policy For Troubled Industries, Institute For International Economics, Washington, D.C., 1986. For a more detailed study of the thirty-one cases, see: Hufbauer, Berliner & Elliott, Trade Protection In The United States: 31 Cases, Institute for International Economics, Washington D. C., 1986.

as a cause of injury separate from imports. Most of the Commissioner's, however, seemed disposed to consider such a shift separately, an alternative to imports as a cause of injury, although Commissioner Stern was careful to say it required analysis. Indeed, Vice Chairman Michael Calhoun responded to the industry's argument by drawing a conceptual distinction between a shift in demand reflecting an over-all structural decline or other change in an industry and a pure shift to imports. Section 201, he points out, is not a "industrial relief" but an "import relief" measure. Query, does this conceptual distinction of itself explain why a change in demand that redounds overwhelmingly to the benefit of imports should not still be an occasion for "escape clause" relief?[65] Would it change your answer if the domestic industry had failed to take any corrective action knowing that the shift was likely to occur, or had it responded with a patently inferior product.

(8) Recall that the working party in the *Hatter's Fur* Case said that it was not permissible under Article XIX to withdraw a concession "in order to promote the . . . development of domestic production of a new or novel type of product" which foreign suppliers had introduced to the domestic market. On the other hand, the United States countervailing duty legislation,[66] as sanctioned by the GATT Subsidies Code,[67] authorizes the imposition of a countervailing duty against any subsidized import if because of the latter "the establishment of an industry in the United States is materially retarded." United States "escape clause" legislation contains no such provision. Should the latter and Article XIX be revised or interpreted to permit relief in such cases? From an economic viewpoint is there a difference between the "escape clause" and the countervailing duty law? Could one make a political argument for the revision?

[D] Assistance to Workers and Firms Injured By Increased Import Competition

In addition to the "escape clause" as a devise for assisting American firms to adjust to increased import competition, there are two programs under which direct financial and other assistance may be given to firms and to workers ostensibly to aid them in adjusting to injurious import competition. Labelled "Trade Adjustment Assistance" these programs were first established under the

---

[65] To his credit the Vice Chairman goes on to explain more fully why the shift to smaller fuel efficient cars was a cause of injury separate from imports. He pointed out that in the period 1978-1979, with the start of the recession, the demand for large cars fell by more than the overall decline in demand so that sales of small cars actually increased and that, in 1979, domestic small car sales increased by an even greater amount, while sales of imports declined. The growth in small car demand was, in short, moving overwhelmingly toward small domestic cars. Then, between the first half of 1979 and the first half of 1980, the trend was reversed for two reasons. First, by 1980 demand for small cars had caught up with domestic production capabilities. (*e.g.*, Chevrolet Chevette was operating at or above their capacity). Second, other domestic manufacturers were experiencing serious recall problems (*e.g.*, Chrysler's Volarie and Aspen) or major adverse publicity regarding product safety (Ford Pinto).

[66] 19 U.S.C Section 1671(a)(2)(C).

[67] Article 2, Note 4 of the Agreement On Interpretation And Application Of Article VI, XVI and XXIII Of The General Agreement On Tariffs And Trade, GATT, BISD 26th Supp. (1980) at page 57.

Trade Expansion Act of 1962 were then liberalized in the Trade Act of 1974 and have proceeded fitfully ever since. In 1981[68] the Reagan Administration persuaded Congress to change the method of paying and the level of benefits, changes that have been retained in the several subsequent renewals of the program. The last of these — the 1988 Act — extends both programs through 1993 essentially along the lines of the 1981 enactment but with a number of interesting new features.

Both programs have come in for severe criticism. Worker assistance has, according to its critics, served more as an extended unemployment insurance program than as an incentive for worker adjustment to new competitive conditions. Direct assistance to firms has had a marginal impact. Be that as it may, a review of both programs and the criticisms leveled at them is necessary to a fuller understanding of what mechanisms may be useful in facilitating the adjustment to changing conditions of international trade.

Worker Assistance

The Secretary of Labor, acting in response to a petition, is required to certify as eligible for worker readjustment assistance any group of workers in a firm or "subdivision" thereof if he finds that: the sales or production of that firm have decreased; that a significant proportion of all workers in the firm or "subdivision" have been totally or partially separated; and that increased imports have "contributed importantly" to the separation. "Contributed importantly" is defined as "a cause which is important, but not necessarily more important than any other cause". In spite of an aborted attempt in 1981 to conform this latter requirement to the escape clause "substantial cause" standard (*i.e.*, not less important than any other cause), these criteria have remained unchanged since 1974. The 1988 Act, reversing several court decisions, extends the program's coverage to employees of firms supplying inputs to a company that has been injured by import competition.

Once a group of workers have been certified, individual workers within the group who have been employed by their firm at least 26 weeks during the 52 weeks preceding their separation, can apply for one or more of the following types of assistance; a weekly cash payment known as a trade readjustment allowance (TRA), an allowance to cover the costs of training, a job search allowance or a relocation allowance.

Under the 1974 Act, the TRA was equal to the lesser of 70% of the workers own average weekly wage or 100% of the average weekly manufacturing wage. If the worker was also receiving unemployment insurance or training assistance, or both, his TRA would be reduced if the combination of all benefits, plus any wages earned exceeded 80% of his weekly wage or 130% of the average manufacturing wage, whichever was less. TRA payments continued for up to 52 weeks with an additional 26 weeks for certain elderly workers and workers in training.

The 1981 changes reduced the amount of the TRA to the applicable unemployment insurance rate and provided that TRA payments were to commence only after the worker had exhausted his unemployment insurance. Also the 52 week

---

[68] Omnibus Budget Reconciliation Act, Pub. L. 97-35, 95 Stat. 357, (1981).

maximum for TRA payments was reduced by the number of weeks the worker had received unemployment compensation. An additional 26 weeks of TRA payments could be made, however, if necessary to allow the worker to complete an approved training program. The 1981 amendments also reduced the amount of the TRA by any income deductible under the applicable state unemployment insurance law and required that the worker be enrolled in, or have completed, a *job search* program approved by the Secretary. The 1988 Act takes this latter requirement one step further. To be eligible for TRA the worker must have enrolled in or, since his separation, completed a *job training* program approved by the Secretary. The 1988 Act provides, however, that training allowances (not TRA) may be paid while the worker is receiving unemployment compensation payments. The 1988 Act also provides funds to assist State's in establishing retraining programs for "displaced workers," a category which could include worker's eligible for trade adjustment assistance but is much more inclusive.

A major innovation of the 1988 Act is a mandate to the Secretary of Labor to establish one or more "demonstration projects" to test the feasibility of a "Supplemental Wage Allowance" program. Under that program any worker eligible to receive TRA payments who can find employment at a weekly wage less than he was receiving before his separation from the import impacted firm, will be offered the option of taking his TRA or taking the new job and receiving from the Government a supplemental payment. That payment would equal the lesser of (i) the TRA which he would otherwise receive or (ii) the difference between 80% of his prior wage and the wage he will receive on the new job.[69]

Other forms of assistance that eligible workers may receive are: an allowance to cover the costs of an approved training program, and, within limits, travel and subsistence for separate maintenance while in training; 90% of the necessary expenses of searching for a job, including travel and subsistence up to a limit of $800; and 90% of the cost of relocating himself and his family to the site of a new job, if the Secretary finds that the worker cannot be expected to secure suitable employment within the commuting area where he resides.

Finally, the 1988 Act creates a Trade Adjustment Assistance Trust Fund in which the proceeds from a uniform *ad velorum* fee imposed on all but a few imports into the United States are to be deposited. Monies from the Trust Fund are to be used to finance both worker and firm adjustment assistance and certain other trade programs. The amount of the fee is to be set periodically by the President based on estimates of the amount of money needed for the programs

---

[69] For example, suppose that a worker before separation from his import impacted job was earning $700 per week, that his TRA, which is equal to his unemployment insurance benefits, is $500 per week and that the new job would pay $400 per week. Eighty percent of his prior wage equals $560 an amount which exceeds his new wage by $160 per week. Since this difference is less than the TRA he would otherwise receive, his supplemental payment is $160. This amount combined with his pay from the new job gives the worker a total income of $560, or $60 per week more than his TRA. Moreover, the supplemental payment begins immediately with the new job, while he will receive his TRA only after his unemployment insurance benefits run out. On the other hand, he runs the risk that if he is laid-off from the new lower paying job his unemployment insurance benefits will probably be lower than if he takes those benefits immediately. Also if the second lay-off is not caused by import competition he foregoes any future TRA.

it is intended to support but may not exceed .15% *ad velorum*. The President is instructed to seek GATT approval of the fee. The Trust Fund will go into effect upon receipt of that approval but no later than 2 years following enactment of the 1988 Act, unless the President certifies that implementation without GATT approval would be contrary to the national economic interest.

During the five year period 1976-1980, before the 1981 changes took effect, 1,313,349 workers had been certified. After the 1981 changes took effect this dropped to 179,869 workers for the four year period 1981-85. Total TRA payments for 1976-1980 equalled $2,433,000,000, dropping to $1,656,300,000 for the period 1981-85. For 1976-1980 training allowances totaled $19 million, relocation allowances $2.6 million and other benefits $600,000. For the years 1981-85 training allowances rose to $51.4 million, relocation allowances to $10.1 million and other benefits $1 million.

Of the 1,320,685 workers who received TRA benefits in 1976-1981, 47,790 or 4% entered approved retraining programs. After the 1981 changes, this jumped to 31% for the three years 1982-84. Of those who in 1976-1981 started training, 36% completed the training and 21% of the latter were actually placed in new jobs. During the three years 1982-84 46% of those who started training completed their programs, but only 8.7% of the latter were placed in new jobs.[70]

Not surprisingly unionized workers benefited from these programs far more extensively than non-unionized workers. For the period April 3, 1975 through June 30, 1982, union workers received 83% of all TRA payments, representing nearly five times the amount paid non-union workers. Also 67% of these payments went to auto and steel workers, with apparel, textile, footwear, metal and electronics workers picking-up most of the remainder.[71]

The TRA program has been broadly criticized as not effectively promoting the transfer of labor from industries whose optimal response to import competition lies in either retrenchment or labor displacing technological change. The criticism is based upon a number of facts. The complicated causality test for eligibility has too often produced inordinate delays in the issuance of eligibility certifications. Seventy-one percent of the workers surveyed in a GAO study had returned to work before receiving their first TRA payments.[72] Moreover, under the original scheme of the 1974 Act, overwhelming numbers of beneficiaries used their TRA payments as supplemental unemployment insurance, rather than treating those benefits as support while engaged in retraining and searching for alternative employment. They viewed the payments as compensation to tide them over a temporary lay-off until recalled to their original jobs — a time for leisure activity and an odd-job or two. Two major factors combined to produce this result. A disproportionate number of beneficiaries were highly paid unionized workers covered by supplemental unemployment insurance. With these supplemental payments added to their TRA, a substantial number of beneficiaries suffered

---

[70] Lawrence and Litan, Saving Free Trade; A Pragmatic Approach, Brookings Institution, Washington D.C. (1986) pages 56 and 58.

[71] Dorn, Trade Adjustment Assistance: A Case Of Government Failure, 2 Cato Journal 865, 879-880 (1982).

[72] General Accounting Office, Restricting Trade Act Benefits to Import-Affected Workers Who Cannot Find A Job Can Save Millions (GAO, 1980).

minimal pay reductions during layoff. Since for these same workers most alternative employment would have entailed a substantial pay reduction, their optimal strategy was to sit tight and hope to be recalled to their old jobs. Indeed, according to the GAO, 85% of TRA beneficiaries through late 1978 did in fact return to their old jobs.[73]

It would not appear that the 1981 changes improved the situation very much. The number of beneficiaries fell dramatically. That, however, does not demonstrate the absence of a need to facilitate the orderly transfer of a significant number of workers to new jobs. Certainly it does not prove that a properly crafted program could not contribute to that adjustment. While the post 1981 emphasis on retraining increased the number of workers who sought and completed that training, the drop in the percentage who secured alternative employment indicates that the new emphasis did not materially improve the overall rate of readjustment, probably because the deferral of TRA payments until the worker's unemployment insurance ran out, caused many workers to defer new job searches. Again, this is evidence of how seriously the program has been plagued by rules that act as a disincentive to the very adjustment they are intended to promote. Most notably, not until the experiments mandated by the 1988 Act did the law take any cognizance whatsoever of perhaps the most important disincentive to worker readjustment — the reduced wages that too many TRA beneficiaries face if they take alternative employment.

Assistance to Firms

Upon application to the Secretary of Commerce, a firm may be certified as eligible for financial and other assistance if the Secretary finds that a significant number of the firm's workers have been partially or totally separated, that its production or sales have decreased or that sales or production of an article accounting for 25% of its business have decreased and that increased imports have "contributed importantly" to the separation of its employees and to the decline in its sales or production. "Contributed importantly" has the same meaning as with worker adjustment assistance. Once certified the firm may apply for several forms of assistance, but, in doing so, must submit an economic adjustment proposal. The proposal must, in the Secretary's judgment, be reasonably calculated to contribute to the firm's adjustment, adequately take account of the worker's interests and demonstrate the firm's willingness to use its own resources for economic development.

Once the proposal is approved the firm may receive technical assistance, loans or loan guarantees for the acquisition or upgrading of its physical plant or for working capital.

Participation in this program has not been widespread. While in 1977 the GAO estimated that over 14,000 manufacturing firms may have been hurt by imports,[74] between 1976-1980 only 972 firms were certified. These firms received $53.4 million in technical assistance and $272 million in financial assistance. For the

---

[73] *Id.*, page 10.

[74] Comptroller General of the United States, General Accounting Office, Report to the Congress: Adjustment Assistance To Firms Under The Trade Act Of 1974 — Income Maintenance Or Successful Adjustment? ID-78-53, page 9.

period 1981-85 the number of certified firms increased to 1,624 and the amount of technical assistance to $79.9 million. Financial assistance, however, declined to $112.2 million.[75]

Several major criticisms have been levelled at the program. Applicant firms have too often found it difficult to show significant worker lay-offs and an absolute decline in production or sales and at the same time give reasonable assurances that any loan they receive will be repaid. More seriously, however, the law does not require firms to shift investments to more competitive sectors of the economy. As a consequence the program has too often been used merely to keep marginal operations alive.

NOTES AND QUESTIONS

(1) Note the provisions of the 1988 Act authorizing the levy of a import "fee" of up to .15% to support trade adjustment assistance programs. Obviously, Congress wanted to expand those programs but, unlike "escape clause" relief, that expansion would require funding from the United States' treasury. Protectionism, in other words, is politically much cheaper for Congress than effective adjustment assistance. Hence, Congress seized upon the import "fee" as a way to minimize adjustment assistance appropriations. How might Congress have accomplished the latter purpose without resorting to a special "fee" requiring GATT approval? What might be done with existing quotas in order to facilitate an expanded trade adjustment assistance program?

(2) Under the law governing trade adjustment assistance for workers the Secretary of Labor must find that increased imports have caused the separation of a significant proportion of all workers in a firm or subdivision of a firm, including the group of workers seeking certification for that assistance. In *International Union, UAW v. Marshall*,[76] the court upheld the Secretary's determination that for the automobile industry this finding had to be made plant by plant, and could not be based solely upon a showing that the company as a whole had discharged a significant proportion of its workers because of increased import competition. The critics have claimed that the delays caused by this approach are among the program's principal failings. Evaluate the Secretary's position. Are the reasons for a causality test under the "escape clause" equally applicable in the case of trade adjustment assistance? Consider the further possibility that if an industry can prove growing unemployment and can otherwise qualify for "escape clause" relief, all separated workers in that industry would be eligible to receive trade adjustment assistance merely upon a showing that the experience of the particular firm from which they were separated conformed to the overall industry experience.

---

[75] Lawrence and Litan, Saving Free Trade; A Pragmatic Approach, Brookings Institution, Washington D.C. (1986) at page 56.

[76] 584 F. 2d 390 (D.C. Cir., 1978) (remanded for a further determination), 627 F. 2d 559 (D.C. Cir., 1980) (Secretary's determination upheld).

(3) Successful adjustment, even with adjustment assistance, often requires an industry and its workers to take hard measures. Does this suggest the need for the government to adopt an "industrial policy" for any industry seeking "escape clause" relief and adjustment assistance. An "industrial policy" means a planned series of measures devised principally by the government with which the industry would have to comply in order to receive the assistance sought.

With more resources available and in light of the political power of the industry, what is such a policy likely to contain? The experience of the carbon steel industry is of some note here. In 1984, after the ITC found that imports had badly damaged the domestic industry, and the President promised to negotiate VRA's, Congress stepped in and by law conditioned the President's authority to enforce those VRA's on the industry reinvesting "substantially all of its net cash flow" in modernizing its plant. It did this in spite of the fact that everyone of the firms which, between 1975-1981, had invested most heavily in steel production had by 1984 either vanished through bankruptcy or forced merger or were close to bankruptcy.[77]

"Industrial policies" pose other problems. In an industry such as apparel with many small firms, enforcement is extremely difficult. Japan's experience with its policy for downsizing the textile industry is instructive. Despite government purchases of surplus spinning looms, required registration of existing spindles and looms, and the banning of unregistered equipment, new producers continued to enter the industry. The estimated number of new illegal (unregistered) looms in production almost exactly cancelled the effective subsidies to reduce capacity.[78] Certainly enforcement of an "industrial policy" is not going to be made any easier when it is attached to protectionist measures that promise high profits.

Observe also how the problem of enforcing an "industrial policy" can increase the dangers of collusion. Consider a firm for whom "escape clause" relief has raised the price of its product 15%-20% and it proceeds to make its investment and employment decisions on that basis. Subsequently the President removes the "escape clause" relief well before its scheduled expiration because other firms in the industry have not shed capacity or modernized as required by a mandated "industrial policy." Plainly, such a prospect virtually invites firms in an industry to minimize the risks of early termination of relief by tacitly coordinating their pricing, investment and marketing activities.

§ 5.02 Subsidies and Countervailing Duties: The GATT and United States Legislation

Introduction

Subsidies pose a grievous problem for the international trading community There is a shared sense that subsidies, no less than tariffs or quantitative restrictions, can divert resources away from their most efficient or valued use. There i also a growing fear that competitive subsidizations may become — or have alread become — a contemporary replacement for the competitive devaluations — th

---

[77] Lawrence and Litan, op cit at page 90.
[78] Id., page 94.

"beggar-thy-neighbor" attitude — that so devastated the world economic order in the years between World Wars I and II. Yet, the impulse to subsidize persists.

In part, this propensity reflects the economic uncertainties of the post-1974 period. Faced with sluggish growth interspersed with periods of sharp and sometimes severe cyclical downturns, governments have found it difficult to resist turning to subsidies as a way of expanding exports and curtailing imports. Also subsidy schemes can, especially in the case of developing countries, become entangled with other more affirmative and urgent policy objectives that are not easily abandoned merely because they also have a trade distorting aspect.[1]

More fundamentally, however, the propensity to subsidize lies in the very nature of modern government. To quote Article 11 of the GATT Subsidies Code:[2]

> . . . subsidies other than export subsidies are widely used as important instruments for the promotion of social and economic policy objectives and . . . [therefore it was not the intent of the Code] to restrict the right of

----

[1] For example, export subsidies may frequently constitute a far better means of fostering the development of an infant industry than a protective tariff. If the rules of the international game permit the latter, the case against export subsidies tends to become something less than persuasive. Other examples include currency retention schemes and multiple exchange rate systems. Under a foreign currency retention scheme an exporter is allowed to keep scarce foreign exchange rather than surrender it to his nation's monetary authorities under the latter's exchange control system. Depending upon the system, the foreign exchange may be sold in a free market where it is likely to command a higher price than the official rate at which it would otherwise have to be surrendered. Alternatively, it may be used to import goods for which foreign exchange would otherwise not be available. Whatever the system, the possibility of keeping the scarce foreign exchange provides an important incentive to export. It may also permit the individual exporter to lower his export price while still realizing the same profit measured in domestic currency. Multiple exchange rate practices involve the establishment of different official rates for different transactions; typically unfavorable rates for imports that compete with domestic production and highly favorable rates for exports likely to encounter stiff competition abroad. For example, suppose that in the absence of exchange controls a market dictated exchange rate would be ten units of local currency to $1. Suppose that under a system of exchange controls the government sets the rate at 15:1 for certain export transactions. Local exporters would then receive 50% more local currency for each export sale, or, more importantly, be able to reduce prices up to one-third while still maintaining their per unit margin in terms of local currency. In short, both of these schemes may find their justification in a nation's broader monetary and development policies but both are very likely to entail a significant incentive to export.

[2] In the 1974-79 Multilateral Trade Negotiations (Tokyo Round) the contracting parties to the GATT negotiated an "Agreement On The Interpretation And Application Of Articles VI, XVI, And XXIII Of The General Agreement On Tariffs And Trade" dealing with subsidies and countervailing duties. The Agreement is commonly known, and is hereinafter referred to, as the "GATT Subsidies Code" (GATT, BISD 26th Supp., (1980) at page 56. As of October 15, 1988 the following were signatories to the Code; Australia, Austria, Brazil, Canada, Chile, Egypt, the EEC, Finland, Hong Kong, India, Indonesia, Israel, Japan, Korea, New Zealand, Norway, Pakistan, Philippines, Spain (now part of the EEC), Sweden, Switzerland, Turkey, the United States, Uruguay and Yugoslavia. In addition, 22 GATT members and 6 non-GATT members have "observer status" in the Committee on Subsidies and Countervailing Measures. Excerpts from the Code are in the Documentary Supplement.

signatories to use such subsidies to achieve these and other important policy objectives. . . .[3]

From a strictly practical view, of course, domestic subsidies[4] can have as significant an impact on international trade flows as export subsidies. Thus the point is clear. While cognizant of the dangers of unconstrained subsidization, no nation has been willing to forego the use of subsidies to achieve those social and economic objectives that it believes cannot be accomplished through market forces. As with so many other issues, no nation will readily give-up its own agenda but no nation can escape the fear of what might happen to the international economic order if all nations persisted in that reluctance.

Finally, as we shall see, the subject is fraught with great theoretical uncertainty and extraordinary empirical complexity. Indeed, there is very respectable opinion suggesting that complexity alone justifies ignoring the problem altogether. In spite of that opinion, however, the question has taken on powerful political and unfortunately ethical overtones that virtually guarantee against any escape.

In light of all of this, it is not surprising that what has emerged in GATT is a body of sometimes contradictory, often indeterminate, rules and a set of procedures which leave a good deal of room for national maneuvering, but have nevertheless increasingly forced nations to respond to the adverse effects of their subsidies on the welfare of others. The adequacy of those rules and procedures is a matter to which we will pay some attention in the ensuing materials

[A] The Provisions of the General Agreement and the Subsidies Code

The centerpiece of GATT on the subject of subsidies is Article XVI as elaborated by the so-called Subsidies Code to which the EEC (Twelve) and twenty-three other GATT members are now signatories. In addition, Articles III:4, III:8 and XXIII are important. There is also Article VI that deals with the imposition of countervailing duties.

Article XVI

Subsidies

Section A—Subsidies in General

1. **If any contracting party grants or maintains any subsidy, including any form of income or price support, which operates directly or indirectly to increase exports of any product from, or to reduce imports of any product into, its territory, it shall notify the contracting parties in writing of the extent and nature of the subsidization, of the estimated effect of the**

---

[3] Among the other "important policy objectives" mentioned by the Code are: the elimination of regional economic disparities; restructuring particular sectors of the economy under socially acceptable conditions; sustaining employment and encouraging retraining; encouraging research and development; implementing development program in less developed countries; redeploying industry to avoid congestion and environmental problems.

[4] For a discussion of the distinction between "domestic" and "export" subsidies see page 401 *infra*.

subsidization on the quantity of the affected product or products imported into or exported from its territory and of the circumstances making the subsidization necessary. In any case in which it is determined that serious prejudice to the interests of any other contracting party is caused or threatened by any such subsidization, the contracting party granting the subsidy shall, upon request, discuss with the other contracting party or parties concerned, or with the Contracting Parties, the possibility of limiting the subsidization.

Section B—Additional Provisions on Export Subsidies

2. The Contracting Parties recognize that the granting by a contracting party of a subsidy on the export of any product may have harmful effects for other contracting parties, both importing and exporting, may cause undue disturbance to their normal commercial interests, and may hinder the achievement of the objectives of this Agreement.

3. Accordingly, contracting parties should seek to avoid the use of subsidies on the export of primary products. If, however, a contracting party grants directly or indirectly any form of subsidy which operates to increase the export of any primary product from its territory, such subsidy shall not be applied in a manner which results in that contracting party having more than an equitable share of world export trade in that product, account being taken of the shares of the contracting parties in such trade in the product during a previous representative period, and any special factors which may have affected or may be affecting such trade in the product.

4. Further, as from 1 January 1958 or the earliest practicable date thereafter, contracting parties shall cease to grant either directly or indirectly any form of subsidy on the export of any product other than a primary product which subsidy results in the sale of such product for export at a price lower than the comparable price charged for the like product to buyers in the domestic market. Until 31 December 1957 no contracting party shall extend the scope of any such subsidization beyond that existing on 1 January 1955 by the introduction of new, or the extension of existing, subsidies.

Article XVI divides subsidies into three groups; (i) export subsidies of primary products, (ii) export subsidies of non-primary products and (iii) domestic subsidies. The regime applicable to export subsidies is more restrictive than that applicable to domestic subsidies. Within the export subsidy category, the regime governing non-primary products is more restrictive than that for primary products.

"Export subsidies" are those the eligibility for which is expressly tied to the exportation of goods. For example, if a production subsidy is available only to aid the production of goods for export, it is an "export" subsidy; if available for the production of goods destined for both export and domestic sale, it becomes a "domestic" subsidy (*e.g.* GATT Subsidies Code, Annex A, paragraph (d)).[5]

A primary product is:

> any product of farm, forest or fishery, or any mineral,[6] in its natural form or which has undergone such processing as is customarily required to prepare it for marketing in substantial volume in international trade.[7]

In one GATT Panel proceeding the EEC contended that a subsidy granted on the chief primary component — durum wheat — of a processed export product — pasta — was to be governed by the less restrictive rules applicable to subsidies on primary products.[8] The Panel rejected the argument, concluding that the subsidy was governed by the rules applicable to non-primary products.

Domestic Subsidies Under the General Agreement

Section A, which technically applies to all types of subsidies, is the only part of Article XVI applicable to domestic subsidies. It draws no distinction between primary and non-primary products nor does it flatly prohibit any subsidy. It functions, instead, as centerpiece in a four-part regime to which a number of other provisions contribute.

(1) Section A requires that GATT be notified of any subsidy that has the effect of increasing exports from or reducing imports by the subsidizing country and mandates consultations with any party claiming that the subsidy has "seriously prejudiced" its interests. To prove such an increase in exports or decrease in imports it is necessary to show that exports are higher or imports lower than would have been the case in the absence of the subsidy.[9] This showing, however, is aided by the general presumption that any subsidy that tends to increase production will, in the absence of off-setting measures, have the effect of increasing exports or curtailing imports.[10]

(2) Article III:4 mandates that imports be treated the same as domestic products with respect to all laws, regulations and requirements affecting their sale.[11] The

---

[5] Documentary Supplement.

[6] The provisions of the Subsidies Code regarding primary products excludes "minerals" thereby substantially broadening the amount of trade governed by the more rigorous rules on export subsidies for non-primary products. Footnote to Article 9 of the Code.

[7] See Ad Article XVI, Section B, of the General Agreement in the Documentary Supplement.

[8] General Agreement on Tariffs and Trade, Report of the Panel on European Economic Community — Subsidies on Export of Pasta Products, SCM/43, 19 May 1983. Panel Report not adopted by Subsidies Committee. Case settled by agreement between U.S. and EEC. See also United States' reservation upon signing the Declaration of 21 November 1958 Extending the Standstill Provisions of Article XVI:4. Under that reservation the United States confirmed its "understanding that this Declaration shall not prevent the United States as part of its subsidization of exports of a primary product (*i.e.*, cotton), from making a payment on an exported processed product (*i.e.*, cotton textiles) . . . which has been produced from such primary product. . . ."

[9] GATT, BISD, Vol. II at pages 34, 44 (1952).

[10] GATT, BISD, Vol. II at pages 34, 44, (1952).

[11] Article III:4 provides, in relevant part, as follows: "The products of the territory of any contracting party imported into the territory of any other contracting party shall be

impact of this requirement as a potential constraint on domestic subsidies, however, has been substantially undercut by the express exception for "subsidies to domestic producers" contained in Article III:8(b).[12] Nevertheless Paragraph 4 applies to all other types of subsidies. For example, subsidies paid to Italian farmers to purchase Italian manufactured tractors and other farm machinery was construed as a subsidy to purchasers, not producers, and fell outside the scope of the 8(b) exception.

(3) Recall that the Article XXIII remedies are available whenever "benefits" accruing to one party under the GATT are being "nullified or impaired" by the action of another "whether or not [the latter actions] conflict with the provisions of [the General Agreement]." In other words, Article XXIII remedies are available even against actions which are not illegal under GATT. Since the numerous GATT negotiating rounds have given rise to an extensive net work of expected "benefits," any subsidy which, in the words of Section A, Article XVI, "seriously prejudices" one party's interests is also likely to impinge upon that party's expected "benefits." Hence, any claim that a subsidy has caused "serious prejudice," even if the subsidy does not violate GATT, is likely to be accompanied by a claim of "nullification and impairment" under Article XXIII. The latter, in turn, opens up remedial possibilities that can be far more stringent than the consultation requirement of Article XVI:1.

(4) Lastly, there is Article VI:3 and 6. While couched in terms of a limitation, Article VI:3 effectively authorizes the imposition of a countervailing duty equal to the amount of the subsidy granted, "directly or indirectly, on the manufacture, production or export" of any imported product. In other words, it applies to any export that benefits from either a "domestic" or "export" subsidy, provided that the country of importation:

> . . . determines that the effect of the subsidization is such as to cause or threaten material injury to an established domestic industry, or is such as to retard materially the establishment of a domestic industry. (Article VI:6(a))

We will review the application of this injury requirement when we examine the U.S. countervailing duty statutes.

Export Subsidies Under the General Agreement: Primary Products

In separating export subsidies on *primary* from *non-primary* products, Section B of Article XVI reflects one of the dominant and more persistent realities of world trade. The farm subsidy programs of the EEC and the United States in particular, have driven domestic prices for many agricultural products far above world prices and have created massive surpluses. This, in turn, has generated pressures to export. But exports require subsidies because otherwise domestic producers could

---

accorded treatment no less favourable than that accorded to like products of national origin in respect of all laws, regulations and requirements affecting their internal sale, offering for sale, purchase, transportation, distribution or use. . . ."

[12] Article III:8(b) provides as follows: "The provisions of this Article shall not prevent the payment of subsidies exclusively to domestic producers, including payments to domestic producers derived from the proceeds of internal taxes or charges applied consistently with the provisions of this Article and subsidies effected through governmental purchases of domestic products.

not meet world prices and governments could not increase foreign sales sufficiently to make a dent in their politically embarrassing agricultural surpluses. In no other area of international trade has competitive subsidization become so widespread and the allocation of production been so distorted.

Thus, while fully cognizant of the problem (Article XVI, Section B, Paragraph 2), the most these nations would concede is the undertaking in Paragraph 3 that subsidization could not result in any of them "having more than an equitable share of world export trade in [any] product." This is an elusive standard, and one to which we shall return.

Export Subsidies Under the General Agreement: Non-Primary Products

With regard to export subsidies on non-primary products Paragraph 4, which was added in 1957, constituted a commitment to the eventual (*i.e.*, "the earliest practicable date" after January 1, 1958) elimination of all such subsidies which resulted in prices for export lower than the comparable domestic price (dual pricing). The last sentence of the Paragraph then added a so-called "standstill agreement" prohibiting the introduction of new or the extension of existing subsidies through December 31, 1957. An Interpretive Note (Ad Art. XVI:4) recorded the intention of the Contracting Parties to extend the "standstill" if an agreement prohibiting subsidies had not been reached by the January 1, 1958 target.

In point of fact, no agreement was reached, but the "standstill" was extended through 1967. During this period, France proposed a "declaration" giving effect to the basic prohibition contained in Article XVI:4. This so-called "Giving Effect" declaration was to come into force only after it had been signed by the members of the EEC, Canada and the United States and then only with respect to trade between the signatories. Eventually the required signatures were obtained. In practical effect this meant that the prohibition contained in Article XVI:4 applied principally to trade among the major industrialized nations, including Japan, and not to most of the developing countries. Implicitly this constituted a recognition by GATT that the overvalued currencies of some developing countries might justify subsidies on exports of non-primary products.

The Subsidies Code

Part I of the GATT Subsidies Code contains detailed undertakings regarding the administration of national countervailing duty statutes. Part II of the Code deals with subsidies. Reflecting the ambivalence that surrounds the whole subject of subsidies, Article 8 (General Provisions) establishes the basic scheme of the Code, as follows:

Article 8. - Subsidies - General Provisions

1. Signatories recognize that subsidies are used by governments to promote important objectives of social and economic policy. Signatories also recognize that subsidies may cause adverse effects to the interests of other signatories.

2. Signatories agree not to use export subsidies in a manner inconsistent with the provisions of this Agreement.

3. Signatories further agree that they shall seek to avoid causing, through the use of any subsidy

(a) injury to the domestic industry of another signatory,

(b) nullification or impairment of the benefits accruing directly or indirectly to another signatory under the General Agreement, or

(c) serious prejudice to the interests of another signatory.

4. The adverse effects to the interests of another signatory required to demonstrate nullification or impairment or serious prejudice may arise through:

(a) the effects of the subsidized imports in the domestic market of the importing country;

(b) the effects of the subsidy in displacing or impeding the imports of like products into the market of the subsidizing country; or

(c) the effects of the subsidized exports in displacing the exports of like products of another signatory from a third country market.

The reader will recognize that, with respect to *domestic subsidies*, Paragraphs 3 and 4 of Article 8 effectively codify the relationship between GATT Article XVI, Section A and GATT Article XXIII described above, with one modification. Paragraph 4(c) makes explicit that one form of "serious prejudice" to which a subsidy may give rise is the displacement of export sales into third country markets. While the extent to which Paragraphs 3 and 4 apply to exports of primary products is still a matter of some dispute (see *EEC Wheat Flour* Case below), those paragraphs are the only operationally significant provisions of the Code applicable to *domestic subsidies*. At this point, however, the reader should also examine Article 11 [13] entitled "Subsidies Other Than Export Subsidies."

With regard to *export subsidies on non-primary products*, Article 9 of the Code implements the basic prohibition contained in Article XVI:4 of the General Agreement. It also codifies the demise of the "dual pricing" requirement.[14] It simply states:

Article 9 - Export Subsidies on Products Other than Certain Primary Products

Signatories shall not grant export subsidies on products other than certain primary products.

Paragraph 2 then refers to a list of practices in an Annex to the Code that are illustrative of export subsidies; the so-called "Illustrative List."[15] We need not

---

[13] Documentary Supplement.

[14] The "dual pricing" requirement was always of dubious merit because it is quite possible for exports to sell at prices no lower than the comparable domestic product and still be the recipients of an "export" subsidy. For example, the domestic product might also be receiving a subsidy but in a form that differed substantially from the export subsidy, or competition in the domestic market might, at least for short periods of time, dictate non-subsidized prices as low as the subsidized export price.

[15] Documentary Supplement.

delay here to discuss the list but will allude to it from time to time in the ensuing materials.

Article 10 of the Subsidies Code *governs export subsidies on primary products.* In addition to repeating the "equitable share" limitation of GATT Article XVI:3, Article 10 contains a number of refinements which are more fully considered in the *EEC Wheat Flour* Case below.

Procedure Under the Subsidies Code

The Subsidies Code establishes a three step process for resolving disputes over subsidies between signatories to the Code. First, the Code provides that if one signatory believes that another has either (i) granted an export subsidy in manner inconsistent with the Code or (ii) granted *any* subsidy which has injured the complainant's domestic industry, nullified or impaired the latter's benefits or caused serious prejudice to its interests, the complaining party may demand that the other signatory enter into "consultations" in an effort to find a mutually acceptable solution to the matter (Article 12). Second, if consultations fail, either party may have the matter submitted to "conciliation" through the "good offices" of the Committee on Subsidies [16] (Articles 13 and 17).

Finally, should "conciliation" fail, either party may ask for the establishment of a panel [17] to review the facts and to present findings to the Committee on Subsidies concerning the rights and obligations of the parties (Article 18). If on the basis of the panel's report the Committee finds that an export subsidy was granted in violation of the Code or that any subsidy has, in fact, caused injury, serious prejudice or nullification or impairment, the Committee is authorized to make recommendations to the parties in dispute. Should those recommendations not be accepted the Committee may authorize such "countermeasures" as it deems appropriate (Article 13). [18]

[B] Of "Equitable Share," Market Displacement, "Undue Disturbance" of World Markets and Production Subsidies

Recall that panel reports to the contracting parties are only recommendations and do not, in any formal sense, represent GATT law unless the report is accepted by the contracting parties or the GATT Council, acting under a consensus rule. The same is true of panel reports to the Subsidies Committee under the Subsidies Code. In the *EEC Wheat Flour* Case the United States blocked Committee acceptance of the panel report set-out below and that report, therefore, cannot be taken as authoritative. Nevertheless, it is a good vehicle for exploring some of the interpretive difficulties presented by the "equitable share" limitation on subsidies of primary products. It also illustrates rather well some of the problems that can occur under the style and approach characteristic of many GATT adjudications.

---

[16] The Committee is formally known as the Committee on Subsidies and Countervailing Measures and is composed of representatives of each of the signatories to the Code (Article 16).

[17] Panels are to consist of three to five persons, preferably governmental but not necessarily so, who are not citizens of either party to the dispute. Panel members are to sit in their "individual capacities" and not as government representatives.

[18] Articles 12-18 of the Subsidies are found in the Documentary Supplement.

EUROPEAN ECONOMIC COMMUNITY
SUBSIDIES ON EXPORTS OF WHEAT FLOUR

General Agreement on Tariffs and Trade

Doc. No. SCM/42

23 March 1983

Report of the Panel

[In this case the United States charged that EEC subsidies in the form of "refunds" on exports of wheat flour, resulted: (i) in the EEC having more than an equitable share of the world export trade in wheat flour, a violation of Article 10:1 & 2(a) of the Subsidies Code; (ii) in prices materially below those of other suppliers, a violation of Article 10:3 of the Code; and (iii) in nullification or impairment of U.S. benefits (Article 8 of the Code.).

The EEC's internal price system for wheat flour consisted of a series of formulae which set a "target" price for *wheat* sold within the EEC. As part of this system a "threshold price" for *wheat flour* was calculated each year and that price served as the internal EEC price standard. Since that price was invariably higher than prices offered by suppliers from outside the EEC, a levy was imposed on all *flour* imports equal to the difference between the "threshold price" and a "hypothetical" import price. The latter was based upon the most favorable price available on world markets adjusted to c.i.f. Rotterdam. Then, to off-set the disadvantage that EEC flour exporters — many of whom were millers — would face because of the high internal EEC price for flour or for raw wheat, the EEC made available to these exporters a "refund" purportedly designed to off-set the difference between the established price for *wheat flour* within the Community and prices prevailing in markets outside the EEC. Specifically, three factors were used in calculating these export refunds (i) common *wheat* prices prevailing in the various EEC markets, (ii) the quantity of *wheat* required for the production of *wheat flour* and (iii) the possibilities and conditions for the sale of *wheat flour* in the market to which the *flour* was to be exported.]

The EEC Violated the "Equitable Share"
Requirement of Article 10:1 of the Code

Code Provisions

Article 10

1. In accordance with the provisions of Article XVI:3 of the General Agreement, signatories agree not to grant directly or indirectly any export subsidy on certain primary products in a manner which results in the signatory granting such subsidy having more than an equitable share of world export trade in such product, account being taken of the shares of the signatories in trade in the product concerned during a previous representative period, and any special factors which may have affected or may be affecting trade in such products.

2. **For purposes of Article XVI:3 of the General Agreement and paragraph 1 above:**

    (a) more than an equitable share of world export trade shall include any case in which the effect of an export subsidy granted by a signatory is to displace the exports of another signatory bearing in mind the developments on world markets.

United States Arguments

[[In determining the proper "previous representative period," the United States, relying on the words "normally" and "normal" in Article 10:2(c) and citing GATT precedents,[19] contended that the three most recent calendar years could not be used because EEC subsidies had completely distorted trade patterns during that period. Instead the U.S. proposed as a reference period the three marketing years preceding establishment of the EEC's Common Agricultural Policy (CAP) (*i.e.* 1958/59 - 1961/62), even though this required the Panel to look back 20 years.

To prove that the EEC system had, in fact, displaced exports by other GATT members within the meaning of Article 10:2(a), the United States offered data showing that between its proposed reference period and the most recent period (*i.e.*, average for the three years 1978/79 - 1980/81), the EEC's share of the world market had increased rather dramatically at the expense of Australia, Canada and the United States (See: Findings of the Panel). These data included only commercial sales of wheat flour and not "special transactions," such as sales under Public Law 480 (PL 480 or the "Food for Peace Program"). The United States also presented statistics to demonstrate displacement in a number of specific national markets. (See Notes following the Report).

In a relatively stagnant market divided among four suppliers, the US argued, so dramatic an increase in one supplier's share necessarily proved displacement of other suppliers and this displacement was the result of EEC export subsidies.]

EEC Counter-Arguments

[The EEC countered by challenging the U.S. choice of a previous representative period. Because Article 10 of the Subsidies Code did not make export subsidies unlawful the grant of subsidies could not, the EEC argued, be thought to render a market abnormal.[20]

The EEC also argued that the U.S. data on displacement was flawed by the omission of PL 480 sales which were generally on very advantageous terms

---

[19] Article 10:2(c) provides that: "a previous representative period shall normally be the three most recent calendar years in which normal market conditions existed." The United States cited GATT, BISD 3rd Supp., (1955) paragraph 19, page 226 and GATT, BISD 9th Supp., (1961) Annex II(b)(ii), page 194.

[20] The EEC also noted that in the Tokyo Round negotiations, Australia had taken the U.S. position (MTN/NTM/W/217/Rev.1) and that a number of delegations, including the United States, had opposed the idea.

(*e.g.*, 5% down payment, balance payable up to forty years at 4%-5% interest).[21]

The core of the EEC response, however, turned on the issue of causality. It had to be proven, the EEC emphasized, that it was the subsidy which had displaced trade flows. For this purpose other factors which might have influenced the U.S. loss of market share had to be considered, especially when examining data over so long a period as that envisaged by the United States. These other factors included: the expansion of United States flour exports under PL 480 at the expense of its commercial exports; U.S. withdrawal from markets for political reasons; the substitution of raw wheat for flour purchases as a result of increased local milling capacity.

Other factors influencing the growth of EEC market share included: growth in inward processing traffic (IPT), which did not involve refunds; the existence of markets with traditional ties to the Community based upon historic or special economic and financial conditions; and the smallness and volatility of many markets which gave European suppliers a shipping and marketing advantage.[22]]

EEC "Prices Materially Below Those of Other Suppliers" In Violation of Article 10:3 of the Code

Code Provision

Article 10

3. **Signatories further agree not to grant export subsidies on exports of certain primary products to a particular market in a manner which results in prices materially below those of other suppliers to the same market.**

United States Arguments

[The United States contended that the use of a subsidy as high as 75% of the US representative f.o.b. price combined with the EEC's complete dominance of world flour markets established a strong presumption of material price undercutting. The presumption was supported by evidence from several specific tenders in key markets during 1980 and 1981,[23] and data on export

---

[21] In an intriguing aside the EEC stated that: "In including concessional sales in the world trade' figure, the Community's intention was not to bring [such sales] under the discipline of Article XVI of the GATT and Article 10 of the Code — although that question could well be examined in GATT. It was [only] a question of . . . equity."

[22] The EEC representative also charged that the US allegations ignored a number of additional facts:

— that the "exclusion" of traditional United States exports was due, in part, to the chronic saturation of United States milling facilities, which for years had been functioning at more than 100 per cent capacity — so much so that United States operators were sometimes unable to deliver the quantities tendered for in third countries;

— that US exporters lacked the trade network necessary to gain access to certain of the markets from which the US appears to have been excluded.

[23] According to the US there are relatively few public tenders in the world wheat flour trade; business is usually conducted through private arrangements. Exact price data is therefore hard to come by. In addition, given the lack of success of U.S. flour exporters in competing with subsidized EEC exports, U.S. exporters had refrained from bidding in many cases.

unit values for 1976-1981. While no continuous export price data for wheat flour were readily available and unit values did not show prices offered on individual transactions, that data did, according to the U.S., indicate convincingly the lower EEC price levels caused by export subsidies.[24] The U.S. also argued that the level of EEC export subsidies were habitually higher than could be accounted for by the difference between world and internal EEC prices for wheat.]

EEC Counter-Arguments

[The EEC questioned the reliability of the U.S. data; the evidence based on specific tenders was, it claimed, incomplete and data based on export unit values were unreliable. The EEC also denied that EEC refunds were considerably in excess of the difference between world prices and internal EEC prices. Moreover, North American flours, the EEC contended had certain qualities (ash, moisture and protein content) which made them more expensive but less well suited than European flour to local bread-making methods and U.S. flour mills were at a transport cost disadvantage because they could not use regular shipping lines but only charters which made deliveries in small quantities impracticable.]

"Nullification or Impairment" of U.S. Benefits and "Serious Prejudice" to US Interests: Article 8 of the Code.

Code Provisions

Article 8

3. **Signatories further agree that they shall seek to avoid causing, through the use of any subsidy:**

* * * *

    (b) **nullification or impairment of the benefits accruing directly or indirectly to another signatory under the General Agreement; or**

    (c) **serious prejudice to the interests of another signatory.**

4. **The adverse effects to the interests of another signatory required to demonstrate nullification or impairment or serious prejudice may arise through:**

* * * *

    (c) **the effects of the subsidized exports in displacing the exports of like products of another signatory from a third country market.**

---

[24] According to the U.S., in fifty-seven out of sixty months of the 1976-80 period at least one, and often several, EEC member States had priced wheat flour exports to all destinations at levels below those of the United States. Even in cases where the EEC was nearer to the countries of destination its proximity gave it no competitive advantage. Therefore, in the absence of export subsidies, its prices would still normally be higher than those of the U.S.

United States Arguments

[The United States argued that Article 8:3(c) of the Code required that the EEC "seek to avoid" causing "serious prejudice" to the interests of another signatory and that since, under Article 8:4(c), "serious prejudice" might arise through the displacement effect of subsidized EEC exports — an effect that the United States' had demonstrated — the EEC had violated its obligations under Article 8:3(c). This also laid a basis for a claim of nullification and impairment under Article XXIII of the GATT. Here the U.S. cited Article 8:4, Footnote 26.[25]

Also, the U.S. relied on Australia's case against the EEC sugar export subsidy system[26] to argue that, because the EEC system lacked pre-established limitations on production, prices and export refunds, it was a "permanent source of uncertainty" in world flour markets and, as such, the cause of "serious prejudice" to the interests of other exporters within the meaning of Article 8:3(c) of the Code. This uncertainty was compounded by the fact that the internal EEC flour price used as a base for the "refund" was arbitrarily selected from nine or ten prices that were, in turn, derived from wheat prices and not actual market prices for flour. Then, in deriving those prices, the EEC made allowances for transportation, bagging, weighing, etc. which bore no relation to the actual cost of those services. No importer or competing exporter could, the U.S. said, anticipate the amount of the subsidy or the resulting EEC bid.]

EEC Counter-Arguments

[The EEC contended that in relying on Article 8:4(c) to establish "serious prejudice," the U.S. had disregarded Footnote 28[27] which indicated that Article 10 was the exclusive authority for control of export subsidies on primary products. Furthermore, the U.S. argument regarding the absence in the EEC system of "pre-established limits on production, prices or refunds" was not, according to the EEC, founded on anything in the Code. The EEC "could not accept" this attempted "modification of its obligations."]

Findings By the Panel

4.3 . . . The Panel concluded that the granting of refunds by the EEC on exports of wheat flour must be considered a form of subsidy and subject to the provisions of Article XVI of the General Agreement as interpreted and applied by the Code.

---

[25] The Note in question reads as follows: "Signatories recognize that nullification or impairment of benefits may also arise through the failure of a signatory to carry out its obligations under the General Agreement or this Agreement. Where such failure concerning export subsidies is determined by the Committee [on Subsidies] to exist, adverse effects may . . . be presumed to exist. The other signatory will be accorded a reasonable opportunity to rebut this presumption."

[26] In that case the GATT Panel concluded that because of the absence of any pre-established limitations on the amount of the subsidy, the EEC's system was a permanent source of uncertainty in world sugar markets and a threat of "serious prejudice" within the terms of Article XVI:1. For a fuller discussion of the case see page 422, note 6, *infra.*

[27] The Note is question provides: "The problem of third country markets so far as certain primary products are concerned is dealt with exclusively under Article 10 below."

* * * *

A. Article 10:1 & 2 of the Code (Equitable Share)

1. Shares of world export trade in wheat flour

4.7. In examining shares of world export trade, the Panel considered global exports from all sources, to all markets, on the basis of statistics compiled by the International Wheat Council in its Record of Operations. . . . [T]he Panel [also] considered that it was difficult to exclude special transactions entirely from an analysis of the market, and that in this case, it was not necessary, or appropriate, to do so in reaching a determination as to equitable share.[28]

4.8. In light of the provisions of Article 10:2(c) of the Code, the Panel first compared world market shares in the three most recent crop years prior to the US complaint under the Code, *i.e.*, 1977/78, 1978/79 and 1979/80 with market shares in 1980/81.

4.9. The market share of the EEC over this period was:

> 1977/78 - 54 per cent
> 1978/79 - 57 per cent
> 1979/80 - 62 per cent
>
> 1977/80 - 58 per cent - Average
> 1980/81 - 66 per cent

4.10. . . . In absolute terms, the net increase in EEC shipments in 1980/81 over the previous three-year average was 903,667 metric tons, a 26 per cent increase.

4.11. The Panel was of the view that while the three most recent year period was in many ways instructive . . . it did not in itself provide a fully satisfactory basis for determining "equitable share." Market shares in this period, as indeed for virtually any period in at least the last twenty years, had been affected by the application of export subsidies[29] and other developments in the market, the full import of which could be properly taken into account only by examining other periods as well.

---

[28] In recent years, such special transactions have represented about one-fifth of world wheat flour export trade. In the case of the United States they have accounted for more than two thirds of the country's total wheat flour exports; between one fourth and one third in the case of both Australia and Canada; and for about one tenth in the case of the EEC, although the EEC figure is limited to outright gifts. The Panel, while being cognizant of the issues involved therein, did not regard it as necessary to draw conclusions of general application in this case. If one excludes special transactions, the magnitude of changes in the market is amplified, but the basic pattern of market changes is similar whether they are included or not. On the other hand, given the volume of special transactions and its importance in overall market developments, the Panel was of the view that these shipments could not be ignored.

[29] See Report of the Working Party on Other Barriers to Trade, adopted by the Contracting Parties on 3 March 1955. (GATT, BISD. 3rd Supp. (1956) at page 266). Member States of the EEC had applied export subsidies for a certain period before 1967. Since that time the EEC export refund system has been operated by the Commission on a Community-wide basis.

4.12. After examining a number of other possibilities of representative periods the Panel found that while there were some differences between the three most recent years and earlier periods, the fundamental picture of market developments tended to be consistent.

4.13. If, for example, one compares the relative positions in the world market during the three years prior to the Community-wide application of export subsidies, with the last three years, the overall increase in the EEC shipments and share of the market (which itself had only increased by 3 per cent) was significant.

[Here the Panel sets forth a table comparing average exports, expressed in tons of wheat equivalent, for the three years 1963/64 - 1965/66 with the average for the years 1978/79 - 1980/81. The Table shows the following:

Australia: exports declined from 691,000 to 116,000 tons (83% decline); market share fell from 11% to 2% of world market (82% decline).

Canada: exports declined from 1.137 million tons to 686,000 tons (40% decline); market share fell from 18% to 11% of world market (39% decline).

United States: exports declined from 2.462 million tons to 1.448 million tons (41% decline); market share fell from 40% to 18% of world market (55% decline).

EEC: exports increased from 1.465 million tons to 3.936 million tons; (169% increase); market share rose from 24% to 62% of world market (158% increase).

All Others: exports declined from 430,000 tons to 188,000 tons (56% decline); market share fell from 7% to 3% of world trade (57% decline).]

4.15. It is evident therefore that the EEC share of world exports of wheat flour has become larger over a time period when payment by the EEC of export subsidies was the general practice.

2. Developments in the Wheat Flour Market

(a) General Observations - Basic Features
of the World Flour Market

4.16. Before examining particular phenomena which might be regarded as "special factors" [under] . . . Article 10, the Panel considered a number of general features which in its view were of fundamental importance in understanding developments in the world wheat flour market and the role of export subsidies therein.

(i) There has been a significant trend . . . toward increased domestic milling capacity throughout the world. This meant that in the past twenty years the wheat flour market has grown very slightly . . . while that of wheat has more than doubled. . . .

(ii) . . . [R]elatively little world trade in wheat flour takes place on the basis of the free play of the market. In recent years, the bulk of EEC and US shipments ([80% of] . . . total world exports . . .) were made either under export subsidies or under non-commercial transactions.

(iii) . . . [T]he world wheat flour market might in some respects be characterized as chaotic due to the existence of a few important markets with greatly varying imports from one year to another, a large number of small markets, some of which import only on an irregular and unpredictable basis, the absence of recognized world prices, and the sometimes broad price difference in a given market for a given type and quality of wheat flour.

(iv) The opening of lines of credit at highly reduced interest rates and/or other forms of government supported deals . . . have sometimes been the major factor influencing the conclusion of transactions. This practice may have been particularly relevant in the Egyptian market in recent years, the largest single market for flour.

(b) Special Factors

4.17. . . . The Panel considered in [detail] . . . a number of special factors, including those presented by the EEC, [which] may have had a bearing on market shares.

(i) Political Developments

4.18. Political developments, such as embargos or changes in diplomatic relations, have played an important role at times in hindering U.S. flour sales . . . and in affecting relative market shares as between the EEC and the U.S.[30] . . . After no shipments to the USSR in 1977/78 and 1978/79, EEC exported 123,348 metric tons in 1979/80 and 702,651 metric tons in 1980/81. Substantial EEC increases in volume terms in 1980/81 over the previous three year average were registered in the following markets where the US exports were disadvantaged on political grounds: USSR, 661,000 metric tons; Libya, 117,000 metric tons; Angola, 76,300 metric tons; total - 854,300 metric tons.

(ii) Non-commercial sales

4.20. . . . [D]uring the period under review the levels of wheat flour entering international trade, and [the proportion of imports accounted for by shipments made,] under conditions not conforming to usual commercial practices . . . were considerable. The Panel considered that [this] . . . could have important consequences for the commercial market . . . notwithstanding agreed mechanisms for limiting such consequences within individual markets.

4.21. . . . [O]ne of the possible effects of large concessional sales was . . . market creation, i.e., the development of an import requirement . . . at levels higher than would otherwise have occurred under purely commercial conditions. The Panel found however that conclusions as to the impact on changing market shares of such an effect were less than clear.

4.22. . . . [A]bout one-forth of the wheat flour market was accounted for by a large number of small markets including [some] . . . which enter[ed] the international market only on an irregular and unpredictable basis. The . . . existence of regular shipping lines from EEC member States to most of these countries could be an important factor in permitting the transportation of small [irregular] quantities . . . at reasonable costs. . . .

---

30 The Panel mentions, Angola, Cuba, Libya, Vietnam, North Korea and, as a direct result of the U.S. grains embargo, the USSR in 1979/80, and, in particular, in 1980/81.

4.23. The Panel, [while] aware of . . . other factors which might be of . . . relevance to [the] development of market shares, [found that] the effects of such factors, *inter alia,* historical links, cultivation of "traditional" markets, particular taste or dietary demands, trade practices . . . increased domestic milling capacity . . . are difficult to establish with any assurance.

4.25. . . . Apart from some 10 per cent produced from imported, higher quality wheat, EEC flour entering international trade is produced from domestically grown soft wheat which on the world market commands a lower price than the hard, higher protein product. . . . The Panel found however that EEC wheat flour was not "lower priced" without the benefit of the export subsidy. . . . The Panel therefore considered that the quality of EEC wheat flour, per se, was not a factor which helped explain the EEC increase in market share.

4.27. . . . [I]n a market situation in which there is downward pressure on prices,[31] the EEC export refund mechanism may provide the EEC trader with a certain advantage vis-a-vis other suppliers, in that it subsidizes the export to the extent necessary to meet lower price levels of wheat flour. This may further contribute to the downward pressure on prices.

3. Market Displacement

4.28. . . . [D]espite the considerable increase in EEC exports, market displacement in the sense of Article 10:2(a) was not evident in the seventeen markets presented by the U.S. and examined by the Panel.

4.29. . . . [W]hen viewed over the time period suggested by the U.S. (from 1959/60)[32] there were several markets[33] in which in the earlier three year period the US was in a stronger position than the EEC, whereas in the most recent three years the EEC was in the stronger position. These markets however had changed considerably in size and nature over such a long period [that] . . . displacement in the sense of Article 10:2 (a) was not evident. There were a number of markets[34] where U.S. commercial shipments had not been particularly significant in the earlier years, and in which the EEC has in recent years obtained all or most of the commercial growth. Finally, in Jamaica the EEC share has increased but not so much at the expense of the US as of other suppliers. Jamaica is a declining market where the EEC has been able to maintain and sometimes increase its volume of exports and thus obtain a relatively larger share of the market. The Panel found in its examination of individual markets that it could not rule out the possibility that the application of EEC export subsidies had resulted in reduced sales opportunities for the United States.

[31] The relationship between wheat and wheat flour prices in the face of a trend toward domestic milling has had an effect in this regard, as had the situation of relative over supply for much of the period under review. Large volumes of non-commercial transactions have probably had a price depressing influence as well, not withstanding international understandings intended to limit their effect on normal commercial sales.

[32] The Panel was of the opinion that the use of the years 1959/60 or 1963/64 as the starting year would not affect its findings.

[33] Chile, Israel, Nigeria, Philippines, Saudi Arabia (stronger position only in 1978/79 and largely through inward processing trade in 1979/80), Sierra Leone, Trinidad and Tobago, Zaire, Barbados.

[34] Egypt, Sri Lanka, Syria, Yemen, Lebanon, Jordan, Cameroon.

B. Article 10 (Price Undercutting)

4.30. The Panel examined the U.S. argument that EEC export subsidies on wheat flour are applied in a manner which results in prices materially below those of other suppliers to the same market in violation of Article 10:3 of the Code.

4.31. The Panel noted that three of the eight specific cases[35] presented by the U.S. were qualified as being "reported" or "estimated." As the Panel was not in a position to ascertain the accuracy of these three cases it did not consider them further.

4.32. As regards the remaining five cases, the Panel considered that as the offers were made in response to specific tenders, there was a certain presumption that the transactions were comparable for purposes of Article 10:3.

4.33. The Panel noted that in all five cases the EEC prices were lower.

* * * *

4.35. . . . [With regard to] . . . the U.S. argument that export unit values provided evidence of price undercutting, [the Panel noted] . . . that wheat flour was not a homogeneous product, that differences in qualities would lead to price differences, . . . that [the market lacked] . . . reasonable price stability . . . [and that the] quantities [shipped] by suppliers from the exporting countries under consideration [were not comparable]. Consequently the Panel was of the opinion that . . . export unit values [could not be used] in the particular case before it.

C. Nullification or Impairment; Serious Prejudice

[4.36. Because it was unclear whether Article 8(c) concerning adverse effects in third country markets applied to subsidies on primary products, the Panel declined to make any finding with respect to nullification or impairment, or serious prejudice, beyond the findings under Article 10, implicit in Sections A and B above.[36]]

Panel Conclusions

5.1 - 5.3. [In spite of the fact that] . . . EEC export refunds for wheat flour [constituted subsidies] . . . subject to Article XVI of the General Agreement . . . [and the fact] . . . that the EEC share of world exports [had] increased considerably . . . while the share of the U.S. and other suppliers has decreased, the Panel . . . was unable to conclude . . . [that these circumstances resulted] in the EEC "having more than an equitable share" in terms of Article 10. [This was because of] . . . the highly artificial levels and conditions of trade in wheat flour, the complexity of . . . the markets, including the interplay of a number of special factors, the relative importance of which it was impossible to assess, and, most importantly, the difficulties inherent in the concept of "more than equitable share."

---

[35] The U.S. also presented two cases from 1975 and 1976. As these cases predated the entry into force of obligations under Article 10:3, the Panel did not include them in its examination.

[36] The Panel also took into account that in this case the United States complaint was largely based upon its contention that practices by the EEC were inconsistent with its obligations under Article 10, and that adverse effects were therefore presumed to exist.

5.4. The Panel concluded that, despite the considerable increase in EEC exports, market displacement in the sense of Article 10:2(a) was not evident in the seventeen markets examined by the Panel.

5.5. With regard to . . . Article 10:3, the Panel found that . . . there was not sufficient grounds to reach a definite conclusion as to whether the EEC . . . subsidies . . . resulted in prices materially below those of other suppliers to the same markets.

5.6 - 5.7. The Panel was not convinced, however, that the application of EEC export subsidies had not caused undue disturbance to the normal commercial interests of the United States in the sense of Article XVI:2 [and it enjoined] . . . the EEC . . . to limit the use of subsidies on the exports of wheat flour.

5.8.- 5.9. Finally . . . the Panel considered [the subsidization] . . . and other aspects of trade in wheat flour to be highly unsatisfactory and was concerned over what this implied for the effectiveness of the legal provisions in this area . . . [I]t found it anomalous . . . that the EEC which, without the application of export subsidies would generally not be in a position to export substantial quantities of wheat flour, had over time . . . become by far the largest exporter. [It also recommended] . . . improved transparency and possibly other forms of multilateral co-operation . . . [and suggested] that solutions . . . could only be found in making the pertinent provisions of the Code more operational, stringent and effective in application. . . .

NOTES AND QUESTIONS

(1) Observe that the payments to exporters in the EEC *Wheat Flour* Case were called a "refund" and purported to be simply a means of returning to exporters the difference between the world price and the higher artificially fixed price they had to pay for wheat flour because of the EEC's system for supporting the domestic price of wheat (Item (i) in the formula) and protecting domestic millers (item (ii) in the formula). Against this background consider the following:

(a) What feature of the refund scheme renders it a subsidy? Note the argument made by the United States regarding the method of adjusting the price of wheat in computing the refund on flour exports. Had payments to exporters been strictly limited to the added costs incurred by them because of the artificially maintained domestic price of flour, should the refund have been construed as a proscribed subsidy? If so why — because otherwise the exporter could not compete on the world market?

(b) Although not directly applicable, how might the principles underlying Paragraph (d) of the Illustrative List of export subsidies on non-primary products[37] affect your answer to the questions in (a) above. To illustrate the principles of Paragraph (d), suppose a government provided lumber

---

[37] Documentary Supplement.

to all manufacturers of furniture for export at a price of $180 per 1,000 board feet while the same lumber would cost a manufacturer who sells his product domestically $220 per 1,000 board feet. Under Paragraph (d) the differential would constitute a subsidy on furniture exports unless the manufacturer would have to pay at least $180 to acquire the same lumber on the world market. In that event the differential would not be a subsidy.

(2) Consider Paragraphs 4.10 and 4.18 of the Panel Report. The United States confronted a very difficult "equitable share" argument if it were confined to a comparison between shipments of wheat flour in 1980-81 and the average of shipments during the most recent three year period. Combined commercial and special sales by the EEC in 1980-81 exceeded the average annual tonnage shipped during the immediately preceding three year period by 903,667 metric tons; an increase of 8 percentage points (58% to 66%) or a overall 14% increase in the EEC's share of the world market. However, 95% (854,300 metric tons) of this increase represented increased sales to markets from which the United States had "voluntarily" withdrawn for political reasons. Moreover, in spite of that withdrawal total U.S. volume in 1980-81 was only 7% (102,000 tons) less than the average of the preceding three years.

To meet this problem the United States argued that the most recent three year period was "abnormal" because of EEC's subsidies. In a highly technical response, the EEC contended that since Article 10 does not purport to ban primary product subsidies, a subsidized market could not be considered "abnormal." Now, consider the aggregate tonnages with which we are dealing. For 1980-81 EEC shipments totaled 4,404,000 metric tons (66% of the world market) while the average for the immediately preceding three years was 3,500,000 tons (58% of the world market). For the United States the comparable figures were 1,394,000 tons (21% of the world market) and 1,496,000 tons (25% of the world market). Drawing upon your general knowledge regarding world wheat production, how might you have used these aggregate figures to persuade the Panel that it should look beyond the immediately preceding three years as a reference period?

(3) The Panel was, of course, sensitive to the import of these aggregate figures (Paragraphs 4.11, 4.15, and especially the dramatic figures in Paragraph 4.13). Yet, after comparing (1) changes in market shares between 1980-81 and the average for the three years immediately preceding 1980-81 with (2) changes based on various earlier representative periods, the Panel concluded that the "fundamental picture of market developments tended to be consistent." (Paragraph 4.12). Has the Panel without justifying its position effectively accepted the EEC's legal argument regarding the appropriate reference period? If so, the United States has virtually lost the case on the "equitable share" question (Article 10 of the Code), has it not? Explain.

This is not untypical of much decision making by GATT Panels. There is a tradition that fears being too "legalistic." Instead, Panel's have often tended to adopt a style of decision making vividly described by Hudec as "vague, almost impressionistic . . . that merely suggest the ruling" being made.[38] How do you

---

[38] Hudec, Reforming GATT Adjudication Procedures: The Lessons Of The DISC Case, 72 Minn. L. Rev. 1443 (1988).

evaluate this approach in the context of the instant case? Return to this question after considering the Notes that follow.

(4) Consider next the Panel's "General Observations;" the growth of domestic milling capacity, the absence of a true world market in wheat flour, the chaotic state of that market and widespread use of low interest loans. Consider also the Panel's discussion of "political developments" and of "Non-commercial sales" as a "special factor" within the meaning of Article 10.

Now, consider the core of the U.S. "equitable share" argument; that EEC sales had displaced U.S. exports within the meaning of Article 10:2(a) of the Code. To prove displacement the U.S. relied on both aggregate figures (Paragraph 4.13 of the Report) and on a comparison of the average market shares for the three year period immediately preceding the establishment of the CAP (*i.e.*, 1959/60 - 1961/62) with the average for the three years 1978/79 - 1980/81, in nine national markets where the U.S. had lost its strong position. The data on seven of those markets are set-forth in Table II below.[39]

---

[39] The other two mentioned by the Panel were Sierra Leone and the Philippines. For Sierra Leone the amounts were insignificant. The Philippines presents a special case since the United States lost market share on commercial sales but not when Special Sales are included. Thus, the overall market declined from annual average of 139,867 metric tons in 1959/60 - 1961/62 to an annual average of 39,067 metric tons in 1978/79 - 1980/81. In the earlier period when special sales were only 3% of the market, Canada (56.4%) and the United States (39.8%) were the principal suppliers to the commercial market. The EEC had only .6% of that market. In the later period Special Sales increased to 65% of all imports. By reason of that fact the United States' increased its share of the combined market to 46%, but fell to 3.5% of the commercial market. The EEC increased its share of the commercial market to 35.7%, Canada dropped out altogether and Australia stepped in and took 60.8% of all commercial sales. The difficulty of reading this data as evidence of displacement is implicit, of course, in the Panel's decision that no sharp line could be drawn between the EEC's commercial sales and the U.S. special sales under PL 480.

Table II

Changes in Market Share: Pre-CAP Compared With
Latest Period

National Market	Annual Average 1959/60 - 1961/62	Annual Average 1978/79 - 198/81
Markets That Increased		
Israel		
Metric Tons	5,233 (95% Spec.)	26,100 (0 Spec.)
U.S.	100%	.3%
EEC	0%	99.7%
Nigeria		
Metric Tons	81,200 (8% Spec.)	81,967 (0 Spec.)
U.S.	59.6%	6.8%
Canada	38%	0%
EEC	.2%	93.2%
Saudi Arabia		
Metric Tons	84,833 (0 Spec.)	531,067 (0 Spec.)
Australia	6%	.1%
U.S.	91.7%	38.4%
EEC	2.2%	60.7%
Markets That Declined		
Barbados		
Metric Tons	15,033 (0 Spec.)	8,267 (3% Spec.)
Canada	33%	49.6%
U.S.	43%	3%
EEC	24%	47.4%
Chile		
Metric Tons	85,000 (42% Spec.)	32,100 (31% Spec.)
Canada	5.5%	0%
U.S.	77.4%	31%
EEC	15.4%	69%
Trinidad-Tobago		
Metric Tons	79,833 (0 Spec.)	3,333 (0 Spec.)
Canada	52.7%	37%
U.S.	41.4%	0
EEC	5.9	63%
Zaire		
Metric Tons	49,000 (57% Spec.)	9,833 (61% Spec
Canada	18.7%	0
U.S.	69.5%	74.6%
EEC	4%	25.4%
Other	7.8%	0

Observe (i) that in the four markets (Nigeria, Saudi Arabia, Barbados, Trinidad-Tobago) which never had any significant special transactions (PL 480) the United States virtually dropped out (Barbados, Trinidad-Tobago) or suffered a sharp decline in market share (Saudi Arabia[40] and Nigeria). Observe also that only in those three markets (Chile, Philippines and Zaire) where both the pre-CAP reference period and the latest three year period was marked by significant special sales did the United States remain a major supplier, gaining slightly in the Philippines and Zaire but dropping sharply in Chile. Finally, note Israel where the elimination of special sales meant the virtual elimination of the U.S. as a supplier.

With this and the aggregate data before it, with no evidence of any market in which the U.S. had experienced a substantial gain in market share but with its general observations and the political and other considerations in mind, the Panel concluded that "[t]hese markets . . . had changed considerably in size and nature over such a long period [that] . . . displacement in the sense of Article 10:2 (a) was not evident." (Paragraph 4.29)

What does this mean? Was the Panel saying that over so long a term (20 years) it simply was not possible to judge what constituted "displacement" in a market characterized by rapid and not readily predictable changes? If so, has the Panel effectively declared Article 10:2 of the Code a dead letter?

Alternatively, was the Panel saying that a violation of Article 10 can only occur where truly commercial sales lose market share to subsidized sales and cannot occur where both parties to a dispute are engaged in competitive subsidizations and one emerges the winner? Note, in this respect, the Panel's statement about the "difficulties inherent in the concept more than equitable share' " (Paragraph 5.3). Difficulties there may be, but did the Panel needlessly exacerbate those difficulties by adopting (arguably) a particular, and limiting, view of the function of international law in disputes of this type? Here return to the discussion of the function of international law, page 309, *et seq.*, *supra* notes 9–11.

(5) What do you make of the following statements by the Panel:

. . . that it [the Panel] could not rule out the possibility that the application of EEC export subsidies had resulted in reduced sales opportunities for the United States. (Paragraph 4.29) and

. . . it [was] anomalous . . . that the EEC which, without the application of export subsidies would generally not be in a position to export substantial quantities of wheat flour, had over time . . . become by far the largest exporter. (Paragraph 5.8)

In light of these statements had the EEC fulfilled its obligation of seeking "to avoid" (Code Article 8:3) displacing U.S. sales (Code Article 8:4(c)? Note the EEC

---

[40] The EEC first became an important factor in the Saudi market around 1966-67. By 1969-70 its market share had risen to 25% with the U.S. at 69%. Through the 1970's the EEC's share hovered between 35% and 39% and the U.S. between 53% and 64%. Then in 1978-79 the EEC's share rose precipitously to 50%, the U.S. declining to 50%. Thereafter the EEC's position continued to improve until, due to a large volume of inward processing trade arrangements, it reached 70% of the market in 1979-80, dropping off to 30% in 1980-81.

response. It argued that Article 8 of the Code was inapplicable to the displacement effect of subsidies on primary products. Article 10:2(a) alone controlled. The Panel refused to address the issue. How would you approach the question?

(6) The *Australian-EEC Sugar* Case is a notable decision. There a GATT Panel found that EEC subsidies of sugar exports constituted a permanent sources of uncertainty in world sugar markets and hence posed a threat of serious prejudice in terms of Article XVI:1. Since Australia had not presented a detailed submission as to what benefits under the General Agreement had been nullified or impaired the Panel declined to make any determination under Article XXIII. According to the Panel the EEC sugar subsidy system, which consisted of a refund very much like that for wheat flour, exhibited three basic defects which rendered it a source of market uncertainty: (i) the method of subsidizing EEC sugar producers through production quotas had no predictable limits and had produced ever increasing surpluses within the Community; (ii) all sugar produced under quotas within the EEC which could not find a domestic market were eligible for an export subsidy, a commitment backed by very substantial budgetary resources, and (iii) while the amount of the refund was generally set at the difference between the Community intervention price and the spot price on the Paris sugar exchange it had, in the most recent period, exceeded that amount and had been growing rapidly precisely at a time when the world price was declining. Contrast this decision in both style and scope to that in the *Wheat Flour* Case.

(7) The effect on international trade flows of domestic production subsidies masquerading as a refund to producers is nicely illustrated by the U.S. case against the EEC's system of production aids on various canned fruits.[41] The EEC argued that no subsidy was involved since the production aids paid to EEC producers of canned fruit simply reimbursed them for the additional costs incurred in purchasing fresh fruit at an artificially established minimum price for EEC growers. The production aid was equal to the difference between a "computed" EEC price for canned fruit and the average duty-free price of the comparable imported product. The "computed" price was, in turn, the sum of (i) a "hypothetical" free market price for fresh fruit within the EEC (ii) the amount added to the free market price in determining the growers' minimum price and (iii) the estimated cost of processing fresh into canned fruit. The Panel rejected the EEC's argument. Explain why.

> Assume, for example, that the duty free price at which one could import from the U.S. into the EEC the *fully processed canned* equivalent of one bushel of peaches was $8; that the "hypothetical" free market price of fresh peaches in the EEC was $5 per bushel; the grower's add-on was $2 per bushel; the cost in the EEC of canning one bushel of peaches $4, and the cost in the United States $3.

Also the U.S. argued that because the system of minimum prices for growers would stimulate increased production of fresh fruit in the EEC it too constituted a subsidy that "upset the competitive relationship" between imported and EEC produced canned fruit. The Panel rejected this argument. Considering the possible

---

[41] GATT, Report of the Panel in European Economic Community - Production Aids Granted On Canned Peaches, Canned Pears, Canned Fruit Cocktail And Dried Grapes L/5778, 20 February 1985.

effects that the minimum prices for growers was likely to have on European canner's costs do you agree with the Panel?

The Panel went on to conclude that although the grant of production aids did not violate any provision of the GATT (See Article XVI:1) it did result in the "nullification and impairment" of benefits that the United States had reason to expect under several GATT tariff negotiating rounds.[42]

NOTE ON TAXATION AND THE GATT SUBSIDIES RULES — THE DISC CASE

There are two problems of tax administration that have become entangled with the GATT subsidy rules. One concerns border tax adjustments (*i.e.*, remission of taxes upon export or import), the other the "territorial" principle of income taxation.

Border Tax Adjustments

When a product is exported and is exempted by the country of export from the payment of a tax or if, upon exportation, the tax is refunded, Article VI:4 of the General Agreement provides that the importing country may not levy a countervailing or anti-dumping duty against that product, provided the tax in question is one that is " . . . borne by the like product when destined for consumption in the [exporting] country." In much the same language an Interpretive Note (Ad Article XVI) also makes clear that such an exemption or refund is not to be considered a subsidy.[43]

The key requirement is that the refund or exemption relate to a tax "borne by [a] like product." This has resulted in a two-fold classification of taxes into "direct" and "indirect taxes." "Direct taxes," such as income and social security taxes, are those levied "directly" on a firm or individual. "Indirect taxes," such as sales, other excise and value-added taxes are those levied on a specific product and hence only "indirectly" on firms or individuals. Since only "indirect taxes" are "borne by [a] like product," it is only refunds of and exemptions from such taxes that are declared by Ad Article XVI to be non-subsidies and are protected by Article VI:4 from the imposition of countervailing duties.

The historical rationale for this disparate treatment of "indirect" and "direct" taxes was the assumption that only "direct" taxes were absorbed by the seller (*i.e.*, were part of the seller's costs); that "indirect taxes" (*e.g.*, sales or other excise taxes) were always "forward-shifted" (*i.e.*, passed on in the price to the buyer). Under this assumption, "indirect" taxes were not thought of as entering into the seller's "costs" and hence remission of those taxes was not a "subsidy" nor did it give the seller a competitive advantage. Indeed, since the imported product was likely to

---

[42] This Panel Report was never approved by the GATT Council. The U.S. and the EEC reached a negotiated settlement. The U.S. then agreed to removal of the Report from the Council agenda.

[43] Article XVI does not address the issue directly.

be subject to sales and other excise taxes in the country of importation, remission of the exporting country's sales or excise tax was, under the forward-shifting assumption, necessary to avoid taxing the import twice. To countervail the remission would be tantamount to double taxation. On the other hand, since it was traditionally thought that "direct taxes" were rarely if ever completely forward shifted an exemption or refund would constitute an impermissible incentive to export and a fully countervailable subsidy.

Needless to say it has often been charged that these GATT rules are unfair to U.S. exporters. The U.S. government relies heavily on non-refundable direct taxes while American exporters have to compete with suppliers from countries that rely more on refundable indirect taxes.[44] Furthermore, both the theory that indirect taxes are fully forward shifted and that direct and indirect taxes differ in this respect, have now been very largely discredited.[45] Reflecting, in part, a sense of unfairness and these theoretical misgivings, the United States, in 1971, undertook to extend income tax relief to its exporters through use of the Domestic International Sales Corporation, or DISC.[46]

The Territorial Principle of Income Taxation

The second and perhaps more telling problem which precipitated the DISC legislation was the higher income taxes that United States exporters were forced to pay because of differences in the tax treatment of "tax haven" export transactions by several of America's principal competitors.

A "tax haven" country offers low or zero income tax rates to foreign firms doing business there. By locating a branch or subsidiary in a "tax haven" and then selling to the subsidiary at a low price and causing the latter to resell to the ultimate foreign buyer in what is otherwise a purely paper transaction, an exporter can limit taxes on its export profits to the low "tax haven" rates, provided the laws of its own country permit it to do so. For many years several European countries following the so-called "territorial principle" made no attempt to tax income earned by the "tax haven" subsidiary and imposed no more than a token tax on earnings remitted to the home country. In the case of the United States, on the other hand, Subpart F of the Internal Revenue Code subjected the income of "tax haven" subsidiaries to immediate U.S. taxation if the subsidiary conducted no manufacturing or substantial sales operations in the "tax haven" country. As a result of these differences, most U.S. exporters were paying higher income taxes on their export earnings than many of their European competitors. It was this discrepancy that the DISC was intended to correct.

---

[44] Many economists have argued that this doesn't make any difference because it is compensated for in the exchange rate. That view, however, has recently been challenged. See: Hamilton and Whalley, Border Tax Adjustments And U.S. Trade, 20 J. of Int'l Economics 377, (1986).

[45] A good exposition of the theoretical problems posed by the traditional theory is to be found in The United States Submission on Border Tax Adjustments to Working Party No. 4 of the Council on Border Tax Adjustments, OECD, February 16, 1966, C/WR 4(66) 4 reprinted in App. 93-116 to the Supreme Court Record in *Zenith Radio Corp. v. United States*, 437 U.S. 443, 98 S. Ct. 2441, 57 L. Ed 337 (1978).

[46] The ensuing summary of the DISC and related legislation and the background of the GATT Review of those laws is adapted from Robert E. Hudec, Reforming GATT Adjudication Procedures: The Lessons Of The DISC Case, 72 Minn L. Rev. 1443 (1988).

Under the DISC legislation[47] U.S. exporters could create a separate domestic corporation, a DISC, that would have no assets, no employees, and no independent business function. Exporters could sell goods to their DISC and then have the DISC resell to the ultimate foreign buyer. Profits from the two-step sale could then be divided between the DISC and its parent company following one of several statutory formulae under which income taxes on a certain portion of the profits *attributable to the DISC* were deferred.

Deferral did not mean total forgiveness. But the liability for taxes on these profits was suspended as long as they were retained by the DISC, no interest was charged on the suspended liability and firms soon began to treat the yearly tax savings as a permanent gain reportable as corporate earnings. Taxes on up to 25% of total export profits could thus be deferred, a figure later reduced to about 17%-18%. The subsidy implicit in this deferral was, in turn, justified by the United States as an equivalent of the subsidy implicit in the lax European rules governing "tax haven" companies.

The Disc Case

Following passage of the DISC legislation, the EEC, in 1972, requested bilateral consultations under Article XXIII:1 of the GATT. The U.S. responded with a similar request for consultations with France, Belgium and the Netherlands claiming that the latters' use of the "territorial principle" of taxation resulted in the same subsidy for exporters as the DISC. In 1973 the EEC invoked Article XXIII:2 and asked for a GATT ruling on its claim that the DISC violated Article XVI:4. The U.S. responded with a request for a similar ruling on its claims against France, Belgium and the Netherlands. The Council agreed to the appointment of a Panel but the five person Panel was not actualiy appointed until 1976. The Panel's four Reports were submitted to the Council in November of that year.

All four reports were written in traditional GATT style as earlier described by Hudec (see p. 418, fn. 38, *supra*). The impressionistic style aside, however, the Panel did conclude that, standing alone, the tax deferral feature of the DISC was a subsidy and that the "bi-level pricing" requirement of Article XVI:4 had been met. DISC, in other words, violated GATT. Then, in the cases against France, Belgium and the Netherlands, the Panel concluded that the latter's tax laws also ran afoul of GATT Article XVI:4. As to the U.S. contention that the European violations of Article XVI:4 were a defense to the charges against the DISC, the Panel remarked only that one violation did not justify another. At no time, however, did the United States attempt to make a similar defense of DISC as an off-set to the asserted unfairness of the GATT rules on border tax adjustments.[48]

---

[47] Revenue Act of 1971, Pub L. 92-178, 85 Stat. 535. What remains of the law is presently codified in Internal Revenue Code Sections 991-997.

[48] It is to be noted that in 1978 the United Supreme Court in *Zenith Radio Corp. v. United States*, 437 U.S. 443, 98 S. Ct. 2441, 57 L. Ed. 337 (1978), upheld an interpretation of the United States countervailing duty law that conformed with the GATT rules on border tax adjustments. *Zenith* had argued that because those rules were based upon "false economic assumptions," they should be rejected by the court. The Court, however, declined this invitation. The legislative history, embodying the traditional economic assumptions described above, was according to the Court too well settled to permit of such judicial innovation. In addition, the Court noted that economists "do not agree on the ultimate

When the Panel's several Reports came to the Council the U.S. agreed not to block Council approval of the DISC Report if the Reports on the French, Belgian and Dutch laws were also approved. The latter countries, however, backed by other members, refused and a stalemate ensued that effectively continued until 1984.

The contemporary importance of this stalemate lies chiefly in its core causes and what those causes reveal about the system of GATT adjudication. In realistic economic terms the U.S. case against the European tax laws was hard to refute. A territorial tax system with lax rules on inter-company pricing could, in fact, be used to reduce a tax on exports below the level of tax imposed on identical domestic sales. The Europeans made no serious effort to refute the American economic argument. They relied instead on the legislative record. The governments who accepted Article XVI:4 had clearly intended to allow territorial taxing systems; systems in widespread use for a very long time.

In point of fact both positions were correct. The adoption of Article XVI:4 was not intended or expected to force a major reform of the world's income tax laws. Yet without reform, taxation under the territorial principle had left open a huge loophole in what was intended as a legal obligation banning all export subsidies on non-primary products. This conflict posed a formidable challenge to the GATT system of adjudication.

The issue was whether the GATT Panel could devise a legal theory distinguishing the DISC from territorial taxing systems that was both persuasive enough to withstand U.S. objections — or at least strip those objections of their principled foundation — while putting in place concepts that might energize other processes, within or without GATT, to close the loophole. A legal theory that would not discard historical expectations but set the stage for those expectations to catch up with economic reality. Indeed, this in part, has happened with the adoption by many European countries of stricter rules on inter-company pricing and "tax-havens." But the GATT process cannot take credit for that progress.

In the end, employing the traditional impressionistic style of decision making, working from a traditional "technocratic" mind-set rather than the broader jurisprudential outlook required to fashion a more adequate legal theory, the GATT system of adjudication failed in the DISC case. Again, the fear of being too legalistic rendered the system too unsophisticated for the task at hand.[49] Not until 1981 was any further progress made in resolving the dispute. In that year a compromise was reached under which all four Reports would be approved but with an "understanding" that territorial tax laws were consistent with Article XVI:4, thus eviscerating the case against the Europeans. Due to a last ditch effort by the U.S. to interpret this understanding so as to keep DISC alive, the case did not finally come to a close until 1984.

---

effect of remitting indirect taxes" and those effects would, in all events, be difficult to measure. In addition, despite the problematic quality of the theory underlying the GATT rules they were reaffirmed in the GATT Subsidies Code. (See Paragraphs (e) through (h) of the Illustrative list.)

[49] One of the more important legacies of the case was the establishment of a legal staff within the GATT Secretariat. A member of that staff now works with each Panel.

Nevertheless, the 1981 understanding did eventually allow a distinction to be drawn between territorial tax laws and the DISC. The latter was a "domestic" tax haven whereas the European systems employed "foreign" tax havens. Accordingly, in 1984 Congress repealed DISC and substituted something called the Foreign Sales Corporation (FSC). Under the FSC exporters obtain substantially the same tax benefits as under DISC except that export sales must, in conformity with the territorial principle, be run through a foreign-based sales corporation.

[C]   Some Contrasting Theories about Subsidies

At this point a theoretical interlude is needed to put what has already been studied into sharper perspective and to lay a better foundation for examining the U.S. countervailing duty law. What follows, therefore, are three contrasting views concerning the efficacy of national governmental measures designed to off-set the effect of subsidies on imports and of international efforts to constrain subsidization more broadly.

Countervailing Duties and International Trade

Warren F. Schwartz

*1978 Sup. Ct. Rev. 294**

I believe that no convincing case can be made for having a countervailing duty law.[50] The notion that a country, to improve its own welfare or to enhance efficiency throughout the world should nullify the effect of foreign subsidization is based upon fundamental misconceptions about the origins and effects of the action of national governments which affect international trade. To say that such laws cannot be justified on [efficiency grounds does not imply that we] . . . should not have them. . . . In the field of international trade (and elsewhere) there are important provisions which are asserted to be efficiency enhancing but whose real raison d'etre is the distribution of wealth they effect. If costs can be imposed on foreign firms, or the quantity of the goods they can sell in the United States can be limited, domestic competitors will derive benefits in the form of higher prices and more sales. If a distributional theory justifying these benefits is accepted then there can be no quarrel with them. . . .

Although the competition of foreign firms which benefit from subsidies is characterized as "unfair" by those advocating such laws, no explanation of why the competition is unfair is offered. It may be thought to be obvious from the fact that a benefit which leads to competitive advantage is conferred. But firms throughout the world are subject to a wide range of governmentally imposed costs

---

[50] I have argued this at length before. See Schwartz & Harper, The Regulation Subsidies Affecting International Trade, 70 Mich.L.Rev. 831 (1972). For a contrary view recommending a selective approach, see Barcelo, Subsidies And Countervailing Duties — Analysis and A Proposal, 9 Law & Pol. in Int'l Bus. 779 (1977).

and receive a great variety of governmentally conferred benefits both of which affect their behavior. A coherent theory of "fairness" would have to define a standard by which the net of these costs and benefits is to be judged. I know of no way of doing this and am unaware of any effort to develop such a standard by those supporting countervailing duty laws. In any event, considerations of national and international efficiency are usually advanced to justify the imposition of countervailing duties. I now turn to these.

I begin with the extreme case where the justification for imposing a countervailing duty is presumably the strongest. Suppose a country decides to increase its exports and provides a large cash payment for each unit exported. It is plain that consumers in the country to which the goods are exported are unambiguously better off. If the subsidy leads to greater sales it is because a portion of it is passed on to consumers in the form of lower prices. The importing country as a whole is also better off. The domestic resources previously used to manufacture the goods which are now imported are shifted to their next highest valued use. Since that value is by definition greater than the cost of the imported goods (or else they would not be imported) the country as a whole is richer by the amount of the difference.

Undoubtedly, American competitors of the foreign firm receiving the subsidy are worse off. But so are all firms which are under sold by competitors. What is necessary to justify government intervention is a reason why this harm should be prevented. The reason usually advanced is that the payment of the subsidy "distorts" the "true" costs of the foreign firm and thus leads to a misallocation of resources. This argument, however, is unpersuasive.

First, in a hypothetical case, a country decides to make a payment to increase its exports. For such a decision to be rational, it must be believed that the amount of money received for the goods in the absence of the subsidy understates the social value of the goods to the country from which they emanate. Thus there is too little incentive to produce the goods. When private transactions do not take account of all costs and benefits so that the incentive structure does not yield the socially desirable outcome an "externality," is said to exist. To assure that these externalities are taken into account is one of the principal roles of governments. A variety of explanations could justify export subsidization on externality grounds. "Pioneer" exporting firms may generate information about the market abroad which is disseminated throughout the country of export — much of it without the receipt of payment equal to its value. The pioneer firm may create consumer acceptance which extends to products of other manufacturers in the industry or indeed to all products emanating from the country. If externalities of this kind exist and government intervention leads to the production of a more "efficient" quantity of goods and services than would be produced in the absence of governmental action then, by definition, there can be no objection on efficiency grounds to the payment of the subsidy.

Of course, the foreign country could make a mistake and pay "too much" subsidy. It is not clear, however, even in principle what it means to say that a "mistake" was made. Given the theoretical and practical difficulties of assessing how the foreign government has determined that a given quantity of externalities exist, it is quite uncertain what we mean by "getting it right." In any event, having another country either assume that the country of export always gets it entirely "wrong" — the approach of the present law — or trying to determine the magnitude of the mistake made by the country of origin seems unwise indeed. This is so especially because the costs of error in dealing with the externalities are largely borne by the country paying the subsidy. There may be a diminution in international efficiency but that is because the country of export (if it does make a mistake) has misallocated its own resources. The importing country is plainly ahead to the extent that the subsidy is passed on to its consumers.

The second basic difficulty in justifying the imposition of countervailing duties on efficiency grounds is that it is not plain what yardstick should be used for deciding whether a subsidy has been paid. Take even my simple case of a direct cash payment for every unit exported. Suppose larger cash payments per unit exported are being paid on other goods which require similar resources for their production. Or assume that the domestic consumption of certain goods is subsidized in the same amount that is paid on export. What emerges, as more complications are added, is that the production and consumption of goods are subject to an enormously complex array of governmental measures which either increase or decrease the private costs and benefits of the people making the consumption and production decisions. The likely direction of change in the allocation of resources, if one governmental measure is introduced and everything else is held constant, can be predicted. But whether the overall effect of governmental action is more or less "neutral" before or after the change is a question of extraordinary complexity.

Furthermore, neutrality in the sense that it is employed in the analysis of subsidies may be the wrong end to pursue. The concept postulates firms and individuals having various skills and preferences with respect to resources without regard to government. It is, however, plain . . . that some of the "gains of trade" which lead to efficient specialization in production and consumption cannot be realized in the absence of government intervention. The costs and benefits generated by a country's efforts to deal with the interdependencies that will not be taken into account in private transactions are as important an element in defining international efficiency as those manifested in private market transactions.

What all this means is that the price at which a good is offered in a foreign market is the product of private and public efforts to achieve efficiency in the country of origin. Efficient allocation of the world's resources requires that all of these costs be taken into account — not only those which are manifested in private transactions.

I thus believe that the notion of neutrality which underlies the efficiency case for nullifying foreign subsidization is undefinable in terms which can be implemented in any workable legal scheme. It is moreover, not a goal worth pursuing. Finally, if it is both desirable and attainable, it is the country granting the alleged subsidy which has the incentives and the means for achieving it.

Subsidies and Countervailing Duties — Analysis and A Proposal

John J. Barcelo, III
9 Law & Pol. in Int'l Bus. 779 at 790 (1977)*

The divergences from full internal efficiency[51] and the nonefficiency objectives discussed above[52] provide a justification for some form of government intervention in the market either to correct the distortion or to achieve the nonefficiency objective.

In the case of market distortions, where output is unduly restricted because of monopoly power, external economies, or market rigidities, the appropriate intervention would be a government aid to production. This might be accomplished either through a subsidy paid to domestic production or through a subsidy paid on the export of the product in question. Both would increase production and tend to equate marginal cost with marginal value.[53]

Economists have demonstrated, however, that where a distortion arises in the domestic sector, as those discussed above do, the most efficient policy would call for intervention at the domestic rather than the trade level. . . . As Denton and O'Cleireacain put it: "Distortions should be tackled as closely as possible to their source."[54]

The production subsidy causes output to expand as it should and allows trade to occur at a uniform price in the international and domestic markets. An export subsidy, while capable of expanding production, would at the same time open up a price difference between the domestic and international markets for the product in question.[55] Since the subsidy causes the domestic price to rise above the world

---

* Copyright © 1977 by Law & Pol'y in Int'l Bus. Reprinted by permission.

[51] Earlier in the article, the author identifies three typical examples of such divergences: (1) imperfect competition (*i.e.* firms with market power to increase price above cost; for a fuller explanation of this phenomenon see Section 5.03[B] *infra* page 478, et seq.); (2) market externalities such as those mentioned by Schwartz in the excerpt above; and (3) market rigidities where, usually as a result of institutional arrangements (*e.g.*, labor union bargaining strategy), supply and demand do not react smoothly to price inducements. - Ed.

[52] Under this heading the author offers, as an illustrative list, policies designed to achieve a more equitable distribution of income, to become self-sufficient in a product important to national defense, to maintain a certain portion of the population in agricultural production or to avoid sudden economic dislocation in certain sectors. - Ed.

[53] Again for a fuller explanation for why efficiency is achieved where marginal cost is equal to price (*i.e.*, "marginal value") see Section 5.03[B], *infra*. - Ed.

[54] G. Denton & S. O'Cleireacain, Subsidy Issues In International Commerce (1972).

[55] The export subsidy causes a greater amount of the total domestic production to be exported, and thus leaves a smaller amount for home consumption. This tends to drive a wedge between the two prices, and the tendency continues until the price gap equals the amount of the subsidy. A producer makes the same profit on export sales as he does on domestic sales when the price difference between the two just equals the subsidy. H. Johnson, Optimal Trade Intervention In The Presence Of Domestic Distortions, In Trade, Growth And The Balance Of Payments, at page 22-23 (Baldwin et al. eds., 1965).
It is implicitly assumed in this analysis that the subsidizing country would impose either an import prohibition or a tariff to prevent imports of the product in question from

price, it prevents consumers from purchasing at the low world price, thereby causing a consumption loss and distribution inefficiency. In some cases the consumption loss could even out-weigh the production gain, so that intervention in the trade sector would reduce overall welfare. In all cases, intervention in the trade sector would be less than optimal. Therefore, the existence of domestic inefficiencies does not represent a serious qualification of free trade principles. Domestic, not trade measures should be applied to correct domestic distortions.

Similarly, domestic intervention should be the preferred method of achieving nonefficiency objectives. . . . For example, if income redistribution is the objective, investment subsidies to depressed regions, and production subsidies to depressed industries are preferable to export subsidies for these same regions or industries. The latter may be used to encourage production, but they also cause unnecessary consumption losses through distribution inefficiency. The same pattern follows for an agricultural policy designed to keep workers on the farm or a national defense policy designed to assure self-sufficiency.

In summary, export subsidies can be soundly condemned as contrary to the principles of economic efficiency and in general cannot be defended as necessary to correct preexisting domestic distortions or to achieve nonefficiency objectives. On the other hand, domestic subsidies may be either efficiency enhancing or distorting or may be instrumental in the achievement of a nonefficiency national objective. Consequently, domestic subsidies cannot be so categorically opposed on the basis of efficiency principles.[56]

. . . The discussion above is based on the underlying premise that removal or avoidance of any given divergence from the optimal conditions of full economic efficiency will automatically improve welfare, even if the utopian state of perfect efficiency is not reached. This is not necessarily correct. Once it is established that distortions and divergences will continue to exist even after any particular liberalizing policy is implemented, an unavoidable condition of the real world, a single liberalizing step is no longer unequivocally beneficial. This is known as the problem of the second best in economic literature. . . .

The second best problem occurs in a simple form where market imperfections directly offset each other, so that the removal of only one would actually worsen efficiency. . . . More complex, secondary effects set into motion by any primary policy because of the cross elasticities between products and possibly even changes

---

undercutting its subsidy program. If this were not done and transportation costs were negligible, all the domestic production would be exported and all the domestic demand would be met by imports, in both cases at a single world price. This would be a wholly irrational scheme.

[56] Later Barcelo follows through on his general observations with the recommendation that importing countries should be permitted to countervail export subsidies without proof of "material injury" to domestic producers (p. 799) but that a showing of injury should be required before an importing country could countervail "selective" domestic subsidies on exportable products (p. 842 et. seq.). Later he was to advocate an injury prerequisite for all countervailing duty actions. See: Barcelo, Subsidies And Countervailing Duties And Antidumping After The Tokyo Round, 13 Cornell Int'l L. J. 257 (1980) and also Barcelo, An "Injury-Only Regime" (For Imports) And Actionable Subsidies, In Interface III. Wallace, Loftus & Kirkorian, eds. (1984). - Ed.

in the exchange rate can also result in a net distortion of efficiency, even though the primary effect has a beneficial tendency.

Despite these technical possibilities [it is still appropriate to draw conclusions] . . . about the efficiency enhancing or distorting effects of policies based on their *primary* effect without returning each time to a discussion of the second best problem, unless [a particular issue involves an] . . . obvious difficulty with offsetting distortions. This approach can be justified on several grounds. First, it is useful to have an analysis of policy choices which would lead to the maximization of potential world income as an ideal or model solution. Second, since the long-run objective is to remove all market imperfections, it seems appropriate to favor policies whose primary effect is efficiency enhancing so long as there are no obvious offsetting and irremediable counter-distortions. . . . Third, [with] the removal of distortions on as generalized a level as possible, on all products and sectors of the economies of all countries, but especially distortions of a high magnitude, [s]econdary effects . . . can be presumed to be minimal as compared with the primary effect. Finally . . . [e]mpirical evidence does not indicate any reaso⟩ o suspect that the distortions created by export subsidies are generally counterbalanced by roughly equal and irremediable market imperfections acting in the opposite direction. . . .

Subsidies in International Trade

Gary Clyde Hufbauer & Joanna Shelton Erb
Institute for International Economics, pages 5, 8 (1984)*

An economist might . . . ask why the international community should concern itself with the subsidy practices of its member nations. After all, if one nation wishes to subsidize production or exports in the name of infant-industry arguments, second-best policies, or simply to assuage particular industries, isn't the resulting economic distortion principally the misfortune of the subsidizing nation? This question becomes especially pointed when an importing country can enjoy the advantage of cheaper goods made possible by another country's subsidy practices. To be sure, the producers in one country might, with the assistance of public subsidies, drive out foreign producers, capture their markets and later make good any losses through monopolistic pricing. . . . But shouldn't the international community require evidence of monopolistic intent or result before authorizing countermeasures? Put simply, apart from clear instances of grasping monopoly, why would the international community be the keeper of national export morals?

The answer is also simple: unbridled and competing national subsidies can undermine world prosperity. Whatever the analytic merits of a purist free trade turn-the-other-cheek approach, the Great Depression taught the world that protective policies can quickly and destructively spread from nation to nation. Because the concentrated interests of producers command greater political

---

support than the diffuse interests of consumers, national governments find it much easier to emulate the vices of protection than the virtues of free trade. This lesson has prompted the international community to fashion guidelines that distinguish between acceptable and unacceptable national subsidy measures and to codify those guidelines both in bilateral treaties and in multilateral agreements . . . Robert Baldwin has ably summarized the negotiating history since the 1930s:

> The 1930s experience with export subsidies as well as with competitive devaluation, which has the effect of a general export subsidy and import surcharge, apparently convinced the GATT founders that export subsidies exacerbate international political tensions and should be eliminated. Though consumers in the importing country gain from export subsidization by other nations, domestic producer groups in the importing countries are forced to curtail output and incur a producer-surplus loss. . . . The view that domestic producers are somehow more entitled to domestic compared to foreign markets is still widely held by the general public. Thus, in the case of export subsidies, it was not necessary for the founders of GATT to implement their international political objective with regard to this distortion only gradually (as with tariffs) and export subsidies were banned outright.

Firms do not like to surrender markets for any reason, and certainly not to another firm that is aided by its government. If the international community cannot discipline subsidy practices, nations may be caught up in a wasteful spiral of escalating emulation. . . .

NOTES AND QUESTIONS

(1) Schwartz makes much of the fact that the importing country is always "better-off" whenever another country subsidizes its exports even though particular industries within the importing country may, as a result, be worse-off. This, he says, holds true even if the subsidy exceeds anything that might be justified on efficiency grounds, such as off-setting market externalities. Are you convinced? Or, does the assertion depend upon how you define a nation's economic welfare and does that definition, in turn, depend upon a very particular perspective? Do Barcelo and Hufbauer suggest an alternative perspective? Note that while Barcelo and Hufbauer can still be read as addressing themselves to a nation's economic welfare, to what extent is their perspective on how to assess that welfare a function of the political dynamics of contemporary international economic relations?

(2) Schwartz again correctly points out the difficulties of knowing whether any particular subsidy does or does not contribute to efficiency (*i.e.*, does not distort trade). Is that necessarily an argument against either a national countervailing duty law or a broader international effort to regulate subsidies? How does the *Wheat Flour* Case bear on this question? Consider both the changing pattern of global trade in wheat flour from 1962 to 1981 as well as the basic formula used by the EEC in fixing its export "refunds."

(3) As Schwartz and Barcelo both point out, nations use *domestic subsidies* to improve efficiency and to pursue non-efficient but nevertheless worthwhile

domestic social objectives. If the former are non-trade distorting and the latter are within the exclusive competence of the granting nation as a sovereign state, what rationale is there for the international regulation of *domestic subsidies* merely because they happen to benefit exports, which, in any event, leaves the importing nation better-off? Is the case for regulation confined solely to the case where *domestic subsidies* are in point of fact a blatant effort at export expansion undertaken at the expense of other more efficient non-subsidized producers? If, as the panel decision in the *Wheat Flour* Case can be read to suggest, even *export subsidies* which meet this test cannot always be readily identified, is there any justification whatsoever for the international regulation of domestic subsidies, even if we accept the broader perspective that Hufbauer employs? Are you persuaded by Hufbauer's answer to this?

[D] Treatment of Subsidized Imports Under United States Law: Imposition of Countervailing Duties

1. Overview of U.S. Legislation

In General

Following is an overview of United States countervailing duty legislation as it stands after being substantially amended by the Omnibus Trade and Competitiveness Act of 1988 ("1988 Act"). Under that legislation all subsidized imports fall into one of two broad categories as follows:

(1) Subsidized imports that may not be subject to a countervailing duty unless it is first established that they caused or were likely to cause "material injury" to the domestic industry. This includes all imports that would otherwise enter the United States duty free [57] and all imports that come from a country entitled to the benefits of the GATT Subsidies Code (hereinafter referred to as "Code Countries"). The Code Countries are:[58] (i) signatories to the Code, (ii) any non-signatory country that has assumed obligations substantially equivalent to those imposed by the Code, and (iii) any country that is party to an agreement with the United States which requires that its exports to the United States be given Code treatment.[59]

(2) All other subsidized imports (hereinafter referred to as imports from "non-Code countries"). In these cases countervailing duties are to be imposed without considering whether they injured domestic producers.[60]

---

[57] 19 U.S.C. Section 1303.

[58] 19 U.S.C. Section 1671(b).

[59] The countries are: El Salvador, Honduras, Liberia, Nepal, North Yemen, Paraguay and Venezuela. See. S. Rep. 249, 96th Congress. 1st Sess. at 45.

[60] These categories are the result of history. Section 1303 had its origins in the Tariff Act of 1930 (46 Stat. 687) which contained no injury requirement. Then when GATT was framed, a finding of "material injury" was made a pre-condition to the imposition of both countervailing and antidumping duties (Article VI:6(a)). Under the Protocol of Provisional Application, however, the United States proceedings under Section 1303 were exempt from this requirement. On the other hand, Section 1303 only applied to imports that were otherwise dutiable. When the Trade Act of 1974 (88 Stat. 2049) extended Section 1303 to all non-dutiable imports irrespective of source, the amendment was not entitled to the

These two categories of cases are governed by two separate substantive provisions. Imports from *non-Code countries* come under 19 U.S.C. Section 1303(a)(1) which provides in pertinent part as follows:

Sec. 1303(a). Levy of Countervailing Duties (1) . . . whenever any [non-Code] country . . . shall pay or bestow, directly or indirectly, any bounty or grant upon the manufacture or production or export of any article manufactured or produced in such country . . . then upon the importation of such article or merchandise into the United States, whether the same shall be imported directly from the country of production or otherwise, and whether such article or merchandise is imported in the same condition as when exported from the country of production or has been changed in condition by remanufacture or otherwise, there shall be levied and paid . . . in addition to any duties otherwise imposed, a duty equal to the net amount of such bounty or grant. . . .

Subsidized imports from *Code countries* fall under Section 1671 of Title 19. The section divides administrative responsibility for the law between the International Trade Commission (ITC) and what is called the "administering authority" — currently, the International Trade Administration (ITA) of the Department of Commerce. It provides that (i) if the administering authority (ITA) determines that a Code Country, or other defined party in such a country, is providing a subsidy with respect to the "manufacture, production, or exportation" of imported merchandise and (ii) if the ITC determines that a U.S. industry is "materially injured, or threatened with material injury," or that establishment of a U.S. industry is "materially retarded" because of the subsidized imports, then, the imported merchandise shall be assessed a countervailing duty "equal to the amount of the net subsidy." In addition, the provisions of Section 1671(a)(2), requiring an injury determination by the ITC, apply to subsidized imports from *non-Code Countries* that would otherwise enter duty-free.

Material Injury

Since the "material injury" test in countervailing duty cases is the same as in dumping cases we shall defer a more detailed examination of that test until after we have reviewed the dumping problem (See Section 5.03). It is worth noting here, however, that "material injury" is defined as "harm which is not inconsequential, immaterial, or unimportant."[61] This is a lower standard than the "serious injury" standard which governs in "escape clause" proceedings. Moreover, under the "escape clause" the ITC must not only find that the domestic industry has suffered "serious injury" but that imports were a cause of that injury "no less important than any other cause."[62] The absence of this language in the countervailing duty

---

Protocol exemption and it was necessary to apply the GATT injury requirement to those imports. Then in 1979 the United States became a party to the GATT Subsidies Code which, following Article VI:6(a), included an injury requirement. That requirement, however, was only applicable to Code Countries. Hence Section 1671, which was added by the Trade Agreements Act of 1979, Pub. L. 96-39, 93 Stat. 151.

   [61] Section 1677(7).

   [62] Section 202(b)(1)(B) of the Trade Act of 1974 as amended by Section 1401(a) of the Omnibus Trade and Competitiveness Act of 1988 (19 U.S.C. 2252(b)(1)(B)).

law means that in such a case, unlike an "escape clause" proceeding, the ITC does not weigh the adverse effect of subsidized imports against other factors which may have contributed to the domestic industry's problems.[63] Indeed, a countervailing duty may be imposed even though the subsidized imports contributed only marginally to that industry's overall decline.

Definition of Subsidy

While Section 1303 uses the words "bounty or grant" and Section 1671 refers to "subsidies," Section 1677(7) makes clear that this difference has no operative effect. Nowhere, however, does the statute attempt to provide a general definition of a "subsidy." Instead Section 1677(5)(A) provides a non-exclusive illustrative list of what will be deemed subsidies as follows:

Sec. 1677. Definitions; Special Rules. For Purposes of this Subtitle —

* * * *

(5) Subsidy

(A) **In General. The term "subsidy" has the same meaning as the term "bounty or grant" as that term is used in section 1303 of this title and includes, but is not limited to, the following:**

  (i) **Any export subsidy described . . . [in the Illustrative List attached to the GATT Subsidies Code]**

  (ii) **The following domestic subsidies if . . . paid or bestowed directly or indirectly on the manufacture, production, or export of any class or kind of merchandise:**

  (I) **The provision of capital, loans, or loan guarantees on terms inconsistent with commercial considerations.**

  (II) **The provision of goods or services at preferential rates.**

  (III) **The grant of funds or forgiveness of debt to cover operating losses sustained by a specific industry.**

  (IV) **The assumption of any costs or expenses of manufacture, production, or distribution.**

The Conduct of an Investigation

The following Table sets out the steps involved in a countervailing duty investigation relating to imports from a Code Country or imports that would otherwise enter duty free. For imports where no injury determination is required, these procedures are modified as appropriate. Since the procedures in anti-dumping cases (19 U.S.C. 1673a-h) track those in countervailing duty cases very closely the Table covers both, although the procedures shown in the Table apply to all anti-dumping cases regardless of the source of the imports.

In structure these procedures are very largely the result of two GATT Codes. As already noted, Part I of the Subsidies Code pertains to countervailing duty

---

[63] Consult 19 CFR Section 207.27.

actions. There is also the GATT Anti–Dumping Code initially negotiated during the Kennedy Round [64] and then revised and superceded by the Code negotiated during the Tokyo Round [65] (Unless otherwise indicated all references herein to the GATT Anti-Dumping Code are to the Tokyo Round document). Both the Subsidies and the Anti-Dumping Code were addressed to a number of perceived abuses under then existing European, Canadian and American legislation. The Codes sought: to assure that cases were resolved quickly (generally within one year) in order to prevent domestic producers from using those laws to harass their import competition; to assure that the injury question and the subsidy or dumping question were addressed simultaneously so that cases in which there was no evidence of injury could be disposed of quickly; and to ensure that the proceedings were open and fair and that all decisions were made a matter of public record.

---

[64] Agreement On Implementation Of Article VI Of The General Agreement On Tariffs And Trade, June 30, 1967, GATT BISD, 15th Supp.,(1968) at page 24.

[65] Agreement On Implementation Of Article VI Of The General Agreement On Tariffs And Trade, April 12, 1979, GATT, BISD, 26th Supp., (1980) at page 171.

Table III

COUNTERVAILING DUTY PROCEDURES
(Variations under the anti-dumping law shown in [brackets])

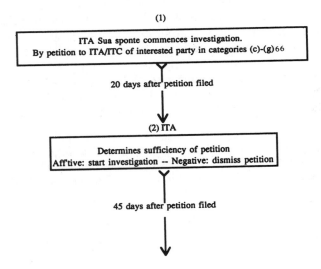

(1)

| ITA Sua sponte commences investigation.
By petition to ITA/ITC of interested party in categories (c)-(g)66 |

20 days after petition filed

(2) ITA

| Determines sufficiency of petition
Aff'tive: start investigation -- Negative: dismiss petition |

45 days after petition filed

66"Interested Party" is defined as: (a) a foreign producer or exporter of merchandise under investigation, or a U.S. importer of that merchandise or a trade association a majority of whose members are such importers, (b) the government of a country in which that merchandise was produced, (c) a producer or wholesaler in the United States of a like product, (d) a union representing workers in an industry producing a like product in the United States, (e) a trade association a majority of whose members produce or wholesale a like product in the United States, (f) a trade association a majority of whose members are interested parties under categories (c)–(e), and (g) in the case of a processed agricultural product any trade association representative of processors and producers, or processors and growers. 19 U.S.C. Section 1677(9).

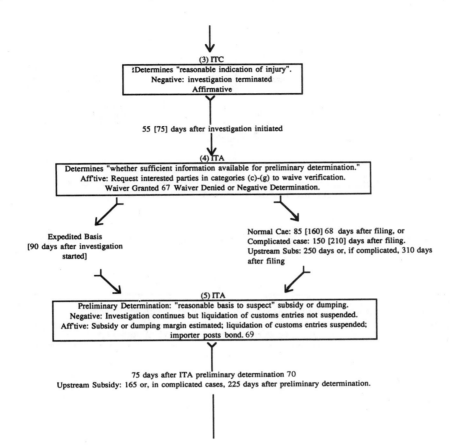

(3) ITC
¦Determines "reasonable indication of injury".
Negative: investigation terminated
Affirmative

55 [75] days after investigation initiated

(4) ITA
Determines "whether sufficient information available for preliminary determination."
Aff'tive: Request interested parties in categories (c)-(g) to waive verification.
Waiver Granted 67 Waiver Denied or Negative Determination.

Expedited Basis
[90 days after investigation
started]

Normal Cae: 85 [160] 68 days after filing, or
Complicated case: 150 [210] days after filing.
Upstream Subs: 250 days or, if complicated, 310 days
after filing

(5) ITA
Preliminary Determination: "reasonable basis to suspect" subsidy or dumping.
Negative: Investigation continues but liquidation of customs entries not suspended.
Aff'tive: Subsidy or dumping margin estimated; liquidation of customs entries suspended;
importer posts bond. 69

75 days after ITA preliminary determination 70
Upstream Subsidy: 165 or, in complicated cases, 225 days after preliminary determination.

67 This waiver process has never been invoked, and is unlikely to be used in the future because of the tight time limitations to which countervailing duty proceedings are already subject.

68 Shortened to 100 or 120 days for a two or more time offender who manufactures "short life-cycle" merchandise defined in 19 U.S.C. 1673h(b)(4) as merchandise determined by ITC as likely to be "outmoded" within four years.

69 When goods are imported into the United States they "enter" into customs; a customs "entry" is established. When the duty or other charges against those goods is paid the entry is "liquidated," although the goods may have been released to the importer under bond well before "liquidation" occurs. To suspend liquidation of entries upon issuance of a preliminary countervailing duty or anti-dumping determination, therefore, means that the entry will not be liquidated until a final determination is made and, if affirmative, the countervailing or anti-dumping duty paid. To get possession of the goods in the meantime, the importer must post a bond equal to the amount of the estimated countervailing or anti-dumping duty.

70 In an anti-dumping case the party losing a preliminary determination may petition for an extension of up to 135 days from the date of that determination.

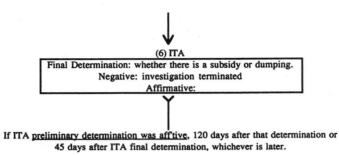

There are a number of additions to or variations on these procedures that deserve comment.

Retroactive Orders in Critical Circumstances. Upon a timely allegation, the ITA is required to determine whether a case is attended by "critical circumstances." Such a case is one in which there have been "massive imports" of the merchandise "over a relatively short period" and either "reason to suspect" a violation the GATT Subsidies Code or, in a dumping case, a history of dumping accompanied by evidence that the importer should have known that the exporter was dumping. Neither "massive" nor "relatively short period" are defined by the statute.

Nevertheless, an ITA finding of critical circumstances before[71] or after[72] issuance of an affirmative preliminary determination (Step (5) above), requires

---

[71] For this to occur the allegation must have been made at least 20 days before the Preliminary Determination is due. 19 C.F.R. Sections 353.40 (dumping) and 355.29 (countervailing duty).

[72] In this case the critical circumstance decision will be made one–month after the allegation is made. 19 C.F. R. Sections 353.40 (dumping) and 355.29 (countervailing duty).

that the resulting ITA order suspending the liquidation of customs entries be retroactively applied to all unliquidated entries of merchandise entering customs in the 90 day period prior to that order. Likewise, if a "critical circumstance" determination is made in connection with an affirmative final determination (Step (6) above), the order suspending the liquidation of entries must be retroactively applied to all entries made within 90 days prior to the first suspension order.[73] Lastly, if the ITA finds "critical circumstances," the ITC in its final injury determination (Step (7) above) must decide whether retroactive application of the countervailing or anti-dumping duty is necessary to prevent the "effectiveness of [that] duty" from being "materially impaired." If the ITC finds that such application is not necessary, any prior retroactive application of an order suspending liquidations is eliminated (19 U.S.C. 1671d(c)(3) and 1673d(c)(3)).[74]

Termination and Suspension of Investigations. In addition to terminating a subsidy or dumping investigation at the various points noted in the chart, the ITA and the ITC may terminate the investigation upon the withdrawal of the petition by the petitioner or *sua sponte* if the investigation was begun on the ITA's own initiative. If, however, the withdrawal of the petition or the *sua sponte* termination was precipitated by the ITA's "acceptance" of the foreign government's agreement to limit exports of the subsidized or dumped product to the United States (*i.e.*, *quantitative restriction agreement*), the ITA must first make a special "public interest" determination. This means that, after consulting with domestic producers and consumers, the ITA must conclude that the agreement will be no less beneficial to producers and no less harmful to consumers or to the "international economic interests of the United States" than the imposition of a countervailing or anti-dumping duty.

In addition, negotiators of the GATT Subsidies and Anti-Dumping Codes sought to encourage the settlement of countervailing duty and anti-dumping cases through agreements with exporters and foreign governments (see Article 4:5 of the Subsidies Code and Article 7 of the Anti-Dumping Code). They also subjected these agreements to rules designed to prevent their abuse and improve their transparency. In response to the Code initiatives the U.S. countervailing duty and anti-dumping legislation not only provides for the termination of an investigation upon "acceptance" of a *quantitative restriction agreement* (see above), but also authorizes the ITA to *suspend* an investigation upon "acceptance" of any of the following types of agreements: (i) a *subsidy elimination agreement* under which the foreign government granting, or the exporters receiving, a subsidy undertake, within six months, to eliminate or off-set the subsidy completely or to stop exporting to the United States altogether; (ii) a *dumping elimination agreement* under which the exporters charged with dumping agree either to eliminate the

---

[73] This means that if the ITA's preliminary determination was affirmative, the liquidation of all entries made on or after a date 90 days prior to that determination will be suspended. If, however, the preliminary determination was negative, the 90 days is measured only from the date of the ITA's final, rather than its preliminary, determination.

[74] This provision for retroactive application of countervailing duties has a very differential impact. For many imports the time between entry and liquidation is so short that retroactivity catches relatively few imports entered before a proceeding has begun. Where, however, the Customs Service takes its time, retroactivity can affect a substantial volume of goods entered prior to the commencement of a countervailing duty proceeding.

dumping margin through an immediate revision of their prices or to stop exporting to the United States within six months; (iii) with regard to subsidies, an *injury elimination agreement* whereby the foreign government agrees to eliminate the injurious effect of its subsidy either by restricting exports to the United States or by off-setting 85% or more of its subsidy and preventing suppression or undercutting of the U.S. domestic price; (iv) with regard to dumping, an *injury elimination agreement* with exporters which will prevent the dumped imports from undercutting or suppressing the U.S. domestic price and will assure an 85% reduction in the margin of dumping on future imports. *Injury elimination agreements* may be used as the basis for suspending countervailing duty and anti-dumping investigations only in complex cases and only if the ITA concludes that the agreement would be more beneficial to the domestic industry than continuation of the investigation. In the case of all of these agreements, the ITA must consult with the parties to the investigation, must find that the agreement is in the "public interest" as defined above and must conclude that it can be effectively monitored.

Procedurally, ITA acceptance of any of these agreements has the effect of suspending any further investigation by it or the ITC. If the ITA "accepts" an agreement before issuing a preliminary determination in the case (Step 5) it must automatically issue an affirmative determination. However, in the case of a *subsidy or dumping elimination agreement*, the liquidation of customs entries is not suspended as would otherwise be the case with an affirmative preliminary determination.

On the other hand, in the case of an *injury elimination agreement*, liquidations are suspended for twenty days. Within that 20 days any party to the investigation under categories (c)-(g) (See note 66, p. 438 *supra*) may ask the ITC to determine whether the "injurious effect" has, in fact, been eliminated. This determination must be made within 75 days. If the answer is negative, liquidations are suspended and the investigation proceeds. If the answer is that the "injurious effect" is actually being eliminated, the suspension of liquidations is terminated and all importers are released from their bonds. If no request for a review is made, the suspension of liquidations and release of bonds goes forward.

Finally, if within 20 days of the notice of suspension of the investigation by reason of either a *subsidy/dumping elimination agreement* or an *injury elimination agreement*, the foreign government accused of granting a subsidy, any substantial exporter of an allegedly dumped product or any party to the investigation under categories (c)-(g), requests that the investigations continue, the ITA and the ITC must comply. However, even if their final determinations are affirmative (Steps (6) and (7) of the chart), no final countervailing or anti-dumping duty order will issue if the agreement is still in effect, is having its intended impact and all the parties are fulfilling their obligations.

Preventing Circumvention of Countervailing Duty Orders. To prevent the circumvention of countervailing and anti-dumping duty orders the 1988 Act included a number of new provisions. The first is directed at the possibility of a foreign exporter circumventing an order by importing components of the product subject to the order and assembling them in the United States.[75] The second

---

[75] Pub. L. 100-418, Section 1321, adding a new Section 781(a) to the Tariff Act of 1930, 19 U.S.C. 1677j(a).

provision deals with the possibility of an exporter of components seeking to circumvent an order against those components by performing the assembly operation abroad.[76] In either case the statute authorizes the ITA to broaden its orders to cover the components of the product that is subject to the order (first case) or to cover products assembled abroad from components that have been interdicted by an order (second case). Before doing so, however, the ITA must find that "the difference between the value of" the interdicted item and the component or assembled product is "small." It must also take into account trade patterns; whether the manufacturer or exporter of the item sought to be subjected to a more inclusive order is related to the party doing the assembly; and whether imports of that item increased after the initial countervailing or anti-dumping duty order was issued. Finally, where a countervailing or anti-dumping duty has been assessed against an imported component of a product assembled in the United States (the "downstream product"), provision is made for monitoring imports of the latter to assure against circumvention of the order against the components.[77]

[2] Some Core Problems in Identification of Countervailable Subsidies: "Specificity Test" and Efficiency Norm

Schwartz puts it well:

> It is plain . . . that some "gains of trade" which lead to efficient specialization in production and consumption cannot be realized in the absence of government intervention.

One simply cannot, in other words, divorce a nation's comparative advantage in privately traded products or services from the entire socio-economic infrastructure upon which the production or supply of those goods and services depend — highways, ports, police, the level of scientific research, the educational system, etc. In most trading nations these inputs are, in large measure, provided by government. As such, they constitute "domestic subsidies" since, if the government didn't provide them, private producers would have to do so if they expected to hold their competitive position in foreign and domestic markets.

Yet, for practical and theoretical reasons it would be folly to try and countervail all of these "subsidies" even if it were possible to trace them into particular exports. Accordingly, the ITA, and before it the Treasury Department, devised a "specificity test." Drawing upon the language of what is now 19 U.S.C. Sec. 1677(5)(A), the ITA countervails only subsidies provided to a "specific enterprise or industry or group of enterprises or industries."[78] If the subsidy fails the test — if it is "generally available"[79] — it is treated as though it were part of the non-countervailable government benefits that form a nation's infrastructure. The cases that follow illustrate how the ITA, under the supervision of the courts, and with

---

[76] Pub. L. 100-418, Section 1321, adding a new Section 781(b) to the Tariff Act of 1930, 19 U.S.C. 1677j(b).

[77] Pub. L. 100-418, Section 1320, adding Section 780 to the Tariff Act of 1930, 19 U.S.C. 1677i.

[78] See page 436 *supra* for full text of 19 U.S.C. Section 1677(5)(A).

[79] "Generally available" is short-hand term representing the flip side of "specific." See Section 1677(5)(B).

one instance of Congressional intervention, have applied this test to a variety of situations.

CABOT CORPORATION v. UNITED STATES

United States Court of International Trade
620 F. Supp. 722 (1985)

[Plaintiff, a United States producer of carbon black, filed a complaint with the ITA alleging that producers of carbon black imports from Mexico had received from the Mexican government a multitude of bounties or grants within the meaning of 19 U.S.C. Section 1303; Mexico not being a Code Country. In its final countervailing duty determination the ITA found that some of the grants constituted countervailable subsidies. It concluded, however, that the government's provision of *carbon black feedstock* to the Mexican producers at below world market prices and its provision of natural gas at rates below those charged residential users did not constitute a countervailable domestic subsidy. Plaintiff sought judicial review of that decision.

Carbon black is an elemental carbon used primarily in the rubber industry, but also in the production of paints, inks, plastics and carbon paper. It is produced from a petroleum derivative feedstock, commonly known as *carbon black feedstock* which is a residue that collects at the "bottom" of the catalytic cracking tower after gasoline and other lighter distillates have been removed. For this reason carbon black feedstock is sometimes called "catcracker bottoms."

Catcracker bottoms are a unique product — their only commercial use worldwide is by the carbon black industry — and they represent the major cost of producing carbon black. In the case of Mexican carbon black, two Mexican producers — Hules Mexicanos and Negromex — had geared their plants to the use of feedstock from Petroleos Mexicanos (PEMEX), the government owned petroleum company of Mexico. Because of the inherent nature of the product and the current levels of technology in Mexico, no enterprise or industry in Mexico, other than these two carbon black producers, could make commercial use of PEMEX catcracker bottoms. Both had located their plants close to PEMEX refineries in order to reduce transportation costs.

In addition, Mexico had adopted a comprehensive strategic plan (the National Industrial Development Plan) designed to promote the industrial growth of Mexico through 1990. Pursuant to the Plan, PEMEX sold its catcraker bottoms to the two Mexican carbon black producers at substantially below "world market" prices. The firms also received natural gas from PEMEX at the rate for industrial users which was less than for residential uses.]

CARMAN, JUDGE.

. . . Plaintiff contends that the term "bounty or grant" in section 1303 is to be broadly construed and includes essentially every governmental program which "bestow[s] an unfair competitive advantage on a foreign company as against U.S.

producers of the products." Defendant opposes this proposition, arguing that programs or benefits which are generally available within the exporting country are not countervailable. . . .

. . . Since any industrial user in Mexico could purchase carbon black feedstock and natural gas at the same price, the ITA viewed PEMEX's provision of these inputs at well below world market prices as not constituting a countervailable practice. The ITA view was based on . . . a rule which has evolved within the administrative agency and was adopted by the court in *Carlisle Tire & Rubber Co. v. United States.*[80] . . . Two other decisions of this court, however, have rejected the rule as contrary to the countervailing duty statutes. . . . *Agrexco, Agricultural Export Co. v. United States,*[81] . . . and *Bethlehem Steel Corp. v. United States,*[82] . . . . This Court thus faces considerable controversy regarding the rule that generally available benefits provided within the relevant jurisdiction are not countervailable.

* * * *

In *Carlisle*, the court upheld the ITA's interpretation of section 1303 as being reasonable. . . . Apparently the ITA and the court in *Carlisle* viewed the non-countervailability of generally available benefits as the opposite side of the coin from the countervailability of benefits conferred upon a specific class. There is a distinction, however, which has not been clearly deciphered by the ITA or in prior judicial opinions, but which disrupts the apparent symmetry of the two sides of the coin.

The distinction that has evaded the ITA is that not all so-called generally available benefits are alike — some are benefits accruing generally to all citizens, while others are benefits that when actually conferred accrue to specific individuals or classes. Thus, while it is true that a generalized benefit provided by government, such as national defense, education or infrastructure, is not a countervailable bounty or grant, a generally available benefit — one that may be obtained by any and all enterprises or industries — may nevertheless accrue to specific recipients. . . .

The court in *Carlisle* recognized the absurdity of a rule that would require the imposition of countervailing duties where producers or importers have benefited from general subsidies, as "almost every product which enters international commerce" would be subject to countervailing duties. . . . Alternatively, the court in *Bethlehem* recognized the absurdity of a law that would transform an obvious subsidy into a non-countervailable benefit merely by extending the availability of the subsidy to the entire economy. . . . Thus, although a bounty or grant is preferential in nature, bestowed upon an individual class, the generally available benefits rule as developed and applied by the ITA is not an acceptable legal standard for determining the countervailability of benefits under section 1303. The appropriate standard focuses on the *de facto* case by case effect of benefits provided to recipients rather than on the nominal availability of benefits.

---

[80] 5 C.I.T. 229, 564 F.Supp. 834 (1983).
[81] 604 F. Supp. 1238 (1985).
[82] 590 F.Supp. 1237 (1984).

The case must therefore be remanded for further investigation and redetermination.

. . . The programs [before the Court] appear to effect specific quantifiable provisions of carbon black feedstock and natural gas to specific identifiable enterprises. That additional enterprises or industries can participate in the programs, whether theoretically or actually, does not destroy the programs as subsidies. The programs are apparently available to all Mexican enterprisers, but in their actual implementation may result in special bestowals upon specific enterprises.

Once it has been determined that there has been a bestowal upon a specific class, the second aspect of the definition of bounty or grant requires looking at the bestowal and determining if it amounts to an additional benefit or competitive advantage. If so, the benefit might fit within one of the illustrative examples of 19 U.S.C. Sec. 1677(5)(A)(ii). The ITA, however, prematurely concluded that "the provision of carbon black feedstock and natural gas clearly involves the provision of goods within the meaning of section [1677(5)(A)(ii)(II)]"[83] . . . that is, the subsidy example of providing goods or services at preferential rates. The ITA asserted, "[t]he standard contained in subsection (ii)(II) is 'preferential,' which normally means only more favorable to some within the relevant jurisdiction than to others within the jurisdiction." Thus, concluded the ITA, "even if carbon black feedstock and natural gas were not generally available, we would not find this rate to be a subsidy, because this rate is not preferential."

The ITA has engaged in a tautology, merely extending its generally available benefits rule into the illustrative example of subsection (ii). Although preferential pricing clearly is a countervailable subsidy, subsection (ii), as only one such example of a subsidy, does not include all pricing programs for carbon black feedstock and natural gas that are additional benefits or competitive advantages within the scope of section 1303.[84]

---

[83] For full text see page 436 *infra*.

[84] Plaintiff argues that a price below the world market price is per se a countervailable benefit. The matter is more complex. The availability of inputs at low prices to foreign producers may be the result of various non-countervailable factors such as comparative advantage. See T. Pugel, The Fundamentals Of International Trade And Investment, In Handbook of International Business 1-2, 4 (I. Walter ed. 1982). The facts of this case indicate that the Mexican carbon black producers have located themselves (although perhaps pursuant to the NIDP) to take advantage of available carbon black feedstock with specific qualities. This arrangement might allow PEMEX to sell a by-product which would otherwise go unsold. Thus, prices below the world market price or the export price may simply be the result of a symbiotic industrial relationship. Further, PEMEX's refusal to sell carbon black feedstock abroad to plaintiff might be on account of limited Mexican domestic supply. On the other hand, "generally available" benefits are not necessarily the result of the exercise of comparative advantage. It cannot be concluded merely on the basis of nominal availability and absent further investigation that the prices for carbon black feedstock and natural gas as set by PEMEX are the result of factors such as excess supply and low production cost. See contra Note, Upstream Subsidies and U.S. Countervailing Duty Law: The Mexican Ammonia Decision And The Trade Remedies Reform Act Of 1984, Law and Pol'y in Int'l Bus. 263, 291 & n. 126 (1985).

NOTES AND QUESTIONS

(1) In the 1988 Act Congress codified the first holding in the *Cabot* Case in what is now 19 U.S.C. Section 1677(5)(B) as follows:

In applying subparagraph (A), the administering authority, in each investigation shall determine whether the bounty, grant or subsidy in law or in fact is provided to a specific enterprise or industry, or group of enterprises or industries. Nominal general availability, under the terms of the law, regulation, program, or rule establishing a bounty, grant, or subsidy, of benefits thereunder is not a basis for determining that the bounty, grant or subsidy is not, or has not been, in fact provided to a specific enterprise or industry, or group thereof.

In *Carlisle Tire and Rubber Co. v. United States, supra* the Court of International Trade upheld the ITA's determination that a Korean tax law allowing accelerated depreciation on equipment in use longer than twelve hours a day was available to the "entire business community of Korea" and hence was not countervailable. *Carlisle* had argued that the twelve hour use requirement effectively limited the usefulness of this law to a few Korean companies. Has the 1988 amendment effectively over-ruled the result in *Carlisle*? If so, since virtually every tax benefit sets some minimum qualifying conditions which if not met disqualifies a taxpayer, where is the line to be drawn? Or is it necessary to draw a line?

(2) *Bethlehem Steel Corp. v. United States,*[85] involved a South African law that allowed any company which maintained a government approved employee training program an income tax deduction equal to 200% of the program's expenses. While there was no evidence of how many companies had qualified for the deduction, Judge Watson, in affirming the ITA's decision not to countervail steel imports from a company with a qualified program, had the following to say:

those acts of a government which are fundamentally adverse to the purely economic self-interest of business enterprises are not subsidies. Decisions to reduce or eliminate the adverse effects of those acts are simply forms of a decision as to the desired extent of the adverse effect. The level of the adverse effect is transformed into a positive benefit only when a select group is freed from the adverse effect while others are not. That is an act of subsidy by means of selective relief from an adverse condition.

Didn't the deduction free a "select group" (*i.e.*, all companies having approved training programs) from the adverse effect of the South African tax law? Under 19 U.S.C Section 1677(5)(B), wouldn't the ITA have had to discover how many companies actually benefited from the law? Suppose there were only five companies? What result under Judge Watson's test? Again, where is the line to be drawn? After all, the DISC was a subsidy to hundreds of companies.

(3) Once more, is it necessary to draw the kind of line that the company argued for in *Carlisle*, that Section 1677(5)(B) and Judge Watson seem to require? Given that it is not possible to "disentangle all the effects of governmental action upon costs to determine whether the costs faced by a particular industry are real or

---

[85] 590 F. Supp. 1237 (CIT, 1984).

distorted,"[86] should our attention not focus more sharply on the underlying political justification for countervailing duties? With this in mind may it not be appropriate to countervail those domestic programs which tend to focus on economic activities likely to have a significant affect on a nation's trading patterns and which can be traced into particular product lines and there measured with some rough accuracy. Are these not the principal hallmarks of those governmental actions that are most likely to contribute to the fearful potential of a world caught-up in an never-ending competitive cycle of deliberate distortions of international trade? Tested by some such rationale was the ITA or the court closer to getting it right in the *Cabot Case*? Did the court get it right in *Carlisle*? In *Bethlehem Steel*?

(4) *Agrexco, Agricultural Export Co. v. United States*,[87] represents a particularly formalistic application of the "specificity test." There the ITA determined that an Israeli government research and development program for roses was not countervailable because the results of the program's research and development projects were widely disseminated through-out the world and were as readily available to American as to Israeli growers. The court reversed on the ground that the program was primarily for the benefit of rose producers, a specific industry.

In yet another case the ITA concluded that a West German program that provided "direct payments" to employees to enable them "to change jobs through the improvement of skills" was not countervailable because it "was available to all industries or employees."[88] At the same time the ITA warned that a similar retraining program conducted by the European Coal and Steel Community (ECSC) might be considered a countervailable subsidy.[89]

Can the latter decision be squared with the result in *Bethlehem Steel*? Does it and the decision in the *Agrexco* case illustrate how the "specificity" test as articulated in *Cabot* can be over-inclusive.

(5) In *PPG Industries, Inc. v. United States*,[90] the court upheld ITA's refusal to countervail a Mexican program under which any Mexican firm with registered long-term debt payable to financial institutions or suppliers abroad in foreign currency could purchase dollars to make principal payments on the debt at a "controlled" exchange rate. The ITA had found that the program was "available to all Mexican firms with foreign indebtedness; [was] not targeted to a specific industry or enterprise . . . or to companies located in specific regions . . . [and was] not tied in any way to exports." Is this a case illustrating how the "specificity test" can be "underinclusive?" See also a later decision in *PPG Industries, Inc. v. United States*.[91]

(6) The assistance to the carbon black industry in the *Cabot* Case clearly constituted the "provision of goods" within the meaning of 19 U.S.C.

---

[86] The quoted phrase is from Tarullo, *Beyond Normalcy In The Regulation Of International Trade*, 100 Harv. L. Rev. 547 at 559 (1987).

[87] 604 F. Supp. 1238 (CIT, 1985).

[88] *Certain Steel Products From The Federal Republic Of Germany*, 47 Fed. Reg. 39,345, 39349-50 (1982).

[89] *Certain Steel Products From Belgium*, 47 Fed. Reg., Appendix 3 at 39324.

[90] 662 F. Supp. 258 (CIT, 1987).

[91] 712 F. Supp. 195 (CIT, 1989).

1677(5)(A)(ii)(II). However, was the court correct is saying that the ITA was engaged in a tautology by concluding that even if the Mexican program constituted assistance to a specific industry it was nevertheless not the provision of goods "at preferential rates" and hence not countervailable? In this connection again examine Paragraph (d) of the Subsidies Code Illustrative List[92] and the hypothetical case in Note (1)(b) of the Notes and Questions following the *Wheat Flour* Case (page 417 *supra*). See also footnote 84 of the court's opinion.

The ITA's "specificity" test is a pragmatic device for sorting-out those forms of government intervention in private markets that constitute countervailable subsidies and those that do not. Such a test, however, requires reading into the rather sparse interdictions of the countervailing duty law the grant of considerable administrative discretion to sort-out what is otherwise a difficult, if not intractable, problem. Yet, in the following case the Court of Customs and Patent Appeals (now the Court of Appeals for the Federal Circuit) interpreted the structure of that law — perhaps inadvertently — in a way that set the stage for Congress to enact what could arguably be considered far reaching limitations on that discretion. The wisdom of such a move is an issue of some moment.

ASG INDUSTRIES, INC. v. UNITED STATES

United States Court of Customs and Patent Appeals
610 F. 2d. 770 (1979)

[In this pre-Subsidies Code case, the Treasury concluded that low-interest loans, cash grants and tax credits received by float glass manufacturers in West Germany under various regional development programs could not be regarded as bounties or grants within the meaning of 19 U.S.C. 1303. The benefits had the effect of offsetting disadvantages which would prevent industry from moving to less prosperous regions; the recipient glass producers sold a preponderance of their production in the West German home market (not less than 80 percent and up to 99%); the level of exports to the United States was a small percentage of total exports; and the amount of assistance received was less than 2 percent of the value of float glass produced. On this record Treasury held that the U.S. producers had failed to establish that the benefits received by the German manufacturers had any distorting effect on international trade.

The Customs Court [now the Court of International Trade] upheld the Treasury determination, concluding that, while the statutory language was mandatory ("there shall be levied"), Congress did not intend "that all assistance given by foreign governments" be considered bounties or grants. Citing the circumstances relied upon by Treasury, and the fact that United States production and exports

---

[92] Documentary Supplement.

(especially to West Germany) had increased while West German exports to the U.S. had decreased, the Customs Court found that, although the assistance was more than de minimis (a point conceded by the Government), "the bounties [did] not appear to have induced the sale of merchandise in such quantities or value as would tend to distort international trade." The American producers then appealed.]

Before MARKEY, CHIEF JUDGE, and RICH, BALDWIN, MILLER and PENN, JUDGES.

MILLER, J.

Essentially, appellants argue that, since the countervailing duty statute is mandatory, once the Secretary has determined that foreign manufacturers are receiving any benefit from their government, a countervailing duty must be imposed. The Government. . . argues that. . . Congress intended countervailing duties to be imposed only against those programs and actions of a foreign government that has been shown to distort international trade and that [for this purpose] the following factors [had to be considered]: . . . (1) the *ad valorem* size of the benefits; (2) the level of exports from the foreign country of goods receiving the benefits; and (3) whether the benefit programs had a positive effect on these exports.

 . . . [T]he Government's concession that the benefits under the regional development programs are not *de minimis* establishes, *prima facie*, that [the first] factor is met. The finding by Treasury that up to 20 percent of the goods are exported likewise establishes that the second factor is met.[93] As to whether the benefit programs had a positive effect on exports, Treasury's finding that "the amount of assistance provided by the regional incentive programs is less than 2 percent of the value of float glass produced" does not, without more, overcome a presumption that such benefits had a positive effect, or would have a potentially positive effect, on exports, particularly when compared to the average ad valorem rate of duty of 8.2 per cent during the year involved (1974). . . . In 42 Fed.Reg. 23146-47 (1977), [Treasury determined] . . . that while ordinarily, benefits of [.2% *ad valorum*] . . . might be considered de minimis in relation to the value of the merchandise they were "significant" when compared to the regular duty rate (up to .75 percent on an *ad valorem* basis.)

* * * *

Congress also made clear its understanding that "the present [countervailing duty] statute is mandatory in terms.". . . . This demonstrates that, except for the waiver provision in the 1974 Act, the Secretary has not had any discretion to not impose a countervailing duty once it has been determined that a bounty or grant is being paid or bestowed. [And by requiring] . . . that the Secretary reach a final countervailing duty determination within one year of the filing of a petition (19 U.S.C. 1303(a)(4)), Congress [sought] . . . to put an end to Treasury Department practice calculated "to stretch out or even shelve countervailing duty investigations for reasons which have nothing to do with the clear and mandatory nature

---

[93] Treasury set forth no basis for its finding that "the level of exports to the United States is a small percentage of the amount exported."

of the countervailing duty law.". . . . To permit the Secretary to place a narrow or restricted interpretation on "bounty" or "grant" as a basis for a negative countervailing duty determination would clearly frustrate the Congressional purpose of "assuring effective protection of domestic interests from foreign subsidies. . . ."

* * * *

Despite a clear expression of Congressional intent that an injury test not be employed, the Secretary impliedly injected one into this case. . . . The Senate-House Conference Report on H.R. 10710 declares that the waiver provision "is not to be construed as the intent of congress [to] . . . inject an injury concept into countervailing duty cases regarding durable goods. . . ."[94]

Accordingly, . . . we hold that, for purposes of the countervailing duty law, the benefits bestowed by West Germany upon float glass manufacturers under the regional development programs were bounties or grants.

At the same time . . . appellants' proposed test (any benefit, that is not *de minimis* . . . requires a countervailing duty) ignores the clear wording of the statute. Once it has been determined that a bounty or grant is being paid or bestowed, 19 U.S.C. 1303(a)(1) provides that "there shall be levied . . . a duty equal to the net amount of such bounty or grant.". . . . Such language implies that certain deductions may be made from the actual payments to calculate the net bounty or grant and that all relevant circumstances are to be taken into account.

We note that earlier court opinions have not been precise in distinguishing between "bounty or grant" and "net amount of each bounty or grant." Nevertheless, a difference has been implicit from the opinions. In *Zenith*, although the Supreme Court held that Japan was not conferring a bounty or grant, the Court actually determined that there was no net bounty or grant upon which countervailing duties could be imposed. The Court stated[95] . . . that:

> . . . the 1897 statute did provide for levying of duties equal to the *"net amount"* of any export bounty or grant. And the legislative history suggests that this language, in addition to establishing a responsive mechanism for determining the appropriate amount of countervailing duty, was intended to incorporate the prior rule that *non-excessive remission* of indirect taxes would not trigger the countervailing requirement at all; [Emphasis added.]

The Court clearly indicated that an excessive remission of tax would give rise to a bounty or grant.

Although the Secretary apparently made a feeble attempt to calculate the amount of the net bounty or grant involved here, the statement that "[t]he German Government has advised the Treasury Department that these benefits have the effect of offsetting disadvantages which would discourage industry from moving to and expanding in less prosperous regions" is totally inadequate. If a factual basis were shown for such an assertion, it might be concluded that no net bounty or

---

[94] Conf. Rep. No. 93-1644, 93d Cong., 2d Sess. 45, reprinted in [1974] U.S. Code Cong. & Admin. News, *supra*, at 7390.

[95] 437 U.S. at 452–53, 98 S. Ct. at 2446.

grant was involved. However, contrary to the dissenting opinion, the statement that Treasury was "advised" is hardly a factual basis supporting the conclusion that there was no bounty or grant. . . . Once it is established that a foreign manufacturer is receiving payments such as those here involved . . . from its government, a countervailing duty must, absent a waiver by the Secretary, be imposed unless, in considering all circumstances surrounding the payment, certain deductions can be established resulting in no net benefit to the manufacturer. These deductions must be established by facts[96] — not by mere allegations of the foreign government or of the enterprises receiving the bounty or grant.

* * * *

In view of all the foregoing, we reverse the judgment of the Customs Court and remand for further proceedings consistent with this opinion.

MARKEY, CHIEF JUDGE, with whom RICH, JUDGE, joins dissenting.

The case comes to us on appeal from the grant of summary judgment to defendant. . . . Nothing in the state of the law . . . precludes the Secretary's acceptance of another government's advice that its payment merely offset disadvantages of moving. Nor has appellant shown anything to suggest that the advice accepted here was untrue. Absent a clear legal basis . . . the courts should avoid even an appearance of directing the Secretary to disregard statements of sovereign foreign governments with which he and our government must deal daily on a wide variety of matters.

The legal posture on appeal might be different if it could be said that appellants had established on the record an excess in the government payment over the foreign manufacturer's costs incurred in meeting his government's goals. If proved, that excess might or might not constitute a bounty. Its absence means there is no support whatever in the present record for the majority's assertion that a bounty was here paid.

* * * *

[Further] concerning the determination of the existence or nonexistence of a bounty, the Congress unquestionably left to the Secretary the clear discretion to decide. . . . Naked of [statutory] guidance . . . the Secretary has assertedly employed a guideline of his own devising, *i.e.*, the presence or absence of distortions and of barriers to trade caused by the challenged payments. Though "distortions" and "barriers" are terms undefined . . . the Secretary's approach to the exercise of his discretion is in my view perfectly reasonable.

---

[96] If the Treasury Department cannot, with its expertise, establish the necessary facts, a countervailing duty must be imposed, although a challenge may be brought later by the importer. Because the importer is in a better position to obtain these facts from the foreign manufacturer, once a *prima facie* case has been established by evidence that payments such as those here involved are being made, the domestic manufacturer should not (contrary to the dissenting opinion) have the burden of obtaining evidence of deductions necessary to negate its own *prima facie* case. Also, we note that under 19 U.S.C. 1303(a)(5), the Secretary is permitted to estimate the net bounty (*i.e.*, estimate the necessary deductions), and his expertise will play a part in this estimate as long as there is a factual basis to support it.

In all events, [it] . . . appears far more reasonable than that set forth in the majority opinion. . . . The majority opinion's effective equation of every payment to a foreign manufacturer . . . with a bounty is an approach not recommended by reason. It is creative of chaos. Administrative, diplomatic, and judicial channels would be clogged if every payment to every manufacturer were presumptively a bounty. . . .

Moreover, if a bounty could exist without adverse effect on international trade, who cares? What would there be to shout about on the international stage.

* * * *

Though the absence of adverse effects on international trade should raise no ruckus on the international stage, payments to those who export to our country can raise deep domestic disturbances. Respecting such payments, congressional response . . . consists of just three elements. (1) If those payments are determined by the Secretary to be a bounty, he must impose countervailing duties . . . ; (2) injury or non-injury to American business shall not be a factor in determining whether a bounty is being paid; and (3) American manufacturers can obtain judicial review of the Secretary's determination that a bounty was not paid.

The majority opinion recognizes that Congress disdained the "injury concept," but, with no authority . . . the majority opinion then converts the rejected concept of injury to domestic business into "injury to United States trade." It then accuses the Secretary of "injecting" the latter concept into countervailing duty cases and of erroneously employing "an injury (to United States trade) test." The complete answer is, "Certainly! That is the name of this game. It is precisely the trade relationships of the United States with other countries that constitute the *raison d'etre* for our countervailing duty laws."

After seeming to reject appellants' assertion that any payment requires a countervailing duty, the majority opinion says that once it is established that a foreign manufacturer is receiving payments such as those here involved from its government, a countervailing duty, *must* . . . be imposed, unless there is no net benefit. The majority then requires a virtual audit by the Secretary of a foreign manufacturer's operations, to establish whether a payment exceeded the manufacturer's cost (here of moving), and, if so, by how much. . . . The majority opinion would thus insist that a bounty was paid (but no countervailing duties would be imposable) when a payment is equal to or less than the costs of moving. . . . I cannot see the value in creating even the potential for requiring investigation of every payment made to a foreign manufacturer, nor can I estimate the hoards of government employees, buildings, and paper supplies, involved in meeting that potential.

Earlier court opinions have not distinguished "bounty" from "net amount" in the manner suggested in the majority opinion because there is no such distinction there. If the Secretary finds a bounty, he must calculate or estimate the net in determining the countervailing duty. If there be a payment exceeding expenses, that excess may or may not adversely effect world trade. If it doesn't, there is no bounty. But if there is zero excess, *i.e.*, zero "net," there is also zero "bounty," and there is nothing to countervail. *In law*, a payment resulting in no net benefit cannot be held a "bounty" countervailable under [Section 1303].

* * * *

The one clear point in the majority opinion, to me at least, is the view that all payments . . . are (at least in gross) bounties, and that proof of payment alone imposes on the Secretary a burden to prove that there is no net amount to be countervailed. That view cuts the Gordian knot of frustration (by defining "bounty" as any *non-de minimus* payment) but it severely restricts the Secretary's discretion . . . ignores the statutory presumption of correctness, and would require a trial *de novo* to determine net amount in every suit challenging a negative countervailing duty determination. More importantly, by rejecting the Secretary's right to rest his discretionary bounty determination on the presence or absence of adverse effects on world trade, the majority opinion opens a ponderous Pandora's box which only Congress or the Supreme Court, after long travail, may close.

NOTES AND QUESTIONS

(1) The concept of "net bounty" or "net subsidy," as used by the majority in *ASG Industries*, is scarcely a necessary reading of 19 U.S.C. 1303 which stipulates that the countervailing duty must be "equal to the net amount of [any] bounty or grant." Even less persuasive is the majority's use of the Supreme Court's decision in *Zenith Radio Corp. v. United States, supra*, page 425, fn. 48. In *Zenith* the Supreme Court upheld the Secretary's decision, following the GATT rules discussed earlier, not to countervail excise taxes remitted by Japan on exports of electronic products to the United States. The amount remitted was exactly equal to the tax. It was a "non-excessive remission" and, therefore, according to the Court, not a "bounty or grant" within the meaning of Section 1303.

The decision rested largely on the legislative history of Section 1303. From the beginning, according to the Court, Congress understood that only when the amount remitted exceeded the amount of the domestic "indirect" taxes levied against the exported product was a countervailing duty to be imposed. Unfortunately in the course of describing this history Justice Marshall several times refer to the "excessive" portion of any remission as the "net bounty" that could be legitimately countervailed. At no time, however, can he be read as saying that the entire remission, including the "non-excessive" portion, constituted a Section 1303 "bounty" that was then to be "netted out" in computing the countervailing duty. Yet, this is precisely how the majority in *ASG Industries* attempts to read the *Zenith* opinion. Contrary to that reading, it seems clear that to Justice Marshall only the excess remission would constitute a Section 1303 "bounty or grant" — a subsidy. This is underscored by the Justice's assertion that even if not "compelled" by the legislative history, the Secretary's interpretation was entirely "reasonable" in light of the statutory purpose which was to:

> . . . offset the unfair competitive advantage that foreign producers would otherwise enjoy from export subsidies paid by their governments.

If the distortion of competition in international trade is the key to identifying a countervailable subsidy, then it would seem clear, *under the assumption the indirect taxes are always forward shifted,* that a non-excessive remission of such taxes can never constitute a subsidy.

Now, if you follow the principle of *Zenith* and assume that the German Government was correct in saying that payments to the West German glass manufacturers in the *ASG Industries* case only offset the costs of moving their operations to a less well developed area of the country, did those payments constitute a subsidy under either 19 U.S.C. 1303 or 19 U.S.C. 1671(a)? In answering, consider the likely effect of the payments on competition in the American market if you also assume that without the payments the West German producers would not have moved. How do you answer the majority's position that the Treasury had written an injury requirement into Section 1303?

(2) As Chief Judge Markey pointed out, the majority, by transforming the question of whether the German government's payments were a "subsidy" into a question of whether they were to be deducted (*i.e.*, "off-set") in computing the "net-subsidy," dealt what was potentially a body blow to the Secretary's (now the ITA's) discretion. Given the uncertainties and the level of sophistication necessary in determining what should be a countervailable subsidy — and Congress' traditional and sensible reluctance to devising a comprehensive definition — that move was problematic at best. What made it worse, however, was that before the final opinion was handed down by the court, Congress in the Trade Agreements Act of 1979 stipulated in Paragraph (6) of 19 U.S.C. 1677 the following:

(6) Net Subsidy. For the purpose of determining the net subsidy, the administering authority may subtract from the gross subsidy the amount of —

    (A) any application fee, deposit, or similar payment paid in order to qualify for, or to receive, the benefit of the subsidy,

    (B) any loss in the value of the subsidy resulting from its deferred receipt, if the deferral is mandated by Government order, and

    (C) export taxes, duties, or other charges levied on the export of merchandise to the United States specifically intended to offset the subsidy received.

In explaining this provision the Report of the Senate Finance Committee states:

The list is narrowly drawn and is all inclusive. For example, offsets under present law which are permitted for indirect taxes paid but not actually rebated, or for increased costs as a result of locating in an underdeveloped area, are not now permitted as offsets.[97]

What does this all mean? To be fair the Secretary traditionally treated the added costs of moving to depressed or underdeveloped regions as an off-set from any government payments designed to cover those costs. See *Michelin Corporation v. United States.*[98] But isn't the upshot of the *ASG Industries* Case, combined with Congress' action, to forestall any possibility of treating those payments as "non-subsidies?" If so, can you square the statute with the principles underlying Article

---

[97] S. Rep. No. 96-249, 96th Cong., 1st Sess. 86, reprinted in 1979 U.S. Code Cong. & Admin. News, p. 472. The House Committee report also states that the list to be considered is all inclusive. H.R. Rep. No. 96-317, 96th Cong., 1st Sess. 74 (1979).

[98] 2 ITRD 143 at 158 (1981).

VI:4 of the GATT Paragraph (d), of the Subsidies Code's Illustrative List and the *Zenith* Case?

Consider the case of non-industry specific payments to firms to offset the costs of special technical training programs that the recipient firms would not otherwise have carried out. Suppose that in addition to such payments, the foreign government provided the same training through specially established public schools or other training centers. Are the payments to firms now to be considered "subsidies" and therefore countervailable because not included in the Section 1677(6) list of permissible offsets? Or is the ITA still free to decide whether they are not "subsidies," under either its "trade distortion" or its "generally available" test? If not, the majority opinion in *ASG Industries* worked a major change in the law, did it not? "Curiouser and Curiouser."

[E]   Government Equity Participation In State-Owned Enterprises

BRITISH STEEL CORPORATION v. UNITED STATES
and
ALLEGHENY LUDLUM STEEL CORP., *et al.*, Defendant-Intervenors

United States Court of International Trade
605 F. Supp. 286 (1985) and 632 F. Supp. 59 (1986)

Background

[The case against British Steel Corporation (BSC) was one of 132 cases (38 antidumping and 94 countervailing duty cases) filed by American steel producers in January 1982 against exporters from nine European countries[99] and from Brazil and South Africa. The difficulties that gave rise to these cases started with the world-wide recession of 1974–75 when declining demand through-out the industrialized world caused steel production to fall-off drastically. For example, U.S. production fell from 111.4 million tons in 1973 to 80 million tons in 1975. Initially both American and European producers thought the decline was a normal cyclical phenomenon and were confident that world steel requirements would, by the mid 1980's, support significant increases in plant capacity. By 1977, however, it was clear the large surge in world-wide demand was not going to occur. At the same time, American producers were feeling the effects of increased import penetration especially from Europe. In 1976, while struggling to get back on its feet, the American industry faced an increase in imports of 19% over the 1975 level. In 1977 while U.S. consumption grew only 7%, imports increased by 35% over the prior year's level, capturing nearly 18% of the total U.S. market. In response, the U.S. industry demanded protective quotas. The Carter Administration, however, believed that countervailing duty and antidumping actions would solve the problem. A number of cases were filed, but as those cases progressed it appeared that the remedies likely to be invoked would completely close the American market to most European imports. In January 1978, therefore, the administration instituted a so-called "trigger price mechanism"[100] and the

---

[99] Belgium, France, West Germany, Italy, Luxembourg, the Netherlands, Roumania, Spain and the United Kingdom.

[100] This mechanism was a price-based monitoring system which established a series of pricing levels below which imported steel products could not be sold without "triggering" an antidumping investigation.

pending cases were withdrawn. While initially helpful, by 1980 the U.S. industry had become disenchanted with the "trigger" price program; the prices, they said, were set too low and were no longer an effective curb on surging imports. Nevertheless, the Administration persisted but only after receiving European assurances that upwardly revised trigger price levels would be strictly observed. The revised program lasted eighteen months. Rampant violations, the lack of staff to monitor and enforce the program and continued growth in imports led to the massive filing of new countervailing duty and anti-dumping cases in January 1982, including Allegheny Ludlum's case against BSC. Shortly thereafter the trigger price program was abandoned.[101]

In its petition against BSC, Allegheny Ludlum asked for the imposition of countervailing duties on imports of several stainless steel products produced by BSC. The petition charged that BSC, formed in 1967 through the nationalization of fourteen private producers and wholly owned by the British Government, had been subsidized by that Government through equity infusions in each fiscal year 1974/75 through 1981/82 and by the conversion of outstanding loans to equity in fiscal year 1971/72 and again in 1981/82. The ITA concluded that the equity infusions up through 1976/77 and the 1971/72 loan conversion were not subsidies. They were not, according to the ITA, "inconsistent with commercial considerations" even though BSC had posted losses in each of the years 1974/75 through 1976/77. From 1977 on, however, the company's losses continued to increase. On this record ITA concluded that equity infusions in the period 1977/78 through 1981/82 and the loan conversion in 1981 were "inconsistent with commercial considerations" and constituted countervailable subsidies. Most of the money received in 1977/78 was used by BSC to cover current operating losses and for working capital.

Then in 1978 BSC adopted a plan of radical restructuring that called for drastic reductions in obsolete and redundant productive facilities, upgrading and streamlining plants that were to be retained, replacing obsolete equipment with new technologies, laying-off workers and implementing a wide range of other cost-cutting measures. From 1978/79 through 1981/82 the equity infusions and loan conversions were used not only to cover current operating losses but also to purchase new equipment, modernize existing plants and to underwrite plant closing and worker severance costs, all in accord with the restructuring plan.

The percentage value of these subsidies for fiscal year 1981/82 was fixed by ITA at 18.09% *ad valorum* representing the *grant value* of the equity infusions used for loss coverage in that year plus the grant value of prior year equity infusions carried forward under ITA methodology.[102] To this ITA then added 1.22% *ad*

---

[101] This summary of the circumstances surrounding the BSC case is taken largely from Barshefsky, Mattice & Martin, Government Equity Participation In State-Owned Enterprises: An Analysis Of The Carbon Steel Countervailing Duty Cases, 14 Law & Pol. in Int'l Bus. 1101-1113 (1983).

[102] To determine the amount of the subsidy implicit in the equity infusions ITA first calculated the difference between the British Government's rate of return on its equity investment in BSC and the average rate of return on all industrial equities in Britain (the difference being called the "rate of return shortfall"). This "shortfall" would ordinarily have been treated as the amount of subsidy received by BSC. Since, however, the British

valorum for training and regional development grants received by BSC during the period under investigation. The total proposed countervailing duty was thus 19.31% ad valorum. That duty, however, was to be applied only to imports of stainless steel plate, the ITC having concluded that subsidized imports of other types of stainless steel from BSC had not injured the U.S. industry.

BSC then challenged ITA's decision before the Court of International Trade. In the first case (*British Steel I*, 605 F. Supp. 286 (1985)) the Court upheld the ITA's finding that equity infusions, including loan conversions, during the restructuring period (1978/79 through 1981/82) constituted countervailable subsidies. The Court, however, remanded the case with orders for ITA to reconsider its decision regarding the 1977/78 equity infusions and to recalculate the subsidies for all of the years covered by the investigation in accordance with a new methodology which ITA had adopted in another case.[103] In its remand proceeding ITA affirmed its earlier conclusion that the 1977/78 equity infusions constituted subsidies. It also decided that, except for amounts used to cover operating losses, the subsidies for each of the years 1977/78 through 1981/82 should be amortized over a fifteen year period representing the average useful life of renewable physical assets in the U. S. steel industry. Plaintiff BSC again challenged the ITA's decision (*British Steel II*, 632 F. Supp. 59) on a number of grounds set-forth below.]

BRITISH STEEL I (1985)

(Equity Infusions for Restructuring, 1978/79 - 1981/82)

NEWMAN, SENIOR JUDGE:

* * * *

I

The Statutory "Commercial Considerations" Standard

* * * *

[Agreeing with ITA that the funds provided BSC during the restructuring period were provided on "terms inconsistent with commercial considerations" the Court observed:]

Government had experienced a negative return on its investment in most of the years under investigation, the "rate of return shortfall" exceeded the amount of the subsidy that would have resulted had the equity infusions been treated as outright grants. For this reason ITA capped its subsidy calculation at the grant equivalent of the equity infusions. Under ITA methodology an equity infusion, in contrast to a grant, is a payment with some potential for return, either in the form of dividends, retained earnings or increased value of the firm. A grant is were no such potential exists. See, *Hercules, Inc. v. United States*, 673 F. Supp 454 (CIT, 1987).

[103] The revised methodology was set-forth in a "Subsidies Appendix" to the ITA decision in *Cold-Rolled Carbon Steel Flat-Rolled Products From Argentina*, 49 Fed. Reg 18006 at 18016 (April 26, 1984).

The annual reports and accounts of BSC for fiscal years 1974/75 through 1981/82 paint a bleak picture of a company burdened, in the face of a severe economic recession, with, among other things, redundant/obsolescent plants and equipment, a redundant work force, and poor industrial relations. In 1978, BSC initiated a program of radical restructuring . . . in the hope of attaining a competitive position in domestic and foreign markets.

Nonetheless, even by the end of fiscal year 1981/82, BSC was still not out of the financial "woods," as evidenced by [the fact that in that year it] . . . had incurred a huge loss of 358 million pounds after interest and taxation, and before extraordinary items. . . .

Against this dismal financial background, ITA . . . stated in its notice of final affirmative countervailing duty determinations (48 Fed.Reg. at 19049):

> Our treatment of government equity investment in a company hinges essentially on the soundness of the investment. . . .

> For the purpose of determining whether BSC represented a sound investment . . . we primarily considered BSC's cash flow from operations, including interest, but excluding government grants. Our analysis also included BSC's operating results and computations of BSC's current ratio (current assets divided by current liabilities). On the basis of these tests, we considered investment in BSC to be inconsistent with commercial considerations from fiscal year 1977/78 through 1981/82.

* * * *

In response to BSC's contention that ITA should not countervail against funding for restructuring because restructuring eliminates excess capacity, alleviating a form of trade distortion — consistent with the goals of our countervailing duty law and the GATT Subsidies Code — ITA stated (48 Fed.Reg. at 19053):

> . . . Our statutory obligations are carefully defined and mandatory in nature. Whenever it is determined that subsidized imports are injuring the domestic industry . . . we are required by domestic law, and authorized by the Code, to impose appropriate countervailing duties. . . . [A]n equity investment provided on terms inconsistent with commercial considerations, . . . [is] countervailable, regardless of whether some of the funds received from these capital infusions were used for restructuring or to purchase assets now idle as a result of restructuring. . . .

Although Article 11 of Part II of the Code does provide, among other things, that a signatory's right to provide domestic subsidies for purposes of restructuring are not precluded by the Code, it does not exempt such subsidies from countervailing duties. Therefore, regardless of whether restructuring subsidies serve to alleviate other trade distortions, countervailing against such benefits is wholly consistent with the Code and our statute.

Plaintiffs also argue here that since the Trade Agreements Act of 1979 was intended to remedy trade distortions and funds expended for restructuring are intended to reduce or eliminate trade distortions, ITA misapplied the "commercial considerations" standard prescribed by the statute. However, plaintiffs' "trade distortion" theory is plainly without merit. See *ASG Industries, Inc. v. United States,*[104] . . . *ASG Industries, Inc. v. United States*[105] . . . .

* * * *

ITA found that the U.K. government received a rate of return on its BSC investment lower than the average return on equity investment for the country as a whole (including returns on both successful and unsuccessful investments). Clearly, given BSC's deteriorating financial condition and precarious situation, no private sector investor expecting a reasonable return on his investment within a reasonable time would have given any consideration whatever to investing in BSC during the period of its restructuring. As aptly stated in defendants' memorandum at 22:

> The imperatives which committed the British government to saving BSC were not based upon the normal and usual commercial considerations of the market place. They were based upon a need to shore up a failing steel industry which would "recapture its home market share from imports and establish inroads to the export market," and thus strengthen an economy weakened by a worldwide recession, low productivity, obsolescent industries, and poor industrial relations, not to mention such other factors as national pride and the government's commitment to maintain its steel industry.

The Court also strongly disagrees with plaintiffs' contention that in determining whether government funds were provided on terms inconsistent with commercial considerations, the "rationality" of the structuring must be considered. While government investment in its state-owned enterprises may indeed be rational in terms of national policy, such investment may not be consistent with commercial considerations, depending upon the soundness and terms of the investment. However, neither the reasonableness of the action taken by the government, nor the results ultimately achieved (viewed in retrospect), are pertinent to the "commercial considerations" test.

II

Redundancy and Closure Funds

Plaintiffs claim . . . ITA erred in determining that funds provided specifically for closure of inefficient plants and discharge of "redundant" work force (redundancy and closure funds) are countervailable since such funds do not benefit, either directly or indirectly, "manufacture, production or export." See 19 U.S.C. 1671(a)(1) and 1677(5)(B). In plaintiffs' view, funds provided to shut down excess capacity and eliminate unnecessary jobs are for purposes that are the very antithesis of "manufacture, production or export," and thus are not countervailable under any circumstances.

* * * *

The apparent purpose of . . . closing obsolete facilities, eliminating excess capacity and laying off unnecessary workers, is to reduce costs and enhance the

---

[104] 67 CCPA 11, C.A.D. 1237, 610 F. 2d 770 (1979).
[105] 82 Cust.Ct. 101, C.A.D. 4797, 467 F. Supp. 1200 (1979).

competitiveness of the remaining enterprise. As a company becomes more cost efficient and thereby more price competitive, there is a direct benefit to the manufacture, production or export of all the firm's products. Thus, the use of government funds to finance improved efficiencies and competitive posture obviously provides direct benefits to BSC's manufacture, production or export. Whatever laudable objectives motivated the provision of funds for restructuring, the effect of the U.K. government's action was not only to assure the survival of a company that otherwise would be bankrupt, but to make the company more competitive in the market place. . . . [I]n *Zenith Radio Corporation v. United States,* [106] . . . the Supreme Court specifically . . . observed [that] " . . . the countervailing duty was intended to offset the unfair competitive advantage that foreign producers would otherwise enjoy from export subsidies paid by their governments" [107] . . . .

* * * *

In sum, . . . [b]y providing massive funding to help BSC eliminate obsolete facilities and unneeded labor, the British government reduced BSC's cost of producing steel and gave BSC precisely the kind of unfair competitive advantage that Congress sought to equalize through the application of countervailing duties.

Further, the Court agrees with defendants' contention that since the equity investments in BSC benefited all of its remaining manufacturing and exporting operations, it is unnecessary to trace the use of such funds or to find that they directly related to enhanced product competitiveness. "General financial benefit to the production is sufficient to support a determination of subsidy and a quantification of exact competitive benefit to the products need not enter into the allocation of the benefit." *Michelin Tire Corporation v. United States* [108] . . . .

Finally, plaintiffs attack what they claim to be ITA's assumption that funds received by BSC are "fungible," *viz.*, "government funds invested in a firm enter one large pool that may be used for any purpose that the firm desires". . . . Plaintiffs insist that viewing money as fungible violates the countervailing duty law's requirement of "precisely calculated duties on particular products." The Court agrees with intervenors' argument that although the funds received by BSC were untied to specific assets and treated by BSC as fungible, such funding is countervailable on a pro rata basis to the production of a particular product like stainless steel plate. If prorating were not allowed, a program could readily escape countervailing duties simply by the government's direction that its grants be used for "general" purposes. The short of the matter is ITA properly allocated a share of the funds provided to BSC for redundancy and closure costs to the products benefitted, including a proration to stainless steel plate.

---

[106] 437 U.S. 443, 98 S. Ct. 2441, 57 L. Ed. 2d 337 (1978).
[107] 437 U.S. at 437 at 455-56, 98 S. Ct. at 2447-48.
[108] 4 CIT 252, 255 (1982).

III

Funds for Purchase of Capital Assets Prematurely Taken Out of Use in the Course of Capacity Reduction

Further . . . plaintiffs contend that ITA is prohibited from imposing countervailing duties over a period of years upon subsidized funding used by BSC to acquire capital assets prematurely taken out of use in the course of capacity reductions incident to restructuring. In plaintiffs' view, even assuming ITA correctly found that assets were initially acquired with funds provided on terms "inconsistent with commercial considerations," all benefits to "manufacture, production, or export" abruptly cease when an asset is taken out of use, and from that point on there is no subsidy to countervail. Thus, according to plaintiffs, ITA erred in imposing countervailing duties over the full fifteen year anticipated useful life of assets prematurely retired. . . .

The Court cannot agree with plaintiffs' hypothesis. . . . Plaintiffs' argument confuses the benefit conferred by the use of the asset with the benefit conferred by the use of the subsidy to acquire the asset. Plainly, after an asset is taken out of service, the asset itself does not continue to provide a benefit to the firm. Nevertheless, . . . the competitive benefit of funds used to acquire [the] asset does not cease . . . [but] continues to contribute to the firm's remaining assets. Subsidies for the purchase of capital assets bestow a benefit to the recipient firm by relieving it not only of the immediate costs normally incurred in acquiring such assets (thereby freeing up other funds for other uses), but also by relieving the firm of the continuing annual costs of acquiring an asset. . . .

* * * *

Plaintiffs also insist that after an asset is retired there is no continuing obligation to repay a loan used to acquire the asset since under standard commercial practice a repayment obligation is accelerated and the remaining balance becomes due and payable at the time of the asset's retirement. However, acceleration clauses applicable to loan defaults, relied upon by plaintiff to prove their point, are entirely inapposite to premature retirement of assets. In brief, after retirement of its assets, BSC did not repay the funds to the government and had no obligation of repayment, and accordingly BSC continued to benefit from the subsidy.

BRITISH STEEL II (1986)

(Equity Infusion 1977/78 and Amortization Methodology)

NEWMAN, SENIOR JUDGE.

* * * *

The Commercial Reasonableness of the British Government's Equity Infusions in BSC in FY 1977/78

. . . In [our earlier decision] . . . this court . . . reviewed the financial history of BSC and found that for FYs 1978/79 through 1981/82 ". . . no private sector investor expecting a reasonable return on his investment within a reasonable time would have given any consideration whatever to investing in BSC during the period of its restructuring."

On remand, ITA applied the same "reasonable investor" criterion . . . [to the] equity infusions in FY 1977/78. . . . [In addition to financial data] the ITA considered such additional factors as the substantial cost of forming BSC, leading to unfavorable financial results for the first few years of the company's existence; the enormous social costs borne by BSC because of the British government's policy decisions, such as keeping high-cost plants open to preserve jobs; BSC's massive losses; the extremely bleak prospects of the company expressed by its own chairman in BSC's 1976-77 annual report; and the dismal outlook for the world steel market in general.

Based on its analysis . . . ITA [concluded that] ". . . a reasonable investor in 1977 would not have considered British Steel . . . a reasonable commercial investment."

The court finds substantial evidence in the record [to sustain this decision]. . . .

Plaintiffs argue that ITA's "reasonable investor" test is irrelevant to [its situation]. . . . [T]he British government, unlike an outside investor, could not simply abandon BSC and incur no further losses if it decided to close the firm, and therefore the steps the British government took as the sole investor in the corporation were reasonably taken to minimize its prospective losses. In short, plaintiffs contend that the overall operating results and financial ratios of a loss-incurring company are irrelevant to the issue of whether the British government's equity infusions were inconsistent with commercial considerations within the purview of the statute.

[To the contrary ITA contends that] . . . the term "commercial considerations" — [requires that] . . . the British government's equity infusions in BSC . . . [be judged] from the standpoint of the reasonable outside investor. . . . As stated by ITA:

. . . When a firm's shares are not traded publicly, there is no market-determined price. Therefore, the Department must rely on information available to an investor at the time of the investment as a means of determining the commercial reasonableness of investments in the company.

* * * *

In connection with the instant litigation, BSC commissioned an economic analysis by Dr. Joseph W. McAnneny of Economists, Incorporated. Predicated on his analysis, Dr. McAnneny submitted the following arguments concerning ITA's methodology:

First, [under] . . . ITA's . . . test six integrated U.S. steel producers with unfavorable operating results in 1981-84 would . . . [not have been] able to attract capital. Yet, during [that] period . . . all raised debt and equity capital in significant amounts.

Second, ITA has created a *per se* rule . . . [which] conflicts with observed market behavior where frequently corporations reorganize around their profitable assets, rather than terminate all productive facilities.

Finally, ITA's . . . test focuses primarily on recent . . . financial performance to the exclusion of other relevant data, and neglects to consider possible remedies that a firm might take to reposition itself in a market or reduce operating costs and restore profitability.

In view of the foregoing shortcomings of ITA's test . . . McAnneny . . . proposes [two] alternative [tests] . . . for determining whether investment in a loss-incurring corporation is inconsistent with commercial considerations.

(1) The corporation should continue to operate (and the investor should continue to cover operating losses) for facilities where revenues exceed the variable costs of production and make some contribution to coverage of fixed expenses. . . . [This test he maintains] permits ITA to assess the commercial reasonableness of equity infusions from the standpoint of the interest of the British government and BSC's management in minimizing its losses. [He] . . . also posit[s] that U.S. investors and lenders "customarily" inject funds in failing companies to minimize their losses, irrespective of any expectation of future profits.

(2) The investor should undertake all new investment schemes (or fund to completion existing investment schemes) where the discounted cash flows from the investment exceed the cost of the investment (*viz.*, the net present value or "NPV" of specific projects or ventures are greater than zero).

Based on the application of the foregoing tests, McAnneny argues that investments by the British government in FY 1977/78 in BSC were consistent with "commercial considerations."

Capital-Raising Experiences of Six U.S. Steel Companies

[The Court dismissed McAnneny's study of the capital-raising experiences of the six largest integrated U.S. steel companies on the ground that he (1) used a different time period, 1982-84, for his comparison of the returns on equity of the United States producers thereby failing to consider differences in economic climate, market conditions and investor expectations, (2) failed to take into account differences in the financial history of BSC and the domestic companies, and (3) erroneously assumed that ITA looked only at BSC's performance for the two preceding fiscal years, when in fact ITA had considered BSC's financial history back to 1973/74. McAnneny's conclusions thus were "sheer speculation"].

"Variable Cost Test"

. . . The theory [behind McAnneny's "variable cost" test] is that . . . [i]f a firm whose revenues did exceed its variable costs were to cease production, it would be foregoing revenue that could have helped to defray fixed costs. Accordingly, even though a firm may not be earning enough to cover its total costs (fixed plus variable), it would be economically rational to continue operations so that the overall loss would be minimized by the additional revenues. McAnneny maintains that equity funds used to help cover BSC's operating losses are not subsidies if BSC was covering its variable costs at the time.

As aptly pointed out by defendants, the variable cost test may be a useful analytical tool for the owner-manager as a means of deciding whether (and for how long) to continue operating a loss-incurring company, but the test is inapposite to investment decisions by private investors. . . . [W]hile it may be perfectly rational for an owner to sustain loss-minimizing operations, it would not be commercially reasonable for an investor to provide funds for that purpose without adequate assurance of the future profitability of the enterprise and a return on his investment within a reasonable time. The record supports no such assurances for BSC in 1977/78. Under these circumstances, ITA properly rejected application of the variable costs test.

The court stresses here that equity infusions in loss-incurring companies do not per se confer a subsidy, and defendants have not so argued in this case. Defendants . . . point out ITA found that equity investments in BSC in years prior to 1977/78 were consistent with commercial considerations despite the fact that the company was sustaining substantial losses.

* * * *

Net Present Value Test

. . . McAnneny observes that under standard principles of economic analysis, the commercial reasonableness of capital expenditures by BSC on new projects must properly be judged against an evaluation of the NPV of each project. Thus projects whose discounted cash flows show a positive NPV are commercially justified; projects whose cash flow show a negative NPV are not. According to plaintiffs, NPV analysis focuses upon whether investment in a new project is commercially worthwhile (positive), and it is irrelevant whether a capital project (or some combination of projects) returns the corporation to overall profitability. In support of NPV analysis, plaintiffs make reference to "concrete market examples" of private companies that had suffered heavy losses in successive years and nevertheless continued to make new capital investments.

Defendants, however, correctly observe that . . . BSC furnished [NPV] analyses only of individual projects without any evaluation of those projects in terms of their effect upon BSC's overall operations and income-producing prospects.

While unquestionably NPV analyses were of importance to BSC's management, they were relevant to an outside investor only to the extent that the analyses showed how the investments in the individual projects would affect the overall operations and future profitability of BSC. Stated differently, from the investor's point of view, an investment would not be commercially reasonable if overall the company may still constantly lose money and never provide a reasonable return no matter how justifiable a company's decision respecting individual projects analyzed on the basis of NPV.

As stated by ITA in its remand results . . .

. . . The Department agrees that a profit-maximizing company . . . when making its managerial decisions . . . will attempt to set production at a level where marginal revenue equals marginal cost and will select among capital projects by comparing the net present values of alternative projects. However, . . . the Department believes tests of individual project decisions present too limited an appraisal of a company's overall condition to be the bases of the Department's methodology for evaluating purchases of equity. Such purchases relate to a company's operations as a whole, not just individual activities. . . . For example, if a company is losing a billion dollars annually on all its investments and a new project provides a positive net return of $200 million, the company overall would still be losing $800 million annually and is, therefore, probably a bad equity investment.

* * * *

In sum, the court finds ITA's determination that the British government's investments in BSC in FY 1977/78 were inconsistent with commercial considerations, predicated upon its reasonable investor test, is supported by substantial evidence and otherwise in accordance with law.

ITA's Methodology for Valuing the Benefits from Equity Infusions

* * * *

. . . Under [its] revised methodology, ITA allocated the subsidies arising from the British government's equity infusions over 15 years, irrespective of the use to which the funds were put. Such allocation period subsumed a stream of benefits lasting the average useful life of integrated steel-producing assets, as determined by the United States Internal Revenue Service.

ITA [explained that it had] . . . considered various allocation periods including a variety of fixed time periods and the average life of long-term debt for a company or country, but ha[d] concluded that there are no economic or financial rules that dictate the choice of any one particular allocation period. Therefore, the Department ha[d] chosen a standard period . . . openly stat[ing] that its choice [was] arbitrary . . . [but] reasonable . . . [It also] offers predictability in the outcome of Department proceedings and . . . [will] eliminate inconsistent results between companies and countries.

Plaintiffs vigorously object to [this method with respect to] . . . subsidy funds that were not used to acquire long-lived assets[109] . . . . [That method, they

---

[109] Only a portion of the subsidy funds provided by the British government during FYs 1977/78 through 1981/82 were used for the acquisition of capital assets.

contend, contravenes generally accepted accounting principles (GAAP) and fails to reflect the commercial and competitive benefit of the equity infusions.[110] Specifically, plaintiffs argue that:

    1) The benefit of funds used to purchase assets prematurely retired must be expensed in the year of retirement.

    2) The benefit of funds used to cover operating losses must be expensed in the year of receipt.

    3) The benefit of funds used to cover redundancy and closure costs must be fully recognized in the year the decision is made to close the facility.

* * * *

The legislative history of the Trade Agreements Act of 1979 shows that Congress recognized the concept of allocating the benefits of subsidies over a number of years. . . .

Significantly, the Senate's report states that in allocating the benefit of the subsidy "a reasonable period based on the commercial and competitive benefit to the recipient as a result of the subsidy must be used"[111] . . . .

After careful review of ITA's methodology . . . the court is constrained to conclude that linking the commercial and competitive benefit of the subsidies at issue to the 15-year average useful life of capital assets in the U.S. steel industry, while administratively convenient, is unreasonable and not in accord with Congressional intent.

* * * *

ITA itself has conceded that the life of capital assets does not necessarily relate to the economic benefits of subsidy funds:

    [W]e recognize first that physical assets are often a fairly small part of the cost of doing business, and second that even in highly capital intensive industries the benefit of funds received has no particular relationship to the life of the machinery.[112]

* * * *

As previously noted, plaintiffs maintain that the subsidies in dispute must be allocated in accordance with GAAP. Interestingly, [while] . . . it is clear that Congress intended that GAAP should be used where the funds provide an enterprise with capital equipment or a plant, . . . nothing in the legislative history . . . suggest[s] that Congress expected that the value of a subsidy not used for acquiring assets be related to either the useful life of capital assets or to GAAP. . . . [While] the commercial and competitive benefit of these subsidies continue beyond the year of receipt and into subsequent accounting periods . . .

---

[110] Plaintiffs do not challenge the 15-year allocation period as applied to subsidy funds used to acquire long-lived assets.

[111] S. Rep. 249, 96th Cong., 1st Sess., at 85-86, 1979 U.S. Code & Ad. News at 381, 472-473.

[112] "Subsidies Appendix" to *Cold-Rolled Carbon Steel Flat-Rolled Products From Argentina*, 49 Fed. Reg. 18006, 18018 (April 26, 1984). (Final).

the [court] in . . . *Michelin Tire Corp. v. United States, Slip Op.* 83-136 at 3 . . . admonished against the use of valuation techniques that do not provide "a basic correspondence of the subsidy to the benefit." "Expensing" the "non-capital" subsidies at issue in accordance with GAAP would not provide [such] a correspondence . . . and consequently GAAP should not be applied under the circumstances of this case.

Although previously rejected by ITA . . . intervenors nonetheless suggest that the benefit of the subsidies in question should be allocated on the basis that they relieve BSC of the necessity for issuing long term debt on a commercial basis. Intervenors' hypothesis is that the commercial and competitive benefit of the subsidies is not the specific uses to which the funds were put, "but rather in being able to avoid the alternative commercial cost of obtaining the funds. . . ."

Intervenors' proposal . . . comports with the following observations in *Michelin Tire Corp., supra, Slip Op.* 83-136, regarding the benefits of a subsidy:

> . . . For a business, the direct consequences of receiving a gift of money normally are the elimination of the necessity of looking elsewhere for those funds and paying the price required by the alternative source of funds. The normal alternative sources of funding for business enterprises are two — the sale of shares in the business, carrying with it the obligation to share the profits, or the incurring of debt, carrying with it the obligation to repay the creditor with interest.

* * * *

In summary, while the court need not at this juncture pass upon the merits of intervenor's suggested allocation technique . . . the court ineludably [sic] concludes that ITA's 15-year allocation methodology . . . is neither supported by the record nor Congressional intent. . . . [T]his action must be remanded to ITA for further consideration of other "viable options". . . .

British Government's Forgiveness of Indebtedness

In 1981, the British government forgave 509 million pounds in long-term indebtedness owed by BSC to the National Loans Fund. . . . ITA treated the loan forgiveness as an additional equity investment amortizable over 15 years . . . at an interest rate of 17.11 percent, representing the 1981 United Kingdom domestic corporate bond rate plus a risk premium. The weighted average interest rate on BSC's existing loans in 1981 was 11.57 percent.

Plaintiffs . . . urge that inasmuch as the interest rates on the existing loans were fixed, absent the British government's forgiveness, BSC would have continued to pay 11.57 percent — not a rate based on what new capital would have cost BSC in 1981, *viz.*, 17.11 percent. Plaintiffs also challenge ITA's 15-year allocation period . . . since the remaining life of the loans in question was substantially shorter than 15 years and ITA inexplicably refused to use the repayment schedules associated with the forgiven loans.

The court fails to perceive any reasonable basis for [using] . . . what it would have cost BSC to obtain new financing in 1981. . . . Absent the loan forgiveness, BSC undoubtedly would have continued to pay 11.57 percent interest on its existing loans, and most assuredly BSC would not have refinanced its debt at a cost of 17.11 percent, which refinancing is implicit in ITA's methodology . . . [This implication] is, in the words of the United States Supreme Court, "economically senseless." *Matsushita Electric Industrial Co. Ltd. v. Zenith Radio Corp* [113] . . . .

    . . . [T]his action is remanded to ITA for revaluation of the benefits of the 1981 debt forgiveness consistent with the foregoing opinion.

NOTES AND QUESTIONS

    (1) Effective March 1, 1986 the U.S. and the EEC signed an agreement limiting certain European steel imports into the United States. Relying on this agreement the ITA, in August 1986, revoked its countervailing duty order with respect to all such imports entering after March 1. That, however, left imports for 1985/86 potentially subject to countervailing duties. Nevertheless, the Government moved to vacate the judgment in the *British Steel* Case and to have the case dismissed as moot. BSC opposed this effort. After a good deal of maneuvering, the Court, in July of 1987 and at the request of both parties, suspended proceedings on the Government's motion to vacate having been advised that the parties were still actively pursuing settlement. Finally, in May of 1988 a settlement agreement was reached and in June the court, at the parties' request, dismissed the case with prejudice (10 ITRD 1488). Under the agreement, BSC, without admitting liability, agreed to pay a stated sum on the unliquidated entries, to be offset against existing cash deposits. Under the heading "Privatization" ITA agreed that:

> In any future countervailing duty investigation . . . the Department will consider the effect of any sale of all or any part of British Steel Corporation on any government benefits allegedly received by British Steel prior to any such transaction.

    In 1989 BSC was, in fact, privitized. As of this writing, however, the ITA has yet to announce new methodologies on the points covered by the Court's remand order, although some modifications are pending. See Notice of Proposed Rule-Making, 54 Fed. Reg. 23366 (May 31, 1989).

    (2) According to *British Steel II* the "reasonable investor" envisioned by ITA, and by the court, as the final arbiter of whether the British Government's equity infusions were commercially sound, consists of a private investor contemplating a *first time purchase* of an equity position in the company. On the other hand, BSC argued that this model was not relevant to the situation confronting the British Government both in 1977/78 and presumably after adoption of the restructuring plan. Unfortunately Judge Newman's opinion is not very precise regarding the breadth of BSC's contention. In British Steel I, however, the court, quoting from what seems to be ITA's response to the BSC position, leaves the impression that BSC was arguing that, in the case of the British Government, "commercial

---

[113] 437 U.S. 443, 106 S. Ct. 1348, 89 L. Ed. 2d 538 (1986).

reasonableness" had to be judged on the basis of a wider set of both macro-economic considerations — saving an entire national industry and strengthening a recession weakened economy — and essentially political factors, "national pride" and a political commitment to nationalization. Assuming, that some such implication can be read into BSC's position, do these polar opposites — ITA's uncommitted private outsider and BSC's government as sui generis — exhaust the possible perspectives from which to judge the commercial soundness of the British Government's infusions? Or, is it possible to refashion ITA's "reasonable investor" into a private party — thus an investor stripped of the wider imperatives to which governments must respond — but a private party responsive to some of the financial considerations that the British Government could hardly ignore? In answering, consider the three criticism's of ITA's standard offered by McAnneny in *British Steel II*. They are suggestive, are they not?

(3) From the alternative perspective suggested by the discussion in Note (2), consider McAnneny's "variable cost test" (*British Steel II*). According to McAnneny's model, equity holders in a firm experiencing continuing operating losses will, instead of shutting the company down and liquidating the assets, keep covering the losses with new money so long as revenues cover variable costs and make some contribution towards fixed costs. What McAnneny describes is not untypical of a firm contemplating a reorganization. For any company experiencing continuing losses, the complete cessation of operations followed by a liquidation is likely to result in massive losses to equity holders. Yet the failure to cover fixed costs is likely to mean that the company is either in trouble with its creditors or, in the longer run, faces a worsening competitive position through depletion and obsolescence of its physical plant. Under these circumstances, if revenues can cover variable costs (wages, raw materials and supplies, current maintenance, etc.), the equity owners often stand to lose far less by putting-in new money (*i.e.*, covering operating losses including debt) and then either attempting to come to some accommodation with creditors through a formal reorganization proceeding or engaging in radical restructuring or a combination of both; a pattern of private investor behavior, in short, that bears more than passing resemblance to what the British Government was apparently attempting to do with BSC. ITA's only response to this line of argument is to advert to its "reasonable investor" test.[114] Nevertheless, there is at least a partial answer to McAnneny's approach, is there not? Perhaps it proves too much? On this point consider separately:

(i) The infusions in 1977/78 before adoption of the restructuring plan. Is there not a fatal flaw in McAnneny's attempted analogy?

(ii) The infusions after adoption of the restructuring plan. Here the analogy is much closer is it not? Note that by 1984/85 the restructuring of BSC was complete. In that year the company earned a profit and has continued to do so in each of the ensuing years. Identify the relevance of McAnneny's net present value (NPV) analysis to this aspect of the problem.

---

[114] We are never told by either ITA or the Court why ITA's "reasonable investor" would have made equity investments in all years prior to 1977/78, even though the company had sustained losses in each of those years, and why that investor would suddenly cease doing so in 1977/78. We are not even offered a theory of investor behavior that might explain this discontinuity.

(4) BSC contended (*British Steel I*) that equity infusions spent directly on closing obsolete facilities, eliminating excess capacity and laying off workers were not subsidies on the "manufacture, production or export" of steel products and were therefore not countervailable. In answer to this the court serves-up an economic bromide: "As a company becomes more cost efficient and thereby more price competitive," the court opines, "there is a direct benefit to the manufacture, production or export of all the firm's products." This argument is readily answered by a point made by ITA in *British Steel II*: "The Department agrees," ITA conceded, "that a profit-maximizing company . . . will attempt to set production at a level where marginal revenue equals marginal cost and will select among capital projects by comparing the net present value of alternative projects."

Recall that these cases involved only BSC imports of stainless steel plate. If what ITA says is true — as it is — why would BSC, as the court implies, charge less than the profit maximizing price for plate merely because, through plant closures, it had reduced its costs on some other product? In the context of BSC's actual situation what the court was predicting is that as BSC, through restructuring, succeeded in cutting its losses on one product line it would turn around and start loosing money on another product line (stainless steel plate) by selling below cost. Such behavior remains utterly improbable even if there are fairly strong cross-elasticities of demand between the two products.

The only case in which the court's rationale makes some sense is in the case of an equity infusion used directly to meet plant closure and redundancy costs of factories producing stainless steel plate. There the cost reduction effect of the subsidy would allow BSC to sell at a lower profit maximizing price. Whether this actually occurred, however, is impossible to tell without evidence which the court dismissed as irrelevant.

Even in this narrow case where a loss reduction can lead to lower prices the question persists whether the countervailing duty law ought to apply? Certainly, the gains to efficiency are real (no one is taking business away from the most efficient producer). That being the case, one can only say that the subsidy is trade distorting if one also believes that all changes in established trade patterns must flow only from private initiative. If so, then shouldn't all government efforts to reposition its economy in world markets, including infrastructure support, be banned? Or, is there some more comprehensive global–systemic (*i.e.*, political) justification for countervailing such subsidies?

(5) The foregoing questions still leave open a broader set of issues which require some further comments regarding the context in which the case arose. The precipitous decline in world wide demand for steel in 1974-75 hit the European steel industry as hard, if not harder, than the American. Between 1974 and 1978 European steel production fell by 20%, 100,000 workers were laid-off and another 100,000 were on shorter work schedules. In 1975 alone European plant capacity utilization fell to 60% compared with Japan's 74% and the U.S. 77%. The official European response to these conditions was along two lines.

First, national governments increased their direct involvement in the financing and management of the steel industry. Steel in Britain had long since been nationalized. In the Fall of 1978 the French Government carried-out a program which, through the intermediation of the major government owned French banks, effectively put France's steel industry under direct government control. Shortly thereafter Belgium nationalized its two largest steel enterprises. By 1979, steel in Britain, Belgium, France and Italy representing 50% of total EEC production was under government control. With this control — and even where control was less direct — came government resources. The final countervailing duty determinations in the cases filed against European steel in January 1982 present a catalogue of virtually every form of government assistance imaginable.[115]

Second, in 1977 the Commission of the European Coal and Steel Community (ECSC) implemented what became known as the Davignon Plan. Initially, the Plan set either mandatory or "guidance" prices for internal sales by EEC producers at levels well in excess (20+%) of then prevailing market prices. By 1980 these price controls were superceded by a system of production quotas which had the general effect of keeping prices up and freezing individual producers into the relative market position they held between 1977 and 1980. To then buffer the EEC market against foreign imports the Commission in December 1977 set "basic prices" for imports at a level generally about 7% below the prescribed "guidance price" for EEC producers. As in the case of the U.S. "trigger price mechanism," imports below the "basic price" were subject to an accelerated "antidumping" investigation. These latter quickly led to a series of agreements with steel exporting countries — not including the United States — that effectively assured foreign producers their traditional share of the Community market but no more.

The Plan had several effects. It permitted European steel manufacturers to compete aggressively outside the ECSC because a relatively stable (and high) rate of return was assured them by the internal price control system. In addition, the quota system by freezing internal deliveries generally to ratios established on the basis of 1977-1980 sales, provided an additional incentive to export sometimes, it has been argued, at prices below cost.[116]

Now, of course, we do not have enough data to judge whether the perspectives and the analysis suggested in Notes (2), (3) and (4) would have made a significant difference to the outcome in the *British Steel* cases. Plainly, however, they would have lessened the chance of an affirmative determination. Against this background consider the following:

---

[115] The assistance included: capital grants, loan guarantees, preferential loans, assumption of financing costs, interest relief grants, exemptions from real property tax, social security payment exemptions, exemptions from capital registration tax, reimbursements from federal taxes based on percentages of capital investment, government equity participation, cancellation of debt, readaptation and retraining assistance, reimbursement of worker training costs, benefits for early retirement, expenses incurred in employee layoffs, relocation and moving expenses, subsidization of employee wages, assistance for plant operating expenses, funds for loss coverage, funds for introducing new technologies, preferential transportation rates, regional development grants, export incentive programs, European Investment Bank (EIB) loans, European Coal and Steel Community (ECSC) industrial investment loans, ECSC loan guarantees and ECSC and EEC labor assistance. 47 Fed. Reg. 39, 304-93. Summarized in Barchefsky, Mattice & Martin, op. cit at page 1111.

[116] See, *Note, The Concrete Reinforcement Bars Case And The Davignon Plan: Judicial Endorsement Of The ECSC's Crisis Policies*, 14 J. of Int'l Law & Econ. 559 (1980).

(a) When viewed in the larger context of the ills that had befallen the steel industry world-wide, could ITA, as a matter of policy, have taken the chance of the negative determination which might have resulted had it proceeded along the lines of our critique?

(b) Are the principles and ostensible purposes of the countervailing duty law a fit instrument for addressing this type of world-wide perturbation in international markets? If not, would it be accurate to say that the countervailing duty law in such a setting functioned principally as an instrument with which the American industry could goad the U.S. government into a more concerted effort at negotiating a general settlement of the problem?

(c) Review, in this connection, the provisions of the Omnibus Trade and Competitiveness Act of 1988 specifically authorizing the ITA and the ITC to suspend countervailing duty investigations upon "acceptance" of certain types of agreements with foreign countries. While originating in the GATT Anti-dumping and Subsidy Code negotiations, do these statutory provisions implicitly recognize this "coercive" function of the countervailing duty law?

(d) If so, that law can no longer be sold as simply a matter of "fair trade," can it? In fact, in this setting, subsidization is scarcely the problem at all, is it? At most it is only a symptom of a more fundamental ailment.

(e) From this perspective, what are the drawbacks to the "coercive" use of the countervailing duty law? Is it misleading? Does it contribute to a proper focus on the problems needing attention? Were the people who would have to pay for it all — steel using industries and their workers, U.S. exporters of products made from steel, the American consumer — properly represented in the process? Was proper consideration given to the impact that the settlements precipitated by these actions would have on the U.S. balance of payments and the value of the dollar? Has Congress seen to it that these factors are given proper consideration?

(f) Is there any way conceptually to break out from the countervailing duty law cases of this type in which the subsidy phenomenon is merely symptomatic of a deeper problem in the structure of the world economy?

§ 5.03 The Problem of Dumping

[A] Overview of the GATT Provisions and the United States Anti-Dumping Statute]

GATT Article VI and the Anti-Dumping Code

Drawing upon existing U.S. statutes the drafters of the ITO charter included an anti-dumping provision which, with some modifications, was carried over into Article VI of the GATT as follows:

Article VI

Anti-dumping and Countervailing Duties

1. The contracting parties recognize that dumping, by which products of one country are introduced into the commerce of another country at less than the normal value of the products, is to be condemned if it causes or threatens material injury to an established industry in the territory of a contracting party or materially retards the establishment of a domestic industry. For the purposes of this Article, a product is to be considered as being introduced into the commerce of an importing country at less than its normal value, if the price of the product exported from one country to another

   (a) is less than the comparable price, in the ordinary course of trade, for the like product when destined for consumption in the exporting country, or,

   (b) in the absence of such domestic price, is less than either

   (i) the highest comparable price for the like product for export to any third country in the ordinary course of trade, or

   (ii) the cost of production of the product in the country of origin plus a reasonable addition for selling cost and profit.

Due allowance shall be made in each case for differences in conditions and terms of sale, for differences in taxation, and for other differences affecting price comparability.

Paragraph 2 stipulates that an anti-dumping duty may not exceed the so-called "margin of dumping" as described in Paragraph 1. Paragraph 6 empowers the contracting parties to authorize the imposition of an anti-dumping duty in so-called third party dumping cases.[1] At this point be sure you can state clearly the Article VI definition of dumping.

As already noted, at the Kennedy Round the contracting parties adopted an Anti-Dumping Code[2] that was superceded by a Tokyo Round Code (hereinafter all references are to the latter).[3] As of October 15, 1988 there were, in addition to the EEC with its twelve members, twenty-three other signatories to the Code.[4]

---

[1] Thus, country A may be authorized to impose an anti-dumping duty against imports from country B if the latter by dumping its exports to country C has injured an industry in that country which also exports to country A.

[2] Agreement On Implementation Of Article VI Of The General Agreement On Tariffs And Trade, June 30, 1967, GATT, BISD, 15th Supp., (1968) at page 24.

[3] Agreement On Implementation Of Article VI Of The General Agreement On Tariffs And Trade, April 12, 1979, GATT, BISD 26th Supp., (1979), page 171.

[4] These were: Australia, Austria, Brazil, Canada, Czechoslovakia, Egypt, Finland, Hong Kong, Hungary, India, Japan, Korea, Mexico (ad referendum), New Zealand, Norway, Pakistan, Poland, Rumania, Singapore, Sweden, Switzerland, the United States and Yugoslavia.

Many of the Code provisions, containing procedural reforms to which signatories are required to conform, have already been covered in our discussion (*supra* page 436) of the U.S. countervailing duty legislation.[5] Also in a manner similar to the GATT Subsidies Code (see *supra* page 406), Article 14 of the Anti-Dumping Code establishes a GATT "Committee on Anti-Dumping Practices" to oversee Code reporting requirements, provide a forum for signatories to consult on the Code's operations and administer the system established for the settlement of disputes. Under Article 15 any party claiming that benefits accruing to it under the Code are being nullified or impaired or that Code objectives are being impeded by another party can demand consultations with the latter. If consultations don't solve the problem, the Committee, upon the request of either party, is required to lend its good-offices to help the parties "develop a mutually acceptable solution." If that effort fails, either party may request the Committee to appoint a panel. The panel's formation and the conduct of its proceedings are governed by the general GATT provisions on settlement of disputes under Article XXIII:2.[6]

In addition, the Code contains a number of more substantive provisions governing the determination of whether imports are being dumped (Article 2), whether a domestic industry has been "materially injured" (Article 3) and what is the relevant "industry" (Article 4). The latter two Articles will be considered when we turn to the injury requirement in Section 5.04 *infra*.

Article 2, on the other hand, contains a number of points worth noting because they illustrate some of the complexities of comparing a foreign producer's home market price with its export price. First, Article 2:1 & 4 restate with some elaboration the Article VI definition of dumping. Second, in keeping with GATT tradition, Article 2:2 confines "like products" to those sharing the same physical characteristics[7] and does not include "directly competitive or substitutable products."[8] Third, Article 2:3 stipulates that if a product has its origin in one country but is exported from another to the nation conducting a dumping investigation, the home market price will ordinarily be the domestic price in the

---

[5] These include rules on the initiation and subsequent conduct of an anti-dumping investigation (Article 5), rules granting foreign producers and others the right to be notified, to be consulted, to present evidence to have evidence from other sources made available to them, rules on the maintenance of trade secrets and on the right to conduct investigations in each others territories (Article 6), rules on the use of "price undertakings" (*i.e.*, undertakings by foreign producers to revise their prices in order to eliminate the injurious effect of dumping. (Article 7), rules concerning the imposition and collection of anti-dumping duties (Article 8), the duration of anti-dumping duties (Article 9), provisional measures and retroactivity (Article 10 and 11).

[6] These provisions are elaborated upon in the Understanding Regarding Notification, Consultation, Dispute Settlement And Surveillance adopted by the Contracting Parties 28 November 1979, L/4907, GATT, BISD 26th Supp., page 210.

[7] Article 2:2 of the Code defines "like product" as "a product which is identical, *i.e.*, alike in all respects to the product under consideration" or, in the absence of an identical product, a product which has "characteristics closely resembling those of the product under consideration."

[8] See: The Australian Subsidy On Ammonium Sulfate, Report adopted by the Contracting Parties, 3 April 1950 (GATT/CP. 4/39), BISD Vol II, (1950) set-out at page 271 *supra*. Also compare GATT Article III:4 with Article III:2 and Ad Article III:2.

country of export not the country of origin unless the export is a mere transshipment. Fourth, if there is no export price or that price is unreliable because the exporter and the importer are related, Article 2:5 & 6 sanction the U.S. practice of substituting for the export price the price of first resale to an independent buyer in the importing country, properly adjusted for the importer's costs and profit. Finally, Article 2:6 requires that all price comparisons be based on sales made as close to the same time as possible, at the same level of trade; "normally the ex-factory level," and restates the allowances listed in GATT Article VI.

The U.S. Anti-Dumping Statutes

The principal U.S. anti-dumping statute is codified at 19 U.S.C. Sections 1673 *et seq.*[9] Somewhat elliptical in its definition of dumping, Section 1673, the law's principal operative provision, states in relevant part as follows:

Sec. 1673. Imposition of anti-dumping duties

If —

(1) the administering authority determines that a class or kind of foreign merchandise is being, or is likely to be, sold in the United States at less than its fair value, and

(2) the Commission determines that —

(A) an industry in the United States —

(i) is materially injured, or

(ii) is threatened with material injury, or

(B) the establishment of an industry in the United States is materially retarded,

by reason of imports of that merchandise or by reason of sales (or the likelihood of sales) of that merchandise for importation.

then there shall be imposed upon such merchandise an anti-dumping duty . . . in an amount equal to the amount by which the foreign market value exceeds the United States price for the merchandise. . . .

———————

"Fair value" is nowhere defined. In the absence of a definition, the only clue in the statute as to what constitutes dumping is found in the measure of the anti-dumping duty. Dumping occurs, in other words, if foreign merchandise is imported at a "United States price" that is less than its "foreign market value." "United States price" is either what the statute calls the "purchase price" or the "exporter's sales price." The "purchase price" is the price at which the merchandise is purchased from the foreign firm for exportation to the United States

———————

[9] The first U.S. anti-dumping statute was enacted as Section 801 of the Revenue Act of 1916. That act interdicted only predatory dumping based on the foreign producer's intentions. It has proven to be unenforceable.

whether that firm is the producer of the goods or merely a reseller.[10] The "exporter's sales price" is the price at which the merchandise under investigation is sold *in the United States* to an independent purchaser by or for the account of the exporter.[11] The "purchase" price will be used as the "United States price" unless the person importing the goods is related to the foreign producer or reseller in one of the ways specified by the statute.[12] In that event, the importer becomes an "exporter" and the "exporter's sales price" is used as the "United States price." Both the "exporter's sales price" and the "purchase price" will be increased by (i) the cost of packing the goods for shipment to the United States if those costs are not already included in the price, (ii) the amount of any refund of or exemption from import duties or taxes granted by the country of exportation (iii) the amount of refunded excise taxes imposed by the country of export that are included in the price and (iv) the amount of any countervailing duty levied by the United States against the goods.[13] They will be reduced by the costs of bringing the goods from the place of shipment abroad including any U. S. import duties and foreign export duties or charges levied against the merchandise if those costs are included in the price.[14] In other words both the purchase price and the exporter's sales price are adjusted back to an "ex factory" price. In addition, the exporter's sales price will be reduced by the exporter's costs of selling the goods in the United States and any pre-sale costs that the exporter might have incurred in assembling or processing the goods in the United States.[15]

There are three alternative ways of ascertaining the "foreign market value" of the goods under investigation. First, the preferred way is to use the price at which the same or similar merchandise is sold in the country of exportation "in the usual wholesale quantities and in the ordinary course of trade for home consumption."[16] Second, if there are no sales to the home market or if those sales are so small in relation to exports as to destroy the validity of any comparison with the United States price, then the price in sales from the county of exportation to third countries is used to establish the "foreign market value" of the goods under investigation.[17] Each of these two reference prices are subject to such adjustments as are necessary to reflect any added packing costs that would have been incurred if the goods had been exported to the United States[18] and to reflect any differences in the circumstances of sale between the goods under investigation and those being used to establish the foreign market value of the latter, including differences in

---

[10] 19 U.S.C. Section 1677a(b).

[11] 19 U.S.C. Section 1677a(c).

[12] Section 1677(13) provides that the importer of the goods is an "exporter" if: (i) the importer is the foreign producer's or exporter's principal or agent, (ii) the importer controls, through stock ownership or otherwise, any interest in the foreign producer's or exporter's business, (iii) the foreign producer or exporter controls any interest in any business conducted by the importer, or (iv) any third party holds 20% or more of the voting power or control over both the importer and the foreign producer or exporter.

[13] 19 U.S.C. Section 1677a(d)(1).

[14] 19 U.S.C. Section 1677a(d)(2).

[15] 19 U.S.C. Section 1677a(e).

[16] 19 U.S.C. Section 1677b(1)(A).

[17] 19 U.S.C. Section 1677b(1)(B).

[18] 19 U.S.C. Section 1677b(1).

standard wholesale quantities.[19] Third, if foreign market value cannot be established by reference to either home market or third country export sales or if those sales are at prices below the cost of production, then a "constructed value," equal to the cost of production plus general expenses (*i.e.*, selling expenses and overhead) and profit[20] is used to establish the foreign market value of the goods under investigation. There are also special rules for ascertaining the foreign market value of sales by multinational corporations and in cases where the country of exportation has a state controlled economy.[21]

[B] Introduction to the Economics of Dumping: The Theory of International Price Discrimination

At the beginning of this Chapter we examined the behavior of sellers as a group depicted by the industry marginal cost or supply curve and the behavior of buyers as a group depicted by the industry demand curve. We observed how, in a competitive market, the interaction of buyers and sellers each behaving as depicted will result in a market clearing equilibrium price. Finally, we noted how, under free-trade, assuming transportation costs were not prohibitive, competitive markets will yield a "world" price. "Dumping," on the other hand, occurs where instead of a world price, producers in one country charge a *higher* price in their home market than they charge in exporting to other national markets; they price discriminate between markets. Of course, "reverse dumping" can occur where the home market price is less than the export price, but that possibility rarely raises any concern. It is the image of foreign producers "dumping" low priced products on the importing country's markets that is thought to be a problem. Indeed, as the pejorative connotations of the word itself — "dumping" — indicate, there is a pervasive tendency to treat such behavior as an evil — as "unfair" trade or, as the U.S. statute puts it, selling at "less than the fair value" of the goods. Intuitively, of course, the reader might ask why a nation would object to its citizens buying something for less than what foreigners must pay. Be that as it may, and putting intuition aside for the moment — but only for the moment — we can only understand why producers engage in international price discrimination, why importing nations object and whether they should do so, by looking beyond *industry* behavior to the behavior of *individual producers* within an industry operating in a monopolistic or oligopolistic market as contrasted with a competitive market.

The Parameters: Demand and Its Elasticity,
Marginal Revenue and Marginal Cost

To begin this inquiry consider an industry composed of many firms selling a standardized product the demand for which is shown in the first two columns of Table I.

---

[19] 19 U.S.C. Section 1677b(4).
[20] 19 U.S.C. Sections 1677b(a)(2), 1677b(b) and 1677b(e).
[21] 19 U.S.C. Section 1677b(c) and (d).

Table I

Demand, Total Revenue and Marginal Revenue

Price ($000)	Quantity Demanded ($000)	Total Revenue ($000)	Marginal Revenue ($000)
$45	500,000	$22,500	$____
44	520,000	22,880	+380
43	540,000	23,220	+340
42	560,000	23,520	+300
41	580,000	23,780	+260
40	600,000	24,000	+220
39	620,000	24,180	+180
38	640,000	24,320	+140
37	660,000	24,420	+100
36	680,000	24,480	+ 60
35	700,000	24,500	+ 20
34	720,000	24,480	− 20
33	740,000	24,420	− 60
32	760,000	24,320	−100
31	780,000	24,180	−140
30	800,000	24,000	−180
29	820,000	23,780	−220
28	840,000	23,520	−260
27	860,000	23,220	−300
26	880,000	22,880	−340
25	900,000	22,500	−380

From what we have already learned, we know that, as the price of the industry's product rises, consumers, as a group, will, as Table I shows, buy less from the industry. Conversely, as the price declines, consumers will increase their purchases of the industry's product. The quantity demand will rise. This is shown as a linear demand curve (D) in Figure 1.

Price and Output: The Parameters of the Market[22]

Figure 1

Price and Output: The Parameters of the Market

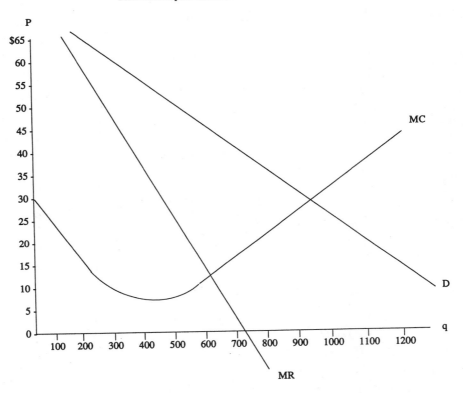

[22] The inverse relationship between price and quantity reflected in Table I and by the left to right downward slope of the demand curve in Figure 1, assumes that other things which might effect the demand for a product are being held constant. If, for example, peoples' preference for the industry's product relative to other uses of their money rises as their incomes rise, one might find that a general rise in incomes within the society was accompanied by a rise in both the price and the quantity demanded. This phenomenon, however, could only be accurately depicted by drawing a new demand curve lying to the right of the present curve (D) in Figure 1. Also note, we have used a straight line or linear demand curve. Of course demand curves are not necessarily linear. Since, however, the principles with which we are concerned will not be affected by the difference, we will stay with the linear form in order to simplify exposition.

Consider next the fourth column in Table I; the statement of the industry's marginal revenue. This column shows the amount of revenue that would be added to or subtracted from the industry's total revenue by the sale of an additional 20,000 units of output, which, under our assumed linear demand curve, will be the additional amount sold with each successive $1 reduction in price. Observe, that as the price is lowered from $45 to $35, total revenue increases with each successive $1 reduction, but at a reduced rate (marginal revenue is positive but declining). For each $1 reduction in the range from $34 to $25 total revenue declines at an increasing rate (marginal revenue is negative and increasingly so). The explanation for this is to be found in the price "elasticity" of the demand curve. Elasticity is the effect that a change in price will have on the quantity demanded at any point on the demand curve. If a given price increase (or decrease) elicits an inverse and proportionally greater change in the quantity demanded, demand at that point on the curve is said to be price "elastic." If, however, a change in price elicits a proportionally lesser inverse change in the quantity demanded, demand is classified as "inelastic." Here consult Table II.

Table II

Elasticity of Demand
(Price Range $25 - 45)

	(Col. 1) Price	(Col. 2) Percent Change in Price	(Col. 3) Percent Change in Quantity	(Col.4) Elasticity of Demand
	$45	2.22%	4.0%	1.8%
	44	2.27	3.85	1.7
	43	2.33	3.7	1.59
	42	2.38	3.57	1.5
Elastic	41	2.44	3.45	1.41
Demand	40	2.5	3.33	1.33
	39	2.56	3.23	1.26
	38	2.63	3.13	1.19
	37	2.7	3.03	1.12
	36	2.77	2.94	1.01
Unity	35	2.86	2.86	1.0
	34	2.94	2.78	.95
	33	3.03	2.70	.89
	32	3.13	2.63	.84
	31	3.23	2.56	.79
Inelastic	30	3.33	2.5	.75
Demand	29	3.45	2.44	.71
	28	3.57	2.38	.67
	27	3.70	2.33	.63
	26	3.58	2.27	.59
	25	4.0	2.22	.56

Observe that for each $1 change in price (increase or decrease) between $25 and $34, the percentage of that change (column 2) exceeds the percentage change in the quantity demanded (column 3). More precisely, as column 4 shows, each 1% change in price over this range yields an inverse change in quantity demanded of less than 1%. Demand is "inelastic" with the result that as price is increased the additions to revenue from that increase more than offset the loss in revenue from a decline in the quantity sold (*i.e.*, total revenue rises). Conversely, as *price is lowered* the loss in revenue from that reduction is not offset by increased sales (total revenue declines).

At the same time, for each price change between $36 - $45 the percentage of that change (column 2) is less than the inverse percentage change in quantity demanded (column 3). In this range, each 1% change in price elicits an inverse change in the quantity demanded of more than 1% (column 4). Demand is "elastic." At $35, elasticity reaches "unity" (a 1% change in price evokes a 1% inverse change in the quantity demanded). Also, if the price is anywhere above $35, a *decrease* in price will increase the industry's total revenue. If the price is anywhere below $35, an *increase* in price will increase the industry's total revenue. At $35 the industry's total revenue is maximized.

Now, return to Figure 1 and note that we have plotted the industry marginal revenue curve (MR). Remember that the marginal revenue curve (MR) is a derivative of the demand curve (D). The way to read the marginal revenue curve, therefore, is to draw a horizontal line from each dollar amount on the price axis (p) to where that line intersects the demand curve (D) and then, from that point, draw a vertical line down to the marginal revenue curve (MR). By doing this you will observe that as price decreases and sales increase within the "elastic" range of the demand curve (*i.e.*, from $45 to $35), marginal revenue is positive (*i.e.*, MR lies *above* a horizontal line drawn from $0 on the price axis (p)) but is declining in amount. Now pick a point on the price axis (p) about half-way between $34 and $35. From that point move out along a horizontal line until it intersects the demand curve (D). Next move along a vertical line downward from D to the marginal revenue curve (MR) and note how the vertical line intersects MR exactly where the price axis (p) shows $0. In other words, at somewhere between $34 and $35, marginal revenue reaches $0. Verify this by examining the marginal revenue column in Table I. From that point on, the industry's demand curve enters the "inelastic" range (*i.e.*, any price reduction from $34+ to $25 will reduce total revenue). Hence, marginal revenue is negative and lies below a horizontal line drawn from $0 on the price axis (p). That line, of course, also serves as the horizontal quantity axis (q).

Lastly, in Figure 1 we have plotted the industry's marginal cost curve (MC) at various levels of output. As already noted marginal cost is the increase in total costs resulting from each additional unit of output.[23] In Figure 1 we have assumed the typical U shaped marginal cost curve.

_____

[23] Note what is meant by marginal cost. Marginal costs are those costs that vary with output. But variability is a property that cannot be ascertained without reference to time. Once a producer has made a decision to invest in plant and equipment and is obligated to service its debt or pay rent or depreciate its assets, these latter costs are, for a time thereafter, fixed costs. They must in all events be met even if the company produces nothing. Hence, if a producer seeks to maximize profits (*i.e.*, the excess of total revenue over total costs) in the short run, the only costs that will affect profits as a result of a decision to increase or decrease output are costs which vary with different levels of output. Fixed costs cannot be made to vary in this fashion and are, therefore, irrelevant to the output

Now, having defined the several curves shown in Figure 1 we can turn to examining how our hypothetical industry is likely to behave under varying conditions. In so doing, it is important to keep in mind that the curves shown in Figure 1 represent *industry wide* conditions and that what we now propose to examine is how, under those conditions, *individual producers* will behave.

Pricing Under Competition

The first basic principle to keep in mind is that the individual producer will maximize its profits by carrying production to the point where its marginal cost precisely equals its marginal revenue. If at any level of output the cost of the last unit produced — marginal cost — is less than the revenue derived from that unit — marginal revenue — there is still profit to be made by increasing production. If, however, the cost of the last unit produced exceeds the revenue derived from that unit, the production of that last unit results in reducing the producer's profit and should be discontinued. Profit is maximized at an output where MC = MR.

Secondly, while in Figure 1 we have plotted the *industry's* demand, marginal revenue and marginal cost curves, we have also stipulated that our industry is composed of many producers competing with each other. As a first approximation, competition exists where because of a multiplicity of producers no one producer so controls supply that he can exercise power over price. Consider the thousands of corn farmers in Iowa. Anyone of them may, at some time, withhold his crop from the market. That would doubtless diminish the amount of corn offered for sale. But the quantity withheld will represent so small a fraction of the total supply and its impact on price will be so infinitesimal that we can, for all practical purposes, treat the single farmer as wholly without power over price. Stated another way, if under competition, no one producer can measurably change price by increasing or decreasing output, each producer in making its output decision must take the price as given throughout the full range of the output possibilities from which it must choose. It is what we call a "price taker." As a "price taker" each producer will, as price rises, offer more to the market allowing buyers, facing an increase in aggregate supply, to pay less. Conversely as price falls, producers will offer less to the market compelling buyers to pay more.

---

decision. Yet those costs don't go away. If they are not met the producer will eventually go out of business. This reality suggests the need for an alternative time horizon. In the longer run all costs, including capital and equipment costs, vary with the producer's output decisions. A producer does not invest in a new plant unless it reasonably expects to use that plant to produce additional output and the decision to build becomes a function of a decision regarding the long-term output of the firm. There is, in other words, a distinction between short-run and long-run marginal costs and unless the producer has no fixed costs, long-run marginal costs will exceed short-run marginal costs. The question remains, which of these is the appropriate point of reference in ascertaining how producers will behave under varying circumstances? Managers don't ignore fixed costs. However, our purpose is to analyze producer pricing decisions. Those decisions are typically made with considerable frequency in response to changing market conditions with fixed costs as given. Accordingly, the marginal cost curve (MC) in Figure 1 can be taken as representing the short-run marginal costs of the industry. Finally, it should be noted that among the costs included in a producer's longer run marginal costs is the amount necessary, in a competitive capital market, to induce investment in the firm; what can roughly and somewhat inaccurately be called "profit."

Now, observe that since, under competition, no one producer can influence the market price, each producer will recognize that no matter how much he increases or decreases output he will get exactly the same revenue from each unit of output he offers to the market; he will get the market price. This also means that, for the individual producer, each additional unit offered to the market will add to total revenue an amount exactly equal to the market price; marginal revenue will equal price. Stated another way, from the *viewpoint of the individual producer* under competition, the demand curve, as a statement of how much buyers will buy, is not the left to right downward sloping curve shown in Figure 1, but is, for all practical purposes, a flat horizontal line equal to the then prevailing market price. From the *individual producer's view*, buyers will buy all he is willing to supply. As a derivative of this horizontal demand curve, the marginal revenue curve of the *individual producer* is likewise a flat horizontal line equal to the then prevailing market price.

Now, precisely how much will each individual producer offer to the market under these conditions? We have already given the answer. Each producer, seeking to maximize profits, will increase (or decrease) output until the cost of the last unit it produces — its marginal cost — is equal to its marginal revenue, namely the market price.

What this means is that by combining all of the marginal cost curves of producers in the industry into a single *industry* marginal cost curve, we can specify exactly how much the *industry as a whole* will supply at varying prices; we can specify the *industry* supply curve. Thus, in Figure 1 the *industry* marginal cost curve (MC) is also the *industry* supply curve (S). Then, as we have already noted, under competition, the market clearing or equilibrium price will be where the industry supply curve (S) intersects the industry demand curve (D). In Figure 1 the equilibrium price will be $25 per unit and 900,000 units will be purchased.

Finally, note that since all the producers in the industry will maximize profits by operating at a point where their marginal costs equal their marginal revenue and, under competition, all will have the same marginal revenue (*i.e.*, the market price), it follows that, under competition, all the producers in the industry will operate at the same marginal cost. It may be that the outputs of various producers at that marginal cost differ; some will produce 5,000 units, some 7,000 units, etc. Producers will, in other words, differ in the scale of operations at which cost is equal to price. This will, in turn, have an important bearing on the structure of the industry and upon the absolute magnitude of the industry's marginal costs. But, at any given point in time, the marginal costs of all producers will, under competition, be the same and will equal price. In Figure 1, it will be $25. In other words, under competition, price, as a measure of the value society assigns a product when compared with alternative ways of using its resources, will be exactly equal to the cost of producing the product. If price, as such a measure of value, covers the cost of supplying the product to society but no more, we can legitimately say that society has attained an "efficient" solution to the problem of supplying its needs.

Pricing Under Monopoly

Now, contrast the situation of the *individual producer* in a monopolistic market. A monopolist is a seller who can change the price at which his product is sold by

changing the quantity he offers to the market. If the monopolist reduces the quantity offered, price will rise. If he increases the quantity offered, price will decline. Power over price is the essence of the economic concept of monopoly.

Suppose all the producers in our hypothetical industry, either by agreement (*i.e.,* a cartel) or by merger, placed themselves in a position to regulate aggregate industry output. From this collective perspective and with the collective power in their hands, the industry managers would immediately recognize that at $25 per unit the *industry* was not maximizing profits. Consider at this point Figure 2 which replicates the demand, marginal revenue and marginal cost curves from Figure 1.

Figure 2

Price and Output Under Monopoly.

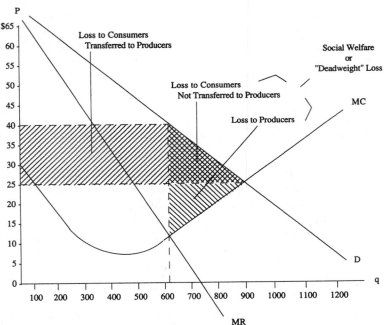

As Figure 2 illustrates, the managers of the cartel or merged firm will immediately see that at $25 per unit the cartel's (*i.e.,* industry's) marginal cost far exceeds its marginal revenue and having the power to curtail output they will do so. As they cut back output, price will rise with some buyers dropping out of the market altogether and others curtailing their purchases. This will continue until the managers see that the cartel's (industry's) marginal cost is equal to its marginal revenue. At that point price and output would stabilize. According to Figure 2 output would be 600,000 units (q) and price $40 (p) and the cartel would reap a monopoly profit. This latter is measured by the difference between the loss producers suffer by reducing output (left cross-hatched triangle marked "loss to

producers") and that which they gain by a transfer from consumers (right cross hatched quadrangle in Figure 2.)

Later in Chapter 7, when we study the transnational operation of the U.S antitrust laws, we will want to explore the social consequences of this kind of power over price more thoroughly; why monopoly power is thought to be an evil Suffice it here to note several points. First, a monopolized market imposes on society a net welfare or deadweight loss together with certain opportunity costs that it does not incur under competition; costs borne by consumers and producers alike, costs related to the reduced demand for inputs to the monopolist's production, costs associated with the establishment and maintenance of monopoly power.

Second, observe that if our hypothetical monopolist is a cartel, it must, in order to reduce overall industry output, impose upon each member of the cartel production limit, a quota. Observe also that since costs are always positive, the point on the demand curve at which the cartel's (i.e., industry's) marginal revenue equals its marginal cost must necessarily lie on the "elastic" portion of that curve (i.e., where marginal revenue is also positive). This, in turn, means that each producer in the cartel has a strong incentive to cheat on the cartel by increasing output and lowering price. Cartel's are, in other words, notoriously unstable and must invariably establish some mechanism to fix quotas and police against cheating. These mechanisms are never costless. Moreover, even if our hypothetical monopolist was created by the merger of previously competitive firms and as such, can prevent cheating, mergers are a far more complex and costly affair to bring-off.

Lastly, when our monopolist, whether a cartel or a merged firm, starts to raise the price from $25 to $40 and reap the monopoly profit, its market becomes very attractive to others; to firms abroad, to domestic producers of other products with comparable technologies and even to completely new firms. We now have a sophisticated global capital market which is highly responsive to such opportunities. Again, monopoly power tends to be an unstable commodity, as often as not sustainable over long periods of time only through governmental fiat.[24]

Pricing Under Oligopoly

Now, of course, the blatant globe-girdling cartels or the market devouring single firm monopolies of the past are no longer the problem they once were. In some significant part this is because cartels and monopolies are illegal under both the U.S. and EEC antitrust laws and many of the global cartels that existed before World War II were broken-up by the Justice Department. As a consequence oligopoly is increasingly the order of the day both in the United States and abroad More and more markets are being served by a handful of firms, one of whom may

[24] A further reason why cartels tend to be unstable lies in the possibility of non-price competition. Even if cheating on the cartel price is successfully controlled, individual members may resort to non-price competition — better services, longer warranties improved quality, etc. — in order to engross to themselves a larger share of the cartel's profit. Taken to the extreme this could actually continue until the members' costs rise to the cartel price stripping the cartel of any monopoly profit and producing, in effect, a fully competitive industry.

emerge as the industry leader but, if so, will be closely tracked by two or three others, with a number of smaller companies on the fringe. In this state of affairs and because of the fear of anti-trust prosecution, the potential for supra-competitive pricing lies in the subtler and less readily detectable possibility of interdependent pricing or "tacit collusion."

Consider the seller in a market of one hundred sellers of roughly the same size who increases his output by 20%. That increase will raise total industry output by only .2 of 1%, an amount too small to measurably reduce the market price. It is an action his competitors can safely ignore. Contrast this with a firm that confronts only two competitors of approximately equal size. If this firm reduces price to a level that increases its sales by 20%, it will cause its competitors' sales to decline if they don't do likewise. While the magnitude of the decline will depend upon the elasticity of demand, it could reach dimensions which the competitors could not afford to ignore. Accordingly, if the price cutter's strategy includes taking short-term losses to enhance market share, his competitors' will likely match his price and effectively take away the gain from increased sales, rendering his strategy hazardous in the extreme. Thus, in a concentrated market suppliers will be required to make their pricing decisions in anticipation of the likely responses of others — they must think and act interdependently — and will be less likely to initiate price reductions than sellers in a highly fragmented market. There is, potentially at least, an implicit floor on price. But if that is so, competitors in a concentrated market will also see an opportunity to raise price in order to capture, each for himself, a share of the resulting monopoly profit. Certainly no one will want to be left out.

Lawyers and economists are generally agreed that theoretically, and stated in broad terms, concentrated markets may give rise to this "tacit" interdependent, supra-competitive pricing done without any agreement whatsoever. They are sharply divided, however, over the nature and extent of the danger. To some, interdependent, supra-competitive pricing is the only type of pricing behavior likely to be rational once an industry reaches a requisite level of concentration and other reinforcing conditions are met. This is especially so if there is one firm in the industry dominant enough to exercise price leadership. Others tend to stress the additional factors that must accompany concentration before such separately arrived at, interdependent pricing decision can, in fact, become the only rational mode of firm behavior. To this group, the probability of such a convergence is sufficiently remote to warrant a much more permissive approach to the problem.

It is unnecessary for our present purposes to enter into this debate. The critical point is to understand how the possibilities for international price discrimination (dumping) depend upon these market structures and what incentives to discriminate they supply. They are also helpful in evaluating those explanations of dumping which are used to justify an anti-dumping policy and they highlight some of the welfare affects of such a policy.

The Necessary Conditions for Price Discrimination

Here consult Figure 3.

Figure 3

Price Discrimination Between Home and Export Markets

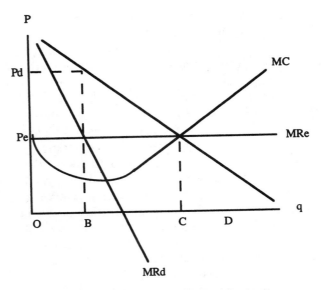

Figure 3 shows the industry demand (D) and marginal revenue curves (MRd) for the foreign producer's home market; the foreign producer's own marginal costs (MC); and the price in a particular export market (Pe). Also, on the assumption that the price in the export market is a competitive price, Figure 3 shows the foreign producer's marginal revenue from that market (MRe) as equal to price (*i.e.*, he is a "price taker" in the export market). Now observe that at the competitive export price (Pe) the foreign producer maximizes his profit at point C on the quantity (q) axis (*i.e.*, output OC). This is where his marginal cost equals his marginal revenue from exports (MC=MRe). But next observe the point where the marginal revenue from exports (MRe) intersects the marginal revenue on domestic sales (MRd). For all output from O to point B the domestic marginal revenue (MRd) lies above the export marginal revenue (MRe) (*i.e.*, MRd exceeds MRe). This means that for OB units of output the revenue the foreign producer could potentially obtain by selling to his home market exceeds the revenue he could obtain by exporting. We say *potentially*. The key is that the producer must have sufficient power over price in his home market to take advantage of the higher domestic marginal revenue (MRd); he must have monopoly or oligopoly power. If he does have that power he will obviously sell OB units of output to the home market at price Pd and will export BC units of output at price Pe. Since Pd exceeds Pe he will be dumping.

To underscore how the power to charge a monopoly or other supra-competitive price in the home market is a necessary condition for dumping, consult Figure 4.

Figure 4

Competitive Home Market: Absence of Incentive to Discriminate

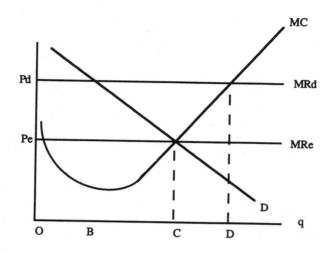

Observe that in Figure 4 we are assuming that the foreign producer is operating in a competitive market at home (*i.e.*, he lacks the power over price). Hence, we have had to re-draw his domestic marginal revenue curve (MRd). It is no longer the backward sloping curve shown in Figure 3, but is essentially a horizontal line equal to the competitive price in the home market (Pd). He is a "price taker" in that market as well as in the export market. If, under these conditions, the home market price (Pd) exceeds the export price (Pe), his domestic marginal revenue (MRd) would exceed his marginal revenue from exports (MRe). He, would, as a consequence, maximize profits by increasing output from point C to point D where MC=MRd and selling all of that output at home. Why export if he can sell all of his output at a higher price at home? Conversely, if the competitive export price exceeded the competitive home price he would produce where MC=MRe and would export all of that output at the prevailing export price. This is precisely the pattern encountered and explained in Figure 4 of Chapter 3.

At this point the reader will, of course, observe that if the foreign producer can, because of his monopoly power, sell at home at a higher price than that prevailing in the export market, there is a real danger that producers located outside the home market will enter that market and drive the price down to the competitive level. For this reason very frequently international price discrimination can occur only if the home market of the foreign producer is protected by tariffs and other barriers to trade, a point rather dramatically illustrated by the dumping cases against European steel.[25] Also, while largely for ease of exposition, we have assumed that the export market was competitive, that need not be so. Even if the export market were oligopolistic or monopolistic and the foreign producer held some or all of

---

[25] See page 456, note 5, *supra*.

the power over price, he would discriminate if the elasticity of demand in the two markets differed.

Lastly, thus far we have assumed a profit maximizing foreign producer; one who sells at no less a price than that necessary to cover his marginal costs. Under this assumption, a foreign producer will, as we have seen, price discriminate only if he has power to set a monopoly or other supra-competitive price in his home market. On the other hand, price discrimination could occur if the foreign producer sells at marginal cost at home and then exports at a price below marginal cost. In that event the home and export markets could both be competitive. But, as we shall see, this is a hazardous pricing strategy and precisely when and why it is likely to occur and with what consequence for the importing country's economy is a matter we will examine at some length below.

[C] The Economic Costs of an Antidumping Policy and the Claim of "Unfair" Competition

Here we return to the simple intuitive question asked earlier; what possible reason would an importing country — in our case the United States — have for objecting to its citizens buying something more cheaply at home than what foreigners must pay abroad? The answer is complex. It requires identifying the benefits that the U.S. as an importing country can derive from dumping. It is also necessary to examine not only the rationality of the many claims concerning the dangers of dumping, but to place those claims into a broader institutional and political context.

Recall that under both GATT and U.S. legislation dumping may be interdicted by an anti-dumping duty only upon proof that the imports materially injured the domestic industry. To meet this requirement the dumped imports must command a sufficient position in the relevant U.S. market to cause more than a de-minimus sales loss to U.S. producers. That, in turn, should[26] translate into a showing that the market share of the dumped imports sufficed to put downward pressure on the U.S. price.[27] Legally relevant dumping, in other words, should occur only when there is evidence that foreign producers command some degree of market power. Yet dumping which reaches this magnitude — this threshold of illegality — is precisely the level of dumping likely to make the United States, as a whole, better-off. Schwartz, in referring to subsidies, states the point succinctly:

> The domestic resources previously used to manufacture the goods which are now imported [because of the lower dumped price] are shifted to their next highest valued use. Since that value is by definition greater than the cost of imported goods (or else they would not be imported) the [importing] country as a whole is richer by the amount of the difference.

---

[26] We say "should." The reader will want to examine some of the cases in Section 5.04 and inquire whether the ITC is in fact properly implementing this legal requirement.

[27] Theoretically U.S. producers might lose out to imports solely by reason of non-price competition (better salesmanship, service, product quality, etc.), rather than through lower prices. But even so the analysis does not change. These advantages are not costless to producers. Therefore, if they lead to a loss of sales by U.S. producers it only means that imports without these advantages — imports identical in every respect to the domestic product — will sell for less than the latter.

In addition, of course, importers and consumers unequivocally benefit from dumping. Anti-dumping duties — for which the importer alone is legally responsible — result in higher costs to importers, fewer imports and consequently higher prices to consumers through the reduction in supply and the partial forward shifting of the duty. If facing the threat of an anti-dumping duty, foreign producers unilaterally, or by agreement with ITA, raise their U.S price to match the supra-competitive home market price, the effect is the same; higher costs to consumers and a welfare loss to the nation as a whole through a misallocation of resources.[28]

It is also to be remembered that consumers of a dumped import include other United States industries that use the import in their productive process. As the studies of the steel import quotas show,[29] higher costs visited upon these users by an anti-dumping policy can translate into higher product prices, increased import competition and a loss of exports for those industries. If the quantity of imports interdicted by that policy is large enough it can also have macro-economic effects. In the short run, restrictions on dumped imports can strengthen the U.S dollar which will increase total U.S. imports and decrease total U.S. exports exacerbating the losses suffered by the direct users of the dumped imports.

At this point, before turning to the arguments usually given in favor of an anti-dumping policy, the normative and political implications of the economic costs of that policy need to be given a fuller statement. First, it is a basic reality that, except for the most cynical purveyors of naked protectionism, political acceptance of an anti-dumping policy for the United States turns on the creditability of the claim that it will preserve "fair competition." This is not an economic postulate but a normative one. Dumping is not playing by the rules of the game. To sustain that claim, of course, one must articulate the normative standards upon which the rules of the game are based and precisely under what circumstances dumping violates those standards. To this issue we shall turn shortly. Here, the point to note is that the normative argument, at the very threshold, can be perverse. "Fair competition" when used as a normative appeal in political argument evokes not just popular allegiance to fairness and justice but also an allegiance to competition and the powerful linkage that history has forged in the American mind between America's economic success and the competitive process. We may want "fair" competition, but it is competition nevertheless.

In this light consider the case of foreign producers faced with an anti-dumping investigation where the American market is basically competitive. There are three possibilities.

First, their share of the American market may be small enough that their sales will be found not to have injured the American industry. In that case they will simply go on dumping because dumping is necessary to meet the competition.

---

[28] For most industries in the industrialized world, their primary market is the home market. Accordingly, the possibility that faced with a U.S. anti-dumping investigation these industries will choose to lower the home market price (*i.e.*, forego some of the monopoly profit being earned at home rather than lose sales to the U.S.) is remote. This is especially so if the American market is already characterized by oligopoly pricing (*e.g.*, steel).

[29] See: Mendez, *The Short-Run Trade And Employment Effects Of Steel Import Restraints*, 20 J. of World Trade Law 554 (1986).

Alternatively, they may be found to have possessed enough market power to satisfy the minimal injury test but not enough to alter materially the prevailing price in the American market. In that case, the American market will remain essentially competitive after *an affirmative dumping determination*, and the foreign producers will, with one exception,[30] have to withdraw from that market. Dumping was necessary to meet the competitive price in the American market so that the imposition of an anti-dumping duty or the raising of their price to the home market monopoly price will drive them out. The anti-dumping law, in other words, will have served only to weaken competition in the American market.

Third, faced with an imminent or an actual affirmative dumping determination, the foreign producers may, unilaterally or by agreement with the ITA, raise their price to the home market price or suffer the imposition of an anti-dumping duty. If this occurs, and the *foreign producers continue selling* in the American market, it will mean that those producers possessed genuine supra-competitive pricing power in that market but did not fully exploit that power (*i.e.*, they dumped) until threatened with an anti-dumping investigation. There could be several reasons for this reluctance, but whatever the reason the basic effect of the anti-dumping law in such a case is to destroy the very competition which, in its normative appeal, it purports to foster. Moreover, even if the American market was plagued by supra-competitive pricing before the foreign producers raised their price or suffered an anti-dumping duty, the anti-dumping law could only exacerbate the competitive weakness of that market.

In this connection, recall the economic rents reaped by the Japanese automobile companies as a result of the VRA's on exports to the United States. With this experience in mind, one could readily hypothesize conditions under which foreign producers would invite an anti-dumping investigation in order to mask a move toward monopoly or oligopoly pricing in sales to the United States and then, in response to that investigation, voluntarily raise their price to the home market monopoly price rather than have those rents taxed away by an anti-dumping duty. In all events, it is clear that in many cases, the anti-dumping law's answer to "unfair" competition is not "fair" competition, but monopoly.

In this respect it is unlike any other law on the books. There are, of course, a host of statutes which, in the name of some non-efficiency postulate of public welfare, visit monopoly power on the American people. But, those laws invariably rest their political case on the virtues of regulated monopoly over competition. The anti-dumping law, on the other hand, rests its political case on the virtues of "fair" competition, while potentially surrendering the nation to the vagaries of an wholly unregulated monopoly the very existence of which depends upon conditions in a market that lies largely beyond American control — the foreign producers' home market.

[D] The Claims in Support of an Anti-Dumping Policy

What then has led the United States and most industrialized nations of the world to adopt laws that interdict international price discrimination? Particularly

___
[30] The only exception would be if the dumped product was being sold below the foreign producer's marginal cost, an extraordinary case which we will nevertheless examine below.

why has dumping received such a bad name — "unfair" trade? It is certainly not "unfair" to consumers. Is it merely political rhetoric employed by domestic industries to mask a naked redistribution of wealth from consumers to themselves? Clearly, in a number of cases that is all it is. Traditionally, however, the economic literature sought to distinguish at least three types of dumping. Jacob Viner, whose seminal work[31] has long influenced thinking on the subject, divided dumping into: (i) sporadic, (ii) short run or intermittent, and (iii) long-run or continuous dumping. Viner thought that only short-run or intermittent dumping was potentially harmful to the welfare of the importing country. The basic problem with such a classification for the law is that it depends upon information normally available only ex post — after the dumping has come and gone. Be that as it may the classification is a useful starting point and leads us into the whole problem of producer pricing strategies.

While Viner did not fully develop the economic rational behind his categories, he apparently thought "sporadic" dumping was largely unpredictable and of such short duration that it would not affect investment and employment decisions by producers in the importing country and therefore would not result in any misallocation of resources.[32] To attempt to interdict this type of dumping would be pointless and it would be wasteful to incur the transactions costs of doing so. Likewise, according to Viner, long-run or continuous dumping would only demonstrate that the foreign producer who engaged in dumping was the more efficient producer. To levy an anti-dumping duty in that case would not only be trade distorting but would undermine the competitiveness of the importing country's market in ways we have already noted. Long-run dumping is "fair" free trade.

Viner's final category — intermittent or short-run dumping — constituted the only type of international price discrimination that he thought could be injurious to the importing country and should be interdicted. Again, Viner's economic rational is not entirely clear. At one point his concern appears to be that if such dumping drove resources — capital and labor — out of the domestic industry the short-term efficiency gains from cheaper imports could be off-set by the long-term misallocation of resources when the dumping stopped. At another point, however, he seems to be concerned less with a longer-term misallocation than with the temporary idling or under-utilization of resources, a very different set of circumstances.

As already noted, the difficulty in fashioning a policy response to short-run or intermittent dumping is to know, at the point where the dumping starts, whether it will be short-term, intermittent and harmful or long-term, continuous and beneficial to the importing country. For that matter continuous dumping, say three to five years, can suddenly stop and have the same misallocative effect as intermittent dumping. Time based categories are of only limited utility in fashioning a policy. Indeed other laws may address the potential harm of

[31] Jacob Viner, Dumping: A Problem In International Trade, Chicago, University of Chicago Press, 1923.

[32] Much of the analysis under this heading is based on Dale, Anti-dumping Law In A Liberal Trading Order, St. Martin's Press, New York, 1980.

intermittent dumping — especially the temporary idling or under-utilization or resources — more effectively.

We turn then to the matter of foreign producer strategies. First, a fundamental distinction must be drawn between foreign producers who are exporting at prices below marginal cost and those who are covering their costs or better (*i.e.*, taking advantage of a supra-competitive price in the importing country market). There is simply no case for an anti-dumping law where the export price is at or above the producer's marginal costs.

Consider several worst case scenarios from the viewpoint of the U.S. as the importing country. Assume that foreign producers engaged in dumping can, because of their superior efficiency and without selling below marginal cost, drive U.S. producers out of business altogether or cause substantial under-utilization of U.S. plant capacity and unemployment. Assume further that once their U.S. competition is destroyed they intend to extract a supra-competitive price from the American market or intend to discontinue all sales to the U.S., leaving this country with a costly misallocation of resources. Assume also that with the U.S. industry out of business the foreign producers' government could use the threat of an embargo as a political weapon against the U.S.

The reader will appreciate that these possibilities attend *all free-trade*. They are the risks inherent in opening national markets to foreign competitors who have a comparative advantage. That those competitors also have the power to charge a higher monopoly price in their home market is wholly irrelevant. Their comparative advantage alone is responsible for the plight of the U.S. industry and the problem should be handled as such.

If the American industry needs temporary protection so that it can adjust to foreign competition, the "escape clause" is the answer. If we fear that foreign producers will foist a supra-competitive price on the American market, the anti-trust laws are the appropriate remedy. If we believe that the U.S. should not become unduly dependent upon foreign sources for some strategic or otherwise vital product, the case should be made on that ground and the necessary protective measures imposed, rather than invoking the spurious rhetoric of "unfair" trade and employing a potentially inappropriate remedy.[33] If the U.S. industry believes that the social costs of foreign competition (unemployment, idle plants, depressed communities, etc.) outweigh the benefits of free trade to consumers and to the nation as a whole, it should be compelled to prove its case. If it succeeds, we should negotiate a tariff increase or extend "escape clause" relief to the industry. If it fails, the domestic industry's claim is naked protectionism. Any law that would arm that claim with normative underpinnings — a search for "fairness" — is intellectually bankrupt; a cynical pretext to hide a naked redistribution of wealth.

Thus, the "problem of dumping," if there is one, is confined to situations in which the foreign producers' dumping is at prices below marginal cost. There are

---

[33] In this case since the anti-dumping duty is not set according to the margin of protection that the American industry needs to off-set the foreign producers' comparative advantage, it is very likely either to be excessive or wholly inadequate to achieve its purposes.

several possible explanations for such a pricing strategy. The foreign producers may be trying to get a foothold in the American market; they may be a new industry, have a new product or the American market may have just become unprotected. Under these circumstances the below cost pricing is bound to be relatively short-term. If they can only penetrate the U.S. market by continuous below cost pricing it means that the U.S. industry has the comparative advantage and the foreign producers will quickly withdraw. If they succeed in penetrating the market they will raise their price to cover marginal costs and, once again, we will be back in the "fair" free-trade case. More importantly, by what normative precept is such a strategy "unfair." It is widely practiced by American industry and is generally viewed as desirable; it brings competitive vigor to the market and expands consumer product choices.

Another oft-cited reason for below cost pricing is the desire to unload surplus production. Here it is necessary to explicate the case carefully. Temporary surpluses can reflect nothing more than the foreign producers' miscalculation of current demand. Anxious not to compromise the monopolistic structure of their home market by lowering price and increasing sales, those producers may turn to the export market. Rather than write the surpluses off as a total loss or incur added storage costs they may be willing to export at prices below cost. In this limited context below cost sales are likely to be a very short-term phenomenon posing essentially no cognizable threat of misallocating the importing country's resources. Moreover, in this setting an anti-dumping law is virtually certain to be ineffective; the dumping will have come and gone before the requisite petition can be filed, the claim investigated and an anti-dumping duty imposed.

This type of short-term surplus dumping, however, is to be contrasted with the far more complex problem of periodic dumping by highly cyclical industries with chronic over-capacity. Steel is the classic example. Capital intensive, with long lead times for plant construction and with national prestige on the line, the world steel industry has for many years been plagued with over-capacity that tends to exacerbate — at least in public perception — the adversities attendant each cyclical downturn in demand. Moreover, the structure of the industry has led to supra-competitive pricing in virtually every national market. In cyclical down-turns the Europeans and Japanese in particular are prone to increase the margin of "apparent" over-capacity by turning their own markets over to explicit government sponsored cartel arrangements (e.g., the Davignon plan). In sum, for steel — or for any other industry similarly positioned — the stage is always set for international price discrimination.

On the other hand, this discriminatory potential does not necessarily mean that export sales will be made at prices below marginal cost. The prevalence of sticky oligopoly pricing raises a distinct possibility (especially in the case of sales to the United States) that foreign producers are fully capable of enhancing their share of the American market without having to sell below cost. If so, any divergence between their home and export prices is wholly irrelevant. It is just another case of free-trade working as intended.

Nevertheless, one could postulate conditions under which foreign steel producers — or producers in any other comparable industry — would find it worthwhile to engage in below cost export sales especially during a recession. Large fixed costs, government regulations that make lay-offs costly (*e.g.*, British redundancy payments), production necessary to maintain a quota position in government sponsored cartels (*e.g.*, the Davignon Plan), to mention a few factors, could, in the short run, render the costs of curtailing production at home greater than the losses incurred in exporting at below marginal cost. Trade under these circumstances can legitimately be labelled "unfair;" a classic "beggar-thy-neighbor" effort to shift the burden of recession onto another's shoulder's. Indeed, it maybe thought "unfair" even without a recession; the effort of one nation to shift the social costs of its own chronic over-capacity onto another.

Having said all this, the difficulty with using this possibility to support an anti-dumping policy is that dumping has nothing whatsoever to do with the problem. Sales below cost, not price discrimination, is the mechanism used to shift the burden of recession or of chronic over-capacity from one nation to another. If shifting is "unfair" it remains so without dumping. True, monopoly power in the home market — a necessary condition of dumping — combined with price discrimination might legitimately be seen by export markets as a signal for cases to watch; cases with a high potential for the export of excess production at prices below cost. But suspicion is not proof, a matter on which we shall have more to say. Even if the suspicion is proven, the appropriate remedy is a duty based on the margin of below cost pricing, not the difference between a foreign producer's home and export prices.

Yet another concern cited as justification for an anti-dumping policy is the fear of "predatory" dumping; a close cousin to the chronic surplus dumping we have already encountered. The claim is that the phenomenon of international price discrimination is likely somehow to be tied to a strategy of below marginal cost export sales made with the intent of driving American producers out of business and thereafter extracting a monopoly profit from the American market. In an apparent effort to forge some logical link between price discrimination and predatory pricing, this claim is often accompanied by what we might call the "war chest" theory. Foreign producers engaged in dumping, so it is said, come armed with home market monopoly profits which they can draw upon to mount a protracted price war which their American competitors, lacking such resources, cannot sustain, *e.g.*, plaintiffs argument in *Matsushita Electric Industrial Co,., Ltd. et al. v. Zenith Radio Corporation et. al.*[34]

Unfortunately, nothing in the fact that foreign producers must be capable of earning home market monopoly profits before they will engage in dumping, explains why they would risk dissipating those profits on a price war in the United States. Only if they calculate that their chance of winning the war is sufficiently great and that the resulting monopoly profits from the U.S. market will both cover their losses and yield a greater than competitive return thereafter will they risk throwing their home market profits away. Certainly a decision to price discriminate standing alone doesn't indicate that they have decided to take that risk. Quite the contrary, we have already noted the inherent instability of monopolistic arrangements. Based on this fact virtually every authority, representing nearly every viewpoint on the spectrum of antitrust philosophy, has expressed profound

---

[34] 475 U.S. 574, 106 S. Ct. 1348, 89 L. Ed. 2d. 538 (1986). Set out in greater detail in Chapter 7.

scepticism regarding the underlying rationality of predatory pricing. The Supreme Court in the *Matsushita* case summarized as follows:

> The success of any predatory scheme depends on *maintaining* monopoly power for long enough both to recoup the predator's losses and to harvest some additional gain. Absent some assurance that the hoped–for monopoly will materialize and that it can be sustained for a significant period of time "[t]he predator must make a substantial investment with no assurance that it will pay off[35] . . . . For this reason, there is a consensus among commentators that predatory pricing schemes are rarely tried, and even more rarely successful [Citations omitted]. [N]owhere in the recent outpouring of literature on the subject do commentators suggest that [predatory] pricing is either common or likely to increase." *Northeastern Telephone Co. v. American Telephone and Telegraph Co.*[36]

> These observations apply even to predatory pricing by a *single firm* seeking monopoly power. . . . [A] conspiracy [involving a number of firms] is incalculably more difficult to execute than an analogous plan undertaken by a single predator. . . . Precisely because success is speculative and depends on a willingness to endure losses for an indefinite period, each conspirator has a strong incentive to cheat, letting its partners suffer the losses necessary to destroy the competition while sharing in any gains if the conspiracy succeeds (emphasis by the Court).

Now, of course, all the studies and all the authoritative opinions cited by the Court focus on American firms. Arguably they reflect a business ethos unique to the United States; an ethos in which each firm possess a high order of managerial autonomy and managers tend to pursue relatively short-term profit making strategies. Perhaps, for this reason, we should be cautious and not assume that the Court's assessment of predation can be automatically applied to other countries. The Japanese, for example, tend to follow much longer-term strategies. They operate in an industrial system geared to a complex set of reciprocal inter-company relationships fashioned under sometimes subtle — sometimes not so subtle — government guidance. They may judge the possibilities for successful predation differently, have different profit expectations, and may operate under constraints against cheating unknown to American companies.

Even conceding, however, that for U.S. trade policy purposes the Court's assessment should be received with caution, the point remains that mere proof that foreign producers charge a higher price in their own market than they do in the U.S. constitutes no evidence whatsoever of predation. It does not prove that the U.S. price is below marginal cost. Without evidence of below cost pricing there can be no evidence of predation, whether intended or not. In fact, predatory pricing can just as readily exist in the absence of dumping. In sum, to the extent an antidumping policy is designed to interdict predatory behavior, it simply is not responsive to the very problem it purports to address.

[35] The Court at this point is quoting from Easterbrook, Predatory Strategies And Counterstrategies, 48 U. Chi. L. Rev. 263, 268 (1981). Ed.
[36] 651 F. 2d. 76, 88 (2d. Cir., 1981) cert. denied 455 U.S. 943, 102 S. Ct. 1438, 71 L.Ed.2d 654 (1982).

Finally, there may be something else at work to explain a law whose ostensible policy justification is utterly problematic and yet evokes such normative fervor. No small part of the growing protectionism in the United States is fueled by a sense that other nations in their trade relations are not playing the game as it "ought" to be played. Either the formal rules that exist are inadequate — they do not comport with our sense of fair play — or they are not enforced properly or the requisite proof of violation is too costly to obtain or is too easily concealed. Subtle protectionist measures against American exports, especially by the Japanese, concealed subsidies, predatory strategies, industrial targeting, blatant threats of retaliation when we protest violations of existing rules, all combine to lend credence to a feeling that the United States has been victimized by the very free-trade regime it so long championed. There is, of course, much hypocrisy in this. The "fair-traders" conveniently tend to ignore our protectionist subtleties, our industrial targeting, our subsidies and our open defiance of established rules. Much of the argument is contrived; propaganda by industries that have simply failed to maintain their international competitiveness. Nevertheless, the sentiment exists and appears to grow.

In this climate an anti-dumping policy with its overtones of fair play may actually serve another unarticulated purpose. Proof of dumping is by no means uncomplicated. The adjustments necessary to compare a producer's home with its export price can reach levels of complexity that makes the entire process look contrived. Nevertheless, decisions do appear to be based on evidence and evidence, however complicated, is generally available. The form, at least, is credible. Too often, on the other hand, evidence of subsidies, of industrial targeting, of below cost pricing, of predatory intent is far more difficult to obtain and far more difficult to interpret persuasively. We have difficulty even defining when a subsidy is trade distorting, what constitutes industrial targeting or what goes into the computation of a company's costs.

Now, against this background return to the basic point of the prior discussion. A *per se* ban on price discrimination tied to an injury requirement can sweep far more broadly than any rational justification for an antidumping law might warrant. It can catch the suspected but unprovable predatory pricing or subsidy scheme. It can interdict a plan to deliberately target an American industry with devises — whether subsidies or otherwise — that are easily hidden. Practically speaking, in other words, dumping may often serve as a convenient proxy for what we suspect but cannot prove. That dumping rationally has nothing whatsoever to do with the vices that an antidumping statute can catch, is quite beside the point. The normative baggage — the patina of "unfairness" — that accompanies an affirmative dumping decision tends to squelch any residual doubts that supporters of an antidumping policy might entertain about the legitimacy of using such a proxy.

One cannot, of course, pretend that devices of this sort are unprecedented in our law. We use the tax law to catch illegal gambling. RICO — ostensibly an anti-crime measure — is used to harass unions engaged in publicizing management failures. Yet, the point to remember is who pays; the consumer — including American industries whose competitive life depends upon the dumped product — the competitiveness of our markets and the wealth of the nation as a whole.

To sacrifice the welfare of so many to a mere suspicion unaccompanied by proof is precisely the kind of cynical use of law that undermines the basic integrity of all government and of our allegiance to the rule of law. Worse, there are alternative and legitimate ways to protect those who would, if we had proof, be the victims of what we can only suspect.

If the United States and other nations are to repeal their anti-dumping laws because their interdiction of international price discrimination is far too sweeping, the question remains what type of law might be put in their place to interdict sales made below marginal cost. We have identified at least two circumstances where such an interdiction could be justified — periodic below cost sales by industries with chronic over capacity and by industries engaged in predatory pricing. Arguably, of course, all cases of predatory pricing should be left to the anti-trust laws. But that would still leave the below marginal cost chronic surplus disposal sales for the trade law to take care of, provided such a law could be properly crafted (*i.e.*, would not interdict below cost market entry sales).

In fashioning such a law there are two practical difficulties. As with Viner's time based classification of dumping, it is hard to know, at the point where below cost sales first occur, what their purpose may be; predation, surplus disposal or market entry. Purpose is notoriously easy to mask. The second problem is the inherent complexity of determining whether sales are actually being made below marginal costs. Some have suggested using average costs as a proxy, but even average cost determinations are not without difficulty.

For these reasons a somewhat modified "escape clause" would seem to offer an elegant solution. Both the countervailing duty and anti-dumping laws are, of course, measures intended to safeguard American industry from certain practices thought to be trade distorting or otherwise unfair. The "escape clause," however, sweeps more broadly. It seeks to safeguard American industry against all forms of foreign competition legitimate or otherwise and no inquiry into motive or purpose or the producer's prices or costs is necessary. The "escape clause" finds its justification for this in the open, honest admission that an American industry is being hurt by imports and needs protection and then by making that protection time limited, digressive and capable of being tied to such adjustments as the domestic industry needs to make in order to meet international competition. This would appear to offer a much more honest and rational approach to the phenomenon of international price discrimination than the current anti-dumping law.

For example, if applied to a case such as steel, where there is world-wide over capacity to which the American companies contribute, "escape clause" relief could be tied to a retrenchment program for the American industry. This could be extended to foreign producers as well, through an agreement that would scale the timing and level of "escape clause" relief to those producers' efforts. "Escape clause" relief can also be tailored to the length of the business cycle where, as frequently occurs, recession is a key element leading foreign producers to sell excess production below cost.

Moreover, while use of the "escape clause" would avoid the need to ascertain whether foreign producers were selling below cost, the injury requirement will generally secure against premature interdiction of cases where, in fact, below cost sales are part of a market entry strategy. Indeed, one could justify drawing a line between legitimate market entry and illegitimate predatory or chronic surplus disposal strategies at precisely the point where imports begin to seriously injure the American industry. This approach would also avoid the difficult, if not futile, inquiry into the foreign producers' motives. This is not to suggest that if evidence of below cost sales is in fact available, it would be irrelevant. It would appropriately influence the form, timing and extent of relief granted. But the right to relief would not be conditioned upon the availability of that evidence.

This, of course, does not mean that the "escape clause" as it now stands is wholly adequate to the task we suggest it might perform. Perhaps the "serious injury" standard as currently framed is too rigorous, a question we consider below. The MFN and compensation requirements of Article XIX of the GATT maybe thought to render "escape clause" relief too inflexible. If so, that is a matter to be addressed in the context of an international "safeguards" code. The essential fact is that we are dealing here with a "safeguards" problem, not a dumping problem. We have a "dumping" problem only because we have an antidumping policy.

§ 5.04 "Material Injury"

[A] The Statute

The reader will recall that before an antidumping duty may be imposed on any imports or a countervailing duty levied against imports from a Code Country, the International Trade Commission (ITC) must determine that "by reason" of those imports (i) an American industry has been "materially injured," or (ii) is "threatened with material injury" or (iii) the establishment of an American industry has been "materially retarded."[1] This requirement tracks Article VI of the GATT as amplified in both the GATT Subsidies and Antidumping Codes. For purposes of both countervailing duty and antidumping cases, Paragraph (7) of 19 U.S.C. Section 1677 provides a definition of "material injury" and lays down rules that the ITC is to follow in making its determination. While the statutory definition does not find express sanction in either of the GATT Codes, many, but not all, of the statutory rules track the Codes closely.

Under the statute the term "material injury" means "harm which is not inconsequential, immaterial, or unimportant."[2] Subparagraph (B) of Paragraph (7) then sets forth the following basic factors that the Commission is to consider. Subsequent Subparagraphs amplify on each.

[B] Volume and Consequent Impact

In making [preliminary and final determinations in countervailing duty and antidumping cases, under] . . . this title, the Commission, in each case —

(i) shall consider —

    (I)   the volume of imports of the merchandise which is the subject of the investigation,

---

[1] 19 U.S.C. Sections 1671(a)(2) and 1673(a)(2).
[2] 19 U.S.C. Section 1677(7)(A).

(II)   the effect of imports of that merchandise on prices in the United States for like products, and

(III)   the impact of imports of such merchandise on domestic producers of like products, but only in the context of production operations within the United States; and [3]

(ii)   may consider such other economic factors as are relevant to the determination regarding whether there is material injury by reason of imports.

* * * *

Under Subparagraph (C) the Commission, in evaluating the volume of imports, must decide whether any increase, absolute or relative to domestic consumption, is "significant."[4] In evaluating the effect of imports on prices the Commission is to consider (i) whether there has been "significant price underselling" by the imports, (ii) whether imports depress prices to a significant degree (*i.e.*, price depression), or (iii) prevent price increases that would otherwise have occurred (price suppression).[5] Subparagraph C, clause (iii) continues as follows:

* * *

(iii) Impact on affected domestic industry

In examining the impact required to be considered under subparagraph (B)(i)(III), the Commission shall evaluate all relevant economic factors which have a bearing on the state of the industry in the United States, including, but not limited to —

(I)   actual and potential decline in output, sales, market share, profits, productivity, return on investments, and utilization of capacity,

(II)   factors affecting domestic prices,

(III)   actual and potential negative effects on cash flow, inventories, employment, wages, growth, ability to raise capital, and investment,[6] and

(IV)   actual and potential negative effects on the existing development and production efforts of the domestic industry, including efforts to develop a derivative or more advanced version of the like product.

The Commission shall evaluate all relevant economic factors described in this clause within the context of the business cycle and conditions of competition that are distinctive to the affected industry.

---

[3] These factors track Article 6:1 of the GATT Subsidies Code and Article 3:1 of the GATT Antidumping Code.

[4] 19 U.S.C. Section 1677(7)(C)(i).

[5] 19 U.S.C. Section 1677(7)(C)(ii). All the points listed in this paragraph are based on Article 6:1 of the Subsidies Code and Article 3:1 of the Antidumping Code.

[6] These provisions track Article 6:3 of the Subsidies Code and Article 3:3 of the Antidumping Code.

The statute goes on (i) to prohibit treating any one of the factors listed above as "necessarily giv[ing] decisive guidance" in making the Commission's determination;[7] (ii) to require that imports from different countries be cumulated if they meet certain conditions[8] — a provision we examine more closely *infra* 0000; (iii) to prohibit making a negative injury determination on agricultural products merely because the prevailing price is above the minimum support price;[9] and (iv) to require that in the case of countervailing duties the Commission take into account the nature of the subsidy, especially if it is an export subsidy that violates the GATT Subsidies Code.[10]

Turning next to determinations of whether the domestic industry is "threatened with material injury," the statute lists the following factors that the Commission is to consider:[11] (i) nature of the subsidy, (ii) an increase in or the existence of unused foreign productive capacity that is likely to result in increased imports, (iii) a "rapid" increase in import penetration of the U.S. market, (iv) the probability of imports causing price depression or suppression, (v) increase in domestic inventories, (vi) the existence of underutilized foreign productive capacity, (vii) "any other demonstrable adverse trends" that indicate that imports, whether or not actually being made, will cause injury, (viii) the potential for product-shifting, (See Section 5.04[B], Note 2 *infra*), (ix) again the possibility for product shifting between raw agricultural products and products processed therefrom, and (x) the potential negative effects on a domestic industry's development efforts, including efforts to develop a more advanced product. In addition, an affirmative determination of "threatened" injury must be based on evidence showing that the threat "is real and that actual injury is imminent."[12]

Lastly, in connection with "threatened" injury determinations, the statute contains a mandate to consider dumping in third-country markets,[13] to cumulate[14] and contains instructions on handling negligible imports.[15]

---

[7] 19 U.S.C. Section 1677(7)(E)(ii). See also Article 6:2 of the Subsidies Code and Article 3:2 of the Antidumping Code.

[8] 19 U.S.C. Section 1677(7)(C)(iv). No comparable provision in the GATT Codes.

[9] 19 U.S.C. Section 1677(7)(D). No comparable provision in the GATT Codes.

[10] 19 U.S.C. Section 1677(7)(E)(i). Footnote 1 to Article 6:1 of the GATT Subsidies Code.

[11] 19 U.S.C. Section 1677(7)(F)(i)(I)-(X). The GATT Codes make no distinction between the factors to be considered in an "actual" injury determination and the factors applicable to a "threatened" injury determination. The Antidumping Code, however, contains language similar to that in Section 1677(7)(F)(ii) (see Footnote 12 and accompanying text) and then provides that "threatened" injury cases must be "studied and decided with special care." (Article 3:7).

[12] 19 U.S.C. Section 1677(7)(F)(ii). See also Article 3:6 of the Antidumping Code.

[13] 19 U.S.C. Section 1677(7)(F)(iii). None of the subjects referred to in this paragraph are dealt with in the GATT Codes, although the principle of taking third-country dumping into account may find some sanction in Article VI:6(b) of the GATT.

[14] 19 U.S.C. Section 1677(7)(F)(iv).

[15] 19 U.S.C. Section 1677(7)(F)(v).

[C] Select Problems in the Application of the "Material Injury" Requirement

What follows are summaries of three ITC decisions that raise some of the more interesting issues with which the commission has had to grapple in carrying-out its statutory mandate. Instead of setting-out the views of the dissenting Commissioners in the summaries, those views are used in the Notes and Questions that follow to highlight the issues.

CERTAIN WELDED CARBON STEEL PIPES AND TUBES FROM INDIA, TAIWAN AND TURKEY

("Steel Pipe Case")

International Trade Commission

Investigations Nos. 731-TA-271 through 273 (Final)

USITC Publication 1839 (April, 1986)

In this antidumping case the Commission issued (1) an *affirmative* injury determination in the case of "standard" steel pipes from India and Turkey and (2) a *negative* injury determination in the case of "line" steel pipes from Turkey and Taiwan. In each case the vote was 4-2. In the case of "standard" pipe, three Commissioners (Stern, Eckes and Lodwick) found a present material injury and one Commissioner (Rohr) found a threat of injury. In the case of "line" pipe, two of these Commissioners (Stern and Lodwick) found no present or threatened injury and two (Eckes and Rohr) found a threat of material injury. The two negative votes were then joined by two Commissioners (Liebeler and Brunsdale) who dissented overall. "Standard" and "line" pipe could not, they concluded, be separated (*i.e.*, they were "like" products) and no American industry had been injured or threatened with injury by any of these imports.

The majority concluded that "standard" and "line" pipe were different products because the latter was made of higher grade steel, required additional testing and was thicker in the larger diameters.[16] "Line" pipe was used primarily in transporting gas, oil or water in utility distribution systems while "standard" pipe was used for "low pressure" conveyance in plumbing, aid-conditioning, sprinkler and other similar systems. The period covered by the investigation was January 1982 through December 1985.

Standard Pipe (Majority View). In assessing the volume, price and other impact of imports from India and Turkey, the majority cumulated these imports with each other and with imports from Singapore, the Philippines, and the People's Republic of China. It also cumulated Thai imports even though an anti-dumping order had been issued against those imports in late January 1986.

---

[16] This conclusion was based on the decision in an earlier case, Certain Welded Carbon Steel Pipes And Tubes From Thailand And Venezuela, Investigation No. 701-TA-242 (Preliminary), USITC Publication 1680 (April, 1985) at page 7.

As far as the condition of the domestic industry was concerned, it had shown "reasonable" performance through 1981 but suffered a serious set-back in 1982 as measured by all significant indicators, including production and shipment levels, capacity utilization, and employment. Then, between 1982 and 1984, while domestic consumption of standard pipe rose 45% (decreasing marginally in 1985) and domestic producer's output, shipments and capacity utilization also increased, the latter increases were substantially below the increase in consumption. Also, employment and hours worked declined between 1982 and 1984 (increasing slightly in 1985). The industry as a whole suffered net operating losses in 1982, 1983 and 1984. And while the industry showed a modest operating income in 1985, four firms registered losses, the largest number to do so during the entire period 1982-1985. On this basis the majority concluded that the domestic industry was experiencing "material injury."

Turning to whether imports were the cause of this injury, the majority noted that in 1982 there were no imports from the countries subject to cumulation, that in 1983 those imports represented a "negligible" percentage of domestic consumption (i.e., there was "negligible" import penetration), that those imports rose "significantly" in 1984 and "dramatically" in 1985.

[Note: While the Commission Report marks the import penetration (i.e., percent of domestic consumption) for dumped imports from India as confidential, total Indian imports, including non-dumped, was less than .001% of domestic consumption in 1984 and .9% in 1985. The figures for Turkey were .1% in 1984 and 1.5% in 1985. The percentages for the other imports subject to cumulation were: China 0% in 1984 less than .05% in 1985;[17] Philippines 0% in 1984, .1% in 1985; Singapore less than .05 in 1984, .3% in 1985, Thailand less than .05% in 1984, 1.4% in 1985. The total market penetration for all cumulated imports thus were something less than .2% for 1984 and something between 4.2% and 4.9% for 1985, depending upon the actual numbers for India and China.]

With regard to U.S. producer's price, the Commission's data showed that prices rose from 1983 to 1984 and then declined in 1985. For the service center/distributor market, prices in the last three months of 1985 were "substantially" below prices in the same period of 1984 and approximately the same as 1983. The end-user market showed a similar trend. In all instances for which the Commission had information, Indian standard pipe undersold domestic pipe by up to 11% and Turkish standard pipe undersold domestic pipe by up to 15%. Also data on the weighted average price showed sales from Turkey and India at least 13% below the weighted average price in sales by domestic producers. In this price sensitive market the increased volume of imports accompanied by consistent underselling and a coincident decline in domestic producers' prices was, the majority concluded, an indication of price depression due to imports.

Lastly, the majority noted that in order to improve the domestic industry's "chances of recovery," the U.S., in 1985, had negotiated VRAs for standard pipe with the largest foreign suppliers. No agreements were concluded with suppliers

[17] The Commission report identifies any percentage less than .05% as such, without giving the precise amount.

from India and Turkey. Yet, in 1985, domestic producers lowered their prices and "continued to operate at a loss, in significant part because of the impact of the cumulated ["dumped"] imports." Those imports were thus "a source of material injury to the domestic industry."

Commissioner Rohr based his conclusion that the domestic industry was "threatened" with material injury on the following evidence: the rapid increase in imports from Turkey and India, the recent increase in Turkish productive capacity, the existence of underutilized capacity in both Turkey and India, the absence of any indication that price underselling would not continue and the VRA's as an incentive to continued underselling.

Line Pipe (Negative Determination by Commissioners Stern and Lodwick). After cumulating imports from Turkey and Taiwan and concluding that, in terms of capacity utilization, employment and financial health, the line pipe industry was very much in the same condition as the standard pipe industry (conclusions with which Commissioners Eckes and Rohr concurred), Commissioners Stern and Lodwick found that those difficulties were not caused by imports from Taiwan and Turkey. The bases for this conclusion were: (i) while those imports increased, this increase was small in comparison to domestic consumption and was only 10% of the increase in total imports, (ii) that notwithstanding the increase in imports from Taiwan and Turkey domestic producers share of domestic consumption increased from 53% in 1984 to 57% in 1985, (iii) domestic prices did not decline in 1985 and inspite of some underselling by imports, domestic producers costs declined by substantially more than prices, yielding a 10% improvement in those producers' gross margin, and (iv) the absence of any evidence of lost sales.

In addition, Commissioners Stern and Lodwick thought that the low level of market penetration, the existence of a substantial commitment by Taiwan to supply pipe to the China Petroleum Corporation and the relatively high capacity utilization rates exhibited by Turkish producers, foreclosed a finding that the domestic industry was "threatened" with material injury by imports from Taiwan and Turkey.

Line Pipe (Commissioners Eckes and Rohr). While not challenging the negative determination with regard to present injury, Commissioners Eckes and Rohr contradicted Commissioners Stern and Lodwick on nearly every point regarding the "threat" of injury. To this end they relied on the increase in import penetration by Taiwan pipe from .4% of domestic consumption in 1984 to 1.3% in 1985, the substantial unused productive capacity in Taiwan, uncertainty as to the length of the commitment to the China Petroleum Corporation and especially the incentive to export to the United States provided by the VRAs. In the case of Turkey the case was weaker. There were no imports from 1982-84 and while the Report marks the market penetration figure for 1985 as confidential, those imports totaled slightly over 7,000 tons or .02% of total imports, the latter representing 43% of domestic consumption. Nevertheless, the shrinking Mid-East market, the ability to shift production from standard to line pipe and the VRAs convinced Commissioners Eckes and Rohr that Turkish imports "threatened" the U.S. industry.

OIL COUNTRY TUBULAR GOODS
FROM CANADA AND TAIWAN
("Tubular Goods Case")

International Trade Commission

Investigation Nos. 701-TA-255 (Final)
and 731-TA-276-277 (Final)

USITC Publication 1865
(June 1986)

In this case a majority of the Commission (Commissioners Stern, Eckes, Lodwick and Rohr), found that the domestic tubular goods industry had been materially injured by (1) subsidized imports from Canada and (2) dumped imports from both Taiwan and Canada. The majority made no determination regarding the threat of injury. Two Commissioners (Liebeler and Brunsdale) dissented. Brunsdale found no present or threatened injury in either case and Liebeler found no present or threatened injury from subsidized Canadian imports but declined to rule on the dumped imports.

"Oil country tubular goods" (OCTG) consist of casings, tubings and drill pipes used in drilling oil and gas wells and transporting oil and gas to the surface. The period covered by the investigation was January 1982 through December 1985.

In reaching their decision the majority cumulated the subsidized imports from Canada with those from Israel but refused to cumulate Argentine imports because the latter were then under a countervailing duty order that dated back to November 1984 which was too remote in time. The majority also cumulated dumped imports from Canada, Taiwan and Israel. Imports from Israel were then under separate countervailing and antidumping duty investigations. In addition, Commissioners Eckes and Lodwick cross-cumulated the dumped and subsidized imports, but noted that their decision did not change because of doing so. Commissioners Stern and Rohr found it "unnecessary" to cross-cumulate. Commissioners Liebeler and Brunsdale refused to cross-cumulate.

Majority Decision. 1981 was, the majority noted, an "extremely prosperous year" for the domestic tubular goods industry. Then in 1982 and 1983 the industry's condition declined dramatically — sales and profits fell, plants and whole firms shut down. While 1984 brought some improvement the general decline continued in 1985. Thus, U.S. consumption decreased by 66% between 1982 and 1983, rose in 1984, then declined by 23% in 1985, ending up 32% below 1982. Domestic production and net sales closely tracked these movements. The production figure for 1985 was 22% below the 1982 level and net sales in 1985 were approximately $1 billion compared with $2 billion in 1982. Capacity utilization showed the same pattern, declining to 10% in 1983, rising to 32% in 1984 and falling to 27% in 1985. Also, while profitable in 1982, the industry incurred operating losses in 1983, 1984 and 1985, although the losses declined from $217 million in 1983 to $111 million in 1985. On this record the majority concluded that the domestic tubular goods industry was experiencing "material injury."

In finding that subsidized imports from Canada were a cause of the injury, the majority relied on the fact that those imports, after being cumulated with imports from Israel, had steadily increased in absolute terms, had increased as a percent of total imports and as a percent of domestic consumption. While the report marks these percentages as confidential, Commissioner Liebeler in her dissent notes that market penetration never exceeded 6%. At the same time, while the domestic industry's share of the U.S. market had increased in 1985, it had not reached the 55% share enjoyed in 1983. Also, while aggregate imports had declined in 1985 — largely because of VRA's with major foreign suppliers — the cumulated imports under investigation had increased, suggesting that the latter "maybe replacing that of restrained countries and inhibiting U.S. producers' sales."

With regard to price, the majority noted that prices fell from 1983 to 1985, a "depression," it concluded, that "resulted in part from the presence of unfairly traded imports in the market." Next, however, the majority noted that the Commission's investigation showed "close pricing with mixed underselling and overselling." It then concludes:

> We recognize that there have been several causes of injury to the domestic OCTG industry during the period of investigation, including decreased demand for the product. However, the Commission is not to weigh causes in an antidumping or countervailing duty investigation. . . . It is possible for both declining demand and unfairly traded imports to materially injure an industry. In fact, the imports might result in relatively greater injury to an industry facing a downturn in demand.[18]

With regard to the dumped imports from Canada and Taiwan, the majority report is very brief, relying on essentially the same pattern of evidence as was relied upon for the subsidized imports; namely, steady absolute increases and increased market penetration by the imports under investigation, compared with declines in total imports; close pricing with mixed under and over selling; and the VRA's.

CERTAIN STEEL WIRE NAILS
FROM KOREA
("Korean Nails Case")

International Trade Commission

Investigation No. 701-TA-145 (Preliminary)

USITC Publication 1223
(March 1982)

In this preliminary determination case a unanimous Commission decided that there were reasonable indications that subsidized imports from Korea had materially injured the domestic industry. Commissioners Stern and Calhoun filed

---

[18] USITC Publication 1865 at pages 11-12.

separate views on the question of whether, under the GATT Subsidies Code and the statute, the Commission could render a decision based solely on the effect of imports on the domestic industry or whether they had to find specifically that it was the subsidy given the imports that caused the injury. Neither Commissioner thought the question decisive in the instant case.

The products in question consisted of seven categories of nails made from steel wire that were differentiated by the coatings applied (*e.g.*, hot or electrogalvanized, vinyl, cement or phosphate coated). While approximately fifty U.S. companies were engaged in making one or more of these seven categories, fifteen firms produced nearly 96% of the nails in question. The Commission declined to use the continuum principle in order to include other types of nails in its investigation. That principle holds that where a group of products are only slightly distinguishable from each other in terms of physical characteristics and use, the "like" product will be defined as all products in the group. The Commission decided instead to define "like" product as the narrowest group of products for which there was actual information available.

With regard to material injury and condition of the domestic industry the Commission made the following points:

Imports increased from less than .5% of domestic consumption in 1973 (1,000 tons) to 12% in 1978 (109,000 tons). In spite of the fact that imports declined to 92,000 tons in 1979 and then to 76,000 tons in 1980, an even sharper drop in domestic consumption resulted in imports holding at 11% of that consumption. Then, in 1981, imports increased to 115,000 tons (51% increase). At the same time domestic consumption continued to drop so that Korean imports increased to 19% of consumption.

With regard to prices, U.S. producers alleged that Korean nails were the price leaders in the U.S. market and that there had been "destructive" price cutting in an effort to maintain sales. This was confirmed by Commission data showing that since the second quarter of 1979 imported nails of the one type for which data were gathered undersold the domestic product by weighted average margins ranging from .4% to 6.9%. Also, the price of Korean nails declined from January-March 1979 to October-December 1981, precisely as the trigger price index for nails increased by 10% and the Bureau of Labor Statistics index increased by 31%. Evidence of price suppression was found in the fact that (i) Korean imports had undersold the domestic product in every quarter since April of 1979, (ii) in that period the price of domestically-produced nails increased at a slower rate than the [overall] producer price index and (ii) simultaneously the price of Korean nails decreased slightly.

With regard to the condition of the domestic industry in the period 1979-1981, the Commission noted that while Korean market penetration was increasing (see above), domestic production declined by 76,000 pounds [sic] or 27%, the ratio of inventories to production increased steadily and the ratio of production to capacity declined from 52% to 48%. Also, the average number of employees declined by 33% (from 1,946 to 1,300 workers). Finally, of the fifteen U.S. firms supplying profit-and-loss information, representing 96% of reported U.S. production in 1981, four firms reported losses in 1979, and seven in 1980. In 1981, five firms reported losses, overall gross profit for the fifteen firms declined and eight plants closed or filed for Chapter 11 reorganizations. On this record the Commission decided that there were reasonable indications that the domestic industry had suffered material injury by reason of subsidized imports.

NOTES AND QUESTIONS

(1) Both the *Steel Pipe* Case and the *Tubular Goods* Case can be understood only against the background of the total world-wide collapse of crude oil prices and the consequent wholesale curtailment of oil drilling and the capping of less productive wells. We will return to the broader question of how such events should be viewed in the context of a "material injury" determination. For the moment, however, observe that by 1985 both the standard pipe and the line pipe industries were making a comeback. Domestic consumption of standard pipe was up almost 45% over 1982, domestic producers' output, shipments and capacity utilization had increased and the industry experienced a modest 1% operating profit. As Commissioners Stern and Lodwick noted, the picture for the line pipe industry was even more encouraging. In other words demand was still weak, but on the rebound.

1985 was, of course, the critical year in judging the impact of the Indian and Turkish imports of standard pipe, since they were negligible in 1983 and reached only about .2% of domestic consumption in 1984. Against this background the question facing the ITC was what effects were the Turkish and Indian imports likely to have on the domestic industry's recovery if those imports, after being cumulated with other imports, commanded, at most, 4.5% to 4.9% of the domestic market.

(a) The ITC reported that there were at least 23 known U.S producers of standard pipe and that eight different importers handled Indian imports and eight Turkish imports. In addition, there were importers from other foreign sources commanding between 54% and 55% of the U.S. market. Absent concrete evidence to the contrary, the market certainly appeared to be competitive. Even assuming some form of coordination between the importers of Turkish and Indian pipe, how significant an effect in such a market would sellers supplying 4.5% to 4.9% likely have on the prevailing market price? Absent that coordination we are speaking about the threat of inquiry from eight firms supplying in total 4.5% of the market. What a threat! Nevertheless, compare this likely effect with the effect other foreign producers could, as a group, have had.

(b) Recall, we know that "dumping" does not confer a cost advantage on the dumper. Yet, the ITC reported Indian pipe underselling domestic pipe by up to 11% and Turkish pipe by up to 15%. These findings were based on very sketchy evidence, some of it purely anecdotal. That problem aside, however, given your answer to (a) above, what might this evidence suggest about the ability of the domestic industry to meet the market demand at the prevailing market price? If this was the case, does it mean that *legally* the injury suffered by the domestic industry could not be attributed to Indian and Turkish imports?

(c) Again in light of your answer to (a) above, are there alternative explanations for the price underselling by the producers of Indian and Turkish pipe? In answering, consider the implications of the following facts: the fact that Turkish and Indian imports commanded a very modest share of the U.S. market, the fact that the foreign producers apparently had some unused productive capacity, the world-wide downturn in oil prices and the VRA's. Is this like the steel case? If not, should we worry about the foreign producers' objectives?

(2) At the threshold of the case, the ITC faced a difficult problem of product definition. Should standard and line pipe be treated as separate products or as one product. The majority separates them on the strength of differences in physical characteristics and use. Yet, Commissioners Eckes and Rohr expressed concern with the possibility of foreign producers employing unused line pipe productive capacity to make standard pipe — engaging in what is known as product shifting. The dissenters are more pointed. In arguing that line and standard pipe should be treated as one product, Commissioners Liebeler and Brunsdale stated:

> When there is a high degree of commonality of inputs in the production of two products, it may be impossible for domestic firms to segregate those inputs in such a manner that they are able to analyze the performance of each product separately. This occurs, for example, when two products are (or can be) produced using the same equipment and the same labor. . . . More generally, when the domestic supply-side substitutability between two products is very strong . . . then the appropriate analysis . . . should focus on the product line consisting of both products. . . . [T]estimony from the petitioner [i.e., domestic industry] now confirms . . . that standard and line pipe can be made on the same equipment and using the same labor.[19]

Against this background consider the following:

(a) The purpose of the analysis, of course, is to determine whether dumped imports caused "material injury." In light of this purpose, which approach — the majority's physical characteristics and use analysis or the dissent's production process analysis — is the more appropriate?

(b) Note that the maximum market penetration ratio for line pipe from Turkey and Taiwan in 1985 was 1.4%. Had these line pipe imports been combined with standard pipe imports having a market penetration ratio of 4.9%, the resulting combined rate of market penetration would have been 3.9%. With this figure in mind, revisit the issue posed in Question 1(a) above? In doing so, note Commissioners Stern's and Lodwick's negative determination regarding "line" pipe. How confident can we be of any causality analysis which draws a distinction between a 1.4% and

---

[19] Commissioners Liebeler and Brunsdale cite for support 19 U.S.C. 1677(4)(D) which provides as follows: "The effect of subsidized or dumped imports shall be assessed in relation to the United States production of a like product if available data permit the separate identification of production in terms of such criteria as the production process or the producer's profits. If the domestic production of the like product has no separate identity in terms of such criteria, the effect of the subsidized or dumped imports shall be assessed by the examination of the production of the narrowest group or range of products, which includes a like product, for which the necessary information can be provided.

3.9% rate of market penetration? Contrast the market penetration rates in the *Korean Nails* Case.

(3) Consider the majority's decision to cumulate standard pipe imports from Turkey and India with each other and with dumped imports from Singapore, Philippines, China and Thailand. 19 U.S.C Section 1677(7)(C)(iv) would seem to require cumulation of imports from all of these countries with the possible exception of Thailand.[20] Thai imports were already subject to an anti-dumping order. They were not, in the words of the statute, imports "subject to investigation." The majority ignored this fact because the order issued against the Thais was of very recent date (January 1986). The dissenters, on the other hand, refused to cumulate the Thai imports. Who was right? In answering consider the following:

(a)   Explain why it might be sensible to cumulate dumped imports from other countries that are then under investigation?

(b)   One way of reading the statute is to say that the mandate to cumulate imports "subject to investigation" did not, by negative implication, prevent the ITC from cumulating other imports if the Commission thought it appropriate to do so. Consider then, whether it was appropriate. If imports are already subject to an antidumping order presumably the remedy is in place and they are no longer a threat to the domestic industry. But in the Thai case the remedy was not in place until January 1986 and the Commission had to decide whether the domestic industry suffered injury during the three years prior thereto. Does this justify treating the Thai imports in the prior years (1982-85) as part of the imports responsible for the injury to domestic producers in those years? In answering assume that in the antidumping case against Thailand, imports from Turkey and India were cumulated with Thai imports. Also note that in the *Tubular Goods* Case the majority refused to cumulate Argentine imports because the antidumping order was issued in November 1984. It was too remote in time.

(c)   If inclusion of the Thai imports was not appropriate, how do you read the statute? Should it now be read as containing a negative implication: imports subject to an existing antidumping order shall not be cumulated?

(d)   Note, if the Thai imports are excluded, the combined market penetration rate for cumulated line and standard pipe imports drops to 2.7% Again, revisit your answer to Question 1(a) above.

(4) In the *Tubular Goods* Case Commissioners Eckes and Lodwick cross-cumulated the dumped imports from Taiwan and Canada with the subsidized imports from Canada. The argument for doing so is that where a domestic industry claims to be suffering injury by reason of "unfairly" traded imports, all such imports contributing to the injury ought to be considered, whether the

---

[20] 19 U.S.C. Section 1677(7)(C)(iv) provides as follows: "For purposes of clauses (i) and (ii), the Commission shall cumulatively assess the volume and effect of imports from two or more countries of like products subject to investigation if such imports compete with each other and with like products of the domestic industry in the United States markets."

unfairness lies in the receipt of a subsidy or in price discrimination. *Bingham & Taylor Division, Virginia Industries Inc. v. United States.*[21] Are you persuaded? Consider that the international law under which the United States purports to act, establishes two quite separate legal regimes for subsidized goods (the Subsidies Code) and dumped goods (the Antidumping Code). Does this suggest that injury by reason of dumping cannot be equated with injury by reason of a subsidy? More fundamentally the purpose of those regimes is, in part, to regulate national countervailing duty and antidumping proceedings to protect the interests of those accused of such practices. From the perspective of the accused, who controls subsidies and who controls dumping? Suppose a country, in response to a countervailing duty investigation, chooses to eliminate the subsidy as an irritant in its relations with the United States. Can cross-cumulation frustrate this objective? If the United States wants to encourage such action, does cross-cumulation make it more difficult to do so?

Perhaps the difficulty really lies in the problematic quality of the antidumping law. The fact imports are dumped neither adds to nor detracts from the injury that the domestic industry might suffer if the same imports were "fairly" traded. Under this view it is perverse to add dumped imports to subsidized imports in a countervailing duty action. Unlike dumping, the subsidy can make a difference; it can cause an injury that non-subsidized imports would not cause. Note that the Subsidies Code provides that: "It must be demonstrated that the subsidized imports are, *through the effects of the subsidy*," causing injury within the meaning of this Agreement." Likewise, the Antidumping Code requires a showing that injury is caused "through the effects of dumping." If you accept the problematic view of the antidumping law, could it not be argued that cross-cumulation is contrary to the international obligations of the United States?

(5) In their dissent in the *Steel Pipes* case, Commissioners Liebeler and Brunsdale pointed to a fundamental problem with the majority's conclusion that the domestic industry was "materially injured." The industry, they noted, was undergoing a basic re-structuring. The picture for the large integrated producers and for the smaller non-integrated firms was quite different. Thus, between 1982 and 1985 integrated producers' sales declined by 25%, non-integrated producers' sales increased 28%. Several integrated producers scaled down or closed plants, while non-integrated producers expanded their plant capacity. Non-integrated firms were profitable through-out the 1982-1985 period with gross profits as a percent of sales ranging from 15.6% to 18.1% and operating income between 6% and 7.7%. The financial condition of the integrated producers was just the opposite. While Commissioners Liebeler and Brunsdale do not tell us which segment was the larger, they conclude from this that, since it is injury to the industry, not a segment of the industry, that must be established, it was "not clear that the industry as a whole [had been] materially injured."

With the foregoing facts in mind, return to the evidence used by the majority to demonstrate that pipe imports from India and Turkey had caused price underselling in the American market. Remember that evidence was based on very partial returns. Using a combined line and standard pipe market penetration ratio

---

[21] 815 F. 2d 1482 (Fed. Cir. 1987) (cross cumulation upheld).

of between 3.9% (Thai imports included) and 2.7% (Thai imports excluded) revisit Question 1(b) and (c) above. What was, very likely, going on?

If there was any problem to be addressed in the *Steel Pipe* Case, it was a safeguards problem, was it not?

(6) Recall the majority's admission in the *Tubular Goods* Case that undoubtedly declining demand had a great deal to do with the condition of the domestic industry. However, the Commission went on to point out, it was "not to weigh causes in an antidumping or countervailing duty investigation." Is this a sufficient answer to the problem? Article 3:4 of the Antidumping Code provides:

> There may be other factors which at the same time are injuring the industry, and the injuries caused by other factors must not be attributed to the dumped imports.**22**

Does compliance with this injunction necessarily require that the Commission weigh the relative impact of imports and of declining demand on the domestic industry in the same fashion as was done in the *Automobile* Case under the "escape clause?" In answering assume that the market penetration of cumulated imports from Canada, Taiwan and Israel was something slightly over 2.2% in 1983, about 3.9% in 1984 and 6% in 1985.**23** Could it be said that the Commission's decision does precisely what Article 3:4 prohibits? Again, if there was any problem, it was a safeguard's problem, was it not?

(7) Return to the question of whether, and how, the "serious injury" standard of the "escape clause" might be changed in order to make it a more responsive instrument for interdicting below marginal cost imports which can be legitimately labelled "unfair" trade (*i.e.*, chronic surplus disposal and predatory pricing) and, at the same time, not interdict below cost market entry imports. The "material injury" standard as applied by the Commission in the *Steel Pipe* Case and the *Tubular Goods* Case would seem to go too far. Those decisions can legitimately be challenged as protectionism pure and simple. Note, however, that in all three cases studied, domestic demand had undergone a severe downturn and imports were capturing an increasing share of the domestic market even as that market showed some signs of recovering. Recall the test suggested earlier under the "escape clause;" namely that if, during periods of declining demand or cyclically weak demand, imports exhibit a non-trivial increase in market share, they would be presumed a legally sufficient cause of any injury suffered by the domestic industry unless that injury was clearly attributable to other factors unrelated to

---

22 Among the other factors listed in a footnote to Article 3:4 are "contraction in demand or changes in the patterns of consumption."

23 While the Commission Report marks the volume of imports from Taiwan as confidential we can use these assumptions because the Report gives the figures for Canada and Israel. Thus, we know that imports from the latter two countries were 5.9% of domestic consumption in 1985, 3.8% in 1984 and 2.2% in 1983. Next, Commissioner Liebeler stated that the aggregate for the three countries never exceeded 6%. We use that figure for 1985 because the Commission says that the market penetration rate by the cumulated imports increased in each of the years under investigation. This also means that the rate for imports from Taiwan were .1% in 1985 and less than that in the earlier years. Hence we assume an aggregate market penetration rate for all three countries of slightly over 2.2% in 1983, 3.9% in 1984 and 6% in 1985.

either the imports or to general macro-economic conditions. Apply this test to the three cases discussed in this section. Does it show promise as a reformulation which might allow repeal of the antidumping statute?

CHAPTER 6

PRESCRIPTIVE JURISDICTION

*Introduction: An Historical Note
and a Basic Perspective*

In this Chapter we begin to explore the problem of defining the people and events that may properly be made subject to national law when all or some of those events occur or people reside outside the territory of the prescriptive State. Understandably, in addressing this subject, courts and commentators sometimes refer to the "extra-territorial" effect of law. The lack of precision in that reference, however, too often serves only to mislead. We shall not use the word here. If any reference is necessary, "transnational" effect of law comes closer to the mark.

The subject is "prescriptive jurisdiction" or "competence to prescribe." As such, it must be distinguished from "personal" and "subject-matter" jurisdiction. The latter pertain to the power of national courts.[1] "Prescriptive jurisdiction," on the other hand, pertains to the power of a sovereign State to prescribe the substantive law governing particular conduct and it does not matter whether that law emanates from the legislature, the executive or the courts of the sovereign. It is the sovereign power itself, not the power of courts as components of the institutional sovereign, that is at issue.

I

In the world today, as throughout the modern era, law emanates principally from and is applied through the official organs of politically independent, nominally equal sovereign States. Sovereignty, in turn, is generally attributed only to political organizations that exhibit an effective power of governance over the people who live and events which occur within a defined geographical area. Nineteenth Century writers saw it clearly. The only law that could have effect within the territory of a truly sovereign State was, they said, law emanating from the official organs of that State. If one then observes a world community composed of numerous States each possessing these attributes and if the stability of that structure is thought to be desirable, a normative precept logically ensues. A political organization that is sovereign over the people of one territory cannot be and, with structural stability in mind, ought not claim to be sovereign — to prescribe and apply rules — over people in the territory of another sovereign state. Quite naturally, in other words, national law-making authority is thought of as territorially bound and territoriality emerges as a normative principle which tends to render any claim that transgresses its limits a cause for diplomatic protest,

---

[1] "Personal jurisdiction" pertains to whether a national court has power over the particular parties to a dispute; "subject-matter" jurisdiction concerns the authority of a national court to entertain a particular class or type of dispute.

retaliation or even war. Moreover, if all of this sounds a bit abstract and archaic, one need only observe that the "territorial principle" comes to the modern world supported by some of the most compelling allegiances known to the human race; to a land, to a people, to institutions, a language and a history; to all that makes a Nation.

On the other hand, if sovereignty is territorial, law is functional, and increasingly, in the modern world, the territorial principle has come into conflict with the very nature of law itself. More and more national governments use law to regulate and otherwise redirect private behavior in accord with social values and national policies that would not otherwise be accomplished if individuals were left to pursue their own ends. In this role, law tends, by the logic of its function, to claim a "right" to govern any people and any event necessary to the achievement of its objectives and to reject as irrational any limitation — territorial or otherwise — that might frustrate those objectives. Consider, for example, an antitrust law intended to secure the benefits of competitive markets to consumers living within or businesses trading from a particular territory. Logically that function implies a claim of right to proscribe anticompetitive behavior by any buyer or any seller anywhere in the world once it is shown that their behavior would, in fact, deny the benefits of competition to the consumers and traders intended to be protected.

No less than with the territorial principle, such national claims to transnational prescriptive power are at times undergird by powerful popular sentiments. A popular sense of great purpose or urgent necessity is the very stuff from which the modern regulatory State draws its sustenance. In such a setting, certain pragmatic realities, rather than abstract precepts, are likely to be the chief force for moderation and restraint. A lack of power, in fact, to enforce its law or a fear of retaliation by other sovereigns, or a concern lest a lack of self-restraint encourage others to tender matching claims on behalf of hostile policies are likely to be the principal restraints upon the fuller assertions of a national competence to prescribe. And because this is so, these pragmatic realities must find a place in the substance of legal doctrine.

If the conflict between the territorial principle and the expansive tendencies of the modern regulatory State furnishes the essential setting for a contemporary study of prescriptive jurisdiction, the complexity and importance of the subject can be fully appreciated only by reference to the incredible increase that has occurred since World War II in the volume and ease with which things, money, people and ideas — the inevitable objects of national regulation — move across national boundaries. We have already noted the extraordinary expansion in world trade that has occurred since the end of World War II.[2] Also, since the War, the free world has fashioned a single, global capital market. Virtually nothing can occur in any major center of that market without having an immediate effect on centers, even whole economies, elsewhere. In like manner the elaboration and development of the multinational corporation has vastly enhanced the ease and frequency with which people, goods, money and ideas can and do move across national boundaries.

---

[2] Chapter 3, page 189 *supra*.

These developments have contributed enormously to the economic well-being of the nations that are part of the system. Precisely because of this success, however, each participant has a greater stake in the system as a whole and may face a greater temptation or feel a greater need to regulate it in ways designed to enhance or protect its own interests; ways bound to conflict with the regulatory efforts of other nations.

Lastly, as we have already taken note, there is a festering problem lying just under the surface of this record of rising prosperity. Nations whose people constitute nearly one half of the human race have been largely left out of the post-war experience. Even were this problem solved in the near future, the disparity has already engendered a climate of bitterness and disappointment certain to yield widening claims to national prescriptive power. That, in the past, such claims have enhanced neither global welfare nor the real welfare of their proponents is beside the point. They are acts of political desperation and, as such, intrude a new and volatile element into any effort at ordering the world economy through law.

Now, as all that we have thus far studied indicates many of these conflicts can best be contained through direct negotiation at a political level. The General Agreement on Tariffs and Trade (GATT), the International Monetary Fund (IMF), the United Nations Conference on Trade and Development (UNCTAD), the United Nations Law of the Sea Conference are only some of the more notable institutional manifestations of this reality. Yet, the political process can only operate at a certain level of generality. There still remains the task of working out, day-to-day, case-by-case the precise meaning of any political arrangement. There is, in addition, the task of dealing with matters upon which political consensus or compromise cannot be reached; where the most to be hoped for is the minimizing of conflict. These tasks, in the end, must be left largely to national institutions, especially courts, working within a framework of subtle interaction between a national and a customary international law of prescriptive jurisdiction. Moreover, for one trained in the common law, there is always the abiding question of whether some points of conflict might better be left to the incremental and more flexible processes of customary law than to the more ambitious and oft-times rigid generalizations of "positive" law, whether treaty or statute.

II

If complexity is the first condition to be recognized in any contemporary study of prescriptive jurisdiction, the second is the inadequacy of the law as it now stands; the law which must be the point of departure for any such study.

There are, for this purpose, two, as yet, quite separate bodies of law; so-called "public" international law and "private" international law or, in Anglo-American parlance, the Conflict of Laws. Under the influence of Vatel, it was, by the middle of the 19th Century, a generally accepted principle that international law, as such, pertained only to relations between sovereigns; hence the appellation "public" international law. There remained, however, that vast body of law employed largely by domestic courts in dealing with disputes arising out of private transnational relations; "private" international law. In the works of both Continental and Anglo-American writers there was, throughout much of the 19th Century, no sharp discontinuity between these two. By the latter decades of that century, however, a complete separation had occurred, at least in Anglo-American jurisprudence. One no longer spoke of "private" international law, but of the "Conflict of Laws," and under the tutelage of Austinian positivism, the latter had become domestic law pure and simple. The result of this separation was telling.

With regard to "public" international law, the 1935 Harvard Research[3] identified five general principles which the international community had come to recognize as bases upon which a nation might apply its criminal law to particular conduct, as follows:

— the "territorial principle," (the conduct took place in the national territory);

— the "nationality principle" (the person committing the offense was a citizen);

— the "protective principle" (the conduct was injurious to a fundamental national interest);

— the "universality principle," (the offender was in custody);

— the "passive personality principle" (the victim was a citizen).

Of these, the Harvard study concluded, the "territorial principle" is "everywhere regarded as of primary importance and of fundamental character." The "nationality principle," although universally accepted, was marked by wide differences in use. The others did not, according to the study, command wide acceptance and only when used as a basis for punishing pirates did the "universality principle" command any significant recognition at all.

We will, of course, take a closer look at these principles. While the Harvard study was concerned only with the criminal law, the ensuing materials illustrate how insistently they have been applied to nearly all forms of public regulation of private conduct. At this juncture, however, it is important to observe that these principles treat the problem of prescriptive jurisdiction not as though it involved choosing between conflicting sovereign claims to prescriptive authority but solely as though it involved determining if one sovereign's claim, viewed unilaterally, was legitimate. The rules are framed and applied from an entirely "unilateral perspective;" a perspective ill equipped to deal with modern reality.

Nevertheless, throughout the 19th Century and well into this Century, this unilateral approach, with the "territorial principle" as touchstone, worked reasonably well. It was applied only to those laws pursuant to which national public institutions directly intervened in private affairs either through the courts or through the exercise of some form of prerogative power. This so-called "public" law, in turn, performed a very limited social function. Apart from Constitutional law, the principal forms of domestic "public" law were the criminal law and the revenue laws.

Throughout most of the 19th Century, national revenue laws took the form almost exclusively of customs and other excise duties. The purpose of such laws could largely be accomplished by levies against imports or exports or other local exchanges of goods or as a condition upon the grant of a right to own local property

---

[3] Harvard Research on International Law: Jurisdiction With Respect to Crime, 29 Am. J. Int L., Supp. 1, 435 (1935).

or practice a profession locally or maintain a local craft or business establishment. Their purpose, in other words, could largely be accomplished within the confines of strictly local taxable events and, as such, were unlikely to come into conflict with the laws of other sovereigns.

The same was also true of the criminal law. Reflecting the then dominant "laissez faire" theory of the state, national criminal laws were largely confined to punishing for those traditional breaches of the peace, or depredations against property, which society has always found minimally necessary for the maintenance of order. Again the purpose of these laws could largely be accomplished within the confines of local occurrences offering few opportunities for conflict with foreign law. The unilateral perspective tended to conform to the realities of international life.

There were, of course, exceptions. Ships posed a particular problem never fully answered by subsuming the ship into the territory of the nation whose flag it flew. Competence to prescribe for conduct aboard ship, to punish for causing collisions at sea, to regulate the relationship between the shipowner and the crew and, on occasion, to control use of the ship itself, were issues that tended to bedevil the "law of the flag." The same was true of mail and telegraphic frauds, where the sender was in one nation and the victim in another. Fraud against the government, crimes against ambassadors and other diplomats and treason could also, on occasion, lead governments to legislate with respect to conduct in another nation's territory. To meet these latter situations the protective and nationality principles were devised. Since, however, the need for such departures from the territorial principle were universally felt by all governments, they posed no serious point of conflict so long as confined to such shared necessities.[4]

If the prevailing "public" law regimes of the 19th Century posed few challenges to the "territorial principle," and were reasonably well suited to a unilateral analytic approach, the same was not true for "private" international law. People, things and money, then as now, moved across national boundaries. Contracts were made in one place to be performed in another; banks lent money to borrowers and corporations sold securities to investors throughout the Western world; equipment manufactured in one country broke down and caused injuries to people in another.

On the other hand, courts were chosen to resolve disputes arising out of these far flung affairs on the basis of party convenience or according to rules of "personal" jurisdiction that took little note of the substantive law that might properly govern the courts' deliberations. The result was predictable. When courts

---

[4] If there was any strong impulse to give extended effect to a nation's general criminal law, it stemmed from the desire of Western nations to protect their own citizens against the vagaries of alien systems that were not considered part of the civilized world. While dangerous in its potential for conflict, this pre-emptive impulse, sanctioned by the nationality principle, was rarely called for in the case of citizens living or traveling within the Western community. Since it was the practice of this community alone that gave shape to international law, any conflict with the prescriptive claims of "uncivilized" sovereigns could, insofar as the content of that law was concerned, be ignored. Within the relevant community, in other words, the conflict simply did not occur with a regularity that might have threatened the efficacy of the system.

so selected turned to the substance of their task, they quickly discovered that any principle commanding them to judge solely according to their own substantive law, was unworkable. Such parochialism could too often yield judgments contrary to the clear, and sometimes expressed, expectations of the parties. It threatened to intrude a new and unpredictable element into the planning of private affairs. It tended to encourage forum shopping and, on occasion, gave offense to the interests or sensibilities of foreign sovereigns. Even as legal theorists laid down the "territorial principle" in terms which seemed to preclude the application in any territory of any law other than that of the territorial sovereign, they confronted a need to circumvent their own premises. Practical justice and the good order of the international community required no less. The conflict between the territorial principle, on the one hand, and law, as an ordering device and a functional expression of social values, on the other, was already apparent even in the laissez-faire atmosphere of the 19th Century.

The history of the effort in Anglo-American jurisprudence to deal with this conflict properly begins with the publication, in 1834, of Joseph Story's great treatise on the Conflict of Laws.[5] Drawing upon the work of the 17th Century Dutch commentator Huber, Story acknowledged the territorial principle in the preclusive terms which by then had become customary. Then, however, he argued that the proper approach to the conflict of laws that would inevitably arise was expressed in the notion of "comity;" the idea that all sovereigns have a stake in the larger order of the international community which may, on occasion, require that they set aside their claim to preclusive power within their own territory and render deference to the laws of another State. Deference, he thought, was dictated by the stake that each nation had in the good order of all. Story wrote:

> The true foundation on which the administration of international law must rest is that the rules, which are to govern, are those which arise from mutual interest and utility, from a sense of the inconveniences which would result from a contrary doctrine, a sort of moral necessity to do justice, in order that justice may be done to us in turn.[6]

To Story, "comity" was, quite plainly, the working out of the needs of the international community; a normative underpinning to all international law. It partook of the character of "public" law. "It is not," [he said] "the comity of the courts, but the comity of the nation, which is administered." Nor, to Story, did comity have a content from which judges might deduce specific doctrine. Story's was the method of the common law. As a reference to the efficacy of using foreign law and to the values and pragmatic goals consonant with that use, comity was discoverable in the decisions of the common law courts. As such, it served to explain, to lend coherence, and to direct the further application of those decisions.

> It is not the comity of the courts, but the comity of the nation which is administered, and ascertained in the same way, and guided by the same reasoning, by which all other principles of the municipal law are ascertained and guided.[7]

---

[5] J. Story, Commentaries On The Conflict Of Laws (1834).

[6] *Id.* at page 34.

[7] *Id.* at page 37.

Simple, coupled with an imaginative apprehension of basic values and pragmatic realities, all of this has a very contemporary ring. Story's sensitivity to the public stake in the resolution of private disputes evidences a certain disdain for the distinction between public and private international law. In its tie to the common law method — the incremental working through of experience in a changing context — lies a flexibility that bespeaks the creative growth of law. Our task today would have been very different had the law of prescriptive jurisdiction, in the years since Story wrote, been built upon his seminal insights. Unhappily, this did not occur.

Starting with the latter half of the 19th Century and continuing well into the early decades of this Century, Anglo-American legal thought was decisively influenced by Austinian Positivism. According to Austin, law was "sovereign command" — essentially legislative command. To fit this definition, the common law was said to be a closed system of extant rules which the judges were only empowered to discover and apply. As a system of extant rules, it continued to exist only at the sufferance of the sovereign legislature, and hence assumed the aspect of a legislative command, albeit an indirect one.

One can readily discern why, under the tutelage of so crabbed a jurisprudence, Storian internationalism withered. In the hands of those great Austinians, Dicey in England and later Joseph Beale in the United States, the Conflict of Laws became municipal law pure and simple, and municipal law uninstructed, at least in theory, by state practice or by any reciprocal concern for the common values and goals of the international community. That something called "law" might be drawn out of the shared values, customs and needs of a community of independent sovereign states, or that something called "law" might serve those needs and reinforce those values, were propositions which the Austinians all but disdained. Moreover, if law were "sovereign command" and sovereignty was territorial, the "territorial principle" necessarily assumed a decisive place in the development of Conflicts doctrine.

Yet, these stoic theorists had chosen as their subject the "conflict of laws;" a subject uniquely borne of the need to choose between contending laws. It was a subject created by the stubborn unwillingness of people to confine their affairs to the constricting boundaries of a single State and their propensity to plan those affairs by reference to laws that were not necessarily the law of the courts to which their disputes were referred.

The device used by Dicey and Beale to reconcile theory with this reality was pure period piece. They developed the doctrine of "vested rights." Once the "territorial sovereign," through its law, had "vested" the rights of the parties to a dispute, it was for the "forum" sovereign, as an exercise of its own sovereign power, to recognize, *not a foreign law*, but a "vested" private right. All that remained, under such a structure, was to identify the "true" territorial sovereign whose law would fix those rights. Again, the "territorial principle" was vindicated. It was for the "forum" sovereign, through its own Conflicts rules, to make that determination.

What followed, in the works of Dicey and Beale, was an elaborate series of mechanistic, but not unimaginative rules for selecting the State whose law should give rise to the "vested rights" that the forum was to vindicate. In contract disputes it was generally the place of contracting; in tort, the place of the wrong; in debtor-creditor disputes, the situs of the debt; in family matters the place of "domicile" and so forth. In form, this was a system for choosing law. But the mechanistic character of the rules, the tendency to assign preclusive authority to the law selected, the denial of any creative "law-making" role to the courts, all tended to deprive the system of any aspect of reasoned judicial choice, at least any broad-based choice encompassing public policy or the needs of the international order.

There were two important exceptions to this system. First, courts in the "forum" State would not enforce any "vested" right offensive to some fundamental precept of the "forum" sovereign embodied in the latter's *public policy* or *ordre public*. Secondly, since enforcement of the penal and revenue laws of a State were typically at the instance of the State itself, such laws could not be run through the saving fiction of the "vested" private rights theory. Hence, it became universal dogma that the courts of one State would not recognize much less enforce the *penal* or *revenue* laws of another.

These last two exceptions help explain the persistence with which courts and commentators, even after the modern revolution in Conflicts doctrine, have tended to answer all questions pertaining to the prescriptive reach of regulatory legislation by reference to the traditional rules of "public" international law. It is as though such legislation, as "public" law, with an implication of strong "public policy," could not be entrusted to the choice of law process of "private" international law. Yet, the propensity to ignore that process poses a major obstacle to the development of a more adequate law of prescriptive jurisdiction. The potential for conflict between the "public" laws of two sovereign States, each undergirded by strong public policies, and the need to choose between these two laws, describes precisely the principal problem confronting the law of prescriptive jurisdiction today. Certainly no adequate law will develop so long as courts and commentators withdraw all such conflicts from any broad-based system of reasoned choice and consign them automatically to the constructs of traditional "public" international law; to a unilateral perspective dominated by the "territorial principle" and developed primarily with 19th Century criminal law in mind.

In spite of its mechanistic approach the Bealian system for the choice of law did, in a fashion and for a time, work. So long as the community of Western nations subscribed to a large body of common legal principles and shared a strong aversion to State direction of private affairs, the settlement of the "choice of law" problem in any single private controversy was unlikely to threaten any strongly held governmental view or overriding State interest. At least the threats were rare enough to permit a system of mechanical rules, devised without regard for the policies underlying the relevant substantive law, to operate reasonably well.

By the early decades of this Century the system began to crack. It floundered badly when called upon to deal with the effects on private arrangements of a number of 20th Century perturbations that heralded the end of laissez-faire. With the rising concern for distributive justice came the break up of the policy consensus that characterized the substance of so much 19th Century private law in the West. Legal heterogeneity became even more pervasive as, in the years following World War II, a host of new non-Western nations joined the community of States, each with its own unique indigenous and colonial tradition and its own experience with modernization. By mid-Century the fundamental conditions upon which the Bealian system depended for its continued serviceability were simply no longer in place.

Equally important, starting with the second decade of this Century, the older Bealian system was subjected to a merciless scholarly critique. At one level, the critics were able to show that the older system was neither as productive of certainty nor as principled as it pretended to be. They dissected the cases to demonstrate that too often the rules yielded perverse results. From this they argued that the system's apparent serviceability depended heavily upon the willingness of judges to escape or manipulate the rules in order to reach sensible results. The vagaries of characterization, manipulation of the substance-procedure distinction, the adjustable contours of the "public policy" exception, the "renvoi" were only some of the devices that robbed the system of its vaunted claim to certainty and principled neutrality. More telling, this false claim of certainty not only concealed the result oriented character of many court decisions, it concealed the bases used in deciding upon those results. It fostered, they said, decisions designed to serve undisclosed social purposes chosen according to unrevealed criteria.

For our purpose the most telling consequence of this critical onslaught was the dispelling of the territorial myth. It cut Conflicts doctrine loose from the false search for the "true" or single legitimate territorial sovereign. In so doing it also forestalled the tendency to force doctrine into a unilateral mode and emphasized the need to formulate comprehensive principles to guide in a process of reasoned choice. We need not pause here to review the rich, and at times heated, debate that took place and continues to take place as courts and commentators work to sharpen the content of that process. Some of the debate is reflected in the materials that follow. Here we note only that, disagreement aside, there has emerged a substantial consensus around certain basic social values that should enter into a process of reasoned choice; the need to fulfill party expectations, to render results as predictable as possible, to simplify the judicial task, and perhaps most important, the need to secure to governments a proper regard for their interests and to foster, through a kind Storian mutual respect and reciprocity, a system in which the conflicting interests of States can be resolved without threatening those vital interests which, if not respected, tend to invite reprisal and the break down of order.

III

Against the background of this all too brief historical sketch, it should be plain that we now stand at a critical point in the evolution of our thinking about prescriptive jurisdiction. The prospect is for ever burgeoning national claims of power to regulate transnational economic and business relationships and for increasing conflicts among those claims. Yet, in the effort to contain these conflicts, traditional public international law, with its unilateral perspective and its preoccupation with the territorial principle, is a manifestly inadequate instrument even though it cannot be ignored. To test this the reader will want to observe in the ensuing materials how often it is clear that one nation cannot logically accuse the other of an "extraterritorial" jurisdiction without, at the same time, logically defeating its own claim to "territorial" jurisdiction or, *vice versa*, how often the accuser's claim to "territorial" authority is equally available to its protagonist. Where this occurs — and in a transnational setting it occurs with frequency — traditional "public" international law is no law at all. Worse, its unilateral perspective and purportedly neutral principles serve too often to conceal what is essentially a policy oriented choice of law. If any law is to exist, in other words, it must be predicated upon a broadly based paradigm of choice, capable of treating true conflicts between basic national values and interests differently from mere conflicts of pride and sovereign pretension, and capable, unapologetically, of weighing conflicting values and interests according to prevailing international practice and the practical political and economic goals of the international community.

So fundamental a reorientation has begun, having received a hopefully powerful impetus in the new Restatement (Third) of the Foreign Relations Law of the United States. But this is only the beginning. Most of the experience available to guide in elaborating a broadly based system of reasoned choice is far from definitive. It has not been universally accepted. It has been concerned, almost exclusively, with the law of private disputes; the law of contracts, of torts, and of property. If increasingly those laws have come to embody distinctive national policies and social values — in only a limited sense are they "private" law — they are nevertheless often very different from the regulatory law that is of concern here. A nation may attach public importance to a rule of comparative negligence, a rule that voids an unconscionable contract, or a wrongful death statute. Rarely, however, do such matters rank in public importance with laws designed to assure an economic system based upon competitive markets, or to curtail fraud in the sale of securities or to secure compliance with a nation's international monetary policies or to prevent trading with an enemy. Laws of this latter kind, whether invoked directly by public authority or derivatively in the settlement of private disputes, reflect national interests and evoke ethical and political values with an intensity rarely found in the mandates of the more traditional areas of so-called "private" law. As such, conflicts between such regulatory enactments are likely to be far less amenable to resolution through reasoned principles and more threatening to the good order of the international community.

To begin exploring how far we have come and where we may go, we start, in this Chapter, by exploring some recurrent themes: the traditional international law of prescriptive jurisdiction; an emerging U.S. foreign relations law on the subject, including the changes wrought by the Restatement; and the relationship between this emerging body of foreign relations law and both customary international law and treaties. In later Chapters, the ideas developed here are given a wider testing through an examination of the transnational reach of the anti-trust laws, export control and corrupt practices legislation, to mention a few.

§ 6.01 The Traditional "Public" International Law

In this section we examine the traditional public international law of prescriptive jurisdiction as applied to the criminal law. The propensity of courts and commentators to extend these rules to non-criminal forms of economic regulation will become obvious in subsequent chapters.

THE S.S. LOTUS

France v. Turkey

Permanent Court of International Justice, 1927

P.C.I.J. Ser. A., No. 10.

* * * *

The Facts

* * * *

On August 2nd, 1926, just before midnight, a collision occurred between the French mail steamer *Lotus*, proceeding to Constantinople, and the Turkish collier *Boz-Kourt*, between five and six nautical miles to the north of Cape Sigri (Mitylene). The *Boz-Kourt*, which was cut in two, sank, and eight Turkish nationals who were on board perished. After having done everything possible to succour the shipwrecked persons, of whom ten were able to be saved, the *Lotus* continued on its course to Constantinople, where it arrived on August 3rd.

At the time of the collision, the officer of the watch on board the *Lotus* was Monsieur Demons, a French citizen, lieutenant in the merchant service and first officer of the ship, whilst the movements of the *Boz-Kourt* were directed by its captain, Hassan Bey, who was one of those saved from the wreck.

As early as August 3rd the Turkish police proceeded to hold an inquiry into the collision. . . . On August 5th, Lieutenant Demons was requested by the Turkish authorities to go ashore to give evidence. Th[is] examination . . . led to the . . . arrest of Lieutenant Demons . . . and Hassan Bey, amongst others [on a charge of manslaughter].

As a result of [French protests against the arrest and trial of M. Demons] . . . the two Governments appointed their plenipotentiaries with a view to the drawing up of [a] special agreement to be submitted to the . . . [Permanent Court of International Justice at The Hague]. . . . This special agreement was signed at Geneva on October 12th, 1926.

[According to the special agreement the Court was asked to decided two questions as follows:

(1) Has Turkey acted in conflict with the principles of international law by instituting joint criminal proceedings in pursuance of Turkish law against M. Demons, officer of the watch on board the *Lotus* at the time of the collision?

(2) Should the reply be in the affirmative, what pecuniary reparation is due to M. Demons ?]

The Law

* * * *

The prosecution was instituted in pursuance of Turkish legislation. The special agreement does not indicate what clause or clauses of that legislation apply. . . .

[But], even if the Court must hold that the Turkish authorities had seen fit to base the prosecution of Lieutenant Demons upon . . . Article 6 [of the Turkish Penal Code][1] the question submitted to the Court is not whether that article is compatible with the principles of international law; it is more general. The Court is asked to state whether or not the principles of international law prevent Turkey from instituting criminal proceedings against Lieutenant Demons under Turkish law. Neither the conformity of Article 6 in itself with the principles of international law nor the application of that article by the Turkish authorities constitutes the point at issue; it is the very fact of the institution of proceedings which is held by France to be contrary to those principles. . . .

* * * *

The French government [also] contends that the Turkish Courts, in order to have jurisdiction, should be able to point to some title to jurisdiction recognized by international law in favor of Turkey. On the other hand, the Turkish Government takes the view that . . . Turkey [has] jurisdiction whenever such jurisdiction does not come into conflict with a principle of international law.

The latter view seems to be in conformity with the special agreement itself. According to . . . [that] agreement, it is not a question of stating principles which would permit Turkey to take criminal proceedings, but of formulating the principles, if any, which might have been violated by such proceedings.

This way of stating the question is also dictated by the very nature and existing conditions of international law.

International law governs relations between independent States. The rules of law binding upon States therefore emanate from their own free will as expressed in conventions or by usages generally accepted . . . and restrictions upon the independence of States cannot therefore be presumed.

* * * *

According to the . . . [French view, however,] . . . the exclusively territorial character of law constitutes a principle which, except as otherwise expressly provided, would, *ipso facto*, prevent States from extending the criminal jurisdiction of their courts beyond their frontiers; the exceptions in question, which include for instance extraterritorial jurisdiction over nationals and over crimes directed against public safety, would therefore rest on special permissive rules forming part of international law.

Adopting, for the purposes of the argument, this standpoint . . . it must be recognized that, in the absence of a treaty provision, its correctness depends upon whether there is a custom having the force of law establishing it. The same is true

---

[1] Article 6 of the Turkish Penal Code, Law No. 765 of March 1st, 1926 (Official Gazette No. 320 of March 13th, 1926), provided that:

Any foreigner who, apart from the cases contemplated by Article 4, commits an offense abroad to the prejudice of Turkey or of a Turkish subject, for which offense Turkish law prescribes a penalty involving loss of freedom for a minimum period of not less than one year, shall be punished in accordance with the Turkish Penal Code provided that he is arrested in Turkey. The penalty shall however be reduced by one third and instead of the death penalty, twenty years of penal servitude shall be awarded.

as regards the applicability of this system — assuming it to have been recognized as sound — in the particular case. It follows that, even from this point of view, before ascertaining whether there may be a rule of international law expressly allowing Turkey to prosecute a foreigner for an offense committed by him outside Turkey, it is necessary to begin by establishing both that the system is well-founded and that it is applicable in the particular case. Now, in order to establish the first of these points, one must, as has just been seen, prove the existence of a principle of international law restricting the discretion of States as regards criminal legislation.

Consequently, whichever of the two systems described above be adopted, the same result will be arrived at in this particular case: the necessity of ascertaining whether or not under international law there is a principle which would have prohibited Turkey, in the circumstances of the case before the Court, from prosecuting Lieutenant Demons.

The Court will now proceed [to consider that question]. . . . The arguments advanced by the French Government . . . are, in substance, the three following:

(1) International law does not allow a State to take proceedings with regard to offenses committed by foreigners abroad, simply by reason of the nationality of the victim; and such is the situation in the present case because the offense must be regarded as having been committed on board the French vessel.

(2) International law recognizes the exclusive jurisdiction of the State whose flag is flown as regards everything which occurs on board a ship on the high seas.

(3) Lastly, this principle is especially applicable in a collision case.

As regards the first . . . contention, [it] only relates to the case where the nationality of the victim is the only criterion on which the criminal jurisdiction of the State is based. Even if that argument were correct generally speaking — and in regard to this the Court reserves its opinion — it could only be used in the present case if international law forbade Turkey to take into consideration the fact that the offense produced its effects on the Turkish vessel and consequently in a place assimilated to Turkish territory in which the application of Turkish criminal law cannot be challenged, even in regard to offenses committed there by foreigners. But no such rule of international law exists. No argument has come to the knowledge of the Court from which it could be deduced that States recognize themselves to be under an obligation towards each other only to have regard to the place where the author of the offense happens to be at the time of the offense. On the contrary, it is certain that the courts of many countries, even of countries which have given their criminal legislation a strictly territorial character, interpret criminal law in the sense that offenses, the authors of which at the moment of commission are in territory of another State, are nevertheless to be regarded as having been committed in the national territory, if one of the constituent elements of the offense, and more especially its effects, have taken place there. . . . Consequently, once it is admitted that the effects of the offense were produced on the Turkish vessel, it becomes impossible to hold that there is a rule of international law which prohibits Turkey from prosecuting Lieutenant Demons because of the fact that the author of the offense was on board the French ship. Since, as has already been observed, the special agreement does not deal with the provision of Turkish law under which the prosecution was instituted, . . . there is no reason prosecution may . . . [not] be justified from the point of view of the so-called territorial principle.

It has been sought to argue that the offense of manslaughter cannot be localized at the spot where the mortal effect is felt; for the effect is not intentional and it cannot be said that there is, in the mind of the delinquent, any culpable intent directed towards the territory where the mortal effect is produced. In reply to this argument it might be observed that the effect is a factor of outstanding importance in offenses such as manslaughter, which are punished precisely in consideration of their effects rather than of the subjective intention of the delinquent. But the Court does not feel called upon to consider this question, which is one of interpretation of Turkish criminal law. It will suffice to observe that no argument has been put forward and nothing has been found from which it would follow that international law has established a rule imposing on States this reading of the conception of the offense of manslaughter.

* * * *

The second argument put forward by the French Government is the principle that the State whose flag is flown has exclusive jurisdiction over everything which occurs on board a merchant ship on the high seas.

It is certainly true that — apart from certain special cases which are defined by international law — vessels on the high seas are subject to no authority except that of the State whose flag they fly. . . . But it by no means follows that a State can never in its own territory exercise jurisdiction over acts which have occurred on board a foreign ship on the high seas. . . . All that can be said is that by virtue of the principle of the freedom of the seas, a ship is placed in the same position as national territory; but there is nothing to support the claim according to which the rights of the State under whose flag the vessel sails may go farther than the rights which it exercises within its territory properly so called. . . . If, therefore, a guilty act committed on the high seas produces its effects on a vessel flying another flag or in foreign territory, the same principles must be applied as if the territories of two different States were concerned. . . .

This conclusion could only be overcome if it were shown that there was a rule of customary international law which, going further than the principle stated above, established the exclusive jurisdiction of the State whose flag was flown.

The cases in which the exclusive jurisdiction of the States whose flag was flown has been recognized would seem . . . to have been cases in which the foreign State was interested only by reason of the nationality of the victim. . . .

As regards conventions expressly reserving jurisdiction exclusively to the State whose flag is flown, . . . it should be observed that these conventions relate to matters of a particular kind, closely connected with the policing of the seas, such as the slave trade, damage to submarine cables, fisheries, etc., and not to common-law offenses. Above all it should be pointed out that the offenses contemplated by the conventions in question only concern a single ship: it is impossible therefore to make any deduction from them in regard to matters which concern two ships and consequently the jurisdiction of two different States.

* * * *

It only remains to examine the third argument advanced by the French Government and to ascertain whether a rule especially applying to collision cases has grown up, according to which criminal proceedings regarding such cases come exclusively within the jurisdiction of the State whose flag is flown.

In this connection, the Agent for the French Government has drawn the Court's attention to the fact that questions of jurisdiction in collision cases, which frequently arise before civil courts, are but rarely encountered in the practice of criminal courts. He deduces from this that, in practice, prosecutions only occur before the courts of the State whose flag is flown and that circumstance is proof of a tacit consent on the part of States and, consequently, shows what positive international law is in collision cases.

In the Court's opinion, this conclusion is not warranted . . . [t]he rarity of . . . judicial decisions . . . merely show[s] that States ha[ve] often, in practice, abstained from instituting criminal proceedings, and not that they recognized themselves as being obliged to do so. . . .

So far as the Court is aware there are no decisions of international tribunals in this matter; but some decisions of municipal courts have been cited. [With respect to those decisions it] . . . will suffice to observe that, as municipal jurisprudence is . . . divided, it is hardly possible to see in it an indication of the existence of the restrictive rule of international law which alone could serve as a basis for the contention of the French Government.

In support of [its theory, France has] . . . contended that it is a question of the observance of the national regulations of each merchant marine and that effective punishment does not consist so much in the infliction of some months imprisonment upon the captain as in the cancellation of his certificate as master, that is to say, in depriving him of the command of his ship.

In regard to this, the Court must observe that in the present case a prosecution was instituted for an offense at criminal law and not for a breach of discipline. Neither the necessity of taking administrative regulations into account . . . nor the impossibility of applying certain disciplinary penalties can prevent the application of criminal law and of penal measures of repression.

The conclusion at which the Court has therefore arrived is that there is no rule of international law in regard to collision cases to the effect that criminal proceedings are exclusively within the jurisdiction of the State whose flag is flown.

Having thus answered the first question submitted by the special agreement in the negative, the Court need not consider the second question, regarding the pecuniary reparation which might have been due to Lieutenant Demons.

For these reasons, the Court . . . gives, by the President's casting vote — the votes being equally divided — judgment to the effect . . . [that] Turkey, by instituting criminal proceedings . . . against Lieutenant Demons . . . has not acted in conflict with the principles of international law.

Dissenting Opinion by M. Loder

Turkey argues from . . . [the] facts that M. Demons . . . is guilty of manslaughter and that . . . this offense took place on board the *Boz-Kourt* because it was there that the effects of the alleged negligence were felt. She therefore contends that the wrongful act having taken place on board the Turkish ship, its author is amenable to the jurisdiction of the Turkish Courts. . . . The question of the localization of the offense is therefore of capital importance for the purposes of the decision of the dispute before the Court.

It is clear that the place where an offense has been committed is necessarily that where the guilty person is when he commits the act. The assumption that the place where the effect is produced is the place where the act was committed is in every case a legal fiction. It is, however, justified where the act and its effect are indistinguishable, when there is a direct relation between them; for instance, a shot fired at a person on the other side of a frontier; a parcel containing an infernal machine intended to explode on being opened by the person to whom it is sent. The author of the crime intends in such cases to inflict injury at a place other than that where he himself is.

But the case which the Court has to consider bears no resemblance to these instances. The officer of the *Lotus*, who had never set foot on board the *Boz Kourt*, had no intention of injuring anyone, and no such intention is imputed to him. In these circumstances, it seems to me that the legal fiction whereby the act is held to have been committed at the place where the effect is produced must be discarded.

* * * *

The general rule that the criminal law of a State loses its compelling force and its applicability in relation to offenses committed by a foreigner in foreign territory . . . has indeed undergone modifications and has been made subject to exceptions. . . . But according to a generally accepted view, this is not the case as regards the high seas. There the law of the flag and national jurisdiction have retained their indisputable authority to the exclusion of all foreign law or jurisdiction. . . .

This applies with especial force to the case now before the Court. The accusation against Lieutenant Demons is that whilst navigating his ship he gave an order for a wrong manoeuvre. The rules for navigation which he was obliged to follow were those contained in his national regulations. He was responsible to his national authorities for the observance of these rules. It was solely for these authorities to consider whether the officer had observed these rules, whether he had done his duty, and, if not, whether he had neglected their observance to such a degree as to have incurred criminal responsibility. It consequently seems to me that Turkey, in arrogating to herself jurisdiction over the acts of a foreign officer doing duty on the high seas on a ship carrying a foreign flag, has acted in contravention of . . . international law.

On these grounds I regret that I am unable to concur with the Court in its present judgment.

Dissenting Opinion by Lord Finlay

* * * *

It was argued for Turkey that the *delit* committed by Demons was committed on board the *Boz-Kourt* when by a faulty manoeuvre of his she was struck by the

Lotus, and as the *Boz-Kourt* was a Turkish ship she must, it was said, be regarded as part of Turkish territory, and the delit was therefore committed on Turkish territory as much as if it had been committed on shore within the territorial limits of Turkey.

This is a new and startling application of a metaphor and, if it is held good, it would mean that if there is a collision on the high seas between the Turkish vessel and a ship of any other nationality, any of the officers and crew of that other ship may be arrested in any Turkish port and put on trial before a Turkish court on a criminal charge of having caused the collision by their negligence. This view appears to be based on a misconception of the proposition that a ship on the high seas may be regarded as part of the territory of the country whose flag she flies.

Turkey's case is that the crime was committed in Turkish territory, namely, on a Turkish ship on the high seas, and the Turkish Courts therefore have a territorial jurisdiction. A ship is a movable chattel, it is not a place; when on a voyage it shifts its place from day to day and from hour to hour, and when in dock it is a chattel which happens at the time to be in a particular place. The jurisdiction over crimes committed on a ship at sea is not of a territorial nature at all. It depends upon the law which for convenience and by common consent is applied to the case of chattels of such a very special nature as ships. It appears to me to be impossible with any reason to apply the principle of locality to the case of ships coming into collision for the purpose of ascertaining what court has jurisdiction; that depends on the principles of maritime law. Criminal jurisdiction for negligence causing a collision is in the courts of the country of the flag, provided that if the offender is of a nationality different from that of his ship, the prosecution may alternatively be in the court of his own country.

* * * *

Turkey, however, has another ground upon which she contends that there was jurisdiction. . . . Turkey asserts that the trial of Demons before the Turkish Courts was justified by Article 6 of the Turkish Penal Code, above set out. . . . The passing of such laws to affect aliens is defended on the ground that they are necessary for the "protection" of the national. Every country has the right and the duty to protect its nationals when out of their own country. . . . The Law of Nations [however] . . . does not recognize the assumption of jurisdiction for "protection;" there never has been any such general consent by the nations as would be required to make this doctrine a part of international law. Any State which finds it necessary to acquire such a power should by convention get the consent of the other States affected.

* * * *

Of course, every country has the right to protect the persons and the property of its citizens. If a wrong is done, the State may demand redress and enforce it, but the assertion that any State can by any law of its own assume criminal jurisdiction in respect of alleged crimes committed abroad or on the high seas is a new one. The government of the country of the injured person may call upon the government of the country where the injury was committed to have the offenders punished in due course by law, but it cannot make laws for their punishment in its own courts, except in pursuance of a convention with the other Power affected.

In my opinion, both the grounds on which Turkey has tried to support the conviction are unsound and France is entitled to the judgment of this Court.

* * * *

NOTES AND QUESTIONS

(1) According to Judge Loder, would Turkey have had jurisdiction to try M. Demons under Turkish law if he had been charged with intentionally ordering the helmsman of the *Lotus* to ram the *Boz-Kourt*? Suppose Demons had stood on the bridge of the *Lotus* and shot and killed a seaman aboard the *Boz-Kourt*? Does this mean Turkey would have jurisdiction to try M. Demons under the Turkish law of murder but not manslaughter?

(2) Assume that under both French and Turkish law manslaughter is defined as the involuntary killing of a human being in the course of performing an unlawful act (*i.e.*, in M. Demons' case, negligent operation of the *Lotus*) and consider the following:

    (a) If one accepts France's contention that M. Demons' offense was not committed on Turkish territory, where, in light of this definition of manslaughter, was it committed? Apart from the special argument with regard to collisions at sea (see below), why should this be so?

    (b) In *Treacy v. Director of Public Prosecutions*,[2] defendant challenged his conviction for blackmail under the Theft Act of 1968. He argued that having mailed, in England, a letter containing, in the words of the statute, an "unwarranted demand with menaces" to his victim in Germany his conduct could not constitute an offense against English law because it occurred on German rather than English territory. In rejecting this contention the House of Lords, two Lords dissenting, was of the view, as expressed by Lord Diplock, that when Parliament defines a crime in words containing no geographical limitation, and "where the definition of [the] offense contains the requirement that the described conduct of the accused be followed by described consequences," then the act of Parliament will, under the rules of international comity, be denied application only if "*neither* the conduct *nor* its harmful consequences took place in England." Thus, with respect to blackmail, it was sufficient, his Lordship observed, that "*either* the physical acts were done *or* their consequences took effect in England." Dissenting, Lord Morris of Borth-y-Gest emphasized that since, under the common law of England, criminal jurisdiction did not extend to acts committed on land abroad, the question was whether the appellant made an "unwarranted demand with menaces" in England. The making of such a

---

[2] [1971] A.C. 537.

demand could not occur, his Lordship said, "until it [was] communicated to the person who was unjustifiably menaced. . . . If the demander puts his menacing demand into writing and entrusts the post . . . to deliver it to his victim he will not have made his demand unless and until his letter arrives. . . . If a person went on to a remote and deserted shore and spoke words involving an unwarranted demand with menaces it would be fanciful to suggest that he had committed an offense under [the Theft Act]." Hence, with regard to the defendant, his offense was not committed in English territory and was not subject to English law.

Unless there is some intrinsic difference between blackmail and manslaughter how would France's argument in Lotus have fared under Lord Morris' analysis? Which should it be: only the place where the defendant acted, only the place where his act had its criminal effect, or both? Does the majority in either the PCIJ or the House of Lords help you answer that question?

(3) In light of the *Lotus'* definition of the outer limits of the territorial principle, consider the following decisions:

(a) In *Rocha v. United States*,[3] defendant aliens were convicted of filing false visa applications with the U.S. Consulate in Mexico in violation of 18 U.S.C. Section 1546. The visas were subsequently issued by the Consul in Mexico and were used by the defendants to gain entry into the United States. The conviction, the Ninth Circuit concluded, was valid under both the "protective principle" and the "territorial principle," the latter because it "rested not only upon the act abroad, but also on the effect it produced within the boundaries of the United States, namely the aliens' subsequent successful entrance at the border upon a document allegedly procured by fraud." For this purpose the court relied on *Strassheim v. Daly*.[4]

(b) In *United States v. Pizzarusso*,[5] the Second Circuit likewise rejected the defendant's jurisdictional challenge to a conviction for the making of false statements in a visa application to the American Consul in Montreal. The visa was subsequently issued by that Consul and used by the defendant to enter the U.S. Unlike the Ninth Circuit, however, the Second Circuit, per Judge Medina, relied solely on the "protective principle," pointedly disagreeing with the Ninth Circuit's reliance on the "territorial principle." Under *Lotus*, who had it right, the Ninth Circuit or the Second Circuit?

(c) In *Strassheim v. Daly, supra*, relied upon by the *Rocha* court, defendant Daly was indicted by Michigan for delivering used equipment to the State of Michigan under a contract that called for new machinery and for bribing a State official to remain silent when the old equipment arrived. When he made the false pretense by signing the contract and when he mailed the bribe to the State official, Daly was in Illinois and

[3] 288 F. 2d 545 (9th Cir. 1961).
[4] 221 U.S. 280, 31 S. Ct. 558 (1910).
[5] 388 F. 2d 8 (2d Cir., 1968).

the court assumed that he took no action in Michigan in furtherance of his unlawful scheme. In upholding Michigan's demand for Daly's extradition, Justice Holmes stated that "the usage of the civilized world" would warrant Michigan in punishing Daly although he had "never set foot in the state" until after the crime was complete:

Acts done outside a jurisdiction, but intended to produce and producing detrimental effects within it, justify a state in punishing the cause of the harm as if he had been present at the effect. . . .

Was the *Rocha* court's reliance on this statement well founded?

(4) Next, examine the following decisions, and consider the soundness of the outer limits of the "territorial principle" as articulated by *Lotus*:

(a) *Pizzarusso* and *Rocha.*

(b) *United States v. Layton*,[6] arose out of the notorious Jonesville murders in Guyana. The court in that case concluded that, under either the "protective principle," the "nationality principle" or the "territorial principle," the United States had jurisdiction to apply American law to defendant Layton, an American citizen, charged with murdering Congressman Leo Ryan at the Port Kaituma airport in Guyana. The "territorial principle" was available, according to the court, because the "alleged offenses were intended to produce and did produce harmful effects within this nation." Assume that the victim was not a Congressman but a private American citizen domiciled in California but temporarily resident in Guyana and that the accused was a Guyanian whom the State of California sought to prosecute under a criminal statute containing no explicit geographical or territorial limitation. These assumptions would appear to eliminate reliance on either the "protective" or the "nationality principle," leaving only the "territorial principle." What result under the court's reasoning in *Layton*? How do you evaluate that result? Does *Lotus* appear to draw a sensible line in such a case?

(c) In *United States v. Columba-Colella*,[7] defendant, a British subject and permanent resident of Mexico, entered into an agreement in Juarez, Mexico with one Keith, a U.S. citizen, to sell a car which Keith had already stolen from its owner in El Paso, Texas and to split the proceeds of sale. Keith had informed the defendant of the theft prior to their agreement. After being arrested by Mexican police with the keys in his possession, the defendant was turned over to U.S. authorities and charged with receiving a stolen vehicle in foreign commerce in violation of 18 U.S.C. Section 2313. The Fifth Circuit concluded that the indictment could not be sustained under either the "protective"[8] or the

---

[6] 509 F. Supp. 212 (N.D. Cal., 1981).

[7] 604 F. 2d 356 (5th Cir., 1979).

[8] With respect to the "protective principle" the court, while conceding that defendant's conduct "affected a United States citizen," held that was not sufficient to sustain use of that principle because "there was no interference with a governmental function." The case was contrasted with *United States v. Fernandez*, 496 F. 2d 1294, (5th Cir. 1974) where jurisdiction to prosecute for fencing in Mexico social security checks stolen from Americans in the United States was sustained under the "protective principle."

"territorial" principle. With regard to the latter, the court noted that while the accused's agreement to fence the car followed Keith's crime, it was legally unrelated to the latter and was not a "constituent element of Keith's act." Good *Lotus*? If so, does it make any sense to draw the line at this point?

(5) It has often been charged that the "effects" doctrine is pernicious. It can give rise to excessively expansive claims to prescriptive jurisdiction (see especially, Chapter 7). Return to the position taken by France and M. Loder to the effect that only the State in which the defendant was located at the time he performed the illegal act can claim to have prescriptive jurisdiction under the "territorial principle." Expansive notion, is it not, when coupled with a charge of a conspiracy to commit the unlawful act? For this purpose consider the following cases in which the Coast Guard acted under 14 U.S.C. Section 89(a). That Section gives the Coast Guard authority to board and search "any vessel . . . subject to the jurisdiction or to the operation of any law of the United States," and then to arrest any person if "it appears that a breach of the laws of the United States . . . is being or has been committed, by [that] person."

(a) In *United States v. Cardena*,[9] the Coast Guard arrested the Colombian crew of a Colombian freighter on the high seas some 200 miles off the Florida coast and charged the crew with a conspiracy to import marijuana into the United States in violation of 18 U.S.C. Sections 846 and 963. Rejecting defendants' argument that the vessel and its crew were not, at the time of arrest, "subject to the operation" of U.S. law within the meaning of 14 U.S.C. Section 89(a), the court relied upon the "territorial principle." Certain of defendant's co-conspirators had, the court noted, committed acts in "furtherance of the conspiracy within [the] territorial limits" of the United States.

(b) In *United States v. Postal*,[10] the court invoked the "territorial principle" in upholding the high seas arrest of the crew of a Cayman Islands vessel on a charge of conspiracy to import marijuana because, acting in furtherance of the conspiracy, one of the conspirators purchased and outfitted the vessel in Florida.

Suppose a conspiracy is alleged between the defendants arrested aboard a foreign vessel on the high seas and persons in the United States, the latter responsible, under the terms of the alleged conspiracy, for taking delivery of, and distributing the drugs in the United States. Aided by the conspiracy charge would that fact not suffice, under M. Loder's and the French version of the "territorial" principle, to allow all the defendants, including those who had never set foot in the United States, to be tried according to U.S. law? If so, hasn't the French version of the "territorial" principle become something like the Berlin Wall, insofar as it is intended to guard against the overly expansive consequences of the "effects" doctrine? On the question of conspiracy consult: *Ford v. United States*,[11] *Rivard v. United States*,[12] *Marin v. United States*.[13]

---

[9] 585 F. 2d 1252 (5th Cir. 1978).
[10] 589 F. 2d 862 (5th Cir. 1979).
[11] 273 U.S. 593, 47 S. Ct. 531 (1927).
[12] 375 F. 2d 882 (5th Cir. 1967).
[13] 352 F. 2d 174 (5th Cir. 1965).

(6) Recall that a majority of the Judges in *Lotus* concluded that M. Demons' offense was committed in both French and Turkish territory. This, in turn, demonstrated that there was no rule of international law rendering the exercise of prescriptive jurisdiction by Turkey unlawful. Hence it was lawful. Note further that Lord Finlay would not have quarrelled with the majority's conclusion, if territory had meant land. He quarrels with calling the *Boz-Kourt* Turkish territory, at least for the purpose of judging whether ships' officers involved in collisions at sea were criminally responsible. It is a misuse, he says, of a mere "metaphor." Now, re-examine M. Loder's opinion? Did he need to quarrel with the majority's use of the "effects" doctrine. Could he not very profitably have joined Lord Finlay? If so, how would you reshape his argument? Is it persuasive? Note that Article 6 of the Convention on the High Seas[14] reverses the *Lotus* decision insofar as prosecutions arising out of collisions between vessels on the high seas are concerned. To the same effect is Article 97 of the United Nations Convention on the Law of the Sea.[15]

If, having reformulated M. Loder's position, you find that he and Lord Finlay are more persuasive than the majority, it means, does it not, that framing the issue solely in terms of whether Turkey's claim of jurisdiction was justified (*i.e.*, taking a unilateral perspective) and judging that claim by the mechanical application of a general principle (*i.e.*, the criminality of an act is determined by the law of the nation in whose territory it occurs), is far less persuasive than a process of making a reasoned choice between the law of France and the law of Turkey? But if this so, you are suggesting, are you not, that we should abandon the way we have historically thought about these issues? In short, consider the possibility that both M. Loder and Lord Finlay were hampered by traditional methodology and were, implicitly at least, pushing toward a new approach that has now received the blessings of The Restatement (Third) of the Foreign Relations Law of the United States.

(7) Sections 402 and 403 of The Restatement (Third) of the Foreign Relations Law of the United States contain general principles which are then refined in the specific context of jurisdiction to tax, to apply the antitrust and securities laws, to control foreign subsidiaries and to seek discovery.

Section 402. Bases of Jurisdiction to Prescribe

Subject to Section 403, a state may, under international law, exercise jurisdiction to prescribe law with respect to

(1) (a) conduct, that wholly or in substantial part, takes place within its territory;

(b) the status of persons, or interests in things, present within its territory;

(c) conduct outside its territory which has or is intended to have substantial effect within its territory;

[14] 450 U.N.T.S. 82, 13 U.S.T. 2312, TIAS No. 5200).
[15] A/Conf. 62/122, 7 October 1982.

(2)   the activities, interests, status, or relations of its nationals outside as well as within its territory; and

(3)   certain conduct outside its territory by persons not its nationals that is directed against the security of the state or against a limited class of other state interests.

Section 403. Limitations on Jurisdiction to Prescribe

(1)   Even when one of the bases for jurisdiction under Section 402 is present, a state may not exercise jurisdiction to prescribe law with respect to a person or activity having connections with another state when the exercise of such jurisdiction is unreasonable.

(2)   Whether exercise of jurisdiction over a person or activity is unreasonable is determined by evaluating all relevant factors, including:

(a)   the link of the activity to the territory of the regulating state, *i.e.* the extent to which the activity (i) takes place within the regulating state, or (ii) has substantial, direct, and foreseeable effect upon or in the territory;

(b)   the connections, such as nationality, residence, or economic activity, between the regulating state and the persons principally responsible for the activity to be regulated, or between that state and those whom the law or regulation is designed to protect;

(c)   the character of the activity to be regulated, the importance of regulation to the regulating state, the extent to which other states regulate such activities, and the degree to which the desirability of such regulation is generally accepted;

(d)   the existence of justified expectations that might be protected or hurt by the regulation;

(e)   the importance of the regulation to the international political, legal or economic system;

(f)   the extent to which the regulation is consistent with the traditions of the international system;

(g)   the extent to which another state may have an interest in regulating the activity;

(h)   the likelihood of conflict with regulation by other states.

(3)   When it would not be unreasonable for each of two states to exercise jurisdiction over a person or activity, but the prescriptions by the two states are in conflict, each state has an obligation to evaluate its own as well as the other state's interest in exercising jurisdiction, in light of all the relevant factors, Subsection (2); a state should defer to the other state if that state's interest is clearly greater.

What might the outcome have been in *Lotus* under the Restatement?

Return to Note (4) and reconsider your evaluation of the outer limits of the "territorial" principle as defined by *Lotus*. Would the Restatement cause you to change your appraisal?

§ 6.02 Some Experiments in the Joinder of Public and Private International Law: Seamen's Welfare Legislation and the Regulation of Foreign Shipping Under United States Labor Law

In 1948, 53% of this nation's foreign trade was carried in American flag vessels. By 1960, the figure was less than 12% with only a slight decline since. The reason for this loss of competitiveness, begun well before World War II, is that the costs of constructing and operating American vessels under the constraints of existing legislation exceed those borne by the ships of virtually every other maritime nation: higher registration rates, higher rates of taxation on ship income, more costly safety and other regulations, the requirement that many American flag vessels be built and repaired in high-cost American dockyards and, most important to our purpose, higher labor costs. By law, American flag vessels must generally be manned by American crews whose wages range from 2 1/2 to 4 times higher than the wages paid most foreign seamen. The welfare costs of an American crew — social security, pension, injury and sickness benefits — can run 25 to 30% higher than the cost of benefits payable to a foreign crew. Again, by law, American ships must often carry one-third again as many crewmen as ships registered under foreign flags.

In the face of these costs, American shipowners, in order not to relinquish ownership of their vessels, have increasingly placed their ships under so-called foreign "flags of convenience." A "flag of convenience" country, according to a British Committee under the chairmanship of Lord Rochdale (the "Rochdale" Report[1]), is typically a small country with no conceivable national economic or military requirement for the tonnage entered upon its registry. It will register, at modest rates, vessels owned or controlled by non-citizens, will permit those vessels to be manned by non-nationals and will make access to and transfer from its registry easy. In addition, a "flag of convenience" country will typically subject ship income to very low rates of taxation, if any, and may lack the power or the administrative capacity to police national and international regulations pertaining to crew wages and living conditions, safety and officer competence. As a matter of policy, these countries also tend, according to the Report, to exercise little or no control over the companies that own their vessels.[2]

---

[1] Committee of Inquiry into Shipping; Report - Chairman, Lord Rochdale, London, May 1970.

[2] Using these characteristics as a guide, the OECD reported that of the approximately 36,000 commercial vessels in the world in 1960, having a gross registered tonnage of over 129 million tons, approximately 12%, by tonnage, were registered in "flag of convenience" countries. (OECD, Maritime Transport Committee, Maritime Transport 1971, Part V, reprinted in 4 J. of Mar. Law and Comm. 231 (1973)). By 1971 this had risen to over 19%. By 1977, 28% of the worldwide gross registered tonnage of 393 million tons was registered under "flags of convenience." Even this figure tends to understate the effect of the phenomenon. In 1977, 34%, by tonnage, of the world tanker fleet and 30% of the ore and bulk carriers were under "open-registries." Nearly 80% of world trade is carried by these two types of vessels. In 1960, 71%, by tonnage, of the vessels flying "flags of convenience" were registered in Liberia, 27% in Panama and 3% in Honduras. As of 1977, Liberia, with approximately 80% of the "convenience" fleet, and Panama with 13% continued to be the principal countries of registry. By the mid 1960s, however, Honduras had changed its policy and was replaced by Cyprus and Singapore with about 6% of the fleet. American,

Understandably, the American merchant fleet's loss of competitiveness has been a matter of deep concern to American seamen and their unions. In the view of these seamen the flight of American owned vessels to foreign registries, without change in beneficial ownership, represents a visible and flagrant attack on their jobs. In their concern, American seamen have been joined by maritime unions in other developed countries. Largely as a result of pressure brought by these unions on their governments and of a growing "third world" hostility to "flags of convenience," the 1958 Geneva conference included in the Convention on the High Seas,[3] Article 5 as follows:

> Every State shall fix the conditions for the grant of its nationality to ships, for the registration of ships in its territory, and for the right to fly its flag. Ships have the nationality of the State whose flag they are entitled to fly. There must exist a genuine link between the State and the ship; in particular, the State must effectively exercise its jurisdiction and control in administrative, technical and social matters over ships flying its flag.[4]

While successful in promoting a "genuine link" requirement in the High Seas Convention, the alliance between the maritime unions in the West and the developing nations of the world is problematic at best. The latter, especially the Group of 77 working through the UNCTAD Shipping Committee, look upon "flags of convenience" as a "front" which Western nations have used to perpetuate their dominance of world shipping notwithstanding their loss of competitiveness in the maritime labor market. Their solution is to force a return of vessels now registered under "flags of convenience" to the country of beneficial ownership — to prohibit registration in a country without a "genuine link" to the vessel — confident that if deprived of this "front," competitive forces would compel Western owners to sell many of their vessels to developing countries. This is scarcely the goal sought by Western seamen and their unions.[5]

Ironically, the American Government's behavior suggests that the Group of 77's strategy is well-founded. The Government has refused to side with American unions in the latters' efforts to organize foreign seamen. It opposed inclusion of a "genuine link" requirement in the High Seas Convention and has joined with other Western governments in opposing resolutions offered by the Group of 77 in the UNCTAD Shipping Committee.[6] Fearful that American shipowners would, in fact, sell if compelled to operate under the American flag and concerned lest this entail a loss of control over vessels that might be needed in a national emergency, the American Government has steadfastly taken the view that open foreign registries which permit continued American ownership are essential to

---

West German, Japanese, Greek, and Hong Kong shipping companies are the principal beneficial owners of these vessels.

[3] 13 U.S.T. 2312, T.I.A.S. No. 52, 450 U.N.T.S. 82.

[4] Under the U.N. Law of the Sea Convention (A/CONF. 62/122, 7 Oct. 1982) the language of Article 5 of the High Seas Convention has been retained by Article 91, except that the last clause thereof ("in particular . . ., etc.") was removed to, and elaborated upon in, a separate Article 94 without any express tie back to the "genuine link" requirement of Article 91.

[5] Juda, World Shipping, UNCTAD, and the New International Economic Order, 35 Int. Org. 493 (1981).

[6] See page 554, note 6 infra.

national security. Thus, the United States Maritime Commission has, for some time, required that before an American shipowner could receive Commission consent to a transfer of a vessel from American to foreign registry, it had to agree to place the vessel under Government control in the event of an emergency. The Commission has also convinced American owners to give voluntarily similar assurances covering newly built ships initially registered under foreign flags, while all of the major "flag of convenience" countries have, by agreement, undertaken not to contest U.S. government orders requisitioning vessels beneficially owned by American citizens.

This is the background for a study of the two lines of cases that follow. Both lines are concerned broadly with the competitive effect of foreign shipping upon the U.S. merchant marine and upon American seamen. The first line of cases treats with the so-called Jones Act,[7] under which a seaman injured in the course of his employment may sue his employer in common law negligence rather than settle for the traditional admiralty remedy of maintenance and cure that would be available without proof of fault. Not all of the Jones Act cases that follow involved ships flying "flags of convenience." Nevertheless, they are of a piece with the "flag of convenience" problem and the changing attitude of the Supreme Court cannot be understood or evaluated apart from that problem. Indeed, only when viewed in that context can one clearly discern the impact of these decisions on the interaction between international law and domestic statutes as elements in the law of prescriptive jurisdiction.

The second line of decisions arises out of direct efforts by American maritime unions to redress their loss of jobs to foreign shipping by attempts to organize foreign seamen. Here, the lessons of the Jones Act cases are extended to the more directly regulatory sphere.

[A] The "Jones Act" Cases

The Jones Act provides in pertinent part as follows:

Any seaman who shall suffer personal injury in the course of his employment may, at his election, maintain an action for damages at law with a right of trial by jury. . . . Jurisdiction in such actions shall be in the court of the district in which the defendant employer resides or in which his principal office is located.[8]

---

[7] 41 Stat. 1007, 46 U.S.C. Section 688.

[8] It has been held that "resides" in this statute refers to any state in which a corporate defendant is licensed to do business, *Pure Oil Co. v. Suarez*, 384 U.S. 202, 86 S. Ct. 1394 (1966). Also a Jones Act claim may be joined with an admiralty libel action and thus governed by the more liberal admiralty venue rules. *Brown v. C.D. Mallory & Co.*, 122 F. 2d 98 (3rd Cir. 1941).

LAURITZEN v. LARSEN

United States Supreme Court
345 U.S. 751, 73 S. Ct. 921 (1953)

[Respondent Larsen, a Danish seaman, while temporarily in New York joined the crew of the Randa, a ship of Danish flag registry, owned by petitioner Lauritzen, a Danish citizen. Larsen signed the ship's articles, written in Danish, providing that the rights of crew members would be governed by Danish law and by the employer's contract with the Danish Seamen's Union, of which Larsen was a member. He was negligently injured aboard the Randa, while in Havana harbor and brought suit under the Jones Act in the District Court for the Southern District of New York. Petitioner Lauritzen contended that Danish law was applicable and that, under that law, respondent had received all of the compensation to which he was entitled. Entertaining the cause, the District Court, in a decision affirmed by the Circuit Court of Appeals, ruled that American rather than Danish law applied and the jury rendered a verdict of $4,267.50. The Supreme Court reversed.]

MR. JUSTICE JACKSON delivered the opinion of the Court.

Denmark has enacted a comprehensive code to govern the relations of her shipowners to her seagoing labor which by its terms and intentions controls this claim. . . . The shipowner, supported here by the Danish Government, asserts that the Danish law supplies the full measure of his obligation and that maritime usage and international law as accepted by the United States exclude the application of our incompatible statute.

That allowance of an additional remedy under our Jones Act would sharply conflict with the policy and letter of Danish law is plain. Both assure the ill or injured seafaring worker the conventional maintenance and cure. . . . [But] the two systems are in sharpest conflict as to treatment of claims for disability. . . . Such injuries Danish law relieves under a state-operated plan similar to our workmen's compensation systems . . . [which] depend not upon fault or negligence but only on the fact of injury and the extent of disability. Our own law makes no such compensation in the absence of fault or negligence. [W]hen such fault or negligence is established by litigation, it allows recovery for elements such as pain and suffering not compensated under Danish law and lets the damages be fixed by jury. In this case, since negligence was found, United States law permits a larger recovery than Danish law.

Respondent does not deny that Danish law is applicable to his case. The contention . . . is rather that "A claimant may select whatever forum he desires and receive the benefits resulting from such choice" and "A ship owner is liable under the laws of the forum where he does business as well as in his own country." This contention . . . is not based on any explicit terms of the [Jones] Act . . . [but] upon the literal catholicity of its terminology.

If read literally, Congress . . . has extended our law and opened our courts to all alien seafaring men injured anywhere in the world in service of watercraft of every foreign nation — a hand on a Chinese junk, never outside Chinese waters, would not be beyond its literal wording.

But Congress in 1920 wrote these all-comprehending words, not on a clean slate, but as a postscript to a long series of enactments governing shipping. . . . While some [of these enactments] have been specific in application to foreign shipping and others in being confined to American shipping, many give no evidence that Congress addressed itself to their foreign application. . . . By usage as old as the Nation, such statutes have been construed to apply only to areas and transactions in which American law would be considered operative under prevalent doctrines of international law.

* * * *

This doctrine of construction is in accord with the long-heeded admonition of Mr. Chief Justice Marshall that "an Act of Congress ought never to be construed to violate the law of nations if any other possible construction remains. . . ." And it has long been accepted in maritime jurisprudence that ". . . if any construction otherwise be possible, an Act will not be construed as applying to foreigners in respect to acts done by them outside the dominions of the sovereign power enacting. . . ."

This is not, as sometimes is implied, any impairment of our own sovereignty, or limitation of the power of Congress. . . . On the contrary, we are simply dealing with a problem of statutory construction rather commonplace in a federal system by which courts often have to decide whether "any" or "every" reaches to the limits of the enacting authority's usual scope or is to be applied to foreign events or transactions.

Respondent places great stress upon the assertion that petitioner's commerce and contacts with the ports of the United States are frequent and regular, as the basis for applying our statutes to incidents aboard his ships. But the virtue and utility of sea-borne commerce lies in its frequent and important contacts with more than one country. If, to serve some immediate interest, the courts of each were to exploit every such contact to the limit of its power, it is not difficult to see that a multiplicity of conflicting and overlapping burdens would blight international carriage by sea. Hence, courts of this and other commercial nations have generally deferred to a non-national or international maritime law . . . [which] in such matters as this does not seek uniformity [but] . . . aims at stability and order through usages which considerations of comity, reciprocity and long-range interest have developed to define the domain which each nation will claim as its own. . . . The criteria, in general, appear to be arrived at from weighing of the significance of one or more connecting factors between the shipping transaction regulated and the national interest served by the assertion of authority. It would not be candid to claim that our courts have arrived at satisfactory standards or apply those they profess with perfect consistency. But in dealing with international commerce we cannot be unmindful of the necessity for mutual forbearance if retaliations are to be avoided; nor should we forget that any contact which we hold sufficient to warrant application of our law to a foreign transaction will logically be as strong a warrant for a foreign country to apply its law to an American transaction.

In the case before us . . . [three] nations can claim some connecting factor with this tort — Denmark, because . . . the ship and the seaman were Danish nationals; Cuba, because the tortuous conduct occurred and caused injury in Cuban waters; [t]he United States . . . because the seaman had been hired in and was returned to the United States, which also is the state of the forum. We therefore review the several factors which, alone or in combination, are generally conceded to influence choice of law to govern . . . a maritime tort claim, and the weight and significance accorded them.

Place of the Wrongful Act The test of location of the wrongful act or omission [the *lex loci delecti commissionis*], however sufficient for torts ashore, is of limited application to shipboard torts, because of the varieties of legal authority over waters she may navigate . . . [and hence is] usually modified by the more constant law of the flag. The locality test . . . [in all events] affords no support for the application of American law in this case.

Law of the Flag. Perhaps the most venerable and universal rule of maritime law relevant to our problem is that which gives cardinal importance to the law of the flag. This Court has said that the law of the flag supersedes the territorial principle, even for purposes of criminal jurisdiction of personnel of a merchant ship, [and] . . . [o]n this principle . . . we concede a territorial government . . . only concurrent jurisdiction of offenses aboard our ships. . . . Some authorities reject, as a . . . fiction, the doctrine that a ship is constructively a floating part of the flag-state, but apply the law of the flag on the pragmatic basis that there must be some law on shipboard, that it cannot change at every change of waters, and no experience shows a better rule than that of the state that owns her.

It is significant to us here that the weight given to the ensign overbears most other connecting events in determining applicable law . . . [and hence is] of such weight in favor of Danish and against American law in this case that it must prevail unless some heavy counterweight appears.

Allegiance or Domicile of the Injured. Until recent times there was little occasion for conflict between the law of the flag and the law of the state of which the seafarer was a subject, for the long standing rule . . . was that the nationality of the vessel for jurisdictional purposes was attributed to all her crew. Surely during service under a foreign flag some duty of allegiance is due. But, also, each nation has a legitimate interest that its nationals and permanent inhabitants be not maimed or disabled from self-support. . . . We need not, however, weigh the seamen's nationality against that of the ship, for here the two coincide without resort to fiction . . . [Respondent's] presence in New York was transitory and created no such national interests in, or duty toward, him as to justify intervention of the law of one state on the shipboard of another.

Allegiance of the Defendant Shipowner. Until recent times [the nationality principle applied to the owners] . . . was not a frequent occasion of conflict [with the law of the flag], for the nationality of the ship was that of its owners. But it is common knowledge that in recent years a practice has grown, particularly among American shipowners, to avoid stringent shipping laws by seeking foreign registration eagerly offered by some countries. Confronted with such operations, our courts on occasion have pressed beyond the formalities of more or less nominal foreign registration to enforce against American shipowners the obligations which our law places upon them. But here again the utmost liberality in disregard of formality does not support the application of American law in this case, for it appears beyond doubt that this owner is a Dane by nationality and domicile.

Place of Contract. Place of contract, which was New York, is the factor on which respondent chiefly relies to invoke American law. . . . But this action does not seek to recover anything due under the contract or damages for its breach.

The place of contracting in this instance, as is usual to such contracts, was fortuitous. A seaman takes his employment, like his fun, where he finds it; a ship takes on crew in any port where it needs them. The practical effect of making the *lex loci contractus* govern all tort claims during the service would be to subject a ship to a multitude of systems of law, to put some of the crew in a more advantageous position than others, and not unlikely in the long run to diminish hirings in ports of countries that take best care of their seamen.

But if contract law is nonetheless to be considered, we face the fact that this contract was explicit that the Danish law and the contract with the Danish union were to control. . . . We are aware of no public policy that would prevent the parties to this contract, which contemplates performance in a multitude of territorial jurisdictions and on the high seas, from so settling upon the law of the flag-state as their governing code. This arrangement is so natural and compatible with the policy of the law that even in the absence of an express provision it would probably have been implied. . . .

Inaccessibility of Foreign Forum. It is argued, and particularly stressed by an *amicus* brief, that justice requires adjudication under American law to save seamen expense and loss of time in returning to a foreign forum. This might be a persuasive argument for exercising a discretionary jurisdiction to adjudge a controversy; but it is not persuasive as to the law by which it shall be judged. . . .

Confining ourselves to the case in hand, we do not find this seaman disadvantaged in obtaining his remedy under Danish law from being in New York instead of Denmark. . . . There is not the slightest showing that to obtain any relief to which he is entitled under Danish law would require his presence in Denmark or necessitate his leaving New York. And, even if it were so, the record indicates that he was offered and declined free transportation to Denmark by petitioner.

The Law of the Forum. It is urged that, since an American forum has perfected its jurisdiction over the parties and defendant does more or less frequent and regular business within the forum state, it should apply its own law to the controversy between them. The "doing business" which is enough to warrant service of process may fall quite short of the considerations necessary to bring extraterritorial torts to judgment under our law. . . . We have held it a denial of due process of law when a state of the Union attempts to draw into control of its law otherwise foreign controversies, on slight connections because it is a forum state. The purpose of a conflict-of-laws doctrine is to assure that a case will be treated in the same way under the appropriate law regardless of the fortuitous circumstances which often determine the forum. Jurisdiction of maritime cases in all countries is so wide and the nature of its subject matter so far-flung that there would be no justification for altering the law of a controversy just because local jurisdiction of the parties is obtainable.

This review of the connecting factors which either maritime law or our municipal law of conflicts regards as significant in determining the law applicable to a claim of actionable wrong shows an overwhelming preponderance in favor of Danish law.

In apparent recognition of the weakness of [its] . . . legal argument, a candid and brash appeal is made by respondent and by amicus briefs to extend the law to this situation as a means of benefiting seamen and enhancing the costs of foreign ship operations for the competitive advantage of our own. We are not sure that the interest of this foreign seaman, who is able to prove negligence, is the interest of all seamen or that his interest is that of the United States. Nor do we stop to inquire which law does whom the greater or the lesser good. The argument is misaddressed. It would be within the proprieties if addressed to Congress. Counsel familiar with the traditional attitude of this Court in maritime matters could not have intended it for us.

The judgment below is reversed and the cause remanded to the District Court for proceedings consistent herewith.

Reversed and remanded.

MR. JUSTICE BLACK agrees with the Court of Appeals and would affirm its judgment.

* * * *

ROMERO v. INTERNATIONAL TERMINAL OPERATING COMPANY

United States Supreme Court
358 U.S. 354, 79 S. Ct. 468 (1959)

[Petitioner was a Spanish citizen, employed in Spain as a crew member of a Spanish flag vessel for a voyage which was to begin and end in Spain. The vessel was owned by a Spanish corporation and Petitioner was injured while the ship was in the port of New York. In affirming the lower courts' dismissal of Petitioner's Jones Act complaint, Justice Frankfurter, writing for the Court, stated with regard to the claim against the Spanish owner]:

* * * *

We are not here dealing with the sovereign power of the United States to apply its law to situations involving one or more foreign contacts. But in the absence of a contrary congressional direction, we must apply those principles of choice of law that are consonant with the needs of a general federal maritime law and with due recognition of our self-regarding respect for the relevant interests of foreign nations in the regulation of maritime commerce as a part of the legitimate concern of the international community. . . . The controlling considerations are the interacting interests of the United States and of foreign countries, and in assessing them we must move with the circumspection appropriate when this Court is adjudicating issues inevitably entangled in the conduct of international relations. . . ."

* * * *

In *Lauritzen v. Larsen* the injury occurred in Havana and the action was brought in New York. [Petitioner] Romero was injured while temporarily in American territorial waters. This difference does not call for a difference in result. . . . Although the place of injury has often been deemed determinative of the choice of law in municipal conflict of laws, . . . [t]o impose on ships the duty of shifting from one standard of compensation to another as the vessel passes the boundaries of territorial waters would be not only an onerous but also an unduly speculative burden, disruptive of international commerce and without basis in the expressed policies of this country. The amount and type of recovery which a foreign seaman may receive from his foreign employer while sailing on a foreign ship should not depend on the wholly fortuitous circumstances of the place of injury.

[MR. JUSTICE BLACK, in dissent, notes that, in his view, the decision in *Lauritzen v. Larsen* was based:]

. . . on the Court's concepts of what would be good or bad for the country internationally rather than on an actual interpretation of the language of the Jones Act. . . . Such notions, weak enough in *Lauritzen*, seem much weaker still in this case . . . I cannot but feel that, at least as to torts occurring within the United States, Congress knew what it was doing when it said "any seaman" and I must dissent from today's further and, I believe, unjustifiable reduction in the scope of the Jones Act.

HELLENIC LINES LTD. v. RHODITIS

United States Supreme Court
398 U.S. 306, 90 S. Ct. 1731 (1970)

[Respondent, Rhoditis, a Greek citizen, sued under the Jones Act for injuries sustained aboard the Greek vessel, Hellenic Hero, while the latter was docked in New Orleans. Rhoditis was serving aboard the Hellenic Hero under a contract made in Greece, providing that Greek law and a Greek collective-bargaining agreement were to govern the employment relationship and that all claims arising out of that contract were to be adjudicated by a Greek court. Petitioner, Hellenic Lines, Ltd., owner of the Hellenic Hero, was a Greek corporation with its largest office in New York. More than 95% of the company's stock was owned by a Greek citizen who, since 1945, had been domiciled in Connecticut and who had managed the company out of its New York office. The Hellenic Hero was engaged in regularly scheduled runs between American ports and ports in the Middle East, Pakistan and India. All of its income was derived from cargoes either originating or terminating in the United States. The District Court, sitting without a jury, rendered judgment for the seaman, and the Court of Appeals affirmed.]

MR. JUSTICE DOUGLAS delivered the opinion of the Court.

The Jones Act speaks only of "the defendant employer" without any qualifications. In *Lauritzen v. Larsen* . . . however, we listed seven factors to be considered in determining whether a particular shipowner should be held to be an "employer" for Jones Act purposes. . . .

Of these seven factors it is urged that four are in favor of the shipowner and against jurisdiction: the ship's flag is Greek; the injured seaman is Greek; the employment contract is Greek; and there is a foreign forum available to the injured seaman.

The *Lauritzen* test, however, is not a mechanical one. . . . The significance of one or more factors must be considered in light of the national interest served by the assertion of Jones Act jurisdiction.[8] Moreover, the list of seven factors in *Lauritzen* was not intended as exhaustive. As held in *Pavlov v. Ocean Traders Marine Corp.,* . . . and approved by the Court of Appeals in the present case, . . . the shipowner's *base of operations* is another factor of importance in determining whether the Jones Act is applicable; and there well may be others.

In *Lauritzen* the injured seaman had been hired in and was returned to the United States, and the shipowner was served here. Those were the only contacts of that shipping operation with this country.

The present case is quite different.

[The owner of petitioner Hellenic Lines, Ltd.] became a lawful permanent resident alien in 1952. We extend to such an alien the same constitutional protections of due process that we accord citizens. . . . The injury occurred here. The forum is a United States court. [The owner's] base of operations is New York. The *Hellenic Hero* was not a casual visitor; rather, it and many of its sister ships were earning income from cargo originating or terminating here. We see no reason whatsoever to give the Jones Act a strained construction so that this alien owner, engaged in an extensive business operation in this country, may have an advantage over citizens engaged in the same business by allowing him to escape the obligations and responsibility of a Jones act "employer." The flag, the nationality of the seaman, the fact that his employment contract was Greek, and that he might be compensated there are in the totality of the circumstances of this case minor weights in the scales compared with the substantial and continuing contacts that this alien owner has with this country. If . . . the liberal purposes of the Jones Act are to be effectuated, the facade of the operation must be considered as minor, compared with the real nature of the operation and a cold objective look at the actual operational contacts that this ship and this owner have with the United States. By that test the Court of Appeals was clearly right in holding that petitioner Hellenic Lines was an "employer" under the Jones Act.

---

[8] Judge Medina speaking for the Court of Appeals for the Second Circuit, correctly stated the problem in the following words: "[T]he decisional process of arriving at a conclusion on the subject of the application of the Jones Act involves the ascertainment of the facts or groups of facts which constitute contacts between the transaction involved in the case and the United States, and then deciding whether or not they are substantial. Thus each factor is to be weighed' and 'evaluated' only to the end that, after each factor has been given consideration, a rational and satisfactory conclusion may be arrived at on the question of whether all the factors or group of facts must be tested in the light of the underlying objective, which is to effectuate the liberal purposes of the Jones Act." *Bartholomew v. Universe Tankships, Inc.,* 263 F. 2d 437, 441.

Affirmed.

MR. JUSTICE HARLAN, with whom THE CHIEF JUSTICE and MR. JUSTICE STEWART join, dissenting.

I dissent from today's decision. . . . [It] is supported neither by precedent, nor realistic policy, and in my opinion is far removed from any intention that can reasonably be ascribed to Congress.

Lauritzen . . . announced that the law of the flag, "the most venerable and universal rule of maritime law," would in Jones Act cases "overbear most other connecting events in determining applicable law . . . unless some heavy counter-weight appears. . . ."

Such a counterweight would exist only in circumstances where the application of the American rule of law would further the purpose of Congress. While some legislation in its purpose obviously requires extension beyond our borders to achieve national policy, this is not so, in my opinion, with an Act concerned with prescribing particular remedies, rather than one regulating commerce or creating a standard for conduct.

The only justification that I can see for extending extraterritorially a remedial-type provision like [the Jones Act] is that the injured seaman is an individual whose well-being is a concern of this country. It was for this reason that *Lauritzen* recognized the residence of the plaintiff as a factor that should properly be considered in deciding who is a "seaman" as Congress employed that term in [the Jones Act]. . . .

Lauritzen in enumerating these factors ("contacts") as independent consider-ations, was attempting to focus analysis on those factors that are the necessary ingredients for a statutory cause of action: first, as a matter of statutory construc-tion, is plaintiff within that class of seamen that Congress intended to cover by the statute? and, second, is there a sufficient nexus between the defendant and this country so as to justify the assertion of legislative jurisdiction? In other words the Court must define "seaman" and "employer" as those words are used in [the Jones Act]. In this regard the situs of the accident or the vessel's contacts with this country by virtue of its beneficial ownership or the frequency of calls at our ports simply serves as an adequate nexus between this country and defendant to assert jurisdiction in a case where congressional policy is otherwise furthered. But no matter how qualitatively substantial or numerous these kinds of contacts may be, they have no bearing in themselves on whether Jones act recovery is appropriate in a given instance. For transactions occurring aboard foreign-flag vessels that question should be answered by reference to the plaintiff's relationship to this country.

Viewed in this perspective, today's decision and decisions of several lower courts that have taken the phenomenon of "convenient" foreign registry as a wedge for displacing the law of the flag, . . . have, I believe, misconstrued these basic premises on which *Lauritzen* was founded. This is underscored by the fact that the *Lauritzen* allusion to the practice of American owners of finding a "convenient" flag "to avoid stringent shipping laws by seeking foreign registration eagerly offered by some countries," . . . lifted out of context, has acquired a dynamism and become the justification for recovery by foreign seamen simply on the ground that convenient "registry" somehow circumvents an obligation that Congress desired to impose on all owners within its jurisdiction.

This underlies today's decision . . . Jones Act [l]iability is only one factor that contributes to the higher cost of operating an American flag vessel. Indeed, recognizing the insurance factor, it is doubtful that this factor is a significant contribution to the competitive advantage of foreign flag ships especially given the higher crew wages. . . .

Even were Jones Act liability a significant uncompensated cost in the operation of an American ship, I could not regard this as a reason for extending Jones Act recovery to foreign seamen when the underlying concern of the legislation before us is the adjustment of the risk of loss between individuals and not the regulation of commerce or competition.[10]

Today's decision suggests that courts have become mesmerized by contacts, and notwithstanding the purported eschewal of a mechanical application of the *Lauritzen* test, they have lost sight of the primary purpose of *Lauritzen* which, as I conceive it, was to reconcile the all-embracing language of the Jones Act with those principles of comity embodied in international and maritime law that are designed to "foster amicable and workable commercial relations."

NOTES AND QUESTIONS

(1) Justice Jackson's work in *Lauritzen v. Larsen* exhibits at least three critical features. First, the Justice draws upon both traditional public international law and choice-of-law principles. Yet, the case is never treated as posing a choice-of-law problem in the strict sense. While concluding that Danish, rather than American law, ought to govern plaintiff's recovery, Justice Jackson in fact, dismisses plaintiff's complaint because the sovereign United States had not prescribed a rule of law upon which the plaintiff could predicate his claim for relief. Plaintiff had failed to state a claim upon which relief could be granted (Rule 12(b) (6), Fed. R. Civ. P.). In other words, confronted with a classic problem in prescriptive jurisdiction, steadfastly recognizing it as such throughout the opinion, Justice Jackson uses the rules of both public and private international law as clues to the underlying factors — the values and interests — upon which the decision should turn and then, drawing upon an emerging methodology of private international law, forges a mechanism for working those factors into a coherent decision.

---

[10] The Second Circuit quite properly relied on the beneficial ownership of the ship to permit recovery in *Bartholomew v. Universe Tankships, Inc.*, 263 F. 2d 437 (2d Cir. 1959), where the injured plaintiff was an American domiciliary. *Bartholomew*, unfortunately, apprehended what I conceive to be unintended reverberations in Justice Jackson's *Lauritzen* language which it all but echoed: "looking through the facade of foreign registration and incorporation to the American ownership . . . is essential unless the purposes of the Jones Act are to be frustrated by American shipowners intent upon evading their obligations under the law by the simple expedient of incorporating in a foreign country and registering their vessels under a foreign flag." 263 F.2d 437, 442.

Second, beyond the methodological innovation is the perspective from which the opinion is written. "[T]he virtue and utility of seaborne commerce," the Justice writes, "lies in its frequent and important contacts with more than one country." Then, he continues:

> If, to serve some immediate interest, the courts of each were to exploit every such contact to the limit of its power, it is not difficult to see that a multiplicity of conflicting and overlapping burdens would blight international carriage by sea. Hence, courts of this and other commercial nations have generally deferred to a non-national or international maritime law . . . [which] in such matters as this does not seek uniformity [but] . . . aims at stability and order through usages which considerations of comity, reciprocity and long range interest have developed to define the domain which each nation will claim as its own. . . .

This is the global perspective, true Storian "systemic comity," and a predicate for "law as rational process," not "law as rules."

The third important feature of the opinion is the way Justice Jackson takes as a point of departure for his statutory analysis, Justice Marshall's statement that: "an Act of Congress ought never to be construed to violate the law of nations if any other possible construction remains. . . ."

(2) Against this background, consider Justice Douglas' work in *Rhoditis*. While purporting to apply Justice Jackson's methodology, Justice Douglas makes no reference whatsoever to international law. To him the task at hand was a straightforward matter of statutory interpretation. Moreover, contrast the perspective from which the opinion is written. All that seems to matter are those interests of the United States that the Justice finds reflected in the statute or perhaps elsewhere (see below). Gone is Justice Jackson's insistence on reading the statute through the filter of a presumed Congressional intention not to violate international law. The question, therefore, is how far these differences may have influenced the outcome in the two cases. In examining that question, consider the material in the notes that follow.

(3) Compare *Patterson v. The Bark Eudora,*[11] *Sandberg v. McDonald (The Talus)*[12] and *Strathearn S.S. Co. Ltd. v. Dillon.*[13] While the Supreme Court in each case purports to rely upon the same rule of international law, in all the cases that rule is clearly ameliorated by invocations of "comity." To what extent does comity, as an express element of the rule, effectively change the rule from a mechanical test based on a unilateral perspective into a mandate for a reasoned choice of law based on a broader perspective?

> (a) In *The Bank Eudora* several seamen (nationality unspecified) sued a British vessel for back wages that included advances previously paid in New York at the beginning of their voyage. The U.S. statute under which they sued made such advances unlawful, and gave seamen the right to recover their wages in full (no deduction for the advances) after being earned. By its terms the statute applied " . . . to foreign vessels while

[11] 190 U.S. 169, 23 S. Ct. 821 (1903).
[12] 248 U.S. 185, 39 S. Ct. 1, 84 (1918).
[13] 252 U.S. 348, 40 S. Ct. 350 (1920).

in the waters of the United States as [well as] to vessels of the United States." The owners contended that if applied to a foreign vessel, the statute would violate international law. The Court rejected the argument relying on *Wildenhus' Case* [14] to the effect that under international law all merchant vessels, of whatever nationality, are subject to the law of the "ports to which they go" and that only as a matter of comity do such vessels enter under an implied consent of the sovereign to honor the flag state's jurisdiction over matters internal to the vessel. That consent being only implied, it could, the Court emphasized, be withdrawn at any time, as Congress had expressly done in the statute sued upon. The Court also thought that exempting foreign vessels from the statute would "embarrass domestic vessels in obtaining their quota of seamen," a practical consideration that "presumably appealed to Congress" and "justified" its extension of the statute to foreign ships.

(b)   In *Sandberg v. McDonald (The Talus)*, foreign crewmen aboard foreign vessels temporarily in American ports, sought to recover one-half of the wages thus far earned by them, even though under their employment contracts all wage payments were to be postponed until the end of the voyage. The seamen relied upon Section 4 of the Seamen's Act of 1915 which stipulated that, upon demand, "seamen aboard U.S. vessels" and every "*seaman on a foreign vessel while in harbors of the United States*" was entitled to receive one-half of the wages earned to that point in the voyage. The statute also voided any contrary contractual provision. The ship's master conceded the seamen's right to receive one-half their pay, but insisted upon deducting certain advances made in Liverpool. The seamen charged that the deduction violated the anti-advancement statute involved in *The Bark Eudora* (re-enacted as Section 11 of the Seamen's Act of 1915). The Court concluded that Section 11 was not

---

[14] In *Wildenhus' Case (Mali v. Keeper of the Common Jail of Hudson County, New Jersey)*, 120 U.S. 1 (1887)), the Belgian Consul, by writ of habeas corpus, sought the release of one Wildenhus, a Belgian national, who was in defendant's custody on a charge of murdering a fellow Belgian during a quarrel below decks of a Belgian ship docked in Jersey City. In affirming the lower courts' denial of the writ, the Supreme Court noted that under "the law of civilized nations" a merchant vessel entering the port of another state "subjects itself to the law of the place to which it goes." Nevertheless, the Court added, "experience had shown that commerce would benefit if the local government would abstain from interfering with the internal discipline of the ship." Thus, among "civilized nations" it was understood that "all things done on board, which affected only the vessel, or those belonging to her, and did not involve the peace or dignity of the country or the tranquility of the port, should be left . . . to be dealt with by the authorities [and according to the law] of the nation to which the vessel belonged." This principle had, the Court admitted, been embodied in a treaty with Belgium. Nevertheless, the Court concluded that the writ should not issue since Wildenhus' crime impaired the "tranquility of the port." Unlike the "mere disputes or quarrels of seamen," or acts which "relate only to the discipline of the ship," murder is a crime whose "gravity awaken[s] a public interest as soon as [it] . . . become[s] known." In the case of a murder "inquiry is certain to be instituted at once . . . and the popular excitement rises or falls as the news spreads. . . . It is not alone the publicity of the act, or the noise and clamor which attend it, that fixes the nature of the crime, but the act itself."

applicable to advance payments made in a foreign country pursuant to contracts entered into abroad. According to Justice Day, the Court would not presume an intent by Congress to "take over the control of contracts and [attendant] payments" by foreign vessels, unless made "while [the vessels] were in our ports." A contrary reading would, the Justice added, only result in futility. Foreign countries "would continue to permit such contracts and advance payments no matter what our declared law or policy" might be.

(c) *Strathearn S.S. Co. v. Dillon* also involved a suit for half-wages under Section 4 by foreign seamen aboard a foreign vessel while in a U.S. port. The owners refused the seamen's wage demand. This time, a unanimous Court decided that, unlike Section 11, Section 4 was available to foreign seamen notwithstanding contrary stipulations in their contracts of employment, all of which were made abroad and valid where made. Both Section 4 and Section 11 applied to "foreign vessels while in the waters (Section 11) or harbors (Section 4) of the United States." But Section 4 expressly provided that the United States' courts were to be open to [foreign seamen], and voided all contrary contractual provisions. These differences sufficed, the Court thought, to establish Congress' intent to apply the section to all foreign vessels while in U.S. ports, adding that a contrary construction would "have a tendency to prevent the employment of American seamen, and to promote the engagement of those who were not entitled to sue for one-half wages," a result that would scarcely "subserve" Congress' purpose.[15]

Are *Sandberg* and *Strathearn* distinguishable (i) as a matter of statutory interpretation (ii) with regard to the potential for conflict with foreign law, (iii) as an assessment of the relative importance of the interests of both the U.S. and foreign countries that were at stake? How sensitive is Justice Douglas to these considerations? Shortly after the decision in *Sandberg*, several proposals were made in Congress to extend Section 11 to advancements made by foreign vessels in foreign ports. These were met by a "storm of diplomatic protests" and the bills died in Congress. *Benz v. Campania Naviera Hidalgo, S.A.*[16]

---

[15] In a memorandum circulated by Justice Brandeis, but not handed down as the opinion of the Court, the Justice noted the British Government's protest against the application of Section 4 to British vessels and then reviewed the legislative history. He concluded that Congress, intent on forestalling continued American losses to competition by foreign vessels, thought that foreign seamen if entitled to receive one-half their pay upon reaching an American port would desert their foreign ships unless the latter improved wages and working conditions. These objectives were not, the Justice thought, barred by the customary rule that the "rights and duties of officers and crew were, like matters of internal discipline, to be determined" according to the law of the flag. The latter rule applied only with the consent of the sovereign of the port, and that consent could be withdrawn at any time.

[16] 353 U.S. 138, 144, 77 S.Ct. 699, 703 (1957). In *Cunnard S.S. Co. v. Mellon*, 262 U.S. 100, 43 S.Ct. 504 (1923), the Court, relying upon the principles in *Wildenhus' Case* and in *The Bark Eudora*, upheld a Treasury Regulation which, in implementing the Prohibition Act, prohibited all foreign vessels entering U.S. territorial waters from carrying intoxicating liquors whether as sea-stores or as cargo, even if the liquor was kept by the ship under seal

(4) Between the decision in *Lauritzen v. Larsen* and the decision in *Hellenic Lines Ltd. v. Rhoditis*, the United States entered into four separate conventions prepared in Geneva by the First United Nations Law of the Sea Conference, including the Convention on the High Seas.[17] Much of the subject matter of these Conventions has now been incorporated into the comprehensive United Nations Convention on the Law of the Sea.[18] Now, suppose Rhoditis had been injured while the Hellenic Hero was still on the high-seas bound for the port of New Orleans and consider the following:

(a) Would the rationale offered by Justice Douglas for his decision in *Rhoditis* have warranted a different result? If the result would *not* differ, then note that Article 6 of the 1958 High Seas Convention provides that ships shall sail under the flag of one State only and shall "be subject to its exclusive jurisdiction on the high seas," save for "exceptional cases" provided for by treaty or "these articles."[19]

(b) If, because of the High Seas Convention, Justice Douglas would simply not have extended Jones Act relief to seamen injured on the high seas, how strong are the U.S. interests he says are at stake in the case, or how convincing the intent he attributes to Congress?

(5) If, as Justice Douglas suggests, Jones Act liability may be a significant competitive factor, how would you characterize Greece's interest in having the seamen compensated solely in accordance with Greek Law? Was Greece's interest more or less compelling than Denmark's interest in *Lauritzen*? Was the U.S.

---

guaranteeing that it would not be consumed by passengers or crew or otherwise sold while the vessel remained in a U.S. port. Once again, foreign governments protested. Typical of these was a Note filed by the Dutch Government which admitted the "jurisdictional power of a nation over foreign ships entering its territorial waters," but argued "that international comity and the exigencies of international intercourse require that the exercise of this power [be] . . . limited to matters which involve . . . the peace or dignity of the country or the public order or safety of the port. . . ." Liquor "as cargo or sea-stores on board a foreign vessel . . . can never," the Dutch Government said, "affect the public order and safety of the port . . . whereas interference on the part of the United States with such cargo or stores would bring about a serious limitation of [Dutch] . . . freedom of commerce and navigation. . . ." (Note of the Netherlands Minister to the Secretary of State, June 1, 1923; Department of State Press Release, February 16, 1927 pp. 4-5).

[17] 13 U.S.T. 2312, TIAS No. 5200, 450 U.N.T.S. 82.

[18] A/Conf. 62/122, 7 October 1982. The High Seas Convention is one of several conventions on the law of the sea signed at Geneva in 1958. By its terms the High Seas Convention is declarative of customary international law. The United States has not signed the United Nations Convention on the Law of the Sea, and is, therefore, still bound by the terms of the High Seas Convention since Article 311 of the U.N. Convention states: "this Convention shall prevail, as between States parties, over the Geneva Conventions on the Law of the Sea of 29 April, 1958." Moreover the United States has recognized that many parts of the U.N. Convention, including the Articles listed in this Note (4), are declarative of customary international law.

[19] The exceptions pertain to pirate ships (Articles 19 and 22), slavers, certain ships refusing to show a flag (Article 22) and hot pursuit (Article 23). Warships are "completely immune" from any jurisdiction "other than the flag State." (Article 8). These provisions are all carried over substantially unchanged by Articles 92, 95, 105, 110 and 111 of the U.N. Convention.

interest in applying the Jones Act, as that interest is defined by Justice Douglas, any more compelling in *Rhoditis* than in *Lauritzen*? Viewed in terms of the broader systemic interests and values, including the benefits to international commerce mentioned in *Lauritzen*, how would you assess the arguably competing interests of Greece and of the United States, the latter as defined by Justice Douglas? Is any of this of interest to Justice Douglas?

(6) Would the Executive, or Congress or American shipowners have necessarily agreed that the Jones Act recovery in *Rhoditis* served the national interest? Recall that, in the Geneva Conference that drafted the High Seas Convention, the United States opposed the "genuine link" requirement. The Executive's position was set forth in a brief submitted to the NLRB in 1961 stating that "the flag, as a ready recognizable and accepted standard must be preferred pragmatically to any other, that in accordance with that standard, the indirect financial interest of American citizens in a foreign registered ship may not deprive a vessel of its status as a national of the state whose flag it is flown." (Cited in *Empressa Hondurena de Vapores S.A. v. McLeod.* [20]) Also, the United States in opposing a resolution before the UNCTAD Shipping Committee which called for the "phasing-out of "open-registries," joined other developed countries in opposing any attempt to establish "the economic elements of a genuine link between ships and the flag state by an internationally legally binding instrument." [21]

Note also Justice Douglas, in dissenting from the Court's refusal to extend National Labor Relations Act jurisdiction to foreign flag vessels beneficially owned by American companies, accuses the majority of the Court of "shifting from all taxpayers to seamen alone the burden of financing an Executive policy of assuring an adequate American-owned merchant fleet for federal use during national emergencies." [22]

The *Rhoditis* episode might fairly be said to underscore how the process upon which Justice Jackson had embarked, and the process implicit in the Restatement (Third) of the Foreign Relations Law of the United States is not without its hazards. Once judges and commentators had come to recognize the need to move away from the older mechanical rules of the First Restatement of the Conflict of Laws, there ensued a lively debate and a vast literature on the "choice of law process." For our purposes among the more significant of the leading commentators — and one keenly aware of the dangers illustrated by the *Rhoditis* decision — was Professor Brainerd Currie, whose "state interest analysis" — and the opposition which it evoked — are particularly germane to any study of the problems that an extension of the *Lauritzen* analysis to a broader range of regulatory legislation is likely to encounter. Consider then the following excerpt from one notable essay by Professor Currie.

---

[20] 300 F.2d 222, 225 (2d Cir., 1962).

[21] TD/B/C.4 (S.-III)/Misc. 2, at page 23 (1981).

[22] *McCulloch et. al, v. Sociedad Nacional de Marineros de Honduras et. al.*, 372 U.S. 10, 83 S. Ct. 671 (1963), discussed *infra* at page 564.

Brainerd Currie, MARRIED WOMEN'S CONTRACTS: A STUDY IN CONFLICT-OF-LAWS METHOD

25 U. CHI. L. REV. 227 (1958)*

The final alternative, or set of alternatives [to the older Bealian method], is offered by the high-minded, transcendent, and form-free counsels of those who tell us that the choice should be of "the more effective and more useful law," or of the law that fulfills the demands of justice in the particular situation, or of the law that fulfills the "needs and interests of the community," or the law that produces acceptable results. . . . The inescapable fact remains that [these approaches] have proved ineffective. . . . This cardinal disappointment is due in part to the intractable character of the problem itself. It is due in part to the fact that the proffered solutions undoubtedly beg the question; for the original question, at least — *i.e.*, the question as it stood prior to the erection by the Territorialists of a structure of false questions — was precisely: What is the just result? It is due in part to the fact that the approach attributes to courts a freedom and a competence that they do not possess; for courts are committed to the administration of justice under law, and the constraint of that commitment is not likely to be thrown off simply because the law in question may seem to the court old-fashioned, unwise, unjust or misguided. . . .

* * * *

I think it is clear that we cannot accept any conflict-of-laws method that proceeds on such premises. . . . [In] the context of live issues of policy . . . the suggestion is an alarming one. It is simply not the business of courts to substitute their judgment for that of the legislature. The content of the law to be applied must be inquired into, to be sure, and one of the grievous faults of the traditional system is its treatment of that content as immaterial, but the inquiry should be in aid of a determination of the scope of legislative policy and of the ways in which that policy is to be implemented, not an instrument for undermining that policy. . . .

* * * *

[The author at this point draws a distinction between "false conflict cases" and "true conflict cases." The "false conflict" cases] . . . do not involve conflicting interests of the respective states. It is perfectly clear what the result should be in each. Either state, though approaching the case with no other purpose than to advance its own interests, would reach that result. . . .

* * * *

[Professor Currie then turns to the "true conflict" situation.] Paradoxically, the problem is insoluble with the resources of conflict-of-laws precisely because it is a true problem of a conflict of interest. . . . The policies [of the affected states] are in direct conflict. Who is to say which is the more important, or the more deserving, or the more enlightened? Not even the United States Supreme Court is in a position to do so. Certainly it is not for the courts of one state to sacrifice local policy because they feel that it is relatively old-fashioned or misguided. . . .

---

* * * *

The sensible and clearly constitutional thing for any court to do, confronted with a true conflict of interests is to apply its own law. In this way it could be sure at least that it is consistently advancing the policy of its own state. It should apply its own law . . . simply because the court should never apply any other law except when there is a good reason for doing so. That so doing will promote the interests of a foreign state at the expense of the interest of the forum state is not a good reason. Nor is the fact that such deference may lead to a conjectural uniformity of results among the different forums a good reason, when the price for that uniformity is either the indiscriminate impairment of local policy in half of the cases or the consistent yielding of local policy to the policy of a foreign state.

In yet another essay Professor Currie had the following to say:

I know that courts make law, and that in the process they "weigh conflicting interests" and draw upon all sorts of "norms" to inform and justify their action. I do not know where to draw the line between the judicial legislation that is "molecular," or permissible and that which is "molar" or impermissible. But assessment of the respective values of the competing legitimate interests of two sovereign states, in order to determine which is to prevail is a political function of a very high order. This is a function that should not be committed to courts in a democracy.

A REJOINDER

Currie's "government interest analysis" with its forum preference corollary has not gone unchallenged. Professor Von Mehren,[23] had this to say:

. . . [Professor Currie's] . . . methodology builds on an avowed view of the appropriate role of the judicial process; courts are not agencies to "weigh" and choose between truly conflicting interests of different states. . . . [T]he methodology [also] assumes — though this attitude perhaps never becomes explicit — that a Hobbesian state of nature exists as between the communities relevant for legal purposes even though contemporary life, in so many of its aspects, is not confined within a single jurisdiction. Finally . . . the approach apparently does not recognize that, in any given multistate situation, a jurisdiction may have not only policies expressed in domestic rules that would be forwarded by applying those rules in a given case, but also policies (peculiar to or of special importance in multistate transactions as distinguished from wholly domestic transactions) that likewise have a claim to application in the particular case.

In my own thinking about the choice-of-law problem I am not prepared to accept what I take to be Professor Currie's position on these three points; consequently I must reject his general proposition. . . .

---

[23] Book Review, 17 J. Legal Ed. 91, 94-95, 96-97 (1964).

If his teaching were ever fully accepted and became the exclusive basis for handling choice-of-law problems American thinking would, in my judgment, have adopted a point of view that is in its way as narrow and as dogmatic as the approach of the original Restatement which Currie so effectively attacks . . . [and would] tend to fasten upon the international and the interstate communities . . . a legal order characterized by chaos and retaliation.

Later Currie did concede that when courts inquire into the "scope of legislative policy and of the ways in which that policy is to be implemented," they should proceed as a "restrained and enlightened forum." Judge Traynor, in a notable commentary on this addendum to Currie's initial position, suggests that, in its strict form, the "forum preference principle" as a device to avoid "interest weighing seems to strike at the heart of the judicial process." But, the Judge went on, in his call for a "restrained and enlightened forum," Currie recognized the need for balancing the opposing interests of states against each other and that some sort of weighing of interests was inevitable. M. Traynor, Conflict of Laws: Professor Currie's Restrained and Enlightened Forum, 49 Calif. L. Rev. 945 (1961).

NOTE

Return to *Lotus* and the "territorial" principle — or for that matter to any of the rules noted by the Harvard Research — and consider some of the problems that Professor Currie discusses as well as the problem of uncertainty and the susceptibility of the newer methodology to manipulation at the hands of judges with their own agenda. The fault of the older rules lies in their unilateral perspective and their tendency to invite a mechanical application having no relation whatsoever to the interests at stake in the prescriptive jurisdictional question. In other words, their weakness is in being treated as rules; as sufficient answers to the jurisdictional problem. Perhaps, therefore, they might better be treated as beginning points in a process; not as rules, but as presumptions to be overcome. Thus, the outer limits of the "territorial principle" as defined by *Lotus* might be treated as a presumption that any substantive law that does not fall within those limits is presumptively inapplicable unless a strong case can be made for its application based on all of the considerations listed by the Restatement. With this in mind return to the following cases and test whether the suggestion helps overcome some of the problems of the newer methodology.

— *Rocha v. United States* and *United States v. Pizzarusso*

— Our variation on *United States v. Layton*

— *United States v. Columba-Colella*

— *Hellenic Lines, LTD. v. Rhoditis*

[B] Efforts to Organize Foreign Seamen

McCULLOCH et. al. v. SOCIEDAD NACIONAL de MARINEROS de HONDURAS, et. al

An Introductory Note

[This decision covers three companion cases that stem from a petition filed in 1959 with the National Labor Relations Board (the "Board") by the National Maritime Union of America (NMU) against the United Fruit Company (United Fruit) as the sole stockholder of Empressa Hondurena de Vapores, S.A. (Empressa), a Honduran company. The petition asked the Board to certify the approximately 335 seamen employed by Empressa on its Honduran flag vessels as a bargaining unit under the National Labor Relations Act (the "Act")[24] and to order an election in which those seamen would decide whether they wanted to be represented by the NMU, by Sindicato Maritimo Nacional de Honduras (Sindicato), an Honduran union which had intervened in the action, or no union at all. At the time the seamen, all but one of whom (a Jamaican) were Honduran citizens, were represented by Sociedad Nacional de Marineros de Honduras (Sociedad) another Honduran union which was invited to intervene in the Board proceedings but declined to do so. Empressa — the employer — did, however, intervene.

According to the Court, Honduras had a long established and comprehensive system of laws governing Honduran registered vessels. Under those laws Empressa was required to negotiate with Sociedad which, since 1941, had been the recognized bargaining representative of its seagoing employees. The latest contract between Empressa and Sociedad dated from 1957, provided for a union shop, contained a "no-strike" and a "no lock-out" clause, and established a scale for determining wages, hours, maintenance and cure, vacation and other benefits. Also, under Honduran law, only a union whose membership was at least 90% Honduran nationals and whose "juridic personality" was recognized under Honduran law could represent seamen aboard Honduran registered ships. Obviously NMU could not meet these requirements.

The ships on which the seamen served, although owned and operated by Empressa and registered in Honduras, were all time-chartered to United Fruit and were used to carry United Fruit products from South and Central America to the United States. On return trips the vessels carried freight for various United Fruit subsidiaries and occasionally for other shippers. Although Empressa's directors were all elected by United Fruit, there were no interlocking directors and no officers in common. Empressa maintained its own records, property and, according to the Board, "appeared to function as a distinct corporate entity." As owner and operator of the vessels, Empressa was responsible for putting fully equipped, provisioned and manned ships to sea, for paying all wages and for disciplining the crew. As time-charterer,

---

[24] National Labor Relations Act, 49 Stat. 449 (1935), as amended by Pub. L. No. 101, 80th Cong., 1st Sess., 1947, and Pub. L. No. 257, 86th Cong., 1st Sess., 1959; 29 U.S.C. Sections 151-68.

United Fruit determined what voyages the ships were to make, their ports of call, their stay at each port and their cargoes. On these matters United Fruit dealt directly with the captain of each vessel. If dissatisfied with the handling of a ship, however, or with the performance of its officers or crew or its mechanical condition, United Fruit held Empressa responsible for taking the necessary corrective action. Organizationally, United Fruit's direction of the vessels was in the hands of its Marine Division. As such, the ships were fully integrated into United Fruit's shipping operations which included a number of U.S. flag vessels owned outright or chartered by United Fruit from its U.S. subsidiaries.

Under these facts, the Board decided that Empressa was engaged in "commerce" within the meaning of Section 2(6) of the Act[25] and that its shipping operations "affected commerce" within the meaning of Section 2(7) of the Act.[26] Hence, the Board concluded it had jurisdiction under Section 9(c) of the Act to order the requested election among Empressa's seamen. Responsibility for conducting the election was delegated to the Board's Regional Director in New York.[27]

Under Section 7 of the Act, as it now reads, employees are guaranteed "the right to self organization, to form, join, or assist labor organizations, to bargain collectively through representatives of their own choosing, and to engage in other concerted activities for the purpose of collective bargaining or other mutual aid or protection" . . . Under Section 8(a) of the Act it is an "unfair labor practice for an employer . . . to interfere with, restrain, or coerce employees in the exercise of the rights guaranteed in Section 7." Under Section 9(a), representatives selected by a majority of the employees in an appropriate unit serve as the "exclusive representatives of all the employees" in that unit "for the purpose of collective bargaining in respect to rates of pay, wages, hours of employment, or other conditions of employment. . . ." Under Section 9(c), if a petition is filed with the Board by an "employee or group of employees . . . or labor organization acting in their behalf," alleging that while a substantial number of employees wish to be represented for collective bargaining purposes, their employer declines to recognize their representative, the Board is to investigate and, if appropriate, hold a hearing on the petition. If the Board finds "upon the record of such hearing that . . . a question of representation exists, it shall direct an election by secret ballot and shall certify the results thereof."

Following issuance of the Board order, Empressa, in two separate cases, sued the Regional Director in an effort to prevent the election. The District Court

---

[25] Section 2(6) of the Act stipulates in relevant part as follows: "The term "commerce" means trade, traffic, commerce, transportation, or communication among the several states or . . . between any foreign country and any State, Territory, or the District of Columbia. . . ."

[26] Section 2(7) of the Act provides as follows: "The term "affecting commerce" means in commerce, or burdening or obstructing commerce or the free flow of commerce, or having led or tending to lead to a labor dispute burdening or obstructing commerce or the free flow of commerce."

[27] In the proceedings before the Board the Executive Branch filed an *amicus* brief supporting Empressa's challenge to the Board's jurisdiction.

denied Empressa's request for an injunction but was reversed on appeal by the Second Circuit in an opinion by Friendly J. Meanwhile, the District Court in the District of Columbia, acting upon the application of Sociedad, enjoined the members of the Board from carrying out their order. The Supreme Court granted certiorari in all three cases. What follows are excerpts from the opinions by the Board, the Second Circuit and the Supreme Court.]

The Board Decision

UNITED FRUIT COMPANY AND NATIONAL MARITIME UNION OF AMERICA

134 NLRB No. 25, November 17, 1961
1961 CCH NLRB Decisions Paragraph 10,620

With respect to the companies' arguments upon the foreign flag law and other international law doctrines and upon certain treaties and conventions between the United States and Honduras, such matters were dealt with in *West India Fruit & Steamship Company, Inc.*[28] In that case, it was held that the presence of such matters did not necessarily preclude the Act's coverage of a given maritime operation. . . . [N]one of these cases support the proposition that the underlying stock or other beneficial ownership and, thus, ultimate control of a foreign corporation or its operations by domestic United States interests necessarily bring the foreign corporation or its operations within the coverage of the Act. . . . It is the commerce of this nation, not of foreign nations, with which the Act is concerned. . . . In following the Supreme Court's decision in *Lauritzen v. Larsen*, the Board has pointed out that the test of jurisdiction given commerce literally within Section 2(6) of the Act is whether there existed substantial contacts between the "foreign" maritime operation and important United States interests. The problem is to evaluate the many aspects of the operation and to determine whether or not the shipping involved is essentially that of this nation and not that of a foreign nation which the exigencies of international trade have brought in contact with the United States. . . .

* * * *

The facts . . . show that the maritime operations before us come literally within the Act's definition of commerce as they encompass in large part, transportation and trade between foreign countries and States of this nation. They further demonstrate that the relationship between [United Fruit] . . . and Empressa is one in which the affairs of the subsidiary are designed essentially to further the shipping operations of the parent and not one in which Empressa is considered an independent undertaking whose success or failure is gauged by its role in the open market. Supporting this conclusion are inter alia, (1) that Empressa's capital, expenditures and other substantial changes [sic?] in operations are tied to [United

---

[28] 130 NLRB No. 46.

Fruit's] . . . sea-going transportation needs, both present and projected, (2) that Empressa, with but few possible exceptions, time-charters its vessels to [United Fruit] . . . only and does not look to the open market for business, and (3) that Empressa's vessels are utilized by [United Fruit] . . . as an integral and necessary part of its fleet of vessels and not chartered as an alternative to acquiring vessels elsewhere or only to meet particular contingencies that may arise. Thus, the record shows that Empressa's maritime operations are a part of a single integrated maritime operation under the continuous, direct control and either direct or ultimate ownership of [United Fruit] . . . and are an essential part of a sea-going enterprise located in and directed from the United States and engaged in the commerce of this nation as described in Section 2(6) of the Act. It is also evident, and we find, that Empressa through its immediate authority and control over hiring and other terms and conditions of employment and [United Fruit] . . . through its control of Empressa and of the vessels and their operations are joint employers of the employees covered by the petition.

[T]he companies' motion to dismiss on jurisdictional grounds [is] . . . denied.

The Second Circuit's Decision

EMPRESSA HONDURENA DE VAPORES, S.A., v. McLEOD

300 F. 2d 222 (2d Cir. 1962)

Before LUMBARD, CHIEF JUDGE and FRIENDLY and MARSHALL, CIRCUIT JUDGES.

FRIENDLY, CIRCUIT JUDGE.

The defendant [Regional Director's] position proceeds from the basis that Section 9(c) of the Act authorizes direction of an election if the Board has determined that "a question of representation affecting commerce exists" . . . Literally the words cover the case. Yet the Board would hardly insist that the words apply to everything within their literal reach; we have not heard it suggested that the Board considers its power to extend to the stevedores who load Empressa's ships in Honduras although they are engaged in "commerce" quite as much as the seamen who man them. Neither do we suppose the Board would think it could direct an election among miners employed by a wholly owned subsidiary of an American company abroad, even though the ore was shipped to the United States and American employees of the parent were objecting to what they regarded as unfair wage competition arising from lack of effective organization among the foreign miners, although again the words literally apply. . . .

The problem of workers directly engaged in transportation is more difficult; the stevedores stay on the piers, the miners remain in the mines, but the seamen come to the United States and return. The Board is right in saying the scope of its power in respect of the latter is not to be determined by the simple notion that a Honduran registered ship is a floating piece of Honduran territory; that is a mere "figure of speech" whose fictitious character was exposed long ago, *Wildenhus' Case*[29] . . . .

Although Article 10 of the Treaty,[30] which requires the United States to recognize Empressa's vessels as vessels of Honduras, also is not the end of our investigation, it surely must be the beginning. As was said with respect to the Jones Act in *Lauritzen v. Larsen,* . . . "Perhaps the most venerable and universal rule of maritime law relevant to our problem is that which gives cardinal importance to the law of the flag" . . . How "cardinal" the importance is and how much "weight" should be given must depend, in the absence of clear expression by Congress, on what other factors of foreign and United States interest are present, and on the nature of the United States statute sought to be applied, taking particular account of the danger that an attempt to apply our law may result in a collision with the foreign sovereign.

> [Here Judge Friendly reviews *Lauritzen, Romero* and *Gerradin v. United Fruit,*[31] in which the Second Circuit held that an American seaman hired in New York by a Honduran registered vessel and injured on the high seas, could maintain an action under the Jones Act against an American demise-charterer of the vessel.]

* * * *

It is with this background that we come to *Benz v. Compania Naviera Hidalgo S.A.*[32] . . . It involved the SS. Riviera, owned by a Panamanian corporation, sailing under the Liberian flag, and manned by a foreign crew, principally German and British, who had signed a British form of articles at Bremen, Germany. While the Riviera was in Portland, Oregon, loading a cargo of wheat destined for India, crew members struck because of a wage dispute, and picketed the vessel. The picketing was later continued by three American unions. The shipowner's action, in which federal jurisdiction was predicated on diverse citizenship, sought damages from these unions and their representatives, under Oregon law. The defense was that the Labor Management Relations Act had preempted the field; the Supreme Court held the defense unfounded. The opinion, by Mr. Justice Clark, stated:

> Our study of the Act leaves us convinced that Congress did not fashion it to resolve labor disputes between nationals of other countries operating ships under foreign laws. The whole background of the Act is concerned with industrial strife between American employers and employees.

The Board seeks to distinguish *Benz* on the ground that it involved no such indirect American ownership and no such regular coming and going from American ports as here. . . . Stress is laid upon the sentence in the *Benz* opinion, "The

---

[29] 120 U.S. 1, 7 S.Ct. 385, 30 L.Ed. 565 (1887).

[30] Article X of the Treaty of Friendship, Commerce and Consular Rights between Honduras and the United States, 45 Stat. 2618 (1927), provides that merchant vessels flying the flags and having the papers of either country "shall, both within the territorial waters of the other High Contracting Party and on the high seas, be deemed to be the vessels of the Party whose flag is flown."

[31] 60 F. 2d 927 (2d Cir. 1932).

[32] 353 U.S. 138, 77 S. Ct. 699, 1 L. Ed. 2d 709 (1957).

only American connection was that the controversy erupted while the ship was transiently in a United States port and American labor unions participated in its picketing" . . . As against these respects in which the instant case is stronger than *Benz* for the application of the Labor Act, there is at least one in which it may be weaker. As Mr. Justice Douglas pointed out in his dissent, the *Benz* case did not directly involve the application of the panoply of labor regulation embodied in Sections 7, 8, 9 and 10, but only the provisions of Section 303 of the Taft-Hartley Act relating to picketing, there wholly on American soil; it is hard to believe that a foreign government would be, or under international practice would have any right to be, concerned with whether the rights of their ships to damages for such picketing were governed by Federal or state law. Here, on the other hand, application of Sections 7, 8, 9 and 10 of the National Labor Relations Act would involve the risk of continuous conflict between the United States and Honduras with respect to labor conditions which, though of more interest to the United States than those in *Benz*, are still Honduras' "primary concern" . . .

The case made by plaintiff's complaint goes far beyond the flying of the Honduran flag, important as *Lauritzen* teaches that to be. In this case there are also the Honduran citizenship of the crews, the employment of the crews in Honduras under Honduran articles, the vessels' regular visits to Honduras, the Honduran corporate identity — admittedly not fictitious — of the owner, the long recognition of and contract with a Honduran union, and the provisions of Honduran law regulating labor matters. Though the vessels are engaged in the foreign commerce of the United States, they are also engaged in the foreign commerce of Honduras. The only United States contacts not matched by Honduran ones are United Fruit's stock ownership and its direction and use of the voyages; these are substantially outweighed, for the purpose here at issue, by Honduras' interest.

* * * *

[O]n the allegations of the complaint, the conflict between United States and Honduran law would be constant; far from dealing only with incidents while the ships were in American waters, the Board would be regularly applying the shifting standards of its own decisions, and those of American courts and American legislators, to conduct in Honduras, where the bargaining between Empressa and its employees had always taken place; it would be endeavoring to enforce its will on matters that Honduras, with a better claim, regards as for itself to decide. . . . The case is appropriate for application of Mr. Justice Jackson's warning that "in dealing with international commerce we cannot be unmindful of the necessity for mutual forbearance if retaliations are to be avoided; nor should we forget that any contact which we hold sufficient to warrant application of our laws to a foreign transaction will logically be as strong a warrant for a foreign country to apply its law to an American transaction" . . .

Our belief that the Labor Act should not be held applicable in a case such as this is reinforced by [Article 5, of] the Geneva Convention on the High Seas. . . . Discussion seems to have been centered on what happens if the "genuine link" does not exist:[33] neither the text nor such explanatory materials as we have found

---

[33] The "genuine link" requirement as adopted was less stringent than proposals made by such governments as the United Kingdom and the Netherlands and by the International

say specifically what happens if the conditions of the final sentence are met. Yet, since it was deemed so important to insist upon the existence of a "genuine link" and the flag state's effective exercise of "jurisdiction and control in administrative, technical and social matters over ships flying its flag," it would be unreasonable to conclude that when all this had been done other states do not owe some obligations of respect.

* * * *

We realize that American unions understandably desire to organize vessels which they conceive to be in substance a part of this country's merchant marine, and that attempts to implement that desire can lead to a breach of the industrial peace which the Board is bound to promote. . . . Therefore, we recognize that a controversy between an American union and Empressa could lead or tend to lead "to a labor dispute burdening or obstructing commerce or the free flow of commerce" carried on by American flag ships, as well as directly obstructing commerce carried on by foreign ones. However, that scarcely is decisive — the question still is how far Congress intended to permit the Board to intervene in what would normally be the affairs of a foreign government in order to prevent this . . . obstruction. [W]e see no basis for believing Congress would have chosen to solve the problem by an exercise of jurisdiction which would create such a conflict with a foreign government as would seem inevitable here.

* * * *

The order denying a temporary injunction is reversed.

The Supreme Court Decision

McCULLOCH ET. AL. v. SOCIEDAD NACIONAL DEMARINEROS DE HONDURAS Et. Al.

United States Supreme Court
372 U.S. 10, 83 S. Ct. 671 (1963)

Mr. Justice Clark delivered the opinion of the Court.

Labor Conference, "which would have enabled states other than the flag state to withhold recognition of the national character of a ship if they considered that there was no "genuine link" between the state and the ship." Report of the Committee on Foreign Relations, 106 Cong. Rec. 10382 (1960). The Senate was told that the effect of the language as adopted in Geneva is that "no state can claim the right to determine unilaterally that no genuine link exists between a ship and the flag state," but "nevertheless, there is a possibility that a state, with respect to a particular ship, may assert before an agreed tribunal, such as the International Court of Justice, that no genuine link exists. In such event, it would be for the Court to decide whether or not a genuine link existed." *Id.*

* * * *

The question of application of the laws of the United States to foreign-flag ships and their crews has arisen often and in various contexts. As to the application of the National Labor Relations Act and its amendments the Board has evolved a test relying on the relative weight of a ship's foreign as compared with its American contacts.

Six years ago [however,] this Court considered the question of the application of the Taft-Hartley amendments to the Act in a suit for damages "resulting from the picketing of a foreign ship operated entirely by foreign seamen under foreign articles while the vessel [was] temporarily in an American port." *Benz v. Compania Naviera Hidalgo. . . .* We held that the Act did not apply, searching the language and the legislative history and concluding that the latter "inescapably describes the boundaries of the Act as including only the workingmen of our own country and its possessions."

It is contended that this case is nonetheless distinguishable from *Benz* in two respects. First, here there is a fleet of vessels not temporarily in United States waters but operating in a regular course of trade between foreign ports and those of the United States; and, second, the foreign owner of the ships is in turn owned by an American corporation. We note that both of these points rely on additional American contacts and therefore necessarily presume the validity of the "balancing of contacts" theory of the Board. But to follow such a suggested procedure to the ultimate might require that the Board inquire into the internal discipline and order of all foreign vessels calling at American ports. Such activity would raise considerable disturbance not only in the field of maritime law but in our international relations as well. In addition, enforcement of Board orders would project the courts into application of the sanctions of the Act to foreign-flag ships on a purely *ad hoc* weighing of contacts basis. This would inevitably lead to embarrassment in foreign affairs and be entirely infeasible in actual practice. The question, therefore, appears to us more basic; namely, whether the Act as written was intended to have any application to foreign registered vessels employing alien seamen.

Petitioners . . . have been unable to point to any specific language in the Act itself or in its extensive legislative history that reflects such a congressional intent. Indeed, the opposite is true as we found in *Benz*, where we pointed to the language of Chairman Hartley characterizing the Act as "a bill of rights both for *American* workingmen and for their employers." . . . We continue to believe that if the sponsors of the original Act or of its amendments conceived of the application now sought by the Board they failed to translate such thoughts into describing the boundaries of the Act as including foreign-flag vessels manned by alien crews. Therefore, we find no basis for a construction which would exert United States jurisdiction over and apply its laws to the internal management and affairs of the vessels here flying the Honduran flag, contrary to the recognition long afforded them not only by our State Department but also by the Congress.[34] In addition,

---

[34] Here Justice Clark cites Article X of the Treaty of Friendship, Commerce & Consular Rights between Honduras and the United States, quoted by Judge Friendly at page 562, footnote 30 *supra*. - Ed.

our attention is called to the well-established rule of international law that the law of the flag state ordinarily governs the internal affairs of the ship. . . . The possibility of international discord cannot therefore be gainsaid. Especially is this true on account of the concurrent application of the Act and the Honduran Labor Code that would result with our approval of jurisdiction. Sociedad, currently the exclusive bargaining agent of Empressa under Honduran law, would have a head-on collision with N.M.U. should it become the exclusive bargaining agent under the Act. This would be aggravated by the fact that under Honduran law N.M.U. is prohibited from representing the seamen on Honduran-flag ships even in the absence of a recognized bargaining agent. Thus even though Sociedad withdrew from such an intramural labor fight — a highly unlikely circumstance — questions of such international import would remain as to invite retaliatory action from other nations as well as Honduras.

The presence of such highly charged international circumstances brings to mind the admonition of Mr. Chief Justice Marshall . . . that "an act of congress ought never to be construed to violate the law of nations if any other possible construction remains. . . ." Since neither we nor the parties are able to find any such clear expression, we hold that the Board was without jurisdiction to order the election. This is not to imply, however, "any impairment of our own sovereignty, or limitation of the power of Congress" in this field. . . . In fact, just as we directed the parties in *Benz* to the Congress, which "alone has the facilities necessary to make fairly such an important policy decision," . . . we conclude here that the arguments should be directed to the Congress rather than to us.

Mr. Justice Goldberg, took no part in the consideration or decision of these cases.

Mr. Justice Douglas, concurring.

I had supposed that the activities of the American labor organizations whether related to domestic vessels or to foreign ones were covered by the National Labor Relations Act, at least absent a treaty which evinces a different policy.[35] . . . But my views were rejected in *Benz v. Compania Naviera Hidalgo*, and, having lost that cause in *Benz*, I bow to the inexorable result of its extension here, though not without some misgivings. The practical effect of our decision is to shift from all the taxpayers to seamen alone the main burden of financing an executive policy of assuring the availability of an adequate American-owned merchant fleet for federal use during national emergencies.

---

[35] It is agreed that Article XXII of the Treaty of Friendship, Commerce, and Consular Rights between the United States and Honduras, 45 Stat. 2618 (1927), and Article X of the Convention with Liberia of October 7, 1938, 54 Stat. 1751, 1756, grant those nations exclusive jurisdiction over the matters here involved.

NOTES AND QUESTIONS

(1) According to the Board, Empressa's shipping operations came within the reach of the Act because those operations had (i) more contact with the United States than with Honduras? (ii) weightier contacts with the United States than with Honduras? or (iii) because . . . ? How did the Board go wrong, according to Judge Friendly? according to Justice Clark? Judge Friendly, while not reversed, did not fair so well either, why? What seemed to be the Supreme Court's principal concern?

(2) In *Peninsular & Occidental Steamship Company, Green Trading Company and Seafarer's International Union of North America*,[36] the Board asserted jurisdiction to hear an unfair labor practice complaint by a union against a Liberian corporation, owner of a Liberian flag vessel, the S.S. Florida. The company had allegedly responded to the union's efforts to organize the predominantly alien crew of the Florida by interrogating and threatening the crew with dismissal, putting them under surveillance and demanding that they refuse to testify at Board hearings. Prior to 1955, the S.S. Florida, a cruise ship operating out of Miami to ports in the Caribbean, had been owned by a U.S. corporation and flew the U.S. flag. When the ship began to lose money the American corporate owner formed a Liberian subsidiary to which it transferred the vessel. The subsidiary promptly entered the ship on the Liberian registry and then chartered the vessel to yet another Liberian subsidiary of the American owner. The second subsidiary then time-subchartered the ship back to the former corporate American owner which continued to operate it out of Miami. The ship had never been in Liberian waters although it was inspected by agents of the Liberian Government.

Assuming there was no Liberian union to which the crew of the S.S. Florida could belong and that Liberian law did not confer upon the crew a right to organize comparable to that found in the Act, how would the Board's decision have fared upon appeal after the Supreme Court's *McCulloch* decision? Might the Board's decision have had a better chance if Judge Friendly's *McCulloch* opinion were the controlling authority?

(3) Even if Justice Douglas was correct in charging that the Court in *McCulloch* capitulated to the Executive, isn't his complaint mistimed, if not misplaced, after his *Rhoditis* opinion? Might Justice Douglas have found support for his position in Professor Currie's methodology?

(4) Note that Judge Friendly thought that an assumption of Board jurisdiction in *McCulloch* would have violated Article 5 of the 1958 High Seas Convention. Would the same hold true in *Peninsular and Oriental Steamship Co.*? Assume, in the latter case, that the Executive had abandoned its position regarding "flags of convenience," how would you deal with the Article 5 problem? Recall, in this connection, that the rule of construction employed in *Lauritzen v. Larsen*, was intended to reconcile domestic statutes with customary international law only to

---

[36] 132 NLRB No. 1., (1962).

the extent possible. In the case of treaties, however, the later in time rule prevails.**37**

§ 6.03 United States' Export Controls

Generally it is the policy of the United States to encourage export trade with most of the countries of the world. Necessarily, however, in the context of a world divided along ideological lines and characterized, until very recently, by a "cold-war," by periodic "hot" wars such as the Korean and Vietnam conflicts and by tensions that arise when other nations are perceived by the United States to be acting in a manner hostile to its interests and those of its allies, the United States has, as one might expect, placed limits on the right of individuals to export to certain proscribed foreign countries. Beyond this the United States has also from time to time attempted to control exports originating in some friendly foreign country when the exports are destined for a proscribed country and are undertaken by a corporation subject to the control of a U.S. company. Needless to say these latter attempts in particular have given rise to a number of serious jurisdictional disputes between the United States and its allies.

The principle legislative authority for controlling exports is the Export Administration Act of 1979 (EAA).**1** While recognizing that controls are at times necessary, the Act also recognizes that, unless used judiciously, controls could undermine the economic well being of the United States and the stability of the entire free world. Accordingly, the Act authorizes the President to institute a system of export controls but only where necessary to achieve certain specified objectives and then only after full consideration has been given to the impact of such controls on the United States economy.**2**

---

37 In this connection note that in *United States v. Postal*, 589 F.2d 862 (5th Cir., 1979) the court held that the High Seas Convention was not self-executing, had not been implemented by legislation and was hence not, under the Supremacy Clause (Article VI, cl. 2), a rule of municipal law sufficient, in the courts of the United States, to over-ride the so-called Kerr-Frisbie rule, barring an unlawfully arrested accused from raising a due process challenge to the court's jurisdiction. (pages 874-878). Under this rationale are we back to the Justice Marshall's rule of construction?

1 50 U.S.C. 2401 et seq. The Export Administration Act (EAA) was extensively amended by the Export Administration Amendments Act of 1985, Pub. L. 99-64, 98 Stat. 120 (July 12, 1985) and by the Omnibus Trade and Competitiveness Act of 1988, Pub. L. 100-418, 102 Stat. 1107 (August 23, 1988). At times, the Export Administration Act has lapsed and the regulations implementing the act have been maintained under the International Emergency Economic Powers Act, 50 U.S.C. 1701 et. seq. In addition to the EAA, control of the exportation of arms and munitions is provided for in a completely separate regulatory scheme operated by the State Department under the authority of the Arms Export Control Act, Pub. L. 90-629, c. 1, Section 1, October 22, 1968, 81 Stat 1321 as amended, 22 U.S.C. 2751 et. seq. See especially 22 U.S.C. 2778.

2 In enacting the Export Administration Act of 1979 Congress acknowledged:
"Exports contribute significantly to the economic well- being of the United States and the stability of the world by increasing employment and production in the United States, and by earning foreign exchange thereby contributing favorably to the trade balance. The restriction of exports from the United States can have serious adverse effects on the balance

Under the EAA controls may be imposed by the President "only to the extent necessary" to achieve one or more of the following three objectives:[3]

(A)   to restrict the *export of goods and technology* which would make a significant contribution to the military potential of any other country or combination of countries which would be detrimental to the national security of the United States;

(B)   to restrict the export of *goods and technology* where necessary to further significantly the foreign policy of the United States or to fulfill its declared international obligations; and

(C)   to restrict the export of *goods* where necessary to protect the domestic economy from the excessive drain of scarce materials and to reduce the serious inflationary impact of foreign demand.

The authority to prohibit or curtail exports of goods or technology applies to any export that is "subject to the jurisdiction of the United States" or "exported by any person subject to the jurisdiction of the United States." Also note that exports of technology may only be controlled for national security or foreign policy reasons. Only exports of goods can be controlled for short supply reasons. Moreover, the President may not prohibit or curtail exports for foreign policy reasons under contracts entered into prior to the notice of his intention to impose controls unless the President certifies to Congress that:

(A)   a breach of the peace poses a serious and direct threat to the strategic interest of the United States

(B)   [prohibiting or curtailing exports] . . . will be instrumental in remedying the situation posing the direct threat, and

(C)   the export controls will continue only so long as the direct threat persists. Section 6(m).[4]

In addition, the 1985 Amendments to the Act bar application of controls for foreign policy reasons to donations intended to meet basic human needs. The Act also includes specific mandated controls on certain items such as nuclear explosives and crime control instruments.

---

of payments and on domestic employment, particularly when restrictions applied by the United States are more extensive than those imposed by other countries." 50 U.S.C. 2401(2).

[3] The Act defines the term "good" as "any article, natural or man made substance, material, supply or manufactured product, including inspection and test equipment, and excluding technical data." Section 16(3). The term "technology" is defined as "the information and know-how (whether in tangible form, such as models, prototypes, drawings, sketches, diagrams, blueprints, or manuals, or in intangible form, such as training or technical services) that can be used to design, produce, manufacture, utilize, or reconstruct goods, including computer software and technical data, but not the goods themselves." Section 16(4). In addition, the term exports is very broadly defined to include any transfer to any person within the U.S. with knowledge or intent that goods or technology will be shipped to an unauthorized recipient. Section 16(5)(C).

[4] The only exercise to date of the President's authority under this section was to stop shipments of scuba gear to Iran. Presidential Determination 87-20 of September 23, 1987, 52 Fed. Reg. 36749.

The Licensing System

The EAA is implemented through regulations establishing a complex licensing system administered by the Department of Commerce. Licenses are granted primarily on the basis of the goods or technology listed on the Commodity Control List (CCL) and the country to which the exports are being shipped. Established by the Secretary of Commerce, the CCL sets forth the licensing requirements for each commodity listed. For licensing purposes foreign countries are divided into seven groups designated by the symbols "Q," "S," "T," "V," "W," "Y," and "Z." Canada is not included in any country group. The country groups include:

Q - Rumania

S - Libya

T - North, Central, and South America, Bermuda and the Caribbean, except Canada and Cuba

V - All countries not included in any other country group (except Canada)

W - Hungary, Poland

Y - Albania, Bulgaria, Czechoslovakia, Estonia, Laos, Latvia, Lithuania, Mongolian People's Republic, U.S.S.R.

Z - Cuba, Cambodia, North Korea, Vietnam

In addition, there are three broad categories of licenses. First, a "general license" is a license in name only. Where the Regulations permit the export of any commodity or technology to a particular foreign country subject to the requirement of a "general license," it means that the exporter is free to ship the item abroad without applying to the Department for any license or other permission. Most U.S. exports move under general licenses. A general license, however, is only applicable to the export of commodities or technical data under the licensing jurisdiction of the Department of Commerce.

Second, a "validated license" authorizes a specific export and is issued pursuant to an application by the exporter. Validated licenses are granted on a case-by-case basis for a single transaction and are generally valid for only two years. Finally, a "special license" is a type of validated license that authorizes multiple exports issued pursuant to an application by the exporter. Special licenses include:

1. Distribution licenses which authorize multiple exports and reexports to eligible countries for a period of two years subject to extension and renewal. A distribution license may be used for all countries in Country Group T and V, except Afghanistan, Iran and the Peoples Republic of China. The regulations emphasize that exporters granted distribution licenses must be reliable, experienced and capable of adhering to export control requirements.

2. Project Licenses authorize multiple exports for specified ongoing activities for a period of one year, subject to renewal. Specific activities under a project license include substantial capital expansion to a new or existing plant, programs for maintenance, repair, and operating supplies to an existing facility, and programs for supplying material to be used in the production of other commodities for sale. The regulations make certain

commodities ineligible for a project license (*e.g.* all projects involving shipments to Iran or Libya)

3. Service Supply licences which enable U.S. exporters to export spare or replacement parts for goods previously exported

In general, all exports and reexports of goods and technology to Country Group Z require a "validated license" for foreign policy reasons with certain exceptions including humanitarian shipments of donated goods for basic human needs and some publications, recordings and films. For Country Groups Q, W and Y virtually all non-public technical data requires a "validated license" for national security reasons. Most exports to free world destinations are made under a "general license" unless the commodity is controlled for national security reasons.

In addition to limitations placed on exports to specific countries or country groups, the Act includes a special provision for exports to controlled countries[5] of goods, technology, and industrial techniques developed by funds appropriated to the Department of Defense. The purpose of this section is to provide an assessment to determine whether the export of any goods, technology, or techniques will significantly increase the present or potential military capability of any controlled country and to insure that notice of the proposed exports is given to the Secretary of Defense so that the Secretary may determine whether the exports will significantly increase the military capability of a controlled country.

Violations of the Export Administration Act

For willful violations of the EAA or any regulation promulgated thereunder, Section 11(b) of the Act provides:

(1) whoever willfully violates or conspires to or attempts to violate any provision of this Act . . . or any regulation, order or license issued thereunder, with knowledge that the exports involved will be used for the benefit of, or that the destination or intended destination of the goods or technology involved is, any controlled country or any country to which exports are controlled for foreign policy purposes —

(A) except in the case of an individual, shall be fined not more than five times the value of the exports involved or $1,000,000, whichever is greater; and

(B) in the case of an individual, shall be fined not more than $250,000, or imprisoned not more than 10 years, or both.

Civil penalties up to $10,000 may also be imposed for each violation of the Act or its regulations in addition to or in lieu of any other penalty which may be imposed.

In *United States v. Mechanic*,[6] goods for which validated licenses were required but had not been obtained, were interdicted at the Houston airport after being checked-in for a flight to Zurich, Switzerland but before they had actually been exported. The erstwhile "exporters" were then charged under a regulation that

[5] Controlled country for purposes of this section means the Soviet Union, Poland, Rumania, Hungary, Bulgaria, Czechoslovakia, and such other countries as may be designated by the Secretary of Defense. 2403-1(d)

[6] 809 F. 2d 1111 (5th Cir., 1987)

made any "attempt to bring about, a violation of the [EAA]" a criminal offense. This regulation, defendants argued, exceeded the authority delegated to the Department of Commerce by the statute. The Fifth Circuit disagreed stating:

> To construe [the power to prohibit or curtail exports] . . . too narrowly eviscerates the congressional purpose of preventing U.S. goods and technology from reaching those who might use them to our detriment. . . . [A]n effective means of controlling the exportation of listed items is to stop smugglers as they approach the border, to confiscate the items, and to impose sanctions for their almost-successful efforts. . . . Otherwise, [as the Ninth Circuit] correctly observed "[n]o crime would be committed until the smuggler stepped across the border, but at that point, the violator would be outside the jurisdiction of the law enforcement officers and courts directed to penalize him for the crime."[7]

International Cooperation in Export Control: The Coordinating Committee (CoCom)

CoCom was founded in 1949 as an informal strategic trade control coordinating mechanism participated in by NATO member governments (excluding Iceland) plus Australia and Japan. There are no formal treaties or other formal agreements that underlie CoCom. Rather, the Committee operates by unanimous agreement and any measures promulgated must be implemented by laws or regulations of the participating governments before they acquire legal effect.

CoCom is concerned with preserving the shared security interests of its participants in controlling strategic exports to a number of countries. Its objectives include:

a. to achieve agreement on strategic criteria for controls

b. to formulate detailed lists of embargoed commodities and technical data

c. to coordinate efforts to achieve effective enforcement of the embargo

The United States, as well as most other nations, bases its commodity control list on the CoCom lists. The significance of CoCom was reflected in the 1988 amendments to the Export Administration Act. Section 5(b)(2)(A) was added which states in part:

> No authority or permission may be required under this section to export to any country, other than a controlled country, any goods or technology if the export of the goods or technology to controlled countries would require only notification of participating governments of the Coordinating Committee.

Recognition of the importance of CoCom in facilitating cooperation in export control has resulted in efforts by the United States and other countries to strengthen CoCom. A meeting of CoCom participants was held in 1988 at Versailles at which the participants affirmed the basic principle that each country has the responsibility to ensure effective enforcement of CoCom-agreed controls on its exports. An agreement was reached to rationalize the control lists by concentrating on those goods or technologies that are strategically significant (in

[7] *Id.* at page 1114. The Fifth Circuit is quoting from *United States v. Gurrola-Garcia,* 547 F. 2d 1075 at 1077 (9th Cir., 1976).

effect streamline the control lists). The rapidly changing events in Eastern Europe will have a significant impact on CoCom's streamlining task.

The Prescriptive Reach of Export Controls

As noted the EAA grants the President authority to impose export controls on goods and technology "subject to the jurisdiction of the United States." This language has been the basis for controlling U.S. origin goods and technology, including reexports. In addition, controls over foreign made products of U.S. technology and foreign made products containing U.S. parts rely on this authority. The Act also authorizes the President to control exports by any "person subject to the jurisdiction of the United States." This language has been the basis for regulating exports of wholly foreign origin goods or technology by foreign entities controlled by U.S. persons. The use of these authorities by the Administration has, from time to time, given rise to some rather acrimonious disputes between the United States and its allies, the latest being the so-called Russian pipeline dispute.

In 1980, several Western European countries agreed to buy large quantities of natural gas from Siberia. Many companies, including some U.S. firms, competed for the right to build a pipeline that would transport the gas from Siberia to Europe. The trade deal was worth somewhere between $11-$15 billion. With the advent of martial law in Poland in 1981, President Reagan exercised his authority under the EAA to impose an embargo on the export of oil and gas equipment and technology to the USSR citing the "Soviet Union's heavy and direct responsibility for the repression in Poland."[8]

The embargo was extended in June 1982 to specifically include foreign subsidiaries and licensees of U.S. companies. Although the embargo remained in effect until November 13, 1982, a number of companies violated the embargo which led the United States to impose sanctions.

THE DRESSER CASE

Dresser (France) S.A. Appellant

**Decision and Order of Assistant Secretary
for Trade Administration**

**On Appeal of Hearing Commissioner's Denial of Motion
to Vacate August 26, 1982 Temporary Denial Order**

Case No. 632, November 1, 1982

47 Fed. Reg. 51463 (November 15, 1982)

. . . Dresser (France) S.A. (appellant) and Dresser Industries, Inc. (intervenor), have appealed the initial decision of Hearing Commissioner Thomas W. Hoya, rendered September 30, 1982, denying appellant's motion to vacate the August 26, 1982 Temporary Denial Order (TDO) [as amended] denying export privileges

---

[8] 47 Federal Register 141 (1982)

[to Dresser (France)]. . . . [F]or the reasons discussed below, I deny appellant's appeal.

Factual Background

. . . [O]n September 28, 1981, appellant, a French corporation which manufactures compressors and pumps for the oil and gas industry and which is owned and controlled by a United States manufacturing corporation, Dresser Industries, Inc., signed a contract with Creusot-Loire, a French company, and V/O Machinoimport, a Soviet agency, for the delivery of 21 gas compressors for use in building the oil and gas pipeline currently being constructed between the Soviet Union and Western Europe. Appellant's manufacture of the . . . compressors is based on technology obtained from Dresser, Inc. pursuant to a license agreement between those two entities. On December 30, 1981, in response to Soviet behavior concerning Poland, the Commerce Department issued regulations under the Export Administration Act (EAA), . . . forbidding export to the Soviet Union of U.S.-origin commodities and technical data for oil and gas transmission and refinement. . . . Export controls under the EAA were further extended by the Department . . . on June 22, 1982, to forbid export to the Soviet Union of non-U.S.-origin commodities and technical data by U.S.-owned or controlled foreign firms. In addition, the June regulations forbid the export to the Soviet Union of foreign produced goods of U.S. technical data where the right to use the data is subject to a licensing agreement between the foreign entity and an entity subject to United States jurisdiction. . . . Like the December regulations, the June regulations were expressly issued in furtherance of U.S. foreign policy in response to Soviet interference in the affairs of Poland.

Because of these regulations, Dresser Industries, Inc. ordered Dresser France to cease the manufacture of the compressors produced for the Soviet contract and not to deliver any compressors already manufactured. Dresser France complied, until on August 26, 1982, three days after the issuance of a French Government requisition order for the compressors, the company delivered three compressors . . . for shipment to the Soviet Union. On that same day, August 26, 1982, at the request of the Department, the Hearing Commissioner issued an ex parte TDO temporarily denying all export privileges to Dresser France. In its request, the Department stated that Dresser France was under investigation for possible violation of the EAA and . . . cited the danger that Dresser France might, in the future, make an export similar to the delivery of the three compressors then under investigation. The Hearing Commissioner found that the issuance of the TDO was required in the public interest to facilitate enforcement of the Act and Regulations and to permit completion of the Department's investigation. . . . On September 7, 1982, the Hearing Commissioner, at the request of the Department, modified the TDO to limit its coverage only to U.S.-origin commodities and technical data relating to oil and gas exploration, production, transmission or refinement. Since that date, there has been no further delivery by Dresser France to the Soviet Union of compressors under the Soviet contract. On September 30, 1982, the Hearing Commissioner issued his initial decision denying appellant's motion to vacate the August 26 TDO. On October 15, 1982 the Department issued a formal charging letter against appellant for violation of the June regulations.

Decision

* * * *

This appeal[9] presents three dispositive questions for decision which will be addressed in turn:

1. Was the issuance of the August 26, 1982 TDO in compliance with the pertinent regulations?

2. Are the June regulations in compliance with the Export Administration Act, as amended, under which they were issued?

3. Was the implementation of the regulations in this case by issuance of the ex parte TDO in violation of the Due Process clause of the Fifth Amendment?

* * * *

1. Was the issuance of the August 26, 1982 TDO in compliance with the pertinent regulations?

The regulation governing the issuance of an *ex parte* TDO . . . states [that]. . . .

. . . [t]he Department may request the [issuance of such an] . . . order on an *ex parte* basis . . . to any person against whom other administrative or judicial proceedings relating to export control are pending, or who is under investigation for violation of the Act. . . . The . . . [order] may issue . . . upon a showing that [it] . . . is required in the public interest to permit or facilitate enforcement of the Act . . .; to avoid circumvention of such administrative or judicial proceedings or to permit the completion of an investigation. The order shall be issued initially only for such period of time, ordinarily not exceeding 30 calendar days, as may be required to complete the administrative or judicial proceeding, or to complete the investigation.

* * * *

. . . It was no secret by August 26, 1982 that Dresser France had delivered for shipment to the Soviet Union three of the 21 compressors called for by the contract, an act which the Department characterizes as a possible violation of the EAA. Appellant has since stated that it intends to complete manufacture and delivery of the remaining 18 compressors. . . .

Given this expressed intention, the issue is whether theTDO can aid the Department in its enforcement responsibilities under the EAA . . . by precluding or making more difficult the completion of appellant's Soviet contract. . . .

---

[9] Under 15 CFR 388.22 the Assistant Secretary may, on appeal, reverse the Hearing Commissioner's order on the following grounds:

(1) That a necessary finding of fact is omitted, erroneous or unsupported by substantial evidence of record;

(2) That a necessary legal conclusion or finding is contrary to law;

(3) That prejudicial procedural error occurred; or

(4) That the decision or the extent of sanctions is arbitrary, capricious or an abuse of discretion. Ed.

[Appellant asserted that the TDO could serve no enforcement purpose because it already had all the U.S.-origin technology needed to complete the Soviet contract. Commerce contended that there was a substantial uncertainty as to whether this was the case.]

Upon review of the record I conclude that there is uncertainty [on this point] . . . [and therefore] . . . the TDO may well facilitate enforcement by either precluding completion of the contract or making completion more difficult by requiring appellant to seek necessary commodities and technology from non-U.S.-origin sources. For example, appellant's contractual schedule for delivery . . . calls for 7 compressors, in addition to the 3 already delivered prior to the August 26 TDO, to have been transmitted by October 2, 1982. . . . Apparently, none of these 7 compressors have been delivered . . . suggesting that perhaps not all necessary U.S. technology or commodities were received by appellant and that the TDO is affecting completion of the contract.

Further, appellant nowhere states that it has all of the commodities necessary for completion of the contract. The TDO may, by shutting off the flow of U.S.-origin commodities as of August 26, have the effect of requiring appellant to seek goods necessary for completion of the contract from other than U.S. sources. The apparent inability of appellant to meet its contractual delivery schedule lends support to this possibility.

. . . Certainty that the TDO is making an impact on the completion and/or shipment of the 18 compressors is not required to justify issuance of a TDO.[10] This conclusion also addresses appellant's charge that the TDO was "punitive." . . . Precisely what is meant by "punitive" is never explained by appellant, but apparently appellant means the TDO was issued to punish it for the delivery of the three compressors under its Soviet contract rather than to forestall future violations or aid in the investigation.

Because I determine that this TDO properly is designed to forestall future violations and fulfill its intended role . . . appellant's "punitive" argument falls. . . .[11]

The TDO was not designed to punish appellant, indeed, no substantive violations have yet been proven. There is no question, and the Department does not dispute, that appellant may well suffer damage as a result of the imposition of the TDO. Whether damage may be suffered, however, is not the pertinent inquiry in determining whether the TDO was properly issued. All TDO's by their nature can

---

[10] Additionally, given the contractual relationship between Dresser France and the Soviet firm V/O Machinoimport, the possibility of other future violations being precluded by the TDO cannot be gainsaid.

[11] For similar reasons, appellant's additional argument that it is being impermissibly punished for acts compelled by the French government, fails. As discussed in the text, this case involves the issuance of a TDO to permit the completion of the investigation of appellant and to forestall any future regulatory violations. This case does not involve the imposition of penalties on appellant for conduct done under compulsion of the French government in violation of U.S. law. Accordingly, the defense of foreign compulsion is inapplicable. In light of this disposition, I need not address the parties' other arguments and factual determination requests concerning whether appellant was legally compelled by the French government to deliver the three compressors under the Soviet contract.

impose some injury on their recipients as an unavoidable consequence of their purpose which is to prevent future violations and facilitate an ongoing investigation. Furthermore, on September 7, 1982, the TDO was modified to limit its scope. . . .

This narrowing . . . is evidence of the Department's desire to tailor the TDO to fulfill the purposes of [the regulations] . . . rather than to punish appellant. For the above-stated reasons, the TDO complies with the pertinent regulation.

2. Are the June regulations in compliance with the Export Administration Act, as amended, under which they were issued?

The essential question here is whether the June regulations fall within the intent of Congress expressed in the EAA as amended in 1979. The June regulations were promulgated pursuant to section 6 of the EAA. . . . That section concerns foreign policy controls and gives the President the authority to prohibit or curtail the exportation of any goods or technology "subject to the jurisdiction of the United States or exported by any person subject to the jurisdiction of the United States" to the extent necessary to further U.S. foreign policy.[12] Appellant argues that Congress by amending the EAA in 1979 did not intend for the executive branch to be able to direct activities of foreign companies controlled by U.S. firms or control the use of U.S. technology after it leaves this country.

. . . In attempting to discern the Congressional intent behind a statute it is axiomatic that the primary authority is the wording of the statute itself.[13] The wording of the statute demonstrates that Congress intended section 2405 to have an extraterritorial effect. . . .

The Senate Banking Committee considered an amendment to the EAA which would have prohibited foreign policy controls on non-U.S. origin exports of foreign subsidiaries of U.S. companies except in international economic emergencies. . . . The committee failed to adopt this amendment, taking note of a letter from the State Department in opposition to that amendment urging that the President be allowed to retain the flexibility he had under the existing legislation to impose foreign policy controls on subsidiaries. The committee recognized "that claims to U.S. jurisdiction over such exports are not likely to go unchallenged by the governments of the countries in which such subsidiaries are located." . . . Nevertheless, the Committee chose not to adopt the Amendment and it was withdrawn.

The House also considered the question of extraterritoriality within the context of the national security section of the statute (section 2404) and determined to grant the President the authority to control the reexport of U.S. goods by foreign entities. The House specifically chose to delete an initial provision of the 1979 amendments which would have forbidden the imposition of conditions by the United States with respect to the reexport of U.S.-origin items shipped to COCOM (Coordinating Committee) countries. In offering the amendment deleting this provision, Congressman Lester Wolfe (D-N.Y.) stated:

---

[12] 50 U.S.C. App. 2405(a).

[13] Additionally, the Commerce Department's interpretation of the 1979 amendments to the EAA as embodied in the December and June regulations is entitled to grate weight in light of the Commerce Department's legislatively assigned responsibility to implement the EAA. *Caterpillar Tractor Co. v. United States*, 589 F.2d 1040, 1045 (Ct. Cl. 1978).

. . . this amendment deletes the section in the bill which prohibits the United States from attaching any condition onto the reexport of goods that the United States has exported to any one of our COCOM allies. I do not believe that we should prohibit ourselves from utilizing them (reexport controls) if we feel it is necessary. I feel eliminating the possibility of using reexport controls could create an enormous loophole through which third country transfers could legally be made.[14]

Thus the jurisdictional reach of the national security section of the EAA was intended to include extraterritorial application of controls. The House's use of identical jurisdictional language in the foreign policy control section demonstrates an intent to permit the President to impose similar extraterritorial controls in the foreign policy area. The final version of the bill passed by both houses of Congress retained this identical jurisdictional language.

Therefore, both houses of Congress demonstrated the intent to permit the President to impose extraterritorial foreign policy controls similar to those in the regulations challenged here. There is nothing in the statute or its legislative history to indicate that Congress did not intend foreign policy controls to be implemented extraterritorially as they are in the challenged regulations.

* * * *

Finally, a recent vote in the House of Representatives lends additional support to the position that the June regulations were within the reach of the EAA.[15]

Appellant argues at great length that these regulations are unprecedented. However, whether the President has instituted similar export control mechanisms in the past does not alter the wording of the statute, the legislative history and the recent House of Representatives vote. . . . The June regulations do not violate the EAA.[16]

---

[14] 125 Cong. Rec. H 7664-65 (daily ed. Sept. 11, 1979).

[15] On September 29, 1982, the House of Representatives voted on the issue of whether to terminate the December and June regulations. Supporters of the bill made many of the same arguments raised by appellant attaching the extraterritorial reach of the June regulations. The House rejected the version of the bill which would have eliminated outright the December and June regulations. Instead, the House voted to rescind the December and June regulations in 90 days provided that within that period the President certifies that the Soviet Union is not using forced labor in the construction of the pipeline. The vote of the House of Representatives thus sustains the December and June regulations unless the President certifies that the U.S.S.R. is not using slave labor on the pipeline. 128 Cong. Rec. H 7915, 7918, D 1294 (daily ed. Sept. 29, 1982). Certainly the initial proposal presented a clear opportunity for at least the House of Representatives to state that the December and June regulations were not within the purview of the EAA and the will of the legislature. This legislative refusal to reverse the executive's implementation of the EAA lends support to my analysis of the Congressional intent behind the EAA.

[16] Appellant also complains that the June regulations have been applied in an improperly retroactive manner—forbidding the export of products of U.S. technology that were transmitted to the licensee prior to written assurances being required of it. Regardless of when the U.S.-origin technology inherent in the production of the compressors may have been transmitted to Dresser France, the TDO is designed only to prevent the future export to the Soviet Union of the compressors, and any other item falling within the regulations.

3. Was the implementation of the regulations in this case by issuance of an ex parte TDO in violation of the Due Process Clause of the Fifth Amendment?

The parties do not dispute that the TDO in this case was implemented . . . prior to the issuance of a formal charging letter or a hearing on the merits. The question is whether such a procedure violates due process protections.

Even assuming, *arguendo*, that the due process clause is applicable to protect appellant and that a property interest cognizable under the Fifth Amendment is involved, under certain circumstances the governmental seizure of a property interest without a prior hearing is constitutional. The standard for justifying such governmental behavior has been set out by the Supreme Court in *Fuentes v. Shevin*, 407 U.S. 67, (1972):

> . . . the seizure has been directly necessary to secure an important govern-mental or general public interest. Second, there has been a special need for very prompt action. Third, the State has kept strict control over its monopoly of legitimate force; the person initiating the seizure has been a governmental official responsible for determining, under the standards of a narrowly drawn statute, that it was necessary and justified in the particular instance.

See also *Calero-Toledo v. Pearson Yacht Co.*, 416 U.S. 663 (1974). Clearly the effectuation of governmental foreign policy goals is an important governmental interest. Congress passed section 6 of the EAA and the Commerce Department promulgated the December and June regulations in furtherance of this interest. The need for prompt action to preclude possible future export violations has been demonstrated. Finally, the actual issuance of the TDO was done by the appropri-ate Commerce Department official and comported with the procedure set out in [the Regulations] . . . I note also that appellant received a hearing on the merits of the TDO less than 30 days after its August 26 issuance. Thus under the *Fuentes* standard the *ex parte* TDO was proper.

Further, the Supreme Court has held on more than one occasion that the government is entitled to terminate benefits and recoup monies from individuals without first providing a pre-deprivation hearing. See *Califano v. Yamasaki*, 442 U.S. 682 (1979); *Mathews v. Eldridge*, 424 U.S. 319 (1976). Additionally, both *Horne Brothers, Inc. v. Laird*, 463 F.2d 1268 (D.C. Cir. 1972), and *Gonzales v. Freeman*, 334 F.2d 570 (D.C. Cir. 1964), cited by appellant in support of its argument, stand for the proposition that there can be a temporary suspension of an important right prior to the provision of a hearing if the governmental interest involved justified such a procedure. The governmental interest of protecting the integrity of its export controls in furtherance of foreign policy objectives as applied in this case justifies the *ex parte* TDO procedure . . . utilized here. The Due Process Clause of the Fifth Amendment has not been violated by the issuance of the August 26 TDO against appellant.

The question of imposition of punishment for behavior not in violation of statute or regulation at the time it occurred is not before us. Beyond this, "Congressional legislation or regulations adopted pursuant thereto, whether prospective or retrospective in applica-tion, often have economic consequences which may be inconsistent with a party's reasonable expectations. Such inconsistencies are not equivalent to unconstitutionality as to . . . enactments (in dispute)." *Springdale Convalescent Center v. Mathews*, 545 F.2d 943, 955. (5th Cir. 1977).

* * * *

. . . [T]he appeal of Dresser France and Dresser Industries, Inc. from the September 30, 1982 initial decision of the Hearing Commissioner denying their motion to vacate the Temporary Denial Order is denied.

NOTES AND QUESTIONS

(1) Recall the Harvard Studies list of traditional international law principles governing the exercise of prescriptive jurisdiction in criminal matters. Under which, if any, of those principles could the United States justify the TDO against Dresser France.

(2) Restatement (Third) of the Foreign Relations Law of the United States, Section 414 provides as follows:

> **Section 414. Jurisdiction with Respect to Activities of Foreign Branches and Subsidiaries**
>
> **(1) Subject to Section 403 [17] and 441, [18] a state may exercise jurisdiction to prescribe for limited purposes with respect to activities for foreign branches of corporations organized under its laws.**
>
> **(2) A state may not ordinarily regulate activities of corporations organized under the laws of a foreign state on the basis that they are owned or controlled by nationals of the regulating state. However, under Section 403 and subject to Section 441, it may not be unreasonable for a state to exercise jurisdiction for limited purposes with respect to activities of affiliated foreign entities**
>
> **(a) by direction to the parent corporation in respect of such matters as uniform accounting, disclosure to investors, or preparation of consolidated tax returns of multinational enterprises; or**
>
> **(b) by direction to either the parent or the subsidiary in exceptional cases, depending on all the relevant factors, including the extent to which**
>
> **(i) the regulation is essential to implementation of a program to further a major national interest of the state exercising jurisdiction;**

---

[17] See page 537 *supra*.

[18] Section 441 deals with the "foreign compulsion doctrine" in the following terms:

(1) In general, a state may not require a person

(a) to do an act in another state that is prohibited by the law of that state or by the law of the state of which he is a national, or

(b) to refrain from doing an act in another state that is required by the law of that state or by the law of the state of which he is a national.

(2) In general, a state may require a person of foreign nationality

(a) to do an act in that state even if it is prohibited by the law of the state of which he is a national; or

(b) to refrain from doing an act in that state even if it is required by the law of the state of which he is a national.

(ii)   the national program of which the regulation is a part can be carried out effectively only if it is applied also to foreign subsidiaries;

(iii) the regulation conflicts or is likely to conflict with the law or policy of the state where the subsidiary is established.

(c)   In the exceptional cases referred to in paragraph (b), the burden of establishing reasonableness is heavier when the direction is issued to the foreign subsidiary than when it is issued to the parent corporation.

Recall Professor Currie's view of the perspective that national courts will, or may even be bound to take regarding conflicts between policies of their own legislature and those of legislatures in other states. Recall also the legislative history concerning the prescriptive reach of the EAA contained in the Assistant Secretary's *Dresser* Opinion. Is there any question as to what the result would be if an American court were called upon to pronounce on whether issuance of the TDO in the *Dresser* Case conformed to the requirements of the Restatement? See Reporters' Notes 3 and 4 regarding the conflicts with other nations engendered by claims to jurisdiction over foreign subsidiaries of American companies under EAA and other legislation.

(3) In light of your response to Question (2) consider the decision of a French Court in another much noted confrontation between the United States and France, the *Fruehauf* Case.

FRUEHAUF CORPORATION V. MASSARDY[19]

Court of Appeals of Paris, 14th Chamber
Decision of May 22, 1965
La Gazette du Palais, Paris, 1965.II, pp. 86-90

In December 1964 Fruehauf-France, S.A., a French company in which the Fruehauf Corporation (United States) held a two-thirds stock interest, signed a contract with Automobiles Berliet, S.A., another French company, for delivery of 60 "Fruehauf" vans, valued at 1,785,310 francs, for eventual delivery to the People's Republic of China. The first deliveries were to be made in February 1965. In January 1965 the U.S. Treasury Department issued an order directing the Fruehauf corporation to suspend execution of the contract as violating the U.S. transaction control Regulations.[20]

---

[19] Prepared by the editors of International Legal Materials based upon an English translation provided by Mrs. Rita E. Hauser. 5 ILM 476
[20] 31 Code of Federal Regulations sec. 505.01 *et seq.*]

When Fruehauf-France approached Automobiles Berliet about rescinding the contract, Berliet refused. Fearing that failure to perform the contract would weaken the company's position to obtain future contracts from its largest customer (Berliet) and subject the company to suit for damages, the French minority directors on February 15, 1965, instituted a proceeding against the Fruehauf corporation and the American directors before the Tribunal of Commerce of Corbeil Essonnes. On February 16 the President of the Tribunal appointed a temporary administrator to head Fruehauf-France, S.A., for three months and to execute the contract.

The Fruehauf Corporation appealed to the Court of Appeals of Paris. The Court of Appeals in a decision of May 22, 1965, affirmed the order of February 16, 1965. Among the considerations cited by the Court of Appeals in its decision were:

> The evidence demonstrates, without serious question, not only the clear and present interest Fruehauf-France, S.A. has in the execution of a contract made with its principal customer, Berliet, S.A., which accounts for about 40 per cent of its exports, but above all the catastrophic results which would have been produced, on the eve of delivery date, and which would be felt even today, if the contract had been breached, because the buyer would be in a position to demand of its seller all commercial damages resulting therefrom, valued at more than five million francs, following upon the break-off of its dealings with China.
>
> . . . these damages, which Fruehauf Corporation or Fruehauf-International [the United States parent companies] did not indicate any intention of assuming, would be of such an order as to ruin the financial equilibrium and the moral credit of Fruehauf-France, S.A. and provoke its disappearance and the unemployment of more than 600 workers; . . . in order to name a temporary administrator the judge-referee must take into account the interests of the company rather than the personal interests of any shareholders even if they be the majority.

What impact would (should) this judgment have in any action brought by the United States to impose criminal penalties on either Fruehauf Corporation or Fruehauf-France for carrying through with the sale to Berleit knowing the goods were destined for Communist China? See Section 441 of the Restatement. In light of your answer and the likelihood of similar foreign responses to other U.S. attempts at controlling foreign subsidiaries of U.S. companies, what basic purpose is served by the expansive claim to jurisdiction contained in the EAA?

(4) What impact would the principles stated in the Restatement have in a statutory case such as the *Dresser* case, even assuming the Restatement purports to reflect an emerging international law on this subject? Recall the principle discussed in *Lauritzen v. Larson* regarding the impact of international law on statutorily prescribed jurisdictional claims.

(5) Section 8 of the EAA authorizes the President to issue regulations prohibiting any "United States person," with respect to activities in interstate or foreign commerce, from taking certain actions in furtherance of any boycott fostered by one foreign country against another foreign country, if the latter is not itself the subject of a U.S. mandated boycott. Among the prohibited actions are refusing

to do business in or with the boycotted country, refusing to employ any person on the basis of race, religion, sex or national origin and the giving of certain specified types of information. These "anti-boycott" provisions are, of course, directed primarily at preventing American firms from being used to further the Arab boycott against Israel. In Section 8 the term "United States person" was defined to include "any United States resident or national (other than an individual resident outside the United States and employed by other than a United States person), any domestic concern" (including a domestic subsidiary of a foreign concern), and "any foreign subsidiary or affiliate of any domestic concern which is controlled in fact by such domestic concern." In furtherance of this statutory mandate the Department of Commerce has published a detailed definition of "United States person" with some nine illustrations; a definition of "controlled in fact" with 11 illustrations; and a definition of "activities in interstate or foreign commerce of the United States" accompanied by 20 illustrations. 15 CFR Section 469.1.

(6) After some very delicate diplomacy by then Secretary of State George Shultz, the Department of Commerce, on November 13, 1982, rescinded the export controls on oil and gas equipment and technology imposed on December 30, 1981 and June 22, 1982. The Department then moved to vacate the TDO against Dresser France. An order granting the motion was signed on November 16, 1982.[21]

---

[21] 47 Fed. Reg. 52490 (November 22, 1982).

CHAPTER 7

THE UNITED STATES ANTITRUST LAWS AND TRANSNATIONAL BUSINESS

Introduction

In this Chapter we consider the extent to which the American antitrust laws apply to a wide variety of transnational business arrangements. Again, the subject is prescriptive jurisdiction. As such, it has been a rich mine of material for the international lawyer. Yet, it is not a subject for which international law, standing alone, offers an analytic framework adequate to an understanding or a critique of the issues. This is all the more so as the analysis of prescriptive jurisdiction moves away from its more traditional perspective into a new rational choice mode with an emphasis on both the likely and actual consequences of particular business conduct. Substantive antitrust law with its attendant economic principles, political values and institutional presuppositions must, in other words, be an integral part of the subject.

On the other hand, neither can questions of transnational antitrust enforcement be divorced from the teachings of international law regarding the orderly arrangement of power among sovereign states and the nurturing of a more inclusive and viable global economic order. Indeed, because antitrust is concerned with regulating the structure of the markets that ultimately determine the direction and vigor of international trade and capital movements, it is an integral part of any study of trade policy or of the measures that affect international capital flows. It makes no sense whatsoever for the nations of the world to attempt to regulate and eventually eliminate governmental barriers to trade and capital movements only to have private arrangements, driven by the allure of monopoly profits, step-in and re-divide the world into closed, national markets. Ultimately, if the world is ever to realize the welfare gains that free trade and the free movement of capital make possible, markets must be kept open and competitive. We are long past the point where any nation can remain sanguine in the face of the adverse effects that closed, non-competitive markets maintained by other nations can have on their own welfare and on the emergence of a more viable international economic order.

The question, in short, is not whether antitrust enforcement is important to global welfare, the only question is how we can best manage that enforcement in the context of the oft-times diverse interests of separate and still very jealous nation states. If, in this setting, restraint in the application of any one nation's law is sometimes necessary, that must only be for tactical reasons. It cannot reflect some deeper conviction that the question of whether to have an antitrust policy should be left to the idiosyncratic proclivities of each nation's economic and legal culture.

To treat so broad a subject within the limited confines assigned to it here necessarily involves a compromise. This Chapter cannot and does not purport to offer detailed instruction into either substantive antitrust law or antitrust economics. Lest these be ignored, however, the first Section, building on the economic principles discussed in Chapters 3 and 5, sets out certain core principles, few of which are seriously questioned and all of which should be mastered as an essential foundation for the ensuing analysis. Section 2 then gives a broad overview of certain basic principles of antitrust law. In both Sections where controversy tends to shroud either economic principles or legal doctrine, the materials merely note the fact without attempting a resolution except as the courts may have settled on one side or the other of the dispute.

The antitrust laws with which are principally concerned are Section 1 and Section 2 of the Sherman Act,[1] Section 1 of the Wilson Tariff Act,[2] and Section 7 of the Clayton Act.[3] These provide as follows:

Sherman Act

(15 U.S.C. Sections 1 & 2.)

Section 1. Every contract, combination in the form of trust or otherwise, or conspiracy, in restraint of trade or commerce among the several States, or with foreign nations, is declared to be illegal. Every person who shall make any contract or engage in any combination or conspiracy hereby declared to be illegal shall be deemed guilty of a felony. . . .

Sec. 2. Every person who shall monopolize, or attempt to monopolize, or combine or conspire with any other person or persons, to monopolize any part of the trade or commerce among the several States, or with foreign nations, shall be deemed guilty of a felony. . . .

Wilson Tariff Act

(15 U.S.C. Sections 8 through 11)

[The Wilson Tariff Act declares illegal any contract, combination or conspiracy, between persons engaged in the importation of articles into the United States from a foreign country, if the contract, combination or conspiracy is intended to restrain lawful trade in, or increase the price in the United States of, the imported article or of any manufacture into which the imported article enters.]

---

[1] Act of July 2, 1980, c. 647, 1 et seq. 26 Stat. 209, 15 U.S.C. Sections 1-7 as amended.
[2] Act of Aug. 27, 1894, c. 349 Section 73, 28 Stat. 570, 15 U.S.C. Sections 8-11 as amended.
[3] Act of Oct. 15, 1914, c. 323, 1 et seq. 38 Stat. 730, 15 U.S.C. Sections 12-26, as amended. For the fuller text of these statutes, see the Documentary Supplement.

Section 7 of the Clayton Act

(15 U.S.C. Section 18)

Section 7. No person engaged in commerce or any activity affecting commerce shall acquire, directly or indirectly, the whole or any part of the stock or other share capital and no person subject to the jurisdiction of the Federal Trade Commission shall acquire the whole or any part of the assets of another person engaged also in commerce or in any activity affecting commerce, where in any line of commerce or in any activity affecting commerce in any section of the country, the effect of such acquisition may be substantially to lessen competition, or tend to create a monopoly. No person shall acquire, directly or indirectly, the whole or any part of the stock or other share capital and no person subject to the jurisdiction of the Federal Trade Commission shall acquire the whole or any part of the assets of one or more persons engaged in commerce or in any activity affecting commerce, where in any line of commerce or in any activity affecting commerce, in any section of the country, the effect of such acquisition, of such stocks or assets, or of the use of such stock by the voting or granting of proxies or otherwise, may be substantially to lessen competition, or tend to create a monopoly.

[The balance of Section 7 exempts from its provisions stock acquisitions for the purpose of investment, of forming subsidiaries and branches, for certain line extensions by common carriers or incident to mergers approved by other Federal agencies such as the Federal Communications Commission, Interstate Commerce Commission, etc.[4]]

§ 7.01   The Core Learning; The Economics

In Section 1 and Section 2 of the Sherman Act, the Wilson Tariff Act and again in Section 7 of the Clayton Act, Congress has expressed its policies in broad terms. It has, in the words of the Supreme Court, fashioned "a charter of freedom . . . [with] a generality and adaptability comparable to that found to be desirable in Constitutional provisions." *Standard Oil Company of New Jersey v. United States.*[1] As in the case of the Constitution, therefore, the bulk of our antitrust law has been developed by the courts. While the critical words differ — Section 1 proscribes "restraints of trade," Section 2 "monopolizing" and Section 7 mergers that "substantially lessen competition" — the central theme is the same. All are directed at forestalling the acquisition or exercise of monopoly power in any market within their ambit and to assuring that those markets, whether they pertain to goods, or services, to money or ideas (*i.e.*, technology), operate as the full and free play of competitive forces dictate.

---

[4] For the jurisdiction of the Federal Trade Commission see Section 11 of the Clayton Act. Under Section 5 of what is commonly called the Federal Trade Commission Act (15 U.S.C. Section 45 et. seq.) the Commission is empowered, by the issuance of cease and desist orders, to prevent any person, partnership or corporation not subject to the jurisdiction of other stated regulatory agencies "from using unfair methods of competition in or affecting commerce and unfair or deceptive acts or practices in or affecting commerce."

[1] 221 U.S. 1 (1911).

[A] Competition and Monopoly

[NOTE: At this point the reader should return to § 5.03[B] pages 478 through 487 and review the basic principles governing the pricing behavior of firms in competitive, monopolistic and oligopolistic markets. One cannot make much sense of the antitrust laws without a firm grasp of these principles and, without them, the discussion of antitrust enforcement against transnational business arrangements, becomes almost incomprehensible.]

As we noted in Chapter 5, chief among the advantages of monopoly power is the opportunity it affords sellers to enhance profits (the excess of total revenue over total costs) by raising price above costs. In a competitive market, on the other hand, if any one seller attempts to raise price, his customers will find other sellers willing to sell at the lower equilibrium price. Under monopoly, in other words, consumers will pay more than they would under competition[2] and when this happens society will incur certain opportunity costs which, because they would not be incurred under competition, are properly viewed as losses to the social welfare. Moreover, monopoly results in a wealth transfer from consumers to the monopolistic seller.

To understand these consequences, more rigorously consult Figure 1, which is an exact replica of Figure 2 in Chapter 5.

---

[2] If this is observed not to be the case, that is usually because (1) by improperly defining the relevant market, one has attributed to the single seller a power over price that does not in fact exist or (ii) there are potential competitors standing in the wings ready to enter the market if the monopolist in fact exercises his power.

Figure 1

Price and Output Under Monopoly.

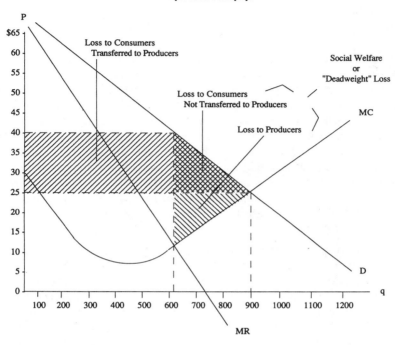

First, note the *double-hatched triangle* marked "Loss to Consumers Not Transferred to Producers." The horizontal side of the triangle shows the quantity by which consumers will reduce their purchases because of the price rise; the vertical side shows the various prices at which they would have made the lost purchases. The area of the triangle represents, therefore, the aggregate value "lost" to consumers by reason of the cartel. We say "lost" because the cartel price has caused consumers to put their resources to some alternative use and because, had the market been operating competitively, consumers would have purchased the industry's product in preference to that alternative. The value represented by this loss of preference is an opportunity cost recovered by no one, not even the cartel, and as such is a deadweight loss to society.

Next, consider the *cross-hatched triangle* marked "Loss to Producers" and lying immediately below the double-hatched triangle discussed above. The horizontal side of the lower triangle measures output that could have been produced at a cost below the price the market was willing to pay. The entire area of the triangle, therefore, represents the value of production that is simply lost to society because of the monopolist's decision to curtail output. Together the two triangles represent a "deadweight" welfare loss imposed on society by the monopoly.

Finally, note that the monopolistic producer's gain is measured by the excess of the *cross-hatched rectangle* marked "Loss to Consumers Transferred to

Producers" over the "Loss to Producers" (*cross-hatched triangle* discussed above). The *rectangle* is substantially larger than the *triangle*. This excess is the gain that induces monopolistic behavior and is of special interest to the student of international antitrust. The fact that consumers continue to purchase the industry's product at the cartel price (*i.e.*, base of the *rectangle*), means that they still value the industry's product more highly than the alternatives and they are still getting that higher value. All that has occurred is that the difference between what these consumers are willing to pay (*i.e.*, the cartel price) and what, under competition, they would have been required to pay — the difference is called "consumer surplus" — has been captured by the cartel rather than being left with consumers. This is a wealth transfer from consumers to producers. Classical economics postulated that since there was no basis in economic theory for saying that this wealth in the hands of consumers was of greater social utility than in the hands of the monopolist producer, society had suffered no lost opportunity and no "social cost" could be assigned to the transfer, as such, so long as both buyers and sellers were part of the same society. Increasingly, however, there are economists who argue both sides of this point. Be that as it may, the point for us is that, even under the classical theory, in an international setting where the consumers are in one country and the producers in another, the transfer cannot be so easily ignored.

Traditional economic analysis stopped at this point, ignoring the obvious fact that the opportunity to obtain this lucrative transfer payment is likely to attract resources into efforts by sellers to establish and maintain monopoly power. For example, as we have already explained,[3] since costs are always positive, the output at which the monopolist's Marginal Revenue equals its Marginal Cost must necessarily lie on the "elastic" portion of the Demand curve (*i.e.*, where Marginal Revenue is also positive). This means, in the case of a cartel, that each member of the cartel has a strong incentive to cheat by lowering price and increasing output. Typically, therefore, cartels must establish some mechanism to fix quotas and to police against cheating and these mechanisms are never costless.

Moreover, even if the cartel successfully controlled cheating, individual members might resort to non-price competition — better services, longer warranties, improved quality, etc. — in order to capture for themselves a larger share of the cartel's profit. Taken to the extreme this could actually continue until the members' costs rose to the cartel price level, producing, in effect, a fully competitive industry. The point is, however, that if under price competition consumers were unwilling to bid up the price of the product in order to obtain these improvements in quality, that means they value those improvements less highly than some alternative use of their money, alternatives which by reason of the cartel, they are now compelled to forgo. Since, the cartel does not capture this value, it only adds to the deadweight loss visited upon society.

Lastly, a reduction in the industry's output will also reduce the industry's demand for inputs (raw materials, equipment, labor, etc.). This, in turn, will lower the price of those inputs (assuming competitive suppliers) and will result in their diversion to less valued alternative uses. Again, by diverting resources away from their highest valued use the cartel imposes a loss upon society.

---

[3] Chapter 5 at page 486.

In sum, the American antitrust laws rest on a core of theoretical learning which teaches that competitive markets are the best mechanism for assuring that the Nation's productive resources are used efficiently. Efficiency, in turn, is viewed as a social good for it assures that in a world in which resources are not unlimited, those resources will be put to their highest valued use at least cost.

In positing this core learning we need not pause to consider how fully the framers, or the courts in their early encounters with the Sherman and Clayton Acts, understood the theoretical relationship between competitive markets and economic efficiency. What we do know, however, is that the Sherman Act was passed at a time when ever increasing segments of the American economy were being monopolized by the great "trusts." The framers plainly viewed these combinations with alarm and responded by interposing the virtues of competition against the evils of monopoly. In so doing, it is certainly arguable that they were animated as much by the perceived dangers that great concentrations of economic power posed for a democratic polity as upon a refined appreciation of the economic costs of monopoly. To the extent this was the case, the framers struck a note that continues to find its way into much contemporary discussion of antitrust policy; the recurrent idea that the thing to fear is private economic power *per se* (*i.e.*, size alone), and that the antitrust laws are as much a bulwark of small enterprise as a charter of economic efficiency.

While it is not our purpose here to explore the merits of this recurrent theme in the context of the domestic application of the antitrust laws, it is nevertheless a theme to which the student of these materials must be sensitive. It surfaces repeatedly in decisions regarding the law's transnational reach. In its most extreme form it tends to convert antitrust law from a measure concerned with preserving the competitive structure of markets to one concerned with guarantying individual survival in the market. In this extreme form it threatens to turn antitrust law into a law of fair competition or even an extended body of commercial tort law. Even if this reading of the American antitrust tradition can be justified in the domestic setting, it is highly problematic in the transnational setting where market size and structure, the effects of international trade and political context differ widely from nation to nation. To read into U.S. law something more than a strict efficiency rationale can appear — especially to foreigners who do not share the American tradition — as nothing but a device for projecting American business ethics into foreign markets and for arming American companies with a weapon to use against their foreign competitors. Moreover, only by reason of its efficiency rationale can a strong antitrust policy lay claim to being of universal concern; to having a place in a liberal international economic order and to being something more than a parochial American contrivance.

Now, of course, the blatant globe-girdling cartels or the market devouring single firm monopolies that so preoccupied the framers of the Sherman Act are no longer the problem. Antitrust enforcement and economic circumstance have combined to transform the American economy so that oligopoly is increasingly the order of the day. While, as we have noted,[4] lawyers and economists are generally agreed that theoretically, and stated in broad terms, concentrated oligopolistic markets may give rise to interdependent, supra-competitive pricing without any agreement

---

[4] Chapter 5 at page 487.

whatsoever between the firms involved (*i.e.*, "tacit" collusion), there are sharply diverging views on the nature and extent of the danger and how it should be handled under the antitrust laws. One group sees the danger as very real. In their view, interdependent, supra-competitive pricing is likely to be the only rational form of pricing behavior for a company once its industry reaches a requisite level of concentration and certain other reinforcing conditions are met. According to this group the proper antitrust response is to break up already overly concentrated industries and prohibit presently fragmented industries from becoming concentrated. The law should, in other words, remove the fundamental conditions that make supra-competitive pricing rational.

Others tend to stress the additional factors that must accompany concentration before such separately arrived at, interdependent pricing decisions can, in fact, become the only rational pricing strategy for a firm. To this group, the probability of the right convergence of the factors is sufficiently remote to warrant taking a wholly different approach to the problem. At most, they argue, the general theory shows that as an industry becomes more concentrated it becomes increasingly possible for sellers to engage in actual "price-fixing" without requiring any detectable machinery of collusion or enforcement. But the mere possibility is not proof. Accordingly, they emphasize the need for antitrust authorities to identify industries in which this type of collusive pricing is most likely to occur and then only prosecute members of a suspect industry for "price fixing" under Section 1 of the Sherman Act if, upon further investigation, evidence of actual collusion is uncovered or there is sufficient evidence of "tacit collusion" judged according to a number of indicia pertaining to market shares, demand elasticities, industry wide pricing practices, profit patterns, information exchanges and the like.

While it is unnecessary for us to enter into this debate, it is necessary to understand when and why oligopolistic markets pose a cognizable danger of visiting monopoly costs upon society and upon whom those costs are, in the context of particular transnational arrangements, likely to fall.[5] To this end it is

---

[5] Note that as a first approximation we defined a competitive market as one having many suppliers no one of which possessed power over price. Yet, in addressing the problem of oligopolistic markets we postulated the opposite. Having thus relaxed our basic definition of competition, the question remains whether, in the context of an oligopolistic market, the twin models of competition and monopoly remain a valid framework for analyzing the behavioral tendencies of firms in an industry and the social consequences of that behavior. The answer is clear; the analytic framework remains in all essential respects valid. Whether or not one agrees that interdependent pricing is the preeminent form of rational pricing strategy in a concentrated industry, the crucial point is that if conditions are propitious and concentration produces a higher than competitive price, then our model of cartel behavior is the apposite analytic framework. Producers will curtail output, prices will rise and the same costs will be visited upon society, although the cost associated with establishing and maintaining the higher price may be less or at least different than in the case of the explicit cartel. A more interesting question, peripheral to our subject, is how close the industry will actually be able, under either theory, to bring industry output to where industry marginal cost equals industry marginal revenue and how long, if at all, such a condition can be sustained without overt collusion. On the other hand, if conditions are not propitious and concentration does not yield a pattern of interdependent supra-competitive pricing, our competitive model sets the framework. This holds true even if we postulate that one or more of the firms in the industry commands a sufficient

necessary first to specify with particularity the level of industry concentration that is sufficient to trigger a legitimate concern for supra-competitive pricing. While a number of indices have been devised and tested for this purpose, the most widely accepted, at present, is the Herfindahl Hirschman Index (HHI).

The HHI is calculated by summing the squares of the market share of each firm included in the relevant market. This has the virtue of including the fringe, while giving greater weight to the larger firms. For example, if an industry consists of six firms, three of which supply approximately 30% of the market each, one 4% of the market and two 3% each, the result is an index of 2,734 ($30^2 + 30^2 + 30^2 + 4^2 + 3^2 + 3^2$). Contrast this with another six firm industry in which four firms supply approximately 17% of the market each and two firms 16% each. In this case the Index drops to 1,668 ($17^2 + 17^2 + 17^2 + 17^2 + 16^2 + 16^2$). A completely monopolized industry, of course, has an Index of 10,000.

Later, in considering certain core legal concepts, we shall indicate the HHI index levels which, according to the Justice Department, give rise to a cognizable danger of supra-competitive pricing. Here, however, it is necessary to emphasize that a high level of industry concentration alone is not enough. There are other economic factors that serve both as danger signals and perhaps as necessary conditions to a finding that interdependent, supra-competitive pricing is sufficiently probable to warrant legal intervention. For convenience these can be grouped under several headings: the price elasticity of demand, the rate of entry, the problem of "cheating" and the nature of the product.

The Price Elasticity of Demand

A monopoly price must always lie on the elastic portion of the demand curve. If over time, therefore, the prevailing price in an industry has remained inelastic that would constitute telling evidence that interdependent or collusive pricing is not occurring. Conversely, while persistence over time of a highly elastic price is not equally probative of collusion, that persistence certainly points to the need for a closer look at the industry.

The Rate of Entry

One element that can effect demand elasticity is the promptness with which new firms can, in response to a price increase, enter an industry and take business away from existing firms. This, in turn, suggests a number of possibilities.

---

market share to materially effect price by increasing or decreasing output. Observe that if price is already in the elastic portion of the demand curve but industry marginal revenue still lies below marginal cost (*i.e.*, there is increased profit to be had by raising price), each firm in the industry has a positive incentive to let others take the lead in reducing output. Only if it is virtually certain that the dynamics of interdependent behavior or tacit collusion are so strong that mutual forbearance will hold until industry output is reduced to the profit maximizing point (*i.e.*, MC = MR), does price leadership become genuinely tenable, and even then, the incentive to cheat may be irresistible. On the other hand, if the industry is operating on the inelastic portion of the demand curve, while the initial benefits of a price rise may be sufficient to assure a pattern of mutual forbearance, once price reaches the "elastic" portion of the curve the dynamics change; the incentive to cheat enters, price leadership as a strategy and the idea of a floor on price reductions become increasingly problematic. While this is not to suggest that interdependent, supra-competitive pricing will never occur, it does emphasize that in addition to a high level of concentration other economic conditions must be propitious before the danger becomes real.

— In an industry where a new entrant is likely to encounter higher long-run costs than existing firms (*i.e.*, barriers to entry) the likelihood of collusive pricing is greater at lower levels of concentration than in an industry where entry can be relatively rapid.

— In an industry with high entry costs, any increase in concentration accompanied by an increase in the frequency and rate of new entrants strongly suggests the presence of supra-competitive pricing. On the other hand, if entry into an industry is relatively easy, the absence of any increase in the rate of entry incident to a rise in concentration strongly suggests that interdependent or collusive pricing is not occurring, even if the absolute level of concentration is high.

The Problem of Cheating

Recall that the possibility of tacit monopoly pricing by a concentrated industry rests upon the assumption that individual price cutting will be constrained through a mutual fear of retaliatory cuts. This assumption, in turn, attributes to each supplier the belief that his cuts cannot be concealed; that his competitors will find him out. If, on the contrary, suppliers believe that their "cheating" on the tacit cartel price can be concealed, the substantial short term gains to be had from cheating virtually assure the attempt. Among the factors to consider, therefore, in assessing the dangers of supra-competitive pricing is the ease with which cheating can be concealed. The more difficult the concealment, the greater the danger of tacit collusion. In making this assessment the following are some useful indicators:

— On the selling side the more concentrated the industry the more difficult it will generally be to conceal cheating.

— On the buying side the converse is true. It is easier for a seller to keep his "price shaving" confidential by blaming buyer idiosyncrasies for buyer defections from traditional suppliers if a single large scale buyer defects than if a large number of small buyers are involved.

— Because price cutting in an industry where demand is rising will have a less noticeable effect on competitors, cheating can be more readily concealed and hence more widespread than in an industry facing a static or declining demand.

— If fixed costs constitute a high proportion of an industry's total costs, the resulting vulnerability of firms to market changes, particularly to reductions in demand, will increase the benefits of supra-competitive pricing and reduce the incentives to cheat.

— Where it is customary to award business on the basis of sealed bids, cheating is more difficult to conceal.

— All theories concerning interdependent or collusive pricing presume that suppliers will not only have an incentive to match each others' price movements, but can do so with relative ease. The more difficult matching movements become the greater the need for some more readily detectable overt mechanism to police the cartel. Thus, the more the technical specifications of a product vary from order to order the easier it will be to conceal price cutting under cover of asserted differences in product quality or design.

Nature of the Product

If an industry sells a highly fungible product, the principal form of competition will be price competition and collusive pricing the principal means of increasing profits. If, however, other forms of competition loom large (*e.g.*, product quality and service), collusive pricing may only succeed in enlivening these other forms of non-price competition. Since ultimately these alternatives, if vigorous enough, can bid away the entire monopoly profit inherent in a supra-competitive price, that prospect alone may be strong enough to discourage even the initial attempt at an interdependent pricing strategy. In short, the less standardized or fungible the product the smaller the danger that a concentrated industry will be able to engage successfully in interdependent or collusive pricing.[6]

Lastly, a word concerning the strengths, the limitations and the uses to be made of this analytic framework. We speak, of course, as though we have perfect information; as though we know the precise dimensions of the industry demand curve, its marginal revenue and marginal cost curves; that we can measure the precise elasticity of demand, have a readily defined industry, know the trade-offs between price and non-price competition, can accurately compare the relative costs of established firms and of new entrants and more. In the actual enforcement of the antitrust laws these are matters to be established by evidence. That evidence maybe very difficult to obtain, if it exists at all. The probative value of such evidence as does exist maybe highly problematic and may admit of more than one interpretation. Even that interpretation can, at times, engage subtle and highly controverted points of theory. Moreover, the complexity and uncertainty of the evidentiary setting in which judgment must be made constitutes an open invitation to subjectivity and the unexamined predicate. In the end, no serious student of antitrust can escape the discomfiting sense that at times judgments so confidently asserted are little better than educated guesses.

In spite of all this, the principles discussed above are central to any serious effort at rational decision making. They identify the critical questions that must be addressed. They help locate the evidence that must be uncovered. They postulate the central relationships that will determine, if not the precise degree, the essential direction of human behavior. Above all else, as a heuristic design — a statement of the tendencies inherent in the relationship between observable phenomena — they are fundamentally true. Hence, any decision made in disregard of these principles, whether out of disbelief or a fear that their operation is too shrouded in evidentiary ambiguity to be credited, is a decision all but certain to yield those unintended effects that can only frustrate whatever object the decision maker may have set himself.

---

[6] This theoretical possibility appears not to have received any systematic empirical testing, and intuitively may be thought to run counter to conditions in some oligopolistic industries such as automobiles.

§ 7.02 The Core Learning; The Law

[A] Some Points of General Reference: Market Definition and the "Rule of Reason"

With this core of economic learning in mind we turn to take a closer look at Section 1 and Section 2 of the Sherman Act and Section 7 of the Clayton Act. Under all three sections, the initial and sometimes decisive task is to define the relevant market. Power over price — monopoly power — does not exist in the abstract, a point sadly ignored in some important international antitrust cases. It exists, if at all, only between particular sellers and particular buyers engaged, or potentially engaged, in the exchange of some particular economic good, whether it be goods, services, money or technology.

Stated otherwise, for purposes of antitrust analysis it is sheer nonsense to talk about the American "export market" in a particular product. Accordingly, while in this study we will usually take the market definition as given, it is important to recognize that in defining the relevant participants in the market — the buyers and the sellers — commercial function and geography are critical factors, especially the latter. If sellers of a product in a particular geographical area can increase price without attracting an immediate inflow of the product from other more distant sellers, the market can generally be defined by reference to that limited geographical area. But this test presents difficulties. Where the extent of the inflow is a function of factors other than governmentally imposed barriers to trade,[1] the suspected monopolist who has already raised his price may argue that he is not a monopolist by pointing to distant competitors that only his monopoly price have induced into the local market. The only guard against this danger is to recognize it and to use as a corrective a number of more practical indicia such as historical trade patterns, industry perceptions, actual differences in transportation costs, consumer loyalties and the like.

The next general point to note concerns the ambiguous yet necessary interposition of a "Rule of Reason." Section 1 of the Sherman Act speaks of "contracts" and "combinations" in restraint of trade and Section 2 of "monopolizing." If "restraint of trade" and "monopolizing" are equated with the restraint of competition, every contract, in one sense, restrains trade. If a buyer is restrained by his contract from purchasing identical goods from a competing seller, even one offering a lower price, the contract restrains competition among sellers. Yet, it would be absurd to think that every contract is outlawed by the antitrust laws. Hence, the courts have devised a "Rule of Reason." It is only an "unreasonable" or "undue" restraints of trade that those laws reprehend.

Manifestly, a concept of this sort is a flexible vessel. Not surprisingly there are decisions in which "reasonableness" turns not on economic factors but upon the effect that a challenged business conduct is thought to have on the survival of small enterprises or upon the assumed dangers of economic power as such. More often, however, the "Rule of Reason" serves as a bridge between the language of the

---

[1] Where, as often happens in the international setting, governmentally imposed barriers to trade are chiefly responsible for curtailing inflow, the definition is perhaps more certain. One can speak quite realistically of the European market or the Brazilian market.

antitrust statutes and the core economic learning. Used strictly in this way, the question to be asked under a "Rule of Reason" inquiry is not whether the individual trader's competitive freedom has been restrained, but whether a restraint upon the individual's freedom is likely to impair the full and vigorous operation of competitive forces within the relevant market. Difficulties of measurement aside, if the restraint on the individual does not pose a cognizable threat to market competition, or if it promises to perfect the market, the restraint is ignored; it is a "reasonable" restraint. If it does pose such a threat, it will fail to pass muster under the "Rule of Reason."

Finally, certain types of business arrangements are classified as *per se* "unreasonable." Again, we shall encounter cases applying the *per se* classification to certain types of conduct for reasons other than their necessary effect on market competition. But, in the narrower context with which we are concerned, the *per se* rule operates to establish one or more conclusive presumptions concerning the anti-competitive effect of the arrangement in question that would otherwise require proof.

To illustrate, consider a price-fixing agreement among some, but not all, of the suppliers to a particular market. Before that agreement could actually result in a market price different than the equilibrium price under competition (*i.e.*, actually restrain competition) two conditions would have to be met. First, the price actually fixed by the agreement would have to be higher than the marginal cost of the firms' that were parties to the agreement. It would have to be a supra-competitive price. Second, in order for the first condition to be met, the aggregate market share of the parties to the agreement would have to be large enough to confer upon them the power to raise price above cost and to render them relatively impervious to the lower price that non-parties to the agreement, if any, would doubtless offer. In effect, therefore, when the courts declared price fixing agreements *per se* violations of the Sherman Act, they established a conclusive presumption that these conditions had been met. They rendered it unnecessary to actually prove that the parties to the agreement had the power to exact a supra-competitive price from the market and had actually done so. Proof of the agreement was proof of the offense and the trial of a price fixing case was transformed from that of an antitrust case (*i.e.*, an inquiry into the agreement's effect on the market) into the trial of a conspiracy case (*i.e.*, did the parties collude).

Now, while the reasons assigned for constructing these conclusive presumptions may sometimes differ, there are certain recurring themes. Again, consider the price-fixing agreement. The first conclusive presumption (*i.e.*, that the parties charged a supra-competitive price) rests initially on the theoretical point that if, in fact, the conspirators had power over price there could be no competitive price with which to establish the violation. At the very least, proof would be difficult. Moreover, even if one could approximate a competitive price and even if it were shown at trial that the agreed upon price were no higher, there could be no guarantee that it would remain that way. To the contrary, it may be presupposed that the agreement was not an idle exercise and that the participants intended, sooner or later, to raise price above the competitive level. Under these circumstances, if actual proof of supra-competitive pricing were required, the courts and the antitrust enforcement authorities would carry an almost impossible burden of continually policing the arrangement.

The second conclusive presumption (*i.e.*, that the parties had power over price) rests upon at least two presuppositions; that the purpose of the agreement was to raise price and that careful businessmen would not engage in such an undertaking unless reasonably assured that they possessed the market power necessary for success. However, suppose they were mistaken? On this point the courts have never been very clear. But one may assume that a rule foreclosing any defense based upon mistake or misjudgment would serve several purposes. It would be a prophylactic; a rule to discourage the attempt. It would add certainty to the law and would simplify the trial of such cases, with judicial economy being perhaps the foremost justification.

In sum, a number of basic reasons have been used to justify raising a conclusive presumption that certain types of conduct impair the full and free operation of competition in the relevant market; are *per se* anti-competitive. For the student of international antitrust, the point to keep in mind is that even if these justifications are persuasive in the domestic context, their fitness in the international setting is a matter deserving careful scrutiny.

[B]   Section 1 of the Sherman Act

Section 1 of the Sherman Act pertains to concerted action between two or more firms. As such, it is the section which outlaws the classic "price-fixing" cartel. Other than naked "price-rigging," however, suppliers may agree or conspire to exercise monopoly power in other ways. They may divide the market into territories in which each is to be the sole supplier. Where each would, under competition, sell a line of complementary or otherwise related products, they may agree to assign to each member the exclusive right to sell one or more products in the line. They may channel all their sales through a common sales agency. They may, through trade associations or cooperative research and development efforts, exchange information which enables them to set a common price or divide up the market.

Also, there are varieties of vertical restraints. A firm at one level in the chain of distribution (*e.g.*, the manufacturer) may fix the price at which downstream firms (*e.g.*, distributors) must resell a product, or may assign each downstream firm an exclusive territory or forbid those firms from selling except at stated locations. Broadly these practices may be categorized as "collusive" because they present two potential dangers. Where competition among downstream firms is necessary to the maintenance of competition in the relevant market, the upstream firm — the manufacturer — may be acting only as cloak for what is otherwise collusion among the downstream companies. Similarly, the restraints imposed by the upstream firm may be a device for policing a cartel among upstream firms. All of these arrangements, if they have the effect of enabling the participants to exercise power over price, or if classified as per se "unreasonable," are outlawed by Section 1 of the Sherman Act as contracts, combinations and conspiracies "in restraint of trade."

Another group of practices that may run afoul of Section 1 of the Sherman Act, can be broadly classified as "exclusionary" practices. They are designed to attain, rather than exercise, monopoly power by either driving existing competitors out of the market or preventing potential competitors from entering. Examples include, efforts by traders at one level in the chain of distribution to induce traders at another level to refuse to deal with their actual or potential competitors (*i.e.*, concerted refusals to deal or group boycotts); attempts by a trader to deny competitors access to a market by acquiring all the existing distribution outlets or requiring his distributors to deal only in his product; attempts to foreclose competitors from obtaining essential supplies through long term "requirements contracts" or exclusive distributorship arrangements. There is also "tying," whereby a merchant with market power over one product conditions the sale or lease of that product (the "tying" product) to the purchase or lease of another item (the "tied" product). While tying has traditionally run afoul of Section 1 (see also Section 3 of the Clayton Act), opinion is quite divided on the extent to which these arrangements can really have the monopolizing tendency attributed to them or whether they more often serve other pro-competitive purposes.

[C] Section 2 of the Sherman Act

Section 2 of the Sherman Act is, as the words imply, directed principally at the single firm monopolist. As noted earlier, the framers of the Act were preoccupied with certain large and highly visible "trusts" often formed, according to popular opinion, by ruthless predation. Reflecting this focus, the courts early backed away from punishing a business that, without hint of unethical conduct, had grown to monopoly proportions through superior business acumen, or the dictates of scale economies or by the accident of position (*e.g.*, the first into a market or the first to acquire an important technology). The phrases used, make the point: Monopoly "thrust upon" a firm did not violate the law. Monopoly "deliberately" obtained did. Monopoly acquired through "superior skill, foresight and industry" was acceptable. Monopoly resulting from conduct "not honestly industrial" was not. While suggestive, these phrases do no more than underscore that it is not "monopoly" as such but "monopolizing" that offends the Sherman Act.

Without attempting to explore the intricacies of this distinction, a few of the steadier benchmarks are worth noting. Early it was settled that monopoly power acquired or maintained by conduct involving two or more firms which also ran afoul of Section 1 of the Sherman Act would suffice to sustain a parallel charge of "monopolizing" under Section 2. (*e.g.*, monopoly power acquired by way of a merger of two or more firms, a territorial division agreement, or an exclusive dealing arrangement with suppliers or buyers). Section 2 has also traditionally been held to interdict any predatory conduct by a single firm resulting in the acquisition or maintenance of monopoly power which would, because of the absence of any concert of two or more actors, escape the reach of Section 1 (*e.g.*, predatory pricing, threatening or engaging in tortious conduct).

When, however, one turns to some of the more expansive interpretations of "monopolizing" the boundary becomes far less clear. The most notable of these interpretations is that formulated by Judge Learned Hand in *United States v. Aluminum Co. of America*,[2] who concluded that "monopolization" was established upon a showing of monopoly achieved and maintained over time by a course of conduct which, although wholly ethical, was nevertheless "deliberate" and which tended to keep competitors from entering into or expanding their share

---

[2] 148 F.2d 416 (2d Cir. 1945).

of the market; a "deliberateness" test. In practical effect, however, Judge Hand's test tended to include what it purported to exclude. It has, as a consequence, invited retreat. In its stead, later decisions have tended to place greater emphasis on whether a defendant's conduct had the necessary effect of raising entry barriers or otherwise excluding competitors and whether it was pursued with that specific purpose in mind.

Lastly, Section 2 of the Sherman Act interdicts both "attempts[s] to monopolize" and combinations and conspiracies "to monopolize." The latter simply catches "monopolizing" or "attempts to monopolize" in which two or more firms are involved. The interdiction of "attempt[s] to monopolize" is designed to reach the unsuccessful effort at obtaining monopoly power but is significantly constrained by the need to prove a "specific intent." The nature of that proof is a point to which we shall return in the materials that follow.

[D] Section 7 of the Clayton Act

Enacted in 1914, restrictive court interpretations of Section 7 of the Clayton Act — asset acquisitions were held excluded — prevented that Section from having any significant impact on American merger law until amended in 1950. Moreover, despite a waive of mergers between 1920 and 1929, the inherent difficulties of maintaining monopoly power without actively excluding new entrants, Sherman Act curtailment of the more blatant forms of "exclusionary" conduct, the success of earlier attacks on cartelization, all combined to transform the merger problem confronting the Nation as it emerged from World War II. It was no longer a matter of forestalling the creation of new monopolistic giants, but rather a matter of dealing with mergers which, while leading to increased industrial concentration, were likely to fall far short of vesting in any one firm true monopoly power. Accordingly, the genesis of modern American merger law may be traced back to 1948 when the Supreme Court handed down its decision in *United States v. Columbia Steel*.[3] There the Court turned aside the Justice Department's effort, relying upon Sections 1 and 2 of the Sherman Act, to prevent Columbia Steel, a subsidiary of United States Steel, from acquiring Consolidated Steel, one of the largest independent fabricators of steel building frames on the West Coast. Two points emerged from the decision. It was plain that the Court lacked anything approximating a coherent theory by which to judge the likely market effects of a non-monopolistic merger. Second, the decision was read to say that such mergers could not be reached under either Section 1 or Section 2 of the Sherman Act, with the consequence that the nation appeared to be wholly without any law that would effectively prevent increased concentration in already concentrated industries.

Largely as a reaction to *Columbia Steel*, Congress in 1950 amended Section 7 of the Clayton Act. The asset acquisition loophole was closed and other language added that appeared intended to give the section wider compass. More importantly, while it was clear that Congress' theoretical grasp of the oligopoly problem was no greater than the Court's, the legislative history made plain that Congress deemed the growing concentration of American industry to be a problem and intended the Court to address the problem.

---

3 334 U.S. 495, 69 S. Ct. 1107 (1948).

At first the task did not proceed smoothly. Too often the Court seemed unable to grasp the difference between concentrated and fragmented markets or to understand fully the kind of anticompetitive conduct that might result from an oligopolistic market structure.[4] Moreover, the government always won. Then, in 1974 the Court handed the Government its first defeat since the 1950 amendments. It upheld the merger of two coal producers which, in one market, increased the share of the largest firm from 45% to 49% and, in the other, from 44% to 53%. In both markets the absolute number of producers was declining. Because the acquired firm's coal reserves were heavily committed under long term supply contracts, it could not, the Court concluded, be viewed as a significant factor in competition for future business. *United States v. General Dynamics Corp.*[5] Market share was just the starting point for analysis; a threshold measure of concentration. Once that threshold was crossed it was necessary, the Court said, to assay the competitive significance of that measure in light of the total economic context of the merger being judged.

In the years since, the basic approach laid down in *General Dynamics* has remained intact. This being so, it is unnecessary for our present purposes to trace the changing and sometimes contradictory course of the Court's decisions under that approach.[6] It suffices for our immediate purposes to turn to the Merger

---

[4] See especially *Brown Shoe Co. v. United States*, 370 U.S. 294 (1962) 82 S.Ct. 1478. Following *Brown Shoe*, the Court started searching for simplifying assumptions (mergers creating firms with a 30% market share were presumptively anti-competitive). *United States v. Philadelphia National Bank*, 374 U.S. 321, 83 S.Ct. 1283 (1964). One year later it seemed to back-off this approach and, according to Justice Stuart in dissent, contradict itself. *United States v. Von's Grocery Company*, 384 U.S. 270 (1966).

[5] 415 U.S. 486, 94 S.Ct. 1186 (1974).

[6] All of the cases referred to in the text related to so-called "horizontal mergers;" mergers between two or more firms that were, at the time, competitors in the relevant market. Three other types of mergers, however, have occupied the courts and should be noted.

First, there are so-called "market extension mergers;" a merger between firms who are not current competitors but whose separate operations may so affect competitive conditions in one or more markets that a merger between them may have an anticompetitive effect. (*e.g.*, two firms market the same product in different geographical markets, or sell, in the same geographical market, different items at different ends of the industry's product line or different items using a closely related technology). At the core of concern with these "market-extension" combinations is the fact that because the dangers of collusive or interdependent pricing can depend greatly upon the existing market participants perceived freedom from new entrants, the danger of supra-competitive pricing can never be fully appraised without taking account of potential competitors standing in the "wings." If there is evidence that a "perceived potential entrant" plays an important role in constraining collusive pricing any merger through which that potential entrant actually enters a new geographical or product market by acquiring an established firm, rather than entering de-novo, is a merger that requires close scrutiny.

Second there are the so-called "vertical mergers" where a firm acquires a supplier or customer. On the pro-competitive side, vertical mergers may help reduce costs, aid in avoiding an upstream or downstream monopolist or an already integrated supplier or customer. On the other hand, vertical mergers can also be used to foreclose other non-integrated competitors from access to markets or to sources of supply, to reduce the likelihood of new entry or to assist in the process of minimizing price competition through product differentiation.

Guidelines first promulgated by the Justice Department in 1968, revised in 1982 and again in 1984.[7] These Guidelines may be taken as either a fair distillation of the law as it now appears or the law as it is likely to develop.

For our purposes there are three points to note about the Guidelines; (i) the use of the Herfindahl Hirschman Index (HHI) to measure industry concentration; (ii) the specification of various thresholds of concentration that are to be used as a guide to further inquiry regarding the industry's potential for supra-competitive pricing and (iii) the identification of the other economic factors that should enter into that inquiry.

Using the HHI Index the Guidelines divide industries into three categories and within each category identify those levels of increased concentration which are likely to result in the Department challenging the merger, provided the other economic circumstances warrant the challenge.

Table I

Justice Department Merger Guidelines

Categories of Industries

	Post Merger Index	Increase Not likely to Invite Challenge	Increase Likely to Invite Challenge
Category 1	Below 1,000	[No challenge except in "extraordinary circumstances"]	
Category 2	1,000-1,800	Less than 100 Index 100 Index Points	More than 100 Index Points
Category 3	Above 1,800	Less than* 50 Index Points	50-100 Index Points Investigate 100 or more Index Points Challenge

---

Third, there are "conglomerate mergers" in which a firm operating in one product market acquires one or more firms operating in wholly unrelated product markets. Unique to the conglomerate merger is the danger of reciprocity where both potential customers of and potential suppliers to an independent firm are part of a conglomerate which conditions purchase of the independent's product on the latter's undertaking to purchase its inputs from the conglomerate. Despite periodic public interest, government efforts to break up some of the more notable conglomerates have not been attended with great success.

[7] CCH Trade Regulation Reports, Paragraph 13,301 at page 20,551 et. seq.

More specifically, the Guidelines provide as follows:[8]

. . . [M]arket share and concentration data provide only the starting point for analyzing the competitive impact of a merger. Before determining whether to challenge a merger, the Department will consider all other relevant factors that pertain to its competitive impact. [See below for discussion of these other factors.]

The general standards for horizontal mergers are as follows:

(a) Post-Merger HHI Below 1000. Markets in this region generally would be considered to be unconcentrated . . . [and] the Department will not challenge mergers falling in this region except in extraordinary circumstances.

(b) Post-Merger Between 1000 and 1800. Because this region extends from the point at which the competitive concerns associated with concentration are raised to the point at which they become quite serious, generalization is particularly difficult. The Department, however, is unlikely to challenge a merger producing an increase in the HHI of less than 100 points.[9] The Department is *likely* to challenge mergers . . . that produce an increase in the HHI of more than 100 points, unless the Department concludes, on the basis of the post-merger HHI, the increase in the HHI and . . . [the other] factors [discussed below] . . . that the merger is not likely substantially to lessen competition.

(c) Post Merger HHI above 1800 . . . Additional concentration resulting from mergers [in markets within this region] is a matter of significant competitive concern. The Department, however, is unlikely to challenge mergers producing an increase in the HHI of less than 50 points [and] . . . is likely to challenge mergers . . . that produce an increase . . . of more than 50 points, unless . . . the [other factors indicate] that the merger is not likely substantially to lessen competition. However, if the increase in the HHI exceeds 100 and the post-merger HHI substantially exceeds 1800, only in extraordinary cases will such factors establish that the merger is not likely substantially to lessen competition.

Leading Firm Proviso . . . Notwithstanding [the foregoing] standards, the Department is likely to challenge the merger of any firm with a market share of at least one percent with the leading firm in the market, provided the leading firm has a market share that is at least 35 percent. [In its review of such a case] the [only other factors] . . . the Department will consider . . . [pertain to (i) changing market conditions, (ii) the financial condition of firms in the market (iii) special factors affecting foreign firms and (iv) ease of entry.[10]

---

[8] *Id.* at page 20,560.

[9] As examples of mergers likely to produce increases in concentration close to the 100 point threshold, the Guidelines list mergers between firms with the following market shares: 25% and 2%; 16% and 3%; 12% and 4%; 10% and 5%; 8% and 6%; and two 7% firms. *Id.* at page 20,560.

[10] Recall the example given earlier of a six firm industry in which four firms supply approximately 17% of the market and two firms 16% each. In this case the HHI is 1,668.

As the Guidelines make clear the Department does not treat its HHI thresholds as conclusive of the decision to challenge a merger. All other relevant factors will be considered. Thus, in addition to the factors already discussed [11] the Guidelines make the following points:

(i) Because market share analysis is based on historical evidence, current market share data can, if the market is undergoing rapid changes, either overstate or understate a firm's future competitive significance. For example, the development of an important new technology which, depending upon whether it is available to the firms involved in the merger or not, can substantially change the competitive effect of the merger from that indicated by the raw HHI numbers.

(ii) If a firm is in a chronically poor financial condition, that will tend to diminish the future competitive significance of any merger involving that firm, especially in a market experiencing a long-term decline in demand.

(iii) The smaller the qualitative difference between an industry's product and the "next best" substitute excluded from the relevant market or the closer the "next most distant" seller is to the market, the less the danger of collusion.

(iv) If the industry product is highly differentiated or the industry spatially disbursed, the Department will examine consumers' qualitative perception of the product and the relative geographic proximity of the firms and will be less favorably disposed toward mergers between firms whose products or plants are good substitutes for each other.

(v) If the industry has a history of collusion or of mandatory delivered prices, or of engaging in the exchange of price or output information, or of standardizing product variables, this history will mitigate against approval of any merger.

(vi) Any evidence of non-competitive industry performance, especially evidence showing that the leading firms have experienced relatively stable market shares or a declining aggregate share combined with profit rates in excess of firms in comparable industries, will mitigate against approval of any merger.

Lastly the Guidelines comment on certain "Special Factors Affecting Foreign Firms," as follows:

In this example the six firms are of nearly equal size yet the industry remained in Category 2 because the four largest firms command less than 70% of the market. This illustrates how the Guidelines account for the "fringe effect" that can be material in assessing the dangers of collusion. Where, as in the example, there are post-merger two firms not in the top four but of nearly the same size as the top four, the Department is less fearful of an increased propensity to collude than if there were a much smaller fringe. Compare the following: Industry A: Seven firms: four with 17% of market; one with 16%; one with 14%; one with 2%. Pre-merger Index: 1612. Merger: 14% firm with 2% firm = four with 17%; two with 16%. Post Merger-Index: 1668 (Category 2). Increase: 56 Index Points. Industry B: Pre merger: Same as Industry A. Pre-merger Index: 1612. Merger: 16% firm with 14% firm = one firm with 30%; four with 17%; one with 2%. Post-merger Index: 2060 (Category 3). Increase: 448 Index Points.

[11] Section 7.01 at page 593 *supra.*

Actual import sales, shipment data, or capacity in some cases may tend to overstate the relative competitive significance of foreign firms. This will be the case, for example, if foreign firms are subject to quotas. . . . [G]enerally [such firms] cannot increase imports into the United States in response to a domestic price increase. In the case of restraints that limit imports to some percentage of the total amount of the product sold in the United States . . . a domestic price increase that reduces domestic consumption would actually reduce the volume of imports into the United States. . . . Less significant, but still important factors, such as other types of trade restraints and changes in exchange rates, also may cause actual import sales and shipment data to overstate the future competitive significance of foreign firms. To the extent [this occurs] . . . the relative competitive significance of domestic firms concomitantly will be understated.

In addition, limitations on available data concerning the amount of foreign capacity that would be devoted to the United States in response to a "small but significant and nontransitory" increase in price may require the Department to use market share data that understates the true competitive significance of foreign competitors. Despite the inability to obtain [precise quantitative] data . . . the Department will consider strong qualitative evidence that, for example, there is significant worldwide excess capacity that could readily be devoted to the United States [12] . . . .

For the student of international antitrust, the important point to note is that while formally these Guidelines apply only to mergers, they are potentially of broader interest. Insofar as the prescriptive jurisdictional test for the transnational application of the U.S. antitrust laws is a substantive test, every application will involve an economic inquiry. The question will be whether, in light of the industry structure and attendant economic circumstances, the conduct or arrangement being challenged raises a cognizable danger of collusive supra-competitive pricing or of conferring upon the participants a power over price.

More specifically, the Guidelines lay down certain threshold measures of industry concentration that are thought to raise a cognizable danger of collusive pricing. They then identify other economic circumstances that can affect the probability of successful collusion. Accordingly, if, in an international case, the threshold were crossed not by merger but by, for example, an explicit agreement to collude, one could, with some certainty, conclude that a significant element in the requisite jurisdictional nexus had been established. If, on the other hand, the threshold were not crossed or if other economic factors suggested that the risk of supra-competitive pricing was minimal, that would, in turn, suggest that the agreement had a purpose unrelated to the exaction of a monopoly profit from the American economy and would compel a much closer inquiry into whether any purpose of the antitrust laws would be served by interdicting the arrangement. In this way the Guidelines, as reflective of a broader learning about oligopolistic

---

[12] CCH Trade Regulation Reports, Paragraph 13,103, at pages 20,561-20,562.

markets, have a utility extending to virtually any transnational business conduct or arrangement involving firms in a concentrated industry. At the same time, we do not suggest that the Guidelines can invariably or automatically be given this extended application. They only offer benchmarks which raise issues that must be addressed in any sensible attempt to define the prescriptive reach of American antitrust law.

§ 7.03 Restraints in the American Market: The "Effects Doctrine"

An Historical Note

Among the earliest judicial pronouncements on the transnational reach of the American antitrust laws was the opinion by Justice Holmes in *American Banana Co. v. United Fruit Co.*[1] According to conventional wisdom, the *American Banana* decision, although not expressly over-ruled, no longer reflects the law.[2] This is doubtless correct, if one considers only the holding of the case. Nevertheless, Justice Holmes' opinion contains a number of intriguing elements that help put into historical perspective our continuing concern with the joinder of the public international law of prescriptive jurisdiction with the rational choice mode of private international law. As we shall see this perspective has more than passing contemporary relevance in the antitrust context.

American Banana, an Alabama corporation, sued United Fruit, a New Jersey company, for treble damages under the Sherman Act alleging that, long before plaintiff was established, United Fruit had monopolized the banana trade between the United States and Central and South America and the West Indies. To this end, United Fruit had bought-up the property and businesses of several of its competitors, with provision against their resuming the trade, made contracts with still others regulating the quantity and price of bananas to be purchased from growers and acquired a controlling interest in yet other competitors. It then organized a company which sold to the United States at a fixed price all the bananas of the combining parties.

In 1903, one McConnell, started a banana plantation in Panama (then part of Colombia) and was, the complaint alleged, promptly notified by United Fruit that he must either combine or stop building the rail line necessary to export his produce. Two months later, allegedly at defendant's instigation, the governor of Panama recommended to his government that Costa Rica be allowed to administer the territory through which the railroad was to run, even though that territory had been awarded to Colombia in an arbitration agreed to by treaty. In November 1903, Panama declared its independence from Colombia claiming that its boundary with Costa Rica was that settled by the arbitration award.

In June 1904, the plaintiff — American Banana — bought out McConnell and went on with building the railroad. In July of that year, Costa Rican soldiers, again

---

[1] 213 U.S. 347, 29 S. Ct. 511, 53 L. Ed. 826 (1909).

[2] *Industrial Inv. Development Corp v. Mitsui & Co.*, 594 F.2d 48, 52 (5th Cir. 1979); cert. denied 445 U.S. 903 (1980); *Hunt v. Mobil Oil Corp.*, 550 F.2d 68, 74 (2d Cir., 1977) cert. denied 434 U.S. 984 (1977); Areeda & Turner, 1 Antitrust Law, at 261; Atwood & Brewster, 1 Antitrust & American Business Abroad, at 144.

allegedly instigated by the defendant, seized the plantation along with a cargo of supplies and then stopped construction of the railway and operation of the plantation. In August 1904, one Astua, by ex parte proceedings, obtained a judgment from a Costa Rican court declaring the plantation to be his, although the property was within the jurisdiction of Panama. The plaintiff tried to induce the government of Costa Rica to withdraw its soldiers and also tried to persuade the United States to intervene, but was thwarted in both efforts, allegedly by United Fruit. The government of Costa Rica remained in possession of plaintiff's property down to the bringing of the law suit.

Finally, the complaint alleged that not only had United Fruit deprived plaintiff of the use of its plantation and railway but had also driven purchasers out of the market and by buying from other producers at "high prices," had prevented plaintiff from buying for export.

On this complaint the district court dismissed for failure to state a claim. The Court of Appeals affirmed and the Supreme Court did likewise.

In his opinion for the Court, Justice Holmes starts by suggesting that plaintiff's case depended on "several rather startling propositions." All the acts causing damage were done outside the United States and it is, the Justice opines, "the general and almost universal rule . . . that the character of an act as lawful or unlawful must be determined wholly by the law of the country where the act is done."[3] Then, the Justice continues:

> Law is a statement of the circumstances, in which the public force will be brought to bear upon men through the courts. But the word commonly is confined to such prophecies or threats when addressed to persons living within the power of the courts. A threat that depends upon the choice of the party affected to bring himself within that power hardly would be called law in the ordinary sense.

In line with this conception of law, statutes, the Justice argues, should be construed "as intended to be confined in [their] operation and effect to the territorial limits over which the lawmaker has general and legitimate power." In the case of the Sherman Act "the improbability of the United States attempting to make acts done in Panama or Costa Rica criminal is obvious."

A further impediment to plaintiff's suit, Justice Holmes concluded, was to be found in the fact that "not only were the acts of the defendant in Panama or Costa Rica not within the Sherman Act, but they were not torts by the law of the place, and therefore were not torts at all, however contrary to the ethical and economic postulates of that statute." The "fundamental reason," the Justice continues:

> . . . why persuading a sovereign power to do this or that cannot be a tort is . . . [because] . . . it is a contradiction in terms to say that, within its jurisdiction, it is unlawful to persuade a sovereign power to bring about a result that it declares by its conduct to be desirable and proper. . . . It makes the persuasion lawful by its own act. The very meaning of sovereignty is that the decree of the sovereign makes law. . . .

---

[3] The Justice did admit to some exception to the rule namely in the case of regions subject to no sovereign such as the high seas, or no law recognized by civilized countries, cases of piracy and cases immediately affecting the national interest.

Finally, "as to the buying at a high price, etc.," the Justice asserts that "it is enough to say that we have no ground for supposing that is was unlawful in the countries where the purchases were made." In sum, "giving to this complaint every reasonable latitude of interpretation," the Justice was of the opinion that it alleged no case under the Sherman Act and "disclose[d] nothing that [the Court could] suppose to have been a tort where it was done."

Two years after *American Banana*, Justice Holmes authored the Court's decision in *Strassheim v. Daily*.[4] In that case the Court upheld Michigan's jurisdiction to indict Daily on a charge of having delivered used equipment to the State under a contract calling for new machinery and for bribing a State official to remain silent. When Daily made his fraudulent promise by signing the contract and when he mailed the bribe to the State official, the Court assumed that he was in Illinois and took no action in Michigan in furtherance of his unlawful scheme. On these facts the Justice wrote:

> Acts done outside a jurisdiction, but intended to produce and producing detrimental effects within it, justify a state in punishing the cause of the harm as if [it] had been present at the effect. . . .

While cryptic style may leave meaning in doubt, it would seem, under the facts of *Strassheim*, that Holmes' invocation of the "effects" doctrine would fit squarely within the "territorial principle" as interpreted by the Permanent Court of International Justice in the *Lotus Case*.[5] Daily's actions in Illinois not only had an "effect" in Michigan but that "effect" was a "constituent element of the crime charged."

Can *Strassheim v. Daily* be reconciled with *American Banana*? Perhaps the Justice simply changed his mind two years later. But before reaching that conclusion a number of additional points should be noted.

First, plaintiff American Banana asserted two separate causes of action, one under the Sherman Act, the other in tort. Under the then prevailing "vested rights" theory of private international law (conflicts of law) the controlling choice of law rules were characterized as "jurisdiction selecting" and the almost universally accepted rule was that the law of the place of the tort governed. In American Banana's case both the acts causing the injury and the injury itself occurred in Costa Rica and Panama. The latter were clearly the place of the alleged tort.

On the other hand, if the cause of action under the Sherman Act were characterized as a matter of "public" law, that would warrant applying to the case the traditional jurisdictional precepts of public international law, including the "effects" doctrine articulated by Holmes in *Strassheim*. In short, the case can be seen as placing before the Court a rather classic challenge to the traditional public-private law dichotomy; a single set of facts giving rise to a claim that could legitimately be characterized under either heading but with potentially disparate results.

---

[4] 221 U.S. 280, 31 S. Ct. 558 (1911).

[5] *The S.S. Lotus, France v. Turkey*, Permanent Court of International Justice, P.C.I.J. Ser. A, No. 10 (1927). See Chapter 6, page 525 *supra*. Recall also *United States v. Pizarusso*, 388 F. 2d 8 (2d Cir. 1968) in which Judge Medina criticized the Ninth Circuit's reliance on *Strassheim v. Daily in Rocha v. United States*, 288 F. 2d 545 (9th Cir. 1961), Chapter 6 at page 533, note 3(b).

Now, without intending to attribute such a design to Justice Holmes, it is worth observing nevertheless that the Court reached a result which readily conformed to the prevailing private international law rule but which, under the principles of public international law, was far more problematic. In addition, at least two circumstances can be cited to justify the Court's choice of a result mandated by private, not public, international law.

First, contrast *Strassheim v. Daily*. That case involved an extradition proceeding brought by public authority (State of Michigan) in aid of its own criminal prosecution on a charge which, if proven, would doubtless have offended the law of Illinois as well as the law of Michigan. *American Banana*, on the other hand, involved an action by one private party against another with the plaintiff asserting what, for all practical purposes, looked like a traditional common law tort action converted into a "public" matter only by the intervention of a then somewhat novel — and by no means widely accepted — regulatory measure — the Sherman Act — whose principal impact on the case was the trebling of damages.

Second, in its complaint the plaintiff charged the following: (i) that prior to defendant's incorporation there were many companies engaged in importing bananas into the United States and "that active competition producing reasonable prices existed" (Record p. 49), (ii) that while the acts with which defendant was charged all involved foreign properties and firms engaged in production abroad the purpose of those acts was to restrain and monopolize the trade in bananas "between Central America, South America and the West Indies, on one part, and the United States of America, on the other" (Record p. 50) including raising the price at which the fruit was sold in the United States, (iii) that they succeeded in this purpose and (iv) that the producer conspiracy involved "the great majority of the companies importing bananas into the United States." Certainly these allegations speak to an "effect" within the United States and certainly that "effect" was a constituent element of the offense charged: monopolizing the market for bananas in the United States. The jurisdictional elements relied on in *Strassheim v. Daily* all appeared to be present.

Observe, however, that the substantial injury suffered by the plaintiff flowed not from these "effects" but from their causes; defendant's destruction of plaintiff's plantation, railroad and other assets in Panama. The essential nexus between defendant's actions and plaintiff's injury was the tortious conduct in Panama and not the monopolization of the American market. In short, if the jurisdictional issue in *American Banana* is viewed as turning on which system of international law — public or private — should control, a result based on a characterization of the dispute which best captures the essential relationship between the conduct complained of and the injury suffered would seem more than defensible. The lesson lies, of course, in the folly of having to make such a choice. Nevertheless, so long as two systems persist, *American Banana* also serves to remind us that no prospective jurisdictional issue can be decided without taking into account the differing perspectives that the two systems can bring to the problem.

Lastly, *American Banana* should be contrasted with *United States v. Sisal Sales Corp.* [6] In the latter case the Justice Department charged three American banks

---

[6] 274 U.S. 268 47 S.Ct. 592 (1927).

and two other American corporations with violations of Section 1 and Section 2 of the Sherman Act. The defendant's organized, under Mexican law, the Commission Exportadora de Yucatan. With loans from the defendant banks and with aid of favorable Mexican legislation obtained by or at the instance of the banks, the Commission Exportadora became the sole purchaser of sisal from producers in the Yucatan. Defendant Sisal Sales Corp., then became the exclusive selling agent for Commission Exportadora in all markets of the world, including the United States. Sisal was then the principal staple used in the manufacture of rope and binder twine and 80% of all sisal sold in the United States came from the Yucatan. The trial court relying on *American Banana* dismissed the complaint for failure to state a cause of action. The Supreme Court reversed observing that "the circumstances of the present controversy are radically different from those presented" in *American Banana*. "Here we have a contract, combination and conspiracy entered into by parties within the United States and made effective by acts done therein. The fundamental object was control of both importation and sale of sisal in complete monopoly of both internal and external trade and commerce therein. The United States complained of a violation of their laws within their own territory by parties subject to their jurisdiction, not merely of something done by another government at the instigation of private parties." Is the purported distinction between Sisal and American Banana convincing? Or, is their a more telling distinction? Explain.

[A] The Contemporary View: The "Effects" Doctrine

UNITED STATES v. ALUMINUM CO. OF AMERICA

United States Court of Appeals, Second Circuit
148 F.2d 416 (1945)

[In this action, the United States charged the Aluminum Co. of America ("Alcoa") a Pennsylvania corporation, with monopolizing interstate and foreign commerce in the manufacture and sale of "virgin" aluminum ingots in violation of Section 2 of the Sherman Act. The Government also charged Alcoa and Aluminium Limited ("Limited"), a Canadian corporation, with participation in the "Alliance," a Swiss based cartel of aluminum producers. Under the Alliance, production quotas were established for all members. Participation by Alcoa and Limited in this arrangement, the Government alleged, constituted a violation of Section 1 of the Sherman Act. The District Court held for the defendants on both counts and dismissed the complaint. The United States appealed, and the Supreme Court, lacking a quorum of six Justices qualified to hear the case, referred the appeal to the Court of Appeals for the Second Circuit pursuant to 15 U.S.C. Section 29.

Alcoa was established in 1888 and had engaged ever since in the production and sale of "virgin" aluminum ingots and, since 1895, in the fabrication of that metal into many finished and semi-finished products. Through the acquisition of patents and patent licenses which greatly reduced production costs Alcoa enjoyed a legal monopoly in the production of "virgin" ingots until approximately 1909. From 1909 to 1912, through agreements with foreign producers and by restrictive covenants in agreements with electric power companies, Alcoa perpetuated that monopoly. In 1912 the United States sued to enjoin these practices. The resulting consent degree declared many of the agreements unlawful and enjoined their performance. Against this background the Second Circuit turned to the charge that over the next twenty eight years, 1912-1940, Alcoa had continued to monopolize the American market in "virgin" aluminum ingots in violation of Section 2 of the Sherman Act.]

Before L. HAND, SWAN and AUGUSTUS N. HAND, CIRCUIT JUDGES.

L. HAND, CIRCUIT JUDGE.

[*Monopolization of the Domestic Market*]

It is undisputed that throughout this period "Alcoa" continued to be the single producer of "virgin" ingot in the United States; and the plaintiff argues that this without more was enough to make it an unlawful monopoly. It also takes an alternative position: that in any event during this period "Alcoa" consistently pursued unlawful exclusionary practices, which made its dominant position certainly unlawful, even though it would not have been, had it been retained only by "natural growth." . . . "Alcoa's" position is that the fact that it alone continued to make "virgin" ingot in this country did not, and does not, give it a monopoly of the market; that it was always subject to the competition of imported "virgin" ingot, and of what is called "secondary" ingot; and that even if it had not been, its monopoly would not have been retained by unlawful means, but would have been the result of a growth which the Act does not forbid, even when it results in a monopoly. We shall first consider the amount and character of this competition; next, how far it established a monopoly; and finally, if it did, whether that monopoly was unlawful under Section 2 of the Act.

[Judge Hand starts his review of Alcoa's share of the U.S. "virgin" aluminum ingot market by noting that in 1912 that share stood at 91%, had throughout the period 1912-1940 exceeded 80% except for a dip to 68% in 1921, to 72% in 1913 and again in 1922 and had averaged 90% in each of the years 1938-40. He then considers and rejects Alcoa's contention that these percentages should be reduced by adding to the definition of the relevant market, sales of "secondary" aluminum (*i.e.*, ingots manufactured from aluminum scrap). The Judge continued:]

We conclude therefore that "Alcoa's" control over the ingot market must be reckoned at over ninety per cent; that being the proportion which its production bears to imported "virgin" ingot. If the fraction which it did not supply were the product of domestic manufacture there could be no doubt that this percentage gave it a monopoly — lawful or unlawful, as the case might be. The producer of so large a proportion of the supply has complete control within certain limits. . . .

The case at bar is however different, because, for aught that appears there may well have been a practically unlimited supply of imports as the price of ingot rose. Assuming that there was no agreement between "Alcoa" and foreign producers not to import, they sold what could bear the handicap of the tariff and the cost of transportation. . . . For the period of eighteen years — 1920-1937 — they sold at times a little above "Alcoa's" prices, at times a little under; but there was substantially no gross difference between what they received and what they would have received, had they sold uniformly at "Alcoa's" prices. While the record is silent, we may therefore assume — the plaintiff having the burden — that, had "Alcoa" raised its prices, more ingot would have been imported. Thus, there is a distinction between domestic and foreign competition: the first is limited in quantity, and can increase only by an increase in plant and personnel; the second is of producers who, we must assume, produce much more than they import, and whom a rise in price will presumably induce immediately to divert to the American market what they have been selling elsewhere. It is entirely consistent with the evidence that it was the threat of greater foreign imports which kept "Alcoa's prices where they were, and prevented it from exploiting its advantage as sole domestic producer; indeed, it is hard to resist the conclusion that potential imports did put a "ceiling" upon those prices. Nevertheless, within the limits afforded by the tariff and the cost of transportation, "Alcoa" was free to raise its prices as it chose, since it was free from domestic competition, save as it drew other metals into the market as substitutes. Was this a monopoly within the meaning of Section 2? The [trial] judge found that, over the whole half century of its existence, "Alcoa's" profits upon capital invested, after payment of income taxes, had been only about ten per cent, and, although the plaintiff puts this figure a little higher, the difference is negligible. . . . This assumed, it would be hard to say that "Alcoa" had made exorbitant profits on ingot, if it is proper to allocate the profit upon the whole business proportionately among all its products — ingot, and fabrications from ingot. . . .

There are however, two answers to any such excuse; [first] . . . it is no excuse for "monopolizing" a market that the monopoly has not been used to extract from the consumer more than a "fair" profit. The Act has wider purposes. . . . Congress . . . did not condone "good trusts" and condemn "bad" ones; it forbad all. Moreover, in so doing, it was not necessarily actuated by economic motives alone. It is possible, because of its indirect social or moral effect, to prefer a system of small producers, each dependent for his success upon his own skill and character, to one in which the great mass of those engaged must accept the direction of a few. These considerations, which we have suggested only as possible purposes of the Act, we think the decisions prove to have been in fact its purposes.

[Second] [i]t is settled, at least as to Section 1, that . . . all contracts fixing prices are unconditionally prohibited, the only possible difference between them and a monopoly is that while a monopoly necessarily involves an equal, or even greater, power to fix prices, its mere existence might be thought not to constitute an exercise of that power. That distinction is nevertheless purely formal. . . . As soon as [the monopoly] began to sell, . . . it must sell at some price and the only price at which it could sell is a price which it itself fixed. Thereafter the power and its exercise must needs coalesce. Indeed it would be absurd to condemn such contracts unconditionally, and not to extend the condemnation to monopolies; for the contracts are only steps toward that entire control which monopoly confers: they are really partial monopolies.

* * * *

We hold that "Alcoa's" monopoly of ingot was of the kind covered by Section 2.

It does not follow because "Alcoa" had such a monopoly, that it "monopolized" the ingot market: it may not have achieved monopoly; monopoly may have been thrust upon it. . . . [And] it is unquestionably true that from the very outset the courts have at least kept in reserve the possibility that the origin of a monopoly may be critical in determining its legality. . . . This notion has usually been expressed by saying that size does not determine guilt; that there must be some "exclusion" of competitors; that the growth must be something else than "natural" or "normal"; that there must be a "wrongful intent," or some other specific intent; or that some "unduly" coercive means must be used. At times there has been emphasis upon the use of the active verb, "monopolize," as the judge noted in the case at bar. . . . What engendered these compunctions is reasonably plain; persons may unwittingly find themselves in possession of a monopoly, automatically so to say: that is, without having intended either to put an end to existing competition, or to prevent competition from arising when none had existed; they may become monopolists by force of accident. . . . The most extreme expression of this view is in *United States v. United States Steel Corporation.*[7] . . . But, whatever authority [that] case does have was modified by the gloss of Cardozo, J., in *United States v. Swift & Co.*[8] . . . when he said "Mere size . . . is not an offense against the Sherman Act unless magnified to the point at which it amounts to a monopoly . . . but size carries with it an opportunity for abuse that is not to be ignored when the opportunity is proved to have been utilized in the past." "Alcoa's" size was "magnified" to make it a "monopoly"; indeed, it has never been anything else; and its size, not only offered it an "opportunity for abuse," but it "utilized" its size for "abuse," as can easily be shown.

[At this point Judge Hand reviews the history of Alcoa noting that its lawful monopoly had ended in 1909, that between 1912 and 1934 it expanded from two plants producing 42 million pounds to five plants producing 327 million pounds, that it had twice forestalled efforts by other companies to enter the industry, and that while it had stimulated demand and opened up new uses for the metal, it had also made "sure that it could supply what it had evoked." After agreeing that Alcoa had always conducted its business with "skill energy and initiative" and disclaiming any intent to charge the Company with "moral dereliction," the Judge states and then answers the question in the following terms:]

. . . The only question is whether [Alcoa] falls within the exception established in favor of those who do not seek, but cannot avoid, the control of a market. It seems to us that that question scarcely survives its statement. It was not inevitable that it should always anticipate increases in the demand for ingot and be prepared to supply them. Nothing compelled it to keep doubling and redoubling its capacity before others entered the field. It insists that it never excluded competitors; but we can think of no more effective exclusion than progressively to embrace each new opportunity as it opened, and to face every newcomer with new capacity already geared into a great organization, having the advantage of experience, trade connections and the elite of personnel. Only in case we interpret "exclusion" as limited to manoeuvres not honestly industrial, but actuated solely by a desire to

---

[7] 251 U.S. 417, 40 S. Ct. 293, 64 L. Ed 343, 8 A.L.R. 1121.
[8] 286 U.S. 106, p. 116, 52 S. Ct. 460, 463, 76 L. Ed. 999.

prevent competition, can such a course, indefatigably pursued, be deemed not "exclusionary." So to limit it would in our judgment emasculate the Act; would permit just such consolidations as it was designed to prevent.

* * * *

[In reaching this conclusion] [w]e disregard any question of "intent." Relatively early in the history of the Act [it was established that although] . . . the primary evil was monopoly, the Act also covered preliminary steps, which, if continued, would lead to it. These may do no harm of themselves; but if they are initial moves in a plan or scheme which, carried out, will result in monopoly, . . . the law will nip them in the bud. For this reason conduct falling short of monopoly, is not illegal unless it is part of a plan to monopolize. . . . To make it so, the plaintiff must prove what in the criminal law is known as a "specific intent;" an intent which goes beyond the mere intent to do the act. [But that showing is unnecessary under Section 2 where, as in Alcoa's case, the defendant possess monopoly power, because] . . . the monopolist must have both the power to monopolize, and the intent to monopolize. . . . [N]o monopolist monopolizes unconscious of what he is doing. So here, "Alcoa" meant to keep, and did keep, that complete and exclusive hold upon the ingot market with which it started. That was to "monopolize" that market, however innocently it otherwise proceeded. So far as the judgment [below] held that it was not within Section 2, it must be reversed.

* * * *

[Conspiracy with Foreign Producers]

. . . We have [thus far,] omitted consideration of any supposed conspiracy between "Alcoa" and . . . foreign producers to protect its domestic monopoly, because it will be more convenient to deal with this as part of the organization of "Limited," and of Alcoa's use of "Limited" both before and after 1931 when the "Alliance" was founded. . . . The plaintiff's position in general is that "Alcoa" was independently a party to such combinations until the advent of the "Alliance." We do not understand, however, that it asserts that this continued thereafter, except in so far as "Limited" is to be understood as always acting as Alcoa's agent or affiliate.

[Limited was incorporated in Canada in 1928 for the purpose of taking over all but two[9] Alcoa properties outside the United States. In exchange for these properties, Limited issued its stock in a one to three ratio to Alcoa's shareholders. While at first the two companies had common officers, by 1931 this had ceased and formal separation of the companies was complete. At the time of the litigation, two American families, Davis and Mellon, and the officers and directors of Alcoa (11 individuals in all), owned 48.9% of Alcoa's shares and 48.5% of Limited shares. Arthur V. Davis, Chairman of Alcoa was the largest shareholder in both companies.

In 1931 Limited became a member of the Alliance, a Swiss corporation, whose operations are described in detail in the following excerpt from Judge

---

[9] A Dutch Company owning bauxite deposits in Dutch Guiana and a Canadian power transmission company supplying Alcoa's plant in Messena, N.Y.

Hand's opinion. The Government attempted to show that Alcoa itself was a member of the Alliance because of its relationship with Limited. It presented evidence of a number of transactions between the two companies which tended to prove that they did not deal at arm's length. The Government also attempted to prove that Alcoa had taken part in the formation of the Alliance, relying mainly on statements by other witnesses concerning declarations by Arthur V. Davis, a cable from Edward K. Davis, Arthur's brother and an officer of Limited, to another officer of that company, the fact that Edward was the originator of the Alliance and the alleged "improbability that the Alliance would have been set-up without the active cooperation of Arthur," especially since he was in Europe talking to foreign producers when the Alliance was first suggested. The Government also introduced evidence to establish that prior to 1928 Alcoa had made agreements with foreign producers concerning price.]

The [Defendants] in answer to all this evidence swore that "Limited" had been organized for three reasons, quite different from controlling prices in the United States. First, there was at that time a growing nationalism in the British Empire — where Alcoa sold most of its foreign aluminum — which manifested itself in the slogan: "Buy British," and which would be better satisfied, if the properties were owned by a Canadian corporation, even though its shareholders were American. Next, Alcoa had neglected its foreign properties — relatively — and they would better prosper under a management, singly devoted to them. Finally, the time was coming when Arthur V. Davis wished to take a less active part in company affairs [and it avoided the problem of having to choose between Edward and another officer of the company as Arthur's successor].

* * * *

Upon the whole evidence the [trial] judge found that by 1935 "Limited" had become altogether free from any connection with Alcoa and that Alcoa had had no part in forming the "Alliance," or in any effort at any time to limit imports, to fix their price, or to intervene in price fixing "cartels" in Europe — except the early ones. . . . Considering the interests in "Limited" which Arthur V. Davis and both the Mellons had, it would perhaps have taxed our credulity to the breaking point to believe that they knew nothing about the formation of the "Alliance." Arthur V. Davis did not go as far as that; and that he and the Mellons should have put into the hands of Edward K. Davis the whole management of "Limited," does not appear to us to pass the bounds of reasonable entertainment . . . Alcoa had had collisions in plenty with plaintiff and others before 1931. . . . It was not unreasonable to believe that Arthur V. Davis and the Mellons, seeing that some kind of "cartel" might be an inescapable incident to continuing business abroad, wished in 1931 to keep Alcoa as far removed from it as possible. Even so, the question remains whether Alcoa should be charged with the "Alliance" because a majority of its shareholders were also a majority of "Limited's" shareholders; or whether that would be true, even though there were a group, common to both, less than a majority, but large enough for practical purposes to control each. It is quite true that in proportion as courts disregard the fictitious persona of a corporation — as perhaps they are increasingly disposed to do — they must substitute the concept of a group of persons acting in concert. Nevertheless, the group must not be committed legally except in so far as they have assented as a body, and that assent should be imputed to them only in harmony with the ordinary notions of delegated power. The plaintiff did not prove that in 1931, to say nothing of 1936, there was not a substantial minority in each company made up of those who held no shares in the other; and the existence of the same majority in the two corporations was not enough by itself to identify the two. Alcoa would not be bound, unless those who held the majority of its shares had been authorized by the group as a whole to enter into the "Alliance;" and considering the fact that, as we shall show, it was an illegal arrangement, such an authority ought convincingly to appear. It does not appear at all. . . . Except when there is evidence that those in nominal control of one of two corporations, exercised no independent decisions, but followed the directions of the other, they should be treated as juridically separate. Indeed, were it not so, a minority of shareholders would always be compelled to see to it that a majority — perhaps even a controlling fraction — of the shares did not pass to a confederated group who had a similar control over another corporation. For these reasons we conclude that Alcoa was not a party to the "Alliance," and did not join in any violation of Section 1 of the Act, so far as concerned foreign commerce.

Whether "Limited" itself violated that section depends upon the character of the "Alliance." It was a Swiss corporation, created in pursuance of an agreement entered into on July 3, 1931, the signatories to which were a French corporation, two German, one Swiss, a British, and "Limited." The original agreement, or "cartel," provided for the formation of a corporation in Switzerland which should issue shares, to be taken up by the signatories. This corporation was from time to time to fix a quota of production for each share, and each shareholder was to be limited to the quantity measured by the number of shares it held, but was free to sell at any price it chose. The corporation fixed a price every year at which it would take off any shareholder's hands any part of its quota which it did not sell. . . . Nothing was said as to whether the arrangement extended to sales in the United States. That question arose very shortly after the agreement was made, and Edward K. Davis took the position that the United States was included, relying upon [the] absence of any exception in the general language. His interpretation would seem to have been plainly right, not only for the reason he gave, but because otherwise there would have been no occasion for the "Conversion Clause."[10] However, the other shareholders overruled him, and until 1936, when the new arrangement was made, imports into the United States were not included in the quotas.

* * * *

The agreement of 1936 abandoned the system of unconditional quotas, and substituted a system of royalties. Each shareholder was to have a fixed free quota

[10] This clause provided that any shareholder could exceed its quota to the extent that it sold aluminum converted in the United States or Canada from ores delivered to it in either of those countries by persons situated in the U.S. The clause was intended to permit Limited, without charge to its quota, to receive bauxite or alumina (an intermediate product) from Alcoa, to smelt it into aluminum and deliver it back to Alcoa. Obviously, unless the agreement otherwise applied to such sales, the clause was, as Judge Hand intimated, unnecessary. - Ed.

for every share it held, but as its production exceeded the sum of its quotas, it was to pay a royalty, graduated progressively in proportion to the excess; and these royalties the "Alliance" divided among the shareholders in the proportion to their shares. . . . Although this agreement, like its predecessor, was silent as to imports into the United States, when that question arose during its preparation, as it did, all the shareholders agreed that such imports should be included in the quotas. . . . The shareholders continued this agreement unchanged until the end of March, 1938, by which time it had become plain that, at least for the time being, it was no longer, of service to anyone. Nothing was, however, done to end it, . . . [and the] "Alliance" itself has apparently never been dissolved; and indeed it appeared on the "Proclaimed List of Blocked Nationals" of September 13, 1944.

Did either the agreement of 1931 or that of 1936 violate Section 1 of the Act? The answer does not depend upon whether we shall recognize as a source of liability a liability imposed by another state. On the contrary we are concerned only with whether Congress chose to attach liability to the conduct outside the United States of persons not in allegiance to it. That being so, the only question open is whether Congress intended to impose the liability, and whether our own Constitution permitted it to do so: as a court of the United States, we cannot look beyond our own law. Nevertheless, it is quite true that we are not to read general words, such as those in this Act, without regard to the limitations customarily observed by nations upon the exercise of their powers; limitations which generally correspond to those fixed by the "Conflict of Laws." We should not impute to Congress an intent to punish all whom its courts can catch, for conduct which has no consequences within the United States. *American Banana Co v. United Fruit Co.* [supra]; *United States v. Bowman*[11] . . .; *Blackmer v. United States*[12] . . . On the other hand, it is settled law — as "Limited" itself agrees — that any state may impose liabilities, even upon persons not within its allegiance, for conduct outside its borders that has consequences within its borders which the state reprehends; and these liabilities other states will ordinarily recognize. *Strassheim v. Daily* [supra]; *Lamar v. United States*[13] . . .; *Ford v. United States*[14] . . . Restatement of Conflict of Laws, Section 65. It may be argued that this Act extends further. Two situations are possible. There may be agreements beyond our borders not intended to affect imports, which do affect them, or which affect exports. Almost any limitation of the supply of goods in Europe, for example, or in South America, may have repercussions in the United States if there is trade between the two. Yet when one considers the international complications likely to arise from an effort in this country to treat such agreements as unlawful, it is safe to assume that Congress certainly did not intend the Act to cover them. Such agreements may on the other hand intend to include imports into the United States, and yet it may appear that they have had no effect upon them. That situation might be thought to fall within the doctrine that intent may be a substitute for performance in the case of a contract made within the United States; or it might be thought to fall within the doctrine that a statute should not be interpreted to cover acts abroad which have no consequence here. We shall not

[11] 260 U.S. 94, 98, 43 S. Ct. 39, 67 L. Ed. 149.
[12] 284 U.S. 421, 437, 52 S. Ct. 252, 76 L. Ed 375.
[13] 240 U.S. 60, 65, 66, 36 S. Ct. 255, 60 L. Ed 526.
[14] 273 U.S. 595, 620, 621, 47 S. Ct. 531, 71 L. Ed 793.

choose between these alternatives; but for argument we shall assume that the Act does not cover agreements, even though intended to affect imports or exports, unless its performance is shown actually to have had some effect upon them. Where both conditions are satisfied, the situation certainly falls within prior decisions as *United States v. Pacific & Artic R. & Navigation Co.*[15] . . .; *Thomsen v. Cayser*[16] . . . and *United States v. Sisal Sales Corp.*[17] . . . It is true that in those cases the persons held liable had sent agents into the United States to perform part of the agreement; but an agent is merely an animate means of executing his principal's purposes, and, for the purposes of this case, he does not differ from an inanimate means; besides, only human agents can import and sell ingot.

Both agreements would clearly have been unlawful, had they been made within the United States; and it follows from what we have just said that both were unlawful, though made abroad, if they were intended to affect imports and did affect them. Since the shareholders almost at once agreed that the agreement of 1931 should not cover imports, we may ignore it and confine our discussion to that of 1936: indeed that we should have to do anyway, since it superseded the earlier agreement.

The [trial] judge found that it was not the purpose of the agreement to "suppress or restrain the exportation of aluminum to the United States for sale in competition with Alcoa." By that we understand that he meant that the agreement was not specifically directed to "Alcoa," because it only applied generally to the production of the shareholders. If he meant that it was not expected that the general restriction upon production would have an effect upon imports, we cannot agree for the change made in 1936 was deliberate and was expressly made to accomplish just that. It would have been an idle gesture, unless the shareholders had supposed that it would, or at least might, have that effect. The first of the conditions which we mentioned was therefore satisfied; the intent was to set up a quota system for imports. The [trial] judge also found that the 1936 agreement did not "materially affect the . . . foreign trade or commerce of the United States;" apparently because the imported ingot was greater in 1936 and 1937 than in earlier years. We cannot accept this finding, based as it was upon the fact that, in 1936, 1937 and the first quarter of 1938, the gross imports of ingot increased. It by no means follows from such an increase that the agreement did not restrict imports; and incidentally it so happens that in those years such inference as is possible at all, leads to the opposite conclusion. It is true that the average imports — including "Alcoa's" — for the years 1932-1935 inclusive were about 15 million pounds, and that for 1936, 1937 and one-fourth of 1938 they were about 33 million pounds; but the average domestic ingot manufacture in the first period was about 96 million and in the second about 262 million; so that the proportion of imports to domestic ingot was about 15.6 per cent for the first period and about 12.6 per cent for the second. We do not mean to infer from this that the quota system of 1936 did in fact restrain imports, as these figures might suggest; but we do mean that nothing is to be inferred from the gross increase of imports. We shall dispose

---

[15] 228 U.S. 87, 33 S. Ct. 443, 57 L. Ed 472.
[16] 243 U.S. 66, 37 S. Ct. 353, 61 L. Ed 597, Ann. Cas. 1917D, 322.
[17] 274 U.S. 268, 47 S. Ct. 244, 56 L. Ed 731.

of the matter therefore upon the assumption that, although the shareholders intended to restrict imports, it does not appear whether in fact they did so. Upon our hypothesis the plaintiff would therefore fail, if it carried the burden of proof upon this issue as upon others. We think, however, that, after the intent to affect imports was proved, the burden of proof shifted to "Limited." In the first place a depressant upon production which applies generally may be assumed, *ceteris paribus*, to distribute its effect evenly upon all markets. Again, when the parties took the trouble specifically to make the depressant apply to a given market, there is reason to suppose that they expected that it would have some effect, which it could have only by lessening what would otherwise have been imported. If the motive they introduced was over balanced in all instances by motives which induced the shareholders to import, if the United States market became so attractive that the royalties did not count at all and their expectations were in fact defeated, they to whom the facts were more accessible than to the plaintiff ought to prove it, for a prima facie case had been made. Moreover, there is an especial propriety in demanding this of "Limited," because it was "Limited" which procured the inclusion in the agreement of 1936 of imports in the quotas.

There remains only the question whether this assumed restriction had any influence upon prices, *Apex Hosiery Co. v. Leader*[18] . . . To that *Socony-Vacuum Oil Co. v. United States*[19] . . . is an entire answer. It will be remembered that, when the defendants in that case protested that the prosecution had not proved that the "distress" gasoline had affected prices, the court answered that that was not necessary, because an agreement to withdraw any substantial part of the supply from a market would, if carried out, have some effect upon prices, and was an unlawful as an agreement expressly to fix prices. The underlying doctrine was that all factors which contribute to determine prices, must be kept free to operate unhampered by agreements. For these reasons we think that the agreement of 1936 violated Section 1 of the Act.

* * * *

NOTES AND QUESTIONS

(1) Judge Hand's "intent" and "effects" test has become the touchstone for determining the prescriptive reach of the United States antitrust laws. In exploring the several possible interpretations of that test, it must first be noted that the relevant market was, for purposes of Judge Hand's analysis, the United States market in "virgin" aluminum ingots, including both ingots produced domestically and sold in interstate commerce and ingots produced abroad and imported into the United States.

It is generally agreed that the Judge was intent upon excluding from the prescriptive reach of the Sherman Act, actions by foreigners abroad whose impact in the American market was wholly unintended or, if intended, failed in that

---

[18] 310 U.S. 469, 60 S. Ct. 982, 84 L. Ed 1311, 128 A.L.R. 1044.
[19] 310 U.S. 150, 60 S. Ct. 811, 84 L. Ed 1129.

purpose. Consistent with this latter, most authorities have interpreted the decision to exclude actions by foreigners abroad with an intended but wholly insubstantial impact on the American market. There must be an intended and "substantial affect."[20] Once this point is reached, however, opinion divides.

One school contends that the whole of Judge Hand's purpose was merely to exclude the unintended or *de minimis* foreign restraint on American commerce. Accordingly, they argue, if the requisite intent is shown, the "effects" branch of the test is met if the action abroad pertains to goods or services which enter, or in the absence of the foreign restraint, would have entered, the stream of commerce feeding the American market.[21] Most pointedly, this school rejects the need to show that the foreigners' actions had any anti-competitive effect on the American market. There is, they say, no substantive content to the test whatsoever.We may, therefore, legitimately label this position as espousing a "mechanical effects" test.[22]

Another view, however, would bring actions by foreigners abroad within the prescriptive ambit of the American antitrust laws only upon proof that the consequence or "effect" of those actions upon the United States market violated the law; were anti-competitive. Since the anti-competitive "effect" that must be shown is a constituent element of the offense charged, this point of view also reads Judge Hand as adapting to economic legislation the co-called "objective territorial principle" of public international law laid down in the *Lotus Case, supra*. So interpreted, prescriptive jurisdiction quite plainly engages substance.[23]

It is worth noting that Section 415 of the Restatement (Third) of the Foreign Relations Law of the United States is ambiguous on this question and apparently deliberately so.[24] Comment d notes that opinion is divided "as to whether intent to interfere with the commerce of the United States without an actual anti-competitive effect" will support an exercise of antitrust jurisdiction. The Comment then goes on to indicate that the matter remains unresolved and that the Restatement "takes no position" on the question.

---

[20] Fugate, I Foreign Commerce and the Antitrust Laws, at page 71.

[21] This school of thought would also contend that even if the foreigners' actions abroad do not directly pertain to goods or service in the stream of American commerce, the "effects" test is met if the products to which those actions pertain bear a relationship to other goods and services that do enter the stream and if, through this relationship, the foreign restraint has some not insubstantial impact on the latter (*e.g.*, a cartel abroad that fixes the price of materials entering into the manufacture abroad of goods exported to the United States).

[22] For one of the clearer expressions of this view, see Rahl, American Antitrust And Foreign Operations: What is Covered?, 8 Cornell Int'l Law J. 1 (1974)).

[23] This position is taken in the Report of the Attorney General's National Committee to Study the Antitrust Laws, 76 (1955).

[24] Section 415, Subsection (2) of the Restatement (Third) of the Foreign Relations Law of the United States provides as follows: "Any agreement in restraint of United States trade that is made outside of the United States, and any conduct or agreement in restraint of such trade that is carried out predominantly outside of the United States, are subject to the jurisdiction to prescribed of the United States, if a principal purpose of the conduct or agreement is to interfere with the commerce of the United States, and the agreement or conduct has some effect on that commerce."

In evaluating these differing interpretations consider the following:

(a) Recall that Alliance sales to the United States had increased in absolute terms, but had declined as a percent of the total U.S. market. Yet, according to Judge Hand, neither an absolute increase nor a percentage decrease sufficed to establish whether the Alliance had the requisite "effect" on U.S. commerce. Indeed, the Judge notes that on this evidence the case would have had to be dismissed for lack of jurisdiction. Only a shifting of the burden of proof from the Government to defendant Limited saved the Government's case. If proof of imports constituting 12-15% of the U.S. market did not establish the "effect" required for Sherman Act jurisdiction what kind of "effect" was the Judge looking for?

(b) Recall Judge Hand's analysis of Alcoa's historic pricing behavior. In the years prior to formation of the Alliance, import prices closely tracked Alcoa's prices and he (the Judge) could "assume" that "had Alcoa raised its prices, more ingot would have been imported." It is against this background that he describes the Alliance as a "depressant on production." What does this suggest was the substantive economic impact of the Alliance on the American market? In structural terms what kind of market was the Judge dealing with?

(c) Now, consider the evidence that Judge Hand suggests Limited would have had to supply in order to prove the absence of an "effect" on commerce under his jurisdictional test. How does that evidence relate to the economic impact on the U.S. that Judge Hand ascribes to the foreign producers who were in the Alliance? In view of your answer, how would you characterize his "effects" test? Was it a "mechanical test" or, with the burden of proof reversed, did Limited have to prove that the Alliance had no anti-competitive "effect" on the U.S. market?

(2) Alliance's quota and then royalty system, as a mechanism for controlling supply, constituted a classic price-fixing device proscribed as a *per se* offense under Section 1 of the Sherman Act. *Socony-Vacuum Oil Co. v. United States.*[25] Recall the several conclusive presumptions that underlie the classification of price-fixing as a per se offense: (i) the presumption that the conspirators will charge a supra-competitive price and (ii) that they have the market power to do so. With this in mind, consider the following:

(a) Recall, that the participants in the Alliance, at no time, supplied more than 12-15% of the American market. It may be doubted that, in and of itself, that market share was sufficient to confer on the Alliance a power over price. Yet, Judge Hand ascribes to the Alliance a power to influence price. Is his analysis more in keeping with the presumptions of the *per se* rule or with a structural analysis under the "Rule of Reason?" In answering keep in mind that Judge Hand was writing well before modern theories of oligopoly pricing had been fully developed.

---

[25] 310 U.S. 150, 60 S.Ct. 811 (1940).

Yet, his opinion clearly apprehends some of the possibilities with which modern theory is concerned. Explain.[26]

(b)   Again return to the type of evidence the Judge suggests Limited would have had to supply under its burden of proof to show that the Alliance did not have the "effect" requisite to the exercise of jurisdiction. To which of the *per se* presumptions is that evidence directed? In other words, under the Judge's jurisdictional test, the presumption is rebutable, is it not? If so, which presumption?

(c)   Suppose that instead of Alcoa with a 85% market share, that share of the market was divided among six or seven independent and highly competitive U.S. firms each of approximately the same size and that the five foreign producers composing the Alliance accounted for the remaining 15% of the market. This would mean that the industry had a pre-Alliance HHI of approximately 1178 and a post-Alliance HHI of 1258 (80 point increase). Under these circumstances Limited could readily, could it not, have supplied the evidence Judge Hand called for in order to prove that the Alliance did not have the "effect" on the American market that his jurisdictional test required? Explain.

(d)   If under Judge's Hand's "effects" test at least one of the presumptions is rebutable, the *per se* rule has undergone a subtle transformation, has it not? If so, can you account for the Judge's reliance on *Socony-Vacuum*?

(3) Recall that Judge Hand cited *Strassheim v. Daily* as support for his "effects" doctrine? Could the exercise of jurisdiction under our hypothetical in Note 2(c) be squared with that decision? If not, what does that say about a "mechanical," non-substantive "effects" test? Could such a test be squared with the "territorial principle" of international law as applied in the *Lotus* Case? Can Judge Hand's decision be squared with that principle?

(4) On the face of it, a "jurisdictional test" that implicates the substantive merits of a case may seem anomalous. Not only does it appear conceptually untidy, but may raise vexing procedural problems. On the other hand, perhaps this so only because we tend to be careless with the word "jurisdiction" and too often fail to distinguish between "prescriptive" and "subject-matter jurisdiction?" Consider the following:

(a)   Subject-matter jurisdiction is a question to be settled at the outset of litigation because in its absence the court may lack either statutory or constitutional authority to proceed to adjudicate the merits of a dispute. On the other hand, a challenge to the merits is a challenge directed at the plaintiff's substantive legal rights without regard to the authority of a particular court to vindicate those rights.[27] If in answer to the

---

[26] The difficulty of the task Judge Hand assigned Limited is illustrated by the fact that if before formation of the Alliance, Alcoa commanded 85% of the United States market and five foreign producers each 3%, the industry would have had a HHI of 7,270. If the Alliance were treated as similar to a merger of the foreign producers, the industry HHI would have risen to 7,450, an increase of 180 index points.

[27] It may be true that on occasion a challenge to the merits of the plaintiff's claim and a challenge to the court's authority turn on common questions of fact or that the subject

plaintiff's claim based upon an alleged violation of the Sherman Act, the defendant asserts that the conduct complained of lay outside the prescriptive reach of that Act, is that assertion more in the nature of a challenge to the plaintiff's substantive right or more like a challenge to the court's authority divorced from the merits of the plaintiff's right?[28]

matter of the plaintiff's case may have some bearing on the court's authority over that case. These similarities, however, are merely accidents of the way we sometimes choose to describe the competence of various courts within our system. They should not be allowed to conceal the fundamental distinction between prescriptive and subject-matter jurisdiction.

[28] To illustrate how "subject-matter" jurisdictional label may have contributed to the confusion surrounding the Alcoa "effects" test compare *Fleischmann Distilling Corp. v. Distillers Company Ltd.*, 395 F. Supp. 221 (S.D.N.Y., 1975) with *National Bank of Canada v. Interbank Card Association*, 666 F.2d 6 (2d Cir., 1981). In *Fleischmann* two United States companies acting as American distributors for defendant's Black & White Scotch charged that the termination of their long-standing distributorships was part of a conspiracy between defendant Distiller's and its subsidiaries in violation of Section 1 of the Sherman Act. Defendant moved to dismiss for lack of subject matter jurisdiction (Rule 12 (b)(1)) and for failure to state a claim upon which relief could be granted (Rule 12 (b)(6)). In denying defendant's motion to dismiss for lack of subject matter jurisdiction, the court found two allegations sufficient to meet the Alcoa "intent" and "effects" test: (i) defendant sold Scotch whiskey in the United States through exclusive distributors, and (ii) that such sales "embody a continuous stream of commerce among the States and with foreign nations." In support of its motion under Rule 12(b)(6), defendant relied upon the absence of any allegation that the termination and replacement of plaintiffs by other distributors restrained competition in the sale of Scotch whiskey in the United States. According to defendant's uncontroverted affidavits Black & White Scotch was, in 1953, the leading Scotch on the American market, but had since then declined precipitously (*e.g.*, between 1959 and 1972 Black & White shipments dropped by 54% while Scotch sales generally increased by 185%) so that even if Black & White had commanded 100% of the U. S. market in 1959, by 1972 it commanded less than 15%. The court denied defendant's motion (treated as motion for summary judgment) noting that: "replacement of one distributor with another may be unlawful if. . . in furtherance of a horizontal conspiracy to establish market dominance or monopoly." Since the complaint implicitly made out a case of price fixing or of an attempt to monopolize, that sufficed, the Court thought, to withstand summary judgment because "these latter practices being illegal *per se* are presumed to involve public injury eliminating the necessity for specific allegations to that effect."

In *Interbank*, on the other hand, plaintiff, successor by merger to one of two Canadian banks licensed to operate a "Mastercharge" system in Canada, sued defendant Interbank, a United States corporation. The latter had cancelled plaintiff's license because the other Canadian licensee had refused to approve transfer of the license from plaintiff's predecessor to plaintiff. The right to withhold approval was reserved in the license agreement. Its exclusion from the Canadian credit card market, plaintiff argued, violated Section 1 of the Sherman Act. While the Second Circuit affirmed the trial court's dismissal of the complaint, it held that the latter had erred on two points. (1) The trial court had turned back a challenge to its jurisdiction on the ground that Canadian credit card holders used those cards to purchase goods in the United States (*i.e.*, those cards were in the stream of U.S. commerce). This, the Second Circuit concluded, was the wrong test. (2) The Second Circuit held that there was, indeed, a lack of jurisdiction under the Alcoa "effects" test because plaintiff had failed to submit evidence that the "challenged restraint has, or is intended to have any anticompetitive effect upon United States commerce, either commerce within the United

(b) Observe, that in *American Banana* the decision appealed from and affirmed by the Supreme Court was a dismissal of the complaint for a failure to "[set]-forth a cause of action." In *United States v. Sisal Sales Corp. supra* the case came to the Court in the same procedural posture. In *Alcoa* Judge Hand poses the "jurisdictional" question as follows:

Did either the agreement of 1931 or that of 1936 violate Section 1 of the Act? The answer does not depend upon whether we shall recognize as a source of liability a liability imposed by another state. On the contrary we are concerned only with whether Congress chose to attach liability to the conduct outside the United States of persons not in allegiance to it.

Does this sound like subject-matter jurisdiction?

(c) If both Justice Holmes and Judge Hand understood that the issue before them was not a question of "subject matter" jurisdiction but a question that went to the merits of the controversy, then quite plainly the substantive content of the antitrust laws in a case with substantial foreign elements might well be different from the content of those laws in a wholly domestic case.

(4) This last observation raises two points. First, the Sherman Act, of course, interdicts only restraints that pertain to an exchange of goods, service, money or technology in the American market or restraints that pertain in someway to the export of such items from the United States. Also the amount of U.S. commerce affected by the restraint must be more than de-minimus. For the purpose of assuring that these requirements are met, a "mechanical effects" test is probably as good as any. And for expositional clarity, the question of whether that "mechanical" nexus has been met can be designated a question of "subject-matter jurisdiction, although that is not an entirely appropriate usage. That, however, is not the jurisdictional question to which Judge Hand was addressing himself, if we are correct in our suggestion that the Judge's test went to the merits of the case.

This, in turn, raises a further question. What is the function of the Judge's test? If, in any case, a "mechanical" nexus between the alleged offense and the foreign commerce of the United States is established (*i.e.*, there is subject-matter jurisdiction), and all that remains is to decide the case on the merits, what possible need is there for an additional "jurisdictional" inquiry if that inquiry also goes to the merits? The answer is clear. The prescriptive "jurisdictional" inquiry under Judge Hand's "effects" test changes the substantive standard that would otherwise govern the merits of the case. In Alcoa, the Alliance was a classic price-fixing cartel — what the Justice Department's new Guidelines for International Operations calls a "naked restraint."[29] As such, it would normally be judged under a strict

_____

States or export commerce." Even if cancellation of plaintiff's license resulted in increased concentration in the Canadian credit card market through higher fees to Canadian merchants and fewer Canadian credit card holders, the Second Circuit found the record devoid of any evidence showing how these events would have had an anti-competitive effect on United States commerce.

[29] U.S. Department Of Justice Antitrust Enforcement Guidelines For International Operations, BNA Antitrust and Trade Regulation Report, Vol 55, No. 1391, Special Supplement at page S-6.

per se rule. Not so under the Hand "effects" test as we have construed it. Through the intervention of the Judge's prescriptive jurisdictional test the *per se* rule has become subtly and substantively transformed. Or stated otherwise, through the intervention of international law, the substantive content of U.S. law has been changed.

That raises the second point. Is this a proper function of international law? In thinking about this question, recall that the *per se* rule forecloses any defense to a price-fixing charge based upon the conspirators' miscalculation of market power. In the domestic setting, the possibility of such a miscalculation can be ignored partly on the normative ground that the law ought to deter all such attempts and a conclusive presumption of power serves that deterrent purpose. The presumption may also serve the cause of judicial economy. In the transnational setting, however, ought the law so readily dispense with actual proof of the power to impose the social costs of monopoly upon the United States? If not, the intervention of international law to transform domestic law can be readily justified. In other words, the central question, which cuts across a host of potential transnational business arrangements, becomes whether actual proof of market power should or should not be required when the antitrust law operates in the larger global context. This is a question to which we will repeatedly return.

The intervention of international law — the formal interposition of a prescriptive jurisdictional analysis — may not be the only way that substantive antitrust doctrine is transformed when dealing with transnational business arrangements. What follows is one of the more intriguing of recent Supreme Court decisions. While one can not make too much of the point, there is at least some hint that, along with strongly held views about predatory pricing more generally, the transnational setting of the case may have influenced the way the Court framed the issues.

MATSUSHITA ELECTRIC INDUSTRIAL CO. LTD, et al. v. ZENITH RADIO CORP. et al.

United States Supreme Court
475 U.S. 574, 106 S. Ct. 1348, 89 L. Ed. 2d 538 (1986)

[In this case, which was begun in 1974, Zenith Radio and National Union Electrical Corp (NUE) — successor to Emerson Radio Company — sued twenty-one Japanese manufacturers and Japanese owned American distributors of consumer electronic products (CEP's), alleging that starting in 1953 defendants had conspired to drive American firms out of the American CEP market. The gist of the alleged scheme consisted of fixing artificially high prices for television receivers sold by defendants in Japan and, at the same time, fixing prices for receivers exported to the United States so low as to cause plaintiffs substantial losses. Indeed, NUE had dropped out of the U.S. market by 1970. The district court granted defendants' motion for summary judgment on the grounds (i) that some of the offenses charged did not cause any injury to plaintiffs and (ii) that the more plausible inference from the evidence of price-cutting in the U.S. was that defendants were simply competing vigorously in the American market.

The Court of Appeals reversed, concluding that a reasonable fact-finder could draw the following conclusions from the evidence.

(i)   That the Japanese market for CEP's was ologopolistic enabling a small number of producers by regularly exchanging price and other information to raise prices and reap supra-competitive profits.

(ii)   Defendant's had higher fixed costs than their American competitors and therefore a greater need to operate at near full capacity.

(iii)   Defendant's plant capacity exceeded the needs of the Japanese market.

(iv)   By formal agreement with the Japanese government, defendants fixed minimum prices for the American market; the so-called "check prices."

(v)   Defendants agreed that each would use no more than five distributors to distribute their products in the United States; the so-called "five-company" rule.

(vi)   Defendants undercut their own "check-prices" by a series of rebate schemes which they then tried to conceal from U.S. Customs (to avoid customs and antidumping regulations) and from the Japanese government.

In reaching these conclusions the Court of Appeals apparently relied heavily on Plaintiff's expert, a Dr. DePodwin who summarized his views along the following lines.

The injuries suffered by the American CEP industry must be viewed in the context of defendants' generally collusive scheme that embraced the American and the Japanese domestic market. This scheme increased the supply of television receivers to the U.S. and restricted supply in Japan. If the defendants had competed in both markets, they "would have sold more in [Japan] and less in the United States," domestic "prices would have been lower and export prices . . . higher" so that fewer receivers would have been exported to the U.S. and the U.S. market price would have risen. In other words, as a consequence of the defendants' collusive behavior in the Japanese market, there was an influx of receivers into the U.S. at "depressed prices" which "cut the rates of return" on U.S. receiver production "to so low a level as to make such investment uneconomic."

The Japanese defendants appealed and the Supreme Court on a 5-4 vote reversed.]

JUSTICE POWELL delivered the opinion of the Court

* * * *

II

We begin by emphasizing what respondents' [American plaintiffs'] claim is *not*. Respondents cannot recover antitrust damages based solely on an alleged cartelization of the Japanese market, because American antitrust laws do not regulate the competitive conditions of other nation's economies. *United States v. Aluminum Co. of American [supra]* . . . 1 P. Areeda & D. Turner, Antitrust Law, P236d (1976). Nor can respondents recover damages for any conspiracy by petitioners to charge higher than competitive prices in the American market. Such conduct would indeed violate the Sherman Act, *United States v. Trenton Potteries Co.*,[30] . . . *United States v. Socony-Vacuum Oil Co.*[31] . . . but it could not injure respondents; as petitioners' competitors, respondents stand to gain from any conspiracy to raise the market price in CEP's. . . . Finally for the same reason, respondents cannot recover for a conspiracy to impose non-price restraints that have the effect of either raising market price or limiting output. . . . Thus neither petitioners alleged supra-competitive pricing in Japan, nor the five company rule . . . can by themselves give respondents a cognizable claim against petitioners for antitrust damages. . . .

Respondents nevertheless argue that these supposed conspiracies, if not themselves grounds for recovery of antitrust damages, are circumstantial evidence of another conspiracy that *is* cognizable: a conspiracy to monopolize the American market by means of pricing below the market level.

The Court of Appeals found that respondents' allegation of a horizontal conspiracy to engage in predatory pricing,[32] if proved, would be a *per se* violation of Section 1 of the Sherman Act. . . . Petitioners do not appeal from that

---

[30] 273 U.S. 392 (1927).

[31] 310 U.S. 150, 223 (1940).

[32] Throughout this opinion, we refer to the asserted conspiracy as one to price "predatorily." This term has been used chiefly in cases in which a single firm, having a dominant share of the relevant market, cuts its prices in order to force competitors out of the market, or perhaps to deter potential entrants from coming in. [Citations omitted.] In such cases, "predatory pricing" means pricing below some appropriate measure of cost. [Citations omitted.] There is a good deal of debate, both in the cases and in the law reviews, about what "cost" is relevant in such cases. We need not resolve this debate here, because unlike the cases cited above, this is a Sherman Act Section 1 case. For purposes of this case, it is enough to note that respondents have not suffered an antitrust injury unless petitioners conspired to drive respondents out of the relevant markets by (i) pricing below the level necessary to sell their products, or (ii) pricing below some appropriate measure of cost. An agreement without these features would either leave respondents in the same position as would market forces or would actually benefit respondents by raising market prices. . . . We do not consider whether recovery should ever be available on a theory such as respondents' when the pricing in question is above some measure of incremental cost. See generally Areeda & Turner, Predatory Pricing and Related Practices Under Section 2 of the Sherman Act, (discussing cost-based test for use in Section 2 cases). As a practical matter, it may be that only direct evidence of below-cost pricing is sufficient to overcome the strong inference that rational businesses would not enter into conspiracies such as this one. See Part IV-A, *infra*.

conclusion. The issue in this case thus becomes whether respondents adduced sufficient evidence in support of their theory to survive summary judgment. . . .

III

To survive petitioners' motion for summary judgment, respondents must establish that there is a genuine issue of material fact as to whether petitioners entered into an illegal conspiracy that caused respondents to suffer a cognizable injury. Fed. Rule Civ Proc. 56(e); *First National Bank of Arizona v. Cities Service Co.*[33] . . . This showing has two components. . . . Respondents charge petitioners with a whole host of conspiracies in restraint of trade . . . [but] [e]xcept for the alleged conspiracy to monopolize the American market through predatory pricing, these alleged conspiracies could not have caused respondents to suffer an antitrust injury. . . . Therefore, unless, in context, evidence of these "other" conspiracies raises a genuine issue concerning the existence of a predatory pricing conspiracy, that evidence cannot defeat petitioners' summary judgment motion.

Second, the issue of fact must be "genuine." Fed. Rules Civ. Proc. 56(c), (e) . . . It follows from this . . . that if the factual context renders respondents' claim implausible — if the claim is one that simply makes no economic sense — respondents must come forward with more persuasive evidence to support their claim than would otherwise be necessary. . . .

Respondents correctly note that "[o]n summary judgment the inferences to be drawn from the underlying facts . . . must be viewed in the light most favorable to the party opposing the motion." *United States v. Diebold, Inc.*[34] . . . But antitrust law limits the range of permissible inferences from ambiguous evidence in a Section 1 case. Thus, in *Monsanto Co. v. Spray-Rite Service Corp.*[35] . . . we held that conduct as consistent with permissible competition as with illegal conspiracy does not, standing alone, support an inference of antitrust conspiracy[36] . . . Respondents in this case, in other words, must show that the inference of conspiracy is reasonable in light of the competing inferences of independent action or collusive action that could not have harmed respondents. . . .

* * * *

IV

A

A predatory pricing conspiracy is by nature speculative. Any agreement to price below the competitive level requires the conspirators to forgo profits that free competition would offer them. The forgone profits may be considered an investment in the future. For the investment to be rational, the conspirators must have a reasonable expectation of recovering, in the form of later monopoly profits, more than the losses suffered. As then-Professor Bork, discussing predatory pricing by a single firm, explained:

---

[33] 391 U.S. 253, 288-289 (1968).
[34] 369 U.S. 654, 655 (1962).
[35] 465 U.S. 752 (1984).
[36] *Id.* at 764.

Any realistic theory of predation recognizes that the predator as well as his victims will incur losses during the fighting, but such a theory supposes it may be a rational calculation for the predator to view the losses as an investment in future monopoly profits (where rivals are to be killed) or in future undisturbed profits (where rivals are to be disciplined). The future flow of profits, appropriately discounted, must then exceed the present size of the losses.[37] . . .

. . . As this explanation shows, the success of such schemes is inherently uncertain: the short-run loss is definite, but the long-run gain depends on successfully neutralizing the competition. Moreover, it is not enough simply to achieve monopoly power, as monopoly pricing may breed quick entry by new competitors eager to share in the excess profits. The success of any predatory scheme depends on maintaining monopoly power for long enough both to recoup the predator's losses and harvest some additional gain. Absent some assurance that the hoped-for monopoly will materialize, and that it can be sustained for a significant period of time, "[t]he predator must make a substantial investment with no assurance that it will pay off."[38] . . . For this reason, there is a consensus among commentators that predatory pricing schemes are rarely tried, and even more rarely successful[39] . . .

These observations apply even to predatory pricing by a single firm seeking monopoly power. In this case, respondents allege that a large number of firms have conspired over a period of many years to charge below-market prices in order to stifle competition. Such a conspiracy is incalculably more difficult to execute than an analogous plan undertaken by a single predator. The conspirators must allocate the losses to be sustained during the conspiracy's operation, and must also allocate any gains to be realized from its success. Precisely because success is speculative and depends on a willingness to endure losses for an indefinite period, each conspirator has a strong incentive to cheat, letting its partners suffer the losses necessary to destroy the competition while sharing in any gains if the conspiracy succeeds. The necessary allocation is therefore difficult to accomplish. Yet if conspirators cheat to any substantial extent, the conspiracy must fail, because its success depends on depressing the market price for all buyers of CEP's. If there are too few goods at the artificially low price to satisfy demand, the would-be victims of the conspiracy can continue to sell at the "real" market price, and the conspirators suffer losses to little purpose.

Finally, if predatory pricing conspiracies are generally unlikely to occur, they are especially so where, as here, the prospects of attaining monopoly power seem slight. In order to recoup their losses, petitioners must obtain enough market power to set higher than competitive prices, and then must sustain those prices long enough to earn in excess profits what they earlier gave up in below-cost prices.

---

[37] R. Bork, The Antitrust Paradox 145 (1978). See also McGee, Predatory Pricing Revisited, 23 J. Law & Econ. 289, 295-297 (1980).

[38] Easterbrook, Predatory Strategies And Counterstrategies, 48 U. Chi. L. Rev. 263, 268 (1981).

[39] See, e.g., Bork, supra, at 149-155; Areeda & Turner, Predatory Pricing And Related Practices Under Section 2 Of The Sherman Act, 88 Harv. L. Rev. 697, 699 (1975); Easterbrook, supra; Koller, The Myth Of Predatory Pricing-An Empirical Study.

See *Northeastern Telephone Co. v. American Telephone & Telegraph Co., supra,* at 89.[40] . . . Two decades after their conspiracy is alleged to have commenced, petitioners appear to be far from achieving this goal: the two largest shares of retail market in television sets are held by RCA and respondent Zenith, not by any of petitioners. . . . Moreover, those shares, which together approximate 40% of sales, did not decline appreciably during the 1970's. . . . Petitioners' collective share rose rapidly during this period, from one-fifth or less of the relevant markets to close to 50%.[41] Neither the District Court nor the Court of Appeals found, however, that petitioners' share presently allows them to charge monopoly prices; to the contrary, respondents contend that the conspiracy is ongoing — that petitioners are still artificially depressing the market price in order to drive Zenith out of the market. The data in the record strongly suggest that that goal is yet far distant.

* * * *

Nor does the possibility that petitioners have obtained supra-competitive profits in the Japanese market change this calculation. Whether or not petitioners have the means to sustain substantial losses in this country over a long period of time, they have no motive to sustain such losses absent some strong likelihood that the alleged conspiracy in this country will eventually pay off. The courts below found no evidence of any such success. . . . More important, there is nothing to suggest any relationship between petitioners' profits in Japan and the amount petitioners could expect to gain from a conspiracy to monopolize the American market. In the absence of any such evidence, the possible existence of supra-competitive profits in Japan simply cannot overcome the economic obstacles to the ultimate success of this alleged predatory conspiracy.

B

In *Monsanto*, we emphasized that courts should not permit fact finders to infer conspiracies when such inferences are implausible, because the effect of such practices is often to deter procompetitive conduct. . . . Respondents, petitioners' competitors, seek to hold petitioners liable for damages caused by the alleged conspiracy to cut prices. Moreover, they seek to establish this conspiracy indirectly. . . . But cutting prices in order to increase business often is the very essence of competition. Thus, mistaken inferences in cases such as this one are especially costly, because they chill the very conduct the antitrust laws are designed to protect. . . .

In most cases, this concern must be balanced against the desire that illegal conspiracies be identified and punished. That balance is, however, unusually one-sided in cases such as this one. . . . [E]conomic realities tend to make predatory pricing conspiracies self-deterring [and] . . . unlike predatory pricing by a single firm, successful predatory pricing conspiracies involving a large number of firms can be identified and punished once they succeed, since some form of minimum price-fixing agreement would be necessary in order to reap the benefits of

---

[40] 651 F.2d 76 (1981)(2d Cir.), *cert. den.* 455 U.S. 943, 102 S.Ct. 1438, 71 L. Ed. 2d 654 (1982).
[41] 723 F. 2d at 316.

predation. Thus, there is little reason to be concerned that by granting summary judgment in cases where the evidence of conspiracy is speculative or ambiguous, courts will encourage such conspiracies.

* * * *

The decision of the Court of Appeals is reversed, and the case is remanded for further proceedings consistent with this opinion

It is so ordered

[C] The "Effects" Doctrine: Some Foreign Reactions

Much of the foregoing material is designed to show how a "substantive effects" doctrine is more likely than any "mechanical effects" approach to keep the Sherman Act interdictions within the boundary set by the most widely accepted jurisdictional precept of international law — the objective territorial principle. In spite of this, the fact remains that not even the most punctilious regard by the American courts for the territorial principle of international law is likely to banish all foreign criticism of American antitrust enforcement. This is certainly so with the Uranium case, among the most bitterly protested exercises of American jurisdiction in recent years. *In Re Uranium Antitrust Litigation; Westinghouse Electric Corporation.* [42]

Part of this is doubtless a problem of language exacerbated by politics. If American lawyers seem unable to settle upon the precise meaning of Judge Hand's

---

[42] 480 F. Supp. 1138 (N.D. Ill., 1979) aff'd on the jurisdictional issue 617 F.2d 1248 (7th Cir. 1980). In its complaint Westinghouse alleged that twenty domestic and nine foreign corporations conspired to fix the price of uranium in the world market. The alleged meetings at which Westinghouse claimed prices were agreed upon took place in France, Australia, South Africa, Illinois, the Canary Islands and England. In light of the scope of the alleged conspiracy and the proportion of world uranium trade under the control of the defendants, one could scarcely quarrel with the conclusion that Westinghouse's complaint, on its face, sufficed to make out a case of jurisdiction under a "substantive effects" test. The fault, if any, lay in the court's willingness to decide the jurisdictional issue upon motions to dismiss when the denial of those motions effectively meant the entry of default judgments against certain key, non-appearing foreign defendants, and when, from the arguments of several governments appearing as amicus-curae, one might have concluded that a substantial question of jurisdiction existed under principles of comity, notwithstanding the facial sufficiency of Westinghouse's complaint under the "effects" test. On the other hand, both the trial court and the appeals court were properly concerned with the difficulty of addressing the comity issue and delaying judgment on the merits. Not only had several key defendants refused to appear, those same defendants, in open defiance of the court, were engaged in a most unseemly rush to remove all their assets from the United States and virtually all had mounted determined efforts to resist discovery abroad in several instances aided by eleventh hour foreign legislation. The court, in other words, confronted an extraordinarily difficult problem in case management in a politically and emotionally charged setting, all of which requires that any criticism be tendered with great diffidence. Underlying this entire unfortunate episode was also the fact that the cartel which was the subject of Westinghouse's attack had been formed largely in retaliation for certain blatantly protectionist regulations issued by the U.S. Atomic Energy Commission closing the U.S. market to all foreign uranium.

"effects" test and are capable of expanding it beyond the limits set by the "territorial principle" of international law, one would hardly expect foreign governments to concede a narrower interpretation that might undermine their claim of American overreaching. But the problem is far more complex than this. In the end, it may point to the inadequacy of the international law upon which Judge Hand seemed to rely and to the need for a broader formulation, more nearly attuned to the underlying elements of the problem.

To better appraise this possibility it is first advisable to take a closer look at some foreign reactions to American enforcement policies. For this purpose we shall consider principally the British position because the British have tended to lead the protest. Recurrently, the British Government has contended that, for antitrust purposes, a foreign state lacks prescriptive jurisdiction with respect to actions carried out in Great Britain by non-citizens of the foreign State.[43] Not only have the British taken this position with respect to American antitrust jurisdiction, they have done so with regard to the antitrust provisions of the Treaty of Rome. *Aide-Memoire of October 20, 1969 from the Government of the United Kingdom to the Commission of the European Communities.*[44]

Not long after submission of this Aide-Memoire, the EEC Commission found Imperial Chemical Industries Ltd. of London (ICI) and a number of other companies, which together were the principal suppliers of dye stuffs to the Common Market, guilty of "a concerted practice" to fix prices in sales to that market. ICI took the case to the Court of Justice of the European Communities contending inter alia that it was domiciled outside the Community, that all of its actions were taken outside the Community and that, therefore, the Commission lacked jurisdiction over it notwithstanding the fact that its actions had an "effect within the Common Market." The Court rejected these contentions noting that "the price increases took place in the Common Market . . . affected competition between producers operating on this market [and were] . . . therefore practices carried out directly within the Common Market." The Court then added: "By availing itself of its power of direction over its subsidiaries established in the Common Market, plaintiff [ICI] was able to apply its decision on that market." *Imperial Chemical Industries Ltd. v. Commission.*[45] This last statement was just enough to cast doubt on whether the Court had actually adopted a full-fledged "effects" doctrine, although the Court went on to reject the argument that the illegal conduct in the Common Market was the "conduct of [ICI's] subsidiaries, not its own."

Then in late in 1988 the Court of Justice handed down its decision in *The Wood Pulp Cartel* Case[46] upholding a decision of the Commission imposing fines

---

[43] See, Note from the British Embassy at Washington (Note 196), presented to the United States Department of State on July 27, 1978, requesting the latter to present the British Government's views to the National Commission for the Review of Antitrust Laws and Procedures. [1979] British Yearbook of Int'l Law, at page 390).

[44] [1967] Brit. Prac. Int'l L. 58.

[45] Court of Justice of the European Communities, Case No. 48/69, July 14, 1972. Recueil Vol. XVIII, 1972-5, at page 619.

[46] *Re: Wood Pulp Cartel: A. Ahlstrom OY et. al v. E.C. Commission,* Court of Justice of the European Communities, Cases No. 89/85, 104/85, 114/85, 116-117/85, 125-129/85, 27 September 1988, [1988] 4 CMLR 901.

against forty-one wood-pulp producers and two of their trade associations — including a U.S. Webb-Pomerene Association — for price-fixing in sales to the EEC, all in violation of Article 85[47] of the Treaty of Rome. The defendants had their registered offices in Sweden, Finland, Canada and the United States and supplied approximately 60% of the total wood-pulp consumed in the Common Market. A substantial portion of the sales were made by the defendants direct to customers in the EEC without involving subsidiaries, agents or other intermediaries located in the Market. In answer to the defendant's argument that under both Article 85 and international law, the EEC lacked jurisdiction to subject the defendant's to the strictures of that Article, the Court of Justice had the following to say:

. . . [T]he main sources of supply of wood pulp are outside the Community, in Canada, the United States, Sweden and Finland and that the market therefore has global dimensions. Where wood pulp producers established in those countries sell directly to purchasers established in the Community and engage in price competition in order to win orders from those customers, that constitutes competition within the Common Market.

It follows that where those producers concert on the prices to be charged their customers in the Community and put that concertation into effect by selling at prices which are actually co-ordinated, they are taking part in concertation which has the object and effect of restricting competition within the Common Market within the meaning of Article 85 of the Treaty.

Accordingly, it must be concluded that . . . the Commission has not made an incorrect assessment of the territorial scope of Article 85.

The applicants have submitted that the decision is incompatible with public international law . . . [insofar as the application of Article 85] was founded exclusively on the economic repercussion within the Common Market of conduct . . . which was adopted outside the Community.

. . . [A]n infringement of Article 85, such as the conclusion of an agreement which has had the effect of restricting competition within the Common Market, consists of conduct made up of two elements, the formation of the agreement . . . and the implementation thereof. If the applicability of prohibitions laid down under competition law were made to depend on the place where the agreement . . . was formed, the result would obviously be to give undertakings an easy means of evading those prohibitions. The decisive factor is therefore the place where it is implemented.

---

[47] Article 85 of the Treaty of Rome provides in pertinent part as follows: "1. The following shall be prohibited as incompatible with the Common Market: all agreements between enterprises, all decisions by associations of enterprises and all concerted practices which are apt to affect trade between the Member States and which have as their object or effect the prevention, restriction or distortion of competition within the Common Market, in particular those consisting in: (a) [price fixing] . . . (b) the limitation or control of production, markets, technological development or investment; (c) [market division] . . . (d) [certain types of discrimination] . . . (e) [tying]."

Accordingly the Community's jurisdiction to apply its competition rules to such conduct is covered by the territoriality principle as universally recognised in public international law.[48]

The British certainly are not so inept as to think that their position has been accepted by either the United States or the European Economic Community, or, for that matter, by any other nation with a reasonably well developed antitrust law.[49] Yet the British Government persists. Plainly in that persistence there is something more at work than a commitment to a nice point of law. Perhaps it has something to do with antitrust as such. On this point consider next the British Protection of Trading Interests Act of 1980.

UNITED KINGDOM
PROTECTION OF TRADING INTERESTS ACT OF 1980
(1980 c. 11)

Under Section 1 of the Act, the Secretary of State for trade may order:

. . . any person in the United Kingdom who carries on business there . . . [not to comply with any] measures [that] have been or are proposed to be taken [under foreign law for the purpose of] regulating or controlling international trade . . . [if] those measures, insofar as they apply . . . to things done or to be done outside the territorial jurisdiction of [the issuing country] . . . by the person carrying on business in the United Kingdom, are damaging or threaten to damage the trading interest of the United Kingdom.

The Secretary's orders may be special or general (e.g., he may interdict all orders emanating from a specified matter pending abroad), absolute or conditional, and

---

[48] *Id. at 940-941.* It should be noted that in his opinion to the Court, the Advocate General M. Darmon alluded to the *Lotus* Case especially the requirement that the "effect" of any action must be a "constituent element of the offense" before that "effect" would warrant the exercise of jurisdiction under the territorial principle. This limitation, the Advocate General opined, "would have no bearing" on the instant case. Article 85 prohibits any agreement which has the "effect" of preventing, restricting or distorting competition within the Common Market. "Is not," he asks, "such an effect necessarily a constituent element of the offense?" *Id. at 922.*

[49] See: Section 98(2) of the German Law of 1957 against restraints on competition. The High Court of Berlin, affirmed by the Federal Supreme Court of Germany has held that where a United States subsidiary of Bayer A.G., a German company, acquired the organic pigments division of Allied Chemical Corporation (ACC) another U.S. company, the merger had to be notified under Section 23 of the German Law. During the relevant period Bayer had only 4.4% and 3.5% of the German organic pigments market while ACC had only .14% and .23%. The court nevertheless thought that the merger would have perceptible affects on the German market within the meaning of Section 98(2) and therefore had to be notified. Bayer maintained that the merger would improve its competitive position in that market. This was held not to be relevant to the requirements of notification but went to the merits of whether the merger was subject to the prohibitions of Section 214 of that law.

may be annulled by Parliament. The Secretary may require any person in Britain or carrying on business there to inform him of any measure potentially subject to his interdiction. A failure to comply with a Secretary's order is punishable by fine, except as to acts of non-compliance by non-citizens of Britain or by foreign corporations done outside the United Kingdom (Section 3 of the Act).

While apparently the "measures" which the Secretary may interdict do not include "judgments" of foreign courts, they do include all regulations and orders of administrative agencies (*e.g.*, a cease and desist order by the Federal Trade Commission), and possibly all intermediate court orders such as temporary restraining orders and preliminary injunctions.

Section 2 of the Act confers authority on the Secretary of State for Trade to bar compliance with certain juridical or administrative orders to produce commercial documents located outside the territory of the issuing authority or to furnish documentary evidence. Section 4 limits the authority of British courts to assist foreign courts in obtaining evidence in Great Britain and Section 5 prohibits those courts from entertaining any proceeding to recover sums payable under a foreign judgment if the latter calls for "multiple damages" or pertains to a restraint of competition. That section also bars registration of such judgments in Britain and is retroactive.

Lastly, Section 6 of the Act contains a so-called "claw-back" provision as follows:

(1) **This section applies where a court of an overseas country has given a judgment for multiple damages [i.e., a "judgment for an amount arrived at by doubling, trebling or otherwise multiplying a sum assessed as compensation"] against:**

    (a) **a citizen of the United Kingdom and Colonies; or**

    (b) **a body corporate incorporated in the United Kingdom or in a territory outside the United Kingdom for whose international relations Her Majesty's Government in the United Kingdom are responsible; or**

    (c) **a person carrying on business in the United Kingdom;**

    (in this section referred to as a "qualifying defendant") and an amount on account of the damages has been paid by the qualifying defendant either to the party in whose favor the judgment was given or to another party who is entitled as against the qualifying defendant to contribution in respect of the damages.

(2) **Subject to subsections (3) and (4) below, the qualifying defendant shall be entitled to recover from the party in whose favor the judgment was given so much of the amount referred to in subsection (1) above as exceeds the part attributable to compensation.**

(3) **Subsection (2) above does not apply where the qualifying defendant is an individual who was ordinarily resident in the overseas country at the time when the proceedings in which the judgment was given were instituted or a body corporate which had its principal place of business there at that time.**

(4) Subsection (2) above does not apply where the qualifying defendant carried on business in the overseas country and the proceedings in which the judgment was given were concerned with activities exclusively carried on in that country.

(5) A court in the United Kingdom may entertain proceedings on a claim under this section notwithstanding that the person against whom the proceedings are brought is not within the jurisdiction of the court.

(6) The reference in subsection (1) above to an amount paid by the qualifying defendant includes a reference to an amount obtained by execution against his property or a company which (directly or indirectly) is wholly owned by him.

NOTES AND QUESTIONS

(1) Suppose you are counsel for an American company that controls approximately 40% of the relevant U.S. market but also does business in Great Britain. Suppose also that your client has received a very attractive proposal to purchase all of the assets of its principal competitor, a British firm that currently supplies 20% of the U.S. market, that all of the assets to be purchased are located in England and that you can arrange the closing for London. Assuming that the FTC would either order your client not to go through with the acquisition or, having acquired the assets, to divest itself of the purchase, would such an order be interdictable? What arguments could be made in favor of interdiction?

(2) If assured by English counsel that the prospect of actually receiving such an interdiction were strong, would you advise your client to go through with the purchase? In this connection consider the "foreign compulsion" doctrine, discussed *infra* p. 691, *et. seq.* [50]

(3) Suppose a French firm, participant in a world-wide price-fixing conspiracy that was negotiated entirely outside the United States, is successfully sued by an American customer in an American court for treble damages based upon the price of goods manufactured in France but purchased from a wholly-owned American sales subsidiary of the French defendant? If the French firm also sold its product

----

[50] Briefly that doctrine immunizes from antitrust liability any person whose violation of U.S. antitrust law is the result of a direct "command of foreign law or of a foreign governmental official, acting pursuant to law," at least if the acts constituting the violation are taken in the country whose law commands them. *InterAmerican Refining Corp. v. Texaco Maracaibo, Inc.,* 307 F.Supp. 1291 (D. Del. 1970). In its Guidelines on International Operations, the Department of Justice has indicated that it will not prosecute anticompetitive conduct compelled by a foreign sovereign provided (i) non-compliance with the foreign government's mandate would entail substantial penalties or loss of benefits for the private parties involved, (ii) the anticompetitive conduct is genuinely compelled — not merely encouraged or tolerated — and (iii) the conduct has not occurred wholly or primarily in the United States. U.S. Department of Justice Antitrust Enforcement Guidelines for International Operations, BNA Antitrust & Trade Regulation Report, Vol. 55, No. 1391, Special Supplement, November 10, 1988 at page S-23.

in Great Britain, could it sue the American plaintiff in London under Section 6 of the Protection of Trading Interests Act? Suppose the goods were purchased direct from the French firm, "F.O.B. [designated French port]?"

(4) Suppose the American court awarded compensatory damages of $1 million, trebled to $3 million but that the American antitrust plaintiff had actually been able to recover by execution against the French defendant's assets in the United States only $1.5 million. How much would the French firm recover in the British court?

(5) If the American company had no assets in Britain, would that deter the suit? (See European Economic Community Convention on Jurisdiction and the Enforcement of Judgments,[51] discussed Chapter 11, page 956, note 12.)

(6) Can Section 6 be squared with the traditional British position regarding the international law of prescriptive jurisdiction in antitrust matters? Does it matter? Suppose, as is likely, the British will continue to maintain their traditional position on international law while giving Section 6 its broadest possible application. How would you assess such behavior? Does it indicate that international law is no law at all, that the British are prone to self-serving hypocrisy, or that international law may, at times, perform functions quite different from most municipal laws; that it does not necessarily set out rules for determining the outcome of disputes?

NOTE

THE FOREIGN CARTEL — A WIDER PERSPECTIVE AND A PROBLEM

An inquiry into the appropriateness of the *per se* rule in dealing with foreign based collusive arrangements may be aided by placing the price-fixing problem into a broader perspective.

Most governments, not excluding the United States, from time to time embrace policies that favor a certain tolerance of cartel arrangements, especially if accompanied by more direct forms of governmental regulation. Cartels, it is sometimes said, may assist in ameliorating the problem of "ruinous competition" or of volatile markets. It may enable an industry to exploit scale economies more fully. There is also the argument from the second best and the idea that cartels can be a useful way of compelling a socially desirable redistribution of wealth; compelled cross-subsidization. In the purely domestic case these considerations are irrelevant to the treatment of price-fixing under the antitrust laws because Congress has effectively said so. Where Congress has found these, and other reasons of policy, persuasive it has granted the affected industry a measure of exemption from antitrust liability. And precisely because Congress has shown its disposition, from time to time, to exempt certain segments of the economy from market discipline,

---

[51] 25 Off. J. European Commission (No. L. 388) 1 (1982).

the courts have refused to interject these policy considerations into the structure of antitrust doctrine in any domestic case not otherwise exempted by Congress.

Moreover, while *Socony-Vacuum* has withstood the test of time insofar as arrangements that have no other apparent purpose than to "rig" prices are concerned,[52] not all arrangements which necessarily fix prices between competing firms are subject to *per se* interdiction. When two firms in an industry merge, the resulting substitution of one uniform selling price for the competing prices that theretofore existed, results not in a *per se* interdiction, but a Rule of Reason inquiry focusing on whether the merger is likely to enhance the dangers of collusive pricing by the industry as a whole. The reason is that the substitution of a single price for theretofore competing prices is the result of a broader structural adjustment in the industry which may even enhance competition. Even where this potential benefit is problematic, mergers which do not raise a cognizable danger of monopoly pricing can be useful curbs upon managerial complacency and may reflect the kind of entrepreneurial energy that the law ought to encourage. In like manner, partial mergers, such as joint ventures in research and development[53] or in market extension, are treated under a Rule of Reason even though again these arrangements can result in the substitution of a single price for what, without the merger, would be separate pricing. Where, however, two or more competing firms in an industry merge only their selling operations the traditional presumptions of the per se interdiction tend to speak more surely. Not only is the likelihood of scale economies more problematic, but there is a strong suspicion that the sole purpose of the cooperative arrangement may be to cover blatant collusion. The classic cartel has, at times, been structured in precisely this fashion. But even in this situation, the cases evidence a certain flexibility where significant scale economies, genuine improvements in market performance or other pro-competitive possibilities seem to merit modification of a strict *per se* approach.[54]

---

[52] *Socony-Vacuum* has been extended to include arrangements that fix the elements of, rather than the final price to buyers (*e.g.*, distributors agreement not to grant short-term credit to retailers, *Catalano, Inc. v. Target Sales, Inc.*, 100 S. Ct. 1925 (1980)); agreement among automobile dealers on a uniform "list-price," even though customers invariably bargained and cars were never sold at that price, *Plymouth Dealer's Association of Northern California v. United States*, 279 F.2d 128 (9th Cir., 1960).

[53] In 1984 Congress enacted the National Cooperative Research Act of 1984, 15 U.S.C. Sections 4301-4305 (Supp. II 1984) requiring that, for antitrust purposes, joint research and development activities be judged under a Rule of Reason that balances the pro-competitive benefits of the arrangement against its potential anti-competitive effects and eliminates the tripling of actual damages.

[54] See, *Broadcast Music, Inc. v. CBS*, 441 U.S. 1 (1979) where the Court opted for a Rule of Reason approach in dismissing a Section 1 price fixing charge against BMI, who, as the non-exclusive licensee of authors, composers and other copyright owners, had given broadcasters and other users of those works a "blanket license" to perform an entire designated repertory upon payment of a uniform fee. Also in *Chicago Board of Trade v. United States*, 246 U.S. 231 a Rule of Reason analysis was employed to uphold a Board of Trade Rule which prohibited after hour trades at any price other than the closing price on the Exchange (*i.e.* price fixing). In *Appalachian Coal Inc., v. United States*, 288 U.S. 344 (1933) the Court approved the establishment of an exclusive selling organization by 137 companies accounting for almost 75% of all production in the Appalachian region. This decision, however, probably cannot be construed to have survived *Socony-Vacuum*. In

Manifestly, the American courts cannot differentiate between "good" foreign cartels and "bad" foreign cartels, by casting about among the various policy considerations which may, from time to time, have persuaded Congress to exempt certain domestic industries from antitrust liability. But to say they lack such authority, does not mean they are bound to a strict application of the *per se* rule in determining upon the proof required for a judgment of illegality. They cannot be insensitive to the possibility that behind a foreign cartel lie the self-same policy objectives of a foreign government that Congress has sometimes evidenced in its treatment of domestic cartels. And constrained by the laws and policies of a foreign power, it may not always be possible to assign to foreign firms the intentions, the motives or other of the behavioral assumptions upon which domestic applications of the *per se* rule depend or to accord to the social values or to considerations of judicial economy the same weight as in the wholly domestic case. Indeed, if strict adherence to these behavioral assumptions, social values and institutional considerations is sometimes found inappropriate to the purely domestic case, it is unlikely that they will be found any the less so in the international setting. Flexibility in one fairly invites flexibility in the other. Against this background consider the following problem.

PROBLEM

The Swedish Crystal Glassware Industry

The Swedish cut crystal glassware industry has for several years been experiencing growing unemployment and declining profits. It is an industry with high fixed costs and excess capacity. The Swedish government has decided that it must do something to minimize the dislocations likely to occur as the industry makes the changes necessary to assure its continued viability. The government does not, however, want to make the industry permanently dependant upon government subsidies. It has, therefore, enacted a protective tariff which is to be progressively phased out over a six year period. Informally it also encouraged the major Swedish manufacturers (four in number) to enter into an agreement fixing for each manufacturer a quota based upon the latter's historical share of total Swedish

---

National Society of Professional Engineers v. United States, 435 U.S. 679 (1978), the Court examined an ethical canon prohibiting society members from engaging in competitive bidding under the Rule of Reason, concluding that the canon could not pass muster under that Rule. Then in *Arizona v. Maricopa County Medical Society*, 457 U.S. 332, 102 S. Ct. 2466 (1982), the Court engaged in some rather vigorous advocacy of the per se doctrine. Nevertheless it took pains to indicate why it thought the Society's claim of a pro-competitive effect lacked substance. In *NCAA v. Board of Regents*, 468 U.S. 85 (1984) the Court had before it an agreement among NCAA member schools restricting the number of college football games that could be televised. Relying mainly on BMI, the Court held that, since some cooperation between schools was necessary for college athletics to function at all, use of a per se rule was inappropriate. It then went on to conclude that the agreement could not pass muster under the Rule of Reason. *NCAA* indicates that *Maricopa County* was not really a retreat from *BMI*.

production. Traditionally, all of the members of this cartel have exported their products to the United States. When the cartel was formed their combined share of the American market was at its historical high of approximately 20% with no one member having more than six percent of that market.

Under the terms of the cartel agreement all exports, including exports to the United States, are expressly chargeable to each firm's quota. The reason for this is that several foreign markets served by the Swedish industry, *not including the United States*, are highly concentrated and collectively members of the cartel hold a strong position in those markets. They fear that if an exemption from each firm's quota were created for exports to the United States, members might find it easier to "cheat" on the cartel by using the United States as a transshipment point for sales to those markets.

Two years following establishment of the cartel, Tracy-Lord, a major American department store, sued the individual members of the cartel alleging an illegal price-fixing conspiracy in violation of Section 1 of the Sherman Act.

(1) Assume that in that law-suit the following additional facts were adduced:

   (i)   Prior to establishment of the cartel 12 firms, four in the United States and eight in Sweden, France, Ireland and Austria regularly supplied the American market, and that total sales in the United States by these firms for the five years preceding the cartel's formation had increased at about 3% each year from approximately $80 million to $92 million; with about 2% annual growth in the two years since the cartel started operating;

   (ii) Before establishment of the cartel the largest non-Swedish supplier in the U.S. market accounted for 15% of the market, one firm 12%, three firms commanded about 10% each, two 8% each and one 7%.

   (iii) During the five years prior to the cartel's establishment and in the two years since, prices for most of the industry's products increased at about the same rate as the wholesale price index;

   (iv) The industry has exhibited a moderate degree of product differentiation but not sufficient to impair operation of the cartel's quota system;

   (v)   80% of the American market is currently supplied by foreign firms all of which could rapidly increase their production by 5% or more and all of which face roughly the same transportation and other costs in gaining access to that market;

   (vi) There are no quotas or voluntary restraint agreements (VRAs) against imports of cut crystal glassware and the MFN tariff is bound under GATT at 2% *ad velorum*.

   (vii) Cut crystal glassware is, to some extent, in competition with other less expensive types of "pressed" and "blown" glassware. According to the best estimates sales of these latter products would likely increase by 2%-3% in response to a 5% increase in the price of cut crystal glassware.

(2) To what extent are the several presuppositions and policy considerations that underlie the *per se* presumptions applicable to this case? If, in the law suit by Tracy-Lord, the Swedish companies move for summary judgment claiming a

lack of prescriptive jurisdiction under the Alcoa "effects" doctrine, what should the court do?

(3) In its Antitrust Guidelines for International Operations (hereinafter "Foreign Operations Guidelines") the Justice Department makes the following general statement:

> As a general matter, the Department uses two modes of analysis: per se condemnation and case-by-case examination under a "rule of reason." The Department condemns as per se unlawful "naked" restraints of trade that are so inherently anticompetitive and so rarely beneficial that extensive analysis of their precise competitive effects is unnecessary. The Department considers a restraint to be naked if it is a type of restraint that is inherently likely to restrict output or raise price and is not plausibly related to some form of economic integration (by contract or otherwise) of the parties' operations that in general may generate procompetitive efficiencies. The most common examples of naked restraints of trade are price-fixing and bid-rigging schemes among competitors. The Department prosecutes naked restraints of trade among competitors as criminal violations under the Sherman Act.

Surely, our Swedish glass-makers cartel is, under the Department's definition, a "naked restraint." There are no evident efficiencies to be had. Presumably, in encouraging the cartel as a substitute for a direct subsidy, the Swedish government expected that in some foreign markets the Swedish companies would have sufficient market power to reap supra-competitive profits. Surely the cartel is within the reach of the U.S. antitrust laws under the "mechanical" stream of commerce test; the only apparent jurisdictional test that the Department uses anywhere in its Guidelines. Assume, therefore, that were a court in the Tracy-Lord suit to adopt the Justice Department's position, it would have to deny the Swedish companies' motion for summary judgment. With this in mind consider the following:

(a) How does that outcome compare with your answer to the question in Note (2) above?

(b) When the Justice Department says that "naked restraints" are so "rarely beneficial that extensive analysis of their precise competitive effects is unnecessary," rarely beneficial to whom? To the American consumer? If so, is the American consumer's welfare even at issue in the Swedish cartel case, even if the impact on that welfare is judged by the Justice Department's own standards (*i.e.*, the Merger Guidelines)? Perhaps the problem here is that the Justice Department, in a document on International Operations, has ignored international law?

(c) There still remains the problem of the third country markets from which the Swedish firms collectively might well have the power to exact a supra-competitive price. We know the Justice Department is not concerned about those markets,[55] but should the U.S. as a matter of its larger foreign economic policy be concerned? If so, how should the U.S. go about expressing that concern? Is Tracy-Lord or the U.S. Department of Justice the proper instrument for giving effect to that concern?

---

[55] See Foreign Operations Guidelines at page S-21 and discussion page 682 *infra*.

(4) Suppose that in lieu of making an agreement setting quotas, the shareholders of the member companies exchanged their stock in those companies for the stock of a single new holding company the directors of which then controlled the production and pricing policies of the four operating companies, roughly allocating business among the latter in the same manner as the cartel? Assume all of the facts noted above, what result, in this latter case, under Section 7 of the Clayton Act? How is the Justice Department likely to respond (see the Merger Guidelines).[56] Again, there is a problem, is there not, when U.S. international antitrust policy is formulated without careful regard — or even understanding — of international law?

(5) Turn the last question around and review the traditional British position on the international law governing prescriptive jurisdiction in antitrust matters. There is a problem, is there not, when international lawyers formulate positions on such matters without a full appreciation of the role antitrust should play in the larger international economic order?

[C] Of International "Comity:" An Initial Approach

TIMBERLANE LUMBER CO. et al. v.
BANK OF AMERICA, N.T. & S.A. et al.

United States Court of Appeals, Ninth Circuit
549 F. 2d 597 (1976)

Before BROWNING and CHOY, CIRCUIT JUDGES, and GRAY, DISTRICT JUDGE.

---

[56] See also Foreign Operations Guidelines, *Id.* at page S-28, Case 4 "Merger of Two Foreign Firms," discussed by the Justice Department in the following terms: "Beta Corporation and Delta Corporation are among the leading diversified electronics companies in Country A. They are two of the most significant producers outside the United States of product X, a highly advanced and complex electronic device possessing important and unique capabilities. Beta and Delta together supply approximately 60 percent of all X consumed in the United States, accounting for more than $110 million in annual sales. Each company has at least $15 million (book value) in assets located in the United States, although none of these assets are used to produce or sell X. Both companies' facilities for producing X are located in Country A. Beta and Delta each make sales of X in the United States through agreements with independent distributors. There are no quotas or other governmentally-imposed trade restraints constraining sales by Beta and Delta in the United States. Beta has announced that it intends to purchase all of the stock of Delta. After conducting a preliminary investigation the Department has determined that the relevant market for the sale of X in which Beta and Delta compete is highly concentrated and that concentration will increase substantially as a result of the merger. It therefore appears that the merger could have an anticompetitive effect in the United States unless other factors, such as significant likely entry into the market in response to a price increase, would make the post-merger exercise of market power unlikely or unless procompetitive efficiencies that would result from the merger outweigh any threat of anticompetitive harm to U.S. consumers." Might an analysis of our hypothetical Swedish cartel along the lines of this obviously correct approach, been more responsive to the larger systemic problem that the U.S. confronts in the transnational application of its antitrust law?

CHOY, CIRCUIT JUDGE:

Four separate actions arising from the same series of events, were dismissed by the same district court and are consolidated here on appeal. The principal action is *Timberlane Lumber Co. v. Bank of America* (Timberlane action), an antitrust suit alleging violations of Sections 1 and 2 of the Sherman Act . . . and the Wilson Tariff Act.

The other three are diversity tort suits brought by employees of one of the Timberlane plaintiffs for individual injuries allegedly suffered in the course of the extended anti-Timberlane drama. Having dismissed the Timberlane action [under the Act of State doctrine and for lack of subject-matter jurisdiction] the district court dismissed these three suits on the ground of *forum non conveniens.* We vacate the dismissal of all four actions and remand.

The basic allegation of the Timberlane plaintiffs is that officials of the Bank of America and others . . . conspired to prevent Timberlane . . . from milling lumber in Honduras and exporting it to the United States, thus maintaining control of the Honduran lumber export business in the hands of a few select individuals financed and controlled by the Bank.

There are three affiliated plaintiffs in the Timberlane action. Timberlane Lumber Company is an Oregon partnership principally involved in the purchase and distribution of lumber at wholesale in the United States and the importation of lumber into the United States for sale and use. Danli Industrial, S.A., and Maya Lumber Company, are both Honduran corporations, incorporated and principally owned by the general partners of Timberlane. Danli held contracts to purchase timber in Honduras, and Maya was to conduct the milling operations to produce the lumber for export. (Timberlane, Danli, and Maya will be collectively referred to as "Timberlane.")

The primary defendants are Bank of America Corporation (Bank), a California corporation, and its wholly-owned subsidiary, Bank of America National Trust and Savings Association, which operates a branch in Tegucigalpa, Honduras. Several employees of the Bank have also been named and served as defendants. . . . Other defendants have been named, but have not been served, . . . [including] two Honduras corporations . . . and Michael Casanova, a citizen of Honduras (together referred to as "Casanova"). The Timberlane complaint [also] identified two co-conspirators not named as defendants . . . [including one] Jose Caminals Galego (Caminals), a citizen of Spain, [who] is described as an agent or employee of the Bank in Tegucigalpa.

The conspiracy sketched by Timberlane actually started before the plaintiffs entered the scene. The Lima family operated a lumber mill in Honduras, competing with . . . Casanova, in . . . which the Bank had significant financial interests. The Lima enterprise was also indebted to the Bank. By 1971, however, the Lima business was in financial trouble. . . . [As a result, various of Lima's assets, including its milling plant, passed to Lima's creditors: Casanova, the Bank, and a group of Lima employees who had not been paid the wages and severance pay due them. Under Honduran law, the employees' claim had priority].

Enter Timberlane, with a long history in the lumber business, in search of alternative sources of lumber for delivery to its distribution system on the East

Coast of the United States. After study, it decided to try Honduras. In 1971, Danli was formed, tracts of forest land were acquired, plans for a modern log-processing plant were prepared, and equipment was purchased and assembled for shipment from the United States to Danli in Honduras. Timberlane became aware that the Lima plant might be available and began negotiating for its acquisition. Maya was formed, purchased the Lima employees' interest in the machinery and equipment in January 1972, despite opposition from the conspirators, and re-activated the Lima mill.

Realizing that they were faced with better-financed and more vigorous competition from Timberlane and its Honduran subsidiaries, the defendants and others extended the anti-Lima conspiracy to disrupt Timberlane's efforts. The primary weapons employed by the conspirators were the claim still held by the Bank in the remaining assets of the Lima enterprise under the all-inclusive mortgage Lima had been forced to sign and another claim held by Casanova. Maya made a substantial cash offer for the Bank's interest in an effort to clear its title, but the Bank refused to sell. Instead, the Bank surreptitiously conveyed the mortgage to Casanova for questionable consideration, [and] . . . Casanova immediately assigned the Bank's claim and its own on similar terms to Caminals, who promptly set out to disrupt the Timberlane operation.

Caminals is characterized as the "front man" in the campaign to drive Timberlane out of Honduras. . . . Having acquired the claims of Casanova and the Bank, Caminals went to court to enforce them, ignoring throughout Timberlane's offers to purchase or settle them. Under the law of Honduras, an "embargo" on property is a court-ordered attachment, registered with the Public Registry, which precludes the sale of that property without a court order. Honduran law provides, upon embargo, that the court appoint a judicial officer, called an "interventor" to ensure against any diminution in the value of the property. In order to paralyze the Timberlane operation, Caminals obtained embargoes against Maya and Danli. Acting through the interventor, since accused of being on the payroll of the Bank, guards and troops were used to cripple and, for a time, completely shut down Timberlane's milling operation. The harassment took other forms as well: the conspirators caused the manager of Timberlane's Honduras operations, Gordon Sloan Smith, to be falsely arrested and imprisoned and were responsible for the publication of several defamatory articles about Timberlane in the Honduran press.

As a result of the conspiracy, Timberlane's complaint claimed damages then estimated in excess of $5,000,000. Plaintiffs also allege that there has been a direct and substantial effect on United States foreign commerce, and that defendants intended the results of the conspiracy, including the impact on United States commerce.

> [The court here considers the district court's dismissal of Timberlane's suit under the "Act of State" Doctrine. That court apparently concluded that Timberlane's injury resulted principally from the Honduran government's enforcement of defendant's security interest in Maya's plant, and that under the "Act of State" doctrine a U.S. court was barred from reviewing such governmental actions. The Appeals Court concluded that this constituted an "erroneous" application of the doctrine.]

There is no doubt that American antitrust laws extend over some conduct in other nations. . . . That American law covers some conduct beyond this nation's borders does not mean that it embraces all, however. Extraterritorial application is understandably a matter of concern for the other countries involved. . . . Our courts have recognized this concern and have, at times, responded to it, even if not always enough to satisfy all the foreign critics. . . . In any event, it is evident that at some point the interests of the United States are too weak and the foreign harmony incentive for restraint too strong to justify an extraterritorial assertion of jurisdiction. What that point is or how it is determined is not defined by international law. . . . Nor does the Sherman Act limit itself. . . . It is the effect on American foreign commerce which is usually cited to support extraterritorial jurisdiction. *Alcoa* set the course. . . . [But] [e]ven among American courts and commentators . . . there is no consensus on how far the jurisdiction should extend. The district court here concluded that a "direct and substantial effect" on United States foreign commerce was a prerequisite, without stating whether other factors were relevant or considered. . . .

* * * *

[Also] . . . in several of the cases and commentaries employing the "effects" test, is the suggestion that factors other than simply the effect on the United States are weighed, and rightly so. As former Attorney General (then Professor) Katzenbach observed, the effect on American commerce is not, by itself, sufficient information on which to base a decision that the United States is the nation primarily interested in the activity causing the effect. "[A]nything that affects the external trade and commerce of the United States also affects the trade and commerce of other nations, and may have far greater consequences for others than for the United States."[57] . . .

The effects test by itself is incomplete because it fails to consider other nations' interests. Nor does it expressly take into account the full nature of the relationship between the actors and this country. Whether the alleged offender is an American citizen, for instance, may make a big difference; applying American laws to American citizens raises fewer problems than application to foreigners. . . .

American courts have, in fact, often displayed a regard for comity and the prerogatives of other nations and considered their interests as well as other parts of the factual circumstances, even when professing to apply an effects test. To some degree, the requirement for a "substantial" effect may silently incorporate these additional considerations, with "substantial" as a flexible standard that varies with other factors. The intent requirement suggested by *Alcoa*, . . . is one example of an attempt to broaden the court's perspective, as in drawing a distinction between American citizens and non-citizens.

The failure to articulate these other elements in addition to the standard effects analysis is costly, however, for it is more likely that they will be overlooked or slighted in interpreting past decisions and reaching new ones. . . .

A tripartite analysis seems to be indicated. As acknowledged above, the antitrust laws require in the first instance that there be *some* effect — actual or

---

[57] Katzenbach, Conflicts on an Unruly Horse, 65 Yale L.J. 1087 1150 (1956).

intended — on American foreign commerce before the federal courts may legitimately exercise subject matter jurisdiction under those statutes. Second, a greater showing of burden or restraint may be necessary to demonstrate that the effect is sufficiently large to present a cognizable injury to the plaintiffs and, therefore, a civil *violation* of the antitrust laws. . . . Third, there is the additional question which is unique to the international setting of whether the interests of, and links to, the United States — including the magnitude of the effect on American foreign commerce — are sufficiently strong, vis-a-vis those of other nations, to justify an assertion of extraterritorial authority.

It is this final issue which is both obscured by undue reliance on the "substantiality" test and complicated to resolve. An effect on United States commerce, although necessary to the exercise of jurisdiction under the antitrust laws, is alone not a sufficient basis on which to determine whether American authority *should* be asserted in a given case as a matter of international comity and fairness. In some cases, the application of the direct and substantial test in the international context might open the door too widely by sanctioning jurisdiction over an action when these considerations would indicate dismissal. At other times, it may fail in the other direction, dismissing a case for which comity and fairness do not require forbearance, thus closing the jurisdictional door too tightly — for the Sherman Act does reach some restraints which do not have both a direct and substantial effect on the foreign commerce of the United States. . . .

What we prefer is an evaluation and balancing of the relevant considerations in each case — in the words of Kingman Brewster, a "jurisdictional rule of reason." Balancing of the foreign interests involved was the approach taken by the Supreme Court in *Continental Ore Co. v. Union Carbide & Carbon Corp.* [*infra* page 691]. . . . Similarly in *Lauritzen v. Larsen* [*supra*, page 541] . . . the Court used a like approach. . . .

The elements to be weighed include the degree of conflict with foreign law or policy, the nationality or allegiance of the parties and the locations or principal places of business of corporations, the extent to which enforcement by either state can be expected to achieve compliance, the relative significance of effects on the United States as compared with those elsewhere, the extent to which there is explicit purposes to harm or affect American commerce, the foreseeability of such effect, and the relative importance to the violations charged of conduct within the United States as compared with conduct abroad.

A court evaluating these factors should identify the potential degree of conflict if American authority is asserted. A difference in law or policy is one likely sore spot, though one which may not always be present. Nationality is another; though foreign governments may have some concern for the treatment of American citizens and business residing there, they primarily care about their own nationals. Having assessed the conflict, the court should then determine whether in the face of it the contacts and interests of the United States are sufficient to support the exercise of extraterritorial jurisdiction.

We conclude, then, that the problem should be approached in three parts: Does the alleged restraint affect, or was it intended to affect, the foreign commerce of the United States? Is it of such a type and magnitude so as to be cognizable as a violation of the Sherman Act? As a matter of international comity and fairness, should the extraterritorial jurisdiction of the United States be asserted to cover it? The district court's judgment found only that the restraint involved in the instant suit did not produce a direct and substantial effect on American foreign commerce. That holding does not satisfy any of these inquiries.[58]

The Sherman Act is not limited to trade restraints which have both a direct and substantial effect on our foreign commerce. Timberlane has alleged that the complained of activities were intended to, and did, affect the export of lumber from Honduras to the United States — the flow of United States foreign commerce, and as such they are within the jurisdiction of the federal courts under the Sherman Act. Moreover, the magnitude of the effect alleged would appear to be sufficient to state a claim.

The comity question is more complicated. From Timberlane's complaint it is evident that there are grounds for concern as to at least a few of the defendants, for some are identified as foreign citizens: . . . Moreover, it is clear that most of the activity took place in Honduras, though the conspiracy may have been directed from San Francisco, and that the most direct economic effect was probably on Honduras. However, there has been no indication of any conflict with the law or policy of the Honduran government, nor any comprehensive analysis of the relative connections and interests of Honduras and the United States. Under these circumstances, the dismissal by the district court cannot be sustained on jurisdictional grounds. We, therefore, vacate the dismissal and remand the Timberlane action.

OCCIDENTAL PETROLEUM CORP. v. BUTTES GAS & OIL CO.

District Court for the Central District of California
331 F. Supp. 92 (1971),
aff'd. 461 F. 2d 1261 (9th Cir.,1972),
cert. denied 409 U.S. 950, 93 S. Ct. 272 (1972)

[Plaintiff Occidental Petroleum Corp. obtained from one of the Trucial States, Umm Al Quywayn ("Quywayn"), a concession to explore for and develop petroleum resources in an ocean area up to a point within three miles of Abu Musa, an island lying off the coast of Quywayn. Defendant Buttes, also an American corporation, having failed to obtain the concession granted Occidental obtained a concession from an adjoining Trucial State, Sharjah. At that time Sharjah, according to plaintiff, claimed sovereignty over Abu Musa and over a territorial sea extending only three miles from the island. When

---

[58] Our separation in the foreign commerce context between the degree of restraint necessary for establishing subject matter jurisdiction as opposed to that required to a state a claim is, of course, not duplicated in the interstate setting, for there a "substantial" restraint is in any event necessary for the establishment of jurisdiction itself. Nevertheless, since the interstate cases provide a standard for both jurisdiction and the statement of a claim . . . they thus offer some guidance for determining the degree of restraint necessary to support a claim for relief in the foreign commerce context as well.

Occidental discovered oil in an ocean area approximately nine miles from Abu Musa, Buttes, according to the complaint, commenced a number of maneuvers designed to establish that its concession from Sharjah and Sharjah's sovereignty extended twelve miles seaward of the island, an area encompassing Occidental's discovery. These maneuvers, however, were forestalled when Great Britain, which had control over the foreign relations of both Quywayn and Sharjah, withheld its approval of Sharjah's claims. Whereupon, according to Occidental, Buttes went to the National Iranian Oil Co. and induced that company to claim that Abu Musa and a twelve mile seaward area belonged to Iran and then induced Great Britain to ask that Occidental refrain from drilling in the area until the question of sovereignty was settled. When Occidental refused, Great Britain allegedly sent planes and ships to harass Occidental's drilling operations, to board its equipment and then, by threatening the ruler of Quywayn with exile, caused the latter to order cessation of Occidental's operations. This effectively meant termination of Occidental's rights since the concession automatically expired unless Occidental was able within four years to prove discovery of oil "in commercial quantities."

At this point, Occidental filed suit against Buttes charging that the latter had conspired with the several governments involved to restrain U.S. foreign commerce in violation of Section 1 of the Sherman Act. The governmental conspirators were not made parties to the suit. Defendant Buttes moved to dismiss inter alia for failure to state a claim upon which relief could be granted and for lack of subject-matter jurisdiction. In support of this latter motion Buttes contended that Occidental had failed to allege any "substantial anti-competitive effect upon United States commerce." Its relatively small size within the industry as compared to Occidental, the limited and speculative character of Occidental's concession, the vastly greater amounts of Persian Gulf oil being imported into the United States by other companies demonstrated, Buttes argued, that its conduct could not possibly have had any anti-competitive effect on the U.S. market. The district court rejected this last contention, although it later concluded that Occidental's suit was barred by the "Act of State" doctrine. On this latter point alone the district court's decision was affirmed by the Ninth Circuit.

In rejecting the argument that it lacked "subject-matter" jurisdiction because Butte's allegedly illegal conduct had no "substantial anti-competitive effect" on U.S. commerce, the district court had the following to say]:

An "affect" is a necessary element of *jurisdiction* . . . a direct and substantial "affect" is necessary for Sherman Act violations. The problem arises when the standards of illegality (which might be modified to promote foreign trade) are confused with the jurisdictional feature of the "affect on foreign commerce" (emphasis in original).

In reviewing the cases, Von Kalinowski notes the confusion evident therein:

The cases that used the word "affect" have said that a restraint must (1) "directly affect," or (2) "substantially affect," or (3) "directly and substantially affect," or (4) simply "affect" the flow of foreign commerce. . . .

He concludes that "[t]he better view would seem to be that any effect that is not both insubstantial and indirect will support federal jurisdiction under Section 1."

The interference with plaintiff's business of extracting and importing oil into the United States alledged in the complaint, is certainly a "direct" effect on our foreign commerce. On this basis, the court is disposed to hold that the complaint alleges a sufficient effect on foreign commerce.

Moreover, since the standard urged by defendants is largely coterminous with the scope of proof required to establish plaintiff's section 1 case on the merits, dismissal now on the grounds that the standard has not been met would be premature. In urging dismissal, defendants stress [the economic factors noted above]. . . . These are matters that would appear to bear upon proof of plaintiffs' claims of antitrust violations; they cannot serve at this stage to defeat jurisdiction.

NOTES AND QUESTIONS

(1) *Timberlane* has been much noted and generally applauded for bringing "comity" into the determination of the antitrust laws' prescriptive reach.[59] Yet, Judge Choy's principal, if unwitting, achievement may in the end lie in quite another direction. In his tripartite analysis the Judge appears to have separated "subject matter" jurisdiction (Step 1) from prescriptive jurisdiction (Steps 2 and 3) and to have utterly, and appropriately, trivialized "subject-matter" jurisdiction. If this is so, should not Timberlane's complaint have been dismissed under the second step in Judge Choy's tripartite analysis? Stated otherwise, was the Ninth Circuit premature in remanding for a further inquiry under the comity doctrine (Step 3)? Is the same not true for Occidental's complaint? Do we really have enough information to answer?

(2) In considering these questions, it is necessary to examine the substance of the antitrust charge against the defendants in each of these cases. In both

---

[59] In its International Operations Guidelines, the Justice Department ". . . recognizes that considerations of comity among nations . . . properly play a role in determining the recognition which one nation allows within its territory to the legislative, executive or judicial acts of another nation . . . [Accordingly] [w]here the defense of foreign sovereign compulsion does not apply, the Department [will] attempt to balance the interests of the U.S. Government in preserving competitive markets and protecting U.S. consumers and the interests of the affected foreign sovereign in promoting its laws and policies." The Guidelines also state that in making its determination the Department will take into account the following factors: (1) the relative significance, to the violation alleged, of conduct in the United States compared with conduct abroad; (2) the nationality of the persons involved; (3) the presence or absence of a purpose to affect U.S. consumers or competitors; (4) the relative significance and foreseeability of the effects of the conduct on the U.S. as compared to the effects abroad; (5) the existence of reasonable expectations that would be furthered by the action; and (6) the degree of conflict with foreign law or articulated foreign economic policies. BNA, Antitrust and Trade Regulation Report, Vol. 55, No. 1391, Special Supplement, November 10, 1988 at page S-22.

Timberlane and *Occidental* defendants were charged with exclusionary acts. Of these, Occidental's charge against Buttes fits rather clearly into one of the more familiar categories; the group boycott or concerted refusal to deal. One classic form of group boycott is where traders at one level in the chain of distribution (*e.g.*, manufacturers), intent upon excluding a potential competitor or driving an existing competitor out of business, induce traders at another level (*e.g.*, wholesalers) to discontinue dealing with the target firm. *Fashion Originators Guild v. FTC.*[60] They may do this by threatening to withhold their business unless the latter complies or they may use other more subtle methods of persuasion. The inducement employed is not important and there need be no more than one trader seeking to exclude the target competitor, so long as that trader succeeds in persuading others not to deal with the target firm. *Klor's Inc., v. Broadway-Hale Stores, Inc.*[61]

Plainly, Occidental's charge against Buttes fits this pattern. By fomenting a quarrel regarding sovereignty over Occidental's concession area, Buttes, it was alleged, was able to persuade Great Britain to induce the ruler of Quywayn, as Occidental's "supplier," to stop the latter's drilling operations. Bank of America's conduct in *Timberlane* is more difficult to categorize. Aside from the alleged destruction of Timberlane's property and the harassment of its employees, it may be questioned whether Bank of America's refusal to accept Timberlane's preferred repayment of the Lima debt and its resort to the Honduran courts sufficed to cross over some threshold between a perfectly proper exercise of business prerogative — analogous to a unilateral refusal to deal — and improper predation. Assuming, however, that taken in context Timberlane succeeded in making out a threshold case of predation, then the boycott precedents would seem apposite *a fortiori*.

Against this background consider the Supreme Court's decision in *Klors*. Klors, a small retail store in San Francisco operating next door to Broadway-Hale, a major department chain, and competing with the latter in the sale of nationally advertised brands of household appliances, sued for treble damages under Section 1 of the Sherman Act, alleging that Broadway-Hale had used its "buying power" to induce appliance manufacturers such as General Electric, Admiral, Zenith and others not to sell to it or to sell on highly discriminatory terms. Broadway-Hale did not dispute these allegations, but moved for summary judgment on the basis of unchallenged affidavits showing that there were numerous competing retailers selling the same appliances within a few blocks of both Klors' and Broadway-Hale's store and that consequently plaintiff could not allege or prove an injury to the public (*i.e.*, any anti-competitive affect in the relevant market). Defendant's motion was granted by the trial court and affirmed by the Ninth Circuit. The Supreme Court reversed. Writing for the Court, Justice Black, after reviewing certain earlier cases, noted:

> The Court [in those cases] recognized that there were some agreements whose validity depended on the surrounding circumstances. It emphasized, however, that there were classes of restraints which from the "nature or character" were unduly restrictive and hence forbidden. . . .

---

[60] 312 U.S. 467, 61 S. Ct. 706 (1941).
[61] 359 U.S. 207, 79 S. Ct. 705 (1959).

Group boycotts, or concerted refusals by traders to deal with other traders, have long been held to be in the forbidden category.

They have not been saved by allegations that they were reasonable in the specific circumstances, nor by a failure to show that they "fixed or regulated prices, parcelled-out a limited production, or brought about a deterioration in quality". . . .

Plainly, the allegations of this complaint disclose such a boycott. This is not a case of a single trader refusing to deal with another . . . [nor an agreement to establish] . . . an exclusive distributorship. Alleged . . . is a wide combination . . . of manufacturers, distributors and a retailer. This combination . . . interferes with the natural flow of commerce. It clearly has by its "nature" and "character" a "monopolistic tendency." As such it is not to be tolerated merely because the victim is just one merchant whose business is so small that his destruction makes little difference to the economy . . .[62]

In spite of some ambiguity in *Klors'* and the Court's recent rejection of the *per se* approach to a claim that expulsion of a member from a wholesale purchasing cooperative constituted a group boycott in violation of Section 1,[63] we can, for present purposes, treat the naked boycotts of the type involved in *Occidental* and *Timberlane* as *per se* violations of that Section.[64]

(3) With the foregoing as background, return to Justice Black's *Klors'* opinion. The Justice expresses a concern for the "monopolistic tendency" of boycotts. "[M]onopoly can surely thrive," he argues, "by the elimination of small . . . businessmen, one at a time as it can by driving them out in large groups." This seems intended as a statement of probabilities. If so, are the probabilities

---

[62] 79 S. Ct. pages 709-710.

[63] *Northwest Wholesale Stationers, Inc. v. Pacific Stationery and Printing Co.*, 472 U.S. 284, 105 S. Ct. 2613 (1985).

[64] See *Silver v. New York Stock Exchange*, 373 U.S. 571, 83 S. Ct. 1246 (1963) and *United States v. General Motors Co.*, 384 U.S. 127, 86 S. Ct. 1321 (1966)). Indeed, even while the Court in *Northwest Wholesale Stationers* was cautioning that not every group boycott was so devoid of possible pro-competitive effect as to warrant per se treatment, it distinguished the exclusionary action in that case from those naked schemes to "disadvantage competitors by 'either directly denying or persuading or coercing suppliers . . . to deny relationships the competitors need in the competitive struggle.'" In the case of these latter, *per se* interdiction would continue to be appropriate. As examples of such naked schemes the court listed *inter alia*: denial of necessary access to exchange members (*Silver*); denial of important sources of news (*Associated Press v. United States*, 326 U.S. 1 (1945)) and denial of wholesale supplies (*Klors*). Here, however, a cautionary note. There is some suggestion in *Northwest Wholesale Stationers, supra* of a possible predisposition in the Court to subject group boycotts to per se interdiction only upon some showing of market power. See pages 296-297. It is also well to note that an explicit boycott need not be as blatantly offensive as the actions with which Buttes, Bank of America or Broadway-Hale were charged. The target of a boycott may, for example, be engaged in false advertising or cheating customers or producing an inferior, even dangerous, product and the boycott may be intended as a measure of industry self-regulation. Only, however, if such self regulation falls within the necessary boundaries of some statutory mandate for industry self-regulation and only if it is conducted in a procedurally fair manner will it escape per se interdiction. *Silver, supra, Northwest Wholesale Stationers, supra.*

comparable to the economic probabilities or the presuppositions regarding human behavior that underlie the *per se* interdiction of price fixing?[65] How do they differ?

(4) To the extent that the antitrust laws are intended to protect the competitive structure of markets, would the *per se* interdiction of Buttes' or Bank of America's conduct, on the basis of Justice Black's rationale, meet the prescriptive jurisdictional test laid down in *Alcoa*? In answering make the following assumptions:

    (i)   That both defendants were interested in securing to themselves or to companies under their control regular sources for the supply of lumber or oil in order to strengthen their competitive position in the relevant United States market;

    (ii)   That in spite of supplies available from other sources, Quywayn and Honduras were among the cheapest and most accessible sources to the respective defendants;

    (iii)   That each deliberately sought to reserve those sources exclusively to itself;

    (iv)   That at the time of their actions neither controlled more than 5% of the relevant American market and that both faced strong competition from multiple and equally low-cost sources of supply.

(5) If, in economic terms, Justice Black's argument leaves something to be desired, and if we cannot really bring either *Timberlane* or *Occidental* within the prescriptive reach of *Alcoa's* "effects" test (*i.e.*, the strict objective territorial principle; See Note (6) below) are there nevertheless ethical postulates here — rules of the game — that bear upon the law's purpose of preserving competitive markets? If so, then perhaps we have to extend the reach of the antitrust laws beyond the constraints of those principles and, in so doing, engage Judge Choy's Step 3: a comity analysis.

Before taking that step, however, recall Professor Currie's skepticism regarding the ability of courts of law to engage in the subtle choices that the factors listed by Judge Choy might well require. As a device to overcome some of that skepticism — to lend structure and discipline to the process — consider the possibility of starting the analysis with a presumption — a strong presumption — that the United States will not exercise antitrust jurisdiction in any case that

---

[65] Alternatively, perhaps Justice Black can be read as providing a rationale for a rule under which proof of a specific intent to drive a competitor out of business would, without more, make out an illegal "attempt to monopolize" under Sec. 2 of the Sherman Act (*i.e.*, that an "intent" to drive the competitor out is sufficient to establish an "intent" to create a monopoly.) The difficulty with any such rule is that evidence of acts alone — even acts as blatantly predatory as Buttes' and Bank of America's — have traditionally been thought inadequate to show an intent to create a monopoly without some consideration of the probability of success. Perhaps no refined inquiry into the remaining competition is warranted if the predator seems bent on his purpose by fair means or foul, *Lessig v. Tidewater Oil Co.*, 327 F.2d 459 (9th Cir., 1964) cert. denied 377 U.S. 993, 84 S.Ct. 1920 (1964) and see Turner, Antitrust Policy and the Cellophane Case, 70 Harv. L. Rev. 281, 305 (1956). But even then, it is doubtful that one can, upon the basis of the act alone, ascribe to the act a purpose to create monopoly if the achievement of monopoly power lies beyond practical attainment.

lies outside the boundaries set by the strict objective territorial principle, unless the plaintiff can demonstrate some need, rooted in American foreign economic policy, that is compelling enough to overcome the presumption. Alternatively, the presumption might be set aside if application of the U.S antitrust laws would have some positive effect and there is no real reason in either policy or basic considerations of fairness not to exercise jurisdiction. With this scheme in mind consider the following:

(a) The conduct with which the defendants were charged in *Timberlane* and *Occidental*, if proven, certainly raise serious ethical problems. However, how might the ethics of that conduct be relevant to the antitrust law's purpose of preserving open and competitive markets?

(b) Now, in judging whether these ethical concerns — this link between ethics and markets — is compelling enough to set aside the presumption that jurisdiction was lacking in *Timberlane* and *Occidental*, consider first *Timberlane*. Recall that, in addition to their antitrust claim, plaintiffs sued for malicious prosecution, abuse of process and theft of personal property. After dismissing the antitrust action the district court also dismissed these suits on forum non-conveniens grounds. The Ninth Circuit agreed that viewed separately from the antitrust claim this was appropriate. The "torts took place in Honduras . . . [the Appeals Court noted], most of the witnesses and evidence are apparently based there, as are two of the plaintiffs, and Honduran law would have to be applied."[66] However, because the antitrust claim was being remanded the Appeals Court instructed the district court to hear the tort claims as well. Certainly, U.S. tort law is as sensitive to American ethical traditions as the antitrust laws. If, therefore, the U.S. choice of law process is prepared to consign to Honduran law and Honduran courts the task of judging and possibly punishing the *Timberlane* defendants for their ethical transgressions what possible basis would there be for applying the U.S. antitrust law to the case when it is clear that those transgression have no anticompetitive "effect" in the American market? Is there, in other words, any reason to set aside the presumption against jurisdiction in that case? Perhaps the sensitivity exhibited (arguably) by Justice Holmes' to the impact of private international law on these matters is worth emulating? See discussion of *American Banana v. United Fruit, supra* page 606.

(6) After Judge Choy's valiant initiative, the *Timberlane* Case had a tortured history. On remand the District Court, purporting to undertake the comparative interest analysis under the third prong of Judge Choy's jurisdictional test, and after noting that Honduran lumber imports into the U.S. were insubstantial and their effect "upon competitive conditions in the U.S. . . . . *de minimus*," concluded that *Timberlane's* lawsuit was:

. . . essentially a group of separate tort actions which were deemed unsuccessful in Honduran courts [and were then] repackaged as an antitrust case in an

---

[66] 549 F. 2d at 616.

attempt to subvert prudent and traditional limits upon applications of our laws to foreign conduct and actors.[67]

The case then went back to the Ninth Circuit which, in affirming the District Court's dismissal of the case, also undertook a comparative interest analysis in which it pointed out that Honduran lumber imports into the United States constituted .07%, .02% and .04% of total U.S. imports by volume for the years 1970-1972 respectively and constituted .011%, .004% and .008% of total U.S. lumber consumption in those same years.[68] Valiant but, in light of *Alcoa*, did we need the third prong of Judge Choy's test at all?

(7) Consider at this point *Industrial Investment Development Corp. ("IID") v. Mitsui & Co. Ltd.*[69] In 1970, IID entered into a joint venture with an Indonesian company (Telagas Mas), calling for the establishment of an Indonesian company to which IID was to provide the equipment, capital, and technical skills necessary to exploit a timber concession in Borneo which Telagas Mas had obtained from the Indonesian government. By July 1971 Telagas Mas and IID had negotiated a so-called forestry agreement with the Government. The agreement provided that the lumbering concession would terminate if the partners to the joint venture failed to cooperate or carry out their duties prior to the issuance of a "cutting" license. Before issuance of the license the world price of lumber began to rise. This rise, according to IID, prompted Mitsui — a customer and creditor of Telagas Mas — to organize and finance secretly an effort by dissident shareholders to take control of Telagas Mas. The effort was ultimately successful and, once in control, the new management refused to cooperate further with IID. Thereupon the Indonesian government terminated the concession. IID then sued Mitsui charging that by driving it out of the logging and lumber products business in Indonesia, Mitsui had violated Sections 1 and 2 of the Sherman Act. The complaint also charged Mitsui with tortious interference with contractual relations and Telagas Mas with breach of contract. Defendants moved to dismiss, contending *inter alia* that the case was beyond the "extra territorial reach" of the antitrust laws, and that the suit was barred by the "Act of State" doctrine. The district court granted the motion on "Act of State" grounds alone. The Fifth Circuit reversed, remanding for consideration of defendants' alternative contentions, noting that IID's injury could be traced directly to Mitsui's predatory acts independent of any decision that the Indonesian government may have taken. Nothing in the complaint intimated that Mitsui's conduct had adversely affected competition in the American lumber market, although plaintiff did at one point claim an intention to import "agathis" logs into the U.S. The case continued for over thirteen years, returning three more times to the Fifth Circuit. Only on the last appeal did the court finally dismiss on the basis of a jury finding that any imports that plaintiff might have made "would constitute an insignificant percentage of the market."[70] Assuming that IID's alleged intention to import logs into the U.S. would have satisfied a "mechanical" stream of commerce test, without evidence of any

[67] *Timberlane Lumber Co. v. Bank of America National Trust & Savings Ass'n.*, 574 F. Supp. 1453 at 1463 (N.D. Cal., 1983).
[68] 749 F. 2d 1378 at page 1385 (9th Cir. 1984).
[69] 594 F. 2d 48 (5th Cir. 1979).
[70] 855 F.2d 222 at 227 (5th Cir. 1988)

substantive anticompetitive effect on the relevant U.S. lumber market it seems clear that IID was using the U.S. antitrust laws simply to protect its investment abroad against the allegedly unfair competitive methods of foreign rivals. Should the antitrust laws be used in this way? In answering, consider two points. Under U.S. conflicts law, what law would govern IID's claim of tortious interference with its joint venture agreement? From a broader systemic perspective, do actions like this advance the goal of securing open and competitive markets worldwide, especially in dealing with countries, like Japan, whose enthusiasm for such markets is something less than overwhelming?

(8) Return to *Occidental*; it is simply a suit by one American company against another. Does that argue for setting aside our presumption against jurisdiction? After all, if proven, Butte's conduct is scarcely conducive to the kind of competition that will enhance the efficient use of world resources. Moreover, one may doubt that any other remedy was available to Occidental. On the other hand, there is another critical element in the case. Identify it. How should that affect the decision of whether to exercise jurisdiction? Perhaps without that element in the case, *Occidental* illustrates at least one situation where we might set aside the presumption against any antitrust jurisdiction not in strcict conformity with the objective territorial principle on the gound that there may be some benefit from hearing the case and no harm is likely to come from doing so?

§ 7.04   The Division of International Markets and More

UNITED STATES v. TIMKIN ROLLER BEARING CO.

United States Supreme Court
341 U.S. 593, 71 S. Ct. 971 (1951)

[In this case the United States charged the Timkin Roller Bearing Co. ("American Timkin"), British Timkin Ltd. ("British Timkin"), a company partially owned by American Timkin, and Societe Anonyme Francaise Timkin ("French Timkin"), a company jointly owned by American and British Timkin, with conspiring to restrain the foreign commerce of the United States in violation of Section 1 and Section 3 of the Sherman Act. American Timkin was the sole defendant in the case.

The district court[1] characterized each of the conspirators, as of the time of trial, as the "dominant company" in the sale and manufacture of "tapered roller bearings" within their respective territories. "Tapered roller bearings" are one form of "anti-friction" bearing of which there are two basic types: "ball bearings" and "roller bearings." "Roller bearings" are either of the "tapered" or "regular" type.

With regard to the relevant product market the district court offered the following somewhat ambiguous description: (i) Tapered roller bearings compete with other types of anti-friction bearings ("ball" and "regular roller"), and to some extent with "friction" bearings, but "because of their . . .

---

[1] 83 F. Supp. 284, (N.D. Ohio, 1949).

applicability for particular use, enjoy freedom from competition, just as for certain definite uses, ball bearings are free from competition;" (ii) such competition as exists between different types of "anti-friction" bearings, is present only up to the point of adoption in the design of a particular type of equipment, all replacements thereafter must be of the same size and type; (iii) 95% of all roller bearing sales are for original installation in new equipment, and only 5% for replacement purposes. During the period 1941-45, American Timkin sold between 71% and 82% of all "tapered roller bearings" sold in the United States, while its share of the total "anti-friction" bearing market in the United States hovered around 25%. For the period 1927 to 1947, British Timkin supplied between 70% and 90% of the "tapered roller bearing" market in Great Britain but only 20% of the total "anti-friction bearing" market. For French Timkin the comparable figures for 1947 were 80% and 10%.

In 1909 American Timkin granted British Timkin's predecessor company (hereinafter also referred to as "British Timkin") an exclusive license to manufacture and sell tapered roller bearings under patents then, or in the future, owned by American Timkin in Great Britain, Continental Europe and various British dependencies, excluding Canada. American Timkin also agreed not to sell in British Timkin's territory. The 1909 agreements also required British Timkin to sell only anti-friction bearings manufactured under the licensed patents and bearing the "Timkin" trademark. It too agreed not to sell outside its licensed territories. American Timkin was granted the right to use any improvements that British Timkin might make in the basic patents. British Timkin was permitted to determine its own selling price. The 1909 agreements remained in force until the basic patents expired in 1924 at which point the patent licensing agreements were superseded by two, five-year agreements preserving essentially the division of territories worked-out in 1909 with the same conditions attached.

Up to this point British and American Timkin were wholly separate and independent companies. In 1927, American Timkin and one Michael Dewar, an officer of British Timkin's parent company, each acquired a 50% interest in British Timkin. All of the voting stock, however, was held by Dewar who ran the company's affairs throughout the period relevant to the lawsuit. The next year, 1928, British and American Timkin entered into a comprehensive series of 10-year agreements which basically tracked the exclusive territorial licensing and other provisions of the 1909 and 1924 agreements. The parties agreed to keep each other informed of any technological developments to which they were privy, and British Timkin agreed to assign to the American company any patents obtained by it in the latter's territories. Also in 1928, British and American Timkin jointly established French Timkin to which British Timkin turned over all of its rights to sell under the "Timkin" trademark in France, its colonies and dependencies.

In 1938 the basic 1928 agreements were renewed for a term that was intended to continue through 1965. The Government's lawsuit, however, intervened.

In actual operation the companies' evidenced a considerable determination not to be drawn into each other's territories. For example, the American company refused an Australian Government request to establish a plant in Australia and, when under wartime pressures, the American Company took to filling orders for use in new equipment from the British Company's customers, it did so at prices generally higher than in sales to its own customers. This was viewed by the district court as evidence of the American Company's determination not to exploit its competitive power in British Timkin's territory. Indeed, American Timkin went so far as to pressure one of its major customers into discontinuing the practice of buying large quantities from the American Company and reselling to customers in the British company's territory.

On this record the district court concluded that the three Timkin companies had restrained the foreign commerce of the United States by (1) allocating trade territories throughout the world; (2) fixing prices on products sold by any one party into the territory of the other; (3) assisting in protecting each other's markets and eliminating competition from outsiders, and (4) participating in foreign cartels which restricted exports from the United States. These restraints all constituted, in the court's opinion, violations of Section 1 of the Sherman Act. In its opinion the court also concluded that the restraints were "unreasonable *per se*."

In response to the argument that all of the restraints were merely ancillary to a joint venture (*i.e.*, partners don't have to compete with each other) the district court noted that British and French Timkin were independently managed by Dewar, that the restrictive arrangements originated in 1909 long before there was a joint venture and that the only change that took place in 1927 was American Timkin's acquisition of a stock interest in British Timkin and later in French Timkin. The execution of the 1928 contracts did not, the court thought, "mark the beginning of new business contacts, they merely extended the restrictive arrangements which had existed for almost twenty years between potential competitors." On appeal, the Supreme Court modified and affirmed.]

MR. JUSTICE BLACK delivered the opinion of the Court.

* * * *

Appellant . . . contends that the restraints of trade so clearly revealed by the District Court's findings can be justified as "reasonable," and therefore not in violation of the Sherman Act, because they are "ancillary" to allegedly "legal main transactions," namely, (1) a "joint venture" between appellant and Dewar, and (2) an exercise of appellant's right to license the trademark "Timkin."

We cannot accept the "joint venture" contention. That the trade restraints were merely incidental to an otherwise legitimate "joint venture" is, to say the least, doubtful. The District Court found that the dominant purpose of the restrictive agreements into which appellant, British Timkin and French Timkin entered was to avoid all competition either among themselves or with others. Regardless of this, however, appellant's argument must be rejected. Our prior decisions plainly establish that agreements providing for an aggregation of trade restraints such as those existing in this case are illegal under the Act. . . . The fact that there is common ownership or control of the contracting corporations does not liberate them from the impact of the antitrust laws. . . . Nor do we find any support in reason or authority for the proposition that agreements between legally separate persons and companies to suppress competition among themselves and others can be justified by labeling the project a "joint venture." Perhaps every agreement and combination to restrain trade could be so labeled.

Nor can the restraints of trade be justified as reasonable steps taken to implement a valid trademark licensing system, even if we assume with appellant that it is the owner of the trademark "Timkin" in the trade areas allocated to the British and French corporations. Appellant's premise that the trade restraints are only incidental to the trademark contracts is refuted by the District Court's finding that the "trademark provisions [in the agreements] were subsidiary and secondary to the central purpose of allocating trade territories." Furthermore, while a trademark merely affords protection to a name, the agreements in the present case went far beyond protection of the name "Timkin" and provided for control of the manufacture and sale of anti-friction bearings whether carrying the mark or not. A trademark cannot be legally used as a device for Sherman Act violations. Indeed, the Trade Mark Act of 1946 itself penalizes use of a mark "to violate the antitrust laws of the United States."

We also reject the suggestion that the Sherman Act should not be enforced in this case because what appellant has done is reasonable in view of current foreign trade conditions. The argument in this regard seems to be that tariffs, quota restrictions and the like are now such that the export and import of anti-friction bearings can no longer be expected as a practical matter; that appellant cannot successfully sell its American made goods abroad; and that the only way it can profit from business in England, France and other countries is through the ownership of stock in companies organized and manufacturing there. This position ignores the fact that the provisions in the Sherman Act against restraints of foreign trade are based on the assumption, and reflect the policy, that export and import trade in commodities is both possible and desirable. Those provisions of the Act are wholly inconsistent with appellant's argument that American business must be left free to participate in international cartels, that free foreign commerce in goods must be sacrificed in order to foster export of American dollars for investment in foreign factories which sell abroad. Acceptance of appellant's view would make the Sherman Act a dead letter insofar as it prohibits contracts and conspiracies in restraint of foreign trade. If such a drastic change is to be made in the statute, Congress is the one to do it.

Finally, appellant attacks the District Court's decree as being too broad in scope. . . . The more vigorous objection, however, is made to those portions of the decree relating to divestiture of appellant's stockholdings and other financial interests in British and French Timkin.

MR. JUSTICE DOUGLAS, MR. JUSTICE MINTON and I believe that the decree properly ordered divestiture. Our views on this point are as follows: Appellant's interests in the British and French companies were obtained as part of a plan to promote the illegal trade restraints. If not severed, the intercompany relationships will provide in the future, as they have in the past, the temptation and means to engage in the prohibited conduct. These considerations alone should be enough to support the divestiture order. . . . But there are other considerations as well.

The decree should not be overturned unless we can say that the District Court abused its discretion. Absent divestiture, it is difficult to see where other parts of the decree forbidding trade restraints would add much to what the Sherman Act by itself already prohibits. And obviously the most effective way to suppress further Sherman Act violations is to end the intercorporate relationship which has been the core of the conspiracy. For these reasons, MR. JUSTICE DOUGLAS, MR. JUSTICE MINTON and I cannot say that the District Court abused its discretion in ordering divestiture.

Nevertheless, a majority of this Court . . . believe that divestiture should not have been ordered by the District Court. Therefore, it becomes necessary to . . . [modify] the decree. As so modified, the judgment of the District Court is affirmed.

It is so ordered.

Judgment modified and affirmed.

MR. JUSTICE FRANKFURTER, dissenting.

The force of the reasoning against divestiture in this case fortifies the doubts which I felt about the Government's position at the close of argument and persuades me to associate myself, in substance, with the dissenting views expressed by MR. JUSTICE JACKSON. Even "cartel" is not a talismanic word, so as to displace the rule of reason by which breaches of the Sherman Law are determined. Nor is "division of territory" so self-operating as a category of Sherman Law violations as to dispense with analysis of the practical consequences of what on paper is a geographic division of territory.

While *American Banana Co. v. United Fruit Co.,* . . . presented a wholly different set of facts from those before us, the decision in that case does point to the fact that the circumstances of foreign trade may alter the incidence of what in the setting of domestic commerce would be a clear case of unreasonable restraint of trade.

Of course, it is not for this Court to formulate economic policy as to foreign commerce. But the conditions controlling foreign commerce may be relevant here. When as a matter of cold fact legal, financial, and governmental policies deny opportunities for exportation from this country and importation into it, arrangements that afford such opportunities to American enterprise may not fall under the ban of a fair construction of the Sherman Law because comparable arrangements regarding domestic commerce come within its condemnation.

MR. JUSTICE JACKSON, dissenting.

I doubt that it should be regarded as an unreasonable restraint of trade for an American industrial concern to organize foreign subsidiaries, each limited to serving a particular market area. If so, it seems to preclude the only practical means of reaching foreign markets by many American industries.

The fundamental issue here concerns a severely technical application to foreign commerce of the concept of conspiracy. It is admitted that if Timkin had, within its own corporate organization, set up separate departments to operate plants in France and Great Britain, as well as in the United States, "that would not be a conspiracy. You must have two entities to have a conspiracy." Thus, although a single American producer, of course, would not compete with itself, either abroad or at home, and could determine prices and allot territories with the same effect as here, that would not be a violation of the Act because a corporation cannot conspire with itself. Government counsel answered affirmatively the question of the Chief Justice: "Your theory is that if you have a separate corporation that makes the difference?" Thus, the Court applies the well established conspiracy doctrine that what it would not be illegal for Timkin to do alone may be illegal as a conspiracy when done by two legally separate persons. The doctrine now applied to foreign commerce is that foreign subsidiaries organized by an American corporation are "separate persons," and any arrangement between them and the parent corporation to do that which is legal for the parent alone is an unlawful conspiracy. I think that result places too much weight on labels.

But if we apply the most strict conspiracy doctrine, we still have the question whether the arrangement is an unreasonable restraint of trade or a method and means of carrying on competition in trade. Timkin did not sit down with competitors and divide an existing market between them. It has at all times, in all places, had powerful rivals. It was not effectively meeting their competition in foreign markets, and so it joined others in creating a British subsidiary to go after business best reachable through such a concern and a French one to exploit French markets. Of course, in doing so, it allotted appropriate territory to each and none was to enter into competition with the other or with the parent. Since many foreign governments prohibit or handicap American corporations from owning plants, entering into contracts, or engaging in business directly, this seems the only practical way of waging competition in those areas.

The philosophy of the Government, adopted by the Court, is that Timkin's conduct is a conspiracy to restrain trade solely because the venture made use of subsidiaries. It is forbidden thus to deal with and utilize subsidiaries to exploit foreign territories, because "parent and subsidiary corporations must accept the consequences of maintaining separate corporate entities," and that consequence is conspiracy to restrain trade. But not all agreements are conspiracies and not all restraints of trade are unlawful. In a world of tariffs, trade barriers, empire or domestic preferences, and various forms of parochialism from which we are by no means free, I think a rule that it is a restraint of trade to enter a foreign market through a separate subsidiary of limited scope is virtually to foreclose foreign commerce of many kinds. It is one thing for competitors or a parent and its subsidiaries to divide the United States domestic market which is an economic and legal unit; it is another for an industry to recognize that foreign markets consist of many legal and economic units and to go after each through separate means. I think this decision will restrain more trade than it will make free.

NOTES AND QUESTIONS

(1) *Timkin* has and continues to be read as declaring territorial division agreements between actual or potential competitors ("horizontal restraints") *per se* violations of Section 1 of the Sherman Act. Accord: *United States v. Sealy,*

Inc.,[2] and *United States v. Topco Associates, Inc.*[3] As between independent firms such a rule seems quite unexceptional. Market division agreements can be even more pernicious than price-fixing. They can foreclose not only price but non-price competition (quality, service, etc.), may be less vulnerable to cheating and simpler to operate. But Timkin introduces a further dimension to the problem. Precisely how far that decision reaches to interdict territorial division agreements (or price-fixing) among related companies ("an intra-enterprise arrangement") is a matter which until recently was shrouded in ambiguity. In 1984, however, the Supreme Court in *Copperweld Corp. v. Independence Tube Corp.*[4] undertook to clarify the issue but in so doing may be read as leaving matters as problematic as before.

In 1972 Lear Siegler, Inc. sold Regal Tube Co., ("Regal") a manufacturer of structural steel tubing used in heavy equipment, cargo vehicles and construction to Copperweld Corp. ("Copperweld") which thereafter managed Regal as a wholly owned subsidiary. One David Grohne was the Vice President and General Manager of Regal while it was a division of Lear Siegler. After the sale of Regal, Grohne set out to establish his own steel tubing company which he called Independence Tube Corp. In mid-February 1973, Yoder Co. accepted Independence's offer of a contract under which Yoder would construct a steel tubing plant for Independence. Two days later Yoder cancelled the agreement having in the meantime received a letter from Copperweld stating that Copperweld would be "greatly concerned if [Grohne] contemplates entering the structural tube market . . . in competition with Regal Tube" and promising to take "any and all steps . . . necessary to protect our rights under the terms of our purchase agreement . . . with Lear Siegler." In addition to contacting Yoder, Copperweld and Regal repeatedly contacted banks that were considering financing Grohne's enterprise, real estate firms with whom Grohne had discussed obtaining plant space and prospective suppliers and customers of Grohne.

Independence then sued Copperweld, Regal and Yoder charging a conspiracy in violation of Section 1 of the Sherman Act, tortious interference with its contractual relationships and breach of contract. The jury found that Yoder was not part of the conspiracy but was guilty of a breach of contract. They also found that Regal, but not Copperweld, was guilty of tortious interference with at least one potential customer of Grohne. That left Regal and Copperweld as the only conspirators under the Section 1 charge. On that charge Independence was ultimately awarded treble damages of nearly $7.5 million. The Court of Appeals affirmed and the Supreme Court reversed after reviewing the "intra-enterprise conspiracy doctrine" and concluding that a company and its wholly owned subsidiary "are incapable of conspiring with each other for purposes of Section 1 of the Sherman Act." The Court cautioned, however, that it was not deciding "under what circumstances, if any, a parent may be liable for conspiring with an affiliated corporation it does not completely own."

Two points from Chief Justice Burger's opinion for the Court are of note. First, in reviewing the cases to which the intra-enterprise conspiracy doctrine had

---

[2] 388 U.S. 350, 87 S. Ct. 1847 (1967).
[3] 405 U.S. 596, 92 S. Ct. 1126 (1972).
[4] 467 U.S. 752, 104 S. Ct. 2731 (1984).

traditionally been attributed, the Chief Justice concluded that "a finding of intra-enterprise conspiracy was in all but perhaps one instance unnecessary to the result."[5] Second, a parent and its wholly owned subsidiary had, the Chief Justice concluded:

> . . . a complete unity of interest. Their objectives are common, not disparate; their general corporate actions are guided or determined not by two separate corporate consciousnesses, but one.

With this characterization in mind the Chief Justice then went on to suggest that the result reached by the Court was largely commanded by the language of the Sherman Act. He explained:

> It cannot be denied that Section 1's focus on concerted behavior leaves a "gap" in the Act's proscription against unreasonable restraints of trade. . . . An unreasonable restraint of trade may be effected not only by two independent firms acting in concert; a single firm may restrain trade to precisely the same extent if it alone possesses the combined market power of those same two firms. Because the Sherman Act does not prohibit unreasonable restraints of trade as such — but only restraints effected by a contract, combination or conspiracy — it leaves untouched a single firm's anticompetitive conduct (short of threatened monopolization) that may be indistinguishable in economic effect from the conduct of two firms subject to Section 1 liability.
>
> . . . Congress left this "gap" for eminently sound reasons. Subjecting a single firm's every action to judicial scrutiny for reasonableness would threaten to discourage the competitive enthusiasm that the antitrust laws seek to promote. . . . Moreover, whatever the wisdom of the distinction, the Act's plain language leaves no doubt that Congress made a purposeful choice to accord different treatment to unilateral and concerted conduct. . . . [In addition] any anticompetitive activities of corporations and their wholly owned subsidiaries meriting antitrust remedies may be policed adequately without resort to an intra-enterprise conspiracy doctrine. A corporation's initial acquisition of control will always be subject to scrutiny under Section 1 of the Sherman Act and Section 7 of the Clayton Act. . . . Thereafter, the enterprise is fully subject to Section 2 of the Sherman Act . . .[6]

---

[5] Here the Chief Justice identifies as the single exception *Kiefer-Stewart Co. v. Joseph E. Seagram & Sons, Inc.*, 340 U.S. 211 (1951). In all the other cases, including *Timkin*, the affiliated conspirators, according to the Chief Justice, had at one time been independent companies and, while not free from ambiguity, the terms and circumstances by which one acquired the other were either outright violations of Section 1 (*United States v. Yellow Cab Co.*, 332 U.S. 218 (1947)), or evidence of a design "to effectuate restrictive practices" (*Timkin* 467 U.S. at 765.).

[6] Justice Stevens, joined by Justices Brennan and Marshall in dissent, observed somewhat ironically that the Court, in announcing a new *per se* rule in order to protect cooperative efforts between parent and subsidiary that would enhance their integration and competitive strength — efforts which a Rule of Reason analysis had all along protected — chose to do so in a case involving "the type of restraint that has precious little to do with effective integration between parent and subsidiary corporations." The sole purpose of the challenged conduct in Copperweld was "to exclude a potential competitor of the subsidiary from the market."

(2) The Justice Department in Case 9 of its Guidelines on International Operations[7] has gone the Supreme Court one step further.

A Multinational Operation

Alpha Corporation is a large multinational corporation headquartered in New York City. Alpha manufactures printing machines in New Jersey. It exports its printing machines only to Latin American countries. It uses non-U.S subsidiaries to manufacture and sell its products throughout the rest of the world. Although Alpha's patents . . . expired years ago, Alpha and its subsidiaries collectively have retained a dominant position in most markets because of their superior sales and service organizations, know-how, and low manufacturing costs.

Alpha's system of management involves a strong "profit center" concept. Individual subsidiaries are judged by their ability to make sales in their assigned territories. Normally, when an order comes in to one Alpha subsidiary from the assigned territory of another, the recipient sends it on, or suggests that the customer contact directly the subsidiary assigned to that territory.

[Alpha's subsidiaries are: Alpha U.K., once wholly owned, now 60% owned by Alpha servicing the U.K, Ireland and all Commonwealth countries except Canada; Beta Corp., a wholly owned Canadian subsidiary servicing Canada; Alpha GmbH acquired 38 years ago from four investors who still hold 44% of the stock (Alpha holds 56%) servicing the rest of world except the United States and markets reserved to Alpha U.K. and Beta Corp. Alpha plans to sell-off an additional 7% interest in Alpha GmbH and 50% of Beta Corp.]

Discussion

. . . [After noting *Copperweld*, the Department states:] The Court [in that case] declined to decide whether the same result would apply where a subsidiary is less than wholly-owned. In the Department's view, however, the policies underlying the Sherman Act . . . support the conclusion that a parent corporation and any subsidiary corporation of which the parent owns more than 50 percent of the voting stock are a single economic unit under common control and are thus legally incapable of conspiring with one another within the meaning of section 1. If a parent company controlled a significant but less than majority, share of the voting stock of a subsidiary, the Department would make a factual inquiry to determine whether the parent corporation actually had effective working control of the subsidiary.

In this case, prior to any stock divestitures, the Department would view Alpha and its subsidiaries as a single economic entity . . . Alpha's sale of its majority interests in the German and Canadian subsidiaries would probably not change that conclusion. [It] would retain . . . apparent effective working control of both subsidiaries. . . . If it appeared that Alpha relinquished effective working control over either subsidiary, however, then . . . any

---

[7] BNA, Antitrust and Trade Regulation Report, Vol. 55, No. 1391, Special Supplement, November 10, 1988 at page S-37.

agreement between [Alpha and that subsidiary] . . . would be subject to normal antitrust rules under section 1 of the Sherman Act.

Would *Timkin* be immunized against antitrust prosecution under the Justice Department's Guidelines?

(2) Chief Justice Berger talks of a "gap" in the Sherman Act. A "gap" there certainly is. Turn the Justice Department's Case around and consider a large multinational corporation headquartered, say in Western Europe, that commands a dominant position — say 60% — in a highly concentrated U.S. market and also occupies a comparable position in the Canadian and perhaps other national markets. Assume, that the company achieved dominance strictly by internal growth (no acquisitions or other concerted activity) and, much like Alpha in the Justice Department's Case, by low manufacturing costs and superior sales and service organizations and know-how. Assume further that the company does all its manufacturing in Western Europe but sells to non-European markets exclusively through wholly owned sales subsidiaries incorporated in each of those markets. These subsidiaries are under strict orders, carefully policed by the parent company, not to engage in any selling activity outside their assigned national territories and are required to refer any customer inquiries from outside their territory to the subsidiary in whose market the potential customer is located. With the courts having backed away from Judge Hand's "deliberateness" test of monopolization, it is very doubtful that our hypothetical multinational could ever be called to account under Section 2 of the Sherman Act so long as it acquired no companies and engaged in no efforts to eliminate, or forestall the entry of, competitors by means other than completely ethical, albeit aggressive, business conduct. Now, the Court and the Justice Department have announced that Section 1 likewise is not available. The company is entirely free to completely eliminate what might possibly be the most viable competitive force available to the American market; the Canadian subsidiary. At least that would seem to be the case.

By way of contrast, in Case 4 of its Guidelines for International Operations, the Justice Department indicates that it would very likely challenge a 100% stock acquisition by one European based company of another such company where combined the two companies would command approximately 60% of an otherwise concentrated U.S. market.[8]

(3) Perhaps now that the Supreme Court and the Justice Department have spoken in such unequivocal terms we should simply leave the matter. But, inspite of the fact that a wholly-owned subsidiary is, as the Justice Department notes, hard to distinguish from a partially owned but wholly-controlled subsidiary, the Court has still left the door open for retreat. Moreover, Chief Justice Burger to the contrary notwithstanding, the language of the Sherman Act certainly does not dictate the result in *Copperweld*. Nothing in that language compelled the Chief Justice to characterize the interaction of parent-subsidiary as "unilateral" rather than "concerted" action. And there is an altogether different analytic perspective that can be brought to bear on the matter of intra-company activity.

---

[8] BNA, Antitrust and Trade Regulation Report, Vol. 55, No. 1391, Special Supplement, November 10, 1988 at page S-28.

Particularly, in international business the selection of the form through which business is conducted usually reflects considerations having nothing whatsoever to do with antitrust law; tax considerations, the desire to shield corporate assets located in one country from the risks of doing business in another, or foreign laws that require local incorporation or local capital participation. It certainly would not be sound antitrust policy to ignore all these considerations and force companies engaged in transnational business to abandon separate incorporation solely because of antitrust concerns? On the other hand, it would be equally unsound to sweep away all concern for the threat that large multinational enterprises operating through subsidiaries can present to the maintenance of open and competitive markets, markets vital to the free-flow of trade and capital upon which a viable international economic order depends. In short, an analytic perspecitve different from the all or nothing approach taken by Chief Justice Burger in *Copperweld* and in the *Timkin* debate is needed.

(4) *Timkin* came to the Supreme Court as just one more among the many post-war cases brought by the Department of Justice as part of its vigorous and generally successful campaign to breakup the great international cartels formed in the more tolerant atmosphere of the 1920's and early 1930's.[9] While each cartel was distinctive, all involved a deliberate and continuing campaign by a group of unrelated firms to gain world-wide control of the technology necessary to the attainment of economic monopoly and through patent pooling, cross-licensing, trademark licensing and the like to divide the world into exclusive territories. This resulted in the monopolization of the American and other national markets all in violation of both Sections 1 and 2 of the Sherman Act. While *Timkin* involved patent licensing, promises to cross-license future patents and to exchange know-how, a division of territories reinforced by price-fixing and threats of boycott, the nature of the competition that the *Timkin* companies sought to suppress was not comparable to that suppressed in the other cartel cases? Explain. In answering, consider why the Justice Department did not charge American Timkin with violating Section 2 of the Sherman Act?

(5) The most frequently encountered type of restraint on intra-brand competition is the so-called "vertical restraint." And while *Timkin* involved horizontal restraints the distinction between vertical and horizontal restraints is not theoretically, as we shall see, as clear as it may at first appear. As noted earlier a "vertical restraint" is where a merchant at one level in the chain of distribution (*e.g.*, a manufacturer) imposes upon a merchant at another level (*e.g.*, a distributor) a restraint that typically consists of one or more of the following: (i) placing an upper or lower limit on the latter's resale price ("resale price maintenance"), (ii)

---

[9] The titanium cartel, *United States v. National Lead Co.*, 63 F. Supp. 513 (S.D.N.Y. 1945) aff'd 322 U.S. 319 (1947); the dyestuff and heavy chemical cartel, *United States v. General Dyestuff Corp. et. al.*, 57 F. Supp. 642 (S.D.N.Y., 1944); the cartel controlling tungsten and other carbide-based materials for tool and die-making, *United States v. General Electric Co., et. al.* (the "Carbolloy Case"), 80 F. Supp. 989 (S.D.N.Y., 1948); the incandescent lamp cartel, *United States v. General Electric Co., et. al.*, 82 F. Supp. 753 (D.N.J., 1949); the chemical cartel, *United States v. Imperial Chemical Industries Ltd., et. al.*, 100 F.Supp. 504 (S.D.N.Y.,1951); but see the unsuccessful prosecution of the cellophane cartel, *United States v. E. I. Dupont de Nemours.,et. al.*, 118 F. Supp. 41 (D. Del., 1953) aff'd 351 U.S. 377, 76 S. Ct. 994 (1956).

prohibiting sales to customers outside a prescribed geographic territory ("territorial restraint") or to particular classes of customers ("customer restraint") (iii) restricting the number and location of places from which the distributor may do business ("locational restraint"). Other vertical restraints include exclusive distributorships, "exclusive dealing" requirements (*e.g.*, a distributor may handle only products of a single manufacturer), full-line forcing and long-term supply and requirements contracts. Vertical territorial, resale price, customer and locational restraints, to the extent they impact market competition, are generally "collusive" in their effect. The other types of vertical restraints tend to be more "exclusionary" than "collusive." All, however, may, under proper conditions, be no more than devices by which potentially competing downstream merchants (distributors) use the up-stream merchant (manufacturer) as a cover for their horizontal collusion or to get rid of rivals. Alternatively, if such restraints are widely used in an industry they maybe a device for policing a cartel or "tacit" horizontal collusion among up-stream firms.

In the earliest case, *Dr. Miles Medical Co. v. John D. Park & Sons Co.*,[10] the Supreme Court, declared resale price maintenance illegal, evidencing in its decision, a strong sense that such measures were nothing more than an indirect means of price fixing. Not until 1967 did the Court in *United States v. Arnold Schwinn & Co.*,[11] extend this reasoning to territorial and customer limitations on sales by distributors and franchise retailers for their own account,[12] declaring such restraints to be *per se* illegal.

In the meantime economists began to point out some good (*i.e.*, "pro-competitive") reasons why manufacturers might impose minimum resale price and other limits on distributors and retailers. Facing strong competition from other products, perhaps attempting to penetrate a new market, a manufacturer could well decide that the best way to enhance his market share was to improve his distributors' "point-of-sale" services (showrooms, repair services, inventories and the like) or to increase local distributor advertising and other promotional activities. If improved "point-of-sale" services and better promotion were truly the road to greater profitability, one might expect distributors to initiate such improvements on their own. In both practice and theory, however, that prospect is likely to founder on the "free-rider" problem. The more profitable an expanded service or advertising effort, the more tempting it becomes for an individual distributor to let other distributors pay for the advertising, the showrooms, the inventories of spare parts or service facilities and then undercut the latter's price. The manufacturer could, of course, by contract, require each distributor to mount a more vigorous service or advertising effort and will typically do so. But it may be far more effective to establish a system of economic incentives to induce the desired effort. To this end, territorial, customer and locational restraints and even resale price maintenance can be very useful. Just as distributors will be prepared to compete by cutting prices and "free-riding" on each other's service and promotional efforts they will, if foreclosed from price competition, compete

---

[10] 220 U.S. 373 (1911).

[11] 388 U.S. 365, 87 S. Ct. 1856 (1967).

[12] Distributors could sell only to franchise retailers within their territory and franchised retailers could sell only to consumers.

against each other for a larger share of the aggregate difference between the market price and the wholesale cost of all goods sold by increasing their point-of-sale service and their promotional efforts. In fact, they will continue to do so until the marginal cost of those services equals the excess of the market price over the wholesale cost of the goods. Thus, by foreclosing price competition among distributors (*i.e.*, eliminate the "free-rider" problem) the manufacturer can establish an optimal level of distributor services and promotional activity.

In postulating an explanation for vertical restraints that undercuts the theory that such arrangements are merely devices to conceal or police horizontal collusion or ways of excluding competitors from the market, economics does not suggest that the latter can never occur. Obviously, under proper market conditions, the elimination of *intra-band* competition may seriously increase the dangers of supra-competitive pricing in the *inter-brand* market.[13] Nonetheless, in positing a "non-collusive" explanation for vertical restraints, economics has severely under-cut the tendency to analogize those restraints uncritically to horizontal price fixing or territorial division agreements. Thus, a decade after the unhappy *Schwinn* decision, *Continental T. V. Inc. v. G.T.E. Sylvania, Inc.*,[14] came to the Court. Sylvania, having suffered a decline in its national market share for television sets to about 2%, undertook, in 1962, to reorganize its distribution system by radically cutting back on the number of franchised dealers, requiring each dealer to sell only from one authorized location and reserving to itself the right to franchise additional dealers in that area. The new system apparently paid off. Within three years Sylvania had increased its market share to approximately 5%. In 1965, Sylvania, over the objections of its San Francisco dealer (Continental T.V.), decided to franchise another dealer in that city while refusing Continental permission to open a new location in Sacramento. When Sylvania sued to recover for unpaid merchandise, Continental cross-claimed contending that the locational clause in its contract constituted a *per se* violation of Section 1. The district court, relying on *Schwinn*, agreed. On appeal the Supreme Court concluded that *Schwinn* should be overruled. Writing for the Court Justice Powell noted that "vertical restrictions [can] promote interbrand competition by allowing the manufacturer to achieve certain efficiencies in the distribution of his products." By these restraints he can, the Justice observed, induce retailers to invest the capital and labor needed to exploit a new product and to engage in the promotional, service and repair activities upon which the "goodwill and competitiveness" of an established product may depend. Yet, because of what the Justice called "market imperfections such as the so-called 'free-rider' effect these services might not be provided by retailers in a purely competitive situation, despite the fact that each retailer's benefit would be greater if all provided the services than if none did."[15]

[13] It has some times been thought that resale price maintenance will also adversely affect inter-brand competition by prohibiting distributors from cutting prices to meet that competition. One must ask, however, why a manufacturer, intent upon increasing market share through expanded point-of-sales service, will not be as responsive to changes in his competitor's prices as any of his distributors.

[14] 433 U.S. 36, 97 S. Ct. 2549 (1977).

[15] More recently in *Business Electronics Corporation v. Sharp Electronics Corporation*, 108 S. Ct. 1515 (1988), the Supreme Court, while continuing to view strictly enforced resale price maintenance arrangements as *per se* violations of Section 1, refused to apply that rule

(5) *G.T.E. Sylvania* and *Timkin* have much in common. They both pertain to intra-brand restraints. While it is far from certain that the Court's decision to adopt a Rule of Reason approach to vertical intra-brand territorial restraints can necessarily be extended to the horizontal form, *United States v. Topco Associates, Inc.,*[16] it is nevertheless, useful to reconsider *Timkin* in light of the vertical restraint cases. The division of territories in *Timkin* was plainly "horizontal" was it not? Yet, might the *Timkin* companies have had either the same "pro-competitive" reasons or the same "anti-competitive" reasons for not competing with each other as Topco's members or Sylvania's distributors? How does one discern which purpose is the activating purpose? Use your imagination to ask what reasons, other than those discussed by the Court, might have actuated the *Timkin* companies' territorial restraints. What objective economic circumstances are suggestive? In answering, consider the Department of Justice Vertical Restraint Guidelines set out in the footnote.[17] What more do you need to know about the

in a case where a supplier agreed with one of its distributors to terminate another distributor for pricing too low where there was no evidence of an agreement on the price levels that the remaining distributor would charge.

[16] 405 U.S. 596, 92 S. Ct. 559 (1972). Topco, was a cooperative association of small and medium seized supermarket chains that purchased and distributed nearly one thousand different items to its members, mostly under brand names owned by Topco. The gravamen of the Government's charge was that the member companies acting through Topco were guilty of a continuing conspiracy to refrain from selling Topco brand products outside the marketing territory assigned them, all in violation of Section 1. Aggregate sales by Topco members were exceeded only by the three largest chains, A & P, Safeway and Kroger, although in no marketing territory did a Topco member's share exceed 15%. The average was 6% and the lowest 1.5%, although the Court thought that in some areas Topco members were "in as strong a competitive position . . . as any other chain." Topco answered the Section 1 charge by arguing that its "private label" vastly improved the ability of small grocery chains to compete with the big chains but that the label could only have this effect if the stores whose efforts were necessary to promote the label were assured of reaping its full benefits; an elliptical yet plain reference to the "free-rider" problem. The Court rejected the argument. The assignment of exclusive territories to Topco members, Justice Marshall wrote, was not a vertical but an "historic horizontal restraint" and hence a *per se* violation of Section 1.

[17] To dispel what it said was considerable uncertainty about the law of vertical restraints and of the Government's enforcement policies in the area, the Department of Justice in 1985 issued its "Vertical Restraint Guidelines." (See, CCH Trade Regulation Reports, P. 13,105 at page 20,575 et. seq.) The Guidelines cover territorial and customer restraints, exclusive dealing arrangements and tying. As a general matter the Guidelines state: "Vertical restraints are likely to facilitate collusion only if (after the imposition of the restraints) relatively few dealers account for most sales of the product in the geographic area, relatively few suppliers account for most of the sales in the geographic area, and the practice is widely used by large suppliers in [that] area." More specifically with regard to customer and territorial restraints and exclusive dealing the Department first defines the primary market (up-stream level) and the secondary market (downstream market in which the restraint is applied) and then outlines a two-step procedure: The first step involves an initial "market structure screen" to eliminate quickly restraints not likely to have any anti-competitive effect. The second step consists of a more carefully structured rule of reason inquiry. Under the "market structure screen," if a particular arrangement passes any one of four tests, the Department will not challenge the restraint. The tests are based on the VRI (the sum of the squares of the market share of each firm that is a party to a contract

roller-bearing industry? If, upon fuller analysis, you conclude that the *Timkin* companies' arrangement was anti-competitive, does the intra-company nature of those arrangements still concern you? What remedy should the Court decree? Does *Copperweld* make any sense?

§ 7.05   Restraints of Export Trade

[A]   The Scope of United States' Interests; A Preliminary Excursus

While the following case takes us back to the years 1929 through 1948 and we will later want to consider whether the same result would be reached under current law, it is nevertheless a rich resource for study. Given the increasing protectionist climate surrounding world trade and the uncertainties of the EEC situation after 1992, many of the practical problems which the defendants claimed necessitated their arrangements, have a very contemporary ring. More importantly, Judge Wyzanki's opinion raises a number of very basic questions of principle concerning the role that the U.S. antitrust laws should play in the world economy today; questions, whether answered by recent legislation or not, will not go away.

UNITED STATES v. MINNESOTA MINING & MANUFACTURING CO. et al.

United States District Court (Massachusetts)
92 F. Supp. 947 (1950)

WYZANSKI, DISTRICT JUDGE.

Findings of Fact

Introduction

[The Complaint] . . . charges defendants with violations of Sections 1 and 2 of the Sherman Act, . . . with respect to foreign trade and commerce in coated abrasives. . . . There are six defendants. The first four are domestic manufacturers of coated abrasives: Minnesota Mining and Manufacturing Company, Behr-Manning Corporation, The Carborundum Company and Armour and Company.

---

containing the restraint) and the "coverage ratio" (*e.g.*, if 10 suppliers each commanding 5% of the primary market use the restraint in their distributorship agreements, the coverage ratio of that market is 50%). The four tests are: (i) the firm using the restraint has 10% or less of the relevant market, (ii) a VRI under 1,200 and a coverage ratio in the same market of less than 60%, (iii) A VRI below 1,200 in both relevant markets, and (iii) a coverage ratio below 60% in both markets. For restraints not screened out at this initial step the more careful Rule of Reason analysis begins with an examination of entry conditions in the market (the easier the entry, the less concern that the restraint will have an anti-competitive effect) and then proceeds to an examination of a number of factors, many of which are similar to those considered under the Merger Guidelines, such as product homogeneity, history of collusion, availability of inputs for small or entering firms, intent, etc.

The fifth is Durex Abrasives Corporation — hereafter called the Export Company. It was originated on May 23, 1929 under the Webb-Pomerene Act[1] . . . by the first four defendants and five other former domestic manufacturers of coated abrasives. [These latter have now dropped out of the picture]. . . . The sixth is The Durex Corporation — hereafter called Durex. It also was organized by the same companies on May 23, 1929 and, as will appear later, is a corporation holding securities of foreign companies and holding foreign patents.

Prior to May 1929 the . . . nine domestic manufacturers of coated abrasives were engaged individually in the export of coated abrasives from the United States to many foreign countries, including the British Commonwealth of Nations, Germany and France. Their total sales in 1928 exceeded $3,295,000. The rate of export was increasing in 1929 and amounted to over 86% of the total dollar value of all United States exports of coated abrasives. Several of these domestic manufacturers had foreign patents and were engaged in research with the object of securing other patents. There is no satisfactory evidence that in 1929 either the export or the related patent business was conducted at either an out-of-pocket loss or at what proper accounting would show to be a loss.

In May 1929 the nine domestic manufacturers adopted a three-pronged program, each prong of which will be considered separately. . . .

Creation of the Export Company

The nine domestic producers formed the Export Company . . . to engage solely in export trade, as the term . . . is defined in the . . . Webb-Pomerene Act. The nine subscribed to the stock in the approximate proportion that those companies had exported coated abrasives in 1927 and the first ten months of 1928. However, the stock is now owned by the four manufacturing defendants. . . .

On the same day the Export Company was formed, the nine companies entered into an Export Agreement. Each company agreed to export only through the Export Company, with certain exceptions. This provision was canceled in October 1948. However, the member companies have not solicited any foreign business since 1948 but have continued to refer inquiries to the Export Company. And Minnesota, which is the only member that has actually made shipments, has dealt only with the foreign plants of American manufacturers and in each case has accounted to the Export Company . . . for the profit.

The territory of the Export Company . . . [includes] all the countries of the world except the United States and its territories and possessions. . . . The Export Company was to purchase its requirements of coated abrasives from the

---

[1] Under the Webb-Pomerene Act (31 U.S.C. Sections 61-65) competing American companies, through the formation of a corporation or other association, can combine their export operations and obtain a limited antitrust exemption. The exemption applies only to the export of "goods, wares, or merchandise." No exemption is provided if the single export operation has an anticompetitive effect in the United States or injures domestic competitors of the association members. An association seeking an exemption under the Act must file its articles of agreement and annual reports with the FTC, but preformation approval by the FTC is not required. Compare the Webb-Pomerene Act with the Export Trading Company Act of 1982, discussed in Chapter 2 *supra*. - Ed.

shareholders in proportion to their holdings of stock in the Company. [There were also provisions governing member withdrawal.[2]] . . .

Upon beginning business in 1929, the Export Company established its principal office in this country. It established a European sales manager with offices in Europe to direct the sales in Continental Europe and a sales manager in this country to handle export sales to other countries. . . .

The Export Company has purchased all its coated abrasive products on direct order from its member companies. It has . . . had three methods of distribution. One was through distributors in foreign countries with whom it made contracts. . . .

A second method was for the Export Company to sell coated abrasives to domestic exporters for export to foreign countries. These sales to American exporters have been in the neighborhood of only $150,000 to $200,000 annually. There is no evidence that the Export Company has rejected any firm order placed by any American exporter [except] . . . once in 1941 and again in January 1948. These [however] were isolated cases not reflecting a policy of the Export Company to decline to meet the needs of competing American exporters.

The third method the Export Company has used to sell coated abrasives has been through foreign subsidiaries which operate warehouses stocking American coated abrasives available for immediate delivery to distributors and others.

In seeking export business, the Export Company has always been in competition with many foreign manufacturers who have ties of nationality, local preference and sometimes of governmental subsidies or low labor costs.

The Export Company has also been in competition with American producers who are not members of the Export Company. Their export volume and their share of the market have risen steadily, increasing from 17.7% of the total American exports of abrasives in 1929 to 39.7% in 1948. This growth has occurred despite the Export Company's policy followed until 1947 of discouraging foreign distributors from handling competing products of American origin and its policy of occasionally cutting prices to meet American competition abroad. Despite these occasional cuts in price the regular practice of the Export Company has been to sell coated abrasives at prices substantially higher than those of its American competitors. There is no reason to believe that any American producer had any difficulty in obtaining foreign distributors for coated abrasives. From the record of increased sales of American competitors and from the interest of American exporters in securing defendants' products in the United States for export abroad it is transparent that at least in some foreign areas and at some times when some types of American abrasives could have been sold at some profit defendants preferred to sell abrasives made in Durex's foreign subsidiaries.

---

[2] A party to the Agreement desiring to withdraw prior to December 31, 1954 might do so on one year's notice but had to agree to refrain from competing with the Export Company until after December 31, 1956. After December 31, 1954 a party might withdraw by giving two years' notice. On June 1, 1944 the required term of the agreement not to compete was extended to December 31, 1966. - Ed.

* * * *

In meeting competition in foreign markets, the Export Company's representatives have constantly sought favorable modifications of import restrictions, dollar shortages, discriminatory tariffs and the like. The Company has sought to sell abrasives made in the United States when they could be sold as profitably as abrasives made in its foreign subsidiaries. With this object in mind, the Export Company has consistently instructed its representatives to steer to it business which could be as profitably handled by the Export Company as by a Durex subsidiary.

Creation of Durex and Its Subsidiaries

As already stated above on May 23, 1929 the same nine domestic producers of coated abrasives that formed the Export Company also formed Durex. Both the Export Company and Durex have had the same representatives of their member companies serving on their boards of directors and have had the same persons as executive officers, but not the same employees or sales forces. The assets and records of the two companies have not been co-mingled. The charter of Durex prohibits it from owning securities of any company engaged in importing into the United States.

In 1929 Durex formed and acquired 84% of the stock of Durex Abrasives, Ltd., which operated a coated abrasives plant in Great Britain. In 1930 Durex formed and acquired all the stock of Canadian Durex Abrasives, Ltd., which operates a . . . plant in Canada. In 1935 Durex acquired a plant in Germany.

The formation of Durex and its English and Canadian subsidiaries was motivated by the recrudescence of economic nationalism after World War I. American manufacturers found that the establishment of foreign branch factories was a convenient way to hurdle wartime economic restrictions, to save transportation expenses and import duties, to overcome prejudice respecting imported goods, to take advantage of local sentiment and regulations furthering local enterprise and to comply with local patent laws.

The German subsidiary reflects the impact of the even more aggressive type of economic nationalism characteristic of Hitler's Germany. . . .

Durex now has completed plans for . . . one other foreign coated abrasives plant . . . in Australia to be operated by a subsidiary it organized in 1945 . . . [and] has under consideration plans for converting machinery in existing tape plants in South America and for a tape plant in South Africa.

Patent Agreements

On May 23, 1929 the nine member companies entered into what is here called "the main patent agreement." The general scheme was for each member company to license Durex under all its foreign patents relating to coated abrasives but to reserve rights to fix prices and standards of manufacture for patented products. The particular method can be illustrated with reference to waterproof sandpaper. Minnesota agreed to license Durex under its foreign patents relating to waterproof sandpaper; the other members agreed to assign to Minnesota foreign patents covering waterproof sandpaper inventions; Durex was to have a license under the assigned patents; and if the assignor withdrew from the main patent agreement it was to have non-exclusive licenses under the patents. With respect to foreign patents relating to discs, Carborundum had the same position as Minnesota had with respect to foreign patents relating to waterproof sandpaper.

On January 3, 1933 Behr-Manning and Durex and Armour and Durex entered into substantially similar license agreements relating to foreign patents covering respectively electrocoated sandpaper and heat-treated garnet abrasives.

A member's participation in the main patent agreement could be terminated only by a two years' notice served after December 31, 1954 or by dissolution, bankruptcy or certain defaults of a member. If a membership in the agreement terminated, the withdrawing member was obliged until December 31, 1950 to grant licenses on new patents; and the termination had no effect on outstanding licenses of old patents.

Concurrently with the execution of the main patent agreement each member gave the promised license to Durex. . . . With the exception of sales to the Export Company . . . this was an exclusive license not only for foreign manufacture but also for export sale from the United States. On its part, Durex agreed not to import into the United States any product in which the patented inventions were used and to pay royalties and to abide by specified customary obligations of a license, as well as the prices and standards stipulated by Minnesota.

After securing these licenses, Durex granted sublicenses with similar reservations to its subsidiaries each of which was given a license which was virtually exclusive except that it was limited to manufacture and sale in that subsidiary's country. . . .

In 1941 the . . . license agreements were each terminated and the main patent agreement was modified in these among other respects. . . . [T]he member companies agreed to make available to Durex . . . exclusive rights under all foreign patents . . . [and gave-up] their reserved rights to fix prices and standards . . . Durex agreed to assign on demand to Minnesota, Carborundum and Behr Manning, respectively, any United States patents acquired by Durex [on certain products] . . . and to all the members on a non-exclusive basis any other United States patents acquired by Durex . . . [Upon termination] [a]ny foreign patents which Durex might have acquired from other sources . . . were to go to Minnesota, Carborundum and Behr-Manning . . . who were required to grant the other members non-exclusive licenses thereunder. All Durex's other foreign patents were to become the joint property of the member companies. The term of the main patent agreement was extended to December 31, 1964 and for a period of not less than two years thereafter.

Relations between the Export Company and Durex Subsidiaries

Neither Durex nor any of its subsidiaries has made any agreement with the Export Company or any domestic or foreign manufacturer covering imports into the United States or commerce within the United States.

In some situations where economic and political situations curtailed the Export Company's opportunity to export profitably it arranged for a Durex subsidiary to supply the particular export.

Beginning in 1930 the Export Company arranged with Durex's British subsidiary to supply British Crown Colonies, British India, Egypt, Palestine, Iraq, Iran, Arabia and British Oceania possessions. . . . The Export Company has not, however, abandoned attempts to sell in those areas.

* * * *

In 1932 the Export Company arranged with Durex's British subsidiary to supply Durex coated abrasives in Australia and New Zealand. . . . These arrangements were made after a sharp fall of the Export Company's shipments . . . in the depression years 1930-1932 . . . [and] after discriminatory or preferential changes in . . . tariffs and . . . the sharp fall in the value of the pound. Several times after 1933 the Export Company considered abrogating the arrangements but the tariff and foreign exchange situation made it more economical to supply the market through Durex's British subsidiary. In 1939 Durex notified . . . [its] distributors [in the area] that the arrangement with the Export Company was terminated. However, the outbreak of World War II with its embargoes, currency difficulties and the like frustrated that announced termination.

The sales of Durex's British subsidiary to Australia and New Zealand from 1933 through 1946 were generally well over $150,000 a year, and indeed in 1941 over $400,000. The Canadian subsidiary's sales in this area exceed $750,000 in 1948. Meanwhile the Export Company made virtually no sales in this market; its Australian volume dropped from over $191,000 in 1929 to less than $3,100 in 1948. . . .

* * * *

From March 24, 1937 through 1940 the Export Company acted under a formal "general agency agreement" whereby the British subsidiary of Durex supplied coated abrasives to such of Export's European distributors as Export designated at a commission of 10% payable to Export. The reasons were difficulties of dollar exchange, import restrictions, customer preference and sometimes mere convenience. The sales thus handled in each of the four years 1937-1940 were [all] under $27,000. . . . In the same years the Export Company's sales to the same countries . . . [ranged from $153,000 to $590,000].

* * * *

In 1937 the Export Company agreed with Durex's German subsidiary to have the latter sell certain of its products in Hungary, Poland, Roumania, Bulgaria, Denmark and Italy for a commission of 10% (after 1939, 5%) payable to the Export Company in Reichsmarks or blocked account currency. The reason for this arrangement was that these countries lacked dollar funds, had import restrictions and often were under German influence. After Germany invaded Czechoslovakia and the U.S.S.R. took over the Baltic states those countries were supplied by Durex's German subsidiary. . . .

From 1939 until 1948 Durex had no control over Durex's [German subsidiary]. . . . In the latter half of 1949 the Export Company made a new 10% commission agreement with that . . . subsidiary covering Hungary, Czechoslovakia and Yugoslavia. These "iron curtain" countries presented problems of currency and import restriction.

On June 6, 1946, the Export Company agreed with Durex's Canadian subsidiary that, at a 10% commission (reduced in 1948 to 7 1/2%) payable to Export, the Canadian subsidiary should supply abrasives to designated Export distributors. So far Export has designated Australian distributors and two Dutch distributors. The Australian customers were included because the British subsidiary of Durex could not supply them; the Dutch were included because they were unable to obtain dollar exchange for all their requirements of coated abrasives from the United States.

. . . These findings must be read together with the records of the purely internal business done during the same period of time by these same British, Canadian and German Durex subsidiaries. As illustrative, it should be noted that taken together the external and internal sales of the Durex British subsidiary increased from under $1,680,000 in 1938 to over $5,488,000 in 1948 (while the Export Company's exports to Britain fell from over one million dollars in 1929 to less than nine thousand dollars in 1948 and while the Export Company was discontinuing all its own distributors in England). It is not shown at what rate of profit the British subsidiary did business in these years. [But for the years] . . . 1936 and 1937, . . . on a business of $4,270,000 stockholders holding 84% of the stock received dividends of $1,540,076 or at a rate of over 42% of the gross sales. The combined external and internal sales of the Durex Canadian subsidiary increased from under $518,000 in 1938 to over $2,035,000 in 1948 (while the Export Company's exports to Canada fell from over $423,000 in 1928 to less than $69,000 in 1948). With respect to the German situation it will be enough to observe that in 1948 Durex's German subsidiary sold half a million dollars' worth of coated abrasives while the Export Company sold none in the German or "iron curtain" areas.

However, if it be material at the same time that there was a decline in the exports of coated abrasives from the United States to the British Commonwealth of Nations there was an increase in the exports of raw materials and supplies. Whereas in 1929 there were exports of only $67,000 of raw materials to Durex's British subsidiary and none to Durex's Canadian subsidiary, by 1948 the respective figures were over $685,000 and $434,000.

Opinion

Relying on Sections 1 and 2 of the Sherman Act, the Government in Count 2 complains of the combined action in the field of foreign commerce of the dominant American manufacturers of coated abrasives. Defendants answer that they took these joint steps to preserve and expand their foreign markets which were disappearing in the face of foreign countries' tariffs, quotas, import controls, dollar shortages, foreign exchange restrictions, local preference campaigns and like nationalistic measures. . . . They gladly concede that before May 1929 they exported from the United States substantial quantities of coated abrasives to many parts of the world including the United Kingdom, Canada, Australia, New Zealand, Germany and the countries now behind the "iron curtain;" that they do not do so in the same volume any longer; and that they supply substantial quantities of abrasives to those same areas from factories located abroad in which they are jointly beneficially interested. But they say, and their exhibits are offered to show, that the reason that they no longer make substantial exports from the

United States to those areas is that they cannot do so profitably because of the economic and political barriers that others have erected. The diminution of their American exports to those areas, they allege, is not the consequence of their design or desire or conduct. The fault lies not in themselves but in their destiny determined by the machinations of foreign rulers and by the desires of foreign peoples.

With part of the defendants' argument there can be no legitimate quarrel. It is axiomatic that if over a sufficiently long period American enterprises, as a result of political or economic barriers, cannot export directly or indirectly from the United States to a particular foreign country at a profit, then any private action taken to secure or interfere solely with business in that area, whatever else it may do, does not restrain foreign commerce in that area in violation of the Sherman Act. For, the very hypothesis is that there is not and could not be any American foreign commerce in that area which could be restrained or monopolized.

[This being so] . . . it is legitimate for defendants to show such political and economic conditions, if they exist. . . . [T]he nub of the case, [therefore] is . . . whether defendants' political and economic exhibits, . . . taken together with the other evidence in the case, prove that defendants could not have profitably exported from the United States a substantial volume of coated abrasives to the areas supplied by their jointly owned factories located in England, Canada and Germany. To answer this factual question it is necessary to examine the situation in some of the principal areas so supplied.

The most significant area because of the large volume of actual and potential business is the United Kingdom. Defendants' contention is that after 1929 it was impractical to continue to export . . . to Britain because of Empire preference measures including official tariff restrictions and the more subtle aspects of a "Buy British" campaign. . . .

It is not claimed that the United Kingdom imposed a legal ban upon imports of abrasives. Nor is it asserted that economically no American coated abrasives could be profitably exported to the British market. . . . Stated another way this means, as we shall see, only that it was more profitable to make abrasives in Britain than to export them to Britain.

In support of their position defendants place great reliance on two points: first, that the prices at which they sold goods they made in England were much lower than the prices at which the sold goods they made in the United States and landed in England . . . and second, that in Australia and New Zealand — countries which have been subjected to the same economic and political factors that affected the British market but where defendants had no joint manufacturing subsidiary — neither they nor their American competitors could sell a large volume of American-made abrasives.

A difficulty with the tabular comparison of defendants' prices for American-made and British-made abrasives is that it shows merely prices set by defendants. It does not show respective rates of profit. If there are large profits included in the prices set, then the table shows nothing more than that defendants could make large profits with American-made goods and even larger profits with British-made goods. And this possibility is by no means fanciful. The net profits in the prices set for defendants' British-made goods were at a higher than 42% rate in 1937. . . . Suppose the unrevealed net profits in the prices set for defendants' American-made goods were equally high. Then defendants would still have had a not unattractive rate of profit if they had reduced prices on their American-made goods to the level of their prices on British-made goods. And if it is further supposed that Durex's British subsidiary had not existed, presumably a respectable fraction of its business of millions of dollars a year would have gone to the Export Company selling the same goods at the same prices.

Defendants' reference to Australia and New Zealand is buttressed by statistics for the years 1929 through 1932. . . . During those years Durex subsidiaries did not manufacture in or ship to that area. Yet the exports from the Export Company to Australia fell from $191,999 to $61,000, and to New Zealand from $43,000 to $3,000. . . . [By comparison] the decline in the same years of the Export Company's trade with Great Britain . . . was from $1,045,000 to $26,000. One can hardly maintain therefore that the Australian experience proves that the decline in the Export Company's commerce with the United Kingdom was attributable not to defendants but to factors universal in the British Commonwealth of Nations. . . .

Defendants make some other points worth answering.

They note that their American competitors did not succeed in selling a large volume of American goods either to those parts of the British Empire where Durex had factories or to other parts where Durex neither had factories nor shipped goods. And defendants say that this shows that after 1929 the Empire markets were closed to American goods. The reason that the argument is invalid . . . is that it does not prove that if Durex competition had not existed the market could not have been reached by both the Export Company and its American competitors . . . [and] it does not appear that American competitors' abrasives were ever as of good quality or as much in demand as defendants' abrasives, or . . . that the American competitors get much less business from the British Commonwealth now than they secured in a normal pre-depression year.

* * * *

Next, defendants urge that they have always preferred to sell products made in their American factories. . . . Of course, no one doubts that if it were equally profitable to get British business for . . . [American] factories and . . . receive payment in dollars [rather than] . . . pounds, defendants would elect the former. The fact that defendants used their British factories therefore justifies an inference that under the political and economic conditions in the United Kingdom defendants found it less profitable to sell from the United States factories than from the United Kingdom factories. It does not, and nothing else in the case can, justify a finding of fact that if defendants had not themselves established joint foreign factories it would have been legally or economically impossible to sell at some profit a substantial volume of defendants' American-made coated abrasives.

In short this Court finds as an ultimate fact that defendants' decline in exports to the United Kingdom is attributable less to import and currency restrictions of that nation and to the preferential treatment afforded to British goods by British customers than to defendants' desire to sell their British-made goods at a large profit rather than their American-made goods at a smaller profit and in a somewhat (but not drastically) reduced volume.

The Canadian situation does not differ from the British in substance. . . .

The only other market which deserves special notice in this opinion is Germany and its former satellites. In 1934 it became apparent that although abrasives could be exported from the United States to Germany the shippers could receive only blocked marks in payment. . . . And the situation grew progressively worse in Germany and Eastern European countries as the Nazi power increased and spread in 1938-1939 to Austria, Czechoslovakia and Poland. Drastic as these measures were they did not absolutely prohibit the export of American abrasives at some profit to the German controlled area because triangular or barter trade was a possibility open to defendants. But it is not necessary to rest on that point. For after the cessation of hostilities five years ago the Nazi restrictions disappeared. There is no showing that now or at any time since 1945 it has been impossible for American abrasives to be exported to the German area at a profit.

There is not much left to this case once the Court has by its ultimate finding of fact rejected defendants' argument that not they but foreign principalities and powers make it impossible to export American abrasives in substantial volume at a profit to large parts of the British Commonwealth of Nations and Germany.

Prima facie there could hardly be a more obvious violation of Section 1 of the Sherman Act than for American manufacturers controlling four-fifths of the export trade of an industry to agree not to ship to particular areas but to do their business there through jointly owned foreign factories. It is, in statutory language, a "combination . . . or conspiracy, in restraint of trade or commerce . . . with foreign nations."

One aspect of this restraint has operated upon the commerce with foreign nations of the four manufacturing defendants and of the Export Company. The restraint has consisted in their united forbearance from supplying to certain areas American-made goods when other companies owned jointly by the manufacturing defendants could supply to those same areas equivalent foreign-made goods. To achieve the restraint they have not merely established jointly owned foreign factories. They have also by a concert of action conformed to arrangements not to export from the United States to those areas. These arrangements have included the temporary or permanent decision of the Export Company not to ship to areas where Durex subsidiaries could ship or sell more profitably; the formal agreement from May 1929 through October 1948 of each of the American manufacturing defendants not to export except through the Export Company; and the practice of all of these manufacturing defendants since that date to refrain from making individual exports, with the minor exception of a few exports by Minnesota to foreign plants of American companies. Such a concert constituted a conspiracy within the intendment of Section 1 of the Sherman Act.

Another aspect of this restraint has operated upon the commerce with foreign nations of defendants' American competitors in the coated abrasives industry. The restraint has consisted in the effect of defendants' jointly owned foreign factories' precluding their American competitors from receiving business they might otherwise have received from the markets served by these jointly owned foreign factories. It may be that the American competitors would not have received all or most of the business of these subsidiaries. The competitors might not have got the business because they may have made inferior products or may have been less aggressive merchants. The business, if it had not gone to Durex subsidiaries, might have gone in whole or in large part to the Export Company. But such speculation is unnecessary. When a dominant group of American manufacturers in a particular industry combine to establish manufacturing plants in a foreign area to which the evidence shows that it is legally, politically and economically possible for some American enterprises to export products in reasonable volume, then it is not necessary in an injunction suit brought by the Government to show that particular American competitive enterprises would have exported profitably to that area. The showing of the combination together with the showing of the possibility of profitable American exports in reasonable volume proves a violation of Section 1 of the Sherman Act. *Cf. United States v. United States Alkali Export Ass'n.* [3] . . .

It is no excuse for the violations of the Sherman Act that supplying foreign customers from foreign factories is more profitable and in that sense is, as defendants argue, "in the interests of American enterprise" . . . Financial advantage is a legitimate consideration for an individual non-monopolistic enterprise. It is irrelevant where the action is taken by a combination and the effect, while it may redound to the advantage of American finance, restricts American commerce. For Congress in the Sherman Act has condemned whatever unreasonably restrains American commerce regardless of how it fattens profits of certain stockholders. Congress has preferred to protect American competitors, consumers and workmen.

Nor is it any excuse that the use of foreign factories has increased the movement of raw materials from American to foreign shores. We may disregard the point that the books are not in balance when raw materials actually transported are set off against finished products potentially transported. It is more significant that Congress has not said you may choke commerce here if you nourish it there.

Nor is it any excuse that . . . in many markets, South American, for example, defendants have been expanding their export business and that in almost all markets defendants' American competitors have been getting a constantly larger share of the available business. What defendants are charged with is restraining not eliminating export trade. If defendants had never joined to operate factories abroad, both their and possibly their competitors' export trade would have been considerably greater.

Nor is it any excuse that American export trade might have been equally adversely affected if there had been — or if there should now be — established plants in Great Britain, Canada and Germany by one or more of the manufacturing defendants acting independently. Such suppositious individual action would, it is true, be a restraint upon American commerce with foreign nations. But such a restraint would not be the result of a combination or conspiracy. Hence it would not run afoul of Section 1 of the Sherman Act. Nor would it, so far as now appears, have the purpose or effect of promoting one company's monopoly in violation of

---

[3] 86 F.Supp. 59, 70, 76 (S.D.N.Y).

Section 2 of the Sherman Act. Indeed the decree to be entered in this case will expressly contemplate allowing just such individual operation of foreign factories. For nothing in this opinion can properly be read as a prohibition against an American manufacturer seeking to make larger profits through the mere ownership and operation of a branch factory abroad which is not conducted as part of a combination, conspiracy or monopoly.

[At this point Judge Wyzanski suggests that in addition to charging a restraint of "foreign commerce," the Justice Department might amend its complaint to charge a "combination in restraint of commerce among the several States" in violation of Section 1 of the Sherman." He explains]:

. . . The intimate association of the principal American producers in day-to-day manufacturing operations, their exchange of patent licenses and industrial know-how, and their common experience in marketing and fixing prices may inevitably reduce their zeal for competition inter sese in the American market. And [since such] . . . a combination of producers . . . has not the benefit of the statutory immunity of the Webb-Pomerene or any other Act of Congress . . . [i]t may . . . be subject to condemnation regardless of the reasonableness of the manufacturers' conduct in the foreign countries . . .[4]

* * * *

In view of the conclusion that defendants violated Section 1 of the Sherman Act in their establishment of Durex and its manufacturing subsidiaries in England, Canada and Germany there is no occasion to consider any possible violation of Section 2 of the Sherman Act by Durex or its subsidiaries.

The Government contends that this Court should decree the termination of the American abrasives manufacturers' joint control not only of Durex and its foreign manufacturing and other subsidiaries but also of the Export Company organized under the Webb-Pomerene Act.

[This Judge declined to do. An injunction against the Export Company was an "adequate remedy." Nevertheless, the Judge concluded that if the Export Company was to continue some changes had to be made. The manufacturers' agreement not to withdraw from the group or at least not to export independently at any time before 1966 was unreasonably long. The Export Company's practice of establishing prices 10% to 30% higher for competitive American exporters than for the unit's own foreign distributors could continue only so long as justified by the costs of certain added services the distributors allegedly performed. He concludes:]

* * * *

Purged of their connection with Durex, Durex subsidiaries and the whole Durex program . . . the Export Agreement and the Export Company will not be in violation of the Sherman Act. . . .

Decree for plaintiff in accordance with this opinion.

---

[4] Apparently the Justice Department never picked-up on the Judge's suggestion. - Ed.

NOTES AND QUESTIONS

(1) Judge Wyzanski finds the defendants' guilty of violating section 1 of the Sherman Act because they conspired to restrain two categories of trade. Define them.

(2) Note that up until 1929 Minnesota, Behr-Manning, Carborundum, and Armour had each been separately engaged in exporting their products in competition with each other. Suppose in that year, each had separately established manufacturing subsidiaries in Great Britain, Canada and Germany, assigning exclusive foreign territories to each subsidiary and separately discontinuing exports to those territories. On this evidence would Judge Wyzanski have found any, or all, of the defendants guilty of either of the trade restraints identified in your answer to Note (1) above? He tells you.

(3) Assume, that prior to the formation of the Export Company each of the defendants established a separate foreign manufacturing subsidiary in Britain, Canada and Germany and that each discontinued any export sales into the exclusive territories assigned those subsidiaries. Next, assume that later, through an asset merger, they combined the separate subsidiaries into a single manufacturing operation, one in Canada, one in Great Britain and the other in Germany and that they continued their policy of not exporting to the foreign markets reserved to those companies. The question is, all other conditions being the same, would the combining of foreign manufacturing operations have increased, decreased or have had no effect on U.S. exports as they existed immediately before the manufacturing operations were combined? Specifically consider the following:

(a) How would the combination affect direct exports by the defendants themselves?

(b) How would the combination affect exports by other American companies? In answering, note that Judge Wyzanski concluded that the combined manufacturing operations (*i.e.*, Durex subsidiaries) were probably more profitable for the defendants than their own direct exports. This could be because:

(i) The subsidiaries had lower costs or because . . .?

(ii) If the latter, what impact would that likely (certainly) have on exports by other American companies? Note that the other American companies had apparently been steadily increasing their share of American exports.

(iii) If the Durex subsidiaries could manufacture at lower costs, application of the U.S. antitrust laws to bar the combination would raise, would it not, a very basic question of principle? Explain.

In short, if the establishment of separate foreign manufacturing subsidiaries and the discontinuance of exports in competition with those subsidiaries would not constitute an illegal restraint of trade, can the combination of those subsidiaries constitute an illegal restraint? If not, then consider the next Note.

(4) Turning to the Export Company, note that it would have been perfectly legal if the defendants, without establishing foreign manufacturing subsidiaries, had

merely formed the Export Company and discontinued direct exports in competition with that Company. With this and your answer to Note (3) in mind, it would appear that Judge Wyzanski's holding is that:

(a) The defendants could *combine their foreign manufacturing operations* and individually discontinue exporting (Note 3);

(b) Defendants could *combine their foreign export operations* (Export Company) and individually discontinue exporting; but

(c) Defendants could not *combine their foreign manufacturing operations* and discontinue their *combined export operations.*

Are you persuaded?

(5) Drawback from the technical analysis of the previous Notes and consider what purpose the defendants may have had in mind when they established their three-way combination; Durex, the Export Company and the Patent Agreement. What further information do you need to either confirm (or refute) your suspicions? In answering, consider the discussion of the *Timkin* case. There is some evidence in Judge Wyzanski's opinion relevant to this point. Is it consistent with your worst suspicions?

(6) If your worst suspicions are confirmed, that would raise some very fundamental issues which the ensuing materials are intended to explore.

[B] Contemporary Developments

[1] The Justice Department Guidelines

In the Introduction to its Guidelines For International Operations, the Department of Justice had the following to say:

> The U.S. antitrust laws are the legal embodiment of our nation's commitment to a free market economy. The competitive process, unimpeded by privately and governmentally imposed barriers, ensures the most efficient allocation of our resources and the maximization of consumer welfare. In enforcing the U.S. antitrust laws, the U.S. Department of Justice . . . focuses its resources on protecting U.S. consumers from anticompetitive conduct. The Department does not seek to reach anticompetitive conduct that has no effect, or only a remote effect, on U.S. consumer welfare.[5]

Elsewhere the Guidelines take note of the fact that, under the Foreign Trade Antitrust Improvement Act which added a new Section 6a to the Sherman Act (see discussion *infra*), U.S. antitrust jurisdiction extends to conduct that has a direct effect on the export trade of persons engaged in that trade in the United States. Nevertheless, the Guidelines state: the "Department is concerned only with adverse effects on competition that would harm U.S. consumers by reducing output or raising prices."[6]

---

[5] BNA, Antitrust & Trade Regulation Report, Vol. 55, No. 1391, Special Supplement, November 10, 1988 at page S-3.

[6] *Id.* at page S-21. If the U.S. Government is financing the exports, then the Justice Department is concerned with conduct that restrains export trade.

In short, the Department appears to have embraced two basic ideas. First, that the U.S. Government should be concerned with the social costs of monopoly only to the extent they impose opportunity costs on consumers. From what you know of monopoly theory, is this sound? Second, those costs can safely be ignored if borne by foreign consumers.

This latter position appears to reflect a number of considerations. First, that the protection of foreigners is first and foremost properly the business of the foreigners' own law. Second, it may reflect a certain responsiveness to repeated foreign accusations of overreaching in United States antitrust enforcement. Underlying both of these considerations may be the thought that other nations should be free, without instruction or intervention by the United States, to construct their own economic and political institutions along lines dictated by their own social values and traditions. Lastly, the Department may be responding to repeated claims by American business groups that U.S. antitrust laws disadvantage them in competition with foreign firms that suffer under no such regulatory threat. This latter claim raises a host of questions and is utterly problematic at best. It seems to suggest that a law forcing companies to compete makes them less competitive. Be that as it may, the Justice Department's position should be placed into a broader context. Consider the following problem.

PROBLEM

Suppose all of the American producers of a product entered into an international cartel with their leading foreign competitors under which (i) the American producers divided up certain *foreign markets* among themselves agreeing not to export in competition with each other in those markets and (ii) agreed collectively to refrain from exporting to other specified foreign markets in competition with the foreign members of the cartel, while the latter, in turn, gave comparable undertakings *inter se* and with respect to the markets reserved to the Americans. The agreement also provided that it was to have no application to the U.S. market and there was, in fact, no appreciable diminution of competition among the parties — United States and foreign — in that market. Suppose, that as a result of this arrangement the quantity of United States exports declined significantly while each American participant's export profits increased? If, upon finding no restraint of trade affecting U.S. consumers,[7] the Justice Department took no action in this case, consider some broader issue.

---

[7] The Guidelines do note that "the export conduct of U.S. firms conceivably could have [an anticompetitive effect on the U.S. market] if supply in the relevant U.S. and foreign export markets were fixed or highly inelastic and U.S. firms accounting for a substantial share of the domestic market agreed on the level of their exports in order to reduce supply and raise prices in the United States. Second, it could have such an effect if conduct that ostensibly involved exports were actually designed to affect the price of products that were to be sold or resold in the United States." *Id.* at page S-21. The second case described by the Guidelines appears to echo Judge Wysanki's suggestion to the Justice Department in *Minnesota Mining.*

(1) Practically, the Government of the United States must continuously be engaged in improving its own citizens' access to foreign business opportunities, or protecting them against the loss of those opportunities. Can this be effectively done by a policy that broadly professes indifference to any loss of welfare by foreign citizens at the hands of American companies?

(2) Can any policy which would be indifferent to the cartel described in the Problem while professing concern for American consumers avoid being discredited?

(3) How widely applicable is the assumed capability of foreign governments to protect their own citizens from the depredations of American enterprise? Where they are capable (*e.g.*, EEC), comity may well dictate restraint, but then in that case the American companies are less likely to embark on such ventures.

(4) From a purely nationalistic perspective, can the United States with its interest in a well functioning world economy, afford to ignore cartels of this type? Consider, in this connection the basic economic principles underlying the General Agreement on Tariffs and Trade (GATT) and the specific measures taken by the members of the GATT in furtherance of those principles. Observe, that when the nations of Western Europe embarked upon the creation of a "common-market" they deemed it essential to include in the treaty establishing that market, two provisions (Articles 85 and 86 of the Treaty of Rome) which bear important similarities to the Sherman Act and have, through rigorous enforcement, rendered antitrust a significant component of EEC law. What is the relationship between "free trade" and "antitrust" that seems to have guided European thinking? Does the Justice Department appear to have ignored the European experience?

(5) Is adherence to the Justice Department's position necessary in order for United States antitrust enforcement to conform with the "territorial principle" of prescriptive jurisdiction under international law? Would the British even argue the point?

[2] The Foreign Trade Antitrust Improvement Act (Section 6a of The Sherman Act): Some Interpretive Problems

The Department of Justice's 1977 Guidelines on International Operations,[8] took the position that the U.S. antitrust laws should be confined to protecting U.S. consumers — the position carried over in the 1988 Guidelines — and "to protect[ing] American export and investment opportunities against privately imposed restrictions."[9] The view expressed by the 1977 Guidelines was accepted by Congress when it enacted the Foreign Trade Antitrust Improvements Act of 1982[10] adding a new Section 6a to the Sherman Act as follows:

Section 6a. This Act shall not apply to conduct involving trade or commerce (other than import trade or import commerce) with foreign nations unless—

---

[8] Department of Justice, Guidelines on Antitrust and International Operations, January 26, 1977.

[9] It is with this latter function that the 1988 Guidelines take issue, confining the Department's interest in restraints of export trade only if they are likely to result in higher prices in the American market or apply to U.S. government financed exports. See text accompanying Note 6, *supra.*

[10] Pub. L. 97-290, Title IV, 96 Stat. 1246, October 8, 1982.

   (1)   such conduct has a direct, substantial, and reasonably foreseeable effect—

      (A)   on trade or commerce which is not trade or commerce with foreign nations, or on import trade or import commerce with foreign nations; or

      (B)   on export trade or export commerce with foreign nations, of a person engaged in such trade or commerce in the United States; and

   (2)   such effect gives rise to a claim under the provisions of this Act, other than this section.

      If this Act applies to such conduct only because of the operation of paragraph (1)(B), then this Act shall apply to such conduct only for injury to export business in the United States. [11]

In its report on the proposed amendment [12] the House Judiciary Committee noted that since *Alcoa* "it has been relatively clear that it is the situs of the effects as opposed to the conduct, that determines whether United States antitrust law applies." Then noting with approval the Justice Department 1977 Guide, which it characterizes as faithful to the teachings of *Alcoa*, the Committee Report continues:

> The intent of . . . [the proposed amendment] is to exempt from the antitrust laws conduct that does not have the requisite domestic effects. . . . While [the amendment] . . . preserves antitrust protections in the domestic market-place for all purchasers, regardless of nationality or the situs of the business, a different result will obtain when the conduct is solely export-oriented. Thus, a price-fixing conspiracy directed solely to exported products or services, absent a spillover effect on the domestic marketplace . . . would normally not have the requisite effects on domestic or import commerce. Foreign buyers injured by such export conduct would have to seek recourse in their home courts.

> If such solely export-oriented conduct affects export commerce of another person doing business in the United States, both the Sherman and FTC Act amendments preserve jurisdiction insofar as there is injury to that person. Thus, a domestic exporter is assured a remedy under our antitrust laws for injury caused by unlawful conduct of a competing United States exporter. But a foreign firm whose non-domestic operations were injured by the very same export oriented conduct would have no remedy under our antitrust laws. This result is assured by the Committee's inclusion of the final sentence in the Sherman Act amendments. . . .

---

[11] 15 U.S.C. Section 6a.

[12] House Committee on the Judiciary, Report on H.R. 5235, H.R. Rep. No. 686, 97th Cong., 2d Sess., pages 5-12 (1982) reprinted in [1982] United States Code Cong. and Ad. News, 2490-2497).

[Lastly], to make certain that the bill . . . was not intended to confer jurisdiction on injured foreign persons when that injury arose from conduct with no anti-competitive effects in the domestic marketplace . . . [the] Committee added language . . . to require that the "effect" providing the jurisdictional nexus must also be the basis for the injury alleged under the antitrust laws. . . .

THE CASE OF THE SUNKIST ORANGES

In *Pacific Coast Agricultural Export Association v. Sunkist Growers, Inc.,*[13] plaintiffs, a Webb-Pomerene Association composed of seven fruit exporting companies and M-C International Inc., an independent fruit exporter, charged Sunkist, an association of citrus growers in Arizona and California, with having restrained and monopolized the export trade in oranges from Arizona and California to Hong Kong, all in violation of Section 1 and Section 2 of the Sherman Act. Over 75% of the oranges grown in Arizona and California were produced by Sunkist growers and marketed through various Sunkist regional exchanges and, internationally, through its Export Department.[14]

Until 1966 Sunkist made virtually no direct sales to Hong Kong. Rather, its Export Department sold to a variety of American exporters who resold to Hong Kong importers. Chief among these exporters were the plaintiffs for whom Sunkist was the principal source of supply. In 1966 Sunkist decided to start making direct sales to Hong Kong. It terminated its arrangements with the plaintiffs and entered into a contract with Reliance Commercial Enterprises, Inc. (Reliance). The latter was an established citrus broker in the Far East. Under its contract with Sunkist, Reliance was to act as the American company's exclusive agent in Hong Kong, soliciting and transmitting orders from Hong Kong importers, arranging for letters of credit and otherwise representing Sunkist's interests in the Crown Colony. Sunkist through its Export Department was to perform such functions as packing and handling the oranges, booking shipping space and purchasing insurance.

Within six months of the new arrangement, Sunkist succeeded in capturing 70% of what the Ninth Circuit described as the "market for American oranges sold in Hong Kong." By the end of 1967, however, Sunkist's share of those sales had fallen to 60%. By 1971, the year prior to suit, it had fallen to 45% with plaintiffs controlling most of the remaining 55%. Overall, the plaintiff who had once controlled the largest share of American sales to Hong Kong saw that share drop from its pre-1966 high of 18% to about 12%, although an "improving overall" market in Hong Kong meant that by 1970 the aggregate value of sales by at least three association members had exceeded the pre-1966 high.

In upholding the jury's finding that Sunkist had violated Section 1 of the Sherman Act, the Ninth Circuit first noted that "formation of an exclusive agency

---

[13] 526 F. 2d 1196 (9th Cir., 1976) cert denied, 425 U.S. 959, 96 S. Ct. 1741 (1976).

[14] Sunkist is primarily an association of growers whose concerted activities are exempt from the antitrust laws under the Capper-Volstead Act (7 U.S.C. Section 291).

agreement was not illegal *per se* . . . [A] good faith, economically motivated decision to switch exporters, would not subject [Sunkist] to Section 1 liability."[15]

Nevertheless, there was, the court held, sufficient evidence to warrant a jury finding that Sunkist had engaged in an unreasonable restraint of trade citing, for this purpose, termination by Sunkist of most sales to independent U.S. exporters, the booking of shipping space not needed for its own orders, obtaining "shipping advantages," "fraudulently" persuading plaintiffs to surrender their Hong Kong customer lists and supplying Reliance with those lists. If separately each of these actions "could be regarded as reasonable responses to competitive pressures," taken cumulatively, the court concluded, they constituted sufficient evidence to support the jury verdict.

Next, the Ninth Circuit upheld the jury's finding that Sunkist had violated Section 2 of the Sherman Act. The Court commenced this portion of its opinion by concluding that the "relevant market" was correctly defined as " . . . oranges grown in Arizona and California for export to Hong Kong." It then concluded that control ranging from 70% to 45% of that market was sufficient to establish (i) the market power requisite to a showing of monopolization and (ii) the probability of success which, combined with a specific intent, sufficed to make out an illegal "attempt to monopolize." Monopoly power, the court added, was to be seen in the "power to control prices or exclude competition."

Observe that if, in 1966, the Hong Kong market was highly competitive and Sunkist estimated that it could not distribute its oranges at less cost than the plaintiffs, its profit-maximizing strategy would have been to stay out of direct sales to Hong Kong altogether and to continue selling exclusively through plaintiffs. On the other hand, if Sunkist thought that it could be a more efficient distributor than plaintiffs, its profit-maximizing strategy would have been to discontinue selling through plaintiffs and to increase exports to a point where the additional revenue from the increased sales at the competitive Hong Kong price was equal to the marginal cost thereof.

Now, if the Hong Kong market was competitive, it would, of course, have turned the antitrust law on its head to have said that Sunkist, acting on efficiency grounds, could not legally have established an exclusive outlet for its oranges in Hong Kong, just because it meant driving plaintiffs out of the Hong Kong market. Hence, the Ninth Circuit's qualification; Sunkist's decision was perfectly legal if taken in "good faith" and "economically motivated." Obviously what concerned the court were the "rules of the game." If Sunkist, knowing that it was a less efficient distributor than plaintiffs or uncertain of its competitive prowess and anxious to reduce the risk of error, proceeded to defraud the plaintiffs, coerce other suppliers into cutting-off sales to plaintiffs and overbook shipping, then Sunkist's conduct itself served to raise doubts regarding whether plaintiffs exclusion from the Hong Kong market was efficient or inefficient. Against this background consider the interpretive problems posed by Section 6a.

---

[15] 526 F. 2d at 1203.

NOTES AND QUESTIONS

(1) At the threshold, note that the Ninth Circuit upheld the jury's finding that the relevant market was "oranges grown in Arizona and California for export to Hong Kong." Stated this way, without more, it is a very problematic definition, is it not? Explain. In fact Sunkist argued that the definition would "frustrate the Section 2 claim" becauseit describes a "supply, not a distribution, market." In response, the Ninth Circuit pointed out that plaintiffs' complaint charged Sunkist with "monopolizing . . . all or most of the *trade and commerce* in citrus fruits with . . . Hong Kong" (emphasis in the original). Are you completely satisfied with this answer?

(2) Assume that the Ninth Circuit had the economics right and that Sunkist did possess monopoly power in the Hong Kong market. Assume also that it engaged in impermissible exclusionary conduct. Recall, however, that plaintiffs were not driven out of the Hong Kong market altogether. In fact, re-examine the evidence, what hypothesis does it suggest?

Recall also that as a monopolist raises its price along the inelastic portion of the demand curve — usually in the early stages of the monopoly — the volume of sales will decline, but the total value (*i.e.*, total revenue) will rise. Against this background, assume that the aggregate value of United States orange sales to Hong Kong increased, what result under Section 6a, if the evidence also showed that plaintiffs' share of the Hong Kong market declined but the aggregate value of their sales increased more than would have occurred under competition? Could plaintiffs' claim any antitrust injury? Or stated otherwise, under Section 6a is the successful monopolization of a foreign market a potential defense against a Section 1 charge of having partially excluded a competitor from that market? If so, and if foreign consumers can't complain, doesn't Section 6a mean that successful monopolization of a foreign market is also a defense to a Section 2 charge of monopolization.

Reflect further, what would be the better approach to the problems that concerned Congress?

(3) Return to the analysis of *Minnesota Mining*. What result in that case under Section 6a?

(4) *Todhunter-Mitchell & Co v. Annheuser-Busch Inc.,*[16] was among the decisions cited by Congress as constituting an over-reaching of American antitrust jurisdiction and a justification for Section 6a. In that case plaintiff, Todhunter-Mitchell, a Bahamian corporation engaged in blending, bottling and wholesaling a wide variety of beers, wines and liquors, approached National Brands, Inc. Annheuser-Busch's independently owned South Florida wholesaler, with an offer to purchase large quantities of Budweiser for export to and resale in the Bahamas. National Brands, Inc. was anxious to make the sale, but it was vetoed by Annheuser-Busch. The latter already had an established wholesale distributor in the Bahamas, Bahama Blenders. It was company policy to assign an exclusive territory to each of its distributors and to discourage distributors from selling to customers outside that territory.

---

[16] 375 F. Supp. 610 (E.D. Penn. 1974).

After making several offers to National Brands, with the latter each time reluctantly declining, Todhunter-Mitchell, working through a New Orleans ship's chandler, finally succeeded in obtaining the beer from Annheuser-Busch's New Orleans distributor. As soon as the Budweiser began to appear in the Bahamas, Bahama Blenders complained to Annheuser-Busch that "Todhunter-Mitchell . . . have been bringing in Budweiser . . . illegally . . . and offering it at prices below those set by the Bahama's Liquor Association." In his report, an Annheuser-Busch investigator, observed that Todhunter-Mitchell was not a member of the "local Association in Freeport" and was selling Budweiser at 50 cents per case less than Bahama Blenders' price.

After an extensive investigation, Annheuser-Busch located the New Orleans source of the shipment and immediately ordered its New Orleans distributor to discontinue selling to the ship's chandler. Whereupon, Todhunter-Mitchell, unable to obtain any further shipments, sued, charging Annheuser-Busch along with National Brands, Inc., and the New Orleans distributor with a conspiracy in violation of both Section 1 and Section 2 of the Sherman Act. By way of defense, Annheuser-Busch asserted that its refusal to sell to Todhunter-Mitchell was motivated by legitimate marketing considerations relating to quality control and potential over-supply and not by any anti-competitive motive. On this record the court, relying principally on *United States v. Arnold Schwinn & Co.*,[17] concluded that Annheuser-Busch, Bahama Blenders and National Brands were guilty of a horizontal territorial division agreement, a *per se* violation of Section 1. With these facts in mind, consider the following.

(a) *Schwinn* has been superceded by *GTE Sylvania* (discussed *supra* page 667) and Annheuser-Busch's defense certainly seems to echo *GTE Sylvania*. Assume that there was evidence to sustain Annheuser-Busch's claim of quality control, etc. but that there also was evidence suggesting that, under the *GTE Sylvania* Rule of Reason, a defense along these lines might have been difficult to sustain? Identify that evidence. In the face of the evidence, does Section 6a really mean that Todhunter-Mitchell is powerless; without appeal to the American courts to rectify a wrong visited upon it by Americans? Have we come to that! Suppose the Bahamian government tried to prosecute Annheuser-Busch, how long would Bahamians have any imported beer? And what would Washington say?

(b) In *Monsanto Co. v. Spray-Rite Service Corp.*[18] defendant Monsanto was charged with conspiring with other distributors to terminate plaintiff's distributorship because of the latter's practice of giving customers large discounts. Monsanto and its distributors were, plaintiff charged, guilty of a resale price maintenance conspiracy, a per se violation of Section 1. The jury found for plaintiff and the Seventh Circuit affirmed stating that to prove conspiracy plaintiff only had to show that its termination for price-cutting came in response to complaints from other distributors. The Supreme Court disapproved of this evidentiary standard. Something more than distributor complaints was needed to prove a

---

[17] 388 U.S. 365, 87 S. Ct. 1856 (1967).
[18] 465 U.S. 752, 104 S. Ct. 1464 (1984).

conspiracy to set resale prices. There had to be direct evidence of a "conscious commitment to a common scheme,"[19] that "tend[ed] to exclude" the possibility of independent action by the manufacturer and its other distributors. The Court went on to uphold the judgment because there was ample evidence in the record to sustain a jury verdict under the Court's higher standard of proof.

Todhunter-Mitchell, of course, is not a case involving the termination of a distributor for price cutting, but rather a case of excluding a competitor because of price cutting. Assume, as is very likely the case, that there was evidence sufficient to satisfy the *Monsanto* standard of a conspiracy between Annheuser-Busch, Bahama Blenders and Bahama Liquor Association to set a resale price for Budweiser (and other beers) and to exclude Todhunter-Mitchell for under selling that price. Of course, the antitrust laws do not confer on Todhunter-Mitchell any right to be a Budweiser distributor. On the other hand, the facts and circumstances surrounding his exclusion evidence the existence of a conspiracy, rigorously carried-out, to fix resale prices. That conspiracy, in turn, has resulted in a loss of export sales from the United States. Would Section 6a, however, foreclose Todhunter-Mitchell from bringing his suit? Could National Brands have sued Annheuser-Busch and Bahamas Blender for excluding Todhunter-Mitchell from the Bahamas market? What is the likelihood of National Brands bringing such an action?

(5) Contrast *Todhunter-Mitchell* with *AGS Electronics Ltd. v. B.S.R. (U.S.A.) Ltd., and B.S.R. Ltd.*[20] B.S.R., a British firm and its subsidiary B.S.R. (U.S.A.), were manufacturers of record changers and record players. Plaintiff AGS — a Canadian corporation — was the exclusive distributor in Canada and the Far East for Glenburn Corp., an American firm that, until 1975, was B.S.R.'s principal competitor in the United States and allegedly elsewhere in "North America." In that year B.S.R., which then controlled 70% of the U.S. market in "low-end" (*i.e.*, inexpensive) record players, acquired Glenburn which controlled 30% of that market. B.S.R. immediately terminated plaintiff's distributorship and turned all of the Far East and Canadian business in the two product lines over to Keron Trading Ltd., which had theretofore been B.S.R.'s distributor in that region. Plaintiff AGS alleged *inter alia* that the termination of its distributorship was the result of a conspiracy between B.S.R. and Keron motivated by defendants' desire to maintain an artificially high supra-competitive price in violation of Section 1 of the Sherman Act. The court dismissed on the ground that the refusal to deal with plaintiff "clearly had no impact upon American consumers" and on the ground that AGS "failed to allege any anticompetitive impact on American exporters." This latter, the court thought, distinguished the case from Todhunter-Mitchell.

---

[19] 465 U.S. at 764.
[20] 460 F. Supp 707 (S.D.N.Y., (1978)).

§ 7.06 Restraints on Trade and the Problem of Foreign Sovereigns, Foreign Law and Foreign Plaintiffs: Foreign Compulsion, Act of State and More

[A] The "Foreign Compulsion" Doctrine

CONTINENTAL ORE CO. v. UNION CARBIDE AND CARBON CORP.

United States Supreme Court
370 U.S. 690, 82 S. Ct. 1404 (1962)

[In this action plaintiff Continental Ore Co. (Continental), a partnership, alleged that the Vanadium Corporation of America (VCA), Union Carbide and Carbon Corporation (Carbide) and four of the latter's subsidiaries, including Electro-Metallurgical Company of Canada (Electro-Met of Canada) conspired to restrain and monopolize both the United States' and Canadian markets in vanadium products, all in violation of Section 1 and Section 2 of the Sherman Act. Only VCA, Carbide and one of the latter's U.S. subsidiaries was served.

The products in question consist of vanadium ore, which after being mined, is processed into an oxide. The oxide is then converted into ferro-vanadium which is, in turn, used as an alloy in steel production. According to Continental's complaint, between 1933-1949, defendants produced 90% of all oxides and, through the electric furnace method, 99% of all ferro-vanadium manufactured in the United States. In the same period they allegedly accounted for 99% of all sales of these same products.

One Henry J. Lier, founder of Continental, came to the United States in 1938 and through Continental, sought to enter the vanadium business in the United States. These efforts, Continental charged, were all frustrated by defendants. On several occasions, after plaintiff had entered into, or was negotiating, arrangements with other companies to produce ferro-vanadium according to the alumino-thermic process, the defendants, it was alleged, forced these ventures to be abandoned by either refusing to sell or preventing others from selling, the required oxides to Continental or by threatening reprisals against Continental's erstwhile partners. All of these actions by the defendants had the effect, according to Continental, of excluding it from the United States market.

With regard to the Canadian market, Continental offered into evidence a letter dated January 19, 1943, from Continental to a Carbide subsidiary in New York City reciting the fact that the new allocation system in Canada[1]

---

[1] Canada's entry into World War II prompted the Canadian Government to take extraordinary measures to assure optimum availability of strategic materials to Canadian private industries engaged in the war effort. Pursuant to these measures, the Office of Metals Controller was established and given broad powers to regulate the procurement of the materials and to allocate them to industrial users. The Metals Controller enlisted the aid of Electro Met of Canada in early 1943, delegating to it the discretionary power to purchase and then allocate to Canadian industries all vanadium products required by them. The validity of these wartime measures and delegations under Canadian law is not here contested.

had eliminated Continental from the Canadian market, that Continental had inquired about the matter from the Metals Controller for the Canadian Government and that the latter had referred Continental to Electro Met. The trial court struck this letter from the record and rejected Continental's additional offer to prove that it was excluded from the Canadian market by Electro Met of Canada acting as exclusive purchasing agent for the Metals Controller but allegedly operating under the control and direction of Carbide for the purpose of carrying out the overall conspiracy to restrain and monopolize the vanadium industry. Continental also offered to prove that its former share of the Canadian market was divided between Carbide and VCA. The trial court denied this entire line of proof "for the reason that this is a transaction wholly in the hands of the Canadian Government and that whether or not this plaintiff was permitted to sell his material to a customer in Canada was a matter wholly within the control of the Canadian Government."

After trial the jury returned a verdict for defendants. On appeal the Ninth Circuit concluded that the trial court should have directed a verdict for defendants, because Continental had not proven that defendants had caused its ventures to fail. In addition, the Ninth Circuit agreed that proof of Continental's exclusion from the Canadian market had properly been excluded. According to the Appeals Court, even if Electro Met of Canada had acted for the purpose of entrenching the monopoly position of the defendants in the United States or Canada, defendants efforts to persuade and influence the Canadian Government through its agent were not within the purview of the Sherman Act.The Supreme Court reversed, concluding that the Appeals Court had taken too narrow a view of the evidence; that the issue of causality was for the jury. With regard to Continental's exclusion from the Canadian market, the Supreme Court had *inter alia* the following to say]:

MR. JUSTICE WHITE delivered the opinion of the Court.

* * * *

Olsen v. Smith[2] . . . *United States v. Rock Royal Co-op.*[3] . . . and *Parker v. Brown*[4] . . . do not help respondents. These decisions, each of which sustained the validity of mandatory state or federal governmental regulations against a claim of antitrust illegality, are wide of the mark. In the present case petitioners do not question the validity of any action taken by the Canadian Government or by its Metals Controller. Nor is there left in the case any question of the liability of the Canadian Government's agent, for Electro Met of Canada was not served. What the petitioners here contend is that the respondents are liable for actions which they themselves jointly took, as part of their unlawful conspiracy, to influence or to direct the elimination of Continental from the Canadian market. As in *Sisal*,[5] the conspiracy was laid in the United States, was effectuated both here and abroad,

---

[2] 195 U.S. 332, 25 S. Ct. 52, 49 L. Ed 224.

[3] 307 U.S. 533, 59 S. Ct. 993, 83 L. Ed 1446.

[4] 317 U.S. 341, 63 S. Ct. 307, 87 L. Ed 315.

[5] The reference is to *United States v. Sisal Sales Corp.*, 274 U.S. 268, 47 S. Ct. 592 (1927), discussed *supra* page 609. - Ed.

and respondents are not insulated by the fact that their conspiracy involved some acts by the agent of a foreign government.

From the evidence which petitioners offered it appears that Continental complained to the Canadian Metals Controller that Continental had lost its Canadian business. The Controller referred Continental to one of the respondents. But there is no indication that the Controller or any other official within the structure of the Canadian Government approved or would have approved of joint efforts to monopolize the production and sale of vanadium or directed that purchases from Continental be stopped. The exclusion, Continental claims, resulted from the action of Electro Met of Canada, taken within the area of its discretionary powers granted by the Metals Controller and in concert with or under the direction of the respondents. The offer of proof at least presented an issue for the jury's resolution as to whether the loss of Continental's Canadian business was occasioned by respondents' activities. Respondents are afforded no defense from the fact that Electro Met of Canada, in carrying out the bare act of purchasing vanadium from respondents rather than Continental, was acting in a manner permitted by Canadian law. There is nothing to indicate that such law in any way compelled discriminatory purchasing, and it is well settled that acts which are in themselves legal lose that character when they become constituent elements of an unlawful scheme. . . .

The case of *Eastern Railroad Presidents Cong. v. Noerr Motor Freight, Inc.,* [6] . . . cited by the court below and much relied upon by respondents here, is plainly inapposite. The Court there held not cognizable under the Sherman Act a complaint charging, in essence, that the defendants had engaged in a concerted publicity campaign to foster the adoption of laws and law enforcement practices inimical to plaintiffs' business. Finding no basis for imputing to the Sherman Act a purpose to regulate political activity, a purpose which would have encountered serious constitutional barriers, the Court ruled the defendants' activities to be outside the ban of the Act "at least insofar as those activities comprised mere solicitation of governmental action with respect to the passage and enforcement of laws" . . . In this case, respondents' conduct is wholly dissimilar to that of the defendants in *Noerr*. Respondents were engaged in private commercial activity, no element of which involved seeking to procure the passage or enforcement of laws. To subject them to liability under the Sherman Act for eliminating a competitor from the Canadian market by exercise of the discretionary power conferred upon Electro Met of Canada by the Canadian Government would effectuate the purposes of the Sherman Act and would not remotely infringe upon any of the constitutionally protected freedoms spoken of in *Noerr*.

NOTES AND QUESTIONS

(1) While the Court did not explicitly say whether defendants' could have escaped antitrust liability if the Canadian government had directly compelled

---

[6] 365 U.S. 127, 81 S. Ct. 523, 5 L. Ed 2d 464.

Continental's exclusion from the Canadian market, the case has long been understood to imply that that would be the case. In the same vein, the Justice Department in its Guidelines on International Operations states: "A sensible approach to the antitrust laws that accommodates notions of comity and fairness supports the reading of an implied defense to application of the U.S. antitrust laws based on foreign sovereign compulsion." Indeed, the Guidelines suggest that the "implied defense" can be read into the statutes themselves because Congress was legislating "against the background of well recognized principles of international comity among nations." Also the Guidelines argue that it would be unfair to prosecute private firms — American and foreign — whose anticompetitive conduct was not voluntary but the result of governmental compulsion.

At the same time, however, the Guidelines make clear that the Department will forego prosecution only if the circumstances surrounding the foreign sovereign's commands indicate that a refusal to comply "would give rise to the imposition of significant penalties or to the denial of specific and substantial benefits." It is not enough that the anticompetitive conduct is merely encouraged, permitted or consistent with foreign law. Furthermore, the Department will not recognize the defense if the compelled anticompetitive conduct occurred wholly or primarily in the United States.[7]

The Guidelines then discuss the following hypothetical case:

Voluntary Export Restraint[8]

The Association of American X Manufacturers (the "Association"), whose members are suffering from overcapacity, slack demand, and the impact of increased imports of X from Country A, has been seeking legislated import quotas. The Association has publicly announced that its members may also invoke provisions of the U.S. trade laws that could lead to the restriction of imports. U.S. government trade officials have informed officials of the government of Country A about the problem. They have suggested that Country A take action to ease trade relations between the two countries.

In an effort to forestall the imposition of U.S. import quotas and to respond to the concern of the U.S. Government, Country A's Minister of Trade holds separate meetings with the top representatives of each of Country A's five X producers. The Minister asks each producer to reduce its exports to the United States during the coming year by ten percent. The Minister makes it clear that the government of Country A views the reduction of exports to be crucial to Country A's overall trade relationship with the United States.

Each of the five producers of X agrees to reduce its exports to the United States. The Minister advises U.S. trade official of this fact and publicly announces the voluntary restraint program. Each of the five producers of X has a U.S. sales subsidiary.

Discussion

---

[7] Copyright © 1988 by BNA. Reprinted with permission. BNA Antitrust & Trade Regulation Report, Vol. 55, No. 1391, Special Supplement, November 10, 1988 at page S-23.

[8] *Id.* at page S-46

This case raises two questions. First, is there an agreement among the producers of X in Country A? Second, would U.S. antitrust enforcement action be appropriate in view of the involvement of the government of Country A and the request by U.S. Government officials that the government of A act to resolve the trade friction?

As a general matter . . . mere parallel conduct, without more, is not enough to establish agreement. Parallel conduct by competitors in some cases can be equally consistent both with agreement and with independent decision making. A conspiracy may be inferred from parallel conduct, however, where the parties appear to have a rational economic motive for engaging in the conspiracy (*e.g.*, to restrict output and raise price) and it would not be in the economic self-interest of individual firms to engage in the conduct alone.

If it appeared that the Minister of Trade were simply acting as the coordinator for a private conspiracy among Country A's producers of X to restrict exports to the United States, the Department might seek to prosecute this arrangement as an unlawful cartel. The fact that the Minister served as the "hub" of the conspiracy would not insulate the private-party "spokes."

. . . For reasons of comity, however, the Department likely would not challenge a voluntary export restraint that clearly arose from the decision and the official action of the government of Country A in response to specific trade concerns officially expressed by the U.S. government. As a matter of prosecutorial discretion, in deciding whether to challenge such conduct, the Department would consider the potential impact of a U.S. antitrust enforcement action on Country A's national interests as well as on the U.S. government's relationship with the government of Country A. The Department's action in a particular case would depend on the totality of the circumstances.

Observe, that in this case the Department's only apparent concern is whether, if there is an antitrust offense (*i.e.*, parallel conduct amounting to a conspiracy), the foreign government played enough of a role to call it a "government compelled conspiracy." And rightly so, for as the Guidelines state, antitrust prosecution under these circumstances would be "anomalous" if there is genuine government compulsion.[9] Also rightly, the Department is prepared to decide what constitutes compulsion by taking context into account — what is implied when a foreign government expresses a concern for its overall trade relationship with the United States. But that does not answer the question, why in all other cases, as the Guidelines seem to indicate, genuine foreign government compulsion will be a good defense. Consider the following:

(a) Does "comity" require so sweeping an exemption?

(b) The court in *InterAmerican Refining Corporation v. Texaco Maracaibo, Inc.,*[10] had the following to say:

Anticompetitive practices compelled by foreign nations are not restraints of commerce, as commerce is understood in the Sherman Act, because refusal

---

[9] Elsewhere the Guidelines use the word "anomalous" to characterize the prosecution of foreign firms for a conspiracy to restrain trade made necessary by an order of their own government responding to a U.S. request. *Id.* at page S-23.

[10] 307 F. Supp. 1291 (D. Del., 1970) at page 1298.

to comply would put an end to commerce . . . American business abroad does not carry with it the freedom and protection of competition it enjoys here and our courts cannot impose them. . . . Were compulsion not a defense, American firms abroad faced with a government order would have to choose one country or the other in which to do business. The Sherman Act does not go so far.

Are you persuaded?

  (c) The 1977 Justice Department Foreign Operations Guidelines took a very different position from the apparent sweeping exemption announced by the 1988 Guidelines:

Generally, when an unresolvable and direct conflict between the laws of two countries imposes substantial hardship upon the affected party, comity may indicate that the laws of the nation with the more important national interest at stake, based upon its own laws and policies, should prevail.

We believe the United States antitrust laws represent a fundamental and important national policy.The 1977 Guidelines then go on to offer an example. "If the purpose and necessary effect of (the foreign sovereign's) command [is] to create a *per se* antitrust violation in U.S. markets . . . we do not believe comity would require that the United States treat [that] . . . command as controlling here."Is this a more, or less, persuasive position than taken in the 1988 Guidelines? From the viewpoint of preserving the integrity of American antitrust law? from the viewpoint of overall U.S. foreign economic policy?

(2) Should the doctrine laid down in the *Noerr* case be extended to appeals to foreign governments for restrictive laws or other regulations?

NOTE

ANTITRUST AND THE ACT OF STATE DOCTRINE

Closely related to the foreign sovereign compulsion doctrine in its potential effect on the enforcement of the antitrust laws, but not related in its theoretical foundations, is the Act of State doctrine. We will examine the foundations of that doctrine more fully in Chapter 11. Suffice it here to note that the doctrine is a rule of "federal common law" binding on State and Federal courts alike, which bars those courts from judging the legality of foreign "acts of state." Not all actions of a foreign sovereign are "acts of state" and that creates the difficulty. The precise contours of the doctrine are far from certain. In the leading Supreme Court case, *Banco Nacional de Cuba v. Sabbatino,*[11] the Court declared that:

The text of the Constitution does not require . . . the doctrine . . . [but it does] have "constitutional" underpinnings. It arises out of the basic relationships between branches of government in a system of separation of

---
[11] 376 U.S. 398, 84 S. Ct. 923, 11 L. Ed 2d 804 (1964).

powers. . . . [I]ts continuing vitality depends on its capacity to reflect the proper distribution of functions between the judicial and political branches of the Government on matters bearing upon foreign affairs.

Some have read this as meaning that the doctrine is only intended to forestall judicial embarrassment of the Executive in the conduct of foreign relations.[12] Others, while not denying such a purpose, give it a much richer texture, seeing in it elements of justiciability; the "fitness" of particular issues for judicial resolution and a parallel to the "political question" doctrine.[13] Be that as it may, the Act of State doctrine has played an important role in a number of antitrust cases. A brief review of some of the leading decisions is instructive.

In *International Association of Machinists and Aerospace Workers (IAM) v. Organization of Petroleum Exporting Countries (OPEC)*,[14] IAM charged OPEC with a price fixing conspiracy in violation of the Sherman Act, asking both treble damages and injunctive relief. In affirming the district court's dismissal of the complaint on Act of State grounds, the Ninth Circuit observed that for a court to give the relief requested would be tantamount to a U.S. court "instructing a group of foreign sovereigns to alter their chosen means of allocating and profiting from their own valuable natural resources." Other factors which the court thought warranted application of the Act of State doctrine were the potential adverse impact of an adjudication on U.S. relations with the OPEC states generally and on the ability of the Executive to negotiate with the cartel. The strength of the U.S. regulatory interest — enforcement of the Sherman Act — was outweighed by political necessity.

In *Clayco Petroleum Corp v. Occidental Petroleum Corp*,[15] the Ninth Circuit again affirmed the dismissal on Act of State grounds of Clayco's claim that it had been deprived of an oil concession given to Occidental by one of the Persian Gulf Emirates because of the payment by Occidental of a bribe to the local Sultan. The payment, Clayco claimed, violated the Sherman Act, the Robinson Patman Act, the California Business and Professions Code and was a common law tort. As in *OPEC*, the court relied heavily on the fact that the sovereign decision as to who should be granted authority to exploit important natural resources of the state was a matter of significant public, not just private, interest. It also noted the intrusive nature of the inquiry required to prove Clayco's claim — did the Sultan accept a bribe and did that determine his decision. Such an inquiry the court thought, could be highly embarrassing, certainly to the Sultan and possibly to the United States as well.

Very much along the same lines was the decision in *Occidental Petroleum Corp. v. Buttes Gas & Oil Co.*,[16] discussed at length at page 647 *supra*. There the court

---

[12] See Justice Rehnquist writing in *First National City Bank v. Banco Nacional de Cuba*, 406 U.S. 759, 92 S. Ct. 1808, 32 L. Ed 2d 466 (1972).

[13] See Justice Brennen dissenting in *First National City Bank v. Banco Nacional de Cuba, supra*. See also Swan, Act Of State At Bay: a Plea On Behalf Of The Elusive Doctrine, [1976] Duke L. J. 807.

[14] 649 F. 2d 1354 (9th Cir. 1981) cert denied, 454 U.S. 1163 (1982).

[15] 712 F. 2d 404 (9th Cir. 1983) cert. denied 444 U.S. 1040 (1984).

[16] 331 F. Supp. 92 (D.C. Cal. 1971) aff'd, 461 F. 2d 1261 (9th Cir. 1971) cert. denied 409 U.S. 950 (1972).

determined that Occidental could not prevail unless it could prove that the Ruler of Sharjah had issued a fraudulent territorial waters decree because of Buttes' action. Also implicated were the propriety of the actions of the Iranian and British governments, the latter in exercising its supervisory powers over the Persian Gulf Emirates.

In *Hunt v. Mobil Oil Corp.* [17] the Second Circuit held that the Act of State doctrine was applicable because in order for Hunt to prevail on its Section 1 Sherman Act claim it would have to prove that but for the defendant oil companies' (seven in all) conspiracy with the Government of Libya, the latter would not have expropriated Hunt's Libyan oil concession. This would entail a wholesale inquiry into Libyan policy; how Libya treated other companies; what provoked Qadhafi's displeasure; whether or not the concessions Hunt was willing to give would have appeased Qadhafi. The court rejected Hunt's argument that the Act of State doctrine should only be applied where the legality of the foreign sovereign's actions are called into question. Moreover, the State Department had already publicly characterized Qadhafi's action as politically motivated; a reprisal against the United States. A contrary judicial assessment would hardly have helped U.S. relations with that sensitive part of the world.

Contrast these decisions with those in *Timberlane Lumber Co. v. Bank of America N.T.,* [18] *Williams v. Curtiss Wright Corp.* [19] and *Mannington Mills, Inc. v. Congoleum Corp.* [20]

In *Timberlane* the district court, relying principally on the *Buttes* case had concluded that because Timberlane's antitrust injury resulted principally from the Honduran Government's enforcement of the Bank's security interests in the Maya lumber mill, a U.S. court was barred by the Act of State doctrine from reviewing those actions. The Ninth Circuit reversed, concluding that the government action in Buttes was different altogether from that in *Timberlane*. In the latter case Honduras' action consisted only of a judicial proceeding initiated by a private party. There was no charge that any Honduran official was implicated in the defendants' conspiracy or that the Honduran courts had acted other than in strict accordance with Honduran law. Timberlane's claim did not challenge any Honduran law or policy in any way that could embarrass U.S. relations with Honduras. Nor was their any suggestion that those actions "reflected a sovereign decision that Timberlane's efforts should be crippled or that trade with the United States should be restrained."

In *Williams v. Curtiss-Wright Corp.*, Williams charged Curtiss-Wright with a number of improper practices in seeking to monopolize the world-wide market for the sale of surplus J-65 aircraft engines and parts, most of which were purchased by foreign governments. In concluding that the Act of State doctrine did not bar the claim, the Third Circuit rejected Curtiss-Wright's argument that the doctrine prohibited the American courts from scrutinizing a foreign government's motives for refusing to purchase plaintiff's engines. The foreign governments were not implicated in any wrongdoing, nor would their policies be called

---

[17] 550 F. 2d 68 (2d Cir. 1977), cert. denied 434 U.S.984 (1977).
[18] 549 F. 2d 597 (9th Cir. 1976) discussed at page 642 *supra*.
[19] 694 F. 2d 300 (3d Cir. 1982).
[20] 595 F. 2d 1287 (3d Cir. 1979).

into question. They were, according to Williams complaint, as much a victim of Curtiss-Wright unlawful practices as was the plaintiff. Under these circumstances an adjudication would not hinder the conduct of American foreign relations and the U.S. had a strong interest in the full and effective enforcement of its antitrust laws.

Lastly, in *Mannington Mills*, plaintiff charged Congoleum with restraining trade in violation of the antitrust laws by making false and misleading statements about the status and content of certain U.S. patents to foreign patent offices in order to obtain from those offices some twenty-six separate foreign patents. The Third Circuit rejected defendants argument that the Act of State doctrine barred plaintiff's claim because it would require an inquiry into the policies governing issuance of patents by those offices. According to the court, the only foreign governmental action involved was the neutral application of the foreign sovereign's own law. Plaintiff's charge did not call either the legality or the ethics of any foreign official action into question — only Congoleum's conduct was at issue — and the granting of patents was more in the nature of a ministerial function that did not implicate either the policies or the vital interests of a foreign sovereign to the extent that was necessary before the Act of State doctrine could be applied.

The contours of the doctrine are fairly discernable, are they not? Perhaps we should trust the judges to judge, at least in these antitrust cases.[21]

Even if neither the foreign sovereign compulsion or the Act of State doctrine are applicable, the interaction of the antitrust laws with foreign law can raise important and difficult issues concerning how conflicting national interests might properly be reconciled. Consider, in this light the following case.

In *Zenith Radio Corp. v. Hazeltine Research Inc.*[22] the Supreme Court upheld an award of treble damages to Zenith for injuries caused by the refusal of a Canadian patent pool to grant Zenith a license to import American manufactured goods into Canada. Canadian Radio Patents, Ltd. (CRPL) was a pool formed in 1926 by the Canadian subsidiaries of a number of major American companies, including RCA, General Electric and Westinghouse. CRPL was the exclusive licensee of the latters' Canadian patents — some 5,000 in number — and was authorized to grant package sub-licenses principally for manufacture in Canada. Defendant Hazeltine Research had licensed its Canadian patents to CRPL and had participated in pool royalties.

After trying unsuccessfully for many years to obtain from CRPL a sublicense to import its American made products into Canada, Zenith, in 1957, brought an antitrust suit against a number of the largest American participants in the pool, not, however, including defendant Hazeltine Research or CRPL itself. That suit was settled by a grant to Zenith of worldwide licenses on patents owned by the

---

[21] For a perceptive student note on these cases see: The Act of State Doctrine: Reconciling Justice and Diplomacy on a Case-by-Case Basis, 43 U. of Miami L. Rev. 1169 (1989).

[22] 395 U.S. 61, 89 S. Ct. 1562 (1969).

named defendants. But, when Zenith in 1958 began exporting American radio and television products to Canada it was informed by CRPL that it was infringing at least one of Hazeltine Research's patents and that continued sales of the product in Canada would require it to sign CRPL's standard form license agreement which did not permit importation.

This charge of infringement was a genuine bar. CRPL had long maintained a highly effective organization of agents, investigators, trade associations and others to police the market and warn dealers and consumers against trading in unlicensed products. It continued to use this system against Zenith even after settlement of the 1957 lawsuit. In short, CRPL's chief purpose, which it pursued with diligence, was, as the Supreme Court noted, "to protect the manufacturing members and [sub]-licensees from competition by American and other foreign companies seeking to import their products into Canada."[23] When Hazeltine Research sued, charging Zenith with infringing certain U.S. patents, Zenith counterclaimed alleging injury to its export business by reason of a conspiracy between Hazeltine Research and CRPL in violation of Section 1 and Section 2 of the Sherman Act.

The district court dismissed Hazeltine Research's claim of infringement and then, on Zenith's counterclaim, granted the latter $35 million dollars in treble damages and enjoined Hazeltine Research from any continued participation in the restrictive practices of the Canadian pool. This judgment was affirmed by the Supreme Court upon appeal from a judgment of reversal by the Seventh Circuit.[24] The Supreme Court concluded that Hazeltine Research had acted beyond the scope of its patent monopoly when it conspired with CRPL to exclude Zenith from the Canadian market.

Judged according to traditional standards of United States law there is little reason to take exception to this conclusion. Comprehensive patent pools or cross-licensing arrangements that embrace virtually all of the dominant technology in an industry and which operate to divide markets and raise barriers to entry have traditionally been viewed as crossing over the line between the lawful monopoly conferred by the patent and an unlawful restraint of trade condemned by the antitrust laws. See *United States v. Singer Manufacturing Co.*[23] and *United States v. National Lead Co.*[26]

In the *Hazeltine* case, however, the controlling patents were not American, but Canadian. The district court addressed the point only by observing that Canadian patent law did not compel CRPL to refuse Zenith a license to import. While, in its briefs on appeal, Hazeltine Research had asserted its own "good faith" belief that Canadian law required CRPL's non-importation licensing policy, both the Seventh Circuit and the Supreme Court apparently concluded that the district

---

[23] 395 U.S. at 115.

[24] Zenith had also claimed injury at the hands of similar patent pools in Australia and Great Britain in which Hazeltine Research was a participant. The damage portion of those claims was dismissed by the Supreme Court because Zenith failed to prove that had defendant's exclusionary practice not existed it would have exported its product to those markets. The Court did, however, enjoin Hazeltine Research from participating in certain package licensing practices employed by the British and Australian pools.

[25] 374 U.S. 174 (1963).

[26] 63 F.Supp. 513 (S.D.N.Y., 1945) aff'd 332 U.S. 319 (1947).

court's finding eliminated the need for any further concern with Canadian law. There was no foreign compulsion and no need, therefore, to take foreign law into account.

The state of and purposes behind Canadian law were, however, more subtle than the district court's cursory review would admit. As then in effect, the Canadian Combinations Investigation Act[27] authorized the imposition of sanctions against the "use" of a patent that "unduly prevent[ed] . . . or lessen[ed] competition in the production, manufacture, purchase . . . sale . . . or supply of any . . . article or commodity" in trade or commerce.

At the same time, Section 67 of the Canadian Patent Act[28] defined a number of practices as "abuse of a patent" and provided a variety of remedies for those abuses, including compulsory licensing and even patent revocation. Among the abuses listed in sub-section (2) of Section 67 was the failure to "work" a patent in Canada and permitting importation of a patented product that prevented domestic exploitation of the patent. More precisely, sub-section (2) (b) provided that a patent would be deemed abused:

> [I]f the working of the invention within Canada on a commercial scale is being prevented or hindered by the importation from abroad of the patented article by the patentee or persons . . . against whom the patentee is not taking or has not taken any proceedings for infringement. . . .

To this, Section 67(3) of the Patent Act added the following:

> It is declared with relation to every paragraph of subsection (2) that, for purposes of determining whether there has been any abuse of the exclusive rights under a patent, it shall be taken that patents for new inventions are granted not only to encourage invention but to *secure that new inventions shall so far as possible be worked on a commercial scale in Canada without undue delay* (emphasis supplied).

On the face of these provisions alone the American courts in the *Hazeltine* case might have paused to examine further whether CRPL's policy against licensing for importation was, if not compelled by the Canadian Patent Act, a measure positively in line with the economic objectives of that Act. The failure to do so was all the more notable because the Supreme Court relied upon a 1960 report of the Royal Commission on Patents, Copyrights and Industrial Designs, to establish the technological comprehensiveness of CRPL as a patent pool[29] and to confirm the rigor with which CRPL enforced its non-importation policy.[30] What the Court failed to mention, however, was the Commission's further observation that CRPL's policy was in conformity with Canadian law and that, while CRPL would probably not have been subjected to sanctions had it licensed imports, the risk of legal attack could not be discounted. The Commission also noted that CRPL was "not obliged" to grant import licenses "where the patent [was] being commercially worked in Canada," that CRPL licensed on reasonable

---

[27] Can. Rev. Stat., c. 314 (1952) as amended 8-9 Eliz. II c. 485 (1960).

[28] Can. Rev. Stat. c. 203 (1952) as amended 2-3 Eliz. II c. 40 (1953-1954).

[29] [I]t [was] doubtful," the Commission reported, "if anyone could sell in Canada a radio or television receiver" without a CRPL license.

[30] 395 U.S. at 120 n. 16.

terms anyone intending to manufacture in Canada and licensed for import those patented products incapable of being produced in Canada. An earlier investigation by the Commission (1947) had disclosed no illegality in CRPL's operation and no evidence was proffered to the American courts suggesting that CRPL fixed prices, divided territories, suppressed competing patents or discriminated in licensing for Canadian manufacture.

All of this was ignored by the courts in the *Hazeltine* case presumably because at least one American exporter, Zenith, could prove that its exports were foreshortened by CRPL's policy and because the proof of "foreign compulsion" fell short of the standard set out in *Continental Ore*. On the other hand, It would be too easy to dismiss the *Hazeltine* decision as simply a failure by the Supreme Court to appraise foreign law accurately. The case raises fundamental issues concerning the purpose of the antitrust laws, the relationship of those laws to broader tenets of U.S. foreign economic policy and the wisdom of such measures as Section 6a of the Sherman Act.

NOTES AND QUESTIONS

(1) What economic considerations or objectives might explain Canada's apparent tolerance, even encouragement, of CRPL's non-importation policy? Do these objectives necessarily reflect a willingness to tolerate restraints on the competitive vigor of the Canadian market?

(2) Was there any evidence to suggest that Zenith's exclusion from the Canadian market, or any other aspect of CRPL's operations, impaired the competitive efficiency of the Canadian market. Was there any evidence to suggest an anticompetitive effect on the American market? In proving damages Zenith relied almost exclusively on a comparison between its United States and Canadian market shares during the period it was excluded from the latter. In that period Zenith's share of the United States market ranged from 15.6% to 21.7%. Its share of the Canadian market varied from 3.1% to 5.2%. The district court concluded that had Zenith been able to obtain a license from CRPL for its American made goods it would have been able to command 16% of the Canadian market.

(3) If CRPL's policy had no adverse effect on the competitive vigor of any national market, the case would seem to have involved nothing more than a choice between rival American firms. How might the courts have made that choice? Was Canadian law relevant? Was Zenith the only American firm whose profits were at issue in the case? Would Section 6a permit a result consistent with your conclusions.

(4) Take a broader perspective; was this even an antitrust case? If the courts were compelled to regard it as such, at the very least the antitrust analysis might have been placed into the broader context of American foreign economic policy, including policies governing intellectual property. If so, what other body of international and American law might have been considered apposite to a resolution of the antitrust question? How would you reconcile the differences in

approach between that law and traditional Sherman Act concepts? Is the foreign compulsion doctrine adequate to that task or is this a matter for a "comity doctrine?"

(5) The *Hazeltine* decision caused considerable consternation in Canada and evoked a number of strong protests by the Canadian Government. It was, the Canadian's asserted, another example of American over-reaching of its proper antitrust jurisdiction. Is Section 6a responsive to such a claim?

[B] Foreign Plaintiffs: Standing to Sue

In *Pfizer Inc. et. al. v. Government of India et. al.*[31] , the Governments of India, Iran and the Philippines as drug purchasers sued a number of American drug manufacturers for treble damages claiming injury as the result of a conspiracy among defendants that fixed the price, divided markets and made fraudulent claims on the United States patent office with respect to a broad spectrum of antibiotics, all in violation of Section 1 and Section 2 of the Sherman Act. As an affirmative defense, the companies contended that plaintiffs lacked standing to sue because a foreign government was not a "person" within the meaning of Section 4 of the Clayton Act.[32] The Supreme Court rejected the argument, affirming the lower court's determination that plaintiffs had standing.

Defendants argued first that it could be inferred from the "general protectionist and chauvinistic attitude" of the Congress which enacted the Sherman Act that the law was intended to "protect only American consumers." The Supreme Court disagreed. Consistent with the Sherman Act's "expansive remedial purpose," which foreclosed any narrow technical interpretation of the word "persons," Justice Stewart, writing for the Court, noted that "foreign" as well as United States corporations were expressly entitled to sue for treble damages, that the Sherman Act applied as much to "trade 'with foreign nations' " as to interstate commerce and that Congress, by passage of the Webb-Pomerene Act had apparently felt it necessary to create a special exemption from the Sherman Act for American "export cartels." This latter, the Justice thought, signalled the absence of any Congressional intention to limit the "general applicability of the antitrust laws to foreign commerce." In all events the Court added, defendants argument "confuses the ultimate purposes of the antitrust laws with the question of who can invoke their remedies." The treble damage remedy, the Court continued, was intended "to deter violators and deprive them of the 'fruits of their illegality,' and 'compensate victims of antitrust violations for their injuries.' " To deny "a foreign plaintiff the right to sue . . . would," the Court thought, "defeat these purposes." It would "permit a price fixer or monopolist to escape full liability, . . . would deny compensation to certain of his victims, merely because he happens to deal with foreign customers . . . [and] would lessen the deterrent factor of treble damages." Moreover, if "potential anti-trust violators must take into account the full costs of their conduct," American consumers would be benefited.

Next the Court rejected defendants contention that foreign sovereigns, as distinguished from private persons, should, like the United States Government,

---

[31] 434 U.S. 308, 98 S. Ct. 584 (1978).
[32] 15 U.S.C. Section 15.

be denied standing. *United States v. Cooper Corp.*[33] The apposite case, according to the Court, was not *Cooper* but *Georgia v. Evans,*[34] which held that States of the Union were "persons" within the meaning of Section 4. When "a foreign nation enters our commercial markets," the Court wrote "it can be victimized . . . just as surely as a private person or a domestic State. The antitrust laws provide no alternative remedies for foreign nations as they do for the United States."[35]

In dissent, Chief Justice Burger thought that the omission of any reference in Section 4 to foreign sovereigns, coupled with the inclusion of foreign corporations, was dispositive of the question in favor of defendants. He also concluded from the legislative history that the focus of the reference to "foreign commerce" in the Sherman Act was so singularly upon protecting domestic consumers from restraints on imports that any attempt to read those words more broadly "simply belie its lineage." At best, the issue was not considered by Congress and so extraordinary an expansion of potential antitrust liability was a matter, the Chief Justice argued, for Congress not the Court, a point underscored by Justice Powell concurring in the dissent. To say that foreign nations like domestic States would otherwise be powerless to protect themselves, was, according to the Chief Justice, fanciful in light of such evidence as the European antitrust experience and the ample coercive power that other nations had shown themselves capable of exercising.

NOTES AND QUESTIONS

The House Judiciary Committee thought that in the proposed new Section 6a to the Sherman Act it was preserving, in part at least, the Court's *Pfizer* decision. In light of the text of Section 6a and the Committee's comments, consider whether, as purchasers from Sunkist, a Hong Kong importer or the Government of Hong Kong (assuming that as a British Crown Colony that Government had all the attributes of a foreign sovereign)[36] could sue under Section 4 upon proof that Sunkist monopolized or attempted to monopolize the Hong Kong market?

[33] 312 U.S. 600, 61 S. Ct. 742 (1941).
[34] 316 U.S. 159, 62 S. Ct. 972 (1942).
[35] 434 U.S. at page 318.
[36] Pub. L. 97-393, December 29, 1982, 96 Stat. 1964, added a new subsection (b) to Section 4 of the Clayton Act, 15 U.S.C. 15(b) severely limiting a foreign sovereign's right to recover any amount in excess of actual damages. For text, see Documentary Supplement.

CHAPTER 8

UNITED STATES BUSINESS IN FOREIGN COUNTRIES THROUGH FOREIGN DIRECT INVESTMENT

§ 8.01 General Considerations

Introduction

As we have seen in Chapter 2, in contemplating the possibility of exporting its products, the U.S. business enterprise may find that a variety of problems diminish the attractiveness or render infeasible the export route. Such problems could include, among others, high transportation costs, export controls, and import restrictions (*e.g.*, tariffs, quotas, currency restrictions). To some extent these problems can be avoided through the use of licensing arrangements. Similarly, direct participation in the economic life of a foreign country — through establishment of a foreign branch, subsidiary or joint venture — may offer a number of attractions. It avoids, or at least minimizes, the adverse impact of import restrictions. Production of products abroad may greatly facilitate entry into the market of the foreign country as well as those of its neighbors. Lower wages for labor abroad may be an inducement. Affiliation with a local investor or business partner and the employment of nationals of the foreign country may prove to be a significant business asset. Operation in a foreign country may be indispensable for an extractive enterprise, because of the need to have access to minerals and other raw materials to support home industries.

Assuming the presence of these and other inducements, the prospective investor still must consider other factors before deciding to invest abroad. The political stability of the foreign country under consideration, especially if the country is a developing country, may be a factor of overarching importance. An unstable political climate makes long term business planning difficult if not impossible, and a political atmosphere hostile to foreign investments is likely to result in the enactment of (from the point of view of the U.S. investor) unacceptable legislation and regulations. Conversely, a political atmosphere that increasingly favors foreign investment may induce legislation and implementing regulations highly beneficial to foreign investment.

Foreign *direct investment* should be distinguished from *portfolio investment*. The latter includes investments in bonds or small blocks of stock that do not provide the investor with the capacity for control. By contrast foreign direct investment carries with it the capacity for control. One common definition of foreign direct investment employed by the U.S. government is foreign ownership interests of 10% or more in a domestic enterprise.

According to at least one authority, Peter Drucker, international investment has grown to where it has become the dominant factor in the world economy,

705

replacing international trade. Although most of this increase has been portfolio investment, more than a third is now foreign direct investment in manufacturing and financial services.[1]

The great increase in international investment activity came in the post World War II period. From 1960 to 1973, for example, the annual average rate of growth for foreign direct investment was 13 percent; for the period between 1977 and 1979, the rate had increased to between 20 and 26 percent annually. As of 1980, total United States direct investment abroad had reached $213 billion, and foreign direct investment in the United States $65 billion. By 1982 foreign direct investment in the United States had increased to $102 billion, while U.S. direct investment abroad had climbed to $221 billion. Thereafter, the rate of growth in U.S. direct investment abroad slowed considerably, by the end of 1989 total foreign direct investment in the United States had reached $390 billion, and U.S. direct investment abroad had increased to $368.1 billion.

Before a client makes a decision to invest in a particular country, his American attorney must, of course, work closely with local lawyers, bankers and accountants, drawing on their familiarity with the law and local practices, especially to avoid unnecessary bureaucratic tangles and delays. Consultation with local tax experts is especially advisable because in most countries, as in the United States, the tax laws are constantly changing. For counsel not actually located in the country where the contemplated investment will take place, it is impossible to be aware of all the latest developments.

Beyond tax matters, however, there are a host of other questions a prospective United States investor will wish to address in deciding whether to undertake a foreign direct investment. Although the legal aspects of foreign direct investment in developed and developing countries are similar, there are enough differences between the two to warrant separate treatment. Accordingly, we first take up the situation in developed countries and then turn to the developing world.

After the general discussion of foreign direct investment, this Chapter considers particular investment arrangements: the concession or economic development agreement and the contract for construction of industrial works. Then the Chapter turns to an increasingly important form of foreign investment, the international joint venture. Finally the Chapter examines various "profile lowering devices" whereby the foreign investor agrees to certain arrangements that limit or even eliminate its control of the investment in exchange for greater assurance that the investment will not be expropriated or subject to other forms of onerous local control.

Before turning to these matters, however, it is worth noting, largely by way of contrast, that the United States has relatively few controls on foreign investment, at either the federal or state level, except in those few areas of the economy where it is thought that foreign ownership would be undesirable for national security or other reasons. During the 1970s, in response to substantial increases in foreign direct investment and several economic shocks such as rampant inflation and increased interest rates, there were a number of legislative proposals that would have imposed wide-ranging controls and limitations on foreign investment. The

---

[1] Wall Street Journal, May 26, 1987, at 32, col. 3.

ultimate result of this activity, however, was little legislative change. Four statutes are worthy of note. First, the International Investment Survey Act of 1976,[2] calls upon the Executive Branch to conduct, at least every five years, surveys of foreign investment in the United States and to publish the results. Second, the Agricultural Foreign Investment Disclosure Act of 1978,[3] requires foreigners who acquire United States agricultural land to report such ownership to the Secretary of Agriculture. Third, the International Banking Act of 1978,[4] authorizes foreign banks to establish branches or agencies in states under certain conditions. Fourth, the so-called Exon-Florio Amendment of 1988,[5] gives the President authority to block an acquisition by foreigners of a U.S. firm if he determines it would be a threat to national security.

Interestingly, during the 1980s there has been relatively little concern (at least until recently) in Congress or State legislatures with foreign investment. Rather, the focus was on trade problems. The consequent threat of new U.S. trade barriers has, somewhat ironically in light of past concerns, led to increased foreign direct investment by companies anxious to protect or secure a stronger position in the United States market . Lastly, in considering the over-all setting in which foreign investment in the United States occurs, one cannot ignore the limitations on federal and State regulation of foreign participation in the American economy imposed by the United States Constitution. These limitations are discussed at length in Chapter 13. Suffice it here to note that "due process" and "equal protection" remain so far an assurance to the foreigner investing in this country of an economy open and largely free of the discrimination that otherwise plagues and destabilizes the economic climate in so many other nations.

[A]　Direct Investment in Developed Countries

A first question the prospective United States investor contemplating investment abroad will want to ask is whether any provision of law of the host country bars the investment he intends to make. For example, in France, aliens are not permitted to participate in the hydroelectric, aircraft, shipping, publishing and armaments industries. In Canada, federal and provincial legislation limits the ownership by foreigners of such businesses as banking, broadcasting, insurance, securities, and trust companies.

As for those areas of the economy open to foreign investment, it may be necessary to obtain advance approval from a government agency. Foreign investments in France are scrutinized by the Ministry of the Economy, Finance, and Budget. Investment Canada Agency serves a similar role in Canada, although the scope of review is more limited than in France. In France, until 1990 all

France.

---

　[2] 22 U.S.C. Section 3101 et seq.
　[3] 7 U.S.C. Section 3501 et seq.
　[4] 12 U.S.C. Section 3101 et seq.
　[5] 50 U.S.C. App. Section 2170. For a thorough discussion of the Exon-Florio Amendment, see, Alvarez, Political Protectionishm and United States International Investment Obligations in Conflict: The Hazards of Exon-Florio, 30 Va. J. Int'l L. 1 (1989). At this writing the Exon-Florio Amendment is technically not in effect because Congress adjourned in the fall of 1990 without renewing the legislation. It is expected to do so, however, when it returns from its break.

France until 1990

individuals whose place of residence was outside France, all legal entities, whether public or private, whose head office was located outside France, all enterprises in France under direct or indirect foreign control, and all establishments of foreign companies located in France had to obtain advance authorization for their investments, unless the direct investment was subject to a specific exception (*e.g.*, in 1988 the advance authorization requirement was eliminated for investments that create new business enterprises in France). A "direct investment" is defined under French law and practice as one or more operations that individually or together permit one or more individuals or legal entities to create, or to obtain or increase their control over, an enterprise or an ongoing business located in France, or to extend the operation of such an enterprise already under their control. Detailed information regarding the proposed business operation must be submitted to the Ministry. It may also be necessary to obtain special cards equivalent to visas for foreign businessmen.

In January, 1990, however, the French Government further relaxed some of the administrative rules governing foreign investment. For example, investments originating in member states of the European Communities no longer are required to give prior notification to the Finance Ministry, provided that the investor companies have been in existence for three years and have an annual turnover of at least one billion in French francs. Although smaller EC companies still must give advance notice of their investment plans, French authoriites must now reply within two weeks instead of two months, unless the investment is related to defense, public health and public order.

Investments from outside the European Communities in excess of ten million French francs are still subject to a one-month waiting period. They are, however, approved automatically unless French officials question them within that time. In 1989, the government approved all of the 428 applications for foreign acquisitions of French businesses.

Once the United States investor has obtained the necessary permissions and documentation, the legal problems which must be considered in doing business abroad are manifold. These include (1) forms of business organization; (2) maintenance of control of the operation through majority stock ownership or other means; (3) procedures which must be followed, and authorities which must be consulted, in setting up a business operation; (4) restrictions on the repatriation of funds, whether capital, interest, dividends or other earnings such as royalty payments; (5) protection of patents and know-how; (6) taxation; (7) labor relations; (8) antitrust and trade regulation procedures; (9) environmental rules; (10) securities law; (11) limitations on sources of financing — in some countries most of the financing of the acquisition of a local business must come from foreign sources to conserve scarce foreign exchange; (12) methods of dispute settlement.

Moreover, as noted more extensively in Chapter 4, *supra*, pp. 286 *et seq.*, in the Western European context, the U.S. business enterprise must take into account that the European Community has a so-called "supra-national" lawmaking capacity of its own. The European Community has been active in several areas relevant to foreign direct investment, some of the leading developments of which are addressed below.

One major example of European Community lawmaking that we simply note in passing is the regulation on Control of Concentrations Between Undertakings or, as it is commonly called, the merger regulation. The merger regulation, which became effective on September 21, 1990, gives the EC Commission sole authority to review and approve most of the largest corporate mergers, acquisitions, and joint ventures within the European Community, including those involving companies located outside of the Community.

In this section, we take an overview of the forms of business organization, exchange controls, securities laws, the nature and impact of the regulation of labor relations, and methods of taxation. Some of these areas, as well as others, will be examined in greater detail later.

[1] Forms of Business Organization

The two most frequently used forms of business organization are the branch and the locally incorporated subsidiary. A branch is a division of the home company, and is accordingly considered part of a single legal entity that has its head office outside of the host country. A subsidiary is a separate legal entity, distinct from its parent, but subject to the parent's control through the latter's ownership of the subsidiary's stock. From 1966 to 1979, ninety-four percent of the foreign direct investment in the United States, and eighty-five percent of United States direct investment abroad, was accomplished through the subsidiary form of organization. Normally, if a subsidiary's operations are heavily concentrated in or confined to one foreign country, it will be established under the laws of that country. On occasion, however, it may be incorporated under U.S. law to operate in the host country as a foreign corporation. If the subsidiary's operations blanket a number of foreign countries, it will be established either under the law of one of those countries or under U.S. law.

The principal advantage of the branch lies in its ability to back its assets with those of the head office, often making capital and insurance less expensive and easier to obtain. This very advantage, however, carries with it a potential disadvantage. Claims against the branch, such as for product liability, can be satisfied out of the assets of the parent corporation. Indeed, limitation of legal liability is one of the main reasons for using a subsidiary. Another advantage of the subsidiary is that, if established under the laws of the host country, it will be perceived as a local rather than an "American" company. Some countries, developed and developing, have established incentive programs to encourage foreign investment, but normally only host country corporations are eligible for these programs. Such incentives can include, among others, cash grants, tax benefits, and investment guarantees. Some countries may go so far as to bar branch operations. Others require local participation, indirectly barring operations by a branch or a subsidiary incorporated elsewhere. As we shall see later in this chapter, some countries, like Mexico, may require that the foreign investor enter into a joint venture with a local enterprise.

Tax considerations play a major role in any decision whether to establish a branch or a subsidiary. Under the United States' global concept of taxation, all income realized from branch activities will be immediately reflected on the United States federal income tax return. At the same time, the home office can offset domestic profits with the losses and expenses of its foreign branches. United States corporations in the mineral and petroleum extraction industries, for example, often use foreign branch operations to take depletion allowances and deductions for intangible drilling and development costs.

On balance, however, the tax advantages weigh in favor of utilizing the foreign subsidiary as a form of doing business abroad. This is because the United States parent who operates through a subsidiary incorporated abroad has the "tax deferral" advantage. Income of a United States company's foreign subsidiary will normally not be subject to United States taxes until earnings are remitted to the parent shareholder.

If the decision is made to utilize the subsidiary form of doing business abroad, it may be necessary to decide, in a federal country like Canada, whether to incorporate the subsidiary under federal law or under the law of one of the states or provinces. Filing as a federal corporation does not necessarily avoid the application of state or provincial law, and there may be circumstances where state or provincial incorporation is the preferred choice.

Within the subsidiary form of doing business, broadly defined, there are a number of forms of business organizations from which a foreign investor can choose. In countries following the British model, the foreign investor can form a closely held "private" company or a "public" company. In a civil law country the investor may choose between a public corporation or a limited liability company. The limited liability company resembles the British private company and the U.S. closed corporation, with some of the characteristics of a limited partnership. Among the main advantages of limited liability corporations are that they are well suited to a small group of investors, limit the liability of each member to his contribution and usually do not issue shares of stock to members but assign quotas. Quotas are endowed with continuity of existence and allow corporations to be members. Their main disadvantage is that in some countries shares or quotas are not readily transferable.

Other possible forms of business organization include general partnerships, mixed partnerships, limited partnerships, and sole proprietorships. However, these forms are usually not appropriate for large-scale investments.

[2] Exchange Controls

There are a number of governments that maintain elaborate controls on payments received from abroad by residents or citizens, as well as on payments made abroad by residents or citizens. The International Monetary Fund (IMF) publishes an annual report on "exchange restrictions," which briefly summarizes the various exchange controls in effect at the time of publication of the report.

The IMF also imposes a number of limitations on what a national government may do in restricting foreign exchange transactions. Article VIII of the Fund's Articles of Agreement prohibits discriminatory currency practices and enjoins member countries to avoid restrictions on "current payments." In contrast, the IMF Articles contain no restrictions on member states' treatment of capital payments.

Although the United States traditionally has not utilized, and has been philosophically opposed to, exchange controls, beginning in the 1960s the United States

Government adopted a variety of measures in response to severe balance of payments difficulties. These included, among others, (1) an "interest equalization tax" (IET) on the value of foreign securities bought by United States residents which was intended to discourage such purchases; (2) the Department of Commerce Foreign Direct Investment Controls, administered by the Office of Foreign Direct Investments; and (3) the Federal Reserve Board "Voluntary Foreign Credit Restraint Program," designed to restrain loans and investments abroad. After the floating of the dollar and other measures which resulted in a flexible exchange rate system and a revaluation of the dollar, these measures were discontinued. At the present time, the United States does not subject incoming or outgoing capital payments to exchange control, with a few exceptions for national security reasons or to protect vital national interests.

Until recently, the United Kingdom maintained an elaborate system of exchange controls. These were basically administered by the Bank of England and took on particular significance in light of the United Kingdom's importance as a center of international finance. The United Kingdom has now, however, abolished all exchange controls.

Until even more recently, one of the most elaborate systems of exchange controls among the major industrial countries was that maintained by France. Imposed in part as a response to a rapidly worsening balance of trade, and correspondingly weak franc, French regulations required that payments or financial transfers of any kind from a resident to a foreign destination or to a nonresident in France, as well as the importation and exportation of gold, had generally to be authorized by the Ministry of the Economy, Finance and Budget. Also, exchange operations and payments of all kinds between France and foreign countries and between residents and nonresidents in France had, unless otherwise specifically authorized by the Ministry, to be carried out through approved intermediaries or the Postal and Telecommunications Administration. Approved intermediaries were designated by the Ministry of the Economy, Finance and Budget and included most commercial banks.

On March 9, 1989, France abolished all exchange controls for business transactions. Some controls remained for bank transactions of ordinary individuals, but these were eliminated by June 1990.

Exchange controls remain in other countries in Western Europe, but these too have been liberalized and are expected to be abolished as the European Community moves toward 1992.

[3] Securities Law

Securities law is the law that governs trade in stocks, bonds and other marketable securities and is part of the general law of financial services which includes, in addition to securities, banking, insurance, and miscellaneous related sevices such as factoring, mortgage lending and certain leasing operations. Such laws also impact such support industries as accountants and foreign exchange traders. From the perspective of the European Economic Community the free movement of capital and financial services is indispensable to the realization of a single, internal market. As a result, the Community is close to final adoption of a directive[6] (The

---

[6] Article 189 of the Rome Treaty provides: "A directive shall be binding, as to the result to be achieved, upon each member state to which it is addressed, but shall leave to the

Second Banking Directive) which would establish a single EC banking license and thereby permit a bank, established in any member state (the home country), to set up branches in any other member state, subject to regulation by the home country. As originally drafted, the Second Banking Directive would have conditioned third country access to the single market on "reciprocal treatment," *i.e.*, it appeared that a third country (such as the United States) would have to accord to EC credit institutions "mirror image" reciprocity before its own banks could be authorized to do business in a member state of the European community. The EC Commission later modified its position and adopted a "national treatment" standard, under which a non-EC country would only have to accord to EC banks the same competitive opportunities as were available to domestic banks to receive the full benefits of the Second Banking Directive.

The European Community has also adopted or proposed a number of directives relating to the regulation of securities trading. The most relevant to foreign direct investments are a directive on the information that must be published when major holdings in EC companies are acquired or disposed of and a proposed directive on takeover bids for EC public companies. These and other directives establish only minimum standards and are heavily supplemented by the laws of member states, especially those with developed systems of takeover regulation.

France, for example, has recently adopted new securities legislation. The legislation contains a number of measures aimed at protecting French private enterprises against hostile takeovers, such as increasing disclosure requirements for acquisitions. It also broadens the powers of the French Stock Exchange Transactions Commission. For its part the United Kingdom has expressed reservations regarding the proposed EEC directive on takeovers. Of particular concern to the British are the methods of implementation, the apparent lack of flexibility and the likelihood that the directive would generate unnecessary litigation. As the EEC member state with the most mergers and acquisitions, the United Kingdom has a particular interest in this subject.

Directives already adopted by the European Community contain, inter alia, requirements on the establishment in each member state of public registers for important corporate documents, on minimum standards for initial capitalization of a public company, on mergers carried out by the formation of a new company, and on minimum standards for the financial statements of public and private limited liability companies.

[4] Labor Relations

A major factor the U.S. based business enterprise considering doing business abroad must take into account is the legal, economic and social environment surrounding employer-employee relations in the prospective host country. In many of the industrial countries, especially in Western Europe, both blue and

---

national authorities the choice of form and methods." Under this provision, the implementing legislation — not the directive itself — is the enforceable law within member countries. However, the member country itself is under an obligation to enact such implementing legislation, and in several instances where a member country has failed to do so, the Commission has brought a suit against the country before the European Court of Justice, the judicial organ of the Community.

white-collar workers have gained rights which extend far beyond those attained in the United States, while management freedoms have been restricted in many areas. Through a process known as "harmonization," a primary function of the European Community has been to encourage member countries to adjust their laws so that all national law on a particular subject is essentially equivalent and reflects a uniform minimum standard. While, in response to explicit provisions in the Treaty of Rome,[7] the Community has been particularly active in the harmonization of company law, Article 117 of the Treaty instructs the Commission to propose measures for "the improvement of the living and working conditions of labour so as to permit the equalization of such conditions in an improved direction." Pursuant to this provision, the Community has adopted a number of so-called "social policy" directives concerning employer-employee relations.

For example, under one Directive, companies must guarantee that workers not be adversely affected as a result of the transfer or merger of a business which means that workers cannot be dismissed as result of the transfer or merger; all rights granted in a collective bargaining agreement must be maintained; and companies must provide information to and consult with employee representatives on proposed transfers or mergers. A Directive on Mass Dismissals provides for notification and consultation procedures where an employer intends to lay off employees for a reason unrelated to the individual behavior of the employee. In practice these consultation procedures have usually involved some form of collective bargaining on the issue of layoffs.

Proposed Directives have a much more expansive reach than those adopted to date. The Proposed Fifth Directive on Company Structure and Administration would require that public companies be managed by a three-tier system: a management branch (responsible for managing and representing the company); a supervisory branch (responsible for controlling management); and a general meeting of shareholders. Worker participation in the supervisory branch would be required for companies employing over 500 persons. Opposition by European business groups to this proposal has been formidable, and it is unlikely that the proposal will be adopted in the near future.

Similarly, strong opposition from business circles is likely to defeat an EC Commission proposal for a regulation[8] that would create a European limited

---

[7] One objective of the Treaty of Rome, establishing the European Economic Community (EEC), was to assure that companies organized under the laws of one member country would be free to organize branches or subsidiaries in any other member country. In keeping with this goal, the Treaty authorizes the EEC Commission to propose, and the Council of Ministers to adopt, directives requiring that company laws of member countries be essentially equivalent with respect to the rights granted to, and the obligations imposed upon, enterprises doing business in the Community. To take advantage of the Community's provisions on freedom of establishment, an American corporation can organize a subsidiary in, say, the Federal Republic of Germany, and use the subsidiary to establish businesses in all other member states of the Community.

[8] Under Article 189 of the Rome Treaty, a regulation "shall have general application. It shall be binding in its entirety and directly applicable in Member States." Accordingly, a regulation may be enforced directly in the courts of member countries, as well as through Community procedures.

liability company. According to the Commission, the proposed European Company, which would be like a company formed under federal rather than state law in the United States, would facilitate cross-border cooperation between enterprises in different member states. The regulation proposed by the Commission, however, would set forth rules regarding the participation of workers in the decision making process of the European company.

The most expansive, as well as the most controversial, proposed Directive is the so-called Vredeling Proposal. Several member countries of the Community, most notably Belgium and Germany, have legislation that requires employers to provide extensive information to their workers and to consult with them before taking decisions that could affect the workers' jobs. Unions in these countries have consistently charged that multinational corporations have been able to avoid these laws. In order to meet these objections and in an attempt to promote Community-wide compliance, former EC Social Affairs Commissioner Henk Vredeling proposed a new Directive which would require all member states of the Community to adopt worker disclosure and consultation requirements similar to those already in place in Belgium and Germany. Vredeling's proposal would go further than the Belgian and German laws, however, and require that parent companies of Community-based enterprises disclose to their subsidiaries all corporate plans which could conceivably affect the interests of workers in the Community. In its original form of October 24, 1980, the Vredeling Proposal would require, *inter alia*:

— That the management of a "dominant" company in a group forward every six months to the management of its subsidiaries in the Community information on such matters as its payroll, investment program, production and sales, manufacturing and work methods, and any other matter likely to have "a substantial effect on employees' interests." Each subsidiary employing more than 100 people would have to pass on such information to worker representatives without delay;

— That management must inform the subsidiary at least 40 days in advance of any action which could have a major impact on the workers. Workers are then given 30 days to give their opinion. If workers believe that the proposal will affect their jobs, management must initiate direct consultations with the workers concerned.

— That when a subsidiary does not inform or consult with workers, worker representatives must be able to talk directly with the management of the dominant company.

The Vredeling Proposal was subjected to heated objections from a broad sector of business and industry in Europe and the United States. As a result, it was amended. Nonetheless, the amended draft retained its extraterritorial scope. It is unlikely to be adopted by the Council in the near future.

The country in the Community that has gone the furthest in granting rights to employees and imposing restrictions on management is the Federal Republic of Germany. Of particular note is the Co-Determination Law of 1976. Under that law all stock corporations must have at least one labor representative on their supervisory board except for stock corporations with fewer than 500 employees if they are family companies, or are owned by one or a small group of closely related persons. Limited liability companies with fewer than 500 employees need have no supervisory board and therefore have no labor representatives. On the other hand, employees must have an equal number of seats on the supervisory boards of companies with 2,000 employees or more. Any business corporation with a share capital exceeding Deutsche Mark 50 million must have 21 members on its supervisory board, ten each from the shareholders and from the employees and one independent member selected by a simple majority of the other board members.

Equally noteworthy are the constraints placed on employers in personnel matters by the 1972 Work Council Law. For example, entrepreneurs employing more than 20 persons who plan to hire an additional employee must obtain the work council's consent. The work council may insist that new jobs be offered first to current employees. Also, employees have the right to look into their personnel files, to lodge complaints with the work council, and to express their views on measures taken by the employer that concern them. They may ask for an explanation of the way in which their pay is computed. Work councils must be heard prior to giving any notice of discharge to an employee. Any notice given without hearing the views of the work council is void. If an employer and a work council cannot resolve a dispute, it may be referred to a conciliation board or to a separate labor court for decision.

[5] Taxation

Tax considerations are an indispensable component in planning for international business transactions. The subject of U.S. taxation of international business transactions alone is complex enough to require book length treatment, and we do not attempt to cover this subject other than to highlight the need to explore the implications of United States tax laws for international business planning. In addition to tax burdens under United States law, the international practitioner must be aware of possible tax liabilities in the country where the client is contemplating doing business as well as the possible applicability of bilateral treaties designed to avoid double taxation. In this section, we briefly survey some of these considerations.

The United States has entered into income tax treaties with approximately forty countries and has negotiated or is negotiating such treaties with a number of other countries. These treaty countries account for the major portion of international trade with the United States, as well as for the bulk of United States investment abroad.

Most of these treaties are subject to a so-called "savings" clause which provides that the United States has the right to tax its citizens, residents, and domestic corporations as if the treaty had not come into effect. Accordingly, the treaties generally affect only the taxes that may be due the foreign country. Nonetheless, tax treaties may prove beneficial if the United States foreign tax credit mechanism (which is uniformly excepted from the savings clause) fails to resolve the problem of international double taxation. Also, these treaties may help to resolve conflicting concepts of taxable income, conflicting rules on the timing of income and deductions, or conflicting income sourcing rules between the United States and its treaty partner countries.

A basic rule of these treaties is that a resident or enterprise of a treaty country deriving industrial or commercial profits from sources in the other country shall not be subject to taxation by the latter unless it is engaged in a trade or business through a permanent establishment there. The definition of a permanent establishment differs from treaty to treaty, but usually includes a branch, general agency, or fixed place of business. It does not include a subsidiary. The foreign tax, if paid, would be credited against United States tax liability on the foreign income. At a minimum, the permanent establishment concept may help in avoiding the inconvenience of having to file a foreign tax return and may result in a tax savings if the treaty has the effect of eliminating the payment of foreign taxes or if the foreign tax payment would exceed the applicable U.S. tax rate or if the foreign tax could not be taken as a credit against U.S. taxes.

Other important clauses in tax treaties include the "commercial travelers" exemption designed to provide the migrant corporate executive who spends substantial amounts of time during the year in several countries with objective criteria that prevent his income being taxed by two or more jurisdictions; clauses reducing or eliminating foreign tax on investment income, such as dividends, interest, rents, and royalties; and clauses providing that income from personal services (including professional and artistic services) performed for an enterprise of one country, while temporarily residing in the other country, are exempt from taxation in the latter. Most treaties limit the temporary residence to six months, and in some treaties the income exemptions are limited to $3,000 to $10,000 and the consideration must be paid by a nonresident alien or foreign corporate employer. Exemptions are also provided for students, teachers and trainees.

Under these treaties the competent authorities of the treaty parties are to exchange such information as is necessary to carry out the provisions of the treaty and to prevent fraud or fiscal evasion. These treaties also set forth procedures for consultation between the parties regarding the interpretation and application of the treaty.

Depending upon the item and the nature of its operations, a firm doing business in a foreign industrialized country may be subject to a wide variety of taxes. These could include, among others, (1) corporate taxes; (2) an annual capital tax measured by the amount of invested capital; (3) a "turnover tax" based upon sales or turnover of inventory; (4) stamp and registration taxes on the issuance or transfer of stock certificates or on the transfer of real estate; (5) payroll taxes based on either wages or the number of employees; and (6) miscellaneous forms of local taxes.[9]

---

[9] For information regarding doing business in Europe, the best general and most current source is Commerce Clearing House, Common Market Reporter: Doing Business In Europe. Another useful Commerce Clearing House publication is the four volume Common Market Reporter. The Bureau of National Affairs, International Trade Reporter, U.S. Export Weekly And U.S. Import Weekly also contains much helpful information regarding developments in foreign countries of interest to United States investors. For a helpful overview of current developments in the European Community, see Thieffry, Van Doorn, and Lowe, The Single European Market: A Practitioner's Guide To 1992, 7 Boston Col. Int'l and Comp. L. Rev. 357 (1989). With regard to Canada, Volume 1 of the Boston University International Law Review (1982) contains a symposium on foreign investment in Canada. For reports on the Investment Canada Act, see Glover, New, & Lacourciere,

[B] The Developing Countries

Many of the problems a United States investor may face in the developing countries are similar to those it encounters in the developed world. Even as to these problems, however, the investor may find that, while similar in kind, they are of a greater magnitude in the developing world. Other problems are more or less unique to the developing world, *e.g.*, requirements for divestment and high tariffs.

One major complicating factor in the developing countries is the ambivalence many of them feel toward foreign private investment. If one focuses on recent actions taken by the United Nations General Assembly, the developing countries appear to view foreign investment as a form of neocolonialism to be severely constrained in order to ensure that the host country retains control over its national sovereignty. By contrast, a number of developing countries (*e.g.*, Egypt, Sri Lanka, Korea and Taiwan) have enacted national legislation that contains highly favorable provisions for foreign investors, including, in a few cases (Korea, Taiwan), guarantees against expropriation, or at least guarantees that, in the event of expropriation, full compensation in a convertible currency shall be promptly paid; relaxed exchange controls; tax incentives, such as tax holidays, which are partial or complete exemptions from the payment of income tax for a specified period; relief from export duties; and special incentives for foreign investors who intend to establish export oriented industries in the host country. Also, a rather large number of developing countries have entered into bilateral investment treaties or "BITS." The BIT serves to protect foreign investment abroad by establishing a comprehensive framework for nondiscriminatory treatment of foreign investors, dispute settlement procedures, compensation for expropriation, and transfers of funds into and out of the host country.

The United States has been a latecomer to bilateral investment treaties, having signed its first BIT with Egypt on September 29, 1982. Shortly thereafter it signed similar agreements with Panama and Haiti. As of late 1989, the United States had signed ten, and ratified eight, BITS. These treaties afford a substantially greater protection to foreign investment than do the Friendship, Commerce and Naviagation Treaties and have the potential to promote investment abroad in both developed and developing countries.[10]

The debate over the advantages and disadvantages of foreign investment has, unfortunately, generated more heat than light. Those promoting the benefits of foreign investment point out that it brings much needed foreign currency and capital goods to the host country, that it increases employment, both directly in

---

The Investment Canada Act: Foreign Investment In Canada, 41 Bus. Law. 83 (1985); Grover, The Investment Canada Act, 10 Can. Bus. L. J. 75 (1985). The Canada-United States Free Trade Agreement requires a gradual liberalization of Canadian laws on foreign investments. International tax issues are discussed in depth by D. Tillinghast, International Economic Law: Tax Aspects Of International Transactions (2d ed. 1984).

[10] For comment on BITS, see United Nations Centre On Transnational Corporations, Bilateral Investment Treaties (1988); Vandevelde, The Bilateral Investment Treaty Program Of The United States, 21 Cornell Int'l L.J. 201 (1988); Gann, The U.S. Bilateral Investment Program, 21 Stan J. Int'l L. 373 (1986); Comment, Developing A Model Bilateral Investment Treaty, 15 Law and Pol. in Int'l Bus. 273 (1983).

the company established by the foreign investors and indirectly through generating employment in related industries, and that foreign investment transfers technology and know-how or managerial expertise to the host country. In contrast the critics of foreign investment, especially in Latin America, contend that it is a form of neocolonialism. They argue that the foreign investor's interests are in conflict with those of the host country and that the former will attempt to maintain the latter in a state of dependency if possible. In their view, the foreign investor creates imbalances in the local economy because of its emphasis on the extractive industries and primary agricultural products. Further, under this view, the foreign investor excludes nationals of the host country from managerial positions, exacerbates foreign exchange problems through the repatriation of dividends, interest and royalties, competes with local businesses for scarce financing, and enjoys excessive profits through the use of sophisticated accounting procedures.

It is risky to generalize about which view is in the ascendancy at any particular time, especially since there is often a wide gap between rhetoric and practice in developing countries. Moreover, it is important to realize that, regardless of the general attitude among developing countries toward foreign investment, one must focus on the situation in the particular country one is considering for investment purposes. Even if the investment climate appears favorable at the moment, it may change radically with a change of governments. Protection against such abrupt changes in position must therefore be an integral part of any planning for investment.

Some obvious first steps toward such protection would include an examination of any applicable foreign investment laws or bilateral investment treaties. In conducting this search, one must ascertain the extent to which, under the laws of the prospective host country, the foreign investor is able to maintain control over its investment. Thus it is advisable to survey such factors as requirements concerning the amount and form of foreign equity contributions; the necessity and extent of local equity participation; restrictions on the voting rights of equity shareholders; and the extent, in practice, of government interference in the management of business. Labor laws of the developing countries may place severe restraints on the hiring and firing of personnel and limit the number of foreign nationals that may serve in management positions.

There may also be severe constraints on the remittance of profits, royalties, technical service fees, and interest and on repatriation of capital. These constraints may include foreign exchange controls, which may take many forms. The host country may set artificial exchange rates utilizing a two-tier exchange rate, require that the foreign exchange earnings of the enterprise be deposited in the central bank, limit access to foreign exchange based on its own priorities, or otherwise restrict access to foreign exchange. Essential to the viability of any project are guarantees of access to foreign currency for debt servicing and materials essential to constructing and operating the enterprise. Also the ability to import materials may be constrained by tariffs imposed by the host country. High customs duties can increase the costs both of initial capital expenditures and raw materials or components used in the manufacture of products. Obtaining a total or partial exemption from import duties may be crucial to the success of a project.

More generally, with respect to the level of tax liability in the host country, the investor must be aware not only of import duties but also export taxes, personal property and real estate taxes, corporate taxes, including those on income, royalties, dividends, and interest payments, personal income taxes, local and municipal taxes, and value added, sales or other excise taxes. As in the case of investments in developed countries, a tax treaty with the United States may be an important factor, although there are few such treaties with developing countries.

Also of great importance is the host country's treatment of patents, trademarks and know-how. One needs to search the host country's law and practice to ensure the absence of burdensome restrictions on licensing agreements, the availability of protection for industrial property rights, and the ability to control the use and development of technology.

In all of these and other areas, it must be emphasized, one must be aware of the difference between law on the books and law in practice. In developing countries in particular, arbitrary changes in administrative practice or capricious decision making can deny benefits that the investor expected. The laws of the host country themselves may provide government officials with substantial discretion in the decision making process, or such officials may simply arrogate to themselves such authority. In any event the prospective foreign investor is well advised to consider the experience of already established enterprises in the host country.

In addition to research into the law and practice of the host country, there are a number of specific steps the United States investor can take to minimize its risk in developing countries. These include obtaining investment guarantees from the United States and negotiating with the host country's government contractual provisions regarding choice of law, arbitration, and waiver of sovereign immunity and the exhaustion of local remedies defenses.[11]

By way of illustration of some of the points covered above, as well as of some other matters, consider the following:

MEXICO

Law To Promote Mexican Investment
and to
Regulate Foreign Investment

Diario Official, March 9, 1973

ARTICLE 2

For purposes of this law, foreign investment shall be considered that which is undertaken by:

I.   Foreign corporate companies;

II.   Foreign individuals;

III.   Foreign economic entities without legal personality; and

---

[11] For a detailed survey of these steps, see Brower, International Legal Protection Of United States Investors Abroad, A Lawyer's Guide To International Business Transactions (Part III, Folio 6), W. Surrey and D. Wallace, Jr. 2d ed. 1981).

IV. Mexican business enterprises with majority foreign capital or in which foreigners are empowered, by any title, to control the management of the business enterprise.

Foreign investment in the capital of business enterprises, in the acquisition of properties, and in all other operations to which this law refers, shall be subject to the provisions of said law.

ARTICLE 4

The following activities are reserved exclusively for the Government:

(a) Petroleum and other hydrocarbons;

(b) Basic petrochemicals;

(c) Exploitation of radioactive minerals and the generation of nuclear energy;

(d) Mining in cases covered by the law relating thereto;

(e) Electricity;

(f) Railroads;

(g) Telegraphic and wireless communications; and

(h) Other activities established in specific laws.

The following activities are reserved exclusively for Mexicans or for Mexican companies with an exclusion of foreigners clause:

(a) Radio and Television;

(b) Urban and Interurban automotive transportation and transportation on federal highways;

(c) Domestic air and maritime transportation;

(d) Exploitation of forestry resources;

(e) Gas distribution; and

(f) Other activities established in specific laws, or in regulations issued by the Executive Branch of the Federal Government.

ARTICLE 5

Foreign investment shall be permitted in the activities of business enterprises listed below, in the following capital percentages:

(a) Exploitation and use of minerals.

Concessions may not be granted or transferred to foreign individuals or corporate bodies. Foreign investment in companies operating in this area may hold up to 49 percent in the case of exploitation and use of substances subject to ordinary concessions, and 34 percent in the case of special concessions for the exploitation of national mining reserves;

(b) Secondary petrochemicals: 40 percent

(c) Manufacture of automotive components: **40** percent; and

(d) Those established in specific laws or regulations issued by the Executive Branch.

In cases where legal provisions or regulations do not specify a given percentage, foreign investment may hold up to **49** percent of the capital of business enterprises provided it is not empowered, by any title, to control the management of the business enterprise.

The National Commission on Foreign Investment may decide on the increase or reduction of the percentage to which the preceding paragraph refers when it judges this to be in the interest of the country's economy, and it may establish the conditions under which foreign investment will be accepted in specific cases.

The participation of foreign investment in the administration of the business enterprise may not exceed its share of the capital.

When laws or regulations exist for a given activity, foreign investment shall comply with the percentages and conditions specified in such laws or regulations.

ARTICLE 8

Authorization by the corresponding Ministry, according to the economic activity involved, shall be required where one or more of the individuals or companies to which Article 2 refers, in one or several actions, or a succession of actions, acquires . . . more than **25** percent of the capital, or over **49** percent of the fixed assets of a business enterprise. The leasing of a business enterprise or of the essential assets required for its functioning, shall be considered equivalent to the acquisition of assets.

Also requiring authorization are actions by which the administration of a business enterprise is acquired by foreign investors, or by which foreign investment is empowered, by any title, to control the management of the business investment.

The authorization to which this article refers shall be granted when it is considered in the interest of the country, pursuant to ruling by the National Commission on Foreign Investment.

Actions undertaken without such authorization shall be null and void.

ARTICLE 12

The National Commission on Foreign Investment shall have the following powers:

I. To decide, in accordance with Article 5 of this law, the increase or reduction of the percentage of the foreign investment share in the country's different geographical areas or economic activities, when there are no legal provisions or regulations that establish a given percentage or set the conditions under which such investment may be received;

II.   To decide the percentages and conditions in which foreign investment shall be accepted in specific cases where, because of exceptional circumstances, special treatment is called for;

III. To decide on proposed foreign investment in business enterprises established, or to be established, in Mexico, or in new business enterprises;

IV.   To decide on the participation of foreign investment existing in Mexico in new fields of economic activity or in new production lines;

* * * *

ARTICLE 13

In order to determine the advisability of authorizing foreign investment and to establish the percentages and conditions by which it shall be governed, the Commission shall take into account the following criteria and characteristics of the investment:

I.   That it should be complementary to national investment;

II.   That it should not displace national business enterprises that are operating satisfactorily, and that it should not enter fields that are adequately covered by such enterprises;

III. Its positive effects on the balance of payments and, especially, on the increase of Mexican exports;

IV.   Its effect on employment, taking into account job opportunities created and wages paid;

V.   The employment and training of Mexican technical and management personnel;

VI.   The incorporation of domestic inputs and components in the manufacture of its products;

VII. The extent to which it finances its operations with resources from abroad;

VIII. The diversification of sources of investment and the need to foster Latin American regional and subregional integration;

IX.   Its contribution to the development of the relatively less economically developed zones or regions;

X.   That it should not enjoy a monopolistic position in the domestic market;

XI.   The capital structure of the branch of economic activity involved;

XII. Its contribution of technology and its assistance in the country' technological research and development;

XIII. Its effect on price levels and quality of production;

XIV. That it should respect the country's social and cultural values;

XV.   The importance of the activity in question in the context of the country's economy;

XVI. The extent to which the foreign investor is identified with the country's interest and his connection with foreign centers of economic decision; and

XVII. In general, the extent to which it complies with, and contributes to the achievement of national development policy objectives.

ARTICLE 17

Foreigners shall obtain prior permission from the Ministry of Foreign Affairs to acquire real estate and to constitute or modify companies. Said permissions shall be subject to legal provisions in force and to rulings made by the National Commission on Foreign Investment.

ARTICLE 23

The National Registry of Foreign Investments is hereby created, in which shall be registered:

I. Foreign individuals or companies that make investments governed by this law;

II. Mexican companies, a share of whose capital is held by the individuals or entities to which Article 2 of this law refers;

III. Trusts in which foreigners participate and the purpose of which is to conduct operations governed by this law;

IV. Securities representing capital owned by foreigners, or given to them as guarantee;

V. Rulings made by the Commission.

The regulations shall determine the organization of the Registry and establish the form and manner in which information should be provided.

ARTICLE 27

Companies that are obliged to register in the National Registry of Foreign Investment and fail to do so, shall not pay dividends. Neither shall dividends be paid on securities which, though required to be registered in the National Registry of Foreign Investments, are not so registered.

Companies that are obliged to register, and do so, shall be registered ex parte by the competent authorities, or at the request of any of their shareholders.

ARTICLE 28

Actions undertaken in violation of the provisions of this law, and actions that, though required to be registered in the National Registry of Foreign Investments, are not so registered, shall be null and void and shall therefore have no validity before any authority. In addition, offenders shall be fined by the corresponding Government Ministry or Department up to the value of the operation. The fine will be up to 100,000 pesos in those cases where the amount of the violation cannot be determined.

Consider as well the following provisions of the General Resolutions issued by the National Foreign Investment Commission:

SECTION II. FOREIGN PARTICIPATION IN MANAGEMENT

1. The appointment of non-Mexican directors in Mexican corporations having foreign investment is hereby authorized, provided that compliance is given to the paragraph before last of Article 5 of the Law.

SECTION VII. FOREIGN INVESTMENT IN MEDIUM AND SMALL SIZE CORPORATIONS

1. Foreign individuals or entities that meet the requirements set forth in Paragraph 2 below, are hereby authorized to acquire shares of stock or corporate participation in Mexican companies, upon incorporation thereof, representing up to 100% of the capital thereof, provided that any such foreign individuals or corporate entities shall assume the obligation, upon incorporation of the Mexican company, that the latter shall comply with the terms and conditions set forth in Paragraph 3 below.

The above authorization is granted with the exceptions provided for in the first and last paragraphs of Article 5 of the Law.

2. The authorization set forth in the preceding point is granted to foreign individuals and corporate entities, provided:

    a. Their annual consolidated sales shall not exceed US $8,000,000.

    b. Their personnel, including workers, technicians and office employees, shall not exceed 500 people.

    c. They shall assume the obligation to provide to the newly incorporated Mexican company technology that is not available in this country, or if available, is not advanced. For purposes hereof, not advanced technology shall be considered existing technology which is not capable of reducing production costs at levels attainable with technology supplied by the foreign investors referred to herein.

    d. They shall not belong to any foreign economic unit or group exceeding, on a consolidated basis, the limits set forth in paragraphs (a) and (b) above.

3. The authorization set forth in Paragraph 1 above is granted provided, however, that the Mexican companies to be incorporated thereunder will be subject to the following conditions and obligations:

    a. Will be engaged solely in manufacturing or industrial activities and will not operate in service and commerce areas, other than those related to the above activities.

    b. Will not exceed, in domestic sales, the limit determined on an annual basis by the Subcommission for Medium and Small-Sized Industries, pursuant to the presidential decree that regulates said agency.

    c. Will export at least 35% of their total annual production, either directly or through third parties. To this end, each productive year shall commence on the date of the first sale of manufactured goods or products.

   d. Will attain in each productive year a surplus in their balance of trade and a break even point in their balance of payments. To this end, each productive year shall be computed as provided in sub-paragraph (c) above.

   e. Will establish their industrial plants outside zones III-A and III-B, pursuant to the "Decree establishing geographical zones for industrial decentralization and incentive guaranteeing" thereof, published in the Official Gazette on January 22, 1986, or similar zones as may be defined in further legal regulations.

* * * *

SECTION IX. FOREIGN INVESTMENT IN NEW ESTABLISHMENTS

1. For purposes of the Law, a "new establishment" shall be deemed any areas and premises physically separate or different from those establishments already opened and effectively operated by foreign investors to conduct economic, administrative and supplementary activities or any support thereto, with personnel subordinated to said foreign investors or with personnel that, being subordinated to any third parties, may render its services to such foreign investors, regardless of the title, the possession, use or enjoyment of the property.

2. For the same purposes, a "new establishment" shall also be deemed all premises opened and operated by foreign investors to be used in activities other than those already being performed, whether or not related to the manufacture of items already being manufactured or activities already performed in any other premises.

* * * *

SECTION X. FOREIGN INVESTMENT IN NEW AREAS OF ECONOMIC ACTIVITY AND NEW PRODUCT LINES

1. Pursuant to the provisions of Article 12, Section IV and Article 15 of the Law, any and all investments intended to be made in new fields of economic activity or new product lines shall be subject to a prior resolution of the Commission and the prior approval from the Department of Commerce.

2. Foreign investors wishing to start an economic activity or manufacture a product or line of products which imply entering into a new activity or a new product line, as set forth in Paragraphs 3 and 4, must file an application with the Executive Secretary furnishing the required information to determine the advisability of authorizing the respective investment, pursuant to Article 13 of the Law.

3. For purposes of Article 12, Section IV, of the Law, a "new field of economic activity" shall mean:

   a. Any activities other than those effectively conducted by an established foreign investor as of the date it became a foreign investor, pursuant to the provisions of Article 2 of the Law, continuously, at a commercial and not experimental scale, under any required governmental authorizations and approvals, which activities imply entering into a different class under the catalogue included as Exhibit 1 hereof.

    b. Any activities other than those effectively conducted by an established foreign investor, as outlined in the preceding paragraph, which do not imply entering into a different class in the catalogue, will satisfy the demand of a different market or consumer sector.

    c. Any activities not within the classes where the company operates, nor contemplated in the catalogue, provided that such determination is made by the Commission, upon filing the respective application, pursuant to the provision of Paragraph 2 hereof.

4. For purposes of the provisions of Article 12, Section IV, of the Law, "new product lines" shall mean:

    a. A product or group of products other than those actually manufactured by an established foreign investor, as of the date it became a foreign investor, pursuant to the provisions of Article 2 of the Law, continuously, at a commercial and not experimental scale, under any required governmental authorizations and approval, which products imply entering into a different class, under the catalogue included as Exhibit 2 hereof.

    b. A product or group of products other than those actually manufactured by an established foreign investor, as outlined in the preceding paragraph, which do not imply entering into a different class, will satisfy the demand of a different market or consumer sector.

    c. Any products or lines not within the classes where the company operates, nor contemplated in the catalogue, provided such determination is made by the Commission upon filing of the respective application, pursuant to the provisions of Paragraph 2 hereof.

PROBLEMS

(1) Assume that your client, a small but highly innovative computer company with U.S. sales of ten million dollars and 550 employees, wishes to establish a market in Mexico through a subsidiary. It wants to have majority ownership and control of the subsidiary, including a majority of U.S. citizens on the board of directors, because it is anxious to minimize the risk of disclosure of information regarding its intellectual property.

Can your client carry out its wishes? What further information, if any, would you wish to have to better evaluate your client's chances? What plan of action would you propose for your client?

(2) Assume that since 1970 another client of yours that sells chocolate in bars and other forms has done business in Mexico through a wholly owned subsidiary. Concluding that there would be a strong market in Mexico for additional sweet foods, your client wishes to sell a variety of pastries in Mexico, some with a chocolate base and some with other sweetening ingredients.

What problems, if any, might your client face in carrying out its plan? How might they be resolved?

———————————

One form of foreign investment strongly encouraged by the Mexican Government is the so-called *maquiladora* operation. Under this system some of the manufacturing process is performed in the United States and some in Mexico. For its part the Mexican Government permits inputs from the U.S. plant to enter duty free and to be assembled in the *maquiladora* plant on the Mexican side of the border. When the finished product is shipped back to the United States, the U.S. Government imposes a tariff only on the value added to the product in Mexico. No duty is charged on the U.S. source content. The primary benefits of the program to Mexico are that it increases jobs for its citizens and constitutes a major source of foreign exchange — currently the second largest after the petroleum/hydrocarbons industry. The *maquiladora* industry also ranks as the country's most rapidly expanding industrial sector. As a consequence, Mexican foreign investment law expressly permits 100 percent foreign ownership of a *maquiladora* company. Another major benefit for the U.S. investor is that, through the use of low cost Mexican labor and the special customs benefits, it can better compete with foreign competition in the U.S. market. Although it has been criticized as exploiting Mexico and depriving U.S. labor of jobs, the program is generally viewed as highly successful.

Prior to 1982, Mexico scrupulously avoided the imposition of foreign exchange controls. In that year, however, in response to a rapidly worsening foreign debt problem, Mexico established, by presidential decree, a stringent system of such controls and nationalized the banks as well.[12] (They are currently being returned to the private sector.) Also in response to the foreign debt crisis, Mexico, along with other developing countries, engaged in so-called "debt for equity swaps," whereby persons holding a country's external debt, which was selling at a significant discount, could exchange it for local currency at or near the face value of the obligation and use the proceeds for certain stated investment purposes in the debtor country.[13]

In Mexico, one must pay special attention to the regulations implementing the law on foreign investment as well as the law itself. On May 16, 1989, The Regulations of the Law to Promote Mexican Investments and Regulate Foreign Investments were published in the Official Gazette (Diario Official). Under these regulations, which repealed all former administrative investment regulations, 100% foreign ownership of many enterprises with assets of as much as $100 million is permitted. Moreover, a foreign investor that meets certain requirements set forth in the regulations will have its investment proposal approved automatically, without the need of special approval from the National Foreign Investment

———————————

[12] See, *e.g.*, Doing Business In Mexico: The Impact Of Its Financial Crisis on Foreign Creditors And Investors: A Symposium, 18 Int'l Law. 287 (1984).

[13] See also W.P. Streng & J.W. Salacuse, 4 International Business Planning: Law And Taxation, Section 19.11 (1988).

Commission. Among these requirements are that all financing of the project come from outside Mexico, that the business locate outside the congested urban centers of Mexico City, Guadalajara, and Monterrey, and that the business's accumulated foreign exchange flows balance during its first three years of operation. The regulations also cut red tape in other ways and open some previously restricted sectors of the economy.

Although the regulations are designed to increase capital flows into Mexico at a time when foreign bank credit is scarce, skeptics point out that the law itself remains on the books and that the new regulations could easily be revised should the political climate in Mexico change. Accordingly, foreign investors and some Mexican economic officials have long urged that Mexico enact an entirely new law that would eliminate the provisions that restrict foreigners to minority holdings. At this writing, however, it appears that the Mexican government does not have the political strength to ensure passage of such legislation.[14]

§ 8.02 Particular Agreements

At this point, we turn to an examination of two kinds of investment agreements that raise particular problems: the economic development (formerly called concession) agreement and contracts for the construction of industrial works. Both of these types of investment agreements have received considerable attention in recent years, and each, partly as a result of this attention, has undergone considerable evolution.

[A] The Concession or Economic Development Agreement

Concession or economic development agreements are arrangements between foreign investors and host countries for the development of natural resources. Such arrangements have traditionally been referred to as "concession agreements." More recently, the name most commonly applied to such an arrangement has been "economic development agreement," although others have been employed as well. The reasons for this shift in terminology should become apparent from the discussion below.

Under the traditional concession agreement which predominated in the first half of the twentieth century, the foreign investor or concessionaire was given a virtually unrestricted right to exploit one or more natural resources. Typically, the concessionaire was given exclusive rights over a large land area for a period of time as long as 50 or 60 years or more. These exclusive rights commonly covered exploration, exploitation, processing, refining, transportation, storage, marketing, and all other rights and powers appropriate for the conduct of the operation. Payments to the host country from the concessionaire consisted mainly of royalties and were not onerous.

These expansive "concessions" reflected the enormous power of a small group of western industrialized states. The leaders of the non-industrialized countries

---

[14] For a discussion of these regulations and of the changing investment climate in Mexico, see Symposium on the New Environment for Trade and Investment in Mexico, 12 Houston J. Int'l L. 181 (1990).

were often lacking in technological expertise and were sometimes corrupt. Futhermore, the movement for independence that followed World War II and the anti-colonial ideology that accompanied that movement strengthened the position of the developing countries in the United Nations. This strength began to be reflected in General Assembly resolutions. The resolutions of 1962 and 1974, discussed *infra* in Chapter 9, pp. 775-777, are perhaps the best examples of this change. In the 1962 resolution, paragraph 8 stated that "foreign investment agreements freely entered into by . . . sovereign states shall be observed in good faith." By 1974 the Charter on Economic Rights and Duties contained no such provision, stressed instead the concept of national sovereignty over natural resources, and rejected the application of international law to actions by a sovereign state taken with respect to natural resources within its own territory.

This shift of power from the concessionaires to the host countries began as early as the 1950s when an agreement between Saudi Arabia and Aramco introduced the concept of equal profit sharing as compared to the host country taking only 20% or less of the net. The process accelerated in the 1970s with the so-called oil crisis. The embargo in 1974 by the Organization of Petroleum Exporting Countries (OPEC) in the wake of the 1973 war between Israel and Egypt and Syria and the resultant sharp rise in the price of oil ushered in a radical restructuring of arrangements between the host countries and the oil companies. Royalties gave way to income taxation as the primary source of government revenue and the result was that the host countries began to take as much as 80% of the net profits. Other changes in concession agreements also took place, including provisions that required the concessionaire to hire and train local citizens; to guarantee access by local users to such infrastructure as roads, railroads, and communications systems; to build and operate schools, hospitals, and other services for the concessionaire's workers; and to contribute money and personnel to local community development. In some instances the restructuring of the arrangement was so extensive as to leave the concessionaire in the position of being little more than an operator of an oil field under a technical services contract with the country. The host countries also increasingly enacted legislation that subjected the concessionaire to economic and environmental regulation.

The success of the OPEC countries in dealing with the international oil companies led the producers of other raw materials to establish similar cartels. For a variety of reasons, however, these efforts have not been successful. Indeed, for all the reasons that make cartels inherently unstable (see Chapter 7) OPEC itself has come under severe strain. Nonetheless, these strains have not as yet led to any significant changes in the relationship between concessionaires and host countries forged in the cartel's heyday.

The problems of drafting an economic development agreement are manifold. In this section we explore only a few of the most salient problems.[1] To this end consider the provisions of a draft agreement set forth below. Then turn to the following notes and questions.

---

[1] For more elaborate consideration, see Smith & Wells, Negotiating Third World Mineral Agreements (1975); D. Vagts, Transnational Business Problems 445-88 (1986).

AGREEMENT BETWEEN THE UNITED ABU EMIRATES AND THE EXTRATERRESTRIAL ENERGY COMPANY 23 JULY 1990 (selected provisions)[2]

This Agreement is made in the United Abu Emirates, this twenty-third day of July, 1990, between the Government of United Abu Emirates (hereinafter referred to as the "Government") and the Extraterrestrial Energy Company (hereinafter referred to as the "Company") whereby it is agreed between the Government and the Company as follows:—

Article 1. Definitions

For purposes of this Agreement, the following terms shall be defined as set forth below.

    (A) "Economic Development Area" means 8520.66 sq. kms. of that part of United Abu Emirates territory which, for the purpose of identification only, is shown on the map annexed hereto. . . .

    (B) "Petroleum" means crude oil, natural gas, or ozokerite and all other hydrocarbon substances, products, by products, and derivatives.

* * * *

Article 2. Grant

The Government hereby grants to the Company subject to the terms hereinafter set forth, the exclusive rights to explore, search and drill for, produce, store, transport and sell Petroleum within the Economic Development Area. The exclusive right to explore, search and drill for, produce, store, transport and sell Petroleum includes all functions normally associated with such operations.

Article 3. Duration

The duration of this agreement shall be for a period of forty (40) years, starting with the Effective Date.

Article 4. Reservation

The Government reserves the right to search for and obtain any substances other than those exclusively granted by this Agreement within the Economic Development Area, excepting only those areas occupied by wells or other necessary installations of the Company provided always that the right thus reserved by the Government shall be exercised so as not to endanger or interfere with the operations and rights of the Company hereunder. In any grant of such rights so reserved by the Government, the grantee shall be bound by the provisions of this article.

---

[2] This economic development agreement is adapted from an Oil Concession Agreement between the Government of Abu Dhabi and Amerada Hess Exploration, Abu Dhabi Ltd., Occidental of Abu Dhabi Ltd. and Alpha Oil Corporation that appears in II Al Otaiba, The Petroleum Concession Agreements Of The United Arab Emirates, 1939-81, at 156 (1982). The agreement may also be found in D. Vagts, Transnational Business Problems 448 (1986). Copyright © 1986 by Foundation Press. Reprinted by permission.

Article 5. Work Obligations

(A)   The Company shall within six (6) months of the Effective Date commence to explore for Petroleum and shall within eighteen (18) months after the Effective Date complete initial geophysical operations in the Concession Area for the purposes of assessing the prospects of the area for production of Petroleum.

(B)   The Company shall within two (2) years after the Effective Date commence drilling a test well. Having commenced a test well the Company shall proceed with due diligence in accordance with good oil field practice to completion thereof and to completion of any other test well or wells which it may at any time thereafter drill in the Concession Area; provided, however, that in no event shall the aggregate depth of such well or wells be less than thirty thousand (30,000) feet (hereinafter referred to as "Minimum Depth Requirement") unless Crude Oil is discovered in Commercial Quantities before reaching the "Minimum Depth Requirement."

(C)   The Company shall undertake to spend on prospecting, exploration, drilling or development operations, even though Petroleum may have been discovered in Commercial Quantities, the following minimum amounts:

(1) In the first year after the Effective Date U.S. $3 million (Three million).

* * * *

(D)   If the expenditure in any year shall be less than the amounts specified above for such year, the Company shall expend the deficiency during the next succeeding two years in addition to the amounts specified for those years. In the event that the expenditures in any year shall be greater than that required for such year, such excess shall be credited against expenditure obligations for any succeeding year or years.

Article 7. Discovery of Other Minerals

If the Company shall discover in the course of its operations any deposits of minerals other than Petroleum, including , but not limited to, gold, silver, copper, lead, potash, sulphur or salt, the Company shall not work or appropriate the same but shall forthwith inform the Government of the discovery.

* * * *

Article 9. Bonus Payments

The Company agrees to pay to the Government the following amounts at the time and in the manner stated:

(A)   U.S. $4 million (Four million) within thirty (30) days after the Effective Date.

(B)   U.S. $5 million (Five million) within thirty (30) days after the discovery of crude oil in Commercial Quantities.

    (C)   U.S. $4 million (Four million) after regular exports of crude oil have reached and maintained an average rate of 50,000 barrels per day for thirty (30) consecutive days.

    (D)   U.S. $6 million (Six million) after regular exports of crude oil have reached and maintained an average of 100,000 barrels per day for thirty (30) consecutive days.

    (E)   U.S. $6 million (Six million) after regular exports of crude oil have reached and maintained an average of 200,000 barrels per day for thirty (30) consecutive days.

Article 10. Annual Rentals

The Company agrees to pay to the Government the following amounts of annual rentals at the time and in the manner stated:

    (A)   U.S. $100,000 (One hundred thousand) within thirty (30) days after the Effective Date.

    (B)   U.S. $100,000 (One hundred thousand) within thirty (30) days after each anniversary of the Effective Date including the anniversary preceding the date of the discovery of crude oil in commercial quantities.

    (C)   U.S. $100,000 (one hundred thousand) within thirty (30) days after the discovery of crude oil in commercial quantities and each anniversary thereof up to and including the anniversary preceding the export commencement date.

    Such rentals as aforesaid shall be deemed to accrue from day to day and the Company shall be entitled to recover such part of any rental which may have been paid which is referable to periods subsequent to the date of the discovery of Crude Oil in Commercial Quantities and the Export Commencement Date respectively.

Article 11. Royalty Payments

    (A)   The Company shall pay to the Government a (fully expensed) royalty equal to twelve and one half (12 1/2%) per cent of the Posted Price of Crude Oil produced and saved in the Concession Area each year, excluding Crude Oil used by the Company in its operation hereunder, as gauged at the point of export after deducting the basic sediments and water. If the production of Crude Oil during a calendar year shall reach an average rate of one hundred thousand (100,000) barrels per day, the Company shall pay a (fully expensed) royalty of sixteen (16%) per cent of the Posted Price. If the production of Crude Oil during a calendar year shall reach an average rate of two hundred thousand (200,000) barrels per day the Company shall pay a fully expensed royalty of twenty (20%) per cent of the Posted Price. The royalty herein provided shall be paid in whole or in part in kind or in cash at the election of the Government. The election of the Government to take its royalty wholly or partly in kind shall be given by notice in writing to the Company not less than three calendar months prior to the beginning of the calendar year to which such notice applies and shall cover a minimum period of one calendar year. Deliveries in kind hereunder shall be credited against royalties at the prevailing Posted Price.

(B) The royalty accruing to the Government as provided herein in any given calendar quarter shall be paid by the Company on or before the 30th of the following calendar month.

Article 12. Taxation

The Company shall, with respect to its net income from operations under this Agreement, pay a basic income tax at 55%. If the production of Crude Oil during a calendar year shall reach an average of 100,000 (One hundred thousand) barrels per day, the Company shall pay income tax at 65%. If the production of Crude Oil during a calendar year shall reach an average of 200,000 (Two hundred thousand) barrels per day, the Company shall pay income tax at 85%.

Assessment and payment of income tax shall be subject to the following provisions: —

(A) The United Abu Emirates Income Tax Decree shall be supplemented as follows: —

(1) —

     (a) The Company shall determine its income from operations under this Agreement and shall declare and pay the Government its income tax in respect thereof.

     (b) If a separate non-profit making company is formed to carry out any operations under this Agreement, it is hereby agreed that such company shall be deemed to have neither income nor expenses but the Company shall include in its determination under subparagraph (a) above such company's actual income and expenses arising from its operations.

     (c) In the case referred to under (b) above the total income tax due to the Government from the Company as aforesaid for any income tax year shall not be less than the income tax which would have been due if the company had carried out itself all operations under this Agreement.

     (d) In determining the income tax liability of the Company in respect of its net income from operations under this Agreement, no account shall be taken of any income which that Company may derive from costs or expense which it may incur in respect of any other operations in United Abu Emirates whether under a concession agreement or otherwise and the Company shall maintain its financial records accordingly; provided that where costs or expenses are incurred which are common to operations under this Agreement and other operations such costs and expense shall be apportioned between operations in accordance with sound accounting principles.

(2) —

    (a) Taxable income shall be the aggregate value of Petroleum exported or sold by the Company or delivered to the Government as royalty in kind after deducting costs and expenses fairly, properly and necessarily attributable to the operations of the Company in United Abu Emirates computed in accordance with the provisions of the United Abu Emirates Income Tax Decree. But for the purpose of calculating the annual allowances referred to in paragraph (1)(c) of Article 6 of the said Decree the reasonable percentage in respect of intangible assets shall be 5% per annum and in respect of physical assets shall be 10% per annum and this provision shall be deemed to be an agreement of the kind referred to in paragraph (2)(b) of the said Article 6.

    (b) The aggregate value of any Petroleum delivered to the Government as royalty in kind shall be the aggregate of the amounts credited for the purpose of royalties in accordance with Article 11(A) hereof.

    (c) In the event that the Company disposes of any technical information or know-how which has been gained by or used in operations under this Agreement the amount or value of any consideration received by the Company for the disposal shall, so far as it is not taken into account in computing the costs and expenses deducted in determining the taxable income of the Company as aforesaid, be treated for all purposes as part of the Company's taxable income.

(3) In the case of Crude Oil exported by the Company from United Abu Emirates, the aggregate value referred to in paragraph (2) above shall not be less than the amount which results from multiplying the number of barrels of such Crude Oil exported by the applicable Posted Price per barrel.

(4) In the determination of taxable income, nothing in this Agreement shall be construed as permitting the deduction either as an expense of the year or by way of depreciation or amortization of the following items:

    (a) foreign taxation paid on income derived from sources within United Abu Emirates.

    (b) interest or other consideration paid or suffered by the Company in respect of the financing of its operations in United Abu Emirates.

    (c) expenditures in relation to the organizing and initiating of Petroleum operations in United Abu Emirates.

    (d) bonuses paid to the Government under Article 9 of this Agreement.

    (e) rentals to the Government under Article 10 of this Agreement

* * * *

(C) The Government has the right to appoint auditors to examine the books and records of the Company on its behalf.

Article 13. Limit of Taxation

Except for payments provided for in Article 12 hereof, no other or higher taxes, impositions, duties, fees or charges shall be imposed upon the Company or upon its property, privileges or employees or upon the latter's property, privileges or employees within United Abu Emirates, other than those ordinarily imposed and generally applicable to other companies engaged in similar operations in Abu Dhabi. . . .

Article 14. Imports, Exports and Customs

(A) The Company and its contractors shall be entitled to import free of customs duties, or any other import, sale or excise tax now existing or which may later exist, all materials which the Company may need in conducting the operations authorized by this Agreement but excluding goods for personal use of its employees and the materials mentioned in paragraph (B) of this Article. . . .

The Company shall be entitled to export Petroleum produced or manufactured in United Abu Emirates free of customs duties or any export sales, use or excise taxes now existing or which may later exist. The Company and its contractors shall also be entitled to export free of customs duties or any export, sales, use, or excise taxes all materials imported free of duties, taxes and charges under the provisions of this Article.

(B) The classes of goods on which customs duty is payable are: [categories of food, personal effects, etc.]

* * * *

Article 18. Construction and Operation Of Facilities by the Company

Subject to existing prior rights of third parties and applicable laws and regulations, the Company shall have without hindrance in the Economic Development Area and elsewhere in United Abu Emirates all reasonable rights and facilities for the purpose of its operations under this Agreement including, but not limited to:

(A) the right to build, construct, maintain, operate and use all sorts of buildings, installations, communications and transport systems, and engineering works of every description;

(B) the right to construct new roads for motor and general traffic and to make use of existing roads or tracks free of charge or taxes of any kind. Before exercising any of its rights hereunder outside the Economic Development Area the Company shall apply to the Government for its approval and shall submit plans to it of any proposed works. In granting its approval for the construction of any facility suitable for public use, the Government may require that the same be available for public use free of charge provided that such use does not interfere with the operations of the Company.

Article 19. Use of Land by the Company

(A)   Subject to the rights of third parties the Company shall enjoy free of charge such use and occupation of uncultivated lands of United Abu Emirates as it may require for the purpose of its operations.

(B)   If the Company requires for the purpose of its operations any privately owned or cultivated land in United Abu Emirates, the Company may lease with the permission of the Government such land on terms to be arranged with the owners thereof.

(C)   The Company shall not carry on any operations within areas occupied by or devoted to the purpose of mosques, sacred buildings, graveyards, archaeological sites or in the immediate vicinity thereof.

(D)   The Company shall not use, occupy or carry on any operations within any area which may have been or which may from time to time be selected by or on behalf of the Government for defense purposes, for airfields or for wireless or telegraph installations.

Article 20. Employment of Persons

Subject to the applicable laws and regulations in United Abu Emirates, the Government and the Company agree that in selection of employees of various nationalities the efficiency of operations must be given consideration. In selecting its employees in United Abu Emirates the Company agrees that it shall, as far as is consistent with the efficient management of the Company and its undertakings, give first priority to citizens of the United Abu Emirates, second priority to other Arab subjects and third priority to other nationalities which the Government has advised the Company are acceptable.

Article 21. Company's Use of Transport, Communications and Port Facilities

The Company shall be entitled to use in its operations under this Agreement any form of transport, whether by land, water or air, for the movement of its employees, equipment or materials subject to the due observance of all laws and regulations covering the use of such transport.

* * * *

Article 25. Government Representative

(A)   The Government may from time to time nominate one or more of its officials to act on its behalf in all matters relating to this Agreement.

(B)   The Government may nominate two (2) members of the Board of Directors of the Company operating this Agreement.

Article 26. Force Majeure

If the Company is delayed or prevented from carrying on its work in fulfilling any of its obligations under this Agreement by force majeure in United Abu Emirates or elsewhere, the Company shall not be liable in respect of any such failure or delay, and if through force majeure the fulfillment by the Company of any of the conditions of this Agreement be delayed, the period of such delay, together with such period as may be necessary for the restoration of any damage done during such delay, shall be added to the period fixed by the Agreement, provided always that no addition shall be made to the period fixed in Article 4 hereof unless the production or export of Crude Oil by the Company shall be totally suspended for not less than sixty (60) consecutive days through force majeure occurring within United Abu Emirates.

"Force Majeure" as used in this Agreement includes Act of God, war, insurrection, riot, civil commotion, lightening, fire and earthquake.

Article 27. Revisions

The Government of United Abu Emirates will take all steps necessary to ensure that the Company enjoys all the rights conferred by this Agreement. The contractual rights expressly created by this Agreement shall not be altered except by mutual consent of the parties.

Article 28. Relinquishment

(A) The Company: —

  (1) shall relinquish to the Government not less than 25% of the Economic Development Area within three years from the Effective Date and shall further relinquish another 25% of the original size of the Economic Development Area within five years from the Effective Date and shall further relinquish another 25% of the original size of the Economic Development Area within eight years from the Effective Date;

  (2) may at any time relinquish to the Government all or any part of the Economic Development Area upon giving three months notice in writing of their intention to do so. Any area relinquished under this subparagraph shall count towards the Company's obligation under subparagraph (1) above.

(B) The portions so relinquished shall, so far as is reasonably possible, be a block or blocks of sufficient size and convenient shape, taking into account contiguous areas already relinquished and not the subject of a further concession to enable oil operations to be carried out thereon.

* * * *

(C) Upon relinquishment the portions so relinquished shall cease to be part of the Economic Development Area but the Company shall continue during the duration of this Agreement to enjoy the right to use the portions so relinquished for transport and communications facilities and to do so in a manner which shall interfere as little as practicable with any use to which the relinquished portions may be put.

(D) If the Company gives notification of relinquishment of the whole of the Concession Area and the Company has not fulfilled the minimum investment obligation under paragraph (C) of Article 5 hereof, then the

Company shall pay to the Government a sum equal to one-half of the expenditure required thereunder, due prior to such notification, provided that the investment obligation in respect of the year in which such notification is given shall be reduced by the amount thereof apportioned on a daily basis referable to the period after the date of such notification.

Article 29. *Changed Circumstances*

If, in the future, arrangements are made between the Government of United Abu Emirates and any other states in the Middle East or the agent of such Government and the Company or any other company/companies operating in the petroleum industry as a result of which an increase in benefits should accrue generally to all such governments as aforesaid, then the Government and the Company shall review and discuss the changed circumstances within the petroleum industry in order to decide whether any alteration to the terms of this Agreement would be equitable to both parties.

Article 30. *Currency*

(A)   All payments which the Company is required to make hereunder to the Government shall be made in U.S. dollars. Conversion from other currencies into United States dollars shall be effected on the basis of the par values for the time being established under the Articles of Agreement of the International Monetary Fund, or if no par value is established for one or more of the relevant currencies, or if the International Monetary Fund is discontinued, then on the basis of the appropriate rate or rates of exchange recognized by any other internationally accepted authority.

(B)   The Company shall have the right:

    (1)   to maintain and operate bank accounts in whatever currency and wheresoever and freely to retain or dispose of any funds therein;

    (2)   freely to import and export currencies and foreign exchange;

    (3)   freely to exchange such currencies and foreign exchange into other currencies;

    (4)   freely to maintain and operate accounts in its books or records in the name of other persons wheresoever situate;

    (5)   freely to maintain and operate accounts in the books and records of other persons wheresoever situate and the Company shall not be restrained from freely retaining or disposing of any funds or assets outside United Abu Emirates including such funds or assets as may result from its activities in United Abu Emirates.

Article 31. *Operating Company*

(A)   The Company shall have the right from time to time to appoint an operating company to carry out operations under this Agreement on its behalf and shall immediately notify the Government in writing of any such appointment.

(B) The Government shall be entitled to look to and communicate with the operating company as the representative of the Company with regard to operations hereunder and notice to the operating Company shall be deemed to be notice to the Company.

(C) Anything required to be done hereunder by the Company may be done by the operating company on its behalf and any operations or other activities carried out by the operating company in accordance with the terms hereof shall be deemed to be performance hereof by the Company.

(D) The Company may enter into such agreements or make such arrangements with the operating company with regard to its mutual rights, interests, obligations, and liabilities as it may from time to time think fit, but no such agreements or arrangements shall be binding on the Government which shall not be affected with notice thereof.

(E) In the event of the appointment of an operating company being terminated whether by the Company or otherwise, the Company shall immediately give notice of such termination to the Government and may appoint another operating company in its stead.

(F) Notwithstanding the provisions of this Article 31 the Company shall declare and pay its income tax in accordance with the United Abu Emirates Income Tax Decree and Article 12 hereof and shall separately deal with the Government on all matters pertaining thereto.

(G) Nothing herein contained shall be construed as requiring an operating company to act as agent for the Company in the disposition and sale of Petroleum.

Article 32. Government's Option

(A) At any time after the date of discovery of Crude Oil in Commercial Quantities, the Government may by notice in writing to the Company elect either by itself or by an entity it nominates to acquire a non-assignable undivided participating interest of sixty (60%) per cent (or such lesser proportion as the Government shall then determine) in all rights and obligations under this Agreement and in the Concession Area.

(B) The Government shall pay for such participating interest a sum equal to sixty (60%) per cent or such lesser proportion as the Government shall have elected to acquire of the total accumulated costs and expenses recorded in the books of the Company or of the operating company as the case may be as of the date of discovery of Crude Oil in Commercial Quantities (excluding the bonus and rentals paid by the Company before the date of discovery of Crude Oil in Commercial Quantities). The Company shall notify the Government within a period of forty-five (45) days from the date of discovery of Crude Oil in Commercial Quantities of the total amount of such accumulated costs and expenses in order to enable the Government to ascertain the sum it will have to pay if an election under this Article is made. The Government shall have the right to appoint auditors to examine the said books and records of the Company and of the operating company and to verify the said sum on its behalf. Payment of such sum shall be made by the Government in ten equal annual installments together with interest on the outstanding balance at a rate equal to the prevailing rate of discount for the time being of the Federal Reserve Bank of the United States of America plus one percent (1%), calculated from the date six months after the date of discovery of Crude Oil in Commercial Quantities. The first such payment shall be made at one (1) year intervals thereafter.

If the Government acquires a participating interest in this Agreement pursuant to this Article, operations shall be conducted in accordance with the terms of the Operating Agreement to be concluded between the Government and the Company.

Article 33. Arbitration

(A) If any doubt, difference or dispute shall arise at any time between the parties hereto concerning the interpretation hereof or anything herein contained or in connection herewith, or concerning the rights and liabilities of any of the parties hereunder, and if the parties fail to settle it in any other way the same shall be referred to two arbitrators, one of whom shall be chosen by each party and to a referee who shall be chosen by the two arbitrators within sixty (60) days of being requested to do so in writing by either party.

(B) Each party shall nominate its own arbitrator within sixty (60) days after the delivery of a request so to do by the other party, failing which its arbitrator may at the request of the other party be designated by the President of the International Court of Justice. In the event of the arbitrators failing to agree upon a referee, the President of the International Court of Justice may appoint a referee at the request of the arbitrators or either of them.

(C) The decision of the arbitrators or, in the case of a difference of opinion between them, the decision of the referee, shall be final and binding on both parties.

(D) The decision shall specify an adequate period of time during which the party against whom the decision is given shall conform to the decision and that party shall be in default only if that party has failed to conform to the decision prior to the expiry of that period and not otherwise.

(E) The place of arbitration shall be United Abu Emirates or elsewhere at the discretion of the referee.

(F) This Agreement shall have the force of law. It shall be given effect and shall be interpreted and applied in conformity with the principles of law normally recognized by civilized states in general, including those which have been applied by international Tribunals.

Article 34. Arabic and English Texts

This Agreement is drawn in the Arabic and English languages, both texts being authentic. In the event, however, of any difference of interpretation arising between the Arabic and English texts of this Agreement, the English text shall prevail.

NOTES AND QUESTIONS

(1) The Economic Development Agreement excerpted above is a modern agreement in that it is lengthy and complex. The traditional concession agreement was much shorter and less complex. In commenting on this change, Smith and Wells have stated:

> There is much to be said for the traditional form of concession. The agreements are often less complicated and may therefore be easier to administer than some of the newer forms of agreements. The income tax provisions, if well conceived and well drafted, can be relatively straightforward. A country with a weak income tax administration or without a sophisticated governmental body to police an agreement might well prefer a traditional agreement, which raises minimal administrative problems, to one which is so complex that the governmental machinery simply cannot cope with its administration. Government income might well be higher when complex, though purportedly more favorable, financial arrangements are avoided.
>
> Nevertheless, many developing countries have been under pressure to break away from the traditional form of agreement. The pressure has usually been: (1) for increased government participation in the ownership of the enterprise; and (2) for an increased governmental role in the management of the extractive operation. The result has been agreements that differ significantly in structure from the traditional concession arrangements. In most cases, they have been more complex.[3]

(2) Note that the Economic Development Agreement has dropped use of the term "concession." Could it nonetheless be termed a "concession agreement?" What, precisely, constitutes a "concession?" Is it necessary for the concessionaire to own the land or the minerals in question? If this is the test, is it met under this Economic Development Agreement?

(3) As counsel for Extraterrestrial Energy Company, would you be satisfied with the provisions of the Agreement relating to United Abu Emirates' share of the take? How much is the Government entitled to under the Agreement? How much of the Government's take would qualify as income tax for purposes of the U.S. foreign tax credit? How would you redraft the pertinent provisions of the Agreement?

---

[3] Smith & Wells, *Mineral Agreements In Developing Countries: Structures And Substance,* 69 Am. J. Int'l L. 560, 572 (1975).

(4) Note that, in Article 32, the Agreement envisages the Government acquiring a "participating interest" in "all rights and obligations under this agreement and in the Concession Area." What does this entail? Does it mean participation in the management of Company operations? If so, 60% would mean management control. If that is the case, does it necessarily mean that Government appointed personnel are to make the day-to-day management decisions? What alternative interpretation is possible? This is an important point. Is the failure to pin it down a serious defect of the Agreement? Might the Government have wanted it left open? Reflect upon what your answers might tell you about the broader function of such long-term economic development agreements.

(5) Article 3 of the Economic Development Agreement envisages that the Agreement will last for 40 years. The very length of the Agreement may exacerbate problems peculiar to such agreements. For example, the Agreement can be of crucial importance to the economy of the host country, more so than most national legislation or regulation. Yet the Agreement envisages this elaborate economic arrangement remaining unchanged over a lengthy period, even if the host country decides that economic trends would dictate different arrangements. Does or should the existence of the economic development agreement preclude the host country from passing tax, tariff or other economic legislation incompatible with the terms of the agreement? If not, can the Government enter into such an agreement and still fulfill its responsibilities as lawmaker through its formal legislative and executive processes? In this connection reconsider the decision of the House of Lords in *Czarnikow Ltd. v. Rolimpex*, [1979] A.C 351, *supra* Chapter 1. Also note the "choice-of-law clause" in Article 33(G). Is the issue less a question of power than of remedy? Reexamine Article 32. Does it provide the Government a way out of the constraints imposed upon it by the Agreement?

(6) Consider the terms of Article 29, on "Changed Circumstances." From the perspective of counsel for the Company, how would you evaluate the likely future impact of this provision? Is the provision applicable if one other Middle East country and another oil company reach agreement on an economic development agreement more favorable than that between United Abu Emirates and Extraterrestrial Energy, but no other agreement along similar lines is concluded? Is the provision applicable if several such agreements are reached in Asia? If the provision is applicable, what is the extent of the obligations it imposes? Would the Company be obligated to conclude a new agreement with the Government of United Abu Emirates? If the Government and the Company fail to agree on the terms of a new agreement, what happens?

(7) Note that Article 20 on "Employment of Persons" appears to give the Government the authority to reject the Company's selection of certain employees as "unacceptable." Were the Company to accept the government's objection, this might cause it to run afoul of U.S. law.

(8) An important consideration for any company contemplating entering into an economic development agreement is the adequacy of the host country's infrastructure, *i.e.*, roads, transport systems, ports, etc. Consider in this connection Articles 18 and 21 of the Economic Development Agreement. Are they satisfactory from the Company's perspective? If not, how would you redraft them?

(9) Provisions regarding choice of law and choice of forum are normally exceedingly important parts of any international business contract. In an economic development agreement, such provisions are, if anything, even more important because in the absence of such provisions the foreign investor is likely to be governed by local law applied by local tribunals. Consider Article 33 on arbitration. Does it call for international or local arbitration? Is the arbitration likely to take place in United Abu Emirates or at some other location?

An alternative version of an arbitration clause for an economic development agreement might read as follows:

> All disputes of a technical nature arising out of this Agreement shall be settled by a panel of three experts, one to be selected by each party and the third to be selected by the Minister of Petroleum. All disputes of a legal nature shall be finally settled by arbitrators in accordance with the Rules of Conciliation and Arbitration of the International Chamber of Commerce.

What are the advantages and disadvantages of such a provision? Does it raise any issues of interpretation and application? If so, what are they?

(10) With respect to choice of law, note Article 33 (G) and its similarity to Article 38(c) of the Statute of the International Court of Justice which mandates decisions by the court in accordance with "general principles of law recognized by civilized nations." The precise meaning of this provision, however, is not free from doubt. One view, held especially firmly by the socialist countries, is that general principles refer only to principles of customary international law. Another, more widely held view, is that the concept requires a survey of developed legal systems — e.g., common law, civil law, socialist law, Islamic law — in order to ascertain principles of law common to them all.

In the context of an economic development or concession agreement, there is also some question as to whether the reference is only to general principles of contract law or includes all regulatory law bearing on the agreement. If the latter, the practical problems of search and proof become overwhelming.

Several arbitrations of disputes involving concession agreements have referred to general principles of law even absent an express reference thereto in the concession agreement. For example, in *Petroleum Development Ltd. v. Sheikh of Abu Dhabi*,[5] the umpire found that no municipal system of law in Abu Dhabi could be said to exist and that there was no basis on which the law of England could be applied. Instead he found that "principles rooted in the good sense and common practice of the generality of civilized nations — a sort of 'modern law of nature' " should apply.

In a situation where the agreement is between the host country and a consortium of foreign investors from several different countries, the issue may arise whether the "general principles" should be those common to the host country's legal system and those of the investors' countries or to legal systems throughout the world. A concession agreement of September 19, 1954 between Iran and a

---

[4] We are grateful to Keith Highet, member of the New York Bar, for making available to us an unpublished paper by his partner George Kahale, III from which this provision is taken.

[5] [1951] Int'l Rep. 144.

consortium of oil companies of the United States and European Companies faced and resolved this issue. Article 46 of the agreement provided:

> In view of the diverse nationalities of the parties to this Agreement, it shall be governed by and interpreted and applied in accordance with principles of law common to Iran and the several nations in which the other parties to this Agreement are incorporated, and in the absence of common principles, then by and in accordance with principles of law recognized by civilized nations in general, including such of those principles as may have been applied by international tribunals.[6]

Besides the municipal law of the host country or general principles of law, two other possible choices of law have been suggested by tribunals and writers. The first is that the contract itself should be regarded as a self-contained legal system that would resolve all disputes between the parties. What conceptual or practical problems, if any, does this suggestion present?

The other suggestion is that the economic development agreement be governed by international law — that is, treaty law or norms of customary international law as distinct from general principles of law recognized by civilized nations. Some commentators and tribunals have contended that the very nature of a concession agreement, with its many transnational and international aspects, requires that it be analogized to a treaty and subject to principles of customary international law applicable to a treaty, such as *pacta sunt servanda* and *rebus sic stantibus* or changed circumstances.[7] To the contrary it has been argued that only states have rights and obligations under international law, a state can limit its exercise of sovereignty only by an agreement with another state or international organization, and that therefore a state cannot limit its exercise of sovereignty under international law by entering into an agreement with a foreign investor.

How convincing do you find these arguments? Is there a middle position between these two views?

There is little doubt that a host state and foreign investors can choose what system or systems of law should govern the agreement between them. As provided in a resolution adopted by the Institute de Droit International in 1979: "[t]he parties may in particular choose as the proper law of the contract either one or several domestic legal systems or the principles common to such systems or the general principles of law or the principles applied in international economic relations, or international law, or a combination of these sources of law."[8] However, the final choice of law is often the result of intense negotiations that may, in particular cases, reflect the views and interests not only of the host country but also those of the home country or international organizations.

(11) Consider Article 27 of the Agreement. Would it prevent the government from passing tax or customs law that would adversely affect the Company?

---

[6] The Agreement may be found in 2 Hurewitz, Diplomacy In The Near And Middle East, 348 (1956).

[7] See, *e.g.*, Kissam and Leach, Sovereign Expropriation Of Property And Abrogation Of Concession Contracts, 28 Fordham L. Rev. 177, 194-214 (1959).

[8] 58 Ann. Inst. De Droit Int'l, part II, at p. 195.

(12) An alternative method of dispute settlement that may be available under an economic development agreement is arbitration under the auspices of the International Centre for the Settlement of Investment Disputes. For discussion of this kind of arbitration, see *infra*, Chapter 11, p. 960.[9]

[B] International Contracts for Construction of Industrial Works

Developing countries have long recognized the importance of industrialization to economic development. As a consequence increased attention has been paid in recent years to contracts for construction of industrial works. This increased interest resulted in the United Nations Economic Commission for Europe (ECE) producing guides to facilitate international negotiations for such contracts. More recently, the United Nations Commission on International Trade Law (UNCITRAL) has completed a Legal Guide on Drawing Up International Contracts for Construction of Industrial Works.[10] This project greatly exceeds in scope of coverage the guides produced by the ECE.

Contracts for the construction of industrial works (hereinafter called "works contracts") are a hybrid that in some ways resemble contracts for the sale of goods or services but in others partake of foreign direct investment arrangements, especially if, as is often the case, they are undertaken in the form of a joint venture. Works contracts are typically of great complexity, with respect both to the technical aspects of the construction and to the legal relationship between the parties, and normally extend over a period of several years.

As defined in the UNCITRAL Guide, "an industrial works is an installation which incorporates one or more major pieces of equipment and a technological process to produce an output. Examples of industrial works include petrochemical plants, fertilizer plants and hydroelectrical plants." Under works contracts, the contractor is obligated to supply equipment and materials to be incorporated in the works, as well as either to erect the works or to supervise others who do so.

An idea of the complexity of works contracts can be gained by a recitation of the primary topics covered by the UNCITRAL Guide. These include:

---

[9] For further readings and cases on economic development and concession agreements, see A. Fatouros, Government Guarantees To Foreign Investors (1962); Horigan, Foreign Natural Resource Investment, 1 The Law Of Transnational Business Transactions 7-1 (V.P. Nanda, ed. 1987); Mann, State Contracts And State Responsibility, 54 Am. J. Int'l L. 572 (1960); Asante, Stability of Contractual Relations In The Transnational Investment Process, 28 Int'l & Comp. L.Q.401 (1979); Teson, State Contracts And Oil Expropriations: The Aminoil-Kuwait Arbitration, 24 Va. J. Int'l L. 323 (1984); Texaco Overseas Petroleum Co. v. Government of Libyan Arab Republic, 53 Int'l L. Rep. 359, 17 Int'l Leg. Mat. 3 (1977); Libyan-American Oil Co. v. Government of Libyan Arab Republic, 20 Int'l Leg. Mat. 1 (1977); BP Exploration Co. (Libya) Ltd. v. Government of Libyan Arab Republic, 53 Int'l L. Rep. 297 (1977). For a recent "concession agreement" between Syria and oil companies from the Federal Republic of Germany, the Netherlands, and the United States, see 26 Int'l Leg. Mat 1186 (1987).

[10] See UNCITRAL Legal Guide On Drawing Up International Contracts For The Construction Of Industrial Works (1988). For earlier guides, see Guide On Drawing Up Contracts For Large Industrial Works (1973) (ECE/Trade 117); Guide For Use In Drawing Up Contracts Relating To The International Transfer Of Know-How In the Engineering Industry (1970) (Trade/222 Rev.1).

pre-contract studies; choice of contractual approach; procedure for concluding contract; general remarks on drafting; description of works; transfer of technology; price and payment conditions; supply of equipment and materials; construction on site; consulting engineer; subcontracting; inspection and test during manufacture and construction; completion, take-over and acceptance; passing of risk; transfer of ownership of property; insurance; security for performance; delay, defects and other failures to perform; liquidated damages and penalty clauses; exemption clauses; hardship clauses; variation clauses; suspension clauses; termination of contract; supplies of spare parts and services after construction; transfer of contractual rights and obligations; choice of law; and settlement of disputes.

A consideration of all these subjects is greatly beyond the scope of this Section. We will limit our discussion to the following subjects: price and payment conditions; passing of risk; hardship and exemption clauses; choice of law and settlement of disputes.

[1] Price and Payment Conditions

Works contracts raise particularly difficult problems of price and payment. The price will normally cover various aspects of construction by the contractor, *e.g.*, the supply of equipment, materials and services and the transfer of technology. The costs of construction may change over the length of period of the contract, and the extent of construction to be completed may not be precisely ascertainable at the time of conclusion of the contract. Accordingly, it is important that the parties to the contract decide who is to bear the consequences of changes in costs.

There are three main methods of pricing used in works contracts: lump sum, cost reimbursment and unit-price.

Under the *lump sum method*, the parties agree on the total amount to be paid for the construction, and this amount remains constant even if the actual cost of construction turns out to be different from that anticipated at the time of conclusion of the contract. The amount can change, however, if the contract or the law applicable to the contract provides for an "adjustment" of the price or its "revision." "Adjustment" refers to cases where the construction costs become higher or lower after entering into the contract due to changes in the construction required under the contract. "Revision" of the price refers to situations where the nature of the construction remains the same, but economic circumstances have changed dramatically. Examples would be a substantial change in prices of equipment, material or construction services after conclusion of the contract or a sharp change in exchange rates of the currency in which the price is to be paid in relation to other currencies.

Under the *cost reimbursable method*, the exact amount of the price is not known at the time of contracting because the price will consist of the actual costs of construction incurred by the contractor, plus a fee paid him to cover his overhead and profit. This method of pricing requires more detailed contractual provisions than does the lump sum method.

As for the *unit-price method*, here the parties agree on a rate for a unit of construction, and the total contract price depends upon the total number of units actually used. The rate fixed for a construction unit includes an increment for the contractor's profit. The construction unit may take one of several forms, for example, a ton of cement for concrete, an hour of labor in excavation work, or a cubic meter of reinforced concrete.

An example of a provision for "revision" of a *lump sum* price might read as follows:

The agreed price is to be revised if there is an increase or decrease in the costs of . . . The revision is to be made by the application of the formula contained in the appendix to this contract.[11]

The formula set forth in the appendix reads as follows:

The price revision envisaged in Article . . . of this contract is to be made by the application of the following formula:

$$P1 = \frac{Po}{100} \quad (a + b) \quad \frac{M1}{Mo} \quad + \quad c\,\frac{N1}{No} \quad + \quad d\,\frac{W1}{Wo}$$

Where:

P1 = price payable under index clause;

Po = initial price as stipulated in the contract; a, b, c, d, represent the contractually; agreed percentages of individual elements of construction price covered by the index; clause, which add up to 100 (a + b + c + d = 100);

a = proportion of price excluded from adjustment = _____ percent;

b = proportion of [specified materials covered by this weighting] = _____ percent;

c = proportion of [specified other materials covered by this weighting] = _____ percent;

d = proportion of [specified wages covered by this weighting] = _____ percent;

Mo = base level of price indices for materials specified under b;

M1 = comparable level of price indices for materials specified under b;

No = base level of price indices for materials specified under c;

N1 = comparable level of price indices for materials specified under c;

[11] For discussion, see UNCITRAL, Legal Guide On Drawing Up International Contracts For Construction Of Industrial Works, pp. 76-96.

Wo =   base level of price indices for wages specified under d;

W1 =   comparable level of price indices specified under d.

Notes:

— "b," "c" and "d" should be equal to the percentage indicated in paragraph 3 of illustrative provisions; "a" should include the remaining percentage;

— The dates provided for in paragraph 2 and the price indices indicated in paragraph 5 of the illustrative provision should be used for base levels under Mo, No and Wo and comparable levels under M1, N1, W1.

The timing of payments from the purchaser to the contractor is often an issue that arises during the negotiation of a works contract. The contractor will normally demand that progress payments be included and that there be a percentage advance by the purchaser into an escrow account. For its part the purchaser tries to avoid payments tied to specific dates and to substitute payments dependent upon completion of specified segments of the project. The purchaser will also usually insist that these progress payments be no more than 60 to 65 percent of the agreed price so as to ensure the full completion of the project.

Foreign exchange currency restrictions in the purchaser's country may pose a problem. These restrictions may require that some portion of the purchase price be payable in local currency. This may not create too great a problem for the contractor if the portion of the price required to be paid in local currency is not too large and the contractor has costs payable in local currency.

NOTES AND QUESTIONS

(1) What are the advantages and disadvantages of the lump sum method of pricing for a works contract? It has been suggested that this method especially favors the purchaser of industrial works. In what ways? Are there any disadvantages for the purchaser? Might the price to the purchaser be higher in some cases than if the cost reimbursable method were used for the same construction? Under the lump sum method might it be especially important for the purchaser to ensure that the contract precisely specify the scope of the works as well as to monitor closely the construction?

(2) The cost reimbursable method may be especially appropriate when the extent of construction services or materials and the kinds of equipment needed for the construction cannot be accurately anticipated when the contract is concluded. What are the advantages and disadvantages of this method of pricing for the contractor and the purchaser? Are there any ways that a purchaser might be protected under this arrangement? Might the fee of the contractor be structured

in such a way as to give it an incentive to minimize the costs of construction? Can you think of other ways the purchaser could be protected?

(3) In most cases the unit-price method of pricing can be used only in combination with other pricing methods, since it is not suitable for pricing elements of the construction which, by their very nature, cannot be divided into several identical units, for example, equipment. The unit-price method is also not appropriate where it is difficult to control the quantities of units to be used for the construction, e.g., where the techniques of construction are left to the discretion of the contractor.

Under the unit-price method, which party bears the risk of increases in construction costs or gains the benefits from a decrease in those costs? Who bears the risk of an increase of the costs of materials and labor for each unit? Who bears the risk of an increase in the total contract price because of a need to use more units for the construction than anticipated at the time of entering into the contract?

[2] Passing of Risk

The issue of who bears the risk of loss of or damage to equipment and materials to be incorporated in the works or to the works before or after completion looms large in works contracts. Specifically, the issue is who is to bear the loss or damage that may be caused by an accident or by the acts of third persons for whom neither party is responsible. The party bearing a risk of loss or damage will have to bear the financial consequences of the loss or damage without being able to obtain compensation from the other party.

An accident or act of a third party causing loss or damage to the works may also prevent a party from performing his contractual obligations. An example would be if a storm damaged the works during a period when the contractor bears the risk of accidental damage and the contractor is thereby prevented from finishing the works on time. It is important to distinguish the issue of whether the party who has failed to perform his contractual obligations is liable to pay damages to the other party for financial loss from the issue of who should bear the risk of loss or damage caused by the accident or act of the third person. In the example given above, the contractor might be obligated to repair the damage to the works caused by the storm, but not to pay damages to the purchaser for the financial loss arising from his failure to perform if the storm constituted an event which fell within the scope of an applicable exemption clause contained in the works contract.

NOTES AND QUESTIONS

(1) What factors should determine the allocation of risk of loss or damage between the parties? Some factors that have been suggested include which party can better control the circumstances which may result in loss or damage; which party is able to insure the goods at the least cost; and which party can best salvage and dispose of the damaged property. Can you think of any others? Does it really matter, as long as the allocation is clear? Explain.

(2) Assume that you are counsel for the contractor and counsel for the purchaser suggests that the following provision be included in the contract:

> The contractor bears the risk of any loss or damage from any cause whatsoever to any equipment and material supplied by him until their incorporation in the works as well as the risk of any loss or damage from any cause whatsoever to the works themselves until the works are accepted by the purchaser.

What would be your response to this suggestion? If you would not be entirely satisfied with the provision, how would you redraft it?

[3] Hardship and Exemption Clauses

In addition to risks of loss of or damage to property, there are other risks with which the parties to the works contract need to be concerned. There are circumstances beyond the control of the parties that make carrying out obligations of the contract either more onerous or impossible. To use the terminology of the UNCITRAL Guide, such circumstances are covered by hardship or exemption clauses in the contract.

Hardship Clauses

Under the UNCITRAL definition, a hardship clause would apply when a change in economic, financial, legal, or technological circumstances makes the performance of a party's obligations more onerous (has "serious economic consequences" for a party), but does not prevent that performance. An exemption clause applies only when a change of circumstances prevents performance. A hardship clause typically identifies the particular types of hardships for which relief is available and provides for renegotiation to adapt the contract to the new situation created by the hardship.

Recall the cases and statutory materials in Chapter 1 on "commercial impossibility" and the difficulties encountered by merchants in modifying or extricating themselves from contracts when unanticipated circumstances threaten them with substantial losses if they carry out the contract according to its terms. A hardship clause is one means of ameliorating the effect of those doctrines which are fairly typical of most jurisdictions with a well developed commercial law.

The purpose behind a hardship clause is analogous to the doctrine of *rebus sic stantibus* or fundamental change of circumstances in the law of treaties. Article 62 of the Vienna Convention on the Law of Treaties[12] provides:

Article 62. Fundamental Change of Circumstances

(1) A fundamental change of circumstances which has occurred with regard to those existing at the time of the conclusion of a treaty, and which was not foreseen by the parties, may not be invoked as a ground for terminating or withdrawing from the treaty unless:

    (a) the existence of those circumstances constituted an essential basis of the consent of the parties to be bound by the treaty, and

---

[12] UN DOC. A/CONF.39/27, at 289 (1969), reprinted in 8 Int'l Legal Mat. 679 (1969).

    (b)   the effect of the change is radically to transform the extent of obligations still to be performed under the treaty.

(2)   A fundamental change of circumstances may not be invoked as a ground for terminating or withdrawing from a treaty:

    (a)   if the treaty establishes a boundary; or

    (b)   if the fundamental change is the result of a breach by the party invoking it either of an obligation under the treaty or of any other international obligation owed to any other party to the treaty.

(3)   If, under the foregoing paragraphs, a party may invoke a fundamental change of circumstances as a ground for terminating or withdrawing from a treaty it may also invoke the change as a ground for suspending the operation of the treaty.

NOTES AND QUESTIONS

(1) Consider, from the perspective of both the contractor and the purchaser, the advantages and disadvantages of a hardship clause. Is such a clause more likely to favor one party over the other? Are there steps that might be taken in drafting a hardship clause that would minimize the disadvantages of such a clause? Might Article 62 of the Vienna Convention on the Law of Treaties be of any assistance in this connection?

(2) One suggested approach to the drafting of a hardship clause is to provide that a party may invoke the clause only if it demonstrates that one or more of the events enumerated in an exhaustive list has occurred and has resulted in hardship to it as defined in the clause. Examples of events that might be included in such a list are a severe reduction in the size of the purchaser's anticipated market for the output of the works, or an increase in the costs of production (equipment, raw materials, transportation, labor) which results in a severe reduction in the profitability of the works.

(3) It is standard for a hardship clause to provide for the renegotiation of the contract if hardship occurs. An issue for the parties to decide is whether the contract should obligate them only to participate in renegotiations with a view to adapting the contract, or should obligate them as well to adapt the contract after renegotiations. If the latter course of action is chosen, the parties may also agree upon a conciliator to assist them in their efforts to adapt the contract. The parties may also decide to include a provision that, if they fail to reach agreement upon adaptation, the contract will be adapted by a court, arbitral tribunal or third person. In some countries, however, the law does not permit adaptation in judicial or arbitral proceedings.

Exemption Clauses

As indicated above, an exemption clause deals with events which may prevent, permanently or for a period of time, a party from performing his contractual obligations. Such clauses are also often referred to as force majeure clauses.

These events, or "impediments" to use the UNCITRAL Guide's terminology, may be of a physical nature, such as a natural disaster, or they may be of a legal nature, such as a change in the law of the purchaser's country after conclusion of the contract such as new environmental or trade regulations preventing the use of certain equipment, technology or following the agreed upon plan for the project. In order to limit the scope of an exemption clause, the parties sometimes provide that a party failing to perform is exempt only from the payment of damages to the other party.

There are three basic approaches to the drafting of exemption clauses. One approach is to provide only a general definition of exempting events. Another is to provide a general definition coupled with an illustrative or exhaustive list of exempting events. A third approach is to provide an exhaustive list of exempted events without a general definition.

Some exempting events often included in an exemption clause are typical of the standard "force majeure" clause (*e.g.*, natural disasters, war or other military activity, strikes). Others relate to changes in labor, general economic, legal or other technical conditions (*e.g.*, boycotts, slow-downs and occupation of factories by workers, shortages or non-availability of materials and equipment needed for construction, government refusal to grant necessary licenses). The parties may also clarify the scope of an exemption clause by expressly excluding some events. For example, the contract might preclude a party from claiming an exemption if prevented from performing because of its financial position.

NOTES AND QUESTIONS

(1) Consider the three basic approaches to the drafting of exemption clauses. What are the advantages and disadvantages of each? What elements might be included in a general definition of exempting events? If one employs a list approach, either with or without a general definition, should it be illustrative or exhaustive?

(2) The issue of whether government actions should constitute exempting events may be tricky. Such actions may take a variety of forms. Some examples would include export controls imposed by the contractor's country; currency restrictions imposed by the purchaser's country which block payment to the contractor; import controls imposed by the purchaser's country; refusal to grant a license to the contractor by the purchaser's country that precludes him from completing certain parts of the project. What are the arguments for and against including such actions as exempting events?

(3) There may also be a question whether certain other events should be regarded as exempting. For example, if natural disasters such as storms, cyclones,

floods or sandstorms are normal conditions at a particular time of the year at the construction site, should they be regarded as exempting events?

With respect to war or other military activity, air raids near the construction site may create a high risk of danger to the contractor's employees, but not actually prevent them from continuing with the construction. Should a high risk of danger be enough to support an exemption?

[4] Choice of Law and Settlement of Disputes

As we have seen previously in this casebook, and shall see again *infra*, Chapter 11, choice of law and settlement of dispute provisions are indispensable in any international or transnational contract. Such provisions are, if anything, even more important in works contracts. The complexity of such contracts means the likelihood of disputes arising is high, and because such contracts often involve several parties from several different countries (often there is more than one contractor), several systems of law are potentially applicable. The complexity of the works contracts and the various kinds of disputes that may arise under them may call for more complex and varied dispute settlement arrangements than one finds in other transnational contracts.

We consider first choice of law and then turn to settlement of disputes.

Choice of Law

If a works contract is multiparty, the courts of several countries may be competent to decide disputes between the parties. Each country's private international law (conflicts of law) may point to the application of a different system of law and thereby create a high degree of uncertainty as to the precise rights and obligations of the parties. Even if there is agreement that one country's law applies, that country's law may be too general to allow the parties to be confident of their position under the contract.

Through a choice of law provision the parties can seek to eliminate or minimize this uncertainty. It should be noted, however, that the ability of the parties to choose the applicable law may be limited. Under some systems of private international law the autonomy of the parties is limited. For example, no matter what choice the parties might wish to make, the law of the country where equipment or materials are situated may govern the transfer of ownership of that property, and the law of the country where the site is situated may govern the transfer of ownership of the works. Similarly, under some systems of private international law, the parties are only permitted to choose a legal system which has some connection with the contract, such as the legal system of the country of one of the parties or of the place of performance. Accordingly, the parties need to agree upon a choice of law that would be upheld by the rules of private international law in the countries whose courts might be competent to settle their disputes. If the parties agree on an exclusive jurisdiction clause, they should be careful to ensure that a court in the chosen jurisdiction will uphold their choice of law.

Most often the parties will choose the law of the country where the construction is to take place, or the law of the purchaser's country, if that country is different from the country where the construction is to take place. In some cases, however, especially if the law of the country where the construction is to take place is relatively underdeveloped, the parties may choose the law of a third country which is known to them and which is appropriate for settlement of disputes arising from works contracts.

Several different approaches to the drafting of a choice of law clause are possible. One is to provide that only the interpretation of the contract is to be governed by the chosen law. A second is to provide that all disputes arising out of the relationship created by the contract are to be governed by the chosen law. Such a provision might also include an illustrative list of the issues governed by that law. A third is to provide that the chosen law is to govern only the issues listed in the clause. Under this approach the issues not set forth in the clause will be governed by the otherwise applicable rules of private international law.

NOTES AND QUESTIONS

(1) Consider the three approaches to the drafting of a choice of law clause set forth in the immediately preceding paragraph. Under what circumstances might the parties wish to choose one approach over the other?

(2) The United Nations Convention on Contracts for the International Sale of Goods [13] applies to contracts of sale of goods when (i) the parties have their place of business in different states and those states are parties to the Convention, or (ii) the rules of private international law point to the law of a state party.[14] In some instances, therefore, the Convention may apply to transactions under a works contract.[15] The parties may find application of the Convention desirable, but, if they do not, they are able under the Convention to exclude the application of the Convention and, with few exceptions, to derogate from or to vary the effect of any of its provisions.

Settlement of Disputes

The subject of the resolution of international business disputes is extensively discussed *infra*, in Chapter 9. This section will briefly consider some problems that do not often exist in disputes arising under types of contracts other than works contracts.

Disputes under works contracts often concern highly technical matters connected with the construction process and with the technology incorporated in the works. Disputes that arise during the construction must be quickly settled in order not to disrupt the construction. Also, as we saw in our consideration of "hardship

---

[13] UN DOC. A/CONF. 97/19 (1980), reprinted in 19 Int'l Legal Mat. 668 (1980).

[14] Note: By reason of a special declaration, the United States will not apply the Convention in circumstances described in sub (ii).

[15] Application of the Convention may be barred in many works contracts by Article 3(2) which provides that: "This Convention does not apply to contracts in which the preponderant part of the obligations of the party who furnishes goods consists in the supply of labour or other services."

clauses," a works contract may provide for its terms to be changed or supplemented in certain circumstances.

As noted above in the section on hardship clauses, under some legal systems, courts and arbitrators are not competent to change or supplement contractual terms or to substitute their own consent for a consent improperly withheld by a party. Under other legal systems courts and arbitrators may do so only if they are expressly authorized by the parties. Still other legal systems permit arbitrators to make such changes but prohibit courts from doing so. Parties have to keep these variations in mind when drafting dispute settlement clauses and may wish to introduce a system whereby changes may automatically take place, *e.g.*, through provisions whereby the contract price changes automatically when the price levels of equipment, materials, or labor change. Alternatively, the parties might provide for dispute mechanisms other than arbitration or court proceedings.

Dispute settlement mechanisms other than arbitration or court proceedings, such as negotiation and conciliation, are often effective in dealing with disputes that arise under works contracts. A form of dispute settlement employed relatively rarely in the case of other contracts may be especially suitable for works contracts, *i.e.*, proceedings before a referee. The advantages of proceedings before a referee are that they are normally informal, expeditious, and may be tailored to suit the nature of the dispute. The disadvantages are that the proceedings before a referee may provide only limited legal safeguards, and it may not be possible to enforce his decision under some legal systems. In any event the contract should delimit as precisely as possible the authority to be conferred upon the referee and include a list of technical issues that are to be subject to the referee's decision.

Because works contracts often involve several contractors the possibility of multiparty dispute settlement proceedings is great. Accordingly, the dispute settlement clause in a works contract may confer exclusive jurisdiction on a court which has the authority to conduct multiparty proceedings. While arbitration generally lends itself less easily to multiparty proceedings, a well drafted arbitration statute can readily assure that arbitration will take place in such cases.[16] On this score, the Federal Arbitration Act, the United Nations Convention and the UNCITRAL model act are simply out of date.

§ 8.03 The International Joint Venture

Perhaps the most prominent feature of an international joint venture is the sharing of overall management planning and control. With the increased demand from many developing countries and some developed countries for local participation in foreign investors' operations, the international joint venture has become an increasingly popular form of doing business abroad. Indeed, taking a local firm into a joint venture may be the only way a foreign investor can gain access to local supplies or markets. A local firm may also supply the political contacts and cultural expertise that are indispensable to the success of the venture. The following have been suggested as "strategic reasons" for entering into a joint venture:

---

[16] See The Florida International Arbitration Act, Florida Statutes, Section 684.12.

(i) to share the risk; (ii) to obtain productive assets in a foreign market; (iii) to nurture an entity that will buy technology from you; (iv) to obtain a secure source of components or end products; (v) to nurture an entity that will buy components or end products from you; (vi) to enable you to ease out of a line of business, while retaining some participation to protect your source of components; (vii) to obtain management assistance; (viii) to obtain local identity or experience that you believe would be helpful to break into a foreign market; (ix) to comply with a local law requiring a local partner; and (x) to comply with a local law requiring local content.[1]

Peter Druker has suggested that, in the 1990s, businesses will integrate themselves into the world economy though various kinds of "alliances," *e.g.*, minority participations, joint ventures, research and marketing consortia, partnerships in subsidiaries or in special projects, cross-licensing, etc.[2] In his view small and middle-sized businesses will have to "go global" to maintain and develop markets, but rarely will they have the financial or managerial resources to build subsidiaries abroad or to acquire them. Technology and markets, he suggests, will induce firms to enter into such alliances. Today not even a big company can get all the technology it needs from its own research laboratories. Markets, too, are rapidly changing, merging, crisscrossing, and overlapping each other. No longer are they separate and distinct. Lastly, Drucker warns, alliances are difficult to create, maintain, and terminate. They require clarity concerning objectives, strategies, policies, relationships, and people.

Most often international joint ventures take the form of a separate, incorporated entity in which the joint venturers have equity interests. This is especially the case where the joint venture involves a long time commitment which requires a highly structured arrangement. However, if a joint venture is to last only for a limited period of time, or if it is formed for the purpose of engaging in a single transaction, the appropriate form may be a partnership or a contractual joint venture. Some of the advantages of a partnership joint venture include flexibility with respect to capital structure, management, and financial arrangements and less exposure to possible interference from either the host country's or the home country's government.

We will direct our attention to the possibility of an equity joint venture between a United States venturer and a local participant from the private sector. Realize, however, that international joint ventures can consist of various combinations of venturers, including, for example, two U.S. firms, one U.S. venturer and a venturer from a state other than that in which the venture is to take place, and a U.S. firm and the host country's government. Each type of international joint venture may have special problems of its own.

As noted above, by definition a joint venture involves a sharing of control or management. Acceptance of minority ownership, which may be required by the

---

1 These "strategic reasons" are set forth in the outline of a paper delivered by David N. Goldsweig at a panel on "International Joint Ventures: Setting Them Up, Taking Them Apart," held on April 26, 1990, at the Spring Meeting of the American Bar Association's Section on International Law and Practice, New York City.

2 Drucker, the futures that have already happened, "The Economist," October 21, 1989, at 19.

host country's government, does not necessarily mean loss of all control in the joint venture. In some countries as little as twenty-six percent ownership may give the minority owner the right to challenge decisions made by a majority partner, and in any event it is often possible to draft the by-laws in such a way as to require the concurrence of all venturers or a super-majority of votes on specified important questions. It may not be necessary, therefore, for the U.S. venturer to seek a fifty-fifty arrangement, much less fifty-one — forty-nine.

The following organizational structure has been suggested for international joint ventures:

(1) A board of directors which serves as the highest echelon of policy making. The board is often the forum for final resolution of policy disputes between the partners.

(2) A system of internal management, led by a managing director, that runs the venture in the same manner as management runs a conventional company.

(3) A managing partner, who by agreement of the partners will have the responsibility for controlling the company and will act as liaison between the partners and with the internal management of the joint venture.

(4) A system of management control which the partners use to assure themselves that the provisions of the joint venture agreements are being kept, and that the venture's operations are within the original plan. The management control system is used to measure management performance and also gives the partners the means to make their reaction to that performance felt.[3]

Although the majority venturer will normally name the chairman of the board, in developing countries a prominent local business person, otherwise not connected with the venturers, or a host country government official, might be selected as chairman. If the relationship is long-term, the managing partner will normally assume a more passive role and the board of directors will be more active.

An important point to keep in mind is that the management of the joint venture should be independent of the joint venturers. That is, even if the joint venturers provide the management of the joint venture, the key managers should not remain on their parent company's payroll or be part of a parent corporation's organization. Failure to maintain this independence may result in serious conflict of interest problems. Thus, for example, all sales to or purchases from the joint venture by the joint venturers should be negotiated at arms-length and problems should be anticipated and resolved at that time.

Another problem to resolve during the early negotiations between the joint venturers is the extent to which there will be a requirement for super-majority voting of the board of directors or for shareholder meetings or their committees on important issues to protect minority interests. Examples of such issues might include the selection of top managers, changes in the product line, the declaration of dividends, monetary commitments over a certain percentage of net worth, the initiation of lawsuits, and the selection of accountants and lawyers. Requirements for super-majorities should be recorded in the documents establishing the joint

---

[3] T.F. MacLaren & W.G. Marple, Jr. (eds), 4 Eckstrom's Licensing In Foreign And Domestic Operations: Joint Ventures, Section 2.02 (1986).

venture, *i.e.*, in the contract of establishment, or in a partnership agreement, or in a corporate charter, bylaws, or founding resolutions. Routine, day-to-day decisions should be made by the managers of the joint venture free from interference by the joint venturers.

After preliminary negotiations and after having chosen the management structure for the joint venture, the venturers will turn to drafting the joint venture agreement as well as any related agreements such as a licensing agreement or a technical assistance agreement. It has been suggested that the most important clauses in joint venture agreements relate to choice of governing language, choice of law, choice of forum, arbitration, government approvals, renegotiation, withdrawal from the joint venture, force majeure, limitation on liability, restrictions on the transfer of interests to third parties, marketing provisions, trademarks and trade names, and final agreement review by counsel.[4] We have already considered some of these subjects, and others are taken up later in the casebook. For present purposes, we turn to problems associated with the drafting of clauses on government approvals, withdrawal from the joint venture, marketing provisions, and final agreement review by counsel.[5]

Government Approvals

Especially in the developing countries it may be necessary to receive government approval at the national, provincial, or municipal level before an international joint venture can begin operations. It may also be necessary or desirable to obtain special guarantees from the host government regarding such matters as repatriation of profits, taxation of dividends, import and export restrictions, work permits and visas, and expropriation. Responsibility for obtaining these approvals should be specifically assigned in the contract.

QUESTION

Under a joint venture agreement, who should be responsible for obtaining the necessary government approvals? What should be the consequences of a failure to obtain such approvals? As counsel for the U.S. venturer what provisions would you include in the applicable clause?

Withdrawal From or Termination of the Joint Venture

Withdrawal from or termination of a joint venture is often a complex undertaking, and the drafting of the clause for this contingency is accordingly of great importance, especially since the rate of failure for joint ventures under some circumstances may be as high as 50 percent. As we have previously seen in this

---

[4] *Id.*, Section 3.02.
[5] *Id.*, Section 3.02(8).

chapter, termination of business enterprises is often heavily regulated by local law, which should be thoroughly researched. The applicable clause should specify whether the joint venture is for a fixed term or of indefinite duration and the grounds for termination or withdrawal. Depending upon what local law would permit, such grounds might include non-payment of obligations beyond a fixed time; corporate reorganization, dissolution, or bankruptcy of the other venturer; resignation, firing or death of a key member of the venture; and poor financial return over a specified period of time.

As to methods of withdrawing from or terminating a joint venture the following have been suggested as alternatives:

(1) The liquidation of the joint venture at either party's option;

(2) Allowing the withdrawing party to sell its shares in the public market;

(3) A buy-sell option having the following general form. The terminating party sets a price on the shares. The other party then has the option of either buying the shares or selling its own shares to the party wishing to terminate at the stated price;

(4) Withdrawal as a matter of right upon notice. If one party elects to continue the venture, a price which is mutually agreed-upon or determined by an arbitrator or predetermined formula is paid to the withdrawing party. If none of the parties wish to continue, the venture is liquidated;

(5) An option, granted to one party, to sell its interest in the venture to the other party after a fixed period of time and at a price determined by an arbitrator or a predetermined formula. The other party should have the option of liquidating the venture;

(6) An option to buy, given to one party, covering the interest of the other party after a fixed period of time and at a price determined at the time of the exercise of the option;

(7) The sale by a party of its interest to a third party with the other party having a right of first refusal;

(8) A right of first refusal similar to the above, except that one party has the option of selling the entire venture to a third party, unless the other party agrees to buy the interest of the other under the same terms and conditions offered by the third party;

(9) The provisions of state statutes, which govern the dissolution of a joint venture in the event of serious disagreement between the partners. Resort to these statutes should be avoided as it will generally result in high litigation costs and reduced opportunity to exploit the value of the business.

The rights and obligations of the venturers following termination of a joint venture also must be clearly specified. These include the payment of damages and disposition of other payments due, for example, to local personnel; discontinuance of the use of patents, know-how, copyrights, trademarks, and trade names; and the return of equipment and confidential information.

Marketing Provisions

Since normally the joint venture will have been established for the purpose of manufacturing, the issue of restrictions on the export of products may arise between the U.S venturer on the one side and the other venturer and the host country's government on the other. As we have previously seen, the host country's government in particular is likely to resist any restrictions on the export of the venture's products. For its part the U.S. venturer may have established, either through distributorship or licensing agreements or through joint ventures, markets in other countries, and may not wish the products of the venture to compete with its operations in those markets.

A possible compromise on this issue is to provide that the venture can export to those countries in which the U.S. venturer does not have licensees or distributors or joint ventures and list those countries in an appendix to the agreement. It should be noted, however, that restrictions on exports may raise antitrust problems, and these should be checked carefully.

Final Agreement Review by Counsel

Before the venturers close on the joint venture agreement — i.e., sign the agreement in its final form and bring it into effect — local counsel should review the agreement to ensure that it is compatible with the host country's laws on, for example, foreign investment controls, customs, importation of capital, foreign exchange, notarial forms, antitrust, tax incentives, and corporate structure. Similarly, U.S counsel should review the agreement to determine whether it complies with, for example, the Foreign Corrupt Practices Act, anti-boycott legislation, antitrust laws, U.S. export administration laws, U.S. import trade laws and tax laws. U.S. counsel should also review any related arrangements, such as licensing agreements, technical assistance agreements, loan agreements, letters of credit, bonds, guarantees, and escrow agreements.

If the agreement provides for arbitration in a country other than the United States or the host country, it might require an opinion by competent counsel that an arbitral tribunal in that country would accept jurisdiction over disputes arising under the agreement and that the agreement to arbitrate as well as an award by the arbitral tribunal would be enforceable in a court in that country.

PROBLEM

Assume that you are counsel to Admore, a U.S. corporation that is engaged in trilateral negotiations regarding a possible joint venture with Absorbet, an enterprise in the developing country of Valencia, and with the Government of Valencia. Absorbet proposes that the following provisions be included in the joint venture agreement:

1. The Board of Directors of the Company shall consist of eight members of which four shall be appointed by Absorbet, from which the Government of Valencia shall appoint the chairman, and four shall be appointed by Admore,

from which the Government of Valencia shall appoint the Managing Director. The chairman shall have a casting vote.

2. Either Admore or Absorbet may assign its rights or obligations under this agreement as the dictates of business may require.

3. If the performance of any obligation on the part of Admore or Absorbet shall be prevented or delayed by *force majeure* including, without limitation, strikes, embargoes, wars, civil insurrection, riots, floods, or other events beyond their control, either party shall have the right to terminate this Agreement.

4. Absorbet shall be responsible for obtaining all necessary approvals, licenses, and permits from the Government of Valencia.

5. In the event of a dispute arising out of any of the clauses hereunder, or in the case of a breach of any of these clauses, the parties shall try to reach an amicable settlement. Should this fail, the dispute shall be submitted to arbitration, which shall take place at the residence of the opponent to the party seeking arbitration. Both parties shall nominate an arbitrator within a fortnight; should one party fail to do so, the other party shall name the other arbitrator also. Both arbitrators shall name a third arbitrator who shall be a member of the legal profession. The decision of the arbitrators shall be final and both parties agree to abide by the same. The arbitrators shall also decide on each party's share of the expenses of arbitration.

What would be your reaction to these provisions? If you find any of these provisions unsatisfactory, how would you revise them? Draft provisions incorporating your proposed changes. Antitrust and tax considerations[6] also loom large in drafting an international joint venture. Antitrust problems are taken up *supra*, in Chapter 7.

---

[6] A good treatment of tax issues is Klein, Taxation Of International Joint Ventures, T.F. MacLaren & W. Marple, Jr. (ed), 4 Eckstrom's Licensing In Foreign And Domestic Operations: Joint Ventures, Section 6.01 (1986). Additional writings on international joint ventures include: P.B. Fitzpatrick, Transnational Joint Ventures (1989); 4 W.P. Streng & J.W. Salacuse, International Business Planning: Law And Taxation, Section 19.08 (1988) (with draft agreements); United Nations Centre On Transnational Corporations, Arrangements Between Joint Venture Partners In Developing Countries, St/CTC/ser.B2(1987); Clark, Energy And Mineral Joint Ventures In China, The Law Of Transnational Business Transactions, 7A-1 (V.P.Nanda, ed. 1987); ABA, Joint Venturing Abroad - A Case Study (March 1-2, 1984); D. Hall, The International Joint Venture (1984); W. Friedman & J.P. Beguin, Joint International Business Ventures In Developing Countries (1971): Foreign Joint Ventures; Basic Issues, Drafting And Negotiation: A Panel, 39 Bus. Law. 1033 (1983) (with draft agreement); Comment, Protecting The Entrepreneur: Special Drafting Concerns For International Joint Venture Contracts, 14 U.C. Davis L. Rev. 1001 (1981), Carpenter & Smith, U.S.–Soviet Joint Ventures, 43 Bus. Law 79 (1987).

A NOTE ON JOINT VENTURES IN THE SOVIET UNION
AND EASTERN EUROPE[7]

As even the most casual reader of newspaper headlines is aware, extraordinary changes are currently taking place in the Soviet Union. Through a process of economic restructuring (perestroika) and greater openness (glasnost) President Mikhail S. Gorbachev's government has greatly improved relations with the Western democracies and challenged some of the most fundamental tenets of Marxism-Leninism. As part of perestroika the Soviet Union has adopted new laws on and a new approach to joint ventures with Western firms.

Specifically, in January 1987, the USSR Council of Ministers (the highest executive and administrative body in the Soviet Union) issued a decree authorizing equity joint ventures in the Soviet Union between Soviet organizations and Western firms. Prior to issuance of this decree Western firms had been limited in their dealings to contractual arrangements such as countertrade, licensing of technology and know-how, supply of production lines, service agreements, research and development projects and other forms of cooperation.

Under the 1987 decree, however, Western firms faced a number of difficulties. For example, those firms primarily interested in selling products in the Soviet Union itself were required to produce for export and their access to foreign exchange was tied to foreign exchange generated through exports. The decree also limited the foreign partner to a maximum forty-nine percent share of the equity in the joint enterprise, required that both the chairman of the board of directors and the director general, or chief operating officer, be Soviet citizens and that the joint venture's transactions in the Soviet economy be conducted through the intermediary of a Soviet foreign trade organization. The decree also provided that Soviet law was to govern all aspects of the terms of employment of the labor force, except for the wages, vacations, and pensions of foreign specialist employees, and reserved to the Council of Ministers the power to terminate a joint venture which failed to conform to the objectives for which it was created.

Some, although not all, of these difficulties were removed by Council of Minister's decrees issued in December 1988 and May 1989 and by the regulations implementing the decrees. The joint venture is no longer required to produce for export, although a joint venture selling mainly in the Soviet domestic market may

---

[7] We are indebted to Robert Starr, an American lawyer practicing in London, England, for providing us with an unpublished memorandum on "Joint Ventures In The USSR," dated May 1989. Much of the discussion that follows is based on Mr. Starr's memorandum and on a paper, "Soviet Joint Ventures: The Perspectives," delivered by Jeffrey M. Herzfeld, an American lawyer practicing in Paris, France, to the Moscow Conference on Law and Economic Cooperation, held from September 19-21, 1990. For further consideration of Soviet Union ventures, see e.g., Vecchio, Soviet Joint Ventures: Keeping an Eye on the Goalposts, 9 Int'l Financial L. Rev. 37 (1990); International Chamber of Commerce, Guide To Joint Ventures In The USSR (1988); Starr, Back In The USSR, Taxation International 102 (1989); Aronson, The New Soviet Joint Venture Law: Analysis, Issues, And Approaches For The American Investor, 19 L. & Pol'y Int'l Bus. 851 (1987); Carpenter & Smith, U.S. - Soviet Joint Ventures: A New Opening in the East, 43 Bus. Law. 79 (1987). For the Soviet decree on joint ventures, as amended, see 29 Int'l Leg. Mat. 262 (1990).

find it difficult to obtain enough foreign currency to remit profits to a parent corporation or to import materials and supplies necessary for its operations. The Soviet government has announced its intention to move towards convertibility of the ruble, but this will take time and may depend on the success of other measures, such as price reforms, which are currently under sharp attack.

The 1988 decree allows a foreign party to a joint venture to have a majority equity interest, perhaps as high as 100% if the joint venture is to operate in special economic zones, such as one recently created near the Soviet-Finnish border. Moreover, the joint venture no longer has to sell through a foreign trade organization and can sell directly to the public if it wishes. Nor must either the chairman of the board of directors or the director general of the joint venture be Soviet citizens. This can now be decided by negotiation between the joint venturers.

The staff of the joint venture must consist primarily of Soviet citizens. Under the December 1988 decree, however, the joint venturers are free to agree on questions of hiring and dismissal, pay, and incentives, although such decisions may be made only while "observing those rights of citizens provided for in USSR legislative acts." Other aspects of labor relations are subject to severe constraints under Soviet law, but there is apparent room for negotiation on some issues.

Since the Council of Ministers still has authority to terminate a joint venture whose activities are not consistent with the objectives indicated at the time of its creation, considerable thought must be given to drafting the objectives clause. Some objectives favored by the Soviet Government include the satisfaction of domestic requirements for certain types of industrial products, raw materials and foodstuffs, supplying advanced foreign technologies, management expertise, and financial resources to the Soviet economy, the expansion of exports and the reduction of superfluous imports.

Under the 1987 and 1988 decrees and implementing regulations, two basic documents need to be prepared — after disposing of such important preliminary matters as a memorandum of understanding and a feasibility study. These are first, a joint venture agreement and second, a statute or charter. Collectively these are known as foundation documents and govern the relations of the joint venturers and the operation of the joint venture.

Under the 1987 decree the statute must specify:

— the nature of the joint venture and its objectives;

— its "legal address;"

— the names of the parties forming the joint venture;

— the amount of the "authorized fund" (a fund consisting of contributions from the joint venturers which are the basis for the allocation of profits between the parties), the procedure for raising the fund and the venturer's respective interests in the fund;

— the structure, composition and competence of the venture's governing board;

— procedures for management decision making;

— procedures for terminating the venture.

In addition to the foundation documents the venturers may prepare various ancillary agreements such as licensing or supply contracts.

The foundation documents must first be approved by the highest administrative authority of the Soviet venturer and then submitted to the Ministry of Finance for registration. Upon registration the joint venture becomes a legal entity under Soviet law. As of May 1990, approximately 1500 joint ventures had been registered and many more reportedly were under review by the Ministry of Finance. Of these, however, only about 140 joint ventures had commenced operations.

With respect to management the highest governing body of a joint venture is the board. The foundation documents determine the composition of the board and the procedures by which it makes its decisions. The December 1988 decree requires that "fundamental" questions be decided by unanimous vote, but does not define these questions. Accordingly, the parties to a joint venture should define what issues are to be regarded as fundamental. As noted above the parties are now free to choose a foreign national as chairman of the board or as director general of management if they wish.

As to labor relations the 1987 decree required the joint venture to conclude "collective agreements" with trade union organizations formed at the joint venture's enterprise. Under the more liberal 1988 decree, however, it became possible to introduce flexibility into the venture's labor relations through negotiations with different units of the workforce or even with individuals outside the system of collective agreements. It is also necessary to address the special needs of foreign personnel. The Soviet venturer can assist in obtaining any special permits or in arranging accommodations or other matters for foreign personnel.

As indicated above, a joint venture that sells to the domestic market may do so directly or through a foreign trade organization. The same is true for import and export operations. However, importing or exporting from the Soviet Union requires a license from the Ministry of Foreign Economic Relations. The joint venture will want to be assured it can import necessary supplies and export its products. A particular problem with respect to imports may be U.S. and other Western controls on exports to the Soviet Union and other communist countries, especially with respect to so-called "dual use" items, *i.e.*, goods or technical data that have commercial applications but that could be used for military purposes as well.

The current inconvertibility of the Soviet ruble creates a variety of thorny problems. For example, inconvertibility means that the currency conversion rates used in the Soviet Union are artificial. This can distort the income and expenses of the joint venture and may have serious tax implications, especially if the joint venture is export oriented. Another problem may be limited access to hard currency and the resultant inability of the joint venture to remit profits. Although the 1987 decree guaranteed the right to remit profits, this guarantee is meaningless if hard currency is not available. This is particularly a problem for a joint venture selling mainly in the Soviet domestic market.

There are other dimensions to the inconvertibility problem. Not surprisingly, there is a strong interest in obtaining raw materials locally for rubles, since importing raw materials aggravates the hard currency needs of the joint venture. A Soviet regulation, however, authorizes state enterprises to sell to joint ventures for hard currency as well as for rubles. Consequently, joint ventures often have to pay Soviet organizations at least partially in hard currency for raw materials. Another problem is that since August 1990, Soviet citizens have been authorized to hold hard currency. One may accordingly expect employees to demand that joint ventures pay at least part of their salaries in hard currency.

If foreign currency reserves are insufficient to allow the foreign venturer to remit all of its share of the profits, the balance of these profits will be held in accounts with a Soviet bank pending the joint venture earning the additional hard currency needed for further profit remittance. Possible ways to resolve or at least mitigate this problem include lending accumulated rubles to other hard currency investors who require rubles for investment in the Soviet Union, or exports of joint venture products, and countertrade arrangements.

Prior to March 1989, some joint ventures also sought to alleviate the inconvertibility problem by buying and exporting Soviet goods. Since that time, however, a Soviet decree has permitted joint ventures to export only their own production. Moreover, in August 1990, a Soviet decree prohibited joint ventures from selling for hard currency products other than their own even on the Soviet market.

Other approaches to the inconvertibility problem — such as State-sponsored hard currency auctions and a new system of so-called convertibility exchanges, both of which are designed to exchange rubles at market rather than official Gosbank (the central bank of the Soviet Union) rates, as well as the concept of free economic zones — have so far failed to afford much relief. Accordingly, as Jeffrey M. Hertzfeld, an eminent authority in the field, has suggested, the threshold question one asks when contemplating a joint venture in the Soviet Union is not, is there a market for the goods to be produced? Rather, it is, can the investment be made self-financing in hard currency?

Another general problem is the absence of freedom to set prices on the basis of supply and demand. The lack of a realistic pricing system may make valuing the venturer's respective contributions to the authorized fund of the joint venture, upon which their respective shares of the venture's profits are based, extremely difficult. This problem must be resolved through negotiations, since the Soviet decrees and regulations offer little guidance.

Taxation matters are especially complex. After an initial two year "tax holiday" (three in the Far Eastern Economic Area) a two-tier tax system applies to the joint venture. Until 1990, the venture itself paid a thirty percent tax on its profits, and the foreign venturer was subject to an additional twenty percent withholding tax on the profits it repatriates out of the Soviet Union. Soviet tax law, moreover, although apparently applicable to foreign source income of a joint venture, contains no provision for a foreign tax credit. This creates special problems for an export-oriented joint venture. Also, Soviet accounting rules differ significantly from those followed in Western countries. On the other hand, there are indications that taxes are partly or even wholly negotiable.

In 1990, as part of a general Soviet tax reform, the corporate tax rate applicable to joint ventures in which the foreign investment is thirty percent or less was increased to the forty-five percent rate applicable to other Soviet enterprises under the new law. Although the dividend withholding rate was reduced to fifteen percent, it was made payable in the currency of profit remittance rather than the ruble, a substantial new hard currency burden, and withholding tax was imposed as well on the Soviet partner.

Futhermore, the new tax law subjected all enterprises, including joint ventures, to a new excess profits tax, with rates of up to ninety percent on profits exceeding certain limited levels of profitability to be established in each industry by the Supreme Soviet, the highest legislative body in the Soviet Union. These levels of profitability are to be based upon twice the average level of profitability for state enterprises in the given industry.

Tax treaties that the Soviet Union has concluded with a number of countries, including, for example, France, the Federal Republic of Germany, Italy, the United States, and the United Kingdom, may help. For example, most of these Soviet tax treaties exempt royalties from withholding tax. The rules vary, however, from treaty to treaty. Typically, Soviet tax treaties require the Soviet Union to levy a reduced withholding tax of fifteen percent on dividends, but both the U.S. and Swiss treaties do not reduce the otherwise applicable twenty percent withholding taxes on dividends. Similar variations exist with respect to withholding of taxes on royalties and interest payments. These variations should be taken into account by a U.S. joint venturer when deciding where its participation in the joint venture should be based and to which country or countries profits from the joint venture should be remitted. The Soviet tax treaties usually do not contain provisions against "treaty shopping."

The U.S. participant in the Soviet joint venture will also be concerned whether U.S. officials will regard the joint venture as a corporation or a partnership for purposes of U.S. taxation. Although the Soviets have made an effort to give their joint ventures the attributes that a corporation has under U.S. law, the final decision on this point will be made by U.S. officials pursuant to the terms of U.S. laws. Hence the U.S. venturer needs to pay special attention to its negotiations with the Soviet venturer on such matters as duration, transferability of interest, and terms for dissolution of the joint venture.

Even if the joint venture is likely to be considered a partnership under U.S. law, it may be possible to avoid the tax consequences of this status by investing in the joint venture through a subsidiary, possibly one in a tax haven country. It would be necessary to do this, however, in compliance with applicable legislation prohibiting or discouraging tax avoidance.

Under current Soviet law the parties to the joint venture enjoy substantial flexibility with repect to termination or liquidation of the venture. Although the Soviet Law on State Enterprises allows for the liquidation of insolvent enterprises, there is no bankruptcy law as such in the Soviet Union. As noted above, the Council of Ministers has the authority to terminate a joint venture whose operations are inconsistent with the goals and objectives set forth in the foundation documents. Otherwise, the parties to a joint venture have complete freedom to decide how to wind up the affairs of the venture.

Soviet law does require that the duration of the joint venture be specified in the foundation documents but does not expressly prohibit a venture of unlimited duration. One approach to this issue might be to seek agreement on a venture of limited duration but with provision for renewal.

Because Soviet law gives the parties flexibility, the U.S. venturer will want to draft the provisions on termination of the venture with particular care. For example, the U.S. party would want to consider providing an escape mechanism in the event of a breach by the other party or parties, deadlock in voting on crucial matters, or *force majeure* circumstances. Another possibility is to provide for an option to terminate the venture if for reasons beyond the control of the parties, the venture becomes commercially untenable, or a party is unable to fulfill contemplated undertakings, or Soviet law is changed to the disadvantage of the venture or of either party.

The foundation documents should clearly specify the procedure for both voluntary and involuntary liquidations. The U.S. party should, at a minimum, be entitled to its share of the venture's net assets and should receive compensation for the loss of anticipated profits if the venture is subjected to an involuntary liquidation. The U.S. party might also want to seek a first priority on the venture's hard currency assets and to ensure that any rights the joint venture may have acquired to use industrial and intellectual property or the name or logos supplied by the U.S. party are terminated, and that the Soviet party acquires no rights in such property.

The Soviet Union has recently signed investment promotion and protection agreements with Belgium/Luxembourg, France, the Federal Republic of Germany, and the United Kingdom.[8] These agreements provide the foreign investor with various kinds of protection. The agreement with the United Kingdom, for example, provides for fair and equitable treatment and full protection for investments and returns, including *inter alia*, most favored nation treatment for investments and a guarantee of full compensation in the event of expropriation. As of September 1990, discussions were reportedly underway between the United States and the Soviet Union with a view to the conclusion of a similar agreement.

As in any joint venture the provisions on dispute settlement and governing law are exceedingly important and should be specified in the foundation documents. The Arbitration Court at the USSR Chamber of Commerce and Industry (formerly the Foreign Trade Arbitration Commission) has jurisdiction to deal with disputes involving joint ventures between foreign and Soviet parties.

It is possible, however, for the Soviet party to a joint venture to agree to arbitration outside of the Soviet Union. In such proceedings the UNCITRAL Arbitration Rules are often utilized (for more extensive discussion of arbitration, see, Chapter 11, *infra*, p. 957). The parties to a joint venture can also agree to make their relations subject to a law other than Soviet law, except with respect to those matters which Soviet law expressly mandates must be governed by Soviet law. The Soviet Union is a party to the 1958 New York Convention on the Recognition and Enforcement of Foreign Arbitral Awards (as is the United States) and the 1961 European Convention on International Commercial Arbitration. These conventions would govern recognition and enforcement of an arbitral award in the Soviet Union and in other countries that are parties to them.

---

[8] For text and commentary on the four agreements, see 29 Int'l Leg. Mt. 299, 317, 351, 366 (1990).

As of September 1990, a draft of a proposed new Soviet Foreign Investment Law was under active consideration. According to reports, the law was designed to further stimulate foreign investment in the Soviet Union and included the possibility of wholly foreign-owned enterprises and the granting of foreign concessions for natural resource development projects. With respect to joint ventures, the draft reportedly envisaged a system of decentralized and expedited registration at the level of the Union Republics rather than by the Soviet Government, and proposed special incentives for joint ventures in certain high priorty fields such as consumer goods, agricultural processing and storage, medical products and equipment, among others, including extending the joint venture tax holiday to five years, reducing the corporate tax rate to twenty percent, and cutting in half the dividend withholding rate on profit distribution to the foreign investor. At this writing, however, the economic and political situation in the Soviet Union is in extreme flux, and it is impossible to predict with any degree of confidence the fate of this legislation.

PROBLEM

Your client, a fast growing technology company, with operations in state of the art computer hardware and software and highly sophisticated communications equipment, has developed a substantial niche in the United States market and operates abroad through subsidiaries in Italy, France, and the United Kingdom. The company, learning of the new Soviet decrees on joint ventures and their implementing regulations, would like to explore the feasibility of setting up a joint venture in the Soviet Union. It informs you that, in addition to selling in the Soviet Union, it would like to use the Soviet Union as a base for exports to countries in Eastern Europe, especially in light of the political changes underway in those countries.

Your client asks you about the legal aspects of its plans. Please advise.

NOTES AND QUESTIONS

(1) At this writing there is general agreement that Soviet joint ventures, with a few exceptions, have not lived up to expectations. Accordingly, there are reports that the Soviet Union may substantially revise its legislation on joint ventures.

What factors do you think have contributed to this lack of success? Are they primarily problems with the terms of existing law or do they reflect other dimensions of the situation?

(2) The recent changes in Eastern Europe have been even more startling than those in the Soviet Union, and the interest of Western firms in investing in Eastern Europe, especially through joint ventures, has been intense. Eastern Europe, however, cannot be viewed as a monolith, because the prospects for democracy,

free markets, and political stability vary greatly from country to country. At this writing Western interest in joint ventures and other forms of doing business is particularly strong in Hungary, while, by contrast there is little such interest with respect to Rumania. Moreover, on October 3, 1990, West Germany and East Germany were reunited and became a single nation, with the result that future investment in the territory that once constituted East Germany will be governed by the liberal West German approach to foreign investment. There were over 3,300 joint ventures registered in the Eastern European countries by the end of 1989.

§ 8.04   Profile Lowering Devices

Devices for lowering the profile or visibility of a U.S. business in a foreign country, especially a developing foreign country, are useful where the political climate is problematic and the threat of expropriation or other hostile actions is accordingly great. Previously in this chapter we have seen some examples of such devices: new provisions in economic development agreements requiring disinvestment down to minority stock ownership; contracts for the construction of industrial works where the contractor merely supplies equipment or materials for incorporation into the works; and joint ventures, especially those in which the U.S. venturer does not have majority stock ownership. All of these approaches may make the U.S. foreign investor a less visible target for hostile local reaction.

There are other such devices. Management service contracts as an alternative to ownership interests are increasingly common. Under these arrangements the host country government may contract with the foreign firm to run the day-to-day activities of the operating company but deny it any equity involvement. For such service the foreign business may be compensated through a percentage of the operating company's gross sales proceeds or of its net consolidated profits. It might also receive fees for special services such as engineering. Experience has shown, however, that for a foreign firm to be interested in a management service contract, there must be a great potential for sales and profits from the foreign firm's downstream operations that depend on inputs from the project it is managing.

In other instances the foreign firm may have no management responsibilities but merely a straight service contract with the host country government or the local enterprise. A variant of this arrangement is the production sharing agreement. Interpreted literally, a production sharing agreement would cover only arrangements whereby the foreign firm and the host country government share the output of the operation in predetermined amounts. In practice, the term has been applied to any arrangement where there is at least an option that the firm and the government receive their benefits in kind rather than in cash. Such arrangements have been fairly common in Eastern Europe. The Western firms have provided machinery and technical assistance and have accepted part of the venture's production in payment. The great majority of production sharing arrangements, however, have been in the oil industry.

In addition to production sharing arrangements, there are special profit sharing arrangements, *i.e.*, arrangements where the foreign firm's share of the profits is high at the start of a long term enterprise but decreases over time, while that of the host government increases. Utilizing improved techniques of economic forecasting, the arrangement is structured so as to provide for increasing the host government's share of the proceeds at successive stages in the life of the enterprise.

So-called "indigenization" is another profile lowering device. This refers to the use of nationals of the host country in executive and managerial positions as well as in the labor force. Often indigenization is mandated by local law or by contractual arrangements between the foreign firm and the host government.

Still another profile lowering device is multinationalization of the foreign ownership or operation. This reduces the association of the venture with any single foreign nationality, which may be particularly advantageous to the U.S. foreign investor.

The extent to which such profile lowering devices will be necessary or desirable will vary from country to country. In some countries the traditional majority ownership and control arrangement is still available to the foreign investor, although the possibility of a radical change in the local investment environment should always be considered.

CHAPTER 9

INTERNATIONAL CLAIMS FOR ECONOMIC INJURIES
TO ALIENS

Introduction

Expansively defined, the subject of "international claims" would encompass all claims by one state against another alleging that the latter had violated an obligation owed it. A more narrow reading would limit international claims to those covered by the international law of state responsibility for injury to aliens. Even this limited definition, however, would cover a subject substantially more expansive than that which is the focus of this chapter. Here we explore the subject of *state responsibility for economic injuries to aliens*: a subject that has been a focal point of dispute in the 20th century.

Economic injury may take the form of an outright expropriation of alien owned property. Alternatively, it may consist of a diminution in value of an alien's economic interests caused by regulations of the host state. As we shall see later in this Chapter, the distinction between an expropriation, which may require the payment of compensation to an alien, and a diminution of value, which may not, can be difficult to draw.

Assuming that the economic injury is an expropriation, there may still be a debate as to whether the host state is obligated to pay the alien any compensation and, if so, how much. There is the further issue as to who may bring the claim. The traditional law of state responsibility for injuries to aliens holds that the claim belongs to and may only be brought by the state of which the alien is a national — assuming that the alien has exhausted the domestic remedies offered by the host state. Recently, however, international procedures have been developed that allow the alien to bring the claim in his own name against the host state.

As we shall see below, the search for an internationally agreed upon standard for compensation in the event of an economic injury to an alien has proven to be an illusive quest. The reasons for this difficulty are rooted in economics, politics, and the sensitive history of relations between the Western developed states and the developing states, many of which were formerly colonies. Some of the methods employed by states in the effort to reach a concensus on a standard for compensation include the drafting of resolutions in international organizations, especially the General Assembly of the United Nations; the conclusion of bilateral investment agreements; lump sum claims settlement agreements and the awards of national and international claims commissions. To date, however, no global multilateral agreement on foreign investment has been concluded, and none appears imminent, although trade related investment issues are currently on the agenda of the Uruguay Round of the GATT. As a consequence, there has been increasing emphasis on the development of arrangements designed to avoid disputes over expropriation and to provide new avenues for settlement of those disputes that arise.

To place this subject in proper context, the chapter begins with a consideration of the history and evolution of the doctrine of state responsibility for the expropriation of alien-owned property. The chapter then turns to challenges to this doctrine, with particular emphasis on the Calvo Doctrine. It next turns to methods employed to settle these claims, including mobilizing the assets of the expropriating state and lump-sum settlement agreements; determining the validity of claims through such national claims commissions as the United States Foreign Claims Settlement Commission; establishing special tribunals, using as case studies tribunals set up under the World Bank's International Centre for the Settlement of Investment Disputes (ICSID) and the Iranian-United States Claims Settlement Tribunal; and applying economic sanctions. Lastly, the chapter discusses and evaluates methods that both seek to avoid disputes over expropriation and to provide new avenues of settlement for those that do develop. These methods include private investment insurance, national programs of investment insurance such as the Overseas Private Investment Insurance Corporation (OPIC), and multilateral investment guarantee programs, most particularly, the Multilateral Investment Guarantee Agency (MIGA).

§ 9.01   History and Evolution of the Doctrine of State Responsibility for Expropriation of Alien Owned Property

Perhaps any history of the doctrine of state responsibility for expropriation of alien owned property ought to begin with a consideration of the influence of natural rights theory, especially as developed by the English philosopher John Locke during the 17th century. Locke posited the existence of men and women in a state of nature where no one was subjected to the will or authority of another and where all were able to determine their own actions. Because of the dangers and burdens of this state of nature men and women decided to enter into a contract whereby they agreed to establish a political community. While establishing a political community, however, they retained their natural rights of life, liberty, and property. The primary purpose of government under this arrangement was to protect these natural rights, and failure to do so would result in a forfeiture of the right of government to govern.

Locke grounded his natural rights theory on certain basic premises concerning the nature of man. With respect to the natural right to property, Locke was of the view that:

> . . . every man has a property in his own person; this nobody has any right to but himself. The labor of his body and the work of his hands we may say are properly his. Whatsoever, then, he removes out of the state that nature hath provided and left it in, he had mixed his labor with, and joined to it something that is his own, and thereby makes it his property.[1]

---

[1] This quotation is from Chapter V of Locke, The Second Treatise Of Civil Government (Gough ed. 1946).

Note Locke's reference to a right to "property" in one's own person and his concept that, if one alters something through his own labor, it becomes one's own, almost a fusion of the self with creations of the self.

Another strong strand in Anglo-American legal tradition is the utilitarian theories developed by Jeremy Bentham, another English philosopher who wrote in the 18th and early 19th centuries. Defining rights in terms of a teleological perspective that stresses the goal of the common good, Bentham contended that every political decision should be judged by the test whether it produced the greatest good for the greatest number. Bentham's emphasis on the total net sum of the happiness of all of a government's subjects contrasted markedly with the natural rights emphasis on specific basic interests of each individual subject.

At first blush, one might conclude that the utilitarian approach, which was highly influential during the 19th century, would result in less concern for individual property rights than the Lockian analysis. But for most of this time and well into the 20th century as well, the two theories were mutually reinforcing. Although the utilitarians rejected Locke's thesis of inalienable property rights which preceded government and which it was government's primary duty to protect, they argued that private property rights, by securing to individuals their reasonable expectations, were an indispensable condition for productivity and hence a substantial benefit to society. According to utilitarian thinkers of this period, attacks on private property such as governmental confiscation would result in social pains in excess of pleasures. Such attacks would lower productivity because there would be no assurance that the person who produced the product would be able to enjoy the fruits of his labor. For his part, Locke developed utilitarian arguments for property rights, stressing that they would encourage industry.

Despite this strong philosophical support for property rights, acceptance of the principle of compensation for governmental takings was lacking for much of United States history. The original version of the United States Constitution contained no endorsement of the compensation principle, and although the Fifth Amendment to the Bill of Rights did so, the States did not similarly protect property against State governmental activity. As a consequence, during the early days of U.S. history, the States engaged in significant land and wealth confiscation for the building of railroads and other projects.[2]

Moreover, although most States in the United States moved relatively quickly away from this position and towards acceptance of the compensation principle, it was not until the late 19th century that the Supreme Court incorporated the principle of just compensation for a taking into the due process clause of the 14th Amendment. In doing so, the Court noted that some governmental activities fell outside the coverage of the compensation principle because they constituted an exercise of the police power.

With the ultimate victory of the just compensation principle in the United States, an issue arises as to the philosophical underpinnings of this principle.

---

[2] We are grateful to Professor Jeremy Paul of the University of Connecticut School of Law for these observations. For discussion, see Note, The Origins And Original Significance Of The Just Compensation Clause Of The Fifth Amendment, 94 Yale L.J. 694 (1985); M. Horowitz, The Transformation Of American Law 63-66 (1977).

Professor Joseph Sax has argued, for example, that the just compensation principle is more concerned with preventing the arbitrary actions of an unjust sovereign than with the maintenance of the economic status quo.[3] In support of this proposition, Sax notes that western law contains a Christian as well as Roman tradition. Under this thesis the search for a standard of just compensation becomes an effort to serve the concept of justice.

With the advent of the 20th century, the consensus view was that a government's taking of an alien's property required full compensation. Decisions of the Permanent Court of International Justice early in the 20th century confirmed this view. See, *e.g.*, the *Factory at Chorzow*,[4] and *Case Concerning German Interests in Polish Upper Silesia.*[5]

The first major international challenge to this view was by the Bolshevik government in the Soviet Union which took over in 1917 and contended that an alien enters the territory of another state or acquires property there wholly subject to national law. In other words, according to the Soviet perception, international law is simply inapplicable to the issue of what compensation, if any, a government must pay for the taking of an alien's property.

Mexican expropriations between 1915 and 1940 of agrarian and oil properties owned, directly or indirectly, by United States citizens, presented another challenge to the consensus view. The reaction in the United States to these expropriations was sharp, and precipitated an exchange of correspondence between the United States and Mexican governments on the question of compensation.

In 1938, U.S. Secretary of State Cordell Hull wrote to the Minister of Foreign Relations of Mexico and contended that the property of aliens was protected by an international standard.[6] This standard, according to the United States, required, in the case of expropriation of an alien's property, the payment of "prompt, adequate and effective compensation." In addition, Secretary Hull noted, this standard appeared in the constitutions of almost all nations and in particular the constitutions of the American Republics and embodied the principle of "just compensation."

In response the Mexican Minister of Foreign Affairs contended, in support of the expropriation of agrarian properties without payment of compensation, that "[t]he political, social and economic stability and the peace of Mexico depend on the land being placed anew in the hands of the people who work it, that is to say, the future of the nation, could not be halted by the impossibility of paying immediately the value of the properties belonging to a small number of foreigners who seek only a lucrative end." He insisted that international law required only that foreign nationals be treated no less favorably than were nationals, at least in the case of "expropriations of a general and impersonal character like those which Mexico has carried out for the redistribution of land." Nevertheless, he admitted that Mexico had an obligation, "in obedience to her own laws," to "idemnify in

---

[3] Sax, Takings And The Police Power, 74 Yale L.J. 36,58 (1964).

[4] P.C.I.J. Ser. A, No. 17 (1928).

[5] P.C.I.J. Ser. A, No. 7, p. 32 (1926).

[6] For the exchange of notes between the United States and Mexico, see Hackworth, Digest of International Law, Vol. III, 655-61 (1942).

an adequate manner; but the doctrine which she maintains on the subject, which is based on the most authoritative opinions of writers of treatises on international law, is that the time and manner of such payment must be determined by her own laws."

With respect to the "equality of treatment" standard advanced by Mexico, Secretary Hull stated that "[t]here is now announced by your Government the astonishing theory that this treasured and cherished principle of equality, designed to protect both human and property rights, is to be invoked, not in the protection of personal rights and liberties, but as a chief ground of depriving and stripping individuals of their conceded rights. It is contended, in a word, that it is wholly justifiable to deprive an individual of his rights if all other persons are equally deprived, and if no victim is allowed to escape. . . ."

The two countries eventually agreed to settle the United States claims for compensation of both the agrarian and the oil properties. In settling, however, both countries retained their conflicting positions on what international law required.

Another challenge to the consensus view was raised by the Rumanian law of July 30, 1921, which expropriated the land of a substantial number of Hungarians located in Transylvania, a territory which had been part of the former Kingdom of Hungary. Unlike Mexico, Rumania did not deny the existence of an international principle concerning compensation, only its content. Specifically, Rumania argued that it was financially impossible for it to pay full compensation, immediately and in cash. Instead, under the Rumanian legislation, the amount of compensation was determined on the basis of the assessed value of the land in 1913. This amount was to be paid not in cash but in non-transferable government bonds bearing interest at the rate of five percent, and redeemable in fifty years.[7]

As refined by later practice and statements, the "prompt, adequate and effective" standard invoked by Secretary Hull has come to mean full compensation of "fair market value" and "value . . . as a going concern." It also has been interpreted to require "speedy compensation in convertible foreign exchange equivalent to the full value thereof. . . ." See the so-called Hickenlooper Amendment, *infra*, p. 808.

The challenge to the consensus view became more intense following World War II. As a result of decolonization, many new states came into being and this "Third World" became a new majority in the United Nations. On December 14, 1962, at its Seventeenth Session, the General Assembly adopted Resolution No. 1803 (XVII) on Permanent Sovereignty Over Natural Resources. The vote was 87 in favor, 2 opposed, with 12 abstentions (primarily the Soviet Union and Eastern European countries). The United States voted for the resolution. In pertinent part the preamble and the operative parts of the Resolution provide:

The General Assembly

Considering that it is desirable to promote international cooperation for the economic development of developing countries, and that economic and financial

---

[7] For discussion of the Rumanian case, see F. Garcia-Amador, The Changing Law Of International Claims, 307-309 (1984).

agreements between the developed and the developing countries must be based on the principles of equality and of the right of peoples and nations to self determination,

Considering that the provision of economic and technical assistance, loans and increased foreign investment must not be subject to conditions which conflict with the interests of the recipient State,

Considering the benefits to be derived from exchanges of technical and scientific information likely to promote the development and use of such resources and wealth, and the important part which the United Nations and other international organizations are called upon to play in that connection,

Attaching particular importance to the question of promoting the economic development of developing countries and securing their economic independence,

Noting that the creation and strengthening of the inalienable sovereignty of States over their natural wealth and resources reinforces their economic independence, . . .

Declares that:

1. The right of peoples and nations to permanent sovereignty over their natural wealth and resources must be exercised in the interest of their national development and of the well-being of the people of the State concerned.

2. The exploration, development and disposition of such resources, as well as the import of the foreign capital required for these purposes, should be in conformity with the rules and conditions which the peoples and nations freely consider to be necessary or desirable with regard to the authorization, restriction or prohibition of such activities.

3. In cases where authorization is granted, the capital imported and the earnings on that capital shall be governed by the terms thereof, by the national legislation in force, and by international law. The profits derived must be shared in the proportions freely agreed upon, in each case, between the investors and the recipient State, due care being taken to ensure that there is no impairment, for any reason, of that State's sovereignty over its natural wealth and resources.

4. Nationalization, expropriation or requisitioning shall be based on grounds or reasons of public utility, security or the national interest which are recognized as overriding purely individual or private interests, both domestic and foreign. In such cases the owner shall be paid appropriate compensation, in accordance with the rules in force in the State taking such measures in the exercise of its sovereignty and in accordance with international law. In any case where the question of compensation gives rise to a controversy, the national jurisdiction of the State taking such measures shall be exhausted. However, upon agreement by sovereign States and other parties concerned, settlement of the dispute should be made through arbitration or international adjudication. . . .

* * * *

8. Foreign investment agreements freely entered into by or between sovereign States shall be observed in good faith; States and international organizations shall strictly and conscientiously respect the sovereignty of peoples and nations over their natural wealth and resources in accordance with the Charter and the principles set forth in the present resolution. . . .

Third World states continued their attack on the traditional view and, on December 12, 1974, the General Assembly adopted Resolution No. 3281 (XXIX), the Charter of Economic Rights and Duties of States. The vote was 120 to six. The dissenters were five Western European countries and the United States. Ten abstentions were from Western Europe, Canada, Israel and Japan. In a separate vote on article 2(c) of the Charter, the count was 104 in favor, 16 opposed, with six abstentions. Article 2 of the Charter provides:

ARTICLE 2

1. Every State has and shall freely exercise full permanent sovereignty, including possession, use and disposal, over all its wealth, natural resources and economic activities.

2. Each State has the right:

    (a) To regulate and exercise authority over foreign investment within its national jurisdiction in accordance with its laws and regulations and in conformity with its national objectives and priorities. No State shall be compelled to grant preferential treatment to foreign investment;

    (b) To regulate and supervise the activities of transnational corporations within its national jurisdiction and take measures to ensure that such activities comply with its laws, rules and regulations and conform with its economic and social policies. Transnational corporations shall not intervene in the internal affairs of a host State. Every State should, with full regard for its sovereign rights, co-operate with other States in the exercise of the right set forth in this subparagraph;

    (c) To nationalize, expropriate or transfer ownership of foreign property in which case appropriate compensation should be paid by the State adopting such measures, taking into account its relevant laws and regulations and all circumstances that the State considers pertinent. In any case where the question of compensation gives rise to a controversy, it shall be settled under the domestic law of the nationalizing State and by its tribunals, unless it is freely and mutually agreed by all States concerned that other peaceful means be sought on the basis of the sovereign equality of States and in accordance with the principle of free choice of means.

NOTES AND QUESTIONS

(1) Consider the terms of Resolution 1803 (XVII). Do they primarily reflect the views of the United States, the Third World, or the Soviet Union on the question of compensation for the taking of an alien's property? As noted above, the United States voted for the Resolution. If you were the General Counsel for a United States multinational corporation with substantial investments in the Third World, would you be satisfied with the Resolution?

(2) What attitudes on international law and expropriation are reflected in Article 2 of the Charter of Economic Rights and Duties of States?

(3) Do either Resolution 1803 or the Charter of Economic Rights and Duties of States address the *standard* of compensation to be paid in the event of an expropriation? Note that both the Resolution and the Charter speak in terms of "appropriate compensation." Does either specify what it means by this term?

The U.S. Department of State has expressed its view of what the "prompt, adequate, and effective" standard requires. For example, with respect to the meaning of the term "adequate," the then director of the Office of Investment Affairs, Bureau of Economic and Business Affairs, Department of State, stated:

> Once it appears that a "taking" of American-owned property has occurred or is about to occur, it is the longstanding and continued position of the United States Government that international law requires payment of fair market value, calculated as if the expropriatory act had not occurred or was not threatened. Since market value is often not directly ascertainable, and since there usually are no recent sales of comparable properties to refer to, market value generally must be approximated by indirect methods of valuation. There are at least three methods.

> *The going-concern approach* attempts to measure earning power (and so encompasses elements such as loss of future profits which may be based on projections of past earnings or estimates of future earnings), and in the view of the United States Government generally best approximates market value. We recognize that there may be circumstances in which application of this method is impracticable, or where it might operate unfairly — for example, where an investment has a limited history of operating results, or where expropriation occurs after significant costs are incurred but before a revenue-generating stage is reached. This method of valuation is also vulnerable to governmental actions which adversely affect profitability, such as increased taxes, threat of cancellation of contractual or concessionary rights, or withdrawals of privileges. We believe that such actions taken for the purpose of, or which have the effect of, unfairly influencing compensastion may not properly be allowed.

> *The replacement cost* of the property at the time of expropriation less actual depreciation, a standard which is likely to yield an amount substantially greater than book value but which does not take into account earning capacity, is of limited use in valuing intangibles, and, in our view, is generally less acceptable in most circumstances than the going-concern approach.

> *Book Value*, or some variation of it, which (unlike the replacement-cost approach) values assets at acquisition cost less depreciation, is a figure which

in most cases bears little relationship to their actual value. We believe this to be the least acceptable method for valuation of expropriated property.

We recognize that no single method of valuation is valid under all circumstances. The method or combination of methods most likely to provide just compensation for expropriated property varies, and depends upon the attendant circumstances of the particular case. We also recognize that nonmonetary aspects of settlements — for example, assured access to sources of supply, preferential pricing, or new arrangements for the provision of technical or other services on a contractual basis — may in certain instances constitute elements of compensation.[8]

In the State Department's view, the "prompt" part of the standard is satisfied if there is payment of interest from the time of the taking of the property to the date of payment of compensation unless there is an inordinate delay. Since the interval between the time of taking and the time of the award is often substantial, the payment of an appropriate interest rate is necessary if the award is to be adequate.

By its terms the "prompt, adequate, and effective" formula has not received an imprimatur from any international tribunal or multilateral treaty. Dean Gann has concluded, however — in a study of two arbitration decisions of the International Centre for Settlement of Investment Disputes, four international arbitration decisions involving expropriations of the interests and property of various international oil companies, two decisions of the Iran-United States Claims tribunal, and one U.S. Court decision — that "the valuation methods applied by the tribunals are consistent with the Department of State's interpretation of the appropriate methods of valuation under the standard of 'adequate' compensation."[9] Does this lend support to the U.S. position that "prompt, adequate, and effective" remains the standard? Conclusive support? Persuasive support?

(4) There have recently been concluded a number of bilateral investment treaties — more than 200 by recent count — between developed and developing states that contain the "prompt, adequate and effective" standard among their provisions.[10] At this writing the United States has signed ten and ratified eight such treaties. As noted in Chapter 8, *supra*, the Soviet Union has recently signed such agreements with Belgium/Luxembourg, France, The Federal Republic of Germany, and the United Kingdom. Many of the parties to these treaties voted in favor of the Charter of Economic Rights and Duties of States.

Earlier treaties of Friendship, Commerce and Navigation (FCN) were concluded largely between developed states, although the United States has six such treaties with developing countries. Characteristically, these FCN treaties protect property owners against expropriation without compensation.

Moreover, several developing countries have enacted laws that encourage foreign investment by providing expressly for compensation upon expropriation

[8] Smith, *The United States Government Perspective On Expropriation And Investment In Developing Countries*, 9 Vand J. Transnat'l. L. 517, 519-20 (1976).
[9] Gann, *Compensation Standard For Expropriation*, 23 Colum. J. Transnat'l L. 615, 649-50 (1985).
[10] For a comprehensive listing of such agreements, see International Chamber of Commerce, Bilateral Treaties For International Investment (1977) updated.

of approved investments. Some of these laws specify the method to be used in calculating the value of the property taken, and others provide for arbitration if there is a failure to agree on the amount to be paid. The International Centre for the Settlement of Investment Disputes, p. 960, *infra*, publishes a multi-volume loose leaf service that keeps current the Investment Laws of the World.

How much support, if any, do these developments give to the U.S. position that "prompt, adequate, and effective" remains the standard? As their economic conditions greatly worsened during the later 1970s and the 1980s many developing countries became increasingly desperate for capital inflows. How, if at all, does this fact affect the persuasiveness of these developments as support for the U.S. position?

(5) In *Texaco Overseas Petroleum Co.,/California Asiatic Oil Co. v. Government of the Libya Arab Republic* (1977),[11] the sole arbitrator, in finding that Libya's expropriation of the property of alien oil companies without payment of compensation violated international law, ruled that Resolution 1803 (XVII) reflected customary international law because only it had the support of a majority of member states of the United Nations representing all of the major economic groups. In contrast, the arbitrator noted, the Charter of Economic Rights and Duties of States was supported by a majority of states but not by any of the developed countries with market economies which carry on the largest part of international trade.

Do you agree? What arguments might be made on behalf of the supporters of the Charter of Economic Rights and Duties that it, rather than Resolution 1803 (XVII), reflected the applicable law?

(6) In *Banco National de Cuba v. Sabbatino*,[12] Mr. Justice Harlan observed:

> There are few if any issues in international law today on which opinion seems to be so divided as the limitations on a State's power to expropriate the property of aliens. There is, of course, authority, in international judicial and arbitral decisions, in the expressions of national governments, and among commentators for the view that a taking is improper under international law if it is not for a public purpose, is discriminatory, or is without provision for prompt, adequate, and effective compensation. However, Communist countries, although they have in fact provided a degree of compensation after diplomatic efforts, commonly recognize no obligation on the part of the taking country. Certain representatives of the newly independent and underdeveloped countries have questioned whether rules of state responsibility toward aliens can bind nations that have not consented to them and it is argued that the traditionally articulated standards governing expropriation of property reflect "imperialist" interests and are inappropriate to the circumstances of emergent states.

> The disagreement as to relevant international law standards reflects an even more basic divergence between the national interest of capital importing and capital exporting nations and between the social ideologies of those countries

---

[11] 17 Int'l Leg. Mat. 3 (1978), 53 Int'l Law Reps. 389 (1979).
[12] 376 U.S. 398, 428-29, 84 S. Ct. 923, 940-41, 11 L. Ed. 2d 804 (1962).

that favor state control of a considerable portion of the means of production and those that adhere to a free enterprise system.

As demonstrated by the adoption of the Charter of Economic Rights and Duties of States, the differences of opinion referred to by Justice Harlan are still present today. If opposition by the western developed countries has prevented the Charter of Economic Rights and Duties of States from becoming customary international law, does it necessarily follow that the propositions set forth in Resolution 1803 remain valid? Or is it appropriate to conclude that there now is no international law on point at all?

Does the foregoing raise a broader jurisprudential point as to what is "international law" in this context? Should the law be defined in narrow "positivist," "law as rules" terms? For example, from a functional perspective, to what extent, if any, should the following factors play a role in determining the compensation to be paid for the taking of alien property? Would (should) it make a difference whether these factors were being considered by a domestic court, an international tribunal, or a United Nations conference attempting to draft a multilateral treaty on foreign direct investment?

    (a)   the purpose behind the expropriation, such as whether it was part of a plan to effect major structural changes in the expropriating state's economy;

    (b)   the amount of foreign exchange available to the expropriating country to pay compensation in convertible currency rather than in local inconvertible currency;

    (c)   the absence of discrimination against alien owners of property in the amount of compensation paid;

    (d)   the scope of the expropriations — that is, whether they affected only a small sector of the economy as compared to several major industries — and the financial position of the host country;

    (e)   the presence of attractive alternative investment opportunities for a foreigner in the expropriating country;

    (f)   the amount and reasonableness of past profits of the foreign investor;

    (g)   the waiver of claims that the expropriating country may have against the foreign investor or against the state of the foreign investor's nationality;

    (h)   the extent to which the foreign investment has contributed to the economic development of the expropriating country;

    (i)   the environmental damage the foreign investment has caused over a period of years.

(7) The United States and some other capital-exporting states have refused to agree to any change in the "prompt, adequate and effective" standard. They argue, *inter alia*, that this standard is solidly based both on the moral rights of property and on the needs of an effective international system of private investment. They argue further that, whatever objections might be made to investment arrangements made during the colonial period, the traditional standard should apply to

arrangements made between investors and independent governments negotiated in good faith on a commercial basis. From a Third World perspective, what response might be made to these arguments?

(8) Section 712 of Restatement (Third) of The Foreign Relations Law of the United States provides:

Section 712. State Responsibility for Economic Injury to Nationals of Other States

A state is responsible under international law for injury resulting from:

(1) a taking by the state of the property of a national of another state that

(a) is not for a public purpose, or

(b) is discriminatory, or

(c) is not accompanied by provision for just compensation;

> **For compensation to be just under this subsection, it must, in the absence of exceptional circumstances, be in an amount equivalent to the value of the property taken and be paid at the time of taking, or within a reasonable time thereafter with interest from the date of taking, and in a form economically usable by the foreign national;**

(2) a repudiation or breach by the state of a contract with a national or another state

(a) where the repudiation or breach is (i) discriminatory; or (ii) motivated by noncommercial considerations, and compensatory damages are not paid; or

(b) where the foreign national is not given an adequate forum to determine his claim of repudiation or breach or is not compensated for any repudiation determined to have occurred; or

(3) other arbitrary or discriminatory acts or omissions by the state that impair property or other economic interests of a national of another state.

(a) Does the Restatement's formulation fully support the "prompt, adequate and effective" standard?

(b) In Comment d to Section 712, and Reporters' Note 3, the Restatement (Third) suggests that, in order for payment to be "just," it must be, in the absence of "exceptional circumstances," for the full value of the property, usually fair market value, if that can be determined, and should take into account "going concern" value because a willing purchaser would be receiving that value. One method of determining going concern value is to calculate the present value of the future earnings of the enterprise. The Restatement suggests further that, although compensation should be in convertible currency without restriction on repatriation, payment in bonds may be permissible if they bear interest at an economically reasonable rate and if there is a market for them through which their equivalent in convertible currency can be realized.

As an example of "exceptional circumstances" permitting deviation from the standard of compensation set forth in Section 712, the Restatement refers to national programs of agricultural land reform. Unlike nationalizations of investments in natural resources or of a going business concern, takings of agricultural land typically do not generate funds from which the government could pay compensation. Hence, it often would be impossible to carry out the reform if full compensation had to be paid. The Restatement also notes, however, that the United States has consistently rejected such an exception, as have a number of scholars, and that no international tribunal has ruled on this exception. (See Section 712, Reporters' Note 3.)

Might there be other instances of "exceptional circumstances" permitting deviation from the standard of compensation suggested by the Restatement? Consider, for example, *United States v. Pink*, discussed *infra*, Chapter 12, p. 1069. What "exceptional circumstances" in Pink resulted in the foreign creditors of the Russian Insurance Company receiving no compensation for the loss of their interests? Are they analogous to those that may pertain to the expropriation of a U.S. foreign investment?

(c)   Suppose a taking arises out of a revolutionary situation that would make it difficult to find a purchaser for the expropriated enterprise. Should the investor be limited to a recovery of the net asset value of its enterprise? See *Banco Nacional de Cuba v. Chase Manhattan Bank.*[13]

(9) Although it is generally agreed that a taking must be for a public purpose, this issue has seldom arisen in international claims practice. The concept of "public purpose" is broad, and other states are reluctant to challenge a host country's determination on this issue. As an example of a taking that would violate this requirement, Section 712, Comment e, of the Restatement (Third) of the Foreign Relations Law of the United States posits a seizure of alien owned property by a dictator or oligarch for personal use.

U.S. courts have also been reluctant to challenge legislative determinations that the public interest is served by exercise of the power of eminent domain. See, *e.g., Hawaii Housing Authority v. Midkiff.*[14]

(10) An issue that has arisen often is whether a host country's actions constitute a "taking" or merely economic or other forms of regulation. According to Section 712, Comment g, Restatement of the Foreign Relations Law of the United States, a "taking" results when a host country subjects:

. . . alien property to taxation, regulation, or other action that is confiscatory, or that prevents, unreasonably interferes with, or unduly delays, effective enjoyment of an alien's property or its removal from the territory . . . [of] a state. A state is not responsible for loss of property or for other economic

[13] 658 F.2d 875 (2d Cir. 1981).
[14] 467 U.S. 119 (1984).

disadvantage resulting from bona fide general taxation, regulation, forfeiture for crime, or other action of the kind that is commonly accepted as within the police power of states, if it is not discriminatory . . . and is not designed to cause the alien to abandon the property to the state or sell it at a distress price. As under United States constitutional law, the line between "taking" and regulation is sometimes uncertain.

Reporters' Note 6 of Section 712 of the Restatement suggests that "in general" the line between a taking and a regulation in international law is similar to that drawn by the U.S. Supreme Court for purposes of the Fifth and Fourteenth Amendments to the Constitution.

If so, it is noteworthy that the Supreme Court has recognized that it has been unable to develop any general formula for distinguishing between a taking and a regulation and that the outcome depends upon the particular facts of each case. See, *e.g.*, *Penn. Central Transportation Co. v. New York City*. [15] Less charitably, one scholar has characterized the Supreme Court's decisions in this area as "a welter of confusing and apparently incompatible results." [16] Although it is possible to identify certain broad factors that are relevant to determining when there has been a taking for Fifth Amendment purposes — such as the magnitude of the economic impact of the regulation on the claimant, the extent to which it interferes with distinct investment-backed expectations, and the nature of the governmental action in question (a physical invasion normally is deemed a "taking") — there remains a "crazy-quilt pattern of Supreme Court doctrine" on the taking problem. [17] The classic statement is that of Justice Holmes in *Pennsylvania Coal v. Mahon*: [18]

> The general rule at least is, that while property may be regulated to a certain extent, if regulation goes too far, it will be recognized as a taking.

Holmes gave no guidance, however, as to when a regulation would be regarded as going "too far." In *Agins v. City of Tiburon*, [19] the Court, while upholding a zoning ordinance, stated by way of dictum that it might constitute a taking "if the ordinance does not substantially advance legitimate state interests . . . or denies an owner economically viable use of his land."

Handing down the first of three major decisions in 1987, the Court in *Keystone Bituminous Coal Association v. DeBenedictis*, [20] stated that it would uphold regulations enacted "to arrest what [the legislature] perceives to be a significant threat to the common welfare" when that threat outweighs the impact of the regulation on the affected property owner. In that case, Pennsylvania's Bituminous Mine Subsidence and Land Conservation Act, since 1966, had prohibited mining that caused subsidence damage to public buildings, homes, and cemeteries. The State Department of Environmental Resources required that 50 percent of the coal

---

[15] 438 U.S. 104, 98 S. Ct. 2646, 58 L. Ed. 2d 631 (1978).

[16] Sax, *Takings And The Police Power*, 74 Yale L.J. 36 (1964).

[17] For Discussion, see Field, *Supreme Court's Views As To What Constitutes Taking Within Meaning Of Fifth Amendment's Command That Private Property Not Be Taken For Public Use Without Just Compensation*, 57 L. Ed.2d 1254 (1978).

[18] 260 U.S. 393, 415 (1922).

[19] 447 U.S. 255, 260 (1980).

[20] 107 S. Ct. 1232, 1248 (1987).

beneath such protected structures be kept in place in order to provide that support. Keystone Bituminous Coal Association alleged that the act forced them to leave 27 million tons of coal in place in support. Because they owned it but could not mine it, they claimed this resulted in an unconstitutional taking of private property. The Court rejected this claim on the grounds, among others, that, in acting to protect the public's interest in health, the environment and the fiscal integrity of the area, the state was exercising its police power to abate activity akin to a nuisance and that the association's deprivation of property rights was not sufficiently significant to satisfy the "heavy burden placed upon one alleging a regulatory taking." One commentator has interpreted Keystone as construing this "heavy burden" to be met only if a landowner can show "(1) it is not merely difficult, but impossible to make a profit on the land as restricted, and (2) the regulation does not serve a legitimate general and substantial public interest in the health, environment and fiscal integrity of the area."[21] Query, has the Court silently reversed *Pennsylvania Coal?*

If this heavy burden is met, the Court held, in the second of the landmark 1987 decisions, that an action for compensation, as well as for declaratory and injunctive relief, could be maintained. The rationale of *First English Evangelical Lutheran Church v. County of Los Angeles,*[22] was that an invalidation of a regulation is only a prospective remedy; it does not provide any remedy at all for the denial of the use of private property that has already occurred. It is important to note, however, that the Court did not find that a taking had occurred in *First English.* Rather, it remanded the case to the state courts for a determination of this issue. By way of dictum the Court intimated that a court could still decide that a compensable taking had not occurred if the public need for the regulation was sufficiently great.

Under the facts in *First English* this would appear a close issue. There, the church sued the County of Los Angeles over an interim ordinance that prohibited most development on its property. Flooding had destroyed the Church's summer camp, and the county had temporarily designated the property, located along a creek, as a flood protection area. The Court stated:

> We have no occasion to decide . . . whether the court might avoid the conclusion that a compensable taking had occurred by establishing that the denial of all use was insulated as part of the state's authority to enact safety regulations.

Lastly, in *Nollan v. California Coastal Commission,*[23] the Court displayed a willingness to scrutinize carefully the purported public interest behind state regulations, at least where the regulations involve a physical intrusion on private property and thereby interfere with a landowner's right to exclude others. In *Nollan,* the California Coastal Commission had required that landowners dedicate to the public the right to transit their private beach before receiving a permit to rebuild a beach house into a permanent residence. The Nollan's beach was in a strip of private beaches separating two public beaches by about six-tenths of a

---

[21] Callies, *Takings Clause — Take Three,* 73 A.B.A.J. 48, 52 (November 1, 1987).
[22] 107 S. Ct. 2378 (1987).
[23] 107 S. Ct. 3141 (1987).

mile. The California Court of Appeal had held this was a valid exercise of the commission's police power under its statutory duty to protect the California coast.

The Supreme Court reversed. While noting that land use regulations do not effect "takings" if they substantially advance legitimate state interests and do not deny an owner the economically viable use of his land, the Court concluded there was no nexus between California's interests and the condition attached to the Nollan's beach house redevelopment. The Court stated:

> It is quite impossible to understand how a requirement that people already on the public beaches be able to walk across the Nollan's property reduces an obstacle to viewing the beach created by the new house. It is also impossible to understand how it lowers any "psychological barrier" to using the public beaches, or how it helps to remedy any additional congestion on them caused by construction of the Nollans' new house.

At the same time the Court indicated that if there is an "essential nexus" between the regulation and what the landowner intends to do with the property, it may be deemed not to constitute a taking. For example, if the Commission had attached to the permit some condition that would have protected the public's ability to see the beach in spite of the construction of the new house — such as a height or width restriction, or a ban on fences, or even a requirement that the Nollans provide a viewing spot on their property for passersby — the Court indicated the regulation would have been upheld.

Under international law, the Restatement (Third) notes, a test suggested by some to distinguish a taking from a regulation is whether it is applied only to alien enterprises. This test is not useful, however, if there are no comparable locally-owned enterprises in the host country.

Another suggested test is the extent to which the government action deprives the foreign investor of effective control over the enterprise. Accordingly, government appointment of an "intervenor" or "receiver" to manage the enterprise might constitute a taking.

(11) "Creeping expropriation" is an expression applied to state taxation and regulatory measures that have a major adverse impact on the economic viability of an enterprise. One of the more thorough discussions of "creeping expropriation" is Judge Holtzman's concurring opinion in *Starrett Housing Corp. v. Islamic Rep. of Iran.*[24] As examples of circumstances which so impair the economic viability of a business as to give rise to a "taking or expropriation," Judge Holtzmann suggests the following:

(i)   measures which force the owner to flee the country and thus deprive it of the effective management and control of its property;

(ii)   measures which deny the owner access to its funds and profits;

(iii)   coercion and intimidation forcing the owner to sell at unfairly low prices;

(iv)   interference with the owner's access to needed facilities and supplies; and

---

[24] 4 Iran-U.S. C. 122, 23 Int'l Leg. Mat. 1090 at page 1124 (1984).

(v) appointment of conservators or administrators to manage the property in the enforced absence of the owner.

The circumstances cited by Judge Holtzmann would all appear to go "too far," in Justice Holmes' words, and deny the foreign investor all use of his property without a demonstrated public need for such measures. But what if the host country were to adopt regulations along the lines of those at issue in *Keystone* and *First Church*? The owners may not have had to "flee the country" but were they not deprived of "management and control" and "access" to their property? Is forcing an owner "to sell at unfairly low prices" any different than prohibiting a sale altogether (*Keystone*)? If the rule is that where the public purpose is substantial enough to outweigh the loss to the owner no "taking" occurs and no compensation is required under the 5th and 14th amendments, then consider whether a regulation to prevent surface subsidence (*Keystone*) or establish flood control (*First Church*) is more substantial than land reform or saving scarce foreign exchange or compelling a foreign investor to bring in local ownership or relinquish management control to nationals of the host country. In short, can Section 712, Comment g (*supra*, page 783, note 10) of the Restatement (Third) be squared with the U.S. Constitution?

(12) The issue of discrimination also has arisen with some degree of frequency. Again, in the words of the Restatement (Third), Section 712, Comment f:

> Discrimination implies unreasonable distinctions. Takings that invidiously single out property of persons of a particular nationality would be unreasonable; classifications, even if based on nationality, that are rationally related to the state's security or economic policies might not be unreasonable. Discrimination may be difficult to determine where there is no comparable enterprise owned by local nationals or by nationals of other countries, or where nationals of the taking state are treated equally with aliens but by discrete actions separated in time.

United States courts have held that the expropriation of U.S. properties by Cuba violated international law because, inter alia, the purpose was to retaliate against U.S. nationals for acts of the U.S. Government and was directed against U.S. nationals exclusively. See the discussion of these cases in the section on Act of State, *infra*, pages 1083 *et seq*. In contrast, see the decision in *Kuwait v. the American Independent Oil Co. (AMINOIL)*[25] for a ruling that nationalizing one company but not another did not violate international law when there was no discrimination on the basis of the nationality of the two companies and there were "adequate reasons" for distinguishing between them.

(13) It is generally, though not uniformly, agreed that a breach by a state of its contract with a foreign national does not, *ipso facto*, raise an issue of international law. Rather, the prevailing view seems to be that a violation of international law arises only if the state breaches or repudiates the contract for governmental motives, as compared to commercial, and fails to pay compensation. In any event, failure of a state to provide an adequate forum to determine whether there had been a breach of contract under the host country's law would constitute a denial

---

[25] 21 Int'l Leg. Mat. 976, 1019-1020 (1982).

of justice in violation of international law. But compare discussion by the House of Lords in *Czarnikow Ltd. v. Rolimpex*,[26] discussed in Chapter 1, *supra*.

Concession or development agreements involving the exploitation of natural resources raise especially sensitive issues. Such contracts have in the past become symbols of interference with a state's sovereignty over its natural resources, yet recovery of the alien's large capital investment requires a long period of contractual security. In an effort to safeguard their capital investment, foreign investors have sometimes sought to "internationalize" the contract by providing that it shall be governed by "general principles of the law of nations" or "principles of the law of [the host country] not inconsistent with international law." Foreign investors have also tried to protect their capital through so-called "stabilization" clauses which prohibit the host country from expropriating the foreign investor's property during the term of the contract.[27] Some less developed states have resisted such clauses on the ground that they derogate from the state's inalienable sovereignty, especially that over its natural resources. How persuasive do you find this argument? What might be the response of the foreign investor or his home country?

Several arbitral decisions have held that a state that expropriates property contrary to a stabilization clause has engaged in wrongful conduct under international law and is obliged to provide reparation to the foreign investor instead of mere compensation. In one case, *Texaco Overseas Petroleum Co./California Asiatic Oil Co. v. Libya, supra*, page 780, the tribunal awarded restitution in integrum or specific performance as the appropriate form of reparation. According to the sole arbitrator in the *Texaco* case, specific performance was the normal form of reparation under both Libyan and international law, and it is inapplicable only to the extent that restoration of the *status quo ante* is impossible. Two other arbitral decisions explicitly reject restitutio in integrum as an appropriate remedy. See *BP Exploration Co. v. Libya*,[28] and *Libyan American Oil Co. v. Libya*.[29]

Assuming that most national legal systems grant specific performance as the normal remedy in breach of contract cases, does it follow that specific performance is an appropriate remedy for an international arbitral tribunal to grant? What arguments can be made for and against such a conclusion?

§ 9.02 Diplomatic Intervention and Espousal: The Calvo Doctrine

As we saw in the preceding section, the Mexican Government, in its dispute with the United States over expropriation of agrarian land, contended that its only obligation under international law was one of non-discrimination against foreign investors. This contention reflects a special Latin American attitude toward international law and the protection of aliens. It reflects as well an unhappy experience of those countries with repeated diplomatic and military intervention

---

[26] [1979] A.C. 351.

[27] For discussion of stabilization clauses, see the majority and concurring opinions in *Kuwait v. American Independent Oil Co.*, 21 Int'l Leg. Mat. 976 (1982).

[28] 53 Int'l L. Rep. 297 (1979).

[29] 20 Int'l Leg. Mat 1, 86 (1981).

during the 19th century by developed countries, especially the United States, on behalf of foreign investors. In response to this experience, an Argentine jurist, Carlos Calvo (1824-1906), developed the Calvo Doctrine, which claims that an alien doing business in a foreign country is entitled only to non-discriminatory treatment and to rights and remedies available under domestic law.

The Calvo Doctrine has been endorsed by several Inter-American conferences, and was incorporated into such regional legal instruments as the Treaty of Commerce and Navigation (1865) and the Convention on Rights and Duties of States (1933). Article 9 of the latter instrument provides: "Nationals and foreigners are under the same protection of the law and the national authorities and the foreigners may not claim rights other or more extensive than those of the nationals." The United States, although a party to the Convention on Rights and Duties of States, made a reservation to Article 9.

According to Garcia-Amador, the function of the Calvo Doctrine was to prevent abuse of the right of diplomatic protection; it was not intended as a "bar to those international claims based on breaches of well-established international obligations regarding the treatment of aliens."[1] Hence, the Calvo Doctrine does not postulate a complete, absolute equal status between nationals and aliens. In contrast, the Calvo Clause, which appears in Latin American Constitutions and statutes, as well as in contracts between Latin American Governments and foreign investors, seeks to eliminate the institution of diplomatic protection. As stated by Garcia-Amador, "the clause develops and complements the doctrine to the point of perfecting the principle of equality between nationals and aliens; in other words, it is only when incorporated with the clause that the principle provides for complete total equality."[2] . . .

An example of a Calvo Clause was involved in the *North American Dredging* case set forth below.

UNITED STATES OF AMERICA (NORTH AMERICAN DREDGING CO. OF TEXAS) v. UNITED MEXICAN STATES

United States Mexican Claims Commission, 1926
Opinions of Commissioners Under the Convention
Concluded September 8, 1923 Between the
United States and Mexico, 1926-27,
4 U.N. Rep. Int'l Arb. Awards 26

[Article 18 of an agreement between the North American Dredging Company and the Government of Mexico to dredge a port provided:

The contractor and all persons who, as employees or in any other capacity, may be engaged in the execution of the work under this contract either directly

---

[1] Garcia-Amador, Calvo Doctrine, Calvo Clause, 8 Encyclopedia Of Public International Law 62 (R. Bernhardt, ed. 1985).
[2] *Id.*, at 63.

or indirectly, shall be considered as Mexicans in all matters, within the Republic of Mexico, concerning the execution of such work and the fulfillment of this contract. They shall not claim, nor shall they have, with regard to the interests and business connected with this contract, any other rights or means to enforce the same than those granted by the laws of the Republic to Mexicans, nor shall they enjoy any other rights than those established in favor of Mexicans. They are consequently deprived of any rights as aliens, and under no conditions shall the intervention of foreign diplomatic agents be permitted, in any matter related to this contract.

In an opinion by VAN VOLLENHOVEN, the Commission considered the validity of this Calvo Clause:]

* * * *

13. The Commission is fully sensible of the importance of any judicial decision either sustaining in whole or in part, or rejecting in whole or in part, or construing the so-called "Calvo Clause" in contracts between nations and aliens. It appreciates the legitimate desire on the part of nations to deal with persons and property within their respective jurisdictions according to their own laws and to apply remedies provided by their own authorities and tribunals, which laws and remedies in no wise restrict or limit their international obligations, or restrict or limit or in any wise impinge upon the correlative rights of other nations protected under rules of international law. . . .

14. Reading [Article 18] as a whole, it is evident that its purpose was to bind the claimant to be governed by the laws of Mexico and to use the remedies existing under such laws. . . . It did not take from him his undoubted right to apply to his own Government for protection if his resort to the Mexican tribunals or other authorities available to him resulted in a denial or delay of justice as that term is used in international law. In such a case the claimant's complaint would be not that his contract was violated but that he had been denied justice.

[The Commission concluded that the claim should be dismissed.]

20. Under Article 18 of the contract the present claimant is precluded from presenting to its Government any claim relative to the interpretation or fulfillment of this contract. If it had a claim for denial of justice, for delay of justice or gross injustice, or for any other violation of international law committed by Mexico to its damage, it might have presented such a claim to its Government, which in turn could have espoused it and presented it here. Although the claim as presented falls within the first clause of Article I of the Treaty, describing claims coming within this Commission's jurisdiction, it is not a claim that may be rightfully presented by the claimant to its Government for espousal and hence is not cognizable here, pursuant to the latter part of paragraph 1 of the same Article I.

21. It is urged that the claim may be represented by claimant to its Government for espousal in view of the provision of Article V of the Treaty, to the effect "that no claim shall be disallowed or rejected by the Commission by the application of the general principle of international law that the local remedies must be exhausted as a condition precedent to the validity or allowance of any claim." This provision is limited to the application of a general principle of international law to claims that may be presented to the Commission falling within the terms of

Article I of the Treaty, and if under the terms of Article I the private claimant cannot rightfully present its claim to its Government and the claim therefore cannot become cognizable here, Article V does not apply to it, nor can it render the claim cognizable, nor does it entitle either Government to set aside an express valid contract between one of its citizens and the other Government. . . .

NOTES AND QUESTIONS

(1) Decisions of arbitral tribunals on the Calvo Clause have not been uniform. Compare the *North American Dredging* case with the *Mexico Union Railway, Ltd. (Great Britain v. Mexico), Mexico — Great Britain Claims Commission, 1930*,[3] in which the majority of the Commission stated that no person could "deprive the Government of his country of its undoubted right to apply international remedies to violations of international law committed to his hurt . . . for the government the contract is *res inter alios acta*, by which its liberty of action cannot be prejudiced." See also Commissioner Nielsen's dissenting opinion in *International Fisheries Co. Claim (United States v. Mexico)*,[4] which stated that the *Dredging* case "contains nothing of any consequence with which I agree."

After the United States reached a lump-sum settlement of $40,000,000 with Mexico in 1942 on a variety of claims, Congress, through the Settlement of Mexican Claims Act,[5] established a three-person American-Mexican Claims Commission, a purely national commission. This commission re-examined the *North American Dredging* case and disagreed with the rationale of the international commission as to the Calvo Clause and rendered an award in favor of the Dredging Company.[6] In the opinion of the Commission, Article V of the 1923 Convention was controlling. No significant international arbitral decisions concerning the Calvo Clause have been rendered since the 1930s.

(2) If the injured individual, after the wrong, but before espousal of the claim by his state, voluntarily waives or settles the claim, this is generally regarded as effective. Should it make any difference then, if the settlement or the waiver takes the form of a Calvo Clause?

(3) Assuming that a foreign investor has exhausted all local remedies in seeking compensation for economic injury and has renounced his right to diplomatic protection through a Calvo Clause, what right, if any, does the state of the foreign investor's nationality have to pursue a claim against the host state? Is the claim of the state purely derivative, or does the state have interests to protect that go beyond individual claims subject to the Calvo Clause? Can you identify any such interests, or are the state claims and the private claims essentially identical?

---

[3] 5 U.N. Rep. Int'l Arb. Awards 115.

[4] General Claims Commission, 1931 [1930-31] 207, 226, 4 U.N. Rep. Int'l Arb. Awards 691, 704 (1931).

[5] 56 Stat. 1058.

[6] Bishop, International Law 817, fn. 83 (3d ed. 1971).

Assume that a "Calvo Clause" waived claims for immunity or redress from torture. Would such a clause be viewed as valid under international law? If not, is there some reason that economic rights are more waivable? If so, should there be any limits on the waivability of economic rights? From an international perspective, should a sovereign state have total power to define "property" vis-a-vis aliens and other sovereign states? What constraints, if any, might be put on such a power?

With the above questions in mind, what is your reaction to a suggestion that the Calvo Clause should bar a foreigner from seeking intervention by his government, but not that government from intervening on its own initiative?

(4) As noted previously, the Calvo Clause may appear in various forms: in a contract with an alien, in a country's constitution, or in a statute that applies to all aliens in all situations. Another version of the Calvo Clause appears in Article 27 of the Convention on the Settlement of Investment Disputes, see Documentary Supplement. Should the form in which the Calvo Clause appears make any difference as to its validity and effect?

(5) Section 202 of the Restatement (Second), Foreign Relations Law of the United States would validate the Calvo Clause if (1) the interests affected are economic, (2) the investor in fact receives national treatment and (3) there is a bona fide remedy in the national courts that satisfies the requirements of procedural justice. By contrast Section 713 of the Restatement (Third) of the Foreign Relations Law of the United States is more cautious. In Comment g, the section merely notes that the United States rejects the Calvo Clause and regards companies that submit to a Calvo Clause as waiving rights that are not theirs to waive. Reporters' Note 6 adds that "[a]rbitrators during the 1920's left the effectiveness of such a provision in doubt."

Is either of these formulations an accurate codification of current law and policy? How would you codify international law on the Calvo Clause?[7]

§ 9.03   Methods of Settlement and Avoidance of Disputes

In this section we turn to methods that have been employed to settle post-war disputes over expropriations as well as to techniques that have been developed to minimize the possibilities of expropriation and therefore resultant disputes. The two areas are not mutually exclusive, because some of the new methods designed to settle international claims often serve to prevent such disputes from arising in the first place.

The first of these methods — lump-sum agreements, together with the use of such national claims commissions as the United States Foreign Claims Settlement Commission — combine the diplomatic negotiation of an international agreement with national adjudication of the validity of individual claims. The resulting

---

[7] For further reading on the Calvo Clause, see Shea, The Calvo Clause (1955); Freeman, *Recent Aspects Of The Calvo Doctrine And The Challenge To International Law*, 40 Am. J. Int'l L. 121 (1946); *Note, The Calvo Clause: Its Current Status As A Contractual Renunciation Of Diplomatic Protection*, 6 Texas Int'l L. Forum 289 (1971).

agreements have normally been for less than "prompt, adequate, and effective" compensation as otherwise favored by the U.S. Government.

Special tribunals, the second method of dispute settlement, have included arbitral tribunals established under the Convention on the Settlement of Investment Disputes Between States and Nationals of other States — a convention concluded under the auspices of the International Bank for Reconstruction and Development (the "World Bank") — and the Iran-United States Claims Settlement Tribunal. The Convention seeks to establish a permanent mechanism for the resolution of investment disputes. The Iran-United States Claims Settlement Tribunal, while an *ad hoc* institution for resolving disputes between Iran and the United States as well as between Iran and U.S. nationals, has a significance that extends far beyond the boundaries of those disputes because of the circumstances under which the tribunal was established, its terms of reference, and the composition of its bench.

The use of economic sanctions — the third method of dispute settlement, through such national legislation as the so-called Hickenlooper Amendment — involves an element of coercion not found in the other methods. Partly as a consequence it is the most controversial of these methods.

We leave for the next section a consideration of national and international investment guaranty programs.

[A] Lump-Sum Settlements

One of the earliest and most controversial of the lump-sum settlement agreements was the so-called Litvinov Assignment whereby the Soviet Union released and assigned to the United States certain funds in this country out of which claims by U.S. nationals based on expropriation of their property in the U.S.S.R. could be paid.[1]

National claims commissions established under United States law have often been used to adjudicate the validity of the claims of individuals and corporations and to disburse to successful claimants whatever sums may be or become available. Usually such distributions are on a pro rata basis. In the case of the Litvinov Assignment, for example, some of the claims against the Soviet Union were satisfied through proceedings before the International Claims Commission, established in the Department of State by the International Claims Settlement Act of 1949,[2] converted into a separate executive agency in 1954 and transferred in 1980 to the Department of Justice. The FCSC, along with a War Claims Commission, also heard claims against the Soviet Union. *Foreign Claims Settlement Commission*

Most of the work of the FCSC has involved the adjudication of claims arising out of expropriations since World War I by Communist countries of Eastern Europe and elsewhere. The Commission has no general authority to adjudicate international claims. Rather, its authority comes from specific statutes which authorize the Commission to adjudicate all claims against a particular country. Pursuant to these statutes, the Commission has adjudicated claims against such

---

[1] A discussion of the Litvinov Assignments may be found in *United States v. Belmont*, Chapter 12, *infra*, p. 1068 and *United States v. Pink*, Chapter 12, *infra*, p. 1069.

[2] 64 Stat. 13, as amended, 22 U.S.C. 1622a-g (1986).

countries as Poland, Czechoslovakia, Hungary, Rumania, Bulgaria, Yugoslavia, the German Democratic Republic, Cuba, and China.

The process of obtaining compensation for American citizens normally involves three separate departments of the United States government. As noted above, the Foreign Claims Settlement Commission evaluates the evidence and determines whether the private claimant has established a valid claim under international law and within the terms of the authorizing statute, and determines the amount of the loss. However, unless and until the Department of State has negotiated a lump-sum or other settlement with the country that has confiscated the property, there is no money available to pay the award. Although the usual pattern is for the Commission to adjudicate claims after a lump sum agreement has been concluded, in several instances the United States has employed the device of pre-adjudication. Under this procedure the Commission adjudicated claims against Bulgaria, Hungary and Rumania before any settlement agreements were concluded. The same procedures were followed in the case of Cuba, although no settlement agreement is in sight. The primary purposes of pre-adjudication are to afford a hearing on claims while evidence and testimony are fresh and to inform the Executive Branch of the nature and magnitude of the claims before negotiations toward settlement begin. Upon conclusion of a claims settlement agreement, the Department of Justice distributes funds in accordance with awards certified to Treasury by the Foreign Claims Settlement Commission.

The amount of money a United States national ultimately recovers on his claim against a foreign country may depend heavily upon whether that country or its nationals have funds in this country that can be blocked or vested by the United States Government. Depending upon the presence or absence of such funds, the percentage paid on each adjudicated claim, especially against Communist nations, has varied greatly, *e.g.*, Yugoslavia (90%) and Rumania (40%).

Reluctance on the part of a state to freeze or seize foreign assets can result in greatly diminished recovery. As pointed out by Professor Richard Lillich in his book, International Claims: Postwar British Practice (1967), the United Kingdom's desire to maintain its position as an international banking center made it reluctant to block bank accounts of foreign governments in order to induce them to conclude a claims settlement. Consequently, the ultimate settlements reached with six Eastern European countries and with Egypt were much less generous than comparable United States settlements, *e.g.*, 10% of claims in the case of Yugoslavia.

SARDINO V. FEDERAL RESERVE BANK OF NEW YORK

United States Court of Appeals, Second Circuit
361 F.2d 106 (1966), cert. denied
385 U.S. 898, 87 S. Ct. 203, 17 L. Ed.2d 130 (1966)

[This case was one of many that arose after Cuba expropriated property owned, directly or indirectly, by United States corporations. Plaintiff, a

Cuban citizen and resident, had a savings account in a New York bank. He was unable to obtain funds from that account in Cuba because the U.S. Cuban Assets Control Regulations, issued under the Trading with the Enemy Act, prohibited transfer outside of the United States of property owned by Cuban nationals without specific authorization. No such authorization was forthcoming. Accordingly, Sardino brought an action requesting that the court order a license to be issued or a declaration that none was required. The district court dismissed the complaint for failure to state a claim. The Court of Appeals affirmed.

After holding that the Regulations were authorized by the Trading with the Enemy Act, and that the Act was not an unconstitutional delegation of legislative power, the court turned to Sardino's argument that the Regulations, as applied, deprived him of his property without due process of law in violation of the Fifth Amendment.]

Before LUMBARD, CHIEF JUDGE, FRIENDLY and SMITH, CIRCUIT JUDGES

FRIENDLY, CIRCUIT JUDGE:

* * * *

The contention that Sardino has not been deprived of his property stresses that the Government has not taken over the bank account but has merely placed a temporary barrier to its transfer outside the United States. Indeed, the barrier is said to be not merely temporary but partial. Without a license Sardino can use the account to pay customs duties, taxes or fees owing to the United States, a state, or any instrumentality of either,[3] . . . or can have the sum belonging to him invested in securities listed on a national securities exchange or issued by the United States, a state, or an instrumentality of either,[4] . . . [T]he Regulations also permit remittance not in excess of $100 a month for necessary living expenses, but only through payment to a blocked account of a Cuban bank in the United States,[5] . . . Sardino effectively replies that he owes no customs duties, taxes or fees; that securities purchased at his instruction would be blocked to the same extent as the savings account; and that there would be little incentive for a Cuban bank to make monthly payments to him in Havana when the corresponding payments to it in the United States were blocked. . . . The due process clause speaks in terms not of taking but of deprivation; we find it hard to say there is no deprivation when a man is prevented both from obtaining his property and from realizing any benefit from it for a period of indefinite duration which may outrun his life. . . .

[The court then rejected the Government's argument that the Constitution confers no rights on nonresident aliens owning property in the United States. The opinion continued:]

It does not follow, however, that in dealing with the property of an alien the United States must be blind to the acts of the country of which he is a national; the Constitution protects the alien from arbitrary action by our government but

---

[3] 31 C.F.R. Section 515.510.
[4] 31 C.F.R. Section 515.513.
[5] 31 C.F.R. Section 515.521.

not from reasonable response to such action by his own. . . . Hard currency is a weapon in the struggle between the free and the communist worlds; it would be a strange reading of the Constitution to regard it as demanding depletion of dollar resources for the benefit of a government seeking to create a base for activities inimical to our national welfare. The Supreme Court's approval of wartime seizure of assets of a non-enemy alien "as a means of avoiding the use of the property to draw earnings or wealth out of this country to territory where it may more likely be used to assist the enemy than if it remains . . . in the hands of this government" . . . is broad enough to justify the refusal of a license to Sardino.

Still other considerations support the constitutionality of the freezing order. Cuba has adopted a program expropriating property within its territory owned by designated American nationals, with a system of compensation holding out only an "illusory" possibility of payment. See *Banco Nacional de Cuba v. Sabbatino*, [p. 1084, *supra*]. . . . There is a long history of governmental action compensating our own citizens out of foreign assets in this country for wrongs done them by foreign governments abroad. A famous instance is the Litvinov Assignment . . . the Treaty of Berlin,[6] . . . terminating World War I with Germany, confirmed the retention of vested enemy property in the control of the United States until the German government had satisfied all war claims of our citizens; the Supreme Court has said "it does not matter whether this action was taken simply to secure claims of American citizens against Germany or was regarded as the rightful withholding of spoils of war." *Guessefeldt v. McGrath*,[7] . . . The treaties of peace with Bulgaria, Hungary and Roumania at the end of World War II provided that any property of their nationals, blocked long before we were at war,[8] . . . should vest in an agency or officer designated by the President and, after payment of debts owed by the owner, should be used to pay claims of United States nationals against the three countries[9] . . . . While these had been enemy countries, it is not clear that this was crucial. See *Guessefeldt v. McGrath, supra*; 2 O'Connell, International Law 846-48 (1965). In any event Congress followed the same course to compensate United States citizens for Czechoslovakian expropriations occurring after the war, setting up a fund out of the proceeds of Czech-owned steel mill equipment ordered here in 1947 and blocked and sold in 1954 by the Secretary of the Treasury[10] . . . .

Congress has already taken steps to determine the claims of our nationals against Cuba,[11] . . . although without as yet providing for their payment. In *Propper v. Clark*,[12] . . . the Court noted that a pre-war freezing order served the salutary purpose of immobilizing the assets of foreign nationals until our Government could determine whether they were needed "to compensate our citizens or ourselves for the damages done by the governments of the nationals affected." This would seem a rather clear intimation that if Congress should ultimately

---

[6] 42 Stat. 1939, 1940-1941 (1921).

[7] 342 U.S. 308, 313-314, 72 S. Ct. 338, 96 L. Ed. 342 (1952).

[8] Exec. Order No. 8389 of April 10, 1940.

[9] 22 U.S.C.A. Sections 1631a, 1614a.

[10] 22 U.S.C.A. Sections 1642a, 1264c, and 1642; see 1958 U.S. Code Cong. & Ad. News 3299, 3301.

[11] 22 U.S.C.A. Section 1643.

[12] 337 U.S. 472, 484, 69 S. Ct. 1333, 1340, 93 L. Ed. 1480 (1949).

choose to apply the blocked assets of Cuban nationals to that purpose, the Fifth Amendment would not stand in its way. The unquestioned right of a state to protect its nationals in their persons and property while in a foreign country, see 1 Oppenheim, International Law Section 319, at 686-87 (8th ed. Lauterpacht 1955), must permit initial seizure and ultimate expropriation of assets of nationals of that country in its own territory if other methods of securing compensation for its nationals should fail [13] . . . . To be sure, Congress has not yet chosen to invoke the ultimate sanction, having indeed eliminated a provision for the sale of certain Cuban assets to pay the expenses of administering the claims program.[14] . . . Such commendable forbearance should not be understood as connoting lack of power. . . .

NOTES AND QUESTIONS

(1) Castro shows his stripes and talks about exporting the Cuban revolution to South and Central America. The Cuban Government starts harrassing American business and takes over some American owned property. The U.S. responds by cutting back Cuba's sugar quota. Cuba retaliates by expropriating U.S. properties in Cuba without paying compensation. The U.S. retaliates for the Cuban expropriations by expropriating Cuban property located in the United States without compensation. Cuba, according to the Second Circuit in *Sabbatino*, violated international law. How about the United States? And what about the U.S. Constitution? *Sardino* holds that the U.S.'s uncompensated expropriation can pass muster under the "due process" clause. But can it pass muster under the Second Circuit's (and Executive Branch's) view of international law?

(2) Suppose, before any settlement is made with Cuba, Congress adopts legislation mandating that all property of Cuban nationals and residents in this country be used to satisfy claims of American citizens for property they previously owned in Cuba. Would, as suggested by the Court in *Sardino*, this clearly be constitutional as applied to someone in Sardino's position? If so, would it violate the international law standard used by the Second Circuit in its Sabbatino decision? the standard espoused by the Executive Branch?

(3) Assume that the United States reaches a settlement with Cuba of all major pending issues. The terms of the settlement include extending the United States lease on the naval base in Guatanamo Bay in perpetuity. In return assume that the United States takes the following actions:

    (a)   Waives all claims of United States' citizens arising out of the expropriation of their property by the Cuban government and releases the blocked Cuban assets in this country. Would the United States' claimants be able to bring suit in the U.S. courts for a taking of their property? In any event, drawing on the Supreme Court decisions discussed above, what

[13] See Colbert, Retaliation In International Law 63-69 (1948).
[14] See 79 Stat. 988 (1965) amending 78 Stat. 113 (1964), and 1965 U.S. Code Cong. & Ad. News 3581, 3583-3584.

arguments would you, as counsel for these claimants, make in support of the proposition that the United States has a constitutional obligation to compensate the American owners for their loss? Does it help to know that, in the United Kingdom's 1959 settlement with Egypt, resolving claims from expropriations that followed the Suez taking and military activity by Britain, France and Israel against Egypt, Parliament appropriated sums to better the outcome for the individual claimants? See also the facts related in *Banco Nacional de Cuba v. Sabbatino, infra*, p. 1086.

(b)   In the alternative, assume that the United States reaches a lump-sum settlement with Cuba equal to the value of the blocked Cuban owned assets in the United States. These assets are to be used to satisfy claims of United States citizens against Cuba but the total value of the assets is substantially less than the amount owed the claimants as determined by the Foreign Claims Settlement Commission. Hence, as part of the agreement with Cuba, the United States waives all unsatisfied claims that its citizens may have against Cuba. Again, would any of the claimants be able to bring suit in the U.S. courts for a "taking" of their property requiring compensation under the Fifth Amendment?

(c)   Again, assume a lump-sum settlement with Cuba and a waiver of all U.S. citizen claims against Cuba, but nothing is said about paying those claims out of the proceeds of the settlement. Suppose then that the United States government refuses to distribute those proceeds to the claimants, there being no statute requiring such distribution. Would this constitute a taking? See *Aris Gloves, Inc. v. United States*,[15] *Blagge v. Balbalch*.[16] Cf. *Dames and Moore v. Regan, infra*, p. 1021, and *Causey v. Pan American World Airways*[17] (plaintiffs have right to compensation if their claims have been reasonably impaired by limitation on liability in Warsaw Convention).

(d)   If the United States citizens in any of the circumstances described in paragraphs (a), (b) and (c) have no constitutional claim against the United States government, what does that say about the international law standard so-long espoused by the Executive Branch?

(4) In *United States v. Commodities Trading Corp.*,[18] the Court ruled per Justice Black that compensation for whole grain pepper requisitioned during World War II could be constitutionally paid at price levels set pursuant to wartime price regulations. The Court rejected the argument that, since Commodities Trading Corporation had the right to withold its pepper from the market in order to get higher prices after the end of the war and the lifting of price controls, the true market value of the requisitioned pepper exceeded the wartime prices. In the Court's view fulfillment of the congressional purpose and the necessities of the wartime economy required that the ceiling prices be the measure of compensation. The Court also rejected claims that compensation below the cost of the pepper was unconstitutional, arguing that market value is the constitutional standard.

---

[15] 420 F. 2d 1386 (Ct.Cl. 1970).
[16] 162 U.S. 439, 457 (1896).
[17] 684 F. 2d 1301 (4th Cir. 1982).
[18] 339 U.S. 121 (1950).

(Note the contradictory attitude the Court takes towards markets.) Justices Frankfurter and Jackson dissented. In light of the decision in *Commodities Trading Corp.*, is U.S. law as firmly commited to the "prompt, adequate and effective" standard as the U.S. Government is in international forums?

(5) Reflect on the difficulties raised by the foregoing questions and consider also Justice Harlan's statement in *Sabbatino* quoted at page 780 *supra*. Does all this not suggest that the traditional "prompt, adequate and effective" compensation standard is something less than law under the strict traditional account of law as rules? At this point review the discussion of the several functions of international law in Chapter 4 (page 309 notes 9-12) and consider the function that the traditional standard may play in the settlement of disputes over the taking of alien owned property. From this perspective is it important to preserve the rigid standard espoused by the Executive Branch? If so, how should that affect the role of national courts in these kinds of disputes?

[B] Special Tribunals

The use of international tribunals for the resolution of international business disputes is extensively examined in Chapter 11 of this casebook. Here we examine two examples of arbitral tribunals that can truly be termed "special" in the sense that they represent innovative approaches to the settlement of disputes over foreign investments. Both the arbitral tribunals established under the World Bank's Convention on the Settlement of Investment Disputes Between States and Nationals of Other States and the Iran-United States Claims Settlement Tribunal afford the individual foreign investor standing to hold the host country accountable before an international tribunal. In the case of arbitration under the World Bank Convention's auspices, moreover, the home country of the foreign investor is excluded from appearing before the tribunal. These tribunals have been controversial, however, and we will examine the reasons for this controversy.

CONVENTION ON THE SETTLEMENT OF INVESTMENT DISPUTES BETWEEN STATES AND NATIONALS OF OTHER STATES

The International Bank for Reconstruction and Development or the World Bank was created after World War II. Its first task was to assist in the reconstruction of Europe. Later it turned to work for the economic advancement of developing countries.

Because the World Bank wished to facilitate the international flow of private capital for economic development, it occasionally participated in the arbitration or mediation of disputes. In an effort to develop more effective institutions for resolving disputes arising out of foreign investment, the World Bank during the 1960s drafted the Convention on the Settlement of Investment Disputes Between States and Nationals of Other States, which created the International Centre for the Settlement of Investment Disputes (ICSID). ICSID in turn constitutes a framework for arbitration between states and foreign investors. This framework includes a set of arbitration rules and procedures as well as a stand-by panel of arbitrators.

Proceedings may be commenced under the Convention by any Contracting State or national of a Contracting State who files a request which sets forth the nature of the dispute and indicates that jurisdictional requirements have been satisfied. Mere ratification does not constitute consent by a state to arbitrate under the Convention. Additional steps are required. These may include consenting in advance by domestic legislation, by a separate agreement between Contracting States, or by an agreement between a Contracting State and a national of another Contracting State. Alternatively, consent may be given through an *ad hoc compromis* to settle a particular investment dispute.

The Convention became effective in 1966, having received the requisite number of ratifications. As of January 1, 1988, there were 89 parties to the Convention, including the United States. However, of the Latin American countries, only Ecuador, Guyana and Paraguay had become parties. By 1985 eighteen disputes had been referred for resolution by panels of arbitrators drawn from ICSID's roster. Several had been settled by the parties and five had been disposed of by opinions of arbitrators. Two had been referred to conciliation proceedings. Although at first the opinions were not published, recently several have been published, and there is hope that the Centre will eventually build a body of case law.[19]

Consider now the portions of the Convention excerpted in the Documentary Supplement and apply them to the questions asked below.

NOTES AND QUESTIONS

(1) Assume that you are counsel for an investor who is contemplating investing in a country that is a party to the World Bank convention. What advantages, if any, do you find in the ICSID procedure as compared to other possible methods of dispute settlement, *e.g.*, traditional arbitration, home country courts, host country courts? Do you find any disadvantages? See, *e.g.*, Articles 42 and 55 of the Convention.

(2) How does ICSID look from the perspective of a host country? Why have Latin American countries resisted becoming parties to the Convention? What advantages, if any, do the ICSID procedures afford for a host country? Would Libya, for example, have been better off proceeding under ICSID than before the sole arbitrator in *Texaco Overseas Petroleum Co./California Asiatic Oil Co. v. Government of the Libyan Arab Republic, supra*, p. 780 note 5?

(3) Note that the Convention does not define the term "investment." This omission of a definition was deliberate. Its purpose was to allow ICSID to accommodate both traditional types of investment in the form of capital

------

[19] See, *e.g.*, *AGIP v. People's Republic of the Congo*, 21 Int'l Leg. Mat. 726 (1982) and *Benevenuti et Bonfant v. People's Republic of the Congo*, 21 Int'l Leg. Mat. 740 (1982); *Liberian Eastern Timber Corporation (LETCO) v. The Government of the Republic of Liberia*, 26 Int'l Leg. Mat. 647 (1987); *Amco v. Republic of Indonesia*, 27 Int'l Leg. Mat. 1281 (1988).

contributions and new types of investments, including service contracts and transfers of technology.[20]

Was this a wise decision? Would ordinary sales that involved substantial supplier credits constitute an investment? Might the parties to a foreign investment arrangement define the term themselves?[21]

(4) Consider Article 26 of the Convention, which states that a Contracting State may require, as a precondition to arbitration, that the private investor exhaust local administrative remedies. Suppose the investor exhausts such remedies without success. What then is the task of the arbitral tribunal? Is it merely to review the fairness of local proceedings, or is the investor to be given a *de novo* hearing on the merits of its claim?[22]

(6) For a case where a United States court held that consent to submission of a specific dispute to ICSID barred an investor from suing the host country in United States courts, see *Maritime Intl. Nominees Establishment v. the Republic of Guinea.*[23]

(7) Under Article 54 of the Convention, recognition of an award rendered pursuant to the convention's procedures is assured. However, Article 55 of the Convention allows each Contracting State's national law to decide issues of immunity from execution. In *Liberian Eastern Timber Corporation v. Liberia,*[24] the court held that the assets of Liberia against which execution was sought were immune from execution under the U.S. Foreign Sovereign Immunities Act. On November 16, 1988, however, Congress passed Public Law 200-669, Section 3 of which added a new section (6) to Section 1610(a) of the Foreign Sovereign Immunities Act, which provides that a foreign state shall not be immune from the jurisdiction of U.S. Courts when the cause of action is to enforce a judgment "based on an order confirming an arbitral award rendered against the foreign state, provided that attachment in aid of execution, or execution, would not be inconsistent with any provision in the arbitral agreement."[25]

(8) On December 6, 1988, the United States ratified eight bilateral investment treaties (BITS). A major innovation of the BITS is their guarantee to the investor, if negotiations or nonbinding third-party dispute resolution procedures fail, of the right to arbitrate the dispute before a neutral third party, usually the International Centre for the Settlement of Investment Disputes.[26]

---

[20] For further discussion, see Delaume, *Economic Development And Sovereign Immunity*, 79 Am. J. Int'l. L. 319, 339, fn. 76 (1985).

[21] See Gopal, *International Centre For Settlement Of Investment Disputes*, 14 Case W. Res. J. Int'l L. 591, 598-600 (1982).

[22] As of 1982, ICSID had not proven to offer the advantages of speed and simplicity. As of that time, the average period for an arbitration to be completed, either by a final award or settlement, was three years. See Gopal, *supra*, at 594.

[23] 693 F. 2d 1094 (D.C. Cir. 1982), *cert. denied*, 104 S. Ct. 71 (1983).

[24] 659 F. Supp. 606 (S.D.N.Y. 1986).

[25] See 28 Int'l Leg. Mat. 398 (1989).

[26] For a comprehensive overview of the BITS, see Vandevelde, *The Bilateral Investment Treaty Progam Of The United States*, 21 Cornell Int'l L. J. 201 (1988).

THE IRAN-UNITED STATES CLAIMS TRIBUNAL

In *Dames & Moore v. Regan, infra*, p. 1021, we shall note that, as part of the Algiers Accords which led to the release of 52 Americans held hostage in Iran, the United States and Iran agreed to the establishment of a new international arbitral tribunal, the Iran-United States Claims Tribunal. This part of the Accords, known as the Claims Settlement Agreement, provides in Article II(1) that the Tribunal has jurisdiction, inter alia, over "claims of nationals of the United States against Iran and claims of nationals of Iran against the United States, and any related counterclaims . . . aris[ing] out of debts, contracts . . . expropriations or other measures affecting property rights." Article II(2) of the Agreement gives the Tribunal jurisdiction over "official claims of the United States and Iran against each other arising out of contractual arrangements between them for the purchase and sale of goods and services."

Under Article III of the Claims Settlement Agreement, the Tribunal consists of nine members (three appointed by the United States, three appointed by Iran, and three third-country arbitrators chosen by the six party appointed arbitrators) or such larger multiple of three as the two governments may agree upon. Claims may be decided by the full panel or by a panel of three members as the President of the Tribunal determines. By Presidential order three chambers have been created to hear claims arising under Article II(1) and (2) of the Agreement.

Jurisdiction of the Tribunal over an American expropriation claim depends on a showing that the dispute was "outstanding" as of January 19, 1981 and that the claim is owned by a United States "national." A claim is owned by a United States national (i) if the claimant is a citizen of the United States or a corporation at least 50% owned by U.S. citizens and formed under the laws of a United States' jurisdiction or (ii) if the claimant is a juridical person in which United States' nationals as defined in (i) above have an ownership interest sufficient to control the company and the company is not otherwise entitled to bring a claim. The claim must be against "Iran," *i.e.*, the Government of Iran, including any agency, political subdivision, instrumentality, or controlled entity thereof. Excluded from the Tribunal's jurisdiction are all claims "arising under a binding contract between the parties specifically providing that any dispute thereunder shall be within the sole jurisdiction of the competent Iranian courts in response to the Majlis position."

Under Article V of the Claims Settlement Agreement, the Tribunal is required to decide all cases "on the basis of respect for law, applying such choice of law rules and principles of commercial and international law as the Tribunal determines to be applicable, taking into account relevant usages of the trade, contract provisions and changed circumstances."

Before the Tribunal the United States Government represents claimants whose claims total less than $250,000. Claims over that amount are presented by private counsel for the claimant. The United States Government also, of course, presents any claims that the United States is bringing in its own name. On May 13, 1990, the United States and Iran concluded a settlement agreement that covered the remaining U.S. claims under $250,000 and the U.S. Government's own claim against Iran for repayment of fifteen loans made between 1955 and 1967 as part of the U.S. long-term economic development assistance program in Iran. The settlement agreement was confirmed by an award from the Tribunal. The claims of U.S. nationals of less than $250,000 that were covered by the award and settlement agreement were then formally transferred by the U.S. Department of State to the Foreign Claims Settlement Commission for adjudication.

At this writing the Tribunal has rendered approximately two dozen awards that bear on expropriation issues.[27] In particular the Tribunal has addressed three general areas: (1) the type of conduct that gives rise to state responsibility for expropriation; (2) the standards that govern the compensation to be paid to the foreign investor for expropriated property; and (3) the methods of valuation to be used to quantify damages.

With respect to the type of conduct that gives rise to state responsibility for expropriation, the Tribunal, in most of the cases brought before it, has had to deal with situations where there was no formal taking announced by the Government of Iran. Rather, the claimants have argued that the Government of Iran has taken certain actions that amount to a taking *de facto*. The Tribunal has consistently ruled that interference by the Government of Iran with the alien's enjoyment of the incidents of ownership — examples include the use or control of the property, or the income and economic benefits derived therefrom — constitutes a compensable taking. In these holdings the Tribunal has most often applied a test of "reasonableness," *i.e.*, an "unreasonable" interference with the alien's property rights is sufficient to amount to an expropriation. The Tribunal has focused on a wide range of ownership rights, including the right to appoint directors and participate in management; the receipt in the ordinary course of business of financial and commercial information from the business; receipt of income or other distributions; and other aspects of ownership. The replacement of the owners' or directors' management with representatives appointed by the Government of Iran has consistently resulted in the Tribunal's finding that an expropriation has taken place at the point when the former managers are no longer able to participate in the management.

By contrast, where no governmental managers have been appointed, claimants have had more difficulty proving that there has been an expropriation. For example, a claimant's continued attempts to participate in the management of the company through its minority of two directors on the seven person board of directors was the basis for the Tribunal's determination that there had been no expropriation, even though the board adopted a policy, over the objections of these two directors, which expressly and totally excluded the foreign shareholder from any participation in dividends. The Tribunal only awarded the claimant the amount of cash dividends that had not been paid as declared, up to the jurisdictional cutoff date of January 19, 1981.

As to the standards that govern the compensation to be paid to the foreign investor for expropriated property, the Tribunal has consistently upheld, over the

---

27 The following discussion is based largely on Current Developments In Expropriation And Compensation: A Preliminary Survey Of Awards Of The Iran-United States Claims Tribunal, a paper delivered by Charles N. Brower, U.S. Judge, Iran-United States Claims Tribunal, at the Winter Meeting of the ABA Section of International Law & Practice, Dec. 12, 1986, St. Thomas, U.S. Virgin Islands.

dissent of the Iranian judges, the traditional principle of "prompt, adequate and effective" compensation. Although some of the Tribunal's rulings on the applicable standard of compensation have been based on the Treaty of Amity, Economic Relations, and Consular Rights Between the United States of America and Iran, *signed* 15 August 1955, which entered into force 16 June 1957,[28] and which the Tribunal has held to be still in force, the Tribunal has also expressly held that customary international law supports the "prompt, adequate and effective standard." The most extensive discussion of the requirements of customary international law is the Tribunal decision set out below.

SEDCO, INC. and NATIONAL IRANIAN OIL COMPANY AND IRAN

Award No. ITL 59-129-3 (27 March 1986)[29]

* * * *

III. Conclusions of the Tribunal

The Parties disagree on the applicability of the Treaty of Amity to this Case. The Tribunal notes, however, that in *Phelps Dodge Corp. and Islamic Republic of Iran*,[30] . . . the Tribunal held that Article IV (2) of the Treaty was "clearly applicable to [the investment at issue in that Case] at the time the claim arose" and that "whether or not the Treaty is still in force today, it is a relevant source of law on which the Tribunal is justified in drawing in reaching its decision." We find the reason set forth in that Award, at 14-16, convincing and therefore conclude that the rule of law set forth in Article IV (2) of the Treaty is applicable to the issue of compensation due Claimant in the present case for the taking of its property on 22 November 1979.

It is nonetheless necessary, however, to consider what is the applicable standard of compensation under customary international law due to Respondents argument that the said Article simply incorporates customary law as it may exist from time to time. . . .

Although Respondents argue otherwise, it is the Tribunal's conclusion that "the overwhelming practice and the prevailing legal opinion" before World War II supported the view that customary international law required compensation equivalent to the full value of the property taken. See Dolzer, New Foundations of the Law of Expropriation of Alien Property.[31] . . . It is only since those days that this traditional legal standpoint has been challenged by a number of States and commentators.

Assessment of the present state of customary law on this subject on the basis of the conduct of States in actual practice is difficult, *inter alia*, because of the

---

[28] 284 U.N.T.S. 93, T.I.A.S. 3453, 8 U.S.T. 900.

[29] Reprinted in 25 Int. Leg. Mat. 629 (1986). See also extensive separate opinion by the United States Judge, 25 Int'l Leg. Mat. 636.

[30] Award No. 217-99-2 (19 March 1986).

[31] 75 Am. J. Int'l L. 553, 558-559 (1981).

questionable evidentiary value for customary international law of much of the practice available. This is particularly true in regard to "lump sum" agreements between States (a practice often claimed to support the position of less than full compensation), as well as to compensation settlements negotiated between States and foreign companies. Both types of agreements can be so greatly inspired by non-judicial considerations — *e.g.*, resumption of diplomatic or trading relations — that it is extremely difficult to draw from them conclusions as to *opinio juris*, *i.e.*, the determination that the content of such settlements was thought by the States involved to be required by international law. The International Court of Justice and international arbitral tribunals have cast serious doubts on the value of such settlements as evidence of custom. As this Tribunal itself has stated in another context, "considerations underlying settlements often include factors other than elements of law." *United States of America and Islamic Republic of Iran.*[32] . . . The bilateral investment treaty practice of States, which much more often than not reflects the traditional international law standard of compensation for expropriation, more nearly constitutes an accurate measure of the High Contracting Parties' view as to customary international law, but also carries with it some of the same evidentiary limitations as lump sum agreements. Both kinds of agreements involve to some degree bargaining in a context to which "*opinio juris*" seems a stranger.

Those arguing that there has been an erosion of the traditional international law standard of full compensation often cite also resolutions and declarations of the United Nations General Assembly. Respondents in this Case, for example, refer in particular to the Declaration on the Establishment of a New International Economic Order and the Charter of Economic Rights and Duties of States ("Charter"), as well as the earlier Resolution 1803, of 14 December 1962, on Permanent Sovereignty over Natural Resources.

United Nations General Assembly Resolutions are not directly binding upon States and generally are not evidence of customary law. Nevertheless, it is generally accepted that such resolutions in certain specified circumstances may be regarded as evidence of customary international law or can contribute — among other factors — to the creation of such law. . . .

There is considerable unanimity in international arbitral practice and scholarly opinion that of the resolutions cited above, it is Resolution 1803, and not either of the two later resolutions, which at least reflects, if it does not evidence, current international law. . . .

The pertinent part of Resolution 1803 provides:

Nationalization, expropriation or requisitioning shall be based on grounds or reasons of public utility, security or the national interest which are recognized as overriding purely individual or private interests, both domestic and foreign. In such cases the owner shall be paid *appropriate* compensation in accordance with the rules in force in the State taking such measures in the exercise of its sovereignty and *in accordance with international law*. In any case where the question of compensation gives rise to a controversy, the national jurisdiction of the State taking such measures shall be exhausted.

---

[32] Decision No. Dec 8-a1-FT (14 May 1982) reprinted in 1 Iran-U.S.C.T.R. 144 at 151.

However, upon agreement by sovereign states and other parties concerned, settlement of the dispute should be made through arbitration or international adjudication . . . (Emphasis added.)

This provision has been argued, on the one hand, to express the traditional standard of compensation with different words and, on the other hand, to signify an erosion of this standard.

Those learned writers who have argued, however, that the adoption of Resolution 1803, against the background of general recognition of the permanent sovereignty of States over natural resources, evidenced or brought about a change in customary international law so that less than full compensation should be the applicable standard, have focused mainly on the possible impact of the Resolution on the issue of compensation in the context of a formal systematic large-scale nationalization, *e.g.*, of an entire industry or a natural resource, a circumstance not argued by either of the Parties to have been present in the instant case.

Opinions both of international tribunals and of legal writers overwhelmingly support the conclusion that under customary international law in a case such as here presented — a discrete expropriation of alien property — full compensation should be awarded for the property taken. This is true whether or not the expropriation itself was otherwise lawful. . . .

NOTES AND QUESTIONS

(1) This decision reflects an extraordinarily formalistic conception of law — law as some autonomous body of rules formulated out of only those special elements of social behavior that qualify somehow (unexplained) as the only legitimate building blocks of law. Test this concept. Explain why an almost universal pattern of lump-sum settlements of less than full-value is not probative of a legal principle. Because it is the product of bargaining or the desire of both sides to normalize relations? At least in the context of large-scale expropriations accompanying a major political upheaval, might not those considerations add to the pattern's weight as probative of law?

(2) Why are bilateral investment treaties more reliable evidences of the law than lump-sum settlements? The Tribunal speaks of the parties' expectations. Are you persuaded?

(3) Does the Tribunal's reasoning mask an otherwise intractable conflict of interests, the settlement of which was implicit in the Algerian Accords establishing the Tribunal? If this is so, what authoritativeness does one attribute to the Tribunal's decisions?

(4) Alternatively, recall the wider functional possibilities for international law discussed in Chapter 4. How might the Tribunal's work be thought to contribute to one or more of these possibilities?

(5) The Tribunal has been cautious in the remedies it has made available to claimants. In theory, remedies could include restitution or specific performance

or even punitive damages. In practice, however, virtually all of the Tribunal's decisions have focused solely on the return to the claimant of the value of the property interest lost. The Tribunal has ruled, moreover, that full compensation must be awarded whether or not the expropriation itself is otherwise lawful. It thereby rejected Iran's claim that there should be a two-tiered system of compensation, providing "partial" compensation in lawful expropriations and "full" compensation in unlawful ones.

(6) In calculating the amount of compensation for an expropriation, the Tribunal has recognized that valuation of the expropriated property must exclude any diminution in value caused by the fact of expropriation or by events that occurred subsequent to the expropriation. At the same time the Tribunal has recognized that the value of the claimant's business would be reduced by the generally pessimistic business outlook that preceded the actual expropriation.

Where, precisely, should an international tribunal draw the line? The United States Supreme Court has permitted recovery based on reasonable uses but not speculative uses. Would this precedent permit a host country to argue persuasively that valuation based on a continued right to own property or a business enterprise without government intervention is speculative? Recent U.S. Supreme Court decisions suggest that citizens operating a business in a regulated industry have less right to compensation where regulations are made more stringent because their investment-backed expectations under such circumstances are less reasonable. See, *e.g., Connelly v. Pension Benefit Guaranty Corporation,*[33] and *Ruckelhaus v. Monsanto Co.*[34]

In determining the fair market value of a claimant's enterprise, the Tribunal has taken into account both the present value of reasonably ascertainable future profits as well as any outstanding obligations. The Tribunal has not yet, at this writing, adopted a particular financial theory of valuation. Methods based on price/earning ratios, discounted cash flow techniques, actual share prices, and other criteria have been suggested. In practice claimants have been well served by using two or more corroborating valuation models.[35]

[C] Economic Sanctions

The backdrop to the so-called Hickenlooper Amendment, named after its sponsor Senator Hickenlooper, of Iowa, was the 1962 expropriation by a Brazilian state of assets of a local subsidiary of ITT. Because the expropriation took place shortly before a contemplated visit by Brazil's President to the United States in search of further financial assistance, congressional reaction was especially hostile. Critical comments in both Houses of Congress precipitated the introduction by Senator Hickenlooper of an amendment to the Foreign Assistance Act of 1962. Although opposed by the President and Secretary of State, it became Section 620(e)(1) of the Foreign Assistance Act of 1962 as amended. The current version

---

[33] 106 S. Ct. 1018 (1986).

[34] 467 U.S. 986 (1984).

[35] For a recent discussion of the Tribunal's decision making process, see Crook, *Applicable Law In International Arbitration: The Iran-U.S. Claims Tribunal Experience,* 83 Am. J. Intl L. 278 (1989).

of the Hickenlooper Amendment[36] may be found in your Documentary Supplement.

In pertinent part the Hickenlooper Amendment requires the President to suspend economic assistance to the government of any country that expropriates property owned by U.S. citizens or business enterprises, repudiates contracts with U.S. citizens or business enterprises, or engages in so-called "creeping expropriation" of property owned by U.S. citizens or business enterprises, if the foreign government fails within a "reasonable time" (as defined under the Act) to "take appropriate steps, which may include arbitration, to discharge its obligations under international law toward such citizen or entity, including speedy compensation for such property in convertible foreign exchange, equivalent to the full value thereof as required by international law." Such suspension is to continue until the President is satisfied that appropriate steps are being taken.

Until amended by the Foreign Assistance Act of 1973,[37] to provide for waiver when certified by the President to be in the national interest, the Hickenlooper Amendment contained a no-waiver clause. Before the 1973 change, the amendment had been invoked only once, against Ceylon in 1963, although its application was threatened to several other countries, including Argentina, Brazil, Indonesia and Peru. Since the 1973 revision the Amendment has been invoked only once-against Ethiopia in 1979.

Congress has enacted other legislation along the Hickenlooper Amendment model. For example, it has prohibited the President from granting trade preferences under the Trade Act of 1974,[38] . . . to less developed countries that expropriate U.S. property. Also, several statutes bar U.S. representatives on international bank governing boards from supporting loans to expropriating states.[39]

NOTES AND QUESTIONS

(1) As noted above the Executive Branch has been firmly opposed to the Hickenlooper Amendment and has worked assiduously to avoid its application. For example, with respect to the dispute between International Petroleum Company, Ltd. (IPC), a wholly owned subsidiary of Standard Oil of New Jersey, and Peru in 1969, the Nixon Administration contended that resort to Peruvian administrative remedies and ongoing negotiations constituted "appropriate steps" adequate to make invocation of the Amendment unnecessary. Why, do you suppose, has the Executive Branch been so opposed to the Hickenlooper Amendment?

[36] 22 U.S.C.A. Section 2370(e)(1).

[37] P.L. No. 93-183, 87 Stat. 722 (1973).

[38] 88 Stat. 2066 as amended, 19 U.S.C.A. Section 2462(b)(3).

[39] 22 U.S.C.A. Sections 283r, 284, 285a. For an excellent discussion of these and other U.S. economic sanctions, see B. Carter, International Economic Sanctions: Improving The Haphazard U.S. Regime (1988).

(2) In *Requiem for Hickenlooper*,[40] Professor Lillich suggests that the 1973 revision has made the Hickenlooper Amendment a dead letter, and indeed the Amendment has been invoked only once since that date. Should the Amendment therefore be revoked? What arguments might be made for and against revocation?[41]

(3) Note that the Hickenlooper Amendment requires that states receiving U.S. financial assistance must, in the event of expropriation, discharge their "obligations under international law . . . including speedy compensation for such property in convertible foreign exchange, equivalent to the full value thereof as required by international law. . . ." Does Hickenlooper prescribe the international law standard? If so, how would you evaluate the Amendment's provisions in light of the material you studied earlier in this chapter? What alternative interpretation can be given to the Amendment?

(4) Does the Hickenlooper Amendment require the foreign investor to exhaust any available local remedies before sanctions can be imposed against the host country?

[D] Investment Guaranty Programs

Not surprisingly the private investor would like insurance against expropriation and other risks of doing business abroad. For United States investors such insurance may be available through certain private insurance companies or the Overseas Private Investment Corporation (OPIC), a self-supporting corporation wholly owned by the United States Government. The Convention Establishing the Multilateral Investment Guarantee Agency (the MIGA Convention) has recently been concluded under the auspices of the World Bank. We consider insurance and OPIC programs first and then turn to the MIGA.

[1] Private Insurance[42]

The background to private political risk insurance lies in marine insurance coverage provided to exporters and shipping lines. This coverage has a long history and, as might be expected, Lloyds of London has played a leading role in providing this coverage. More broadly based coverage was developed about ten to fifteen years ago, and drew some additional participants like the American International Group.

This more recent coverage initially offered, and still consists primarily of, protection against confiscation, expropriation, or nationalization of assets or fixed investments. Other coverages that have become available include, most notably, protection against loss arising from government actions which interfere with the delivery of goods or the performance of other contract obligations.

---

[40] 69 Am. J. Int'l L. 97 (1975).

[41] For a recent consideration of the Hickenlooper Amendment, see Vandevelde, *Reassessing The Hickenlooper Amendment*, 29 Va. J. Int'l L. 115 (1988).

[42] The following discussion is based largely on a paper, New Developments In Private Political Risk Insurance And Trade Finance, delivered by Douglas A. Paul, Vice President, American International Group, at the winter meeting of the American Bar Association, Section of International Law & Practice, Dec. 12, 1986, St. Thomas, U.S. Virgin Islands.

In addition to the political risk insurance coverage, the private sector also provides a market for export credit insurance which protects against a private buyer's failure to pay for goods or service. Although there is some overlap in the nature of the risks insured under the two programs, these coverages are perceived by the market as quite separate, primarily because Lloyds underwriting syndicates have agreed, through internal regulation, not to insure against commercial default or financial guaranty type exposures.

With respect to political risk insurance, there is a distinction between the Lloyds and the non-Lloyds, or company market. Lloyds consists of hundreds of underwriting syndicates under separate management, some of which choose to participate in various types of political risk insurance. Brokers handle requests for insurance on a one-by-one basis and first gain support and negotiate terms and conditions with syndicates specializing in political risk insurance. These brokers then, on the strength of the "leaders" participation, attract other syndicates to sign on for a percentage of the risk exposure.

The "company" market operates through reinsurance "treaties" (i.e., agreements between participating reinsurers). These commit participating reinsurers to a specific percentage of each and every transaction underwritten by the primary or "lead" underwriter. Lloyds syndicates, along with their direct business, participate as reinsurers on most political risk treaties. These treaties are annually renewable by participating reinsurers, although reinsurers remain on the risk till expiration for all policies written during that treaty year.

Although the high hazard nature of political risk insurance requires broad reinsurance, overall participation in this market is rather thin. Also, the annual nature of treaty negotiations and individual risk decision-making renders this market quite fragile.

[2] The Overseas Private Investment Corporation

Designed to complement the coverage of private political risk insurance — although private insurance companies also view them as somewhat competitive — are national programs.[43] Primary among these in the United States is the insurance offered through the Overseas Private Investment Corporation (OPIC), a semiautonomous agency. Created by the Foreign Assistance Act of 1969,[44] OPIC is a continuation of an earlier Agency for International Development (AID) program. In addition to expropriation, OPIC also insures against losses resulting from currency exchange controls.

Insurance coverage by OPIC involves, in effect, a tripartite arrangement. That is, as a condition of OPIC issuing insurance to the investor, the Agency must first enter into an agreement with the host country. The most fundamental provision of this agreement is the host government's acceptance of OPIC's claim to subrogation — the right in OPIC to compensation from the host government for the funds it has had to pay to the investor. This agreement also characteristically requires that the U.S. investor obtain the approval of the foreign government

---

[43] For a discussion of national insurance programs in various countries, see T. Meron, Investment Insurance In International Law (1976).

[44] 83 Stat. 809, 22 U.S.C. Sections 2191-2200a, as amended by 95 Stat. 1021 (1981).

before OPIC will issue a guaranty. Arbitration is often required in the event of a dispute between OPIC and the host country over the agency's right to receive compensation as subrogee. However, many Latin American states, particularly those that assert the Calvo Clause, resist inter-governmental arbitration. As a consequence OPIC has relatively few such agreements with Latin American countries.

The insurance contract between OPIC and the U.S. investor provides the actual insurance coverage. These contracts contain both "specific terms and conditions," applicable to the specific transaction, and printed "general terms and conditions," which represent OPIC's general policy. The most important item in OPIC's "general terms and conditions" is the definition of "Expropriatory Action." Disputes under the contact between OPIC and the investor are resolved by arbitration, and the number of such arbitrations has given rise to a rich jurisprudence.

The three main issues in these disputes have been "whether there was an expropriatory action by the host state, whether OPIC may invoke any defense under the contract, and what date should be designated as the date of expropria-tion."[45] With respect to the issue of whether there was an expropriatory action by the host state, OPIC has denied claims on the ground that the claimant's business mismanagement was the real cause of its failure rather than acts of the government. In at least one case an arbitral tribunal disagreed with OPIC's contention. OPIC has also resisted claims of "creeping expropriation," finding that government harassment was only a prelude to a later act constituting the "real" expropriation such as a government taking legal control of the operation of the enterprise.

In relying on defenses under the contract with the investor, OPIC has claimed that the host country's actions were essentially regulatory in nature and were not part of an overall scheme directed against the investor. Arbitral tribunals have upheld this claim. OPIC also resisted a claim by ITT that it was obligated to pay for Chile's expropriation of ITT's Chilean telephone subsidiary on the ground that ITT's clandestine political actions had contributed to this expropriation. How-ever, the arbitrators held that these activities did not violate the insurance contract and therefore did not affect coverage under the policy.[46]

Determining the precise date of the expropriation has been the most hotly contested issue arising from claims under the contract, except for the issue of whether there has been an expropriation. Here OPIC has viewed expropriation as a discrete event — such as a takeover of the enterprise by government agents — rather than a process continuing over time. Moreover, arbitration panels have upheld OPIC's view that depreciation in the value of the enterprise caused by the host government's action must be taken into account when valuing the invest-ment. In the view of one commentator, "since the value of the enterprise generally declines as the governmental interference increases, application of this theory adds insult to injury by valuing the enterprise at its lowest ebb."[47] . . .

---

[45] Koven, Expropriation And The "Jurisprudence" Of OPIC, 22 Harv. Int'l L.J. 269 (1981).

[46] Matter Of The Arbitration Between International Tel. And Tel. Corp. Sud America And OPIC, 14 Int'l Leg. Mat. 1307 (1974).

[47] Koven, op cit. at 318.

The goals behind OPIC political risk insurance are multifaceted. One goal is to shelter the private investor to some extent from the often tempestuous controversies among states as to what the customary international law of expropriation is or should be, as well as from the expense, delay, and inconvenience of prosecuting claims against foreign states for these kinds of losses. Another is to develop strong, private "free enterprise" sectors in foreign countries so that they can resist Communism and be generally more sympathetic to the United States. Preference is to be given to projects in friendly less developed countries that have annual per capita incomes of less than $680 in 1979 U.S. dollars. At the same time OPIC is required to avoid insuring projects that would reduce employment in the United States by setting up "runaway plants" abroad.

The OPIC program has been highly controversial. The Nixon Administration contemplated its eventual replacement by private insurance programs, and sponsored amendments in 1974 that would have put OPIC, after an interim period of collaboration with private insurers, out of the business of managing expropriation risks by December 31, 1979. Further legislative amendments in 1978, however, continued OPIC coverage. Among the charges made against OPIC are that it favors big business at the expense of small business; that it makes no meaningful contribution to economic development; that it does not reach the poorest nations; that it is not needed to help U.S. business compete with other national systems; that it encourages the flow of jobs abroad; and that it encourages State Department intervention in foreign economic disputes.[48]

INVESTMENT GUARANTY AGREEMENT BETWEEN THE UNITED STATES AND INDONESIA

January 7, 1967

18 U.S.T. 1850, T.I.A.S. No. 6330, 692 U.N.T.S. 109 (selected provisions).

* * * *

2. The procedures set forth in this Agreement shall apply only with respect to guaranteed investments in projects or activities approved by the Host Government.

3. If the Guaranteeing Government makes payment to any investor under a guaranty issued pursuant to the present Agreement, the Host Government shall, subject to the provisions of the following paragraph, recognize the transfer to the guaranteeing Government of any currency, credits, assets, or investment on account of which payment under such guaranty is made as well as the succession of the Guaranteeing Government to any right, title, claim, privilege, or cause of action existing, or which may arise, in connection therewith.

4. To the extent that the laws of the Host Government partially or wholly invalidate the acquisition of any interests in any property within its national territory by the Guaranteeing Government, the Host Government shall permit such investor and the Guaranteeing Government to make appropriate arrangements pursuant to which such interests are transferred to an entity permitted to

---

[48] See e.g., House Committee On Foreign Affairs, Hearings On Extension And Revision Of Overseas Private Investment Insurance Programs, 97th Cong., 1st Sess. (1981).

own such interests under the laws of the Host Government. The Guaranteeing Government shall assert no greater rights than those of the transferring investor under the laws of the Host Government with respect to any interest transferred or succeeded to as contemplated in paragraph 3. The Guaranteeing Government does, however, reserve its rights to assert a claim in its sovereign capacity in the eventuality of a denial of justice or other question of state responsibility as defined in international law.

5. Amounts in the lawful currency of the Host Government and credits thereof acquired by the Guaranteeing Government under such guaranties shall be ac- *non-discri* corded treatment neither less nor more favorable than that accorded to funds of nationals of the Guaranteeing Government deriving from investment activities like those in which the investor has been engaged, and such amounts and credits shall be freely available to the Guaranteeing Government to meet its expenditures in the national territory of the Host Government.

6. (a) Differences between the two Governments concerning the interpretation of the provisions of this Agreement shall be settled, insofar as possible, through *settlement* negotiations between the two Governments. If such a difference cannot be resolved within a period of three months following the request for such negotiations, it shall be submitted, at the request of either Government, to an ad hoc arbitral tribunal for settlement in accordance with the applicable principles and rules of public international law. . . .

(b) Any claim, arising out of investments guaranteed in accordance with this Agreement, against either of the two Governments, which, in the opinion of the other, presents a question of public international law, shall, at the request of the Government presenting its claim, be submitted to negotiations. If at the end of three months following the request for negotiations the two Governments have not resolved the claim by mutual agreement, the claim, including the question of whether it presents a question of public international law, shall be submitted for settlement to an arbitral tribunal. . . .

NOTES AND QUESTIONS

(1) What effect, if any, does Article 6 of the U.S.-Indonesia Investment Guaranty Agreement have on Indonesia's liabilities? On the U.S. investor's rights?

(2) Under Article 6 of the agreement, would OPIC, as subrogee, be obliged to exhaust local remedies prior to the initiation of arbitration? *probably not but should try (w/in 3 months).*

(3) What are the advantages and disadvantages of OPIC insurance arrangements from the perspective of the U.S. Investor, the U.S. Government and the host country?

(4) Article VI, paragraph 3, of OPIC's agreement with Brazil[49] provides:

3. There shall be excluded from the negotiations and the arbitral procedures herein contemplated matters which remain exclusively within the internal

---

[49] 18 U.S.T. & O.I.A. 1807, T.I.A.S. No. 6327.

jurisdiction of a sovereign state. It is accordingly understood that claims arising out of the expropriation of property of private foreign investors do not present questions of public international law unless and until the judicial process of the Recipient Country has been exhausted, and there exists a denial of justice, as those terms are defined in public international law.

What effect does this provision have on OPIC's rights as subrogee?

(5) Are there any problems in OPIC entering into an insurance arrangement when the host country is a party to the Convention on the Settlement of Investment Disputes Between States and Nationals of other States? See the discussion of the Convention and ICSID *supra*, page 799.

(6) Are there situations where OPIC might be required to pay a U.S. investor and yet not be entitled to recover as Subrogee under its agreement with the host country?

(7) OPIC has been subrogated to private investors' claims in a number of cases being brought before the Iran-United States Claims Tribunal, see *supra*, page 802.

(8) Consider the discussion of the disputes OPIC has had with U.S. foreign investors over whether there has been an "expropriatory action" by the host state which requires OPIC to compensate them pursuant to the terms of the contract. Do the positions OPIC has taken in these disputes support the "prompt, adequate, and effective" standard of compensation?[50]

[3] Convention Establishing the Multilateral Investment Guarantee Agency (the MIGA Convention)[51]

Foreign direct investment flows to less developed countries declined markedly during the 1980s. For example, after reaching a high of U.S. $17.24 billion in 1981, direct investment flows to less developed countries fell to U.S. $11.86 billion in 1982 and to U.S. $7.80 billion in 1983. Although they have increased slightly in subsequent years, at this writing they have not even regained their 1982 level.

This decline has been caused by a number of interrelated factors. These include, for example, the increasingly heavy debt of developing countries; a worldwide recession that stopped the growth of local markets and reduced demand for new investment for import substitution purposes; a sharp drop in the price of commodities that adversely affected investment in the extractive sector; and increasing protectionism in the developed countries that adversely impacted export oriented industries in the less developed countries. Other, long range trends have also

---

[50] For further information on OPIC, see Note, Encouraging Investment In LDC's: The United States Investment Guaranty Program, 8 Brooklyn J. Int'l L. 365 (1982); Koven, Expropriation And The "Jurisprudence" Of OPIC, 22 Harv. Int'l L.J. 269 (1981); Adams, The Emerging Law Of Dispute Settlement Under The United States Investment Insurance Program, 3 Law & Pol. Int'l Bus. 101 (1971).

[51] Much of the material in this section is based on a paper, Factors Influencing The Flow Of Foreign Investment And The Relevance Of A Multilateral Investment Guarantee Scheme, delivered by Ibrahim F.I. Shihata, Vice President and General Counsel, the World Bank, on December 12, 1986, at the Winter Meeting of the ABA's Section of International Law and Practice, held in St. Thomas, U.S. Virgin Islands.

caused a decline in foreign direct investment in less developed countries. These include, among others, labor's declining share in production resulting from increased shifts to automated and technology based industries. This, in turn, has adversely affected the comparative advantage that less developed countries otherwise derive from their low labor costs. Further eroding the competitive position of the many less developed countries, and hence their attractiveness to foreign investors, has been the rise in production costs due to persistently high rates of inflation and low levels of technical education.

The most important factor, for present purposes, contributing to the decline in foreign direct investment in the less developed countries, has been the perception of high and increasing political risks in these countries, especially risks related to expropriation and the imposition of controls on the convertibility and transfer of funds. As we have seen above, national insurance programs like OPIC are designed to minimize and mitigate these risks. *Overseas Private Ins.Cos.*

The purpose of a global agency for investment insurance is to improve the worldwide investment climate, especially though not exclusively that of less developed countries, and to combine the offering of guarantees against non-commercial risks with broader service and advisory functions. The primary means to achieve this purpose is by providing guarantees against non-commercial risks in a more comprehensive and effective manner than that which is available under present circumstances. *purpose of OPIC*

The possibility of the World Bank establishing an international agency that would provide insurance to investors against non-commercial risks had been under consideration since the late 1940s.[52]

For a variety of reasons early proposals for such an agency were not adopted. With the slow growth in official development assistance and the declining trends in commercial lending, the World Bank in 1981 revised the proposal for a global investment guarantee agency operating under the Bank's auspices. After a number of studies and consultations, the Bank's Executive Directors, in June 1985, held twenty sessions of meetings as a "Committee of the Whole" to consider a draft of the Convention Establishing the Multilateral Investment Guarantee Agency (the MIGA Convention). On October 11, 1985, the Bank's Board of Governors adopted a resolution opening the MIGA Convention for signature by member governments of the Bank and Switzerland. *MIGA 1985*

The United States has ratified the MIGA Convention, and it is now in force.[53]

The objective of the Multilateral Investment Guarantee Agency (MIGA) is to encourage the flow of investments for productive purposes among its member countries especially to less developed member countries. To meet this goal, MIGA will guarantee and reinsure eligible investments against losses resulting from non-commercial risks. In addition the Agency will engage in a broad range of promotional activities. The four categories of non-commercial risks covered by Article *MIGA's objective*

---

[52] Much of this description of MIGA is taken from Shihata, *The Settlement Of Disputes Regarding Foreign Investment: The Role Of The World Bank, With Particular Reference To ICSID And MIGA*, 1 Am. U.J. Int'l L. and Pol. 97, 106-116 (1986).

[53] For the MIGA Operational Regulations, see 27 Int'l Leg. Mat. 1227 (1988). For the MIGA Standard Contract Of Guarantee and General Conditions Of Guarantee For Equity Investment, see 28 Int'l Leg. Mat. 1233 (1989).

Risks covered

11 of the MIGA Convention are: (1) the transfer risk resulting from host government restrictions on currency conversion and transfers; (2) the risk of loss resulting from legislative or administrative actions or omissions of the host government which deprive the foreign investor of ownership, or control of, or substantial benefits from his investment; (3) the repudiation or breach of government contracts in cases where the investor has no access to a competent judicial or arbitral forum, or faces unreasonable delays in such a forum, or is unable to enforce a judicial or arbitral decision issued in his favor; and (4) the risk of armed conflict and civil disturbance.

Requirements

For an individual investor to be eligible for the Agency's guarantee he must be a national of a member country. Corporate investors, to be eligible, must either be incorporated and have their principal place of business in a member country, or the majority of their capital must be owned by nationals of a member country. Eligible investors may include both public and private sector corporations and member governments and joint ventures among them. Eligibility may even, under certain conditions, be extended to nationals of the host country if they transfer the assets to be invested from abroad; a measure intended to help reverse capital flight.

Like OPIC and other national insurance agencies, MIGA, after paying a claim, would assume the rights that the indemnified investor acquired against the host country as a result of the event giving rise to his claim. Although, under the Convention, MIGA could ultimately have recourse to international arbitration to enforce such subrogated rights, the drafters of the Convention hoped that MIGA's involvement in a conflict would facilitate an amicable settlement. The hope is that MIGA, as an impartial third-party, may be able to moderate the conflicting claims of the investor and the host country and increase the likelihood of a settlement.

MIGA is designed to complement national, regional, and private non-commercial risk insurance rather than compete with it. Accordingly, MIGA will emphasize guaranteeing investments from member states without an investment guaranty program, co-guaranteeing investments with national and regional agencies, providing reinsurance for national and regional agencies, guaranteeing investments that fail eligibility tests of national and regional programs, and participating in arrangements for reinsurance with private insurance companies in member states.

NOTES AND QUESTIONS

(1) If the MIGA Convention were widely adopted, it would greatly increase the amount of investment guarantees available. If such insurance is widely available, would it mean that a nation had less to lose by expropriating? If so, would this call into question the financial integrity of the MIGA program? What steps might be taken by MIGA to minimize such risks? Will an agency such as MIGA prove capable of taking such steps? Would you favor extending MIGA to cover guarantees of international bank loans?

(2) A key component of the MIGA program is its definition of the risks to be covered. An excessively broad definition would result in a large number of successful claims and endanger the financial integrity of the program. On the other hand, an excessively narrow definition might make the MIGA insurance unattractive to foreign investors, especially those with access to national insurance programs. An extensive commentary on the MIGA Convention published by the World Bank (the "Commentary") contains the following observation regarding the Convention's definition of the expropriation risk:

> 14. Article 11(a)(ii) defines the expropriation risk. It would encompass measures attributable to the host government such as nationalization, confiscation, sequestration, seizure, attachment and freezing of assets. The phrase "any legislative or administrative action" in the provision includes measures by the executive, but not measures taken by judicial bodies in the exercise of their functions. Measures normally taken by governments to regulate their economic activities such as taxation, environmental and labor legislation as well as normal measures for the maintenance of public safety, are not intended to be covered by this provision unless they discriminate against the holder of the guarantee. In defining these measures, the Agency's practice would not be meant to prejudice the rights of a member country or of investors under bilateral investment treaties, other treaties and international law.

Does this definition strike you as too broad, too narrow or just about right?

(3) The unusual, indeed unique, voting provisions in the MIGA are described at pages 18-19 of the Commentary:

> 63. The voting structure of the Agency reflects the view that Category One and Category Two countries have an equal stake in foreign investment, that cooperation between them is essential, and that both groups of countries should, when all eligible countries become members, have equal voting power (50/50). It is also recognized that a member's voting power should reflect its relative capital subscription. The Convention, therefore, provides that each member is to have 177 membership votes plus one subscription vote for each share of stock held by it (Article 39(a)). The number of membership votes is computed so as to ensure that if all [World] Bank members joined the Agency, developing countries as a group would have the same voting power as developed countries as a group. In order to protect the minority group before such equality is reached, this group would receive, during the three years after entry into force of the convention, supplementary votes which would allow it to have as a group 40 percent of the total voting power. These supplementary votes would be distributed among the members of the group concerned in proportion to their relative subscription votes and would be automatically increased or decreased, as the case may be, so as to maintain the 40 percent voting power of the group (Article 39(b)). Even during the transition period, such supplementary votes would be canceled whenever the group reached 40 percent of the total voting power through subscription and membership votes. In any case, supplementary votes would be canceled at the end of the three-year period. During this three-year period, all decisions of the Council and the Board would be taken by a special majority of at least

two-thirds of the total voting power representing at least fifty-five percent of total subscriptions, except if a specific decision was subject to a higher majority under the Convention, in which case, the higher majority would be controlling (Article 39(d)). An example of the latter would be certain amendments to the Convention (Article 59(a)).

64. During the third year after entry into force of the Convention, the Council is required under Article 39(c) to review the allocation of shares and to be guided in its decisions by three principles: (a) the voting power of members is to reflect actual subscriptions and membership votes; (b) the shares originally allocated to countries which have not signed the Convention at the time of the review are to be made available for reallocation so as to make possible voting parity between developing and developed members; and (c) the Council will take appropriate measures to facilitate the members' subscriptions to the shares allocated to them. The purpose of the reallocation is in time to achieve voting parity between both groups on the basis of relative subscription and membership votes.[54]

---

[54] For further comment on the MIGA Convention, see I.F.I. Shihata, MIGA And Foreign Investment (1988). Shihata, *The Multilateral Investment Guarantee Agency*, 20 Int'l Law. 485 (1986); Shihata, *MIGA: A Fresh Investment For Cooperation*, 26 EFTA Bull. 6-7 (1985). Also, in 1970 an Inter-Arab Investment Guarantee Corporation was established. For an early description of this arrangement, see *Arab Investment Guarantee Corporation — A Regional Investment Insurance Guarantee Corporation*, 6 J. World Trade L. 185 (1972).

CHAPTER **10**

THE INTERNATIONAL MONETARY SYSTEM[1]

Introduction

As noted by Richard Edwards, "in a strict sense, the international monetary system is not a 'system.' It is a network of formal and informal agreements, arrangements, procedures, and customs which over time have evolved, or been purposefully developed, and which interrelate with each other."[2] Moreover, this "network" is a subject of great complexity, a discussion of which is far beyond the scope of this Chapter. Our purpose here is rather to give a brief survey of some salient aspects of international monetary affairs and to highlight significant legal issues.

As we saw in Chapter 3, *supra*, money and goods are inextricably intertwined in international trade. Consider the position of a U.S. exporter who wishes to export its product to a buyer in Europe. If the buyer is located in a country in Eastern Europe, the payment for the U.S. exporter's product might be in the form of some goods the buyer produces. This would constitute a barter arrangement and would not require any international payments.

In most cases, however, the parties to an international sales contract will want to settle their accounts in money. The contract will be denominated in either the currency of the buyer or the seller. That decision is a function of who is to take the exchange risk. (See Chapter 1, page 28, note 2.) Then the party whose currency *is not chosen* will have to use his own currency to purchase the currency of the contract. For example, if the seller is a U.S. firm and the buyer a German firm and the contract is denominated in dollars, the buyer in Germany will use his deutsche marks to purchase dollars (normally from a bank) and pay the seller. If the contract is denominated in deutsche marks, the American seller will normally take the deutsche marks paid to him by the buyer and purchase dollars with which to pay his workers, suppliers, etc.

Note that the bank or some other kind of money changer performs a key function in this sales transaction. To perform it effectively the money changer must keep on hand several types of currencies. These currencies, however, may fluctuate widely in value, and these changes in value may have a profound effect on international trade. For example, if the United States persistently imports more from Germany than it exports — thus running a deficit in its balance of trade with Germany — and Germany exports more to the United States than it imports — thus running a surplus in its balance of trade with the U.S. — the value of the dollar, relative to the deutsche mark, will decline and that of the deutsche mark,

---

[1] We are grateful to Professor Cynthia C. Lichtenstein for helpful comments regarding this chapter.

[2] R. Edwards, Jr., International Monetary Collaboration, Article xxii (1985).

relative to the dollar, will increase, at least in the absence of countervailing capital flows or in the absence of governmental intervention to maintain currency values at a stable ratio of exchange.

The effect of this decline in the value of the dollar is to make German imports more expensive for U.S. citizens because they must pay more dollars to buy the same number of deutsche marks. Conversely it will be cheaper for citizens of Germany or the citizens of other countries with highly valued currencies to import U.S. goods. Leaving aside for the moment a host of other variables, such as the quality of U.S. and German goods, if the value of the dollar declines and that of the mark increases, the balance of trade will begin to shift in favor of the United States.

If, however, there is governmental intervention by a central bank, the exchange rate between the U.S. dollar and the deutsche mark may not change. Thus, for example, if the Federal Reserve Bank, as the U.S. monetary authority, intervenes in the foreign exchange market to buy up the excess dollars, the value of the dollar in relation to the deutsche mark will not change. In order for the Federal Reserve to purchase dollars, however, it must sell gold or convertible foreign exchange. This requires that the U.S. government maintain reserves of gold and foreign currency. If the reserves are inadequate to the task, the Federal Reserve will have to borrow, either from other countries, from commercial banks, or, since World War II, from the International Monetary Fund. The net result of this activity may be a deflationary impact on the U.S. economy.

As we shall see later in this Chapter, an issue that economists heatedly debate is whether fixed or floating exchange rates are superior. But as Kenneth Dam has pointed out:

> The term "fixed rates" is sometimes misunderstood by those unfamiliar with the foreign exchange market. All exchange rates are determined in the marketplace, between willing buyers and sellers (though sometimes national foreign exchange controls preclude some people from buying and force other people to sell.) But under a fixed rate regime, national monetary authorities enter the market either on the buying or the selling side to assure that the market rate bears a close relationship to an officially specified rate. This latter rate is ofter referred to as the official rate, and the effect of such exchange market intervention is to peg the market rate to the official rate. If there is no obligation to intervene, exchange rates are said to float, and the system is said to be a floating (or fluctuating) rate system.[3]

Be that as it may, floating exchange rates do create a substantial measure of uncertainty for the traders of goods. In particular, the seller who enters a contract denominated in the buyer's currency will be concerned lest that currency depreciate sharply between the date of the contract and the date payment is due. To guard against this contingency, the seller may resort to hedging in the foreign exchange markets with futures contracts. While the principal reason for the adoption of a fixed exchange rate system at Bretton Woods was to prevent the competitive devaluations that contributed so significantly to the great depression of the 1930s, fixed exchange rates, it was also thought, would avoid the transaction costs of

---

[3] K. W. Dam, The Rules Of The Game 8 (1981).

hedging as well as the general uncertainty associated with fluctuating rates, thereby facilitating international trade. For reasons we consider below, however, this certainty and stability have proven to be elusive goals, in part because they have come into conflict with the desire of states to pursue domestic economic and social goals with minimal outside interference.

Nevertheless, it was primarily the competitive devaluations of currencies, and the proliferation of exchange controls, in the 1930s and the devastating effect that those measures had on world trade that led the allies, after the war, to construct a new international monetary system at Bretton Woods, New Hampshire.

Against this background we turn to a brief history of the proceedings at Bretton Woods, focusing especially on the problems that led the nations of the world to agree on the need for a new approach. Next we undertake a conspectus of the International Monetary Fund Agreement, exploring the original understanding of the drafters, the collapse of the original system, and its reform. Then we consider the system in operation, highlighting such matters as convertibility, regulation of national exchange controls, the problem of liquidity, and Fund stand-by arrangements. Lastly, we examine some examples of the Fund Agreement in U.S. courts, with a side glance at court decisions in other countries.

[Note. To better understand the ensuing discussion the reader should return to Chapter 3 and review the materials there concerning the operation of foreign exchange markets, the effects of governmental intervention in those markets and the system of balance of payments accounting. These subjects are discussed at pages 199 through 210.]

[A] Before Bretton Woods

The period before Bretton Woods can be usefully divided into two parts. The precise time the first began is uncertain, but it ended with the start of World War I and is generally regarded as encompassing the life of the gold standard. The second is the twenty years between the two world wars and is commonly associated with the gold exchange standard, although, as pointed out by Kenneth Dam,[4] that system actually was in operation only from roughly 1925 to 1931.

The gold standard is the quintessential example of a fixed rate system.[5] Moreover, at least in theory if not in practice, the gold standard constituted a self–adjusting system whereby balance of payments deficits were automatically corrected. The gold standard allowed for the free import and export of gold without limitation. Moreover, national treasuries would accept gold bullion and turn it into gold coins as well as reverse the process upon demand. The gold standard also served the functions of backing the official national currency and permitting circulation of an official gold coin.

The cornerstone of the gold standard was the right of a private party to move freely from gold to currency and back again and to freely import or export gold. The government, through its central bank, facilitated such transactions by redeeming at a fixed rate and without limit the official currency in gold coin. Britain played the key role under the gold standard. A large trading nation, Britain

---

[4] K. W. Dam, The Rules Of The Game 6 (1981).

[5] Much of the discussion that follows relies heavily on Dam, *supra*, Note 2, at 24–70.

was also the center for the world's organized commodities markets, especially the world's gold market. It also was the world's principal creditor nation with over 50 percent of its current savings going into foreign investment in some years. Because of these and other factors sterling was widely used as the currency in which international obligations were discharged, even between third countries. The Bank of England served as central banker to the world, and London as a financial center was the principal source of liquidity for the international monetary system of the time.

The key attribute of the gold standard, however, was not gold flows but fixed exchange rates. During the time of the gold standard, rates were truly fixed, not just pegged, subject to change, as they were under the Bretton Woods system. From 1897 to 1914, there were no changes of parities between the currencies of the United States, Britain, France, and Germany along with a number of smaller European countries.

The most important contributor to the success of the gold standard, however, was not fixed exchange rates, which, like gold itself, were regarded as a means and not an end. Rather, the most crucial factor was the great expansion of trade and the flow of private foreign investment that took place during the period the gold standard was in effect. Despite its many successes the gold standard era came to an abrupt halt with the outbreak of World War I. Efforts to reconstruct it after the war ultimately proved a failure, and the period between the wars was an unstable one for international monetary affairs.

At the end of World War I only the United States was firmly on the gold standard. Among the major European belligerents, only Britain had a currency strong enough to make a return to the prewar parities thinkable. Nonetheless, although exchange ratios between the dollar and the pound had been effectively pegged during the war, the pound floated from 1919 to 1925. Under this float the pound first depreciated against the dollar and then gained in value up to the reestablished previous parity. Currencies of other major belligerents, however, depreciated beyond any possibility of stabilization at the prewar parity.

In 1925 Britain removed its embargo on the export of gold. The effect of this was to put Britain back on the gold standard at the prewar parity with the United States, with a resultant overvaluation of the pound. The devastating consequences for the British economy of this return to the gold standard with an overvalued pound was compounded by the French franc's stabilization at an undevalued rate. By 1928, moreover, most of the other principal countries of the world seeking to stabilize their currencies, had returned to the gold standard. This revival of the gold standard, however, did not last long. It had depended on large-scale U.S. capital exports, which helped to provide the stabilizing countries with the required liquidity. In 1928 diversion of funds into short-term financing of the New York Stock exchange boom brought this flow of capital exports to a virtual halt. The decline in U.S. capital exports, along with the growth of French reserves and their conversion into gold, brought substantial pressure to bear on the British pound. Because Britain's gold reserves were inadequate, and Britain suffered from an overvalued currency as well, the Bank of England began to lose substantial amounts of gold so that, in 1931, the British government suspended payments of gold against legal tender currency, thereby leaving the gold standard.

With the suspension of gold payments, sterling depreciated sharply against all gold standard currencies. The currencies of countries in the British Commonwealth, as well as those of countries that held their reserves primarily in sterling, depreciated in tandem with the pound. The British had effected a devaluation of their currency by letting sterling float. In 1932 Britain decided to create an Exchange Equalization Account, which permitted intervention in the foreign exchange markets while insulating the domestic money supply from the otherwise direct influence of those transactions. In effect Britain had turned to a managed float of its currency. This set a precedent for later developments, as did the United Kingdom's purposeful insulation of its domestic economy from the international monetary system.

For its part, the United States, through the incoming Roosevelt Administration, decided to bring about a depreciation of the dollar in foreign exchange markets in order to increase foreign demand, especially for internationally traded agricultural commodities, and thereby force up prices. Early in its term the Administration had shown its intention to manage the foreign exchange value of the dollar by imposing exchange controls and a gold export embargo, thereby taking the dollar off the gold standard, and by ordering delivery of private holdings of gold coin, bullion, and certificates to the Federal Reserve. In order to further his Administration's currency depreciation policy, Roosevelt next launched a gold buying program and intentionally undermined the London World Economic Conference of 1933, which had been the forum for the negotiation of a stabilization arrangement among the United States, Britain, and the gold standard countries.

The gold-buying program proved successful in depreciating the dollar against gold as well as against the gold standard currencies, and in late January 1934 the president acted to peg the gold price at $35 per ounce. With the return of the United States to the gold standard, the world was effectively divided into monetary blocks. Upon collapse of the 1933 World Economic Conference, European countries adhering to the gold standard had formed a "gold block" and those countries whose currencies tended to float with sterling formed a "sterling bloc." The gold block currencies were considerably overvalued with respect to both sterling area currencies and the dollar. When Belgium devalued its currency by 28 percent in March 1935, and France left the gold standard in September 1936, the attempt to remain on the gold standard collapsed.

Because devaluation was a sensitive political issue in France, the French Government sought some kind of international arrangement to accompany its devaluation. The result was the so-called Tripartite Agreement, actually a series of separate declarations by the French, U.S. and British governments. This represented a move toward multilateralism and toward a recognition that exchange rates were a matter of international and not merely domestic concern. Although the agreement did facilitate cooperation among exchange authorities, it ultimately was unsuccessful as a stabilizing mechanism. The French franc resumed its depreciation in 1937. The sterling-dollar rate remained relatively stable until mid-1938 and then was pegged through foreign exchange intervention until late August 1939 just before the outbreak of World War II.

Perhaps the most serious departure from the pre-1914 gold standard during the interwar years was the attempt to break the link between domestic economic conditions and the international economy through exchange controls. During the 1930s, by use of direct controls on private transactions, many governments attempted to prevent changes in international price levels from generating payment imbalances. Specifically, they required exporters and other recipients of foreign exchange to surrender their foreign exchange earnings to the central bank where it would be made available at an official rate of exchange to private parties. It was, in effect, a rationing scheme for foreign exchange, whose price no longer reflected supply and demand. The motivation behind it was to allow governments to pursue inflationary policies while avoiding the losses in gold that would otherwise occur. Exchange controls tended to discriminate against capital transactions in favor of trade transactions because of the notion that the gold standard, or in its absence any existing set of exchange rates, was threatened by rapid movements of short-term money. By the time of Bretton Woods it was the conventional wisdom that government controls on capital transactions were not only compatible with a stable international monetary system but actually a prerequisite to it. The contrast with the pre-1914 system — in which capital flows in and out of Britain were viewed as a principal method of adjustment facilitating the gold standard — is striking.

In his commentary on lessons to be drawn from the interwar experience,[6] Kenneth Dam points out that by the end of the 1930s the gold standard had become a symbol of an undesirable constraint on government management of domestic economies. At the same time periods when the gold standard was not generally in effect were regarded as highly unstable. The effort, then, of those who sought, during World War II, to design a new international monetary system was to gain the fixed rate benefits of the gold standard without subjecting national economies to its constraints. According to Dam, in seeking to fulfill this goal, they acted on the basis of conclusions not fully supported by the evidence of the interwar period. Nor did they take into account all of the lessons that the interwar experience afford.

For example, the conventional wisdom of the day believed that the strength of the gold standard lay in its pegging of exchange rates. The breakdown of the gold standard came about, according to this view, not because gold standard discipline on domestic economic policy was lacking but rather because countries allowed their exchange rates to float. This vastly oversimplified analysis of the gold standard and the interwar period led to the Bretton Woods preference for fixed rates and its distaste of floating rates which were viewed as engendering destabilizing speculation and disequilibrating short-term capital flows. The historical evidence for these conclusions is slim.

Another lesson from the interwar period drawn by the drafters of Bretton Woods was that competitive depreciation of currencies is a prime evil to be avoided. The United States and Britain were the offenders most open to this charge.

A primary example of a lesson from the interwar period that wasn't learned by the drafters of Bretton Woods, according to Kenneth Dam, was the inherent vulnerability of any gold exchange standard. The major vulnerabilities are

---

[6] K.W. Dam, *supra*, Note 2, at 60-70.

twofold. One is the weakness arising out of the ability of a central bank to vary the proportions of foreign exchange and gold, held as reserve assets, and the other is the ability of a central bank to shift its foreign exchange assets held in the form of one reserve currency (*e.g.*, pounds sterling) to another reserve currency (*e.g.*, the dollar).

With respect to the first vulnerability, the primary risk for a central bank holding its reserves in foreign exchange rather than gold was that the reserve currency might depreciate in terms of gold. Such a depreciation might take place either because of a devaluation of the reserve currency in terms of gold or because the country whose currency was being held as a reserve — sometimes called a "reserve center" — elected to leave the gold standard, permitting its currency to float downward.

The probability at any given time of the depreciation of a reserve currency determines the willingness of central banks to hold obligations denominated in that currency in preference to gold. The probability of depreciation, in turn, depends on three principal factors. The first is the domestic economic policies of the reserve currency countries; if they are inflationary, depreciation is likely to occur. The second is the present level of the exchange rate, which, by definition under a gold standard, is a fixed rate against other currencies on that standard. If the reserve currency is significantly overvalued, then depreciation is a strong possibility. The third factor is the ratio of the reserve center's liabilities relative to its reserve assets (*i.e.*, its ability to defend the value of its currency). The liabilities of a reserve center consist of obligations of the government held by foreign central banks as well as private obligations, such as private bank deposits or commercial paper, readily convertible into gold. The reserve centers holdings of gold and convertible foreign exchange are its reserve assets. As the liabilities of a reserve center grow too large relative to its reserve assets, the willingness of foreign central banks to hold that currency may lessen or even disappear.

This last factor was the major cause of Britain's abandoning the gold standard in 1931. Although Britain maintained a generally conservative domestic economic policy during the 1925-31 period, and although it managed to prevent the ratio of net liabilities to gold from rising until 1931, its net liabilities substantially exceeded its gold reserve. During a particularly difficult moment in this respect there was, in effect, a run on the British gold bank.

Britain's difficulties were compounded by the second major vulnerability of the gold standard, *i.e.*, the ability of a central bank to shift its foreign exchange assets held in the form of claims on one reserve center to claims on another reserve center. Increasingly during the 1925-31 period both foreign private institutions and central banks held part of their foreign exchange reserves in New York. Although this reduction in foreign balances in London lowered the net liquid liabilities of Britain and thus future claims on British gold, it also tended to reduce the Bank of England's gold holdings. The ability of foreign central banks to convert sterling balances into gold resulted in a decreasing percentage of reserves held in foreign exchange, whether in London or New York. The resultant demands on gold created a gold shortage and a liquidity crisis. Intergovernmental lending through central banks proved unequal to the task of saving the system under these conditions.

[B]   A Conspectus of the IMF Agreement

[1]   The Original Understanding

It should be remembered that the plans for postwar international economic organization envisaged separate international institutions for an international monetary fund, an international bank for reconstruction and development, and an international trade organization.[7] As we have seen in Chapter 4, *supra*, efforts to establish an international trade organization failed because the Truman Administration feared that the Senate would refuse to give its advice and consent to ratification. The General Agreement for Tariffs and Trade, an Executive Agreement instead of a treaty, took its place.

The International Bank for Reconstruction and Development (the World Bank), created at Bretton Woods, had as its principal purpose the providing of capital to the war ravaged European economies and for the economic advancement of the developing countries. It is the sister institution to the International Monetary Fund.

The primary movers in planning an international monetary organization were the British and U.S. governments. Each advanced quite different plans. One plan was the product of Harry Dexter White, Assistant to the U.S. Secretary of the Treasury; the other was the creation of the renowned British economist, Lord John Maynard Keynes, a special consultant to the British Treasury. The two plans were in agreement on a number of points but also contained major differences.

Points of agreement included the need for a new international institution staffed by professional economists; the desirability of relatively stable exchange rates as compared to floating rates; the need for a measure of international control over devaluations; and the avoidance of competitive devaluations; the adoption by countries of policies that would achieve balance of payments equilibrium over the long term; and international codes of good conduct banning many of the restrictive and retaliatory practices of the interwar years, either in the monetary arrangements themselves or in other instruments like the proposed trade charter.

As to differences between the two plans, Professor Edwards has observed:

> The most serious differences between the two plans related to the manner in which resources would be provided to countries facing balance-of-payments deficits and the magnitude of the resources to be provided. Lord Keynes, representing a prospective deficit nation, wanted a substantial volume of credit available at the request of a member. In his plan, entitled "Proposals for an International Currency (or Clearing) Union," the international institution would provide this credit by creating a new form of international money, called "bancor." The Currency Union was conceived as a central bank for government central banks. The Union would extend overdraft rights to deficit countries and would credit surplus countries with an equivalent amount in bancor. Then, when a surplus country went into deficit, it could use its bancor balance to offset this deficit. The aggregate total of overdraft rights to be authorized under Lord Keynes' plan was estimated at U.S. $26 billion. Since

---

[7] The discussion in this Section of the Chapter draws heavily from R. Edwards, Jr., *supra*, Note 1, at 4-43.

in practice the only major country likely to run a significant surplus in the immediate postwar period was the United States, the plan was, in effect, a prescription for a $26 billion long-term line of credit from the United States to the rest of the world.

For the United States, as the prime potential creditor, the idea of a $26 billion line of credit was unacceptable. It feared that an overdraft approach, even with safeguards, might cause the United States to lose control over the size of its obligations. The United States wanted to limit the magnitude of its liability to finance the adjustment processes of other countries. And it wanted authority in the international institution to require deficit countries to adopt policies that would restore their international accounts to balance. The limited liability would be protected by deficit states obtaining the currencies they needed to settle international accounts, not simply by means of credits from other members monitored by an international institution, but instead from a finite fund owned and managed by the international institution itself and composed of gold and national currencies. Each member of the organization, which Mr. White called a "Stabilization Fund," would contribute an agreed amount of its own currency and gold. These resources would form a pool on which a deficit country could draw if it were prepared to comply with the conditions imposed by the international authority. The total amount of the fund would be at least U.S. $5 billion. The contributions of the member countries would be determined by a formula related to an appraisal of their general economic strength, with the obligation of the United States being less than $3.5 billion.[8]

After two years of negotiations, differences between the two plans were resolved at Bretton Woods in July 1944, when 44 nations adopted the Articles of Agreement for the International Monetary Fund. These Articles most closely followed the White plan. However, as we shall see below, the First Amendment to the Agreement in 1969 adopted many of the features of Keynes' "bancor" proposal. Also, as we shall see in the next section of this Chapter, a Second Amendment to the IMF's Articles, which entered into force on April 1, 1978, rejected a fundamental premise of the Articles of Agreement as originally drafted, namely, the necessity for relatively stable exchange rates, and ushered in an era of floating rates.

As set forth in Article I of the Articles of Agreement, the purposes of the IMF are:

(i) To promote international monetary cooperation through a permanent institution which would provide the machinery for consultation and collaboration on international monetary problems.

(ii) To facilitate the expansion and balanced growth of international trade and to contribute thereby to the promotion and maintenance of high levels of employment and real income and to the development of the productive resources of all members as a primary objective of economic policy.

(iii) To promote exchange stability, to maintain orderly exchange arrangements among members, and to avoid competitive exchange devaluations.

---

[8] *Id.*, at 7.

(iv) To assist in the establishment of a multilateral system of payments for current transactions between members and in the elimination of foreign exchange restrictions which hamper the growth of world trade.

(v) To give confidence to members by making the general resources of the Fund temporarily available to them under adequate safeguards, thus providing them with an opportunity to correct maladjustments in their balance of payments without resorting to measures destructive of national or international prosperity.

(vi) In accordance with the above, to shorten the duration and lessen the degree of disequilibrium in the international balances of payments of members.

Similarly, the "recognizing" clause at the beginning of new Article IV states as the goals to be sought by the International Monetary System, the following:

Recognizing that the essential purpose of the international monetary system is to provide a framework that facilitates the exchange of goods, services, and capital among countries, and that sustains sound economic growth, and that a principal objective is the continuing development of the orderly underlying conditions that are necessary for financial and economic stability, each member undertakes. . . .

The primary functions that flow from these purposes are threefold: "(1) administration of a large pool of monetary assets to which members could have access to finance balance of payments deficits; (2) administration of a system of 'special drawing rights;' and (3) administration of the 'rules of good conduct' relating to exchange rate arrangements, currency controls, and other matters, and of a system of consultations on domestic and international policies affecting economic growth, employment, and monetary and financial stability."[9]

Under the original Articles of Agreement, the Fund sought to limit members' tendency to resort to currency devaluations as a reaction to balance of payments difficulties. Before 1978, the Articles required each member to establish a "par value" for its currency expressed either in terms of gold or in terms of a U.S. dollar of specified gold content. Thus, the Articles established an official exchange rate for each member's currency, with an allowed variance of 1%. To maintain the agreed par value, a member had a choice. It could either intervene in foreign markets by buying or selling foreign currencies or it could impose currency controls. Only if a member's balance of payments were in "fundamental disequilibrium" (an obvious open-ended criterion) could its par value be changed (*i.e.*, devaluated). Such a change could be made only after "consultation" with the IMF.

The consultation requirement allowed the Fund to express its views on the desirability of a change in par value and to suggest other measures, including changes in domestic economic policies (*e.g.*, control of inflation, adjustment of development priorities and fiscal restraint), to help the members resolve their problems. If the Fund objected to a change in par value, a member would be ineligible to use the resources of the Fund unless the Fund decided to the contrary. As we shall see in the next Section of this chapter, these arrangements did not always work satisfactorily in practice.

---

[9] *Id.*, at 12.

As noted above, the First Amendment to the Articles of Agreement in 1969 created "special drawing rights" or SDRs, which expanded the supply of currency available to solve balance of payments difficulties. With the creation of SDRs, the General Resources Account of the Fund consisted of national currencies, special drawing rights, and gold. The contribution of each of the original members to this account was determined by a formula designed to reflect the importance of the member's currency in the international economy. This contribution or quota determined the size of subscriptions to the Fund, drawing rights in the General Resources Account, the share in the allocation of SDRs, and voting power. The Fund reviews quotas at least every five years in order to determine whether they should be increased or decreased.

The SDR is a form of fiat money issued by the Fund and usable only by monetary authorities and other official agencies. Under Articles XV-XXV, members participating in the Special Drawing Rights Department agree to exchange SDRs for a freely usable currency, *i.e.*, a currency widely used for making payments for international transactions and widely traded in the principal exchange markets. Under applicable procedures, a holder of SDRs notifies the Fund that it wishes to exchange SDRs for one of several national currencies recognized by the Fund as freely usable. The Fund then designates a participating member to accept the SDRs and to provide a freely usable currency in exchange. The value of the SDR is determined by an index based on a basket of national currencies. The exchange rate between the SDR and the designated currency is based on the market rate exchange rate between that currency and the index. There are also limits on the circumstances under which SDRs may be drawn upon. There are also repayment requirements.

Under Article VIII, Section 9(a), and Article XXX, Section (d), the Fund places limits on a member's use of exchange controls. A member is not permitted, unless it has the approval of the Fund, to impose restrictions on the making of payments and transfers for current transactions (*e.g.*, payments on letters of credit for the importation of goods). No such restrictions, however, apply to transfers of capital. Moreover, even as to current transactions, Article XIV allows a member to avail itself of "transitional arrangements" under which it may "maintain and adapt" restrictions that were in effect when it became a member.

Although member countries are to eliminate restrictions on current transactions as soon as they are able, there are still two types of IMF members: "Article XIV countries" and "Article VIII countries." As of 1985 about three-fifths of the IMF members had not yet accepted the obligations of Article VIII. To be sure Article XIV does place limits on a member's currency controls — they can be used only for balance of payments purposes and must be controls in place when the country becomes a member. Moreover, there is no authority to devise wholly new controls. Lastly, Article VIII, Section 2, provides that other countries shall not enforce contracts violating exchange controls maintained by members consistently with the Articles of Agreement, an Article whose effect has been the subject of considerable litigation in U.S. courts.

At this writing, the IMF has 152 members which include most members of the United Nations (the Soviet Union is not currently a member but is contemplating membership). Under the Articles of Agreement the Fund has a legal status separate from its members and enjoys substantial immunities. The Fund has two primary organs: The Board of Governors and the Executive Board. Each member appoints one Governor to the Board of Governors. There are 20 Executive Directors on the Executive Board, with five being appointed by the members having the largest quotas, namely, in order, the United States, the United Kingdom, the Federal Republic of Germany, France, and Japan. The remaining 15 are elected for two year terms in accordance with a complex rating formula. In accordance with Article XII, the Board of Governors has delegated extensive powers to the Executive Board.

Voting in the IMF is on a weighted basis, depending on national quotas and SDRs, rather than on a "one nation, one vote" basis. Although most decisions are to be taken by majority vote, special voting procedures apply to certain actions of the Fund. In practice most decisions have been taken on the basis of consensus rather than formal votes.

The head of the Fund's secretariat is the Managing Director, who is selected by the Executive Directors. The Managing Director and the secretariat are international civil servants who owe their allegiance to the Fund rather than to any member country.

Collapse and Reform: The Jamaica Agreement and After

As noted in the previous section of this Chapter, the original Articles of Agreement of the IMF established a system of exchange rates based on par values.[10] These par values were stated in terms of gold or the U.S. dollar of the gold weight and fineness in effect in 1944. When the Bretton Woods Agreement was negotiated, the U.S. dollar was the most widely used currency in international transactions and was subject to the fewest restrictions. During the period from the date the original Articles entered into force until August 15, 1971, the United States bought and sold gold in transactions with foreign monetary authorities, on their demand, at prices based on $35 ω ounce. Although a member could, with the approval of the Fund, change the par value of its currency to correct a fundamental disequilibrium in its balance of payments, the Fund encouraged members to attempt to correct a disequilibrium by other means. These included, for example, control of government budget deficits, control of price and wage inflation, and control of the size of the domestic money supply.

In practice the system did not always work as envisaged in original Article IV. Many developing countries never established par values for their currencies. Some countries failed consistently to maintain market exchange rates within prescribed margins. The impact of those deviations from the system — when engaged in by developing countries or smaller industrial countries — was not significant. Eventually, however, strains on the parity relationship among currencies of the larger industrial countries led to the collapse of the par value system.

The major strains on the par value system began in the 1960s. At that time the British pound sterling, the French franc, the deutsche mark, and other major currencies became convertible, and restrictions on capital movements were reduced. Many widely used currencies were devalued or revalued. Political as well

---

[10] The following discussion is derived largely from *id.*, at 491-535.

as economic considerations significantly affected the magnitude and timing of some of these changes.

In particular, a 1967 devaluation of the pound sterling of 14.3 percent took place in a crisis atmosphere, since at the time many countries held sterling in their reserves, and the devaluation demonstrated the risks of holders relying on the stability of par values. More important, in terms of undermining the Bretton Woods system, was the deterioration during the 1960s of the U.S. balance of payments because of the costs of the war in Vietnam, an ambitious social program —a "war on poverty"— massive U.S. foreign investments, the costs of NATO, changes in the world economy, and other problems. The dollar was badly overvalued, and a major devaluation of the dollar or revaluation of other currencies was clearly called for.

On the other hand, a substantial dollar devaluation would have resulted in a major loss in the value of their reserves by the industrialized countries. All held the bulk of their monetary reserves in dollars. Moreover, continuing U.S. deficits were the principal source of growth in those reserves. The deficits, in other words, were essential to growth in international liquidity. The system was in crisis. The United States took a variety of steps to counter the downward pressure on the dollar in exchange markets, including intervention in exchange markets, controls on capital movements such as the interest equalization tax and controls on the financing of foreign investment by U.S. residents. These proved unavailing, and demands to convert dollars into gold grew exponentially. Finally, on August 15, 1971, President Nixon dramatically announced several decisions. Because of the increased demand for gold, the United States would "suspend temporarily the convertibility of the dollar into gold or other reserve assets." The United States would not continue to buy or sell foreign currencies in the exchange markets for the purpose of maintaining official parities between the dollar and other currencies. Also, the United States imposed an import tariff surcharge and adopted a wage-price freeze and a cutback in government spending.

Strictly speaking the United States did not violate the IMF Agreement by refusing to buy and sell gold in exchange for dollars. However, when the United States declined freely to buy and sell gold on demand of foreign monetary authorities, it was obligated, under Article IV as it then stood, to intervene in the exchange markets to maintain rates within the required margins of the parity relationships. Other countries also failed to intervene to maintain the established exchange rates. Thereby, they too violated the original Article IV.

Several attempts were thereafter made to preserve the system through realignment of exchange rates. These were unsuccessful in correcting the balance of payments problem of the United States and Britain. Finally, on March 16, 1973, the European Economic Community and the so-called Group of Ten (consisting of the leading industrial countries) jointly announced that the central banks of their countries would withdraw from the role of buying and selling currencies in the markets in order to maintain stable rates with the dollar. With this action the Bretton Woods par value system collapsed.

The collapse ushered in an era of floating rates. The float, however, was always "managed" in that central banks tried to maintain some control over rate movements. These efforts were taken unilaterally and sometimes were not even

832 INT'L BUSINESS & ECONOMIC RELATIONS

publicly announced. The exchange rate policies of IMF members differed substantially and highlighted the need for negotiations on a new Article IV. These began in 1972.

France and the United States took the lead in these negotiations with diametrically opposed positions. France favored a return to a system of stable exchange rates. By contrast the United States strongly favored an unequivocal right of IMF countries to float their currencies without the requirement of special authorization. The United States supported provisions that would permit it to rely primarily on private markets rather than actions of government officials to determine exchange rates, while reserving the right to intervene to maintain order in the exchange markets.

Negotiations attempting to resolve these differences between the French and U.S. positions continued into 1975. Finally, on November 17, 1975, France and the United States announced that they had reached agreement on a new Article IV. The Interim Committee of the Board of Governors of the International Monetary Fund adopted the new Article IV, in slightly revised form, at its meeting in Kingston, Jamaica, in January 1976. It was incorporated into the Second Amendment to the Articles of Agreement of the IMF and is now in force.

NOTES AND QUESTIONS

(1) Consider the terms of new Article IV in Documentary Supplement and address the following questions.

    (a) Under Article IV, Section 1, are the United States and other IMF members obligated to promote exchange rate stability? Is the United States obligated to adopt monetary and fiscal measures to reduce its budget and trade deficits?

    (b) Jacques de Larosiere, then Managing Director of the IMF, stated on November 14, 1978, that "a member which persists in inflating rapidly or in growing at a rate far below that of its potential output may not be fulfilling its obligations under Article IV, even though it may not appear to be contributing to exchange market disturbance in some overt way." Was he correct? What provisions of Article IV could be cited in support of this statement?

    (c) Suppose a country in order to finance a large budgetary deficit adopts high interest rate policies that attract savings from abroad and engender expectations of continuing exchange rate appreciation. Could this constitute a violation of Article IV, Section 1?

(2) At present, more IMF members maintain stable rates between their currencies and the currency of at least one other IMF member than use any other technique. Usually the currency pegged against is a convertible currency widely used in international trade, e.g., the U.S. dollar, the French franc, or the British pound. Most of the countries using this arrangement are developing countries. In contrast, currencies that have floated independently from the time of the collapse

of the Bretton Woods exchange rate system include, among others, the U.S. dollar, the Canadian dollar, the Japanese yen and the British pound. Under Article IV, Section 2(b), the Fund has stated as a principle: "Members should take into account in their intervention policies the interests of other members, including those of the countries in whose currencies they intervene." Although the statement uses the precatory "should" rather than the mandatory "shall," it reflects a widely shared view of the proper conduct of market intervention.

(3) Since adoption of the Second Amendment the United States has engaged in several policy shifts regarding when it will intervene to counter disorderly conditions in the exchange markets. At one point the Reagan Administration stated it would intervene only when disorder in exchange markets became "severe." In response to protests from other IMF members the administration returned to the "disorder" test but still did not intervene frequently.

On the other hand, the United States on occasion has agreed with other economically powerful countries to engage in joint action to maintain or change currency exchange rates. For example, in the September 1985 "Plaza Agreement" on economic policy, the so-called G-5 countries (France, the Federal Republic of Germany, Japan, the United Kingdom, and the United States) stated that "exchange rates should better reflect fundamental economic conditions than has been the case" and that "in view of the present and prospective changes in fundamentals, some further orderly appreciation of the main nondollar currencies against the dollar is desirable." The G-5 countries reported that they stood "ready to cooperate more closely to encourage this when to do so would be helpful." Similarly, on February 1987, the G-5 countries plus Canada noted that "[e]xchange rate adjustments have occurred which will contribute importantly in the period ahead to the restoration of a more sustainable pattern of current acounts." They pledged regularly to "examine, using performance indicators, whether current economic developments and trends are consistent with the medium-term objectives and projections and consider the need for remedial action." The objectives and projections specified involved "the following key variables: growth, inflation, current-trade balances, budget performance, monetary conditions, and exchange rates." In conclusion:

> The ministers and governors agreed that the substantial exchange rate change since the Plaza Agreement will increasingly contribute to reducing external imbalances and have now brought their currencies within ranges broadly consistent with underlying economic fundamentals, given the policy commitments summarized in this statement. Further substantial exchange rate shifts among their currencies could damage growth and adjustment prospects in their countries. In current circumstances, therefore, they agreed to cooperate closely to foster stability to exchange rates around current levels.[11]

Have we come full circle, back to the fixed rate regime envisaged at Bretton Woods?

---

[11] Dep't of State Bull., April 1987, at 31-32.

[2]   The System In Operation

Convertibility

It has been suggested that "a paradigm of a freely convertible currency would have the following characteristics:"

(1) The issuing state in no way restricts the right to hold the currency. Both residents and nonresidents are permitted to hold the currency with no restrictions on the amount of the currency held or the form in which it is held (coins, paper money, bank balances, notes).

(2) The issuing state in no way restricts the manner in which the currency can be exchanged by a holder of it for the currency of another state. The issuing state does not restrict the manner in which its currency can be acquired. That is, the currency can be bought and sold in private markets in the issuing state or in other states.

(3) The issuing state in no way restricts the currency for which its currency can be exchanged. It imposes no limits on the foreign currencies that a holder of its currency, whether a resident or a nonresident, may hold, buy, or sell.

(4) The issuing state does not restrict the uses that can be made of its currency by a nonresident holder. That is, a nonresident can use the currency for the same purposes for which a resident holder can lawfully use it.[12]

In contrast a "paradigm of a comprehensive system of exchange controls would have the following characteristics:"

(1) Residents are not permitted to transfer the state's currency to nonresidents except with the state's permission and this permission, in a paradigm regime, is granted on a case-by-case basis. Nonresident holders of the state's currency are not permitted to transfer their holdings to other nonresidents except with permission.

(2) Nonresident holders of the state's currency are not permitted to transfer their holdings to residents except in approved transactions. A nonresident holding the state's currency may be "blocked" from using the currency even for purchase of goods and services in the issuing state. The uses that a nonresident holder may lawfully make of the currency are circumscribed by regulations.

(3) Residents are not permitted to hold foreign currencies except with the state's permission and this permission, in a paradigm regime, is granted on a case-by-case basis. A resident acquiring foreign currency (for example, in an export transaction) is required to sell that currency to a government agency, licensed dealer, or the central bank. Foreign currency must be purchased through such an agency, licensed dealer, or central bank. Government policies determine the availability of foreign currencies for particular uses.[13]

No currency currently fits exactly within these paradigms. The U.S. dollar, the deutsche mark, and the British pound come closest to the paradigm of a freely

---

[12] R. Edwards, J.R., *supra*, Note 1, at 381.
[13] *Id.*, at 382.

convertible currency. The currencies of some developing countries and socialist countries almost match the paradigm of a currency under comprehensive exchange controls. Most currencies fall somewhere in between the two extremes. This portion of the Chapter briefly considers the impact of the IMF Articles on the concept of "convertibility."

As we have seen earlier in this Chapter, a majority of IMF members have not yet accepted the obligations of Article VIII, Sections 2, 3, and 4. They rely instead on the "transitional arrangements" of Article XIV, Section 2. However, those members who have accepted the obligations of Article VIII include the larger free market industrialized countries of the world as well as many other countries. Section 2(a) of Article VIII prohibits, in the absence of approval by the Fund, a member from imposing restrictions on the making of payments and transfers for current international transactions. The purpose of this prohibition is to ensure that currency restrictions in a purchaser's state do not prevent or delay receipt of payment by the foreign seller or creditor.

Section 3 of Article VIII prohibits members, except as authorized by the Articles of Agreement or by the Fund, to engage in discriminatory currency arrangements or multiple currency practices. Different exchange rates for different classes of transactions can have essentially the same effect as taxes and subsidies upon trade in the goods or services affected. Multiple exchange rates may also be used by national authorities to limit the amount of foreign exchange provided for imports of low priority items.

QUESTIONS

Consider the text of Sections 2 and 3 of Article VIII [14] in light of the questions set forth below.

(1) Under Section 2(a) of Article VIII, may a member country prohibit its residents from using its own currency to settle current international transactions if that currency is demanded by a foreign seller?

(2) Suppose a member limits the importation of particular commodities, or requires that exporters and importers insure all risk of loss with local insurance companies. Would these actions violate Section 2(a)?

(3) Note that Section 2(a) regulates only payments and transfers for current international transactions. Section 3 of Article VI explicitly permits member country regulation of international capital movements. Article XXX(d) defines payments for current transactions.

Assume that a local company, planning to expand its operations, purchases new machinery from abroad and decides to have the installation done by a foreign firm. Are payments made for the machinery and its installation payments for "current" transactions?

---

[14] Documentary Supplement.

(4) In 1982 many residents of the United States held certificates of deposit issued by Mexican commercial banks denominated in U.S. dollars and payable in Mexico. In regulations effective August 13, 1982, Mexican authorities decreed "pesofication" of these certificates, *i.e.*, the obligations were to be paid in pesos at a rate of 70 pesos to the dollar. This rate was different from other exchange rates between the peso and the dollar at the time — the lawful free rate exceeded 105 pesos to the dollar. Under Section 3 of Article VIII did the Mexican authorities require IMF approval for these actions?

Regulation of National Exchange Controls

Under Article VIII, a member that believes it must impose restrictions, multiple currency practices, or discriminatory arrangements prohibited by Section 2(a) or Section 3 can seek to obtain the approval of the Fund. Fund approval renders such actions consistent with the obligations of these sections. Members that have opted for the transitional regime of Article XIV must get the Fund's approval for "new" restrictions. Failure to obtain approval from the Fund may subject a member to the sanctions applicable to violations generally.

Fund approval is often sought for balance of payments purposes. The Fund has indicated that it will grant approval only when it is satisfied that balance of payments measures are necessary and that their use will be temporary.

A practice the Fund has often approved is currency restrictions affecting foreign travel. Restrictions on the amount of exchange to be used by a resident for travel are adopted not only to control travel expenditures but primarily to prevent avoidance of controls on capital movements, *e.g.*, the resident while abroad purchases an investment security for cash.

Even in an emergency situation the IMF's policy is not to approve restrictions unless the particular measures are reasonable. For example, the Fund reacted negatively to Mexico's multiple exchange rate system introduced in 1982, and, through prolonged discussion, induced Mexico to amend its system. As amended the new multiple currency system was approved by the Fund for a temporary period.

The Fund has also approved currency restrictions imposed solely for reasons of national or international security. The Fund has expressly declined, however, to become a forum for the discussion of the political and military considerations leading to enactment of national security measures. Examples of measures approved by the Fund on national security grounds include the restrictions imposed in November 1979 and intensified in April 1980 by the United States against Iran during the hostage crisis.

During the 1960s and early 1970s, the United States took a number of measures designed to control capital flows as a response to balance of payment difficulties. These included, among others, programs to expand exports; the reduction of government expenditures abroad; an Interest Equalization Tax on foreign securities bought by U.S. residents; the Department of Commerce Foreign Direct Investment Controls; and the Federal Reserve Board "Voluntary Foreign Credit Restraint Program." The latter two measures were designed to restrain loans and investments abroad. After the floating of the dollar and other measures taken in

1971 resulted in a flexible exchange rate system, the U.S. Government decided that these measures were no longer necessary and discontinued them.

The Problem of Liquidity

Liquidity becomes a problem, of course, only when there is a lack of it. Perhaps the classic example of lack of liquidity or "illiquidity" is the plight of some U.S. farmers who have thousands of acres of rich farmland but insufficient money in the bank to pay their bills for, say, fertilizers or equipment. Their solution to this problem of illiquidity has been to mortgage some of their land as security for a loan which they then use to pay their bills. Similarly, governments have bills to pay. In international trade, if a country's imports exceed its exports, foreign creditors may want to be paid in their own currency or in a widely internationally used currency. If they accept payment in the importing country's currency, they will want to exchange it for other currencies.

As we have previously seen, a country may wish to maintain the value of its currency by supporting it on the world exchange markets. To support the value of its currency a country uses its monetary reserves to buy its currency on the world exchange markets. This has the effect of increasing the demand for its currency and hence the price of that currency. If a country runs out of reserves, it may seek to borrow from other countries or from international organizations. A principal function of the IMF is to provide this kind of credit to countries with balance of payments problems. If the credit available to countries for this purpose fails to grow with growth in international trade and investment flows, then we can say that there is a problem of international liquidity. Indeed, the lack of international liquidity was a major contributing cause of the great 1930s depression. Also the dependence of the world on U.S. deficits as a source of needed liquidity (the supply of gold was limited) combined with uncertainties regarding the continued value of the dollar which such deficits engendered, was a major cause of the collapse of the IMF par value system.

[3] The Quota System

Most of the resources of the Fund come from the subscriptions or quotas that members are required to pay and, to a lesser extent, from borrowings. A brief description of this quota system follows in the next subsection. These fund resources constitute a pool of assets upon which members can draw to meet balance of payments needs. "Quotas" represent the contributions of member countries to this pool, a contribution determined in accordance with a formula designed to reflect the importance of the member's currency in the world economy. A general review of quotas at least every five years may result in an increase or a decrease of a member country's quota. Also, a member country can request at any time that the Fund adjust its quota. The member's quota determines the size of its subscription to the Fund, drawing rights on the Fund under both regular and special facilities, its share in allocations of special drawing rights, and voting power.

Twenty-five percent of each member's quota must be paid in reserve assets (gold or convertible foreign exchange), the remaining seventy-five percent in the member's own currency. If a member purchases from the IMF, it uses its own currency to purchase the currencies of other members or SDRs held by the General Resources Account of the Fund. Under a prescribed time schedule, a member must buy back its own currency with SDRs or currencies specified by the Fund. When the Fund has holdings of a member's currency not the result of such purchases, and the amount of these holdings is less than the member country's quota, the difference is called the reserve tranche. A member has the option either to use or to retain a reserve tranche position. To make a purchase in the reserve tranche, a member country must have a balance of payments need, but its purchase is not subject to challenge, or to economic policy conditions, or to repurchase requirements.

In addition to the reserve tranche, a member country may make purchases in four credit tranches, each equivalent to twenty-five percent of its quota. For a substantial period of time a member country could make purchases under credit tranche policies only up to 100 percent of its quota. The Fund's Executive Board determines whether the proposed use of the funds purchased would be consistent with the provisions of the Articles and with Fund policies. The uses in all of such cases must be for the support of economic measures designed to overcome a member's balance of payments difficulties. Recently, however, the Fund has waived this limit in response to the need to finance the efforts of some members to remedy structural payments imbalances.

In addition to the credit tranche, the Fund administers the Extended Fund Facility, under which it provides assistance to members to meet their balance of payments deficits for longer periods and in amounts larger in relation to quotas than under the credit tranche. Members receiving assistance under the Extended Fund Facility generally have serious payment imbalances reflective of structural defects in production and trade, and are willing to commit themselves to comprehensive corrective policies over periods of two or three years. The IMF also has a Policy on Enlarged Access to the Fund's resources that permits the Fund to approve stand-by or extended arrangements for a member that needs balance of payments financing in excess of the amount available to it in the four credit tranches or under the Extended Fund Facility.

Finally, the Fund maintains two permanent facilities for specific purposes — the facility for compensatory financing of export fluctuations and the buffer stock financing facility. The compensatory financing facility helps members experiencing temporary shortfalls in export proceeds. The buffer stock financing facility assists the financing of members' contributions to international buffer stocks of primary products when members with balance of payments problems participate in such arrangements under commodity agreements.

The General Arrangements to Borrow

As we saw above the United States and the other major industrial countries have accepted the convertibility obligations of Article VIII, Sections 2, 3, and 4. Shortly after this acceptance it became apparent that these countries might occasionally require large quantities of foreign currencies for interventions in the exchange markets. To meet this need, on January 5, 1962, the IMF Executive Board adopted a formal decision entitled "General Arrangements to Borrow" (GAB).[15]

---

[15] The following discussion of the GAB is derived largely from *id.*, at 287-91.

In its original form the GAB assured the Fund that, in accordance with prescribed conditions, it could borrow from the ten industrial countries [16] that were parties to the GAB if the Fund's General Resources Account needed the currencies to supply a member of the group. Prior to an amendment to the GAB in 1983 the benefits of the arrangement were limited to the Group of Ten. The GAB was designed to ensure that none of these ten members would be denied access to the Fund's resources because the General Resources Account lacked the necessary currencies.

In 1983 the GAB was amended to permit the Fund to finance exchange transactions requested by IMF members that are not members of the Group of Ten if certain conditions are met. These conditions are, however, more demanding than those that apply when the beneficiary is a member of the Group of Ten. The 1983 amendment also authorized the Swiss National Bank to be a participating institution in the GAB, i.e., it can take part in the poll of participants on whether to loan to the Fund and can rely on the credit worthiness of the Fund and not just the beneficiary country for repayment.

If a member country of the IMF wants to obtain funding from the GAB, it first consults the Managing Director of the Fund and then the members of the GAB. The Managing Director in turn consults with the members of the GAB to ascertain the amount they are willing to loan to the Fund in the particular case. After these consultations a "proposal for calls" is drafted. For the proposal to become effective both the participants in the GAB and the IMF's Executive Board must approve it. In the absence of unanimous agreement among the participants, there may be a binding weighted vote taken within the group.

Special Drawing Rights

As we have seen, the First Amendment to the Articles of Agreement in 1969 created special drawing rights or SDRs in order to expand the supply of currency available to solve balance of payments difficulties. In part the creation of the SDR came about because of a realization that the GAB was too ad hoc and only useful for developed countries' liquidity needs.[17]

Prior to creation of the SDR the conventional wisdom was that any new reserves created through the IMF, especially any new reserve asset, had to be "backed" by some other asset such as a claim by the Fund on national governments but not convertible into underlying assets like gold. This lack of backing caused many central and private bankers to view SDRs as "funny money" not fully competitive with gold and reserve currencies as international reserves.

Reluctance to accept the new asset derived in part from the fact that SDRs would not be used directly by deficit countries but rather, like gold, would be used to obtain foreign exchange for market intervention. A creditor country accepting SDRs from a debtor country had to give up convertible currency. Hence, under

---

[16] The ten countries participating in the GAB are: United States, United Kingdom, Canada, France, Italy, Japan, Netherlands, Belgium, Federal Republic of Germany, and Sweden.

[17] Part of this discussion of SDRs is derived from Kenneth Dam, *supra*, Note 2, at 151-168.

Article XXIII, section 1, first, a Fund member was not required to participate in the SDR system, and initially ten members did not become participants.

Under the First Amendment to the Articles of Agreement, a Member was "expected" to use SDRs only in case of a balance of payments need but this need was not made a legal requirement. An SDR use by any participant was legally unchallengeable at the time of use. Only after use could the presence or absence of need be raised as an issue.

In addition to the need requirement other limitations were placed on the use of SDRs that were not present for gold or the dollar. For example, the number of potential holders was strictly limited. From the beginning and to the present day the private sector could not hold SDRs. Only participants in the SDR facility and the Fund itself can hold SDRs. Also, by a qualified majority of 85 percent of the total voting parties, the Fund could permit nonmember countries, nonparticipating members, and "institutions that perform functions of a central bank for more than one member," such as the Bank of International Settlements located in Basle, Switzerland, to hold and use SDRs.

Even among the potential holders of SDRs the types of transactions permitted were strictly limited to the use of SDRs to obtain an equivalent amount of freely usable currency. A participant cannot use SDRs to give foreign aid to another participant, or to lend to it, or to pledge its SDRs as security for a loan.

By contrast there are a number of permissible uses of SDRs in transactions between participants and the Fund. For example, the Fund may accept SDRs in repurchases of a member's currency from the Fund and payment of all charges including the interest component on drawings of currency.

The valuation of the SDR is determined on the basis of a basket of five currencies — the U.S. dollar, the deutsche mark, the French franc, the Japanese yen, and the pound sterling. In a "transaction with designation" another member, designated by the Fund, provides currency in exchange for SDRs. The Fund designates members to provide currency in exchange for SDRs on the basis of the strength of their balance of payments and reserve positions. A member's obligation to provide currency does not extend beyond the point at which its holdings are three times the total allocations.

Fund Stand-By Arrangements

As we have seen above, drawing rights beyond the reserve tranche are conditional. Accordingly, members have sometimes needed to obtain advance assurances from the Fund that drawings will be permitted in the future if necessary. Advance understandings to this effect between a member and the Fund are called "stand-by arrangements" or "extended arrangements."

Article V, Section 3(a) of the Articles of Agreement expressly authorizes the Fund to adopt policies on the use of stand-by arrangements. Under Article XXX(b) a stand-by arrangement is defined as "a decision of the Fund by which a member is assured that it will be able to make purchases from the General Resources Fund in accordance with the terms of the decision during a specified period and up to a specified amount." Drawings under stand-by arrangements are permitted over a period of up to three years.

"Extended Arrangements" are a special class of stand-by arrangement. They almost always run for the maximum period of three years, are normally for larger amounts in relation to quotas than are other stand-by arrangements, have a longer repurchase period, and involve lower charges. The Extended Fund Facility, discussed above, is a special set of rules for this class of arrangement. The primary purpose of extended arrangements is to make resources available to members, especially developing countries, for balance of payments support while they pursue economic programs designed to rectify structural defects in production and trade.

Under the procedure for obtaining a stand-by or extended arrangement a country submits, in a letter of intent to the Fund, a program to correct its balance of payments problems.[18] For its part the IMF undertakes a comprehensive review of the applicant's economy and the policies that affect its international and external financial position. The IMF Executive Board, in response to the member's letter of intent and with the benefit of the recommendation of the Managing Director and the report on the Fund's review of the applicant's economy, adopts a decision approving the stand-by or extended arrangement.

The Doctrine of Conditionality

The terms of stand-by and extended arrangements are often the subject of intense negotiations between the IMF staff and the country's monetary authorities. The scope of these negotiations includes the correction of domestic policies that adversely impact the country's external financial position. Many of the policies the IMF staff urges countries to adopt may be unpopular domestically. Moreover, the wisdom of these policies has been the subject of sharp debate among economists. Dissatisfaction with conditions imposed by the IMF led many developing countries to bypass the Fund and turn to commercial banks for their loans. This was a major contributing factor to the third world debt crisis. Recently, Argentina bypassed the IMF and obtained a $1.25 billion loan from the World Bank without first agreeing on an economic program with the Fund. This procedure was unusual if not unprecedented.[19]

The stand-by arrangement and the extended arrangement have a unique legal status. The member's letter of intent and the Fund's decision regarding the arrangement do not constitute a contract between the member and the Fund. The failure of a country to achieve the results stated in its letter does not even permit the interruption of the right to purchase within the first credit tranche. However, stand-by and extended arrangements permitting drawings beyond the first credit tranche are subject to performance clauses. Observance of the performance criteria guarantees a member the right to make drawings under the arrangement. Failure to abide by these performance criteria renders the country's right to make further drawings under the arrangement automatically interrupted without the need for any action by the Executive Board. This aspect of the Fund's financial assistance is referred to as the doctrine of conditionality.

---

[18] For a copy of the 1981 arrangement with India, see R. Edwards, Jr., *supra*, Note 1, at 251-63.

[19] Wall St. J., Sept. 26, 1988, at 3, Col. l.

Because stand-by and extended arrangements include a statement of economic policy intentions with performance monitored by the IMF, they have been important to other creditors of the member subject to the arrangement. The World Bank has usually conditioned its lending on the conclusion by the borrower of a stand-by or extended arrangement with the IMF, and commercial banks sometimes make loans contingent upon the borrowing country concluding a stand-by or extended arrangement with the Fund.

The European Monetary System

Under Article IV, Section 2(b)(ii) of the Articles of Agreement, IMF members may choose "cooperative arrangements by which members maintain the value of their currencies in relation to the value of the currency or currencies of other members." Those member states of the European Economic Community that participate in the European Monetary System (EMS) have chosen to act under this provision.

The purpose of the EMS is to assure close monetary cooperation among members with a view to stabilizing exchange rates among EEC currencies. This is seen as necessary for economic integration and as a prelude to economic and monetary union. At this writing ten member states of the EEC participate in the EMS.

A European currency unit (ECU) is the denominator (numeraire) for the EMS exchange rate mechanism. Each participating country, in concert with the other participants, sets an official central rate for its currency and agrees to intervene in the market to contain rate fluctuations within an agreed narrow range.

The primary legal issues involved in the establishment and operation of the EMS include:

> Defining the terms of [the] obligations to intervene in the market to contain rate fluctuations within the agreed narrow range, the countries upon which those obligations fall, and the currencies to be used.

> Establishing procedures to assure that underlying economic and monetary policies of the participating countries are consistent with the agreed official central rates and that central rates are changed when they impede balance-of-payments adjustment for any of the participating countries.

> Determining responsibilities and coordinating policies in managing the rates between EMS currencies and the U.S. dollar (and other actively traded currencies).

> Arranging financing for market interventions and establishing rules on how profits and losses from market interventions are to be shared.[20]

With respect to managing rates between EMS currencies and the dollar, there is currently a working understanding between U.S. monetary authorities and issuers of actively traded EMS currencies that market rates between the dollar and these currencies will float in response to market forces with official interventions taking place to maintain orderly trading conditions and to prevent excessive

---

[20] R. Edwards, Note 1, at 538-39.

movements in rates. European central banks thus face the challenge of maintaining the agreed rate relationship among their currencies while ensuring orderly trading conditions in the joint float of their currencies against the dollar. The U.K. pound sterling, Swiss franc, Japanese yen, and Canadian dollar also float in relation to the EMS currencies.

[4] The Fund Agreement In The Courts

In any discussion of the IMF Articles of Agreement in national courts, the key provision to consider is Section 2(b) of Article VIII:

> Exchange contracts which involve the currency of any member and which are contrary to the exchange control regulations of that member maintained or imposed consistently with this Agreement shall be unenforceable in the territories of any member. In addition, members may, by mutual accord, cooperate in measures for the purpose of making the exchange control regulations of either member more effective, provided that such measures and regulations are consistent with this Agreement.

Article VIII(2)(b) rejects, at least in part, the traditional view of conflict of laws that exchange control regulations, like tax and penal laws, are entitled to recognition only in the territory of the state that issued them. Under Article VIII(2)(b), if, in a court of a member country entertaining an action to enforce a contract, the defendant alleges that the contract is inconsistent with the exchange control regulations of another member country, the court has to decide, among other things, (1) whether the regulation is applicable to the case before the court; (2) whether the control was imposed or maintained consistently with the Articles of Agreement; (3) whether the contract is an "exchange contract" under Article VIII(2)(b); and (4) whether the contract "involves the currency" of the member imposing the regulation. Now consider the following cases.

WESTON BANKING CORP. v. TURKIYE GUARANTI BANKASI, A.S.

Court of Appeals of New York
67 N.Y. 2d 315, 442 N.E. 2d 1195 (1982)

JASEN J.

On this appeal, we are asked to decide whether, in light of the Act of State doctrine and the Bretton Woods Agreement, a Panamanian bank can maintain an action in this State against a Turkish bank on the basis of a promissory note that designates New York as the proper jurisdiction for resolution of any disputes. . . .

The promissory note which plaintiff, Weston Banking Corporation, a Panamanian banking corporation, seeks to enforce was signed by representatives of the defendant on July 9, 1976 in Istanbul, Turkey. Pursuant to its terms, defendant bank undertook an obligation to repay plaintiff principal in the amount of 500,000 Swiss francs, plus interest calculated at 9% per annum. The interest was to be paid semiannually and the principal was due on July 9, 1979. The note also provided that: "Payment of principal and interest shall be made at the offices of the Chemical Bank . . . New York City, New York, U.S.A., by means of a cable transfer to Switzerland in Lawful currency of the Swiss Federation." Such payments were to be "made clear of all restrictions of whatsoever nature imposed thereon, by outside bilateral or multilateral payment agreements or clearing agreements which may exist at the time of payment and free and clear of and without deductions for any taxes, levies, imposts . . . imposed . . . by the Republic of Turkey".

Under the terms of the note, the defendant designated Chemical Bank, International Division, New York City, as its legal domicile and accepted the jurisdiction of New York courts "in the event of judicial or extrajudicial [sic] claims or summons of any nature". The holder was also given the option to bring suit against the maker in the Turkish courts. The final paragraph of the note indicates that the note "is issued under communique number 164, published by the Ministry of Finance."

Communique No. 164 amended Decree No. 17 of the Turkish Ministry of Finance. The decree allows banks in Turkey to open convertible Turkish lira deposit accounts (CTLDs) when the bank obtains foreign currency by borrowing or through deposits. The bank is required under Turkish law to transfer the foreign currency to the Central Bank of Turkey. The Central Bank credits the privately owned bank with the equivalent amount of Turkish lira. These amounts are then available for investment by the bank. This program was apparently designed to encourage Turkish banks to seek foreign investments and to help stabilize the Turkish balance of payments by making available to the Turkish government more foreign currency. The banks benefited because the Turkish government covered any costs incurred by a fluctuation in the exchange rates between the currencies.

In July, 1976, the defendant Turkish bank borrowed 500,000 Swiss francs from the plaintiff bank and used these funds to establish a CTLD. As the interest became due, payments were made in Swiss francs at Chemical Banks' International Division in New York City. However, when the note was presented for payment in July, 1979, defendant refused to pay the principal on the ground that the then existing Turkish banking regulations barred it from paying back the loan in Swiss francs. . . .

It is not disputed that the defendant failed to pay the principal amount due plaintiff. Nor is the validity of the underlying note disputed. The heart of the defenses raised is that Turkish monetary regulations enacted subsequent to the date of the note make it legally impossible for the defendant bank to repay the loan in Swiss francs and that plaintiff's only "recourse is to be repaid in Turkish lira." Furthermore, the defendant contends that the promulgation of this regulation is an Act of State and as such is beyond the review of New York courts. Similarly, defendant argues that the policy of the United States, as incorporated in the Bretton Woods Agreement,[21] . . . is to refrain from any interference with the monetary regulations of signatory countries. . . .

---

[21] 22 U.S.C. Section 286, 59 Stat. 512, 60 Stat. 1411.

Turning then to the facts of this case, we must determine whether the note and the regulation which defendant contends restricts the repayment of the promissory note require application of the Act of State doctrine. The note was executed in Istanbul, Turkey, and states that it is "issued under Communique number 164" of the Turkish Ministry of Finance. Defendant contends that this makes the note subject to all Turkish monetary controls, even those enacted subsequent to the date of the note. Plaintiff, on the other hand, points out that Communique No. 164 merely authorizes Turkish banks to engage in this type of transaction and that the note specified that repayment is not subject to regulation by the Turkish government. We would add that the note requires payment to be made at Chemical Bank in New York City and designates New York law to be controlling.

We conclude that on these facts the Act of State doctrine does not constitute a defense to plaintiff's action to recover on this note. A debt is not located within a foreign State unless it has the power at the instance of an interested party to enforce or collect. . . .

Here, the debt is equally capable of being enforced against the defendant's assets in New York as it is capable of being enforced against its assets in Turkey, and the State of Turkey has no power to enforce collection of this debt. The mere fact that this suit might have been commenced in Turkey, instead of New York, does not bar the action. Indeed, the note provides that New York shall be the proper jurisdiction for dispute resolution. Such a provision naturally contemplates enforcement of any judgment which would resolve the dispute. Thus, the Act of State doctrine does not bar this action.

Whether or not extraterritorial effect will be given to the Turkish regulation depends on whether it controls the issue presented to this court and whether it is consistent with the policies of this state. . . . The initial inquiry must be to ask what the regulation provides.

Defendant has provided the court with translated and certified copies of all pertinent Turkish law and plaintiff has raised no claim concerning the propriety of these documents. Our reading of those regulations, whether individually or as representative of a continuous Turkish monetary policy, indicates that there is no per se ban imposed on all Turkish banks preventing them from paying this type of promissory note with foreign currency. The record indicates that the directive of the Ministry of Finance does not bar payment of the note, but, rather, establishes a program under which CTLDs could be restructured through the Turkish Central Bank. Defendant's own counsel in responding to plaintiff's inquiry about the effect of the restructuring program stated: "The Central Bank is obligated to pay interest only after CTLDs are included in the restructuring under the CTLD Credit Agreement. All CTLDs not included in the restructuring will remain obligations of the commercial banks in Turkey with which they are made." Plaintiff denies ever agreeing to have this note included in the restructuring program. Defendant makes no claim that the note was included in the restructuring program. Defendant makes no claim and offers no proof to the contrary; in fact, the record is devoid of any indication that the regulations on which defendant relies are applicable to this note.

Thus, we need not reach the question of whether these regulations comport with this State's policy so that they should be given extraterritorial application. It is sufficient to note that defendant has failed to introduce any documentation to support its contention that Turkish law forbids the payment of a promissory note designating that payment shall be made in Swiss francs at a bank incorporated in the United States.

This failure of proof also reaches to the validity of defendant's claim that the Bretton Woods Agreement bars this action. The Bretton Woods Agreement . . . is an international treaty to which both the United States and Turkey are signatories. The purpose of the Agreement, as stated in Article I is to promote international monetary co-operation, exchange stability and "[t]o assist in the establishment of a multilateral system of payments in respect of current transactions between members and in the elimination of foreign exchange restrictions which hamper the growth of world trade." (Art I. [iv.].)

The defendant relies on Article VIII (Section 2, subd. [b]) of the Agreement as a defense to this action, which provides that "[e]xchange contracts which involve the currency of any member and which are contrary to the exchange control regulations of that member maintained or imposed consistently with this Agreement shall be unenforceable in the territories of any member." This article renders unenforceable any agreement involving the currency of a member State which is contrary to "that member's currency control regulations." The promissory note involved here obligated the defendant to repay the plaintiff the principal sum loaned in Swiss francs and not Turkish lira.

Were the currency regulations to ban payment in foreign currencies when a CTLD was liquidated, a different case would have been presented. In this case, however, the regulation merely permits a Turkish bank to restructure the debt. As we previously stated, there is no proof, in this record, that if the debt were not restructured, the bank would be barred from repaying the plaintiff in Swiss francs as required by the terms of the note. Therefore, although we recognize the validity of the Bretton Woods Agreement and its potential controlling effect over international currency transactions, on the record before us, we do not find it to be applicable. . . .

Accordingly, the order of the Appellate Division should be affirmed.

MEYER, J. (dissenting).

The International Monetary Fund (Bretton Woods) Agreement of 1945 to which the United States and Turkey are signatories, the mandate of Section 11 of the Bretton Woods Agreements Act[22] . . . that "the first sentence of Article VIII, Section 2(b), of the Articles of Agreement of the Fund . . . "shall have full force and effect in the United States", the legislative history of that Congressional enactment, the supremacy clause of the United States Constitution and the decision of the United States Supreme Court in Kolovrat v. Oregon,[23] established beyond peradventure that the applicability of the first sentence of Article VIII (Section 2, subd. [b]) presents a question of Federal not State law. . . .

If Article VIII (Section 2, subd. [b]) applies, neither the Act of State doctrine referred to by the majority and the Appellate Division nor the intention of the

---

[22] 22 U.S.C. Section 286b, 59 Stat. 516.
[23] 366 U.S. 187, 81 S. Ct. 922, 6 L. Ed. 2d 218.

parties to free it from Turkish regulation, relied upon by the Appellate Division, are relevant. The starting point for analysis is rather the Appellate Division's statement[24] . . . that "Communique No. 164, under which the note was issued, imposes no conditions on repayment; it simply authorizes issuance of a note payable in foreign currency" and the statement of the majority in this Court[25] "that defendant has failed to introduce any documentation to support its contention that Turkish law forbids the payment of a promissory note designating that payment shall be made in Swiss Francs at a bank incorporated in the United States." Does the record bear out those conclusions?. . . .

. . . The question is not whether Communique No. 164 in so many words imposed a condition upon payment, but whether the Turkish regulatory system, of which the Communique (which is entitled "Communique on Decree No. 17 Regarding Protection of the Value of Turkish Currency") is but a part, establishes an exchange control regulation within the meaning of Article VIII (Section 2, subd. [b]) of the Agreement.

When the documents are examined together with the affidavit explaining the relationship between them there can be no question but that it does, the more particularly so because plaintiff has submitted no contrary documents or opinions concerning Turkish law. Thus, the affidavit [accompanying defendant's motion, annexes laws] which put all foreign exchange, by whomever owned, at the disposal of the Ministry of Finance and limited spending of exchange to that authorized by the Ministry. The affidavit attaches also copies of Communique Nos. 2, 145 and 164 promulgated pursuant to Decree No. 17 and recounts that through these communiques the CTLD system was established to attract foreign exchange into Turkey through deposits for three years or longer paying very high interest, which, however, were required under Communique No. 145 to be paid over to the Central Bank of Turkey in return for the equivalent in Turkish lira. It attaches as well a copy of plaintiff's order to its Swiss bank by which it made the deposits that are the consideration for the notes sued upon, which acknowledged that the deposits were made subject to Turkish regulations requiring the Swiss francs to be paid over to the Central Bank of Turkey.

As defined by Decree No. 17 foreign exchange includes all foreign currencies "and instruments of any kind assuring payment in these currencies" and, as already noted, the decree puts all foreign exchange by whomever owned at the disposal of the Ministry of Finance and limits spending of foreign exchange to expenditures authorized by the general or special permission of the Ministry. By decision of the Ministry as relayed to defendant by letter of December 19, 1977, permission to repay principal of CTLDs in foreign exchange was canceled. Clearly, therefore, the documentation accompanying defendant's cross motion . . . establishes that Turkish law forbids the Swiss franc payment for which, by this action on the note, plaintiff sues.

That conclusion does not end the inquiry, however, for there remains the question whether the Bretton Woods Agreement makes the note unenforceable by our courts. The answer must be in the affirmative if (1) payment is contrary

---

[24] 86 A.D. 2d 544, 545, 446 N.Y.S. 2d 67.
[25] Pp. 325-326, 456 N.Y.S. 2d 688, 442 N.E. 2d 1199.

to Turkish regulation, (2) the regulation is maintained consistently with the Agreement, (3) Turkish currency is involved and (4) the note is an "exchange contract" within the meaning of Article VIII (Section 2, subd. [b]).

The first three factors are not open to serious question. That the repayment of Swiss francs called for by the note (or the payment of a dollar-equivalent judgment on the note) is contrary to the Turkish regulation is demonstrated beyond question by attachments to defendant's [affadavit]: June 26, 1979 request for Ministry permission to pay the notes when due in Swiss francs, the Central Bank's July 9, 1979 reply advising that the Ministry had denied the request and placed the notes "within the scope of rescheduling" for payment, and of defendant's September 14, 1979 voucher remitting to Central Bank for remittance to plaintiff the then equivalent in Turkish lira of 500,000 Swiss francs.

Plaintiff suggests that the regulation is not maintained consistently with the Agreement because the purpose of the agreement is to promote exchange stability, because Article VIII (Section 2, subd. [a]) provides that "no member shall, without approval of the Fund, impose restrictions on the making of payments and transfers for current international transactions," and because paragraph (a) of Section 1 of Article V requires members to avoid manipulating exchange rates in order to prevent effective balance of payment adjustments or to gain an unfair competitive advantage over other members. The argument overlooks the provisions of Section 2 of Article XIV which permits "restrictions on payments and transfers for current international transactions" during the "post-war transitional period" even though not approved by the Fund, and the powers of the Fund under Section 4 of that Article to make representations that such controls be withdrawn, and under Section 2 of Article XV to compel withdrawal of a member whose regulations offend against the Agreement's provision. Plaintiff presents nothing to suggest that Turkey has violated Article IV, to indicate that the Turkish regulation first imposed in 1930 and amended postwar many times is not a permitted transitional period restriction, or indeed that if [that is not so] the restriction has not been approved by the Fund. Consistency of the regulation in question may be inferred from the failure of the Fund to take any action against Turkey with respect to it, as it had done, for example, in 1954 with respect to Czechoslovakia the more so because, despite the offer of the Fund[26] . . . to advise whether a particular control is consistent, as well as on any other aspect of Article VIII (Section 2, subd. [b]), plaintiff has presented nothing to establish inconsistency.

There is involvement of Turkish currency, moreover, even though the note in suit is payable in New York in Swiss francs. The note recited that it was issued under Communique No. 164, the title of which is "Communique on Decree No. 17 Regarding Protection of the Value of Turkish Currency" and Weston's deposit order to its Swiss bank noted the requirement that the Swiss francs be "brought into the republic of Turkey according to regulations established by the Ministry of Finance in Turkey whereby the Swiss francs have to be paid to the central bank of the republic of Turkey." "Involve" carries such connotations as "entangle", "implicate", "embroil", "connect" and "affect". Because the purpose of the first sentence of Article VIII (Section 2, subd. [b]) is to protect the limited controls

---

[26] Reprinted at 14 Fed. Reg. 5208.

which the Agreement permits by reversing the private law doctrine under which such controls had previously been largely circumvented by the courts, involvement of the currency should be read in terms of the interest of the country whose regulation is in issue rather than of the parties. Moreover, Weston, having paid over its Swiss francs with the understanding that they were destined for the Turkish Central Bank and that the note was to be governed by a decree protecting Turkish currency, should not be heard to argue that Turkish currency is not affected, implicated or embroiled in the transaction.

A more difficult problem is whether the note is an exchange contract within the meaning of the agreement. I do not blink the fact that *Zeevi & Sons v. Grindlay Bank (Uganda)*[27] . . . held that a "letter of credit is not an exchange contract" and that *Banco Do Brasil, S.A. v. Israel Commodity Co.*[28] . . . inclined to the view that it would do violence to the text of the section to interpret it as including "all contracts affecting any members' exchange resources." The narrow interpretation thus arrived at is, however, inconsistent not only with the more expansive reading given the agreement in *Banco Frances e Brasileiro v. Doe*[29] . . . and *Perutz v. Bohemian Discount Bank in Liquidation*[30] but also with the conclusion reached by the courts of at least one other State[31] and commentators.[32] Although

---

[27] 37 N.Y. 2d 220, 229, 371 N.Y.S. 2d 892, 333 N.E. 2d 168, *cert. den.*, 423 U.S. 866, 96 S. Ct. 126, 46 L. Ed. 2d 95.

[28] 12 N.Y. 2d 371, 375-376, 239 N.Y.S. 2d 872, 190 N.E.2d 235, *cert. den.*, 376 U.S. 906, 84 S. Ct. 657, 11 L. Ed. 2d 605.

[29] 36 N.Y. 2d 592, 370 N.Y. 2d 534, 331 N.E. 2d 502, *cert. den.*, 423 U.S. 867, 96 S. Ct. 129, 46 L. Ed. 2d 96.

[30] 304 N.Y. 533, 110 N.E. 2d 6.

[31] *Confederation Life Assn. v. Ugalde*, 164 So. 2d 1, 3 (Fla.), *cert. den.*, 379 U.S. 915, 85 S. Ct. 163, 13 L. Ed. 2d 186; *Sun Life Assur. Co. of Canada v. Klawans*, 165 So. 2d 166 (Fla.); *contra Theye y Ajuria v. Pan-Amer. Life Ins. Co.*, 245 La. 755, 766-767, 161 So. 2d 70, *cert. den.*, 377 U.S. 997, 84 S. Ct. 1922, 12 L. Ed. 2d 1046; see *Pan-Amer. Life Ins. Co. v. Raij*, 164 So. 2d 204 (Fla.), *cert. den.*, 379 U.S. 920, 85 S. Ct. 275, 13 L. Ed. 2d 334; *Blanco v. Pan-American Life Ins. Co.*, 221 F. Supp. 219, 228-229; see, also, Gold, The Cuban Insurance Cases And The Articles Of The Fund and The Paradise Article, *infra*, discussing the above cases.).

[32] The other country cases are discussed in Gold, The Fund Agreement In The Courts ([1962], pp. 1, 43, 64 and 72); Gold, The Fund Agreement In The Courts (Parts VIII-XI [1976], pp. 9, 28, 50, 73, 87, 102, 139); Gold, The Fund Agreement In The Courts (Part XII [1977]); and Gold, The Fund Agreement In The Courts (Part XIV [1979]). From the report and discussion in those articles it appears that though the courts of England originally adopted a broad view of "exchange contract" (Gold [1976]), pp. 43-50), they now take the narrower view (Gold [Part XIII], pp. 205-220. However, the broader view is excepted by the highest courts of France (Gold [1962], pp. 146, 153; Gold [Part XII], p. 221), Germany (Gold [1976], pp. 78-79), the Netherlands (Gold [1962], p. 116), Austria (*id.*, p. 90), Luxembourg (*Id.*, p. 94) and Hong Kong (*Id.*, p. 87). (Baker, Enforcement Of Contracts Violating Foreign Exchange Control Laws, 3 Int. Trade L. J. 247, 273 ff; Gold, *op cit.*, *passim*; Gold, International Monetary Fund And Private Business Transactions, p. 24; Mann, Legal Aspect Of Money [4th ed.], pp. 389, 391; Meyer, *Recognition Of Exchange Controls After the International Monetary Fund Agreement*, 62 Yale L. J. 867, 885; Paradise, *Cuban Refugee Insureds And The Articles Of Agreement Of The International Monetary Fund*, 18 U. of Fla. L. Rev. 29, 55 ff; Pohn, *International Law—Court Refuses To Put Export-Import Contract Within Bretton Woods Agreement*, 15 Syracuse L. Rev.

there are contrary views the majority view reads "exchange contracts" as used in the Agreement, in light of the legislative history of the provision, broadly enough to encompass a transaction based in contract which involves exchange or affects the balance of payments or exchange resources of a member nation.

Because, as the foregoing discussion shows, the note in suit is governed by Turkish regulations and the Bretton Woods Agreement and the Bretton Woods Agreements Act proscribe enforcement of the note by the courts of this State in contravention of those regulations, I would grant defendant's cross motion for summary judgment dismissing the complaint.

NOTES AND QUESTIONS

(1) Is it clear from the discussion in the Weston case how one distinguishes between an "exchange contract" and one that simply involves foreign exchange?

(2) In *Vishipco Line v. Chase Manhattan Bank*,[33] ten Vietnamese corporations and an individual Vietnamese citizen sued Chase Manhattan Bank for breach of contract. Plaintiffs had maintained piastre demand deposit accounts at Chase's Saigon branch in 1975 and claimed that Chase had breached its deposit contracts with them when it closed the doors of its Saigon branch on April 24, 1975, because of the Communist insurgency, and subsequently refused to make payment in New York of the amount owed. Reversing the district court the Second Circuit Court of Appeals rejected various defenses raised by Chase, including the Act of State doctrine. It found the Act of State doctrine inapplicable because, upon Chase's departure from Vietnam, the deposits no longer had their situs in Vietnam at the time of the confiscation decree. The Vietnamese decree nationalizing the Vietnamese banking industry provided that "[a]ll . . . banks . . . will be confiscated and from now on managed by the revolutionary administration." The court did not consider Article VIII(2)(b). Should it have? If it had, would it have reached a different result?[34]

(3) Courts in some other countries (the Federal Republic of Germany, for example) have interpreted "exchange contracts" more expansively than have U.S. courts to include, for example, a contract for the sale of merchandise, a commission contract relating to the refining of maize, and a contract for transfer of shares

100, 102; Williams, *Extraterritorial Enforcement Of Exchange Control Regulations Under The International Monetary Fund Agreement*, 15 Va. J. Int. Law 319, 332 ff; Williams, *Enforcement Of Foreign Exchange Control Regulations In Domestic Courts*, 70 Am. J. Int. L. 101, 106, n. 31; Williams, *Foreign Exchange Control Regulation And The New York Court Of Appeals*, 9 Cornell Int. L. J. 239, 243; Note, 63 Col. L. Rev. 1334, 1336.

[33] 660 F. 2d 854 (2d Cir. 1981), *cert. denied*, 459 U.S. 976 (1982).

[34] For other cases that consider the liability of home offices of U.S. banks for obligations of their foreign branches in the event of foreign governmental expropriation or exchange control measures, see, *e.g.*, *Citibank v. Wells Fargo Asia, Ltd.*, 58 U.S.L.W. 4639 (May 29, 1990); *Trinh v. Citibank, N.A.*, 850 F.2d 1164 (6th Cir. 1988), cert den. 110 L. Ed.2d 282 (1990); and *Edelmann v. Chase Manhattan Bank, N.A.*, 861 F. 2d 1291 (1st Cir. 1988).

in a company.[35] What problems, if any, does this inconsistency of interpretation pose for realization of the objectives sought to be achieved by Article VIII, Section 2(b)? How would you define these objectives?

(4) In *Libra Bank v. Banco Nacional de Costa Rica*[36] the court held that the burden of proof is on a party challenging a contract as contrary to the exchange regulations of a member country to demonstrate that the control regulations are maintained or imposed consistently with the IMF Articles. According to the court, a party could meet this burden in either of two ways. It could show either that the restrictions had the approval of the Fund or that they were upon capital as opposed to current transactions and therefore Fund approval was unnecessary.

BANCO FRANCES e BRASILEIRO S.A. v. DOE

Court of Appeals of New York
36 N.Y. 2d 592, 331 N.E. 2d 502 (1975),
cert. denied, 412 U.S. 867,
96 S. Ct. 129, 46 L. Ed. 2d 96 (1975)

JASEN, J.

The principal question before us is whether a private foreign bank may avail itself of the New York courts in an action for damages for tortious fraud and deceit and for rescission of currency exchange contracts arising from alleged violations of foreign currency exchange regulations.

Plaintiff, a private Brazilian bank, brings this action for fraud and deceit, and conspiracy to defraud and deceive, against twenty "John Does" defendants whose identities are unknown to it. The gravamen of plaintiff's complaint is that these defendants over a period of approximately six weeks participated in violation of Brazilian currency regulations, in the submission of false applications to Banco-Brasileiro of Brazil, which the plaintiff relied upon, resulting in the improper exchange by the Bank of Brazil of cruizeiros into travelers checks in United States dollars totaling $1,024,000. . . .

It is an old chestnut in conflict of laws that one state does not enforce the revenue laws of another. By way of rationale, an analogy is drawn [between] foreign penal laws, extrastate enforcement of which is denied (see *The Antelope*),[37] . . . and foreign tax assessments, judicially expanded also to include foreign currency exchange regulations. The analogy . . . traces from Lord Mansfield's now famous dictum in an international smuggling case that "no country ever takes

---

[35] For an excellent discussion of these cases, as well as for thoughtful comments on the overall role of Article VIII, Section 2(b), see Ebke, Article VIII, Section 2(b), *International Monetary Cooperation And The Courts*, 23 Int'l Law. 677 (1989). See also Zamora, *Recognition Of Foreign Exchange Controls In International Creditors' Rights Cases*, 21 Int'l Law. 1055 (1987).

[36] 570 F. Supp. 870 (S.D.N.Y. 1983).

[37] 10 Wheat [23 U.S.] 66, 6 L. Ed. 268.

notice of the revenue laws of another."[38] . . . . But the modern analog of the
revenue law rule is justifiable neither precedentially nor analytically. . . . In the
international sphere, cases involving foreign currency exchange regulations,
represent perhaps the most important aspect of the revenue law rule. This
assumes, of course, that a currency exchange regulation, normally not designed
for revenue purposes as such, but rather, to prevent the loss of foreign currency
which in turn increases the country's foreign exchange reserves, is properly
characterizable as a revenue law[39] . . . . At any rate, it is for the forum to
characterize such a regulation and in this State the question would appear to have
been resolved for the present at least by *Banco de Brasil v. Israel Commodity Co.*[40]
. . . .

But even assuming the continuing validity to the revenue law rule and the
correctness of the characterization of a currency exchange regulation thereunder,
United States membership in the International Monetary Fund (IMF) makes
inappropriate the refusal to entertain the instant claim. The view that nothing in
Article VIII (Section 2, subd. [b]) of the Bretton Woods Agreements Act[41] . . .
requires an American court to provide a forum for a private tort remedy, while
correct in a literal sense (see *Banco do Brasil v. Israel Commodity Co., supra*), does
not represent the only perspective. Nothing in the Agreement prevents an IMF
member from aiding, directly or indirectly, a fellow member in making its
exchange regulations effective. And United States membership in the IMF makes
it impossible to conclude that the currency control laws of other member States
are offensive to this State's public policy so as to preclude suit in tort by a private
party. Indeed, conduct reasonably necessary to protect the foreign exchange
resources of a country does not offend against international law. (Restatement 2d,
Foreign Relations Law of the United States, Section 198, comment b.) Moreover,
where a true governmental interest of a friendly nation is involved — and foreign
currency reserves are of vital importance to a country plagued by balance of
payments difficulties — the national policy of co-operation with Bretton Woods
signatories is furthered by providing a State forum for suit.

The *Banco do Brasil* case relied upon by the Appellate Division is quite
distinguishable. There the Government of Brazil, through Banco do Brasil, a
government bank, sought redress for violations of its currency exchange regulations incident to a fraudulent coffee export transaction. Here, the plaintiff is a
private bank seeking rescission of the fraudulent currency exchange transactions
and damages. And no case has come to our attention where a private tort remedy
arising from foreign currency regulations has been denied by the forum as an
application of the revenue law rule and we decline so to extend the *Banco do Brasil*
rationale. Thus, in the instant case we find no basis for reliance upon the revenue
law rule to deny a forum for suit. Moreover, where the parties are private, the
"jealous sovereign" rationale is inapposite . . . even as it might seem inapposite

---

[38] *Holman v. Johnson*, 1 Cowp. 341, 342.

[39] Contra, *Kahler v. Midland Bank* [1950] A.C. 24; Dicey, Conflict of Laws [7th ed.],
p. 920.

[40] 12 N.Y. 2d 371, 377, 239 N.Y.S. 2d 872, 875, 190 N.E. 2d 235, 237, *cert. den.*, 376
U.S. 906, 84 S. Ct. 657, 11 L. Ed. 2d 605.

[41] 60 U.S. Stat. 1401, 1411.

in the Banco do Brasil situation where the sovereign itself, or its instrumentality, asks redress and damages in a foreign forum for violation of the sovereign's currency laws. . . .

Accordingly, the order of the Appellate Division should be modified in accordance with the views here expressed and the action remitted to the Supreme Court, New York County.

WACHTLER, J. (dissenting). . . .

I believe that the relief sought here, albeit indirectly through plaintiff bank, is an aspect of the Brazilian government's sovereign management of the economy of its own country. This is not a matter involving the resolution of private rights as those rights are defined under the laws of a foreign State. Were that so our courts would not withhold judicial sanction even if the definition of such private rights were somewhat different from our own, "unless some sound reason of public policy makes it unwise for us to lend our aid". *Loucks v. Standard Oil Co.*[42] . . . .

There is no allegation in this complaint that defendants intended to or succeeded in defrauding plaintiff of foreign currency exchange in the private rights sense. On the contrary, from all that appears, defendants obtained no more United States dollars in consequence of their alleged fraud than they would have been entitled to receive at the then currently effective exchange rate for the Brazilian cruzeiros which they exchanged with plaintiff bank. The gravamen rather is that the fraud and deceit practiced by the defendants induced plaintiff bank to violate Brazilian currency exchange regulations, thereby exposing that bank to consequent penalties which would be imposed by the Brazilian Government.

It has long been recognized that the courts of one jurisdiction will not enforce the tax laws, penal laws, or statutory penalties and forfeitures of another jurisdiction. . . .

In previous cases our court held that governmental foreign exchange regulation may present an aspect of the exercise of sovereign power by a foreign State to implement its national fiscal policy. Thus, in *Banco do Brasil v. Israel Commodity Co. (supra)*, we decided that our courts were not open to enforce a Brazilian foreign currency exchange regulation. Although the regulation in that case was characterized as a revenue measure, the essence of the matter was that we declined to enforce what we considered to be an exercise of Brazil's sovereign power. Whether a regulation denominated "currency exchange regulation" has or does not have a revenue-producing effect, it must be presumed to have been adopted to accomplish fiscal regulation and ultimate economic objectives significantly similar to, if not identical with, the objectives which underlie what would be characterized as revenue measures — namely, governmental management of its economy by a foreign country. Accordingly, the result is not determined by the threshold appearance of the particular law sought to be enforced or whether such law be denominated by the foreign government as a penal law or a revenue law or otherwise. The bottom line is that the courts of one country will not enforce the laws adopted by another country in the exercise of its sovereign capacity for the purpose of fiscal regulation and management. . . .

---

[42] 224 N.Y. 99, 110 N.E. 198, 201.

Nothing in the Bretton Woods Agreements Act or in any other agreement between the United States and Brazil of which we are aware, . . . mandates a complete abrogation of the normal conflicts rule or requires our courts affirmatively to enforce foreign currency regulations, as we are invited to do in the present case. This distinction was expressly recognized and held to be dispositive in *Banco do Brasil* (*supra*), in which we said:[43] "An obligation to withhold judicial assistance to secure the benefits of such contracts [*i.e.*, those violative of the foreign currency control regulation] does not imply an obligation to impose tort penalties on those who have fully executed them.". . . .

The appellant seeks to distinguish our decision in *Banco do Brasil* on the ground that the plaintiff in that case was recognized as an instrumentality of the Brazilian Government. I find this unpersuasive. As Judge Cardozo noted in the *Loucks* case (*supra*), a statute will be deemed to reflect the Sovereign's interest if it "awards a penalty to the state, or to a public officer in its behalf, or to a member of the public, suing in the interest of the whole community to redress a public wrong. . . . The purpose must be, not reparation to one aggrieved, but vindication of the public justice."[44] . . . . Whenever vindication of the public interest is sought at the instance of a third person, as here by plaintiff bank, of necessity such third party must show "aggrievement" or no cause of action will lie. But any such formulation is incomplete.

The core of the issue here is enforcement of a Brazilian currency exchange regulation. The only "reparation" sought by this plaintiff is for damages sustained in consequence of violation. Damages which are wholly attributable to the violation of such a regulation, although alleged to have been occasioned by defendants' fraud, do not convert the action to one solely for private reparation. The ultimate economic reality, of granting relief to the plaintiff bank, would be the imposition on defendants of sanctions for violation of currency exchange controls.

I recognize that this case is not an instance of recourse sought by a foreign country in our courts for the direct enforcement of its foreign currency exchange regulations, as would be the case were the Brazilian Government seeking here to recover penalties from either Banco-Brasileiro or from the defendants. The rights of private parties will be significantly affected; it is alleged that plaintiff bank has suffered and will suffer detriment in its private capacity in consequence of the fraud and deceit of defendants. The resolution of the issue posed by the motion to dismiss does not depend on the incidental, inescapable fact that private rights have already been, and would be affected by the judicial relief sought. Rather, the determinative factor is that the primary objective and the ultimate practical effect of the relief sought would be the enforcement of the currency regulation system of a foreign country. Our courts are not open for the accomplishment of that end, and that it may be sought through private intermediaries does not change the result. It matters not whether enforcement is sought directly or indirectly[45] . . . .

---

[43] 12 N.Y. 2d p. 376, 239 N.W.S. 2d, p. 874, 190 N.E. 2d, p. 237.

[44] *Loucks v. Standard Oil Co., supra*, 224 N.Y. pp. 102-103, 120-103, 120 N.E. p. 198; *cf. Huntington v. Attrill, supra*, 146 U.S. pp. 673, 681-682, 13 S. Ct. 224.

[45] Dicey & Morris, Conflict of Laws [8th ed.], *op. cit.*, pp. 160-161.

I consider the plaintiff's complaint as an attempt to utilize the judicial machinery of our courts to enforce the exercise of the sovereign power by the Government of Brazil. I believe that our courts, under traditional and established principles, are not available for this purpose.

The majority, however, argues that the time may have come for a change in what historically has been the applicable rule. I recognize that strong arguments can be mounted for a change in view of the increased frequency and importance of international commerce and the significantly different perspective in today's world in which one nation views another nation and its interests. In my opinion, however, the responsibility for any change lies with our Federal Government rather than with the highest court of any single State. Change, if at all, in my view, would better come at the hands of the State Department and the Congress, through the negotiation of international agreement or otherwise in the discharge of the constitutional responsibility of the Federal Government "to regulate commerce with foreign nations" (*cf.* Bretton Woods Agreements Act). A fitting sense of judicial restraint would dictate that the courts of no single State should enunciate a change, however large that State's relative proportion of foreign commerce may be, particularly since the authoritative effect thereof would necessarily be confined to the borders of that State.

Accordingly, I believe the order of the Appellate Division should be affirmed.

NOTES AND QUESTIONS

(1) In his dissent in *Banco Frances*, Judge Wachtler concludes that any change in the traditional conflict of laws rule precluding one state from enforcing the "revenue law" of another should come "at the hands of the State Department and the Congress." What arguments might be advanced against this proposition? Might one reasonably conclude that, in cases involving currency exchange restrictions, the political branches of the federal government have already changed the rule?

(2) Are the decisions in *Banco Frances* p. 851 and *Vishipco,* p. 850, consistent as a matter of principle?

(3) The IMF does not publicly announce whether a given measure of exchange control has been approved. It will respond, however, to an inquiry from a national court as to whether a particular exchange restriction is consistent with the Articles of Agreement. An opinion by the Fund that a particular control is not maintained or imposed consistently with the Articles is conclusive; an opinion that the control is maintained or imposed consistently with the Articles is entitled to great weight but the national court makes the final decision.

(4) On occasion an IMF member may impose exchange controls solely for national security purposes. Under an Executive Board Decision, a member state must report such controls to the Fund. Unless the Fund informs the member state within 30 days after notification that it is not satisfied that such restrictions are imposed solely for security purposes, "the member may assume that the Fund has

no objections to the imposition of the restrictions." During the Iranian hostage crisis of 1979, the United States imposed restrictions on transfer of Iranian dollar assets held in the United States or in foreign branches of U.S. banks. The Fund did not disapprove these controls within thirty days after it received notification of them. Accordingly, it was contended in litigation in France and the United Kingdom that the U.S. controls were restrictions maintained consistently with the Articles of Agreement.[46]

---

[46] For discussion, see Edwards, *Extraterritorial Application Of The U.S. Iranian Assets Control Regulations*, 75 Am. J. Int'l L. 870 (1981). For comments highly critical of the IMF practice on national security controls, see Lichtenstein, *The Battle For International Bank Accounts: Restrictions On International Payments For Political Ends And Article VIII of the Fund Agreement*, 19 N. Y. U. J. Int'l L. & Pol. 981 (1987). For general discussions of International Monetary Law, besides those already cited in this Chapter, see J. Gold, Legal And Institutional Aspects Of The International Monetary System (1984); The IMF And Stabilization: Developing Country Experience (T. Killich, ed. 1984); Restatement (Third) of the Foreign Relations Law Of The United States, Sections 821-823 (1987).

CHAPTER 11

RESOLUTION OF INTERNATIONAL BUSINESS DISPUTES

Introduction

In structuring international business transactions, as in any business situation, one should make every effort to avoid disputes arising between the parties concerning the terms and implementation of the transaction. Such an effort, while important in the context of an entirely national transaction, acquires a special sense of urgency when events, parties and goods transcend or cross national borders. If such an effort fails, resolution of the resultant disputes may pose particularly difficult problems.

The method of dispute resolution chosen will depend in large part on the political, economic and social milieu of the transaction out of which the dispute arises. The litigious American attorney may be surprised to learn that a decidedly different attitude toward adjudication prevails in the Orient, although there are some signs that this attitude may be changing. In both Japan and the People's Republic of China, there is a marked preference for avoiding formal dispute resolution mechanisms, such as litigation and arbitration. For example, in China, arbitration or adjudication is usually resorted to only after the exhaustion of three other methods. These are: "(1) friendly negotiations, involving extended discussion of a dispute between involved parties; (2) consultation, involving the assistance of the Foreign and Economic Trade Arbitration Commission; and (3) conciliation, where one of these two organizations makes a non-binding recommendation to the disputing parties."[1]

To be sure, under Article 86 of the new Chinese Code of Civil Procedure, foreigners are guaranteed access to Chinese courts, and equal treatment with their Chinese opponents, subject to the condition that reciprocal rights are available in the courts of the foreigner's country. (Article 87). Further, with the radical changes taking place in China's legal system, courts may play a larger role in the dispute settlement process. Nonetheless, the emphasis in China toward avoiding adjudication and arbitration and maintaining informal methods of dispute resolution is likely to continue.

The same may be said of Japan. Although Japan, unlike China, is a modern, industrial state, long-standing tradition and cultural mores maintain a dislike of litigation. Submitting a dispute to court is considered as a last resort; preference is given to social settlements through compromise or conciliation. Litigation in court is viewed as a failure of society and individuals to maintain harmony through traditional means. This societal attitude is reflected in contractual terms that the western attorney may find startling. For example, a dispute settlement

---

[1] *China's Legal Development: Annotated Bibliography*, 22 Colum. J. Trans. L. 175, 214-18 (1983).

clause in a Japanese contract may read: "If in the future disputes arise between parties with regard to the rights and duties provided in this contract, the parties will *confer in good faith*" (emphasis added).[2] The Japanese business person may resist the insertion of a clause, standard in American contracts, calling for adjudication or arbitration in the event of a dispute and indeed view a proposal for such a clause as an expression of lack of trust. The western attorney must, in short, be prepared to be flexible with respect to methods of dispute settlement.

This Chapter begins its consideration of methods to resolve international disputes with a discussion of informal methods, *i.e.*, negotiation, mediation, and conciliation. It then turns to adjudication and arbitration, the formal methods of dispute resolution and those most familiar to the western international business lawyer.

§ 11.01 Informal Methods of Dispute Settlement: Negotiation, Mediation and Conciliation

The most informal method of dispute settlement, and one that has received a considerable amount of attention in recent years, is negotiation. Negotiation involves efforts by the parties to a contract to resolve the dispute themselves without the assistance of a third party. Recent studies of negotiating techniques have emphasized the desirability of reaching resolutions of disputes that take into account the important interests of all parties rather than impose terms on an unwilling weaker party.[3]

According to one view, mediation is a method "by which third persons seek to dissolve a dispute without imposing a binding decision." It would be incompatible with this notion to "recommend the terms" of a settlement and to "mobilize such strong political, economic, social, and moral pressures upon one or both parties as to leave little option but that of 'voluntary acquiescence'."[4]

Other commentators would distinguish "mediation" from "conciliation" on the basis that only in the case of conciliation does the third party make recommendations to the parties to the dispute. Under this approach, "conciliation" would in turn be distinguished from arbitration by the binding nature of an arbitral award as compared with the recommendatory character of a conciliation proposal. Other features of conciliation that distinguish it from arbitration include the desire of parties to settle their disputes amicably, as compared with the adversarial nature of arbitration, and the requirement that all parties participate in conciliation proceedings, whereas arbitration can continue even if one of the parties fails to appear or to produce certain documents.

---

[2] Quoted in Lansing and Wechselbatt, *Doing Business In Japan: The Importance Of The Unwritten Law*, 17 Int'l. Law. 647 (1983).

[3] See, *e.g.*, R. Fisher & W. Uryl, Getting To Yes: Negotiating Agreement Without Giving In (1981).

[4] Quoted in J. Barton, J. Gills Jr., V. Li & J.H. Merryman, Law And Radically Different Cultures 721 (1983).

There is disagreement whether conciliation has a greater potential for encouraging settlement than does arbitration. Some practitioners believe that conciliation is usually a waste of time and merely delays the start of arbitration. Be that as it may, in some countries, especially as we have seen above in the Orient, conciliation is preferred to arbitration, and parties may be required under national law to attempt conciliation before resorting to arbitration. In 1980, the United Nations Commission on International Trade Law (UNCITRAL), a subsidiary organ of the General Assembly, adopted Conciliation Rules, which per article 1 "apply to conciliation of disputes arising out of or relating to a contractual or other legal relationship where the parties seeking an amicable settlement of their dispute have agreed that the UNCITRAL Conciliation Rules apply."

A unique method, called administrative guidance, characterizes the Japanese approach to dispute settlement. As described in a recent study, "administrative guidance occurs when administrators take action of no coercive legal effect that encourages regulated parties to act in a specific way in order to realize some administrative aim."[5]

Under the administrative guidance approach, Japanese officials do not formally promulgate administrative orders, regulations, or local ordinances that have binding effect on legal relationships between the parties. Rather, they rely on "voluntary" compliance with their attempts to modify the behavior of the parties, although to be sure these officials have a variety of devices to accomplish their goals, including rewarding those who comply with their suggestions.

These pressures are often employed to induce the parties to bargain out or negotiate a resolution of complex problems of resource allocation. As an aid to such private ordering of disputes, the government officials may attempt to reallocate bargaining power between parties in a way to encourage serious good faith bargaining. Foreigners, however, may be disadvantaged by this process, partly because they are excluded from the "old boy" network of former and current government officials.

Although Japanese courts traditionally held challenges to administrative guidance to be non-justiciable, recent decisions have recognized that the process involves an exercise of public authority and thus is reviewable in court. The primary standard of review employed by Japanese courts is whether, during a period when an agency is applying pressure, there was a reasonable expectation that the dispute could be settled by the mutual agreement of the parties. Once such an expectation is no longer present, the further application of administrative guidance is impermissable.

As noted previously, the emphasis in China has traditionally been on negotiation and mediation as methods of dispute settlement. Each contracting enterprise is supposed to organize its work in such a way as to avoid disputes. However, China's Economic Contract Law, effective July 1, 1982, envisages, in Articles 48, 49, and 50, substantial use of arbitration and the courts for settlement of disputes, even, in cases involving foreigners, reference to an arbitral tribunal in a third country. Whether this will come to pass, or mediation will continue to be the primary method of dispute settlement, remains to be seen.

---

[5] Young, *Judicial Review Of Administrative Guidance: Governmentally Encouraged Consensual Dispute Resolution In Japan*, 84 Colum. L. Rev. 923 (1984).

Finally, although the forms and rhetoric differ, these foreign attitudes may not be completely alien to the American lawyer's experience, if one takes account of the fact that only a very small percentage of law suits filed in this country actually go to trial and final judgement, the phenomenon of negotiating in the "shadow" of a lawsuit is pervasive, and in its psychological and tactical dynamics may not be as far removed from other legal cultures as might first appear.

Whatever other methods of dispute settlement may be used or attempted, litigation in national courts will continue to play a major role in the settlement of international business disputes. In the transnational transaction context, however, there may be several substantial hurdles to be crossed if adjudication is to succeed as a method of dispute settlement. These include, among other things, obtaining personal jurisdiction over the defendant; sovereign immunity; choice of forum and choice of law; problems in international discovery; and recognition and enforcement of foreign judgments.

§ 11.02   Obtaining Personal Jurisdiction

Introduction

In Chapter 6 and elsewhere we considered the subject of prescriptive jurisdiction. There we note, by way of a footnote, the distinction between "prescriptive jurisdiction," "personal jurisdiction," and "subject matter jurisdiction." We turn now to a discussion of personal jurisdiction and the most current approaches to defining the various categories of jurisdiction.

The Restatement (Third) of the Foreign Relations Law of the United States, Section 401 has the following to say regarding categories of jurisdiction:

401. Categories of Jurisdiction

Under international law, a state is subject to limitations on

> **(a)   jurisdiction to prescribe, *i.e.*, to make its law applicable to the activities, relations, or status of persons, or the interests of persons in things, whether by legislation, by executive act or order, by administrative rule or regulation, or by determination of a court;**

> **(b)   jurisdiction to adjudicate, *i.e.*, to subject persons or things to the process of its courts or administrative tribunals, whether in civil or in criminal proceedings, whether or not the state is a party to the proceedings;**

> **(c)   jurisdiction to enforce, *i.e.*, to induce or compel compliance or punish noncompliance with its laws or regulations, whether through the courts or by use of executive, administrative, police, or other nonjudicial action.**

In a Comment to Section 401, it is pointed out that the Restatement does not deal with the question of "subject matter jurisdiction", *e.g.*, the authority of a particular court to hear a given dispute, the character of a dispute as a "case or controversy" under Article III of the U.S. Constitution or other constitutional or statutory requirements for the jurisdiction of federal or state courts. As so defined, subject matter jurisdiction will, in this casebook, be discussed only as it occurs as an incidence of certain Constitutional doctrines considered in Chapters 2 and 13.

It is important to note, however, that issues of personal jurisdiction or jurisdiction to adjudicate, to use the Restatement's terminology, arise under both international and national law. As pointed out by the Restatement, "[t]raditionally, public international law dealt with judicial jurisdiction only when exercised on governmental initiative, and treated such jurisdiction as ancillary to jurisdiction to prescribe. The jurisdiction of courts in relation to private controversies was not an important concern of public international law, even when its exercise had transnational implications".[1]

With the realization of the disfunctional nature of the dichotomy between public and private international law, a subject treated extensively in Chapter 6, states have expressed greater interest in the exercise by national courts of judicial jurisdiction in private transactions. Gradually there has evolved a distinction between exercises of judicial jurisdiction that states regard as "reasonable" and those they consider "exorbitant." The precise dividing line between "reasonable" and "unreasonable" exercises of jurisdiction isn't clear at this time; courts and commentators have increasingly been attempting to draw the line.

Most of these attempts have taken place at the national level, although there has been some international activity recently. We first consider adjudicatory jurisdiction in the United States and then the law and practice in selected foreign countries. A primary issue posed is whether it is possible to deduce from national practice regarding judicial jurisdiction general principles of law suitable for incorporation into international law.

[A] Adjudicatory Jurisdiction in the United States

[1] Historical Development and An Overview: Some Comparative Examples

The traditional bases for the exercise of adjudicatory jurisdiction in the United States over natural persons have been consent and presence. In principle, consent as a basis for jurisdiction is straightforward enough; in practice, the issue has arisen whether a party "truly" consented to a court's jurisdiction or whether he was subject to overweaning bargaining power or was duped into consenting because of lack of understanding of standard consent clauses. This issue will be explored more extensively in the later section of this chapter on choice of forum and choice of law.

Presence as a basis for adjudicatory jurisdiction is derived from the territorial notion of jurisdiction and, as stated by Justice Holmes in *McDonald v. McGee*,[2] . . . from the concept of physical power over a defendant. From this it followed that the mere service of a summons and complaint upon a defendant temporarily within a state was sufficient to confer jurisdiction upon a court. Such service was

---

[1] Restatement (Third) of the Foreign Relations Law of the United States. Part IV, Chapter 2, "Jurisdiction To Adjudicate," Introductory Note at page 304.
[2] 243 U.S. 90, 91 (1917).

also sufficient to give notice to a defendant. However, with development of the concept that domicile alone was sufficient to bring an absent defendant before a court, notice of the proceeding became a separate requirement that had to be met to satisfy the constitutional demands of due process.

The theoretical basis of adjudicatory jurisdiction over a corporation has closely paralleled that over an individual, but not without difficulty. A corporation, viewed as a person for purposes of the due process clause of the 14th Amendment, was deemed to have its "domicile" in the state of incorporation. Corporations were also considered to be present, and therefore subject to jurisdiction, where they were "doing business," and many court decisions addressed the issue of the amount of activity sufficient to constitute doing business.

In *Pennoyer v. Neff*[3] . . . the Supreme Court treated this territorialist approach to personal jurisdiction as a due process limitation upon the states. In *Pennoyer*, Mitchell, an Oregon lawyer, had won an Oregon default judgment against Neff for $300 in attorney's fees. Neff, who lived in California, had been "served" by publication in an Oregon newspaper — it was unclear whether he had also been notified by mail, as required by Oregon statute. Neff's land in Oregon was sold to Pennoyer in satisfaction of the judgment. In response Neff sued Pennoyer in a federal court in Oregon to recover the land, contending that the sale was invalid because the state court had lacked jurisdiction over him. In agreeing with Neff's contention, the Supreme Court stated:

> . . . where the entire object of the action is to determine the personal rights and obligations of the defendant, that is, where the suit is merely in personam, constructive service . . . upon a non-resident is ineffectual for any purpose. Process from the tribunals of one State cannot run into another State, and summon parties there domiciled to leave its territory and respond to proceedings against them. Publication of process and notice within the State where the tribunal sits cannot create any greater obligation upon the non-resident to appear. Process sent to him out of the State, and process published within it, are equally unavailing in proceedings to establish his personal liability.

In the landmark case of *International Shoe Company v. State of Washington*[4] . . . the Supreme Court rejected the *Pennoyer* approach, which required the defendant to be present in the forum state at the time of service, in favor of defining the due process limitation as an element of a fair trial. There the court considered the quantity of activity in a state constitutionally required before causes of action unrelated to those activities could be asserted against the corporation. The Court upheld the assumption of jurisdiction by a State court in Washington in a suit to recover payments owed to a State unemployment compensation fund brought by the State against a foreign corporation which employed 13 salesmen in the state. The general principles stated by the Court have become the touchstone for the later development of jurisdictional requirements:

> Whether due process is satisfied must depend rather upon the quality and nature of the activity in relation to the fair and orderly administration of the laws which it was the purpose of the due process clause to ensure. . . . The

---

[3] 95 U.S. 714 (1878).
[4] 326 U.S. 310 (1945).

obligation which is here sued upon arose out of [defendant corporation's activities within the state]. It is evident that these operations establish sufficient contacts or ties with the state of the forum to make it reasonable and just, according to our traditional conception of fair play and substantial justice, to permit the state to enforce the obligations which [the foreign corporation] has incurred there.

Under the *International Shoe* analysis, the defendant's contacts serve as a substitute for presence and permit the exercise of jurisdiction when it comports with "fair play." This analysis had the effect of expanding the permissable limits of State jurisdiction over non-residents, both individual and corporate and gave rise to the so-called "long-arm" statute; a legislative enactment specifying the contacts that would allow courts of the forum State to exercise personal jurisdiction. In fact, a few States have been content, in their long-arm statutes, to provide simply that in every suit personal jurisdiction may be exercised so long as its reach does not offend constitutional standards. Until very recently, these constitutional standards were very expansive indeed. Perhaps the outer limit of State court *in personam* jurisdiction was reached in *McGee v. International Life Insurance Co.* [5] . . . where the Supreme Court held unanimously that the issuance and delivery of a single life insurance policy to a California resident, who remitted premiums by mail, allowed the courts of California to exercise jurisdiction in a beneficiary's suit for the policy proceeds. As we shall see in a later section, the Supreme Court has recently pulled back from this outer boundary.

The parent-subsidiary corporate relationship has given rise to several issues of adjudicatory jurisdiction. The most common issue is the amenability of a parent to suit in a State where its subsidiary does business but it does not. In *Canon Manufacturing Co. v. Cudahy Packing Co.* [6] . . . Canon, a North Carolina corporation, brought an action against Cudahy, a Maine corporation, in a North Carolina federal court. Service upon Cudahy was effected through delivery of a summons and complaint to an agent of its wholly owned subsidiary, an Alabama corporation doing business in North Carolina. The Supreme Court affirmed the decision of the district court that the defendant was not "present" in North Carolina for purposes of adjudicatory jurisdiction. The Court rejected the plaintiff's argument that defendant's apparent complete domination of its subsidiary should be sufficient to treat it as identified with a subsidiary for purposes of jurisdiction. Rather, the court noted that the corporate existence was kept distinct in all formal respects and that plaintiff was not attempting to hold defendant liable for an act of its subsidiary but solely for its own conduct. In its decision, which antedates the Federal Rules of Civil Procedure of 1938, the court expressly abjured resolving any "question of the constitutional powers of the State, or of the federal government."

This latter disclaimer allowed State courts, in later decisions, especially in New York, to take an expansive approach in asserting judicial jurisdiction over out-of-state corporate parents, sometimes under the Cannon theory and sometimes on an independent "doing business" theory. Some of these decisions may be read as

---

[5] 355 U.S. 220 (1957).

[6] 267 U.S. 333 (1925).

calling Cannon into question. See, e.g., *Taca International Airlines, S.A. v. Rolls-Royce of England, Ltd.*[7] . . . (Rolls-Royce Ltd. (England) exercised sufficient control over Rolls-Royce, Inc., (Delaware company doing business in New York) to be subject to suit in a New York court on an El Salvadorian company's claim of negligence in the manufacture of an engine in England which, in turn, caused a crash in Nicaragua.), *Frummer v. Hilton Hotels International*[8] . . . (by benefiting from the services of the New York based Hilton Reservation Service, London Hilton was "doing business" in New York in the traditional sense and was subject to suit there for personal injuries suffered in London.)

The New York courts have also asserted an expansive jurisdiction over out-of-state subsidiaries of parent corporations doing business in New York. For example, in *Public Administrator v. Royal Bank of Canada*[9] . . . the public administrator of the County of New York brought an action against the Royal Bank of Canada which did business in New York through its branch there, and also against the Royal Bank of Canada (France) a separately incorporated French entity wholly owned by the Royal Bank of Canada. The court found that the Royal Bank of Canada treated the French subsidiary not as a separate entity but as a fully integrated part of its operations, *i.e.*, its advertising, legal forms and personnel were all centrally controlled by the parent. On the basis of this finding, the court held both parent and subsidiary were liable to be sued in New York.

Summarizing these developments the Court of Appeals for the Second Circuit noted in *Beja v. Jahangiri*[10] . . . that "the New York Court of Appeals has sustained *in personam* jurisdiction . . . over foreign corporations each time it has considered the issue in the past decade" and has "gone very far" toward extending its jurisdiction over foreign corporations "to the fullest constitutional reach."

This record of uniform result was broken in *Delagi v. Volkswagenwerk, A.G.*[11] . . . . There, the New York Court of Appeals held that mere advertising in New York was not enough in itself to subject a German corporation to personal jurisdiction within the state. It also concluded that the foreign corporation was not present for personal jurisdiction purposes because of the activity in the state of a wholly owned New Jersey corporation where the subsidiary's activities were not so completely subject to the control of the parent that the subsidiary was in effect merely a department of the parent.

Even after *Delagi*, New York courts, as well as others, may hold the activities of a subsidiary to constitute business within the forum by the parent. But those seeking to convince a court to uphold such jurisdiction have a difficult burden to bear. They must demonstrate either that the subsidiary has no independent existence in fact and is merely an instrumentality of the parent or that the subsidiary is being used as an agent of the parent corporation within the state so that the acts of the subsidiary are the acts of the parent.

---

[7] 15 N.Y.2d 97, 204 N.E.2d 329, 256 N.Y.S.2d 129 (1965).

[8] 19 N.Y.2d 533, 281 N.Y. S.2d 41, 227 N.E.2d 851, *remitter amended*, 20 N.Y.2d 737, 283 N.Y. S.2d 99, 229 N.E.2d 696 (1967).

[9] 19 N.Y.2d 127, 278 N.Y. S.2d 378, 224 N.E.2d 877 (1967).

[10] 453 F. 2d 959, 962 (1972).

[11] 29 N.Y.2d 426, 328 N.Y. S.2d 653, 278 N.E.2d 895 (1972).

To be sure, this burden may still at times be met. In *Sunrise Toyota Ltd. v. Toyota Motor Company*[12] . . . an action under the antitrust laws and in State contract and tort claims, the court held a Japanese manufacturer subject to *in personam* jurisdiction because the manufacturer wholly owned and closely controlled a New York distributor corporation and held it out as being part of its network. In the view of the court the New York distributor was operating as an agent of its Japanese parent, and the latter was therefore doing business in New York.

Questions also arise with respect to judicial jurisdiction in federal causes of action, *i.e.*, suits arising under federal statutes. These statutes in turn may be divided into those that contain no special jurisdictional or venue provisions and those that do. In the first category of cases it has been held that Rule 4(e) of the Federal Rules of Civil Procedure requires that a federal district court exercise only such jurisdiction as comports with the applicable State long-arm statute. See, *e.g.*, *Arrowsmith v. United Press Int'l.*[13] . . . . In the second category, of course, the Federal statutory standard controls. For example, Section 22(a) of the Securities Act of 1933[14] . . . contains its own long-arm provision, providing that suits to enforce any liability or duty under the act: " . . . may be brought in the district wherein the defendant is found or is an inhabitant or transacts business, or in the district where the offer or sale took place, if the defendant participated therein, and process in such cases may be served in any other district of which the defendant is an inhabitant or wherever the defendant may be found." Similarly, Section 12 of the Clayton Act provides that any suit under the antitrust laws against a corporation "may be brought not only in the judicial district whereof it is an inhabitant, but also in any district wherein it may be found or transacts business; and all process in such cases may be served in the district of which it is an inhabitant, or wherever it may be found." The decisions have expansively interpreted the words "found" and "transacts business" and stressed the relevance of antitrust policy, that is, of the substantive claims asserted by the government, to resolution of the jurisdictional issues. So interpreted, Section 12 has been the basis for U.S. courts holding that alien parents, subsidiaries, and even contracting parties, constituted one business entity for jurisdictional purposes. See *e.g.*, *United States v. Scophony Corp. of America*[15] . . . *Hoffman Motors Corp. v. Alfa Romeo, SPA*[16] . . . . Lastly, under 35 U.S.C. Section 293, suit may be brought in the United States District Court for the District of Columbia against any patentee of a United States patent in an action affecting the patent or rights thereunder.

Perhaps most significantly for our purposes, the Foreign Sovereign Immunities Act[17] . . . discussed more extensively in the next section of this Chapter, provides for long-arm jurisdiction against the instrumentalities of a foreign government. The experience under state long-arm statutes may be significant for interpreting and applying the provisions of the Foreign Sovereign Immunities Act. Also, the

---

[12] 55 F.R.D. 519 (S.D.N.Y. 1972).

[13] 320 F. 2d 219, 224 (2d Cir. 1963).

[14] 48 Stat. 86, as amended, 15 U.S.C.A. Sec. 77 V(a).

[15] 333 U.S. 795 (1948).

[16] 244 F. Supp. 70 (S.D.N.Y. 1965).

[17] Pub.L. 94-583, 90 Stat. 2891 (1976); 28 U.S.C. Sections 1330, 1332(a)(2), (3) and (4) Section 1391(f), Section 1441(d), Sections 1602-1611.

Foreign Sovereign Immunities Act serves as a limit on the assertion of personal jurisdiction by a state court, i.e., if State law goes beyond the reach of the federal act, jurisdiction could not be asserted under the State statute.

When nationwide jurisdiction is conferred by statute, the "minimum contacts" required to sustain jurisdiction over a foreign or, more precisely, an alien defendant are those with the United States as a whole rather than the contacts with the state where the court sits. If the suit against an alien defendant is based upon a right created by a federal statute which contains no express provision for nationwide jurisdiction, the majority of federal courts have rejected the aggregate contacts test on the ground that there is no congressional authorization for it. Some courts, however, have been willing to aggregate contacts even in the absence of express congressional authorization for doing so. The courts have been unwilling to aggregate contacts in diversity cases. Some commentators have proposed that Congress pass legislation, or amend the Federal Rules of Civil Procedure, to make generally available in federal courts a doctrine of national contacts applicable to aliens[18] . . . .

Lastly, some controversial issues of judicial jurisdiction have arisen in European countries. Most controversial has been Article 14 of the French Civil Code, which provides that an "alien, even one not residing in France, may be summoned before the French courts for the fulfillment of obligations contracted by him in France with a French person; he may be brought before the French courts for obligations contracted by him in a foreign country toward French persons." As interpreted by the French courts, jurisdiction under Article 14 depends *exclusively* upon the French nationality of the plaintiff and covers not only contractual situations but also torts, matrimonial matters, and other legal duties. Conversely, Article 15 of the French Civil Code provides that a "Frenchman may be called before a French court for obligations contracted by him in a foreign country, even towards an alien." Under Article 15 as interpreted by the French courts, a foreigner may sue an absent French national in France even if the foreigner is neither domiciled nor a resident in France, and the cause of action sued upon is unrelated to France.

Another form of exorbitant judicial jurisdiction exercised in some European countries was first developed in Germany (see Section 23 of the German Civil Procedure Code) and is based on a defendant's ownership of property in the forum country. Under this approach a defendant who owns property in the forum thereby becomes subject to the *personal jurisdiction* of the courts of that country, and the effect of a judgment ultimately rendered is not limited to the value of the property. Thus, local property worth a relatively insignificant amount — say $300 — may be the basis for a multimillion dollar judgment against the defendant.

On the other hand, the countries on the continent of Europe have long rejected the mere transitory presence of a defendant in their territory as a basis for judicial jurisdiction. In their view, the common law country's exercise of jurisdiction on this basis is exorbitant, and, as we shall see later in this chapter, civil law courts refuse to enforce judgments grounded on such an exercise.

---

[18] See, *e.g.*, Lilly, *Jurisdiction Over Domestic And Alien Defendants*, 69 Va. L. Rev. 85 (1983); Note, *Alien Corporations And Aggregate Contacts; A Genuinely Federal Standard*, 95 Harv. L. Rev. 470 (1981).

Under the Convention on Accession to the Convention on Jurisdiction and the Enforcement of Judgments in Civil and Commercial Matters [19] . . . members of the EEC have renounced the use of exorbitant bases of jurisdiction as against defendants domiciled in the Common Market area, including jurisdiction based solely on the nationality of the plaintiff, the local presence of defendant's property, mere presence of the defendant and (subject to some qualifications) attachment as a basis of *quasi in rem* jurisdiction.

The Common Market Convention, however, is blatantly discriminatory against defendants not resident in the Common Market. Exorbitant jurisdiction against these defendants is strengthened by requirements that each state party to the Convention recognize and enforce judgments which other Common Market countries, using a regular or an exorbitant basis of jurisdiction, render against such defendants.

It is against this background that Section 421 of the Restatement (Third) of the Foreign Relations Law of the United States would limit a state's jurisdiction to adjudicate to exercises of such jurisdiction as are "reasonable." Specifically, Section 421 provides:

Section 421. Jurisdiction to Adjudicate

(1) A state may exercise jurisdiction through its courts to adjudicate with respect to a person or thing if the relationship of the state to the person or thing is such as to make the exercise of jurisdiction reasonable.

(2) In general, a state's exercise of jurisdiction to adjudicate with respect to a person or thing is reasonable if, at the time jurisdiction is asserted:

(a) the person or thing is present in the territory of the state, other than transitorily;

(b) the person, if a natural person, is domiciled in the state;

(c) the person, if a natural person, is resident in the state;

(d) the person, if a natural person, is a national of the state;

(e) the person, if a corporation or comparable juridical person, is organized pursuant to the law of the state;

(f) a ship, aircraft or other vehicle to which the adjudication relates is registered under the laws of the state;

(g) the person, whether natural or juridical, has consented to the exercise of jurisdiction;

(h) the person, whether natural or juridical, regularly carries on business in the state;

(i) the person, whether natural or juridical, had carried on activity in the state, but only in respect of such activity;

(j) the person, whether natural or juridical, had carried on outside the state an activity having a substantial, direct, and foreseeable effect within the state, but only in respect of such activity; or

[19] 25 Off. J., European Communities No. L 388 (1982).

> (k) the thing that is the subject of adjudication is owned, possessed, or used in the state, but only in respect of a claim reasonably connected with that thing.

A defense of lack of jurisdiction is generally waived by any appearance by or on behalf of a person or thing (whether as plaintiff, defendant, or third party), if the appearance is for a purpose that does not include a challenge to the exercise of jurisdiction.

A Comment on Section 421 states categorically that "jurisdiction based on service of process on a person only transitorily in the territory of the state is not generally acceptable under international law." Reporters' Notes following the Comments point out that the bases for judicial jurisdiction set forth in Section 421 have been developed in United States court decisions, including decisions of the Supreme Court and numerous state courts. Reporters' Note 1 also claims that "the modern concepts of jurisdiction to adjudicate under international law are similar to those developed under the due process clause of the United States Constitution. See Reporters' Note 2. The standards here set forth are comparable also to the criteria set out in Order 11 of the Rules of the Supreme Court of the United Kingdom (1983) and to the standards applicable among EEC domiciliaries set forth in the 1968 European Convention on Jurisdiction and the Enforcement of Judgments in Civil and Commercial Matters, as amended in 1978".[20]

In all of this it may be questioned whether any of these cited sources can accurately be described as sources of international law. If not, it may be doubted whether international law limits a state's jurisdiction to adjudicate.

§ 11.02   Recent United States Constitutional Developments

As noted above, the U.S. Supreme Court, in International Shoe, held that due process required that a defendant's contacts with the forum state be such as to "make it reasonable and just, according to our traditional conceptions of fair play and substantial justice," to allow the state to exercise personal jurisdiction over it. Then in *Shaffer v. Heitner*[1] . . . one Heitner, owner of one share of Greyhound stock and a non-resident of Delaware, brought a shareholder's derivative suit in a Delaware Court against Greyhound, a Delaware corporation, its wholly owned subsidiary, and twenty-eight of its officers and directors, none of whom resided in Delaware. Heitner sequestered the Greyhound stock owned by the absent officers and directors since Delaware law made Delaware the situs of all shares in companies incorporated in Delaware, and gave notice by certified mail to the individual defendants at their last known addresses. The defendants appeared specially and contended that *ex parte* sequestration violated due process and that Delaware did not otherwise have sufficient contacts with the defendant for its courts to exercise jurisdiction over them.

The trial court upheld jurisdiction, and the Delaware Supreme Court affirmed. On appeal, the U.S. Supreme Court reversed, holding that the attachment of intangible property alone (*i.e.*, *quasi in rem* jurisdiction) was an insufficient basis

---

[20] 21 Off. J., European Comm., No. L. 304, 18 Int'l Leg Mat. 21 (1979).
[1] 433 U.S. 186 (1977).

for jurisdiction absent the kind of contacts required by *International Shoe* for personal jurisdiction. In so ruling, the court pointed out that "the express purpose of the Delaware sequestration procedure is to compel the defendant to enter a personal appearance. In such cases, if a direct assertion of personal jurisdiction over the defendant would violate the Constitution, it would seem that an indirect assertion of that jurisdiction would be equally impermissable."

Three years later the Court had occasion to consider the implication of *Shaffer v. Heitner* further. In *World-Wide Volkswagen v. Woodson*[2] . . . the issue before the Court was "whether, consistently with the Due Process Clause of the Fourteenth Amendment, an Oklahoma court may exercise in personam jurisdiction over a nonresident automobile retailer and its wholesale distributor in a products liability action, when defendants' only connection with Oklahoma is the fact that an automobile sold in New York to New York residents became involved in an accident in Oklahoma." By a 5 to 4 margin, the Court held that it could not.

Justice White, writing for the majority of the Court, was of the opinion that the concept of minimum contacts in *International Shoe* could be "seen to perform two related, but distinguishable functions. It protects the defendant against the burdens of litigating in a distant or inconvenient forum. And it acts to ensure that the states, through their courts, do not reach out beyond the limits imposed on them by their status as coequal sovereigns in a federal system." While noting that modern transportation and communication had made it much less burdensome for a party to defend himself in a State where he engaged in economic activity, the Court cited "principles of interstate federalism" in holding that the reasonableness of asserting jurisdiction over the defendant had to be assessed with a view to ensuring the orderly administration of laws. According to the Court, the sovereignty of each State implied a limitation on the sovereignty of all other States. The Court went on to suggest that "[e]ven if the defendant would suffer minimal or no inconvenience from being forced to litigate before the tribunals of another State; even if the forum State has a strong interest in applying its law to the controversy; even if the forum State is the most convenient location for litigation, the Due Process Clause, acting as an instrument of interstate federalism, may sometimes act to divest the State of its power to render a valid judgment."

World-Wide Volkswagen did not involve a truly "foreign" defendant, *i.e.*, one from a foreign country rather than a sister State of the United States. Indeed, up to that time only one Supreme Court case had applied the minimum contacts standard of *International Shoe* to an alien defendant. The next case in which the Court did this was *Helicopteros Nationales de Colombia, S.A. v. Hall*[3] . . . . There, petitioner, a Colombia corporation, entered into a contract to provide helicopter transportation for a Peruvian consortium, the alter-ego of a joint venture that had its headquarters in Houston, Texas, during the consortium's construction of a pipeline in Peru for a Peruvian state-owned oil company. Petitioner had no place of business in Texas and never had been licensed to do business there. Its contacts with the State consisted of sending its chief executive officer to Houston to negotiate its contract with the consortium, accepting into its New York bank account checks drawn by the consortium on a Texas bank,

---

[2] 444 U.S. 286 (1980).
[3] 466 U.S. 408 (1984).

purchasing helicopters, equipment, and training sessions from a Texas manufacturer and sending personnel to that manufacturer's facilities for training. After a helicopter owned by petitioner crashed in Peru, resulting in the death of respondents' decedents — United States citizens who were employed by the consortium — respondents instituted a wrongful death action in a Texas state court against the consortium, the Texas manufacturer, and petitioners. The Texas Supreme court upheld the trial court's assertion of personal jurisdiction.

The U.S. Supreme Court reversed. In the view of the majority, petitioner's contacts with Texas were insufficient to satisfy the requirements of the Due Process Clause of the 14th Amendment. The one trip to Houston by petitioner's chief executive officer for the purpose of negotiating the transportation services contract could not be regarded as a contact of a "continuous and systematic" nature and thus could not support an assertion of general jurisdiction. Petitioner's other contacts with Texas, unrelated to the cause of action, were insufficient to constitute the "minimum contacts" required by *International Shoe* for this specific assertion of personal jurisdiction.

Justice Brennan dissented in *Helicopteros*. He agreed with the majority that the respondents' cause of action did not formally arise out of specific activities initiated by petitioners in Texas, but he was of the view that the wrongful death claim filed by the respondents was significantly related to the undisputed contacts between petitioners and the forum. This, Justice Brennan stated, should have been sufficient to uphold the Texas court's assertion of specific jurisdiction over the particular action.

Justice White, author of the *World-Wide Volkswagen* opinion, recently restated the interstate federalism rationale in the case in more qualified terms. In *Insurance Corp. of Ireland v. Compaigne des Bauxites de Guinea*[4] . . . the Court held that Rule 37(b)(2)(A) of the Federal Rules of Civil Procedure does not violate due process when applied to enable a district court, as a sanction for failure to comply with a discovery order directed at establishing jurisdictional facts, to proceed on the basis that personal jurisdiction over the recalcitrant party has been established. Justice White[5] . . . stated in pertinent part:

> It is true that we have stated that the requirement of personal jurisdiction, as applied to state courts, reflects an element of federalism and the character of state sovereignty vis-a-vis other states . . . the restriction on state sovereign power described in *World-Wide Volkswagen Corporation* . . . must be seen as ultimately a function of the individual liberty interest preserved by the Due Process Clause. That Clause is the only source of the personal jurisdiction requirement and the Clause itself makes no mention of federalism concerns. Furthermore, if the federalism concept operated as an independent restriction of the sovereign power of the court, it would not be possible to waive the personal jurisdiction requirement: Individual actions cannot change the powers of sovereignty, although the individual can subject himself to powers from which he may otherwise be protected.

---

[4] 456 U.S. 694 (1982).
[5] See: footnote 10, 456 U.S. at 702.

Most recently, the Court handed down the landmark decision set forth below.

ASAHI METAL INDUSTRY CO., LTD. v. SUPREME COURT OF CALIFORNIA, SOLANO COUNTY, ETC.

United States Supreme Court
480 U.S. 102, 107 S. Ct. 1026, 94 L. Ed.2d 92 (1987)

JUSTICE O'CONNOR announced the judgment of the Court and delivered the unanimous opinion of the Court with respect to Part I, the opinion of the Court with respect to Part II-B, in which the CHIEF JUSTICE, JUSTICE BRENNAN, JUSTICE WHITE, JUSTICE MARSHALL, JUSTICE BLACKMUN, JUSTICE POWELL, and JUSTICE STEVENS join, and an opinion with respect to Parts II-A and III, in which the CHIEF JUSTICE, JUSTICE POWELL, and JUSTICE SCALIA join.

This case presents the question whether the mere awareness on the part of a foreign defendant that the components it manufactured, sold, and delivered outside the United States would reach the forum state in the stream of commerce constitutes "minimum contacts" between the defendant and the forum state, such that the exercise of jurisdiction "does not offend traditional notions of fair play and substantial justice." *International Shoe Co. v. Washington*[6] . . . quoting *Milliken v. Meyer*[7] . . . .

I

On September 23, 1978, on Interstate Highway 80 in Solano County, California, Gary Zurcher lost control of his Honda motorcycle and collided with a tractor. Zurcher was severely injured, and his passenger and wife, Ruth Ann Moreno, was killed. In September 1979, Zurcher filed a product liability action in the Superior Court of the State of California in and for the County of Solano. Zurcher alleged that the 1978 accident was caused by a sudden loss of air and an explosion in the rear tire of the motorcycle, and alleged that the motorcycle tire, tube, and sealant were defective. Zurcher's complaint named, *inter alia*, Cheng Shin Rubber Industrial Co., Ltd. (Cheng Shin), the Taiwanese manufacturer of the tube. Cheng Shin in turn filed a cross-complaint seeking indemnification from its codefendants and petitioner, Asahi Metal Industry Co., Ltd. (Asahi), the manufacturer of the tube's valve assembly. Zurcher's claims against Cheng Shin and the other defendants were eventually settled and dismissed leaving only Cheng Shin's indemnity action against Asahi.

California's long-arm statute authorizes the exercise of jurisdiction "on any basis not inconsistent with the Constitution of this state or of the United States."[8] . . . . Asahi moved to quash Cheng Shin's service of summons arguing the State could not exert jurisdiction over it consistent with the Due Process Clause of the Fourteenth Amendment.

---

[6] 326 US 310, 316, 90 L.Ed. 95, 66 S.Ct. 154, 161 ALR 1057 (1945).
[7] 311 US 457, 463, 85 L.Ed. 278, 61 S.Ct. 339, 131 ALR 1357 (1940).
[8] Cal. Code Civ. Proc. Ann. Section 410.10 (West 1973).

In relation to the motion, the following information was submitted by Asahi and Cheng Shin. Asahi is a Japanese corporation. It manufactures tire valve assemblies in Japan and sells the assemblies to Cheng Shin, and to several other tire manufacturers, for use as components in finished tire tubes. Asahi's sales to Cheng Shin took place in Taiwan. The shipments from Asahi to Cheng Shin were sent from Japan to Taiwan. Cheng Shin bought and incorporated into its tire tubes 150,000 Asahi valve assemblies in 1978; 500,000 in 1979; 500,000 in 1980; 100,000 in 1981; and 100,000 in 1982. Sales to Cheng Shin accounted for 1.24 percent of Asahi's income in 1981 and 0.44 percent in 1982. Cheng Shin alleged that approximately 20 percent of its sales in the United States are in California. Cheng Shin purchases valve assemblies from other suppliers as well, and sells finished tubes throughout the world.

* * *

Primarily on the basis of the above information, the Superior Court denied the motion to quash summons, stating that "Asahi obviously does business on an international scale. It is not unreasonable that they defend claims of defect in their product on an international scale". . . .

The Court of Appeal of the State of California issued a peremptory writ of mandate commanding the Superior Court to quash service of summons. The court concluded that "it would be unreasonable to require Asahi to respond in California solely on the basis of ultimately realized foreseeability that the product into which its component was embodied would be sold all over the world including California.". . . .

The Supreme Court of the State of California reversed and discharged the writ issued by the Court of Appeal. . . . The court observed that "Asahi has no offices, property or agents in California. It solicits no business in California and has made no direct sales [in California]". . . . Moreover, "Asahi did not design or control the system of distribution that carried its valve assemblies into California". . . . Nevertheless, the court found the exercise of jurisdiction over Asahi to be consistent with the Due Process Clause. It concluded that Asahi knew that some of the valve assemblies sold to Cheng Shin would be incorporated into tire tubes sold in California, and that Asahi benefited indirectly from the sale in California of products incorporating its components. The court considered Asahi's intentional act of placing its components into the stream of commerce — that is, by delivering the components to Cheng Shin in Taiwan — coupled with Asahi's awareness that some of the components would eventually find their way into California, sufficient to form the basis for state court jurisdiction under the Due Process Clause.

We granted certiorari. . . .

II

A

The Due Process Clause of the Fourteenth Amendment limits the power of a state court to exert personal jurisdiction over a nonresident defendant. "[T]he constitutional touchstone" of the determination whether an exercise of personal jurisdiction comports with due process "remains whether the defendant purposefully established 'minimum contacts' in the forum State." *Burger King Corp. v. Rudzewicz*[9] . . . quoting *International Shoe Co. v. Washington*[10] . . . . Most recently we have reaffirmed the oftquoted reasoning of *Hanson v. Denckla*[11] . . . minimum contacts must have a basis in "some act by which the defendant purposefully avails itself of the privilege of conducting activities within the forum State, thus invoking the benefits and protections of its laws." *Burger King*[12] . . . . "Jurisdiction is proper . . . where the contacts proximately result from actions by the defendant himself that create a 'substantial connection' with the forum State." *Ibid.*, quoting *McGee v. International Life Insurance Co.*[13] . . . .

Applying the principle that minimum contacts must be based on an act of the defendant, the Court in *World-Wide Volkswagen Corp. v. Woodson*[14] . . . rejected the assertion that a consumer's unilateral act of bringing the defendant's product into the forum State was a sufficient constitutional basis for personal jurisdiction over the defendant. It had been argued in *World-Wide Volkswagen* that because an automobile retailer and its wholesale distributor sold a product mobile by design and purpose, they could foresee being haled into court in the distant States into which their customers might drive. The Court rejected this concept of foreseeability as an insufficient basis for jurisdiction under the Due Process Clause[15] . . . . The Court disclaimed, however, the idea that "foreseeability is wholly irrelevant" to personal jurisdiction, concluding that "[t]he forum State does not exceed its powers under the Due Process Clause if it asserts personal jurisdiction over a corporation that delivers its products into the stream of commerce with the expectation that they will be purchased by consumers in the forum State."[16] . . . .

In *World-Wide Volkswagen* itself, the state court sought to base jurisdiction not on any act of the defendant, but on the foreseeable unilateral actions of the consumer. Since *World-Wide Volkswagen*, lower courts have been confronted with cases in which the defendant acted by placing a product in the stream of commerce, and the stream eventually swept defendant's product into the forum State, but the defendant did nothing else to purposefully avail itself of the market in the forum state. Some courts have understood the Due Process Clause, as interpreted in *World-Wide Volkswagen*, to allow an exercise of personal jurisdiction to be based on no more than the defendant's act of placing the product in the stream of commerce. Other courts have understood the Due Process Clause and the above-quoted language in *World-Wide Volkswagen* to require the action of the defendant to be more purposefully directed at the forum State than the mere act of placing a product in the stream of commerce.

---

[9] 471 US 462, 474, 85 L. Ed 2d 528, 105 S. Ct. 2174 (1985).
[10] 326 US 310, 316, 90 L. Ed 95, 66 S. Ct. 154, 161 ALR 1057 (1945).
[11] 357 US 235, 253, 2 L. Ed 2d 1283, 78 S. Ct. 1228 (1958).
[12] 471 US, at 475, 85 L. Ed 2d 528, 105 S. Ct. 2174.
[13] 355 US 220, 223, 2 L. Ed 2d 223, 78 S. Ct. 199 (1957).
[14] 444 U.S. 286, 62 L. Ed 2d 490, 100 S. Ct. 559 (1980).
[15] *Id.*, at 295-296, 62 L. Ed 2d 490, 100 S. Ct. 559.
[16] *Id.*, 297-298, 62 L. Ed 2d 490, 100 S. Ct. 559 (citation omitted).

* * *

We now find this latter position to be consonant with the requirements of due process. The "substantial connection," *Burger King*[17] . . . *McGee*[18] . . . between the defendant and the forum State necessary for a finding of minimum contacts must come about by an action of the defendant purposefully directed toward the forum State. . . . The placement of a product into the stream of commerce, without more, is not an act of the defendant purposefully directed toward the forum State. Additional conduct of the defendant may indicate an intent or purpose to serve the market in the forum State, for example, designing the product for the market in the forum State, advertising in the forum State, establishing channels for providing regular advice to customers in the forum State, or marketing the product through a distributor who has agreed to serve as the sales agent in the forum State. But a defendant's awareness that the stream of commerce may or will sweep the product into the forum State does not convert the mere act of placing the product into the stream into an act purposefully directed toward the forum State.

Assuming, *arguendo*, that respondents have established Asahi's awareness that some of the valves sold to Cheng Shin would be incorporated into tire tubes sold in California, respondents have not demonstrated any action by Asahi to purposefully avail itself of the California market. Asahi does not do business in California. It has no office, agents, employees, or property in California. It does not advertise or otherwise solicit business in California. It did not create, control, or employ the distribution system that brought its valves to California . . . there is no evidence that Asahi designed its product in anticipation of sales in California. . . . On the basis of these facts, the exertion of personal jurisdiction over Asahi by the Superior Court of California[19] exceeds the limits of Due Process.

B

The strictures of the Due Process Clause forbid a state court from exercising personal jurisdiction over Asahi under circumstances that would offend "traditional notions of fair play and substantial justice". *International Shoe Co. v. Washington*[20] . . . quoting *Milliken v. Meyer*[21] . . . .

We have previously explained that the determination of the reasonableness of the exercise of jurisdiction in each case will depend on an evaluation of several factors. A court must consider the burden on the defendant, the interests of the forum state, and the plaintiff's interest in obtaining relief. It must also weigh in its determination "the interstate judicial system's interest in obtaining the most efficient resolution of controversies; and the shared interest of the several States

---

[17] 471 US, at 475, 85 L. Ed 2d 528, 105 S. Ct. 2174.

[18] 355 US at 223, 2 L. Ed 2d 223,78 S. Ct. 199.

[19] We have no occasion here to determine whether Congress could, consistent with the Due Process Clause of the Fifth Amendment, authorize federal court personal jurisdiction over alien defendants based on the aggregate of national contacts, rather than on the contacts between the defendant and the State in which the federal court sits.

[20] 326 US, at 316, 90 L. Ed 95, 55 S. Ct. 154.

[21] 311 US, at 463, 85 L. Ed 278, 61 S. Ct. 339.

in furthering fundamental substantive social polices." *World-Wide Volkswagen*[22]
. . . .

A consideration of these factors in the present case clearly reveals the unreasonableness of the assertion of jurisdiction over Asahi, even apart from the question of the placement of goods in the stream of commerce.

Certainly the burden on the defendant in this case is severe. Asahi has been commanded by the Supreme Court of California not only to traverse the distance between Asahi's headquarters in Japan and the Superior Court of California in and for the County of Solano, but also to submit its dispute with Cheng Shin to a foreign nation's judicial system. The unique burdens placed upon one who must defend oneself in a foreign legal system should have significant weight in assessing the reasonableness of stretching the long arm of personal jurisdiction over national borders.

When minimum contacts have been established, often the interests of the plaintiff and the forum in the exercise of jurisdiction will justify even the serious burdens placed on the alien defendant. In the present case, however, the interests of the plaintiff and the forum in California's assertion of jurisdiction over Asahi are slight. All that remains is a claim for indemnification asserted by Cheng Shin, a Taiwanese corporation, against Asahi. The transaction on which the indemnification claim is based took place in Taiwan; Asahi's components were shipped from Japan to Taiwan. Cheng Shin has not demonstrated that it is more convenient for it to litigate its indemnification claim against Asahi in California rather than in Taiwan or Japan.

Because the plaintiff is not a California resident, California's legitimate interests in the dispute have considerably diminished. The Supreme Court of California argued that the State had an interest in "protecting its consumers by ensuring that foreign manufacturers comply with the state's safety standards.". . . . The State Supreme Court's definition of California's interest, however, was overly broad. The dispute between Cheng Shin and Asahi is primarily about indemnification rather than safety standards. Moreover, it is not at all clear at this point that California law should govern the question whether a Japanese corporation should indemnify a Taiwanese corporation on the basis of a sale made in Taiwan and a shipment of goods from Japan to Taiwan. . . . The possibility of being haled into a California court as a result of an accident involving Asahi's components undoubtedly creates an additional deterrent to the manufacture of unsafe components; however, similar pressures will be placed on Asahi by the purchasers of its components as long as those who use Asahi components in their final products, and sell those products in California, are subject to the application of California tort law.

World-Wide Volkswagen also admonished courts to take into consideration the interests of the "several States," in addition to the forum state, in the efficient judicial resolution of the dispute and the advancement of substantive policies. In the present case, this advice calls for a court to consider the procedural and substantive policies of other nations whose interests are affected by the assertion of jurisdiction by the California court. The procedural and substantive interests

---

[22] 444 US, at 292 ,62 L. Ed 2d 490, 100 S. Ct. 559.

of other nations in a state court's assertion of jurisdiction over an alien defendant will differ from case to case. In every case, however, those interests, as well as the Federal interest in its foreign relations policies, will be best served by a careful inquiry into the reasonableness of the assertion of jurisdiction in the particular case, and an unwillingness to find the serious burdens on an alien defendant outweighed by minimal interest on the part of the plaintiff or the forum State. "Great care and reserve should be exercised when extending our notions of personal jurisdiction into the international field." *United States v. First National City Bank,*[23] . . . . (Harlan J., dissenting).

Considering the international context, the heavy burden on the alien defendant, and the slight interests of the plaintiff and the forum State, the exercise of personal jurisdiction by a California court over Asahi in this instance would be unreasonable and unfair.

III

Because the facts of this case do not establish minimum contacts such that the exercise of personal jurisdiction is consistent with fair play and substantial justice, the judgment of Supreme Court of California is reversed, and the case is remanded for further proceedings not inconsistent with this opinion.

It is so ordered.

JUSTICE BRENNAN, with whom JUSTICE WHITE, JUSTICE MARSHALL, and JUSTICE BLACKMUN join, concurring in part and in the judgment.

I do not agree with the plurality's interpretation of the stream-of-commerce theory, nor with its conclusion that Asahi did not "purposely avail itself of the California market.". . . . I do agree, however, with the Court's conclusion in Part II-B that the exercise of personal jurisdiction over Asahi in this case would not comport with "fair play and substantial justice". . . . This is one of these rare cases in which, "minimum requirements inherent in the concept of fair play and substantial justice' . . . defeat the reasonableness of jurisdiction even [though] the defendant has purposefully engaged in forum activities.". . . . I therefore join Parts I and II-B of the Court's opinion, and write separately to explain my disagreement with Part II-A.

The plurality states that "a defendant's awareness that the stream of commerce may or will sweep the product into the forum State does not convert the mere act of placing the product into the stream into an act purposefully directed toward the forum State.". . . . The plurality would therefore require a plaintiff to show "[a]dditional conduct" directed toward the forum before finding the exercise of jurisdiction over the defendant to be consistent with the Due Process Clause. . . . I see no need for such a showing, however. The stream of commerce refers not to unpredictable currents or eddies, but to the regular and anticipated flow of products from manufacture to distribution to retail sale. As long as a participant in this process is aware that the final product is being marketed in the forum State, the possibility of a lawsuit there cannot come as a surprise. Nor will the litigation present a burden for which there is no corresponding benefit. A defendant who has placed goods in the stream of commerce benefits economically from the retail

---

[23] 379 US 378, 404, 13 L. Ed 2d 365, 85 S. Ct. 528 (1965).

sale of the final product in the forum State, and indirectly benefits from the State's laws that regulate and facilitate commercial activity. These benefits accrue regardless of whether that participant directly conducts business in the forum State, or engages in additional conduct directed toward that State. Accordingly, most courts and commentators have found that jurisdiction premised on the placement of a product into the stream of commerce is consistent with the Due Process Clause, and have not required a showing of additional conduct.

The plurality's endorsement of what appears to be the minority view among Federal Courts of Appeals represents a marked retreat from its analysis in *World-Wide Volkswagen v. Woodson*[24] . . . . In that case, "respondents [sought] to base jurisdiction on one, isolated occurrence and whatever inferences can be drawn there from the fortuitous circumstance that a single Audi automobile, sold in New York to New York residents, happened to suffer an accident while passing through Oklahoma."[25] . . . . The Court held that the possibility of an accident in Oklahoma, while to some extent foreseeable in light of the inherent mobility of the automobile, was not enough to establish minimum contacts between the forum State and the retailer or distributor.[26] The Court then carefully explained:

> this is not to say, of course, that foreseeability is wholly irrelevant. But the foreseeability that is critical to due process analysis is not the mere likelihood that a product will find its way into the forum State. Rather, it is that the defendant's conduct and connection with the forum State are such that he should reasonably anticipate being haled into Court there[27] . . . .

The Court reasoned that when a corporation may reasonably anticipate litigation in a particular forum, it cannot claim that such litigation is unjust or unfair, because it "can act to alleviate the risk of burdensome litigation by procuring insurance, passing the expected costs on to consumers, or, if the risks are too great, severing its connection with the State." *Ibid.*

* * *

The Court in *World-Wide Volkswagen* thus took great care to distinguish "between a case involving goods which reach a distant State through a chain of distribution and a case involving goods which reach the same State because a consumer . . . took them there."[28] . . . (Brennan, J., dissenting). The California Supreme Court took note of this distinction, and correctly concluded that our holding in World-Wide Volkswagen preserved the stream-of-commerce theory. . . .

In this case, the facts found by the California Supreme Court support its finding of minimum contacts.The Court found that "[a]lthough Asahi did not design or control the system of distribution that carried its valve assemblies into California, Asahi was aware of the distribution system's operation, and it knew that it would benefit economically from the sale in California of products incorporating its components.". . . . Accordingly, I cannot join the plurality's determination that

[24] 444 US 286, 62 L. Ed 2d 490, 100 S. Ct. 559 (1980).
[25] *Id.*, at 295, 62 L. Ed 2d 490, 100 S. Ct. 559.
[26] *Id.*, at 295-296, 62 L. Ed 2d 490, 100 S. Ct. 559.
[27] *Id.*, at 297,62 L. Ed 2d 490, 100 S. Ct. 559.
[28] 444 US, at 306-307, 62 L. Ed 2d 490, 100 S. Ct. 559.

Asahi's regular and extensive sales of component parts to a manufacturer it knew was making regular sales of the final product in California is insufficient to establish minimum contacts with California.

JUSTICE STEVENS, with whom JUSTICE WHITE and JUSTICE BLACKMUN join, concurring in part and concurring in the judgment.

The judgment of the Supreme Court of California should be reversed for the reasons stated in Part II-B of the Court's opinion. While I join Parts I and II-B, I do not join Part II-A for two reasons. First, it is not necessary to the Court's decision. An examination of minimum contacts is not always necessary to determine whether a state court's assertion of personal jurisdiction is constitutional. . . . Part II-B establishes, after considering the factors set forth in *World-Wide Volkswagen Corp. v. Woodson*[29] . . . that California's exercise of jurisdiction over Asahi in this case would be "unreasonable and unfair.". . . . This finding alone requires reversal; this case fits within the rule that "minimum requirements inherent in the concept of fairplay and substantial justice' may defeat the reasonableness of jurisdiction even if the defendant has purposefully engaged in forum activities." *Burger King*,[30] . . . quoting *International Shoe Co. v. Washington*[31] . . . . Accordingly, I see no reason in this case for the Court to articulate "purposeful direction" or any other test as the nexus between an act of a defendant and the forum State that is necessary to establish minimum contacts.

Second, even assuming that the test ought to be formulated here, Part II-A misapplies it to the facts of this case. The Court seems to assume that an unwavering line can be drawn between "mere awareness" that a component will find its way into the forum State and "purposeful availment" of the forum's market. . . . Over the course of its dealings with Cheng Shin, Asahi has arguably engaged in a higher quantum of conduct than "[t]he placement of a product into the stream of commerce, without more. . . .". Whether or not this conduct rises to the level of purposeful availment requires a constitutional determination that is affected by the volume, the value, and the hazardous character of the components. In most circumstances I would be inclined to conclude that a regular course of dealing that results in deliveries of over 100,000 units annually over a period of several years would constitute "purposeful availment" even though the item delivered to the forum State was a standard product marketed throughout the world.

NOTES AND QUESTIONS

(1) Is the decision in *Asahi* a major victory for foreign manufacturers, or have they "won the battle but lost the war"?

(2) In her plurality opinion Justice O'Connor suggests that a court should consider "the procedural and substantive policies of other nations whose interests

---

[29] 444 US 286, 292, 62 L. Ed 2d 490, 100 S. Ct. 559 (1980).
[30] 471 US, at 477-478, 85 L. Ed 2d 528, 105 S. Ct. 2174.
[31] 326 US 310, 320, 90 L. Ed 95, 66 S. Ct. 154 (1945).

are affected by the assertion of jurisdiction by the California court." Does she identify these policies? What, in your opinion, are they?

(3) Suppose the Plaintiff in *Asahi* had not been Cheng Shin, a Taiwanese Manufacturer, but a manufacturer located in California who was seeking indemnity from Asahi. How would (should) the case have been decided?

(4) In the hypothetical in Note (3) California would clearly have a strong interest in entertaining plaintiff's suit, would it not? In *World-Wide Volkswagen* the Court noted that Oklahoma had a strong "interest" in entertaining plaintiffs' suit against defendants. Oklahoma was the place of the accident; personal and property injury occurred there; and medical expenses were incurred there. The plaintiffs in Volkswagen, however, were not residents of Oklahoma. The same was true with respect to the situation in Asahi: the plaintiff was not a resident of California. In every case in which the plaintiff is a resident the state of the forum will have an interest in exercising jurisdiction over defendants. Should this be determinative of the issue whether such an exercise of jurisdiction is constitutional? If the Oklahoma courts had been permitted to exercise jurisdiction over defendants in *World-Wide Volkswagen*, and the California courts in *Asahi*, who ultimately would have borne the costs of the accidents and the litigation?

In commenting on *World-Wide Volkswagen*, Professor Brilmayer has suggested that "the sovereignty concept inherent in the Due Process Clause is not the reasonableness of the burden but the reasonableness of the particular state imposing it."[32] She suggests further that the aspects of state sovereignty involved in *World-Wide Volkswagen* were twofold — self governance and territoriality — and that unrelated contacts were relevant to the first aspect and related contacts to the second. Thus, Professor Brilmayer states, "[s]ystematic unrelated activity, such as domicile, incorporation, or doing business, suggests that the person or corporate entity may safely be relegated to the State's political processes. Related contacts suggest a regulatory and territorial justification . . . the only related contact [in World-Wide Volkswagen] between the litigation and the State of Oklahoma was the occurrence of the injury in the forum. The court obviously did not find this contact sufficient, since it denied jurisdiction."[33]

Might Professor Brilmayer's observations be especially pertinent to the Court's decision in *Asahi*? Why did the Court in *World-Wide Volkswagen* and *Asahi* not find the occurrence of the injury in the forum to be a sufficient contact to support an exercise of personal jurisdiction? Can you think of reasons to support the Court's conclusion other than those advanced in its two opinions?

(5) To what extent, if at all, would you agree that "domestic Due Process standards derived from *International Shoe* and its progeny . . . do not adequately reflect the special considerations affecting jurisdictional claims in international cases."?

(6) Some commentators have interpreted the *Shaffer* decision so as to call into question the continued validity of transient presence as a basis for personal jurisdiction — the basis most often cited by commentators trained in the civil law

---

[32] Brilmayer, *How Contacts Count: Due Process Limitations On State Court Jurisdiction.*

[33] *Id.* at 87-88.

as an example of a common law exercise of exorbitant jurisdiction. In support of this contention these commentators point to *Shaffer's* reliance on minimum contacts as an indication of fairness, reasonableness and substantial justice and its emphasis that naked power, the original rationale for the sufficiency of presence, is no longer sufficient.

Other commentators have rejected this analysis. In their view *Shaffer* merely extends the minimum contacts test from personal jurisdiction to jurisdiction based on presence of property. Since transient presence had always been subject to the minimum contacts test before *Shaffer*, and had never been invalidated under the standard, mere extension of the test to quasi in rem jurisdiction would have no effect on transient presence. Further, these commentators reason, it is not clear that *Shaffer* had anything new to say about the minimum contacts required in personal jurisdiction cases.

On May 29, 1990, in *Burnham v. Superior Court of California, County of Marin*,[34] the Supreme Court unanimously held that service of a California court summons and a divorce petition on a man who was in the state for three days on business and for the purpose of visiting his children did not violate the due process clause of the Fourteenth Amendment. The Justices differed, however, with respect to the test to be applied in this case. Justice Scalia, who was joined by Chief Justice Rehnquist and Justice Kennedy, was of the opinion that long-standing tradition supported the proposition that transitory presence in a state was sufficient, without more, to serve as the basis for personal jurisdiction. Justice Brennan, however, in an opinion joined by Jutices Blackmun, Marshall, and O'Connor, contended that the mere "pedigree" of a jurisdictional rule did not establish that it comported with due process and that an independent inquiry should be made into the fairness of the prevailing in-state rule. Justice Brennan interpreted *Shaffer* as establishing that "all rules of jurisdiction, even ancient ones, must satisfy contemporary notions of due process." Justice Stevens declined to join either the Scalia or the Brennan opinion and wrote a separate concurring opinion. Justice White, who joined Scalia's opinion in part, also wrote a concurring opinion.

None of these opinions addressed the Restatement's suggestion that jurisdiction based on transitory presence is invalid under international law. Should they have?

(7) Attachment of property in a forum state may serve purposes other than that of obtaining quasi in rem jurisdiction over an absent defendant. For example, plaintiff may have already obtained a judgment in one state and seeks to enforce it against unrelated property located in another state. Dictum in the *Shaffer* case suggests that the presence of property by itself is a sufficient basis for an action to enforce a judgment. What is the basis for this conclusion, the full faith and credit clause to the United States Constitution? If so, is the exception inapplicable to foreign country judgments? Does it matter whether the property involved is tangible or intangible or if the defendant did not appear in the first action and wishes to argue that the court rendering the judgment had no jurisdiction?[34]

---

[34] — U.S. —, 110 S.Ct. 2105, — L.Ed.2d — (1990).

[34] The decision in *Shaffer* has prompted an extensive literature, some examples of which include: Hazard, *A General Theory Of State-Court Jurisdiction*, 1965 Sup. Ct. Rev. 241 (anticipating the decision in Shaffer); Casad, *Shaffer v. Heitner: An End To Ambivalence*

Property in a forum state may also be attached before a judgment is obtained elsewhere as security to satisfy any judgment that may be obtained. In *Carolina Power & Light Co. v. Uranex*[35] . . . plaintiff, a North Carolina utility, sought to garnish a debt owed by a California corporation to the French defendant. Although an $85 million dispute between the parties involving a contract for the delivery of uranium concentrates was in arbitration in New York, the defendant had no other assets in the United States. The court concluded that defendant's contacts with California were insufficient under *Shaffer* to permit an adjudication of the underlying claim, but upheld the attachment for purposes of securing payment of a New York arbitration award.

Is the court's distinction consistent with the minimum contacts standard of *Shaffer, World-Wide Volkswagen*, and *Asahi*, insofar as defendant was deprived temporarily of the use of his property? Should different tests be applied to attaching property before judgment and to attaching property to satisfy an existing judgment?

(8) Other Supreme Court decisions besides *Shaffer, World-Wide Volkswagen* and *Asahi* have supported the apparent trend toward more limitations on the assertion of in personam jurisdiction. In *Kulko v. Superior Court*,[36] a resident divorced mother of two filed suit in California, seeking an increase in the support payments made by her former husband, a N.Y. domiciliary. Invoking California's broad long-arm statute, she contended that the father's voluntary act of sending one of the children to reside with her in California was a sufficient contact with the forum. This act, coupled with California's strong interest in the welfare of resident minors, she argued, was sufficient to permit an action for the support of both children, since each resided in California with the father's acquiescence. The California courts sustained personal jurisdiction, but the Supreme Court reversed, on the ground that the defendant's consent to his daughter's change in residence and his provision of air transport did not constitute an act of purposeful availment. The court stressed that the defendant's contact was not "one that a reasonable parent would expect to result in the substantial burden and personal strain of litigating a child support suit in a forum 3000 miles away."

Similarly, the court in *Rush v. Savchuk*,[37] decided the same day as World-Wide Volkswagen, invalidated a Minnesota plaintiff's attachment of the "obligation" that a resident liability insurance company owed to a non-resident defendant. The Minnesota suit was a quasi in rem action in which the plaintiff's claim was for injuries sustained in an automobile accident in Indiana. Plaintiff's theory, based on a specific state statute, was that his claim could be satisfied up to the amount of the liability insurance proceeds. There was no basis for personal jurisdiction

---

In Jurisdiction Theory?, 26 U. Kan., L. Rev. 61 (1977); Silberman, *Shaffer v. Heitner: The End Of An Era*, 53 N.Y.U.L. Rev. 33 (1978); Riesenfeld, *Shaffer v. Heitner: Holding, Implications, Forebodings*, 30 Hastings L. J. 1183 (1979); *Symposium on Shaffer v. Heitner, Held at Brooklyn Law School December 9, 1978*, 45 Brooklyn L. Rev. 493 (1979); *Note, Attachment Jurisdiction After Shaffer v. Heitner*, 32 Stan. L. Rev. 167 (1979); *Note*, 32 U. of Miami L. Rev. 680 (1978).

[35] 451 F. Supp. 1044 (N.D. Cal. 1977).
[36] 436 U.S. 84 (1978).
[37] 444 U.S. 320 (1980).

over the non-resident defendant, but his liability insurer did substantial business in Minnesota and was accordingly amenable to service of process.

The Supreme Court struck down Minnesota's attempt to exercise judicial power. The purchase of a liability policy from a national company doing business in Minnesota and elsewhere was held not to constitute a "contact" within the meaning of *International Shoe*.

(10) At the same time that it has been placing constitutional limitations on state courts' assertions of in personam jurisdiction, the U.S. Supreme Court, in *All State Insurance Co.v. Hague*,[38] and *Phillips Petroleum v. Shutts*,[39] has indicated that few such constraints are applicable to a forum choosing to apply its own substantive state law to a controversy. Several commentators have noted the incongruity between the two standards and have suggested that they should be fully co-extensive. In the colorful language of Professor Silberman, for example, "to believe that a defendant's contacts with the forum state should be stronger under the Due Process Clause for jurisdictional purposes than for choice of law is to believe that the accused is more concerned with where he will be hanged than whether."[40] Do you agree with this suggestion?

§ 11.03   Sovereign Immunity

[A]   The Concept and Its Origins

The idea that the king can do no wrong, or at least cannot be held responsible under law for his actions, has deep historical roots. With the decline of the divine right of kings and the rise of the modern state, the absolute immunity of the king was transferred to the government. In the national context, this immunity was based on the concept of "sovereignty" and was illustrated by Justice Holmes' comment in *Kawananakoa v. Polybank*,[1] that "there can be no legal right as against the authority that makes the law on which the right depends." More pragmatically it has sometimes been argued that the full allowance of law suits against the government would impair governmental efficiency and lead to excessive liabilities.

With respect to the immunity of foreign sovereigns in U.S. courts, however, the theory is quite different. The classic statement is found in Chief Justice Marshall's opinion in *The Schooner Exchange v. McFaddon*.

---

[38] 449 U.S. 302 (1981).

[39] 472 U.S. 797 (1985).

[40] Silberman, *Shaffer v. Heitner: The End Of An Era*, 53 N.Y.U.L. Rev. 33, 88 (1978).

[1] 205 U.S. 349 (1907).

THE SCHOONER EXCHANGE v. McFADDON

United States Supreme Court
11 U.S. (7 Cranch) 116 (1812)

[The issue in this case was whether the French Emperor Napoleon could claim immunity from a libel action in a United States court brought by an American citizen to establish title to an armed French vessel, found within the waters of the United States.]

MARSHALL CH. J., delivered the opinion of the court.

The question has been considered with an earnest solicitude, that the decision may conform to those principles of national and municipal law by which it ought to be regulated. . . .

The jurisdiction of the nation within its own territory is necessarily exclusive and absolute. It is susceptible of no limitation not imposed by itself. Any restriction upon it, deriving validity from an external source, would imply a diminution of its sovereignty to the extent of the restriction, and an investment of that sovereignty to the same extent in that power which could impose such restriction. . . .

The world being composed of distinct sovereignties, possessing equal rights and equal independence, whose mutual benefit is promoted by intercourse with each other, and by an interchange of those good offices which humanity dictates and its wants require, all sovereigns have consented to a relaxation in practice, in cases under certain peculiar circumstances, of that absolute and complete jurisdiction within their respective territories which sovereignty confers.

This consent may, in some instances, be tested by common usage, and by common opinion, growing out of that usage.

A nation would justly be considered as violating its faith, although that faith might not be expressly plighted, which should suddenly and without previous notice, exercise its territorial powers in a manner not consonant to the usages and received obligations of the civilized world. . . .

This perfect equality and absolute independence of sovereigns, and this common interest impelling them to mutual intercourse, and an interchange of good offices with each other, have given rise to a class of cases in which every sovereign is understood to waive the exercise of a part of that complete exclusive territorial jurisdiction, which has been stated to be the attribute of every nation. . . . If, for reasons of state, the ports of a nation generally or any particular ports be closed against vessels of war generally, or the vessels of any particular nation, notice is usually given of such determination. If there be no prohibition, the ports of a friendly nation are considered as open to the public ships of all powers with whom it is at peace, and they are supposed to enter such ports and to remain in them while allowed to remain, under the protection of the government of the place. . . .

But in all respects different is the situation of a public armed ship. She constitutes a part of the military force of her nation; acts under the immediate and direct command of the sovereign; is employed by him in national objects. He has many and powerful motives for preventing those objects from being defeated by the interference of a foreign state. Such interference cannot take place without affecting his power and his dignity. The implicit license therefore under which such vessel enters a friendly port, may reasonably be construed, and it seems to the Court, ought to be construed, as containing an exemption from the jurisdiction of the sovereign, within whose territory she claims the rights of hospitality.

Upon these principles, by the unanimous consent of nations, a foreigner is amenable to the laws of the place, but certainly in practice, nations have not yet asserted their jurisdiction over the public armed ships of a foreign sovereign entering a port open for their reception. . . .

It seems then to the Court, to be a principle of public law, that national ships of war, entering the port of a friendly power open for their reception, are to be considered as exempted by the consent of that power from its jurisdiction.

Without doubt, the sovereign of the place is capable of destroying this implication. He may claim and exercise jurisdiction either by employing force, or by subjecting such vessels to the ordinary tribunals. But until such power be exerted in a manner not to be misunderstood, the sovereign cannot be considered as having imparted to the ordinary tribunals a jurisdiction which it would be a beach of faith to exercise. Those general statutory provisions therefore which are descriptive of the ordinary jurisdiction of the judicial tribunals, which give an individual whose property has been wrested from him, a right to claim that property in the courts of the country, in which it is found, ought not, in the opinion of this court, to be so construed as to give them jurisdiction in a case, in which the sovereign power has impliedly consented to waive its jurisdiction. . . .

If the preceding reasoning be correct, the Exchange, being a public armed ship, in the service of a foreign sovereign, with whom the government of the United States is at peace, and having entered an American port open for her reception, on the terms on which ships of war are generally permitted to enter the ports of a friendly power, must be considered as having come into the American territory, under an implied promise, that while necessarily within it, and demeaning herself in a friendly manner, she should be exempt from the jurisdiction of the country.

If this opinion be correct, there seems to be a necessity for admitting that the fact might be disclosed to the Court by the suggestion of the Attorney for the United States.

I am directed to deliver it, as the opinion of the Court, that the Sentence of the Circuit Court, reversing the sentence of the District Court, in the case of the Exchange be reversed, and that of the District Court, dismissing the libel, be affirmed.

NOTES AND QUESTIONS

(1) Compare Justice Holmes' comment regarding sovereign immunity in *Kawanankoa* with that of Chief Justice Marshall in *The Schooner Exchange*. Are the jurisprudential underpinnings of the two approaches the same?

(2) Did Chief Justice Marshall purport to apply international law in deciding that the Exchange was immune from a libel in admiralty? If so, consider the rationale for the rule of immunity and the values which the Chief Justice argues it serves. What are those values? That it will assure reciprocal treatment for the United States in the courts of other sovereign states? That it is a courtesy which has become habitual among sovereign states? That it serves broader systemic interests? Note that, while the Chief Justice does not use the word, it is very much akin to Storian "comity".

(3) In light of both the theory of foreign sovereign immunity and the values it is intended to serve, what role, constitutionally, may the Executive Branch play in determinations of immunity?

[B] Emergence of the Restrictive Theory of Sovereign Immunity and the Foreign Sovereign Immunities Act

At the international level, the absolute immunity of a state from the jurisdiction of the courts of another state was an established principle of customary international law. It was justified as required for the effective conduct of international relations and the maintenance of friendly relations.

As long as governments played the relatively limited role characteristic of their activities during the 19th Century, this absolute immunity caused no major problems. During the 20th Century, however, governments increasingly engaged in state trading and other commercial ventures. This gave rise to claims that absolute immunity was unfair because it deprived private parties of their judicial remedies when dealing with states, and gave the latter an unfair competitive advantage over private commercial enterprises. This claim was accepted by a federal district court in *The Pesaro*,[2] but in *Berrizzi Brothers Company v. S. S. Pesaro*,[3] the Supreme Court reversed and confirmed the absolute immunity approach.

During the same decade as the Supreme Court's decision in *Pesaro*, other countries accepted these claims and applied a more restrictive theory that denied immunity in cases arising out of commercial transactions by states or involving public vessels used for trade or commerce. The primary manifestation of this trend was the 1926 Brussels Convention on Immunity of State-Owned Vessels.[4] The Convention provides that seagoing merchant vessels owned or operated by states, cargoes owned by them and passengers carried on such vessels, and the states owning or operating the vessels or owning or operating such cargo are to be subject to the same rules of liability with respect to claims relating to such vessels as those applicable to privately owned vessels.

The United States was slow to adopt the restrictive approach to immunity. Moreover, as a matter of practice, the decision as to whether sovereign immunity was to be granted in a particular case was made by the Executive Branch, not the judiciary, unless the Executive determined to remain silent. As the Supreme Court in *Republic of Mexico v. Hoffmann*[5] said: "[I]t is a guiding principle in

---

[2] 277 F. 473 (S.D.N.Y. 1921).
[3] 271 U.S. 562 (1926).
[4] 176 L. N. T. S. 199, 2 Hackworth Digest of International Law 141 (1941).
[5] 324 U.S. 30, 35 (1945).

determining whether a court should exercise or surrender its jurisdiction in such cases, that the courts should not so act as to embarrass the executive arm in its conduct of foreign affairs. . . . It is therefore not for the courts to deny an immunity which our government has seen fit to allow, or allow an immunity on new grounds which the government has seen fit not to recognize." It still remains open whether this position was simply a matter of judicial deference originating in a judicially prescribed sense of self-restraint or whether it represented a more compelling emanation of the Constitution's separation of powers.

As to the restrictive theory of sovereign immunity, the U.S. approach changed in 1952. At that time the Acting Legal Adviser of the Department of State, Jack B. Tate, wrote to the Acting Attorney General, advising that "it will therefore be the Department's policy to follow the restrictive theory of sovereign immunity in the consideration of requests of foreign governments for a grant of sovereign immunity."[6] The procedure followed for the first few years following the Tate Letter was for foreign governments to submit their claims for sovereign immunity to the Department of State and for the Department to decide, without consulting plaintiffs, whether to advise the courts to recognize immunity. This approach was sharply criticized.[7] In response, the State Department's Office of the Legal Adviser began to hold quasi-judicial hearings on whether a particular claim of immunity was within the criteria set forth in the Tate Letter. The criteria set forth in the Tate Letter were not always followed, however. In several instances considerations of foreign policy apparently prompted the State Department to suggest a grant of immunity although application of the Tate Letter criteria indicated a contrary conclusion. We will examine one of the more notable examples of this in *Rich v. Naviera Vacuba, SA, infra.*

During the 1970s the attitude of the Department of State, partly in response to strongly held views on the part of the practicing bar, changed dramatically. The result was the adoption, in 1976, of the Foreign Sovereign Immunities Act, the text of which is set forth in relevant part below.

[C] Some Constitutional and Policy Issues

The Foreign Sovereign Immunities Act (FSIA)[8]

Section 1330. Actions Against Foreign States

(a) **The district courts shall have original jurisdiction without regard to amount in controversy of any nonjury civil action against a foreign state as defined in section 1603(a) of this title as to any claim for relief in personam with respect to which the foreign state is not entitled to immunity either under sections 1605-1607 of this title or under any applicable international agreement.**

(b) **Personal jurisdiction over a foreign state shall exist as to every claim for relief over which the district courts have jurisdiction under subsection (a) where service has been made under section 1608 of this title.**

---

[6] 26 Dept. State Bull. 1984 (1952).

[7] See Cardozo, *Sovereign Immunity: The Plaintiff Deserves A Day In Court*, 67 Harv. L. Rev. 608 (1954).

[8] 28 U.S.C. Section 1330 and Sections 1602-1611.

(c) For purposes of subsection (b), an appearance by a foreign state does not confer personal jurisdiction with respect to any claim for relief not arising out of any transaction or occurrence enumerated in sections 1605-1607 of this title.

Section 1602. Findings and Declaration of Purpose

The Congress finds that the determination by United States courts of the claims of foreign states to immunity from the jurisdiction of such courts would serve the interests of justice and would protect the rights of both foreign states and litigants in United States courts. Under international law, states are not immune from the jurisdiction of foreign courts insofar as their commercial activities are concerned, and their commercial property may be levied upon for the satisfaction of judgments rendered against them in connection with their commercial activities. Claims of foreign states to immunity should henceforth be decided by courts of the United States and of the States in conformity with the principles set forth in this chapter.

Section 1604. Immunity of a Foreign State from Jurisdiction

Subject to existing international agreements to which the United States is a party at the time of enactment of this Act a foreign state shall be immune from the jurisdiction of the courts of the United States and of the States except as provided in sections 1605 to 1607 of this chapter.

RICH v. NAVIERA VACUBA, S.A.

United States Circuit Court of Appeals (Fourth Circuit)
295 F. 2d 24 (1961)

[The factual background of this case is summarized in Cardozo, *Judicial Deference to State Department Suggestions: Recognition of Prerogative or Abdication to Usurper?*[9] In the wake of a series of hijacking incidents involving American and Cuban airplanes and vessels, the United States and Cuba entered into negotiations by diplomatic notes through third parties for their return. In particular, the notes focused on an Electra airplane owned by Eastern Airlines which had been hijacked to Havana on July 24, 1961, and on a Cuban patrol vessel that had been hijacked to Key West. Diplomatic correspondence between the two governments indicated a willingness on both sides to release the airplane and patrol boat. The Cuban Government also expressed a desire to adopt "the most effective measures to avoid in the future the repetition of acts of piracy and seizure of ships and airplanes. . . ." This correspondence was exchanged a few days before the occurrences that gave rise to the *Rich* case.[10]]

---

[9] 48 Cornell L. Q. 461, 464-67 (1963).
[10] See 45 Dept. State Bull. 407-408 (1961) for copies of this correspondence.

PER CURIAM

The vessel Bahia de Nipe sailed on August 8, 1961, from Cuba with a cargo of 5,000 bags of sugar destined for a Russian port. When on August 17 the ship was about 300 miles east of Bermuda the master and ten of his crewmen put the rest of the crew under restraint, turned the vessel towards Hampton Roads, Virginia, and notified the Coast Guard of their intention to seek asylum in the United States. As they crossed the three mile limit and neared the entrance to the Chesapeake Bay, the vessel was met by the Coast Guard and taken to anchorage off Lynnhaven, Virginia.

These proceedings were begun on August 18 by the filing of a libel against the vessel on behalf of two longshoremen who had earlier recovered judgments against the Republic of Cuba and Naviera Vacuba, S.A. The latter owned the vessel before she was taken over by the revolutionary government of Cuba. Shortly thereafter, another libel was filed against the ship and cargo by Mayan Lines, S.A. which had previously recovered judgment by consent in a state court of Louisiana in the sum of $500,000 against the Republic of Cuba. A third libel was filed against the cargo only by the United Fruit Sugar Company which claimed that the sugar belonged to it, having been unlawfully confiscated in Cuba by the revolutionary government. Libels for wages were also filed by the defecting master and the ten crew members. . . .

A number of communications from and on behalf of the Secretary of State addressed to the Attorney General were presented to the court by the United States Attorney. While infelicitously expressed, we think these sufficiently set forth the requisites of a valid suggestion for the allowance of sovereign immunity. . . .

. . . The chief defense, indeed the only one argued by the Government, is that the Republic of Cuba is a sovereign power immune from the jurisdiction of the courts of the United States, and that when the Department of State accepted Cuba's claim of ownership, possession and public operation of the cargo, and so certified to the court and suggested that sovereign immunity be accorded, the court was bound to respect the determination and suggestion of the State Department.

The libellants argue that before sovereign immunity may be granted they should be heard by the court on whether the foreign government is in fact the owner and possessor of the property in question and, as to the ship, whether she was operated by that government not commercially but in a public capacity.

For the libellant, United Fruit Sugar Company, evidence was adduced to prove that the very bags of sugar constituting the cargo were its property, expropriated from the company's plant in Cuba. Accordingly, this libellant asserted that release of the cargo under the doctrine of sovereign immunity, upon the mere certificate of the State Department would deprive it of property without due process of law in violation of the Fifth Amendment. Similar contentions under the Fifth Amendment were advanced by the other libellants.

Despite these contentions, we conclude that the certificate and grant of immunity issued by the Department of State should be accepted by the court without further inquiry. *Ex parte Republic of Peru*[11] . . . . See also *Republic of Mexico*

---

[11] 318 U.S. 578, 63 S. Ct. 793, 87 L. Ed. 1014.

v. Hoffmann[12] . . . . We think that the doctrine of the separation of powers under our Constitution requires us to assume that all pertinent considerations have been taken into account by the Secretary of State in reaching his conclusion.

The fact that the Mayan Line's judgment was rendered in the Louisiana court after a specific waiver of immunity by the Cuban Government, both with respect to liability and enforcement of the judgment, does not significantly distinguish its position from that of the other libellants, in view of the controlling effect that must be given the State Department's action. We do not mean to suggest that the contention raised by this libellant as to the effect to be given the waiver would not be a suitable subject of inquiry in the absence of State Department action. . . .

The order of the District Court is Affirmed.[13]

NOTES AND QUESTIONS

(1) Why would the Department of State support a decision to turn over determinations of immunity, as Section 1602 states, to the courts of the United States? If it is "not for the courts to deny an immunity which our government has seen fit to allow, or to allow an immunity on new grounds which the government has seen fit not to recognize," why not leave determinations of sovereign immunity with the Department? Can you think of any advantages from a foreign policy perspective in having the courts make such determinations?

(2) It is clear that, in passing the FSIA, Congress intended to terminate the practice of suggestions of immunity by the Department of State. Did it intend also to terminate the power of the President to make suggestions of immunity? Could Congress constitutionally do so?

(3) In considering these last two questions, suppose that the *Rich* case arose after passage of the FSIA. Examine Sections 1609 and 1610 (a) (1) & (3) as set out in the footnote.[14] What would be the result? In view of the background of the *Rich*

----

[12] 324 U.S. 30, 65 S. Ct. 530, 89 L. Ed. 729.

[13] After the decision in the *Rich* case, further diplomatic exchanges between the United States and Cuba resulted in the 1973 Memorandum Of Understanding On Hijacking Of Aircraft And Vessels And Other Offenses, 24 U.S.T. 737, T.I.A.S. No.7579.

[14] 1609. Immunity from attachment and execution of property of a foreign state.

Subject to existing international agreements to which the United States is a party at the time of enactment of this Act the property in the United States of a foreign state shall be immune from attachment arrest and execution except as provided in sections 1610 and 1611 of this chapter.

Sec. 1610. Exceptions to the immunity from attachment or execution

(a) The property in the United States of a foreign state, as defined in section 1603(a) of this chapter, used for a commercial activity in the United States, shall not be immune from attachment in aid of execution, or from execution, upon a judgment entered by a court of the United States or of a State after the effective date of this Act, if-

(1) the foreign state has waived its immunity from attachment in aid of execution or from execution either explicitly or by implication, notwithstanding any with-

case how would you assess those results in terms of the fundamental foreign policy interests of the United States?

(4) Section 1330 of the FSIA (the Act) provides that federal district courts shall have both personal and subject matter jurisdiction over civil suits against foreign states (defined elsewhere in the Act as including an agency or instrumentality of a foreign state). The courts have interpreted the personal jurisdiction conferred by the Act as roughly co-extensive with the due process clause of the Fifth Amendment to the Constitution.[15]

(5) The Supreme Court, in *Verlidor B. V. v. Central Bank of Nigeria*[16] interpreted Section 1330 of the FSIA as authorizing a foreign, non-resident plaintiff to sue a foreign state in a U.S. District Court. Since, in such circumstances, there is no diversity of citizenship, the Court, in order to uphold the constitutionality of this provision, had to conclude that all actions authorized by the FSIA constituted a proper exercise of "federal question" jurisdiction. What conceptual difficulties does this conclusion present? Is the substantive law applied in such a case likely to be federal or State law? What pragmatic considerations may have moved the Court?

(6) In spite of the decision in *Verlidor*, might suits between foreigners and foreign governments, especially if the plaintiff is a citizen of the defendant government, raise problems that should at times induce U.S. courts to insist that the case be tried in the courts of other nations? Upon what theory might a court rely in taking that action? What factors should it consider?[17]

[D]   Commercial Activities and the Nexus Problem

Section 1603. Definitions

For purposes of this chapter-

* * * *

    (d)   A "commercial activity" means either a regular course of commercial conduct or a particular commercial transaction or act. The commercial character of an activity shall be determined by reference to the nature of the course of conduct or particular transaction or act, rather than by reference to its purpose.

---

drawal of the waiver the foreign state may purport to effect except in accordance with the terms of the waiver, or

(2) the property is or was used for the commercial activity upon which the claim is based, or

(3) the execution relates to a judgment establishing rights in property which has been taken in violation of international law or which has been exchanged for property taken in violation of international law., or

[15] See, e.g., *East Europe Domestic International Sales Corporation v. Terra*, 467 F. Supp. 383, 387 (S.D.N.Y. 1979).

[16] 461 U.S. 480, 103 S. Ct. 1962 (1983).

[17] See Note, *Suits By Foreigners Against Foreign States In United States Courts: A Selective Expansion Of Jurisdiction*, 90 Yale L. J. 1861 (1981).

(e) A "commercial activity carried on in the United States by a foreign state" means commercial activity carried on by such state and having substantial contact with the United States.[18]

Section 1605. General exceptions to the jurisdictional immunity of a foreign state

(a) A foreign state shall not be immune from the jurisdiction of courts of the United States or of the States in any case—

(1) in which the foreign state has waived its immunity either explicitly or by implication, notwithstanding any withdrawal of the waiver which the foreign state may purport to effect except in accordance with the terms of the waiver;

(2) in which the action is based upon a commercial activity carried on in the United States by a foreign state; or upon an act performed in the United States in connection with a commercial activity of the foreign state elsewhere; or upon an act outside the territory of the United States in connection with a commercial activity of the foreign state elsewhere and that act causes a direct effect in the United States.

The language of Section 1605(a)(2) is similar in many respects to that found in State long-arm statutes. However, unlike courts interpreting and applying such statutes, a court cannot entertain an action brought under the Act until it has determined whether the defendant is engaged in a "commercial" or "sovereign" activity, since a state still enjoys complete immunity with respect to disputes arising out of its sovereign activities. Sections 1603(d) and (e) fail to provide the courts with precise guidance. Hence much litigation has centered on disputes over how the defendant state's activity should be characterized.

Consider, for example, whether the following activities should be characterized as "commercial."

---

[18] The remaining definitions contained in Sec. 1603 are as follows:

For purposes of this chapter

(a) A "foreign state", except as used in section 1608 of this title, includes a political subdivision of a foreign state or an agency or instrumentality of a foreign state as defined in subsection (b).

(b) An "agency or instrumentality of a foreign state" means any entity-

    (1) which is a separate legal person, corporate or otherwise, and

    (2) which is an organ of a foreign state or political subdivision thereof, or a majority of whose shares or other ownership interest is owned by a foreign state or political subdivision thereof, and

    (3) which is neither a citizen of a state of the United States as defined in section 1332(c) and (d) of this title, nor created under the laws of any third country.

(c) The "United States" includes all territory and waters, continental or insular, subject to the jurisdiction of the United States.

(a) A foreign government enters into contracts with U.S. suppliers for the purchase of large quantities of cement in order to build roads, army barracks, public buildings, etc. and is sued for breach of those contracts by the suppliers. *Texas Trading & Milling Corporation v. Federal Republic of Nigeria.*[19]

(b) A suit is brought by a charterer of a ship which was delivering rice against a company owned by a foreign government which had purchased the rice under a U.S. Government concessional sales program (P.L. 480) to recover for breach of an alleged guaranty of demurrage. *Gemini Shipping Inc. v. Foreign Trade Organization.*[20]

(c) A government owned corporation is created to explore and develop the country's hydrocarbon resources. It engages in drilling an exploratory oil well in its territorial waters in an effort to determine if deposits of oil and gas are located offshore. The drilling results in a disastrous oil leakage and oil from the well reaches and badly pollutes U.S. territorial waters and beaches. Owners, both public and private, of the despoiled property sue the foreign government corporation. *Matter of Sedco, Inc.*[21]

(d) A not-for-profit entity, a governmental instrumentality that exists to encourage foreign industrial development, engages in promotional activities and serves as a mediator to bring about the conclusion of a joint venture agreement between plaintiff and another instrumentality of the host country's government. Plaintiff sues both government instrumentalities for alleged breach of, and tortious interference with, the agreement. *Gibbons v. Udaras na Gaeltachta.*[22]

(e) The foreign government causes its own National Oil Corporation to breach a contract for the sale of crude oil to a private firm. *Carey v. National Oil Corporation.*[23]

(f) A labor union brings an action against the Organization of Petroleum Exporting Countries and its member countries seeking monetary and injunctive relief for price-fixing of crude oil prices in violation of the Sherman Anti-Trust Act. *International Association of Machinists and Aerospace Workers v. The Organization of the Petroleum Exporting Countries.*[24]

(g) A foreign government, through a written agreement, grants a U.S. corporation a ten-year license to capture and export rhesus monkeys. The licensing agreement specifies quantities and prices and provides for payment to the foreign government in fixed amounts. Shortly thereafter the world price for rhesus monkeys greatly increases. Two years later the foreign government terminates the agreement, and the U.S. corporation

[19] 647 F. 2d 300 (2d Cir. 1981).
[20] 647 F. 2d 317 (2d Cir. 1981).
[21] 543 F. Supp. 561 (S.D. Tex. 1982).
[22] 549 F. Supp. 1094 (S.D.N.Y. 1982).
[23] 453 F. Supp. 1097 (S.D.N.Y. 1978).
[24] 649 F. 2d 1354 (9th Cir. 1981), *cert. denied*, 454 U.S. 1163 (1982).

brings suit in federal district court. *Mol, Inc. v. Peoples Republic of Bangladesh.* [25]

(h) Mrs. Sanchez, a Nicaraguan citizen and the wife of President Somoza's Minister of Defense, purchases a certificate of deposit for $150,000 from Banco Nacional de Nicaragua, then a privately owned commercial Nicaraguan bank. Nicaragua later develops a critical shortage of foreign exchange, and the Nicaraguan Government adopts foreign exchange regulations severely limiting the use of foreign exchange. Concerned about this shortage of foreign exchange Mrs. Sanchez succeeds in inducing Banco Central de Nicaragua, Nicaragua's central bank, to issue a check for $150,000 in her favor, replacing the certificate of deposit issued by Banco Nacional. Payment on this check, however, is blocked by the new Sandinista Government. and Mrs. Sanchez sues Banco Central. *De Sanchez v. Banco Central de Nicaragua.* [26]

NOTES AND QUESTIONS

(1) Note that Section 1603(d) expressly provides that the test for a commercial activity is based on a "reference to the nature of the course of conduct or particular transaction or act, rather than by reference to its purpose." Is this sharp distinction between the "nature" and the "purpose" of an act workable? Consider, for example, in the preceding material, the *De Sanchez* case in paragraph (h), the *Mol Inc.* case in paragraph (g), and the *International Association of Machinists* case in paragraph (f). Professor Duncan Kennedy,[27] writing on a subject other than foreign sovereign immunity, has suggested that "the state has blurred into the rest of society. . . . There are no distinguishable state functions that aren't sometimes performed by private organizations, and no private functions that aren't sometimes performed by the state."

(2) Consider again the court's decision in *Rich v. Naviera Vacula, S.A., supra,* page 887. Would the acts in question in that case be regarded as "commercial" or "sovereign"? What effect, if any, would (should) a suggestion of immunity from the Executive Branch have?

(3) Professor Joseph Dellapenna[28] has suggested a balancing of interests test for claims involving foreign sovereign immunity. That is, the courts would balance the interest of a private party in having a remedy against the cost of asserting jurisdiction in politically sensitive cases. What do you think of this proposal?

---

[25] 736 F. 2d 1326 (9th Cir. 1984).

[26] 770 F. 2d 1385 (5th Cir. 1985).

[27] D. Kennedy, Legal Education And The Reproduction Of Hierarchy: A Polemic Against The System, 87 (1983).

[28] See J. Dellapenna, Suing Foreign Governments And Their Corporations 163 (1988).

Assuming that the activity can be characterized as "commercial" under Section 1605(a)(2) of the Act, there must be a sufficient nexus between the activity and the United States for American courts to exercise jurisdiction over claims against a foreign state. This exercise of jurisdiction is subject to the due process requirements of the Fifth and Fourteenth Amendments to the U.S. Constitution.

VENCEDORA OCEANICA NAVIGACION, S. A. v. COMPAGNIE NATIONALE ALGERIENNE DE NAVIGATION

United States Court of Appeals (Fifth Circuit)
730 F. 2d 195 (1984)

[The Panamanian owner of a vessel damaged by fire while at sea and towed into an Algerian port brought an action against Algeria and CNAN, an Algerian government corporation in charge of that country's harbor and coastal tugs, alleging that they had tortiously deprived the owner of its vessel. Tugs owned by CNAN had assisted the vessel. Subsequently a dispute arose over the amount that should be posted as security for these services. When agreement could not be reached, CNAN brought court proceedings in Algeria to realize on its security in the vessel. Thereafter, the Algerian government declared the vessel a wreck and ordered the owner to remove it from the Algerian maritime area. Upon the owners' failure to remove — they claimed obstruction by CNAN — their ownership rights in the vessel were declared forfeit under the Algerian maritime code. The owner thereupon commenced this action. The district court dismissed for lack of subject matter jurisdiction.]

Before RANDALL AND HIGGENBOTHAM, CIRCUIT JUDGES, and McDONALD, DISTRICT JUDGE.

[Plaintiff] first argues that the district court erred in failing to find subject matter jurisdiction under the first clause of Section 1605(a)(2). . . . [It] contends that the district court had jurisdiction by virtue of the unrelated continuing business CNAN does in the United States. CNAN does not deny that it does continuing business in the United States, but asserts that jurisdiction under this clause results only where the cause of action arises from business activity carried on in the United States. Because there is no nexus between CNAN's commercial activity and [Plaintiff's] we find that the district court properly dismissed [Plaintiff's] action.

. . . Courts of appeals and district courts have announced widely varying formulations of the jurisdictional scope of this clause, and these formulations may be divided into four categories: (1) a "literal" approach; (2) a "nexus" approach; (3) a bifurcated literal and nexus approach; and (4) a "doing business" approach.

A description of the first category, that favoring a literal approach, is contained in *Gibbons v. Udaras na Gaeltachta*[29] . . . where the court said: "Read literally,

---

[29] 549 F. Supp. 1094 (S.D.N.Y.1982).

'clause 1' requires that the cause of action be directly 'based upon' an act performed by the defendant 'in connection with' that commercial activity. Thus it is arguable that, where the defendant foreign state's commercial activity in the United States, not merely 'based upon' an act performed by the defendant 'in connection with' that commercial activity. Thus it is arguable that, where the defendant foreign state has carried on a commercial activity in the United States, clause 1 confers subject matter jurisdiction over a cause of action based upon an act performed *in the United States* in connection with that activity, but not over a cause of action based upon an act performed abroad in connection with that activity." *Id.* at 1109 n. 5 (emphasis in original). This literal reading of the first clause of section 1605(a)(2) was rejected by the *Gibbons* court, and, on the rare instances where it has been applied by district courts, it has been repudiated by the circuits. See *infra,Sugarman v. Aeromexico, Inc.*[30] . . . . See also *Gemini Shipping v. Foreign Trade Organization for Chemical & Foodstuffs.*[31]

The test set forth by the D.C. Circuit in *Gilson v. Republic of Ireland*[32] . . . seems to fall between a literal and a pure nexus approach. In *Gilson*, the court stated that "[s]ection 1605's 'based upon' standard is satisfied if plaintiff can show a direct causal connection between [the foreign entity's commercial activity in the United States] and the [acts] giving rise to his claims . . . or if he can show that [the commercial activity] is an element of the cause of action under whatever law governs his claims." *Id.* at 1027 n.22. Although the court made this statement in the context of interpreting the second, rather than the first, clause of section 1605(a)(2), its sweep has led at least one court to hold that the Gilson court's definition of "based upon" applies to all three clauses of 1605(1)(2). See *Gibbons v. Udaras na Gaeltachta.* \ . . .[33]

The Third Circuit has adopted a nexus approach more broad than either a literal approach or *Gilson's* requirement that the commercial activity in the United States constitutes or directly causes the occurrence of an element of the cause of action. See *Velidor v. L/PG Benghazi,*[34] . . . and *Sugarman v. Aeromexico, Inc.* In *Sugarman,* the plaintiff alleged that an extended delay at the Acapulco airport before the departure of his Aeromexico flight back home to Newark caused him heart problems. The court found jurisdiction under the first clause of section 1605(a)(2), but apparently the fact that "Aeromexico operations in New York . . . plainly constitute commercial activity carried on in the United States" was not enough. Instead, the court looked for a nexus between Aeromexico's commercial activity in the United States and Sugarman's grievance. In finding subject matter jurisdiction, the court found a nexus between the plaintiff's grievance and Aeromexico's commercial activity from the fact that the delayed flight that was bound for New York City was the return portion of a round-trip flight, and because Sugarman had bought his tickets at a travel agency in New Jersey. . . . See also *Gemini Shipping, supra.*

---

[30] 626 F. 2d 270 (3d Cir.1980).

[31] 647 F. 2d 317, 319 (2d Cir.1981).

[32] 682 F. 2d 1022 (D. C. Cir. 1982).

[33] 549 F. Supp. 1094, 1109 (S.D.N.Y. 1982).

[34] 653 F. 2d 812 (3d Cir.1981), *cert. denied,* 455 U.S. 929, 102 S. Ct. 1297, 71 L. Ed.2d 474 (1982).

In adopting a "nexus" approach, the *Sugarman* court specifically rejected the literal reading given to the first clause by the district court in dismissing Sugarman's claim. The court reasoned that Congress would have been clearer had it wanted to require that "the particular misconduct complained of take place 'in the United States,' " since Congress had been clear in adopting such a requirement in the second clause of section 1605(a)(2). The second clause excepts from immunity an action "based . . . upon an act performed in the United States in connection with a commercial activity of the foreign state elsewhere." The court also relied on the fact that such a limitation would be expected and perhaps required in light of due process considerations when, as in the second clause, the underlying commercial activity takes place outside the United States. But this would not be the expectation when, as in the first clause, "the acts complained of," although themselves extra-territorial, grow out of "a regular course of commercial conduct," 28 U.S.C. 1603(d), which was "carried on in the United States," for in such a case obviously there are no due process problems. . . .

An example of the remaining category, that applying a "doing business" test, is *Rio Grande Transport, Inc.*[35] . . . although the court did not specifically refer to its interpretation by that name. Rio Grande involved a collision in the Mediterranean between a vessel owned by CNAN, and an American-owned ship. The CNAN vessel maintained regular service between northern European ports and Algeria, and on this particular voyage was bound from Algeria to West Germany. Since the acts complained of had no particular nexus to the United States, the first clause applied only if jurisdiction could be based on CNAN's worldwide shipping activities, which had substantial contact with the U.S. The *Rio Grande* court reasoned that Congress's broad definition of "commercial activity" as including a "regular course of commercial conduct" meant that "Congress apparently did not intend to require that the specific commercial transaction or act upon which an action is based have occurred in the United States or have had substantial contact with the United States; only the broad course of conduct must be so connected.". . . . The court reasoned that a broad interpretation of "regular course of commercial conduct" was "consistent with 'Congress' goal of providing access to the courts to those aggrieved by the commercial acts of a foreign sovereign," and therefore found clause one subject matter jurisdiction based on CNAN's business in the United States. *Id.* (quoting *Texas Trading & Milling Corp. v. Federal Republic of Nigeria.*)[36] . . . .

We believe that the Third Circuit's nexus interpretation of the first clause of section 1605(a)(2) is sound and therefore adopt it as our own. We note first that this clause cannot mean what it literally says. . . . A literal reading of the clause would require the act complained of to occur in the United States; "the drafters of the FSIA intended no such niggardly construction." *Gemini Shipping v. Foreign Trade Organization for Chemicals & Foodstuffs, [supra].*

That clause one is not as restrictive as it literally appears, however, does not force us to read it as broadly as [Plaintiff] urges. We regard a nexus approach simply as a more effective means of carrying out the goal of requiring a connection between the lawsuit and the United States that the language of clause one appears

---

[35] 516 F. Supp. 1155 (S.D.N.Y.1981).
[36] 647 F. 2d 300, 313 (2d Cir. 1981).

to embody. A "doing business" test, on the other hand, focuses on the connection between the defendant and the United States; by definition it requires no specific connection between the lawsuit and the United States. Since, as the dissent notes, a "doing business" test is more controversial internationally than a nexus test, we think it likely that Congress specifically intended not to include "doing business" as one of the commercial activity exceptions, and did so in part through its restrictive wording of clause one. We note further that section 1605(a)(3),[37] the expropriation exception, clearly embodies a "doing business" test. That Congress made itself clear there when it meant to include a "doing business" test helps persuade us that Congress did not clearly include a "doing business" test among the commercial activity exceptions on purpose.

> Our adoption of the nexus approach also implements the congressional intent underlying the passage of the Act. This determination is based in part upon the recognition that the Act "starts from a premise of immunity, and then creates exceptions to the general principle."[38] . . . . By codifying the restrictive theory of foreign sovereign immunity in the Act, the Congress sought to strike a delicate balance between those aggrieved by the acts of governmental entities and the sovereignty of foreign states. To interpret the first clause of section 1605(a)(2) as urged by The *Rio Grande* court would be to open the floodgates to any controversy around the world, against any foreign entity "doing business" in the United States. Such an unprecedented assertion of jurisdiction over a foreign state was clearly not the Congressional intent underlying the passage of the Act. . . .

We further believe the Third Circuit's nexus approach to be superior to the approach arguably adopted by the D.C. Circuit in *Gilson*. *Gilson's* test would make

---

[37] Sec. 1605. General exceptions to the jurisdictional immunity of a foreign state:

(a) A foreign state shall not be immune from the jurisdiction of courts of the United States or of the States in any case

* * * *

(3) in which rights in property taken in violation of international law are in issue and that property or any property exchanged for such property is present in the United States in connection with a commercial activity carried on in the United States by the foreign state; or that property or any property exchanged for such property is owned or operated by an agency or instrumentality of the foreign state and that agency or instrumentality is engaged in a commercial activity in the United States;

(4) in which rights in property in the United States acquired by succession or gift or rights in immovable property situated in the United States are in issue; or

(5) not otherwise encompassed in paragraph (2) above, in which money damages are sought against a foreign state for personal injury or death, or damage to or loss of property, occurring in the United States and caused by the tortious act or omission of that foreign state or of any official or employee of that foreign state while acting within the scope of his office or employment; except this paragraph shall not apply to -

(A) any claim based upon the exercise or performance or the failure to exercise or perform a discretionary function regardless of whether the discretion be abused, or

(B) any claim arising out of malicious prosecution, abuse of process, libel, slander, misrepresentation, deceit, or interference with contract rights.

[38] House Report at 17, reprinted in 1976 U.S. Code Cong. & Ad. News 6616.

for a tighter connection between the United States and the lawsuit, but we see no reason for requiring a tighter fit under clause one, as opposed to clause two. The Third Circuit's nexus test better serves the purpose of simply requiring a connection between the lawsuit and the United States.

We also find support for our nexus interpretation in *Arango v. Guzman Travelers Advisors Corp.* [39] . . . where we offered a glimpse of our understanding of the first clause of section 1605(a)(2). In *Guzman*, the Arangos' vacation package was aborted prematurely when Dominican Immigration officials denied them entry into that country when they arrived at the airport in Santo Domingo. The officials compelled the Arango's immediate "involuntary-rerouting" back to the United States, which resulted in substantial inconvenience and economic loss in their effort to get back to the United States. The Arangos brought suit in state court for non-performance of the vacation contract against four defendants, including Compagnia Dominicana de Aviacion ("Dominicana"), the national airline of the Dominican Republic. Dominicana removed the action to federal district court and then moved to dismiss the action, arguing first, that as a foreign sovereign it was immune from the jurisdiction of the court under the provisions of the FSIA, and second, that the Arangos' complaint failed to state a complaint upon which relief could be granted because the misconduct complained of was insulated from judicial scrutiny by the "act of state" doctrine. Without specifying the grounds upon which it relied, the district court granted this motion and dismissed the Arangos' suit against Dominicana. The Arangos appealed, but we dismissed their appeal because their complaint against the remaining defendants was pending; therefore the dismissal against Dominicana had not constituted a final judgment. Although we found it unnecessary to decide whether Dominicana was subject to federal jurisdiction under the FSIA, we offered our interpretation of the first clause of section 1605(a)(2) in order to guide the district court on remand.

In construing this clause, we focused on whether Dominicana was immune from suit in federal court for breach of contract based upon miscarriage and non-performance of the vacation tour under the exceptions to the Act. In considering the applicability of the "commercial activity" exception under the first clause of section 1605(a)(2), we observed that "[t]he focus of the exception to immunity recognized in 1605(a)(2) is . . . *on whether the particular conduct giving rise to the claim in question actually constitutes or is in connection with* commercial activity" . . . (emphasis added). Consequently, we determined that the plaintiff's action for breach of contract was "based upon" the sale of airline tickets and tourist cards by Dominicana in the United States and, consequently, was not barred by foreign sovereign immunity. See also *Matter of Sedco, Inc* [40] . . . . Thus, although we did not label our interpretation of the first clause of section 1605(a)(2) as a "nexus test," our construction of the clause mirrors that of the Third Circuit's in *Sugarman, supra.*

---

[39] 621 F. 2d 1371, 1373 (5th Cir. 1980).
[40] 543 F. Supp. 561, 566 (S.D.Tex.1982).

* * * *

NOTES AND QUESTIONS

(1) Which of the several formulations of the jurisdictional scope of Section 1605(a)(2) reviewed by the Fifth Circuit most likely reflects the intentions of the drafters of the Section? Which is most likely to promote the smooth functioning of the world economy? Consider the example of a U.S. resident who lost his life in a hotel fire in Moscow or who was injured when the roof of a building collapsed in Iran. They both undoubtedly suffered "direct effects"; were they "in the United States?" See *Harris v. VAO Intourist, Moscow*[41] and *Upton v. Empire of Iran.*[42]

(2) How would these phrases apply to a corporation? Would they cover a failure to pay an American corporation overseas, or a foreign corporation in the United States? What about a failure to pay American corporations in the United States upon the presentation of shipping documents in accordance with terms of a contract negotiated abroad? Would they cover an alleged breach outside the United States by a foreign shipowner of a contract made abroad with foreign seamen when the ship sails into a U.S. port and the foreign seamen bring a claim under the Seaman's Wage Act, 46 U.S.C. Sec. 596-97? See *Texas Trading & Milling Corporation v. Federal Republic of Nigeria*[43] and *Velidor v. L/P/G Benghaz.*[44]

[E] Additional Interpretive Problems

The cases have not been in agreement on the issue whether an agreement to arbitrate constitutes a waiver of immunity for purposes of Sections 1605(a)(1), 1610(a)(1) and 1610(d)[45] of the Act. See, *e.g., Ipitrade International, S.A. v. Federal Republic of Nigeria,*[46] (waiver); *Libyan American Oil Company v.*

----

[41] 481 F. Supp. 1056 (E.D.N.Y. 1979).

[42] 459 F. Supp. 264 (D.D.C. 1978), *aff'd mem.*, 607 F. 2d 494 (D.C. Cir. 1979).

[43] 647 F. 2d 300 (2d Cir. 1981).

[44] 653 F. 2d 812 (3rd Cir. 1981).

[45] Sec. 1610. Exceptions to the immunity from attachment or execution.

* * * *

(d) The property of a foreign state, as defined in section 1603(a) of this chapter, used for a commercial activity in the United States, shall not be immune from attachment prior to the entry of judgment in any action brought in a court of the United States or of a State, or prior to the elapse of the period of time provided in subsection (c) of this section, if-

(1) the foreign state has explicitly waived its immunity from attachment prior to judgment, notwithstanding any withdrawal of the waiver the foreign state may purport to effect except in accordance with the terms of the waiver, and

(2) the purpose of the attachment is to secure satisfaction of a judgment that has been or may ultimately be entered against the foreign state, and not to obtain jurisdiction.

[46] 465 F. Supp. 824 (D.D.C. 1978).

Libya,[47] (waiver); *Verlidor v. Central Bank of Nigeria*,[48] (no waiver); *MINE v. Republic of Guinea*,[49] (no waiver). The issue regarding an agreement to arbitrate has now been resolved in favor of waiver by a recent amendment to the Foreign Sovereign Immunities Act (FSIA). See 28 U.S.C. Section 1605(a)(6).

In addition, the provisions of the FSIA dealing with immunity from execution were modified to permit execution on property of foreign states used for a commercial activity in the United States in cases where "the judgment is based on an order confirming an arbitral award rendered against the foreign State, provided that attachment in aid of execution, or execution, would not be inconsistent with any provision in the arbitral agreement." 28 U.S.C. Section 1610(a)(6).

Interpretive problems surround Section 1605(a)(3).[50] Under this section does a claim of right to the property depend upon a previous decision that its taking violated international law? if so, how useful is this provision? Alternatively, does Section 1605(a)(4)[51] require the courts to pass upon the international legality of a taking as part of determining whether to grant or deny a claim of immunity? If so, the Act of State Doctrine (see Chapter 13) may bar the court from passing upon the question of immunity. At least one court has so held. *Empresa Cubana Exportadora De Azucar Y Sus Derivados v. Lanborn & Co., Inc.*[52]

In response, the Section of International Law and Practice of the American Bar Association has recommended that the Act be amended by adding a new Section 1606(b) which would exclude application of the Act of State doctrine by a foreign state in cases where the Act confers jurisdiction upon the federal courts to adjudicate claims for expropriation or breach of contract. The Section suggests that adoption of this proposed new section would remedy an "anomalous situation" in current law.

Do you agree? Consider the materials on the Act of State Doctrine in Chapter 13. Are the goals the doctrine is designed to serve the same as those served by sovereign immunity? Or are the jurisprudential underpinnings of the Act of State doctrine sufficiently separate and distinct from those of sovereign immunity to warrant separate treatment?

On November 8, 1988, Congress adopted Public Law 100-640, which added a new provision to the Federal Arbitration Act. This provision, 9 U.S.C. Section 15, states that "[e]nforcement of arbitral agreements, confirmation of arbitral awards, and execution upon judgments based on orders confirming such awards shall not be refused on the basis of the Act of State doctrine." At this writing Congress has adopted no other statutory modification of the Act of State Doctrine.

Under Section 1605(a)(5)[53] the defense of sovereign immunity is not available to a foreign government in certain kinds of tort actions. One of the limitations

[47] 482 F. Supp. 1175 (D.D.C. Cir. 1981).
[48] 488 F. Supp. 1284 (S.D.N.Y. 1980), *affirmed*, 647 F. 2d 320 (2d Cir. 1981), *reversed on other grounds*, 461 U.S. 480 (1983).
[49] 693 F. 2d 1094 (D.C. Cir. 1982).
[50] For text see note 37, *supra.*
[51] For text see note 37 *supra.*
[52] 652 F. 2d 231 (2d Cir. 1981).
[53] For text see note 37 *supra.*

on a claim under this section is that the cause of action cannot be based upon a commercial activity falling under Section 1605(a)(2) of the Act. These "commercial torts", *i.e.*, causes of action sounding in tort and "based upon a commercial activity" are to be governed solely by Section 1605(a)(2). See *Yessenin Volpin v. Novosti Press Agency.*[54]

Several problems have arisen with respect to ensuring satisfaction of a judgment against a foreign state. Under Sections 1609 and 1610(d)[55] of the Act, no attachment prior to entry of judgment to secure satisfaction of a judgment is permitted absent an explicit waiver of immunity. Accordingly, a foreign state sued under the Act is free to remove its assets from the jurisdiction with impunity. *S & S Machinery Co. v. Masinexportimport.*[56]

Critics have also contended that the provisions of Sections 1610(a) and (b)[57] are unduly restrictive. The Section of International Law and Practice of the

[54] 443 F. Supp. 849 (S.D.N.Y. 1978).
[55] For text see note footnotes 14 and 45, *supra.*
[56] 706 F. 2d 411 (2d Cir. 1983).
[57] Sec. 1610. Exceptions to the immunity from attachment or execution.
(a) The property in the United States of a foreign state, as defined in section 1603(a) of this chapter, used for a commercial activity in the United States, shall not be immune from attachment in aid of execution, or from execution, upon a judgment entered by a court of the United States or of a State after the effective date of this Act if —
　(1) [Immunity has been waived. For text see note 14 *supra*]
　(2) the property is or was used for the commercial activity upon which the claim is based, or
　(3) the execution relates to a judgment establishing rights in property which has been taken in violation of international law or which has been exchanged for property taken in violation of international law, or
　(4) the execution relates to a judgment establishing rights in property-
　(A) which is acquired by succession or gift, or
　(B) which is immovable and situated in the United States: Provided, That such property is not used for purposes of maintaining a diplomatic or consular mission or the residence of the Chief of such mission, or
　(5) the property consists of any contractual obligation or any proceeds from such a contractual obligation to indemnify or hold harmless the foreign state or its employees under a policy of automobile or other liability or casualty insurance covering the claim which merged into the judgment.
(b) In addition to subsection (a), any property in the United States of an agency or instrumentality of a foreign state engaged in commercial activity in the United States shall not be immune from attachment in aid of execution, or from execution, upon a judgment entered by a court of the United States or of a State after the effective date of this Act if-
　(1) the agency or instrumentality has waived its immunity from attachment in aid of execution or from execution either explicitly or implicitly, notwithstanding any withdrawal of the waiver the agency or instrumentality may purport to effect except in accordance with the terms of the waiver, or
　(2) the judgment relates to a claim for which the agency or instrumentality is not immune by virtue of section 1605(a)(2)(3), or (5), or 1605(b) of this chapter, regardless of whether the property is or was used for the activity upon which the claim is based.
(c) No attachment or execution referred to in subsections (a) and (b) of this section shall be permitted until the court has ordered such attachment and execution after having determined that a reasonable period of time has elapsed following the entry of judgment and the giving of any notice required under section 1608(e) of this chapter.

American Bar Association, for example, has noted that Section 1605(a)(5) contains no express provision for execution on a tort judgment (except in the case of an insurance policy) and that a judgment under Section 1610(a)(2) can only be executed against the particular property used for the commercial activity upon which the claim is based. In the Section's view, the Act should be amended to provide for execution of judgment against any property of the foreign state which is used or is intended to be used for a commercial activity in the United States. Such a change would bring United States law into line with new statutes adopted in the United Kingdom and Canada.[58]

A number of countries besides the United States have adopted statutes on sovereign immunity. These include, for example, the United Kingdom, Canada, France, Pakistan and South Africa. In addition, the European Convention of 1972 on State Immunity constitutes a regional effort to come to grips with the problem. Recently, the International Law Association, a private organization of international law scholars and practitioners, adopted a Draft Convention on State Immunity in an effort to bring an international and comparative perspective to the area and to reconcile the different approaches reflected in national legislation.[59]

The text of the International Law Association's Draft Convention is set forth in your Documentary Supplement.[60] In what ways is it similar to or different from the Foreign Sovereign Immunities Act? Does the Draft Convention resolve the issues that have arisen regarding the FSIA? Should the United States support the conclusion of an international convention on state immunity, or should this continue to be a matter governed solely by national legislation? The International Law Commission is curently working on Draft Articles on Jurisdictional Immunities of States and Their Property.[61]

§ 11.04 Service of Judicial Documents and Obtaining Evidence Abroad for use in National Civil Litigation

Introduction

As preceding material in this casebook has made clear, litigation involving persons and evidence located in different countries has become increasingly frequent. With this increase, the need for improvements in "international judicial assistance" — assistance that domestic courts render to courts and litigants in other countries — has become compelling.

Basically, this assistance may take two forms: the service of such judicial documents as a summons and complaint or the obtaining of documentary or testimonial evidence for use in proceedings in the requesting country. Such assistance is necessary for it is well established under international law that neither

---

[58] American Bar Association Section of International Law and Practice, Report to the House of Delegates, August 1984.

[59] International Law Association, Report of the Committee on State Immunity, Report of the Sixtieth Conference 325 (1982).

[60] Documentary Supplement.

[61] See 26 Int'l Legal Mat. 625 (1987).

the service of judicial documents nor the taking of evidence in connection with litigation may be conducted in the territory of a state without that state's consent. Moreover, in the absence of a treaty, states render international judicial assistance only as a matter of comity.

The United States was slow in recognizing the need for international judicial assistance. Its courts looked solely to statutes for guidance and Congress approached international judicial assistance warily. Before 1964 no federal statute dealt with the service of foreign process in the United States, or with the service of American process abroad. With respect to obtaining evidence abroad in aid of litigation pending in this country, courts relied in large part on the procedural devices available for obtaining evidence in the territory of sister States. Statutory provisions for the issuance of letters rogatory — a method whereby a court in one country requests a court in another to assist it in the administration of justice — for the taking of evidence in foreign courts were rare.

Similarly, the United States was slow to recognize the need to conclude treaties and conventions relating to international judicial assistance. It declined several invitations to attend conferences on private international law held at the Hague at the end of the 19th and the beginning of the 20th Centuries, on the ground that constitutional limitations, especially its federal system, precluded its participation. Because of this attitude the United States was not even invited to the first post-World War II session of The Hague Conference, held in October 1951, where the Conference gave itself a permanent character and adopted a charter.

The first major change in this situation came in 1958 when Congress established the Commission on International Rules of Judicial Procedure to study the system of international judicial assistance in the United States and to recommend improvements. After joining forces in 1960 with the Project on International Procedure of the Parker School of Foreign and Comparative Law at Columbia University Law School, the Commission decided to concentrate initially on improving United States' domestic law. It did so on the ground that "internal reforms might obviate the need for international regulation, and that regulation by treaty might invade areas traditionally covered by state law."[1]

By way of reform the Commission and the Columbia Project recommended amending the Federal Rules of Civil and Criminal Procedure and revising those sections of the Federal Judicial Code dealing with the authority of courts to render international judicial assistance. Congress adopted the Commission's recommended changes in their entirety and enacted them into law in 1964. For its part the Supreme Court approved the Commission's proposed amendments to Rule 4 of the Federal Rules of Civil Procedure, providing for alternate methods of service of American judicial documents abroad, and Rule 28(b), governing the taking of depositions abroad and legitimizing the use of letters rogatory in federal civil proceedings. These amendments became effective on July 1, 1963.

The impetus for United States involvement in measures of international reform came from the private sector. In 1963, the American Bar Association and a number of other professional societies urged that the United States become a member of The Hague Conference on Private International Law. Pursuant to a

---

[1] 1 B. Ristau, International Judicial Assistance 10 (1984).

Joint Resolution passed by Congress, the United States joined the Conference in 1964. Since joining the Conference, the United States has become a party to three conventions adopted by the Conference and of interest for our present purposes. These include the Convention on the Service Abroad of Judicial or Extrajudicial Documents in Civil or Commercial Matters, done at the Hague, November 15, 1965,[2] entered into force for the United States, February 10, 1969; the Convention on the Taking of Evidence Abroad in Civil or Commercial Matters,[3] entered into force for the United States, October 7, 1972 and the Convention Abolishing the Requirement of Legalization for Foreign Public Documents, done at The Hague, October 5, 1961, entered into force for the United States, October 15, 1981.[4]

We first consider the problem of the service of judicial documents, both under United States law and international law. Next we turn to the question of obtaining evidence abroad for use in national civil litigation, again under both United States law and international law. In the section on obtaining evidence abroad we also take up the issue of the relationship between the Hague Evidence Convention and other sources of United States law on obtaining evidence.

[A] Service of Judicial Documents

[1] United States Law

In an action brought against a person not resident or present in the state where the action is brought, service of a summons or complaint or similar judicial documents is necessary to commence the action. It does not, however, by itself confer jurisdiction on the court where the process originated; rather, jurisdiction to adjudicate must be established in every case by the law and policies we discussed in § 11.02, *supra*.

United States law on the service of judicial documents in a foreign state, in addition to the Service Convention, which we discuss in the next subsection, consists of Rule 4 and Rule 28(b) of the Federal Rules of Civil Procedure and 28 U.S.C. Sections 1696 and 1781-1784. These provisions may be found in your Documentary Supplement.[5] In addition, a number of States in the United States have comparable rules.[6]

Note the alternative methods of service in a foreign country permitted by Rule 4(i). Further, Rule 4(e) provides for service "under the circumstances and in the manner prescribed by any statute or rule," and Rule 4(d)(7) allows service abroad in the manner prescribed by the law of the State in which the district court is located. If one of these methods is followed, several court decisions have held that such service is effective as a matter of United States law, even if it violates the law of the foreign state where service is made.[7] However, such service may

---

[2] 20 U.S.T. 361, T.I.A.S. No. 6638, 658 U.N.T.S. 163.

[3] 23 U.S.T. 2555, T.I.A.S. No. 7444.

[4] T.I.A.S. 10072, 527 U.N.T.S. 189.

[5] Documentary Supplement.

[6] See, *e.g.*, N.Y.C.P.L.R. Section 328.

[7] See, *e.g.*, *Atlantic Steamers Supply Co. v. International Maritime Supplies Co.*, 268 F. Supp. 1009 (S.D.N.Y. 1967); *ALCO Standard Corp. v. Benalal*, 345 F. Supp. 14, 26 (E.D. Pa. 1972); *Kadota v. Hosoga*, 608 P. 2d 68 (Ariz. App. 1980).

precipitate a diplomatic protest, and the country whose law has been violated is unlikely to enforce a judgment based on the violation. Enforcement may also be difficult in a third country. Court decisions have also held that service violating the law of a contracting party to the Hague Service Convention is not effective service for purposes of United States law.[8]

Rule 4(i)(B) of the Federal Rules of Civil Procedure and 28 U.S.C. Sec. 1781(b)(2) provide for service of process abroad by letters rogatory, transmitted to a foreign court or some other authority. Conversely, 28 U.S.C. Sec. 1781(b)(1) authorizes a United States court or judicial officer, including a United States marshal, to receive and execute a letter rogatory issued by a foreign court. Under 28 U.S.C. Sec. 1781(a), the Department of State is authorized to receive and to transmit letters rogatory. However, the State Department does not perform this function between states that are parties to the Hague Service Convention, since the Department of Justice has been designated as the Central Authority under the convention.

[2] International Law

The United States was an original party to the Hague Convention on the Service Abroad of Judicial and Extrajudicial Documents in Civil or Commercial Matters.[9] As of 1988, 26 states were parties to the Service Convention. In part the United States' strong support for the Convention was due to objections from countries in Europe (for example, Switzerland) to the service of summons and complaints in their countries without utilizing local authorities for purposes of transmission. The primary basis of these objections was that such service violated local law; some objections also raised a claim that international law had been violated, on the ground that such service infringed national sovereignty.

In contrast, most common law countries, including the United States, do not regard service of judicial process as a sovereign act which, if performed in their territory, must be performed by their own government officials. Accordingly, they normally raise no objections to service of process by mail, by personal delivery, or by consuls representing the state of origin of the process. Note, however, that, although the United States permits foreign consuls to serve process in the United States in actions originating in the sending state, it does not normally permit its diplomatic or consular officers to serve judicial process abroad.[10]

From the U.S. perspective the most objectionable practice was a procedure, common among civil law countries, called "notification au parquet." This procedure permitted service on a local official and deemed such service complete and effective regardless of whether the official actually transmitted it to the defendant or whether the defendant otherwise received notice of the pending lawsuit. For provisions of the Convention that address this practice, see Articles 15 and 16.

The Hague Service Convention provides for service of judicial and extrajudicial documents through a central authority established in each party to the convention.

---

[8] See, *e.g.*, *Low v. Bayerische Motorenwerke, A.G.*, 88 A.D.2d 504, 449 N.Y.S.2d 733 (1st Dep't 1982).

[9] Documentary Supplement.

[10] See 22 C.F.R. Section 92.85.

The central authority ensures that service of process is carried out by the authorities of the receiving state, thus obviating claims of intrusion upon the receiving state's territory or of violation of the due process rights of a defendant.

By "extrajudicial documents" the Service Convention refers to documents not involved with a law suit but which may require the intervention of a judicial authority and formal service under the law of the state of origin. Examples would include demands for payments, notices to quit leaseholds, protests of bills of exchange, and possibly consents to adoption or objections to a marriage.

NOTES AND QUESTIONS

(1) Consider Articles 5, 8, 10, and 21 of the Service Convention. Assume that you wish to serve a summons and complaint on a German national in the Federal Republic of Germany, a state party to the Convention that has held the traditional civil law view of service of process. What methods of service would be available to you under the Convention?[11]

(2) Suppose that a state party has filed no objection under Articles 8, 10 or 21 of the Service Convention. Would service on officials of the forum state, such as the Commissioner of Motor Vehicles or the Register of Corporations, be effective, assuming that the defendant in the foreign state party receives actual notice?[12]

(3) Courts in the United States have divided on the issue whether Article 10(a) of the Service Convention allows service of process on defendants in a foreign country by sending a copy of a summons and complaint directly to them by registered mail. Recently, the Federal Court of Appeals for the Eighth Circuit[13] held that it does not, on the ground that the word "send" in Article 10(a) is not equivalent to "service of process" and that Article 10(a) merely provides a method for sending subsequent documents after service of process has been obtained by means of the central authority.

(4) By its terms the Service Convention applies only to civil or commercial litigation, but these terms are not defined in the Convention. There is, moreover, no agreement among states that are parties on the definition of these terms. The United States and Great Britain consider any non-criminal proceeding to be covered by the Convention. France excludes fiscal as well as criminal proceedings. The Federal Republic of Germany apparently excludes any matter that involves the enforcement of "public law." Both France and the Federal Republic have refused to serve legal documents issued by the United States Environmental Agency, the International Trade Commission, and the Federal Trade Commission. Morover, two United States Court of Appeals decisions have suggested that

---

[11] See, *Richardson v. Volkswagenwerk, A.G.,* 552 F. Supp. 73 (W.D. Mo. 1982).

[12] See *Low v. Bayerische Motorenwerke, A.G.,* 88 A.D. 2d 504, 449 N.Y.S. 2d 733 (1st Dep't 1982).

[13] *Bankston v. Toyota Motor Corp.,* 889 F.2d 172 (8th Cir. 1989).

service by mail of an investigative subpoena of a U.S. agency, contrary to the law of the state where it was served, also violates international law.[14]

(5) With respect to the relationship between the Service Convention and other sources of United States law, the Supreme Court recently handed down a significant decision in *Volkswagenwerk Aktiengesellschaft v. Schlunk.*[15] In *Schlunk,* a mother and father were killed in an automobile accident, and their son sued the German manufacturer of the automobile his parents were driving. Plaintiff attempted to serve the German manufacturer through its wholly owned and controlled U.S. Subsidiary. Defendant objected on the ground that it had to be served in accordance with the terms of the Service Convention. This argument was rejected by the Illinois Appellate Court, which ruled that service on the subsidiary complied with the Illinois long arm statute and that no foreign service was required.

The Supreme Court unanimously agreed with the conclusion of the Illinois court, but three members of the Court differed with the six member majority as to the rationale for the holding. Writing for the majority, Justice O'Connor noted that under the terms of Article 1, the Convention applies "where there is occasion to transmit a . . . document for service abroad." According to O'Connor, who cited negotiating history in support of her position, since the Convention does not define the circumstances in which "there is occasion to transmit" a complaint for service abroad, courts must refer to the "internal law of the forum state," and only if the law of the forum requires service abroad, is the Convention mandatory. In this case, since the Illinois courts had held that service on the subsidiary was sufficient under the state law — and defendant had not challenged this determination — the Convention was inapplicable. O'Connor rejected the argument that service abroad was necessary because the subsidiary had to actually send the documents to the German corporation.

Justice Brennan, joined by Justices Marshall and Blackmun, challenged the majority's view that it is the law of the forum that controls whether service must be made abroad. In Brennan's opinion this approach undermines the mandatory quality of the Convention. Rather, he stated, the Convention itself provides a substantive standard for deciding whether service must be made abroad. In the words of Justice Brennan:

> The negotiating history and the uniform interpretation announced by our negotiators confirm that the Convention limits a forum's ability to deem service "domestic," thereby avoiding the Convention's terms. Admittedly, the Convention does not precisely define the contours. But that imprecision does not absolve us of our responsibility to apply the Convention mandatorily, any more than imprecision permits us to discard the words "due process of law," U.S. Const., Amdt. 14, Sec. 1. And however difficult it might be in some circumstances to discern the Convention's precise limits, it is remarkably easy to conclude that the Convention does not prohibit the type of service at issue here. Service on a wholly owned, closely controlled

---

[14] See *Federal Trade Commission v. Compaqnie de Saint-Gobain-Pont-a-Mousson,* 636 F. 2d 1300 (D.C. 1980); *Commodity Futures Trading Commission v. Nahas,* 738 F. 2d 487 (D.C. Cir. 1984).

[15] 486 U.S., 108 S. Ct.2104, 100 L. Ed.2d 722 (1988).

subsidiary is reasonably calculated to reach the parent "in due time" as the Convention requires. . . . That is, in fact, what our own Due Process Clause requires, see *Mullane v. Central Hanover Bank & Trust Co.*[16] . . . and since long before the Convention's implementation our law has permitted such service. . . . This is significant because our own negotiators made clear to the Senate their understanding that the Convention would require no major changes in federal or state service-of-process rules. Thus, it is unsurprising that nothing in the negotiating history suggests that the contracting nations were dissatisfied with the practice at issue here, with which they were surely aware, much less that they intended to abolish it like they intended to abolish *notification au parquet*. And since notice served on a wholly owned domestic subsidiary is infinitely more likely to reach the foreign parent's attention than was notice served *au parquet* (or by any other procedure that the negotiators singled out for criticism) there is no reason to interpret the Convention to bar it. My difference with the court does not affect the outcome of this case, and, given that any process emanating from our courts must comply with due process, it may have little practical consequence in future cases that come before us. But *cf.* S. Exec. Rept. No. 6, at 15 (statement by Philip W. Amram suggesting that Convention may require "a minor change in the practice of some of our States in long-arm and automobile accident cases" where "service on the appropriate official need be accompanied only by a minimum effort to notify the defendant"). Our Constitution does not, however, bind other nations haling our citizens into their courts. Our citizens rely instead primarily on the forum nation's compliance with the Convention, which the Senate believed would "provide increased protection (due process) for American Citizens who are involved in litigation abroad.". . . . And while other nations are not bound by the Court's pronouncement that the Convention lacks obligatory force, after today's decision their courts will surely sympathize little with any United States national pleading that a judgment violates the Convention because (notwithstanding any local characterization) service was "abroad."

It is perhaps heartening to "think that [no] countr[y] will draft its internal laws deliberately so as to circumvent the Convention in cases in which it would be appropriate to transmit judicial documents for service abroad" . . . although from the defendant's perspective "circumvention" (which according to the Court, entails no more than exercising a prerogative not to be bound) is equally painful whether deliberate or not. The fact remains, however, that had we been content to rely on foreign notions of fair play and substantial justice, we would have found it unnecessary, in the first place, to participate in a Convention "to ensure that judicial . . . documents to be served abroad [would] be brought to the notice of the addressee in sufficient time," 20 U.S.T., at 362.

The governments of France, the Federal Republic of Germany, Japan, and the United Kindom sent diplomatic notes urging that the Supreme Court reverse the Illinois Appellate Court and hold that the Service Convention applied in the Schlunk case. Even though Justice O'Connor agreed that the *notification au*

[16] 339 U.S. 306, 314-315 (1950).

parquet violated the Convention, doesn't her rationale open the door for the French to argue to the contrary? What is the status under the Convention of service on the Secretary of State or other designated State official in a suit against a foreign corporation?

[B] Obtaining Evidence Abroad

Introduction

In many instances there is a sharp contrast between the ease with which a foreign litigant can obtain evidence in the United States and the difficulties an American faces in securing evidence in a foreign state for use in the United States. This contrast is based on fundamental differences between the procedural system of the United States and that of most foreign countries, especially those within the civil law tradition.

Under 28 U.S.C. Sections 1781-82, no distinction is made between assistance requested by foreign courts in states parties to the Hague Evidence Convention and assistance requested by courts of other states. U.S. courts may also render assistance to foreign courts in criminal proceedings; to foreign authorities of a judicial character, such as investigating magistrates; and to international tribunals, even if the United States is not a party to the agreement that created the tribunal. Similarly, no special permission is required for execution of the commission of a foreign court to take evidence in the United States and, upon request, a U.S. district court will issue an order directing a witness within the district to give his testimony or produce a document.

Foreign tribunals may address letters rogatory (letters of request under the Hague Evidence Convention) directly to the U.S. court requested to give judicial assistance, or they may be transmitted through diplomatic or consular channels to the Department of State. The Department in turn sends them to the Civil Division of the Department of Justice, which sends them to the appropriate court or other authority, just as it does with letters of request received in accordance with the Hague Evidence Convention.[17] No showing of reciprocity is required for execution of letters rogatory in the United States.

Upon receipt of a letter rogatory, a U.S. district court will normally appoint a commissioner or a U.S. magistrate to preside over the witness's deposition or to conduct the questioning. The commissioner is authorized to obtain a subpoena ordering the witness to appear before him. If the letter rogatory was issued at the request of one party, counsel for the other party is entitled to be present and to cross examine. The grant or denial of execution of a letter rogatory is appealable to the court of appeals.

In contrast to all of this, U.S. requests for evidence abroad can face substantial obstacles, although these have eased somewhat recently. The reason is that in most civil law systems there is significantly less authority than in the United States to search for evidentiary facts. Moreover, unlike the U.S. system, any such authority is vested in the judge rather than in the attorneys and the authority to compel the

---

[17] See Stahr, *Discovery Under 28 U.S.C. § 1782 for Foreign and International Proceedings*, 30 Va. J. Int'l L. 597 (1990); Weiner, *In Search Of International Evidence: A Lawyer's Guide Through the United States Department of Justice*, 58 Notre Dame Law. 60 (1982).

production of evidence generally is far more limited than is the case in the United States. As a result, U.S. discovery techniques are frequently resisted because they are considered to violate deep-seated concepts of procedural justice.[18] We explore these below, first under United States law and then under international law. What follows is a discussion of the law governing efforts by U.S. litigants to obtain evidence from sources abroad.

[1] United States Law

Rule 28(b) of the Federal Rules of Civil Procedure provides that a United States district court may chose among one or more of several alternate methods of obtaining evidence abroad. Under Rule 28(b), it is not necessary for a court to find, before issuing a letter rogatory, that an alternate procedure, such as a commission or a deposition on notice, would be impracticable. Moreover, if use of a commission fails to obtain the evidence sought, then recourse to a letter rogatory is available. Nonetheless, some U.S. courts have required resort to letters rogatory before issuing discovery orders regarding information abroad. Their purpose in doing so has been either to show good will toward the foreign jurisdiction or to secure the view of the court of the foreign state on an asserted claim of privilege or of prohibition against disclosure. Under 28 U.S.C. Section 1783, incorporated by reference in Federal Rule of Civil Procedure 45(e)(2) and Federal Rule of Criminal Procedure 17(e)(2), subpoenas may be issued to persons in foreign states only if they are nationals or residents of the United States. Only the court — not the clerk of court or a grand jury — may issue such a subpoena and then only "if the court finds that particular testimony or the production of the document or other thing by him is necessary in the interest of justice." In a civil proceeding the court must find in addition "that it is not possible to obtain his testimony in admissible form without his personal appearance or to obtain the production of the document or other thing in any other manner." Under 28 U.S.C. Sec. 1784, punishment for contempt may be applied for a failure to comply with a subpoena properly issued to a U.S. national or resident outside the United States. See *Blackmer v. United States.*[19] Also, under 18 U.S.C. Section 1621, a person who swears falsely before any person authorized by U.S. law to administer oaths is guilty of perjury, whether the statement is made within or without the United States.

Pursuant to 28 U.S.C. Section 1782(a), a person whose testimony is sought abroad through letters rogatory or other forms of judicial assistance may invoke any testimonial privileges applicable, both in the requesting state and in the requested state. On the other hand, requirements regarding admissibility of evidence are relaxed regarding evidence obtained abroad. For example, under Rule 28(b) of the Federal Rules of Civil Procedure, evidence obtained through a letter rogatory issued by a United States court is not necessarily excludable because it is not submitted in the form of a verbatim transcript, or because the

---

[18] We are indebted to Professor David J. Gerber of the Chicago Kent School of Law for this point and for his many helpful comments on earlier drafts of this section. For further discussion, see Gerber, Extraterritorial Discovery And The Conflict Of Procedural Systems: Germany And The United States, 34 Am J. Comp. L. 745 (1986).

[19] 284 U.S. 421 (1932).

testimony was not given under oath, or for any similar departure from the requirements for depositions taken within the United States. The court has discretion in such cases, however, and may, in appropriate cases, assign such evidence less probative weight, or even exclude it entirely. The admissibility of such evidence in State courts depends upon the rules of procedure for the particular State concerned.

In proceeding under the Federal Rules of Civil Procedure and applicable federal statutes to obtain evidence from abroad, distinctions between testimonial and documentary evidence and between parties and non-parties should be kept in mind. The use of depositions, under Federal Rule of Procedure 5(d)(3), is the usual method of obtaining testimonial evidence abroad, since evidence obtained merely by affidavit will usually be excluded under the hearsay rule. Under Rule 28 a court is empowered to appoint a master to travel with the parties, supervise the depositions, and make rulings when appropriate. The taking of depositions abroad in the usual domestic manner, however, is dependent upon the willingness of the witness and lack of objection by the foreign state to the proceedings as the performance of an official function within its territory. If such an objection is forthcoming it will be necessary to resort under Rule 28(b)(3) and 28 U.S.C. Section 1781 to a letter rogatory requesting the assistance of the foreign court.

With respect to a *non-party* witness located abroad, the court may issue a subpoena under Rule 45 and 28 U.S.C. Section 1783, if the witness is a U.S. citizen or resident.[20] Its ability to enforce the subpoena will depend upon whether the witness has assets in the United States or later appears here. As to a foreign non-party witness, the cooperation of a foreign governmental agency will be needed and may require a formal request through a letter rogatory.

Under Rule 34 the court may issue a discovery order with respect to *documentary* evidence held by a party and threaten sanctions under Rule 37. Unless a foreign non-party witnesss is willing to produce requested documents voluntarily, it will be necessary to resort to a letter rogatory to secure the assistance of a foreign court or agency.

Cases on extraterritorial document inspection constitute a special case. U.S. courts have divided on the issus whether orders for such inspection violate foreign judicial sovereignty. Recently U.S. courts have tried an alternative approach and have ordered that parties produce the documents in the United States. Such removal orders have consistently been held, at least by U.S. courts, not to represent the exercise of judicial functions on foreign territory. See, for example, *Graco Inc. v. Kremlin, Inc. & SKM.*[21]

Requests of State courts for judicial assistance must be issued in accordance with the terms of the Hague Evidence Convention where the Convention is applicable. Under 28 U.S.C. Sec. 1783, State courts may use the Department of State to transmit requests for judicial assistance from states not parties to the Convention, but they are not required to do so.

---

[20] Subpeonas may, of course, also issue against a "party" to the litigation located abroad who is a U.S. citizen or resident but that is rarely necessary because other sanctions are available against a "party" who refuses to give evidence.

[21] 101 F.R.D. 503, 521 (N.D. Ill. 1984).

SOCIETE NATIONALE INDUSTRIELLE AEROSPATIALE and SOCIETE De CONSTRUCTION D'AVIONS De TOURISM v. UNITED STATES DISTRICT COURT FOR THE SOUTHERN DISTRICT OF IOWA

United States Supreme Court
482 U.S. 522 , 107 S. Ct. 2542, 96 L. Ed.2d 461 (1987)

MR. JUSTICE STEVENS delivered the opinion of the Court.

The United States, the Republic of France, and 15 other Nations have acceded to the Hague Convention on the Taking of Evidence Abroad in Civil or Commercial Matters, *opened for signature,* Mar. 18, 1970.[22] This Convention — sometimes referred to as the "Hague Convention" or the "Evidence Convention" — prescribes certain procedures by which a judicial authority in one contracting State may request evidence located in another contracting State. The question presented in this case concerns the extent to which a Federal District Court must employ the procedures set forth in the Convention when litigants seek answers to interrogatories, the production of documents, and admissions from a French adversary over whom the court has personal jurisdiction.

I

[The petitioners are corporations owned by the Republic of France engaged in manufacturing and marketing aircraft, one of which crashed in Iowa injuring the pilot and a passenger who then sued petitioners in the United States District Court for the Southern District of Iowa, alleging that the aircraft was defective due to petitioners' negligence and that petitioners had committed a breach of warranty. Petitioners answered without questioning the jurisdiction of the District Court. The cases were referred to a magistrate.]

Initial discovery was conducted by both sides pursuant to the Federal Rules of Civil Procedure without objection. Then plaintiffs served a second request for the production of documents pursuant to Rule 34, a set of interrogatories pursuant to Rule 33, and requests for admission pursuant to Rule 36. However, petitioners filed a motion for a protective order. The motion alleged that because petitioners are "French corporations, and the discovery sought can only be found in a foreign state, namely France," the Hague Convention dictates the exclusive procedures that must be followed for pretrial discovery. In addition, the motion stated that under French penal law, the petitioners could not respond to discovery requests that did not comply with the Convention.[23]

---

[22] 23 U.S.T. 2555, T.I.A.S. No. 7444.

[23] Article 1A of the French "blocking statute," French Penal Code Law No. 80-538, provides:

"Subject to treaties or international agreements and applicable laws and regulations, it is prohibited for any party to request, seek or disclose, in writing, orally or otherwise, economic, commercial, industrial, financial or technical documents or information leading to the constitution of evidence with a view to foreign judicial or administrative proceedings or in connection therewith."

"The parties mentioned in [Article 1A] shall forthwith inform the competent minister if they receive any request concerning such disclosures."

The Magistrate denied the motion insofar as it related to answering interrogatories, producing documents, and making admissions. After reviewing the relevant cases, the Magistrate explained:

> To permit the Hague Evidence Convention to override the Federal Rules of Civil Procedure would frustrate the courts' interests, which particularly arise in products liability cases, in protecting United States citizens from harmful products and in compensating them for injuries arising from use of such products.

The Magistrate made two responses to petitioners' argument that they could not comply with the discovery requests without violating French penal law. Noting that the law was originally "inspired to impede enforcement of United States antitrust laws," and that it did not appear to have been strictly enforced in France, he first questioned whether it would be construed to apply to the pretrial discovery requests at issue. Second, he balanced the interests in the "protection of United States citizens from harmful foreign products . . . " against France's interest in protecting its citizens "from intrusive foreign discovery procedures." The Magistrate concluded that the former interests were stronger, particularly because compliance with the requested discovery will "not have to take place in France" and will not be greatly intrusive or abusive. . . .

Petitioners sought a writ of mandamus from the Court of Appeals for the Eighth Circuit. . . . [The latter court denied the mandamus petition, concluding] . . . that "when the district court has jurisdiction over a foreign litigant the Hague Convention does not apply to the production of evidence in that litigant's possession, even though the documents and information sought may physically be located within the territory of a foreign signatory to the Convention." [It also] . . . disagreed with petitioners' argument that this construction would render the entire Hague Convention "meaningless," noting that it would still serve the purpose of providing an improved procedure for obtaining evidence from nonparties. . . . [The court also] rejected petitioners' contention that considerations of international comity required plaintiffs to resort to Hague Convention procedures as an initial matter ("first use") . . . [and] the federal discovery rules only if the treaty procedures turned out to be futile, [arguing] . . . that the potential overruling of foreign tribunals' denial of discovery would do more to defeat than to promote international comity. . . . Finally, the Court of Appeals concluded that objections based on the French penal statute should be considered in two stages: first, whether the discovery order was proper even though compliance may require petitioners to violate French law; and second, what sanctions, if any, should be imposed if petitioners are unable to comply. [It] . . . held that the Magistrate properly answered the first question and that it was premature to address the second. . . .

II

In the District Court and the Court of Appeals, petitioners contended that the Hague Evidence Convention "provides the exclusive and mandatory procedures for obtaining documents and information located within the territory of a foreign signatory.". . . . We are satisfied that the Court of Appeals correctly rejected this extreme position. We believe it is foreclosed by the plain language of the Convention. . . .

[At this point the Court reviews some of the history leading up to adoption of the Hague Evidence Convention.]

* * * *

. . . [In his letter of submittal to the President the Secretary of State fairly summarized the Convention as follows:]

. . . The substantial increase in litigation with foreign aspects arising, in part, from the unparalleled expansion of international trade and travel in recent decades had intensified the need for an effective international agreement to set up a model system to bridge differences between the common law and civil law approaches to the taking of evidence abroad.

Civil law countries tend to concentrate on *commissions rogatories*, while common law countries take testimony on notice, by stipulation and through commissions to consuls or commissioners. . . . The civil law technique results normally in a resume of the evidence, prepared by the executing judge and signed by the witness, while the common law technique results normally in a verbatim transcript of the witness's testimony certified by the reporter.

Failure by either the requesting state or the state of execution fully to take into account the differences of approach to the taking of evidence abroad under the two systems and the absence of agreed standards applicable to letters of request have frequently caused difficulties for courts and litigants. To minimize such difficulties in the future, the enclosed convention . . . is designed to:

1. Make the employment of letters of request a principal means of obtaining evidence abroad;

2. Improve the means of securing evidence abroad by increasing the powers of consuls and by introducing in the civil law world, on a limited basis, the concept of the commissioner;

3. Provide means of securing evidence in the form needed by the court where the action is pending; and

4. Preserve all more favorable and less restrictive practices arising from internal law, internal rules of procedure and bilateral or multilateral conventions.

What the convention does is to provide a set of minimum standards with which contracting states agree to comply. Further, . . . it provides a flexible framework within which any future liberalizing changes in policy and tradition in any country . . . may be translated into effective change in international procedures. At the same time it recognizes and preserves procedures of every country which now or hereafter may provide international cooperation in the taking of evidence on more liberal and less restrictive basis, whether this is effected by supplementary agreements or by municipal law and practice.

III

In arguing their entitlement to a protective order, petitioners correctly assert that both the discovery rules set forth in the Federal Rules of Civil Procedure and the Hague Convention are the law of the United States. . . . This observation, however, does not dispose of the question before us. . . . Initially, we note that at least four different interpretations of the relationship between the federal discovery rules and the Hague Convention are possible. Two of these interpretations assume that the Hague Convention by its terms dictates the extent to which it supplants normal discovery rules. First, the Hague Convention might be read as requiring its use to the exclusion of any other discovery procedures whenever evidence located abroad is sought for use in an American court. Second, the Hague Convention might be interpreted to require first, but not exclusive, use of its procedures. . . . Third, . . . the Convention might be viewed as establishing a supplemental set of discovery procedures, strictly optional under treaty law, to which concerns of comity nevertheless require first resort by American courts in all cases. Fourth, the treaty may be viewed as an undertaking among sovereigns to facilitate discovery to which an American court should resort when it deems that course of action appropriate, after considering the situation of the parties before it as well as the interests of the concerned foreign state. . . .

We reject the first two of the possible interpretations as inconsistent with the language and negotiating history of the Hague Convention. . . .

* * * *

[In particular] two of the articles in Chapter III, entitled "General Clauses," buttress our conclusion . . . Article 23 expressly authorizes a contracting State to declare that it will not execute any letter of request in aid of pretrial discovery in a common law country. Surely, if the Convention had been intended to replace completely the broad discovery powers that the common law courts in the United States previously exercised over foreign litigants subject to their jurisdiction, it would have been most anomalous for the common law contracting Parties to agree to Article 23, which enables a contracting Party to revoke its consent to the treaty's procedures for pretrial discovery. In the absence of explicit textual support, we are unable to accept the hypothesis that the common law contracting States abjured recourse to all pre-existing discovery procedures at the same time that they accepted the possibility that a contracting Party could unilaterally abrogate even the Convention's procedures. Moreover, Article 27 plainly states that the Convention does not prevent a contracting State from using more liberal methods of rendering evidence than those authorized by the Convention. . . .

An interpretation of the Hague Convention as the exclusive means for obtaining evidence located abroad would effectively subject every American court hearing a case involving a national of a contracting State to the internal laws of that State. Interrogatories and document requests are staples of international commercial litigation, no less than of other suits, yet a rule of exclusivity would subordinate the court's supervision of even the most routine of these pretrial proceedings to the actions or, equally, to the inactions of foreign judicial authorities. As the Court of Appeals for the Fifth Circuit observed in *Anschuetz*:

> It seems patently obvious that if the Convention were interpreted as preempt-ing interrogatories and document requests, the Convention would really be much more than an agreement on taking evidence abroad. Instead, the Convention would amount to a major regulation of the overall conduct of

litigation between nationals of different signatory states. . . . [A] treaty intended to bring about such curtailment of the rights given to all litigants by the federal rules would surely state its intention clearly and precisely identify crucial terms. *In re Anschuetz & Co., GmbH.*[24]

The Hague Convention, however, contains no such plain statement of a preemptive intent. We conclude accordingly that the Hague Convention did not deprive the District Court of the jurisdiction it otherwise possessed to order a foreign national party before it to produce evidence physically located within a signatory nation.

IV

While the Hague Convention does not divest the District Court of jurisdiction to order discovery under the Federal Rules of Civil Procedure, the optional character of the Convention procedures sheds light on one aspect of the Court of Appeals' opinion that we consider erroneous. That court concluded that the Convention simply "does not apply" to discovery sought from a foreign litigant that is subject to the jurisdiction of an American court. . . . Plaintiffs argue that this conclusion is supported by two considerations. First, the Federal Rules of Civil Procedure provide ample means for obtaining discovery from parties who are subject to the court's jurisdiction, while before the Convention was ratified it was often extremely difficult, if not impossible, to obtain evidence from nonparty witnesses abroad. Plaintiffs contend that it is appropriate to construe the Convention as applying only in the area in which improvement was badly needed. Second, when a litigant is subject to the jurisdiction of the District Court, arguably the evidence it is required to produce is not "abroad" within the meaning of the Convention, even though it is in fact located in a foreign country at the time of the discovery request and even though it will have to be gathered or otherwise prepared abroad. . . .

Nevertheless, the text of the Convention draws no distinction between evidence obtained from third parties and that obtained from the litigants themselves; nor does it purport to draw any sharp line between evidence that is "abroad" and evidence that is within the control of a party subject to the jurisdiction of the requesting court. Thus, it appears clear to us that the optional Convention procedures are available whenever they will facilitate the gathering of evidence by the means authorized in the Convention, although these procedures are not mandatory. . . .

V

Petitioners contend that even if the Hague Convention's procedures are not mandatory, this Court should adopt a rule requiring that American litigants first resort to those procedures before initiating any discovery pursuant to the normal methods of the Federal Rules of Civil Procedure. . . . The Court of Appeals rejected this argument because it was convinced that an American court's order ultimately requiring discovery that a foreign court had refused under Convention procedures would constitute "the greatest insult" to the sovereignty of that tribunal. . . . We disagree. . . . It is well known that the scope of American

---

[24] 754 F. 2d 602, 612 (1985), cert. pending, No. 85-98.

discovery is often significantly broader than is permitted in other jurisdictions, and we are satisfied that foreign tribunals will recognize that the final decision on the evidence to be used in litigation conducted in American courts must be made by those courts. We therefore do not believe that an American court should refuse to make use of Convention procedures because of a concern that it may ultimately find it necessary to order the production of evidence that a foreign tribunal permitted a party to withhold.

Nevertheless, we cannot accept petitioners' invitation to announce a new rule of law that would require first resort to Convention procedures whenever discovery is sought from a foreign litigant. . . . In many situations the Letter of Request procedure authorized by the Convention would be unduly time consuming and expensive, as well as less certain to produce needed evidence than direct use of the Federal Rules. A rule of first resort in all cases would therefore be inconsistent with the overriding interest in the "just, speedy, and inexpensive determination" of litigation in our courts. . . .

Petitioners argue that a rule of first resort is necessary to accord respect to the sovereignty of states in which evidence is located. It is true that the process of obtaining evidence in a civil law jurisdiction is normally conducted by a judicial officer rather than by private attorneys. Petitioners contend that if performed on French soil, for example, by an unauthorized person such evidence-gathering might violate the "judicial sovereignty" of the host nation. Because it is only through the Convention that civil law nations have given their consent to evidence-gathering activities within their borders, petitioners argue, we have a duty to employ those procedures whenever they are available. . . . We find that argument unpersuasive. If such a duty were to be inferred from the adoption of the Convention itself, we believe it would have been described in the text of that document. Moreover, the concept of international comity requires in this context a more particularized analysis of the respective interests of the foreign nation and the requesting nation than petitioners' proposed general rule would generate. . . .

Some discovery procedures are much more "intrusive" than others. In this case, for example, an interrogatory asking petitioners to identify the pilots who flew flight tests in the [petitioners' aircraft] before it was certified for flight by the Federal Aviation Administration, or a request to admit that petitioners authorized certain advertising in a particular magazine, is certainly less intrusive than a request to produce all of the "design specifications, line drawings and engineering plans and all engineering change orders . . . concerning the leading edge slats for the" [aircraft]. . . . Even if a court might be persuaded that a particular document request was too burdensome or too "intrusive" to be granted in full, with or without an appropriate protective order, it might well refuse to insist upon the use of Convention procedures before requiring responses to simple interrogatories or requests for admissions. The exact line between reasonableness and unreasonableness in each case must be drawn by the trial court, based on its knowledge of the case and of the claims and interests of the parties and the governments whose statutes and policies they invoke.

American courts, in supervising pretrial proceedings, should exercise special vigilance to protect foreign litigants from the danger that unnecessary, or unduly burdensome, discovery may place them in a disadvantageous position. Judicial supervision of discovery should always seek to minimize its costs and inconvenience. . . . When it is necessary to seek evidence abroad, however, the District Court must supervise pretrial proceedings particularly closely to prevent discovery abuses. For example, the additional cost of transportation of documents or witnesses to or from foreign locations may increase the danger that discovery may be sought for the improper purpose of motivating settlement, rather than finding relevant and probative evidence. Objections to "abusive" discovery that foreign litigants advance should therefore receive the most careful consideration. In addition, we have long recognized the demands of comity in suits involving foreign states, either as parties or as sovereigns with a coordinate interest in the litigation. . . . American courts should therefore take care to demonstrate due respect for any special problem confronted by the foreign litigant on account of its nationality or the location of its operations, and for any sovereign interest expressed by a foreign state. We do not articulate specific rules to guide this delicate task of adjudication.

JUSTICE BLACKMUN, with whom JUSTICE BRENNAN, JUSTICE MARSHALL, and JUSTICE O'CONNOR join concurring in part and dissenting in part.

Some might well regard the Court's decision in this case as an affront to the nations that have joined the United States in ratifying the Hague Convention on the Taking of Evidence Abroad in Civil or Commercial Matters. . . . The Court ignores the importance of the Convention by relegating it to an "optional" status, without acknowledging the significant achievement in accommodating divergent interests that the Convention represents. Experience to date indicates that there is a large risk that the case-by-case comity analysis now to be permitted by the Court will be performed inadequately and that the somewhat unfamiliar procedures of the Convention will be invoked infrequently. . . . I fear the Court's decision means that courts will resort unnecessarily to issuing discovery orders under the Federal Rules of Civil Procedure in a raw exercise of their jurisdictional power to the detriment of the United States' national and international interests. The Court's view of this country's international obligations is particularly unfortunate in a world in which regular commercial and legal channels loom ever more crucial.

I do agree with the Court's repudiation of the positions at both extremes of the spectrum with regard to the use of the Convention. Its rejection of the view that the Convention is not "applicable" at all to this case is surely correct. . . . The Court also correctly rejects the far opposite position that the Convention provides the exclusive means for discovery involving signatory countries. I dissent, however, because I cannot endorse the Court's case-by-case inquiry for determining whether to use Convention procedures and its failure to provide lower courts with any meaningful guidance for carrying out that inquiry. In my view, the Convention provides effective discovery procedures that largely eliminate the conflicts between United States and foreign law on evidence gathering. I therefore would apply a general presumption that, in most cases, courts should resort first to the Convention procedures. An individualized analysis of the circumstances of a particular case is appropriate only when it appears that it would be futile to employ the Convention or when its procedures prove to be unhelpful.

I

Even though the Convention does not expressly require discovery of materials in foreign countries to proceed exclusively according to its procedures, it cannot be viewed as merely advisory. The Convention was drafted at the request and with the enthusiastic participation of the United States, which sought to broaden the techniques available for the taking of evidence abroad. The differences between discovery practices in the United States and those in other countries are significant, and "[n]o aspect of the extension of the American legal system beyond the territorial frontier of the United States has given rise to so much friction as the request for documents associated with investigation and litigation in the United States."[25] . . . . Of particular import is the fact that discovery conducted by the parties, as is common in the United States, is alien to the legal systems of civil-law nations, which typically regard evidence gathering as a judicial function.

* * * *

It is not at all satisfactory to view the Convention as nothing more than an optional supplement to the Federal Rules of Civil procedure, useful as a means to "facilitate discovery" when a court "deems that course of action appropriate.". . . . Unless they had expected the Convention to provide the normal channels for discovery, other parties to the Convention would have had no incentive to agree to its terms. The civil-law nations committed themselves to employ more effective procedures for gathering evidence within their borders, even to the extent of requiring some common-law practices alien to their systems. At the time of the Convention's enactment, the liberal American policy which allowed foreigners to collect evidence with ease in the United States . . . was in place and, because it was not conditioned on reciprocity, there was little likelihood that the policy would change as a result of treaty negotiations. As a result, the primary benefit the other signatory nations would have expected in return for their concessions was that the United States would respect their territorial sovereignty by using the Convention procedures.

II

By viewing the Convention as merely optional and leaving the decision whether to apply it to the court in each individual case, the majority ignores the policies established by the political branches when they negotiated and ratified the treaty. . . . The discovery process usually concerns discrete interests that a court is well equipped to accommodate — the interests of the parties before the court coupled with the interests of the judicial system in resolving the conflict on the basis of the best available information. When a lawsuit requires discovery of materials located in a foreign nation, however, foreign legal systems and foreign interests are implicated as well. The presence of these interests creates a tension between the broad discretion our courts normally exercise in managing pretrial discovery and the discretion usually allotted to the Executive in foreign matters.

It is the Executive that normally decides when a course of action is important enough to risk affronting a foreign nation or placing a strain on foreign

---

[25] Restatement (Revised) of Foreign Relations Law of the United States, Section 437, Reporters' Notes 1. p. 35 (Tent. Draft No. 7, Apr. 10, 1986).

commerce. . . . The Convention embodies the result of the best efforts of the Executive Branch, in negotiating the treaty, and the legislative Branch, in ratifying it, to balance competing national interests. As such, the Convention represents a political determination — one that, consistent with the principle of separation of powers, courts should not attempt to second guess.

Not only is the question of foreign discovery more appropriately considered by the Executive and Congress, but in addition, courts are generally ill equipped to assume the role of balancing the interests of foreign nations with that of our own. Although transnational litigation is increasing, relatively few judges are experienced in the area and the procedures of legal systems are often poorly understood. . . . A pro-forum bias is likely to creep into the supposedly neutral balancing process and courts not surprisingly often will turn to the more familiar procedures established by their local rules. . . .

III

The principle of comity leads to more definite rules than the ad hoc approach endorsed by the majority. The court asserts that the concept of comity requires an individualized analysis of the interests present in each particular case before a court decides whether to apply the convention. . . . There is, however, nothing inherent in the comity principle that requires case-by-case analysis. . . .

Comity is not just a vague political concern favoring international cooperation when it is in our interest to do so. Rather it is a principle under which judicial decisions reflect the systemic value of reciprocal tolerance and good will. . . . As in the choice-of-law analysis, which from the very beginning has been linked to international comity, the threshold question in a comity analysis is whether there is in fact a true conflict between domestic and foreign law. When there is a conflict, a court should seek a reasonable accommodation that reconciles the central concerns of both sets of laws. In doing so, it should perform a tripartite analysis that considers the foreign interests, the interest of the United States, and the mutual interests of all nations in a smothly functioning international legal regime.

* * * *

A

I am encouraged by the extent to which the Court emphasizes the importance of foreign interests and by its admonition to lower courts to take special care to respect those interests. . . . Nonetheless, the Court's view of the Convention rests on an incomplete analysis of the sovereign interests of foreign states. The Court acknowledges that evidence is normally obtained in civil-law countries by a judicial officer . . . but it fails to recognize the significance of that practice. Under the classic view of territorial sovereignty, each state has a monopoly on the exercise of governmental power within its borders and no state may perform an act in the territory of a foreign state without consent. . . .

Some countries also believe that the need to protect certain underlying substantive rights requires judicial control of the taking of evidence. In the Federal Republic of Germany, for example, there is a constitutional principle of proportionality, pursuant to which a judge must protect personal privacy, commercial property, and business secrets. Interference with these rights is proper only if "necessary to protect other persons' rights in the course of civil litigation". . . .

Use of the Convention advances the sovereign interests of foreign nations because they have given consent to Convention procedures by ratifying them. This consent encompasses discovery techniques that would otherwise impinge on the sovereign interests of many civil-law nations. In the absence of the Convention, the informal techniques provided by Articles 15-22 of the Convention-taking evidence by a diplomatic or consular officer of the requesting state and the use of commissioners nominated by the court of the state where the action is pending — would raise sovereignty issues similar to those implicated by a direct discovery order from a foreign court. "Judicial" activities are occurring on the soil of the sovereign by agents of a foreign state. These voluntary discovery procedures are a great boon to United States litigants and are used far more frequently in practive than is compulsory discovery pursuant to letters of request.

Civil-law contracting parties have also agreed to use, and even to compel, procedures for gathering evidence that are diametrically opposed to civil-law practices. The civil-law system is inquisitional rather than adversarial and the judge normally questions the witness and prepares a written summary of the evidence. Even in common-law countries no system of evidence-gathering resembles that of the United States. Under Article 9 of the Convention, however, a foreign court must grant a request to use a "special method or procedure," which includes requests to compel attendance of witnesses abroad, to administer oaths, to produce verbatim transcripts, or to permit examination of witnesses by counsel for both parties. . . .

B

The primary interest of the United States in this context is in providing effective procedures to enable litigants to obtain evidence abroad. This was the very purpose of the United States' participation in the treaty negotiations and, for the most part, the Convention provides those procedures.

The Court asserts that the letters of request procedure authorized by the Convention in many situations will be "unduly time consuming and expensive". . . . The Court offers no support for this statement and until the Convention is used extensively enough for courts to develop experience with it, such statements can be nothing other than speculation. . . .

There is also apprehension that the Convention procedures will not prove fruitful. Experience with the Convention suggests otherwise — contracting parties have honored their obligation to execute letters of request expeditiously and to use compulsion if necessary. . . .

There are, however, some situations in which there is legitimate concern that certain documents cannot be made available under Convention procedures. Thirteen nations have made official declarations pursuant to Article 23 of the Convention, which permits a contracting state to limit its obligation to produce documents in response to a letter of request. . . . These reservations may pose problems that would require a comity analysis in an individual case, but they are not so all-encompassing as the majority implies — they certainly do not mean that a "contracting Party could unilaterally abrogate . . . the Convention's procedures". . . . First, the reservations can apply only to letters of request for documents . . . the emerging view of this exception to discovery is that it applied only to "requests that lack sufficient specificity or that have not been reviewed for relevancy by the requesting court. . . . " Thus, in practice, a reservation is not the significant obstacle to discovery under the Convention that the broad wording of Article 23 would suggest.

In this particular case, the "French Blocking Statute" . . . poses an additional potential barrier to obtaining discovery from France. But any conflict posed by this legislation is easily resolved by resort to the Convention's procedures. The French statute's prohibitions are expressly "subject to" international agreements and applicable laws and it does not affect the taking of evidence under the Convention. . . .

The second major United States interest is in fair and equal treatment of litigants. The Court cites several fairness concerns. . . . Courts can protect against the first two concerns noted by the majority — that a foreign party to a lawsuit would have a discovery advantage over a domestic litigant because it could . . . [use] of the Federal Rules of Civil Procedure, and that a foreign company would have an economic competitive advantage because it would be subject to less extensive discovery — by exercising their discretionary powers to control discovery in order to ensure fairness to both parties. . . .

The Court's third fairness concern is illusory. It fears that a domestic litigant suing a national of a state that is not a party to the Convention would have an advantage over a litigant suing a national of a contracting state. This statement completely ignores the very purpose of the Convention. . . . Dissimilar treatment of litigants similarly situated does occur, but in the manner opposite to that perceived by the Court. Those who sue nationals of noncontracting states are disadvantaged by the unavailability of the Convention procedures. This is an unavoidable inequality inherent in the benefits conferred by any treaty that is less than universally ratified.

In most instances, use of the Convention will serve to advance United States interests, particularly when those interests are viewed in a context larger than the immediate interest of the litigants' discovery. The approach I propose is not a rigid per se rule that would require first use of the Convention without regard to strong indications that no evidence would be forthcoming. All too often, however, courts have simply assumed that resort to the Convention would be unproductive and have embarked on speculation about foreign procedures and interpretations. . . . When resort to the Convention would be futile, a court has no choice but to resort to a traditional comity analysis. But even then, an attempt to use the Convention will often be the best way to discover if it will be successful, particularly in the present state of general inexperience with the implementation of its procedures by the various contracting states. An attempt to use the Convention will open a dialogue with the authorities in the foreign state and in that way a United States court can obtain an authoritative answer as to the limits on what it can achieve with a discovery request in a particular contracting state.

C

The final component of a comity analysis is to consider if there is a course that furthers, rather than impedes, the development of an ordered international system. A functioning system for solving disputes across borders serves many values, among them predictability, fairness, ease of commercial interactions, and "stability through satisfaction of mutual expectations". . . . These interests are common to all nations, including the United States.

Use of the Convention would help develop methods for transnational litigation by placing officials in a position to communicate directly about conflicts that arise during discovery, thus enabling them to promote a reduction in those conflicts. In a broader framework, courts that use the Convention will avoid foreign perceptions of unfairness that result when United States courts show insensitivity to the interests safeguarded by foreign legal regimes. Because of the position of the United States . . . many countries may be reluctant to oppose discovery orders of United States courts. Foreign acquiescence to orders that ignore the Convention, however, is likely to carry a pricetag of accumulating resentment, with the predictable long-term political cost that cooperation will be withheld in other matters. Use of the Convention is a simple step to take toward avoiding that unnecessary and undesirable consequence.

NOTES AND QUESTIONS

(1) In *Aerospatiale* the Governments of the United Kingdom, France, the Federal Republic of Germany and Switzerland filed amicus curiae briefs. Of these all but the British brief supported the position that the Evidence Convention was the exclusive method for obtaining evidence located abroad in a state party.[26]

(2) Precisely in what ways does Justice Blackmun disagree with the majority of *Aerospatiale*? Both agree that principles of comity should play an important role in determining whether the Evidence Convention is to be utilized. How do their approaches to principles of comity differ?

(3) The majority of the Court in *Aerospatiale* expressly declines to give lower courts any guidance as to how they should approach the "demands of comity in suits involving foreign states." By contrast, Justice Blackmun suggests that a court "should perform a tripartite analysis that considers the foreign interests, the interests of the United States, and the mutual interests of all nations in a smoothly functioning international legal regime." What examples of these interests does Justice Blackmun give? Can you think of any others?[27]

(4) Justice Blackmun does not expressly mention the interests of the individual litigants. Perhaps he meant for these interests to be subsumed by the interests of the sovereign states involved. Should the interests of the litigants be given greater

[26] See 25 Int'l Legal Mat. 1475 (1986).
[27] See Gerber, *International Discovery after Aerospatiale: The Quest for an Analytical Framework*, 82 Am. J. Int'l L. 521 (1988)

emphasis by a court in deciding whether to employ the Evidence Convention? If so, how would you define those interests?

(5) Justice Blackmun suggests that "there is a large risk that the case-by-case comity analysis now to be permitted by the Court will be performed inadequately and that the somewhat unfamiliar procedures of the Convention will be invoked infrequently. I fear the Court's decision means that courts will resort unnecessarily to issuing discovery orders under the Federal Rules of Civil Procedure in a raw exercise of their jurisdictional power to the detriment of United States' national and international interests." It is too soon after the *Aerospatiale* decision to determine whether Justice Blackmun's concern is justified, but the early returns support his prediction. That is, in three reported cases the courts have decided that recourse to the Evidence Convention procedures was unnecessary. *Benton Graphics v. Uddeholm Corp.*,[28] *Haynes v. Kleinwefers*,[29] *Sandsend Financial Consultants v. Wood.*[30] In *Benton Graphics*, moreover, the court decided that the burden was on the foreign litigant seeking to supplant the federal rules with the Convention procedures to show why particular facts and sovereign interests support using the Convention.

In contrast, the court in *Hudson v. Hermann Pfauter GmbH & Co.*,[31] placed the burden on the party opposing use of the Convention's procedures to demonstrate that such use would frustrate the interests of the United States. Moreover, because the majority of *Aerospatiale* had failed to offer specific guidelines for resolving the choice of law between the Convention and the Federal Rules, the court adopted the approach suggested by Justice Blackmun. Applying this approach the court concluded that the foreign interests at stake were "particularly compelling" and ordered that the Convention's procedures be employed.[32]

As in the case of service of process, many countries regard the taking of evidence as a sovereign act and object to attempts by private parties to perform this function. Also, these countries may object to certain U.S. evidentiary procedures, such as the wide scope of discovery in U.S. litigation, especially of documentary evidence. This distaste for U.S. discovery procedures is often coupled with, and based in part on, disagreement with substantive aspects of U.S. laws, particularly our antitrust laws (see *supra* Chapter 7), as well as objections to overly expansive (in the foreign state's view) claims of prescriptive jurisdiction. Requests for documentary evidence may run afoul too of bank secrecy laws or claims of privileged communication in foreign states. Some commentators have suggested

[28] 118 F.R.D. 386 (D.N.J. 1987).

[29] 119 F.R.D. 335 (E.D. N.Y. 1988).

[30] 743 S.W.2d 364 (Tex. App. Houston [1st Dist.] 1988).

[31] 117 F.R.D. 33, 38 (N.D. N.Y.1987).

[32] For discussion of the *Hudson* case, see Youngblood, *Transnational Discovery And The Hague Evidence Convention: Hudson v. Hermann Pfauter GmbH & Co.*, 117 F.R.D. 33 (N.D. N.Y. 1987), Int'l Practitioner's Notebook 5 (March 1988).

that the United States may be the only country that believes unilateral extraterritorial discovery does not violate international law.[33]

Federal Rule of Civil Procedure 26(b) permits discovery not only of clearly relevant material and admissible evidence, but also of information which would be inadmissible at trial yet "appears reasonably calculated to lead to the discovery of admissible evidence." Foreign court decisions view requests for discovery based on this language as wasteful and intrusive "fishing expeditions." *Radio Corp. of America v. Rawland Corp,*[34] quoted with approval in *Rio Tinto Zinc. Corp. v. Westinghouse Elec. Corp.*[35] The practice of other countries in seeking foreign discovery is to request specific documents or provide detailed interrogatories. The United States stands alone, even among common law countries, in the expansive nature of its discovery practice.[34]

Faced with statutes and directives blocking their discovery orders, U.S. courts have had to decide how to respond. Specifically, they have had to decide whether to impose sanctions, for example under Rule 37 of the Federal Rules of Civil Procedure, against a party to the litigation that fails to produce documents blocked by foreign law. The classic case is *Societe Internationale v. Rogers,*[37] where the Supreme Court held that a Swiss company seeking the return in federal court of property seized by the U.S. Alien Property Custodian during World War II on the ground that it was controlled by German interests could not constitutionally have its suit dismissed, at least where it had made a good faith effort to obtain documents proving it was not German controlled that were blocked by a Swiss penal statute. The Court noted, however, that the burden of proof remained with the Swiss company and that failure to produce these documents might result in a failure to prove its case.

Proceeding in a similar vein, lower federal courts avoided coercing the production of documents located in a foreign jurisdiction whose laws made it illegal to produce them to an American court. Typically, an order requiring production of foreign documents would provide that it should be quashed if production would violate foreign law. See, *e.g., Ings v. Ferguson.*[38] If production was compelled, it was usually in a case where no criminal liability would be imposed for disclosure and the risk of civil liability was "quite remote." See, *e.g., United States v. First National City Bank.*[39]

The cases reflect a distinction, however, between the private or public character of the party seeking discovery. As the above discussion indicates, in cases

---

[33] See 2 J. Atwood & K. Brewster, Antitrust And American Business Abroad Section 15.10 (2d ed. 1981); Rosenthal and Yale-Loehr, *Two Cheers For The ALI Restatement's Provisions On Foreign Discovery,* 16 N.Y.U. Int'l L. & Pol. 1075 (1984).

[34] [1956] 1 Q.B. 618, 649 (Lord Goddard, C.J.).

[35] [1978] 1 ALL E.R. 434, 455.

[34] See Gerber, *Extraterritorial Discovery And The Conflict Of Procedural Systems: Germany And The United States,* 34 Am. J. Comp. L. 745, 761-69 (1986).

[37] 357 U.S. 197 (1958).

[38] 282 F. 2d 149, 152-53 (2d Cir. 1960).

[39] 396 F. 2d 897, 903-05 (2d Cir. 1968). *Cf. United States v. Vetco,* 644 F. 2d 1324, 1326-31 (9th Cir. 1981) (controversy over whether compliance with U.S. civil IRS subpoena required respondent to commit a crime under Swiss law), *cert. denied,* 454 U.S. 1098 (1981).

involving private litigants U.S. courts will normally not require a witness to take action in a foreign country that clearly violates its laws, at least in a situation where the witness has made a good faith effort to comply with the U.S. Court's orders and there is a substantial likelihood of meaningful sanction if he violates the foreign law. When the U.S. Government is the party seeking discovery, the attitude of U.S. courts may be quite different, and several recent decisions have ordered parties or witnesses to take action constituting a crime in a friendly foreign country.[40] Among other justifications the primacy of U.S. interests in enforcing its revenue and penal laws over national sovereignty concerns of foreign nations has been cited in support of these decisions. This rationale has not been accepted by any other country, and reaction to it has been sharp.

[2] International Law

PROVISIONS OF THE HAGUE EVIDENCE CONVENTION[41]

As of 1988, 20 states were parties to the Hague Evidence Convention. Under Article 1 of the Convention three different procedures for obtaining evidence abroad are available: (1) letters of request; (2) the use of consular agents; and (3) the use of commissions. As in the case of the Service Convention, each state party is required to designate a Central Authority to which letters of request seeking assistance in obtaining evidence for use in civil or commercial litigation may be addressed by the courts of other states parties. The Central Authority has the responsibility of ensuring that any letter of request meeting the requirements of the Convention is executed expeditiously, in accordance with the procedures, including measures of compulsion, that are utilized for taking evidence in the requested state's courts.

Nonetheless, there are a number of grounds under the Convention that a state party may cite for refusing to execute a letter of request. Most significant is the provision in Article 23 of the Convention permitting states parties to declare that they will not execute letters of request "issued for the purpose of obtaining pretrial discovery of documents as known in Common Law countries." As of 1986, all states parties except the United States, Czechoslovakia, and Israel had made such a declaration. Some states — the United Kingdom, Singapore, Sweden, the Netherlands, Finland, Norway and Denmark — have expressed their declarations in less sweeping form, stating merely that they will refuse to execute letters of request that lack specificity. Although Article 23 applies only to production of documents, many states, in making the declaration permitted by Article 23, have stated their understanding that it precludes asking a witness to state what documents relevant to the proceeding are in his possession. In two recent and related cases a German court — strictly construing Article 23 of the Convention

---

[40] See, *e.g.*, *United States v. Bank of Nova Scotia*, 691 F. 2d 1384, 1389-91 (11th Cir. 1982) *cert. denied*, 103 S. Ct. 3086 (1983); *SEC v. Banca Della Swizzera Italianna*, 92 F.R.D. 111, 117-19 (S.D.N.Y. 1981); *Marc. Rich & Co. v. United States*, 707 F. 2d 663, 666-70 (2d Cir. 1982), *cert. denied*, 103 S. Ct. 3555 (1983); see also, Harfield, *The Implications Of U.S. Extraterritorial Discovery Proceedings Against Multinational Corporations For The Judiciary*, 16 N.Y.U.J. Int'l L. & Pol. 973, 975 (1984).

[41] Documentary Supplement.

and the German declaration made thereunder — denied a request for production of specified documents, but upheld an order to several witnesses to be examined about the same documents.[42]

Also, as we saw above in our discussion of service of judicial documents, a requested state may refuse to honor a letter of request on the ground that it does not relate to a "civil or commercial" matter. Thus, if the evidence sought concerns both a civil and a criminal or public matter, the requested state may refuse to honor the request. Similarly, a state party to the Convention may distinguish between requests on behalf of private parties involved in administrative, including fiscal, proceedings, which might be honored, and requests from administrative authorities or tribunals, including the U.S. Tax Court, which would probably be refused. The Convention also applies only to requests transmitted by or on behalf of a "judicial authority," and only with respect to evidence to be used in judicial proceedings. Accordingly, there is no obligation to honor a request for evidence to be used by a legislative committee, commission of inquiry, or similar body. Article 11 of the Convention permits non-compliance with requests for evidence on the ground of privilege. The privilege may be based on the law of the requested state, or, more frequently, the laws of both states. Lastly, under Article 12, execution of a letter of request may be refused if it does not fall within the function of the judiciary or if the state of execution "considers that its sovereignty or security would be prejudiced" by executing the request.

Note the difference between Chapters I and II of the Convention. Chapter I is not subject to many significant reservations, but a state party may decline to comply with Chapter II in whole or in part, or subject its acceptance to a series of reservations. For example, the reservations of some states to Chapter II may make it necessary to apply for special permission if a diplomatic officer wants to take the testimony of someone who is not a citizen of the requesting state. The same reservations may require prior approval if an appointed commissioner wants to take evidence in the territory of another state party. Even if such permission is given, it will not necessarily enable a diplomatic officer or appointed commissions to employ compulsion in the case of a recalcitrant witness. Thus the methods of obtaining evidence covered by Chapter II are unlikely to be useful in cases where a state party is expected to resist complying with requests for obtaining evidence. In such cases the letter of request is the method of obtaining evidence most likely to be effective, both because every state party is bound by all the most significant provisions of Chapter I and because Article 10 of Chapter I provides for appropriate measures of compulsion. Also, Article 13 requires a requested state to notify a requesting state of the reasons for a refusal to honor a letter of request.

The decision of the British House of Lords in *Rio Tinto Zinc. Corp. v. Westinghouse Electric Corp.*[43] illustrates some of the difficulties of proceeding under the Convention. There, several suits had been brought against Westinghouse in the United States in response to Westinghouse's failure to meet its

---

[42] *Corning Glass Works v. International Telephone and Telegraph Corp.*, OLG Munchen, 10/31/80, 11/27/80, 1981 Juristenzeitung 538, 540, reproduced in 20 Int'l Leg. Mat. 1049, 1025 (1981).

[43] [1978] A.C. 547, (H.L. (E)).

commitments to furnish uranium to plaintiff utility companies. Westinghouse's defense was commercial impracticability due to a seven-fold increase in the world price of uranium. To support that defense, Westinghouse sought to prove the existence of a world-wide uranium cartel. A U.S. district court, pursuant to Westinghouse's request, transmitted a letter rogatory to the High Court in London, seeking documentary evidence from a British company, not a party to the U.S. action, and testimony from several of its officers, also not parties to the U.S. action. After extensive proceedings the High Court issued an order giving effect to the letters rogatory, and the Court of Appeals affirmed. Upon appeal the House of Lords reversed. As summarized by Reporters' Note 7 to Section 473 of Restatement (Third) of the Foreign Relations Law of the United States, the rulings of the House of Lords included the following:

(i) A statement by the requesting judge that the evidence requested was sought for trial, not just for "pretrial" discovery, was sufficient to overcome Britain's declaration under Article 23, at least where the evidence was specifically identified.

(ii) Requests for production of documents not specifically identified were rejected, on the ground that the Convention and the British implementing legislation did not countenance "fishing expeditions." Only particular documents identified as to date, authorship, and subject would be ordered from non-party witnesses.

(iii) If a letter contained both specific and overly general requests, the letter rogatory would not be rejected as a whole, but the court could separate the acceptable from the unacceptable requests, "blue-penciling" the rest.

(iv) So long as the requests were, in good faith, intended for use in the court from which they emanated, the possibility that the evidence so obtained might be used for discovery in connection with another proceeding was not a ground for denying the request.

(v) A request by the U.S. Attorney General to the U.S. Judge to grant the witnesses immunity, and compel them to testify, notwithstanding a claim of possible self-incrimination, in order to aid the work of a grand jury investigating the uranium cartel, "materially altered the character of the proceedings under the Letters Rogatory," so that it no longer came within the category of "civil and commercial." Moreover, the U.S. investigation of the activities of British companies outside of the United States was "an unacceptable invasion of British sovereignty," within the meaning of Article 12 of the Convention. Accordingly, the letters rogatory were refused in all respects.

Rio Tinto is an excellent example of a case where the party seeking to obtain evidence abroad (Westinghouse) won the battle but lost the war. In particular, *Rio Tinto* demonstrates that political considerations may override the most carefully crafted legal arguments. The Court of Appeals decision in that case had expressly considered and rejected the argument deemed dispositive by the House of Lords, namely, that Justice Department involvement in the case transformed it from a civil to a criminal case, thereby precluding use of the Convention. The House of Lords, however, did not review the arguments concerning United States Government involvement that the Court of Appeals had found persuasive. It is noteworthy that the United Kingdom's Attorney General had intervened in the proceedings before the House in response to requests from four foreign governments (those of Australia, Canada, France and South Africa), all of which had enacted regulations barring the disclosure of any documents concerning the alleged cartel.

It is also noteworthy that *Rio Tinto* involved United States legislation that provides for both civil remedies and criminal penalties. Seeking evidence to prove a cause of action under such legislation necessarily raises the risk that a foreign court will find the Convention inapplicable on the ground that the action should be characterized as criminal rather than as civil or commercial. Actions under such legislation also raise a strong possibility of governmental intervention in the case. Lord Wilberforce's opinion for the House of Lords reflects a strong repugnance for the "extraterritorial" application of United States antitrust laws, a view also held by the British Government. The readers will want to reappraise the pronouncements by the House of Lords and the U.K. Attorney General in the context of the material in Chapter 7 concerning the transnational application of the U.S. anti-trust laws, and ask whether those pronouncements are not utterly self-serving.[44]

As a practical matter, the Convention may provide the only means of obtaining evidence from non-parties to the litigation who reside in other states parties. Moreover, in situations where genuine issues of privilege or compulsion to refuse disclosure are raised, resort to the Convention allows the courts or other authorities of the state where evidence is located to rule on these issues, thus giving guidance to courts in the United States as to whether they should impose sanctions on a party or witness failing to comply with a discovery order.

NOTES AND QUESTIONS

(1) In 1981 the United States became a party to the Hague Convention Abolishing the Requirement of Legalization of Foreign Public Documents. A problem in authenticating foreign official documents sought to be introduced in judicial proceedings had been the laborious process of chain authentication from local officials through national officers to certification through diplomatic channels. The Convention, reproduced in 28 U.S.C. following Rule 44, deals with this problem by providing for a single form of authentication known by the French word Apostille. An Apostille certifies the authenticity of the signature of the person who has signed a document, the capacity in which he has acted, and where appropriate the identity of the seal or stamp which the document bears. Under the Convention each state party designates the authorities competent to issue Apostilles and requires them to keep a record or index of all Apostilles issued.

---

[44] For an extensive discussion of the *Rio Tinto* case, see Augustine, *Obtaining International Judicial Assistance Under The Federal Rules And The Hague Convention On The Taking Of Evidence Abroad In Civil And Commercial Matters: An Exposition Of The Procedures And A Practical Example: In Re Westinghouse Uranium Contract Litigation,* 10 Ga. J. Int'l Comp. L. 101 (1980).

The Convention provides that a foreign document bearing an Apostille issued in the prescribed form is authenticated for use in judicial or other official proceedings in all other states parties. This procedure prevails over more onerous provisions for legalization of foreign documents in preexisting treaties or domestic law.[45]

(2) Some U.S. courts have been unsympathetic to objections from foreign governments to American discovery procedures. The Seventh Circuit, for example, in *In Re Uranium Antitrust Litigation*,[46] castigated foreign governments for presenting briefs on behalf of foreign parties, on the ground that this was an impermissable intrusion into an action between two private parties. Supporters of the expansive U.S. approach have also argued that it encourages disclosure of the truth; that foreigners who benefit from U.S. laws should be required to bear its burdens; and that an expansive approach is necessary to ensure the integrity of U.S. laws, especially economic regulation, and of the American judicial system.

From the perspective of foreign countries, what responses might be made to these arguments? Is the foreign countries' position stronger or weaker when the litigant seeking evidence abroad is the United States Government rather than a private party?

(3) Section 442 of The Restatement (Third) of the Foreign Relations Law of the United States provides in part:

Section 442. Requests for Disclosure: Law of the United States

(1)-

    (a) A court or agency in the United States, when authorized by statute or rule of court, may order a person subject to its jurisdiction to produce documents, objects, or other information relevant to an action or investigation, even if the information or the person in possession of the information is outside the United States.

* * * *

    (c) In deciding whether to issue an order directing production of information located abroad, and in framing such an order, a court or agency in the United States should take into account the importance to the investigation or litigation of the documents or other information requested; the degree of specificity of the request; whether the information originated in the United States; the availability of alternative means of securing the information; and the extent to which noncompliance with the request would undermine important interests of the United States, or compliance with the request would undermine important interests of the state where the information is located.

(2) If disclosure of information located outside the United States is prohibited by a law, regulation, or order of a court or other authority of the state in which the information or prospective witness is located, or of the state of which a prospective witness is a national,

---

[45] See *e.g.*, the Opinion of the Attorney General of California, reproduced in 21 Int'l Leg. Mat. 357 (1982).
[46] 617 F. 2d 1248, 1256 (1980).

(a) a court or agency in the United States may require the person to whom the order is directed to make a good faith effort to secure permission from the foreign authorities to make the information available;

(b) a court or agency should not ordinarily impose sanctions of contempt, dismissal, or default on a party that has failed to comply with the order for production, except in cases of deliberate concealment or removal of information or of failure to make a good faith effort in accordance with paragraph (a);

(c) a court or agency may, in appropriate cases, make findings of fact adverse to a party that has failed to comply with the order for production, even if that party has made a good faith effort to secure permission from the foreign authorities to make the information available and that effort has been unsuccessful.

As explained by the Reporters' commentary, Section 437(1)(a) would effect two clarifications in current U.S. law and practice. First, an order to produce documents or information located abroad would have to be issued by a court, not merely by a private party or by a U.S. Government agency. Second, subsection (1) would require that a request for production of documents, objects, or information located abroad meet a more stringent test of direct relevancy, necessity and materiality than is required for comparable requests for information located in the United States.

Subsection (1)(c) would require a balancing test for a U.S. court's issuance of an order directing production of information located abroad comparable to the balancing test for prescriptive jurisdiction set forth in Sections 402 and 403 of the Restatement (see Chapter 6, *supra*). Would you expect application of this provision to obviate objections from foreign states to U.S. discovery?

(4) Reporters' Note 5 to Section 442 takes the position, in response to foreign statutes blocking production of evidence, that "statutes that frustrate . . . [the goal of assuring that adjudication takes place on the basis of the best information possible] . . . need not be given the same deference by courts of the United States as differences in substantive rules of law." Do you agree? How are foreign countries likely to respond to this position? Should that response make any difference?

(5) How far must a party go under subsection 2(a) of Section 437 to demonstrate its good faith? Is it obliged to seek a court order that the foreign blocking statute not be applied? Would it be obliged to appeal to the court of last resort? Similarly, if a party doing business in a foreign country but subject to the jurisdiction of a U.S. court communicates with that country's government informing it of a subpoena or document request in such a way as to invite a blocking directive, should this constitute bad faith? What, if any, interest does the foreign government have in the determination of this issue?

(6) Note that subsection 2(c) of Section 442 would allow U.S. courts to draw inferences of fact adverse to a party that has failed to comply with an order for production of evidence, even if it has made a good faith effort to do so. What possible reason is there for this provision? Does it deny a litigant a fair trial?

(7) Discovery involving corporate parents and their subsidiaries raise special problems. United States courts have generally held corporations responsible for the production of documents located abroad, even when they were in the possession of their foreign branches or subsidiaries. Other countries, including the United Kingdom, do not hold parent companies responsible for production of records of their subsidiaries, unless the subsidiaries were created only for the purpose of perpetrating a fraud. Conversely, several U.S. courts have issued orders to subsidiaries or branches for the production of records located in the parent corporations abroad. They have done so after a determination that they had jurisdiction over the parent company.[47] It appears that no other country would issue a discovery order under such circumstances.

(8) Attempts to obtain evidence abroad for use in criminal proceedings pose especially difficult problems. The provisions for international judicial assistance in the U.S. Code, 28 U.S.C. Sections 1781-1782, make no distinction between civil and criminal proceedings, and the authority for U.S. courts to issue letters rogatory or commissions is not limited to civil actions. Nonetheless the rise in such transnational crimes as trafficking in drugs and terrorism has increased the need for greater international cooperation in law enforcement. To this end the United States has been concluding treaties of mutual assistance in criminal matters, intensifying the use of letters rogatory, and entering into a variety of less formal arrangements among governments and law enforcement agencies.[48]

---

[47] See, *e.g.*, *United States v. Toyota Motor Corporation*, 569 F. Supp. 1158 (C.D. Cal. 1983); *Cooper v. British Aerospace, Inc.*, 102 F.R.D. 918 (S.D.N.Y. 1984).

[48] For a discussion of these developments, see Ellis and Pisani, *The United States Treaties On Mutual Assistance In Criminal Matters: A Comparative Analysis*, 19 Int'l Law 189 (1985). Also, the Comprehensive Crime Control Act of 1984, Pub. L. 98-473, 18 U.S.C. Sections 3292, 3506 and 3507, contains several provisions concerning the use of international judicial assistance. For an exhaustive survey of problems of international discovery, see I and II B. Ristau, International Judicial Assistance (1984). Also useful are the symposium in 16 N.Y.U. Int'l L. & Pol. 957 (1984); Bishop, *Service Of Process And Discovery In International Tort Litigation*, 23 Tort & Ins. L. J. 70 (1987) Brodegaard, Victory Abroad: A Guide To Foreign Discovery, 14 Litigation 27 (1988) and Oxman, *The Choice Between Direct Discovery And Other Means Of Obtaining Evidence Abroad: The Impact Of The Hague Evidence Convention*, 37 U. of Miami L. Rev. 733 (1983). For a multinational consideration of both the problems of international discovery and those of international service of process, see Report on the work of the Special Commmission of April 1989 on the operation of the Hague Conventions of 15 November 1965 on the Service Abroad of Judicial and Extrajudicial Documents in Civil or Commercial Matters and of 18 March 1970 on the Taking of Evidence Abroad in Civil or Commercial Matters, 28 Int'l Leg. Mat. 1558 (1989).

PROBLEMS

(1) Assume that you are an attorney representing a person who has brought an action in a federal court alleging that defendant's widget was negligently manufactured in Europa. The widget was purchased by plaintiff in the U.S. from a department store to whom it had been sold by defendant's U.S. sales subsidiary. The widget exploded while plaintiff was visiting family in Europa causing her serious personal injury. You determine that you need to obtain the following testimonial and documentary evidence: (a) testimony from M. Kunz, a national of Europa who is President of defendant, a European corporation, regarding the defendant's manufacturing processes; (b) police records in Europa concerning the testimony of eyewitnesses to the accident as well as copies of police records of similar accidents involving defendant's products; (c) the records of H. Bremer, who supplies defendant with several components of its widgets, regarding the process used in manufacturing these components; (d) records of defendant in the First National Bank of Europa concerning certain financial transactions; (e) the testimony of European experts with respect to standards for manufacturing widgets in Europa.

As to these various kinds of evidence, consider the following: (1) what further facts would you like to know, if any, in order to better evaluate your chances of obtaining the evidence? (2) under what U.S. law and procedures would you proceed in attempting to obtain this evidence? (3) what problems of foreign law and practice might you encounter? How would you attempt to resolve them?

(2) Suppose that you are a federal judge who faces the following situation. The U.S. prosecutor has brought an action against several defendants for violation of the federal securities laws. Defendants have substantial financial records located in the Island of Caribe. The bank in the Island of Caribe is a branch of a bank chartered in the United Kingdom that also has branches in many other countries including the United States. The U.S. prosecutor requests that a subpoena be served on the manager of the British Bank's U.S. branch calling for the production of all records relating to the defendants' accounts at the bank in Caribe. The law of Caribe prohibits disclosure of any information regarding accounts in Caribbean banks unless authorized by a court or other governmental body in Caribe. An applicant seeking such authorization must demonstrate that the information sought is relevant to the investigation or prosecution of an identified crime.

(a) Would you grant the U.S. prosecutor's request? If not, might you employ an alternative procedure? If so, which one?

(b) If the appropriate Governmental authority in Caribe declined to authorize disclosure, would you be inclined to employ any of the sanctions authorized by 28 U.S.C. Section 1784 or by Rule 37 of the Federal Rules of Civil Procedure? Why? Why not?

§ 11.05   Choice of Forum and Choice of Law

Introduction

Before beginning this Section, the reader should review the material on personal jurisdiction in Section 2 of this Chapter. As noted in that Section there are a number of grounds on which states may claim jurisdiction over persons and transactions abroad. Consequently, private parties to international business transactions face substantial uncertainty as to which forums may claim jurisdiction over their disputes and which law these forums might apply.

There is little that can be done to relieve such uncertainty with respect to possible tort claims not arising out of some contractual relationship. In such a case no agreement as to forum would be possible until after the tort had occurred, and the enforceability of an attempted agreement would be questionable. With respect to transnational contracts, however, advance planning regarding choice of forum and choice of law may be possible. Moreover, the need for certainty and stability, present in all commercial transactions, is especially great in transnational transactions.

Designation by the parties of a particular court as the forum for settlement of all disputes concerning their contract may constitute consent to that forum's jurisdiction. Such conferral of jurisdiction by the parties upon a court is often called *prorogation*. If the parties go further in their contract and attempt to exclude all other courts from exercising jurisdiction over disputes arising under the contract, the question arises whether an excluded court would recognize the effectiveness of such a provision. This issue is often referred to as a question of *derogation*.

In a prorogation situation where the forum chosen by the parties decides to assume jurisdiction, that court may interpret the parties' choice of forum as a choice of the law of the forum as well. On the other hand, the chosen court may find no such choice implicit in the choice of forum clause and apply its ordinary choice of law rules in determining the applicable law.

The general issue to be addressed in this section is the extent to which private planning regarding choice of forum and choice of law will be honored by national courts. We consider this issue in the two subsections below. A related issue is the extent to which a judgment by a court assuming jurisdiction on the basis of a prorogation clause or, alternatively, a judgment of a court assuming jurisdiction in derogation of a choice of forum clause will be recognized and enforced by the courts of other nations. This issue we consider below in Section 6. Still another related issue — the extent to which national courts will recognize and enforce a choice by private parties of a forum other than a court, namely an arbitral tribunal, and recognize and enforce awards issued by an arbitral tribunal — is treated below in Section 7, the concluding section of this Chapter.

[A]   Choice of Forum

With very few exceptions the forum chosen by the parties to a transnational contract has been inclined to exercise jurisdiction over the dispute and to view the choice of forum clause as submission of the parties to the court's jurisdiction.

The more controversial issue has been whether to recognize and enforce a derogation clause in a private contract that excludes a court from deciding the case over which it otherwise has jurisdiction. The issue is often framed in terms of whether a choice of forum clause can "oust" the jurisdiction of all courts other than those of the forum chosen. This is incorrect. In deciding to honor a choice of forum clause a court exercises its jurisdiction. Its exercise of jurisdiction has simply resulted in a decision to refer the parties to the chosen forum in accordance with the bargain they have made.

Traditionally, British courts have been unwilling to uphold derogation clauses although quite accepting of prorogation clauses. Recently, however, they have had a change of attitude. In *Trendtex Trading Corp. v. Credit Suisse*,[1] the House of Lords upheld a contractual choice of a Swiss forum. In doing so the Lords agreed with the analysis and reasoning of Judge Robert Goff of the Queen's Bench Division.[2] In Judge Goff's view, the choice of forum clause should be honored "unless strong cause for not doing so is shown," the burden of proof to show such strong cause being on the plaintiff. Judge Goff further indicated that, to avoid application of the choice of forum clause, plaintiff would have to prove it would be unjust to enforce it.

Until 1972 most American courts had refused to honor choice of forum clauses. But that year the situation changed abruptly when the Supreme Court handed down the following decision.

THE BREMEN v. ZAPATA OFF-SHORE COMPANY

United States Supreme Court
407 U.S. 1, 92 S. Ct. 1907, 32 L. Ed.2d 513 (1972)

[In this case a German firm (Unterweser) had contracted to have its sea-going tug *The Bremen* tow an off-shore oil drilling rig (the Chaparral) owned by Zapata (an American Oil Company) from Louisiana to a point in the Adriatic Sea off Ravenna, Italy. The tow never got out of the Gulf of Mexico because of a severe storm that damaged the oil rig. When the rig was towed to shore in Tampa, Florida, Zapata brought an admiralty action in the federal district court against Unterweser *in personam* and against *The Bremen in rem* alleging negligence in the towage and breach of contract. The contract of towage had a clause that provided: "Any dispute arising must be treated before the London Court of Justice." Unterweser moved to dismiss on the basis of this clause, but then before the district court could rule on the motion, commenced an action against Zapata seeking damages for breach of contract in the High Court of Justice in London. Zapata's challenge to the jurisdiction of the latter court was overruled by that court on the strength of the choice-of-forum clause. At this point Unterweser faced a dilemma. The district court had not ruled on its motion to dismiss but the six-months time within which

---

[1] 1982 A.C. 679.
[2] [1980] 3 All Eng. L.R. 721.

it was required to file a "limitation of liability" was about to run. Under these circumstances Unterweser filed the limitation, the district court subsequently denied its motion to dismiss and then, upon Zapata's motion, enjoined Unterweser from litigating further in the London court. The district court ruled that having taken jurisdiction in the limitation proceeding, it had jurisdiction to determine all matters relating to the controversy. The Court of Appeals for the Fifth Circuit, sitting *en banc*, affirmed.]

MR. CHIEF JUSTICE BURGER delivered the opinion of the Court.

* * * *

We hold, with the six dissenting members of the Court of Appeals, that far too little weight and effect was given to the forum clause in resolving this controversy. For at least two decades we have witnessed an expansion of overseas commercial activities by business enterprises based in the United States. The barrier of distance that once tended to confine a business concern to a modest territory no longer does so. . . . The expansion of American business and industry will hardly be encouraged if, notwithstanding solemn contracts, we insist on a parochial concept that all disputes must be resolved under our laws and in our courts. . . .

Forum selection clauses have historically not been favored by American courts. . . . Although this view apparently still has considerable acceptance, other courts are tending to adopt a more hospitable attitude toward forum selection clauses. This view, advanced in the well reasoned dissenting opinion in the instant case, is that such clauses are prima facie valid and should be enforced unless enforcement is shown by the resisting party to be "unreasonable" under the circumstances. We believe this is the correct doctrine to be followed by federal district courts sitting in admiralty. It is merely the other side of the proposition recognized by this Court in *National Equipment Rental, Ltd. v. Szukhent*[3] . . . holding that in federal courts a party may validly consent to be sued in a jurisdiction where he cannot be found for service of process through contractual designation of an "agent" for receipt of process in that jurisdiction. . . .

. . . This approach is substantially that followed in other common-law countries including England. It is the view advanced by noted scholars and that adopted by the Restatement of Conflicts of Laws. It accords with ancient concepts of freedom of contract and reflects an appreciation of the expanding horizons of American contractors who seek business in all parts of the world. . . .

There are compelling reasons why a freely negotiated private international agreement, unaffected by fraud, undue influence, or overweening bargaining power, such as that involved here, should be given full effect. In this case, for example, we are concerned with a far from routine transaction between companies of two different nations contemplating the tow of an extremely costly piece of equipment from Louisiana across the Gulf of Mexico, and the Atlantic Ocean, through the Mediterranean Sea to its final destination in the Adriatic Sea. In the course of its voyage, it was to traverse the waters of many jurisdictions. The Chaparral could have been damaged at any point along the route, and there were countless possible ports of refuge. That the accident occurred in the Gulf of

---

[3] [citation].

Mexico and the Barge was towed to Tampa in an emergency were mere fortuities. . . . Manifestly much uncertainty and possibly great inconvenience to both parties could arise if a suit could be maintained in any jurisdiction in which an accident might occur or if jurisdiction were left to any place where the Bremen or Unterweser might happen to be found. . . . There is strong evidence that the forum clause was a vital part of the agreement, and it would be unrealistic to think that the parties did not conduct their negotiations, including fixing the monetary terms, with the consequences of the forum clause figuring prominently in their calculations.[4]

. . . Although their opinions are not altogether explicit, it seems reasonably clear that the District Court and the Court of Appeals placed the burden on Unterweser to show that London would be a more convenient forum than Tampa although the contract expressly resolved that issue. The correct approach would have been to enforce the forum clause specifically unless Zapata could clearly show that enforcement would be unreasonable and unjust, or that the clause was invalid for such reasons as fraud or overreaching. Accordingly, the case must be remanded for reconsideration.

We note, however, that there is nothing in the record presently before us that would support a refusal to enforce the forum clause. The Court of Appeals suggested that enforcement would be contrary to the public policy of the forum under *Bisso v. Inland Waterways Corp.*[5] . . . because of the prospect that the English courts would enforce the clauses of the towage contract purporting to exculpate Unterweser from liability for damages to the Chaparral. A contractual choice of forum clause should be held unenforceable if enforcement would contravene a strong public policy of the forum in which suit is brought, whether declared by statute or by judicial decision. . . . It is clear, however, that whatever the proper reach of the policy expressed in Bisso, it does not reach this case. Bisso rested on considerations with respect to the towage business strictly in American waters, and those considerations are not controlling in an international commercial agreement. . . .

Courts have also suggested that a forum clause, even though it is freely bargained for and contravenes no important public policy of the forum, may nevertheless be "unreasonable" and unenforceable if the chosen forum is *seriously* inconvenient for the trial of the action. . . . [But] we are not here dealing with an agreement between two Americans to resolve their essentially local disputes in a remote alien forum. In such a case, the serious inconvenience . . . to one or both of the parties might carry greater weight in determining the reasonableness of the forum clause . . . or might suggest that the agreement was an adhesive one or that the parties did not have the particular controversy in mind when they made their agreement. . . .

---

[4] Elsewhere in its opinion (Footnote 8) the Court observes that while the limitation of liability fund in the district court in Tampa amounted to $1.39 million dollars, in England the fund would be only slightly in excess of $80,000 and that under English practice (Footnote 15) an English court would, absent an express choice of law clause, treat the choice of forum clause as indicating the parties intent to have English substantive law apply. - Ed.

[5] 349 U.S. 85, 75 S. Ct. 629, 99 L. Ed. 911 (1955).

This case, however, involves a freely negotiated international commercial transaction between a German and an American corporation for towage of a vessel from the Gulf of Mexico to the Adriatic Sea. . . . Whatever "inconvenience" Zapata would suffer from by being forced to litigate in the contractual forum as it agreed to do was clearly foreseeable at the time of contracting. In such circumstances it should be incumbent on the party seeking to escape his contract to show that trial in the contractual forum will be so gravely difficult and inconvenient that he will for all practical purposes be deprived of his day in court. Absent that there is no basis for concluding that it would be unfair, unjust, or unreasonable to hold that party to his bargain.

In the course of his ruling on Unterweser's second motion to stay the proceedings in Tampa, the District Court did make a conclusionary finding that the balance of convenience was "strongly" in favor of litigation in Tampa. However, as previously noted, in making that finding the court erroneously placed the burden of proof on Unterweser to show that the balance of convenience was strongly in its favor. Moreover, the finding falls far short of a conclusion that Zapata would be effectively deprived of its day in court should it be forced to litigate in London. Indeed, it cannot even be assumed that it would be put to the expense of transporting its witnesses to London. It is not unusual for important issues in admiralty cases to be dealt with by deposition. Both the District Court and the Court of Appeals majority appeared satisfied that Unterweser could receive a fair hearing in Tampa by using deposition testimony of its witnesses from distant places, and there is no reason to conclude that Zapata would not use deposition testimony to equal advantage if forced to litigate in London as it bound itself to do. Nevertheless, to allow Zapata opportunity to carry its heavy burden of showing not only that the balance of convenience is strongly in favor of trial in Tampa (that is, that it will be far more inconvenient for Zapata to litigate in London than it will be for Unterweser to litigate in Tampa), but also that a London trial will be so manifestly and gravely inconvenient to Zapata that it will be effectively deprived of a meaningful day in court, we remand for further proceedings.

[JUSTICE WHITE'S concurring opinion is omitted].

JUSTICE DOUGLAS, dissenting.

. . . Respondent is a citizen of this country. . . . If it submitted to the English court, its substantive rights would be adversely affected. Exculpatory provisions in the towage contract provide: (1) that petitioners, the masters and the crews "are not responsible for defaults and/or errors in the navigation of the tow" and (2) that "[d]amages suffered by the towed object are in any case for account of its owners."

Under our decision in *Dixilyn Drilling Corp. v. Crescent Towing & Salvage Corp.* [6] "a contract which exempts the tower from liability for its own negligence" is not enforceable, though there is evidence in the present record that it is enforceable in England. . . .

---

[6] 372 U.S. 697, 10 L. Ed. 2d 78, 79, 83 S. Ct. 967.

Moreover, the casualty occurred close to the District Court, a number of potential witnesses, including respondent's crewmen, reside in that area, and the inspection and repair work was done there. The testimony of the tower's crewmen, residing in Germany, is already available by deposition taken in the proceedings.

All in all, the District Court Judge exercised his discretion wisely in enjoining petitioner from pursuing the litigation in England. I would affirm the judgment below.

NOTES AND QUESTIONS

(1) Justice Douglas explicitly, and the Chief Justice almost so, expresses the view that an American court should not send the parties to another forum under a choice-of-forum clause if the substantive law that would be applied to the case by the chosen forum would violate the public policy of the U.S. Why should this be so? Because by honoring the choice-of-forum clause the American court somehow implicates itself in the enforcement of that policy? In the absence of an adhesion contract or of uneven bargaining power why should the objecting party not be governed by policies which, at least by implication, it agreed to when it consented to the forum clause? Might there not be grounds for distinguishing between policies such as that involved in *The Bremen* case and policies offensive to very basic American concepts of morality and justice?

(2) Is the dispute in *The Bremen* really one of choice of forum or choice of law? In a footnote to his dissent, Justice Douglas suggests that the "instant stratagem of specifying a foreign forum is essentially the same as invoking a foreign law of construction except that the present circumvention also requires the American party to travel across an ocean to seek relief." He notes that the courts have regularly refused to honor choice of law clauses that point to a law contrary to the public policy of the forum. Moreover, he argues that U.S. policy to "discourage negligence by making wrongdoers pay damages" applies fully to the situation in *The Bremen* regardless of the relative bargaining position of the parties.

(3) Forum selection clauses in actions arising under certain federal statutes pose special problems. For example, the Carriage of Goods by Sea Act[7] forbids "[a]ny clause, covenant or agreement . . . lessening" the carrier's liability for negligence, fault or dereliction of statutory duties. The courts have held that, when the Act applies by its terms, a forum selection clause pointing to a forum outside of the United States will not be honored, despite the Supreme Court's holding in *The Bremen*. However, if the Act applies only through incorporation by reference in the contract, a forum selection clause may still be valid.[8]

Similarly, the purpose of the Automobile Dealer's Franchise Act[9] is to equalize the bargaining position of dealers against manufacturers and to compel

---

[7] 49 Stat. 1207 (1936), 46 U.S.C. Section 1300.

[8] For a discussion of the cases, see Williams, *Forum Selection Clauses: Where They Are, Where They Are Going*, 6 Houston J. Int'l L. 1 (1983). Also, see cases collected in Chapter 1 pages 64-65, notes 2 & 3 *supra*.

[9] 70 Stat. 1125 (1956), 15 U.S.C. Sections. 1221-25.

manufacturers to "act in good faith" in performing or terminating franchises. It provides that a dealer may bring suit in any district in which the "manufacturer resides, or is found or has an agent." In *Volkswagen Interamerican, S.A. v. Rohlsen*[10] the court refused to honor a choice of forum clause in a franchise agreement restricting actions to the courts of Mexico. It held that the venue provisions of the Dealer's Act were designed to assure the dealer as accessible a forum as reasonably possible. But query after *Mitsubishi Motors Corp. v. Soler Chrysler-Plymouth Inc.*, set-out *infra* page 966.

(4) Since *The Bremen* was a case arising under federal admiralty jurisdiction, it is not binding on the States or on federal courts sitting in diversity jurisdiction. Nonetheless, with a few exceptions, it has been followed by State courts and federal courts exercising diversity jurisdiction. See, *e.g.*, *Stewart Organization, Inc. v. Ricoh Corp.*,[11] *Benge v. Software Galeria, Inc.*,[12] E. Scoles & P. Hay, Conflict of Laws 355-57 (1982). But see *General Engineering Corp. v. Martin Marietta Alumina, Inc.*[13] (*Erie* requires application of state law in the absence of a federal question or interest).

(5) It is unclear what impact, if any, *The Bremen* will have on the attitudes of foreign courts toward choice of forum clauses. Professor Lowenfeld has suggested:

> . . . As for adjudication abroad — say at buyer's place of business — it is not safe to assume that foreign courts will decline to act just because a clause in the contract points to another forum. Selection of a neutral forum, as in *The Bremen v. Zapata Off-Shore Co.*, may have a slightly better chance of prevailing than choice of the other party's jurisdiction. Moreover, a choice of forum clause is more likely to be given effect in the context of a continuing relation between the parties than in the context of a one-time transaction. Finally, clauses selecting a forum at a traditional center for the trade in question, such as London for sale of ships and most commodities, are more likely to be sustained than a forum chosen without the support of tradition, except where the tradition itself is thought to be oppressive, as in some of the developing countries.[14]

(6) For cases where the courts refused to enforce choice of forum clauses in accordance with *The Bremen* criteria, see *Copperweld Steel Co. v. Demag-Mannesmann-Boehler*,[15] *McDonnell Douglas Corp. v. Islamic Republic of Iran.*[16]

[B] Choice of Law

As we saw in the preceding section, courts, in honoring a choice of forum clause in a transnational contract, may find an implicit choice of law as well. That is, the chosen forum may determine that the parties intended the forum's law to apply to the dispute. Indeed, the parties to a contract may choose a particular

---

[10] 360 F. 2d 437 (C.A. Puerto Rico) cert. denied, 385 U.S. 919 (1966).
[11] 779 F.2d 643 (11th Cir. 1986).
[12] 608 F. Supp., 601 (E.D. Mo. 1985).
[13] 783 F.2d 352 (3d Cir. 1986).
[14] International Private Trade, 1 International Economic Law 119 (2d ed. 1981).
[15] 347 F. Supp. 53 (W.D. Pa. 1972), affirmed 578 F.2d 953 (3d Cir. 1978).
[16] 758 F.2d 341 (8th Cir. 1985).

forum in the expectation that the forum will apply its law. In his dissent in *The Bremen*, Justice Douglas suggested that Unterweser's real goal in seeking a London forum for litigation of the dispute was to gain the benefit of English law on limitations of liability.

Professor Lowenfeld has advised that parties to a transnational contract might wisely decide not to insert a choice of law clause in their contract. If the contract contains elaborate rules, Lowenfeld suggests, "the court or panel may well do what Professor Berman suggests - apply the agreed rules to the facts without reference to the sovereign source of those rules, and this process may be easier than if a particular governing law is chosen." It may especially be easier if the law that would be chosen is ambiguous or subject to varying interpretations, as may be the case with certain provisions of the Uniform Commercial Code. On the other hand, Lowenfeld points out, "it is possible that without a choice of law clause a court in buyer's country would apply its own law — as place of performance, place of damage, 'proper law', or law of forum — and that that law would be harsher on seller." [17]

Lowenfeld suggests further that only the most substantial and longest term contracts justify the kind of research required for the parties to make an intelligent choice of law. Most choice of law clauses, in his view, are "products (i) of drafter's familiarity with a particular body of law; (ii) a desire by a seller — or a large purchaser, or trade association — for uniform interpretation of standard contracts; and (iii) a belief (not inevitable but common) that the choice of law should follow the choice of forum, since the law so chosen will be most familiar to the decision makers." [18]

One of the factors that should go into the decision whether to include a choice of law clause in a transnational contract is whether it is likely to be honored in forums where the dispute may be entertained. British courts have long been hospitable to choice of law clauses, as long as the law chosen by the parties is reasonable. Civil law countries in Europe have been less hospitable, and some countries in Latin America have been hostile.

Although the issue was seldom litigated, the prevailing view in the United States has come to where, with some reservations, the concept of party autonomy and the use of choice of law clauses has been widely accepted. The Restatement (Second) of Conflict of Laws states:

Section 187. Law of the State Chosen by the Parties

    (1) **The law of the state chosen by the parties to govern their contractual rights and duties will be applied if the particular issue is one which the parties could have resolved by an explicit provision in their agreement directed to that issue.**

    (2) **The law of the state chosen by the parties to govern their contractual rights and duties will be applied, even if the particular issue is one which the parties could not have resolved by an explicit provision in their agreement directed to that issue, unless either:**

---

[17] A. Lowenfeld, International Private Trade, 1 International Economic Law 104-05 (2d ed. 1981).
   [18] *Id.* at 105.

(a) **The chosen state has no substantial relationship to the parties or the transaction and there is no other reasonable basis for the parties' choice, or**

(b) **Application of the law of the chosen state would be contrary to a fundamental policy of a state which has a materially greater interest than the chosen state in the determination of the particular issue and which, under the rule of Section 188, [relating to the most significant contacts] would be the state of the applicable law in the absence of an effective choice of law by the parties.**

(3) **In the absence of a contrary indication of intention, the reference is to the local law of the state of the chosen law.**

NOTES AND QUESTIONS

(1) Some scholarly comment in the United States has been highly critical of Section 187. See, *e.g.*, R. Weintraub, Commentary on the Conflict of Laws 355-63 (2d ed. 1980); Sedler, The Contracts Provisions of the Restatement (Second): An Analysis and a Critique.[19]

(2) Section 1-105(1) of the Uniform Commercial Code is also supportive of choice of law clauses:

> **Except as provided hereafter in this section, when a transaction bears a reasonable relation to this state and also to another state or nation the parties may agree that the law either of this state or of such other state or nation shall govern their rights and duties.**

The exceptions to Section 1-105(1) include rights of creditors to sold goods, bank deposits and collections, bulk transfers, investment securities, and certain secured transactions.

(3) By its terms, Section 187 is not limited to transactions within the United States. Nonetheless, it was drafted with national rather than international application in mind. To what extent should Section 187 be applicable to international transactions? Note in this connection that under Section 187(2)(a), one of the limitations on party autonomy is that the choice of law clause will not be effective if "the chosen state has no substantial relationship to the parties or the transaction *and there is no other reasonable basis for the parties' choice. . . .*" (emphasis supplied). Comment f to Section 187 provides as an example of a "reasonable basis for the parties' choice" absent a "substantial relationship" that "when contracting in countries whose legal systems are strange to them as well as relatively immature, the parties should be able to choose a law on the ground that they know it well and that it is sufficiently developed." Do you agree? Should it make any difference if the matter in dispute concerns issues of interpretation or issues of validity of the contract?

---

[19] 72 Colum. L. Rev. 279, 286-98 (1972).

In a transnational transaction context, should the validity of a choice of law clause turn on whether the issue is one of private or public law? Whether the contract is for a simple purchase or sale or for a long-term investment or joint venture?

Comment b to Section 187 suggests that a choice of a law that invalidates the contract should be treated as a mutual mistake and therefore disregarded. Do you agree?

(4) Restatement Section 187(2)(b) has been used to substantially undercut the parties choice of law. Thus in *Southern International Sales v. Potter & Brumfield Division*,[20] the court refused to honor the parties' choice of Indiana law to govern a distributorship agreement between an Indiana manufacturing company and its Puerto Rican distributor. Indiana law permitted a principal to terminate a distributorship for any reason whatsoever. The court relying on Section 187(2)(b) of the Restatement (Second) of Conflicts of Law and the "most significant contacts test" concluded that termination was controlled by the "just cause" requirement of the Puerto Rican Dealer's Contracts Act. Although the equipment sold by the distributor was manufactured in Indiana and shipped from there to Puerto Rico, the court thought that the parties' choice of law "would pale" when seen against the fact that most of the equipment sold by the distributor was sold in Puerto Rico, for Puerto Rican accounts and for use in Puerto Rico after solicitation there and because the distributor signed the contract in Puerto Rico and the application of Indiana law would "frustrate the fundamental policy" of Puerto Rico.

(5) The 1980 United Nations Convention on Contracts for the International Sale of Goods (see *supra*, Chapter 1), allows parties to contracts for the international sale of goods freely to choose some law other than that of the Convention to govern the contract. Similarly, in the European Economic Community, the 1980 Convention on the Law Applicable to Contractual Obligations, which is not yet in force, would also permit unlimited party autonomy.

§ 11.06   Recognition and Enforcement of Foreign Country Judgments

Introduction

Even assuming that a plaintiff succeeds in inducing a national court to exercise personal and subject matter jurisdiction over a transnational dispute, and obtains a favorable judgment, it may prove to be a pyrrhic victory if the defendant has no assets in the country where the judgment is rendered. In such an instance the winning party may be required to invoke the aid of the judicial system in another country to *enforce* his judgment.

In order to do this the winning party may have to bring a proceeding in the receiving state to have the court in the receiving state treat that judgment as its own, enforceable against the other party by whatever means (*e.g.*, levy of execution, contempt) are available under the law of the receiving state for the enforcement of its own judgments. No procedure exists in the United States for the registration of foreign country judgments or for their validation according to the

---

[20] 410 F. Supp. 1339 (S.D.N.Y., 1976).

civil law of exequatur followed by many other countries. Accordingly, enforcement must normally be sought by a separate action on the judgment. In the case of a money judgment this takes the form of an action on the debt represented by that judgment.

It should be noted, however, that as of 1990, 22 states had enacted the Uniform Foreign Money-Judgments Recognition Act.[1] Under the Act, an action on the debt represented by a foreign country judgment may be commenced by a motion for summary judgment.

Certain foreign judgments, *e.g.*, regarding status, are inherently incapable of enforcement by the receiving state, but may nevertheless be "recognized" as conclusive in proceedings brought in that state. Recognition may also occur when a foreign country judgment is used defensively in a case brought in a United States court by the losing party to the foreign proceeding. A foreign country judgment may also be "recognized" as conclusive against the parties to a foreign proceeding or as against third parties on questions of law and fact actually litigated abroad when the latter are raised in a United States court action.

In this Section we will not be considering the recognition and enforcement of sister-State judgments in the United States. A major difference between the enforcement of sister-State judgments and the enforcement of foreign country judgments in the United States is that the Full Faith and Credit Clause of Article IV, Section 1 of the United States Constitution severely limits the authority of a State court to decline enforcement of a sister-State judgment. The Full Faith and Credit Clause does not apply, however, to the recognition and enforcement by U.S. courts of foreign country judgments, and the courts have therefore had greater freedom to decide whether to recognize and enforce foreign country judgments and, if so, under what circumstances.

[A]   The Historical Basis for Recognition in the United States

HILTON v. GUYOT

United States Supreme Court
159 U.S 113, 16 S. Ct. 139, 140 L. Ed.2d 95 (1895)

[In this case the liquidator and surviving members of a French firm brought an action in France against two United States citizens and recovered a judgment. However, with nearly $200,000 remaining unpaid, plaintiffs brought an action in the Circuit Court for the Southern District of New York to enforce the judgment. In their answer, defendants denied that they were indebted to plaintiffs and contended that the French judgment had been procured by fraud. Defendants also filed a bill in equity to enjoin the prosecution of the action. When the plaintiffs won in both actions, defendants, by writ of error and appeal, brought the cases to the Supreme Court.]

---

[1] 13 U.L.A. Ann. 261 (1990).

JUSTICE GRAY, after stating the case, delivered the opinion of the Court.

* * * *

No law has any effect, of its own force, beyond the limits of the sovereignty from which its authority is derived. The extent to which the law of one nation, as put in force within its territory, whether by executive order, by legislative act, or by judicial decree, shall be allowed to operate within the dominion of another nation, depends upon what our greatest jurists have been content to call "the comity of nations." Although the phrase has been often criticized, no satisfactory substitute has been suggested.

"Comity," in the legal sense, is neither a matter of absolute obligation, on the one hand, nor of mere courtesy and good will, upon the other. But it is the recognition which one nation allows within its territory to the legislative, executive, or judicial acts of another nation, having due regard both to international duty and convenience, and to the rights of its own citizens, or of other persons who are under the protection of its laws. . . .

Chief Justice Taney . . . speaking for this court, while Mr. Justice Story was a member of it, and largely adopting his words, said:. . . . "The comity thus extended to other nations is no impeachment of sovereignty. It is the voluntary act of the nation by which it is offered, and is inadmissible when contrary to its policy, or prejudicial to its interest. But it contributes so largely to promote justice between individuals and to produce a friendly intercourse between the sovereignties to which they belong, that courts of justice have continually acted upon it as a part of the voluntary law of nations. It is not the comity of the courts, but the comity of the nation, which is administered and ascertained in the same way, and guided by the same reasoning, by which all other principles of municipal law are ascertained and guided. . . ."

In order to appreciate the weight of the various authorities cited at the bar, it is important to distinguish different kinds of judgments. Every foreign judgment, of whatever nature, in order to be entitled to any effect, must have been rendered by a court having jurisdiction of the cause, and upon regular proceedings, and due notice. In alluding to different kinds of judgments, therefore, such jurisdiction, proceedings, and notice will be assumed. It will also be assumed that they are untainted by fraud, the effect of which will be considered later.

> [In this part of his opinion, Justice Gray discusses various kinds of judgments, the different effect given them depending upon the parties to the cause, and British and early American cases and commentary on the subject. He states:]

Thus a judgment *in rem, adjudicating the title to a ship or other movable property within the custody of the court*, is treated as valid everywhere. . . . A judgment affecting the status of persons, such as a decree confirming or dissolving a marriage, is recognized as valid in every country, unless contrary to the policy of its own law. . . . Other judgments, not strictly in rem, under which a person has been compelled to pay money, are so far conclusive that the justice of the payment cannot be impeached in another country, so as to compel him to pay it again. . . . Other foreign judgments which have been held conclusive of the matter adjudged were judgments discharging obligations contracted in the foreign country between citizens or residents thereof. . . .

The extraterritorial effect of judgments in personam, at law or in equity, may differ, according to the parties to the case. A judgment of that kind between two citizens or residents of the country, and thereby subject to the jurisdiction, in which it is rendered, may be held conclusive as between them everywhere. So, if a foreigner invokes the jurisdiction by bringing an action against a citizen, both may be held bound by a judgment in favor of either. And if a citizen sues a foreigner, and judgment is rendered in favor of the latter, both may be held equally bound.

The effect to which a judgment, purely executory, rendered in favor of a citizen or resident of the country in a suit there brought by him against a foreigner, may be entitled in an action thereon against the latter in his own country — as is the case now before us — presents a more difficult question, upon which there has been some diversity of opinion.

* * * *

. . . [I]t clearly appears that, at the time of the separation of this country from England, the general rule was fully established that foreign judgments *in personam* were *prima facie* evidence only, and not conclusive of the merits of the controversy between the parties. But the extent and limits of the application of that rule do not appear to have been much discussed, or defined with any approach to exactness, in England or America, until the matter was taken up by Chancellor Kent and by Mr. Justice Story.

> [At this point Mr. Justice Gray reviews Kent's and Story's work and more recent American and English decisions, concluding:]

In view of all the authorities upon the subject, and of the trend of judicial opinion in this country and in England, following the lead of Kent and Story, we are satisfied that where there has been opportunity for a full and fair trial abroad before a court of competent jurisdiction, conducting the trial upon regular proceedings, after due citation or voluntary appearance of the defendant, and under a system of jurisprudence likely to secure an impartial administration of justice between the citizens of its own country and those of other countries, and there is nothing to show either prejudice in the court, or in the system of laws under which it was sitting, or fraud in procuring the judgment, or any special reason why the comity of this nation should not allow it full effect, the merits of the case should not, in an action brought in this country upon the judgment, be tried afresh, as on a new trial or an appeal, upon the mere assertion of the party that the judgment was erroneous in law or in fact. The defendants, therefore, cannot be permitted, upon that general ground, to contest the validity or the effect of the judgment sued on.

But they have sought to impeach that judgment upon several other grounds, which require separate consideration. . . .

It is next objected that in those courts one of the plaintiffs was permitted to testify not under oath, and was not subject to cross-examination by the opposite party, and that the defendants were therefore deprived of safeguards which are by our law considered essential to secure honesty and to detect fraud in a witness; and also that documents and papers were admitted in evidence, with which the defendants had no connection, and which would not be admissible under our system of jurisprudence. But it having been shown by the plaintiffs, and hardly denied by the defendants, that the practice followed and the method of examining witnesses were according to the laws of France, we are not prepared to hold that the fact that the procedure in these respects differed from that of our own courts is, of itself, a sufficient ground for impeaching the foreign judgment. . . .

There is no doubt that both in this country, as appears by the authorities already cited, and in England, a foreign judgment may be impeached for fraud. . . .

It has often, indeed, been declared by this court that the fraud which entitles a party to impeach the judgment of one of our own tribunals must be fraud extrinsic to the matter tried in the cause, and not merely consist in false and fraudulent documents or testimony submitted to that tribunal, and the truth of which was contested before it and passed upon by it. . . .

But it is now established in England, by well-considered, and strongly-reasoned decisions of the court of appeal, that foreign judgments may be impeached, if procured by false and fraudulent representations and testimony of the plaintiff, even if the same question of fraud was presented to and decided by the foreign court. . . .

But whether those decisions can be followed in regard to foreign judgments, consistently with our own decisions as to impeaching domestic judgments for fraud, it is unnecessary in this case to determine, because there is a distinct and independent ground upon which we are satisfied that the comity of our nation does not require us to give conclusive effect to the judgments of this and other foreign countries. . . .

By the law of France, settled by a series of uniform decisions of the court of cassation, the highest judicial tribunal, for more than half a century, no foreign judgment can be rendered executory in France without a review of the judgment au fond (to the bottom), including the whole merits of the cause of action on which the judgment rests. . . .

> [In this part of his opinion Justice Gray discusses French authorities and authorities of other civil law countries]

It appears, therefore, that there is hardly a civilized nation on either continent which, by its general law, allows conclusive effect to an executory foreign judgment for the recovery of money. . . .

The reasonable, if not the necessary, conclusion appears to us to be that judgments rendered in France, or in any other foreign country, by the laws of which our own judgments are reviewable upon the merits, are not entitled to full credit and conclusive effect when sued upon in this country, but are prima facie evidence only of the justice of the plaintiff's claim.

In holding such a judgment, for want of reciprocity, not to be conclusive evidence of the merits of the claim, we do not proceed upon any theory of retaliation upon one person by reason of injustice done to another, but upon the broad ground that international law is founded upon mutuality and reciprocity, and that by the principles of international law recognized in most civilized nations, and by the comity of our own country, which it is our judicial duty to know and to declare, the judgment is not entitled to be considered conclusive. . . .

If we should hold this judgment to be conclusive, we should allow it an effect to which, supposing the defendants' offers to be sustained by actual proof, it would, in the absence of a special treaty, be entitled in hardly any other country in Christendom, except the country in which it was rendered.

[The dissenting opinion of Chief Justice Fuller, in which Justices HARLAN, Brewer and Jackson joined, is omitted.]

NOTES AND QUESTIONS

(1) Consider the discussion in Chapter 6, *supra*, page 520 regarding the doctrine of comity. Justice Gray speaks at some length of comity in his opinion in *Hilton*. How would you describe comity? Is it the basis of Justice Gray's decision in *Hilton*? Could it be? Or is the comity concept simply too vague to serve as the basis for a decision whether to recognize and enforce a foreign country judgment?

(2) Consider the legal basis for Justice Gray's opinion. Does he, and the majority of the Court, decide not to recognize and enforce the French judgment on the basis of international law? French law? American federal or state law?

(3) Why should the courts of one country recognize and enforce the judgments of courts in other countries? Professors Trautman and Von Mehren have suggested the following considerations:

> [1] a desire to avoid the duplication of effort and consequent waste involved in reconsidering a matter that has already been litigated; [2] a related concern to protect the successful litigant, whether plaintiff or defendant, from harassing or evasive tactics on the part of his previously unsuccessful opponent; [3] a policy against making the availability of local enforcement the decisive element, as a practical matter, in the plaintiff's choice of forum; [4] an interest in fostering stability and unity in an international single jurisdiction; and [5] in certain classes of cases, a belief that the rendering jurisdiction is a more appropriate forum than the recognizing jurisdiction, either because the former was more convenient or for some other reason its views as to the merits should prevail.[2]

> Can you think of other reasons for recognizing and enforcing foreign judgments?

(4) Justice Gray's opinion in *Hilton* requires reciprocity as a pre-condition for the recognition and enforcement of the French judgment. Did the court reach this conclusion on the ground that it was *required* by international law? Permitted by international law? Precisely what role, if any, did international law play in the court's determination on reciprocity?

(5) What arguments does the Court advance in support of a reciprocity requirement? Are they persuasive? Is a primary purpose of the reciprocity requirement

---

2 Von Mehren & Trautman, *Recognition Of Foreign Adjudications: A Survey And A Suggested Approach*, 81 Harv. L. Rev. 1601, 1603-4 (1968).

to pressure countries like France into recognizing and enforcing judgments rendered by United States courts? Is this purpose likely to be realized?

(6) It is important to note that the reciprocity requirement in *Hilton* does not apply to the enforcement of all foreign judgments. It does not apply to foreign judgments *in rem* or to those relating to status. Nor does it apply to suits between citizens of the foreign country; or to suits by a non-citizen against a citizen of the foreign country; or to a suit where a citizen of the foreign country sues a non-citizen and loses. Under *Hilton*, the reciprocity requirement applies only where a suit by a citizen of the foreign country against a non-citizen results in an *in personam* judgment in favor of the citizen. Does this limited scope undermine the arguments for a reciprocity requirement?

(7) If applicable, a reciprocity requirement raises a number of practical problems. Paramount among these is the difficulty in determining when a reciprocity requirement would be satisfied. Would it be necessary, for example, that the grounds on which a foreign court would sustain a challenge to recognition and enforcement of a United States judgment be *precisely* the same as those developed by *Hilton* and other U.S. court decisions?

(8) *Hilton* was decided before the Supreme Court handed down its decisions in *Erie Railroad Co. v. Tompkins*[3] and *Klaxon Co. v. Stentor Electric Manufacturing Co.*[4] In *Erie*, it will be recalled, the Court held that federal courts have the constitutional obligation to apply the State law of the state in which they sit in diversity cases. The *Erie* doctrine was extended to the law of conflicts by the Court's decision in *Klaxon*. Accordingly, in the absence of federal preemption, by treaty or legislation, federal courts in diversity cases and state courts have been free to follow or reject the reciprocity requirement of *Hilton*. Some have followed *Hilton*, e.g., *Leo Feist, Inc. v. Debmar Publication.*[5] The majority of courts, however, have rejected the reciprocity requirement. See, *e.g., Bergman v. Desieyes,*[6] *Scott v. Scott.*[7]

(9) The French practice of subjecting foreign judgments to "revision au fond," the basis for denying enforcement to the French judgment in *Hilton*, was reversed in 1964 by a decision of the Cour de Cassation.[8]

[B] More on Defenses to Enforcement of Foreign Country Judgments

We have already seen a number of possible defenses to recognition and enforcement of foreign country judgments. In *Hilton* and in a minority of cases following *Hilton*, lack of reciprocity may be a bar. Justice Gray in *Hilton* also notes in passing the noncontroversial proposition that the foreign judgment, to be entitled to any effect, must have been rendered in a court having jurisdiction over the cause of action and in accordance with regular proceedings and due notice to

[3] 304 U.S. 64 (1938).
[4] 313 U.S. 487 (1941).
[5] 232 F. Supp. 623 (E.D. Pa. 1964).
[6] 170 F. 2d 360 (2d Cir. 1948).
[7] 51 Cal. 2d 249, 331 P. 2d 641 (1958).
[8] See Restatement (Third) of the Foreign Relations Law of the United States, Section 481, Reporters' Note 6(c) (1987).

the defendant. By way of dicta, the Court also indicates that "extrinsic fraud," *i.e.*, extrinsic to the matter tried in the case rather than false testimony submitted to the foreign tribunal, would be a defense.

In 1971 the United States Court of Appeals for the Third Circuit further addressed the issue of possible defenses to foreign country judgments.

SOMPORTEX LIMITED v. PHILADELPHIA CHEWING GUM CORP.

The United States Court of Appeals, Third Circuit
453 F. 2d 435 (1971), cert. denied 405 U.S. 1017 (1972)

[Through a New York exporter, a Pennsylvania seller negotiated with a British buyer for the sale of chewing gum in England. The deal went sour and the buyer brought a breach-of-contract action in an English court, asserting jurisdiction on the ground of the English equivalent to a United States long-arm statute. Philadelphia Chewing Gum, through an English solicitor, first made a "conditional appearance" in order to contest personal jurisdiction. After the English Court of Appeals ruled that the appearance was actually unconditional, but allowed the Pennsylvania Company additional time in which to enter the case and contest the merits, the latter decided instead to allow a default judgment to be entered against it for the amount claimed, including loss of good will and attorneys' fees. The British buyer then sought enforcement of the English default judgment in the Federal District Court for the Eastern District of Pennsylvania, which issued an order granting summary judgment to the plaintiff. Defendant appealed.]

Before ALDISERT, GIBBONS and ROSENN, CIRCUIT JUDGES.

ALDISERT, CIRCUIT JUDGE

* * * *

Appellant presents a cluster of contentions supporting its major thesis that we should not extend hospitality to the English judgment. First, it contends, and we agree, that because our jurisdiction is based solely on diversity, "the law to be applied . . . is the law of the state," in this case Pennsylvania law. . . .

Pennsylvania distinguishes between judgments obtained in the courts of her sister states, which are entitled to full faith and credit, and those of foreign courts, which are subject to principles of comity. *In re Christoff's Estate.*[9]

Comity is a recognition which one nation extends within its own territory to the legislative, executive, or judicial acts of another. It is not a rule of law, but one of practice, convenience, and expediency. Although more than mere courtesy and accommodation, comity does not achieve the force of an imperative or

---

[9] 411 Pa. 419, 192 A. 2d 737, cert. denied, 375 U.S. 965, 84 S. Ct. 483, 11 L. Ed. 2d 414 (1964).

obligation. Rather, it is a nation's expression of understanding which demonstrates due regard both to international duty and convenience and to the rights of persons protected by its own laws. Comity should be withheld only when its acceptance would be contrary or prejudicial to the interest of the nation called upon to give it effect. . . .

Thus, the court in *Christoff, supra* . . . acknowledged the governing standard enunciated in *Hilton v. Guyot, supra*. . . .

It is by this standard, therefore, that appellant's arguments must be measured.

Appellant's contention that the district court failed to make an independent examination of the factual and legal basis of the jurisdiction of the English Court at once argues too much and says too little. The reality is that the Court did examine the legal basis of asserted jurisdiction and decided the issue adversely to the appellant.

Indeed, we do not believe it was necessary for the court below to reach the question of whether the factual complex of the contractual dispute permitted extraterritorial service under the English long-arm statute. In its opinion denying leave of defense counsel to withdraw, the Court of Appeal specifically gave Philadelphia the opportunity to have the factual issue tested before the courts; moreover, Philadelphia was allocated additional time to do just that. Lord Denning said ". . . . They can argue that matter out at a later stage if they should so wish." Three months went by with no activity forthcoming and then, as described by the district court, "[d]uring this three month period defendant changed its strategy and, not wishing to do anything which might result in its submitting to the English Court's jurisdiction, decided to withdraw its appearance altogether." Under these circumstances, we hold that defendant cannot choose its forum to test the factual basis of jurisdiction. It was given and it waived, the opportunity of making the adequate presentation in the English Court.

Additionally, appellant attacks the English practice wherein a conditional appearance attacking jurisdiction may, by court decision, be converted into an unconditional one. It cannot effectively argue that this practice constitutes "some special ground . . . for impeaching the judgment," as to render the English judgment unwelcome in Pennsylvania under principles of international law and comity because it was obtained by procedures contrary or prejudicial to the host state. The English practice in this respect is identical to that set forth in both the Federal and the Pennsylvania rules of civil procedure. . . .

Thus we will not disturb the English Court's adjudication. That the English judgment was obtained by appellant's default judgment is as conclusive an adjudication between the parties as when rendered after answer and complete contest in the open courtroom. . . . The polestar is whether a reasonable method of notification is employed and reasonable opportunity to be heard is afforded to the person affected. . . .

English law permits recovery, as compensatory damages in breach of contract, of items reflecting loss of good will and costs, including attorneys' fees. These two items formed substantial portions of the English judgment. Because they are not recoverable under Pennsylvania law, appellant would have the foreign judgment declared unenforceable because it constitutes an . . . action on the foreign claim [which] could not have been maintained because contrary to the public policy of the forum," citing Restatement, Conflict of Laws, Section 445. We are satisfied with the district court's disposition of this argument:

> The Court finds that . . . while Pennsylvania may not agree that these elements should be included in damages for breach of contract, the variance with Pennsylvania law is not such that the enforcement "tends clearly to injure the public health, the public morals, the public confidence in the purity of the administration of the law, or to undermine that sense of security for individual rights, whether of personal liberty or of private property, which any citizen ought to feel is against public policy.". . . .[10]

Finally, appellant contends that since "it maintains no office or employee in England and transacts no business within the country" there were no insufficient [sic] contacts there to meet the due process tests of *International Shoe Co. v. Washington.*[11] It argues that, at best, "the only contact Philadelphia had with England was the negotiations allegedly conducted by an independent New York exporter by letter, telephone and telegram to sell Philadelphia's products in England." In *Hanson v. Denckla*,[13] Chief Justice Warren said: "The application of rule will vary with the quality and nature of the defendant's activity but it is essential in each case that there be some act by which the defendant purposefully avails himself of the privilege of conducting business within the forum State, thus invoking the benefits and protection of its laws." We have concluded that whether the New York exporter was an independent contractor or Philadelphia's agent was a matter to be resolved by the English Court. For the purpose of the constitutional argument, we must assume the proper agency relationship. So construed, we find his activity would constitute the "quality and nature of the defendant's activity" similar to that of the defendant in *McGee v. International Life Ins. Co.*,[13] there held to satisfy due process requirements.

For the reasons heretofore rehearsed we will not disturb the English Court's adjudication of jurisdiction; we have deemed as irrelevant the default nature of the judgment; we have concluded that the English compensatory damage items do not offend Pennsylvania public policy; and hold that the English procedure comports with our standards of due process.

In sum, we find that the English proceedings met all the tests enunciated in *Christoff, supra.* We are not persuaded that appellant met its burden of showing that the British "decree is so palpably tainted by fraud or prejudice as to outrage our sense of justice, or [that] the process of the foreign tribunal was invoked to achieve a result contrary to our laws of public policy or to circumvent our laws or public policy." *Christoff, supra.*

The judgment of the district court will be

Affirmed.

---

[10] *Somportex Limited v. Philadelphia Chewing Gum Corp.*, 318 F. Supp. 161, 169 (E.D. Pa. 1970).

[11] 326 U.S. 310, 66 S. Ct. 154, 90 L.Ed. 95 (1965).

[13] 357 U.S. 235, 253, 78 S. Ct. 1228, 1240, 2 L.Ed. 2d 1283 (1958).

[13] 355 U.S. 220, 78 S. Ct. 199, 2 L.Ed. 3d 223 (1957).

NOTES AND QUESTIONS

(1) Note that the court in *Somportex* rejected appellant's argument that it should not allow recovery for loss of good will and costs, including attorneys' fees, because such recovery could not be had if the action had originally been brought in Pennsylvania. In so ruling, was the court making a choice of law decision, choosing the law of England over the law of Pennsylvania? Was the court's discussion of the public policy of the forum part of this choice of law? Should the court have approached the public policy issue the way it did in an action to enforce a *default* judgment? Should a default judgment be treated differently from other foreign country judgments? Indeed, was the issue of recovery for good will and attorneys' fees a procedural issue to be governed by the law of the forum? For other cases involving the enforcement of foreign country default judgments, see *Tahan v. Hodgson*,[14] *Hunt v. BP Exploration Co. (Libya) LTD.*[15]

(2) Both *Hilton* and *Somportex* make it clear that a foreign court need not follow all of the procedures a U.S. court would consider necessary or desirable. Thus, recognition of a foreign court's judgment will normally not be denied just because the foreign court's procedures were more inquisitorial than adversarial, or because its rules of evidence, its grant of the right to cross examine or to call and swear witnesses differed from what would obtain in an American court. Rather, the touchstone is basic fairness. Examples of practices that will result in a denial of recognition of a foreign judgment include domination of the foreign tribunal by the political branches of the foreign government or by the opposing party, denial to the losing party of access to essential evidence or of a timely opportunity to obtain the assistance of counsel on critical points or of a right to appeal.[16]

(3) Certain types of foreign country judgments raise special problems. For example, the traditional view has long been that a foreign country judgment for taxes and penalties will not be recognized when the recognizing court, under its law, would not have entertained an original action on such a claim. Is this exception justifiable in today's world?

With respect to penal judgments, there may be a definitional problem. For example, should an award for punitive damages in a tort case, or for treble damages in a private antitrust suit, be considered "penal" or a civil money judgment? Similarly, in some civil law countries a tort action for injury to persons or property is not a purely "civil action." That is, it may be brought, in the first instance, by the public prosecutor as a criminal proceeding in order to establish liability. The civil plaintiff may then join the proceeding on the question of damages and receive a money judgment. Is this judgment to be considered "civil" or "penal" for purposes of recognition and enforcement?

(4) Problems may also arise with respect to judgments ordering a conveyance of an interest in real property located outside the rendering court's jurisdiction or adjudicating the validity of a U.S. patent, trade-mark, or copyright. Such judgments have traditionally been denied recognition on the ground that the

---

[14] 662 F. 2d 862 (D.C. Cir. 1981).

[15] 492 F. Supp. 885 (N.D. Texas 1980).

[16] See Restatement (Third) of Foreign Relations Law of the United States, Section 482 (1987).

foreign court lacked jurisdiction of the subject matter. The traditional rule, however, is rapidly breaking down in the case of judgments ordering performance of a contract to sell real property or pertaining to the licensing of patents, trademarks or copyrights. Moreover, United States courts are increasingly refusing to entertain challenges to the subject matter jurisdiction of the rendering court in a contested proceeding where the challenge is based solely upon that court's failure to follow its own jurisdictional rules (*e.g.*, a challenge to the judgment of a "civil" court on the ground that jurisdiction lay with the "commercial" court, or a challenge to the "venue" of the rendering court) unless the defect was patent and a manifest abuse of power by the rendering court. See, in this connection, Restatement, Second Judgments, Sections 1, 11, 12, 69 and 81, relating to interstate judgments. More difficult to resolve are challenges to the "prescriptive competence" of the rendering court under international law in cases based upon a regulatory statute or other law.

(5) In the ordinary case, the court of the receiving state will not require that the foreign court's assertion of jurisdiction meet the receiving state's own non-constitutional "long-arm" jurisdictional requirements. However, special rules pertain to judgments on family law matters. With respect to divorce, jurisdiction is almost universally tied to "domicile," or increasingly, "habitual residence." But unlike ordinary cases the foreign court's assertion that it had jurisdiction over the marriage because the parties were domiciled there is generally subject to scrutiny in the receiving court and tested according to that court's own criteria for domicile, unless the party challenging the determination of domicile is estopped (*e.g.*, party initiating the foreign divorce, both parties had remarried, or too much time elapsed). Some courts have limited this kind of close scrutiny to cases where the foreign court's jurisdiction was based upon the domicile of only one, rather than both, of the parties.

With respect to child custody orders, the Uniform Child Custody Jurisdiction Act,[17] adopted as of 1989 by 44 States, provides for recognition of foreign country as well as sister State child custody orders where the rendering court had jurisdiction because: (i) the child's habitual residence was in that state, or (ii) the child and at least one parent, party to the custody proceeding, had a significant connection with that state; or (iii) the child was present in that state when emergency conditions arose requiring a custody order.

(6) Issues may arise as to the *res judicata* or estoppel effect to be given a foreign country judgment. At a minimum, for there to be any such effect, the judgment must be "final" under the law of the rendering state. Finality is not affected by the possibility of an appeal or by the fact that the judgment may be subject to reconsideration or modification under changed circumstances. Besides the requirement of finality, the only point that is clearly settled is that, as between the immediate parties to the foreign proceedings, United States courts will give a foreign country judgment such *res judicata* effect, and no more, as that judgment would receive in similar circumstances under the law of the rendering state.[18] Even this very limited holding, however, is subject to some important qualifications.

---

[17] 9 U.L.A. 111 (1979).
[18] See Restatement, Second, Conflict of Laws, Section 98, Comment (f).

First, where it is clearly established that under the law of the rendering state the judgment would be accorded collateral estoppel effect as to third parties or in a separate proceeding between the parties, as to questions of law and fact actually litigated, courts in the United States are increasingly giving such judgments the same conclusive effect.[19] This is especially so if the rendering state's law of collateral estoppel is similar to that of the receiving state.

Second, where the foreign law of collateral estoppel is uncertain or difficult of ascertainment, recognition is generally confined to the narrow bounds stated above, except that some courts have been willing to apply their own concepts of collateral estoppel in order to give wider recognition to such judgments. In short, these courts are willing to accord a foreign country judgment such conclusive effect as they would give their own judgments under similar circumstances without close inquiry into the law of the rendering state.[20]

Third, some United States courts have made increasing use of the doctrine of "offensive collateral estoppel," without regard to the law of the rendering state.

Appraise these rules in light of the several considerations supporting the recognition of foreign country judgments listed by Von Mehren & Trautman, *supra.*

(7) Should recognition be withheld from a foreign default judgment where service of process on the defendant did not conform to either (i) the method of service established pursuant to the Hague Convention for the Service Abroad of Judicial and Extra-Judicial Documents in Civil or Commercial Matters,[21] or (ii) the method used was not authorized by the laws of the receiving state? In answering see Article 15 of the Convention.

(8) As discussed *supra,* in Section 5 of this Chapter, United States courts are now hospitable to enforcing agreements to submit disputes between the parties to a specified forum. See *The Bremen v. Zapata Off-Shore Co.*[22] Hence, a judgment rendered by a foreign tribunal other than the one specified in the agreement between the parties may be denied recognition and enforcement by a United States court. As we shall see in the next Section of this chapter, this will also be the case if the parties have agreed to submit their disputes to arbitration instead of a judicial tribunal.

(9) The Uniform Foreign Money-Judgments Recognition Act,[23] which is in force in several States including New York, provides for the recognition and enforcement "in the same manner as the judgment of a sister State which is entitled to full faith and credit" of foreign country judgments which grant or deny the recovery of a sum of money. The Act does not apply, however, to judgments for taxes, fines or penalties, or support judgments in matrimonial or family matters. The Act requires further that the judgment be rendered in a legal system providing impartial tribunals and procedures compatible with due process and

---

[19] See, *e.g., Atlantic Ship Supply, Inc. v. M/V Lucy,* 392 F. Supp. 179 (M.D. Fla. 1975).

[20] See Peterson, Foreign Country Judgments And The Second Restatement Of Conflict Of Laws, 72 Colum. L. Rev. 220 (1972).

[21] 20 U.S.T. 361, T.I.A.S. 6638, (Documentary Supplement page 442).

[22] 407 U.S. 1 (1972).

[23] 13 U.L.A. 271 (Master ed. 1975)

that the foreign court had personal and subject matter jurisdiction. Under the Act a judgment also need not be recognized if obtained by fraud, if the foreign court was a seriously inconvenient forum, if the judgment conflicts with another judgment, violates the public policy of the forum or an agreement to arbitrate.

(10) The approach of countries other than the United States to the recognition and enforcement of foreign country judgments is beyond the scope of this casebook. For a summary of some of these approaches, see C. Platto, Ed., Enforcement of Foreign Judgments Worldwide (1989); Restatement (Third) of the Foreign Relations Law of the United States, Section 481, Reporters' Note 6 (1987). It suffices for present purposes to note that, unlike the Anglo-American common law practice of requiring an action on the foreign country judgment, civil law countries employ a procedure that gives executory force (*exequatur*) to the foreign judgment. In these *exequatur* proceedings, however, a judgment debtor may be able to resist the enforcement of the foreign judgment on a number of grounds, among them lack of reciprocity and violation of local public policy. In some countries, especially France, the concept of local public policy has received an expansive interpretation and application. The concept of reciprocity has also proven difficult in application to U.S. judgments because of the diversity of recognition practices followed by state courts in the United States.

(11) For the United States it has not proven possible to resolve problems of recognition and enforcement of judgments through the conclusion of treaties. The closest the United States has come to doing so was the draft convention initialed in 1977 between the United States and the United Kingdom. However, chances for the adoption of such a convention are remote. Primary resistance to final conclusion of the convention has come from the United Kingdom, which has become skeptical regarding the wisdom of facilitating recognition of U.S. judgments in the United Kingdom because of the high level of United States awards in products liability cases and because of the expansive reach of American antitrust jurisdiction, especially in private antitrust suits involving the possibility of treble damage awards.[24]

(12) The member countries of the European Economic Community have been more successful in that they have concluded a Convention on Jurisdiction and the Enforcement of Judgements in Civil and Commercial Matters.[25] This Convention greatly facilitates the recognition and enforcement of judgments in the Common Market area and severely limits the use of the so-called exorbitant bases of jurisdiction discussed *supra* in Section 2. As also discussed previously, however, the Convention is blatantly discriminatory against defendants not resident in the Common Market and may strengthen the use of exorbitant bases of jurisdiction against them by requirements that each state party to the Convention

---

[24] For a discussion of the draft convention, with additional citations, see Scoles & Hay, Conflict Of Laws 971-73 (1982).

[25] Convention is at Off. J., European Communities, No. L. 304 (1978) and was further amended by the Convention on Accession of the Hellenic Republic to the basic Convention. Off. J. European Communities, No. L. 388 (1982). The European Community and EFTA have also concluded a Convention on Jurisdiction and Enforcement of Judgments in Civil and Commercial Matters. 31 Off. J. European Communities, No. L 319 at page 9 (1988), reproduced in 28 Int'l Leg. Mat. 620 (1989).

recognize and enforce judgments which other Common Market countries, using a regular or an exorbitant basis of jurisdiction, render against non-domiciliary defendants.

The Common Market Convention does permit member states to conclude bilateral conventions with non-member states by which they undertake not to enforce judgments against nationals of the latter if such a judgment would not be enforceable against a local domiciliary. The draft convention between the United States and the United Kingdom would have taken advantage of this option.[26]

§ 11.07　International Arbitration[1]

Introduction

From the subjects covered earlier in this Chapter, as well as other material in this casebook, it should be clear that the *judicial* settlement of international business disputes is an increasingly difficult and often controversial proposition. Jurisdictional requirements may be difficult to meet, and the varying views of states regarding the permissible limits of personal jurisdiction may generate conflict. Assuming that jurisdictional requirements are met, a prospective claimant has numerous opportunities for forum shopping. The problem of forum shopping, as well as the possibility that states will have concurrent jurisdiction over a dispute, is exacerbated by the absence of international rules or procedures for the resolution of disputes regarding personal jurisdiction and the avoidance of multiple litigation. If the dispute is complicated, and involves transactions in several states, a foreign court may hold it cannot enjoin an action taking place outside its territory. Moreover, a foreign court may be authorized only to give a judgment in local (and inconvertible) currency.

Choice of law questions and other procedural issues, including international discovery, become especially complex in transnational litigation. With the increasing involvement of the state in international commercial matters, sovereign immunity and the Act of State doctrine may provide an additional level of complexity. Assuming that a judgment is obtained, obtaining its recognition and enforcement abroad is often difficult if not impossible.

Even within the purely national context, there is now general agreement that alternatives to the judicial settlement of disputes are urgently needed. Delays due to court congestion and time consuming procedures such as discovery, the combative nature of court proceedings, especially in the United States, and cost considerations, among other factors, have led to a broad exploration of alternative methods of dispute resolution.

In the first Section of this Chapter we considered the more informal alternatives to judicial settlement of transnational disputes, namely, negotiation, mediation

---

[26] For discussion of the Inter-American Convention on Extraterritorial Validity of Foreign Judgments and Arbitral Awards of 1979, see Casad, Civil Judgment Recognition And The Integration Of Multiple-State Associations 169-181 (1981).

[1] We are indebted to Daniel M. Price of the Pennsylvania Bar for many helpful suggestions regarding this Section.

and conciliation. We now turn to the method that, with the growth of international trade, has begun to emerge as an increasingly preferred means of resolving international commercial disputes: international arbitration.

Among the principal reasons for the increased resort to arbitration is the reluctance of international firms to submit to each others courts, congestion and delay in the latter, concern over confidentiality — in arbitration awards, at least the facts and the reasons for the award can often be kept off the public record; not so court judgments — and a desire for a dispute-resolution mechanism which can be tailored to the technical and commercial elements of the dispute involved.

This is not to say that international arbitration is a panacea. On the contrary, some commentators have contended that the advantages of international arbitration have been exaggerated and its disadvantages ignored or unduly minimized. The critics point out that arbitration largely retains the disadvantages of judicial proceedings, such as a combative environment and the absence of participation by senior management personnel. Contrary to claims by its supporters, international arbitration may not save the parties money or ensure that settlements will be adhered to without costly resort to formal litigation. Such proceedings, the critics claim, may also have a substantial negative impact on the substantive rights of the parties.

We shall consider the validity of some of these criticisms as we go through the materials in this Section. First, we take up the structure and operation of international arbitral associations and the conduct of international arbitration. Next we turn to some of the crucial points to keep in mind while drafting an arbitration clause. We then explore some issues encountered in enforcing an agreement to arbitrate and conclude with a discussion of problems that arise in enforcing arbitral awards.

[A] The Structure and Operation of International Arbitral Associations and the Conduct of International Arbitration

An "arbitration" proceeding can be either "institutional" arbitration, administered by an organization such as the International Chamber of Commerce or the American Arbitration Association and usually conducted under the rules of the organization, or an "*ad hoc*" arbitration, administered and conducted in a manner specifically defined by the parties. Whatever the type involved, the agreement to arbitrate may be included as a provision in the original commercial contract or drawn up and agreed to by the parties after the dispute has arisen. The way in which the arbitration is structured will of course have an impact on the advantages and disadvantages of international arbitration.

Most often, parties will choose to conduct arbitration under the rules of several well known arbitral institutions. These include, among others, the International Chamber of Commerce (ICC), the American Arbitration Association (AAA), the International Center for the Settlement of Investment Disputes (ICSID), the Arbitration Institute of the Stockholm Chamber of Commerce, and the United Nations Commission on International Trade Law (UNCITRAL). A thumbnail sketch of these institutions follows.

The International Chamber of Commerce (ICC)

Established in 1923, the ICC is the oldest international arbitration center. It is also one of the most active, handling between 300 to 350 cases a year. The ICC Court of Arbitration is misnamed, since it performs only supervisory and administrative tasks; the hearing of cases is performed solely by one or a panel of arbitrators. The ICC Court does, however, scrutinize draft awards for clarity and to ensure that they comply with the formal requirements of the country where rendered.

For certain types of cases the fact that the ICC lacks well defined rules of procedure renders the use of ICC facilities ill-advised. In other cases, the flexibility that the rules allow is highly desirable. Under the ICC rules the parties must enter into an agreement with respect to how the arbitration is to be conducted at a conference before the arbitral hearings. The rules also require that the parties and arbitrators draft and execute "terms of reference," *i.e.*, a document setting forth the facts of the case and the parties' claims and defining the issues to be determined by the arbitral tribunal as well as the procedural rules — sometimes a time consuming and expensive process.

With respect to the composition of the tribunal, the ICC does not maintain a panel of arbitrators. Instead, it maintains and regularly updates a list of names of possible arbitrators. The parties may select a sole arbitrator, or nominate one arbitrator each. Unless the parties reserve the right of nomination to themselves or to the arbitrators that each has designated, the third arbitrator, the chairman of the tribunal, will be selected by the Court of Arbitration. Should the parties fail to agree on the choice of a sole arbitrator, the Court of Arbitration gives the choice to a national committee of a country other than that of either party.

Perhaps the major disadvantage of an ICC arbitration is its cost. Especially when three of them are appointed, the fees of arbitrators can be prohibitive. Both the administrative charges and the arbitrators' fees are based on a percentage of the amount of money in dispute, not on the amount of work performed. Accordingly, if the amount in controversy is high, the cost of arbitration will be high. Further, the rules require that the charges must be paid by one party or the other or by both in equal portions. In practice, plaintiffs often pay the whole amount of the fees because defendants fail to pay their half.

The American Arbitration Association (AAA)

Although its governance is national rather than international, and the overwhelming majority of cases filed with it are domestic arbitrations, the American Arbitration Association offers certain advantages for the conduct of international arbitrations. The Association has a great deal of experience in administering an established set of rules that are more specific than the ICC rules as well as the facility to administer arbitrations under the United Nations Commission on International Trade Law (UNCITRAL) Model Arbitration Rules to be discussed later.

Under the AAA rules an arbitration is initiated by the giving of notice of the intention to arbitrate (Demand) and by filing with the Association. Although an answer is permitted, it is not required; failure to answer constitutes a denial. At the beginning of the hearing, both parties must provide a description of the claims and defenses, proofs, and witnesses. The authority to determine the admissibility of evidence is shared by the parties and the arbitrators. It is not in the sole discretion of the arbitrators. Both parties may examine and cross-examine witnesses, and the arbitrator, at a party's request, has the power to issue a subpoena to compel production of documents and witnesses where authorized to do so by the law of the forum. In contrast to the ICC, the AAA does not require the preparation of terms of reference. Instead, it allows the filing of fairly simple written pleadings and the submission of statements clarifying the issues involved.

Again unlike the ICC, the AAA maintains a large panel of arbitrators from which arbitrators are appointed. From this large panel the AAA prepares, for each case, a list of ten technically qualified individuals and sends it to the parties. Each party may then object to certain individuals, in which case they will be eliminated, and rank the remaining individuals in order of preference. The AAA next determines which individual both parties seem to prefer and invites that person to be the arbitrator. If this person is unavailable, or if no arbitrator proposed is mutually acceptable, the AAA appoints an arbitrator or gives the parties another opportunity to select an arbitrator from another list of proposed arbitrators.

The AAA has concluded important agreements with national arbitral associations in other countries, such as Japan, the USSR, Hungary, Poland, and Greece. These agreements contain various provisions designed to facilitate the use of commercial arbitration in trade between the United States and the other country concerned, and may be incorporated in international commercial contracts between private parties through the use of designated clauses. The clause designated by the Japan-American Trade Arbitration Agreement, for example, provides:

> All disputes, controversies, or differences which may arise between the parties, out of or in relation to or in connection with this contract, or for the breach thereof, shall be finally settled by arbitration pursuant to the Japan-American Trade Arbitration Agreement, of September 16, 1952, by which each party hereto is bound.

A major advantage of the AAA is that it often is considerably less costly than the ICC. The AAA's administrative rate schedule stops at $5 million. Any administrative fees for claims in excess of that amount are determined in negotiations between the parties and the AAA. Theoretically, AAA arbitrators serve without fees. However, in practice, if the arbitration is prolonged, the parties normally agree to pay each arbitrator a fee in the range of $250 to $1,000 a day.

The International Center for the Settlement of Investment Disputes (ICSID)

The ICSID is an innovative intergovernmental agency established in 1966 under the Convention on the Settlement of Investment Disputes Between the States and Nationals of Other States,[2] and specifically designed to resolve investment disputes between sovereign states and foreign investors. It has many features that are attractive to foreign investors. A state is not obligated to use the

---

[2] 17 U.S.T. 1270, T.I.A.S. No. 6090, 575 U.N.T.S. 159.

ICSID even after becoming a party to the Convention. But once a dispute arises, and the state and the other party consent to submit to the ICSID, neither party may withdraw its consent unilaterally. There is no appeal from the tribunal's award, and host states must recognize the award and enforce it as if it were a final judgment. Under Articles 52 and 53 of the Convention, defenses against enforcement of an award must be addressed to the Secretary-General of ICSID and may not be raised in the courts of the recognizing state. U.S. district courts, under 22 U.S.C. Section 1650a, have exclusive jurisdiction to enforce within the United States an award rendered pursuant to the Convention. The provisions of the Federal Arbitration Act do not apply to such awards.

Under applicable procedural rules, if one party to the underlying agreement is a state which is a party to the Convention, the parties may, by consenting in writing, submit disputes to the ICSID. The ICSID's arbitration rules may be amended to suit the particular needs of the parties. In accordance with this flexible procedure, the parties have the choice of selecting arbitrators by consensus or of utilizing the ICSID rules governing the appointment of arbitrators. If the ICSID procedure is used, three arbitrators must be chosen. Each party selects one arbitrator, and the third arbitrator is appointed by agreement of the parties.

As to costs, the appointed tribunal determines its fees within limits set by the ICSID's Administrative Council. The tribunal may allocate the expenses between or among the parties, or the parties may agree in advance on the manner of allocation.

The Arbitration Institute of the Stockholm Chamber of Commerce

Because of its long tradition of arbitration, and its reputation for neutrality, Sweden is often utilized as a center for East-West arbitration. For example, the AAA and the U.S.S.R. Chamber of Commerce, in an agreement entitled "Optional Arbitration Clause for use in Contracts in United States of America - Union of Soviet Socialist Republics Trade - 1977,"[3] jointly recommend that all disputes between parties in their respective countries be arbitrated in Sweden and that such arbitrations be conducted under the UNCITRAL arbitration rules. Similarly, the Stockholm Institute is often utilized for the arbitration of disputes between COMECON (the Council of Mutual Economic Assistance) and business enterprises in the Western industrial countries.

Under the Stockholm Institute's procedural rules, a claimant must submit a written request for arbitration that contains a brief account of the dispute and a statement of the claim, including the claimant's principal evidence. For its part, the respondent must submit a reply that includes a brief comment on the request for arbitration, a statement of the respondent's principal evidence, and counterclaims. The rules do not authorize the parties to participate in the selection of arbitrators. Rather, the chairman of the arbitral tribunal or a sole arbitrator is always appointed by the Stockholm Institute under its rules.

The arbitrator has great discretion to choose among various procedural approaches. However, normally the Swedish law of arbitration applies. Under these

---

[3] 16 Int'l Leg. Mat 444 (1977).

rules, the proceedings are oral and arbitrators have the authority to summon witnesses or apply sanctions to the parties. A party may, under some circumstances, be able to compel testimony or the production of a document by applying to the appropriate district court in Sweden.

The United Nations Commission on International Trade Law (UNCITRAL)

The United Nations Commission on International Trade Law (UNCITRAL), a subsidiary organ of the United Nations General Assembly, is not itself an arbitral institution; nor has it created an arbitral institution. It has, however, developed comprehensive arbitration rules that were adopted by the General Assembly on December 15, 1976. Since these rules exist independently of a permanent arbitral institution, they are often used to give structure to *ad hoc* arbitrations. At the same time, the UNCITRAL rules allow the parties to resort to an agreed upon arbitral institution or individual or, failing such agreement, to the Secretary-General of the Permanent Court of Arbitration at the Hague to resolve problems that cannot be settled by the parties. Such use of the UNCITRAL rules is one method, among others, for the parties to structure some hybrid of *ad hoc* and institutional practices.

Under the UNCITRAL system, the parties may participate in the selection of the sole or third arbitrator. If the parties fail to agree on a sole or third arbitrator and cannot agree to name an appointing authority, either party may ask the Secretary-General of the Permanent Court of Arbitration at the Hague to designate an appointing authority. The appointing authority in turn submits a list to the parties who indicate those names on the list acceptable to them. The appointing authority then appoints a sole or a third arbitrator from among the names approved by the parties. If the parties fail to submit a list of approved names, the appointing authority may exercise its discretion in appointing the arbitrator.

After the arbitrators have been appointed, the parties frame the issues by submitting written statements of the claim and defense and may annex relevant documents. Submission of any further written statements is subject to the approval of the arbitrators. The tribunal also has the power, at any time during the arbitral proceedings, to require the parties to produce documents or other evidence. UNCITRAL rules also give either party the right to require, at any stage of the proceedings, hearings for the presentation of evidence by witnesses, including expert witnesses, or for oral argument. The tribunal has the final authority to decide the manner in which witnesses are examined.

A major advantage of the UNCITRAL Rules is that they are acceptable to the Western industrialized countries, developing countries, and countries with centrally planned economies. With some modifications they are being used by the Iran-U.S. Claims Tribunal — the largest arbitration tribunal since World War II.

[B] Drafting the Arbitration Clause

As already demonstrated by material previously considered in this Chapter, determining the appropriate method and procedures for settlement of disputes is one of the most important steps in any international business transaction. Unfortunately, it is often also one of the most neglected steps. After long and arduous negotiations on the substantive rights and obligations to be included in the contract, the parties may treat the clauses setting forth the dispute settlement procedures almost as an afterthought.

This is a serious mistake. Careful draftsmanship of an international arbitration clause is essential to its effectiveness and enforceability. Moreover, failure to consider all the crucial issues can leave important decisions to the unfettered discretion of the arbitrators. It is particularly risky to rely on a standard uniform arbitration clause that may be well suited to a domestic transaction but woefully inadequate for international arbitration. Model arbitration clauses recommended by leading international arbitration institutions, however, should be closely followed, if you intend to use the facilities of such an institution. Revision of an arbitration institution's model clause will result in courts and arbitrators assuming that the clause was modified for a reason and that perhaps you did not mean to cover "all" disputes.

We can do no more here than highlight some of the primary concerns one should keep in mind while drafting clauses for international arbitration.[4] A crucial first step, however, is for the parties to decide on the types of disputes that will be submitted to arbitration. They should also decide whether they would prefer to have arbitration only if more informal methods of dispute settlement, such as conciliation, fail to resolve the dispute. If the parties wish to have *all* issues that may arise under the contract resolved by arbitration, the arbitral clause should say so explicitly. If they intend to exclude some issues from the arbitration, they should expressly exclude those issues and then provide that all issues arising under the contract and not so expressly excluded shall be settled by arbitration.

Once the issues have been identified, the parties will have to decide whether they wish to resort to *ad hoc* arbitration or institutional arbitration and what rules should apply. The drafting chore becomes considerably more challenging if the parties decide to resort to a purely *ad hoc* arbitration, since they have to start from scratch. To be sure, the UNCITRAL arbitration rules, discussed above, exist independently of a permanent arbitral institution and are used to give structure to ad hoc arbitrations.[5] Nonetheless, it is fair to generalize that *ad hoc* arbitration provides more challenges to the draftsman of the arbitral clause than does arbitration under the auspices of one of the arbitral institutions.

The next step in drafting an arbitral clause is to select a place of arbitration. When the contract is silent, the rules of the arbitral institution or the arbitrators may determine the place of arbitration, but the parties may not be happy with the choice. For example, arbitrators often choose sites in their home countries.

The choice of the place of arbitration may be an especially important step for a number of reasons. The procedural rules of the place chosen will, absent an

---

[4] For more detailed discussion, see McCelland, *International Arbitration: A Practical Guide For The Effective Use Of The System For Litigation Of Transnational Commercial Disputes*, 12 Int'l Law. 83 (1978).

[5] Also modern arbitration statutes will frequently have one or more titles that stipulate the procedures to be followed in conducting an arbitration (See *e.g.*, Florida International Arbitration Act, Chapter 685, Florida Statutes). If ad hoc arbitration is desired, therefore, the drafting task can be substantially eased simply by incorporating the apposite provisions of such a statute into the contract by reference.

alternative specification in the arbitral agreement, normally be applied to fill gaps in the institutional rules. Indeed, in what is surely a highly anachronistic provision, the Model Arbitration Law prepared by UNCITRAL stipulates that the arbitral law of the place of arbitration *must* govern questions of procedure not covered by institutional rules or the agreement of the parties.[6] In addition, the arbitral laws of many countries — and certain provisions of the UNCITRAL Model law — contain so-called "mandatory" provisions from which the parties may not deviate even if they agree to do so. It is critical, therefore, that if the procedural law of the place of arbitration is to govern, the parties choose a place whose laws are compatible with the procedures they hope to follow. Also, the place of arbitration should be in a country whose laws favor arbitration — ideally one that has ratified the United Nations Convention on the Recognition and Enforcement of Foreign Arbitral Awards,[7] — to increase the probability that the agreement to arbitrate and the resulting award can be enforced. Under Title 1 of the Federal Arbitration Act an arbitral award is enforceable only if the parties have stipulated for such enforcement.[8] It may be desirable to exclude judicial review of the award, although it must be remembered that in some countries part or all of the procedure and merits of the dispute may be reviewable by a court, unless the parties expressly exclude such reviews. A wrong choice of the place of arbitration can greatly increase the difficulty in enforcing an award or the inconvenience in conducting the arbitration, especially if the law of the place chosen allows for judicial intervention in the proceedings. In all of this it should be recognized that in designating a place of arbitration, the parties do not necessarily foreclose the possibility of the arbitrators conducting certain of their proceedings in other more convenient places. Normally this right should be expressly reserved in the arbitral agreement unless confirmed by the applicable institutional rules.

The location of the administering institution is not necessarily determinative of where the arbitration will take place. The ICC Court of Arbitration in Paris, for example, administers proceedings in many cities around the world. Often a neutral country is chosen as the place of arbitration, especially in contracts between United States nationals and Soviet trading agencies.

If the contract is otherwise silent, the choice of the place of arbitration may also determine the substantive law applicable to the arbitration. In the absence of a specific choice of law clause, the law of the place of arbitration, both procedural and substantive, may be applied. To promote a measure of predictability of outcome, the parties may select a substantive system of law which is highly

---

[6] Over the last twenty years or so the principal advance in the law and practice of international arbitration has been to make it truly "international;" that is, to allow the parties to fashion their own forum, with their own rules, performing its function in such place as is most suitable to the parties without being tied to the idiosyncracies of any particular nation's arbitral law simply because it is convenient to locate the arbitration in that country. For this very reason mandatory provisions are equally anachronistic.

[7] 21 U.S.T. 2517; T.I.A.S. No. 6997.

[8] 9 U.S.C. Section 9. If the stipulation is contained in the rules (*e.g.*, American Arbitration Association rules) that the parties have elected to follow, that will suffice to meet the statutory requirement.

developed in the subject matter of the contract, *e.g.*, the United Kingdom for admiralty and New York for banking.

Although, as we have seen, arbitral rules usually specify procedures for the appointment of arbitrators, the parties may wish to depart from these rules or to reserve rights to participate in the selection process. If so, the arbitral clause should so indicate. As a rule, the contract does not name specific individuals but instead indicates how many arbitrators will preside over the case, their qualifications, and how they are to be selected.

Other matters that should be covered by the arbitration clause include, among others, selection of the language or languages that are to be used at the proceedings; an express waiver of sovereign immunity; the form which the award is to take, whether the arbitrators will be required to state reasons for their decision; whether the award includes interest; an entry of judgment clause whereby the parties consent to immediate entry of a judgment in a court of competent jurisdiction on the arbitration award; a specification whether the arbitration agreement is without prejudice to any other rights and remedies the parties might have in the jurisdiction where the agreement is to be performed or where the dispute might arise; and such miscellaneous matters as conditions precedent to arbitration such as negotiation, consultation, and conciliation, time limits and designation of how costs are to be allocated.

Under some circumstances, the parties may agree that an arbitrator should have the authority to fill in certain gaps in the contract during the performance of a long term contract. If so, the arbitration clause should so provide explicitly, and the legality of such a clause under the applicable law should be confirmed.

Set forth below, for purposes of illustration, are model arbitration clauses recommended by leading international arbitration institutions.

American Arbitration Association Clause

Any controversy or claim arising out of or relating to this contract, or the breach thereof, shall be settled by arbitration in accordance with the Commercial Arbitration Rules of the American Arbitration Association and judgment on the award rendered by the arbitrator(s) may be entered in any court having jurisdiction thereof.

UNCITRAL Clause

Any dispute, controversy or claim arising out of or relating to this contract, or the breach, termination or invalidity thereof, shall be settled by arbitration in accordance with the UNCITRAL Arbitration Rules as at present in force.

International Chamber of Commerce Clause

All disputes arising in connection with the present contract shall be finally settled under the Rules of Conciliation and Arbitration of the International Chamber of Commerce by one or more arbitrators appointed in accordance with the said Rules.

London Court of International Arbitration Clause

Any dispute arising out of or in connection with this contract, including any question regarding its existence, validity or termination, shall be referred to and finally resolved by arbitration under the Rules of the London Court of International Arbitration, which Rules are deemed to be incorporated by reference into this clause.

[C] Enforcing the Agreement to Arbitrate

Under the common law approach, courts were hostile to efforts to obtain judicial enforcement of either an agreement to arbitrate or an arbitral award once rendered, viewing them as an effort to oust the courts of jurisdiction. Other legal systems, although more hospitable to enforcing agreements to arbitrate and arbitral awards, often discriminated against foreign as compared to national awards.

Even the most carefully drafted arbitration clause will be of little use if domestic courts refuse to recognize its validity and enforce it. The issue may arise in three different ways. First, a party may bring an action on the contract contrary to an arbitration clause requiring all such disputes to be submitted to arbitration. In such a case the defendant may rely on the clause as a bar to the action. Second, one party may initiate arbitration proceedings and the other refuse to appear or participate in the proceedings. Under these circumstances a court may be asked to order the defendant to submit to arbitration. Third, one party may commence an arbitration and the other party may ask the court to enjoin the arbitration on the ground that the dispute is not covered by the arbitration clause, or that the clause is invalid or the dispute is not arbitrable.

With enactment of the Federal Arbitration Act in 1925, however, along with a great number of State statutes and through decisions by the Supreme Court, excerpts from the latest of which are set forth below, the attitude in the United States has changed. As also indicated in the excerpts set forth below, the United States has become a party to the Convention on the Recognition and Enforcement of Foreign Arbitral Awards (the New York Convention),[9] which obligates the United States, subject to certain exceptions, to judicially enforce international agreements to arbitrate and international arbitral awards.

MITSUBISHI MOTORS CORP. v. SOLER CHRYSLER-PLYMOUTH, INC.

United States Supreme Court
473 U.S. 614, 105 S. Ct. 3346, 87 L. Ed 2d 444 (1985)

Justice Blackmun delivered the opinion of the Court.

The principal question presented by these cases is the arbitrability, pursuant to the federal Arbitration Act,[10] and the Convention on the Recognition and

---

[9] 21 U.S.T. 2517, T.I.A.S. No. 6997, Documentary Supplement.
[10] 9 USC Sec. 1, *et seq.*

Enforcement of Foreign Arbitral Awards (Convention), . . . of claims arising under the Sherman Act,[11] . . . and encompassed within a valid arbitration clause in an agreement embodying an international commercial transaction.

I

Petitioner . . . Mitsubishi Motors Corporation (Mitsubishi) is a Japanese corporation which manufactures automobiles and has its principal place of business in Tokyo, Japan. Mitsubishi is the product of a joint venture between, on the one hand, Chrysler International, SA ("CISA"), a Swiss corporation registered in Geneva and wholly owned by Chrysler Corporation, and, on the other, Mitsubishi Heavy Industries, Inc., a Japanese corporation. The aim of the joint venture was the distribution through Chrysler dealers outside the continental United States of vehicles manufactured by Mitsubishi and bearing Chrysler and Mitsubishi trademarks. Respondent . . . Soler Chrysler-Plymouth, Inc. (Soler), is a Puerto Rico corporation with its principal place of business in Pueblo Viejo, Guaynabo, Puerto Rico.

On October 31, 1979, Soler entered into a Distributor Agreement with CISA which provided for the sale by Soler of Mitsubishi manufactured vehicles within a designated area, including metropolitan San Juan. On the same date, CISA, Soler, and Mitsubishi entered into a Sales Procedure Agreement (Sales Agreement) which, referring to the Distributor Agreement, provided for the direct sale of Mitsubishi products to Soler and governed the terms and conditions of such sales. Paragraph VI of the Sales Agreement, labeled "Arbitration of Certain Matters," provides:

> All disputes, controversies or differences which may arise between [Mitsubishi] and [Soler] out of or in relation to Articles I-B through V of this Agreement or for the breach thereof, shall be finally settled by arbitration in Japan in accordance with the rules and regulations of the Japan Commercial Arbitration Association.

Initially, Soler did a brisk business in Mitsubishi-manufactured vehicles. As a result of its strong performance, its minimum sales volume, specified by Mitsubishi and CISA, and agreed to by Soler, for the 1981 model year was substantially increased. In early 1981, however, the new-car market slackened. Soler ran into serious difficulties in meeting the expected sales volume, and by the Spring of 1981 it felt itself compelled to request that Mitsubishi delay or cancel shipment of several orders. About the same time, Soler attempted to arrange for the transshipment of a quantity of its vehicles for sale in the continental United States and Latin America. Mitsubishi and CISA, however, refused permission for any such diversion, citing a variety of reasons,[12] and no vehicles were transshipped.

---

[11] 15 USC Sec. 1, *et seq.*

[12] The reasons advanced included concerns that such diversion would interfere with the Japanese trade policy of voluntarily limiting imports to the United States; that the Soler–ordered vehicles would be unsuitable for use in certain proposed destinations because of their manufacture, with use in Puerto Rico in mind, without heaters and defoggers; that the vehicles would be unsuitable for use in Latin America because of the unavailability there of the unleaded, high-octane fuel they required; that adequate warranty service could not be ensured; and that diversion to the mainland would violate contractual obligations between CISA and Mitsubishi.

Attempts to work out these difficulties failed. Mitsubishi eventually withheld shipment of 966 vehicles, apparently representing orders placed for May, June and July 1981 production, responsibility for which Soler disclaimed in February 1982.

The following month, Mitsubishi brought an action against Soler in the United States District Court for the District of Puerto Rico and under the Federal Arbitration Act and the Convention. Mitsubishi sought an order, pursuant to 9 U.S.C. Sections 4 and 201, to compel arbitration in accord with Section VI of the Sales Agreement. Shortly after filing the complaint, Mitsubishi filed a request for arbitration before the Japan Commercial Arbitration Association.

Soler denied the allegations and counterclaimed against both Mitsubishi and CISA. It alleged numerous breaches by Mitsubishi of the Sales Agreement,[13] raised a pair of defamation claims, and asserted causes of action under the Sherman Act,[14] . . . the Federal Automobile Dealers' Day in Court Act,[15] . . . the Puerto Rico competition statute,[16] . . . and the Puerto Rico Dealers' Contracts Act[17] . . . . In the counterclaim premised on the Sherman Act, Soler alleged that Mitsubishi and CISA had conspired to divide markets in restraint of trade. To effectuate the plan, according to Soler, Mitsubishi had refused to permit Soler to resell to buyers in North, Central, or South America vehicles it had obligated itself to purchase from Mitsubishi; had refused to ship ordered vehicles or the parts, such as heaters and defoggers, that would be necessary to permit Soler to make its vehicles suitable for resale outside Puerto Rico; and had coercively attempted to replace Soler and its other Puerto Rico distributors with a wholly owned subsidiary which would serve as the exclusive Mitsubishi distributor in Puerto Rico.

After the hearing, the District Court ordered Mitsubishi and Soler to arbitrate each of the issues raised in the complaint and in all the counterclaims save two and a portion of a third.[18] With regard to the federal antitrust issues, it recognized that the Courts of Appeals, following *American Safety Equipment Corp. v. J.P. McGuire & Co.*,[19] uniformly had held that the rights conferred by the antitrust laws were "of a character inappropriate for enforcement by arbitration.". . . . The

---

[13] The alleged breaches included wrongful refusal to ship ordered vehicles and necessary parts, failure to make payment for warranty work and authorized rebates, and bad faith in establishing minimum-sales volumes.

[14] 15 USC Sec. 1 *et seq.*

[15] 70 Stat 1125, as amended, 15 USC Sec. 1221 *et seq.*

[16] PR Laws Ann, Tit 10, Sec. 257 *et seq.* (1978).

[17] PR Laws Ann, Tit 10, Sec. 278 *et seq.* (1978 and Supp 1983).

[18] The District Court found that the arbitration clause did not cover the fourth and sixth counterclaims, which sought damages for defamation, or the allegations in the seventh counterclaim concerning discriminatory treatment and the establishment of minimum-sales volumes. Accordingly, it retained jurisdiction over those portions of the litigation. In addition, because no arbitration agreement between Soler and CISA existed, the court retained jurisdiction, insofar as they sought relief from CISA, over the first, second, third, and ninth counterclaims, which raised claims under the Puerto Rico Dealers' Contracts Act; the federal Automobile Dealers' Day in Court Act; the Sherman Act; and the Puerto Rico competition statute, respectively. These aspects of the District Court's ruling were not appealed and are not before this Court.

[19] 391 F. 2d 821 (CA 2 1968).

District Court held, however, that the international character of the Mitsubishi-Soler undertaking required enforcement of the agreement to arbitrate even as to the antitrust claims. It relied on *Scherk v. Alberto-Culver Co.*[20] . . . in which this Court ordered arbitration, pursuant to a provision embodied in an international agreement, of a claim arising under the Securities Exchange Act of 1934 notwithstanding its assumption arguendo that . . . *Wilko v. Swan*[21] . . . which held nonarbitrable claims arising under the Securities Act of 1933, also would bar arbitration of a 1934 Act claim arising in a domestic context.

The United States Court of Appeals for the First Circuit affirmed in part and reversed in part[22] . . . . It first rejected Soler's argument that Puerto Rico law precluded enforcement of an agreement obligating a local dealer to arbitrate controversies outside Puerto Rico.[23] It also rejected Soler's suggestion that it could not have intended to arbitrate statutory claims not mentioned in the arbitration agreement. Assessing arbitrability "on an allegation-by-allegation basis," the court then read the arbitration clause to encompass virtually all the claims arising under the various statutes, including all those arising under the Sherman Act.[24]

Finally, after endorsing the doctrine of *American Safety*, precluding arbitration of antitrust claims, the Court of Appeals concluded that neither this Court's decision in *Scherk* nor the Convention required abandonment of that doctrine in the face of an international transaction. Accordingly, it reversed the judgment of the District Court insofar as it had ordered submission of "Soler's antitrust claims" to arbitration. Affirming the remainder of the judgment, the court directed the District Court to consider in the first instance how the parallel judicial and arbitral proceedings should go forward.

We granted certiorari primarily to consider whether an American court should enforce an agreement to resolve antitrust claims by arbitration when that agreement arises from an international transaction.

---

[20] 417 U.S. 506, 515-520, 94 S. Ct. 2449, 41 L. Ed.2d 270 (1974).

[21] 346 U.S. 427, 74 S. Ct. 182, 98 L. Ed. 168 (1953)].

[22] 723 F. 2d 155 (1983).

[23] Soler relied on PR Laws Ann., Tit. 10, Sec. 278b-2 (Supp. 1983), which purports to render null and void "[a]ny stipulation that obligates a dealer to adjust, arbitrate or litigate any controversy that comes up regarding his dealer's contract outside of Puerto Rico, or under foreign law or rule of law." See *Walborg Corp. v. Superior Court*, 104 DPR 184 (1975). The Court of Appeals held this provision pre-empted by 9 USC Section 2, which declares arbitration agreements valid and enforceable "save upon such grounds as exist at law or in equity for the revocation of any contract." See *Southland Corp. v. Keating*, 465 U.S. 1, 79 L.Ed.2d 1, 104 S.Ct. 852 (1984). See also *Ledee v. Ceramiche Ragno*, 684 F.2d 184 (CA1 1982). Soler does not challenge this holding in its cross-petition here.

[24] As the Court of Appeals saw it, "[t]he question . . . is not whether the arbitration clause mentions antitrust or any other particular cause of action, but whether the factual allegations underlying Soler's counterclaims — and Mitsubishi's bona fide defense to those counterclaims — are within the scope of the arbitration clause, whatever the legal labels attached to those allegations." Because Soler's counterclaim under the Puerto Rico Dealers' Contracts Act focused on Mitsubishi's alleged failure to comply with the provisions of the Sales Agreement governing delivery of automobiles, and those provisions were found in that portion of Article I of the Agreement subject to arbitration, the Court of Appeals placed this first counter-claim within the arbitration clause.

[In Section II the Court rejects Soler's contention that because it falls within the class for whose benefit the federal and local antitrust laws and dealers acts were passed, the arbitration clause cannot be read to contemplate arbitration of those statutory claims since the clause fails to expressly mention those statutes.]

III

We now turn to consider whether Soler's antitrust claims are nonarbitrable even though it has agreed to arbitrate them. . . . Notwithstanding the absence of any explicit support for such an exception in either the Sherman Act or the Federal Arbitration Act, the Second Circuit . . . in *American Safety* reasoned that "the pervasive public interest in enforcement of the antitrust laws, and the nature of the claims that arise in such cases, combine to make . . . antitrust claims . . . inappropriate for arbitration." We find it unnecessary to assess the legitimacy of the *American Safety* doctrine as applied to agreements to arbitrate arising from domestic transactions. As in *Scherk v. Alberto-Culver Co.*, [*supra*] we conclude that concerns of international comity, respect for the capacities of foreign and transnational tribunals, and sensitivity to the needs of the international commercial system for predictability in the resolution of disputes require that we enforce the parties' agreement, even assuming that a contrary result would be forthcoming in a domestic context.

Even before *Scherk*, this Court had recognized the utility of forum-selection clauses in international transactions. In *The Bremen, supra*, [this Court held that] . . . notwithstanding the possibility that the English court would enforce provisions in the towage contract exculpating the German party which an American court would refuse to enforce, this Court gave effect to the choice-of-forum clause. It observed:

> The expansion of American business and industry will hardly be encouraged if, notwithstanding solemn contracts, we insist on a parochial concept that all disputes must be resolved under our laws and in our courts. . . . We cannot have trade and commerce in world markets and international waters exclusively on our terms, governed by our laws, and resolved in our courts.

Recognizing that "agreeing in advance on a forum acceptable to both parties is an indispensable element in international trade, commerce, and contracting," . . . the decision in *The Bremen* clearly eschewed a provincial solicitude for the jurisdiction of domestic fora.

Identical considerations governed the Court's decision in *Scherk*, which categorized "[a]n agreement to arbitrate before a specified tribunal [as], in effect, a specialized kind of forum-selection clause that posits not only the situs of suit but also the procedure to be used in resolving the dispute.". . . . In *Scherk*, the American company Alberto-Culver purchased several interrelated business enterprises, organized under the laws of Germany and Liechtenstein, as well as the rights held by those enterprises in certain trademarks, from a German citizen who at the time of trial resided in Switzerland. Although the contract of sale contained a clause providing for arbitration before the International Chamber of Commerce in Paris of "any controversy or claim [arising] out of this agreement or the breach thereof," Alberto-Culver subsequently brought suit against Scherk in a Federal District Court in Illinois, alleging that Scherk had violated Section 10(b) of the Securities Exchange Act of 1934 by fraudulently misrepresenting the status of the trademarks as unencumbered. The District Court denied a motion to stay the proceedings before it and enjoined the parties from going forward before the arbitral tribunal in Paris. The Court of Appeals for the Seventh Circuit affirmed. . . . This Court reversed, enforcing the arbitration agreement even while assuming for purposes of the decision that the controversy would be nonarbitrable under the holding of Wilko had it arisen out of a domestic transaction. Again, the Court emphasized:

> A contractual provision specifying in advance the forum in which disputes shall be litigated and the law to be applied is . . . an almost indispensable precondition to achievement of the orderliness and predictability essential to any international business transaction. . . .

> A parochial refusal by the courts of one country to enforce an international arbitration agreement would not only frustrate these purposes, but would invite unseemly and mutually destructive jockeying by the parties to secure tactical litigation advantages. . . . [It would] damage the fabric of international commerce and trade, and imperil the willingness and ability of businessmen to enter into international commercial agreements.

* * * *

The *Bremen* and *Scherk* cases establish a strong presumption in favor of enforcement of freely negotiated contractual choice-of-forum provisions. Here, as in *Scherk*, that presumption is reinforced by the emphatic federal policy in favor of arbitral dispute resolution. And at least since this Nation's accession in 1970 to the Convention . . . and the implementation of the Convention in the same year by amendment of the Federal Arbitration Act, that federal policy applies with special force in the field of international commerce. Thus, we must weigh the concerns of *American Safety* against a strong belief in the efficacy of arbitral procedures for the resolution of international commercial disputes and an equal commitment to the enforcement of freely negotiated choice-of-forum clauses.

At the outset, we confess to some skepticism of certain aspects of the *American Safety* doctrine. As distilled by the First Circuit . . . the doctrine comprises four ingredients. First, private parties play a pivotal role in aiding governmental enforcement of the antitrust laws by means of the private action for treble damages. Second, "the strong possibility that contracts which generate antitrust disputes may be contracts of adhesion militates against automatic forum determination by contract." Third, antitrust issues, prone to complication, require sophisticated legal and economic analysis, and thus are "ill adapted to strengths of the arbitral process, *i.e.*, expedition, minimal requirements of written rationale, simplicity, resort to basic concepts of common sense and simple equity." Finally, just as "issues of war and peace are too important to be vested in the generals . . . decisions as to antitrust regulation of business are too important to be lodged in arbitrators chosen from the business community — particularly those from a foreign community that has had no experience with or exposure to our law and values.". . . .

Initially, we find the second concern unjustified. The mere appearance of an antitrust dispute does not alone warrant invalidation of the selected forum on the undemonstrated assumption that the arbitration clause is tainted. A party resisting arbitration of course may attack directly the validity of the agreement to arbitrate. See *Prima Paint Corp., supra.* Moreover, the party may attempt to make a showing that would warrant setting aside the forum-selection clause — that the agreement was "[a]ffected by fraud, undue influence, or overweening bargaining power," that "enforcement would be unreasonable and unjust;" or that proceedings "in the contractual forum will be so gravely difficult and inconvenient that [the resisting party] will for all practical purposes be deprived of his day in court." *The Bremen.* But absent such a showing — and none was attempted here — there is no basis for assuming the forum inadequate or its selection unfair.

Next, potential complexity should not suffice to ward off arbitration. We might well have some doubt that even the courts following *American Safety* subscribe fully to the view that antitrust matters are inherently insusceptible to resolution by arbitration, as these same courts have agreed that an undertaking to arbitrate antitrust claims entered into after the dispute arises is acceptable. See, *e.g., Coenen v. R. W. Pressprich & Co.,*[25] . . . *Cobb v. Lewis,*[26] . . . . And the vertical restraints which most frequently give birth to antitrust claims covered by an arbitration agreement will not often occasion the monstrous proceedings that have given antitrust litigation an image of intractability. In any event, adaptability and access to expertise are hallmarks of arbitration. The anticipated subject matter of the dispute may be taken into account when the arbitrators are appointed, and arbitral rules typically provide for the participation of experts either employed by the parties or appointed by the tribunal. Moreover, it is often a judgment that streamlined proceedings and expeditious results will best serve their needs that causes parties to agree to arbitrate their disputes; it is typically a desire to keep the effort and expense required to resolve a dispute within manageable bounds that prompts them mutually to forgo access to judicial remedies. In sum, the factor of potential complexity alone does not persuade us that an arbitral tribunal could not properly handle an antitrust matter.

For similar reasons, we also reject the proposition that an arbitration panel will pose too great a danger of innate hostility to the constraints on business conduct that antitrust law imposes. International arbitrators frequently are drawn from the legal as well as the business community; where the dispute has an important legal component, the parties and the arbitral body with whose assistance they have agreed to settle their dispute can be expected to select arbitrators accordingly.[27]

---

[25] 453 F. 2d 1209, 1215 (CA 2), *cert. denied,* 406 U.S. 949, 92 S.Ct., 32 L. Ed.2d 337, 2045 (1972).

[26] 488 F. 2d 41, 48 (CA 5 1974). See also, in the present cases, 723 F. 2d, at 168, n. 12 (leaving question open).

[27] See W. Craig, W. Park & J. Paulsson, *supra,* Section 12.03, p. 28; Sanders, Commentary On UNCITRAL Arbitration Rules Section 15.1, in II Yearbook Commercial Arbitration, *supra,* at 203. We are advised by Mitsubishi and amicus International Chamber of Commerce, without contradiction by Soler, that the arbitration panel selected to hear the parties' claims here is composed of three Japanese lawyers, one a former law school dean, another a former judge, and the third a practicing attorney with American legal training who has written on Japanese antitrust law. The Court of Appeals was concerned that

We decline to indulge the presumption that the parties and arbitral body conducting a proceeding will be unable or unwilling to retain competent, conscientious, and impartial arbitrators.

We are left, then, with the core of the *American Safety* doctrine — the fundamental importance to American democratic capitalism of the regime of the antitrust laws. . . . As the Court of Appeals pointed out:

> A claim under the antitrust laws is not merely a private matter. The Sherman Act is designed to promote the national interest in a competitive economy; thus, the plaintiff asserting his rights under the Act has been likened to a private attorney-general who protects the public's interest. . . .

quoting *American Safety.* [28]

The treble-damages provision wielded by the private litigant is a chief tool in the antitrust enforcement scheme, posing a crucial deterrent to potential violators. . . .

The importance of the private damages remedy, however, does not compel the conclusion that it may not be sought outside an American court. Notwithstanding its important incidental policing function, the treble-damages cause of action conferred on private parties by Section 4 of the Clayton Act[29] . . . and pursued by Soler here by way of its third counter–claim, seeks primarily to enable an injured competitor to gain compensation for that injury.

> Section 4 . . . is in essence a remedial provision. It provides treble damages to [a]ny person who shall be injured in his business or property by reason of anything forbidden in the antitrust laws. . . . Of course, treble damages also pay an important role in penalizing wrongdoers and deterring wrongdoing, as we also have frequently observed. . . . It nevertheless is true that the treble-damages provision, which makes awards available only to injured parties, and measures the awards by a multiple of the injury actually proved, is designed primarily as a remedy.

Brunswick Corp. v. Pueblo Bowl-O-Mat, Inc. [30]

After examining the respective legislative histories, the Court in Brunswick recognized that when first enacted in 1890 as Section 7 of the Sherman Act . . . the treble-damages provision "was conceived of primarily as a remedy for '[t]he people of the United States as individuals' " . . . ; when reenacted in 1914 as Section 4 of the Clayton Act . . . it was still "conceived primarily as 'open[ing] the door of justice to every man, whenever he may be injured by those who violate the antitrust laws, and giv[ing] the injured party ample damages for the wrong suffered.' ". . . . And, of course, the antitrust cause of action remains at all times

international arbitrators would lack "experience with or exposure to our law and values." The obstacles confronted by the arbitration panel in this case, however, should be no greater than those confronted by any judicial or arbitral tribunal required to determine foreign law. . . . Moreover, while our attachment to the antitrust laws may be stronger than most, many other countries, including Japan, have similar bodies of competition law. . . .

[28] 391 F. 2d, at 826.
[29] 15 USC Section 15.
[30] 429 US 477, 485-486, 97 S. Ct. 690, 50 L. Ed.2d 701 (1977).

under the control of the individual litigant: no citizen is under an obligation to bring an antitrust suit . . . and the private antitrust plaintiff needs no executive or judicial approval before settling one. It follows that, at least where the international cast of a transaction would otherwise add an element of uncertainty to dispute resolution, the prospective litigant may provide in advance for a mutually agreeable procedure whereby he would seek his antitrust recovery as well as settle other controversies.

There is no reason to assume at the outset of the dispute that international arbitration will not provide an adequate mechanism. To be sure, the international arbitral tribunal owes no prior allegiance to the legal norms of particular states; hence, it has no direct obligation to vindicate their statutory dictates. The tribunal, however, is bound to effectuate the intentions of the parties. Where the parties have agreed that the arbitral body is to decide a defined set of claims which includes, as in these cases, those arising from the application of American antitrust law, the tribunal therefore should be bound to decide that dispute in accord with the national law giving rise to the claim. *Cf. Wilko v. Swan*, [*supra*]. . . . And so long as the prospective litigant effectively may vindicate its statutory cause of action in the arbitral forum, the statute will continue to serve both its remedial and deterrent function.

Having permitted the arbitration to go forward, the national courts of the United States will have the opportunity at the award enforcement stage to ensure that the legitimate interest in the enforcement of the antitrust laws has been addressed. The Convention reserves to each signatory country the right to refuse enforcement of an award where the "recognition or enforcement of the award would be contrary to the public policy of that country." Art. V(2)(b)[31] . . . . While the efficacy of the arbitral process requires that substantive review at the award-enforcement stage remain minimal, it would not require intrusive inquiry to ascertain that the tribunal took cognizance of the antitrust claims and actually decided them.

As international trade has expanded in recent decades, so too has the use of international arbitration to resolve disputes arising in the course of that trade. The controversies that international arbitral institutions are called upon to resolve have increased in diversity as well as in complexity. Yet the potential of these tribunals for efficient disposition of legal disagreements arising from commercial relations has not yet been tested. If they are to take a central place in the international legal order, national courts will need to "shake off the old judicial hostility to arbitration" . . . and also their customary and understandable unwillingness to cede jurisdiction of a claim arising under domestic law to a foreign or transnational tribunal. To this extent, at least, it will be necessary for national courts to subordinate domestic notions of arbitrability to the international policy favoring commercial arbitration. . . .

Accordingly, we "require this representative of the American business community to honor its bargain," *Alberto-Culver Co. v. Scherk*[32] . . . by holding this agreement to arbitrate "enforce[able] . . . in accord with the explicit provisions of the Arbitration Act." *Scherk*, [*supra*]. . . .

---

[31] 21 UST, at 2520.
[32] 484 F. 2d 611, 620 (CA 7 1973).

The judgment of the Court of Appeals is affirmed in part and reversed in part, and the cases are remanded for further proceedings consistent with this opinion.

It is so ordered.

JUSTICE POWELL took no part in the decision of these cases.

JUSTICE STEVENS, with whom JUSTICE BRENNAN joins, and with whom JUSTICE MARSHALL joins except as to Part II, dissenting.

One element of this rather complex litigation is a claim asserted by an American dealer in Plymouth automobiles that two major automobile companies are parties to an international cartel that has restrained competition in the American market. Pursuant to an agreement that is alleged to have violated Section 1 of the Sherman Act . . . those companies allegedly prevented the dealer from transshipping some 966 surplus vehicles from Puerto Rico to other dealers in the American market.

The petitioner denies the truth of the dealer's allegations and takes the position that the validity of the antitrust claim must be resolved by an arbitration tribunal in Tokyo, Japan. Largely because the auto manufacturers' defense to the antitrust allegation is based on provisions in the dealer's franchise agreement, the Court of Appeals concluded that the arbitration clause in that agreement encompassed the antitrust claim. . . . It held, however, as a matter of law, that arbitration of such a claim may not be compelled under either the Federal Arbitration Act or the Convention on the Recognition and Enforcement of Foreign Arbitral Awards.

This Court agrees with the Court of Appeals' interpretation of the scope of the arbitration clause, but disagrees with its conclusion that the clause is unenforceable insofar as it purports to cover an antitrust claim against a Japanese company. . . . Because I am convinced that the Court of Appeals' construction of the arbitration clause is erroneous, and because I strongly disagree with this Court's interpretation of the relevant federal statutes, I respectfully dissent. In my opinion, (1) a fair construction of the language in the arbitration clause in the parties' contract does not encompass a claim that auto manufacturers entered into a conspiracy in violation of the antitrust laws; (2) an arbitration clause should not normally be construed to cover a statutory remedy that it does not expressly identify; (3) Congress did not intend Section 2 of the Federal Arbitration Act to apply to antitrust claims; and (4) Congress did not intend the Convention on the Recognition and Enforcement of Foreign Arbitral Awards to apply to disputes that are not covered by the Federal Arbitration Act.

I

[In this Section JUSTICE STEVENS discusses the scope of coverage of the arbitration clause, noting that it applied only to disputes between Soler and Mitsubishi, while Soler's antitrust claims implicated Chrysler. The Justice also pointed out that the arbitration clause related only to disputes arising under 5 designated articles out of 15 articles in the agreement and then only if the dispute pertained to an alleged breach of those articles. None of Soler's antitrust claims, he contends, fit this description.]

II

Section 2 of the Federal Arbitration Act describes three kinds of arbitrable agreements. Two — those including maritime transactions and those covering the submission of an existing dispute to arbitration — are not involved in this case. The language of Section 2 relating to the Soler-Mitsubishi arbitration clause reads as follows:

> A written provision in . . . a contract evidencing a transaction involving commerce to settle by arbitration a controversy thereafter arising out of such contract . . . or the refusal to perform the whole or any part thereof, . . . shall be valid, irrevocable, and enforceable, save upon such grounds as exist at law or in equity for the revocation of any contract.

The plain language of this statute encompasses Soler's claims that arise out of its contract with Mitsubishi, but does not encompass a claim arising under federal law, or indeed one that arises under its distributor agreement with Chrysler. Nothing in the text of the 1925 Act, nor its legislative history, suggests that Congress intended to authorize the arbitration of any statutory claims.

Until today all of our cases enforcing agreements to arbitrate under the Arbitration Act have involved contract claims. In one, the party claiming a breach of contractual warranties also claimed that the breach amounted to fraud actionable under Section 10(b) under the Securities and Exchange Act of 1934. *Scherk v. Alberto Culver Co.* [*supra*]. But this is the first time the Court has considered the question whether a standard arbitration clause referring to claims arising out of or relating to a contract should be construed to cover statutory claims that have only an indirect relationship to the contract. In my opinion, neither the Congress that enacted the Arbitration Act in 1925, nor the many parties who have agreed to such standard clauses, could have anticipated the Court's answer to that question.

On several occasions we have drawn a distinction between statutory rights and contractual rights and refused to hold that an arbitration barred the assertion of a statutory right. Thus, in *Alexander v. Gardner–Denver Co.*[33] . . . we held that the arbitration of a claim of employment discrimination would not bar an employee's statutory right to damages under Title VII of the Civil Rights Act of 1964 . . . notwithstanding the strong federal policy favoring the arbitration of labor disputes. In that case the Court explained at some length why it would be unreasonable to assume that Congress intended to give arbitrators the final authority to implement the federal statutory policy:

> [W]e have long recognized that "the choice of forum inevitably affects the scope of the substantive right to be vindicated". . . . Respondent's deferral rule is necessarily premised on the assumption that arbitral processes are commensurate with judicial processes and that Congress impliedly intended federal courts to defer to arbitral decisions on Title VII issues. We deem this supposition unlikely.

> Arbitral procedures, while well suited to the resolution of contractual disputes, make arbitration a comparatively inappropriate forum for the final

---

[33] 415 U.S. 36, 94 S. Ct. 1011, 39 L. Ed.2d 147 (1974).

resolution of rights created by Title VII. This conclusion rests first on the special role of the arbitrator, whose task is to effectuate the intent of the parties rather than the requirements of enacted legislation. . . . But other facts may still render arbitral processes comparatively inferior to judicial processes in the protection of Title VII rights. Among these is the fact that the specialized competence of arbitrators pertains primarily to the law of the shop, not the law of the land. . . . Parties usually choose an arbitrator because they trust his knowledge and judgment concerning the demands and norms of industrial relations. On the other hand, the resolution of statutory or constitutional issues is a primary responsibility of courts, and judicial construction has proved especially necessary with respect to Title VII, whose broad language frequently can be given meaning only by reference to public law concepts.[34]

In addition, the Court noted that the informal procedures which make arbitration so desirable in the context of contractual disputes are inadequate to develop a record for appellate review of statutory questions. Such review is essential in matters of statutory interpretation in order to assure consistent application of important public rights.

In *Barrentine v. Arkansas-Best Freight System, Inc.*[35] . . . we reached a similar conclusion with respect to the arbitrability of an employee's claim based on the Fair Labor Standards Act[36] . . . . We again noted that an arbitrator, unlike a federal judge, has no institutional obligation to enforce federal legislative policy [and that]:

    . . . Under the FLSA, courts can award actual and liquidated damages, reasonable attorney's fees, and costs. . . . An arbitrator, by contrast, can award only that compensation authorized by the wage provision of the collective-bargaining agreement. . . . It is most unlikely that he will be authorized to award liquidated damages, costs, or attorney's fees.[37] . . . .

The Court has applied the same logic in holding that federal claims asserted under the Ku Klux Klan Act of 1871,[38] and claims arising under Sec. 12(2) of the Securities Act of 1933, 15 USC Section 771(2), may not be finally resolved by an arbitrator. *McDonald v. City of West Branch,*[39] . . . . *Wilko v. Swan,* [*supra*].

The Court's opinions in *Alexander, Barrentine, McDonald* and *Wilko* all explain why it makes good sense to draw a distinction between statutory claims and contract claims. In view of the Court's repeated recognition of the distinction . . . together with the undisputed historical fact that arbitration has functioned almost entirely in either the area of labor disputes or in "ordinary disputes between merchants as to questions of fact," . . . it is reasonable to assume that most lawyers and executives would not expect the language in the standard

---

[34] 415 U.S., at 56-57, (footnote omitted).
[35] 450 U.S. 728, 101 S. Ct. 1437, 67 L. Ed.2d 641 (1981).
[36] 29 USC Sections 201-219.
[37] 450 U.S., at 744-745, (footnote omitted).
[38] 42 USC Section 1983.
[39] 466 U.S. 284, 104 S. Ct. 1799, 80 L. Ed.2d 302 (1984).

arbitration clause to cover federal statutory claims. [This] . . . in my opinion . . . support[s] a presumption that such clauses do not apply to federal statutory claims.

III

The Court has repeatedly held that a decision by Congress to create a special statutory remedy renders a private agreement to arbitrate a federal statutory claim unenforceable. . . . [Here the Justice repeats the examples discussed in Part II]. The reasons that motivated those decisions apply with special force to the federal policy that is protected by the antitrust laws.

To make this point it is appropriate to recall some of our past appraisals of the importance of this federal policy and then to identify some of the specific remedies Congress has designed to implement it. It was Chief Justice Hughes who characterized the Sherman Anti-Trust Act as "a charter of freedom" that may fairly be compared to a constitutional provision. See *Appalachian Coals, Inc. v. United States*[40] . . . . In *United States v. Philadelphia National Bank*[41] . . . the Court referred to the extraordinary "magnitude" of the value choices made by Congress in enacting the Sherman Act. . . .

* * * *

The Sherman and Clayton Acts reflect Congress' appraisal of the value of economic freedom; they guarantee the vitality of the entrepreneurial spirit. Questions arising under these Acts are among the most important in public law.

The unique public interest in the enforcement of the antitrust laws is repeatedly reflected in the special remedial scheme enacted by Congress. Since its enactment in 1890, the Sherman Act has provided for public enforcement through criminal as well as civil sanctions. The preeminent federal interest in effective enforcement once justified a provision for special three-judge district courts to hear antitrust claims on an expedited basis, as well as for direct appeal to this Court bypassing the Courts of Appeals. . . .

The special interest in encouraging private enforcement of the Sherman Act has been reflected in the statutory scheme ever since 1890. . . . "The Act is comprehensive in its terms and coverage, protecting all who are made victims of the forbidden practices by whomever they may be perpetrated." *Mandeville Island Farms, Inc. v. American Crystal Sugar Co.*[42] . . . .

The provision for mandatory treble damages — unique in federal law when the statute was enacted — provides a special incentive to the private enforcement of the statute, as well as an especially powerful deterrent to violators. . . . [This] is buttressed by the statutory mandate that the injured party also recover costs, "including a reasonable attorney's fee."[43] . . . . The interest in wide and effective enforcement has thus, for almost a century, been vindicated by enlisting the assistance of "private Attorneys General". . . .

[40] 288 U.S. 344, 359-360, 77 L. Ed. 825, 53 S. Ct. 471 (1933).
[41] 374 U.S. 321, 371, 10 L. Ed.2d 915, 83 S. Ct. 1715 (1963).
[42] 334 U.S. 219, 236, 92 L. Ed. 1328, 68 S. Ct. 996 (1948).
[43] 15 USC Section 15(a).

. . . [I]n addition, . . . as we explained in *Blumenstock Brothers Advertising Agency v. Curtis Publishing Co.,*[44] . . . an antitrust treble damage case "can only be brought in a District Court of United States." The determination that these cases are "too important to be decided otherwise than by competent tribunals" surely cannot allow private arbitrators to assume a jurisdiction that is denied to court's of the sovereign States.

The extraordinary importance of the private antitrust remedy has been emphasized in other statutes enacted by Congress. Thus, in 1913, Congress passed a special act guaranteeing public access to depositions in government civil proceedings to enforce the Sherman Act[45] . . . . The purpose of that Act plainly was to enable victims of antitrust violations to make evidentiary use of information developed in a public enforcement proceeding. This purpose was further implemented in the following year by the enactment of Section 5 of the Clayton Act providing that a final judgment or decree in a Government case may constitute *prima facie* proof of a violation in a subsequent treble damage case[46] . . . . These special remedial provisions attest to the importance that Congress has attached to the private remedy.

In view of the history of antitrust enforcement in the United States, it is not surprising that all of the federal courts that have considered the question have uniformly and unhesitatingly concluded that agreements to arbitrate federal antitrust issues are not enforceable. . . .

* * * *

This Court would be well advised to endorse the collective wisdom of the distinguished judges of the Court of Appeals who have unanimously concluded that the statutory remedies fashioned by Congress for the enforcement of the antitrust laws render an agreement to arbitrate antitrust disputes unenforceable. Arbitration awards are only reviewable for manifest disregard of the law,[47] and the rudimentary procedures which make arbitration so desirable in the context of a private dispute often mean that the record is so inadequate that the arbitrator's decision is virtually unreviewable.[48] Despotic decision making of this kind is fine for parties who are willing to agree in advance to settle for a best approximation of the correct result in order to resolve quickly and inexpensively any contractual dispute that may arise in an ongoing commercial relationship. Such informality, however, is simply unacceptable when every error may have devastating consequences for important businesses in our national economy and may undermine their ability to compete in world market prices. Instead of "muffling a grievance in the cloakroom of arbitration," the public interest in free competitive

---

[44] 252 U.S. 436, 440, 64 L. Ed. 649, 40 S. Ct. 385 (1920).

[45] 37 Stat. 731, 15 USC Section 30.

[46] 38 Stat. 731, 15 USC Section 16(a).

[47] 9 U.S.C. Sections 10, 207.

[48] The arbitration procedure in this case does not provide any right to evidentiary discovery or a written decision, and requires that all proceedings be closed to the public. Moreover, Japanese arbitrators do not have the power of compulsory process to secure witnesses and documents, nor do witnesses who are available testify under oath. *Cf.* 9 USC Section 7 (arbitrators may summon witnesses to attend proceedings and seek enforcement in a district court).

markets would be better served by having the issues resolved "in the light of impartial public court adjudication." See *Merrill Lynch, Pierce, Fenner & Smith, Inc. v. Ware*[49] . . . .

IV

The Court assumes for the purposes of its decision that the antitrust issues would not be arbitrable if this were a purely domestic dispute, . . . but holds that the international character of the controversy makes it arbitrable. The holding rests on vague concerns for the international implications of its decision and a misguided application of *Scherk v. Alberto-Culver*, [*supra*]. . . .

International Obligations of the United States

Before relying on its own notions of what international comity requires, it is surprising that the Court does not determine the specific commitments that the United States has made to enforce private agreements to arbitrate disputes arising under public law; [namely the commitments contained in] . . . the Convention on the Recognition and Enforcement of Foreign Arbitral Awards. . . .

. . . [T]he United States, as *amicus curiae*, advises the Court that the Convention "clearly contemplates" that signatory nations will enforce domestic laws prohibiting the arbitration of certain subject matters. . . . This interpretation of the Convention was adopted by the Court of Appeals . . . and the Court declines to reject it. . . . The construction is beyond doubt.

Article II(3) of the Convention provides that the court of a Contracting State, "when seized of an action in a matter in respect of which the parties have made an agreement within the meaning of this article, shall, at the request of one of the parties, refer the parties to arbitration." This obligation does not arise, however, . . . if the dispute does not concern "a subject matter capable of settlement by arbitration," Art II(1). . . . [This] . . . clause plainly suggests the possibility that some subject matters are not capable of arbitration under the domestic laws of the signatory nations, and that agreements to arbitrate such disputes need not be enforced.

This construction is confirmed by the provisions of the Convention which provide for the enforcement of international arbitration awards. . . . If an arbitration award is "contrary to the public policy of [a] country" called upon to enforce it, or if it concerns a subject matter which is "not capable of settlement by arbitration under the law of that country," the Convention does not require that it be enforced. Art. V (2)(a) and (b). Thus, reading articles II and V together, the Convention provides that agreements to arbitrate disputes which are nonarbitrable under domestic law need not be honored, nor awards rendered under

---

[49] 414 U.S. 117, 136, 38 L. Ed.2d 348, 94 S. Ct. 383 (1973). The greatest risk, of course, is that the arbitrator will condemn business practices under the antitrust laws that are efficient in a free competitive market. *Cf. Northwest Wholesale Stationers, Inc. v. Pacific Stationery & Printing Co.*, 472 U.S. 284, 86 L. Ed.2d 202, 105 S. Ct. 2613 (1985), *rev'g*, 715 F. 2d 1393 (CA9 1983). In the absence of a reviewable record, a reviewing district court would not be able to undo the damage wrought. Even a Government suit or an action by a private party might not be available to set aside the award.

them enforced, [a] . . . construction . . . supported by the legislative history of the Senate's advice and consent to the Convention. . . .

* * * *

International Comity

It is clear then that the international obligations of the United States permit us to honor Congress' commitment to the exclusive resolution of antitrust disputes in the federal courts. The Court today refuses to do so, offering only vague concerns for comity among nations. The courts of other nations, on the other hand, have applied the exception provided in the Convention, and refused to enforce agreements to arbitrate specific subject matters of concern to them.[50]

It may be that the subject matter exception to the Convention ought to be reserved — as a matter of domestic law — for matters of the greatest public interest which involve concerns that are shared by other nations. The Sherman Act's commitment to free competitive markets is among our most important civil policies. . . . This commitment, shared by other nations which are signatory to the Convention, is hardly the sort of parochial concern that we should decline to enforce in the interest of international comity. Indeed, the branch of Government entrusted with the conduct of political relations with foreign governments has informed us that the "United States' determination that federal antitrust claims are nonarbitrable under the Convention . . . is not likely to result in either surprise or recrimination on the part of other signatories to the Convention."

Lacking any support for the proposition that the enforcement of our domestic laws in this context will result in international recriminations, the Court seeks refuge in an obtuse application of its own precedent, *Scherk v. Alberto-Culver Co.* [*supra*]. . . .

[In *Scherk*] the Court carefully identified two important differences between the *Wilko* case and the *Scherk* case. First, the statute involved in *Wilko* contained an express private remedy that had "no statutory counterpart" in the statute involved in *Scherk*. . . . [Second] the Court explained:

> Alberto-Culver's contract to purchase the business entities belonging to Scherk was a truly international agreement. Alberto-Culver is an American corporation with its principal place of business and the vast bulk of its activity in this country, while Scherk is a citizen of Germany whose companies were organized under the laws of Germany and Liechtenstein. The negotiations leading to the signing of the contract in Austria and to the closing in Switzerland took place in the United States, England, and Germany, and involved consultations with legal and trademark experts from each of those countries and from Liechtenstein. Finally, and most significantly, the subject

---

[50] For example, the Cour de Cassation in Belgium has held that disputes arising under a Belgian statute limiting the unilateral termination of exclusive distributorships are not arbitrable under the Convention in that country, *Audi-NSU Auto Union A. G. v. S. A. Adelin Petit & Cie.* (1979), in 5 Y.B. Commercial Arbitration 257, 259 and the Corte di Cassazione in Italy has held that labor disputes are not arbitrable under the Convention in that country, *Compagnis Generale Construzioni v. Piersanti* (1980), in 6 Y.B. Commercial Arbitration 229, 230.

matter of the contract concerned the sale of business enterprises organized under the laws of and primarily situated in European countries, whose activities were largely, if not entirely, directed to European markets.

Such a contract involves considerations and policies significantly different from those found controlling in *Wilko*. In *Wilko*, quite apart from the arbitration provision, there was no question but that the laws of the United States generally, and the federal securities laws in particular, would govern disputes arising out of the stock-purchase agreement. The parties, the negotiations, and the subject matter of the contract were all situated in this country, and no credible claim could have been entertained that any international conflict-of-laws problems would arise. In *[Scherk]* . . . by contrast, in the absence of the arbitration provision considerable uncertainty existed at the time of the agreement, and still exists, concerning the law applicable to the resolution of disputes arising out of the contract.

Thus, in its opinion in *Scherk*, the Court distinguished *Wilko* because in that case "no credible claim could have been entertained that any international conflict of laws problems would arise." That distinction fits this case precisely, since I consider it perfectly clear that the rules of American antitrust law must govern the claim of an American automobile dealer that he has been injured by an international conspiracy to restrain trade in the American automobile market.

The critical importance of the foreign law issues in *Scherk* was apparent to me even before the case reached this Court. . . . For that reason, it is especially distressing to find that the Court is unable to perceive why the reasoning in *Scherk* is wholly inapplicable to Soler's antitrust claims against Chrysler and Mitsubishi. The merits of those claims are controlled entirely by American law. . . .

The federal claim that was asserted in *Scherk*, unlike Soler's antitrust claim, had not been expressly authorized by Congress[51] . . . . The fraud claimed in *Scherk* was virtually identical to the breach of warranty claim; arbitration of such claims arising out of an agreement between parties of equal bargaining strength does not conflict with any significant federal policy.

In contrast, Soler's claim not only implicates our fundamental antitrust policies . . . but also should be evaluated in the light of an explicit Congressional finding concerning the disparity in bargaining power between automobile manufacturers and their franchised dealers. In 1956, when Congress enacted special legislation to protect dealers from bad faith franchise terminations, it recited its intent "to balance the power now heavily weighted in favor of automobile manufacturers."[52] . . . . The special federal interest in protecting automobile dealers from over-reaching by car manufacturers, as well as the policies underlying the Sherman Act, underscore the folly of the Court's decision today.

---

[51] Justice Stevens explains this point further as follows: "Indeed, until this Court's recent decision in *Landreth Timber Co. v. Landreth*, 471 U.S. 681, 85 L. Ed.2d 692, 105 S. Ct. 2297 (1985), the federal cause of action asserted in *Scherk* would not have been entertained in a number of federal circuits because it did not involve the kind of securities transaction that Congress intended to regulate when it enacted the Securities Exchange Act of 1934.

[52] 70 Stat. 1125.

V

The Court's repeated incantation of the high ideals of "international arbitration" creates the impression that this case involves the fate of an institution designed to implement a formula for world peace. But just as it is improper to subordinate the public interest in enforcement of antitrust policy to the private interest in resolving commercial disputes, so is it equally unwise to allow a vision of world unity to distort the importance of the selection of the proper forum for resolving this dispute. Like any other mechanism for resolving controversies, international arbitration will only succeed if it is capable of performing well — the prompt and inexpensive resolution of essentially contractual disputes between commercial partners. As for matters involving the political passions and the fundamental interests of nations, even the multilateral convention adopted under the auspices of the United Nations recognizes that private international arbitration is incapable of achieving satisfactory results.

In my opinion, the elected representatives of the American people would not have us dispatch an American citizen to a foreign land in search of an uncertain remedy for the violation of a public right that is protected by the Sherman Act. This is especially so when there has been no genuine bargaining over the terms of the submission, and the arbitration remedy provided has not even the most elementary guarantees of fair process. Consideration of a fully developed record by a jury, instructed in the law by a federal judge, and subject to appellate review, is a surer guide to the competitive character of a commercial practice than the practically unreviewable judgment of a private arbitrator.

Unlike the Congress that enacted the Sherman Act in 1890, the Court today does not seem to appreciate the value of economic freedom. I respectfully dissent.

NOTES AND QUESTIONS

(1) The Supreme Court has recently held that claims brought under Section 10(b) of the Securities Act of 1934,[53] and under the Racketeer Influenced and Corrupt Organizations Act (RICO),[54] are arbitrable and must be sent to arbitration in accordance with the terms of an arbitration agreement. *Shearson/American Express v. McMahon.*[55] Although faced with an entirely domestic case, the Court relied heavily on the rationale in *Mitsubishi* in so ruling. With respect to the Section 10(b) action a majority of five Justices rejected eight federal circuit court opinions that had held *Wilko* (cited in *Mitsubishi*) applicable to Section 10(b) claims brought under the 1934 Act. The majority found that earlier assumptions about the inadequacy of arbitration to protect the rights of investors (as expressed in *Wilko*) were outdated for arbitration procedures subject to the SEC's oversight authority under intervening changes in the regulatory structure of the securities

---

[53] 15 U.S.C. section 78j(b).
[54] 18 U.S.C. section 1961 *et seq.*
[55] 482 U.S. 220, 107 S. Ct. 2332, 96 L. Ed.2d 185 (1987).

laws. Four Justices dissented on this issue. The ruling on the RICO claim was unanimous.

(2) It is important to note that, in addition to the New York Convention and its enabling legislation, Chapter 2 of the United States Arbitration Act,[56] there is Chapter 1 of the Act, which is incorporated by reference into Chapter 2 to the extent it is not in conflict with Chapter 2 or the Convention. Chapter 1, which was utilized prior to 1970, can still be used if the Convention does not apply because the foreign award was made in a country not a party to the Convention. Accordingly, the two chapters must be read together. Our focus, however, will be primarily on the Convention and Chapter 2.

(3) In a footnote (Note 19) to its opinion the majority of the Court stated:

> In addition to the clause providing for arbitration before the Japan Commercial Arbitration Association, the Sales Agreement includes a choice-of-law clause which reads: "This Agreement is made in, and will be governed by and construed in all respects according to the laws of the Swiss Confederation as if entirely performed therein." The United States raises the possibility that the arbitral panel will read this provision not simply to govern interpretation of the contract terms, but wholly to displace American law even where it otherwise would apply. The International Chamber of Commerce opines that it is "[c]onceivabl[e], although we believe it unlikely, [that] the arbitrators could consider Soler's affirmative claim of anticompetitive conduct by CISA and Mitsubishi to fall within the purview of this choice–of–law provision, with the result that it would be decided under Swiss law rather than the U.S. Sherman Act." At oral argument, however, counsel for Mitsubishi conceded that American law applied to the antitrust claims and represented that the claims had been submitted to the arbitration panel in Japan on that basis. The record confirms that before the decision of the Court of Appeals the arbitral panel had taken these claims under submission. We therefore have no occasion to speculate on this matter at this stage in the proceedings, when Mitsubishi seeks to enforce the agreement to arbitrate, not to enforce an award. Nor need we consider now the effect of an arbitral tribunal's failure to take cognizance of the statutory cause of action. . . .

It is doubtful that representations by counsel to the U.S. Supreme Court are binding on Japanese arbitrators sitting in Japan with a contract expressly refering them to Swiss law. Suppose, therefore, the arbitrators decline to consider Soler's antitrust claim and issue an award in favor of Mitsubishi on its contract claims. What should a United States court do should that award be brought here for enforcement? Suppose it was possible to obtain enforcement of that award elsewhere than in the United States. What recourse would Soler have?

(4) Suppose the Japanese arbitrators do decide Soler's antitrust claim adverse to Soler. Assume further that in their award the arbitrators recorded their decision on the antitrust claim, but, as often happens in international arbitration, give no reasons for their decision and omit any statement of the facts upon which they relied in reaching their conclusion. Again assume a favorable award to Mitsubishi on its contract claims and an effort by Mitsubishi to enforce that award in a U.S.

---

[56] 9 U.S.C. Sections 201-208.

Court. How should the U.S. Court handle the antitrust issue? In *Wilko* the Court noted by way of dicta that a court should refuse enforcement of an arbitral award based on a "manifest error of law". Would this standard of review conform to the New York Convention?[57]

(5) Article V of the Convention expressly states that the "competent authority in the country where recognition and enforcement is" sought should decide whether a subject matter is "capable of settlement by arbitration under the law of the country." Article V, however, covers only the recognition and enforcement of arbitral awards. Should it be determinative or even relevant to issues regarding the enforcement of an agreement to arbitrate? How do the two opinions in *Mitsubishi* deal with this issue?

(6) How should the terms "null and void, inoperative or incapable of being performed" of Article II be interpreted? Would they allow a court to decline to enforce an agreement to arbitrate a particular issue on the ground that under the public policy of the forum the issue is not arbitrable? Consider the various arguments advanced by Justice Stevens. Would any of those arguments be cognizable under this provision of Article II of the Convention?

(7) In concluding that the agreement to arbitrate in *Mitsubishi* should be enforced, Justice Blackmun relies heavily on *The Bremen* and *Scherk* decisions and their emphasis on "international comity, respect for the capacities of foreign and transnational tribunals, and sensitivity to the need of the international commercial system for predictability in the resolution of disputes." Tested by this standard do these decisions dictate the outcome in *Mitsubishi*, or, as suggested by Justice Stevens, are they distinguishable?

(8) As noted by Justice Blackmun, several federal circuit court opinions had upheld a post-dispute agreement to arbitrate an antitrust claim. In contrast, the circuit courts had uniformly held invalid a pre-dispute agreement to arbitrate an antitrust claim. What would be the rationale for such a distinction? Is it convincing?

(9) As noted by the Court in *Mitsubishi*, Congress passed Chapter 2 of the Federal Arbitration Act to implement the Convention. In its instrument of ratification, the United States made two reservations permitted by the Convention: that it would apply the Convention only to the recognition and enforcement of awards made in the territory of another state party and that it would apply the Convention only to differences arising out of legal relationships, whether contractual or not, which are considered commercial under United States national law. Section 203 of the Act reflects the latter reservation and provides as well that an agreement or award involving only United States citizens will be deemed not to fall within the Convention unless it "involves property located abroad, envisages performance or enforcement abroad, or has some other reasonable relation with one or more foreign states." Section 203 of the Act grants jurisdiction over Convention cases to the federal courts on the ground that they are "deemed to arise under the laws and treaties of the United States" (*i.e.*, present a "federal question") unlike cases under Title I of the Act for which a showing of diversity or maritime jurisdiction is required. Under Section 206 of the Act, a federal court

---

[57] Documentary Supplement.

can order arbitration pursuant to the agreement, whether the place agreed upon is within or outside of the United States. United States courts, with some exceptions, have interpreted the term "commercial" broadly, excluding only "matrimonial and other domestic relations agreements, political awards and the like." See, e.g., Territory of Curacao v. Solitron Devices Inc.[58] ("economic development agreement" for the establishment of an industrial park and operation of a manufacturing plant between a private U.S. firm and a foreign government deemed "commercial"). But see, B.V. Bureau Wigsmuller v. United States.[59]

(10) As noted above, the United States has made a reservation that it will apply the New York Convention on the "basis of reciprocity" only to *awards* made "in the territory of another Contracting State." Does the reciprocity requirement apply to the enforcement of arbitral agreements as well as awards? How would the reciprocity requirement apply, if at all, in the case of an agreement to arbitrate, or an award issued, in the United States, if one of the parties was a citizen of a nonparty to the Convention? At the time of writing the courts have not decided these questions.

(11) In *Ledee v. Ceramiche Ragno*,[60] the United States Court of Appeals for the First Circuit recently noted that:

> A court presented with a request to refer a dispute to arbitration pursuant to Chapter Two of the Federal Arbitration Act performs a very limited inquiry. It must resolve four preliminary questions:
>
> (1) Is there an agreement in writing to arbitrate the subject of the dispute?
>
> (2) Does the agreement provide for arbitration in the territory of a signatory of the Convention? Convention Articles 1(1), I(3);[61] . . . .
>
> (3) Does the agreement arise out of a legal relationship whether contractual or not, which is considered as commercial? Convention, Article I(3);[62] . . . .
>
> (4) Is a party to the agreement not an American citizen? Or does the commercial relationship have some reasonable relation with one or more foreign states?[63] . . . .

The Court in *Ledee* went on to note that, if a district court resolves these questions in the affirmative, it must order arbitration unless it finds the agreement "null and void, inoperative or incapable of being performed" in accordance with Article II(3) of the Convention. The "null and void" clause would be interpreted narrowly, the court held, to cover "only those situations — such as fraud, mistake, duress, and waiver — that can be applied neutrally on an international scale." It would not be interpreted to cover the "parochial interests of the Commonwealth [of Puerto Rico] or of any state." Hence the Puerto Rico Dealers Act, which would have barred arbitration of issues arising out of the contract in any forum outside

---

[58] 356 F. Supp. 1, 13 (S.D.N.Y. 1973), *aff'd*, 489 F. 2d 1313 (2d Cir. 1973), *cert. denied*, 416 U.S. 986 (1974).

[59] 1976 American Maritime Cases 2514 (S.D.N.Y., 1976).

[60] 684 F. 2d 184, 186 (1982).

[61] 9 U.S.C. Sec. 206.

[62] 9 U.S.C. Sec. 202.

[63] 9 U.S.C. Sec. 202.

of Puerto Rico, would be no bar to enforcement of the parties' agreement to arbitrate such issues in Italy.

Similarly, the courts have found that the requirement to arbitrate is not qualified by a showing that any resulting award would not subsequently be enforced by the courts. A proposal to amend Article II(3) to expressly relate arbitral agreements to enforceable arbitral awards was rejected by the drafters of the Convention. See, *e.g., Rhone Mediterranee Compagnia Francese v. Lauro*[64]
. . . .

(12) With respect to jurisdiction over the parties, under the FAA an agreement to arbitrate in a particular place, coupled with an agreement for the entry of judgment on the award, is such a "consent" to the jurisdiction of any court whose territory encompasses the place of arbitration as to confer upon that court *in personam jurisdiction* over the objecting party in an action under Section 9 to confirm an award. No further contacts with the jurisdiction are required to satisfy "due process." Moreover, in the case of a proceeding in a federal court, state "long arm requirements" do not need to be met. Notice of the proceedings must be served in such a case as provided in Section 9. The same principles apply in the case of a proceeding under Section 4 to compel arbitration where the designated place of arbitration is within the territorial jurisdiction of the court. If, however, the designated place of arbitration is abroad, it is doubtful that an agreement for the entry of judgment on any award emanating from that arbitration would, of itself, constitute such a "consent" to the jurisdiction of a court sitting in the United States as would satisfy due process. In such a case the establishment of in personam jurisdiction over the party objecting to arbitration or resisting confirmation of the award would presumably require a showing of some other minimal contacts (*i.e.,* doing business, ownership of property, etc.) with the forum. This latter point is of special importance in connection with proceedings under the New York Convention.[65]

(13) U.S. court decisions have split on the issue whether pre-award attachment is available in cases arising under the U.N. Convention. Compare, for example, *I.T.A.D. Assocs. v. Podar Bros.,*[66] (availability of pre-arbitration attachment interferes with Convention's goal of uniform standards applied on an international scale) with *Carolina Power & Light Co. v. Uranex,*[67] (pre-award attachment permitted as furthering the goals of the Convention).

(14) The United States has entered into a number of bilateral treaties — typically Treaties of Friendship, Commerce and Navigation — that contain 140 provisions relating to the recognition and enforcement of arbitral agreements and awards. Recently, the United States has negotiated bilateral investment agreements, commonly called "BITS," that contain similar provisions.

(15) In addition to the Federal Arbitration Act, most of the States have statutes on arbitration. See, *e.g.,* The New York Arbitration Act of 1920.[68] The arbitration

---

[64] 555 F. Supp. 481, 485 (D. Ct. Virgin Islands 1982), *aff'd,* 712 F. 2d 50(3d Cir. 1983).
[65] See 9 U.S.C. Section 204.
[66] 636 F. 2d 75 (4th Cir. 1981).
[67] 451 F. Supp. 1044 (N.D. Cal. 1977).
[68] NY Laws Ch. 275.

of international disputes may take place as well pursuant to these State laws. Florida, for instance, has two such acts, one relating to domestic arbitrations, the other to international arbitrations.[69]

[D] Enforcing Arbitral Awards

The bases for enforcement of foreign arbitral awards may vary. Our primary focus in this chapter has been on the Convention on the Recognition and Enforcement of Foreign Arbitral Awards (the New York Convention)[70] and its implementing legislation.[71] We have also briefly considered the Convention for the Settlement of Investment Disputes between States and Nationals of Other States (see *supra*, p. 799) and its implementing legislation.[72] In addition, Friendship, Commerce and Navigation Treaties and Bilateral Investment Treaties (discussed later in this casebook) may require the recognition and enforcement of arbitral awards. Lastly, it should be noted that the United States is a party to the Inter-American Convention on International Commercial Arbitration.

Moreover, the scope of coverage of the New York Convention is wide. As noted above, the Convention applies to awards made in the territory of another state party. Under Article I(1) it also applies to awards "not considered domestic." See *Bergeson v. Joseph Muller Corp.*,[73] (enforcing arbitral award rendered in the United States between two foreign entities).

Section 207 of the Federal Arbitration Act, 9 U.S.C. Sec. 207, provides that:

> Within three years after an arbitral award falling under the Convention is made, any party to the arbitration may apply to any court having jurisdiction under this Chapter for an order confirming the award as against another party to the arbitration. The court shall confirm the award unless it finds one of the grounds for refusal or deferral of recognition or enforcement of the award specified in the said convention.

Under Section 207 of the Act one wishing to enforce an award in the United States need only supply the authenticated original award or certified copy thereof, the original or certified copy of the arbitration agreement, and official or sworn translations, if appropriate, within three years after the award. These procedures apply whether the award is the result of an institutional or *ad hoc* arbitration. United States District Courts have original jurisdiction to hear applications to confirm or challenge awards, which are then tried as motions without jury trial. A judgment of confirmation has the same force and may be enforced as a judgment in an action.

As to defenses against enforcement of an award, U.S. court decisions have ruled that the grounds specified in Article V of the Convention are exclusive. See, *e.g.*, *Fotochrome, Inc. v. Gopal Company, Ltd.*[74] and *Ipitrade Interns., S.A. v. Federal*

---

[69] See, Florida Statutes, Chapters 683 and 684.
[70] Documentary Supplement.
[71] 9 U.S.C. Section 201 *et seq.*
[72] 22 U.S.C. Sections 1650, 1650a.
[73] 710 F. 2d 928 (2d Cir. 1983).
[74] 517 F. 2d 512 (2d Cir. 1975).

Republic of Nigeria.[75] U.S. cases have also held that all defenses are to be construed narrowly, given the pro-enforcement bias of the Convention. Article V of the Convention basically sets forth two kinds of defenses: (1) procedural defects as enumerated in the five lettered subparagraphs contained in Article V(1); and (2) jurisdictional defects set forth in subparagraphs (a) and (b) in Article V(2). The procedural defects have to be raised by the party resisting the enforcement action, who then has the burden of proof.

Alleged procedural defects are often raised by the party resisting enforcement of an award.[76] One or two of these procedural defenses are worth noting for present purposes. For example, with respect to subparagraph (d) of Article V(1), recent federal cases have held that the appearance of bias is not sufficient to raise the defense of evident partiality. The strong public policy favoring arbitration, coupled with the lack of evidence of actual partiality, led the courts to conclude that enforcement of the arbitral awards would not contravene United States public policy.[77]

Subsection (e) of Article V(1) requires that the award be "binding" on the parties rather than "final and enforceable," language often found in commercial treaties. The terms "final" and "enforceable" can cause problems. "Final" implies the completion of all permitted appeals. "Enforceable" implies some kind of court action because arbitral awards are not self-executing. The purpose behind the language "binding on the parties" was to narrow the defense to enforcement of the award. Under this language United States Courts have enforced awards even when an appeal has been pending at the place of arbitration. See, *e.g., Landegger v. Bayerische, Hypotheken Und Wechsel Bank.*[78]

In order to carry out the strong public policy favoring international arbitration expressed in *Scherk v. Alberto-Culver Co., supra,* the courts have construed the public policy defense narrowly. In the words of the United States Court of Appeals for the Second Circuit in *Parson & WH. Ov. Co., Inc. v. Societe G. De L. Du P. (R.)*[79] " . . . the Convention's public policy defense should be [applied] . . . only where enforcement would violate the forum state's most basic notions of morality and justice." In Parsons the court rejected the contention that United States disagreements with Egypt in recent years over foreign policy could be the basis for a public policy exception to the enforcement of a foreign arbitral award made against an American corporation and in favor of an Egyptian corporation. See also *Waterside Ocean Nav. Co. Inc. v. International Nav. Ltd.*[80]

Under Section 10 of Chapter 1 of the Federal Arbitration Act, a court may, on application of a party, vacate an award procured by "corruption, fraud or undue means" or where there was "evident partiality or corruption" of the arbitrators. United States courts have demonstrated a willingness to apply Section 10 defenses

---

[75] 465 F. Supp. 824 (D.D.C. 1978).

[76] For a thorough discussion of these tactics, see McClendon, *Enforcement of Foreign Arbitral Awards in the United States,* 4 NW. J. Int'l L. & BUS. 58, 63-67 (1982).

[77] See, *International Produce Inc. v. A/S Rosshavet,* 638 F. 2d 548 (2d Cir. 1981). and *Fertilizer Corp. of India v. IDI Management, Inc.*

[78] 357 F. Supp. 692 (S.D.N.Y. 1972).

[79] 508 F.2d 969, 974 (1974).

[80] 737 F.2d 150 (C.A.N.Y. 1984).

in the name of public policy to international awards procured by fraud or through the partiality of the arbitrator.

The grounds under Chapter 1 of the Federal Arbitration Act which are found in Section 10 thereof, largely parallel the Convention defenses. Section 9, however, authorizes confirmation of the award only if the arbitration agreement contains a stipulation that a court judgment shall be entered on the award. In most States this poses no particular problem because confirmation may be obtained under State common law procedures, and, not infrequently, courts find various forms of implied consent even in the absence of an "entry of judgment" clause; e.g., if the arbitration was conducted under institutional rules providing for judicial enforcement. Alternatively, in most States a judgment confirming an award may be obtained from a court sitting in the foreign arbitral situs and then the judgment of that court brought into an American court for enforcement.

For a case considering a host of defenses to enforcement of an arbitral award, see *Island Territory of Curacao v. Solitron Devices, Inc.*[81] . . . . There, the district court and court of appeals rejected claims, among others, that the arbitral award should not be enforced because the arbitral tribunal in Curacao had no jurisdiction; that one of the arbitrators was biased; that the enforcement of the award would violate public policy; and that there was no commercial relationship between the parties as required by the New York Convention. Especially noteworthy are the court's rejections of claims that the contract did not create a commercial relationship between the parties because it called for the building of factories in an industrial park vital to the economic development of Curacao and that the enforcement of the award would violate public policy because Curacao had raised the minimum wage two and one-half times contrary to Solitron's understanding that wages would remain "stable".

When the party against whom an arbitral award is made is a foreign state, issues of sovereign immunity (see *supra*, p. 882) or Act of State (see *infra*, Chapter 13, p. 1081) may arise. With respect to sovereign immunity, U.S. courts had divided on the issue whether an agreement to arbitrate outside the United States constituted an irrevocable waiver of sovereign immunity. See, *e.g.*, *Ipitrade International, S.A. v. Federal Republic of Nigeria*,[82] (waiver of immunity under Foreign Sovereign Immunities Act, where Nigeria agreed to ICC arbitration in France under Swiss law); *Verlinden B.V. v. Central Bank of Nigeria*,[83] (consent to arbitrate outside United States does not constitute waiver of immunity in U.S.).

The issue regarding an agreement to arbitrate has now been resolved in favor of waiver by a recent amendment to the Foreign Sovereign Immunities Act (FSIA).[84] In addition, the provisions of the FSIA dealing with immunity from execution were modified to permit execution on property of foreign states used for a commercial activity in the United States in cases where "the judgment is based on an order confirming an arbitral award rendered against the foreign State,

---

[81] 356 F. Supp. 1 (D.C.N.Y.), *aff'd*, 489 F. 2d 1313 (2d Cir.), *cert. denied*, 416 U.S. 986 (1973).

[82] 465 F. Supp. 824 (D.D.C. 1978).

[83] 647 F. 2d 320 (2d Cir. 1981), *rev'd on other grounds*, 461 U.S. 480 (1983).

[84] See 28 U.S.C. Section 1605(a)(6).

provided that attachment in aid of execution, or execution, would not be inconsistent with any provision in the arbitral agreement."[85]

As to the Act of State defense, the court in *Libyan Am. Oil v. Socialist People's Libyan Arab Jamahirya*[86] refused to enforce an award granting compensation for nationalization against a foreign sovereign, on the ground that the Act of State doctrine made the dispute incapable of settlement by arbitration and therefore found an Article V(2)(a) defense. This decision, however, has been rejected by a recent revision of the Federal Arbitration Act, which states that "[e]nforcement of arbitral agreements, confirmation of arbitral awards, and execution upon judgments based on orders confirming such awards shall not be refused on the basis of the Act of State doctrine."[87]

The enforcement of arbitral awards in countries other than the United States raises additional problems. The defenses against enforcement abroad under the Convention are the same as those applied by United States courts. However, Article V(2) defenses — inappropriate subject matter and violations of public policy — are determined by the law of the enforcing forum, which may differ substantially from that of the United States. Also, with respect to Article V(1)(b) (procedural due process) defenses, foreign courts apply their own notions of fairness and justice.

The Yearbooks of the International Council for Commercial Arbitration contain summaries of various countries' arbitration laws and practice. Under some of these arbitration laws, the courts are given much more latitude than are United States courts in overturning awards for procedural defects, errors of law, or even for arbitrariness of fact-finding.[88]

---

[85] 28 U.S.C. Section 1610(a)(6).
[86] 482 F. Supp. 1175 (D.D.C. 1980).
[87] 9 U.S.C. Section 15.
[88] See also Van Den Berg, The New York Arbitration Convention Of 1958, 364-67 (1981).

THE CONSTITUTIONAL AUTHORITY OF THE PRESIDENT AND CONGRESS IN THE MAKING OF FOREIGN POLICY

Introduction

The constitutional allocation of authority to determine America's foreign policy is a subject which, over the last decade or so, has engendered heated debate, especially with regard to the use of armed force, the scope of the President's power to make executive agreements with foreign governments and his power to terminate treaties.[1] While the content of each of these debates differs, depending upon the power or function in question, the text of the constitution, the history and circumstances attending the use of the powers in question and the political values those powers evoke, there are nevertheless recurring themes that should be understood from the start of any study of the subject.

The President is the dominant actor in the formation and execution of American foreign policy. In the "vast external realm" the modern President exercises powers of initiative and administration more extensive and more decisive to the course of the Nation than is generally the case in domestic matters, except perhaps in times of emergency. Yet, the reason for this is not immediately apparent from the constitutional text. The framers, constrained by fears of a too powerful executive, conferred upon the President a limited number of essentially instrumental functions. He was to be commander-in-chief and was to "make treaties" with the "Advice" as well as "Consent" of the Senate. He was to participate in the legislative process by making recommendations and exercising the veto power. He was to nominate and, "by and with the Advice and Consent of the Senate, appoint Ambassadors, Public Ministers and Consuls." He was to "receive Ambassadors and other public Ministers" and was to "take Care that the Laws be faithfully executed" (the "take Care" clause). This was the whole of it.

In contrast, not only was the Senate to share in the making of treaties and appointment of ambassadors, but under the commerce power, the power "to establish a uniform Rule of Naturalization," and to secure copyrights and patents to "Authors and Inventors," Congress was given powers whose exercise would inevitably touch upon, or even permit control of, virtually any movement of goods, people and ideas between the United States and foreign countries. Congress was also empowered "to coin Money and regulate the Value thereof and of foreign Coin," to borrow, to tax and to spend. It was "to declare War," grant "letters of Marque and Reprisal," to "raise and support Armies," to "define and punish

---

[1] See, *e.g.*, The 1973 War Powers Resolution, Pub. L. 93-148, 87 Stat. 555, placing limits on the President's power to employ the armed forces of the United States abroad and *Goldwater v. Carter*, 444 U.S. 996, 100 S. Ct. 533 (1979) discussed page 1036, *infra.*

Piracies and Felonies committed on the High Seas, and Offenses against the Laws of Nations." It was also "to make all Laws necessary and proper for carrying into Execution" not only its own powers but those of the President as well. From an 18th Century, as well as contemporary, perspective, there was scarcely a subject likely to arise in the conduct of our relations with other nations in which the Senate or the Congress was not assigned a policy formulating role.

If the structure of power implicit in the text of the Constitution bears little resemblance to the contemporary scheme of things, the transformation has occurred largely through an elaboration upon the scanty enumerations of Article II. The function of "receiving" foreign ambassadors has been read to give the recognition power to the President. When the constitutional text was read as establishing the executive as the sole "organ," or spokesman, of the Nation in its relations with other states, diplomacy became an exclusive Presidential province. With that came the power to negotiate, the power to state the attitude of the Nation and thereby influence foreign expectations and attitudes, the power to control the flow of information and advice to Congress and the power to affect its perception of events abroad, often decisively. As the power to "make treaties" was extended to non-treaty agreements (*i.e.*, agreements without Senatorial consent) Presidents assumed a vast power to commit the Nation either outright or in "moral" terms that Congress would find hard to deny. When as commander-in-chief Presidents assumed the authority to direct the global disposition of American military forces, they came to possess a vast practical capacity to manipulate the Nation's involvement in the tensions that lead to war.

In short, any President disposed to exercise it, eventually came to have a power of *initiative* in the formulation of foreign policy that exceeded anything he was likely to possess in the domestic sphere. In similar vein, the President's power as commander-in-chief, his power as sole "organ" of the Nation, his responsibilities under the "take Care" clause, abetted by ever broader delegations of authority from Congress, combined to give him a vast discretion in the *administration* of foreign policy.

On the other hand, the constitutional text is not just an historical curiosity. The extensive enumerations of Article I still remain. That the President may exercise a large discretion in the *administration* of policy does not excuse him from conforming his actions to that policy. That he possesses a vast power of policy *initiative* and a large capacity for securing congressional agreement with his initiatives does not necessarily confer upon him an exclusive policy-making authority. The text implies as much, but it is more than the text. An exclusive or plenary authority could scarcely be fitted into a constitutional scheme designed to preserve individual liberty and the basic values of a democratic society. Implicit in the textual Constitution is a recognition that any governmental decision by the concurrent will of Congress and President (or President and two-thirds of the Senate, in the case of treaties) constitutes a more authoritative act of governance than is possible when the President alone decides. This, in turn, reflects a belief that a concurrent decision can be taken as a surer and hence more legitimate expression of the general will — a decision more in consonance with our democratic postulates — and a more considered, and hence legitimate, limitation upon individual liberty. The wisdom, even the necessity, of that concurrence is thus an insistent theme intruding its way into virtually every facet of policy formulation and execution.

But this is not all. It would be anomalous if having devolved upon the President the awesome task of assuming the initiative over foreign policy, constitutional tradition would then deny him altogether any independent power to carry his policies into effect; would invariably require congressional concurrence. No system of government committed to the preservation of liberty and democratic values can survive unless it is also capable, over time, of acting effectively. And there are times, in the conduct of foreign affairs, when speed, secrecy and unity in national expressions are essential to effective governance. Implicit, thus, in the historical assumption of Presidential initiative is the possibility that, on proper occasions, the President would possess a power to act without congressional warrant and even, perhaps, in disregard of the congressional will. And yet, such power is only for proper occasions. One cannot ignore the fact that there are also differences in perceptions, in values and in style between the Executive and Congress; differences endemic to the function, structure and diverse constituancies served by each branch. If, on occasion, these differences may render a shared power inimical to effective governance, in other circumstances they may render a concurrence of will essential to it.

In this richly textured context a preclusive claim to power — of an "inherent" authority to conduct "foreign relations" — has no place. What emerges instead from constitutional text and constitutional tradition is a broad charter reflective of certain basic political values which cannot always be easily reconciled, but which nevertheless establish a framework within which each succeeding generation of Americans must work through that allocation of particular powers that is best designed, by their lights, to secure a workable government for a free society. What follows in the first section of this chapter, therefore, are several leading Supreme Court decisions which reflect not only the scheme of the Constitution and the tensions that lie within it, but the principles and modes of analysis — textual and otherwise — that are to be used in making specific allocative decisions. Next, we turn to an examination of congressional delegations of authority over foreign economic policy to the President in order to consider the constitutionally permissible boundaries of such delegations as well as issues of statutory interpretation that have arisen in this area. Then we focus on the use of treaties and other international agreements in the conduct of foreign economic policy and the respective roles of President and Congress.

§ 12.01   Some Basic Theories Of Presidential Power

YOUNGSTOWN SHEET & TUBE CO. v. SAWYER
(The Steel Seisure Case)

United States Supreme Court
343 U.S. 579, 72 S. Ct. 863, 96 L. Ed. 1153 (1952)

Certiorari to the United States Court of Appeals for the District of Columbia Circuit.

Mr. Justice Black delivered the opinion of the Court.

We are asked to decide whether the President was acting within his constitutional power when he issued an order directing the Secretary of Commerce to take possession of and operate most of the Nation's steel mills. The mill owners argue that the President's order amounts to lawmaking, a legislative function which the Constitution has expressly confided to the Congress and not to the President. The Government's position is that the order was made on findings of the President that his action was necessary to avert a national catastrophe which would inevitably result from a stoppage of steel production, and that in meeting this grave emergency the President was acting within the aggregate of his constitutional powers as the Nation's Chief Executive and the Commander in Chief of the Armed Forces of the United States. The issue emerges here from the following series of events:

In the latter part of 1951 [during the Korean War], a dispute arose between the steel companies and their employees over terms and conditions that should be included in new collective bargaining agreements. [Efforts to resolve the dispute were unavailing]. On April 4, 1952, the Union [the United Steelworkers of America] gave notice of a nation-wide strike called to begin at 12:01 a.m. April 9. The indispensability of steel as a component of substantially all weapons and other war materials led the President to believe that the proposed work stoppage would immediately jeopardize our national defense and that governmental seizure of the steel mills was necessary in order to assure the continued availability of steel. Reciting these considerations for his action, the President, a few hours before the strike was to begin, issued Executive Order 10340 [directing] . . . Secretary of Commerce [Sawyer] to take possession of most of the steel mills and keep them running. The Secretary immediately issued his own possessory orders, calling upon the presidents of the various seized companies to serve as operating managers for the United States. The next morning the President sent a message to Congress reporting his action. Congress has taken no action.

Obeying the Secretary's orders under protest, the companies brought proceedings against him in the District Court, [which court] . . . on April 30 issued a preliminary injunction restraining the Secretary from "continuing the seizure and possession of the plants [and] from acting under the purported authority of Executive Order No. 10340.". . . . On the same day the Court of Appeals stayed the District Court's injunction. . . . Deeming it best that the issues raised be promptly decided by this Court, we granted certiorari on May 3 and set the cause for argument on May 12.

The President's power, if any, to issue the order must stem either from an act of Congress or from the Constitution itself. There is no statute that expressly authorizes the President to take possession of property as he did here. Nor is there any act of congress to which our attention has been directed from which such a power can fairly be implied. . . . There are two statutes which do authorize the President to take both personal and real property under certain conditions. [The Selective Service Act of 1948 and The Defense Production Act of 1950]. However, the Government admits that these conditions were not met and that the President's order was not rooted in either of the statutes. The Government refers to the seizure provisions of one of these statutes (Sec. 201(b) of the Defense

Production Act) as "much too cumbersome, involved, and time-consuming for the crisis which was at hand."

Moreover, the use of the seizure technique to solve labor disputes in order to prevent work stoppages was not only unauthorized by any congressional enactment; prior to this controversy, Congress had refused to adopt that method of settling labor disputes. When the Taft-Harley Act was under consideration in 1947, Congress rejected an amendment which would have authorized such governmental seizures in cases of emergency.

* * * *

It is clear that if the President had authority to issue the order he did, it must be found in some provision of the Constitution. And it is not claimed that express constitutional language grants this power to the President. The contention is that presidential power should be implied from the aggregate of his powers under the Constitution. Particular reliance is placed on provisions in Article II which say that "The executive Power shall be vested in a President" . . . that "he shall take Care that the Laws be faithfully executed," and that he "shall be Commander in Chief of the Army and Navy of the United States."

The order cannot properly be sustained as an exercise of the President's military power as Commander in Chief of the Armed Forces. The Government attempts to do so by citing a number of cases upholding broad powers in military commanders engaged in day-to-day fighting in a theater of war. Such cases need not concern us here. Even though "theater of war" be an expanding concept, we cannot with faithfulness to our constitutional system hold that the Commander in Chief of the Armed Forces has the ultimate power as such to take possession of private property in order to keep labor disputes from stopping production. This is a job for the Nation's lawmakers, not for its military authorities.

Nor can the seizure order be sustained because of the several constitutional provisions that grant executive power to the President. In the framework of our Constitution, the President's power to see that the laws are faithfully executed refutes the idea that he is to be a lawmaker. The Constitution limits his functions in the lawmaking process to the recommending of laws he thinks wise and the vetoing of laws he thinks bad. And the Constitution is neither silent nor equivocal about who shall make laws which the President is to execute. The first section of the first article says that "All legislative Powers herein granted shall be vested in a Congress of the United States. . . ." After granting many powers to the Congress, Article I goes on to provide that Congress may "make all Laws which shall be necessary and proper for carrying into Execution the foregoing Powers, and all other Powers vested by this Constitution in the Government of the United States, or in any Department or Officer thereof."

The President's order does not direct that congressional policy be executed in a manner prescribed by Congress — it directs that a presidential policy be executed in a manner prescribed by the President. The preamble of the order itself, like that of many statutes, sets out reasons why the President believes certain policies should be adopted, proclaims these policies as rules of conduct to be followed, and again, like a statute, authorizes a government official to promulgate additional rules and regulations consistent with the policy proclaimed and needed to carry that policy into execution. The power of Congress to adopt such public policies as those proclaimed by the order is beyond question. It can authorize the taking of private property for public use. It can make laws regulating the relationships between employers and employees, prescribing rules designed to settle labor disputes, and fixing wages and working conditions in certain fields of our economy. The Constitution does not subject this lawmaking power of Congress to presidential or military supervision or control.

It is said that other Presidents without congressional authority have taken possession of private business enterprises in order to settle labor disputes. But even if this be true, Congress has not thereby lost its exclusive constitutional authority to make laws necessary and proper to carry out the powers vested by the Constitution "in the Government of the United States, or any Department or Officer thereof."

The founders of this Nation entrusted the lawmaking power to the Congress alone in both good and bad times. It would do no good to recall the historical events, the fears of power, the hopes for freedom that lay behind their choice. Such a review would but confirm our holding that this seizure order cannot stand.

Affirmed.

[The decision was 6 to 3. While all but two of the concurring Justices — Justices Douglas and Clark were the only exceptions — joined the opinion as well as the judgment announced by Justice Black, all wrote separate opinions. These opinions contain some important ideas.]

MR. JUSTICE FRANKFURTER, concurring.

[The framers] . . . rested the structure of our central government on the system of checks and balances. For them the doctrine of separation of powers was not mere theory; it was a felt necessity. No so long ago it was fashionable to find our system of checks and balances obstructive to effective government. It was easy to ridicule that system as outmoded — too easy. The experience through which the world has passed in our own day has made vivid the realization that the Framers of our Constitution were not inexperienced doctrinaires.

* * * *

The issue before us can be met, and therefore should be, without attempting to define the President's powers comprehensively. I shall not attempt to delineate what belongs to him by virtue of his office beyond the power even of Congress to contract; what authority belongs to him until Congress acts; what kind of problems may be dealt with either by the Congress or by the President or by both; . . . what power must be exercised by the Congress and cannot be delegated to the President. . . .

* * * *

The question before the Court comes in this setting. Congress has frequently — at least 16 times since 1916 — specifically provided for executive seizure of production, transportation, communications, or storage facilities. In every case it has qualified this grant of power with limitations and safeguards. This body of enactments . . . demonstrates that Congress deemed seizure so drastic a power as to require that it be carefully circumscribed whenever the President was vested with this extraordinary authority. . . .

[Thus, in 1947,] [u]nder the urgency of telephone and coal strikes in the winter of 1946, Congress addressed itself to the problems raised by "national emergency" strikes and lockouts. The termination of wartime seizure powers on December 31, 1946, brought these matters to the attention of Congress with vivid impact. A proposal that the President be given powers to seize plants to avert a shutdown where the "health or safety" of the nation was endangered, was thoroughly canvassed by Congress and rejected. No room for doubt remains that the proponents as well as opponents of the bill which became the Labor Management Relations Act of 1947 [Taft-Hartley] clearly understood that as a result of that legislation the only recourse for preventing a shutdown in any basic industry, after failure of mediation, was Congress. Authorization for seizure as an available remedy for potential dangers was unequivocally put aside. . . .

It cannot be contended that the President would have had power to issue this order had Congress explicitly negated such authority in formal legislation. Congress has expressed its will to withhold this power from the President as though it had said so in so many words. . . .

But it is now claimed that the President has seizure power by virtue of the Defense Production Act of 1950 and its Amendments. And the claim is based on the occurrence of new events - Korea and the need for stabilization, etc. — although it was well known that seizure power was withheld by the Act of 1947 and although the President, whose specific requests for other authority were in the main granted by Congress, never suggested that in view of the new events he needed the power for seizure which Congress in its judgment had decided to withhold from him. The utmost that the Korean conflict may imply is that it may have been desirable to have given the President further authority, a freer hand in these matters. Absence of authority in the President to deal with a crisis does not imply want of power in the Government. Conversely the fact that power exists in the Government does not vest it in the President. The need for new legislation does not enact it. Nor does it repeal or amend existing law.

No authority that has since been given to the President can by any fair process of statutory construction be deemed to withdraw the restriction or change the will of Congress as expressed by a body of enactments, culminating in the Labor Management Relations Act of 1947. [Here Justice Frankfurter undertakes a detailed review of the Defense Production Act of 1950 and its subsequent amendments].

* * * *

The legislative history here canvassed is relevant to yet another of the issues before us, namely, the Government's argument that overriding public interest prevents the issuance of the injunction despite the illegality of the seizure. I cannot accept that contention. . . .

Apart from his vast share of responsibility for the conduct of our foreign relations, the embracing function of the President is that "he shall take Care that the Laws be faithfully executed. . . ." Art. II, Section 3. The nature of that authority has for me been comprehensively indicated by Mr. Justice Holmes. "The duty of the President to see that the laws be executed is a duty that does not go beyond the laws or require him to achieve more than Congress sees fit to leave within his power." *Myers v. United States.*[2] The powers of the President are not as particularized as those of Congress. But unenumerated powers do not mean undefined powers. The separation of powers built into our Constitution gives essential content to undefined provisions in the frame of our government.

To be sure, the content of the three authorities of government is not to be derived from an abstract analysis. The areas are partly interacting, not wholly disjointed. The Constitution is a framework for government. Therefore the way the framework has consistently operated fairly establishes that it has operated according to its true nature. Deeply embedded traditional ways of conducting government cannot supplant the Constitution or legislation, but they give meaning to the words of a text or supply them. It is an inadmissibly narrow conception of American constitutional law to confine it to the words of the Constitution and to disregard the gloss which life has written upon them. In short, a systematic, unbroken, executive practice, long pursued to the knowledge of the Congress and never before questioned, engaged in by Presidents who have also sworn to uphold the Constitution, making as it were such exercise of power part of the structure of our government, may be treated as a gloss on "executive Power" vested in the President by Sec. 1 of Art. II. . . .

Down to the World War II period . . . [the] record is barren of instances comparable to the one before us. Of twelve seizures by President Roosevelt prior to the enactment of the War Labor Disputes Act in June, 1943, three were sanctioned by existing law, and six others were effected after Congress, on December 8, 1941, had declared the existence of a state of war. In this case, reliance on the powers that flow from declared war has been commendably disclaimed by the Solicitor General. Thus the list of executive assertions of the power of seizure in circumstances comparable to the present reduces to three in the six-month period from June to December of 1941. . . . [I]t suffices to say that these three isolated instances do not add up, either in number, scope, duration or contemporaneous legal justification, to the kind of executive construction of the Constitution . . . [necessary to justify the action here]. Nor do they come to us sanctioned by long-continued acquiescence of Congress giving decisive weight to a construction by the Executive of its powers. . . .

A scheme of government like ours no doubt at times feels the lack of power to act with complete, all-embracing swiftly moving authority. No doubt a government with distributed authority, subject to be challenged in the courts of law, at least long enough to consider and adjudicate the challenge, labors under restrictions from which other governments are free. It has not been our tradition to envy such governments. In any event our government was designed to have such restrictions. I know no more impressive words on this subject than those of Mr. Justice Brandeis:

> The doctrine of the separation of powers was adopted by the Convention of 1787, not to promote efficiency but to preclude the exercise of arbitrary

---

[2] 272 U.S. 52 (1926), 47 S. Ct. 21, 71 L. Ed. 160.

power. The purpose was, not to avoid friction, but, by means of the inevitable friction incident to the distribution of the governmental powers among three departments, to save the people from autocracy.[3]

* * * *

MR. JUSTICE DOUGLAS, concurring.

[In his opinion Justice Douglas, after emphasizing that the case could not be decided upon the basis of "which branch of government can deal most expeditiously with the present crisis", but only on the basis of "the allocation of powers under the Constitution," stated that "the legislative nature of the action taken by the President [was, to him] . . . clear." Even though the seizure was temporary it constituted, the Justice observed, a "condemnation of property for which the United States must pay compensation." The President, he argued, has no power to "raise revenues." That power "is in the Congress." The President "might seize and the Congress by subsequent action might ratify the seizure. But until and unless Congress acted, no condemnation would be lawful." Thus, he concluded, the "branch of government that has the power to pay compensation for a seizure is the only one able to authorize a seizure."]

MR. JUSTICE JACKSON, concurring in the judgment and opinion of the Court. . . .

* * * *

The actual art of governing under our Constitution does not and cannot conform to judicial definitions of the power of any of its branches based on isolated clauses or even single Articles torn from context. While the Constitution diffuses power the better to secure liberty, it also contemplates that practice will integrate the disperse powers into a workable government. It enjoins upon its branches separateness but interdependence, autonomy but reciprocity. Presidential powers are not fixed but fluctuate, depending upon their disjunction or conjunction with those of Congress. We may well begin by a somewhat over-simplified grouping of practical situations in which a President may doubt, or others may challenge, his power, and by distinguishing roughly the legal consequences of this factor of relativity.

1. When the President acts pursuant to an express or implied authorization of Congress, his authority is at its maximum, for it includes all that he possesses in his own right plus all that Congress can delegate. In these circumstances, and in these only, may he be said (for what it may be worth) to personify the federal sovereignty. If his act is held unconstitutional under these circumstances, it usually means that the Federal Government as an undivided whole lacks power. A seizure executed by the President pursuant to an Act of Congress would be supported by the strongest of presumptions and the widest latitude of judicial interpretation, and the burden of persuasion would rest heavily upon any who might attack it.

---

[3] *Myers v. United States*, 272 U.S. 52, 293.

2. When the President acts in absence of either a congressional grant or denial of authority, he can only rely upon his own independent powers, but there is a zone of twilight in which he and Congress may have concurrent authority, or in which its distribution is uncertain. Therefore, congressional inertia, indifference or quiescence may sometimes, at least as a practical matter, enable, if not invite measures on independent presidential responsibility. In this area, any actual test of power is likely to depend on the imperatives of events and contemporary imponderables rather than on abstract theories of law.

3. When the President takes measures incompatible with the expressed or implied will of Congress, his power is at its lowest ebb, for then he can rely only upon his own constitutional powers minus any constitutional powers of Congress over the matter. Courts can sustain exclusive presidential control in such a case only by disabling the Congress from acting upon the subject. Presidential claim to a power at once so conclusive and preclusive must be scrutinized with caution, for what is at stake is the equilibrium established by our constitutional system.

Into which of these classifications does this executive seizure of the steel industry fit? It is eliminated from the first by admission, for it is conceded that no congressional authorization exists for this seizure. That takes away also the support of the many precedents and declarations which were made in relation, and must be confined, to this category.

Can it then be defended under flexible tests available to the second category? It seems clearly eliminated from that class because Congress has not left seizure of private property an open field but has covered it by three statutory policies inconsistent with this seizure. . . .

This leaves the current seizure to be justified only by the severe tests under the third grouping, where it can be supported only by any remainder of executive power after subtraction of such powers as Congress may have over the subject. In short, we can sustain the President only by holding that seizure of such strike-bound industries is within his domain and beyond control by Congress. . . .

I did not suppose, and I am not persuaded, that history leaves it open to question, at least in the courts, that the executive branch, like the Federal Government as a whole, possesses only delegated powers. The purpose of the Constitution was not only to grant power, but to keep it from getting out of hand. However, because the President does not enjoy unmentioned powers does not mean that the mentioned ones should be narrowed by a niggardly construction. Some clauses could be made almost unworkable, as well as immutable, by refusal to indulge some latitude of interpretation for changing times. I have heretofore, and do now, give to the enumerated powers the scope and elasticity afforded by what seems to be reasonable practical implications instead of the rigidity dictated by a doctrinaire textualism.

The Solicitor General seeks the power of seizure in three clauses of the Executive Article, the first reading, "The executive Power shall be vested in a President of the United States of America." Lest I be though to exaggerate, I quote the interpretation which his brief puts upon it: "In our view, this clause constitutes a grant of all the executive powers of which the Government is capable." If that be true, it is difficult to see why the forefathers bothered to add several specific items, including some trifling ones.

The example of such unlimited executive power that must have most impressed the forefathers was the prerogative exercised by George III, and the description of its evils in the Declaration of Independence leads me to doubt that they were creating their new Executive in his image. . . . I cannot accept the view that this clause is a grant in bulk of all conceivable executive power but regard it as an allocation to the presidential office of the generic powers thereafter stated.

* * * *

[At this point Justice Jackson rejects the Government's argument that the President's seizure of the steel mills was sanctioned by his constitutional powers as "Commander-in-Chief"].

* * * *

The third clause in which the Solicitor General finds seizure powers is that "he shall take Care that the Laws be faithfully executed. . . ." That authority must be matched against words of the Fifth Amendment that "No person shall be . . . deprived of life, liberty, or property, without due process of law. . . ." One gives a governmental authority that reaches so far as there is law, the other gives a private right that authority shall go no farther. These signify about all there is of the principle that ours is a government of laws, not of men, and that we submit ourselves to rulers only if under rules.

The Solicitor General lastly grounds support of the seizure upon nebulous, inherent powers never expressly granted but said to have accrued to the office from the customs and claims of preceding administrations. The plea is for a resulting power to deal with a crisis or an emergency according to the necessities of the case, the unarticulated assumption being that necessity knows no law.

Loose and irresponsible use of adjectives colors all non-legal and much legal discussion of presidential powers. "Inherent" powers, "implied" powers, "inciden-tal" powers, "plenary" powers, "war" powers and "emergency" powers are used, often interchangeably and without fixed or ascertainable meanings.

The vagueness and generality of the clauses that set forth presidential powers afford a plausible basis for pressures within and without an administration for presidential action beyond that supported by those whose responsibility it is to defend his actions in court. The claim of inherent and unrestricted presidential powers has long been a persuasive dialectical weapon in political controversy. While it is not surprising that counsel should grasp support from such unadjudi-cated claims of power, a judge cannot accept self-serving press statements of the attorney for one of the interested parties as authority in answering a constitutional question, even if the advocate was himself. But prudence has counseled that actual reliance on such nebulous claims stop short of provoking a judicial test.

* * * *

Mr. Justice Burton, concurring in both the opinion and judgment of the Court.

[T]his emergency [can be distinguished] from one in which Congress takes no action and outlines no governmental policy. . . . The controlling fact here is that Congress, within its constitutionally delegated power, has prescribed for the

President specific procedures, exclusive of seizure, for his use in meeting the present type of emergency. Congress has reserved to itself the right to determine where and when to authorize the seizure of property in meeting such an emergency. Under these circumstances, the President's order . . . invaded the jurisdiction of Congress. It violated the essence of the principle of the separation of governmental powers. Accordingly, the injunction against its effectiveness should be sustained.

MR. JUSTICE CLARK, concurring in the judgment of the Court.

One of this Court's first pronouncements upon the powers of the President under the Constitution was made by Mr. Chief Justice John Marshall some one hundred and fifty years ago. In *Little v. Barreme*[4] he used this characteristically clear language in discussing the power of the President to instruct the seizure of the *Flying Fish*, a vessel bound from a French port: "It is by no means clear that the president of the United States whose high duty it is to 'take care that the laws be faithfully executed,' and who is commander in chief of the armies and navies of the United States, might not, without any special authority for that purpose, in the then existing state of things, have empowered the officers commanding the armed vessels of the United States, to seize and send into port for adjudication, American vessels which were forfeited by being engaged in this illicit commerce. But when it is observed that [an act of Congress] gives a special authority to seize on the high seas, and limits that authority to the seizure of vessels bound or sailing to a French port, the legislature seem to have prescribed that the manner in which this law shall be carried into execution, was to exclude a seizure of any vessel not bound to a French port." Accordingly, a unanimous Court held that the President's instructions had been issued without authority and that they could not "legalize an act which without those instructions would have been a plain trespass." I know of no subsequent holding of this Court to the contrary.

The limits of presidential power are obscure. However, Article II, no less than Article I, is part of "a constitution intended to endure for ages to come, and consequently, to be adapted to the various crises of human affairs. . . ."

I conclude that where Congress has laid down specific procedures to deal with the type of crisis confronting the President, he must follow those procedures in meeting the crisis; but that in the absence of such action by Congress, the President's independent power to act depends upon the gravity of the situation confronting the nation. I cannot sustain the seizure in question because here, as in *Little v. Barreme*, Congress had prescribed methods to be followed by the President in meeting the emergency at hand.

* * * *

MR. JUSTICE VINSON, with whom MR. JUSTICE REED and MR. JUSTICE MINTON join, dissenting.

* * * *

In passing upon the question of Presidential powers in this case, we must first consider the context in which those powers were exercised. Those who suggest that

---

[4] 6 U.S. (2 Cranch) 170 (1804).

this is a case involving extraordinary powers should be mindful that these are extraordinary times. A world not yet recovered from the devastation of World War II has been forced to face the threat of another and more terrifying global conflict.

Accepting in full measure its responsibility in the world community, the United States was instrumental in securing adoption of the United Nations Charter, approved by the Senate by a vote of 89 to 2. . . . In 1950, when the United Nations called upon member nations "to render every assistance" to repel aggression in Korea, the United States furnished its vigorous support. For almost two full years, our armed forces have been fighting in Korea, suffering casualties of over 108,000 men. Hostilities have not abated. The "determination of the United Nations to continue its action in Korea to meet the aggression" has been reaffirmed. Congressional support of the action in Korea has been manifested by provisions for increased military manpower and equipment and for economic stabilization. . . .

> [At this point the Chief Justice reviews a host of legislative measures including the provision of aid to Greece and Turkey (the "Truman Plan"); adherence to the NATO treaty, the appropriation of $130 billion for defense since the June, 1950, attack in Korea; the appropriation of over $5-1/2 billion for military assistance in fiscal year 1952, to be increased to $7 billion for fiscal year 1953; and an authorization for increasing the armed forces of the United States to over 3.5 million men.]

* * * *

Congress recognized the impact of these defense programs upon the economy. Following the attack in Korea, the President asked for authority to requisition property and to allocate and fix priorities for scarce goods. In the Defense Production Act of 1950, Congress granted the powers requested and, *in addition*, granted power to stabilize prices and wages and to provide for settlement of labor disputes arising in the defense program. . . .

The President has the duty to execute the foregoing legislative programs. Their successful execution depends upon continued production of steel and stabilized prices for steel. Accordingly, when the collective bargaining agreements between the Nation's steel producers and their employees . . . were due to expire . . . the President acted to avert a completed shutdown of steel production. . . . [H]e certified the dispute to the Wage Stabilization Board [as provided for in the Defense Production Act], requesting that the Board investigate [and recommend a] settlement. [As a result, the strike was delayed while the matter was before the Board]. . . . After [the Board] submitted its report and recommendations to the President . . . [the recommendations were accepted by] the Union but rejected by plaintiffs. The Union [then] gave notice of its intention to strike, but bargaining between the parties continued with hope of settlement. After bargaining failed . . . the President issued [his order]. . . . Twelve days passed without action by Congress. On April 21, 1952, the President sent a letter to the President of the Senate in which he again described the purpose and need for his action and again stated his position that "The Congress can, if it wishes, reject the course of action I have followed in this matter." Congress has not so acted to this date.

Meanwhile, plaintiffs instituted this action in the District Court to compel defendant to return possession of the [seized] steel mills. In . . . [that action] Secretary of Defense Lovett swore that "a work stoppage in the steel industry will result immediately in serious curtailment of production of essential weapons and munitions of all kinds." He illustrated by showing that 84% of the national production of certain alloy steel is currently used for production of military-end items and that 35% of total production of another form of steel goes into ammunition, 80% of such ammunition now going to Korea. . . .

Even ignoring for the moment whatever confidential information the President may possess as "the Nation's organ for foreign affairs," the uncontroverted affidavits in this record amply support the finding that "a work stoppage would immediately jeopardize and imperil our national defense.". . . . Accordingly, if the President has any power under the Constitution to meet a critical situation in the absence of express statutory authorization, there is no basis whatever for criticizing the exercise of such power in this case.

* * * *

Admitting that the Government could seize the mills, plaintiffs claim that the implied power of eminent domain can be exercised only after an Act of Congress; under no circumstances, they say, can that power be exercised by the President unless he can point to an express provision in enabling legislation. This was the view adopted by the District Judge when he granted the preliminary injunction. . . .

Under this view, the President is left powerless at the very moment when the need for action may be most pressing and when no one, other than he, is immediately capable of action. Under this view, he is left powerless because a power not expressly given to Congress is nevertheless found to rest exclusively with Congress.

Consideration of this view of executive impotence calls for further examination of the nature of the separation of powers under our triparite system of Government. [In so doing] . . . we must never forget . . . [that cases can] arise presenting questions which could not have been foreseen by the Framers. . . . In such cases, the Constitution has been treated as a living document adaptable to new situations. But we are not called upon today to expand the Constitution to meet a new situation. For, in this case, we need only look to history and time-honored principles of constitutional law — principles that have been applied consistently by all branches of the Government throughout our history. It is those who assert the invalidity of the Executive Order who seek to amend the Constitution in this case.

[Here the Chief Justice commences an extensive review of past executive actions which, he states, "demonstrate that our Presidents have on many occasions exhibited the leadership contemplated by the Framers, when they made the President Commander in Chief, and imposed upon him the trust to "take Care that the Laws be faithfully executed!" These examples include President Washington's enforcement of the national revenue laws when those laws were openly flouted in some sections of Pennsylvania, Washington's

Proclamation of Neutrality, discussed *infra*. President John Adams' extradition of Jonathan Robbins and the circumstances leading to the decision in *In Re Neagle* which he discusses as follows:]

In Re Neagle[5] . . . this Court held that a federal officer had acted in line of duty when he was guarding a Justice of this Court riding circuit. It was conceded that there was no specific statute authorizing the President to assign such a guard. In holding that such a statute was not necessary, the Court broadly stated the question as follows:

> [The President] is enabled to fulfill the duty of his great department, expressed in the phrase that "he shall take Care that the laws be faithfully executed." Is this duty limited to the enforcement of acts of Congress or of Treaties of the United States according to their express terms, or does it include the rights, duties and obligations growing out of the Constitution itself, our international relations, and all the protection implied by the nature of the government under the Constitution?

The latter approach was emphatically adopted by the Court.

> [The Chief Justice's review continues with mention of President Hayes' use of Federal troops during the railroad strike of 1877, Cleveland's use of troops in the Pullman strike of 1895, neither of which actions were authorized by statute, President Taft's decision to withdraw federal oil lands from sale "[i]n aid of proposed legislation," an action approved by the Supreme Court in *United States v. Mid-West Oil*[6] President Wilson's establishment of the War Labor Board during World War I, his seizure of the nation's railroads, President Roosevelt's declaration of a bank-holiday, his acquisition of base-rights from Britain, the decision to protect Iceland from Axis attacks, seizure of strike-bound aviation and shipbuilding plants just before Pearl Harbor, and the seizure after the outbreak of war of five other plants and of the nation's coalmines.]

* * * *

This is but a cursory summary of executive leadership. But it amply demonstrates that Presidents have taken prompt action to enforce the laws and protect the country whether or not Congress happened to provide in advance for the particular method of execution. . . . The fact that temporary executive seizures of industrial plants to meet an emergency have not been directly tested in this Court furnishes not the slightest suggestions that such actions have been illegal. . . .

Focusing now on the situation confronting the President on the night of April 8, 1952, we cannot but conclude that the President was performing his duty under the Constitution to "take Care that the Laws be faithfully executed" — a duty described by President Benjamin Harrison as "the central idea of the office."

The President reported to Congress the morning after the seizure that he acted because a work stoppage in steel production would immediately imperil the safety of the Nation. . . . And, while a shutdown could be averted by granting the price

---

[5] 135 U.S. 1, 10 S. Ct. 658, 34 L. Ed. 55, 1890.
[6] 236 U.S. 459 (1915).

concessions requested by the plaintiffs, granting such concessions would disrupt the price stabilization program also enacted by Congress. Rather than fail to execute either legislative program, the President acted to execute both.

* * * *

The absence of a specific statute authorizing seizure of the steel mills as a mode of executing the laws — both the military procurement program and the anti-inflation program — has not until today been thought to prevent the President from executing the laws. . . .

There is no statute prohibiting seizure as a method of enforcing legislative programs. Congress has in no wise indicated that its legislation is not to be executed by the taking of private property (subject of course to the payment of just compensation) if its legislation cannot otherwise be executed.

Whatever the extent of Presidential power on more tranquil occasions, and whatever the right of the President to execute legislative programs as he sees fit without reporting the mode of execution to Congress, the single Presidential purpose disclosed on this record is to faithfully execute the laws by acting in an emergency to maintain the status quo, thereby preventing collapse of the legislative programs until Congress could act.

* * * *

Plaintiffs place their primary emphasis on the Labor Management Relations Act of 1947, hereinafter referred to as the Taft-Hartley Act, but do not contend that that Act contains any provision prohibiting seizure. . . . [Moreover] plaintiffs admit that the emergency procedures of Taft-Hartley are not mandatory. Nevertheless, plaintiffs apparently argue that, since Congress did provide the 80-day injunction method for dealing with emergency strikes, the President cannot claim that an emergency exists until the procedures of Taft-Hartley have been exhausted. . . . Whatever merit the argument might have had following the enactment of Taft-Hartley, it loses all force when viewed in light of the statutory pattern confronting the President in this case.

> [At this point the Chief Justice reviews the procedures established for the settlement of labor disputes under Title V of the Defense Production Act of 1950.]

* * * *

Accordingly, as of December 22, 1951, the President had a choice between alternate procedures for settling the threatened strike in the steel mills: one route created to deal with peacetime disputes [Taft-Hartley]; the other route specially created to deal with disputes growing out of the defense and stabilization program [Defense Production Act]. There is no question of by-passing a statutory procedure because both of the routes available to the President in December were based upon statutory authorization. Both routes were available in the steel dispute. The Union, by refusing to abide by the defense and stabilization program, could have forced the President to invoke Taft-Hartley at that time to delay the strike a maximum of 80 days. Instead, the Union agreed to cooperate with the defense program and submit the dispute to the Wage Stabilization Board.

Plaintiffs had no objection whatever at that time to the President's choice of the WSB route. As a result, the strike was postponed, a WSB panel held hearings and reported the position of the parties and the WSB recommended the terms of a settlement which it found were fair and equitable. . . . Thereafter, the parties bargained on the basis of the WSB recommendation.

When the President acted on April 8, he had exhausted the procedures for settlement available to him. Taft-Hartley was a route parallel to, not connected with, the WSB procedure. The strike had been delayed 99 days as contrasted with the maximum delay of 80 days under Taft-Hartley. There had been a hearing on the issues in dispute and bargaining which promised settlement up to the very hour before seizure, had broken down. Faced with immediate national peril through stoppage in steel production on the one hand and faced with destruction of the wage and price legislative programs on the other, the President took temporary possession of the steel mills as the only course open to him consistent with his duty to take care that the laws be faithfully executed.

Before and after the *Steel Seizure* case, exponents of an expansive executive power have relied on language by Justice Sutherland in the following case.

UNITED STATES v. CURTISS-WRIGHT EXPORT CORP.

United States Supreme Court
299 U.S. 304, 57 S. Ct. 216, 81 L. Ed. 255 (1936)

[In 1934 Congress adopted a Joint Resolution which provided that "if the President finds that the prohibition of the sale of arms and munitions of war in the United States to those countries now engaged in armed conflict in the Chaco may contribute to the re-establishment of peace between those countries, and if . . . he makes a proclamation to that effect, it shall be unlawful" to make such a sale "except under such limitations and exceptions as the President prescribes." Severe penalties were provided for violation of the Joint Resolution[7] and Presidential Proclamation. The President made such a proclamation. Appellee was indicted for conspiracy to sell arms to Bolivia — a country then engaged in armed conflict in the Chaco. The District Court sustained appellee's demurrer on the ground that the Resolution contained an unconstitutional delegation of legislative power to the President.]

---

[7] Resolution passed by a majority of both Houses of Congress, signed by the President and thus having the force of law. Congressional Research Service, Library of Congress, The Constitution of the United States of America; Analysis and Interpretation, 127-128.

Mr. Justice Sutherland delivered the opinion of the Court. . . .

Whether, if the Joint Resolution had related solely to internal affairs it would be open to the challenge that it constituted an unlawful delegation of legislative power to the Executive, we find it unnecessary to determine. The whole aim of the resolution is to affect a situation entirely external to the United States and falling within the category of foreign affairs. The determination which we are called to make, therefore, is whether the Joint Resolution, as applied to that situation, is vulnerable to attack under the rule that forbids a delegation of the law-making power. In other words, assuming (but not deciding) that the challenged delegation, if it were confined to internal affairs, would be invalid, may it nevertheless be sustained on the ground that its exclusive aim is to afford a remedy for a hurtful condition within foreign territory?

It will contribute to the elucidation of the question if we first consider the differences between the powers of the federal government in respect of foreign or external affairs and those in respect of domestic or internal affairs. . . .

The two classes of powers are different, both in respect of their origin and their nature. The broad statement that the federal government can exercise no powers except those specifically enumerated in the Constitution, and such implied powers as are necessary and proper to carry into effect the enumerated powers, is categorically true only in respect of our internal affairs. In that field, the primary purpose of the Constitution was to carve from the general mass of legislative powers *then possessed by the states* such portions as it was thought desirable to vest in the federal government, leaving those not included in the enumeration still in the states. . . . That this doctrine applies only to powers which the states had is self-evident. And since the states severally never possessed international powers, such powers could not have been carved from the mass of state powers but obviously were transmitted to the United States from some other source. During the colonial period, those powers were possessed exclusively by and were entirely under the control of the Crown. By the Declaration of Independence, "the Representatives of the United States of America" declared the United (not the several) Colonies to be free and independent states, and as such to have "full Power to levy War, conclude Peace, contract Alliances, establish Commerce and to do all other Acts and Things which Independent States may of right do."

As a result of the separation from Great Britain by the colonies, acting as a unit, the powers of external sovereignty passed from the Crown not to the colonies severally, but to the colonies in their collective and corporate capacity as the United States of America. Even before the Declaration, the colonies were a unit in foreign affairs, acting through a common agency — namely, the Continental Congress, composed of delegates from the thirteen colonies. That agency exercised the powers of war and peace, raised an army, created a navy, and finally adopted the Declaration of Independence. Rulers come and go; governments end and forms of government change; but sovereignty survives. A political society cannot endure without a supreme will somewhere. Sovereignty is never held in suspense. When, therefore, the external sovereignty of Great Britain in respect of the colonies ceased, it immediately passed to the Union.

The Union existed before the Constitution, which was ordained and established among other things to form "a more perfect Union." Prior to that event, it is clear that the Union, declared by the Articles of Confederation to be "perpetual," was the sole possessor of external sovereignty, and in the Union it remained without change save in so far as the Constitution in express terms qualified its exercise.

* * * *

It results that the investment of the federal government with the powers of external sovereignty did not depend upon the affirmative grants of the Constitution. The powers to declare and wage war, to conclude peace, to make treaties, to maintain diplomatic relations with other sovereignties, if they had never been mentioned in the Constitution, would have vested in the federal government as necessary concomitants of nationality. . . .

Not only, as we have shown, is the federal power over external affairs in origin and essential character different from that over internal affairs, but participation in the exercise of the power is significantly limited. In this vast external realm, with its important, complicated, delicate and manifold problems, the President alone has the power to speak or listen as a representative of the nation. He makes treaties with the advice and consent of the Senate; but he alone negotiates. Into the field of negotiation the Senate cannot intrude; and Congress itself is powerless to invade it. As Marshall said in his great argument of March 7, 1800, in the House of Representatives:

> The President is the sole organ of the nation in its external relations, and its sole representative with foreign nations. . . . The President is the constitutional representative of the United States with regard to foreign nations. He manages our concerns with foreign nations and must necessarily be most competent to determine when, how, and upon what subjects negotiation may be urged with the greatest prospect of success. For his conduct he is responsible to the Constitution. The committee consider this responsibility the surest pledge for the faithful discharge of his duty. They think the interference of the Senate in the direction of foreign negotiations calculated to diminish that responsibility and thereby to impair the best security for the national safety. The nature of transactions with foreign nations, moreover, requires caution and unity of design, and their success frequently depends on secrecy and dispatch. . . .

It is important to bear in mind that we are here dealing not alone with an authority vested in the President by an exertion of legislative power, but with such an authority plus the very delicate, plenary and exclusive power of the President as the sole organ of the federal government in the field of international relations — a power which does not require as a basis for its exercise an act of Congress, but which, of course, like every other governmental power, must be exercised in subordination to the applicable provisions of the Constitution. It is quite apparent that if, in the maintenance of our international relations, embarrassment — perhaps serious embarrassment — is to be avoided and success for our aims achieved, congressional legislation which is to be made effective through negotiation and inquiry within the international field must often accord to the President a degree of discretion and freedom from statutory restriction which would not be admissible were domestic affairs alone involved. Moreover, he, not Congress, has the better opportunity of knowing the conditions which prevail in foreign countries, and especially is this true in time of war. He has his confidential sources of information. He has his agents in the form of diplomatic, consular and other officials. Secrecy in respect of information gathered by them may be highly necessary, and the premature disclosure of it productive of harmful results.

When the President is to be authorized by legislation to act in respect of a matter intended to affect a situation in foreign territory, the legislator properly bears in mind the important consideration that the form of the President's action — or, indeed, whether he shall act at all — may well depend, among other things, upon the nature of the confidential information which he has or may thereafter receive, or upon the effect which his action may have upon our foreign relations. This consideration . . . discloses the unwisdom of requiring Congress in this field of governmental power to lay down narrowly definite standards by which the President is to be governed. . . .

In the light of the foregoing observations, it is evident that this court should not be in haste to apply a general rule which will have the effect of condemning legislation like that under review as constituting an unlawful delegation of legislative power. The principles which justify such legislation find overwhelming support in the unbroken legislative practice which has prevailed almost from the inception of the national government to the present day. . . .

[B]oth upon principle and in accordance with precedent, we conclude there is sufficient warrant for the broad discretion vested in the President to determine whether the enforcement of the statute will have a beneficial effect upon the reestablishment of peace in the affected countries; whether he shall make proclamation to bring the resolution into operation; whether and when the resolution shall cease to operate and to make proclamation accordingly; and to prescribe limitations and exceptions to which the enforcement of the resolution shall be subject. . . .

[The Court reversed the judgment below and remanded the case for further proceedings. JUSTICE REYNOLDS dissented without opinion.]

NOTES AND QUESTIONS

(1) According to Justice Black the decision to seize the steel mills was a decision that Congress had to make, albeit with the President's assent; it was a legislative decision. In form, however, the decision was manifested in a one-time directive ordering the Secretary of Commerce to seize particular mills. This is certainly not the form legislation normally takes. What was it then, in the nature of the decision, that led Justice Black to call it legislating? Reflect on the broader implications of this characterization for the allocation between President and Congress of the basic Constitutional authority to make decisons for the Nation.

(2) Does Justice Frankfurter agree with Justice Black? What gloss would he lay on Justice Black's sweeping characterization of the function of Congress? Note, also, that Justice Frankfurter finds most of the support for his position in the "Separation of Powers" doctrine. What does he see as the overriding function of that doctrine?

(3) Justice Jackson's opinion is certainly the best known and most often cited of the Court opinions in the *Steel Seizure* case. Notice that the Justice devotes little attention to how the President's action should be characterized: legislative or executive. Yet, his tripartite classification assumes the answer. More telling, his rejection of any thought that the President possesses "inherent" or "plenary" or "implied" or "emergency" powers or that the "executive Power" clause is the source of an independent Presidential authority makes clear, does it not, that he agrees with Justice Black?

This part of the opinion, though less frequently noted, is nevertheless important for it was Justice Jackson, when he was Attorney General of the United States, who invoked these very same "adjectives" to support his conclusion that the President had independent authority to furnish Great Britain with 40 overage destroyers during World War II.[8] Note the function that the Justice assigns these claims. What are the implications of that function? Law as politics? How should that impact the judiciary's perspective on these matters.[9]

The most celebrated part of the Justice's opinion centers on the dynamics of the Presidential-Congressional relationship. In this he may be thought to have a different, perhaps more flexible, conception of the Separation of Powers doctrine than Justice Black. As he articulates it, the doctrine must respond to two, perhaps contradictory, imperatives. What are they?

How expansive is the "zone of twilight"? Suppose that Congress had never addressed the question of whether to give the President authority to seize strike-bound industries, and suppose that, before seizing the steel mills, the President had sent proposed legislation to Congress giving him the necessary authority and underscoring the emergency that faced the Nation. Suppose the bill died in a Senate or House Committee. Could the President, under Justice Jackson's view, act unilaterally? Or, would you have to know more? If the President could act, yet, according to Justice Jackson, possesses no "inherent" or "emergency" powers, what is the source of his power?

(4) Consider next Justice Clark's opinion. Had Congress not considered the question of Presidential seizure of strike-bound plants, would Justice Clark have upheld the President's action in this case? If so, what, according to the Justice, would be the source of his authority to act? Consider Chief Justice Marshall's opinion in *Little v. Barreme* upon which Justice Clark relies heavily. What source of Presidential authority does Marshall rely upon in suggesting that had Congress not legislated on the subject, the President could have ordered seizure of the Flying Fish? Does Marshall's opinion support Justice Clark's theory as to the source of Presidential power to act in the absence of a congressional directive?

(5) Does Chief Justice Vinson in support of the President rely on the text of the Constitution or on some "inherent," "emergency" or "foreign relations" power in the President to act under these circumstances? If it is the latter, why then the elaborate discussion of the legislative measures taken by Congress to support the Korean War, NATO, etc. and why the reliance on *In re Neagle*? In terms of their

---

[8] 39 Op. Atty. Gen. August 27, 1940 at page 484.

[9] The reader should keep these observations in mind when considering Chief Justice Rehnquist's opinion in *Goldwater v. Carter*, *infra* page 1036. Mischievous?

basic theories concerning the nature and sources of Presidential power, is Chief Justice Vinson closer to Justice Clark or Justice Black? In light of this, how does the Chief Justice get around the action Congress had taken in 1947 when it was considering the Taft Hartley amendments to the National Labor Relations Act?

(6) Again suppose Congress had never considered the question of whether to give the President power to seize strike-bound plants. What would have been the likely outcome of the case? Five to four (six to three) in favor of the President? An amplitude of Presidential power without having to resort, except for Justice Clark, to vaque notions of an "inherent" or "plenary" or "foreign relations" or "emergency" power? Miracles of Miracles! The Separation of Powers can survive the vicissitudes of foreign relations!

(7) Viewed against the background of the several opinions in the *Steel Seizure* case Justice Sutherland's work in *Curtiss-Wright* needs a closer look. First, while the Justice's theory concerning the sources of the Federal Government's power over foreign relations has been the subject of considerable criticism,[10] it has nevertheless been clear from the beginning that internationally the United States is one sovereign nation and that the authority to maintain and conduct relations with other sovereign states belongs to the Federal Government alone. Nowhere, however, is this stated in the Constitution. Henkin has illustrated the point and, in so doing, raised a central issue of interpretative method:

> The Constitution does not delegate a "power to conduct foreign relations" to the federal government or confer it upon any of its branches. Congress is given power to regulate commerce with foreign nations, to define offenses against the law of nations, to declare war, and the President the power to make treaties and send and receive ambassadors, but these hardly add up to the power to conduct foreign relations. Where is the power to recognize other states or governments, to maintain or break diplomatic relations,[11] . . . to acquire or cede territory . . . indeed to determine all the attitudes and carry out all the details in the myriads of relationships with other nations that are "the foreign policy" and "the foreign relations" of the United States? The power to make treaties is granted, but where is the power to break, denounce, or terminate them? The power to declare war is there, but where is the power to make peace, to proclaim neutrality in the wars of others, to recognize or deny right to belligerents or insurgents?. . . . Congress can regulate foreign commerce but where is the power to make other laws relating to our foreign relations — to regulate immigration, or the status and rights of aliens, or activities of citizens at home or abroad. . . .? These "missing" powers, and a host of others, were clearly intended for and have always been exercised by the federal government, but where does the Constitution say that it shall be so?

> Traditional interpreters of the Constitution have attempted to find the missing powers by traditional doctrines of Constitutional construction. Foreign affairs powers expressly granted have been held to imply others. . . .

---

[10] Levitan, *The Foreign Relations Power: An Analysis Of Mr. Justice Sutherland's Theory*, 55 Yale L.J. 467 (1946); Lofgren, *United States v. Curtiss-Wright Export Corporation: An Historical Assessment*, 83 Yale L.J. 1 (1973).

[11] How about power to receive ambassadors? - Ed.

Foreign affairs powers . . . have been spun also from general grants of power and from designations read as grants, for example, the ["necessary and proper clause"] (Art. I, sec. 8) or the ["executive Power clause"] (Art. II, sec. 1). Additional powers for the Federal Government might be inferred from their express denial to the States.

The attempt to build all the foreign affairs powers of the federal government with a few bricks provided by the Constitution has not been accepted as successful. It requires considerable stretching of language, much reading between lines, and bold extrapolation from 'the Constitution as a whole' and that still does not plausibly add up to all the power which the federal government in fact exercises.[12]

How would Justice Sutherland fill the lacunae which Henkin purports to find between the Constitutional text, on the one hand, and Constitutional practice and the framers' intention, on the other?

(8) Is Justice Sutherland's concept of the President's "delicate, plenary and exclusive power . . . in the field of foreign relations" somehow linked to, or dependant upon, his theory regarding the sources of the Federal Government's power in that field? If, through a generous interpretation, the enumerations of the Constitution are thought sufficient to establish the plenary authority of the Federal Government over foreign affairs, those enumerations also tend to carry with them a certain allocation of the power between President and Congress. On the face of it, that allocation seems difficult to square with Justice Sutherland's expansive vision of the presidential office.

On the other hand, if you can only explain the foreign relations power of the Federal Government by going outside the text, as Henkin seems to suggest, the allocation of that power between President and Congress is also left substantially free from the constraints of the constitutional text. In this latter event, the question becomes, what allocative principle is to be substituted for instruction from the text itself? Again, Henkin suggests:

It seems to have been assumed [by the framers] that [the undifferentiated bundle of powers inherent in sovereignty] . . . are distributed "naturally," those that are "legislative in character" to Congress, those "executive" to the President, with apparently, also, a judicial foreign affairs power lodged in the federal courts. Perhaps that assumption is "natural" and "logical", but its principle of division is hardly self defining.[13]

(9) Among the earliest attempts at a "natural" allocation of the foreign affairs powers among the several branches of government is Hamilton's famous defense of Washington's Proclamation of Neutrality.[14] In 1793, President Washington determined that the United States should not become embroiled in the war between France and Great Britain and accordingly issued a Proclamation declaring America's neutrality and instructing the several United States' attorneys to prosecute anyone violating the international law of neutrality. Hamilton, in his

---

[12] Henkin, Foreign Affairs And The Constitution, 17-18 (1972).
[13] *Id.* at page 27.
[14] 1 Messages and Papers Of The Presidents 148 (Richardson, Ed.) (1897).

now famous *Pacificus* letters, undertook to defend the constitutionality of the President's actions.

The "executive Power clause" of Article II, Hamilton contended, was more than a designation. It establish[d] . . . that the "executive power shall be vested in a President of the United States." Next, he noted, that same article "delineate[s] particular cases of executive power," and argued that it would not "consist with the rules of sound construction to consider this enumeration of authorities, as derogating from the more comprehensive grant in the general clause, further than as it may be coupled with express restrictions or limitations; as [for example] in regard to the cooperation of the Senate in the appointment of officers, and the making of treaties." Such limitations, he added, were to be "strictly construed." Thus, "[t]he general doctrine of our Constitution . . . is," he concluded, "that the executive power of the nation [interpreted in conformity with other parts of the Constitution, and with the principle of free government] is vested in the President; subject only to the *exceptions* and *qualifications* which are expressed in the instrument." (Emphasis in the original).

With this textual foundation, Hamilton proceeds to explain why issuance of the Proclamation was "naturally" an executive function. First, he states the case against legislative issuance:

> The legislative department is not the *organ* of intercourse between the United States and foreign nations. It is charged neither with *making* or *interpreting* treaties. It is therefore not naturally that member of the government, with regard to foreign powers, or to admonish the citizens of their obligations and duties in consequence; still less is it charged with enforcing the observance of those obligations and duties.

Then, he states the case for executive issuance:

> It appears to be connected with the [executive] department in various capacities. As the *organ* of intercourse between the nation and foreign nations; as the *interpreter* of the national treaties, in those cases in which the judiciary is not competent; . . . as the *power* which is charged with the execution of the laws, of which treaties form a part, as that which is charged with the command and disposition of the public force.[15]

Hamilton's construction is laced with difficulties, is it not? Consider, for example:

(a) If the "executive Power" clause were intended as a general grant, why the "take Care" clause? In this instance, doesn't the specific enumeration tend to swallow-up much the most obvious part of the general grant?[16] If the specific enumerations of Article II were merely convenient devices upon which to hang limitations on otherwise "naturally" exclusive executive powers, again, why the "take Care" clause?

(b) Did Hamilton actually need to argue that the "executive Power" clause was a grant of all "naturally" executive authority in order to mount a

---

[15] 2 The Federalist, to which is added Pacificus, William and Whiting, 318-321, New York 1810.

[16] Consult, Holmes, J. in *Myers v. United States*, 272 U.S. 52 (1926) quoted by Justice Frankfurter at page 1000 *supra*.

successful defense of President Washington's Proclamation?[17] Note that Chief Justice Vinson cites the Proclamation as a case supportive of his theory concerning the President's power to seize the steel mills.[18]

(c)   Is the President's function as "organ of intercourse with foreign nations" in any way derived from or dependent upon the "executive Power" clause? In this connection why would the framers have taken pains to confer on the President the power to receive and send ambassadors if that was thought of as a purely ceremonial rather than substantive function? As author of the phrase, "organ of the nation," from what Article II grant did Marshall appear to adduce that power?[19]

(d)   Is the President, as Hamilton implies, the "sole" interpreter of treaties? Might Congress not be permitted, even required, to interpret whether, under a mutual defense treaty for example, the United States was obligated to go to war? If both President and Congress might claim a power to interpret treaties, how could that function be logically laid, insofar as the President is concerned, upon "the executive Power" clause as "naturally" executive? From what other source might it be derived, as Hamilton seems to admit? If President and Senate must both participate in treaty making, in what, if any, sense does the President do so alone? Taken in that sense does the point actually undermine Hamilton's argument?

(e)   On at least one occasion Congress has, in fact, proclaimed United States neutrality in a foreign war.[20] Under current practice, however, it is highly unlikely that Congress would do so again if the proclamation were intended only to advise foreign governments as to the "existing condition of the nation" under international law. Nevertheless, could Congress not direct the President to issue such a proclamation? Upon what constitutional grant might Congress lay a claim of power to issue that directive? What form might such an order take?

(f)   Washington's Proclamation was far more than a statement informing foreign governments of American policy. In the years since 1792, consistent practice supported by some authority[21] has established that neither the rule of a treaty nor of customary international law may be used as the basis for a criminal conviction in the courts of the United States. Legislation is required. In light of this practice, does it lie within the "nature" of the executive office to, as Hamilton claims, both "admonish the citizens of their obligations and duties [as neutrals]" and "to [enforce] the observance of those obligations and duties." In the years since 1793 Congress has enacted a number of so-called "neutrality acts"

---

[17] See Chief Justice Marshall's theory in *Little v. Barreme*, quoted by Justice Clark *supra* page 1004.

[18] It was the extravagance of Hamilton's claims for the President, not a quarrel over the validity of the Proclamation as such, that led Jefferson to urge that Madison reply to Hamilton's Pacificus letters, which he did in the equally famous Helvidius letters.

[19] See *Curtiss-Wright, supra* page 1009.

[20] Chapter XLI, 1 Stat. 372 (1794).

[21] *Over-the-Top*, 5 F. 2d 838, 845 (D. Conn. 1925).

defining conduct (official and private) deemed contrary to a policy of neutrality and imposing criminal penalties upon those convicted of violating that standard.

(10) Perhaps the foregoing questions serve only to point up the technical difficulties of categorizing particular functions as "naturally" executive or "naturally" legislative. Or, perhaps they reflect a basic flaw in the allocative principle itself; in the idea that there is a "natural" allocation of the bundle of foreign affairs powers of the Federal Government? What is the import for the Hamiltonian principle if both President and Congress may, under appropriate circumstances, interpret treaties; or terminate treaties? (See, *Goldwater v. Carter*, discussed page 1036, *infra*). What implication for the Hamiltonian theory follows from the conclusion that the President may proclaim a policy of neutrality and presumably require executive officers to conform their official conduct to that policy, but only Congress can make the violation of neutrality a crime? Does it help to say that the former is "inherently" executive and the latter "inherently" legislative?

(11) In light of your reflections on these questions which statement concerning the general scheme of the Constitution comes closer to the mark; Chief Justice Taft's statement in *Meyers v. United States*, or Justice Brandeis' dissent in that same case? Taft stated:

> [T]he Constitution was so framed as to vest in the Congress all legislative powers therein granted, to vest in the President the Executive power, and to vest in one Supreme Court and such inferior courts as Congress might establish, the judicial power. From this division, on principle, the reasonable construction of the Constitution must be that the branches must be kept separate in all cases in which they are not expressly blended, and the Constitution should be expounded to blend them no more than it affirmatively requires."[22]

With this Justice Brandeis disagreed:

> The doctrine of the separation of powers was adopted by the convention of 1787 not to promote efficiency, but to preclude the exercise of arbitrary power. The purpose was not to avoid friction, but, by means of the inevitable friction incident to the distribution of the governmental powers among three departments, to save the people from autocracy.[23]

(12) With which of the foregoing statements are the Justices in the *Steel Seizure* case more nearly in accord? In answering return to Note (6). Suppose Congress had said nothing, could you square a different outcome in Steel Seizure in the

---

[22] 272 U.S. at 116.

[23] 272 U.S. at 293. Chief Justice Taft's view seemed to have been substantially eroded by the Supreme Court's decisions in *Humphrey's Executor v. United States*, 295 U.S. 602 (1935), *Weiner v. United States*, 357 U.S. 349 (1958) and *Nixon v. Administrator of General Services*, 433 U.S. 425 (1977). Then, however, came *Immigration and Naturalization Service v. Chadha*, 462 U.S. 919, 103 S. Ct 2764, 77 L. Ed. 2d 317 (1983) and *Bowsher v. Synar*, 478 U.S. 714, 106 S. Ct. 3181, 92 L. Ed 2d 583 (1986), both of which can be read to stand in marked contrast with the Court's latest pronouncement in *Morrison v. Olson*, 487 U.S. 654, 108 S. Ct 2597, 101 L. Ed 2d 569 (1988). Arguably the Supreme Court, in the short span of eleven years, has twice flipped-flopped on its basic understanding of the Separation of Powers doctrine.

event Congress had not acted with Chief Justice Taft's conception of the Separation of Powers Doctrine? If not, then plainly Congress is not the only branch of government with "legislative" power (using Justice Black's definition of the "legislative" power), is it?

(13) Justice Sutherland's sweeping rhetoric obviously lacks a certain precision. Suppose Congress had considered and rejected legislation authorizing the President to prohibit arms sales to countries engaged in the Chaco War and to prosecute anybody violating that prohibition? Did Justice Sutherland mean to imply that under such circumstances the President could have nevertheless issued his proclamation and prosecuted the Curtiss-Wright Export Corp.? If so, what is left of his dictum after the *Steel Seizure* case?

If, on the other hand, Justice Sutherland did not intend to suggest that the President might disregard Congress' rejection of such a law, how does his view of the President's powers over foreign relations differ from that of Chief Justice Vinson; from Justice Clark's view and (perhaps) Justice Burton's view; from Justice Jackson's concept? Consider the foregoing question stated differently. Is it really necessary to go outside the constitutional text — to invoke a Presidential "foreign relations" power — in order to find an amplitude of Presidential authority?

(14) It has been suggested[24] that Steel Seizure was only a "domestic" powers case while Curtiss-Wright dealt with a critical foreign policy question. Why? Because the mills that were seized were all in the United States? Where was Curtiss-Wright when it was prosecuted? Because Curtis-Wright was engaged in exporting its products to South America? Where was much of the steel eventually going? It was to keep it going there that led to the President's decision, wasn't it? Consider, also, how the government argued the case. What was the purpose of the Secretary of Defense's affidavit? Does Chief Justice Vinson's dissent sound like he thought that the President's actions were animated by some domestic problem not a foreign policy crisis?

(15) Reread the quotation from Henkin in Note (7), *supra*, concerning the inadequacies of the constitutional text. Are you persuaded? To the extent that it lies within the prerogative of the interpreter, or to the extent it is his duty, to bring the informing force of the Separation of Powers doctrine to bear on that language, is there any escape from a broad interpretation based "on the Constitution as a whole?" Put more bluntly, didn't Chief Justice Marshall provide a complete answer to Professor Henkin in *McCulloch v. Maryland?*[25] The constitutional text may be deficient in its specifications of the "means" necessary to the conduct of foreign relations. But, by anything other than the most crabbed reading, the Constitutional text is comprehensive in its specification of the subjects to which the "ends" of policy may relate. And to Congress, acting often on Presidential initiative and usually with Presidential assent, is given the power to define the "ends" that may be embraced within most of those subjects. Even the most dedicated Blackian "interpretivist" would readily concede the adequacy of the constitutional text to cover most, if not all, of what needs to be done in the conduct

---

[24] See, *e.g., Attlee v. Laird,* 347 F. Supp. 689 (E.D. Pa. 1972), *aff'd mem.,* 411 U.S. 911 (1973).

[25] 4 U.S. (Wheat) 316, 4 L. Ed. 579 (1819).

of the nation's foreign relations. Professor Henkin simply cannot escape from the text, can he?

(16) Return now to Justice Sutherland's theory concerning the sources of the Federal Government's power over foreign relations. Recall, that with respect to the Government's domestic powers he states that the " . . . purpose of the Constitution was to carve from the mass of legislative powers then possessed by the states such portions as it was thought desirable to vest in the federal government leaving those not included in the enumeration still in the states."

The seminal point of reference, for any examination of this theory, is the early struggles over the constitutionality of Section 25 of the Judiciary Act of 1789 which conferred on the United States Supreme Court appellate jurisdiction over the highest court of a State. In *Martin v. Hunter's Lessee*,[26] the Virginia Court of Appeals declared Section 25 unconstitutional. Among the arguments made was that "the Constitution contemplates the independence of both [State and Federal] governments, and regards the *residuary sovereignty* of the states, as not less inviolable than the *delegated sovereignty* of the United States." Hence, a court of the United States, "belonging to one sovereignty," could not stand in an appellate relationship to the State courts, "which belong to a different sovereignty." The Supreme Court reversed upholding the validity of Section 25. Justice Story commenced his opinion for the Court as follows:

> The constitution of the United States was ordained and established, not by the States in their sovereign capacities but emphatically, as the preamble of the constitution declares, by "the people of the United States." There can be no doubt that it was competent to the people to invest in the general government all the powers which they might deem proper and necessary;. . . . As little doubt can there be, that the people had a right to prohibit to the States the exercise of any powers which were, in their judgment, incompatible with the objects of the general compact; [including the right] . . . to reserve to themselves those sovereign authorities which they might not choose to delegate to either. The constitution was not, therefore, carved out of existing States sovereignties nor a surrender of powers already existing in State institutions, for the powers of the States depend upon their own constitutions; and the people of every State had the right to modify and restrain them. . . . On the other hand, it is perfectly clear that the sovereign powers vested in the State governments, by their respective constitutions, remain unaltered and unimpaired, except so far as they would grant to the government of the United States.

If sovereignty ultimately rests with the people (and rested there from 1776 onward), what remains of Justice Sutherland's effort to trace the Federal Government's power over foreign relations to the British crown?

It may, of course, be true that such foreign relations powers as were delegated by the people to some government were delegated entirely to the Federal Government to the exclusion of the States. One might, in addition, concede *arguendo* that this delegation was broad enough to encompass all of the power necessary to protect and vindicate the interests of the people of the United States in their

---

[26] 1 Wheat. 304 (1816).

relations with foreign sovereigns. But that conclusion must be derived, if at all, from the text of the Constitution itself, read, "as a whole." If it is by the Constitution alone that the people relinquished power, it is the text of the Constitution which alone expresses the scope and content of the powers relinquished. Those powers cannot be discerned by reference to some pre-existing model of sovereign power or by reference to any model external to the Constitution that contemporary theory might contrive. Finally, even if contemporary world conditions seem to necessitate a rewriting of history, a word of caution. If the people are not the source of sovereignty over foreign affairs and if, in that sphere, the Constitution does not express the whole of the powers of the Federal Government, on what basis can it be argued that the Federal government, as against the people, must exercise those powers in conformity to the Constitution (see on this point *Reid v. Covert*, p. 1058, *infra*). Surely one must pause before so readily discarding, as Professor Henkin would have it, the implications of what was the single greatest achievement of the American revolution in the realm of political ideas.

The latest decision by the Supreme Court bearing on the subject of Presidential powers over foreign policy was rendered in the context of a major international crisis.

DAMES & MOORE v. REGAN

United States Supreme Court
455 U.S. 654, 101 S. Ct. 2972, 69 L. Ed. 2d 918 (1981)

[On November 4, 1979, the U.S. Embassy in Tehran was seized and the Americans in it were held hostage by Iranian militants. On November 14, President Carter, citing his powers under the International Emergency Economic Powers Act (IEEPA), declared an emergency and blocked "all property and interests in property of the Government of Iran, its instrumentalities and controlled entities" which are "subject to the jurisdiction of the United States" or "under the control" of persons subject to that jurisdiction. Pursuant to presidential authority, the Office of Foreign Assets Control within the Treasury Department issued a regulation providing that "[unless] licensed or authorized . . . any attachment, judgment, decree, lien, execution, garnishment, or other judicial process is null and void with respect to any property" subject to the President's blocking order. The regulation also provided that any license or authorization could be "amended, modified, or revoked at any time." On November 26, 1979 the President granted a general license allowing certain judicial proceedings against Iran but not the "entry of any judgment or of any decree or order of similar or analogous effect." A later regulation authorized pre-judgment attachments.

On December 19, 1979 petitioner Dames & Moore filed suit in a U.S. District Court against the Government of Iran, the Atomic Energy Organization of Iran and several Iranian banks, alleging that it was owed $3.4 million for services performed under a contract with the Organization before the latter canceled the contract. The District Court issued orders attaching the property of certain Iranian banks that had been blocked under the President's order.

On January 20, 1981 the hostages were released in accordance with an agreement embodied in two Declarations of Algeria. *Declarations of the Government of the Democratic and Popular Republic of Algeria, January 19, 1981.*[27] Under the Declarations, Iran agreed that approximately $3.7 billion of blocked assets would be used to pay immediately all outstanding syndicated loans from American and foreign banks, to negotiate the settlement of its remaining bank debt, and to place $1.4 billion of blocked assets in escrow to cover those settlements. It also agreed to the establishment of an international arbitral tribunal to hear the bulk of the remaining (*i.e.*, non-bank) American claims against Iran and to pay the Tribunal's awards. To secure this latter undertaking, $1 billion of blocked assets was to be placed in a special "security account."

In return for these commitments and release of the hostages, President Carter undertook to bar the prosecution of all claims against Iran by the hostages and certain other Americans, to revoke all American trade sanctions against Iran, to withdraw all claims of the United States then pending before the International Court of Justice, to turn over to the Bank of England all of the blocked assets required for the several escrow and security accounts called for by the agreements and to return the remaining assets to Iran. The President also agreed to "freeze" the American assets of the late Shah and his family and to forestall the pleading of certain defenses should Iran sue to recover those assets. These commitments necessitated several Executive Orders which *inter alia* nullified all judicial attachments against Iranian assets located in the United States and ordered those assets transferred to Iran or to the security account for the payment of the arbitral awards.[28]

When he took office, President Reagan ratified these orders and, in addition, ordered the "suspension" of all actions against Iran pending in the U.S. courts by claimants whose cases were arguably within the jurisdiction of the arbitral tribunal.[29] If the tribunal determined that it lacked jurisdiction over the claim, the claimant could, under the latter order, pursue his judicial remedies. Otherwise the suit would remain suspended until the tribunal either decided that the claim was without merit or granted an award and the award was paid in full, in which event the arbitrators' decision was to act as "a final resolution in discharge of the claim for all purposes."

---

[27] 81 Dep't of State Bull., No. 2047 at 1, 3 (1981).

[28] Exec. Order No. 12,277, 46 Fed. Reg. 7,915 (Jan. 19, 1981); Exec. Order No. 12,279, 46 Fed. Reg. 7,919; Exec. Order No. 12,280, 46 Fed. Reg. 7,921 (Jan. 19, 1981); Exec. Order No. 12,281, 46 Fed. Reg. 7,923 (Jan. 19, 1981). (The blocked assets used to settle the bank claims were all located abroad).

[29] Exec. Order No. 12,294, 46 Fed. Reg. 14,111 (Feb. 24, 1981).

On January 27, 1981, the district court granted Dames & Moore's motion for summary judgment, whereupon Dames & Moore commenced proceedings to satisfy the judgment. Then on May 28th, the district court stayed execution of its judgment and vacated all pre-judgment attachments relying for this purpose on the January Executive Orders. Dames & Moore responded by filing a separate action in which it asked the district court to enjoin the United States and the Secretary of the Treasury from enforcing the President's January orders. The district court dismissed the complaint and petitioner appealed to the Court of Appeals. For its part the Treasury Department ordered that all of the blocked assets be turned over to the Federal Reserve Bank of New York by noon on June 19 for transfer to the Bank of England. Because these issues demanded prompt resolution, the Supreme Court granted certiorari before judgment by the Court of Appeals and heard oral argument on June 24. On July 2 the Supreme Court affirmed the district court's dismissal of the complaint.]

MR. JUSTICE REHNQUIST delivered the opinion of the Court.

* * * *

[B]efore turning to the facts and law which we believe determine the result in this case, we [are] . . . acutely aware of the necessity to rest decision on the narrowest possible ground capable of deciding the case. . . . This does not mean that reasoned analysis may give way to judicial fiat. It does mean that the statement of Justice Jackson — that we decide difficult cases presented to us by virtue of our commissions, not our competence — is especially true here. We attempt to lay down no general "guide-lines" covering other situations not involved here, and attempt to confine the opinion only to the very questions necessary to decision of the case.

Perhaps it is because it is so difficult to reconcile the foregoing definition of Art. III judicial power with the broad range of vitally important day-to-day questions regularly decided by Congress or the Executive, without either challenge or interference by the Judiciary, that the decisions of the Court in this area have been rare, episodic, and afford little precedential value for subsequent cases. The tensions present in any exercise of executive power under the tri-partite system of Federal Government established by the Constitution have been reflected in opinions by Members of this Court more than once. The Court stated in *United States v. Curtiss-Wright Export Corp.*[30] . . . . :

> [Here Justice Rehnquist quotes Justice Sutherland's famous dictum concerning the President's authority over foreign affairs].

And yet sixteen years later, Justice Jackson in his concurring opinion in *Youngstown* . . . focused not on the "plenary and exclusive power of the President" but rather responded to a claim of virtually unlimited powers for the Executive by noting:

> The example of such unlimited executive power that must have most impressed the forefathers was the prerogative exercised by George III, and

---

[30] 299 U.S. 304, 57 S. Ct. 216, 81 L. Ed 255 (1936).

the description of its evils in the Declaration of Independence leads me to doubt that they were creating their new Executive in his image.

As we now turn to the factual and legal issues in this case, we freely confess that we are obviously deciding only one more episode in the never ending tension between the President exercising the executive authority in a world that presents each day some new challenge with which he must deal and the Constitution under which we all live and which no one disputes embodies some sort of system of checks and balances.

* * * *

The parties and the lower courts confronted with the instant questions have all agreed that much relevant analysis is contained in *Youngstown Sheet & Tube Co. v. Sawyer* . . . Justice Black's opinion for the Court in that case . . . recognized that "[T]he President's power, if any, to issue the order must stem either from an act of Congress or from the Constitution itself.". . . . Justice Jackson's concurring opinion elaborated in a general way the consequences of different types of interaction between the two democratic branches in assessing presidential authority to act in any given case.

[Here Justice Rehnquist reviews Justice Jackson's threefold categorization of the President's powers].

. . . Justice Jackson himself recognized that his . . . categories represented "a somewhat over-simplified grouping," . . . and it is doubtless the case that executive action in any particular instance falls, not neatly in one of three pigeon-holes, but rather at some point along a spectrum running from explicit congressional authorization to explicit congressional prohibition. This is particularly true as respects cases such as the one before us, involving responses to international crises the nature of which Congress can hardly have been expected to anticipate in any detail.

In nullifying post-November 14, 1979, attachments and directing those persons holding blocked Iranian funds and securities to transfer them to the Federal Reserve Bank of New York for ultimate transfer to Iran, President Carter cited five sources of express or inherent power. The Government, however, has principally relied on Sec. 1702 of the IEEPA[31] as authorization for these actions. . . .

The Government contends that the acts of "nullifying" the attachments and ordering the "transfer" of the frozen assets are specifically authorized by the plain language of the above statute. The two Courts of Appeals that have considered the issue agreed with this contention. [Discussion of cases omitted.]

Petitioner contends that we should ignore the plain language of the statute because an examination of its legislative history as well as the history of Sec. 5(b) of the Trading With the Enemy Act (hereinafter "TWEA"),[32] from which the pertinent language of Sec. 1702 is directly drawn, reveals that the statute was not intended to give the President such extensive power over the assets of a foreign state during times of national emergency. According to petitioner, once the

---

[31] 50 U.S.C. Section 1702.
[32] 50 U.S.C. App. Section 5(b).

President instituted the November 14, 1979, blocking order, Sec. 1702 authorized him "only to continue the freeze or to discontinue controls". . . .

We do not agree and refuse to read out of Sec. 1702 all meaning to the words "transfer," "compel," or "nullify." Nothing in the legislative history of either Sec. 1702 or Sec. 5(b) of the TWEA requires such a result. To the contrary, we think both the legislative history and cases interpreting the TWEA fully sustain the broad authority of the Executive when acting under this congressional grant of power . . . although Congress intended to limit the President' emergency power in peacetime, we do not think the changes brought about by the enactment of the IEEPA in any way affected the authority of the President to take the specific actions taken here. We likewise note that by the time petitioner instituted this action, the President had already entered the freeze order. Petitioner proceeded against the blocked assets only after the Treasury Department had issued revocable licenses authorizing such proceedings and attachments. The Treasury regulations provided that "unless licensed" any attachment is null and void[33] . . . and all licenses "may be amended, modified, or revoked at any time"[34] . . . As such, the attachments obtained by petitioner were specifically made subordinate to further actions which the President might take under the IEEPA. Petitioner was on notice of the contingent nature of its interest in the frozen assets.

This Court has previously recognized that the congressional purpose in authorizing blocking orders is "to put control of foreign assets in the hands of the President. . . ." Such orders permit the President to maintain the foreign assets at his disposal for use in negotiating the resolution of a declared national emergency. The frozen assets serve as a "bargaining chip" to be used by the President when dealing with a hostile country. Accordingly, it is difficult to accept petitioner's argument because the practical effect of it is to allow individual claimants throughout the country to minimize or wholly eliminate this "bargaining chip" to be used by the President when dealing with a hostile country. Neither the purpose the statute was enacted to serve nor its plain language supports such a result.

Because the President's action in nullifying the attachments and ordering the transfer of the assets was taken pursuant to specific congressional authorization, it is "supported by the strongest of presumptions and the widest latitude of judicial interpretation, and the burden of persuasion would rest heavily upon any who might attack it." *Youngstown.* Under the circumstances of this case, we cannot say that petitioner has sustained that heavy burden. A contrary ruling would mean that the Federal Government as a whole lacked the power exercised by the President . . . and that we are not prepared to say.

Although we have concluded that the IEEPA constitutes specific congressional authorization to the President to nullify the attachments and order the transfer of Iranian assets, there remains the question of the President's authority to suspend claims pending in American courts. Such claims have, of course, an existence apart from the attachments which accompanied them. In terminating these claims through Executive Order No. 12294 the President purported to act

---

[33] 31 CFR Section 535.203(e).
[34] 31 CFR Section 535.805.

under authority of both the IEEPA and 22 U.S.C. Sec. 1732, the so-called "Hostage Act". . . .

We conclude that although the IEEPA authorized the nullification of the attachments, it cannot be read to authorize the suspension of the claims. The claims of American citizens against Iran are not in themselves transactions involving Iranian property or efforts to exercise any rights with respect to such property. An *in personam* lawsuit, although it might eventually be reduced to judgment and that judgment might be executed upon, is an effort to establish liability and fix damages and does not focus on any particular property within the jurisdiction. The terms of the IEEPA therefore do not authorize the President to suspend claims in American courts. . . .

[Justice Rehnquist next quotes the "Hostage Act"[35] passed in 1868 and concludes:]

We are reluctant to conclude that this provision constitutes specific authorization to the President to suspend claims in American courts. Although the broad language of the Hostage Act suggests it may cover this case, there are several difficulties with such a view. The legislative history indicates that the Act was passed in response to a situation unlike the recent Iranian crisis. Congress in 1868 was concerned with the activity of certain countries refusing to recognize the citizenship of naturalized Americans traveling abroad, and repatriating such citizens against their will. . . . These countries were not interested in returning the citizens in exchange for any sort of ransom. This also explains the reference in the Act to imprisonment "in violation of the rights of American citizenship." Although the Iranian hostage-taking violated international law and common decency, the hostages were not seized out of any refusal to recognize their American citizenship — they were seized precisely *because* of their American citizenship. The legislative history is also somewhat ambiguous on the question whether Congress contemplated presidential action such as that involved here or rather simply reprisals directed against the offending foreign country and *its* citizens. . . .

Concluding that neither the IEEPA nor the Hostage Act constitutes specific authorization of the President's action suspending claims, however, is not to say that these statutory provisions are entirely irrelevant to the question of the validity of the President's action. We think both statutes highly relevant in the looser sense of indicating congressional acceptance of a broad scope for executive action in circumstances such as those presented in this case. As noted above . . . the IEEPA delegated broad authority to the President to act in times of national emergency with respect to property of a foreign country. The Hostage Act similarly indicated congressional willingness that the President have broad discretion when responding to the hostile acts of foreign sovereigns. . . .

Although we have declined to conclude that the IEEPA or the Hostage Act directly authorizes the President's suspension of claims for the reasons noted, we cannot ignore the general tenor of Congress' legislation in this area in trying to determine whether the President is acting alone or at least with the acceptance of Congress. As we have noted, Congress cannot anticipate and legislate with regard

---

[35] 22 U.S.C. Section 1732.

to every possible action the President may find it necessary to take or every possible situation in which he might act. Such failure of Congress specifically to delegate authority does not, "especially . . . in the areas of foreign policy and national security," imply "congressional disapproval" of action taken by the Executive. *Haig v. Agee*[36] . . . On the contrary, the enactment of legislation closely related to the question of the President's authority in a particular case which evinces a legislative intent to accord the President broad discretion may be considered to "invite" "measures on independent presidential responsibility," *Youngstown*. . . . (Jackson, J., concurring). At least this is so where there is no contrary indication of legislative intent and when, as here, there is a history of congressional acquiescence in conduct of the sort engaged in by the President. It is to that history which we now turn.

Not infrequently in affairs between nations, outstanding claims by nationals of one country against the government of another country are "sources of friction" between the two sovereigns. *United States v. Pink*[37] . . . To resolve these difficulties, nations have often entered into agreements settling the claims of their respective nationals. As one treatise writer puts it, international agreements settling claims by nationals of one state against the government of another "are established international practice reflecting traditional international theory." L. Henkin, Foreign Affairs and the Constitution 262 (1972). Consistent with that principle, the United States has repeatedly exercised its sovereign authority to settle the claims of its nationals against foreign countries. Though those settlements have sometimes been made by treaty, there has also been a longstanding practice of settling such claims by executive agreement without the advice and consent of the Senate.[38] Under such agreements, the President has agreed to renounce or extinguish claims of United States nationals against foreign governments in return for lump sum payments or the establishment of arbitration procedures. To be sure, many of these settlements were encouraged by the United States claimants themselves, since a claimant's only hope of obtaining any payment at all might lie in having his government negotiate a diplomatic settlement on his behalf. But it is also undisputed that the "United States has sometimes disposed of the claims of citizens without their consent, or even without consultation with them, usually without exclusive regard for their interests, as distinguished from those of the nation as a whole."[39] . . . . It is clear that the practice of settling claims continues today. Since 1952, the President has

---

[36] 453 U.S. 280, 101 S. Ct. 2766, 2774, 68 L. Ed. 2d 640 (1981).

[37] 315 U.S. 203, 225, 62 S. Ct. 552, 563, 86 L. Ed. 796 (1942).

[38] At least since the case of the "Wilmington Packet" in 1799, Presidents have exercised the power to settle claims of United States nationals by executive agreement. See Lillich, The Gravel Amendment To The Trade Reform Act of 1974, 69 Am. J. Int'l L. 837, 844 (1975). In fact, during the period 1817-1917, "no fewer than eighty executive agreements were entered into by the United States looking to the liquidation of claims of its citizens." McClure, International Executive Agreements 53 (1941). See also 14 M. Whiteman, Digest of International Law 247 (1970).

[39] Henkin, *supra*, at 263.

entered into at least 10 binding settlements with foreign nations, including an $80 million settlement with the People's Republic of China.[40]

Crucial to our decision today is the conclusion that Congress has implicitly approved the practice of claim settlement by executive agreement. This is best demonstrated by Congress' enactment of the International Claims Settlement Act of 1949[41] . . . . The Act had two purposes: (1) to allocate to United States nationals funds received in the course of an executive claims settlement with Yugoslavia, and (2) to provide a procedure whereby funds resulting from future settlements could be distributed. To achieve these ends Congress created the International Claims Commission, now the Foreign Claims Settlement Commission, and gave it jurisdiction to make final and binding decisions with respect to claims by United States nationals against settlement funds[42] . . . . By creating a procedure to implement future settlement agreements, Congress placed its stamp of approval on such agreements. Indeed, the legislative history of the Act observed that the United States was seeking settlements with countries other than Yugoslavia and stated that the bill "contemplates that settlements of a similar nature are to be made in the future.". . . .

Over the years Congress has frequently amended the International Claims Settlement Act to provide for particular problems arising out of settlement agreements, thus demonstrating Congress' continuing acceptance of the President's claim settlement authority. [References to legislation on claims agreements with the People's Republic of China, East Germany and Vietnam are omitted.]

. . . Finally, the legislative history of the IEEPA further reveals that Congress has accepted the authority of the Executive to enter into settlement agreements. Though the IEEPA was enacted to provide for some limitation on the President's emergency powers, Congress stressed that "nothing in this Act is intended to interfere with the authority of the President to [block assets], or to impede the settlement of claims of United States citizens against foreign countries.". . . .

In addition to congressional acquiescence in the President's power to settle claims, prior cases of this Court have also recognized that the President does have some measure of power to enter into executive agreements without obtaining the advice and consent of the Senate. [Discussion of *United States v. Pink*, p. 1069, *infra*, omitted.]

Petitioner . . . asserts that Congress divested the President of the authority to settle claims when it enacted the Foreign Sovereign Immunities Act of 1976 (hereinafter "FSIA")[43] . . . . The FSIA granted personal and subject matter jurisdiction in the federal district courts over commercial suits brought by claimants against those foreign states which have waived immunity[44] . . . Prior

---

[40] Those agreements are 30 U.S.T. 1957 (1979) (People's Republic of China); 27 U.S.T. 3993 (1976) (Peru); 27 U.S.T. 4214 (1976) (Egypt); 25 U.S.T. 227 (1974) (Peru); 24 U.S.T. 2654 (1969) (Japan); 16 U.S.T. 1 (1965) (Yugoslavia); 14 U.S.T. 969 (1963) (Bulgaria); 11 U.S.T. 1953 (1960) (Poland); 11 U.S.T. 317 (1960) (Rumania).

[41] 22 U.S.C. Section 1621 et. seq., as amended (1980).

[42] 22 U.S.C. Section 1623(a).

[43] 28 U.S.C. Section 1330, 1602 *et seq.*

[44] 28 U.S.C. Section 1330.

to the enactment of the FSIA, a foreign government's immunity to suit was determined by the Executive Branch on a case-by-case basis. According to petitioner, the principal purpose of the FSIA was to depoliticize these commercial lawsuits by taking them out of the arena of foreign affairs — where the Executive Branch is subject to the pressures of foreign states seeking to avoid liability through a grant of immunity — and (sic) by placing them within the exclusive jurisdiction of the courts. Petitioner thus insists that the President, by suspending its claims, has circumscribed the jurisdiction of the United States courts in violation of Art. III of the Constitution.

We disagree. In the first place, we do not believe that the President has attempted to divest the federal courts of jurisdiction. Executive Order No. 12294 purports only to "suspend" the claims, not divest the federal courts of "jurisdiction." As we read the Executive Order, those claims not within the jurisdiction of the Claims Tribunal will "revive" and become judicially enforceable in United States courts. This case, in short, illustrates the difference between modifying federal court jurisdiction and directing the court to apply a different rule of law. See *United States v. Schooner Peggy*. . . . The President has exercised the power, acquiesced in by Congress, to settle claims and, as such, has simply effected a change in the substantive law governing the lawsuit. Indeed, the very example of sovereign immunity belies petitioner's argument. No one would suggest that a determination of sovereign immunity divests the federal courts of "jurisdiction." Yet, petitioner's argument, if accepted, would have required courts prior to the enactment of the FSIA to reject as an encroachment on their jurisdiction the President's determination of a foreign state's sovereign immunity.

Petitioner also reads the FSIA much too broadly. The principal purpose of the FSIA was to codify contemporary concepts concerning the scope of sovereign immunity and withdraw from the President the authority to make binding determinations of the sovereign immunity to be accorded foreign states. . . . The FSIA was thus designed to remove one particular barrier to suit, namely sovereign immunity, and cannot be fairly read as *prohibiting* the President from settling claims of United States nationals against foreign governments. It is telling that the Congress which enacted the FSIA considered but rejected several proposals designed to limit the power of the President to enter into executive agreements, including claims settlement agreements. It is quite unlikely that the same Congress that rejected proposals to limit the President's authority to conclude executive agreements sought to accomplish that very purpose *sub silentio* through the FSIA. And, as noted above, just 1 year after enacting the FSIA, Congress enacted the IEEPA, where the legislative history stressed that nothing in the IEEPA was to impede the settlement of claims of United States citizens. It would be surprising for Congress to express this support for settlement agreements had it intended the FSIA to eliminate the President's authority to make such agreements.

In light of all of the foregoing — the inferences to be drawn from the character of the legislation Congress has enacted in the area, such as the IEEPA and the Hostage Act, and from the history of acquiescence in executive claims settlement — we conclude that the President was authorized to suspend pending claims pursuant to Executive Order No. 12294. As Justice Frankfurter pointed out in Youngstown, "a systematic, unbroken executive practice, long pursued to the knowledge of Congress and never before questioned . . . may be treated as a gloss on 'Executive Power' vested in the President by Section 1 of Art. II." Past practice does not, by itself, create power, but "long-continued practice, known to and acquiesced in by Congress, would raise a presumption that the [action] has been [taken] in pursuance of its consent. . . ." *United States v. Midwest Oil Co.*,[45] . . . . See *Haig v. Agee*. . . . Such practice is present here and such a presumption is also appropriate. In light of the fact that Congress may be considered to have consented to the President's action in suspending claims, we cannot say that action exceeded the President' powers.

Our conclusion is buttressed by the fact that the means chosen by the President to settle the claims of American nationals provided an alternate forum, the Claims Tribunal, which is capable of providing meaningful relief. The Solicitor General also suggests that the provision of the Claims Tribunal will actually *enhance* the opportunity for claimants to recover their claims, in that the Agreement removes a number of jurisdictional and procedural impediments faced by claimants in United States courts. . . . Although being overly sanguine about the chances of United States claimants before the Claims Tribunal would require a degree of naivete which should not be demanded even of judges, the Solicitor General's point cannot be discounted. Moreover, it is important to remember that we have already held that the President has the *statutory* authority to nullify attachments and to transfer the assets out of the country. The President's power to do so does not depend on his provision of a forum whereby claimants can recover on those claims. The fact that the President has provided such a forum here means that the claimants are receiving something in return for the suspension of their claims, namely, access to an international tribunal before which they may well recover something on their claims. Because there does appear to be a real "settlement" here, this case is more easily analogized to the more traditional claim settlement cases of the past.

Just as importantly, Congress has not disapproved of the action taken here. Though Congress has held hearings on the Iranian Agreement itself, Congress has not enacted legislation, or even passed a resolution, indicating its displeasure with the Agreement. Quite the contrary, the relevant Senate Committee has stated that the establishment of the Tribunal is "of vital importance to the United States"[46] . . . . We are thus clearly not confronted with a situation in which Congress has in some way resisted the exercise of presidential authority.

Finally, we re-emphasize the narrowness of our decision. We do not decide that the President possesses plenary power to settle claims, even as against foreign governmental entities. As the Court of Appeals for the First Circuit stressed, "the sheer magnitude of such a power, considered against the background of the

---

[45] 236 U.S. 459 (1915).

[46] Contrast congressional reaction to the Iranian Agreements with congressional reaction to a 1973 Executive Agreement with Czechoslovakia. There the President sought to settle over $205 million in claims against Czechoslovakia for $20.5 million. Congress quickly demonstrated its displeasure by enacting legislation requiring that the Agreement be renegotiated. . . . Though Congress has shown itself capable of objecting to executive agreements, it has rarely done so and has not done so in this case. S. Rep. No. 97-71, 97th Cong., 1st Sess., 5 (1981).

diversity and complexity of modern international trade, cautions against any broader construction of authority than is necessary." *Chas. T. Main Int'l Inc. v. Khuzestan Water & Power Authority*[47] . . . . But where, as here, the settlement of claims has been determined to be a necessary incident to the resolution of a major foreign policy dispute between our country and another, and where, as here, we can conclude that Congress acquiesced in the President's action, we are not prepared to say that the President lacks the power to settle such claims.

We do not think it appropriate at the present time to address petitioner's contention that the suspension of claims, if authorized, would constitute a taking of property in violation of the Fifth Amendment to the United States Constitution in the absence of just compensation.[48] Both petitioner and the Government concede that the question whether the suspension of the claims constitutes a taking is not ripe for review. . . . However, this contention, and the possibility that the President's actions may effect a taking of petitioner's property, makes ripe for adjudication the question whether petitioner will have a remedy at law in the Court of Claims under the Tucker Act[49] . . . in such an event. . . .

* * * *

It has been contended that the "treaty exception" to the jurisdiction of the Court of Claims[50] . . . might preclude the Court of Claims from exercising jurisdiction over any takings claim the petitioner might bring. At oral argument, however, the Government conceded that Sec. 1502 would not act as a bar to petitioner's action in the Court of Claims. . . . Accordingly, to the extent petitioner believes it has suffered an unconstitutional taking by the suspension of the claims, we see no jurisdictional obstacle to an appropriate action in the United States Court of Claims under the Tucker Act.

The judgment of the District Court is accordingly affirmed, and the mandate shall issue forthwith.

* * * *

Justice Powell, concurring and dissenting in part.

I join the Court's opinion except its decision that the nullification of the attachments did not effect a taking of property interests giving rise to claims for just compensation. . . . The nullification of attachments presents a separate question from whether the suspension and proposed settlement of claims against Iran may constitute a taking. I would leave both "taking" claims open for resolution on a case-by-case basis in actions before the Court of Claims. The facts of the hundreds of claims pending against Iran are not known to this Court and may differ form the facts in this case. I therefore dissent from the Court's decision

---

[47] 651 F. 2d at 814.

[48] Though we conclude that the President has settled petitioner's claims against Iran, we do not suggest that the settlement has terminated petitioner's possible takings claim against the United States. We express no views on petitioner's claim that it has suffered a taking.

[49] 28 U.S.C. Section 1491.

[50] 28 U.S.C. Section 1502.

with respect to attachments. The decision may well be erroneous,[51] and it certainly is premature with respect to many claims.

I agree with the Court's opinion with respect to the suspension and settlement of claims against Iran and its instrumentalities. The opinion makes clear that some claims may not be adjudicated by the Claims Tribunal and that others may not be paid in full. The Court holds that parties whose valid claims are not adjudicated or not fully paid may bring a "taking" claim against the United States in the Court of Claims, the jurisdiction of which this Court acknowledges. The Government must pay just compensation when it furthers the Nation's foreign policy goals by using as "bargaining chips" claims lawfully held by a relatively few persons and subject to the jurisdiction of our courts.[52]

NOTES AND QUESTIONS

(1) In *Dames & Moore v. Regan*, the Court was called upon to reconcile two long-standing and important prerogatives, one belonging to Congress, the other to the President. As the Court observed, the executive has, since the earliest days of the Republic, entered into agreements with foreign governments settling claims of United States citizens against those governments. Some of these settlements have provided for lump-sum payments in which all private claimants share pro-rata, others have provided for the establishment of special tribunals to adjudicate the citizens' claims, with the foreign government undertaking to pay the resulting awards. The making of such agreements would seem an altogether unexceptional exercise of the executive's broader function of giving diplomatic protection to American citizens abroad and has, time and again, been carried-out without benefit of enabling legislation. By a variety of enactments designed to aid implementation of these settlements, Congress, as Justice Rehnquist argued, does seem to have acquiesced in this exercise of presidential authority. (*cf.* Justice Frankfurter concurring in the *Steel Seizure* Case). Moreover, historically many of the agreements were predicated upon an assertion by the United States that, in the events giving rise to its citizens' claims against the foreign government, the latter had breached a duty owed by the foreign government to the sovereign

---

[51] Even though the Executive Orders purported to make attachments conditional, there is a substantial question whether the Orders themselves may have effected a taking by making conditional the attachments that claimants against Iran otherwise could have obtained without condition. Moreover, because it is settled that an attachment entitling a creditor to resort to specific property for the satisfaction of a claim is a property right compensable under the Fifth Amendment, *Armstrong v. United States*, 364 U.S. 40, 80 S. Ct. 1563, 4 L. Ed. 2d 1554 (1960), *Louisville Bank v. Radford*, 295 U.S. 555, 55 S. Ct. 854, 79 L. Ed. 1593 (1935), there is a question whether the revocability of the license under which petitioner obtained its attachment suffices to render revocable the attachment itself.

[52] As the Court held in *Armstrong v. United States*, 364 U.S. 40, 49, 80 S. Ct. 1563, 1569, 4 L. Ed. 2d 1554 (1960): "The Fifth Amendment's guarantee that private property shall not be taken for public use without just compensation was designed to bar Government from forcing some people alone to bear public burdens which, in all fairness and justice, should be borne by the public as a whole. . . ."

United States under the international law of "state responsibility." Although this was not true of all the claims against Iran and may not have been true in every prior case, to the extent the doctrine was applicable, vindication of the United States' rights under that doctrine would seem a proper occasion for the exercise of an independent presidential authority, would it not? If so, under what Constitutional grant of authority?

On the other hand, not only had the President made an agreement with Iran, but he had issued orders nullifying judicial attachments and suspending lawsuits then pending before both Federal and State Courts. Article III of the Constitution confers upon Congress, not the Executive, the power to regulate the jurisdiction of the lower federal courts (*Sheldon v. Sill*,[53]) and the appellate jurisdiction of the Supreme Court (*Ex Parte McCardle*[54]). As the long history of debates over the implicit limits of this power makes plain, it is a formidable power whose exercise can engage some very fundamental issues concerning the role of the judiciary and the rule of law in the American system of government. It is not an authority that is lightly to be delegated to the Executive.[55]

It is these two traditional prerogatives that were brought, potentially at least, into conflict by the settlement with Iran. It was a conflict without precedent. The Government contended that under *United States v. Pink* (discussed *infra* page 1068), the President possessed a broad, virtually unlimited claims settlement power adequate to accomplish all that the agreement with Iran required. *Pink*, however, only upheld the power of the President to nullify rights in property granted to aliens by a State court, in order to make that property available for the settlement of citizen claims pursuant to an agreement with the Soviet Union. Also, cases upholding the Government's right to alien-owned property, as against citizen claims to that property, in cases where the property had been blocked or vested under authority of the Trading with the Enemy Act, were of limited utility. More to the point was the fact that in connection with prior settlements the executive had undoubtedly, from time to time, overridden private objections to the terms of the settlement. But never before had the executive claimed an independent constitutional power to implement a claims settlement agreement by limiting, prohibiting or otherwise foreshortening the authority of the federal courts to adjudicate the merits of citizen claims against the foreign government or to execute their judgments against property of that government, in cases where the courts otherwise had full jurisdiction to act.[56] Against this background consider the following:

---

[53] 8 How. 440, 12 L.Ed. 1147 (1850)

[54] 7 Wall. 506, 19 L.Ed. 264 (1869).

[55] See, generally Hart & Wechsler's The Federal Courts And The Federal System, Bator, Shapiro, Mishkin & Wechsler (2d Ed., 1977), pages 309-375.

[56] There was a highly technical question lurking in the background of many of the suits against Iran, including possibly Dames & Moore, which the Supreme Court was able to avoid and which has never been satisfactorily resolved by the lower courts, but which the Supreme Court may yet be called upon to address. These cases fall into at least three categories. Those in which the Iranian properties were attached prior to the President's blocking order and the property was not immune from attachment under either the Foreign Sovereign Immunities Act (FSIA) or under U.S. treaties with Iran; those in which the attachment of non-immune property occurred after the blocking order; and those involving

(a) Consult the theoretical basis for judicial adherence to executive suggestions of immunity in cases against foreign governments brought prior to enactment of the Foreign Sovereign Immunities Act. (See Chapter 11 at page 886 *supra*). Are you persuaded by now Chief Justice Rehnquist's attempt to draw from this prior practice support for the President's orders in the case against Iran?

(b) Among the reasons why this conflict between the President's claims settlement power and Congress' authority to regulate the jurisdiction of the federal courts had never previously occurred was because, under the doctrine of absolute sovereign immunity that had prevailed for so long, such suits were rarely brought and if brought, readily dismissed. Thus, one of the most important questions raised in *Dames & Moore* concerned the effect on the President's historical claims settlement power that was to be attributed to the shift from the doctrine of absolute sovereign immunity to the doctrine of qualified immunity embodied in the Foreign Sovereign Immunities Act (FSIA) and Congress' decision to vest the determination of immunity in the judiciary under the criteria of the FSIA. Does Chief Justice Rehnquist answer this question to your satisfaction? What is the scenario that Congress most likely had in mind when, having enacted the FSIA, it made clear that enactment of IEEPA was not intended to impede the President's power to settle claims?

(c) Would it have made a difference if instead of "suspending" private suits against Iran, pending their submission to the arbitral tribunal, the President had ordered the suits dismissed with prejudice? If so, how would you distinguish a case that: was brought by a U.S. citizen in a U.S. court after attaching non-immune Iranian assets but before "blocking," was suspended by Presidential order, was taken to the arbitral tribunal and there dismissed for lack of jurisdiction and was then refiled in a U.S. court, but this time without benefit of any Iranian assets from which to satisfy a judgment? Does this case only raise a "takings" clause issue?

(d) The President did, in effect, permanently bar any of the suits by the hostages themselves. Does it matter that those suits were probably barred by sovereign immunity and that some, at least, of the rights likely to be asserted by the hostages were derived from rights conferred upon the United States under its treaties with Iran?

(2) Note the almost agonizing care taken by Chief Justice Rehnquist to find Congressional acquiescence in Presidential claim settlements. If Justice Sutherland's broad dictum is taken at face value, how would he likely have addressed the question of the President's authority? In fact, can we not read the Chief Justice's opinion as a requiem for *Curtiss-Wright*?[57] Notice how he opens his opinion. Any doubt now that *Steel Seizure* was a "foreign relations" case?

---

the attachment of immune property after blocking. The impact of the President's nullification order on the claimant's rights in Iranian property is obviously different in each of these cases. The property in *Dames & Moore* fell into one of the post-blocking categories, the issue of the attached properties' immunity never having been actually litigated.

[57] For additional readings on the Iranian hostage episode see, *Symposium On The Settlement With Iran*, 13 Law. Am. i-xiii (1981); Sager, *The Supreme Court, 1980 Term: Executive Branch Power*, 95 Harv. L. Rev. 91-201 (1981).

(3) As already noted, under Article III of the Constitution, Congress has the power to regulate the jurisdiction of the lower federal courts and the appellate jurisdiction of the Supreme Court. The limits of this quite extraordinary power have never been truly tested. One can readily argue that Congress could not use this power to destroy judicial review of statutes and executive acts that infringed basic constitutional guarantees.[58] Short of that, however, the boundaries of the power are uncertain.

Article 19 of the Canadian-United States Free Trade Agreement[59] establishes arbitration panels that are empowered to hear a claim by one Party to the Agreement — Canada or the United States — that a final countervailing or antidumping duty determination ("final determination") by a national authority of the other Party (*e.g.*, ITA or ITC) erroneously applied the latter's own antidumping or countervailing duty law. Panels are to consist of five persons with each Party choosing two and the four panalists thus designated choosing a fifth panelist. Panel procedures can only be initiated by the Parties. But the parties are required to do so if requested by a person who would otherwise be entitled to judicial review of the final determination. If a panel is requested to review a final determination, there can be no judicial review of that determination and no judicial review of the panel's decision, which is made binding on the Parties.

It has been argued that this procedure violates Article III and the Due Process Clause of the Fifth Amendment to the Constitution because it would deny to a person claiming injury from a final countervailing or antidumping duty determination of a U.S. government agency, the right to seek judicial review of that determination. How far does *Dames & Moore* go toward answering this argument?

In December of 1978, President Jimmy Carter announced his decision to give the one-year notice necessary, by the terms of the treaty, to terminate the 1954 Mutual Defense Treaty with the Republic of China (Taiwan). His constitutional authority to do so on his own initiative was immediately and sharply challenged. The ensuing debate, unlike most of those between the President and the Congress concerning their respective constitutional responsibilities for foreign policy, ended up before the courts when Senator Goldwater and other Senators brought suit against the President.

---

[58] See, generally Hart & Wechsler *op. cit.*, note 55.

[59] 27 Int. L. Mat. 293, signed December 22 and 23, 1987 and January 2, 1988, entered into force January 1, 1989. See also, United States-Canada Free-Trade Agreement Implementation Act of 1988, Pub. L. 100-449, 102 Stat. 1851, 19 U.S.C. Section 2112, 1988 U.S. Code Cong. & Admin. News (102 Stat.) 1851.

GOLDWATER v. CARTER

Court of Appeals for the District of Columbia Circuit
617 F. 2d 697 (1979)

Per curiam

[The court first affirmed the district court's ruling that plaintiffs had standing to maintain the action. It continued:]

Various considerations enter into our determination that the President's notice of termination will be effective on January 1, 1980. . . .

We turn first to the argument, embraced by the District Court . . . that, since the President clearly cannot enter into a treaty without the consent of the Senate, the inference is inescapable that he must in all circumstances seek the same senatorial consent to terminate that treaty. As a matter of language alone, however, the same inference would appear automatically to obtain with respect to the termination by the President of officers appointed by him under the same clause of the Constitution and subject to Senate confirmation. But the Supreme Court has read that clause as not having such an inevitable effect in any and all circumstances. Compare *Myers v. United States*[60] . . . with *In Re Humphrey's Executor v. United States*[61] . . . . In the area of foreign relations in particular, where the constitutional commitment of powers to the President is notably comprehensive, it has never been suggested that the services of Ambassadors — appointed by the President, confirmed by the Senate, and of critical importance as they are to the successful conduct of our foreign relations — may not be terminated by the President without the prior authorization of that body.

The District Court's declaration, in the alternative, that the necessary authority in this instance may be granted by a majority of each house of Congress presumably has its source in the Supremacy Clause of Article VI. The argument is that a treaty, being a part of the "supreme Law of the Land," can only be terminated at the least by a subsequent federal statute.

The central purpose of the Supremacy Clause has been accepted to be that of causing each of the designated supreme laws — Constitution, statute, and treaty — to prevail, for purposes of domestic law, over state law in any form. Article VI speaks explicitly to the judges to assure that this is so. But these three types of supreme law are not necessarily the same in their other characteristics, any more than are the circumstances and terms of their creation the same. Certainly the Constitution is silent on the matter of treaty termination. And the fact that it speaks to the common characteristic of supremacy over state law does not provide any basis for concluding that a treaty must be unmade either by (1) the same process by which it was made, or (2) the alternative means by which a statute is made or terminated.

The constitutional institution of advice and consent of the Senate, provided two-thirds of the Senators concur, is a special and extraordinary condition of the exercise by the President of certain specified powers under Article II. It is not

---

[60] 272 U.S. 52 (1926).
[61] 295 U.S. 602 (1935).

lightly to be extended in instances not set forth in the Constitution. Such an extension by implication is not proper unless that implication is unmistakably clear.

* * * *

The constitution specifically confers no power of treaty termination on either the Congress or the Executive. We note, however, that the powers conferred upon Congress in Article I of the Constitution are specific, detailed, and limited, while the powers conferred upon the President by Article II are generalized in a manner that bespeaks no such limitation upon foreign affairs powers. "Section 2. The executive Power shall be vested in a President. . . ." Although specific powers are listed in Section 2 and Section 3, these are in many instances not powers necessary to an Executive, while "The Executive Power" referred to in Section 1 is nowhere defined. There is no required two-thirds vote of the Senate conditioning the exercise of any power in Section 1.

* * * *

Thus, in contrast to the law making power, the constitutional initiative in the treaty-making fields is in the President, not Congress. It would take an unprecedented feat of judicial construction to read into the Constitution an absolute condition precedent of congressional or Senate approval for termination of all treaties, similar to the specific one relating to initial approval. And it would unalterably affect the balance of power between the two Branches laid down in Articles I and II.

Ultimately, what must be recognized is that a treaty is *sui generis*. It is not just another law. It is an international compact, a solemn obligation of the United States and a "Supreme Law" that supersedes state policies and prior federal laws. For clarity of analysis, it is thus well to distinguish between treaty-making as an international act and the consequences which flow domestically from such act. In one realm the Constitution has conferred the primary role upon the President; in the other, Congress retains its primary role as lawmaker. The fact that the Constitution, statutes, and treaties are all listed in the Supremacy Clause as being superior to any form of state law does not mean that the making and unmaking of treaties can be analogized to the making and unmaking of domestic statutes any more that it can be analogized to the making or unmaking of a constitutional amendment.

The recognized powers of Congress to implement (or fail to implement) a treaty by an appropriation or other law essential to its effectuation, or to supersede for all practical purposes the effect of a treaty on domestic law, are legislative powers, not treaty-making or treaty termination powers. The issue here, however, is not Congress' legislative powers to supersede or affect the domestic impact of a treaty; the issue is whether the Senate (or Congress) must in this case give its prior consent to discontinue a treaty which the President thinks it desirable to terminate in the national interest and pursuant to a provision in the treaty itself. The existence, in practical terms, of one power does not imply the existence, in constitutional terms, of the other.

If we were to hold that under the Constitution a treaty could only be terminated by exactly the same process by which it was made, we would be locking the United

States into all of its international obligations, even if the President and two-thirds of the Senate minus one firmly believed that the proper course for the United States was to terminate a treaty. Many of our treaties in force, such as mutual defense treaties, carry potentially dangerous obligations. These obligations are terminable under international law upon breach by the other party or change in circumstances that frustrates the purpose of the treaty. In many of these situations the President must take immediate action. The creation of a constitutionally obligatory role in all cases for a two-thirds consent by the Senate would give to one-third plus one of the Senate the power to deny the President the authority necessary to conduct our foreign policy in a rational and effective manner. . . .

In short, the determination of the conduct of the United States in regard to treaties is an instance of what has broadly been called the "foreign affairs power" of the President. We have no occasion to define that term, but we do take account of its vitality. The *Curtiss-Wright* opinion, written by a Justice who had served in the United States Senate, declares in oft-repeated language that the President is "the sole organ of the federal government in the field of international relations." That status is not confined to the service of the President as a channel of communication, as the District Court suggested, but embraces an active policy determination as to the conduct of the United States in regard to a treaty in response to numerous problems and circumstances as they arise. . . .

We cannot find an implied role in the Constitution for the Senate in treaty termination for some but not all treaties in terms of their relative importance. There is no judicially ascertainable and manageable method of making any distinction among treaties on the basis of their substance, the magnitude of the risk involved, the degree of controversy which their termination would engender, or by another other standards. We know of no standards to apply in making such distinctions. The facts on which such distinctions might be drawn may be difficult of ascertainment; and the resolution of such inevitable disputes between the two Branches would be an improper and unnecessary role for the courts. To decide whether there was a breach or changed circumstances, for example, would involve a court in making fundamental decisions of foreign policy and would create insuperable problems of evidentiary proof. This is beyond the acceptable judicial role. All we decide today is that two-thirds Senate consent or majority consent in both houses is not necessary to terminate this treaty in the circumstances before us now. . . .

MacKinnon, Circuit Judge, dissenting in part and concurring in part.

I concur in the decision of a majority of my colleagues that the Senators and Representatives who are the plaintiffs in this action possess standing to have their grievance decided by this court, and that the question raised is not a "political" one that we should decline to adjudicate. . . . I disagree, however, with the majority's conclusion on the merits that the Constitution confers the absolute power on the President, acting alone, to terminate this Mutual Defense Treaty. No prior President has ever claimed the absolute power to terminate such a treaty. . . .

The Constitution of the United States establishes a government of three departments, each with enumerated powers. One of the enumerated powers vested in the President is the power to "*make* Treaties, . . . provided two thirds of the Senators present concur. . . ." Art. II, Section 2. (Emphasis added). "Treaties" so made and ratified, together with the Constitution and laws of the United States, become "the supreme Law of the Land. . . ." Art. VI. While the power to "make treaties" is a constitutionally enumerated power, the power to repeal or terminate treaties is not one of the enumerated powers. Yet it is manifest that the termination of treaties is frequently necessary. It must thus be recognized that the power to terminate treaties is one of the *implied powers* that the Constitution implicitly vested in the *Government* when it provided for the "making" of treaties. The facts here present another case involving the power of Congress to legislate under the Necessary and Proper clause, as in *Wayman v. Southard,*[62] . . . where Chief Justice Marshall said: [it] "seems to be one of those plain propositions which reasoning cannot make plainer. The terms of the clause neither require nor admit of elucidation. . . ." Later, Justice Harlan in *Neely v. Henkel,*[63] . . . which held for a unanimous court that the necessary and proper clause applied to the treaty power and treaties executed thereunder, said:

> The power of Congress to make all laws *necessary and proper* for carrying into execution as well the powers enumerated in section 8 of Article I of the Constitution, as all others vested in the Government of the United States, or in any Department or the officers thereof, includes the power to enact such legislation as is appropriate to give efficacy to any stipulations which it is competent for the President by and with the advice and consent of the Senate to insert in a treaty with a foreign power.[64] (Emphasis added).

This clearly recognizes the power of Congress to enact legislation pursuant to the termination clause that President Eisenhower had inserted in the Taiwan Treaty. *Missouri v. Holland*[65] . . . also squarely holds that the necessary and proper clause applies to treaty provisions.

It is thus submitted that since the exercise of the power to terminate treaties, which have the status of the law of the land, requires passage of a repealing law, it is Congress' responsibility under the Necessary and Proper Clause to do so. In Article I, Section 8, the Clause provides:

> The Congress shall have Power . . . To make all Laws which shall be necessary and proper for carrying into Execution the foregoing [enumerated] Powers, and *all other* [implied] *Powers vested by this Constitution in the Government of the United States, or in any Department or Officer thereof.* (Emphasis added).

When Congress passes an act terminating a treaty, it *makes a law*, as is illustrated by the Act of July 7, 1798, the first instance of treaty termination by the United States.

[Judge MacKinnon next undertook a lengthy review of the historical record regarding treaty terminations and concluded that there was ample evidence

---

[62] 10 Wheat. (23 U.S.) 1, 20, 6 L. Ed. 253 (1825).
[63] 180 U.S. 120, 21 S. Ct. 302, 45 L. Ed. 457 (1901).
[64] 180 U.S. at 121, 21 S. Ct. at 306.
[65] 252 U.S. 416, 40 S. Ct. 382, 64 L. Ed. 641 (1920).

to refute the President's claim that this record supported unilateral authority on his part.]

Upon appeal the Supreme Court granted certiorari, vacated the judgment and remanded the case with directions to dismiss the complaint, see *Goldwater v. Carter*.[66] Justices White and Blackmun would have granted the petition for certiorari and set the case for hearing. The other Justices were sharply divided in their reasons for dismissal. For the plurality, Justice Rehnquist (with whom the Chief Justice, Stewart, J. and Stevens, J. concurred) was of the opinion that the issue presented by the petitioners was a "political question" and therefore nonjusticiable "because it involves the authority of the President in the conduct of our country's foreign relations and the extent to which the Senate or the Congress is authorized to negate the action of the President." Although this position is worthy of considerable discussion in its own right, we will leave that task to courses on Constitutional Law.

NOTES AND QUESTIONS

(1) The Constitution is silent as to the termination of statutes, treaties and ambassadorial appointments. According to the Court of Appeals, terminating a treaty is more like firing an ambassador than repealing a statute. Are you persuaded? In answering, consider that ambassadors are officials of the executive branch who report to the President. Treaties are law, presumably binding, in a government under law, on the President as well as others.

(2) But then the Court of Appeals tells us, treaties are not like statutes, they are "sui-generis" because they are also international compacts. Does that explain why the President can't unilaterally terminate (*i.e.*, repeal) a statute but can unilaterally terminate a treaty? Consider the following:

(a) Suppose Congress, overriding a Presidential veto, passes a Joint Resolution directing the President to terminate a treaty. Is the President bound to comply? If so, it would seem that Congress can terminate a treaty — even as an international compact — the same way as it repeals a statute. Are treaties really "sui-generis?"

(b) As the district court pointed out, several provisions of the Mutual Defense Treaty with Taiwan were self-executing or had in fact been executed. If, as the Court of Appeals conceded, only Congress can supersede the rule of a treaty as domestic law, is not the President's ostensible power to terminate the Mutual Defense Treaty truly anomalous? What is the law of the land? the Treaty or no Treaty?

---

[66] 444 U.S. 996 (1979).

(3) Recall the question asked in considering *Curtiss-Wright*. Suppose Congress had considered and rejected a Joint Resolution authorizing the President to embargo military sales to the participants in the Chaco War. Would Justice Sutherland have said that the President could ignore Congress' action, proclaim the embargo and prosecute Curtiss-Wright? We don't know. But we do know the answer that the Appeals Court in *Goldwater* would give to that question. It is an unequivocal "Yes," is it not? After all, when Congress passes a statute or the Senate approves a treaty, we are no longer dealing with a question on which Congress has been silent, especially if, year after year, Congress has affirmed the vitality of the treaty by appropriations and other enabling legislation. In other words, according to the Court in *Goldwater*, the President can ignore Congress. But if Sutherland would have said "Yes," then surely he has been overruled by the *Steel Seizure* case. The court in *Goldwater* doesn't even mention *Steel Seizure*.

(4) Whose version of the Separation of Powers doctrine — Chief Justice Taft's version or Justice Brandeis' version (See page 1018, note 11*supra*) — does the court in *Goldwater* adopt? They make it plain, do they not? In the context of a decision as important as deciding upon the structure of America's military alliances, which version is most in keeping with the basic democratic values of American society? In answering are Jackson and Frankfurter helpful?

(5) After *Steel Seizure*, how can a subordinate federal court state that, while they can't define it, the inherent "foreign affairs power" of the President has "vitality?"

(6) It is noteworthy that a Mutual Defense Treaty, like any treaty of alliance, impinges directly upon Congress' war powers. Does it follow from this that the Separation of Powers doctrine, reinforced by political reality, might require that the President be barred from terminating any such treaty without obtaining the concurrence of either two-thirds of the Senate or a majority of both houses of Congress? Or perhaps that would be too much of "checks and balances"? Would Jackson and Frankfurter agree?

(7) Can the power to terminate a treaty be based on the President's recognition power.[67] Does acceptance of this proposition allow the President to make anything constitutional by making it ancillary to recognition? In considering this question, examine the Supreme Court's opinion in United States v. Pink, *infra*, p. 1068. Does a close reading of that opinion support such a Presidential power?

(8) The district court noted that in most prior instances treaties were terminated by joint action of President and Congress (or Senate). Nevertheless, there are examples of unilateral Presidential terminations. Presidents have unilaterally invoked the termination clause of a treaty under the following circumstances: (i) where the treaty was inconsistent with a subsequently enacted statute, (ii) where the other party to the treaty had committed a material breach which indicated that the purposes of the treaty were no longer capable of being realized, (iii) where circumstances had changed so substantially as to defeat the treaty's basic purposes or materially transformed the obligations to be performed thereunder. (See Article 62 of the Vienna Convention on the Law of Treaties). Are these examples precedent for President Carter's action? Upon what specific grants of power in Article II might the President have relied upon in these prior cases? Are the same

---

[67] See, Brennan, J., dissenting in *Goldwater v. Carter*.

grants available to the President in terminating the Taiwan treaty? Are you persuaded by the Court of Appeal's conclusion that it was impossible to draw a judicially manageable line between cases in which the President could and cases in which he could not unilaterally terminate a treaty?

(9) The Restatement (Third) of the Foreign Relations Law of the United States provides:

Section 339. Authority to Suspend or Terminate International Agreements: Law of the United States

Under the law of the United States, the President has the power

(a)   to suspend or terminate an agreement in accordance with its terms;

(b)   to make the determination that would justify the United States in terminating or suspending an agreement because of its violation by another party or because of supervening events, and to proceed to terminate or suspend the agreement on behalf of the United States; or

(c)   to elect in a particular case not to suspend or terminate an agreement.

In support of this sweeping grant of power to the President, the Restatement cites *Curtiss-Wright*, the Court of Appeals decision in *Goldwater v. Carter*, several Supreme Court cases that establish no more than what subsections (b) and (c) would allow. On this authority, the Restatement then blithely announces: "There would seem to be no constitutional basis for requiring Senate consent to the termination of a treaty, even if it is a mutual defense treaty." Really!

(8) With respect to the President's action, one of the authors of this casebook has expressed his view emphatically:

> In the end, what is the case for the President all about? Manifestly, it is not about efficacy in the conduct of foreign relations. Woven into the fabric of constitutional judgment — in the concepts, the balancing, the lawyers' subtle logic — is a concern for efficacy. And judged by lawyers' logic, the President's case utterly fails. To insist nonetheless that efficacy is still at issue, is to say something very different. It is to say that the Constitution is unworkable, that it is not fit for the modern world. But that is also to say that we cannot remain a free people.[68]

§ 12.02   Delegation Of Congressional Power

Apart from the scope of the President's independent authority over foreign relations there are a number of issues regarding congressional delegations of authority to the President. These arise most acutely on matters of foreign

---

[68] Swan, *The Constitutional Power to Terminate Treaties: Who, When and Why*, 6 Yale Studies In World Pub. Order 159, 235 (1979). For other reading on treaty termination, see, *e.g.*, Riggs, *Termination of Treaties by the Executive Without Congressional Approval: The Case of the Warsaw Convention*, 32 J. Air. & Com. 526 (1966); Comment, *Presidential Amendment and Termination of Treaties: The Case of the Warsaw Convention*, 34 U. Chi. L. Rev. 580 (1967); Scheffer, *Law of Treaty Termination as Applied to the U.S. Derecognition of the Republic of China*, 19 Harv. Int'l L. J. 931 (1978). Symposium, *Goldwater v. Carter*, 6 Yale Studies In World Pub. Order 1 (1979).

economic policy because it is in that area that Congress has been most active thereby limiting the possibilities for independent Presidential action. The first issue is the extent to which Congress is permitted by the Constitution to delegate its authority over foreign economic affairs to the President, an issue upon which one finds a strong admixture of both domestic and foreign affairs concerns.

On the domestic side, the Supreme Court has only twice in the last fifty years struck down a congressional delegation to the executive branch. *Panama Refining Co. v. Ryan*[1] struck down a section of the National Industrial Recovery Act (NIRA) that authorized the President to prohibit the transportation in interstate commerce of petroleum produced in excess of the amount allowed by State regulations. In *Schecter Poultry Corp. v. United States*,[2] the court held unconstitutional a poultry code promulgated under a section of the same Act authorizing the President to approve industry-developed codes of "fair competition" — a term left undefined in the legislation. While subsequent Supreme Court decisions upholding delegations of authority to the executive in New Deal legislation, wartime statutes on price controls and renegotiation, and in postwar measures may seem less stringent, none of these cases involved as unrestrained a delegation to the executive as that involved in the NIRA. Thus, in the purely domestic area the delegation doctrine still retains some viability. The controlling axiom was perhaps best put by Judge Leventhal in *Amalgamated Meat Cutters & Butcher Workers v. Connally*[3] as follows:

> There is no analytical difference, no difference in kind, between the legislative function of prescribing rules for the future that is exercised by the legislature or by the agency implementing the authority conferred by the legislature. The problem is one of limits.

> The key question is not answered by noting that the authority delegated is broad, or broader than Congress might have selected if it had chosen to operate within a narrower range. The issue is whether the legislative description of the task assigned "sufficiently marks the field within which the Administrator is to act so that it may be known whether he has kept within it in compliance with the legislative will."

> The *Yakus*[4] ruling of Chief Justice Stone carries forward the doctrine earlier articulated by Chief Justice Taft in *Hampton* that there is no forbidden delegation of legislative power "if Congress shall lay down by legislative act an intelligible principle" to which the official or agency must conform.

> Concepts of control and accountability define the constitutional requirement. The principle permitting a delegation of legislative power, if there has been sufficient demarcation of the field to permit a judgment whether the agency has kept within the legislative will, establishes a principle of accountability under which compatibility with the legislative design may be ascertained not only by Congress but by the courts and the public.[5]

---

[1] 293 U.S. 399, 55 S. Ct. 241, 89 L. Ed. 446 (1935).
[2] 295 U.S. 495, 55 S. Ct. 837, 79 L. Ed. 1570 (1935).
[3] 337 F. Supp. 737, (D.D.C. 1971).
[4] 321 U.S. 414 (1944). Ed.
[5] *Op. cit.* note 3.

With regard to cases with a strong foreign affairs component the boundaries of the doctrine seem more problematic. In *Curtiss-Wright*, Justice Sutherland drew a distinction which seems to accord more generous boundaries to the scope of delegations in the area of foreign affairs than that permitted with respect to domestic matters. While this distinction has been confirmed by subsequent Supreme Court decisions (see *e.g., Zemel v. Rusk*[6]), its precise operative significance, especially in light of Judge Leventhal's formulation, is at best obscure. Thus, in *Hampton & Co. v. United States*[7] the Supreme Court, when it upheld sections of the Tariff Act of 1922 that authorized the President to modify customs duties when necessary to equalize cost differences between American and foreign goods, invoked the "intelligible principle" standard alluded to by Judge Leventhal. Other cases of similar import upholding aspects of the tariff system include *Marshall Field & Co., v. Clark,*[8] and *Starkist Foods, Inc. v. United States.*[9] Not surprisingly, a number of decisions have stated by way of dicta that Congress' authority to delegate power over foreign commerce to the executive is not unlimited.

Moreover, in *Hampton v. Mow Sun Wong*[10] the Supreme Court ruled that a subdelegation of authority from the President to an administrative agency was unconstitutional. There aliens and others challenged Civil Service Commission regulations excluding all persons except American citizens and natives of Samoa from employment in most positions in the federal civil service. In a five to four decision the Supreme Court held that while there might be overriding national interests which would justify selective federal legislation discriminating against aliens, plaintiffs had been denied equal protection of the law (applicable to Federal government under the "due process" clause) since none of the interests which the government had cited in support of the challenged regulations fell within the responsibilities of the Civil Service Commission. Whether the government had an interest in facilitating treaty negotiations by enabling the President to offer employment opportunities to foreign citizens in exchange for reciprocal concessions or whether it had an interest in creating an incentive for aliens to qualify for naturalization were, the Court held, matters for the President and Congress and not the Civil Service Commission to judge. Accordingly, the Constitution required that any decision to deprive resident aliens of their liberty on these grounds had to be made by the President or by Congress. Any such decision by the Commission had to be justified by reasons that were the proper concern of that agency. It remains to be seen whether *Hampton* will prove to have any seminal force in controlling assignments of power over foreign affairs within the Executive Branch. Shortly after the Court's decision, the President issued an executive order that barred most aliens from the civil service. The constitutionality of that order was upheld by a federal district court in *Mow Sun Wong v. Hampton.*[11]

---

[6] 381 U.S. 1, 85 S. Ct. 1271, 14 L. Ed 2d 179 (1965).
[7] 276 U.S. 394, 48 S. Ct. 348, 72 L. Ed. 624 (1928).
[8] 143 U.S. 649, 12 S. Ct. 495, 36 L. Ed. 294 (1892).
[9] 275 F. 2d 472 (1959).
[10] 426 U.S. 88, 96 S. Ct. 1895, 48 L. Ed 2d 495 (1976).
[11] 435 F. Supp. 37 (N.D. Cal. 1977).

UNITED STATES v. YOSHIDA INTERNATIONAL, INC.

Court of Customs and Patent Appeals [12]
526 F. 2d 560 (1975)

MARKEY, CHIEF JUDGE.

This is an appeal from a judgment of the Customs Court [13] . . . granting Yoshida's motion for summary judgment, and declaring an import duty surcharge invalid. Presidential Proclamation 4074, because it imposed the surcharge, was held to have been beyond the President's delegated powers. The court stated that a delegation of sufficient breadth to encompass the proclamation would have been unconstitutional. We reverse.

Yoshida's merchandise (zippers) was imported from Japan. . . . The government levied, in addition to the standard duty . . . an import duty surcharge of 10% in accordance with item 948.00, which was added to the TSUS [Tariff Schedules of the United States] by Presidential Proclamation 4074. Yoshida challenges only the validity of [that] Proclamation.

During the summer of 1971, the United States was faced with an economic crisis. The nation suffered under an exceptionally severe and worsening balance of payments deficit. The gold reserve backing of the U.S. dollar had dropped from $17.8 billion in 1960 to less than $10.4 billion in June of 1971, reflecting a growing lack of confidence in the U.S. dollar abroad. Foreign exchange rates were being controlled by some of our major trading partners in such a way as to overvalue the U.S. dollar. That action, by stimulating U.S. imports and restraining U.S. exports, contributed substantially to the balance of payments deficit. As one step in a program designed to meet the economic crisis [14] the President issued Proclamation 4074, which . . . [after reciting the circumstances noted above, declared a national emergency and terminated or modified all prior Presidential Proclamations carrying out trade agreements in-so-far as required]:

> . . . to assess a surcharge in the form of a supplemental duty amounting to 10 percent ad valorem[:] . . . provided, however, that if the imposition of an additional duty of 10 percent ad valorem would cause the total duty or charge payable to exceed the total duty or charge payable at the rate prescribed in column 2 of the Tariff Schedules of the United States [the statutory rate], then the column 2 rate shall apply.

---

[12] Now called Court of Appeals for the Federal Circuit.

[13] Now the Court of International Trade.

[14] The Proclamation was part of a "New Economic Policy" which involved suspension of the convertibility of foreign held dollars into gold, reductions in taxes, Federal spending and foreign aid, a 90-day wage-price freeze, and imposition of the surcharge "[a]s a temporary measure." "Address to the Nation Outlining a New Economic Policy: The Challenge of Peace," Public Papers Of The Presidents of the United States, Richard Nixon 1971, 886 (1972), 65 Dept. of State Bull. 253 (1971), New York Times, Aug. 16, 1971, at 14, col. 1. The 90-day freeze, though challenged as based upon an unconstitutional delegation of legislative power in violation of the separation of powers doctrine, was upheld in *Amalgamated Meat Cutters & Butcher Work. v. Connally*, 337 F. Supp. 737 (D.D.C. 1971).

To implement the above language, Proclamation 4074 established [a new] item . . . [in the Tariff Schedule of the United States (TSUS Appendix)].

The President's authority for proclaiming the surcharge was stated in Proclamation 4074 to be " . . . the Constitution and the statutes, including . . . the Tariff Act of 1930, as amended (hereinafter referred to as "the Tariff Act")[15] and the Trade Expansion Act of 1962 (hereinafter referred to as "the TEA"),[16] under [which Acts] the President may, at any time, modify or terminate, in whole or in part, any proclamation made under" his authority.

* * * *

Within less than five months following imposition of the surcharge, a multilateral agreement (The "Smithsonian Agreement" of December 18, 1971) among the major industrial nations was reached which, *inter alia*, gave promise of ending the overvaluation of the U.S. dollar. . . . On December 20, 1971 the import duty surcharge was terminated [by a further Presidential Proclamation].

The main opinion below dealt extensively with the President's termination and emergency powers, finding that neither encompassed the tariff surcharge promulgated in Proclamation 4074.

The President's . . . power, as expressed in the Tariff Act and the TEA . . . to "terminate, in whole or in part," existing proclaimed rates was characterized [by the Customs Court] as twofold: the President may "nullify and bring to an end an entire proclamation" (whereupon the duty rate would revert to one previously established but not terminated, thereby permitting a portion thereof to remain in effect." Thus, said the court, exercise of the termination power affects duty rates:

. . . (1) to increase rates to the highest level, *i.e.*, the statutory rate, or (2) to raise or lower rates to conform to rates which have been established by a prior proclamation. In either of these instances, the rates, to which conformance may be sought, have been previously established either by the Congress (statutory rate) or by a bilateral negotiation embodied in a trade agreement pursuant to statutory authority. In short, the power to fix a new and independent rate [such as the 10% surcharge] requires a greater grant of power than that delegated to the President by the termination authority.

The Government's reliance on the phrase "unless otherwise provided" in general headnote 4(d) of the tariff schedules[17] was met with these words:

In our view that phrase is nothing more than an exception to the provision contained in headnote 4(d). . . . [It] gives the President discretionary authority when terminating a proclamation to specify a rate established in a specific

---

[15] Section 350(a)(6) of the Tariff Act of 1930, 19 U.S.C. 1351(a)(6) provided: "The President may at any time terminate, in whole or in part, any proclamation made pursuant to this section." - Ed.

[16] Section 255(b) of the Trade Expansion Act, 19 U.S.C. 1885(b) at the time provided: "The President may at any time terminate, in whole or in part, any proclamation made under this subchapter." — Ed.

[17] General headnote 4(d) provides: "Whenever a proclaimed rate is terminated or suspended, the rate shall revert unless otherwise provided, to the next intervening proclaimed rate previously superseded but not terminated or, if none, to the statutory rate."

previous proclamation other than the next intervening proclamation and thus avoid an automatic reversion to the next intervening proclaimed rate. . . .

The President's emergency power, as expressed in the Trading With The Enemy Act (TWEA), section 5(b), to "regulate . . . importation . . . of any property in which any foreign country or a national thereof has any interest," said the Customs Court:

> . . . conveys to the President an authority consisting only of a specific mode of regulation, as distinguished from the full and all-inclusive power to regulate foreign commerce. The delegation of the specific regulatory authority, "by means of instructions, licenses, or otherwise," manifestly is restrictive in scope. . . .

> We, therefore, conclude that section 5(b)(1) of the [TWEA] contains such restrictive standards and guidelines as to meet the test of constitutionality, but which, in turn, precludes the President from laying the supplemental duties provided by Presidential Proclamation 4074.

Though recognizing that the power to impose duties "may also serve as a regulatory measure," the Customs Court felt that the power to "regulate" could not, per se, be said to include the power to levy duties. . . .

The "emergency" feature of the TWEA was noted by the Customs Court in these words:

> For legislation delegating restrictive regulatory authority cannot operate, merely upon the declaration of an emergency, to the exclusion of other legislative acts providing procedures prescribed by the Congress for the accomplishment of the very purpose sought to be attained by Presidential Proclamation 4074. . . .

> . . . If the words "regulate . . . importation" were given the construction contended for by the defendant, the President by the declaration of a national emergency could determine and fix rates of duty at will, without regard to statutory rates prescribed by the Congress and without the benefit of standards or guidelines which must accompany any valid delegation of a constitutional power by the Congress. *Hampton & Co. v. United States*[18] . . . .

> The delegation of such an unrestrained and unbridled authority to lay duties, indeed, might well be deemed an abdication by the Congress of its constitutional power to regulate foreign commerce.

Citing *Panama Refining Co. v. Ryan* . . . for the proposition that good motives are not in point, the Customs Court summarized its view by stating:

> . . . [N]either need nor national emergency will justify the exercise of a power by the Executive not inherent in his office nor delegated by the Congress. Expedience cannot justify the means by which a deserving and beneficial national result is accomplished. . . .

The concurring opinion set forth substantial additional portions of the TWEA's legislative history, with this summarization:

---

[18] 276 U.S. at 409.

Thus it can be seen that the amendments to section 5(b) successively extended the President's licensing authority in the areas of foreign exchange, banking and currency transactions and transactions involving property in which foreign countries or nationals have an interest. However, nowhere in the Congressional debates, committee hearings or reports on section 5(b) and the amendments thereto is there even a glimmer of a suggestion that Congress ever intended — or even considered — this section as a vehicle for delegating any of its tariff-making authority.

The sole issue before us is whether the Customs Court erred as a matter of law, in holding that Proclamation 4074 was an *ultra vires* Presidential act. Resolution of the issue requires determination of whether the surcharge imposed by Presidential Proclamation 4074 was within the delegated authority to be found in either (1) the termination provisions of the Tariff Act [or] . . . of the Trade Expansion Act (TEA) . . . or (2) the emergency powers granted by Sec. 5(b) of the Trading With The Enemy Act (TWEA) . . . and if so, whether such a delegation of authority was constitutional.

The people of the new United States in adopting the Constitution, granted the power to "lay and collect duties" and to "regulate commerce" to the Congress, not the Executive. . . . Nonetheless, as the Customs Court recognized in the opinion below, and as other courts and commentators have noted, Congress, beginning as early as 1794 and continuing into 1974, has delegated the exercise of much of the power to regulate foreign commerce to the Executive. . . .

As inferred in *United States v. Curtiss-Wright Export Corp* . . . the President has certain "inherent" powers in the conduct of foreign relations and foreign affairs. Some . . . commentators . . . have cited certain "concurrent" powers he shares with the Congress in those fields. The Supreme Court referred to "pooled" legislative and executive powers in foreign affairs, including delegations of power over foreign commerce, in *Chicago & S. Air Lines Inc., v. Waterman Steamship Corp.*[19] It is nonetheless clear that no undelegated power to regulate commerce, or to set tariffs, inheres in the Presidency.

We are in basic agreement with the Customs Court's interpretation (quoted above) of the termination powers delegated by the Congress in the Tariff Act and in the TEA. [Having "found no delegation" it was unnecessary, the court concluded, to consider the constitutional ramifications "that might obtain" had a delegation been attempted].

We are presented, in this case, with the first reliance upon the TWEA as authority for a Presidential imposition of a temporary surcharge on imports. There being nothing in the TWEA or in its history which specifically either authorizes or prohibits the imposition of a surcharge, and no judicial precedent involving the same, we tread new ground.

Our duty is to effectuate the intent of Congress. In so doing we look first to the literal meaning of the words employed. . . .

The express delegation in Sec. 5(b) of the TWEA is broad indeed. It provides that the President may, during "any" period of national emergency declared by

---

[19] 333 U.S. 103, 110, 68 S. Ct. 431, 92 L. Ed. 568 (1948).

him, through "any" agency he designates, or "otherwise," and under "any" rules he prescribes, by means of instructions, licenses, "or otherwise," "regulate," "prevent" or "prohibit" the importation of "any" property in which "any foreign country or a national thereof has any interest," and that the President may, in the manner provided, take "other and further measures," not inconsistent with the statute, for the "enforcement" of the Act.

The Act authorizes the President to define "any or all" of the terms employed by Congress in Sec. 5(b).

It appears incontestable that Sec. 5(b) does in fact delegate to the President, for use during war or during national emergency only, the power to "regulate importation." The plain and unambiguous wording of the statute permits no other interpretation. . . . [T]he primary implication of any emergency power is that it should be effective to deal with a national emergency successfully. The delegation in Sec. 5(b) is broad and extensive; it could not have been otherwise if the President were to have, within constitutional boundaries, the flexibility required to meet problems surrounding a national emergency with the success desired by Congress.

A question remains, however, as to how the President may regulate importation in a national emergency, *i.e.*, what means of execution of the delegated power is permissible. As appears below, we agree with the Customs Court that the delegation could not constitutionally have been of "the full and all-inclusive power to regulate foreign commerce." We do not believe, however, as the Customs Court apparently did, that only in such a sweeping delegation could authority be found for Proclamation 4074. The choice is not draconian.

The Customs Court, considering a broad delegation unconstitutional in the absence of standards restricting the President's actions thereunder, found such standards in an interpretation of the words "by means of instructions, licenses or otherwise" as words of restriction. . . .

We agree with the Customs Court on the necessity of determining the scope and extent of delegated regulatory power. The question in this context is whether Congress, having itself regulated imports by employing duties as a regulatory tool, and having delegated to the President, for use in national emergencies, the power to regulate imports, intended to permit the President to employ the same regulatory tool, and what, if any limitations lay upon his use thereof.

The opinion below states:

The words "instructions, licenses, or otherwise" contained in Section 5(b)(1) define the nature and mode of the regulatory authority intended to be delegated to the President. These words conform to the phraseology used through the history of the Act in the establishment of a system of *licenses and permits* for the control of property during a time of war and crisis and which have come to be recognized as the hallmark and distinguishing feature of the Act. (Emphasis added by the Appeals Court).

We [disagree]. . . . The words "instructions" and "importation" were not added until 1941. As the concurring opinion below recognizes, the legislative history of the TWEA is silent regarding the reasons for the 1941 insertion of those two words. A statute must be interpreted as a whole, and we cannot reconcile the

Customs Court's restrictive view with the remainder of Sec. 5(b), which authorizes the President to take numerous actions not amenable to "licensing." Recognizing that to impose duties can be to "regulate," the Customs Court nonetheless interpreted the words "the President may . . . regulate . . . importation" as though they read, in effect, "the President may . . . license . . . importation.". . . .

The narrow interpretation adopted by the Customs Court also rests upon disregard of the phrase "or otherwise," which follows "by means of instructions, licenses.". . . . The phrase appears to us to be expansive, not restrictive. The words "or otherwise," if they mean anything, must mean that Congress authorized the use of means which, though not identified, were different from, and additional to, "instructions" and "licenses.". . . .

Demonstrably careful and extensive research into the history of Sec. 5(b) led the author of the concurring opinion below to give weight to the lack of an indication that Congress "intended - or even considered - this section as a vehicle for delegating any of its tariff-making authority." However, we do not find [this] . . . surprising. . . . Having left the battlefield, it would hardly do [for Congress] to dictate all the weapons to be used in the fight. Nor do we find anything in the inconclusive and hurried legislative history of Sec. 5(b) which indicates an intent to prohibit action such as that reflected in Proclamation 4074.

We conclude, therefore, that Congress, in enacting Section 5(b) of the TWEA, authorized the President, during an emergency, to exercise the delegated substantive power, *i.e.*, to "regulate importation," by imposing an import duty surcharge or by other means appropriately and reasonably related, as discussed below, to the particular nature of the emergency declared. Whether a delegation of such breadth as to have authorized Proclamation 4074 would be constitutionally embraced, is determined, however, by the nature of the particular surcharge herein and its relationship to other statutes, as well as by its relationship to the particular emergency confronted.

In its proper concern for adherence to the Constitution, the Customs Court erred, we believe, in its expressed fear that, if Proclamation 4074 were upheld, the President, by "merely" declaring a national emergency, "could determine and fix rates of duty at will, without regard to statutory rates prescribed by Congress.". . . . [P]residential actions must be judged in the light of what the President actually did, not in the light of what he could have done. To this we would add, "and not in the light of what he might do." Each Presidential proclamation or action under Sec. 5(b) must be evaluated on its own facts and circumstances. To uphold the specific surcharge imposed by Proclamation 4074 is not to approve in advance any future surcharge of a different nature, or any surcharge differently applied or any surcharge not reasonably related to the emergency declared.

Proclamation 4074, far from fixing rates in disregard of congressional will, specifically provided, as noted above, "that if the imposition of an additional duty of 10 percent ad valorem would cause the total duty or charge payable to exceed the total duty or charge payable at the rate prescribed in column 2 of the Tariff Schedules of the United States, then the column 2 rate shall apply."

Further, the surcharge was limited to articles which had been the subject of prior tariff concessions and, thus, to less than all United States imports. . . .

With respect to those articles on which no concession had been granted, the congressionally established rates remained untouched. And the limitation to "dutiable" articles meant that no duties were created on goods entitled to free entry under the statute. Far from attempting, therefore, to tear down or supplant the entire tariff scheme of Congress, the President imposed a limited surcharge, and "a temporary measure" . . . calculated to help meet a particular national emergency, which is quite different from "imposing whatever tariff rates he deems desirable."

Reliance by the Customs Court on *Youngstown Sheet & Tube* . . . is misplaced. We do not have here, as was the case in *Youngstown*, what the Customs Court described as "legislative acts providing procedures prescribed by the Congress for the accomplishment of the very purpose sought to be obtained" by a Presidential Proclamation. The surcharge did not run counter to any explicit legislation. We know of no act, other than the TWEA, "providing procedures" for dealing with a national emergency involving a balance of payments problem such as that which existed in 1971.

Congress has provided numerous acts touching upon the regulation of imports. The Tariff Act . . . the Trade Agreements Act of 1934 . . . and the [TEA] all provide tariff-making authority to the President, albeit with various limitations. Those acts were viewed by the Customs Court as indicating a congressional intent that such limitations should apply to any delegation of its tariff making authority. Those acts, however, are applicable to normal conditions on a continuing basis. The existence of limited authority under certain trade acts does not preclude the execution of other, broader authority under a national emergency powers act. Though Sec. 5(b) of the TWEA does overlap the traditional framework of trade legislation, it is not controlling that some of the same considerations are involved. That is to be expected. All deal with foreign commerce. Congress has said what may be done with respect to foreseeable events in the Tariff Act, the TEA, and in the Trade Act of 1974 (all of which are in force) and has said what may be done with respect to unforeseeable events in the TWEA. In the latter, Congress necessarily intended a grant of power adequate to deal with national emergencies. . . . We find it unreasonable to suppose that Congress passed the TWEA, delegating broad powers to the President for periodic use during national emergencies, while intending that the President, when faced with such an emergency, must follow limiting procedures prescribed in other acts designed for continuing use during normal times.

A standard inherently applicable to the exercise of delegated emergency powers is the extent to which the action taken bears a reasonable relation to the power delegated and to the emergency giving rise to the action. The nature of the power determines what may be done and the nature of the emergency restricts the how of its doing, *i.e.*, the means of execution. Though courts will not normally review the essentially political questions surrounding the declaration or continuance of a national emergency, they will not hesitate to review the actions taken in response thereto or in reliance thereon. . . .

It is clear that the surcharge herein had, as its primary purpose, the curtailment, *i.e.*, the regulation, of imports. What was sought was an offset to actions of our foreign trading partners which had led to loss of our favorable balance of trade and to a serious negative balance, as the President's address . . . made plain. Pressure exerted by the surcharge contributed to achievement of a multilateral agreement of major nations, which included a realignment of currency exchange rates. . . . [I]t is purpose, not form, which should govern judicial characterization of a charge on imports. . . . A principal function and necessary effect of the import surcharge in Proclamation 4074 was to regulate imports. Section 5(b) delegated power to "regulate importation." The relationship between the action taken and the power delegated was thus one of substantial identity.

The President's choice of means of execution must also bear a reasonable relation to the particular emergency confronted. . . . That the surcharge herein had overtones of foreign relations and foreign policy seems self-evident. As the world has grown smaller and trade more complex, foreign exchange rates, international monetary reserves, balance of payments, and trade barriers have become increasingly intertwined, with trade barriers being used as tools in furtherance of foreign policy. . . . The Customs Court appreciated that the nature of the surcharge action converged with presidential representation of the United States in the "society of nations" and with the President's efforts to achieve "stability in the international trade position" of our country. The declared national emergency was premised on a prolonged decline in our country's international monetary reserves, the serious threat to our trade position, and our unfavorable balance of payments position. Unlike quotas and other forms of action, a surcharge can obviously be quickly imposed and removed, is not discriminatory among nations affected, and is administratively less complex. Through its impact on imports, the surcharge imposed by Proclamation 4074 had a direct effect on our nation's balance of trade and, in turn, on its balance of payments deficit and its international monetary reserves. We conclude, therefore that the President's action in imposing the surcharge bore an eminently reasonable relationship to the emergency confronted.

* * * *

[The court went on to uphold the constitutionality of the TWEA as interpreted and applied in this case. In doing so the court noted that no one has a constitutional right to engage in trade with foreign nations or to the maintenance of an existing right or duty. The court also stressed that the TWEA was operative only during war or national emergencies, situations which did not lend themselves to easy coverage by specific, detailed guidelines. In emergency situations, only the President was in a position to make the quick, decisive response required. The Court found no grant of "unrestrained and unbridled" authority in Section 5(b) of the TWEA, but pointed out that the courts are prepared to strike down any unreasonable or ultra vires exercise of the power granted in that provision].

NOTES AND QUESTIONS

(1) In *Yoshida*, the Court stated "[i]t is . . . clear that no undelegated power to regulate commerce, or to set tariffs, inheres in the Presidency." Is a flat statement of this kind consistent with the various theories of the President's power expressed in the *Steel-Seizure* decision? Consider the following:

(a) Under appropriate circumstances, could the President not proclaim United States' neutrality in a foreign war, and, as part of maintaining that neutrality, issue an Executive Order prohibiting the export of war material to the belligerents which he would then undertake to enforce through civil proceedings in the courts? Are there other circumstances under which the President might independently "regulate" foreign commerce?

(b) In practical terms, what is the chief constitutional barrier that the President is likely to encounter in taking such action? Again, the *Steel Seizure* decision is instructive, is it not?

(c) Suppose Congress had never enacted or even considered a provision along the lines of Section 5(b) of the Trading With the Enemy Act, could the President upon his independent authority have imposed the 10% surcharge that was at issue in *Yoshida*? How is your answer influenced by the courts' interpretation of the Tariff Act of 1930 and the Trade Expansion Act of 1962?

(d) In *Independent Gasoline Marketers Council v. Duncan*,[20] the court denied the President authority under Section 232(b) of the Trade Expansion Act of 1962 (TEA) to impose a 10 cents per gallon gasoline "license fee" on the ground that its importation threatened national security. The court rejected the executive's assertion that the President had independent authority to impose the fee because of the "national security" aspects of oil product importation. The court found that Congress had explicitly precluded a fee-setting approach in enacting the Emergency Policy and Conservation Act, and that there was nothing in the TEA or other legislative authority cited by the executive to the contrary. For a further discussion of the President's independent powers to regulate foreign commerce through executive agreements, see discussion of *United States v. Guy W. Capps., Inc.*, discussed *infra* page 1072, note 4.

(2) In *Yoshida*, the Customs Court held, and the Court of Customs and Patent Appeals confirmed, that the phrase "unless otherwise provided" in general headnote 4(d) of the tariff schedules did not authorize the President to establish new intermediate rates in conjunction with the statutory authority to terminate in part. It only permitted him to specify a rate established in a specific prior proclamation other than the immediately proceeding one. But doesn't general headnote 4(d) permit the President, without the *proviso*, to reestablish a rate other than the next preceding one simply by terminating a series of prior proclamations? Does the court's reading of the proviso render the headnote redundant?

---

[20] 492 F. Supp. 614 (D.C. 1980).

(3) The two courts also agreed in *Yoshida* that Section 255(b) of the Trade Expansion Act of 1962 provided no authorization for the President to modify duty rates other than by "a mechanical procedure of supplanting or replacing existing rates with rates which have been established by prior proclamations or by statute." In reaching this determination the Customs Court relied heavily on the legislative history of the Act. Specifically, the court noted that Congress rejected a provision in the bill that would have given the President the express authority to terminate and adjust rates to a new rate at any point in the range above the reduced rate but no higher than the rate which would have been applicable if the whole of the proclamation had been terminated. The Congress also failed to enact a Senate amendment that would have authorized a surcharge. In the court's view these deletions demonstrated Congress' unwillingness to grant such expansive discretionary powers to the President because it may have thought that they represented an invalid delegation of legislative power to the executive. Nowhere in this legislative history, however, is there any indication why Congress decided to delete these provisions. Does this mean Congress believed that the President already had such power under Section 255(b), and hence the proposed additions were superfluous? In considering this question, how would you evaluate the argument that Congress might have wished to delegate to the President a power to modify rates in order to assure an efficient, effective and unitary approach to any international crises created by tariff "wars," balance of payment problems, and changes in international monetary policy or because he is less subject to pressure by special interest groups than is Congress? Or, is it more persuasive to think that a provision conferring extensive power on the President in the area of foreign commerce would not go undiscussed by a Congress jealous of its legislative prerogatives? How does enactment of Section 5(b) of the Trading with the Enemy Act bear on your answer? Exactly how expansive a power was the President claiming under Section 255(b)?

(4) Does the Court of Customs and Patent Appeals' interpretation in *Yoshida* of the President's power to modify duty rates under the Trading with the Enemy Act allow the President, simply by declaring a national emergency, to subvert the entire tariff structure, free from any limitations in other tariff acts, and free from judicial review of a declaration of the emergency? Is a narrow interpretation of Section 5(b) of that Act necessary to preserve the integrity of the trade acts or to obviate a finding that Congress has exceeded its constitutional authority to delegate power over foreign trade to the President?

(5) The fact that the Supreme Court has only twice struck down legislation on the ground it contained an unconstitutional delegation of legislative authority to the executive, and the willingness of the courts in the years since to uphold some very broad grants of authority, has led some commentators, as the court in *Yoshida* noted,[21] to treat the so-called "non-delegation" doctrine as a dead letter. But consider another perspective. Recall Judge Leventhal's statement that "concepts of control and accountability define the constitutional requirement." That accountability is not only to the Congress but to "the courts and the public." Consider what must almost invariably happen when a court upholds a statute

---

[21] 526 F. 2d at page 572 note 14 citing 1 K. Davis, Administrative Law Treatise 76 (1958).

against the contention that it contains an impermissible delegation of legislative authority to the executive. *Yoshida* is a good example.

(a) How did the Customs Court in *Yoshida* handle the question of whether the Trade Act of 1930 and the Trade Expansion Act of 1962 violated the "non-delegation" doctrine? What interpretive techniques did the Customs Court use to reach its conclusion? The upshot was, of course, a conclusion that the President lacked the authority he claimed under those statutes. He was clearly held accountable, wasn't he? Reflect on the role that the "non-delegation" doctrine played in the process of holding him accountable.

(b) With regard to Section 5(b) of the Trading With The Enemy Act, can you identify some boundary lines within which the President must stay after this decision?[22]

§ 12.03   Treaties and Other International Agreements

[A]   The Constitutional Status of the Treaty

The first set of questions bearing upon the constitutional status of the treaty concerns the scope of the treaty power. There are three primary issues. Does our system of Federalism impose limits upon the treaty making power; are there areas reserved to the States alone? Does the Constitution contain an implicit limitation on the use of treaties in matters of domestic concern? Finally, are there constraints to be found in specific constitutional guarantees such as the Bill of Rights?

Missouri v. Holland[1] is the leading case on the issue whether the rights reserved to the States under the Tenth Amendment preclude treaty coverage of certain subjects. There, the State of Missouri sought to enjoin a game warden from attempting to enforce the Migratory Bird Treaty Act of 1918. Congress had passed that Act in order to implement a 1916 treaty with Great Britain prescribing closed seasons and other protections for several species of birds during their migrations between the United States and Canada. Missouri argued that the statute was an unconstitutional interference with the rights reserved to the States by the Tenth Amendment and that it had a pecuniary interest as owner of wild birds within its borders. It supported this argument by noting that Congress had earlier passed a statute, without aid of a treaty, regulating the killing of migratory birds within the States and that the lower federal courts had declared that statute an unconstitutional encroachment by the Federal government on a subject reserved to the States.

Writing for the Supreme Court, Mr. Justice Holmes stated that whether or not the earlier lower court decisions had been rightly decided, they "cannot be accepted as a test of the treaty power." On the contrary, he said:

[22] For consideration of some of the issues raised in this section, see, *e.g.*, Pollard & Boillot, The Import Surcharge of 1971: A Case Study Of Executive Power In Foreign Commerce, 7 Vand. J. Transnat'l L. 137 (1973); notes in 29 U. Chi. L. Rev. 177 (1971); 73 Mich. L. Rev. 952 (1975).
[1] 252 U.S. 416, 40 S. Ct. 382, 64 L. Ed. 641 (1920).

[I]t is obvious that there may be matters of the sharpest exigency for the national well being that an act of Congress could not deal with but that a treaty followed by such an act could, and it is not lightly to be assumed that, in matters requiring national action, a power which must belong to and somewhere reside in every civilized government' is not to be found. [In this case] . . . "a national interest of very nearly the first magnitude is involved. It can be protected only by national action in concert with that of another power. The subject matter is only transitorily within the State and has no permanent habitat therein. But for the treaty and the statute there soon might be no birds for any powers to deal with. . . . We are of the opinion that the treaty and the statute must be upheld.

For a time, there was fear in some quarters that *Missouri v. Holland* would permit a vast expansion of the Federal power at the expense of the States. In particular, it was feared that the Federal Government by adhering, through a treaty or executive agreement, to various international human rights conventions could impose on the States a whole new regime of law inimical to States' Rights and subversive of State segregation laws and practices, a regime that Congress either lacked constitutional authority or the political will to impose by legislation. This fear also spawned renewed interest in the so-called "domestic concern" limitation on the treaty power discussed below, and, in the early 1950s, produced a number of proposed constitutional amendments most notably that by Senator John Bricker of Indiana.

In more recent years a number of developments have caused these concerns to subside. The vast growth of Federal power, through expansive interpretations of the "commerce clause," has rendered the kind of "back-door" resort to the treaty power that was used in *Missouri v. Holland* largely unnecessary and inadvisable. With the rise of the civil rights movement, the courts and Congress, the latter acting under the "commerce clause" and Section 5 of the 14th Amendment, have moved directly to change State law and practice.

Another purported limit on the scope of the treaty making power is the so-called "domestic concern" limitation. Echoing Jefferson, Charles Evans Hughes in remarks before the American Society of International Law in 1929 had the following to say:

What is the power to make a treaty? What is the object of the power? The normal scope of the power can be found in the appropriate object of the power. The power is to deal with foreign nations with regard to matters of international concern. It is not a power intended to be exercised . . . with respect to matters that have no relation to international concerns.

* * * *

So I come back to the suggestion I made at the start, that this is a sovereign nation; from my point of view the nation has the power to make any agreement whatever in a constitutional manner that relates to the conduct of our international relations, unless there can be found some express prohibition in the Constitution, and I am not aware of any which would in any way detract from the power as I have defined it in connection with our relations with other governments. But if we attempted to use the treaty-making power to deal with matters which did not pertain to our external relations but to control matters which normally and appropriately were within the local jurisdiction of the States, then I again say there might be ground for implying a limitation upon the treaty-making power that it is intended for the purpose of having treaties made relating to foreign affairs and not to make laws for the people of the United States in their external concerns through the exercise of the asserted treaty-making power. . . .[2]

This statement by Hughes has been interpreted by some to mean that certain matters are not appropriate subjects for agreement with another country because they are our own affair and not the legitimate "concern" of any other country. Noting this interpretation of Hughes' statement by way of dictum, the court in *Power Authority of New York v. Federal Power Commission*,[3] construed a "reservation" which allegedly concerned a matter of purely domestic concern as an expression of the Senate's desires and not as part of the treaty. However, no authoritative determination of the validity of this interpretation has ever been rendered.

Assuming the validity of the domestic concern limitation, one must keep in mind the observation of the Permanent Court of International Justice in the *Tunis-Morocco Nationality Decrees* case.[4] Whether a matter is solely within a nation's domestic jurisdiction is, the court observed, "an essentially relative question; it depends upon the development of international relations." Through customary law, multilateral conventions, international organizations and other less formal international arrangements and processes, the scope of international relations has developed dramatically. The area of affairs that can be deemed of purely domestic concern has greatly narrowed.

As already noted, arguments favoring this limitation have arisen most often in debates over whether the United States should ratify various human rights conventions. In addition to Senator Bricker, the American Bar Association advanced the argument that the United States should not ratify such conventions because they covered matters of purely domestic concern. Not until 1976 did the ABA reverse its earlier opposition and vote in favor of U.S. ratification of the Genocide Convention. It is thus an open question whether the domestic concern limitation on the treaty power currently has much support. In 1971, the Committee on Foreign Relations, in recommending that the Senate consent to ratification of the Genocide Convention,[5] stated in its Report[6] that genocide "cannot help but be of concern to the community of nations" and observed that "if the United States Government is conceded the power to make treaties governing the killing of seals, it is capable of acceding to a treaty on the killing of people."

Another form of constitutional challenge to the scope of the treaty power can arise when a particular treaty is attacked as infringing upon rights guaranteed to

[2] Quoted in L. Henkin, Foreign Affairs & The Constitution 151-55 (1972).
[3] 247 F. 2d 538 (D.C. Cir.), vacated 355 U.S. 64, 78 S. Ct. 141, 2 L. Ed. 2d 107 (1957).
[4] P.C.I.J. Ser. B, No. 4 (1923).
[5] Entered into force for the United States, February 23, 1989. U.S. Treaties In Force On January 1, 1989.
[6] Report of the Senate Foreign Relations Committee (Exec. Rep. No. 92-6) on the Genocide Convention, 92nd Cong. 1st Sess. 1971.

the individual by the Constitution. In *Reid v. Covert*,[7] the Court upheld a challenge to two "executive agreements" — which were treated as equivalent to a treaty — with Great Britain and Japan. The agreements stipulated that United States military courts were to have exclusive jurisdiction over offenses committed in Great Britain or Japan by American servicemen or their dependents. Pursuant to these agreements and the applicable provisions of the Uniform Code of Military Justice, Mrs. Covert and Mrs. Smith, who killed their husbands while the latter were stationed in England and Japan, were each tried by courts-martial. After conviction, the defendants sought their release on writs of habeas corpus. The writ was granted in the case of Mrs. Covert and denied in the case of Mrs. Smith. On direct appeal the Supreme Court affirmed Mrs. Covert's case and reversed Mrs. Smith's. In an opinion joined by the Chief Justice, Justice Douglas and Justice Brennan, Justice Black concluded, *inter alia*, that a military trial of civilians was contrary to Article III, Section 2 of the Constitution and the provisions of the Fifth and Sixth Amendments which assure indictment by grand jury and trial by jury. In separate opinions, Justices Frankfurter and Harlan limited their concurrence to capital cases and refused to concur in so literal a reading of the Constitution.

In the course of his opinion, Justice Black stated that "[t]here is nothing in [the Supremacy Clause (Art. VI cl. 2)] which intimates that treaties and laws enacted pursuant to them do not have to comply with the provisions of the Constitution. . . . It would be manifestly contrary to the objectives of those who were responsible for the Bill of Rights — let alone alien to our entire constitutional history and tradition — to construe Article VI as permitting the United States to exercise power under an international agreement without observing constitutional prohibitions. In effect, such construction would permit amendment of that document in a manner not sanctioned by Article V." Acknowledging that Congress' power to "make rules for the Government and Regulation" of the armed forces (Article I, Section 8, cl. 14) had been construed to authorize statutes establishing a separate system of military justice, that authority, the Court held, could not be extended to civilians. *Reid v. Covert* was a capital case, but later decisions of the Court, such as *Kinsella v. United States Ex Rel. Singleton*[8] have extended *Reid* to non-capital cases.

In spite of Justice Black's sweeping assertions, the student will want to consider *United States v. Pink* and *United States v. Belmont* discussed *infra* page 1068. Following *Reid v. Covert*, the United States entered into a number of Status of Forces Agreements with our allies which provide for trial of American servicemen abroad in foreign courts with stipulated "fair trial" guarantees. Challenges to the constitutionality of these agreements or to the constitutionality of particular trials under their aegis have thus far been turned back by the courts in a number of decisions that are well worth examining.[9] Another related problem concerns the effect that the Constitution's guaranty of "due process" and other requirements of a fair trial may have on the power of the United States to extradite fugitives under our extradition treatise or imprison in the United States persons convicted

---

[7] 354 U.S. 1, 77 S. Ct. 1222, 1 L. Ed. 2d 1148 (1957).

[8] 361 U.S. 234, 80 S. Ct. 297, 4 L. Ed. 2d 268 (1960),

[9] Cases are collected in Stotzky & Swan, *Due Process Methodology and Prisoner Exchange Treaties: Confronting an Uncertain Calculus*, 62 Minn. L. Rev. 733 (1978).

of crimes abroad and returned to this country under the prisoner exchange treatise with Mexico and Canada.[10]

[B]   The Self-Executing Treaty

A distinct although related question concerns the problem of whether a treaty is "self-executing," *i.e.*, purports directly by its own terms to operate as a rule of domestic law rather than simply imposing an international legal obligation upon the United States. Not infrequently a treaty is said to be self-executing only if it gives rise to rights in private individuals. There are serious problems with this. Rarely do treaties confer rights on individuals in so many words. It is typically a matter of interpretation based upon the subject matter of the treaty and the nature of the behavior toward that subject that the treaty enjoins upon the governmental signatories. The more thoroughly the subject of the treaty falls within an area reserved in the signatory countries to private action — or in which private individuals are significant actors — (*e.g.*, treaties concerning the ownership and inheritance of property, family matters, the establishment and carrying-on of business enterprises, trade, the patenting of inventions, etc.) and the more specifically the signatory governments pledge themselves to a course of conduct intended to facilitate, protect or regulate such private matters, the more readily the treaty may be read as conferring rights upon private individuals. But it should be quite apparent that this line of interpretive inquiry does not and cannot answer the question of whether the treaty was intended to operate of its own force as a rule of domestic law. That a treaty creates private rights may be probative of an intent to have the treaty operate automatically as domestic law. But, so long as private rights can also be created by statute, the mere conclusion that the treaty was intended to create private rights does not also demonstrate that the treaty was intended to be the exclusive mode for accomplishing that result superceding the need for a statute.

Conversely, the mere fact that a treaty was not intended to create rights in private individuals does not demonstrate the absence of an intent for it to operate of its own force as domestic law. On this point there is a great deal of confusion and much careless language in the cases. There are many treaties that create no private rights at all and cannot be readily enforced in a court of law. The reason is that absent the conferral of a private legal right it will be difficult, often impossible, for any private individual to surmount the threshold standing and other justiciability requirements that must be overcome before a court can entertain the case. But it would be startling in the extreme to suggest that the mere lack of judicial enforceability deprives a treaty of its force as domestic law; that it was not legally binding on State officials under the Supremacy clause and their oath of office, or upon executive officials under the Supremacy and "take Care" clauses. Certainly, there are a host of statutes which create no private rights and, as a consequence, tend to be insulated from judicial enforcement because of justiciability and prudential standing requirements. Equally certain these statutes are part of the law-of-the-land under the Supremacy Clause, binding upon both State and Federal officials. Why should treaties differ? Nothing in the Supremacy Clause distinguishes between treaties and statutes on this point. And surely the

---

[10] *Id.*

larger conception of a government under law suggests no reason why public officials may ignore treaties because they create no private rights and hence cannot be vouchsafed judicial enforcement, but may not ignore statutes of identical purport. Once again thus, the only distinction between a self-executing and non-self-executing treaty is whether the treaty was intended to operate of its own force as domestic law binding upon public officials, or whether that effect was intended to be contingent upon further legislative action.

One classic case in this area illustrating, in part, some of the confusion which attends the subject is *Sei Fujii v. State of California*,[11] which held that the provisions of the United Nations Charter dealing with human rights were non-self-executing. In pertinent part the California court stated that for a treaty to be self-executing " . . . it must appear that the framers of the treaty intended to prescribe a rule that, standing alone, would be enforceable in the [national] courts . . . " and concluded that the United Nations Charter "pledges the various countries to cooperate . . . " and " . . . represents a moral commitment . . . ," but its provisions " . . . were not intended to supercede existing domestic legislation, and we cannot hold that they operate to invalidate the alien land law [of California]. . . ."

The result and reasoning in *Sei Fujii* has been sharply criticized. And the issue continues to be litigated, as the following case illustrates.

DIGGS v. RICHARDSON

Circuit Court of Appeals (District of Columbia)
555 F.2d 849 (1976)

LEVENTHAL, CIRCUIT JUDGE:

This suit seeks judicial enforcement of a U.N. Security Council resolution which calls upon member states to have no dealings with South Africa which impliedly recognize the legality of that country's occupation of the former U.N. territory of Namibia. The plaintiffs, among whom are American citizens who have been denied admission to Namibia, seek declaratory and injunctive relief prohibiting our government from continuing to deal with the South Africans concerning the importation of seal furs from Namibia. We hold this case to be nonjusticiable.

United Nations Security Council Resolution 301, for which the United States voted, declares South Africa's continued presence in Namibia a breach of international obligations and . . . calls upon all states. . . .

> (d) to abstain from sending diplomatic or special missions to South Africa that include the Territory of Namibia in their jurisdiction;. . . .
>
> (f) to abstain from entering into economic and other forms of relationship or dealing with South Africa on behalf of or concerning Namibia which may entrench its authority over the Territory. . . .

---

[11] 3 Cal. 2d 718, 242 P. 2d 617 (1952).

Plaintiffs contend that this resolution states a binding international obligation of the United States[12] and further contend that the Resolution is self-executing — that, without further legislative or executive action, it has become a part of our judicially enforceable domestic law.

Plaintiffs then call the court's attention to several visits to South Africa in 1973-74 by officials of the U.S. Department of Commerce, who met with South African officials and individuals and discussed the harvesting of seal furs in Namibia. The purpose of these visits and related correspondence was to gather information which would allow the Department of Commerce to decide whether to grant to an American company a waiver of the Marine Mammal Protection Act of 1972, which otherwise prohibits the importation of seal furs. Plaintiffs contend that these contacts were in violation of the U.N. resolution quoted above[13] and ask that the district court enjoin any further contacts of this type and any government approval of fur importation from Namibia.

Various objections to the maintenance of this action are pressed by the Government. Prominent among them is a contention that the plaintiffs lack standing. Government counsel argue that *Diggs v. Shultz*,[14] a decision of this Circuit that recognized standing in similar circumstances,[15] was wrongly decided, and that *Diggs'* approach has been undercut by subsequent Supreme Court decisions. The Government also argues that this case raises a political question not appropriate for judicial resolution. And the Government concedes nothing on the merits: it contends that Security Council Resolutions are not legally binding on U.N. members and that, in any event, the Resolution involved in this case is not self-executing.

The district court dismissed the suit. It suffices for us to affirm on the ground, related to the issue of standing, but analytically distinct, that even assuming there

---

[12] Plaintiffs have adduced correspondence between officials of the State Department and Department of Commerce in which the State Department officials repeatedly state that the United States accepts U.N. Resolution 301 as a correct statement of our obligations under international law.

[13] Plaintiffs cite a letter dated August 2, 1974 from Deputy Secretary of State Robert S. Ingersoll which stated: "We do not believe that an official visit to Namibia by Commerce Department employees or contract personnel, and a possible determination by you regarding South Africa's management of Namibia marine mammal resources can be brought into conformity with the . . . obligations [set forth in Security Council Resolution 301]."

Similarly, a subsequent letter from then Acting Secretary Ingersoll to Secretary of Commerce Robert B. Morton stated: "We believe that U.S. Government approval of an application to import Namibian fur seal skins from South Africa would be contrary to our international legal obligations in that it would necessarily recognize the validity of South African management of Namibian mammal resources."

[14] 152 U.S. App. D.C. 313, 470 F. 2d 461 (1972), *cert. denied*, 411 U.S. 931, 93 S. Ct. 1897, 36 L. Ed. 2d 390 (1973).

[15] In *Diggs*, plaintiffs who had been denied admission to Rhodesia sued to enforce executive orders implementing an economic embargo declared by the U.N. Security Council. Although this Court recognized plaintiff's standing to sue, it denied relief on the ground that a subsequent Act of Congress had abrogated whatever obligation may have existed.

is an international obligation that is binding on the United States[16] . . . the U.N. resolution underlying that obligation does not confer rights on the citizens of the United States that are enforceable in court in the absence of implementing legislation.

* * * *

In determining whether a treaty is self-executing courts look to the intent of the signatory parties as manifested by the language of the instrument, and, if the instrument is uncertain, recourse must be had to the circumstances surrounding its execution.

Applying this kind of analysis to the particular Security Council Resolution on which plaintiffs rely, we find that the provisions here in issue were not addressed to the judicial branch of our government. They do not by their terms confer rights upon individual citizens; they call upon governments to take certain action. The provisions deal with the conduct of our foreign relations, an area traditionally left to executive discretion. . . . The Resolution does not provide specific standards. The "entrenchment" standard of the Resolution, while possibly of such a nature that it might be elaborated by an international tribunal, is essentially the kind of standard that is rooted in diplomacy and its incidents, rather than in conventional adjudication, and is foreign to the general experience and function of American courts. In the absence of contrary indication in the international legislative history, and in the absence of domestic legislation evincing an intention for judicial enforcement,[17] we conclude that the provisions of Resolution 301 involved here do not confer on individual citizens rights that are judicially enforceable in American domestic courts.

Affirmed.

THE DOCTRINE OF SELF-EXECUTING TREATIES AND U.S. v. POSTAL; WIN AT ANY PRICE

By Stefan Riensenfeld
74 Am. J.Int'l L. 892*

The doctrine of self-executing treaties is relevant not only in the law of the United States but also in many other legal systems, including that of the Federal

[16] In holding that the U.N. Security Council Resolution involved here is not self-executing, we avoid the larger questions raised by this case: under what circumstances a Security Council resolution can create a binding international obligation of the United States; whether Article 25 of the U.N. Charter, in which the member nations agree to carry out the resolutions of the Council, can ever give rise to a self-executing resolution; and so on.

[17] Moreover, we do not have here a case where the executive urges that the treaty is self-executing. The State Department has not taken a stand on that issue before this court or in its communications with the parties that are contained in the record.

* Copyright © 1980 by American Journal of International Law. Reprinted by permission.

Republic of Germany, Austria, Switzerland, the European Communities and, since the reform of the preliminary title to the Civil Code, Spain. . . .

From a survey of the copious literature it emerges that the concept of self-executing treaties is in need of clarification. It has separate international and domestic constitutional aspects. . . .

The international aspect deals with the content or nature of the treaty obligation: what is to be accomplished and what is the time frame for such accomplishment. The domestic means for such accomplishment will usually not be of international concern. Of course, whether a treaty aims at the creation of domestically enforceable rights and duties . . . depends on the treaty stipulation and in that respect on the intent of the state parties to the treaty, as ascertained by the applicable international rules of treaty interpretation. The same holds true with respect to the related question, whether such creation should be "forthwith" or "in due course." The view here proposed conforms to the approach of the International Law Commission in its Draft Articles on State Responsibility. The ILC draft nowhere refers to self-executing stipulations but differentiates between treaty provisions requiring the achievement of a specific result and treaty provisions requiring the adoption of a particular course of conduct. In the former case each state has the choice of the appropriate action for the achievement of the stipulated result, although its range of options may be limited by its constitutional law. In such a situation, as the ILC's commentary to proposed Article 21 observes, "the commands of international law . . . stop short at the outer boundaries of the State machinery." As the commentary of the ILC also notes, obligations "of result" are much more common in international law than in internal law. There are, however, cases in which problems of interpretation may arise that sometimes are not easily resolved. Moreover, "it may also be that, within a system of rules governing an institution of international law, there are obligations 'of conduct' or 'of means' alongside other obligations which have the characteristics of any obligation 'of result.' " Of course, even where the obligation is one of result, the precise character of this "result" may still be difficult to determine, especially the question of whether that result consists merely in refraining from certain exercises of jurisdiction or also in providing domestic sanctions. At any rate, that determination concerns the true ambit of the international obligation.

Conversely, the way in which the internal domestic law of a nation must be brought into conformity with the mandates of a treaty provision is a matter governed solely by the constitutional law of each state party. To that extent, the intent of other state parties is irrelevant, and even the treaty making authorities of that state party whose domestic law is involved may have little or no choice according to the governing constitutional provisions.

This is the interface where the constitutional aspects of the doctrine of self-executing treaties come into play. These aspects will vary with the constitutional regime governing the treaty making power. Three main systems must be distinguished in that respect:

(1) In some nations the power to conclude treaties is vested in the executive and any treaty concluded by the executive in conformity with the applicable international rules is binding on the nation. If, however, the treaty provides for the

creation of rights and duties of individuals, separate parliamentary action is necessary to accomplish this effect.

(2) In the United States the treaty making power is shared by the Executive and one House of the legislature. Under appropriate conditions, a treaty so concluded may create rights and duties of individuals or have other domestic effects without legislation unless the treaty concerns specific matters recognized to require action by the entire legislature.

(3) In an increasing number of nations having a bicameral system, the treaty making power is shared by the executive and the entire legislature, at least with respect to treaties affecting subjects that otherwise would require legislative rather than executive action. . . . Unless a different form of action is authorized, as for instance, tacit approval in the Netherlands, the approval is given by means of a statute or concurrent resolution.

* * * *

A survey of the constitutions, cases, and scholarly writings in other countries leads to the conclusion that even in countries in which legislative approval is needed for the conclusion of international treaties, the creation of rights, privileges, duties, and immunities cognizable in domestic courts is primarily a function of the particular treaty provision. The power of parties to invoke it in domestic courts depends upon its import, as determined from its language, context, purpose, negotiating history, and general background. The internal applicability is created *by virtue* of and — save where publication requirements dictate otherwise — *upon* the international entry into effect of the treaty provision with respect to the nation involved. The legislative approval is a condition for the valid conclusion of the treaty. Normally it does not determine the domestic applicability of the treaty provisions. Of course, this does not exclude the possibility that the legislature, in giving approval to the international engagement of the nation, may prescribe its domestic cognizability irrespective of the treaty's mandate. Conversely, where the treaty expressly or by implication provides for domestic protection of the rights and privileges created thereby, the parliamentary approval of its conclusion may not deny such cognizability, unless the legislature is empowered to prescribe internationally valid reservations or is constitutionally authorized to postpone domestic applicability until the passage of further legislation.

This analysis compels a further semantic consequence: Strictly speaking, the term "self-executing" is not a notion whose meaning is determined by international law. The self-executing nature of a treaty provision is a product of international and domestic constitutional rules. Internationally relevant is merely the determination whether the treaty provision in question mandates the cognizability in and protection by domestic tribunals of the rights, duties, privileges, and immunities created thereby. Reservations or interpretative declarations, to the extent that they are internationally permissible and effective, may only any relate to that aspect.

NOTES AND QUESTIONS

(1) In *Diggs v. Richardson*, the court expressly declined to decide whether United Nations Security Council Resolution 301 created a binding international legal obligation of the United States. In assessing the import of this refusal and other aspects of the *Diggs* decision, consider the International Court of Justice's *Advisory Opinion on the Continued Presence of South Africa in Namibia (South West Africa)*,.[18] in which the Court gave an expansive reading to the Council's powers under the UN Charter to issue resolutions creating binding international obligations. "The powers of the Council under Article 24," the Court concluded, "are not restricted to the specific grants of authority contained in Chapters VI, VII, VIII and XII. . . . [T]he Members of the United Nations have conferred upon the Security Council powers commensurate with its responsibility for the maintenance of peace and security. *The only limitations are the fundamental principles and purposes found in Chapter 1 of the Charter.*" (emphasis supplied). Consider also that the United States representative to the Security Council, explaining his affirmative vote for Resolution 301, stated that "the United States accepts [the conclusions of the I.C.J.] which declare . . . that members states are 'under obligation to recognize the illegality of South Africa's presence in Namibia . . . and to refrain from any dealings with the Government of South Africa implying recognition of the legality of . . . such presence and administration. . . .' "[19] Despite the ICJ's opinion, it is fair to say that the scope of the authority of the Security Council to bind member states is not settled.[20] Lastly, note that in holding Resolution 301 to be non-self-executing, Judge Leventhal concluded, *inter alia*, that provisions of the Resolution "do not by their terms confer rights upon individual citizens; they call upon governments to take certain action."

Was the court's refusal to determine whether the Resolution created a binding international legal obligation of the United States a serious defect even given the court's assumption *arguendo*, that it was binding? If so, why?

(2) Why did plaintiffs lose, because (i) Resolution 301 conferred no rights on them, albeit *arguendo* they had standing; (ii) the Resolution did not enjoin upon the United States a course of conduct specific enough for a court to judge whether or not Commerce Department officials had (or proposed) to violate its terms, or (iii) the Resolution, although presumed obligatory, did not enjoin upon the United States a course of conduct specific enough to manifest an intention by the Resolution's framers to have it operate, of its own force, as a rule of domestic law? If it is the first, is there some confusion in the decision? If the second, upon what alternative ground might the court have dismissed the case? Is either the first or second reason dispositive of the third? What does Riesenfeld's analysis suggest on this point? If the third is the real reason, are you persuaded? Note that by its terms Resolution 301 called upon all states to "abstain from sending diplomatic or special missions to South Africa that include the Territory of Namibia in their jurisdiction." What further action was the United States Government required to

---

[18] [1971] I.C.J. Rep. 16.

[19] 65 Dep't State Bull. 609-10 (1971).

[20] See Higgins, *The Advisory Opinion On Namibia: Which U.N. Resolutions Are Binding Under Article 25 of the Charter?*, 21 Int'L & Comp. L.Q. 270 (1972).

take under this provision? Under the tests developed by the International Law Commission and embraced by Riesenfeld, what result?

(3) It is to be noted that the executive branch had in fact taken steps to comply with the obligations of Resolution 301. Explaining the affirmative vote of the United States on Resolution 301, the U.S. Representative to the Security Council noted that "the United States had announced it would officially discourage investment by United States nationals in Namibia, would not make available U.S. Export-Import Bank credit guarantees and other facilities, and would not assist U.S. citizens who invest in Namibia."[21] Following this announcement, the government informed investors of the new policy, and investment was in fact inhibited. Further, the State Department applied the obligations contained in Resolution 301 in advising other administrative agencies on the international ramifications of proposed agency action. How do these facts bear on the question of whether the Resolution was self-executing?

(4) Assuming that the court in *Diggs* was correct in concluding the Resolution 301 was non-self-executing, a further inquiry would seem warranted: Had the Resolution in fact been executed? Is it possible for a treaty to be executed by the executive branch acting on its own authority? Under what head of Presidential power might such action be taken?[22]

[C] Other International Agreements: Executive and Congressional-Executive Agreements

Although it is the only kind of international agreement expressly mentioned in the Constitution, the treaty is utilized much less often by the United States than other types of international agreements. These are the presidential-executive agreement, which is an agreement concluded by the President under his independent constitutional powers, and the congressional-executive agreement, which is an agreement concluded pursuant to statutory authorization or ratified, after conclusion, by statute or Joint Resolution. Most international trade agreements, for example, are congressional-executive agreements concluded pursuant to advance congressional authorization. The Bretton Woods Agreements Act, authorizing U.S. membership in the International Monetary Fund and the World Bank, is an example of congressional ratification after negotiation of an agreement.

There has been relatively little controversy over the use of the congressional-executive agreement in place of the treaty. Many (although by no means all) commentators have accepted the proposition that the two are "functionally equivalent;" that there is no constitutional limit on the use of a congressional-executive agreement in lieu of a treaty. This means that the decision to enter into an international agreement in the form of a treaty rather than executive-congressional agreement is based on political rather than constitutional considerations.

On the other hand, while most agree that the executive, and only the executive, may conclude international agreements (*i.e.*, negotiate and ratify), the debate has

---

[21] 61 Dept State Bull. 609, 610 (1971).

[22] For discussion of various issues in the *Diggs* case, see notes in 18 Harv. Int'l L. J. 375 (1977); 24 Kan. L. Rev. 395 (1976); 24 UCLA L. Rev. 387 (1976).

been heated over the authority of the President to set policy by executive agreements independent of Congress, *i.e.*, through presidential executive agreements. Some have claimed that the President has only such independent authority as he would otherwise have whether acting by executive order, proclamation or by agreement (*i.e.*, the instrumental "agreement-making" power adds nothing to his independent policy-making power), others have relied on the President's authority as Chief Executive or "Commander-in-Chief," to support an expansive power in the President to conclude such agreements where otherwise he could not act unilaterally (*e.g.*, by executive order).

At the same time, the Senate Foreign Relations Committee, in particular, has not always been happy with what it perceives as an Executive disposition to bypass the treaty process in favor of executive agreements, either presidential-executive or congressional-executive agreements. Accordingly, in an effort to strike a compromise between executive and congressional views on the use of treaties versus executive agreements, the Department of State in Department Circular 175[23] has stated *inter alia*, that the procedure to be followed in entering into an international agreement is to be determined by such factors as: whether (a) the agreement involves commitments or risks affecting the nation as a whole; (b) is intended to affect State laws; (c) can be given effect without the enactment of subsequent legislation by the Congress; (d) past practice with respect to similar agreements; (e) Congressional preference; (f) the degree of formality desired; (g) the proposed duration of the agreement, the need for prompt conclusion and the desirability of concluding a routine or short-term agreement; and (h) the general international practice with respect to similar agreements. The Circular goes on to state that in "determining whether any international agreement should be brought into force as a treaty or as an international agreement other than a treaty, the utmost care is to be exercised to avoid any invasion or compromise of the constitutional powers of the Senate, the Congress as a whole, or the President."

During the 1950s this debate resulted in a series of proposed constitutional amendments, many of them sponsored by Senator John Bricker of Ohio. Some of these amendments sought to curtail or regulate executive agreements, and failed by only one vote to obtain the necessary two-thirds assent in the Senate. However, the debate over presidential powers more generally reached its greatest intensity during the Vietnam War and the Watergate crisis. During this period Congress had before it many bills to limit or regulate executive agreements. The only one of these to be adopted was the Case Act of 1972 which requires the President to transmit to Congress all international agreements other than treaties within 60 days after their conclusion. If the President deems public disclosure prejudicial to national security he need only transmit the text to the foreign affairs committees of both Houses. In such a case, the transmittal is made under an injunction of secrecy to be removed only upon notice from the President.[24] The Case Act was amended in 1977 and 1978 to make it applicable to agreements made by any

---

[23] State Department Procedures On Treaties And Other International Agreements, October 25, 1974, 11 FAM 700.
[24] See 1 U.S.C.A. Section 112(b).

department or agency of the United States government and to oral as well as written agreements.[25]

UNITED STATES v. BELMONT

United States Supreme Court
301 U.S. 324, 57 S. Ct. 758, 81 L. Ed. 1134 (1937)

[In 1933 President Roosevelt entered into an agreement (the so-called "Litvinov Assignment") whereby the Soviet Union assigned to the United States all of its claims to property held by American nationals and located in this country. The bulk of this property had, at some time, belonged to Russian citizens and was claimed by the Soviet government under a series of decrees which purported to nationalize all private property owned by its citizens or by Russian companies worldwide. Any amounts recovered by the United States as the Soviet's assignee were to be used to pay off claims of United States citizens against the Soviet Government. These claims, in turn, had arisen principally from the Soviet nationalization of American owned property located in the Soviet Union. The settlement of the American claims was intended to remove one of the principal political roadblocks to United States recognition of the Soviet Government and to the resumption of diplomatic relations between the two countries.

Included in the Assignment was a claim to a sum of money deposited with August Belmont, a private banker in New York, by a Russian corporation which was subsequently nationalized by the Soviet Government. When Belmont refused to pay the money over to the United States, the latter sued in the federal district court. That court held for Belmont on the ground that the United States' claim to ownership of the money was predicated upon a confiscatory nationalization decree issued by the Soviet Government, and that, since the situs of the property was New York, New York public policy would govern and that policy forbade the enforcement of such a decree. The Supreme Court reversed. The "Litvinov Assignment" upon which the United States relied in claiming the money and the recognition and establishment of diplomatic relations with the Soviet Government were, the Court said, "part of one transaction resulting in an international compact" which was well "within the competence of the President" to undertake. The Court then continued]:

* * * *

The assignment and the agreements in connection therewith did not, as in the case of treaties, as that term is used in the treaty making clause of the Constitution (Art. II, Section 2), require the advice and consent of the Senate. A treaty signifies a compact made between two or more independent nations with a view to the public welfare. . . . But an international compact, as this was, is not always a

[25] 1 U.S.C.A. Section 112(a).

treaty which requires the participation of the Senate. There are many such compacts, of which a protocol, a modus vivendi, a postal convention, and agreements like that now under consideration are illustrations. . . .

[Furthermore, while the supremacy of treaties over State law] . . . is established by the express language of cl. 2, Art. VI, of the Constitution [the "Supremacy clause"], the same rule would result in the case of all international compacts and agreements from the very fact that complete power over international affairs is in the national government and is not and cannot be subject to any curtailment or interference on the part of the several states. . . . In respect of all international negotiations and compacts, and in respect of our foreign relations generally, state lines disappear. As to such purposes the State of New York does not exist. . . .

UNITED STATES v. PINK

United States Supreme Court
315 U.S. 203, 62 S. Ct. 552, 86 L. Ed. 796 (1942)

[In this case the United States as the Soviet's assignee under the Litvinov Assignments sought to recover approximately $1 million from the New York Superintendent of Insurance (Pink). These funds were part of a larger amount deposited with the Superintendent prior to the Soviet revolution by the New York branch of a Russian insurance company as security for transactions by that branch. Subsequently, the Soviets nationalized the company. While the branch continued in business for a few years, the Superintendent, acting under the order of a New York court, eventually took possession of the branch's assets and proceeded to pay off all of the insurance company's "domestic creditors" (*i.e.*, those creditors whose claims arose out of business done by the New York branch). The New York court then ordered the Superintendent to use the $1 million remaining to pay off the company's "foreign creditors" and to remit any undistributed balance to the company's board of directors. Before this distribution could be completed, however, the United States sued to obtain the $1 million intending to add the money to the general fund available for the payment of United States citizen claims against the Soviet Government. The New York courts dismissed the suit. The Supreme Court reversed].

MR. JUSTICE DOUGLAS delivered the opinion of the Court.

* * * *

The New York Court of Appeals [has] held . . . that the Russian decrees in question had no extraterritorial effect. If that is true, it is decisive of the present controversy. For the United States acquired under the Litvinov Assignment only such rights as Russia had. . . . But that question of foreign law is not to be determined exclusively by the state court. The claim of the United States based on the Litvinov Assignment raises a federal question. *United States v. Belmont*[26]

------

[26] 301 U.S. 324, 57 S. Ct. 758, 81 L. Ed. 1134 (1937).

. . . . We hold that so far as its intended effect is concerned the Russian decree embraced the new York assets of the First Russian Insurance Co.

The question of whether the decree should be given extraterritorial effect is of course a distinct matter. [But on this question the] . . . holding in the *Belmont* case is . . . determinative of the present controversy unless the stake of the foreign creditors in the liquidation proceeding and the provisions which New York has [made] for their protection call for a different result.

> [The Court then went on to reject the contention that New York public policy and the Fifth Amendment barred the United States from recovering assets in this contest between it and the foreign creditors of the Russian Insurance Company. It emphasized the role that the "Litvinov Assignments" played in the policy of recognition and in resolving tensions between the two countries by settling claims of United States nationals against the Soviet Union, concluding]:

If the President had the power to determine the policy which was to govern the question of recognition, then the Fifth Amendment does not stand in the way of giving full force and effect to the Litvinov Assignment. To be sure, aliens as well as citizens are entitled to the protection of the Fifth Amendment. *Russian Volunteer Fleet v. United States*[27] . . . . A State is not precluded, however, by the Fourteenth Amendment from according priority to local creditors as against creditors who are nationals of foreign countries and whose claims arose abroad. . . . By the same token, the Federal Government is not barred by the Fifth Amendment from securing for itself and our nationals priority against such creditors. And it matters not that the procedure adopted by the Federal Government is globular and involves a regrouping of assets. There is no Constitutional reason why this Government need act as the collection agent for nationals of other countries when it takes steps to protect itself or its own nationals on external debts. There is no reason why it may not through such devices as the Litvinov Assignment make itself whole from assets to go abroad in satisfaction of claims of aliens made elsewhere and not incurred in connection with business conducted in this country. . . . If the priority had been accorded American claims by treaty with Russia, there would be no doubt as to its validity. . . . The same result obtains here. The powers of the President in the conduct of foreign relations included the power, without consent of the Senate, to determine the public policy of the United States with respect to the Russian nationalization decrees. "What government is to be regarded here as representative of a foreign sovereign state is a political rather than a judicial question, and is to be determined by the political department of the government." *Guaranty Trust Co. v. United States*[28] . . . . That authority is not limited to a determination of the government to be recognized. It includes the power to determine the policy which is to govern the question of recognition. Objections to the underlying policy as well as objections to recognition are to be addressed to the political department and not to the courts. Recognition is not always absolute; it is sometimes conditional. . . . Power to remove such obstacles to full recognition as settlement of claims of our nationals . . . certainly is a modest implied power of the President who is the "sole organ of the federal

---

[27] 282 U.S. 481, 51 S. Ct. 229 (1931).
[28] 304 U.S. 126, 137 58 S. Ct. 785, 791, 82 L. Ed. 1224.

government in the field of international relations.". . . . Effectiveness in handling the delicate problems of foreign relations requires no less. Unless such a power exists, the power of recognition might be thwarted or seriously diluted. No such obstacle can be placed in the way of rehabilitation of relations between this country and another nation, unless the historic conception of the powers and responsibilities of the President in the conduct of foreign affairs . . . is to be drastically revised. . . .

[Next, Justice Douglas acknowledged that "even treaties with foreign nations will be carefully construed so as not to derogate from the authority . . . of the States . . . unless clearly necessary to effectuate the national policy." In this instance, the Justice continued, "[e]nforcement of New York's policy . . . would collide with and subtract from the Federal policy," because it would amount to official "disapproval or non-recognition of the nationalization program of the Soviet Government" in the face of "a disavowal by the United States of any official concern with that program." Also, any refusal to enforce "the Litvinov Assignment [would] result in [a] reduction or non-payment of claims of our nationals," thereby "keep[ing] alive one source of friction which the policy of recognition intended to remove." In light of these considerations, New York's policy could not prevail because "power over external affairs is not shared by the States' it is vested in the national government exclusively. . . . And the policies of the States become wholly irrelevant to judicial inquiry, when the United States, acting within its constitutional sphere, seeks enforcement of its foreign policy in the courts."]

NOTES AND QUESTIONS

(1) Do *Belmont* and *Pink* add anything significant to the debate over the scope of the President's power to make international agreements without reference to Congress? Both sides in that debate would concede the President's independent authority to make these particular agreements, wouldn't they? Explain.

(2) *Russian Volunteer Fleet v. United States*,[29] cited by Justice Douglas, held that a Russian corporation which had entered into a contract for the construction of ships subsequently taken over by the United States for use in World War I was entitled to compensation under the Fifth Amendment. As an "alien friend" the corporation was, the Court stated, as much entitled to the protections of the Fifth Amendment as any United States citizen. This has to pose problems, does it not, for Justice Douglas:

    (a) Apparently, in Justice Douglas' mind, the situation in *Russian Volunteer Fleet* was distinguishable from *Pink* because the "taking" from the "alien friends" in *Pink* was for the benefit of American citizens with claims against the Soviet Union rather than solely for the benefit of the U.S. Government. The Fifth Amendment did not foreclose the government

---

[29] 282 U.S. 481, 51 Sup. Ct. 229 (1931).

from granting American citizens what the Justice calls a "priority" or a preference over aliens. Are you persuaded?

(b) How persuasive is the Justice's characterization of the government's action as merely the assignment of a preference among different classes of creditors in a "regrouping of assets" (*i.e.*, a kind of reorganization)? Note that the "alien creditors" had a judicially recognized property right in the particular assets being contested while the American claimants had only an undifferentiated interest in whatever assets the United States might succeed in obtaining by virtue of the very agreement under attack. Note also, that the "alien creditors" in Pink were not accorded any right in the pool of assets accumulated by the United States under that agreement. If this is just like a reorganization it looks like the unsecured creditors (American claimants against the Soviet Union) get everything and the secured creditors get nothing, doesn't it? Or, is it really nothing less than the "taking" of property for a public purpose?

(c) Suppose the persons claiming the funds by reason of the New York court order had been American creditors of the defunct Russian company. Would they have been protected by the Fifth Amendment? Judged according to the risks assumed when they obtained a property interest in the defunct company, would not such "American creditors" have been in exactly the same comparative position *vis-a-vis* the American claimants against the Soviet Government as the "alien creditors" in Pink? Wouldn't an award of priority to the "American creditors" frustrate the purpose of the Litvinov Assignment just as much as the grant of priority to the "alien creditors?" The purpose of the Assignment — settling American claims as a necessary step toward recognition and the resumption of diplomatic relations with the Soviet Union — was clearly important to the decision in Pink, was it not?

(d) If the "American creditors" of the insurance company would not have been protected by the Fifth Amendment, what of Justice Douglas' position in the *Steel Seizure* Case? Perhaps the temporary assumption of managerial control over a steel mill by the Government is a "taking," but the permanent appropriation of a creditor's judicially sanctioned rights in his debtor's property is not a "taking." (Per contra, see, Friendly, J. in *Sardino v. Federal Reserve Bank of New York, infra* page 794). Upon this reading of *Pink* what prospect lies ahead for the disappointed claimants against Iran that so concerned the Court in *Dames & Moore?*

(3) Perhaps the only way to reconcile Justice Douglas in *Pink* with Justice Douglas in the *Steel Seizure* decision is to recognize that an alien is not protected by the Fifth Amendment if the purpose of the "taking" is important enough, but that a citizen is, even when the purpose is the same. If this is so then clearly the President's authority to enter into the Litvinov Assignment without Congressional approval was under Justice's Douglas' *Steel Seizure* analysis very much in doubt, was it not? Recall that in *Steel Seizure*, Justice Douglas concluded that since a "taking" must be accompanied by compensation, and only Congress could appropriate funds for that purpose, only Congress could authorize the "taking."

Certainly, there was no assurance at the time of making the agreement with the Soviets that the government would be required to "take" only alien interests in the assigned property. Can *Pink* be squared with *Dames & Moore*? with *Reid v. Covert*? Consult also *Silesian-American Corp. v. Clark*,[30] (upholding against Fifth Amendment attack the 1941 amendment to the Trading with the Enemy Act authorizing the seizure of property nominally in the hands of a "friendly alien" but "tainted" by enemy control. Congress, the Court emphasized, had specifically authorized compensation for the "friendly" alien who could, after seizure, prove the absence of an enemy "taint."[31]

Perhaps there is some magic in an executive agreement? An *executive agreement* "taking" private property in order to facilitate the recognition of a foreign government is merely a "modest implied" extension of the President's recognition power which he is free to exercise without Congressional warrant, but an *executive order* "taking" private property in order to fight a foreign war is not so modest an extension of his powers as Commander-in-Chief or under the "take Care" clause as to dispense with the need for Congressional authorization? Query? How would you assess the authoritativeness of *Pink* with regard to the scope of the President's incidental authority under the recognition power?

(4) In *United States v. Guy W. Capps, Inc.*,[32] the court refused to give effect to an executive agreement regulating the importation of potatoes from Canada to the United States on the ground that it conflicted with an earlier act of Congress. As an alternative ground for its holding the court said that, "while the President has certain inherent powers under the Constitution . . . the power to regulate interstate and foreign commerce is not among the powers incident to the Presidential office, but is expressly vested by the Constitution in the Congress."[33]

Professor Louis Henkin has criticized this statement of the court in *Capps* as follows:

> Judge Parker's . . . argument is unpersuasive. It takes the narrowest view of the President's power, not even mentioning his foreign affairs powers. Judge Parker finds the President has no power because Congress does. If the President cannot make agreements on any matter on which Congress could legislate, there could be no executive agreements with domestic legal consequences, since, as we have seen, the legislative power of the Congress has few and far limits. If Judge Parker denied the President the power to make executive agreements only as to matters on which Congress has "express" powers to legislate, he was drawing a line between express and implied powers of Congress that makes little sense for any purpose. In either event it is difficult to see why the powers of Congress to legislate are any more relevant to determine the scope of Presidential power to commit the United States by executive agreement than by treaty.[34]

Judge Parker's position and Professor Henkin's critique appear to represent the extremes on this question, do they not? Judge Parker to the contrary

---

[30] 332 U.S. 469 (1947).
[31] *Id.* at 480.
[32] 204 F. 2d 635 (4th Cir. 1953).
[33] 204 F. 2d at 659.
[34] L. Henkin, Foreign Affairs And The Constitution, 181 (1972).

notwithstanding, there surely are many heads of power in Article II that might give the President occasion, where Congress is silent, to make a presidential-executive agreement that effectively "regulates foreign commerce." Professor Henkin, on the other hand, appears to go to the other extreme equating the President's undoubted power to negotiate and sign all international agreements with a power to decide the policy underlying those agreements. There is a problem here, is there not? If the instrumental power cannot be wholly separated from the policy-making power, it is even more impossible to found the whole of the policy-making power on mere possession of the instrumental.

CONSUMERS UNION OF THE U.S. INC. v. KISSINGER

Court of Appeals for the District of Columbia Circuit
506 F. 2d 136 (1974)

McGowan, Circuit Judge:

These consolidated cross-appeals are directed respectively to two declarations made by the District Court in a suit.

Steel imports into the United States increased more than tenfold over the period 1958-68, with the great bulk of imports coming from Japan and the countries of the European Communities. The effect of this development on the domestic steel industry . . . became a matter of widespread concern. In 1968 bills with substantial backing were introduced in Congress to impose mandatory import quotas on steel.

The Executive Branch regarded the problem created by steel imports as temporary in nature and thus amenable to a short-term solution. It concluded, moreover, that unilaterally imposed mandatory quotas would pose a danger of retaliation under the General Agreement on Trade and Tariffs (sic), prove inflexible and difficult to terminate, and have a seriously adverse impact on the foreign relations of the United States. . . . Accordingly, the Executive Branch concluded in 1968 that voluntary import restraint undertakings by foreign producers offered the best hope of alleviating the domestic industry's temporary problems at the least cost to United States foreign, economic and trade policies.

[As a result] . . . State Department officials entered into discussions that lasted from June to December, 1968, and resulted in letters being sent to the Secretary in which the Japanese and European producer associations stated their intentions to limit steel shipments to the United States to specified maximum tonnages for each of the years 1969, 1970, and 1971. [At the urging of the U.S. steel industry, certain members of Congress and several Presidential advisors, the arrangements were then extended for the years 1972-1974].

* * * *

The two 1972 letters are substantially alike. Each states the signatories' intention to limit exports of steel products to the United States both in aggregate tonnage and, within such limits, in terms of product mix. Each represents that the signatories "hold themselves [itself] ready to consult with representatives of the United States Government on any problem or question that may arise with respect to this voluntary restraint undertaking" and expect the United States Government so to hold itself ready. In addition, each states that its undertaking is based on the assumptions that (1) the effect will not be to place the signatories at a disadvantage relative to each other, (2) the United States will take no unilateral actions to restrict exports by the signatories to the United States, and (3) the representatives do not violate United States or international laws.

The original complaint in this action contained two separate and distinct claims. They were respectively denominated "First Claim (Antitrust)" and "Second Claim (Unlawful Action by State Department Officials)."

* * * *

After answers had been filed . . . the parties stipulated that the first claim in the complaint be dismissed with prejudice, and an amended complaint was filed. The violation of law alleged in the amended complaint was that the State Department officials had acted to regulate foreign commerce within the meaning of Article 1, Section 8, Clause 3 of the Constitution, and of the laws relating to the regulation of foreign trade set forth in Title 19 of the U.S. Code, including Sections 301 and 352 of the Trade Expansion Act of 1962. The foreign producer defendants were said to be violating the same laws to the extent that they took steps to effectuate the limitations sought by the defendant State Department officials acting in excess of their authority. . . .

The matter came on for hearing in the District Court . . . [which concluded (1)] that "the Executive has no authority under the Constitution or acts of Congress to exempt the Voluntary Restraint Arrangements on Steel from the antitrust laws" [but (2)] that "the Executive is not preempted and may enter into agreements or diplomatic arrangements with private foreign steel concerns so long as these undertakings do not violate legislation regulating foreign commerce . . . and that there is no requirement that all such undertakings be first processed under the Trade Expansion Act of 1962."

* * * *

Appeals were filed by the State Department defendants and by the domestic and foreign producers. The plaintiff filed a cross-appeal "insofar as any declaration, or ruling on the relief requested, has been decided adversely to the plaintiff."

A substantial portion of the briefs and argument before us has been devoted to the Sherman Act [*i.e.* the "anti-trust issue"]. [But] . . . [w]e think that the issue, for all practical purposes, disappeared from this case when the plaintiff, for reasons best known to itself, stipulated its dismissal with prejudice.

* * * *

We turn, then, to the District Court's . . . [second conclusion that] the actions of the Executive culminating in . . . the letters of intent, [was] . . . not preempted . . . and that there is no requirement that all such undertakings be first processed under the Trade Expansion Act of 1962.". . . .

* * * *

Title III of the Trade Expansion Act of 1962, recognizing that domestic interests of various kinds may be adversely affected by concessions granted under trade agreements, authorizes the making of compensating adjustments of various kinds. Under section 301 . . . [if] the Tariff Commission . . . [a]fter holding public hearings . . . finds injury to domestic industry, the President may under Section 351 increase or impose tariff duties or other import restrictions . . . or alternatively he may under Section 352 negotiate agreements with foreign governments limiting the export from such countries to the United States of the article causing the injury. . . . Sections 301 and 352 . . . are the only provisions expressly identified in the amended complaint as constituting the allegedly preeemptive exercise by Congress of its constitutional power to regulate foreign commerce [and thereby] . . . foreclose the actions of the Executive challenged in this case. [There is] . . . also Section 232. . . . This last is the so-called national security clause which provides that the President shall not decrease or eliminate tariffs or other import restrictions if to do so would impair the national security [and also requires that if he finds that] . . . imports threaten to impair the national security . . . [he is to] "adjust the imports" of the article in question.

What is clear from the foregoing is a purpose on the part of Congress to delegate legislative power to the President for use by him in certain defined circumstances and in furtherance of certain stated purposes. Without such a delegation, the President could not increase or decrease tariffs, issue commands to the customs service to refuse or delay entry of goods into the country, or impose mandatory import quotas. To make use of such delegated power, the President would of course be required to proceed strictly in accordance with the procedures specified in the statutes conferring the delegation. Where, as here, he does not pretend to the possession of such power, no such conformity is required.

The steel import restraints do not purport to be enforceable, either as contracts or as governmental actions with the force of law; and the Executive has no sanctions to invoke in order to compel observance by the foreign producers of their self-denying representations. They are a statement of intent on the part of the foreign producer associations. The signatories' expectations, not unreasonable in light of the reception given their undertakings by the Executive, are that the Executive will consult with them over mutual concerns about the steel import situation, and that it will not have sudden recourse to unilateral steps available to it under the Trade Expansion Act to impose legal restrictions on importation. The President is not bound in any way to refrain from taking such steps if he later deems them to be in the national interest, or if consultation proves unavailing to meet unforeseen difficulties; and certainly the Congress is not inhibited from enacting any legislation it desires to regulate by law the importation of steel.

The formality and specificity with which the undertakings are expressed does not alter their essentially precatory nature insofar as the Executive Branch is concerned. In effect the President has said that he will not initiate steps to limit steel imports by law if the volume of such imports remains within tolerable bounds. Communicating, through the Secretary of State, what levels he considers tolerable merely enables the foreign producers to conform their actions accordingly, and to avoid the risk of guessing at what is acceptable. . . . [N]othing in the process leading up to the voluntary undertakings or the process of consultation under them differentiates what the Executive has done here from what all Presidents, and to a lesser extent all high executive officers, do when they admonish an industry with the express or implicit warning that action, within either their existing powers or enlarged powers to be sought, will be taken if a desired course is not followed voluntarily.

The question of congressional preemption is simply not pertinent to executive action of this sort. Congress acts by making laws binding, if valid, on their objects and the President, whose duty it is faithfully to execute the laws. From the comprehensive pattern of its legislation regulating trade and governing the circumstances under and procedures by which the President is authorized to act to limit imports, it appears quite likely that Congress has by statute occupied the field of enforceable import restrictions, if it did not, indeed, have exclusive possession thereof by the terms of Article I of the Constitution. There is no potential for conflict, however, between exclusive congressional regulation of foreign commerce — regulation enforced ultimately by halting violative importations at the border — and assurances of voluntary restraint given to the Executive. Nor is there any warrant for creating such a conflict by straining to endow the voluntary undertakings with legally binding effect, contrary to the manifest understanding of all concerned and, indeed, to the manner in which departures from them have been treated.

The District Court's order with respect to antitrust exemption is vacated, . . . [but otherwise]:

Affirmed.

LEVENTHAL, CIRCUIT JUDGE (dissenting):

With all respect, I must record my disagreement with the ruling of the majority. . . .

In my view, this case is controlled by Congress's exercise of its plenary authority over the regulation of foreign commerce through passage, over the past forty years, of legislation establishing a comprehensive scheme occupying the field of import restraints. While there is room for a role based on inherent authority of the executive, in this case the actions taken by the President are inconsistent, by fair implication, with the scheme Congress has provided. My point is not that the President has taken the kind of action that Congress had forbidden to the Executive. On the contrary, the statutes passed by Congress established a broad executive discretion, [which make it likely] . . . that the President would have been able to make the findings required by that law. But Congress has made the exercise of executive authority over import restraints dependent on public ventilation of the issues and has prescribed a procedure with safeguards and right of comment by affected interests. The President has concededly not followed that procedure, and this course cannot stand consistently with the statutory pattern.

* * * *

I am not persuaded by the majority's pronouncement that the statutes are not pertinent to the present case because the arrangements . . . did not contemplate the mandate of judicial enforceability. These undertakings by the President and foreign steel producers were carefully structured in considerable detail, obviously after detailed consultation with American steel interests, without exposure to the kind of input by purchasers that would have been provided if the Congressional procedures had been followed. These undertakings are bilateral, and establish obligations. Their bite persists notwithstanding the majority's effort to coat them in bland vanilla. The majority tolerates executive detours around the limits staked by Congress in the field it has occupied. Its concept that a different route is available for executive arrangements discerned as not intended for judicial enforcement is, in my view, unsound.

* * * *

The contention, accepted by the majority, that the President's action is valid, notwithstanding its lack of statutory authorization, is based on two propositions: (1) the action is within the President's independent "foreign affairs" power; and (2) the import restraint achieved as a result of the President's action is not pre-empted by the Congressional regulatory structure.

Though there is no specific Constitutional clause granting the President power to conduct foreign affairs, that power has long been recognized. . . . The President's role in shaping foreign policy is rooted in and enhanced by his ability to communicate with foreign governments in the conduct of diplomacy. . . .

However, to say that executive communications with a foreign national are within the President's foreign affairs role only opens the door to analysis. Here the purpose of the communication was to manage commerce between the United States and the foreign producers involved — a matter over which Congress has plenary power conferred by Article I, Section 8. While it would be too narrow a view of the executive function to say that foreign commercial relations are not a proper subject of executive communications with foreign entities, the executive cannot, through its communications, manage foreign commerce in a manner lying outside a comprehensive regulatory scheme Congress has enacted pursuant to its Article I, Section 8 power. . . .

* * * *

The majority says that the steel import restraints are in harmony with the statutory program because they are not enforceable in courts of law; they are said to be mere precatory expressions. . . .

This response presents an issue that focuses on the nature and effect of the undertakings before us. Turning first to effect, Presidents may engage in many activities that have a perceivable economic impact upon the volume of commodities imported. . . . At one pole would lie general Presidential exhortations — say, to consumers to "Buy American" — or general alarms, announcing that protective legislation will be sought if imports are not contained. Such appeals are valid even though they may have the effect of inhibiting some market behavior, and no one would view them as prohibited by even the strongest Congressional "free trade" legislation. At the other extreme is a Presidential proclamation that foreign-trade commodities will not be allowed to enter, which plainly cannot be reconciled with the existing statutory structure, or legitimated by reference to some aura of "inherent" Presidential authority. In between is a continuum of restrictions. In my view, the comprehensive statutory program constrains some but not all of the activities in this continuum. Here, the undertakings have an economic effect that parallels that of import quotas proclaimed by the President.

Turning to its nature, the Presidential action here goes far beyond a speech or announcement. . . . Far from being mere expressions of desire and intent, these are solemn negotiated bilateral understandings.

The arrangements are . . . the culmination of bilateral discussions that were not only participated in, but initiated by State Department officials. . . .

Obviously, foreign firms that have vigorously marketed their products in the United States do not voluntarily withhold production without some reciprocal aspect indicating that forbearance is to their advantage. Here, the undertakings of the foreign producers rest on Government assurances that disadvantages would be equalized among producers; that the United States Government — or at least the not uninfluential Executive Branch — would not take or start other measures to limit steel imports or increase duties; and that the transaction would not violate any law of the United States.

The specificity of the limitations imposed by the undertakings also indicates that they were the result of bilateral bargaining and agreement.

Significantly, by the terms of the arrangements, the parties contemplate continuing consultations. . . . Does one accompany a unilateral declaration of intent with an offer to "consult" about what he has declared?. . . .

The inference of bilateral undertaking is strengthened when the arrangement is placed in the context of historical practice. Export forbearance of foreign producers has historically been obtained by diplomatic exchange of notes between the United States and foreign governments. The diplomatic notes themselves have referred to an "agreement" or "gentlemen's agreement" to limit shipments.

The majority asserts that, unlike agreements negotiated pursuant to statute, . . . the steel arrangements are unenforceable. But it is by no means clear that the Executive is without sanctions if the producers fail to abide by the arrangements. The very specificity of the limitations described by the letters makes violations easy to detect and the arrangements easy to enforce. That the threat of sanctions may carry considerable weight is indicated by the cooperation of the Japanese producers in making compensatory adjustments when they exceeded the quota for 1969 established by the original agreement. The remedy was a reduction of the 1970 quota by the amount of the overshipment. . . . Similarly, when the Japanese producers exceeded their aggregate quotas for 1972, "consultations" resulted in an agreement by the Japanese producers to charge the 1972 overshipments against 1973 quotas. . . .

If, as the government argues, the President has inherent power to negotiate these and similar restraints, I fail to see why the courts would or should refrain from enforcement if sought. Products shipped to the United States in excess of the restraints might be denied entry, or domestic firms might be enjoined from handling them.

* * * *

Even if judicial enforcement was not contemplated by the parties, the arrangements still embody a restraint. . . . [T]he Executive may call on non-judicial resources if foreign producers violate the arrangements. Actions that would ordinarily be resisted as inconsistent with amicable relations, possibly a call to reduce assistance programs to the country in question, could hardly be assailed in the face of foreign producer bad faith.

A deliberate breach may well have an outcome intermediate between direct judicial enforcement and complete non-involvement on the part of the judiciary. Suppose the President directed customs officials to deny entry to United States ports of commodities violating the undertaking, and suppose such actions were sought to be enjoined. It seems to me entirely likely that the parties might have contemplated both this executive action, and the judicial consequence — on the assumption that the negotiations were valid — that the courts had no basis for holding the executive action invalid.

* * * *

In my view, the steel quotas before us present an import restraint having a composite characteristic, in terms of effect and nature, as to be subject to the procedures and requirements set forth in the Trade Expansion Act of 1962.

This is the critical question in the case — where to draw the line. There is a continuum of restraints, as noted above. In my view, the critical distinction is between executive actions that rest wholly in the domain of appeals and exhortations, and executive actions that culminate in obligations. A good faith agreement with the kind of specificity present here puts an obligation on the foreign producer, in any realistic assessment. Accordingly, I think the executive negotiation and acceptance of these undertakings are activity in a field that has been preempted by Congress, and can only be engaged in by following the procedures set forth in the Congressional enactments.

NOTES AND QUESTIONS

(1) The decision in *Consumers Union* illustrates, does it not, the vast extent of power lurking in the President's function as "organ of the nation?" In light of the extent of the power illustrated here, how might Justice Sutherland have addressed the issue posed in the case? Does the case illustrate the wisdom or folly of Justice Sutherland's dictum?

(2) In contrast to the majority, how does Judge Leventhal define the limits of what the President can accomplish under his power to communicate with foreign governments or with foreign citizens? Is it purely a matter of form? Suppose the Secretary of State had, in secret conversations, merely "informed" representatives of the Japanese steel industry of "his government's favorable attitude toward any move by the Japanese to curtail sales to the United States" and also suppose this

"communication" had been memorialized in a secret document? If Judge Leventhal's test is more than form, does he go too far?

(3) Recall, from a trade perspective, this is the case that gave the green light to Presidentially "negotiated" VRA's.

CHAPTER 13

CONSTITUTIONAL AND OTHER LIMITATIONS ON THE REGULATION OF TRANSNATIONAL BUSINESS

In this Chapter we consider a variety of limitations on the power of Federal and State legislatures and executive agencies to regulate transnational business and on the authority of American courts to resolve disputes relating to that business.

Most of these limitations are rooted in the Constitution; either the text directly (*e.g.*, the "takings" clause of the 5th Amendment and the "due process" clause of the 5th and 14th Amendments) or in some more general structural principle such as the separation of powers doctrine, the principles of federalism or of justiciability. As an example of the latter, the "Act of State" doctrine has "constitutional underpinnings" even though the "text of the Constitution does not require [it]." In addition, federal and state regulation of transnational business has increasingly become the subject of and constrained by treaties and other international agreements entered into by the United States. Finally, in this Chapter we briefly take note of some of the specialized courts established to hear cases involving the application of a variety of statutes to transnational business undertakings.

We begin with a discussion of a doctrine that some would say, in the words of Lewis Carroll's Alice in Wonderland, has become "curiouser and curiouser;" the "Act of State" doctrine.

§ 13.01   The Act of State Doctrine

[A]   Historical Background

The classic statement of the Act of State doctrine is that of the Supreme Court in *Underhill v. Hernandez*:[1]

> Every sovereign State is bound to respect the independence of every other sovereign State, and the courts of one country will not sit in judgment on the acts of the government of another done within its own territory. Redress of grievances by reason of such acts must be obtained through the means open to be availed of by sovereign powers as between themselves.

The facts in *Underhill* involved a revolution that broke out in 1892 in Venezuela. General Hernandez, who commanded certain revolutionary forces, entered and assumed command of the city of Bolivar in August 1892. In October 1892, the United States recognized the revolutionary party as the legitimate government of Venezuela. Underhill, a United States citizen, had built and operated a water works system for Bolivar under a government contract. Hernandez forced Underhill to continue operating the water works system against his will until October

---

[1] 168 U.S. 250, 252 (1897).

1892, when he was allowed to leave the country. Upon his return to the United States Underhill brought an action against Hernandez in a federal court in New York to recover damages for wrongful detention. The lower courts gave judgment for defendant, and the Supreme Court, after granting a writ of certiorari, affirmed.

It should be noted that the basis for Underhill's claim was the tort law of Venezuela and that an alternative defense that Hernandez might have advanced would have been sovereign immunity

In *Oetjen v. Central Leather Co.*[2] plaintiff, a Mexican citizen, raised a claim that seizure by a Mexican general during the Mexican revolution of 1913 violated the Hague Convention of 1907 respecting the laws and customs of war. The Supreme Court questioned whether the Hague Convention applied to a civil war or to the particular conduct there involved, and held for defendant on the basis of the principles enunciated in *Underhill v. Hernandez*. In addition, the court stated that: "To permit the validity of the acts of one sovereign state to be reexamined and perhaps condemned by the courts of another would very certainly imperil the amicable relations between governments and vex the peace of nations."

A case arising out of the same Mexican revolution was *Ricaud v. American Metal Company, Ltd.*[3] There, General Pereyra commanded a brigade of the army led by General Carranza. Plaintiff, American Metal Co., claimed to have purchased in June 1913 a quantity of lead bullion in Mexico from the Penoles Mining Company, a Mexican company. In September 1913, General Pereyra confiscated the bullion from Penoles in exchange for a receipt promising to pay for the lead bullion "on the triumph of the revolution." Pereyra sold the bullion to defendant Ricaud, who sold it to another defendant, and Pereyra used the proceeds of sale to equip his army. The customs collector at El Paso, Texas held the lead bullion in bond, and American Metal Co. brought an action in equity against Ricaud and his purchaser to recover the bullion. The United States District Court in Texas held for plaintiff. The Circuit Court of Appeals certified certain questions to the Supreme Court, which reversed the district court. In so ruling the Supreme Court stated:

> It is settled that the courts will take judicial notice of such recognition, as we have here, of the Carranza government by the political department of our government . . . and that the courts of one independent government will not sit in judgment on the validity of the acts of another done within its own territory. . . . This last rule, however, does not deprive the courts of jurisdiction once acquired over a case. It requires only that when it is made to appear that the foreign government has acted in a given way on the subject-matter of the litigation, the details of such action or the merit of the result cannot be questioned but must be accepted by our courts as a rule for their decision. To accept a ruling authority and to decide accordingly is not a surrender or abandonment of jurisdiction but is an exercise of it. It results that the title to the property in this case must be determined by the result of the action taken by the military authorities of Mexico. . . .

---

[2] 246 U.S. 297, 38 S. Ct. 309, 62 L. Ed 726 (1918).
[3] 246 U.S. 304, 38 S. Ct. 312, 62 L. Ed 733 (1918).

. . . The fact that the title to the property in controversy may have been in an American citizen, who was not in or a resident of Mexico at the time it was seized for military purposes by the legitimate government of Mexico, does not affect the rule of law that the act within its own boundaries of one sovereign state cannot become the subject of reexamination and modification in the courts of another. Such action when shown to have been taken, becomes, as we have said, a rule of decision for the courts of this country. Whatever rights such an American citizen may have can be asserted only through the courts of Mexico or through the political departments of our government. . . .

In *Ricaud*, in contrast to *Oetjen*, there was no claim of a violation of international law.

A more recent example of issues involving the Act of State doctrine is the litigation brought by one Arnold Bernstein. Plaintiff Bernstein alleged that, in 1937, when a German citizen and resident, he was imprisoned by Nazi officials because he was Jewish. These officials forced him to execute documents transferring all the stock of a German corporation, the Arnold Bernstein Line, to a Nazi agent, one Boeger. Boeger took over all assets of the Line and transferred the ship "Gandia" to the defendant, a Belgian corporation. According to plaintiff, defendant, before taking possession, knew that plaintiff was a Jew and that the transfer to Boeger had been coerced. The ship was sunk during the war, while under British control. In 1939 plaintiff got out of Germany by a ransom payment.

In 1946, while a resident of New York, plaintiff brought an action against defendant to recover damages for detention of the vessel along with the proceeds of the insurance on the "Gandia," held on defendant's behalf, in New York. Upon removal of the case by defendant to the Federal District Court, in New York, the attachment of the insurance proceeds was quashed and the complaint dismissed on grounds that the claim was for a wrong done by "the German Government under the Nazi regime" and that, since the confiscation had occurred in German territory, it was "not subject to review in our courts."

In *Bernstein v. Van Heyghen Freres Societe Anonyme*,[4] the Court of Appeals affirmed. The court's opinion, delivered by Judge Learned Hand, stated that the court could not pass upon the validity of the transfer under German law. Judge Hand noted that, under New York choice of law rules, the court would not have to recognize the validity of the German officials' actions if they offended New York "public policy," which was certainly true in this case. However, in Judge Hand's view, the plaintiff's difficulty did not lie in any defect of New York conflict of law rules; rather, his claim was bared by the Act of State doctrine, which was dispositive in this case, unless there was evidence that the U.S. Government had acted in such a way as to relieve the court of the necessity of applying the doctrine. Turning to the evidence on this issue, Judge Hand found that legislation enacted by the allied powers proscribing any application of discriminatory legislation was prospective in application and did not purport retroactively to invalidate earlier German laws. As to provisions in such legislation for restoration of seized property and reparations, these also did not permit domestic courts to pass on

---

[4] 163 F. 2d 246 (2d Cir. 1947).

these questions of validity at the time of the transfer. Rather, this claim was reserved for adjudication along with all other such claims as part of the final settlement with Germany.

A decision to similar effect was rendered by the Court of Appeals in *Bernstein v. N.V. Nederlandsche-Amerikaansche Stoomvaart-Maatschappij.*[5] Subsequent to this decision, however, the Department of State issued a press release, which quoted a copy of a letter from the Acting Legal Adviser stating that it was the government's policy to undo the forced transfers and restore identifiable property to the victims of Nazi persecution and that "the policy of the Executive, with respect to claims asserted in the United States for restitution of such property, is to relieve American courts from any restraint upon the exercise of their jurisdiction to pass upon the validity of the acts of Nazi officials." Thereupon, the Court of Appeals issued a per curiam opinion reversing its earlier decision and allowing the district court to proceed on the case free from any restraints under the Act of State doctrine.[6]

Bernstein's claim against the Holland-America Line was settled. Subsequently, he filed a claim before the Foreign Claims Settlement Commission under the War Claims Act of 1948, as amended, which provided for payment, from funds derived from the vesting of German-owned assets during the war, of compensation to American nationals for property destroyed or taken during the war. He succeeded in obtaining a substantial additional award.[7]

[B] Contemporary Applications of the Doctrine

In 1964 the Supreme Court handed down a decision that still constitutes the most detailed discussion by the Court of the Act of State doctrine.

BANCO NACIONAL DE CUBA v. SABBATINO

Supreme Court of the United States
376 U.S. 398, 84 S.Ct. 923, 11 L.Ed 2d 804 (1964)

MR. JUSTICE HARLAN delivered the opinion of the Court.

[The background to this case involved rapidly deteriorating relations between the United States and Cuba after the takeover of power by Fidel Castro. Increasing U.S. dissatisfaction with the policies of the Castro government led President Eisenhower, pursuant to legislation, to issue an order on July 6, 1960, reducing the sugar quota for Cuba. On the same day, the Cuban Government nationalized many companies in which Americans held interests, including Compania Azucarera Vertientes — Camaguey de Cuba (CAV). Before the nationalization of CAV, the latter had sold a shipload of sugar to Farr, Whitlock, an American commodities broker. Before the sugar was

---

[5] 173 F. 2d 71 (2d Cir. 1949).
[6] 210 F. 2d 375 (2d Cir. 1954).
[7] See 61 Am. J. Int'l L. 1069 (1967).

shipped, however, it was seized by the Cuban Government. This caused Farr, Whitlock to enter into a new contract to buy the shipload from the Cuban Government. Banco Nacional, as the Cuban Government's agent, negotiated bills of lading covering the shipload to Farr, Whitlock who in turn negotiated the bills to its customers and received payment for the sugar. Instead of using these proceeds to pay Banco Nacional, however, Farr, Whitlock turned the proceeds over to CAV in return for the latter's agreement to indemnify it against any liability to Banco Nacional. Banco Nacional then brought an action against Farr, Whitlock for conversion of the bills of lading, seeking also to enjoin Sabbatino, the temporary receiver of CAV's New York assets, from disposing of the proceeds. In response Farr, Whitlock contended that title to the sugar never passed to Cuba because the expropriation violated international law. In response to that defense, Banco Nacional argued that the "Act of State" doctrine foreclosed the U.S. courts from judging the legality of the expropriation and required that those courts uphold Banco Nacional's title to the sugar or the proceeds therefrom.]

* * * *

. . . While acknowledging the continuing vitality of the act of state doctrine, the court [*i.e.*, the District Court] believed it inapplicable when the questioned foreign act is in violation of international law. Proceeding on the basis that a taking invalid under international law does not convey good title, the District Court found the Cuban expropriation decree to violate such law in three separate respects: It was motivated by a retaliatory and not a public purpose; it discriminated against American nationals; and it failed to provide adequate compensation. Summary judgment against petitioner was accordingly granted.

The Court of Appeals,[8] . . . affirming the decision on similar grounds, relied on two letters (not before the District Court) written by State Department officers which it took as evidence that the Executive Branch had no objection to a judicial testing of the Cuban decree's validity. The court was unwilling to declare that any one of the infirmities found by the District Court rendered the taking invalid under international law, but was satisfied that in combination they had that effect. We granted certiorari because the issues involved bear importantly on the conduct of the country's foreign relations and more particularly on the proper role of the Judicial Branch in this sensitive area. . . . For reasons to follow we decide that the judgment below must be reversed. . . .

[After reviewing *Underhill v. Hernandez, Oetjen* and *Ricaud*, Justice Harlan noted that in deciding the present case the Court of Appeals had relied in part upon the so-called Bernstein exception to the unqualified teachings of those cases, and then added:]

* * * *

This Court has never had occasion to pass upon th[at] . . . exception, nor need it do so now. For whatever ambiguity may be thought to exist in the two letters from State Department officials on which the Court of Appeals relied,[9] . . . it is

---

[8] 307 F. 2d 845

[9] 307 F. 2d at 858.

now removed by the position which the Executive has taken in this Court on the act of state claim; respondents do not indeed contest the view that these letters were intended to reflect no more than the Department's then wish not to make any statement bearing on this litigation.

The outcome of this case, therefore, turns upon whether any of the contentions urged by respondents against the application of the act of state doctrine in the premises is acceptable: (1) that the doctrine does not apply to acts of state which violate international law, as is claimed to be the case here; (2) that the doctrine is inapplicable unless the Executive specifically interposes it in a particular case; and (3) that, in any event, the doctrine may not be invoked by a foreign government plaintiff in our courts.

Preliminarily, we discuss the foundations on which we deem the act of state doctrine to rest, and more particularly the question of whether state or federal law governs its application in a federal diversity case.

We do not believe that this doctrine is compelled either by the inherent nature of sovereign authority, as some of the earlier decisions seem to imply, see [*Underhill, supra; American Banana, supra; Oetjen, supra*] or by some principle of international law. If a transaction takes place in one jurisdiction and the forum is in another, the forum does not by dismissing an action or by applying its own law purport to divest the first jurisdiction of its territorial sovereignty; it merely declines to adjudicate or makes applicable its own law to parties or property before it. The refusal of one country to enforce the penal laws of another . . . is a typical example of an instance when a court will not entertain a cause of action arising in another jurisdiction. While historic notions of sovereign authority do bear upon the wisdom of employing the act of state doctrine, they do not dictate its existence.

That international law does not require application of the doctrine is evidenced by the practice of nations. Most of the countries rendering decisions on the subject fail to follow the rule rigidly. No international arbitral or judicial decision discovered suggests that international law prescribes recognition of sovereign acts of foreign governments, see 1 Oppenheim's International Law, Sec. 115aa (Lauterpacht, 8th ed. 1955), and apparently no claim has ever been raised before an international tribunal that failure to apply the act of state doctrine constitutes a breach of international obligation. If international law does not prescribe use of the doctrine, neither does it forbid application of the rule even if it is claimed that the act of state in question violated international law. The traditional view of international law is that it establishes substantive principles for determining whether one country has wronged another. Because of its peculiar nation-to-nation character the usual method for an individual to seek relief is to exhaust local remedies and then repair to the executive authorities of his own state to persuade them to champion his claim in diplomacy or before an international tribunal. . . . Although it is, of course, true that United States courts apply international law as a part of our own in appropriate circumstances, . . . the public law of nations can hardly dictate to a country which is in theory wronged how to treat that wrong within its domestic borders.

Despite the broad statement in Oetjen that "The conduct of the foreign relations of our government is committed by the Constitution to the executive and legislative . . . departments," . . . it cannot of course be thought that "every case

or controversy which touches foreign relations lies beyond judicial cognizance."
Baker v. Carr[10] . . . . The text of the Constitution does not require the act of state
doctrine; it does not irrevocably remove from the judiciary the capacity to review
the validity of foreign acts of state.

The act of state doctrine does, however, have "constitutional" underpinnings.
It arises out of the basic relationships between branches of government in a system
of separation of powers. It concerns the competency of dissimilar institutions to
make and implement particular kinds of decision in the area of international
relations. The doctrine as formulated in past decisions expresses the strong sense
of the Judicial Branch that its engagement in the task of passing on the validity
of foreign acts of state may hinder rather than further this country's pursuit of
goals both for itself and for the community of nations as a whole in the international sphere. Many commentators disagree with this view; they have striven by
means of distinguishing and limiting past decisions and by advancing various
considerations of policy to stimulate a narrowing of the apparent scope of the rule.
Whatever considerations are thought to predominate, it is plain that the problems
involved are uniquely federal in nature. If federal authority, in this instance this
Court, orders the field of judicial competence in this area for the federal courts,
and the state courts are left free to formulate their own rules, the purposes behind
the doctrine could be as effectively undermined as if there had been no federal
pronouncement on the subject.

* * * *

If the act of state doctrine is a principle of decision binding on federal and state
courts alike but compelled by neither international law nor the Constitution, its
continuing vitality depends on its capacity to reflect the proper distribution of
functions between the judicial and political branches of the Government on
matters bearing upon foreign affairs. It should be apparent that the greater the
degree of codification or consensus concerning a particular area of international
law, the more appropriate it is for the judiciary to render decisions regarding it,
since the courts can then focus on the application of an agreed principle to
circumstances of fact rather than on the sensitive task of establishing a principle
not inconsistent with the national interest or with international justice. It is also
evident that some aspects of international law touch much more sharply on
national nerves than do others; the less important the implications of an issue are
for our foreign relations, the weaker the justification for exclusivity in the political
branches. The balance of relevant considerations may also be shifted if the
government which perpetrated the challenged act of state is no longer in existence,
as in the *Bernstein* case, for the political interest of this country may, as a result,
be measurably altered. Therefore, rather than laying down or reaffirming an
inflexible and all-encompassing rule in this case, we decide only that the Judicial
Branch will not examine the validity of a taking of property within its own
territory by a foreign sovereign government, extant and recognized by this country
at the time of suit, in the absence of a treaty or other unambiguous agreement
regarding controlling legal principles, even if the complaint alleges that the taking
violates customary international law.

---

[10] 369 U.S. 186, 211, 82 S. Ct. 691, 707, 7 L. Ed. 2d 663.

There are few if any issues in international law today on which opinion seems to be so divided as the limitations on a state's power to expropriate the property of aliens. There is, of course, authority, in international judicial and arbitral decisions, in the expressions of national governments, and among commentators for the view that a taking is improper under international law if it is not for a public purpose, is discriminatory, or is without provision for prompt, adequate, and effective compensation. However, Communist countries, although they have in fact provided a degree of compensation after diplomatic efforts, commonly recognize no obligation on the part of the taking country. Certain representatives of the newly independent and under-developed countries have questioned whether rules of state responsibility toward aliens can bind nations that have not consented to them and it is argued that the traditionally articulated standards governing expropriation of property reflect "imperialist" interests and are inappropriate to the circumstances of emergent states.

The disagreement as to relevant international law standards reflects an even more basic divergence between the national interests of capital importing and capital exporting nations and between the social ideologies of those countries that favor state control of a considerable portion of the means of production and those that adhere to a free enterprise system. It is difficult to imagine the courts of this country embarking on adjudication in an area which touches more sensitively the practical and ideological goals of the various members of the community of nations.

* * * *

The possible adverse consequences of a conclusion to the contrary of that implicit in these cases is highlighted by contrasting the practices of the political branches with the limitations of the judicial process in matters of this kind. Following an expropriation of any significance, the Executive engages in diplomacy aimed to assure that United States citizens who are harmed are compensated fairly. Representing all claimants of this country, it will often be able, either by bilateral or multilateral talks, by submission to the United Nations, or by the employment of economic and political sanctions, to achieve some degree of general redress. Judicial determinations of invalidity of title can, on the other hand, have only an occasional impact, since they depend on the fortuitous circumstance of the property in question being brought into this country. Such decisions would, if the acts involved were declared invalid, often be likely to give offense to the expropriating country; since the concept of territorial sovereignty is so deep seated, any state may resent the refusal of the courts of another sovereign to accord validity to acts within its territorial borders. Piecemeal dispositions of this sort involving the probability of affront to another state could seriously interfere with negotiations being carried on by the Executive Branch and might prevent or render less favorable the terms of an agreement that could otherwise be reached. Relations with third countries which have engaged in similar expropriations would not be immune from effect.

The dangers of such adjudication are present regardless of whether the State Department has, as it did in this case, asserted that the relevant act violated international law. If the Executive Branch has undertaken negotiations with an expropriating country, but has refrained from claims of violation of the law of nations, a determination to that effect by a court might be regarded as a serious insult, while a finding of compliance with international law would greatly strengthen the bargaining hand of the other state with consequent detriment to American interests.

Even if the State Department has proclaimed the impropriety of the expropriation, the stamp of approval of its view by a judicial tribunal, however impartial, might increase any affront and the judicial decision might occur at a time, almost always well after the taking, when such an impact would be contrary to our national interest. Considerably more serious and far-reaching consequences would flow from a judicial finding that international law standards had been met if that determination flew in the face of a State Department proclamation to the contrary. When articulating principles of international law in its relations with other states, the Executive Branch speaks not only as an interpreter of generally accepted and traditional rules, as would the courts, but also as an advocate of standards it believes desirable for the community of nations and protective of national concerns. In short, whatever way the matter is cut, the possibility of conflict between the Judicial and Executive Branches could hardly be avoided.

* * * *

[A] serious consequence of the exception pressed by respondents would be to render uncertain titles in foreign commerce, with the possible consequence of altering the flow of international trade. If the attitude of the United States courts were unclear, one buying expropriated goods would not know if he could safely import them into this country. Even were takings known to be invalid, one would have difficulty determining after goods had changed hands several times whether the particular articles in question were the product of an ineffective state act.

Against the force of such considerations, we find respondents' countervailing arguments quite unpersuasive. Their basic contention is that United States courts could make a significant contribution to the growth of international law, a contribution whose importance, it is said, would be magnified by the relative paucity of decisional law by international bodies. But given the fluidity of present world conditions, the effectiveness of such a patchwork approach toward the formulation of an acceptable body of law concerning state responsibility for expropriations is, to say the least, highly conjectural. Moreover, it rests upon the sanguine presupposition that the decisions of the courts of the world's major capital exporting country and principal exponent of the free enterprise system would be accepted as disinterested expressions of sound legal principle by those adhering to widely different ideologies.

It is contended that regardless of the fortuitous circumstances necessary for United States jurisdiction over a case involving a foreign act of state and the resultant isolated application to any expropriation program taken as a whole, it is the function of the courts to justly decide individual disputes before them. Perhaps the most typical act of state case involves the original owner or his assignee suing one not in association with the expropriating state who has had "title" transferred to him. But it is difficult to regard the claim of the original owner, who otherwise may be recompensed through diplomatic channels, as more demanding of judicial cognizance than the claim of title by the innocent third party purchaser, who, if the property is taken from him, is without any remedy.

* * * *

It is suggested that if the act of state doctrine is applicable to violations of international law, it should only be so when the Executive Branch expressly stipulates that it does not wish the courts to pass on the question of validity[11] . . . . We should be slow to reject the representations of the Government that such a reversal of the Bernstein principle would work serious inroads on the maximum effectiveness of United States diplomacy. Often the State Department will wish to refrain from taking an official position, particularly at a moment that would be dictated by the development of private litigation but might be inopportune diplomatically. Adverse domestic consequences might flow from an official stand which could be assuaged, if at all, only by revealing matters best kept secret. Of course, a relevant consideration for the State Department would be the position contemplated in the court to hear the case. It is highly questionable whether the examination of validity by the judiciary should depend on an educated guess by the Executive as to probable result and, at any rate, should a prediction be wrong, the Executive might be embarrassed in its dealings with other countries. We do not now pass on the Bernstein exception, but even if it were deemed valid, its suggested extension is unwarranted.

However offensive to the public policy of this country and its constituent States an expropriation of this kind may be, we conclude that both the national interest and progress toward the goal of establishing the rule of law among nations are best served by maintaining intact the act of state doctrine in this realm of its application.

* * * *

The judgment of the Court of Appeals is reversed and the case is remanded to the District Court for proceedings consistent with this opinion. It is so ordered.

[The dissenting opinion of MR. JUSTICE WHITE is omitted.]

NOTES AND QUESTIONS

(1) As indicated in *Sardino v. Federal Reserve Bank of New York*,[12] *supra*, Chapter 9, all Cuban assets in the United States had been frozen as of 1963. Accordingly, any recovery by Banco Nacional would have been held subject to those restrictions. Moreover, in light of the history of international claims settlements, as described in Chapter 9, these funds might ultimately have been applied towards a lump sum settlement of claims against Cuba. Thus, a judgment for Farr, Whitlock invalidating Cuba's seizure of CAV's sugar would have effectively given CAV a preference over other claimants whose properties had been expropriated by Cuba but who were not blessed by the fortuitous presence

---

[11] See Association of the Bar of the City of New York, Committee on International Law, A Reconsideration of the Act of State Doctrine in United States Courts (1959).

[12] 361 F. 2d 106 (2d Cir. 1966).

in the United States of the proceeds from the sale of their property. Does this not raise questions of basic fairness, of due process and equal protection?

(2) Is the opinion of the Court in *Sabbatino* based simply on the proposition that the Act of State doctrine is necessary to ensure that the courts will not "embarrass" the executive branch in the conduct of foreign relations? Alternatively, does the opinion rest on more fundamental ideas concerning the fitness for judicial settlement (justiciability) of the issues the Court was being asked to decide? In answering, recall Justice Harlan's comments on the state of international law on the subject. Return to Chapter 9 and examine the difficulties the courts have encountered in determining when, under the 5th and 14th Amendments of the U.S. Constitution, a compensable taking has occurred (pp. 784–786, 794). Re-examine the *Sardino* decision and the Notes that follow. (*supra*, p. 794). Note that in his opinion Justice Harlan expressly declines to take a position on the "so-called Bernstein exception." Suppose that the State Department had written to the lower courts expressing its view that "under no possible circumstances" could the courts' adjudication of the issue whether Cuba's expropriations of U.S. owned property was illegal under international law interfere with the conduct of U.S. foreign policy? Would Justice Harlan have found the Act of State doctrine inapplicable?

(3) In *First National City Bank v. Banco Nacional de Cuba*,[13] Citibank, in July 1958, loaned to the predecessor of Banco Nacional, $15 million secured by a pledge of United States Government bonds. On September 16, 1960, after Castro had come to power, the Cuban government seized all of Citibank's Cuban branches. The Bank retaliated a week later by calling the loan and selling the collateral securing the unpaid balance. Approximately $1.8 million was left over after the proceeds were applied to the principal and interest on the loan. Banco Nacional sued Citibank to recover that excess and the Bank asserted, by way of set-off and counterclaim, its right to recover its expropriation losses out of the fund.

When it was conceded that Citibank's expropriation losses exceeded $1.8 million, the court dismissed Banco Nacional's complaint. The Court of Appeals reversed. While a petition for certiorari was pending, the Department of State wrote a "Bernstein letter" in which it concluded that "the act of state doctrine should not be applied to bar consideration of a defendant's counterclaim or set-off against the Government of Cuba in this or like cases." In granting certiorari, the Supreme Court vacated the Court of Appeals judgment so that the latter court could consider the views of the Department of State. When the Court of Appeals adhered to its previous opinion, the Supreme Court again granted certiorari, and, in a five to four decision, reversed.

An opinion by Justice Rehnquist, joined by Chief Justice Burger and Justice White, relied primarily on the Bernstein exception and the State Department's letter. In the words of the opinion:

> [I]t would be wholly illogical to insist that such a rule, fashioned because of fear that adjudication would interfere with the conduct of foreign relations, be applied in the face of an assurance from that branch of the Federal

---

[13] 406 U.S. 759, 92 S. Ct. 1808, 32 L. Ed. 2d 466 (1972).

Government which conducts foreign relations that such a result would not obtain. Our holding confines the courts to adjudication of the case before them, and leaves to the Executive Branch the conduct of foreign relations. In so doing, it is both faithful to the principle of separation of powers and consistent with earlier cases applying the act of state doctrine where we lacked the sort of representation from the Executive Branch which we have in this case.

In a concurring opinion, Justice Douglas relied on *National City Bank v. Republic of China*,[14] where the Court held that, by bringing suit in U.S. courts, a foreign sovereign waives immunity on offsetting counterclaims — whether or not related to the sovereign's cause of action. According to Justice Douglas, it would "offend our sensibilities if Cuba could collect the amount owed on liquidation of the collateral for the loan and not be required to account for any set-off." He expressly rejected the Bernstein exception, however, and would have applied the Act of State doctrine to bar any recovery by Citibank that exceeded the amount of Banco Nacional's claim.

Justice Powell, concurring in the judgment, rejected the reasoning of both Justice Rehnquist and Justice Douglas. He rested his opinion instead on the view that the Court in *Sabbatino* had been wrong in applying the Act of State doctrine to a case where the issue was the validity of the expropriation under customary international law.

The dissenting opinion, written by Justice Brennan and joined by Justices Stewart, Marshall, and Blackmun, disagreed with Justice Rehnquist's view that the Bernstein letter had removed any risk of interference with the executive's conduct of foreign affairs should the Court consider whether Cuba's actions had violated international law. The opinion pointed out that the State Department's letter to the Court anticipated a ruling that the Cuban expropriation of Citibank's properties was invalid. In response the dissent quoted the *Sabbatino* opinion: "It is highly questionable whether the examination of validity by the judiciary should depend on an educated guess by the Executive as to probable result and, at any rate, should a prediction be wrong, the Executive might be embarrassed in its dealings with other countries." It pointed out further that "this observation, if anything has more force than in *Sabbatino*, since respondent argues with some substance that the Cuban nationalization of petitioner's properties, unlike the expropriation at issue in *Sabbatino*, was not discriminatory against United States' citizens."

The "crux" of the dissent's disagreement with Justice Rehnquist's support for the Bernstein exception was a rejection of the proposition that the Act of State doctrine was designed primarily to avoid embarrassment to the political branch:

In short, *Sabbatino* held that the validity of a foreign act of state in certain circumstances is a "political question" not cognizable in our courts. Only one — and not necessarily the most important — of those circumstances concerned the possible impairment of the Executive's conduct of foreign affairs. Even if this factor were absent in this case because of the Legal Adviser's statement of position, it would hardly follow that the act of state doctrine

[14] 348 U.S. 356, 75 S. Ct. 423, 99 L. Ed. 389 (1955).

should not foreclose judicial review of the expropriation of petitioner's properties. To the contrary, the absence of consensus on the applicable international rules, the unavailability of standards from a treaty or other agreement, the existence and recognition of the Cuban Government, the sensitivity of the issues to national concerns, and the power of the Executive alone to effect a fair remedy for all United States citizens who have been harmed all point toward the existence of a "political question." The Legal Adviser's letter does not purport to affect these considerations at all. In any event, when coupled with the possible consequences to the conduct of our foreign relations explored above, these considerations compel application of the act of state doctrine, notwithstanding the Legal Adviser's suggestion to the contrary. The Executive Branch, however extensive its powers in the area of foreign affairs, cannot by simple stipulation change a political question into a cognizable claim.

With respect to Justice Douglas's reliance on the *Republic of China* case, that decision, the dissent noted, related to a waiver of sovereign immunity and said nothing about the Act of State doctrine. As to Justice Douglas's statement that it would "offend our sensibilities if Cuba could collect the amount owed on . . . [her claim] and not be required to account for any setoff," the dissent contended that it was "by no means clear that the balance of equity tips in petitioner's favor." In its view Citibank was seeking a windfall at the expense of other claimants whose property Cuba had nationalized, because, if the bank prevailed in this case, it would, in effect, have secured a preference over other claimants who were not so fortunate to have Cuban assets within their reach and whose only relief would be before the Foreign Claims Settlement Commission.

(4) In *Alfred Dunhill of London, Inc. v. Republic of Cuba*,[15] a five Justice majority of the Supreme Court found that the mere refusal of a commercial agency of a foreign government to repay funds mistakenly paid to it did not constitute an Act of State, absent any statute, decree, or resolution of the Cuban Government itself to indicate that Cuba had, as a sovereign matter, decided to confiscate the amounts due. Four Justices supported a "commercial exception" to the Act of State doctrine, *i.e.*, the doctrine should not be extended to include the repudiation of a purely commercial obligation even if the repudiation was made pursuant to official decree.

The four dissenting Justices contended that Cuba's refusal to return the funds did not require a formal decree, order or statute to constitute an Act of State and that no commercial act exception was applicable to this case, since the refusal to pay was part of Cuba's nationalization program.

In the *Dunhill* case, the Court had before it a letter from the Legal Adviser to the Department of State to the Solicitor General stating: "this Department's experience provides little support for the proposition that adjudication of acts of foreign states in accordance with relevant principles of international law would embarrass the conduct of foreign policy. Thus, it is our view that if the Court should decide to overrule the holding in *Sabbatino* so that acts of state would thereafter be subject to adjudication in American courts under international law,

---

[15] 425 U.S. 682, 96 S. Ct. 1854, 48 L. Ed. 2d 30 (1976).

we would not anticipate embarrassment to the conduct of the foreign policy of the United States." The Court declined the invitation.

(5) In its *Sabbatino* opinion the Court states that the "Judicial Branch will not examine the validity of a taking of property within its own territory by a foreign sovereign government . . . in the absence of a treaty or other unambiguous agreement regarding controlling legal principles. . . ." Suppose that at the time of the Cuban expropriations there was a Treaty of Friendship, Commerce and Navigation between the United States and Cuba that provided that property of nationals of the contracting parties in the other state shall not be taken "without prompt payment of just and effective compensation." Would the Court have found the Act of State doctrine inapplicable? Can you make an argument against it doing so? See *Kalamazoo Spice Extraction Co. v. Government of Socialist Ethiopia.*[16] Compare *Callejo v. Bancomer, S.A.*[17]

(6) Consider *United States v. Pink, supra*, page 1068. In light of the Court's decision in *Pink*, and of the freezing of Cuban assets in this country, can you make an argument that the Supreme Court could have reached the same result in *Sabbatino* without invoking the Act of State doctrine or discussing international law regarding expropriation? (For discussion of the varying views regarding international law on expropriation, see *supra*, Chapter 9.)

(7) Reaction to the *Sabbatino* decision from U.S. business and lawyers representing clients with large foreign investments was strongly negative and precipitated a campaign for "repeal" of the decision. The result was Section 620(e)(2) of the Foreign Assistance Act of 1961 as amended, commonly called the Sabbatino Amendment, which may be found in your Documentary Supplement.[18] Reference in that section to "the principles of international law, including the principles of compensation and the other standards set out in this subsection. . . ." is to the Hickenlooper Amendment, Section 620(e)(1) of the Foreign Assistance Act of 1961, as amended, which is discussed *supra*, at page 807.[19] It should be read along with the Sabbatino Amendment. Consider the terms of the Sabbatino Amendment carefully.

(a) Is it likely to be of much assistance to American businesses or persons who are seeking to recover property that has been expropriated abroad or compensation therefor? For example, under the Amendment, can a U.S. citizen avoid application of the Act of State doctrine if the property he is claiming is in the country which expropriated it? See *Banco Nacional de Cuba v. First National City Bank of New York.*[20]

(b) Note the exclusion in the Amendment for claims to property acquired pursuant to an irrevocable letter of credit of not more than 180 days duration issued prior to a confiscation or other taking. For the rationale behind this exclusion, see Restatement (Third) of the Foreign Relations Law of the United States, Section 444, Reporters' Note 7.

---

[16] 543 F. Supp. 1224 (W.D. Mich. 1982), *reversed*, 729 F. 2d 422 (6th Cir. 1984).

[17] 764 F. 2d 1101, 1116–21 (5th cir. 1985).

[18] Documentary Supplement.

[19] Documentary Supplement.

[20] 270 F. Supp. 1004 (S.D.N.Y. 1967), *reversed*, 431 F. 2d 394, 399-402 (2d Cir. 1970), *reversed on other grounds*, 406 U.S. 759 (1972).

(c) In *French v. Banco Nacional de Cuba v. Farr*,[21] the New York Court of Appeals applied the Act of State doctrine in rejecting a claim based on breach of contract by a foreign government. The court held that the Sabbatino Amendment did not apply: "It is plain enough upon the face of the statute — and absolutely clear from its legislative history — that Congress was not attempting to assure a remedy in American courts for every kind of monetary loss resulting from actions, even unjust actions, of foreign governments. The law is restricted, manifestly, to the kind of problem exemplified by the *Sabbatino* case itself, a claim of title or other right to specific property which had been expropriated abroad."[22]

(d) Again review the discussion of international law regarding expropriation in Chapter 9. Is the international law standard that governs application of the Sabbatino Amendment reflective of a worldwide consensus, or does it merely represent a U.S. position on a highly controversial issue?

(8) At the time the Sabbatino Amendment came into force, proceedings in the *Sabbatino* litigation were pending, on remand from the Supreme Court, in the District Court. In *Banco Nacional de Cuba v. Farr*,[23] the court held that the Amendment applied to the case before it and rejected plaintiff's argument that "retroactive" application of the Amendment to this case would be unconstitutional and that the provision in the Amendment giving the President the power to invoke the Act of State doctrine in cases where national foreign policy interests so required violated the doctrine of separation of powers. The court also concluded that the opinion of the Court of Appeals, which ruled in favor of defendant on the international law issues, was binding upon it, because these issues were never reached by the Supreme Court. The Court of Appeals affirmed.[24]

(7) Congress has recently amended the Federal Arbitration Act[25] to place yet another limit on application of the Act of State Doctrine.[26] The Amendment provides: "[e]nforcement of arbitral agreements, confirmation of arbitral awards, and execution upon judgments based on orders confirming such awards shall not be refused on the basis of the Act of State doctrine."

---

[21] 23 N.Y.2d 46, 242 N.E. 2d 704, 295 N.Y.S. 2d 433 (1968).

[22] For a consideration of the relationship between the Act of State doctrine and foreign sovereign immunity, see *supra*, Chapter 11.

[23] 243 F. Supp. 957 (S.D.N.Y. 1965).

[24] 383 F. 2d 166 (2d Cir. 1967). The Act of State Doctrine has been raised as a defense in actions not involving expropriation and between two private parties. A number of these cases have been antitrust claims. The issue in these private actions has been whether the defendant's conduct could be judged without scrutiny of the acts or motives of the foreign government; if so, the Act of State doctrine has been held inapplicable. For discussion, see Restatement (Third) of Foreign Relations Law of the United States, Section 444, Reporters Note 7 (1987).

[25] 9 U.S.C. Sec. 15.

[26] Public Law 100-669, 102 Stat. 3969, approved by the President on November 16, 1988.

ALLIED BANK INTERNATIONAL v. BANCO CREDITO AGRICOLA DE CARTAGO

United States Court of Appeals For The Second Circuit
757 F. 2d 516, cert. denied 106 S. Ct. 30 (1985)

ON REHEARING

MESKILL, CIRCUIT JUDGE:

This matter is before us on rehearing. We vacate our previous decision dated April 23, 1984. We reverse the dismissal of the cause by the United States District Court for the Southern District of New York, Griesa, J. we also reverse the district court's denial of plaintiff-appellant Allied Bank International's (Allied) motion for summary judgment. Both district court rulings were predicated solely on the act of state doctrine. Because that doctrine is not applicable, we remand to the district court for entry of summary judgment for Allied.

I

Allied is the agent for a syndicate of thirty-nine creditor banks. Defendants-appellees are three Costa Rican banks that are wholly owned by the Republic of Costa Rica and subject to the direct control of the Central Bank of Costa Rica (Central Bank). Allied brought this action in February 1982 to recover on promissory notes issued by the Costa Rican banks. The notes, which were in default, were payable in United States dollars in New York City. The parties' agreements acknowledged that the obligations were registered with Central Bank which was supposed to provide the necessary dollars for payment.

The defaults were due solely to actions of the Costa Rican government. In July 1981, in response to escalating national economic problems, Central Bank issued regulations which essentially suspended all external debt payments. In November 1981, the government issued an executive decree which conditioned all payments of external debt on express approval from Central Bank. Central Bank subsequently refused to authorize any foreign debt payments in United States dollars, thus precluding payment on the notes here at issue. In accordance with the provisions of the agreements, Allied accelerated the debt and sued for the full amount of principal and interest outstanding.

The Costa Rican banks moved the district court to dismiss the complaint, claiming lack of subject matter jurisdiction due to sovereign immunity, lack of in personam jurisdiction and insufficiency of process and service. Allied moved for summary judgment. The sole defense raised by appellees in response was the act of state doctrine.

The district court denied all of the motions.[27] . . . . Reasoning that a judicial determination contrary to the Costa Rican directives could embarrass the United States government in its relations with the Costa Rican government, the court held that the act of state doctrine barred entry of summary judgment for Allied.

While the action was still pending before the district court, the parties began to negotiate a rescheduling of the debt. In July 1982, the suit was dismissed by

---

[27] 566 F. Supp. 1440 (S.D.N.Y. 1983).

agreement after the parties stipulated that no issues of fact remained with respect to the act of state doctrine issue. In September 1983, appellees, Central Bank and the Republic of Costa Rica signed a refinancing agreement with the coordinating agent for Costa Rica's external creditors. Fidelity Union Trust Company of New Jersey, one of the members of the Allied syndicate, did not accept the agreement. On behalf of Fidelity, the only creditor that refused to participate in the restructuring, Allied has prosecuted this appeal. The refinancing went into effect nonetheless and appellees have been making payments to the remaining thirty-eight members of the syndicate.

II

In our previous decision, we affirmed the district court's dismissal. We did not address the question of whether the act of state doctrine applied because we determined that the actions of the Costa Rican government which precipitated the default of the Costa Rican banks were fully consistent with the law and policy of the United States. We therefore concluded that principles of comity compelled us to recognize as valid the Costa Rican directives.

Our interpretation of United States policy, however, arose primarily from our belief that the legislative and executive branches of our government fully supported Costa Rica's actions and all of the economic ramifications. On rehearing, the Executive Branch of the United States joined this litigation as amicus curiae and respectfully disputed our reasoning. The Justice Department brief gave the following explanation of our government's support for the debt resolution procedure that operates through the auspices of the International Monetary Fund (IMF). Guided by the IMF, this long established approach encourages the cooperative adjustment of international debt problems. The entire strategy is grounded in the understanding that, while parties may agree to renegotiate conditions of payment, the underlying obligations to pay nevertheless remain valid and enforceable. Costa Rica's attempted unilateral restructuring of private obligations, the United States contends, was inconsistent with this system of international cooperation and negotiation and thus inconsistent with United States policy.

The United States government further explains that its position on private international debt is not inconsistent with either its own willingness to restructure Costa Rica's intergovenmental obligations or with continued United States aid to the economically distressed Central American country. Our previous conclusion that the Costa Rican decrees were consistent with United States policy was premised on these two circumstances.

In light of the government's elucidation of its position, we believe that our earlier interpretation of United States policy was wrong. Nevertheless, if, as Judge Griesa held, the act of state doctrine applies, it precludes judicial examination of the Costa Rican decrees. Thus we must first consider that question.

III

The act of state doctrine operates to confer presumptive validity on certain acts of foreign sovereigns by rendering non-justiciable claims that challenge such acts. The judicially created doctrine is not jurisdictional; it is "a rule of decision under which an act meeting the definition . . . is binding on the court." The applicability of the doctrine is purely a matter of federal law.

It has always been clear that "[t]he act of state doctrine does not . . . bar inquiry by the courts into the validity of extraterritorial takings." *Banco Nacional de Cuba v. Chemical Bank New York Trust Co.*,[28] *Republic of Iraq v. First National City Bank*.[29] It simply "concerns the limits for determining the validity of an otherwise applicable rule of law."

Originally linked with principles of sovereign immunity, the act of state doctrine has more recently been described as "aris[ing] out of the basic relationships between branches of government in a system of separation of powers." The policy concerns underlying the doctrine focus on the preeminence of the political branches, and particularly the executive, in the conduct of foreign policy. . . . Therefore, the applicability of the doctrine depends on the likely impact on international relations that would result from judicial consideration of the foreign sovereign's act. If adjudication would embarrass or hinder the executive in the realm of foreign relations, the court should refrain from inquiring into the validity of the foreign state's act.

The extraterritorial limitation, an inevitable conjunct of the foreign policy concerns underlying the doctrine, dictates that our decision herein depends on the situs of the property at the time of the purported taking. The property, of course, is Allied's right to receive repayment from the Costa Rican banks in accordance with the agreements. The act of state doctrine is applicable to this dispute only if, when the decrees were promulgated, the situs of the debts was in Costa Rica. Because we conclude that the situs of the property was in the United States, the doctrine is not applicable.

. . . [T]he concept of the situs of a debt for act of state purposes differs from the ordinary concept. It depends in large part on whether the purported taking can be said to have "come to complete fruition within the dominion of the [foreign] government.". . . . In this case, Costa Rica could not wholly extinguish the Costa Rican banks' obligation to timely pay United States dollars to Allied in New York. Thus the situs of the debt was not Costa Rica.

The same result obtains under ordinary situs analysis. The Costa Rican banks conceded jurisdiction in New York and they agreed to pay the debt in New York City in United States dollars. Allied, the designated syndicate agent, is located in the United States, specifically in New York; some of the negotiations between the parties took place in the United States. The United, States has an interest in maintaining New York's status as one of the foremost commercial centers in the world. Further, New York is the international clearing center for United States dollars. In addition to other international activities, United States banks lend billions of dollars to foreign debtors each year. The United States has an interest in ensuring that creditors entitled to payment in the United States in United States dollars under contracts subject to the jurisdiction of United States courts may assume that, except under the most extraordinary circumstances, their rights will be determined in accordance with recognized principles of contract law.

---

[28] 658 F. 2d 903, 908 (2d Cir. 1981).
[29] 353 F. 2d 47, 51 (2d Cir. 1965), *cert. denied*, 382 U.S. 1027, 86 S. Ct. 648, 15 L. Ed. 2d 540 (1966).

In contrast, while Costa Rica has a legitimate concern in overseeing the debt situation of state-owned banks and in maintaining a stable economy, its interest in the contracts at issue is essentially limited to the extent to which it can unilaterally alter the payment terms. Costa Rica's potential jurisdiction over the debt is not sufficient to locate the debt there for the purposes of act of state doctrine analysis.

Thus, under either analysis, our result is the same: the situs of the debt was in the United States, not in Costa Rica. Consequently, this was not "a taking of property within its own territory by [Costa Rica]." The act of state doctrine is, therefore, inapplicable.

IV

Acts of foreign governments purporting to have extraterritorial effect — and consequently, by definition, falling outside the scope of the act of state doctrine — should be recognized by the courts only if they are consistent with the law and policy of the United States. *United States v. Belmont*,[30] . . . . *Banco Nacional de Cuba v. Chemical Bank*,[31] . . . *Republic of Iraq*[32] . . . . Thus, we have come full circle to reassess whether we should give effect to the Costa Rican directives. We now conclude that we should not.

The Costa Rican government's unilateral attempt to repudiate private, commercial obligations is inconsistent with the orderly resolution of international debt problems. It is similarly contrary to the interests of the United States, a major source of private international credit. The government has procedures for resolving intergovernmental financial difficulties. . . . With respect to private debt, support for the IMF resolution strategy is consistent with both the policy aims and best interests of the United States.

Recognition of the Costa Rican directives in this context would also be counter to principles of contract law. Appellees explicitly agreed that their obligation to pay would not be excused in the event that Central Bank failed to provide the necessary United States dollars for payment. This, of course, was the precise cause of the default. If we were to give effect to the directives, our decision would vitiate an express provision of the contracts between the parties.

The Costa Rican directives are inconsistent with the law and policy of the United States. We refuse, therefore, to hold that the directives excuse the obligations of the Costa Rican banks. The appellees' inability to pay United States dollars relates only to the potential enforceability of the judgment; it does not determine whether judgment should enter. . . .

The parties agreed below that no questions of material fact remained as to Allied's motion for summary judgment. The act of state doctrine was the only defense raised by the Costa Rican banks to Allied's motion and the only ground for the district court's denial of that motion. Moreover, the doctrine was the sole basis for the district court's dismissal of the action. We hold today that the act of state doctrine is not applicable to this litigation. Therefore, the district court's rulings cannot stand.

---

[30] 301 U.S. 324, 332-33, 57 S. Ct. 758, 761-62, 81 L. Ed. 1134 (1937).
[31] 658 F. 2d at 908-09.
[32] 358 F. 2d at 51.

We vacate our previous decision, reverse the district court's denial of Allied's motion for summary judgment and its dismissal of the action and direct the district court to enter judgment for Allied.

NOTES AND QUESTIONS

(1) As the court in *Allied Bank* indicates, the actions taken by the Costa Rican Government were in response to escalating national economic problems. Specifically, in 1981 Costa Rica was burdened with an enormous foreign debt and with the effects of the worldwide recession, which had depressed the prices of coffee and bananas, its chief exports. Inflation in Costa Rica in 1982 was close to 90%, unemployment exceeded 20%, and foreign debt reached $3.2 billion. Approximately $1.4 billion of Costa Rica's foreign debt was owed to private lenders; the majority were American banks.[33] In light of these facts, how would you evaluate the court's conclusion that Costa Rica's interest in the contracts at issue was "essentially limited to the extent to which it can unilaterally alter the payment terms."?

(2) Contrast *Allied Bank* with *Braka v. Bancomer.*[34] There, certificates of deposit issued by Bancomer, a Mexican commercial bank, provided for generous payments, in U.S. dollars, of principal and interest. Until 1982 Bancomer paid the principal and interest due on these certificates as required by their terms. In 1982, however, the government of Mexico issued two decrees — one nationalizing Mexico's private banks, including Bancomer, and the other establishing a general system of currency controls. Under the currency controls, banks were prohibited from using foreign currency as legal tender and were required to perform all domestic obligations for payments in foreign currency by delivering an equivalent amount in pesos at the prevailing official exchange rate. Since U.S. depositors suffered a substantial loss based on the difference between the sum they received and what they would have received had the CDs been redeemed in dollars or exchanged at a free market rate, some of them brought suit against Bancomer in federal district court. In finding the situs of debt to be in Mexico, and the plaintiffs' claim barred by the Act of State doctrine, the court noted that plaintiffs had contracted to place deposits in a bank in Mexico and that the certificates of deposit expressly named Mexico as the situs of the deposit and as the place where principal and interest were payable. For purposes of drafting international commercial instruments, what lessons should counsel for U.S. parties derive from the decisions in *Allied Bank* and *Braka*? Should application turn on the draftsman art and his clients negotiating leverage? For other Act of State cases wrestling with the situs of debts, see, *Bandes v. Harlow & Jones, Inc.,*[35] *Trinh v. Citibank,*[36] *Edelman v. Chase Manhattan Bank,*[37] *Tecacosh Co., Ltd. v. Rockwell International Corp.*[38]

---

[33] See Canas, *Costa Rica: Another View*, Barron's, July 5, 1982, at 36, col. 2. See also Kallen, *Yes, We Have No Bananas*, Forbes, July 1, 1985, at 97.

[34] 589 F. Supp. 1465 (S.D. N.Y. 1984), *affirmed*, 762 F. 2d 222 (2d Cir. 1985).

[35] 852 F. 2d 661 (2d Cir. 1988).

[36] 850 F.2d 1164 (6th Cir. 1988).

[37] 856 F.2d 322, 861 F.2d 1291 (as amended) (1st Cir. 1988).

[38] 766 F. 2d 1333 (9th Cir. 1985).

(3) Although in *Allied Bank* and *Braka* the court's Act of State analysis focused upon the situs of the bank debts, and under its traditional definition, the Act of State doctrine is applicable only to a sovereign's acts done "within its own territory," the situs of intangible property is a fiction. Recognizing, this, The Restatement (Third) of the Foreign Relations Law of the United States, Section 443, Reporters' Note 4 (1987) states:

> In principle, it might be preferable to approach the question of the applicability of the act of state doctrine to intangible assets not by searching for an imaginary situs for property that has no real situs, but by determining how the act of the foreign state in the particular circumstances fits within the reasons for the act of state doctrine and for the territorial limitation.

Consider the reasons for the Act of State doctrine and how they might apply to the facts in the *Allied Bank* case. Are these issues with broad implications for United States foreign policy touching "sharply on national nerves"? Is *Allied Bank* the kind of case where a court should contrast "the practices of the political branch with the limitations of the judicial process."?

(4) The refusal of the court in *Allied Bank* to apply the Act of State doctrine reflects the court's unwillingness "to set a precedent potentially undermining the sanctity of all United States loan agreements with debtor nations. The court perceived that a judgment in favor of the Costa Rica bank debtors would signify approval of unilateral actions by debtor countries to restructure their private obligations. A judgment in favor of the United States creditor, on the other hand, would afford protection to United States creditors by deterring such unilateral actions." Is there anything in the Supreme Court's opinion in *Sabbatino* that responds to this argument?

(5) The court in *Allied Bank* pointed out that appellees explicitly agreed in the contract that their obligation to pay could not be excused in the event that the Costa Rican Central Bank failed to provide the necessary U.S. dollars for payment. Should this have been determinative on the Act of State issue? Did it amount to a waiver of any defense based on the doctrine? Can application of the Act of State doctrine be waived by an agreement between two parties? See Restatement (Third) of the Foreign Relations Law of the United States, Section 443, Comment e (1987).

(6) What role did the Executive Branch as *amicus curiae* play in the *Allied Bank* proceedings? Did the Executive Branch's brief serve, in effect, as a "Bernstein letter."?

(7) The Executive Branch's *amicus* brief in *Allied Bank* suggested that the executive disfavored unilateral action by debtor countries and instead favored multinational cooperation within the framework of International Monetary Fund (IMF) procedures. Costa Rica's attempted unilateral restructuring of private obligations, the *amicus* brief contended, was inconsistent with this system of international cooperation and negotiation and thus incompatible with U.S. policy. The court accepted this argument. Neither the court nor the *amicus* brief, however, addressed the IMF's approval of Costa Rica's actions. A special lending facility of the IMF provided additional funding for Costa Rica from 1981 through 1984 to help the country meet its debt service. To obtain this funding, Costa Rica

was required to submit to the IMF a detailed statement of its economic objectives and policies for the period of the loan and Costa Rica obtained IMF approval of its operations.**39** Thus it is unclear what degree of involvement with the IMF's system of international cooperation and negotiation would be required for a sovereign's act of restructuring its debt to be consistent with U.S. law and policy.

How might the *Allied Bank* decision affect the negotiating position of private lenders in future negotiations over the restructuring of debts under the IMF system? Suppose, as a matter of policy, the Executive Branch decides that the threat of recourse by individual lenders to the U.S. courts would undermine IMF efforts at restructuring a particular country's international debt and so advises the court? How should the latter respond?

(9) Note that in its first decision the Second Circuit affirmed the district court's dismissal of Allied's action because it determined that Costa Rica's action was fully consistent with U.S. law and policy and therefore "principles of comity compelled us to recognize as valid the Costa Rican directives." Assuming *arguendo* the correctness of the determination that Costa Rica's actions were consistent with U.S. law and policy, does it follow that comity compels a U.S. court to recognize them as valid? What, if any, other factors might the court have employed in its choice of law analysis?**40**

(10) Based on the material in this chapter, what would you say is the theoretical rationale for the Act of State doctrine? One rationale often cited is that the doctrine functions as a special choice of law rule. Restatement (Third) of the Foreign Relations Law of the United States, Section 443, Reporters' Note 1 (1987) states:

> In most cases, the act of state doctrine may be seen as a special rule of conflict of laws. The normal rule of choice of law in most act of state cases would point to application of the law of the state where the act took place; that rule may be disregarded in certain instances where the law thus chosen would violate the strong public policy of the forum, *e.g.*, a policy against expropriation without compensation. . . . The act of state doctrine precludes giving effect to that public policy to deny effect to the foreign law.

Is this statement really only a description of one operative effect that the doctrine might have and not a rationale explaining the doctrine?**41**

Two other rationales have often been advanced: (i) a court should abstain from reaching the full merits of a case when its holding might embarrass the Executive

39 See J. Pippenger, Fundamentals Of International Finance 155-56 (1984).

40 For discussion of the issues raised in Allied Bank as well as of related issues, see Hoffman & Deming, *The Role Of The U.S. Courts In The Transnational Flow Of Funds*, 17 N.Y.U.J. Int'l L. & Pol., 493 (1985); Leech, *International Banking: Effects Of Nationalizations And Exchange Controls*, 8 J. Comp. Bus and Cap. Market L. 123 (1986); Comment, *The Act Of State Doctrine And Foreign Sovereign Defaults On The United States Bank Loans: A New Focus For A Muddled Doctrine*, 133 U. Pa. L. Rev. 469 (1985); Note, *The Act Of State Doctrine: Resolving Debt Situs Confusion*, 86 Colum. L. Rev. 594 (1986); Note, *The Act Of State And Allied Bank*, 31 Vill. L. Rev. 291 (1986). See Tigert, *Allied Bank International: A United States Government Perspective*, 17 N.Y.U.J. Int'l L. & Pol. 511, 523-24 (1985).

41 See, Swan, *Act Of State At Bay: A Plea On Behalf Of The Elusive Doctrine*, [1976] Duke L.J. 807 at 883 (Note 85) and 900 (Note 251).

Branch in its conduct of foreign affairs; (ii) the doctrine is a variant of the constitutional principle that "political questions" are non-justiciable. Are these necessarily mutually exclusive? Or is some of the confusion about the doctrine caused by efforts to cabin it within a single over-arching rationale? Perhaps it is more richly textured than that. Recently, Professor Dellapenna has suggested that the Act of State doctrine constitutes a special deference to specific exertions of state power similar in effect to a judgment by a court. Under this "binding recognition" view, the Act of State doctrine functions as a kind of international full faith and credit clause.[42]

Under which of these rationales, if any, should a court give effect to a "Bernstein letter?"

(10) As the Supreme Court stated in *Sabbatino*, international law does not require application of the Act of State doctrine. Nonetheless, the courts of most countries have exercised judicial restraint in adjudicating challenges to expropriations by foreign states, although they may do so on grounds other than the Act of State doctrine. In 1981 the House of Lords decided to adopt the U.S. view of the Act of State doctrine.[43]

(11) In *W.S. Kirkpatrick & Co. v. Environmental Tectronics Corp. International*,[44] plaintiff firm, an unsuccesful bidder on a contract with the Nigerian Government, sued defendant, the successful bidder, for damages on the ground that the latter obtained the contract by bribing a Nigerian official. Defendant had earlier pleaded guilty to criminal charges under the Foreign Corrupt Practices Act. The District Court dismissed plaintiff's suit on Act of State grounds. The Third Circuit reversed. The Supreme Court affirmed the Appeals Court but on the ground that the case did not properly engage the Act of State doctrine since even if the U.S. courts decided that defendant's receipt of a contract through bribery violated U.S. law, that would not constitute a judgment regarding the legality of the ostensible foreign "act of state" (*i.e.*, the award of a contract to defendant). The contract would still remain in full force and effect irrespective of what a U.S. court might say. That the foreign official may have violated the laws of Nigeria was not an issue before the U.S. courts. That such a violation might render the contract void, was a matter for the Nigerian government under Nigerian law and not an issue for the U.S. courts. Writing for a unanimous Court, Justice Scalia observed that: "Act of state issues only arise when a court *must decide* — that is when the outcome of the case turns upon — the effect of official action by a foreign sovereign."[45]

---

[42] See J. Dellapenna, Suing Foreign Governments And Their Corporations, 268-319 (1988); Dellapenna, *Deciphering the Act of State Doctrine*, 35 Vill. L. Rev. 1 (1990).

[43] See Singer, *The Act Of State Doctrine Of The United Kingdom: An Analysis With Comparison To United States Practice*, 75 Am. J. Int'l L. 283 (1981).

[44] — U.S. — , 110 S.Ct. 701, — L.Ed.2d — (1990).

[45] The writings on Act of State are legion. In addition to those already cited in this chapter, a few examples include: Falk, *Toward A Theory of the Participation of Domestic Courts In The International Legal Order: A Critique Of Banco Nacional de Cuba v. Sabbatino*, 16 Rutgers L. Rev. 1 (1961); Henkin, *The Foreign Affairs Power of the Federal Courts: Sabbatino*, 64 Colum. L. Rev. 805 (1964); Lowenfeld, *Act Of State And Department Of State: First National City Bank*, 66 Am. J. Int'l L. 795 (1972). Report by the Committee on International Law of the Association of the Bar of the City of New York, *The Effect*

§ 13.02 Select Problems in Justiciability

As we saw in the preceding section, the Act of State doctrine represents, in part, a deference by the courts to the political departments in the conduct of foreign relations, a safeguard of the national interest in foreign affairs against judicial interference, even though one not mandated by the Constitution. In the related area of foreign sovereign immunity, which we consider in Chapter 11, the courts deferred for years to Executive Branch "suggestions" of immunity, and exercised an independent role in this area only after Congress passed the Foreign Sovereign Immunities Act in 1976. In Chapter 12, we saw several other examples of the courts' refusing to uphold challenges to the Executive Branch's conduct of foreign affairs. Primary examples would include *Dames & Moore v. Regan, supra,* page 1021, and *Diggs v. Richardson, supra,* page 1060. The following case is an especially controversial example of such judicial deference.

CHICAGO & SOUTHERN AIR LINES, INC. v. WATERMAN STEAMSHIP CORPORATION

Supreme Court of the United States
333 U.S. 103, 68 S. Ct. 431, 92 L. Ed. 568 (1948)

MR. JUSTICE JACKSON delivered the opinion of the Court.

The question of law which brings this controversy here is whether Section 1006 of the Civil Aeronautics Act[1] . . . authorizing judicial review of described orders of the Civil Aeronautics Board, includes those which grant or deny applications by citizen carriers to engage in overseas and foreign air transportation which are subject to approval by the President under Section 801 of the Act[2] . . . .

By proceedings not challenged as to regularity, the Board, with express approval of the President, issued an order which denied Waterman Steamship Corporation a certificate of convenience and necessity for an air route and granted one to Chicago and Southern Air Lines, a rival applicant. Routes sought by both carrier interests involved overseas air transportation[3] . . . between continental United States and Caribbean possessions and also foreign air transportation, Section 1(21)(c), between the United States and foreign countries. Waterman filed a petition for review under Section 1006 of the Act with the Circuit Court of Appeals for the Fifth Circuit.[4] . . . Chicago and Southern intervened. Both the latter and the Board moved to dismiss, the grounds pertinent here being that because the order required and had approval of the President, under Section 801

To Be Given In The United States To Foreign Nationalization Decrees, 19 Record of N.Y.C.B.A. Supp. 5 (1964); Bazyler, *Abolishing The Act Of State Doctrine*, 134 U. Pa. L. Rev. 325 (1986).

[1] 49 U.S.C. Sec. 646, 49 U.S.C.A. Section 646.
[2] 49 U.S.C. Sec. 601, 49 U.S.C.A. Section 601.
[3] Section 1(21) (b), 49 U.S.C.A. Section 401(21) (b).
[4] 159 F. 2d 828.

of the Act, it was not reviewable. The Court of Appeals disclaimed any power to question or review either the President's approval or his disapproval, but it regarded any Board order as incomplete until court review, after which "the completed action must be approved by the President as to citizen air carriers in cases under Section 801."[5] . . . . Accordingly, it refused to dismiss the petition and asserted jurisdiction. Its decision conflicts with one by the Court of Appeals for the Second Circuit. *Pan American Airways, Inc., v. Civil Aeronautics Board*[6] . . . . We granted certiorari both to the Chicago and Southern Air Lines, Inc. (No. 78) and to the Board (No. 88) to resolve the conflict.

Congress has set up a comprehensive scheme for regulation of common carriers by air. Many statutory provisions apply indifferently whether the carrier is a foreign air carrier or a citizen air carrier, and whether the carriage involved is "interstate air commerce," "overseas air commerce" or "foreign air commerce," each being appropriately defined.[7] . . . . All air carriers by similar procedures must obtain from the Board certificates of convenience and necessity by showing a public interest in establishment of the route and the applicant's ability to serve it. But when a foreign carrier asks for any permit, or a citizen carrier applies for a certificate to engage in any overseas or foreign air transportation, a copy of the application must be transmitted to the President before hearing; and any decision, either to grant or to deny, must be submitted to the President before publication and is unconditionally subject to the President's approval. Also the statute subjects to judicial review "any order, affirmative or negative, issued by the Board under this Act, except any order in respect of any foreign air carrier subject to the approval of the President as provided in section 801 of this Act." It grants no express exemption to an order such as the one before us, which concerns a citizen carrier but which must have Presidential approval because it involves overseas and foreign air transportation. The question is whether an exemption is to be implied.

This Court long has held that statutes which employ broad terms to confer power of judicial review are not always to be read literally. Where Congress has authorized review of "any order" or used other equally inclusive terms, courts have declined the opportunity to magnify their jurisdiction, by self-denying constructions which do not subject to judicial control orders which, from their nature, from the context of the act, or from the relation of judicial power to the subject-matter, are inappropriate for review. . . .

The Waterman Steamship Corporation urges that review of the problems involved in establishing foreign air routes are of no more international delicacy or strategic importance than those involved in routes for water carriage. . . .

We find no indication that the Congress either entertained or fostered the narrow concept that air-borne commerce is a mere outgrowth or overgrowth of surface-bound transport. . . .

The "public interest" that enters into awards of routes for aerial carriers, who in effect obtain also a sponsorship by our government in foreign ventures, is not

[5] 159 F. 2d 828, 831.
[6] 121 F. 2d 810.
[7] 49 U.S.C. Section 401(20), 49 U.S.C. Section 401(20).

confined to adequacy of transportation service, as we have held when that term is applied to railroads. . . . That aerial navigation routes and bases should be prudently correlated with facilities and plans for our own national defenses and raise new problems in conduct of foreign relations, is a fact of common knowledge. Congressional hearings and debates extending over several sessions and departmental studies of many years show that the legislative and administrative processes have proceeded in full recognition of these facts. . . .

But when a foreign carrier seeks to engage in public carriage over the territory or waters of this country, or any carrier seeks the sponsorship of this government to engage in overseas or foreign air transportation, Congress has completely inverted the usual administrative process. Instead of acting independently of executive control, the agency is then subordinated to it. Instead of its order serving as a final disposition of the application, its force is exhausted when it serves as a recommendation to the President. Instead of being handed down to the parties as the conclusion of the administrative process, it must be submitted to the President, before publication even can take place. Nor is the President's control of the ultimate decision a mere right of veto. It is not alone issuance of such authorizations that are subject to his approval, but denial, transfer, amendment, cancellation or suspension, as well. And likewise subject to his approval are the terms, conditions and limitations of the order.[8] . . . . Thus, Presidential control is not limited to a negative but is a positive and detailed control over the Board's decisions, unparalleled in the history of American administrative bodies.

Congress may of course delegate very large grants of its power over foreign commerce to the President. . . . The President also possesses in his own right certain powers conferred by the Constitution on him as Commander-in-Chief and as the Nation's organ in foreign affairs. For present purposes, the order draws vitality from either or both sources. Legislative and Executive power are pooled obviously to the end that commercial strategic and diplomatic interests of the country may be coordinated and advanced without collision or deadlock between agencies. . . .

It may be conceded that a literal reading of Section 1006 subjects this order to re-examination by the courts. It also appears that the language was deliberately employed by Congress, although nothing indicates that Congress foresaw or intended the consequences ascribed to it by the decision of the Court below. The letter of the text might with equal consistency be construed to require any one of three things: first, judicial review of a decision by the President; second, judicial review of a Board order before it acquires finality through Presidential action, the court's decision on review being a binding limitation on the President's action; third, a judicial review before action by the President, the latter being at liberty wholly to disregard the court's judgment. We think none of these results is required by usual canons of construction.

In this case, submission of the Board's decision was made to the President, who disapproved certain portions of it and advised the Board of the changes which he required. The Board complied and submitted a revised order and opinion which the President approved. Only then were they made public, and that which

---

[8] 49 U.S.C. Section 601.

was made public and which is before us is only the final order and opinion containing the President's amendments, and bearing his approval. Only at that stage was review sought, and only then could it be pursued, for then only was the decision consummated, announced and available to the parties.

While the changes made at direction of the President may be identified, the reasons therefore are not disclosed beyond the statement that "because of certain factors relating to our broad national welfare and other matters for which the Chief Executive has special responsibility, he has reached conclusions which require" changes in the Board's opinion.

The court below considered, and we think quite rightly, that it could not review such provisions of the order as resulted from Presidential direction. The President, both as Commander-in-Chief and as the Nation's organ for foreign affairs, has available intelligence services whose reports neither are nor ought to be published to the world. It would be intolerable that courts, without the relevant information, should review and perhaps nullify actions of the Executive taken on information properly held secret. Nor can courts sit in camera in order to be taken into executive confidences. But even if courts could require full disclosure, the very nature of executive decisions as to foreign policy is political, not judicial. Such decisions are wholly confined by our Constitution to the political departments of the government, Executive and Legislative. They are delicate, complex, and involve large elements of prophecy. They are and should be undertaken only by those directly responsible to the people whose welfare they advance or imperil. They are decisions of a kind for which the Judiciary has neither aptitude, facilities nor responsibility and which has long been held to belong in the domain of political power not subject to judicial intrusion or inquiry. . . . We therefore agree that whatever of this order emanates from the President is not susceptible of review by the Judicial Department.

* * * *

MR. JUSTICE DOUGLAS, with whom MR. JUSTICE BLACK, MR. JUSTICE REED and MR. JUSTICE RUTLEDGE concur, dissenting.

Congress has specifically provided for judicial review of orders of the Civil Aeronautics Board of the kind involved in this case. That review can be had without intruding on the exclusive domain of the Chief Executive. And by granting it we give effect to the interests of both the Congress and the Chief Executive in this field.

But Congress did not leave the matter entirely to the Board. Recognizing the important role the President plays in military and foreign affairs, it made him a participant in the process. Applications for certificates of the type involved here are transmitted to him before hearing, all decisions on the applications are submitted to him before their publication, and the orders are "subject to" his approval. Since his decisions in these matters are of a character which involve an exercise of his discretion in foreign affairs or military matters, I do not think Congress intended them to be subject to judicial review.

But review of the President's action does not result from reading the statute in the way it is written. Congress made reviewable by the courts only orders "issued by the Board under this Act." Those orders can be reviewed without reference to any conduct of the President, for that part of the orders which is the work of the Board is plainly identifiable.[9] The President is presumably concerned only with the impact of the order on foreign relations or military matters. To the extent that he disapproves action taken by the Board, his action controls. But where that is not done, the Board's order has an existence independent of Presidential approval, tracing to Congress' power to regulate commerce. Approval by the President under this statutory scheme has relevance for purposes of review only as indicating when the action of the Board is reviewable. When the Board has finished with the order, the administrative function is ended. When the order fixes rights, on clearance by the President, it becomes reviewable. But the action of the President does not broaden the review. Review is restricted to the action of the Board and the Board alone.

* * * *

The Board can act in a lawless way. With that in mind, Congress sought to preserve the integrity of the administrative process by making judicial review a check on Board action. That was the aim of Congress, now defeated by a legalism which in my view does not square with reality.

In this petition for review, the respondent charged that the Board had no substantial evidence to support its findings that Chicago and Southern Air Lines was fit, willing and able to perform its obligations under the certificate; and it charged that when a change of conditions as to Chicago and Southern Air Lines' ability to perform was called to the attention of the Board, the Board refused to reopen the case. I do not know whether there is merit in those contentions. But no matter how substantial and important the questions, they are now beyond judicial review. Today a litigant tenders questions concerning the arbitrary character of the Board's ruling. Tomorrow those questions may relate to the right to notice, adequacy of hearings, or the lack of procedural due process of law. But no matter how extreme the action of the Board, the courts are powerless to correct it under today's decision. Thus the purpose of Congress is frustrated.

Judicial review would assure the President, the litigants and the public that the Board had acted within the limits of its authority. It would carry out the aim of Congress to guard against administrative action which exceeds the statutory bounds. It would give effect to the interests of both Congress and the President in this field.

NOTES AND QUESTIONS

(1) The Civil Aeronautics Board no longer exists. Its functions are now performed by the Department of Transportation.

---

[9] The Board had consolidated for hearing 29 applications for certificates to engage in air transportation which were filed by 15 applicants. The President's partial disapproval of the proposed disposition of these applications did not relate to the applications involved in this case. As to them, the action of the Board stands unaltered.

(2) Did the majority opinion in *Waterman* ignore the distinction the Civil Aeronautics Act maintained between foreign and U.S. air carriers? Is it only with respect to the former that issues of foreign policy requiring the President's attention would arise?

(3) Suppose the President had a strong foreign policy reason for adopting the Board's recommendation in favor of Chicago and Southern Airlines. Suppose then, as the dissent would seem to argue was appropriate, the Court determined that the Board's finding that Chicago and Southern was fit, able and willing to perform its obligations was not supported by "substantial evidence." Where would that leave the President?

(4) Suppose that the CAB had denied Waterman the certificate of convenience on arbitrary or discriminatory grounds or that the President had rejected a recommendation of the CAB in favor of an applicant because the applicant had supported a political opponent of the President. Would or should judicial review be available under these circumstances? The Civil Aeronautics Act specifically indicates that a certificate of convenience does not have the status of "property" protected by the due process clause of the Fifth Amendment to the Constitution. Is this dispositive of the issue?

(5) Lower courts have held *Waterman* inapplicable where the action of the Board was beyond the Board's power on the theory that in that circumstance the Board could have placed nothing before the President for his decision. *American Airlines, Inc. v. CAB*,[10] *Pan American World Airways, Inc. v. CAB.*[11]

(6) Is the issue of which of two U.S. carriers should fly to a foreign country solely a private dispute without significance for U.S. foreign policy? Would you favor a process whereby it would be so regarded unless the President would indicate otherwise in overruling a recommendation that a particular air carrier be awarded a certificate? Or should the President make final decisions in such cases on the basis of secret diplomatic and intelligence information at his disposal?

(7) In *Harrisiades v. Shaughnessy*[12] the Court stated that matters relating "to the conduct of foreign relations . . . are so exclusively entrusted to the political branches of government as to be largely immune from judicial inquiry or interference." As applied to Waterman does this statement beg the question? See also *Haig v. Agee.*[13]

NOTE
SPECIALIZED COURTS

In spite of the reluctance of the courts in the foregoing materials to review the legality of Executive Branch or administrative agency action touching upon

---

[10] 348 F. 2d 349, 352 (D.C. Cir. 1965).

[11] 380 F. 2d 770 (2d Cir. 1967), *aff'd by an equally divided Court*, 391 U.S. 461 (1968).

[12] 342 U.S. 580, 72 S. Ct. 512, 96 L. Ed. 586 (1952).

[13] 453 U.S. 280, 101 St. Ct. 2766, 69 L. Ed. 2d 640 (1981).

certain aspects of foreign affairs, in the area of international trade, there has been support for an expansion of the judicial function, coupled with a movement to limit Executive discretion through the establishment of legislative parameters. This movement became especially strong during the late 1970s as the economic importance of international trade became more apparent. The results of this movement can be seen most readily in the work of two specialized courts: The United States Court of International Trade and the United States Claims Court.

The Court of International Trade

Prior to 1980 the Court of International Trade was called the Customs Court. In that year the Customs Court was renamed and reestablished as an Article III court under the United States Constitution.[14] The purpose of Congress in effecting this change was to "create a comprehensive system of judicial review of civil actions arising from import transactions." At the same time Congress sought to improve the effectiveness of judicial review by granting to the new court "all the powers in law and equity of, or as conferred by statute upon, a district court of the United States."[15]

A number of factors led to this restatement and enlargement of the Customs Court's jurisdiction. First, there was a long standing confusion leading to much wasted litigation over the respective spheres of jurisdiction of the Customs Court and the district courts over international trade matters, the latter having jurisdiction over cases not within the exclusive jurisdiction of the Customs Court. Second, the Trade Agreements Act of 1979[16] had provided for increased judicial review of trade issues without specifying implementing procedures. The 1979 Act also expanded the definition of interested parties with standing to sue on various import issues.

The Court of International Trade, whose offices are in New York but which sits throughout the United States, consists of nine judges, appointed by the President with the advice and consent of the Senate. No more than five of the judges may be from the same political party. The President appoints one judge under seventy years of age as chief judge, who may serve until he reaches seventy. Its decisions are appealable to the United States Court of Appeals for the Federal Circuit (formerly the Court of Customs and Patent Appeals) and ultimately to the Supreme Court.

The jurisdiction of the Court of International Trade is more expansive than was that of the Customs Court, both with respect to the number of civil actions over which the court has jurisdiction and the larger number of persons entitled to bring these actions. The Court has exclusive jurisdiction in nine types of civil actions against the U.S. Government. These include (1) contesting the denial by the customs service of a protest against a Service decision; (2) contesting the denial by the Secretary of the Treasury of a petition challenging the appraised value, the classification, or rate of duty of an import; (3) countervailing and antidumping duty actions; (4) adjustment assistance eligibility issues; (5) an order for protective

---

[14] Public Law 96-417, 94 Stat. 1727, 28 U.S.C. Section 1581.

[15] Sen. Report 96-466 on S.1654, the Customs Court Act of 1979, 96th Cong., 1st Sess. at 3.

[16] Pub. L. 96-39, July 26, 1979, 93 Stat. 146, 19 U.S.C. Section 2501, *et seq.*

disclosure of confidential information submitted by a party to a countervailing duty or antidumping proceeding; (6) an action to review the final determination of the Secretary of the Treasury on whether a foreign product is exempt from the application of the Buy American Act; (7) an action to challenge a customshouse broker's license suspension or revocation; (8) administrative rulings, prior to importation of the goods, relating to classification, valuation, rate of duty, marking, etc., but only if the party commencing the civil action demonstrates to the court that he would be irreparably harmed unless given an opportunity to obtain judicial review prior to such importation; (9) other revenue, tariff, or quota laws, and enforcement generally.[17]

Before establishment of the Court of International Trade, the United States brought suit on customs, as on other matters, exclusively in the U.S. district courts. In contrast, the Court of International Trade has exclusive jurisdiction over civil actions arising out of an import transaction and brought by the United States for one of the following purposes: (1) to recover certain types of civil penalties; (2) to recover upon a bond relating to the importation of merchandise required by U.S. law or by the Secretary of the Treasury; (3) to recover customs duties. The Court can also, unlike its predecessor the Customs Court, entertain counterclaims, cross claims and third party actions.

A decision of the Secretary of the Treasury or the administering authority (International Trade Administration of the Commerce Department) or the International Trade Commission is presumed to be correct in any action to contest the denial of a protest or petition or to challenge a decision in a countervailing or antidumping duty proceeding. The burden to prove otherwise is upon the challenger. With respect to several categories of actions, the Court is required to hold a *trial de novo* of the issues. In antidumping and countervailing duty cases, the Court reviews certain government actions to determine whether they were arbitrary, capricious, an abuse of discretion or unlawful. Other government actions are reviewed to determine whether they were supported by substantial evidence in the agency record or were unlawful.[18] Determinations of the agency in trade adjustment assistance cases are considered conclusive if supported by substantial evidence on the record. However, the Court has the authority for good cause shown to order the agency to take further evidence.[19] The Court's review in all other actions is governed by the Administrative Procedure Act (APA). The APA generally establishes a substantial evidence standard for agency action taken on a record and an arbitrary-capricious standard for other agency action.[20] A trial by jury is possible in certain circumstances.

The Court is authorized to enter a money judgment for or against the United States, order a retrial of a case, or issue an injunction. In general the Court "shall possess all the powers in law and equity of, or as conferred by statute upon, a district court of the United States."[21]

---

[17] 28 U.S.C. Section 1581.
[18] 28 U.S.C.A. Section 2640(b), 19 U.S.C.A. Section 1516a.
[19] 28 U.S.C.A. Section 2640(c), 19 U.S.C.A. Section 2395(b).
[20] 28 U.S.C.A. Section 2640(d), 5 U.S.C. Section 706.
[21] 28 U.S.C. Section 1585.

The United States Claims Court

In 1887, through legislation later known as the Tucker Act, which itself followed earlier enactments, Congress established a jurisdictional arrangement covering a broad range of claims against the United States. The basic jurisdictional provision of the Claims Court[22] provides:

> The United States Claims Court shall have jurisdiction to render judgment upon any claim against the United States founded either upon the Constitution, or any Act of Congress or any regulation of an executive department, or upon any express or implied contract with the United States, or for liquidated or unliquidated damages in cases not sounding in tort. . . .

United States district courts have concurrent jurisdiction with the Claims Court over the same subject matter in cases where the claim does not exceed $10,000.[23] Specifically excluded from the Claims Court's jurisdiction is any civil action within the exclusive jurisdiction of the Court of International Trade.[24]

Also, significantly, the Claims Court does not have "jurisdiction of any claim against the United States growing out of or dependent upon any treaty entered into with foreign nations."[25] The term "treaty" has been construed by the Claims Court to cover all forms of international agreements entered into by the United States and not just "treaties" requiring ratification by the President with the advice and consent of the Senate. However, the Supreme Court has interpreted the language "growing out of and dependent upon" narrowly and has required the claim to have a direct and proximate connection with the treaty in order for it to fall within the class excluded from the Court's jurisdiction. Recall that, in *Dames & Moore v. Regan, supra*, p. 1021, the United States Supreme Court indicated that there would be no jurisdictional obstacle to appropriate action in the Claims Court by a corporation wishing to challenge the President's suspension of claims against Iran as an unconstitutional taking. Similarly narrow constructions of the "treaty exception" to the Claims Court's jurisdiction have allowed the Court to decide a variety of cases arising out of international business or economic transactions.

The Claims Court is an Article III court, is located in Washington, D.C., but it may sit throughout the United States.[26] By and with the advice and consent of the Senate, the President appoints sixteen judges, and from their number, a chief judge. Direct appeal from the court's decisions invalidating acts of Congress to the Supreme Court is available.[27] Normally, however, appeal is to the United States Court of Appeals for the Federal Circuit.[28]

---

[22] 28 U.S.C. Section 1491.
[23] 28 U.S.C. Section 1346(a)(2).
[24] 28 U.S.C. Section 1491(b).
[25] 28 U.S.C. Section 1502.
[26] 28 U.S.C. Sections 171 and 173.
[27] 28 U.S.C. Section 1252.
[28] 28 U.S.C. Section 1295.

§ 13.03   Limitations on State Regulation

As we saw in Chapter 12, under Article VI, the Supremacy Clause of the Constitution, a federal statute overrides an inconsistent State law. Similarly, a treaty that has become part of the law of the land also overrides inconsistent State law.

In this section we explore some of the constraints that the Constitution places upon State regulation of transnational business. Constitutional challenges to such regulation usually take one of two forms: that the regulation violates the equal protection clause of the Fourteenth Amendment or that it interferes with U.S. foreign policy, especially that relating to foreign commerce.

[A]   The Regulation of Aliens Engaged in Economic Activity in the United States

BERNAL v. FAINTER

Supreme Court of the United States
467 U.S. 216, 104 S. Ct. 2312, 81 L. Ed. 2d 175 (1984)

JUSTICE MARSHALL delivered the opinion of the court.

The question posed by this case is whether a statute of the State of Texas violates the Equal Protection Clause of the Fourteenth Amendment of the United States Constitution by denying aliens the opportunity to become notaries public. The Court of Appeals for the Fifth Circuit held that the statute does not offend the Equal Protection Clause. We granted certiorari . . . and now reverse.

Petitioner, a native of Mexico, is a resident alien who has lived in the United States since 1961. He works as a paralegal for Texas Rural Legal Aid, Inc., helping migrant farmworkers on employment and civil rights matters. In order to administer oaths to these workers and to notarize their statements for use in civil litigation, petitioner applied in 1978 to become a notary public. Under Texas law, notaries publicly authenticate written instruments, administer oaths, and take out-of-court depositions. The Texas Secretary of State denied petitioner's application because he failed to satisfy the statutory requirement that a notary public be a citizen of the United States. Tex. Rev. Civ. Stat. Ann., Art. 5949(2) (Vernon Supp. 1984) (hereafter Article 5949(2)). After an unsuccessful administrative appeal, petitioner brought this action claiming that the citizenship requirement mandated by Article 5942(2) violated the Federal Constitution.

The District Court ruled in favor of petitioner. . . . It reviewed the State's citizenship requirement under a strict scrutiny standard and concluded that the requirement violated the Equal Protection Clause. The District Court also suggested that even under a rational relationship standard, the State statute would fail to pass constitutional muster because its citizenship requirement "is wholly unrelated to the achievement of any valid state interest. . . ." A divided panel of the Court of Appeals for the Fifth Circuit reversed, concluding that the proper standard for review was the rational-relationship test and that Article 5949(2) satisfied that test because it "bears a rational relationship to the state's interest in the proper and orderly handling of a countless variety of legal documents of importance to the state". . . .

II

As a general matter, a state law that discriminates on the basis of alienage can be sustained only if it can withstand strict judicial scrutiny. In order to withstand strict scrutiny, the law must advance a compelling state interest by the least restrictive means available. Applying this principle, we have invalidated an array of state statutes that denied aliens the right to pursue various occupations. In *Sugarman v. Dougall*[1] we struck down a state statute barring aliens from employment in permanent positions in the competitive class of the state civil service. *In re Griffiths*[2] we nullified a state law excluding aliens from eligibility for membership in the State Bar. And in *Examining Board v. Flores de Otero*[3] we voided a state law that excluded aliens from the practice of civil engineering.

We have, however, developed a narrow exception to the rule that discrimination based on alienage triggers strict scrutiny. This exception has been labeled the "political function" exception and applies to laws that exclude aliens from positions intimately related to the process of democratic self-government. The contours of the "political function" exception are outlined by our prior decisions. In *Foley v. Connelie*[4] . . . we held that a State may require police to be citizens because, in performing a fundamental obligation of government, police "are clothed with authority to exercise an almost infinite variety of discretionary powers" often involving the most sensitive areas of daily life[5] . . . . In *Ambach v. Norwick*[6] . . . we held that a State may bar aliens who have declared their intent to become citizens from teaching in the public schools because teachers, like police, possess a high degree of responsibility and discretion in the fulfillment of a basic governmental obligation. They have direct, day-to-day contact with students, exercise unsupervised discretion over them, act as role models, and influence their students about the government and the political process[7] . . . . Finally, in *Cabell v. Chavez-Salido*[8] . . . we held that a State may bar aliens from positions as probation officers because they, like police and teachers, routinely exercise discretionary power, involving a basic governmental function, that places them in a position of direct authority over other individuals.

The rationale behind the political-function exception is that within broad boundaries a State may establish its own form of government and limit the right to govern to those who are full-fledged members of the political community. Some public positions are so closely bound up with the formulation and implementation of self-government that the State is permitted to exclude from those positions persons outside the political community, hence persons who have not become part of the process of democratic self-determination. . . .

---

[1] 413 U.S. 634, 37 L. Ed. 2d 853, 93 S. Ct. 2842 (1973).
[2] 413 U.S. 717, 37 L. Ed. 2d 910, 93 S. Ct. 2851 (1973).
[3] 426 U.S. 572, 49 L. Ed. 2d 65, 96 S. Ct. 2264 (1976).
[4] 435 U.S. 291, 55 L. Ed. 2d 287, 98 S. Ct. 1067 (1978).
[5] *Id.*, at 297, 55 L. Ed. 2d 287, 98 S. Ct. 1067.
[6] 441 U.S. 68, 60 L. Ed. 2d 49, 99 S. Ct. 1589 (1979).
[7] *Id.*, at 78-79, 60 L. Ed. 2d 49, 99 S. Ct. 1589.
[8] 454 U.S. 432, 70 L. Ed. 2d 677, 102 S. Ct. 735 (1982).

We have therefore lowered our standard of review when evaluating the validity of exclusions that entrust only to citizens important elective and nonelective positions whose operations "go to the heart of representative government." *Sugarman v. Dougall, supra.* "While not retreating from the position that restrictions on lawfully resident aliens that primarily affect economic interests are subject to heightened judicial scrutiny . . . we have concluded that strict scrutiny is out of place when the restriction primarily serves a political function. . . ." *Cabell v. Chavez-Salido, supra,* at 439, (citation omitted).

To determine whether a restriction based on alienage fits within the narrow political-function exception, we devised in *Cabell* a two-part test.

"First, the specificity of the classification will be examined: a classification that is substantially over inclusive or underinclusive tends to undercut the governmental claim that the classification serves legitimate political ends. . . . Second, even if the classification is sufficiently tailored, it may be applied in the particular case only to 'persons holding state elective or important nonelective executive, legislative, and judicial positions,' those officers who 'participate directly in the formulation, execution, or review of broad public policy' and hence 'perform functions that go to the heart of representative government.' "[9] . . . .

III

We now turn to Article 5949(2) to determine whether it satisfies the *Cabell* test. The statute provides that "[t]o be eligible for appointment as a Notary Public, a person shall be a resident citizen of the United States and of this state. . . ." Unlike the statute invalidated in *Sugarman,* Article 5949(2) does not indiscriminately sweep within its ambit a wide range of offices and occupations but specifies only one particular post with respect to which the State asserts a right to exclude aliens. Clearly, then, the statute is not overinclusive; it applies narrowly to only one category of persons: Those wishing to obtain appointments as notaries. Less clear is whether Article 5949(2) is fatally underinclusive. Texas does not require court reporters to be United States citizens even though they perform some of the same services as notaries. Nor does Texas require that its Secretary of State be a citizen, even though he holds the highest appointive position in the State and performs many important functions, including supervision of the licensing of all notaries public. We need not decide this issue, however, because of our decision with respect to the second prong of the *Cabell* test.

In support of the proposition that notaries public fall within that category of officials who perform functions that "go to the heart of representative government," the State emphasizes that notaries are designated as public officers by the Texas Constitution. Texas maintains that this designation indicates that the State views notaries as important officials occupying posts central to the State's definition of itself as a political community. This court, however, has never deemed the source of a position — whether it derives from a State's statute or its Constitution — as the dispositive factor in determining whether a State may entrust the position only to citizens. Rather, this Court has always looked to the actual function of the position as the dispositive factor. The focus of our inquiry has been whether a position was such that the officeholder would necessarily

---

[9] 45 U.S., at 440, 70 L. Ed. 2d 853, 93 S. Ct. 2842.

exercise broad discretionary power over the formulation or execution of public policies importantly affecting the citizen population — power of the sort that a self-governing community could properly entrust only to full-fledged members of that community. . . .

The State maintains that even if the actual function of a post is the touchstone of a proper analysis, Texas notaries public should still be classified among those positions from which aliens can properly be excluded because the duties of Texas notaries entail the performance of functions sufficiently consequential to be deemed "political". . . .

We recognize the critical need for a notary's duties to be carried out correctly and with integrity. But a notary's duties, important as they are, hardly implicate responsibilities that go to the heart of representative government. Rather, these duties are essentially clerical and ministerial. In contrast to state troopers, *Foley v. Connelie* [10] notaries do not routinely exercise the State's monopoly of legitimate coercive force. Nor do notaries routinely exercise the wide discretion typically enjoyed by public school teachers when they present materials that educate youth respecting the information and values necessary for the maintenance of a democratic political system. See *Ambach v. Norwick.* [11] To be sure, considerable damage could result from the negligent or dishonest performance of a notary's duties. But the same could be said for the duties performed by cashiers, building inspectors, the janitors who clean up the offices of public officials, and numerous other categories of personnel upon whom we depend for careful, honest service. What distinguishes such personnel from those to which the political-function exception is properly applied is that the latter are invested either with policy-making responsibility or broad discretion in the execution of public policy that requires the routine exercise of authority over individuals. Neither of these characteristics pertains to the functions performed by Texas notaries.

The inappropriateness of applying the political-function exception to Texas notaries is further underlined by our decision in *In re Griffiths* [12] in which we subjected to strict scrutiny a Connecticut statute that prohibited noncitizens from becoming members of the State Bar. Along with the usual powers and privileges accorded to members of the Bar, Connecticut gave to members of its bar additional authority that encompasses the very duties performed by Texas notaries — authority to "sign writs and subpoenas, take recognizances, administer oaths and take depositions and acknowledgments of deeds.". . . . In striking down Connecticut's citizenship requirement, we concluded that "[i]t in no way denigrates a lawyer's high responsibilities to observe that [these duties] hardly involve matters of state policy or acts of such unique responsibility as to entrust them only to citizens."

IV

To satisfy strict scrutiny, the State must show that Article 5949(2) furthers a compelling state interest by the least restrictive means practically available. Respondents maintain that Article 5949(2) serves its "legitimate concern that

[10] 435 U.S. 291, 55 L. Ed. 287, 98 S. Ct. 1067 (1978).
[11] 441 U.S., at 77, 60 L. Ed.2d 49, 99 S. Ct. 1589.
[12] 413 U.S. 634, 37 L. Ed. 2d 853, 93 S. Ct. 2842 (1973).

notaries be reasonably familiar with state law and institutions" and "that notaries may be called upon years later to testify to acts they have performed. . . ." However, both of these asserted justifications utterly fail to meet the stringent requirements of strict scrutiny. There is nothing in the record that indicates that resident aliens, as a class, are so incapable of familiarizing themselves with Texas law as to justify the State's absolute and classwide exclusion. The possibility that some resident aliens are unsuitable for the position cannot justify a wholesale ban against all resident aliens. . . . Similarly inadequate is the State's purported interest in insuring the later availability of notaries' testimony. This justification fails because the State fails to advance a factual showing that the unavailability of notaries' testimony presents a real, as opposed to a merely speculative, problem to the State. Without a factual underpinning, the State's asserted interest lacks the weight we have required of interests properly denominated as compelling.

V

We conclude that Article 5949(2) violates the Fourteenth Amendment of the United States Constitution. Accordingly the judgment of the Court of Appeals is reversed, and the case is remanded for further proceedings consistent with this opinion.

It is so ordered.

JUSTICE REHNQUIST, dissenting.

I dissent for the reasons stated in my dissenting opinion in *Sugarman v. Dougall*[13] . . . .

NOTES AND QUESTIONS

(1) Note the alternative standards of review that the Court considers in *Bernal*. The Court rejected the rational-relationship test favored by the Court of Appeals for the Fifth Circuit and adopted instead the "strict scrutiny" test followed by the district court. This was a crucial step in the Supreme Court's analysis. As Professor Gerald Gunther has commented, strict scrutiny review is "strict" in theory but usually "fatal" in fact.[14]

(2) In his dissent in *Sugarman v. Dougal*, which he applies to *Bernal*, Justice Rehnquist rejects treating alienage as a "suspect classification." He would limit suspect classification analysis to the race area. In his view "[there] is a marked difference between a status or condition such as illegitimacy, national origin, or race, which cannot be altered by an individual, and the 'status' of the [challengers here]." It is true, of course, that alienage, unlike race, is not an unalterable trait. Moreover, it has long been recognized that aliens may be excluded from voting. On the other hand, there has been a long history of discrimination against aliens,

---

[13] 413 U.S. 634, 649, 37 L. Ed. 2d 830, 93 S. Ct. 2908 (1973).
[14] G. Gunther, Constitutional Law, 675 fn. 6 (11th ed. 1985).

and their inability to vote makes them "politically powerless." Are these sufficient reasons for strict scrutiny of alienage classifications?

(3) Note the Court's discussion of the "political function" exception to the strict scrutiny standard. Justice Marshall describes it as "a narrow exception." Do you agree? Is an exception that the Supreme Court has applied to police officers, teachers, and parole officers appropriately described as "narrow?" Assuming arguendo that a strict scrutiny standard is justified for alienage classifications, how can a political function exception be defended? How great a risk is there that the exception will undermine the standard?

(4) Might the Courts have approached alienage classifications in a different manner? Would the federal interest in immigration support strict scrutiny of state alienage classifications under federal preemption principles? Compare the cases and materials in the next subsection.

(5) State law prohibiting the ownership of land by aliens may constitute a special class. In *Terrace v. Thompson*,[15] the Court upheld a statute of the State of Washington that prohibited aliens — other than those who in good faith had declared their intention to become citizens — from having any title or right to benefit from land. The State had applied the statute to bar Japanese subjects resident in Washington from leasing land from American citizens for a period of five years for agricultural purposes. At the time of the case, federal legislation precluded aliens of Oriental descent from becoming citizens.

The Court rejected two challenges to the constitutionality of the statute. First, it stated that each State's power to deny aliens the right to own land had not been preempted by Congress's exclusive jurisdiction over immigration and second, it concluded that the exercise of such power did not violate equal protection. In denying the equal protection challenge the Court stated that the Washington statute involved the "privilege of owning or controlling agricultural land within the state. The quality and allegiance of those who own, occupy and use the farm lands within its borders are matters of highest importance and affect the safety and power of the state itself." The Court also rejected the argument that because under federal law only free whites and Africans could become citizens, the statute invidiously discriminated against Orientals. Its reasoning was that any naturalization classification made by Congress was presumed to be reasonable.

The *Terrace* decision has never been expressly overruled by the Supreme Court. Its continued viability, however, is questionable in light of two later decisions. First, in *Oyama v. California*,[16] the Court invalidated a state statutory presumption that land transfers to citizens which were paid for by an alien ineligible for citizenship were an illegal attempt to transfer property to that alien. The State attempted to take land conveyed to the citizen, son of an ineligible alien, because the alien father paid the consideration. The Court held that this denied the citizen son equal protection of the law.

Second, in *Takahashi v. Fish & Game Commission*,[17] the Court struck down a provision in the California Fish and Game Code that banned issuance of fishing

---

[15] 263 U.S. 197, 44 S. Ct. 15, 68 L. Ed. 255 (1923).
[16] 332 U.S. 633, 68 S. Ct. 269, 92 L. Ed. 249 (1948).
[17] 334 U.S. 410, 69 S. Ct. ll38, 92 L. Ed. 1478 (1948).

licenses to any person ineligible for citizenship. Federal law then prohibited Japanese from obtaining United States citizenship. The Court held that United States regulation of immigration and naturalization on the basis of racial classifications did not support a State's use of such classification to prevent an alien from earning a living in the same manner as citizens. On the contrary, the Court found that the California statute violated the equal protection clause. In so doing, it rejected an argument that California had a "special public interest" in banning Takahashi's commercial fishing. In the Court's view, "to whatever extent the fish in the three-mile belt off California may be 'capable of ownership' by California, we think that 'ownership' is inadequate to justify California in excluding any or all aliens who are lawful residents of the state from making a living by fishing in the ocean off its shore while permitting all others to do so."

[B] State Interference With U.S. Foreign Policy

On the question of whether a State's laws and practices interfere with United States foreign policy, the classic case is *Zschernig v. Miller*. [19] In *Zschernig* an Oregon statute provided that non-resident aliens could inherit only if (1) there was a reciprocal right for a United States citizen to take property in the foreign country; (2) American citizens in the United States could receive payment from an estate in the foreign country; and (3) foreign heirs would receive the proceeds of the Oregon estate "without confiscation." The statute had been applied by the State courts to deny an inheritance to the heir of an Oregon resident living in East Germany. The Supreme Court held the statute unconstitutional as applied on the ground that it was "an intrusion by the State into the field of foreign affairs which the Constitution entrusts to the President and the Congress."

In so ruling the Court distinguished *Clark v. Allen*. [20] There, in upholding a California inheritance statute that contained a general reciprocity clause, the Court stated that the clause did not on its face intrude on the federal domain and would have only "some incidental or indirect effect in foreign countries." Here, by contrast, the application of the Oregon statute "has led into minute inquiries concerning the actual administration of foreign law, [and] into the credibility of foreign diplomatic statements. . . ." This, in the Court's view, had more than "some incidental or indirect effect in foreign countries" and had "great potential for disruption or embarassment."

In an earlier case, *Kolovrat v. Oregon*,[21] the Court had held that a treaty superseded the Oregon Statute as to Yugoslavian heirs. In *Zschernig* the majority of the Court declined to consider whether the treaty with Germany of 1923 applied to East Germany. In a concurring opinion Justice Harlan found the treaty applicable and rejected the majority's conclusion that application of the statute was unconstitutional. Justice Stewart, in a concurring opinion joined by Justice Brennan, would have found that all three of the statutory requirements on their face were unconstitutional.

Zschernig has been subject to sharp criticism, in part because the majority's opinion failed to define clearly the scope of the new foreign affairs preemption

---

[19] 389 U.S. 429, 88 S. Ct. 664, 19 L. Ed. 2d 683 (1968).
[20] 331 U.S. 503, 67 S. Ct. 1431, 91 L. Ed. 1633 (1947).
[21] 366 U.S. 187, 81 S. Ct. 922, 6 L. Ed. 2d 218 (1961).

doctrine and hence provided little guidance as to when State action may impair foreign policy. The result has been that lower courts have reached inconsistent results in interpreting and applying *Zschernig*. Lower courts have differed, for example, as to whether *Zschernig* constituted simply a warning to the state courts to tone down their rhetoric or whether it required those courts to accept foreign representations concerning the effect of foreign law without inquiring into its actual administration or the credibility of the representations.

Some commentators have also criticized the result in *Zschernig*, on the ground that its conclusion that a State court's inquiry into a foreign country's law in action would embarrass the U.S. Government in the conduct of foreign policy was unfounded. They note that the Solicitor General of the United States, appearing as *amicus curiae* in the *Zschernig* case, after consulting with the State Department, reported that implementation of State reciprocity statutes of the kind involved in the case had had no substantial impact on the conduct of U.S. foreign policy. These critics note further that *Zschernig* in effect puts blindfolds over the eyes of State court justices and prevents them from effectively implementing the law.

Other critics approve of the result in *Zschernig* but not its reasoning. Rather than the federal preemption doctrine, these critics would strike down statutes of the kind in Zschernig on the ground that they infringe other constitutional doctrines, such as equal protection of the law. At this writing, however, the Supreme Court has not had occasion to reconsider the result or rationale of *Zschernig*. [22]

Zschernig may be contrasted with the Court's decision in *De Canas v. Bica*. [23] There the Court upheld the constitutionality of a provision of the California Labor Code which provided that "[n]o employer shall knowingly employ an alien who is not entitled to lawful residence in the United States if such employment would have an adverse effect on lawful resident workers." The statute imposed fines and other sanctions for its violation. While noting that the power to regulate immigration "is unquestionably exclusively a federal power," the Court went on to hold that not every state enactment that dealt with aliens "is a regulation of immigration and thus *per se* pre-empted by this constitutional power, whether latent or exercised" and that California had broad authority under its police power to regulate the employment relationship within the state.

The following cases focus more specifically on possible state interference with foreign commerce.

---

[22] For a recent discussion of the problem presented by Zschernig, see Comment, Iron Curtain Statutes, Communist China and The right to Devise, 32 U.C.L.A. L. Rev. 643 (1985).

[23] 424 U.S. 351, 96 S. Ct. 933, 47 L. Ed. 2d 43 (1976).

BETHLEHEM STEEL CORP. v. BOARD OF COMMRS.

Court of Appeal, Second District, Division 5
276 Cal. App. 2d 221, 80 Cal. Rptr. 800 (1969)

STEPHENS, ACTING P.J. These consolidated appeals are from summary judgments rendered in two superior court actions denying Bethlehem Steel Corporation (Bethlehem) injunctive relief and damages against the Department of Water and Power of the City of Los Angeles (the Department).

Bethlehem sought preliminary injunctions in both cases to prevent performance of the contracts unless they were modified to comply with the California Buy American Act. After a consolidated hearing on the two applications, preliminary injunctions were denied. Following this, Bethlehem filed amended complaints to add claims for damages, and for a declaration that the Department must comply with the California Buy American Act in awarding future public works contracts.

Without answering the amended complaints, defendants in both suits moved the trial court for summary judgments, asserting that the California Buy American Act violated certain international agreements of the United States, and was unconstitutional as a burden on foreign commerce and a denial of due process and equal protection of the law. The Department also contended that the act did not apply to it because Los Angeles is a chartered city and because application of the act would result in a gift of public funds. Summary judgments were entered in both cases against Bethlehem and in favor of defendants.

The California Buy American Act[24] . . . requires that contracts for the construction of public works or the purchase of material for public use be awarded only to persons who will agree to use or supply materials, which have been manufactured in the United States, substantially all from materials produced in the United States.[25]

The crucial and determinative issue presented by these appeals is whether this act, as applied to certain purchases of steel products manufactured abroad, violates the United States Constitution. We have concluded that the California Buy American Act is an unconstitutional encroachment upon the federal government's exclusive power over foreign affairs, and constitutes an undue interference with the United States' conduct of foreign relations.

The United States Constitution itself does not, in so many words, vest in the national government the power to conduct external relations. Instead, it parcels out certain aspects of the foreign affairs power among the political departments. As one writer has pointed out, "the organic provisions delegating such specific powers fall far short of covering comprehensively the whole field of foreign affairs."

---

[24] (Gov. Code 4300-4305).

[25] Government Code section 4303 provides: "The governing body of any political subdivision, municipal corporation, or district, and any public officer or person charged with the letting of contracts for (1) the construction, alteration, or repair of public works or (2) for the purchasing of materials for public use, shall let such contracts only to persons who agree to use or supply only such unmanufactured materials as have been produced in the United States, and only such manufactured materials as have been manufactured in the United States, substantially all from materials produced in the United States.

Whether we must conclude from this that the nation does not possess foreign affairs powers other than those specifically enumerated is answered in an unqualified negative: "As a sovereign power possessed by the nation, the power over foreign affairs is inherent, exclusive, and plenary. It is inherent, since . . . it does not depend for its existence upon the affirmative grants of the Constitution. It is exclusive in the Federal Government, both because of express prohibitions on the states in this field and because only the Union is vested with the attributes of external sovereignty. For national purposes, embracing our relations with foreign nations, we are but one people, one nation, one power. [Footnotes omitted.]"

As stated in *United States v. Curtiss-Wright Export Corp.*:[26] "The broad statement that the Federal government can exercise no powers except those specifically enumerated in the Constitution and such implied powers as are necessary and proper to carry into effect the enumerated powers, is categorically true only in respect of our internal affairs." See also *Burnet v. Brooks.*[27] The powers of external sovereignty do not depend upon the affirmative grants of the Constitution, but are vested in the federal government as necessary concomitants of nationality.

The exclusivity of the federal government's power in this sphere is predicated upon the "irrefutable postulate that though the states were several, their people in respect of foreign affairs were one." *United States v. Curtiss-Wright Export Corp., [supra].* . . . Hence, the external power of the United States is exercisable "without regard to state laws or policies" and "is not and cannot be subject to any curtailment or interference on the part of the several states."

The California Buy American Act, in effectively placing an embargo on foreign products, amounts to a usurpation by this state of the power of the federal government to conduct foreign trade policy. That there are countervailing state policies which are served by the retention of such an act is "wholly irrelevant to judicial inquiry," *United States v. Pink*[28] . . . since "[i]t is inconceivable that any of them can be interposed as an obstacle to the effective operation of a federal constitutional power." *United States v. Belmont*[29] . . . . Only the federal government can fix the rules of fair competition when such competition is on an international basis. Foreign trade is properly a subject of national concern, not state regulation. State regulation can only impede, not foster, national trade policies. The problems of trade expansion or non-expansion are national in scope, and properly should be national in scope in their resolution. The fact that international trade forms the basis of this country's foreign relations is amply demonstrated by the following. At the present time the United States is a party to commercial treaties with 38 foreign nations. In addition, there are tax treaties presently in effect between the United States and 31 countries. The United States is a party to many other international treaties and agreements regulating, directly or indirectly, its commercial relations with the rest of the world. . . . Certainly, such problems are beyond the purview of the State of California. As stated in *United States v. Pink*[30] . . . : "These are delicate matters. If state action could

[26] 299 U.S. 304, 315-316, 81 L. Ed. 255, 260-261, 57 S. Ct. 216.
[27] 288 U.S. 378, 396 77 L. Ed. 844, 852, 53 S. Ct. 457, 86 A.L.R. 747.
[28] 315 U.S. 203, 233, 86 L. Ed. 796, 819, 62 S. Ct 552.
[29] 301 U.S. 324, 332, 81 L. Ed. 1134, 1140.
[30] 315 U.S. 203, 232, 86 L. Ed. 796, 818.

defeat or alter our foreign policy, serious consequences might ensue. The nation as a whole would be held to answer if a state created difficulties with a foreign power."

The argument is nevertheless advanced that until such time as the federal government acts, either by conflicting legislation [31] or international agreement, [32] state legislation is unobjectionable. In *Purdy & Fitzpatrick v. State of California,* [33] our Supreme Court stated: "We need not await an instance of actual conflict to strike down a state law which purports to regulate a subject matter which the Congress simultaneously aims to control. The opportunity for potential conflict is too great to permit the operation of the state law. [Footnote omitted.] A state law may not stand "as an obstacle to the accomplishment and execution of the full purposes and objectives of Congress." *Hines v. Davidowitz.* [34] . . . . Suffice it to say that the force of Bethlehem's argument as is premised upon *City of Pasadena v. Charleville (1932)* [35] . . . and *Heim v. McCall (1915)* [36] . . . has been

---

[31] Our attention has been directed to the federal Buy American Act (47 Stat. 1520, as amended in 63 Stat. 1024). This act does not appear to be in direct conflict with the California act so as to preempt the latter. Conversely, the existence of the federal act cannot serve as a justification for state legislation since, as we have previously stated, it is the sole province of the federal government to act in this sphere. However, in contrast to the California act, the federal act appears to serve as an equalizer in considering foreign invitational bids, rather than as an embargo altogether on such bids. (See Executive Order No. 10582, Dec. 17, 1954, 19 F.R. 8723, as amended by Executive Order No. 11051, Sept. 27, 1962, 27 F.R. 9683.).

[32] It is vigorously asserted by defendants and denied by plaintiff that the Buy American Act is violative of the General Agreement on Tariffs and Trade (GATT, 61 Stat., Pts. 5 and 6, as amended), of which this nation is a signatory. In *Balwin-Lima-Hamilton Corp. v. Superior Court*, 208 Cal. App. 2d 803, 819-820 [25 Cal. Rptr. 798], as one column of a twin pedestal upon which its decision was based, the court held that the California Buy American Act had been superseded by GATT. In *Territory v. Ho*, 41 Hawaii 565 [394 P. 2d 623], similar legislation was invalidated on the premise that it was in conflict with GATT. Since we have concluded that the federal power, whether or not exercised, is exclusive in this field, we find it unnecessary to delve into an extensive analysis of the effect of GATT.

[33] 71 Cal. 2d 566, 577 [79 Cal. Rptr. 77, 456 P. 2d 645].

[34] 312 U.S. 52, 67, 85 L. Ed. 581, 587. An editorial dated October 15, 1964 in the New York Journal of Commerce commented: "Something of a dilemma confronts the present Administration and will also confront any future administration in consequence of the urge that prompts many State Legislatures to enact measures that restrict the flow of international commerce within their borders. . . . The nature of this dilemma was suggested in a Washington dispatch to this newspaper yesterday. In brief, its message was to the effect that Washington's opportunity to win meaningful tariff concessions from foreign countries in the current Kennedy Round may be much curtailed by 'Buy American' or by simply 'Buy Local' laws adopted in many states."

After giving a number of examples, the editorial concludes: "In the circumstances, about the best we can hope is that the State Legislatures will try harder in the future to temper the urge to protect their own producers with realization that the cumulative effect of procurement restrictions among many states can produce impossible rigidities in national policy. Even those who do not approve of the national foreign trade policy should realize that if it is to be determined by the future policies of 50 different entities, there won't be any policy at all."

[35] 215 Cal. 384 10 P. 2d 745.

[36] 239 U.S. 175 60 L. Ed. 206, 36 S. Ct. 78.

rendered extremely doubtful, if not completely emasculated, by *Purdy & Fitzpatrick v. State of California, supra.*

The California Buy American Act, like the Oregon escheat statute in *Zschernig v. Miller*[37] . . . "has more than some incidental or indirect effect in foreign countries,' and its great potential for disruption or embarrassment makes us hesitate to place it in the category of a diplomatic bagatelle."[38] Such state legislation may bear a particular onus to foreign nations since it may appear to be the product of selfish provincialism, rather than an instrument of justifiable policy. It is a type of protectionism which invites retaliative restrictions on our own trade. While the present California statute is not as gross an intrusion in the federal domain as others might be,[39] "it has a direct impact upon foreign relations, and may well adversely affect the power of the central government to deal with those problems." *Zschernig v. Miller*[40] . . . .

Our system of government is such that the interest of the cities, counties and states, no less than the interest of the people of the whole nation, "imperatively requires that federal power in the field affecting foreign relations be left entirely free from local interference." To permit state legislation to concurrently operate in this sphere would very certainly "imperil the amicable relations between governments and vex the peace of nations." *Oetjen v. Central Leather Co.*, . . . see *Ricaud v. American Metal Co.*

The present legislation is an impermissible attempt by the state to structure national foreign policy to conform to its own domestic policies. It illustrates the dangers which are involved if federal policy is to be qualified by the variant notions of the several states. We concluded that the California Buy American Act is an unconstitutional intrusion into an exclusive federal domain.

The judgments are affirmed.

REPPY, J. concurred.

Also, J. I concur in Acting Presiding Justice Stephens' opinion holding the California Buy American Act . . . unconstitutional as an undue interference with the federal government's conduct of foreign relations. I desire to add a few supplementary observations.

---

[37] 389 U.S. 429, 434-435 [19 L. Ed. 2d 683, 688-689, 88 S. Ct. 664].

[38] In a concurring opinion, Justice Stewart observed: "today, we are told, Oregon's statute does not conflict with the national interest. Tomorrow it may. But, however that may be, the fact remains that the conduct of our foreign affairs is entrusted under the Constitution to the National Government, not to the probate courts of the several States." (*Zschernig v. Miller, supra,* at p. 443 [19 L. Ed. 2d at p. 693].).

[39] In *Zschernig,* the court pointed out numerous instances where state courts have delved into "foreign policy attitudes" and noted in some detail how the Oregon statute, as applied, was unconstitutional. Nevertheless, Justice Douglas, in his majority opinion, makes it clear that conceptually such legislation based on its history, as well as its operation, was patently "an intrusion by the State into the field of foreign affairs which the Constitution entrusts to the President and the Congress." (*Zschernig v. Miller, supra,* at p. 432 [19 L. Ed. 2d at p. 687].).

[40] 389 U.S. 429, at page 441, 19 L. Ed. 2d 683 at p. 692. See *Passenger Cases,* 7 How. 283, 12 L. Ed. 702; *Crandall v. Nevada,* 6 Wall. 35, 18 L. Ed. 745, *Kent v. Dulles,* 357 U.S. 116, 2 L. Ed. 2d 1204, 78 S. Ct. 1113.

Juxtaposition of the text of the California Buy American Act alongside those of GATT and the Trade Agreements Act (19 U.S.C. 1351) as amended and extended, not only makes manifest the seriousness of the potential, if not presently actual, interference by California with the federal government's power to conduct its foreign affairs, but lays bare California's unconstitutional intrusion into the congressional power "[t]o regulate Commerce with foreign Nations."[41] . . . .

The power to regulate commerce with foreign nations is an express grant by the people to the federal government. *Gibbons v. Ogden*[42] . . . . "It is an essential attribute of the power that it is exclusive and plenary. As an exclusive power, its exercise may not be limited qualified or impeded to any extent by state action. . . . The power is buttressed by the express provision of the Constitution denying to the States authority to lay imposts or duties on imports or exports without the consent of the Congress.[43] . . . . The Congress may determine what articles may be imported into this country and the terms upon which importation is permitted." University of Illinois v. United States (1932).[44]

K.S.B. TECHNICAL SALES CORP. v. NORTH JERSEY COMM.

Supreme Court of New Jersey
75 N.J. 272, 381 A.2d 774 (1977)

SCHREIBER, J.

This case projects for our review the validity of New Jersey "Buy American" statutes, which generally require use in government purchase contracts of materials produced in this country. The bidding specifications of the North Jersey District Water Supply Commission (Commission) for a water treatment plant contained such a provision. K.S.B. Technical Sales Corp. (K.S.B.), a New York corporation which is a wholly owned subsidiary of a West German manufacturer of pumps and pumping equipment, and Linda Fazio, a taxpayer and resident of the City of Clifton, seek an adjudication that the Buy American condition in the specifications be declared invalid and its statutory foundation unconstitutional.

* * * *

A brief factual summary is in order. The North Jersey District Water Supply Commission, a governmental agency, was created for the purpose of developing a water supply for municipalities in the northern part of the State. . . . It has carried out that function and has been distributing water to eight municipalities in Essex, Hudson and Passaic counties. In 1974 the Commission was ordered to comply with a directive of the State Department of Health to construct a water treatment plant to improve the quality of the water. . . .

---

[41] U.S. Constitution, Art. I, Section 8, cl. 3.
[42] (1824) 22 U.S. (9 Wheat.) 1, 187-189, 6 L. Ed. 23, 68.
[43] Art. 1, Section 10. Cl.2.
[44] 289 U.S. 48, 56-57, 77 L. Ed. 1025, 1028; 53 S. Ct. 509, 510.

For that purpose the Commission submitted specifications to prospective bidders which included a requirement that "[o]nly manufactured products of the United States, wherever available, shall be used in the work in accordance with municipalities and counties Local Public Contracts Law. . . .

State work is governed by N.J.S.A. 52:32-1 which reads as follows:

The State shall make provisions in the specifications for all contracts for state work and for work for which the state pays any part of the cost, that only such manufactured and farm products of the United States, whenever available, be used in such work. . . .

This law has remained unchanged since its adoption in 1932.

A contractor's failure to comply with these provisions may disqualify him from being awarded any public work construction contracts for three years. . . .

The plaintiffs, who, as counsel stated during oral argument, are not particularly concerned with the award of this contract, seek a general declaration that the New Jersey Buy American statute is unconstitutional. The constitutional issues concern the applicability and effect of the General Agreement on Tariffs and Trade made between the United States and foreign countries, the conflict, if any, between the New Jersey Buy American provisions and the foreign affairs power, and the conflict, if any, between the New Jersey Buy American provisions and the Commerce Clause.

THE NEW JERSEY BUY AMERICAN STATUTE AND THE FEDERAL GENERAL AGREEMENT ON TARIFFS AND TRADE (GATT)

[In this section of its opinion the court finds that the New Jersey Buy American Statute is compatible with U.S. GATT obligations. It noted that, although GATT, like a treaty, prevails over State law under the U.S. Constitution, in Article III: 8(a), the GATT expressly exempts the purchases involved in this case from the "national treatment" obligation found in Article III: 1 and 2.][45]

II

THE NEW JERSEY BUY AMERICAN STATUTE AND THE FEDERAL FOREIGN AFFAIRS POWER

Plaintiffs argue that the New Jersey Buy American provisions, . . . even if found not to conflict with GATT, represent an impermissible intrusion by the State into the field of foreign affairs, an area constitutionally reserved to Congress and the President. The Constitution contains no specific grant to Congress to enact legislation to regulate foreign affairs, but existence of such power stemming from national sovereignty has been acknowledged by the Supreme Court. . . .

---

[45] GATT Article III: 8(a) provides as follows: "The provisions of this Article shall not apply to laws, regulations or requirements governing procurement by governmental agencies of products purchased for governmental purposes and not with a view to commercial resale or with a view to use in the production of goods for commercial sale." - Ed.

Plaintiffs rely primarily upon the Supreme Court opinion in *Zschernig v. Miller*[46] . . . for their position that the Buy American provisions constitute an impermissible state invasion of foreign policy.

It is significant that the Supreme Court in *Zschernig* refused to reexamine its ruling in *Clark v. Allen.*[47] In *Clark*, a California statute permitted a nonresident alien to inherit personalty only if there was a reciprocal right on the part of United States citizens to take on the same terms and conditions as citizens of the other nation. The challenge to the statute grounded on its intrusion into the field of foreign affairs was rejected. In *Zschernig*, Mr. Justice Douglas, who had also written the opinion in Clark, pointed out that the California reciprocity statute "did not on its face intrude in the federal domain" and would only have "some incidental or indirect effect in foreign countries."[48]

It is quite clear that the New Jersey Legislature, by means of the statutory provisions under review, has not authorized its local units of government to engage in the sensitive business of evaluating the politics of countries whose citizens seek to market their products in this State. The Buy American provisions apply without any discrimination based on the ideology of the seller's country. Nor is there any evidence to suggest that the political climate in a potential foreign bidder's nation has ever motivated the bids or that its inclusion is predicated on an assessment of the internal policies of any foreign country. If refined inquiries into foreign ideologies entered into the decison to apply or not to apply the condition, there would, of course, be little difficulty in finding a constitutional infirmity of the type condemned in *Zschernig*. But the statute in no way requires, nor should it be construed to permit, such inquiries. We can only conclude the statute does not represent the kind of intrusion into the foreign affairs power condemned in *Zschernig*. . . .

In addition in *Zschernig*, the plaintiffs rely heavily on *Bethlehem Steel Corp. v. Board of Comm'rs of Dept. of W. & P.*[49] . . . . The California court in a 3 to 1 decision declared unconstitutional the California Buy American Act containing an absolute requirement that only materials manufactured in the United States be used. The court likened the California act to the Oregon statute in Zschernig and reasoned that the states have no power to affect foreign commerce, an exclusive federal domain. Referring to the numerous treaties and agreements concerned with the trade which the United States has entered into with foreign nations, including GATT (noting that it was unnecessary to delve into an analysis of that agreement), the court held that the California statute had more than an incidental or indirect effect on foreign affairs.

The California Buy American Act did not have the restricted sphere and more limited impact of the New Jersey statute. . . . Unlike the California Code, N.J.S.A. 52:33-2 and 3 provide that domestic materials need not be used if the cost is "unreasonable" or it is "inconsistent with the public interest" or if it is "impracticable." Nor did the California court consider the express exemption in

---

[46] 389 U.S. 429, 88 S. Ct. 664, 19 L. Ed. 2d 683 (1968), *reh. den.* 390 U.S. 974, 88 S. Ct. 1018, 19 L. Ed. 2d 1196 (1968).
[47] 331 U.S. 503, 67 S. Ct. 1431, 91 L. Ed. 1633 (1947).
[48] 389 U.S. at 433-438, 88 S. Ct. at 667, 19 L. Ed. 2d at 688.
[49] 276 Cal. App. 2d 221, 80 Cal. Rptr. 800 (Ct. App. 1969).

GATT into which the New Jersey legislation fits. This exemption indicates that the Federal government has not foreclosed state action which does not have a significant and direct impact on foreign affairs.

* * * *

THE NEW JERSEY BUY AMERICAN STATUTE AND THE COMMERCE CLAUSE

The United States Constitution empowers Congress "[t]o regulate Commerce with foreign Nations and among the several States."[50] . . . . Although literally the clause authorizes only Congress to Act, it is well settled that, at least in the absence of a finding that Congress has preempted the field, there exists a residuum of power in the states to enact legislation affecting commerce. . . .

* * * *

Controversies involving the implicit proscription against State interference have centered about State attempts to establish, directly or indirectly, economic barriers to forestall free trade among the States and prevent foreign competition. . . .

United States Supreme Court cases explicating the unexercised commerce power have traditionally involved state regulation of activity in the private sector. . . .

Review of such state legislation calls for a balancing of the local public interest against the extent of the burden, and consideration of the availability of less onerous alternatives. . . .

It was not until *Hughes v. Alexandria Scrap Corp.*[51] . . . that the Supreme Court discussed the legal impact of the state's entry into the marketplace as a purchaser of goods, rather than as a regulator of the commercial activities of others. In that case the State of Maryland instituted a program to encourage elimination of abandoned automobiles by paying a subsidy to licensed processors to destroy such vehicles. However, because of an amendment to the Maryland statute nonresident processors had to meet substantially more onerous requirements with respect to the title of the vehicles so that Maryland processors were given a substantial advantage in obtaining the business. An out-of-state processor challenged the amendment as violative of the Commerce Clause. Mr. Justice Powell, writing for the majority, reasoned that commerce created when the state enters the market on its own behalf is not to be equated with a state's interference with the natural functioning of the interstate market "through burdensome regulation."[52] He stated that:

> [U]ntil today the Court has not been asked to hold that entry by the State itself into the market as a purchaser, in effect, of a potential article of interstate commerce creates a burden upon that commerce if the State restricts its trade to its own citizens or businesses within the State.[53] . . . .

---

[50] U.S. Const., Art. I, Sec. 8, cl. 3.
[51] 426 U.S. 794, 96 S. Ct. 2488, 49 L. Ed. 2d 220 (1976).
[52] *Id.* at 805-806, 96 S. Ct. at 2495-2496, 49 L. Ed. 2d at 228, 229.
[53] *Id.* at 808, 96 S. Ct. at 2497, 49 L. Ed. 2d at 231.

Mr. Justice Powell concluded:

Nothing in the purposes animating the Commerce Clause forbids a State, in the absence of congressional action, from participating in the market and exercising the right to favor its own citizens over others.[54] . . . .

Accordingly, he held that the amendment was constitutional. Mr. Justice Stevens in his concurring opinion emphasized the same point by stating that:

It is important to differentiate between commerce which flourishes in a free market and commerce which owes its existence to a state subsidy program. Our cases finding that a state regulation constitutes an impermissible burden on interstate commerce all dealt with restrictions that adversely affected the operation of a free market. This case is unique because the commerce which Maryland has "burdened" is commerce which would not exist if Maryland had not decided to subsidize a portion of the automobile scrap processing business[55] . . . .

Congress has expressed a policy judgment that foreign commerce will not be unduly burdened when the federal government and its agencies prefer domestic products in their purchases. By enacting the Buy American Act, Congress has approved the policy of preferring domestic goods for federal governmental projects. State statutes patterned after the federal act are consonant with that policy. At least when governmental purchases are not to be used in the production of goods for commercial sale, that policy judgment has been impliedly extended to the states through the express exemption in GATT. Although Buy American statutes have been the subject of extensive criticism,[56] . . . it is our function to review the constitutionality, not the wisdom, of statutes. We conclude that N.J.S.A. 52:33-2 and 3 do not violate the Commerce Clause.

NOTES AND QUESTIONS

(1) Is the effort of the court in *K.S.B. Technical Sales* to distinguish *Bethlehem Steel Corp.* successful, or are the two cases simply in conflict? If the latter, which view do you find the more persuasive? In answering, consider the difference in the way the two courts (California and New Jersey) characterize the nature of the state interference in U.S. foreign relations that the U.S. Supreme Court decisions prohibit. Which characterization is more faithful to the basic concerns of the Supreme Court decisions?

(2) Note the heavy reliance by the New Jersey court on the "market participant" exception to the limitations on State action imposed by the "dormant commerce clause." In light of the purposes of the dormant commerce clause, how relevant to the Federal-State relationship, at issue in these cases, is that exception?

---

[54] *Id.* at 810, 96 S. Ct. at 2497, 49 L. Ed. 2d at 231.

[55] Id. at 815, 96 S. Ct. at 2500, 49 L. Ed. 2d at 234.

[56] See, *e.g.*, Knapp, *The Buy American Act: A Review And Assessment*, 61 Colum.L.Rev. 430 (1960); Berliner, *State Buy American Policies—One Vice Many Voices*, 32 Geo. Wash. L. Rev. 584 (1964).

(3) The court in *K.S.B. Technical Sales Corp.* acknowledges that New Jersey's Buy American Act has been sharply criticized on policy grounds but concludes that these objections do not partake of a constitutional dimension. Considering the obvious federal interest in these statutes, why has there been no action forthcoming from the federal government? Should the federal government seek to appear as *amicus curiae* in suits challenging the constitutionality of such laws? Should (could) Congress pass legislation nullifying such State statutes? What are the arguments for and against such federal action?[57]

§ 13.04 State Taxation of Transnational Enterprises

JAPAN LINE, LTD. v. COUNTY OF LOS ANGELES

United States Supreme Court
441 U.S. 434, 99 S. Ct. 1813, 60 L. Ed. 2d 336 (1979)

MR. JUSTICE BLACKMUN delivered the opinion of the court.

This case presents the question whether a State, consistently with the Commerce Clause of the Constitution, may impose a nondiscriminatory ad valorem property tax on foreign-owned instrumentalities (cargo containers) of international commerce.

The facts were "stipulated on appeal," . . . and were found by the trial court . . . as follows:

Appellants are six Japanese shipping companies; they are incorporated under the laws of Japan, and they have their principal places of business and commercial domiciles in that country. . . . Appellants operate vessels used exclusively in foreign commerce; these vessels are registered in Japan and have their home ports there. . . . The vessels are specifically designed and constructed to accommodate large cargo shipping containers. The containers, like the ships, are owned by appellants, have their home ports in Japan, and are used exclusively for hire in the transportation of cargo in foreign commerce. . . . Each container is in constant transit save for time spent undergoing repair or awaiting loading and unloading of cargo. All appellants' containers are subject to property tax in Japan and, in fact, are taxed there.

Appellees are political subdivisions of the State of California. Appellants' containers, in the course of their international journeys, pass through appellees' jurisdictions intermittently. Although none of appellants' containers stays

---

[57] For comments on Buy American Acts, see, *e.g.*, Miller, *Foreign Commerce And State Power; The Constitutionality Of State Buy American Statutes*, 12 Cornell Int'l L.J. 109 (1979); Knapp, The Buy American Act: A Review And Assessment, 61 Colum. L. Rev. 430 (1960); student notes in 52 Calif. L. Rev. 355 (1964), 32 Geo. Wash. L. Rev. 584 (1964), 12 Stan. L. Rev. 355 (1960). An excellent survey of the problems the Buy American Acts and similar public and private practices raise may be found in Bilder, *East-West Trade Boycotts: A Study In Private, Labor Union, State And Local Interference With Foreign Policy*, 118 U. Pa. L. Rev. 841 (1970). See also, Bilder, *The Role Of States and Cities in Foreign Relations*, 83 Am. J. Int'l L. 821 (1989).

permanently in California, some are there at any given time; a container's average stay in the State is less than three weeks.

The containers engage in no intrastate or interstate transportation of cargo except as continuations of international voyages. . . . Any movements or periods of non-movement of containers in appellees' jurisdictions are essential to, and inseparable from, the containers' efficient use as instrumentalities of foreign commerce.

Property present in California on March 1 (the "lien date" under California law) of any year is subject to an *ad valorem* property tax. . . . A number of appellants' containers were physically present in appellees' jurisdictions on the lien dates in 1970, 1971, and 1972; this number was fairly representative of the containers' "average presence" during each year . . . Appellees levied property taxes in excess of $550,000 on the assessed value of the containers present on March 1 of the three years in question. During the same period, similar containers owned or controlled by steamship companies domiciled in the United States, that appeared from time to time in Japan during the course of international commerce, were not subject to property taxation in Japan and therefore were not, in fact, taxed in that country. . . .

* * * *

The California Supreme Court concluded that "the threat of double taxation from foreign taxing authorities has no role in commerce clause considerations of multiple burdens, since burdens in international commerce are not attributable to discrimination by the taxing state and are matters for international agreement.". . . . Deeming the containers' foreign ownership and use irrelevant for purposes of constitutional analysis . . . the court rejected appellants' Commerce Clause challenge and sustained the validity of the tax as applied.

Appellants appealed. We postponed consideration of our jurisdiction to the hearing on the merits. . . .

* * * *

The Constitution provides that "Congress shall have Power. . . . To regulate Commerce with foreign Nations, and among the several States, and with the Indian Tribes"[1] . . . . In construing Congress' power to "regulate Commerce . . . among the several States," the Court recently has affirmed that the Constitution confers no immunity from state taxation, and that "interstate commerce must bear its fair share of the state tax burden.". . . . Instrumentalities of interstate commerce are no exception to this rule, and the Court regularly has sustained property taxes as applied to various forms of transportation equipment. . . . If the state tax "is applied to an activity with a substantial nexus with the taxing State, is fairly apportioned, does not discriminate against interstate commerce, and is fairly related to the services provided by the State," no impermissible burden on interstate commerce will be found. *Complete Auto Transit, Inc. v. Brady*[2] . . . .

---

[1] Art. I, Section 8, cl. 3.
[2] 430 U.S. 274, 279, 97 S. Ct. 1076, 1079, 51 L. Ed. 2d 326 (1977).

Appellees contend that cargo shipping containers, like other vehicles of commercial transport, are subject to property taxation, and that the taxes imposed here meet *Complete Auto's* fourfold requirements. The containers, they argue, have a "substantial nexus" with California because some of them are present in the State at all times; jurisdiction to tax is based on "the habitual employment of the property within the State" . . . and appellants' containers habitually are so employed. The tax, moreover, is "fairly apportioned," since it is levied only on the containers' "average presence" in California. The tax "does not discriminate," thirdly, since it falls evenhandedly on all personal property in the State; indeed, as an *ad valorem* tax of general application, it is of necessity nondiscriminatory. The tax, finally, is "fairly related to the services provided by" California, services that include not only police and fire protection, but also the benefits of a trained work force and the advantages of a civilized society.

These observations are not without force. We may assume that, if the containers at issue here were instrumentalities of purely interstate commerce, *Complete Auto* would apply and be satisfied, and our Commerce Clause inquiry would be at an end. Appellants' containers, however, are instrumentalities of foreign commerce, both as a matter of fact and as a matter of law. The premise of appellees' argument is that the Commerce Clause analysis is identical, regardless of whether interstate or foreign commerce is involved. This premise, we have concluded, must be rejected. When construing Congress' power to "regulate Commerce with foreign Nations," a more extensive constitutional inquiry is required.

When a State seeks to tax the instrumentalities of foreign commerce, two additional considerations, beyond those articulated in *Complete Auto*, come into play. The first is the enhanced risk of multiple taxation. It is a commonplace of constitutional jurisprudence that multiple taxation may well be offensive to the Commerce Clause. . . . In order to prevent multiple taxation of interstate commerce, this Court has required that taxes be apportioned among taxing jurisdictions, so that no instrumentality of commerce is subjected to more than one tax on its full value. The corollary of the apportionment principle, of course, is that no jurisdiction may tax the instrumentality in full.

* * * *

Yet neither this Court nor this Nation can ensure full apportionment when one of the taxing entities is a foreign sovereign. If an instrumentality of commerce is domiciled abroad, the country of domicile may have the right, consistently with the custom of nations, to impose a tax on its full value. If a State should seek to tax the same instrumentality on an apportioned basis, multiple taxation inevitably results. Hence, whereas the fact of apportionment in interstate commerce means that "multiple burdens logically cannot occur," . . . the same conclusion, as to foreign commerce, logically cannot be drawn. Due to the absence of an authoritative tribunal capable of ensuring that the aggregation of taxes is computed on no more than one full value, a state tax, even though "fairly apportioned" to reflect an instrumentality's presence within the State, may subject foreign commerce "to the risk of a double tax burden to which [domestic] commerce is not exposed, and which the commerce clause forbids."

Second, a state tax on the instrumentalities of foreign commerce may impair federal uniformity in an area where federal uniformity is essential. Foreign commerce is preeminently a matter of national concern. . . .

A state tax on instrumentalities of foreign commerce may frustrate the achievement of federal uniformity in several ways. If the State imposes an apportioned tax, international disputes over reconciling apportionment formulae may arise. If a novel state tax creates an asymmetry in the international tax structure, foreign nations disadvantaged by the levy may retaliate against American-owned instrumentalities present in their jurisdictions. Such retaliation of necessity would be directed at American transportation equipment in general, not just that of the taxing State, so that the Nation as a whole would suffer. If other states followed the taxing State's example, various instrumentalities of commerce could be subjected to varying degrees of multiple taxation, a result that would plainly prevent this Nation from "speaking with one voice" in regulating foreign commerce.

* * * *

Analysis of California's tax under these principles dictates that the tax as applied to appellants' containers, is impermissible.

* * * *

First, California's tax results in multiple taxation of the instrumentalities of foreign commerce. By stipulation, appellants' containers are owned, based, and registered in Japan; they are used exclusively in international commerce; and they remain outside Japan only so long as needed to complete their international missions. Under these circumstances, Japan has the right and the power to tax the containers in full. California's tax, however, creates more than the risk of multiple taxation; it produces multiple taxation in fact. Appellants' containers not only "are subject to property tax . . . in Japan," . . . but, as the trial court found, "are, in fact, taxed in Japan.". . . . Thus, if appellees' levies were sustained, appellants "would be paying a double tax". . . .

Second, California's tax prevents this Nation from "speaking with one voice" in regulating foreign trade. The desirability of uniform treatment of containers used exclusively in foreign commerce is evidenced by the Customs Convention on Containers, which the United States and Japan have signed.

Under this Convention, containers temporarily imported are admitted free of "all duties and taxes whatsoever chargeable by reason of importation.". . . . The Convention reflects a national policy to remove impediments to the use of containers as "instruments of international traffic."[3] California's tax, however, will frustrate attainment of federal uniformity. It is stipulated that American-owned containers are not taxed in Japan. . . . California's tax thus creates an asymmetry in international maritime taxation operating to Japan's disadvantage. The risk of retaliation by Japan, under these circumstances, is acute, and such retaliation of necessity would be felt by the Nation as a whole. . . .

Appellees proffer several objections to this holding. They contend, first, that any multiple taxation in this case is attributable, not to California, but to Japan.

[3] 19 U.S.C. Section 1322(a).

California, they say, is just trying to take its share; it should not be foreclosed by Japan's election to tax the containers in full. California'a tax, however, must be evaluated in the realistic framework of the custom of nations. Japan has the right and the power to tax appellants' containers at their full value; nothing could prevent it from doing so. . . .

Appellees contend, secondly, that any multiple taxation created by California's tax can be cured by congressional action or by international agreement. We find no merit in this contention. The premise of appellees' argument is that a State is free to impose demonstrable burdens on commerce, so long as Congress has not pre-empted the field by affirmative regulation. But it long has been "accepted constitutional doctrine that the commerce clause, without the aid of Congressional legislation . . . affords some protection from state legislation inimical to the national commerce, and that in such cases, where Congress has not acted, this Court, and not the state legislature, is under the commerce clause the final arbiter of the competing demands of state and national interests." *Southern Pacific Co. v. Arizona ex rel. Sullivan*[4] . . . .

Finally, appellees present policy arguments. If California cannot tax appellants' containers, they complain, the State will lose revenue, even though the containers plainly have a nexus with California; the State will go uncompensated for the services it undeniably renders the containers; and, by exempting appellants' containers from tax, the State in effect will be forced to discriminate against domestic, in favor of foreign, commerce. These arguments are not without weight, and, to the extent appellees cannot recoup the value of their services through user fees, they may indeed be disadvantaged by our decision today. These arguments, however, are directed to the wrong forum. "Whatever subjects of this [commerce] power are in their nature national, or admit only of one uniform system, or plan of regulation, may justly be said to be of such a nature as to require exclusive legislation by Congress." *Cooley v. Board of Wardens.*[5] . . . . The problems to which appellees refer are problems that admit only of a federal remedy. They do not admit of a unilateral solution by a State.

The judgment of the Supreme Court of California is reversed.

It is so ordered.

---

[4] 325 U.S. 761, 769 (1945).
[5] 12 How. 299, 319 (1852).

NOTES AND QUESTIONS[6]

(1) Prior to *Japan Line* in *Michelin Tire Corp. v. Wages*,[7] the Supreme Court had ruled that imports could be taxed once they were no longer in transit; for example, if they were stored in a warehouse awaiting further distribution within the United States. Judged by the basic considerations that animated the decision in *Japan Lines*, are these two cases distinguishable? In a later case, *Xerox Corp. v. Harris County, Texas*,[8] the Court disallowed local property taxation of goods manufactured in Mexico, shipped to the United States and held in a customs bonded warehouse while awaiting shipment to Latin America. It did so on the ground that such State taxation had been preempted under the Supremacy Clause by Congress' comprehensive regulation of customs duties which was designed to create secure and duty free enclaves under federal control in order to encourage merchants in the United States and abroad to make use of American ports.

(2) In *Japan Lines*, the Court expresses substantial sympathy for the appellees' policy arguments but concludes that they are "directed to the wrong forum." To what forum should the appellees direct their arguments? Congress? The Executive Branch? Both? What do you think the chances of success for such an endeavor would be? And what precisely should the appellees ask Congress or the Executive Branch to do?

(3) Compare *Japan Line* with *Container Corporation of America v. Franchise Tax Board*.[9] There, by a 6-3 vote, the Court distinguished Japan Line, upholding a California corporate franchise tax which employed the "unitary business" principle and formula in applying that tax to corporations doing business both in and outside the State. Under California's law, the tax is based on the proportion of a corporation's total payroll, property and sales that are in California.

The appellant was a Delaware corporation which had a number of overseas subsidiaries incorporated in the countries where they operated. The majority of the Court was of the opinion that the California tax did not violate the "one voice" standard established in *Japan Line*, under which a state tax at variance with federal policy will be struck down if it either implicates foreign policy issues which must be left to the Federal government or violates a clear federal directive. In its view the tax did not create an automatic "asymmetry" in international taxation, since it was imposed on a domestic corporation and not on a foreign entity, and even if foreign nations had a legitimate interest in reducing the tax burden of

[6] For commentary relevant to the issues raised in Japan Line, Ltd, see, *e.g.*, Clark, *Property Taxation Of Foreign Goods & Enterprises — A Study In Inconsistency*, 4 Pepperdine L. Rev. 39 (1976); *Comment, State Taxation Of International Air Carriers*, 57 Nw. U.L. Rev. 92 (1962); *Comment, Limitations On State Taxation Of Foreign Commerce: The Contemporary Vitality Of The Home Port Doctrine*, 127 U. Penn. L. Rev. 817 (1979); *Note, Alternative Theories For Establishing A Federal Common Law Of Foreign Judgments In Commercial Cases: The Foreign Affairs Power And The Dormant Foreign Commerce Clause*, 16 Va. J. Int'l L. 635 (1976). Student notes on Japan Line, Ltd, may be found in 55 Wash. L. Rev. 885 (1980); 15 Tex. Int'l L. J. 13 (1980); and 14 J. Int'l L. & Econ. 153 (1979).

[7] 423 U.S. 276, 96 S. Ct. 535, 46 L. Ed. 2d 495 (1976).
[8] 459 U.S. 145, 103 S. Ct. 523, 74 L. Ed. 2d 323 (1982).
[9] 463 U.S. 159, 103 S. Ct. 2933, 77 L. Ed. 2d 545 (1983).

domestic corporations, the appellant was amenable to being taxed in California one way or another, and the tax it paid was more the function of California's tax rate than of its allocation method. Moreover, the California tax was not preempted by federal law. There was no claim that the federal tax statutes themselves provided the necessary preemption. The requirement in some tax treaties that the Federal Government adopt some form of arm's-length analysis in taxing the domestic income of multinational enterprises is generally waived as to taxes imposed by each of the contracting parties on its own domestic corporations. Tax treaties do not cover the taxing activities of the States, and Congress has never enacted legislation designed to regulate State taxation of income.

The three dissenting Justices (Chief Justice Burger and Justices Powell and O'Connor) believed that *Japan Line* was controlling. Justice Powell, the writer of the dissenting opinion, pointed out that the California tax not only created a substantial risk of international multiple taxation, but had actually resulted in double taxation in that case. With respect to the majority's reliance on the appellant's status as a U.S. corporation, Justice Powell responded that California was taxing the income of the foreign subsidiaries and, although foreign governments might be indifferent about the overall tax burden of an American corporation, they would have legitimate grounds to complain when a heavier tax is calculated on the basis of the income of corporations domiciled in their countries. Such a tax might have the effect of discouraging American investment in their countries. A number of foreign governments had in fact filed complaints with the United States Government. Accordingly, Justice Powell concluded, the California tax was an intrusion on national policy in foreign affairs prohibited by the Constitution.

(4) In *Wardair Canada, Inc. v. Florida Dept. of Revenue*,[10] the Court upheld a Florida tax on aviation fuel used by an air carrier engaged exclusively in foreign commerce, despite the opposition of the United States Government which intervened as *amicus* curiae. The Court first found that the Federal Aviation Act had not occupied the field of international aviation and preempted all State regulation. Second, the Court held that the Florida tax did not violate the Commerce Clause because no explicit foreign policy required the nation to speak with one voice on this issue. Such State taxation was not expressly prohibited by applicable international agreements and at most there was an international aspiration to eliminate all impediments to foreign air travel, including taxation of fuel by political subdivisions. No law to this effect had been proven, however.

Justice Blackmun dissented, on the ground that *Japan Line's* requirement that the nation speak with one voice was dispositive of this case. In his view, the aspiration of the U.S. Government to eliminate all impediments to foreign air travel referred to in the majority opinion demonstrated a federal policy that rendered application of the Florida tax unconstitutional. The majority opinion, Justice Blackmun contended, would frustrate the realization of this policy.

(5) In *Franchise Tax Board of California v. Alcan Aluminum Ltd.*,[11] the Supreme Court ruled unanimously that a foreign parent company had no legal

---

[10] 477 U.S. 1, 106 S. Ct. 2369, 91 L. Ed. 2d 1 (1986).
[11] — U.S. — , 110 S.Ct. 661, 107 L.Ed. 2d 696 (1990).

standing to challenge in federal court a state's taxing method on the income of its U.S. subsidiary when that subsidiary had a plain, speedy, and efficient remedy in that state's courts. The constitutional merits of the foreign commerce issue were not before the Court in this case, although it is likely that the "unitary tax" issue will come before the Court again in the future.

(6) As we have seen above, the federal government has the undoubted authority to adopt legislation or to make treaties or other forms of international agreements relating to foreign relations that bind the States. A related and closer question is whether the federal judiciary has the authority to develop rules to resolve issues of foreign relations in the absence of a constitutional provision giving the courts such lawmaking capacity or of federal legislation or a treaty which they can interpret. In short can the courts create a federal common law of foreign relations?

In *Erie R. Co. v. Thompkins*,[12] the Supreme Court, in holding that a federal court exercising diversity jurisdiction must follow state substantive law, stated that "there is no federal general common law." However, in the decades following *Erie*, the federal courts have proceeded to develop such a law in a number of specialized fields. *Banco Nacionale de Cuba v. Sabbatino, supra*, p. 000, is most often cited in favor of a federal common law of foreign relations. The Court held that the issue of whether the Act of State doctrine applied was to be governed solely by federal law binding on State courts and stating "[i]t seems fair to assume that the Court did not have rules like the Act of State doctrine in mind when it decided *Erie R. Co. v. Thompkins.*" The Court makes it quite clear, moreover, that, while the Act of State doctrine has "constitutional underpinnings," it is not required by the Constitution, nor is it to be found in any federal statute, regulation, or treaty. Rather, it is a judicial doctrine, developed as a matter of "federal common law." The precise basis and scope of this federal common law of foreign relations is still a matter of controversy.[13]

§ 13.05   Limitations on Federal Regulation

From time to time it has been contended that there are limits on the federal government's power to regulate economic affairs which result from the powers reserved to the States under the Tenth Amendment to the Constitution. Today, however, there are few, if any, such limitations upon this power of the federal government.[1]

[A]   Federal Control of the Economic Activities of Aliens

The constitutional analysis applicable to federal control of the economic activities of aliens differs from the analysis applicable to State controls. Thus, in contrast to *Bernal v. Fainter* the courts have generally applied the rational basis test to federal legislative distinctions between citizens and aliens and between different kinds of aliens. Under this test, the distinctions have largely been upheld.

---

[12] 304 U.S. 64, 58 S. Ct. 817, 82 L. Ed. 1188 (1938).

[13] For a thoughtful consideration of the problem, see Maier, *The Basis And Range Of Federal Common Law In Private International Law Matters*, 5 Vand. J. Transnational L. 133 (1971).

[1] J. Nowak, R. Rotunda & J. Young, Constitutional Law 138-81 (2d ed. 1983).

The plaintiffs in *Hampton v. Mow Sun Wong*[2] achieved a pyrrhic victory in challenging regulations of the federal Civil Service Commission (CSC) barring aliens, including lawfully admitted resident aliens, from employment in most positions of federal service. Assuming without deciding that a determination by Congress or the President to exclude all aliens from the federal civil service could be supported by such policy reasons as providing the President with a bargaining chip in treaty negotiations, or giving resident aliens an incentive to become citizens, or even for purposes of administrative convenience, the Supreme Court held that such a determination could not be made by the CSC. Rather the Court said: "due process requires that the decision to impose [this] deprivation of an important liberty [exclusion from employment] be made either at a comparable level of government [Congress or the President]" or, if made by the CSC, on the basis of reasons that are properly the concern of that agency. Shortly following the decision the President issued an executive order confirming the bar on employment of aliens. The legality of the order was upheld by several lower court opinions, *e.g.*, *Vergara v. Hampton.*[3] The Supreme Court did not again rule on the issue.

Challenges to distinctions made by federal law between different kinds of aliens also have been unsuccessful. In *Matthews v. Diaz*,[4] Cuban refugees lawfully admitted to the United States less than five years before at the discretion of the Attorney General and an alien lawfully admitted less than five years before for permanent residence brought a class action challenging the constitutionality of provisions in the supplemental medical plan established as part of the federal Medicare program. These provisions disqualified from benefits all aliens except those who were lawfully admitted for permanent residence and who had resided in the United States continuously for five years prior to their application for enrollment. The Supreme Court reversed the decision of a three-judge district court that held that the five year residency requirement violated equal protection notions inherent in the due process clause of the Fifth Amendment.

The Supreme Court first pointed to "a host of constitutional and statutory provisions" to support its conclusion that the federal government could grant benefits to citizens and deny them to aliens. It then turned to the "real question presented by this case . . . whether the statutory discrimination within the class of aliens — allowing benefits to some aliens but not to others — is permissible." In holding that it was permissible the Court relied in part on the proposition that it is "the business of the political branches of the Federal Government, rather than that of either the States or the Federal Judiciary, to regulate the conditions of entry and residence of aliens." The Court also ruled that "it is unquestionably reasonable for Congress to make an alien's eligibility depend on both the character and duration of his residence."

Another case involving distinctions between classes of aliens was *Narenji v. Civilletti*,[5] where the constitutionality of an executive regulation issued while

---

[2] 426 U.S. 88, 96 S. Ct. 1895, 48 L. Ed. 2d 495 (1976).

[3] 581 F. 2d 1281 (7th Cir. 1978).

[4] 426 U.S. 67, 96 S. Ct. 1883, 48 L. Ed. 2d 478 (1976).

[5] 617 F. 2d 745 (D.C. Cir. 1979).

American diplomats were being held as hostages in Iran was challenged. The regulation required nonimmigrant alien post-secondary school students who were Iranian citizens to report to a local INS office "to provide information as to residence and maintenance of nonimmigrant status," or be subject to deportation. Overruling a district court opinion that found the regulation unconstitutional because it violated the Iranian students' right to equal protection of laws, the court of appeals observed that "classifications among aliens based upon nationality are consistent with due process and equal protection if supported by a rational basis" and held that the regulation met this test.

[B] Due Process and the Fifth Amendment's "Takings" Clause

In *Russian Volunteer Fleet v. United States*,[6] the Supreme Court held that an alien friend is entitled to the protection of the Fifth Amendment prohibition of taking without just compensation, even if his government is no longer recognized by the United States Government. The Court has also stated categorically, with respect to non-resident aliens owning property within the United States, that they "as well as citizens are entitled to the protection of the Fifth Amendment." *United States v. Pink*,[7] *supra*, page 1068. As the *Pink* case demonstrates, however, the Fifth Amendment may afford only uncertain protection if the U.S. Government's action is taken as part of a foreign affairs initiative. Another example of this uncertain protection is found in *Sardino v. Federal Reserve Bank of New York*,[8] *supra*, page 794.

Moreover, the Fifth Amendment's protections apply only to alien "friends." With respect to "enemy aliens," the Trading with the Enemy Act[9] "vested" in the U.S. Government all property held by enemy aliens in the U.S. at the start of both World Wars. The effect of vesting was that title was absolutely transferred to the United States and return of the property, or the payment of part or all of the proceeds of its sale, was at the discretion of the U.S. Government. See, *e.g.*, *United States v. Chemical Foundation, Inc.*[10] Under the Trading with the Enemy Act as originally framed "enemies" were defined to include persons resident or doing business in enemy or enemy occupied territory. As revised during World War II to avoid evasions, the Act covered citizens or residents (including corporations) of neutral territory who were "tainted" with enemy relations. *Clark v. Uebersee Finanz-Korp. A.G.*[11] The constitutionality of the Trading with the Enemy Act has been consistently upheld. See *e.g.*, *Silesian American Corp. v. Clark.*[12]

[C] Treaty Obligations

As we have noted, under Article VI of the Constitution, a treaty is part of the supreme law of the land and, as such, prevails, in case of conflict, over any inconsistent provisions of State law. Treaties also bind the federal government

[6] 282 U.S. 481, 51 S. Ct. 229, 75 L. Ed. 473 (1931).
[7] 315 U.S. 203, 228, 62 S. Ct. 552, 564, 86 L. Ed. 796 (1942).
[8] 361 F. 2d 106 (2d Cir. 1966).
[9] 40 Stat. 411 (1917), as amended, 50 U.S.C.A. Sec. 1, *et seq.*
[10] 272 U.S. 1, 47 S. Ct. 1, 71 L. Ed. 131 (1926).
[11] 332 U.S. 480, 68 S. Ct. 174, 92 L. Ed. 88 (1947).
[12] 332 U.S. 469, 68 S. Ct. 179, 92 L. Ed. 81 (1947).

and, at the international level, the President and, more generally, the United States. Hence, as a practical matter, treaty limitations on federal regulation of transnational business will normally be recognized.

This being said, it should be noted that it has not proven possible to reach agreement on a global, multilateral treaty on the regulation of transnational business. On the other hand, the General Agreement on Tariffs and Trade has a host of provisions relevant to foreign trade with and other forms of doing business in states that are parties. Moreover, the Uruguay round of GATT negotiations is likely to result in a major expansion of the areas covered by the GATT, including trade in services, transactions involving intellectual property and trade related investment problems. Also, the obligations imposed on the U.S. by the Articles of Agreement of the International Monetary Fund are a major constraint on the authority of the U.S. to regulate transnational business. There are, in addition, such international bodies as the Organization for Economic Cooperation and Development (OECD), the International Labor Organization, the United Nations Economic and Social Council (UNESCO), and the United Nations Conference on Trade and Development (UNCTAD). These organizations have been forums for the negotiation of codes of conduct for transnational enterprises. Most of these efforts, however, are still in the drafting stage. Those which have come to completion are usually in the form of guidelines, rather than treaty obligations — so-called "soft law." As a consequence, many of the treaty obligations that limit federal regulation of transnational business are to be found in bilateral agreements.

The most prominent of these bilateral agreements are treaties of Friendship, Commerce and Navigation (FCN), treaties for the avoidance of double taxation, commercial treaties dealing with specific products such as textiles or meat, and, most recently, bilateral investment treaties or "BITs" as they have come to be called.

The purpose of an FCN treaty is to delimit "the rights of citizens of each country to establish and carry on business activities within the other and to receive due protection there for their persons and property."[13] Since World War II, however, the "citizens" involved in foreign investment have increasingly been corporations, and the postwar FCN treaties have been drafted to reflect this fact. Although these treaties are often generically referred to as treaties of "friendship," "commerce," and "navigation," the concern of the post-war FCN treaties has been only secondarily with these subjects. They have been above all else treaties of "establishment." As such their primary purpose has been "the protection of persons, natural and juridical, and of the property and interests of such persons. They define the treatment each country owes the nationals of the other; their rights to engage in business and other activities within the boundaries of the former and the respect due them, their property and their enterprises."[14]

The overarching principle informing these treaties is that of "national treatment." As defined in Article XIV(1) of the Convention of Establishment (the more accurate title) Between the United States and France entered into force, December

---

[13] Walker, *Treaties For The Encouragement And Protection Of Foreign Investment: Present United States Practice*, 5 Am. J. Comp. L. 229, 232 (1956).

[14] Walker, *Modern Treaties Of Friendship, Commerce and Navigation*, 42 Minn. L. Rev. 805 (1958).

21, 1960,[15] the term "national treatment" means that each party to the treaty will accord nationals and companies of the other party, treatment no less favorable than it accords its own nationals and companies. This implies "an open door" for foreign investment, subject, of course, to restrictions on alien ownership of sensitive areas of the economy like banking, communications, defense and, as in the case of Canada, a right to "screen" the entry of foreign investment to ensure that it will be compatible with the economic goals of the host country.[16] Once the foreign investment is permitted, however, all the treaties assure it national treatment. As to investments legally present in the territory, then, discrimination against them based on their alienage is forbidden.

As a supplementary principle, most-favored-nation treatment is assured all aspects of an investment activity. Thus, for example, Article IX of the Convention of Establishment between the United States and France, in addition to ensuring national treatment to certain kinds of nationals and companies of one High Contracting Party residing or doing business in the other, provides that, with respect to nationals and companies not falling within the covered categories, taxation shall not be more burdensome than that to which nationals, companies, and associations of any third country in the same situation may be subject.

In some respects, the FCN treaty may go beyond the protection afforded by the national and most-favored-nation principles. With regard to protection of the laws, access to courts, and other forms of protection of persons and property, these principles are not sufficient, and the treaty alien and his property may need special protection from possible vagaries of national law and administration. This is especially so as to any sequestration or expropriation of property. Here the FCN treaties commonly provide for prompt, just and effective compensation. That is, the compensation must be for the full equivalent of the property taken, paid promptly, and in fully convertible currency. The protections accorded by these FCN treaties, however, may be less secure after the judgement of the International Court of Justice in *Case Concerning Elettronica Sicula S.P.A. (ELSI) (United States v. Italy).*[17]

---

[15] 11 U.S.T. & O.I.A. 2398, T.I.A.S. No. 4625.

[16] Note that under the Canada - U.S. Free Trade Agreement, Canada has agreed to raise substantially the threshold value of acquisitions of Canadian companies by American investors that must receive prior approval. After four years from date of entry into force of the Agreement prior review will only be required if an American investor undertakes a "direct acquisition of control" over a Canadian company with an asset value in excess of $150 million measured in constant dollars. After four years no prior approval will be required for the "indirect acquisition of control." Canadian - U.S. Free Trade Agreement, Chapter 16, Article 1607:3, Annex 1697.3.

[17] 1989, I.C.J. Rep. 15, reprinted in 29 Int'l Leg. Mat. 1109 (1989). For discussion of the case, see Scheffer, *Friendship Treaties' Limitations As Shields For Investors*, Wall St. J., Nov. 7, 1989, at 11.

SUMITOMO SHOJI AMERICA, INC. v. AVIGLIANO

United States Supreme Court
457 U.S. 176, 102 S.Ct. 2374, 72 L.Ed.2d 765 (1982)

CHIEF JUSTICE BURGER delivered the opinion of the Court.

We granted certiorari to decide whether Article VIII(1) of the Friendship, Commerce and Navigation Treaty between the United States and Japan provides a defense to a Title VII employment discrimination suit against an American subsidiary of a Japanese company.

Petitioner, Sumitomo Shoji America, Inc., is a New York corporation and a wholly-owned subsidiary of Sumitomo Shoji Kabushiki Kaisha, a Japanese general trading company or sogo shosha. Respondents are past and present female secretarial employees of Sumitomo. All but one of the respondents are United States citizens; that one exception is a Japanese citizen living in the United States. Respondents brought this suit as a class action claiming that Sumitomo's alleged practice of hiring only male Japanese citizens to fill executive, managerial and sales positions violated both 42 U.S.C. Section 1981 and Title VII of the Civil Rights Act of 1964, as amended.[18] Respondents sought both injunctive relief and damages.

Without admitting the alleged discriminatory practice, Sumitomo moved under Rule 12(b)(6) of the Federal Rules of Civil Procedure to dismiss the complaint. Sumitomo's motion was based on two grounds: (1) discrimination on the basis of Japanese citizenship does not violate Title VII or Section 1981; and (2) Sumitomo's practices are protected under Article VIII(1) of the Friendship, Commerce and Navigation Treaty between the United States and Japan. The District Court dismissed the Sec. 1981 claim, holding that neither sex discrimination nor national origin discrimination are cognizable under that section. *Avigliano v. Sumitomo Shoji America, Inc.*[19] . . . . The court refused to dismiss the Title VII claims, however; it held that because Sumitomo is incorporated in the United States it is not covered by Article VIII (1) of the Treaty. . . .

The Court of Appeals reversed in part[20] . . . . The court first examined the Treaty's language and its history and concluded that the Treaty parties intended Article VIII(1) to cover locally incorporated subsidiaries of foreign companies such as Sumitomo. The court then held that the Treaty language does not insulate Sumitomo's executive employment practices from Title VII scrutiny. The court concluded that under certain conditions, Japanese citizenship could be a *bona fide* occupational qualification for high-level employment with a Japanese-owned domestic corporation and that Sumitomo's practices might thus fit within a statutory exception to Title VII. The court remanded for further proceedings.

We granted certiorari[21] . . . and we reverse.

Interpretation of the Friendship, Commerce and Navigation Treaty between Japan and the United States must, of course, begin with the language of the Treaty

---

[18] 42 U.S.C. Section 2002e et seq.
[19] 473 F. Supp. 506 (S.D.N.Y. 1979).
[20] 638 F. 2d 552 (C.A. 2 1981).
[21] 454 U.S. 962, 102 S. Ct. 501, 70 L. Ed. 2d 377 (1981).

itself. The clear import of treaty language controls unless "application of the words of the treaty according to their obvious meaning effects a result inconsistent with the intent or expectations of its signatories". . . .

Article VIII(1) of the Treaty provides in pertinent part:

> [C]ompanies of either Party shall be permitted to engage, within the territories of the other Party, accountants and other technical experts, executive personnel, attorneys, agents and other specialists of their choice. (emphasis added)

Clearly Article VIII(1) only applies to companies of one of the Treaty countries operating in the other country. Sumitomo contends that it is a company of Japan, and that Article VIII(1) of the Treaty grants it very broad discretion to fill its executive, managerial and sales positions exclusively with male Japanese citizens.

Article VIII(1) does not define any of its terms; the definitional section of the Treaty is contained in Article XXII. Article XXII(3) provides:

> As used in the present Treaty, the term companies' means corporations, partnerships, companies, and other associations, whether or not with limited liability and whether or not for pecuniary profit. Companies constituted under the applicable laws and regulations within the territories of either Party *shall be deemed companies thereof* and shall have their juridical status recognized within the territories of the other Party. (emphasis added)

Sumitomo is "constituted under the applicable laws and regulations" of New York; based on Article XXII(3), it is a company of the United States, not a company of Japan. As a company of the United States operating in the United States, under the literal language of Article XXII(3) of the Treaty, Sumitomo cannot invoke the rights provided in Article VIII(1), which are available only to companies of Japan operating in the United States and to companies of the United States operating in Japan.

The Governments of Japan and the United States support this interpretation of the Treaty. Both the Ministry of Foreign Affairs of Japan and the United States Department of State agree that a United States corporation, even when wholly owned by a Japanese company is not a company of Japan under the Treaty and is therefore not covered by Article VIII(1). . . .

* * * *

Sumitomo maintains that although the literal language of the Treaty supports the contrary interpretation, the intent of Japan and the United States was to cover subsidiaries regardless of their place of incorporation. We disagree.

Contrary to the view of the Court of Appeals and the claims of Sumitomo, adherence to the language of the Treaty would not "overlook the purpose of the Treaty.". . . .

The purpose of the treaties was not to give foreign corporations greater rights than domestic companies, but instead to assure them the right to conduct business on an equal basis without suffering discrimination based on their alienage.

The treaties accomplished their purpose by granting foreign corporations "national treatment" in most respects and by allowing foreign individuals and companies to form locally incorporated subsidiaries. These local subsidiaries are considered for purpose of the Treaty to be companies of the country in which they are incorporated; they are entitled to the rights, and subject to the responsibilities of other domestic corporations. By treating these subsidiaries as domestic companies, the purpose of the Treaty provisions — to assure that corporations of one treaty party have the right to conduct business within the territory of the other party without suffering discrimination as an alien entity — is fully met.

Nor can we agree with the Court of Appeals view that literal interpretation of the Treaty would create a "crazy-quilt pattern" in which the rights of branches of Japanese companies operating directly in the United States would be greatly superior to the right of locally incorporated subsidiaries of Japanese companies. . . . The Court of Appeals maintained that if such subsidiaries were not considered companies of Japan under the Treaty, they, unlike branch offices of Japanese corporations, would be denied access to the legal system, would be left unprotected against unlawful entry and molestation, and would be unable to dispose of property, obtain patents, engage in importation and exportation, or make payments, remittances and transfer of funds. . . . That this is not the case is obvious; the subsidiaries, as companies of the United States, would enjoy all of those rights and more. The only significant advantage branches may have over subsidiaries is that conferred by Article VIII(1).

We are persuaded, as both signatories agree, that under the literal language of Article XXII(3) of the Treaty Sumitomo is a company of the United States; we discern no reason to depart from the plain meaning of the Treaty language. Accordingly, we hold the Sumitomo is not a company of Japan and is thus not covered by Article VIII(1) of the Treaty. The judgment of the Court of Appeals is reversed, and the case is remanded for further proceedings consistent with this opinion.

NOTES AND QUESTIONS

(1) A remarkably disingenuous decision, isn't it? Or is the decision disingenuous only because it tries to make sense of a remarkably silly treaty? Or, is the United States just being hung by its own petard? At this point review the Mexican argument in its dispute with the United States over the expropriation of American owned property in Mexico, Chapter 9, at page 774.

(2) After the Court's holding in *Sumitomo*, how might you advise a client on whether to choose a branch or a foreign subsidiary as the form of business entity abroad?

(3) Consider also whether the *Sumitomo* decision may have implications for issues regarding the so-called "extraterritorial" or transnational application of United States regulatory law.

(4) Does the decison mean that if Sumitomo (N.Y.) is subject to U.S. regulations which, under international law, constitute a taking of property for which compensation is due, the Japanese owners of the company are foreclosed from making

any claim based on that law and may only assert such U.S. constitutional claims that they may have?

(5) Note that because it held that Sumitomo's wholly owned subsidiary was not a company of Japan so as to come within the coverage of the U.S. - Japan FCN Treaty, the Supreme Court expressly declined to interpret the scope of Article VIII(1). In *MacNamara v. Korean Air Lines*,[22] — where defendant operated through branches in the United States — the court interpreted a similar provision in the U.S. - Korea FCN Treaty so as to allow each party to have its businesses in the other country managed by its own citizens but not to exempt those businesses from the coverage of national laws prohibiting intentional discrimination on bases other than citizenship, such as race, national origin, and age. The court also held that, although plaintiff on remand could proceed with his claims of disparate treatment, he could not make the required showing of disparate impact by relying exclusively on statistical evidence of disproportionate effect. Rather, plaintiff would have to prove a subjective intent to discriminate on the part of defendant.

(6) As of October 1985, the United States was a party to 48 FCN treaties of which 25 have come into force since the end of World War II. The most recent FCN treaty, however, was concluded in 1966. Most of the FCN treaties were concluded prior to 1960, and it is generally agreed that, with the dramatic increase in international investment since then, and the emergence of developing countries in the world economy, new bilateral treaties in the investment area are needed.

(7) A rather large number of developing countries have entered into bilateral investment treaties or "BITS." BITS, which are also considered *supra*, Chapter 8, serve to protect foreign investment abroad by establishing a comprehensive framework for nondiscriminatory treatment of foreign investors, dispute settlement procedures, compensation for expropriation, and transfers of funds into and out of the host country.

The United States was a latecomer to bilateral investment treaties, having signed its first BIT with Egypt on September 27, 1983. At this writing the United States has ratified eight BITS. These treaties afford a substantially greater measure of protection to foreign investment than do the FCN treaties and have the potential to promote investment abroad in both developed and developing countries. In comparing the BITS with the FCN treaties, Kenneth Vandevelde has noted the following major differences:

> First, the BITS were to be narrower in scope than the FCNs, focusing exclusively on the protection of foreign investment to the exclusion of provisions on trade, maritime relations, consular relations, and other subjects frequently covered in FCNs. Second, the BITs were to provide greater protection in the area of private investment than that afforded by the modern FCNs. Finally, the BITS were to guarantee investors a right to investor-to-state arbitration of investment disputes before a neutral third party.[23]

---

[22] 863 F. 2d 1135 (3rd Cir. 1988), cert. denied 110 U.S. 349 (Oct. 30, 1989).

[23] Vandevelde, *Reassesing The Hickenlooper Amendment*, 29 Va. J. Int'l L. 115, 163 (1988). For a more wide-ranging survey of BITS, which covers BITS between developed countries other than the United States and developing countries, see Salacuse, *BIT by BIT: The Growth of Bilateral Investment Treaties and Their Impact on Foreign Investment in Developing Countries*, 24 Int'l Law. 655 (1990).

(6) A problem in negotiating bilateral investment treaties is to ensure that their provisions do not conflict with federal statutory controls over economic activities of aliens. Also, as the *Sumitomo* case illustrates, there may be other provisions of federal law that pose problems.

The barriers imposed by the federal government on aliens' entry into economic activity are not extensive. The rationale of such barriers is that there are a few areas of the economy where foreign ownership would be undesirable for national security or other reasons. Some examples of fields where foreign participation is prohibited or severely limited include nuclear facilities, radio and television, U.S. registered commercial aircraft and vessels engaged in the coastal trade, defense contractors, the lease of land and mineral rights possessed by the federal government, and banking operations (special provisions are made for certain types of participation by aliens).

TABLE OF CASES

[Principal cases appear in upper case roman type. All other cases appear in lower case roman type. References are to pages.]

[Principal cases appear in upper case roman type. All other cases appear in lower case roman type. References are to pages.]

[Principal cases appear in upper case roman type. All other cases appear in lower case roman type. References are to pages.]

[Principal cases appear in upper case roman type. All other cases appear in lower case roman type. References are to pages.]

[Principal cases appear in upper case roman type. All other cases appear in lower case roman type. References are to pages.]

[Principal cases appear in upper case roman type. All other cases appear in lower case roman type. References are to pages.]

[Principal cases appear in upper case roman type. All other cases appear in lower case roman type. References are to pages.]

INDEX

D

[References are to pages.]

[References are to pages.]

N

O

P

[References are to pages.]

[References are to pages.]

[References are to pages.]

T

[References are to pages.]

U